HANDBOOK OF STRESS

HANDBOOK OF STRESS
Theoretical and Clinical Aspects
Second Edition

Edited by
Leo Goldberger and Shlomo Breznitz

THE FREE PRESS
A Division of Macmillan, Inc.
NEW YORK
Maxwell Macmillan Canada
TORONTO

Maxwell Macmillan International
NEW YORK OXFORD SINGAPORE SYDNEY

The Free Press
A Division of Macmillan, Inc.
866 Third Avenue, New York, N.Y. 10022

Maxwell Macmillan Canada, Inc.
1200 Eglinton Avenue East
Suite 200
Don Mills, Ontario M3C 3N1

Macmillan, Inc. is part of the Maxwell Communication
Group of Companies.

Printed in the United States of America

printing number

1   2   3   4   5   6   7   8   9   10

Library of Congress Cataloging-in-Publication Data

Handbook of stress : theoretical and clinical aspects/edited by Leo
    Goldberger and Shlomo Breznitz.—2nd ed.
        p.   cm.
    Includes bibliographical references and index.
    ISBN 0-02-912035-7 (cloth)   —ISBN 0-02-912036-5 (pbk.)
    1. Stress (Psychology)   2. Stress (Physiology)   I. Goldberger,
Leo.   II. Breznitz, Shlomo.
    [DNLM: 1. Psychophysiologic Disorders—etiology—handbooks.
2. Stress, Psychological—handbooks.   WM 34 H2364]
BF575.S75H35   1993
155.9′042—dc20
DNLM/DLC
for Library of Congress   92-23125
                                                        CIP

This book is dedicated to
Nancy, Zvia, Jessica, Danny, Ruthie, and *Nurit*
And to the memory of
Eugene Goldberger

Contents

Preface to the Second Edition

A ten-year span between two editions of a general handbook is a long time for most disciplines, but especially in a field such as ours. The proliferation of research in the area of stress makes the attempt to survey its course since the publication of the first edition in 1982 both difficult and rewarding. The volume of stress-related studies is, indeed, staggering and is continuously on the rise. In some ways this reflects the popular belief that ours is the era of stress. It may well be that the fuzziness of the definition of stress is conducive to the spread of stress-focused research, because hardly any aspect of human interaction with the environment is entirely stress free.

We believe that the time is more than ripe for a new edition. While we cannot pretend to have a historical perspective on the main directions of inquiry, we can offer the student of stress a significant cross-section of current developments; a state-of-the-art overview of a number of significant and substantive research areas in the stress/coping domain prepared by some of the most respected authorities in the field.

In planning the new edition of the *Handbook of Stress* our initial aim was simply to invite each of the original contributors to revise and update their chapters. However, it became increasingly clear that this would not be feasible in most instances, nor did we deem it an optimal choice. For one thing, several of our original authors were no longer alive: the father of the modern stress concept, Hans Selye, was gone; the seminal contributions of Irving Janis, Norma Haan, and Harold Proshansky were now but a legacy as well. By and large, their original chapters—along with a few additional ones—had stood the test of time so well that they could be reprinted without revision as classics. In addition, in some instances our original contributors were no longer active in the field or declined our invitation to update their original chapters, though several of our original authors did write completely new and updated chapters—such as Chapters 4, 11, 12, 15, 25, 29, 34, 37, 38 and 39.

An overriding concern was our attempt to increase the usefulness of the current handbook by including at least some representation of newer conceptions, methodological and measurement issues, and overviews of some of the more specialized areas, deemed to be at the cutting edge, in our field. In addition, for some of the topics treated in the first edition, we chose to broaden the perspective by inviting a completely fresh chapter by another expert.

Consequently, the current *Handbook of Stress* is a substantially new book. Though the chapters are still organized around the seven major headings in the 1982 edition, the reader will confront an array of new chapters and, in most instances, new contributors. In fact, with the exception of the half dozen classic chapters, this handbook might well be regarded as a companion rather than a replacement for the original volume.

As in the first edition, the choice of topics for inclusion in the current handbook is constrained by the inevitable space limitation of a one-volume reference work. Had we striven for genuine comprehensiveness, we would undoubtedly be faulted by critics as too sketchy. It is clearly impossible to cover the entire panoply of the stress field and do justice to each topic. Consequently, some topics were left by the wayside. For example (and most obviously) chapters on infancy, childhood and family stressors, and the vast domain of sociocultural variables are clearly missing in the handbook. Equally obvious is the fact that the achievement of "organic unity" by imposition of some sort of shared conceptual scheme for each contributor to follow is artificial, if not unwise. In our view, the vitality of the field inheres precisely in its theoretical diversity, multiple levels of complexity, and potential for emergent ideas as a function of cross-disciplinary fertilization.

The opportunity to take a broader look at one's field of inquiry is rare. The publication of the second edition of the handbook presents such an opportunity. In order to illustrate the contrast between stress research as it appeared a decade ago and as it appears today, we decided to keep our introductory chapter in its original form, but we wish here, in the Preface, to draw the reader's attention to some important recent themes that characterize the stress field as a whole and that have found representation in the current volume as well. The themes do not signal a dramatic departure from earlier trends, but may perhaps be viewed as shifts in emphasis and as pointers to the road ahead.

Issues of definition, so central to most discussions of stress just a decade ago, now appear to be of lesser import. This change is not to be understood as a reflection of greater clarity of the concepts, nor does it suggest an emerging consensus. We would like to think that, as our discipline begins to mature, there is a corresponding growth in the tolerance of its inherent ambiguities.

Yet another indication that the stress field is gradually leaving behind the naive quest for simplicity are the models that are being used by most of the researchers in the field. Gone is the simple environmentally induced stressor and its equally simple corresponding stress response. A host of mediators and intervening variables have now replaced those earlier formulations. For example, one can note a renaissance of interest in personality and individual differences. Researchers have also begun to distinguish between and specify antecedent variables, immediate and long-term reactions within their conceptual and causal flowcharts. The prevalent working assumption is that a multilevel, multidimensional approach is a must.

Furthermore, Lazarus's call for transactional models is certainly gaining support; much of current stress research follows his formulations. Specifically, there is a growing awareness of the need for process-oriented research design, with multiple measures of the key variables.

The methodological sophistication of a significant number of studies appears now to be much greater. This increased rigor reflects awareness of the pitfalls of response contamination, social desirability, and the overall shortcomings of a single-source methodology. Internal reliability of the multitude of measures used, either as independent or dependent variables, is another concern that is being addressed more seriously than before.

Life events scales, so abundant in stress research, are becoming increasingly refined by using the respondents' subjective appraisal of event stressfulness or by taking into consideration situational and personal factors that influence the context of the threat and the variability within event categories. This trend has gone a long way toward bridging the initial, pure stimulus conception and the in-depth clinical interview approach. There has been a corresponding increase in the strength of the correlations found between life events and disorders.

Perhaps the most notable change in emphasis is the growing impact of the biological sciences. Two prominent examples of that influence are the emergence of psychoneuroimmunology and the study of stress-related brain chemistry. Recent technological developments of brain imaging techniques, specifically those like PET and SPECT that allow on-line study of physiological changes in the active brain, may well turn out to be the next bridge between neuroscience and stress research (and a good candidate for a new chapter in the next edition of the *Handbook of Stress*).

Finally, we should mention the apparent resurgence of interest in the traditional topic of emotions and its manifold spectrum. This new popularity suggests that, in the future, stress (essentially comprising the so-called negative emotions) will no longer be viewed as a peculiarly isolated rubric of uncertain conceptual lineage, but will find its appropriate location as a subset of emotions in the scaffold of knowledge. We hope that, as our field makes further progress, the challenges of its complex nature will be matched by the richness of the data in what promises to be an important part of the story of human adaptation.

Above all, we wish to thank our contributors, new and old, for their willingness to participate in this project, particularly because we know full well their crowded schedules. Their generosity in contributing their work to our Handbook is deeply appreciated.

Our appreciation is also extended to our editor at The Free Press, Susan Arellano, for her splendid guidance and warm support throughout the project, to Lilian Schein, director of the Behavioral Science Book Service and a good friend, for her interest and encouragement, and to Anne Stubing for her cheerful secretarial assistance.

Leo Goldberger
Shlomo Breznitz

Preface to the First Edition

The concept of stress and, indeed, research on stress have reached an all-time peak in popularity during the past few years. An ever increasing number of books and journals devoted exclusively to stress are being published, courses and seminars are being offered in this area, and references to stress in the mass media abound. With this heightened awareness of stress—meaning here essentially all that is unpleasant, noxious, or excessively demanding—a concomitant interest in stress reducing techniques, or stress management, has given birth to a new specialty in the health sciences.

The tremendous proliferation of stress literature has made a single, comprehensive text on the subject a forbidding undertaking. Instead, the time seems more than ripe for this handbook, the aims of which are to gather within one volume a wide array of authoritative articles on the many facets of stress; provide researchers and clinicians in the field with a forum for critical reflection on the perennial definitional and conceptual problems and methodological complexities peculiar to stress research and stress treatment; and, ideally, to provide readers with a state of the art overview of those areas in which a body of solid findings exists.

The stress field is a sprawling one, characterized by unevenness and lack of coordination (not unlike many other domains within the behavioral and mental health sciences), with pockets of substantial development separated by faddish, superficial, or one-time forays. We believe there is much to be gained by the student of stress in confronting a cross-section of current developments in the field as a whole.

This volume allows the reader to take stock of where we are and to discern links and overlaps among the several disciplinary lines; cross-fertilization of the multiple perspectives on stress is necessary if the field is to maintain its vitality. The idea for the *Handbook of Stress,* born in our recognition of timeliness of such a reference work, surely would have failed to materialize had it not resonated with our colleagues—the distinguished group of authors whom we invited to contribute chapters summarizing topics closest to their current concerns. Their enthusiasm and ready acceptance of the task testified to the shared purpose of our venture.

In choosing the topics included in the handbook, we faced the obvious constraint of space. We could neither cover all disciplinary perspectives and broad categories—biological, psychological, and sociological—nor be exhaustive within a given perspective or category. The reader will undoubtedly compose his/her own list of missing chapters. Clearly, we had to make choices and though these choices were inevitably biased by our professional training as psychologists, we tried to provide a balanced view at least within the field of psychological stress. In other words, we set out to achieve a balance among theoretical viewpoints, as well as a balance between theory and research. Although not all topics covered in the *Handbook of Stress* have reached the level of maturity that permits a state of the art overview, some were nonetheless included because they have significance for the field.

The volume begins with a brief outline of our own perspective on stress and suggestions for future directions of investigation. Dr. Hans Selye—the pioneer in the field of stress whose ideas and influence are discernible in many of these chapters—provides an appropriate historical introduction. The main body of the handbook consists of seven parts. The headings for each part are self-explanatory and reflect our concern for a balanced treatment of stress. The reader should note that quite a few chapters deal with several aspects of their particular topic—theory, research, and/or clinical issues—and some areas are addressed in more than one chapter, for example, the measurement of both stress and coping and the use of life events scales. Our purpose was to provide more intensive treatment of issues that have a singular, pragmatic value for the stress investigators who would, we thought, welcome ready access to this material.

The *Handbook of Stress* is intended for the professional and the student in the behavioral and mental health fields actively working or interested in the stress area. It should have considerable utility as a reference work—as an aid in locating significant bodies of research; as a guide to metrics, tests, scales, and questionnaires in the stress-coping field; and, for the practicing clinician, as a guide to some of the increasingly popular techniques for the prevention and treatment of stress related disorders. The volume also should be useful as a reference work for general readers who wish to gain familiarity with the current scientific yield in the field of stress.

Finally, it should be noted that the contributors were discouraged from being as expansive as they might have wished and from using an overabundance of tables, figures, and references—this decision reflected our concern with conserving space to allow a wide representation of topics. We are grateful for having had such an impressive group of colleagues cooperate with us and give of their time and expertise in preparing their chapters and we appreciate their forbearance in regard to space constraints and editorial cuts.

Our appreciation also goes to a number of other people whose help was invaluable. At New York University our thanks go to Roberta Gordon, Nancy Koch, Bettie Brewer, and William T. Francis for administrative and secretarial help; at Haifa University, our thanks to Ruth Maos and Dinah Katz. Kitty Moore, senior psychology editor at The Free Press, has our warm gratitude for her advice, support, and enthusiastic interest throughout this project.

Leo Goldberger
Shlomo Breznitz

About the Contributors

LISA G. ASPINWALL is an assistant professor at the University of Maryland at College Park. She obtained her Ph.D. in social psychology from the University of California, Los Angeles, in 1991. In 1987, she was awarded a National Science Foundation Fellowship and a Firestone Medal for Excellence in Research from Stanford University. Her interests include social comparison theory, self-regulation under threat, and preventive health behavior.

ROSALIND C. BARNETT is a senior research associate at the Wellesley College Center for Research on Women. She is the director of the Adult Lives Project, a longitudinal study of work and nonwork stressors and stress mitigators in a sample of dual-earner couples. She received her Ph.D. in clinical psychology from Harvard University. Dr. Barnett co-authored *Lifepoints: New Patterns of Love and Work for Today's Women* (with Grace Baruch and Caryl Rivers), and she is the co-editor of *Gender and Stress* (with Lois Biener and Grace Baruch). She is also the recipient of the Radcliffe College Graduate Society Distinguished Achievement Medal.

SHLOMO BREZNITZ is the Lady Davis Professor of Psychology and founding director of the R. D. Wolfe Centre for the Study of Psychological Stress at the University of Haifa, Israel. He has written extensively in the area of anticipatory fear, false alarms, and health psychology. He is the author of *Cry Wolf: The Psychology of False Alarms,* and editor of *Stress in Israel* and *Denial of Stress.*

JOHN G. CARLSON received his Ph.D. in psychology from the University of Minnesota. Formerly department chairman, he is professor and Director of Health Psychology in the Department of Psychology at the University of Hawaii. He is also Health Sciences Specialist at the Veteran's Administration Medical Center in Honolulu Stress Disorders Laboratory. He is the co-author of *Psychology of Emotion* and co-editor of *International Perspectives of Self-regulation and Health.* He was a Cumberland College Research Fellow at the University of Sydney, Australia, and is a member of the editorial board of *Biofeedback and Self-regulation.*

CATHERINE C. CLASSEN is a postdoctoral fellow at the Department of Psychiatry and Behavioral Sciences, Stanford University School of Medicine. She received her Ph.D. from York University, Toronto. Her doctoral research involved a theoretical and empirical investigation of insight into psychotherapy.

HELEN L. COONS is an assistant professor in the Department of Mental Health Sciences, Hahnemann University, Philadelphia. She received her Ph.D. in clinical psychology from Temple University. Her research focuses on psychosocial aspects of chronic or life-threatening physical conditions for adults and their family members. Dr. Coons currently chairs the Committee on Women and Health, Division of Health Psychology, American Psychological Association.

Paul T. Costa, Jr., is chief of the Laboratory of Personality and Cognition, Gerontology Research Center, National Institute on Aging. He has served as president of Division 20, Adult Development and Aging, of the American Psychological Association, and has published widely on aging, health, and personality. He is co-author of the *NEO Personality Inventory.*

Francis Creed is professor of community psychiatry at Manchester University, England. His M.D. thesis involved the life events method, and he worked with Professor George Brown at Bedford College, London. He has extended his life events research to several physical and psychiatric conditions. Other research interests include the use of hospital day treatment for acute psychiatric illness and work in primary care.

Susan Dermit is assistant professor of psychiatry and behavioral sciences at the School of Medicine at the State University of New York at Stony Brook, where she received her Ph.D. in clinical psychology. Her research has focused on an empirical and behavioral approach to the analysis of individual differences in proneness to coronary heart disease.

Leonard R. Derogatis is professor of Mental Health Sciences and director of the Division of Clinical Psychology at Hahnemann University. After graduate study at Columbia University, he received his Ph.D. from Catholic University. In addition to *Clinical Psychopharmacology* and *Anxiety and Depressive Disorders in the Medical Patient,* he has written over 90 papers and monographs. He has also authored ten psychological tests, including the Hopkins Symptom Checklist (HSCL), the SCL-90-R, the Brief Symptom Inventory (BSI), the Psychosocial Adjustment to illness Scale (PAIS), and the Derogatis Stress Profile (DSP). His major research interests include clinical measurement, psychopharmacology, and clinical health psychology.

Bruce P. Dohrenwend is Foundations' Fund for Research in Psychiatry professor at Columbia University and chief of the Department of Social Psychiatry at the New York State Psychiatric Institute. He received his Ph.D. in social psychology from Cornell University and conducts research on adversity, stress, and other risk factors in the field of psychiatric epidemiology under a Research Scientist Award and other grants from the National Institute of Mental Health. His other awards include the 1980 Distinguished Contributions Award of the Division of Community Psychology, American Psychological Association (with Barbara Snell Dohrenwend); the 1981 Rema Lapouse Award, American Public Health Association (with Barbara Snell Dohrenwend); and the 1990 American Association for the Advancement of Science Prize for Behavioral Science Research.

Leo Eitinger, is professor emeritus at the University of Oslo. He holds both an M.D. and a Ph.D. and has been president of the Norwegian Psychiatric Association and the Scandinavian Psychiatric Congress. He was also a Corresponding Fellow of the American Psychiatric Association. A survivor of the Auschwitz and Buchenwald concentration camps, after the war he returned to Norway to do hospital work. The author of more than 150 publications, Dr. Eitinger was awarded the King's Gold Medal by Olso University for his paper "The Influence of Military Life in Young Norwegian Men's Psychic Life." He has published extensively on the subject of concentration camp survivors.

Nigel P. Field is a postdoctoral fellow with the John D. and Catherine T. MacArthur Foundation's Program on Conscious and Unconscious Mental Processes at the University of California, San Francisco. He received his Ph.D. from York University, Toronto. His publications include, with Richard M. Sorrentino, "Emergent Leadership Over Time: The

Functional Value of Positive Motivation," and, with Mardi J. Horowitz and Charles H. Stinson, "National Disasters and Stress Response Syndromes." His research utilizes thought sampling and cognitive methodologies to study intrusion in post-traumatic stress disorder.

MARJORIE FISKE is emeritus professor of social psychology and the former director of the Human Development and Aging research and doctoral program at the University of California, San Francisco. Among her publications are *Four Stages of Life, Middle Age,* and some 100 articles and chapters in professional books and journals. She holds or has held office in the American Sociological, Psychological, and Gerontological Societies and serves as advisor or board member to several journals and educational organizations. Professor Fiske's major research interests are personal/social change and stress/adaptation in adulthood.

DEBORAH FITZPATRICK is a graduate student in clinical psychology at the University of Waterloo, Ontario. She received her B.A. from McGill University, Montreal.

SUSAN FOLKMAN is professor of medicine at the University of California, San Francisco, and senior scientist at the Center for AIDS Prevention Studies. She received her Ph.D. from the University of California, Berkeley. She worked with Richard Lazarus at Berkeley through 1987, and with him co-authored *Stress, Appraisal, and Coping.* She is conducting research on stress and coping in the context of AIDS.

LEO GOLDBERGER is professor of psychology at New York University and a former director of the Research Center for Mental Health. Following graduate study at McGill University, Montreal, he completed his Ph.D. in clinical psychology at New York University. Dr. Goldberger was the recipient of a National Institute of Mental Health Research Career Development Award in 1960, and he has published extensively in the area of sensory deprivation, personality, and cognitive style. He is the editor of *Psychoanalysis and Contemporary Thought* and the *Stress and Health* series and a co-editor of *The International Library of Critical Writings on Psychology.*

ERIC GRAIG is a lecturer in the sociology department at Queens College in New York City and a doctoral candidate in environmental psychology at the Graduate School and University Center of the City University of New York. His primary interest is in the sociology of knowledge, in particular as it relates to knowledge about social and environmental problems.

RAND J. GRUEN is an assistant professor of psychology, a member of the Center for Neural Science, New York University, and an adjunct assistant professor of psychiatry at New York University Medical Center. After receiving his Ph.D. from the University of California, Berkeley, he completed a three-year fellowship in psychiatry and pharmacology at Yale University School of Medicine. His research involves the psychosocial and biochemical bases of depression and anxiety and the interaction between transmitter systems in the central nervous system.

NORMA HAAN (now deceased) was research scientist at the Institute of Human Development, University of California, Berkeley. She was the author of *Coping and Defending: Processes of Self-Environment Organization* and a number of papers concerned with the accommodation to life stress and stress produced by moral conflict and political dissent. She was co-editor of *Past and Present in Middle Life.*

STEVAN E. HOBFOLL is professor of psychology at Kent State University and director of the Applied Psychology Center. He received his Ph.D. from the University of South Florida. He was formerly on the faculty of Tel Aviv University and Ben Gurion University in Israel. He is a fellow of the American Psychological Association and author of *The Ecology of Stress.* Dr. Hobfoll is editor of *Anxiety, Stress, and Coping: An International Journal* and editor-in-chief of *Series in Applied Psychology: Social Issues and Questions.*

ROBERT R. HOLT received his Ph.D. from Harvard University. He was a clinical psychologist in the Veterans Administration and the director of psychological staff at the Menninger Foundation. He was also director of the Research Center for Mental Health at New York University, where he is emeritus professor of psychology. For many years he held a Research Career Award from the National Institute of Mental Health.

MARDI J. HOROWITZ is professor of psychiatry at the University of California, San Francisco, where he directs the Center for the Study of Neuroses and the John D. and Catherine T. MacArthur Foundation's Program on Conscious and Unconscious Mental Processes. He has received the foundation's Fund Prize, the Strecker Award, the Royer Award, and various outstanding achievement or distinguished scientist awards. His books include *Stress Response Syndromes, States of Mind,* and *Introduction to Psychodynamics: A New Synthesis.*

IRVING L. JANIS (now deceased) was emeritus professor of psychology at Yale University. He was a leading contributor to research on psychological stress, attitude change, and decisionmaking. Janis was author of the well-known book *Stress and Frustration* and co-author (with L. Mann) of the highly influential book *Decision Making.* In recognition of his many theoretical and empirical contributions to scientific psychology, the American Psychological Association presented its Distinguished Scientic Contributions Award to Professor Janis in August 1981. Among Janis's other special honors and awards were the Hofheimer Prize of the American Psychiatric Association (1958), the American Association for the Advancement of Science Socio-Psychological Prize (1967), and election to the American Academy of Arts and Sciences (1974).

EDWARD S. KATKIN is professor of psychology at the State University of New York at Stony Brook. He received his Ph.D. in clinical psychology from Duke University. His research has focused on investigating individual differences in psychophysiological components of emotions, psychopathology, and visceral self-perception and self-control. He is a past president of the Society for Psychophysiological Research and is co-editor (with S. B. Manuck) of the two-volume series, *Advances in Behavioral Medicine.*

RICHARD S. LAZARUS is professor emeritus of psychology at the University of California at Berkeley. His many years of leadership in the research field of stress and coping and his influential conceptual contributions have won him worldwide recognition and honors, including the American Psychological Association's Distinguished Scientific Contribution Award in 1989. Among his numerous publications is his most recent book, *Emotion and Adaptation* (1991).

ELLINOR F. MAJOR is a research psychologist investigating Norwegian non-Jewish concentration camp survivors and their children at the Division of Disaster Psychiatry, University of Oslo/The Norwegian Armed Forces, Joint Medical Services. She graduated from the University of Oslo.

GEORGE MANDLER received his Ph.D. from Yale University. He taught at Harvard University and the University of Toronto before moving to the University of California, San Diego, as founding chair of their Psychology Department. He has been a fellow of the Center for Advanced Study in the Behavioral Sciences, a J. S. Guggenheim Fellow, and he received the William James Award of the American Psychological Association. His books include *The Language of Psychology* (with W. Kessen), *Thinking: From Association to Gestalt* (with J. M. Mandler), *Mind and Emotion, Mind and Body: Psychology of Emotion and Stress,* and *Cognitive Psychology: An Essay in Cognitive Science.*

ROBERT R. MCCRAE is research psychologist in the Section on Stress and Coping, Gerontology Research Center, National Institute on Aging. His research interests include personality structure and assessment, psychological well-being, and aging. He is the co-author (with Paul T. Costa, Jr.) of *Personality in Adulthood.*

BRUCE S. MCEWEN is head of the Laboratory of Neuroendocrinology at The Rockefeller University, where he received his Ph.D. in cell biology. After postdoctoral work in Sweden in neuroscience, he returned to Rockefeller University to work as a neuroscientist with the psychologist, Neal Miller. His research interests center on the neurobiology of stress.

DONALD MEICHENBAUM is professor of clinical psychology at the University of Waterloo, Ontario. He received his Ph.D. from the University of Illinois. One of the founders of Cognitive Behavior Modification, he is the author of several books, including *Cognitive Behavior Modification, Coping with Stress,* and *Stress Inoculation Training.* He is the editor of the Plenum Series on Stress and Coping and serves on the editorial boards of a dozen journals, including *Cognitive Therapy and Research.* Dr. Meichenbaum is a fellow of the Royal Society of Canada and the recipient of the Izaak Killam Fellowship.

SCOTT MENDELSON is a fellow in the Medical Scholars Program at the College of Medicine of the University of Illinois. He received his Ph.D. in psychology at the University of British Columbia. In his doctoral dissertation he evaluated the roles of subtypes of serotonin receptors in the modulation of sexual behavior. He also has been a National Research Service Award Fellow in the Laboratory of Neuroendocrinology at The Rockefeller University.

ANDREW H. MILLER is an assistant professor of psychiatry at the Mount Sinai School of Medicine. He holds an M.D. and was given a Research Scientist Development Award from the National Institute of Mental Health. Dr. Miller has conducted both basic and clinical research on the relationship between the hypothalamic-pituitary-adrenal axis and the immune system. He has also investigated immune function in patients with depression and recently edited a book entitled *Depressive Disorders and Immunity.*

THOMAS W. MILLER is a professor in the Department of Psychiatry and Department of Psychology, University of Kentucky, and chief of the Psychology Service, at the Veterans Administration and University of Kentucky Medical Centers. Dr. Miller received his Ph.D. from the State University of New York at Buffalo, and is a diplomate in clinical psychology of the American Board of Professional Psychology. He is the author of more than 80 articles and several books, including *Stressful Life Events.* His research investigations have addressed child abuve, domestic violence, divorce and separation, airline disasters, and wartime experiences and natural disasters.

RUDOLF H. MOOS is research center scientist and director of the Center for Health Care Evaluation at the Department of Veterans Affairs and Stanford University Medical Centers in Palo Alto, California. He also is a professor in the Department of Psychiatry at Stanford

University. He has written extensively about life stressors and coping processes, has conducted long-term evaluation projects on substance abuse and depression, and has developed a set of scales to measure social environments.

SUZANNE C. OUELLETTE is professor of psychology at the Graduate School and University Center of The City University of New York. She is a faculty member in the Social/Personality Psychology Doctoral Program and directs the Health Psychology Research Training Program at CUNY. She holds graduate degrees in theology (Yale University) and psychology (University of Chicago). She is currently leading two stress research projects, one examining the association between stress and lupus flare in women with lupus and the other on the stress and stress-resistance of volunteers in AIDS work.

LEONARD I. PEARLIN is a research sociologist and professor in the Human Development and Aging Program at the Center for Social and Behavioral Sciences, University of California, San Fransisco. For many years, he has been conducting a program of research in the social origins of stress and coping.

HERBERT S. PEYSER is consultant psychiatrist to the Smithers Alcoholism Center of St. Luke's-Roosevelt Hospital Center, and assistant clinical professor of psychiatry and associate attending psychiatrist at The Mount Sinai Medical Center, New York City. He is chairman of the Committee on Addiction Psychiatry of the New York State Psychiatric Association and is chairman of the Committee on Mental Health of the Medical Society of the State of New York. He received his M.D. from the Columbia University College of Physicians and Surgeons and is a Diplomate of the American Board of Psychiatry and Neurology. Among his publications is *Alcoholism: A Practical Treatment Guide,* to which he both contributed and edited (with S. Gitlow).

AYALA M. PINES is a research associate in the psychology department at the University of California, Berkeley. The co-author of *Experiencing Social Psychology* and *Burnout: From Tedium to Personal Growth.* Dr. Pines has studied and written extensively about burnout.

ROBERT S. PYNOOS is Director, Program in Trauma, Violence and Sudden Bereavement at the UCLA Department of Psychiatry and Biobehavioral Sciences. He was the 1991–1992 President of the International Society for Traumatic Stress Studies. He is co-editor of *Posttraumatic Stress Disorder in Children* and *Preventing Mental Health Disturbances in Childhood.* Dr. Pynoos holds M.D. and M.P.H. degrees and has been chair of the American Psychiatric Association's Corresponding Task Force on Psychiatric Dimensions of Disasters and the William T. Grant Consortium on Adolescent Bereavement. He is the recipient of many awards, including the 1991 National Organization for Victim Assistance, Stephen Schafer Award for outstanding contributions in the field of research.

JUDITH GODWIN RABKIN is research scientist, New York State Psychiatric Institute, and associate professor of clinical psychology, in psychiatry, College of Physicians and Surgeons, Columbia University. She received her Ph.D. in clinical psychology from New York University in 1967 and her M.P.H. degree in epidemiology in 1978 from the Columbia University School of Public Health. In addition to publications in the area of stress research in *Science* and Psychological Bulletin, she has published a study of ethnic density and risk for psychiatric hospitalization in the *American Journal of Psychiatry* and is co-editor (with D. F. Klein) of a volume on research in anxiety.

KAREN G. RAPHAEL is assistant professor of public health (epidemiology) in psychiatry at Columbia University. She received her Ph.D. in psychology from Hofstra University. She is currently involved in a family study on stress, chronic pain, and depression. Additional research interests include issues of mood-congruent recall and reporting biases.

RENA L. REPETTI received her Ph.D. in clinical psychology from Yale University and is an assistant professor in the Department of Psychology at the University of California, Los Angeles. Her research is in the area of stress and coping in the family and, in particular, she has studied the effects of occupational stressors on health and family functioning. Among her recent publications are an article in the *Journal of Personality and Social Psychology* describing the effects of daily workload on marital interaction and an *American Psychologist* article, with Karen Matthews and Ingrid Waldron, on the effects of employment on women's health.

RAY H. ROSENMAN received his A.B. and M.D. from the University of Michigan. At present, he is associate chief of medicine at Mount Zion Hospital in San Francisco and director of cardiovascular research at SRI International in Menlo Park. He has devoted half of his time to clinical cardiology and half to research, and he is co-founder of the type A behavior pattern concept. His studies have been widely published in journals and books, he is author or co-author of four books, and he holds membership in many clinical, research, and honorary societies.

JEANNE A. SCHAEFER is a research health scientist, Department of Veterans Affairs and Stanford University Medical Centers, Palo Alto, California. She is involved in a study of stressors and coping among staff in long-term care. She has authored and co-authored articles that focus on life crises and personal growth, coping with physical illness and life crises, and the evaluation of health care work settings.

SHARON SCHWARTZ is assistant clinical professor in epidemiology at Columbia University, where she received her Ph.D. in sociology and M.S. in epidemiology. Her research focuses on the relationship between social factors and psychiatric disorders.

HANS SELYE (now deceased) was professor at the University of Montreal and president of the International Institute of Stress and the Hans Selye Foundation. His famous and revolutionary concept of stress opened countless new avenues of treatment through the discovery that hormones participate in the development of many degenerative diseases. He was the author of 38 books and more than 1,700 technical articles.

JUDITH T. SHUVAL received her Ph.D. in sociology from Harvard University. She is the Louis and Pearl Rose Professor of Medical Sociology at the Hebrew University of Jerusalem, where she directs the Programme in Medical Sociology at the School of Public Health. She has served as chair of the Israel Sociological Association, on the executive committee of the European Society for Medical Sociology, as consultant to the World Health Organization, and on the editorial board of *Social Science and Medicine* and other professional journals. One of her manny books, *Immigrants on the Threshold* won the prestigious Israel Prize for the Social Sciences. She is also the author of *Social Functions of Medical Practice* (1970), *Entering Medicine: The Dynamics of Transition* (1980), *Newcomers and Colleagues: Soviet Immigrant Physicians in Israel* (1983), and *Social Dimensions of Health: The Israeli Experience* (1992).

ARON W. SIEGMAN is currently professor of psychology and Director of the Behavioral Medicine Program at the University of Maryland, Baltimore County. He has also been on the faculties of Bar-Ilan University and Ben-Gurion University in Israel. He received his

Ph.D. from Columbia University in 1957. He is co-editor (with Stanley Feldstein) of *Nonverbal Behavior and Communication*, (with Theodore M. Dembroski) of *In Search of Coronary-Prone Behavior*, and (with Timothy W. Smith) of *Anger, Hostility, and the Heart*. His recent publications concern the control of emotions and their physiological manifestations.

ANDREW SKODOL is associate professor of psychiatry at the Columbia University College of Physicians and Surgeons and research psychiatrist at the New York State Psychiatric Institute. He is a graduate of Yale University and holds an M.D. from the University of Pennsylvania School of Medicine; he trained as a resident at the Albert Einstein College of Medicine. His research focuses on psychiatric diagnosis and issues of classification, including assessment methods, multiaxial evaluation, and personality disorders. He is the author of *Problems in Differential Diagnosis: From DSM-III to DSM-III-R in Clinical Practice* and co-author of the *DMS-III-R Casebook*.

SUSAN B. SORENSON earned her Ph.D. in clinical psychology at the University of Cincinnati, received post-doctoral training in psychiatric epidemiology, and now teaches and conducts research at the School of Public Health at the University of California, Los Angeles. Her research focuses on public health views of violence prevention and victimization, including homicide, suicide, sexual assault, battering, and child abuse. Since 1986, Dr. Sorenson has taught a graduate-level course on family and sexual violence, and in her clinical practice she works with individuals who have been victimized in some way or who have lost a loved one in a sudden violent manner. In 1990, Dr. Sorenson received the Chaim Danieli Young Professional Award for excellence in service and research in the field of traumatic stress from the Society for Traumatic Stress Studies.

MARVIN STEIN is the Esther and Joseph Klingenstein Professor of Psychiatry at the Mount Sinai School of Medicine. After chairing the department for over 15 years, he resigned to devote his efforts to research. A medical doctor, he is a pioneer in the investigation of brain, behavior, and the immune system, and he has published extensively in this area. He has chaired and served on numerous committees of the National Institute of Mental Health, and he has been president of the American Psychosomatic Society and the Academy of Behavioral Medicine Research.

ALAN M. STEINBERG is a member of the faculty at the Department of Developmental and Cell Biology, University of California, Irvine. He received his Ph.D. from the Department of Psychiatry and Biobehavioral Sciences, University of California, Los Angeles. In addition to his theoretical and empirical contributions to the field of stress research, he teaches biomedical ethics, including legal and ethical issues related to treatment and research with traumatized children and adolescents.

JOHANN M. STOYVA is an associate professor of psychology in the Department of Psychiatry at the University of Colorado Health Sciences Center. He received his B.A. and M.A. at the University of British Columbia and his Ph.D. in psychology at the University of Chicago. His worked has focused on biofeedback and behavioral techniques as applied to stress-related disorders, and he has also studied of sleep, dreaming, and hypnosis. He is a former president of the Biofeedback Society of America and was editor of the society's journal, *Biofeedback and Self-regulation*.

ANN STUEVE is assistant professor of public health, epidemiology, at Columbia University and Research Scientist at the Research Foundation for Mental Hygiene at New York State Psychiatric Institute. She received her M.A. in human development from the University of

Chicago and her Ph.D. in sociology from the University of California, Berkeley. Her research interests focus on the relationships among stress, social support, and psychopathology and on the impact of mental illness on families.

SHELLEY E. TAYLOR is professor of psychology and director of the Health Psychology Program at the University of California, Los Angeles, She received her Ph.D. from Yale University. Her research interests are social cognition and health psychology. Professor Taylor has received several awards for her work, including the American Psychological Association's Distinguished Scientific Award for an Early Career Contribution to Psychology and a Research Scientist Development Award. In addition to her journal articles, she is the author of *Health Psychology* and *Positive Illusions* and a co-author of *Social Cognition.*

ALAN VAUX is associate professor of psychology at Southern Illinois University. He earned a Ph.D. in psychology from Trinity College, Dublin, and an M.A. and Ph.D. in social ecology at the University of California, Irvine. He is the author of *Social Support: Theory, Research, and Intervention* and a fellow of the American Psychological Association.

LARS WEISÆTH, is professor of disaster psychiatry at the University of Oslo and director of the Department of Psychology of the Joint Norwegian Armed Forces Medical Services. He holds an M.D. and has done extensive research on human responses to dangerous situations, the etiology and psychopathology of post-traumatic stress disorder, and preventive psychology, particularly in the area of traumatic stress. He has studied stress among peacekeeping troops in Lebanon and participated in World Health Organization mental health missions to countries at war.

SUSAN K. F. WINE is a graduate student in clinical psychology at the State University of New York at Stony Brook. She has been engaged in research on individual differences in visceral self-perception and on the effects of anti-adrenergic drugs on cardiovascular reactivity to psychological stress.

PART I

INTRODUCTION

Stress Research at a Crossroads

Shlomo Breznitz   Leo Goldberger

ORIENTATION TO STRESS

The proliferation of research on stress over the past two decades makes it difficult to penetrate the universe of discourse in this area. Nonetheless, we shall try to identify the basic themes in the literature.

Stressors are external events or conditions that affect the organism. The description of stressors and their impact on behavior is an open-ended task, and current research considers an increasing number of events and conditions to be stressors. Most of this effort is still in the qualitative domain and parametric investigations are by and large rare.

The stressors themselves impinge on an organism that has specific characteristics of its own. Thus, another open-ended challenge is the systematic exposure of different species to a particular stressor. Such research can provide insight into phylogenetic and evolutionary processes, as well as into the general themes that cut across species boundaries. Within the same species it is, of course, possible to investigate the impact of a given stressor on different organisms, and the study of individual differences is a rapidly growing branch of stress research. The individual differences of most relevance in human research have to do with the *cognitive appraisal* of stressors. In line with Lazarus's (1966: Lazarus & Launier, 1978) formulation, cognitive appraisal plays a major role in the transaction between the person and the potentially stressful environment. Accordingly, researchers have sought to uncover the differential effects of a variety of cognitive styles upon the impact of stressors.

Another central element in the adaptational equation relates to *coping*. After appraising the stressor, the organism will use one or more coping strategies in an attempt to adjust to the situation. A relatively large body of stress research addresses various coping strategies. Here, again, the issue of individual differences and predispositions plays a key role.

Finally, investigators are interested in stress effects themselves. Ranging all the way from minor changes in behavior to dramatic clinical symptoms, such effects are often viewed as the raison d'être for stress research and stress management approaches.

Somewhere between the stressor and its effects lies the subjective, phenomenological experience of stress itself. Although from the individual's point of view experiencing stress is the most germane factor in confronting stressful conditions, such experience lies outside the realm of objective inquiry.

Accordingly, behaviors classified as stress effects can also be categorized as the effects of anxiety, the effects of conflict, etc. Insofar as expressions of emotion, performance deterioration, or symptom manifestations are concerned, stress is interchangeable with these other concepts. Its unique features thus have to be more specifically elaborated.

As this volume illustrates, there is substantial disagreement over the definition of *stress*. Different scholars have different definitions and oftentimes abide by those most suitable to the pursuit of their particular interests. Thus, for instance, Selye's (1956) focus on the nonspecific *general adaptation syndrome* forces an extreme response based definition, and the exact nature of the stressor becomes largely irrelevant. By contrast, Lazarus's (1966) focus on cognitive appraisal presumes that specific kinds of information are operative in appraising a particular stimulus as a stressor. Although this lack of agreement on the definition of stress is seen by some as indicative of a paradigm crisis, the absense of consensus more properly reflects the rapid expansion of stress research in many divergent directions and may be more conducive to future theorizing than a premature closure (see Kaplan, 1964, for a cogent argument on tolerance of ambiguity in the conduct of inquiry).

Whereas diversity in definition and emphasis may be helpful, such is not the case, however, with research tools. One of the main reasons that many basic questions relating to the effects of stress on adjustment remain unresolved is the lack of standardization in choosing the stressor, measuring its parameters and effects, and selecting the subjects for specific experiments. The absence of an adequate taxonomy of stressful situations and the paucity of parametric research in this area make it difficult to compare results from different studies. The systematic accumulation of knowledge cannot proceed without comprehensive, long-term research.

FUTURE DIRECTIONS

Reviewing the state of the art from the vantage point of the *Handbook of Stress,* we can trace some major ideas and biases in stress research. The following review points out broad themes and suggests possible directions for scientific inquirys in the future.

Repeated Exposure to Stressors

From Selye's initial formulation of the general adaptation syndrome to the diametrically opposite notion of *stress inoculation,* the analysis of the potential impact of repeated stressors is at the core of many theories (e.g., Breznitz, 1980; Frankenhaeuser, 1980). Investigators are interested in learning whether repeated exposure to the same stressors will result ultimately in immunization, habituation, or breakdown.

Duration of Exposure to Stressors

Our understanding of adaptation will be seriously deficient as long as we are unable properly to estimate the impact of duration of exposure to stressors on behavior. This need is particularly critical in the analysis of chronic versus acute stressors. In both epidemiological and clinical research on risk factors conducive to somatic as well as psychiatric problems, the relatively minor but everyday stressors seem to be emerging as the main culprit.

Pacing of Stressors

A question related to repetition and duration of exposure is the interstressor interval. What is the rate at which stressors follow one another? Is there a critical threshold in terms of pacing? The *recent life changes paradigm* is a case in point. Proponents of this view argue that different kinds of events produce a cumulative deleterious impact only if they follow one another at a rate above a certain critical level (Breznitz, 1972; Cleary, 1979; Holmes & Masuda, 1974; Lloyd, Alexander, Rice, & Greenfield, 1980).

Recovery from Stress

A crucial but neglected area in understanding stress concerns the temporal characteristics of recovery from stressful encounters. Repeated exposure, duration, and pacing are intimately associated with the recovery function.

THE OPTIMISTIC BIAS

Although stress research is concerned mainly with maladjustment, interest in successful coping is increasingly apparent in the field. The major displacement of focus from the concept of *anxiety*, which relates primarily to an internal, personal problem, to the concept of *stress*, which is basically an external, environmental problem, deserves analysis. In our view, this shift indicates a tendency toward the denial of major and often unmanageable difficulties. Advocates of the new approach argue that since stress is caused by factors "out there," it is necessary only to devise ways to change the stressful features of the environment and all will be well. This view may to a certain extent account for the proliferation in Western societies of simplistic techniques of stress management. In any event, the domain of stress research now puts heavy emphasis on coping. Interest in coping strategies and predispositions, as well as in the teaching of coping skills, indicates an essentially optimistic bias. Whether pursued in the military or in the wide variety of stress inoculation programs, these practices rest on the assumption that given the right tools, one can cope effectively with most sources of stress.

Another sign of this optimistic outlook is the importance accorded the idea of control. Many workers in the field make the value judgment (implicitly or explicitly) that an internal locus of control is preferable to an external one; they argue that self-control can be used effectively to combat the potentially deleterious effects of stress. However, many critical stressors do not leave room for control, and passive acceptance may be the most appropriate coping strategy in such situations (e.g., Lazarus, 1982; Selye, 1956).

THE PSYCHOLOGY OF HEALTH

We suggest that stress research and theory are about to undergo a major change in emphasis—a change that may be yet another expression of the "optimistic bias" just noted. Concern with the negative, illness related impacts of stress will gave way to consideration of stress as a force conducive to health. Although health is still defined primarily as the lack of illness, the absence of symptoms is a very limited and unsatisfactory criterion of well-being. A concept denoting the *opposite* of stress would enrich our way of looking at person-environment interactions. In other words, can the active influence of positive factors in principle enhance health? Just as Lazarus and Launier (1978) posited daily uplifts as the opposite of daily hassles, some events may act as *antistressors*. Indeed, stress itself may produce positive effects. Selye (1974) saw the need to coin the concept of *eustress* essentially to account for certain seemingly harmless or even beneficial stressors. In Chapter 14, Haan, referring to her own research (1977), makes the point that stress can lead to gains as well as losses. (This issue has been examined by Breznitz and Eshel [1982] and by Yarom [1982].) Unless our sense of direction is off the mark, psychology and medicine will see an upsurge of interest along the above lines, and the field of stress will significantly increase its relevance.

REFERENCES

BREZNITZ, S. *The effect of frequency and pacing of warnings upon the fear reaction to a threatening event.* Jerusalem: Ford Foundation, 1972.

————. Stress in Israel. In H. Selye (ed.), *Selye's guide to stress research,* vol. 1. New York: Van Nostrand, 1980.

BREZNITZ, S., & ESHEL, J. Life events: Stressful ordeal or valuable experience? In S. Breznitz (ed.), *Stress in Israel.* New York: Van Nostrand, 1982.

CLEARY, P. J. *Life events and disease: A review of methodology and findings.* Stockholm: Laboratory for Clinical Stress Research, 1979.

FRANKENHAEUSER, M. Psychoneuroendocrine approaches to the study of stressful person-environment transactions. In H. Selye (ed.), *Selye's guide to stress research,* vol. 1. New York: Van Nostrand, 1980.

HAAN, N. *Coping and defending: Processes of self-environment organization.* New York: Academic, 1977.

HOLMES, T. H., & MASUDA, M. Life changes and illness susceptibility. In B. S. Dohrenwend & B. P. Dohrenwend (eds.), *Stressful life events: Their nature and effects.* New York: Wiley, 1974.

KAPLAN, A. *The conduct of inquiry: Methodology for behavioral science.* San Francisco: Chandler, 1964.

LAZARUS, R. S. *Psychological stress and the coping process.* New York: McGraw-Hill, 1966.

————. The costs and benefits of denial. In S. Breznitz (ed.), *The denial of stress.* New York: International Universities, 1982.

LAZARUS, R. S., & LAUNIER, R. Stress-related transactions between person and environment. In L. A. Pervin and M. Lewis (eds.), *Perspectives in interactional psychology.* New York: Plenum, 1978.

LLOYD, C., ALEXANDER, A. A., RICE, D. G., & GREEFIELD, N. S. Life change and academic performance. *Journal of Human Stress,* 1980, *6,* 15–25.

SELYE, H. *The stress of life.* New York: McGraw-Hill, 1956.

————. *Stress without distress.* Philadelphia: Lippincott, 1974.

YAROM, N. Facing death in war: An existential crisis. In S. Breznitz (ed.), *Stress in Israel.* New York: Van Nostrand, 1982.

2

History of the Stress Concept

Hans Selye

NOWADAYS, EVERYONE SEEMS TO BE TALKING about stress. You hear about this topic not only in daily conversation but also on television, via radio, in the newspapers, and in the ever increasing number of conferences, centers, and university courses devoted to stress. Yet remarkably few people define the concept in the same way or even bother to attempt a clear-cut definition. The businessperson thinks of stress as frustration or emotional tension; the air traffic controller, as a problem in concentration; the biochemist and endocrinologist, as a purely chemical event; and the athlete, as muscular tension. This list could be extended to almost every human experience or activity, and, somewhat surprisingly, most people—be they chartered accountants, short-order cooks, or surgeons—consider their own occupation the most stressful. Similarly, most commentators believe that ours is the "age of stress," forgetting that the caveman's fear of attack by wild animals or of death from hunger, cold, or exhaustion must have been just as stressful as our fear of a world war, the crash of the stock exchange, or overpopulation.

Ironically, there is a grain of truth in every formulation of stress because all demands upon our adaptability do evoke the stress phenomenon. But we tend to forget that there would be no reason to use the single word "stress" to describe such diverse circumstances as those mentioned above were there not something common to all of them, just as we could have no reason to use a single word in connection with the production of light, heat, cold, or sound if we had been unable to formulate the concept of energy, which is required to bring about any of these effects. My definition of *stress* is the *nonspecific* (that is, common) *result of any demand upon the body,* be the effect mental or somatic. The formulation of this definition, based on objective indicators such as bodily and chemical changes that appear after any demand, has brought the subject (so popular now that it is often referred to as "stressology") up from the level of cocktail party chitchat into the domain of science.

One of the first things to bear in mind about stress is that a variety of dissimilar situations—emotional arousal, effort, fatigue, pain, fear, concentration, humiliation, loss of blood, and even great and unexpected success—are capable of producing stress; hence, no single factor can, in itself, be pinpointed as the cause of the reaction as such. To understand this point, it is necessary to consider certain facts about human biology. Medical research has shown that while people may face quite different problems, in some respects their bodies

7

respond in a stereotyped pattern; identical biochemical changes enable us to cope with any type of increased demand on vital activity. This is also true of other animals and apparently even of plants. In all forms of life, it would seem that there are common pathways that must mediate any attempt to adapt to environmental conditions and sustain life.

HISTORICAL DEVELOPMENT

Even prehistoric man must have recognized a common element in the sense of exhaustion that overcame him in conjunction with hard labor, agonizing fear, lengthy exposure to cold or heat, starvation, loss of blood, or any kind of disease. Probably he soon discovered also that his response to prolonged and strenuous exertion passed through three stages: first the task was experienced as a hardship; then he grew used to it; and finally he could stand it no longer. The vague outlines of this intuitive scheme eventually were brought into sharper focus and translated into precise scientific terms that could be appraised by intellect and tested by reason. Before turning to contemporary science, it will be helpful to review some of the intervening developments that laid the foundation for the modern theory of stress.

In ancient Greece, Hippocrates, often considered the "father of medicine," clearly recognized the existence of a *vis medicatrix naturae,* or healing power of nature, made up of inherent bodily mechanisms for restoring health after exposure to pathogens. But early investigations were handicapped by the failure to distinguish between distress, always unpleasant, and the general concept of stress, which also encompasses experiences of intense joy and the pleasure of self-expression.

The nineteenth-century French physiologist Bernard (1879) enormously advanced the subject by pointing out that the internal environment of a living organism must remain fairly constant despite changes in the external environment: "It is the fixity of the *milieu intérieur* which is the condition of free and independent life" (p. 564). This comment had enormous impact; indeed, the Scottish physiologist Haldane (1922) was of the opinion that "no more pregnant sentence was ever framed by a physiologist" (p. 427). But this influence was due largely to various meanings that subsequently were read into Bernard's formulation. Actually, inanimate objects are more independent of their surroundings than are living beings. What distinguishes life is adaptability to change, not fixity. Bernard's more enduring legacy was the stimulation of later investigators to carry forward his pioneering studies on the particular adaptive changes by which the steady state is maintained.

The German physiologist Pflüger (1877) crystallized the relationship between active adaptation and the steady state when he noted that "the cause of every need of a living being is also the cause of the satisfaction of that need" (p. 57). The Belgian physiologist Fredericq (1885) expressed a similar view: "The living being is an agency of such sort that each disturbing influence induces by itself the calling forth of compensatory activity to neutralize or repair the disturbance" (p. 34).

In this century, the great American physiologist Cannon (1939) suggested the name "homeostasis," from the Greek *homoios,* meaning similar, and *stasis,* meaning position, for "the coordinated physiologic processes which maintain most of the steady states in the organism" (p. 333). Homeostasis might roughly be translated "staying power." Cannon's classic studies established the existence of many highly specific mechanisms for protection against hunger, thirst, hemorrhage, or agents tending to disturb normal body temperature, blood pH, or plasma levels of sugar, protein, fat, and calcium. He particularly emphasized the stimulation of the sympathetic nervous system, with the resulting hormonal discharge from the adrenal glands, which occurs during emergencies such as pain or rage. In turn, this autonomic process induces the cardiovascular changes that prepare the body for flight or fight.

It was against this cumulative background that, as a medical student, I eventually was drawn to the problem of a stereotyped response to any exacting task. The initial focus of my interest was what I thought of as the "syndrome of just being sick." In my second year of training I was struck by how patients suffering from the most diverse diseases exhibited strikingly similar signs and symptoms, such as loss of weight and appetite, diminished muscular strength, and absence of ambition. In 1936, the problem presented itself under conditions suited to analysis. While seeking a new ovarian hormone, co-workers and I at McGill University injected extracts of cattle ovaries into rats to see whether their organs would display unpredictable changes that could not be attributed to any known hormone. Three types of changes were produced: (1) the cortex, or outer layer, of the adrenal glands became enlarged and hyperactive; (2) the thymus, spleen, lymph nodes, and all other lymphatic structures shrank; and (3) deep, bleeding ulcers appeared in the stomach and upper intestines. Being closely interdependent, these changes formed a definite syndrome (see Figure 2–1).

FIGURE 2–1. Typical triad of alarm reaction: (A) adrenals; (B) thymus; (C) group of three lymph nodes; and (D) inner surface of stomach. The organs on the left are those of a normal rat; those on the right, of a rat exposed to the frustrating psychological stress of being immobilized. Note the marked enlargement and dark discoloration of the adrenals caused by congestion and the discharge of fatty secretion granules; the intense shrinkage of the thymus and the lymph nodes; and the numerous blood covered stomach ulcers in the alarmed rat (*from Selye, 1952:225*).

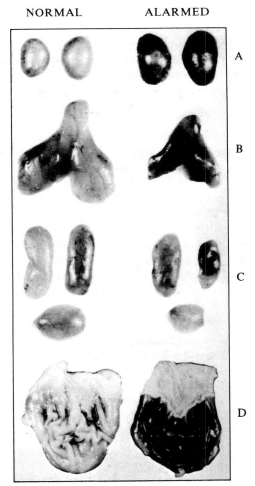

NORMAL   ALARMED

It was soon discovered that all toxic substances, irrespective of their source, produced the same pattern of responses. Moreover, identical organ changes were evoked by cold, heat, infection, trauma, hemorrhage, nervous irritation, and many other stimuli. Gradually, I realized that this was an experimental replica of the "syndrome of just being sick," which I had noted a decade earlier. Adrenal enlargement, gastrointestinal ulcers, and thymicolymphatic shrinkage were constant and invariable signs of damage to a body faced with the demand of meeting the attack of any disease. These changes became recognized as objective indices of stress and furnished a basis for developing the entire stress concept.

The reaction was first described in *Nature* as "a syndrome produced by diverse nocuous agents." Subsequently it became known as the *general adaptation syndrome* (GAS) or *biologic stress syndrome* (Selye, 1936). In the same report, I also suggested the name "alarm reaction" for the initial response, arguing that it probably represented the somatic expression of a generalized call to arms of the body's defensive forces.

THE GENERAL ADAPTATION SYNDROME

The alarm reaction, however, was evidently not the entire response. After continued exposure of the organism to any noxious agent capable of eliciting this reaction, a stage of adaptation or resistance ensues. In other words, a state of alarm cannot be maintained continuously. If the agent is so drastic that continued exposure becomes incompatible with life, the animal dies during the alarm reaction (that is, within the first hours or days). If the organism can survive, this initial reaction is necessarily followed by the *stage of resistance*. The manifestations of this second phase are quite different from, and in many instances the exact opposite of, those that characterize the alarm reaction. For example, during the alarm reaction, the cells of the adrenal cortex discharge their secretory granules into the bloodstream and thus become depleted of corticoid-containing lipid storage material; in the stage of resistance, on the other hand, the cortex becomes particularly rich in secretory granules. In the alarm reaction, there is hemoconcentration, hypochloremia, and general tissue catabolism, whereas during the stage of resistance there is hemodilution, hyperchloremia, and anabolism, with a return toward normal body weight.

Curiously, after still more exposure to the noxious agent, the acquired adaptation is lost. The animal enters into a third phase, the *stage of exhaustion,* which inexorably follows as long as the demand is severe enough and applied for a sufficient length of time. It should be pointed out that the triphasic nature of the general adaptation syndrome gave us the first indication that the body's adaptability, or *adaptation energy,* is finite, since, under constant stress, exhaustion eventually ensues. We still do not know precisely what is lost, except that it is not merely caloric energy: food intake is normal during the stage of resistance. Hence, one would think that once adaptation had occurred and ample energy was available, resistance would go on indefinitely. But just as any inanimate machine gradually wears out, so does the human machine sooner or later become the victim of constant wear and tear. These three stages are reminiscent of childhood, with its characteristic low resistance and excessive response to any kind of stimulus, adulthood, during which the body has adapted to most commonly encountered agents and resistance is increased, and senility, characterized by loss of adaptability and eventual exhaustion, ending with death.

Our reserves of adaptation energy might be compared to an inherited bank account from which we can make withdrawals but to which we apparently cannot make deposits. After exhaustion from excessively stressful activity, sleep and rest can restore resistance and adaptability very close to previous levels, but complete restoration is probably impossible. Every biologic activity causes wear and tear; it leaves some irreversible chemical scars, which accumulate to constitute the signs of aging. Thus, adaptability should be used wisely and sparingly rather than squandered.

Mechanisms of Stress

Discoveries since 1936 have linked nonspecific stress with numerous biochemical and structural changes of previously unknown origin. There has also been considerable progress in analyzing the mediation of stress reactions by hormones. However, the carriers of the alarm signals that first relay the call for adaptation have yet to be identified. Perhaps they are metabolic by-products released during activity or damage, or perhaps what is involved is the lack of some vital substance consumed whenever any demand is made upon an organ. Since the only two coordinating systems that connect all parts of the body with one another are the nervous and the vascular systems, we can assume that the alarm signals use one or both of these pathways. Yet, while nervous stimulation may cause a general stress response, deafferented rats still show the classic syndrome when exposed to demands; so the nervous system cannot be the only route. It is probable that often, if not always, the signals travel in the blood.

The facts that led us to postulate the existence of the alarm signals would be in agreement with the view that the various cells send out different messengers. In that case the messages must somehow be tallied by the organs of adaptation. Whatever the nature of the *first mediator,* however, its existence is assured by its effects, which have been observed and measured. The discharge of hormones, the involution of the lymphatic organs, the enlargement of the adrenals, the feeling of fatigue, and many other signs of stress can all be produced by injury or activity in any part of the body.

Through the first mediator, the agent or situation disruptive of homeostasis eventually excites the hypothalamus, a complex bundle of nerve cells and fibers that acts as a bridge between the brain and the endocrine system (see Figure 2–2). The resulting nervous signals reach certain neuroendocrine cells in the median eminence (ME) of the hypothalamus, where they are transformed into CRF (corticotrophic hormone releasing factor), a chemical messenger that has not yet been isolated in pure form but is probably a polypeptide. In this way, a message is relayed to the pituitary, causing a discharge into the general circulation of ACTH (adrenocorticotrophic hormone).

ACTH, reaching the adrenal cortex, triggers the secretion of corticoids, mainly glucocorticoids such as cortisol or corticosterone. Through gluconeogenesis these compounds supply a readily available source of energy for the adaptive reactions necessary to meet the demands made by the agent. The corticoids also facilitate various other enzyme responses and suppress immune reactions and inflammation, thereby helping the body to coexist with potential pathogens.

Usually secreted in lesser amounts are the pro-inflammatory corticoids, which stimulate the proliferative ability and reactivity of the connective tissue, enhancing the *inflammatory potential.* Thus, they help to build a strong barricade of connective tissue through which the body is protected against further invasion. Because of their prominent effect upon salt and water metabolism, these hormones have also been refered to as *mineralocorticoids* (e.g., desoxicorticosterone and aldosterone). The somatotrophic hormone (STH), or growth hormone, of the pituitary likewise stimulates defense reactions.

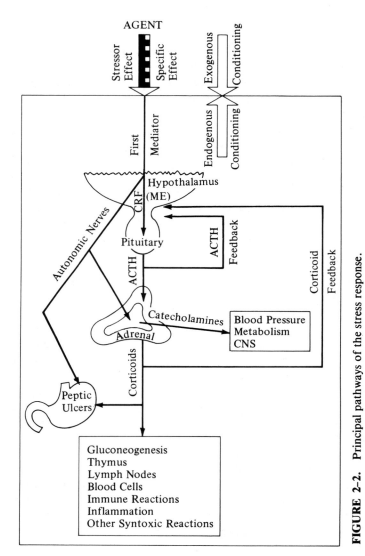

FIGURE 2–2. Principal pathways of the stress response.

This chain of events is cybernetically controlled by several feedback mechanisms. For instance, if there is a surplus of ACTH, a short-loop feedback returns some of it to the hypothalamus-pituitary axis and this shuts off further ACTH production. In addition, through a long-loop feedback, a high blood level of corticoids similarly inhibits too much ACTH secretion.

Simultaneously with all these processes, another important pathway is utilized to mediate the stress response. Hormones such as catecholamines are liberated to activate mechanisms of general usefulness for adaptation. Adrenaline, in particular, is secreted to make energy available, to accelerate the pulse rate, to elevate the blood pressure and the rate of blood circulation in the muscles, and to stimulate the central nervous system (CNS). The blood coagulation mechanism is also enhanced by adrenaline, as a protection against excessive bleeding if injuries are sustained in the state of affairs eliciting stress.

Countless other hormonal and chemical changes during stress check and balance the body's functioning and stability, constituting a virtual arsenal of weapons with which the organism defends itself. The facts known today may lead us to believe that the anterior pituitary and the adrenal cortex play the cardinal roles in stress, but this view probably reflects the active part endocrinologists have taken in elucidating the syndrome. Also, the techniques required to investigate the role of the nervous system are much more complex than those heretofore used. It is considerably easier, for example, to remove an endocrine gland and substitute injected extracts for its hormones than it is to destroy minute nervous centers selectively and then restore their function to determine the role they may play.

Syntoxic and Catatoxic Responses

In the course of human evolution, the body has developed two basic mechanisms for defense against potentially injurious aggressors, whether of external or internal origin. These two types of reactions, on which homeostasis mainly depends, are known as *syntoxic,* from *syn,* meaning together, and *catatoxic,* from *cata,* meaning against. The former help us put up with the aggressor while the latter destroy it. Syntoxic stimuli, acting as tissue tranquilizers, create a state of passive tolerance, which permits peaceful coexistence with aggressors. In the case of catatoxic agents, chemical changes, mainly the induction of destructive enzymes, generate an active attack on the pathogen, usually by accelerating its metabolic degradation.

Corticoids, substances produced by the adrenal cortex, are among the most effective syntoxic hormones. Of these, the best known are the anti-inflammatory group, including cortisone, and related substances that inhibit inflammation and many other defensive immune reactions such as the active rejection of grafted foreign tissues, that is, hearts or kidneys.

The main purpose of inflammation is to prevent the spread of irritants into the bloodstream by localizing them within a barricade. However, when the foreign agent is itself innocuous and causes disease only by inciting an exaggerated defense reaction, the suppression of inflammation is advantageous. Thus, anti-inflammatory corticoids have proved effective in treating diseases whose major complaint is inflammation of the joints, eyes, or respiratory passages.

On the other hand, when the aggressor is dangerous, the defensive reaction should be increased above the normal level. This is accomplished by catatoxic substances carrying a chemical message to the tissues to fight the invader even more actively than usual.

Stressors

The agents or demands that evoke the patterned response are referred to, quite naturally, as *stressors*. Something is thus a stressor to the same degree that it calls forth the syndrome. Stressors, it should be noted, are not exclusively physical in nature. Emotions—love, hate, joy, anger, challenge, and fear—as well as thoughts, also call forth the changes characteristic of the stress syndrome. In fact, psychological arousal is one of the most frequent activators. Yet it cannot be regarded as the only factor, since typical stress reactions can occur in patients exposed to trauma, hemorrhage, etc., while under deep anesthesia. Anesthetics themselves are commonly used in experimental medicine to produce stress, and stress of anesthesia is a serious problem in clinical surgery.

STRESS AND DISEASE

In general, the nervous and hormonal responses outlined above aid adaptation to environmental change or stimuli. Sometimes, however, they are the cause of disease, especially if the state of stress is prolonged or intense. In the latter case, the body passes through successive stages of the GAS, described earlier.

As we have seen, a fully developed GAS consists of the alarm reaction, the stage of resistance, and the stage of exhaustion. Yet it is not necessary for all three stages to develop before we can speak of a GAS; only the most severe stress leads rapidly to the stage of exhaustion and death. Most of the physical or mental exertions, infections, and other stressors that act upon us during a limited period produce changes corresponding only to the first and second stages. At first the stressors may upset and alarm us, but then we adapt to them.

Normally, in the course of our lives we go through these first two stages many, many times. Otherwise we could never become adapted to all the activities and demands that are man's lot. Even the stage of exhaustion does not always need to be irreversible and complete, as long as it affects only parts of the body. For instance, running produces a stress situation, mainly in our muscles and cardiovascular system. To cope with this, we first have to limber up and get these systems ready for the task at hand; then for a while we will be at the height of efficiency in running; eventually, however, exhaustion will set in. This sequence could be compared with an alarm reaction, a stage of resistance, and a stage of exhaustion, all limited primarily to the muscular and cardiovascular systems; yet such an exhaustion is reversible—after a good rest we will be back to normal.

It nevertheless remains true that the adaptive response can break down or go wrong because of innate defects, understress, overstress, or psychological mismanagement. The most common stress diseases—the so-called diseases of adaptation—are peptic ulcers in the stomach and upper intestine, high blood pressure, heart accidents, and nervous disturbances. This is a relative concept, however. No malady is just a disease of adaptation. Nor are there any disease producers that can be so perfectly handled by the organism that maladaptation plays no part in their effects upon the body. Such agents would not produce disease. This haziness in its delimitation does not interfere with the practical utility of our concept. We must put up with the same lack of precision whenever we have to classify a disease. There is no pure heart disease, in which all other organs remain perfectly undisturbed, nor can we ever speak of a pure kidney disease or a pure nervous disease in this sense.

The indirect production of disease by inappropriate or excessive adaptive reactions is well illustrated by the following example drawn from everyday life. If you meet a loudly insulting but obviously harmless drunk, nothing will happen if you take the syntoxic attitude of going past and ignoring him. But if you respond catatoxically, by fighting or even only preparing to fight, the outcome may be tragic. You will discharge adrenalinelike hormones that increase blood pressure and pulse rate, while your whole nervous system becomes alarmed and tense. If you happen to be a coronary candidate, you might end up with a fatal brain hemorrhage or cardiac arrest. In that case, your death will have been caused by your own biologically suicidal choice of the wrong reaction.

MODERN RESEARCH

In this short chapter, it is impossible to give a meaningful sketch of all that has been learned about the structure of stress hormones, the nervous pathways involved, the medicines that have been developed to combat stress, and the diagnostic aids that this approach has offered. Nevertheless, the medical, chemical, and microscopic approaches to the problem have all been extremely fruitful. Since the very first description of the GAS, the most important single discovery was made only recently: the brain produces certain simple chemical substances closely related to ACTH. These substances have morphinelike, painkilling properties, and since they come from the inside (*endo*), they have been called *endorphins*. (I am especially proud that one of my former students, Dr. Roger Guillemin, was one of the three American scientists who shared the 1977 Nobel Prize for this remarkable discovery, although it was made at the Salk Institute quite independently of me.) The endorphins have opened up an entirely new field in medicine, particularly in stress research. Not only do they have antistress effects as painkillers, but also they probably play an important role in the transmission of the alarm signal from the brain to the pituitary, and their concentration is especially high in the pituitary itself. Thus, they may shed some light on the nature of the first mediator.

Significant breakthroughs have also been made with the discovery of tranquilizers and psychotherapeutic chemicals to combat mental disease. These have reduced the number of institutionalized mental patients to an unprecedented low. Also worth mentioning are the enormously potent anti-ulcer drugs that block the pathways through which stress ulcers are produced.

However, all these purely medical discoveries are applicable only by physicians, and the general public cannot use them in daily life without constant medical supervision. Futhermore, most of these agents are not actually directed against stress but rather against some of its morbid manifestations (ulcers, high blood pressure, or heart accidents). Therefore, increasing attention has been given to the development of psychological techniques and behavioral codes that anybody can use, after suitable instruction, to adjust to the particular demands made by his life.

Among these not strictly medical approaches are the relaxation techniques. We should spend a little time each day at complete rest, with our eyes closed and our muscles relaxed, breathing regularly and repeating words that are either meaningless or heard so often that they merely help us not think of anything in particular. This is the basis of Transcendental Meditation, Benson's relaxation technique, and an infinite variety of other procedures. These practices should not be underestimated merely because science cannot explain them; they have worked for so long and in so many forms that we must respect them.

More recently, biofeedback has added a great deal to the psychological approach. A number of highly sophisticated instruments have been developed that inform the user constantly about body changes characteristic of stress, for example, in blood pressure, pulse rate, body temperature, and even brain activity. We do not yet have a scientific explanation for biofeedback, but if people learn to identify, instinctively or through instrumentation, when they are under stress, they can automatically avoid, or at least reduce, their responses.

A SCIENTIFIC ETHICS

The drunk illustration I used earlier shows how certain well-known facts about the demands of everyday life can make clearer some of the principles involved in the unconscious, wired-in stress responses mediated by the neurohumoral system. Yet it is also true that the latter can refine our knowledge of the former. Laboratory observations on the body's methods for fighting distress have already helped us to lay the foundations for a biologically justifiable code of behavior, one designed to achieve the pleasant stress of fulfillment (known technically as *eustress*—from the Greek *eu* meaning good, as in euphemia and euphoria) without the harmful consequences of damaging stress, that is, *distress* (Selye, 1974).

At first it seems odd that the laws governing life's responses at such different levels as the cell, the whole person, and even the nation should be so essentially similar. Yet this type of uniformity is true of all great laws of nature. For example, in the inanimate world, arrangement of matter and energy in orbits circulating around a center is characteristic of the largest celestial bodies, as well as of individual atoms. Why is it that on these opposite levels, the smallest and the largest, the satellites circling a huge planet and the minute electrons around an atomic nucleus, should go around in orbits? We find comparable similarities in the laws governing living matter. Countless phenomena run in cycles, such as the periodically recurring needs for food, water, sleep, and sexual activity. Damage is unavoidable unless each cycle runs its full course.

In formulating a natural code of behavior, these thoughts have fundamental importance. We must not only understand the profound biological need for the completion and fulfillment of our aspirations but also know how to handle these in harmony with our particular inherited capacities. Not everybody is born with the same amount of adaptation energy.

Work: A Biological Necessity

Most people consider their work their primary function in life. For the man or woman of action, one of the most difficult things to bear is enforced inactivity during prolonged hospitalization or after retirement. Just as our muscles degenerate if not used, so our brain slips into chaos and confusion unless we constantly use it for work that seems worthwhile to us. The average person thinks he works for economic security or social status, but at the end of a most successful business career—when he finally has achieved this goal—there remains nothing to fight for. There is no hope for progress and only the boredom of assured monotony. The question is not whether we should or should not work, but what kind of work suits us best.

In my opinion, today's insatiable demand for less work and more pay does not depend so much on the number of working hours or dollars as on the degree of dissatisfaction with life. We could do much, and at little cost, by fighting this dissatisfaction. Many people suffer because they have no particular taste for anything, no hunger for achievement. These, and not those who earn little, are the true paupers of mankind. What they need more than money is guidance.

Without the incentive to work out his role as *homo faber,* a person is likely to seek destructive, revolutionary outlets to satisfy the basic human need for self-assertive activity. Man may be able to solve the age-old problem of having to live by the sweat of his brow, but the fatal enemy of all utopias is boredom. What we shall have to do after technology makes most "useful work" redundant is to invent new occupations. Even this will require a full-scale effort to teach "play professions," such as the arts, philosophy, crafts, and science, to the public at large; there is no limit to how much each man can work on perfecting himself and on giving pleasure to others.

"Earn Thy Neighbor's Love"

Each person must find a way to relieve his pent-up energy without creating conflicts with his fellow men. Such an approach not only insures peace of mind but also earns the goodwill, respect, and even love of our neighbors, the highest degree of security and the most noble status symbol to which the human being can aspire.

This philosophy of hoarding a wealth of respect and friendship is merely one reflection of the deep-rooted instinct of people and animals to collect—a tendency as characteristic of ants, bees, squirrels, and beavers as of the capitalist who collects money to put away in the bank. The same impulse drives entire human societies to build systems of roads, telephone networks, cities, and fortifications, which they view as necessary ingredients of their future security and comfort.

In man, this urge first manifests itself when children start to amass matchboxes, shells, or stickers; it continues when adults collect stamps or coins. This natural proclivity is not artificial. By collecting certain things, one acquires status and security in the community. The guideline of earning love merely attempts to direct the hoarding instinct toward what I consider the most permanent and valuable commodity that man can possess: a huge capital of goodwill that protects him against personal attacks by others.

To live literally by the biblical command to "love thy neighbor as thyself" leads only to guilt feelings because this teaching cannot be reconciled with the laws of objective science. Whether we like it or not, egoism is an inescapable characteristic of all living beings. But we can continue to benefit by the wisdom of this time-honored maxim if, in the light of modern biological research, we merely reword it. Let our guide for conduct be the motto "Earn thy neighbor's love."

REFERENCES

BERNARD, C. *Leçons sur les phénomènes de la vie commune aux animaux et aux végétaux,* vol. 2. Paris: Baillière, 1879.

CANNON, W. B. *The wisdom of the body.* New York: Norton, 1939.

FREDERICQ, L. Influence du milieu ambiant sur la composition du sang des animaux aquatiques. *Archives de Zoologie Experimental et Génerale,* 1885, *3,* 34.

HALDANE, J. S. *Respiration.* New Haven: Yale University Press, 1922.

PFLÜGER, E. Die teleologische mechanik der lebendigen *Natur. Pflüger's Archiv für die gesamte Physiologie des menschen umd der tiere,* 1877, *15,* 57.

SELYE, H. A syndrome produced by diverse nocuous agents. *Nature,* 1936, *138,* 32.

————. *The story of the adaptation syndrome.* Montreal: Acta, 1952.

————. *Stress without distress.* Philadephia: Lippincott, 1974.

————. (ed.). *Selye's guide to stress research,* vol. 1. New York: Van Nostrand, 1980.

PART II

BASIC PSYCHOLOGICAL PROCESSES

3

Why We Should Think of Stress as a Subset of Emotion

Richard S. Lazarus

THE 1980S WITNESSED AN EXPLOSION OF INTEREST in emotion, as reflected by the dozens of books and articles that appeared in the social and biological sciences. It is not clear whether this focus implies a waning of interest in psychological stress or a new awareness of the greater psychological, social, and biological scope of the emotions compared with stress. We should recognize that because stress involves negative emotions, it is part of a larger conceptual whole that includes both positive and negative emotions.

The interest in emotion has been fed by a variety of forces in academic and applied disciplines, the most important of which may be the return of cognitivism and a loosening of the radical behaviorism that dominated the social and biological sciences for most of the century. These changes encourage us once again to study the mind and what is in it, as well as action, Emotions are also a centerpiece of all important human adaptational experiences, as dramatists, novelists, and artists always seem to have understood. One of the most powerful and ubiquitous ways of thinking about emotion is that it plays an essential, functional role in species and individual adaptation. Emotions are also powerful influences on how we think and act and on our social relationships. The discipline of psychology cannot be complete without devoting substantial attention to emotion, what brings it about, and how it affects adaptational outcomes.

This chapter explores the contrasts between stress and the emotions and offers a brief account of a cognitive-motivational-relational theory of the emotions that can enrich our ability to understand and predict the individual emotions and facilitate the concerns of clinical practitioners about the role of emotions in psychopathology and treatment.

STRESS AS A UNIDIMENSIONAL CONCEPT

Why should interest shift from stress to the emotions? What might be the sources of resistance to this change? And why should the transition be encouraged? The answer to the first question arises from the fact that the concept of stress has been embraced since World War II. Until the 1960s, stress had been largely defined as destructive environmental demands, a viewpoint consistent with an epistemology that once dominated academic thought. Though it has been expressed in many ways, this epistemology centers on the belief that explanations must hew closely to what can be observed directly in the environmental stimulus and in the behavioral and organismic response. This residual behaviorism is still a factor in the resistance to the modern readiness to examine what people want and think as powerful causal factors in their reactions.

Until recently, if you asked a social scientist to define stress, the implicit model would be an analogue of Hooke's late seventeenth-century engineering principles (Hinkle, 1973). The external force was called the load; stress was the ratio of the pressure on the object created by the load to the size of the area affected; and strain was the deformation of the object. I should note parenthetically with respect to this use of the term stress, that the smaller the ratio the more the strain, because load distributed over a wide area makes it less destructive. Hooke was concerned with the elasticity of metals, and if one's main concern is building bridges or buildings, it is important to be confident that the load can be carried safely.

Why has this engineering analogy proved so durable in physiology, psychology, and sociology? I can think of three reasons: First, it fulfills social science's penchant for studying observables by reference to environmental stimulus rather than to what is going on the mind. To use Gergen's (1985) dichotomy, with its external and internal referents, the focus is exogenic as opposed to endogenic, which is subjective or phenomenological. A medical variant, drawn from Claude Bernard's concept of homeostasis and reflected in the work of Cannon (1939) and Selye (1956/1976), views stress as the deformation or strain itself—that is, the physiological disturbance in response to load (e.g., Wolff, 1953). In this game of words, Selye used the term stress to mean what Hooke had called strain, and stressor for the noxious agents in the environment; however, the words don't matter as long as we are clear about their referents.

Second, if one is interested in individual differences in resiliency in the face of stress, the idea of elasticity offers a useful analogy between physical objects and persons. Metals and building structures differ in their resistance to environmental loads; because some metals, for example, have the capacity to bend rather than break, the characteristics that make them elastic become important from a practical standpoint. At the psychological level, the measurable traits that underlie these differences likewise become important. Indeed, research on some of these traits has been booming—for example, hardiness (Maddi & Kobasa, 1984; Orr & Westman, 1990), sense of coherence (Antonovsky, 1979, 1987, 1990), optimism (Scheier & Carver, 1987), illusions and self-deceptions (Goleman, 1985; Lazarus, 1983; Taylor, 1989), learned resourcefulness (Rosenbaum, 1990); self-efficacy (Bandura, 1982), and constructive thinking (Epstein & Meier, 1989), among others. Whereas—except for learned helplessness (Petersen, Seligman, & Vaillant, 1988), the emphasis was on negative traits such as anxiety and neuroticism, the same basic variables are more often cast today in terms of their positive reciprocal.

Third, the strong interest in quantification in the social sciences favored a simple conceptualization of stress (or strain). This tendency could be found in the once-popular Yerkes-Dodson law (1908) and the related concept of activation, which Duffy (1941) proposed should replace what she saw as the unnecessary and unwieldy concept of emotion. The dimension of activation was comfortable to psychologists in those days as a result of Lindsley's (1951) ideas, which connected it to drive, mental alertness or torpor, and evidence of correlated physiological activities in the brain (e.g., EEG changes or shifts in the reticular activating system). As a result of this kind of reasoning, stress analysis was usually unidimensional, so that the best one could do with the concept was to evaluate stressors or stress reactions on a scale from low to high.

Late in his career, Selye (1974), who had popularized a physiological version of stress as the general adaptation syndrome (GAS) in which the organismic stress reaction was said to be basically the same regardless of the type of stressor, proposed that there were two types of stress, eustress and distress. The latter was said to be destructive to health, the former not. I also (Lazarus, 1966; Lazarus & Folkman, 1984, 1987) sought to complicate the stress concept by suggesting three types—harm/loss, threat, and challenge. By emphasizing the mediating effects of appraisal and coping in the stress process, which I argued were necessary to help us understand individual differences in reaction to common stressors, a strong case was made for abandoning the simple dimension of activation and replacing it with a cognitive-motivational-relational and process formulation that involved the preceding three types of stress processes.

STRESS AS AN ASPECT OF EMOTION

Leaving aside the factor analytic approach, which reduces emotion to a few simplifying dimensions such as pleasantness and activation, a categorical approach to the emotions identifies a set of negative emotions (such as anger, fright, anxiety, shame, guilt, sadness, envy, jealousy and disgust) and a set of positive emotions (such as happiness, pride, relief, and love). I believe that hope, compassion, and gratitude are also emotions, but for complex reasons their valence is problematic and I shall ignore them here (however, see Lazarus, 1991c). As I said, psychological stress centers on the negative emotions, though the positive emotions often serve as breathers (a break from stress), sustainers (of stressful commitments), and restorers (replenishing damaged resources) (Lazarus, Kanner, & Folkman, 1980).

If we know only that a person is experiencing psychological stress, we have useful information, but it is far more useful to know that a person feels angry, anxious, guilty, sad, happy, proud, relieved, or loving. Each of these emotional states says something different about the conditions being faced and subjectively appraised by the person, that person's goal commitments and beliefs, and how a troubled person-environment relationship is being coped with, all of which are salient features of the emotion process and its outcomes.

For example, depending on our theory of the emotion-generating process, what do we know from observing anger in a person as opposed to pride, guilt, relief, and so on? Anger tells us that the person has experienced a personal slight; pride indicates that the person's self-esteem or ego identity has been enhanced; guilt shows that the person feels blameworthy for a moral transgression; and relief results when a condition of harm or loss, or threat of this, has been removed.

If we observe that a person experiences one emotion frequently, we have learned either that this person often is placed in situations that provoke the emotion or that personality factors, such as goals or beliefs, make that person vulnerable to the particular recurrent emotion. The information derived by expanding our concept of stress to include the emotions is far more revealing about the human condition and its clinical implications than the knowledge afforded by the simpler stress concept. Incidently, this latter implication powers much of the current cognitive therapy of depression, in which the effort is made to change dysfunctional beliefs that lead to chronic or recurrent emotional distress such as depression.

Although stress remains a useful and important concept in the analytic armamentarium of theoreticians, researchers, and practitioners, in the remainder of this chapter I present a brief version of the theoretical analysis of the emotions I have presented elsewhere in a more complete and elaborate form (Lazarus, 1991a, 1991b, 1991c).

A WORKING CLASSIFICATION OF THE EMOTIONS

Though I cannot explain fully in the space available, there are good reasons for excluding some states from the emotion lexicon (see, for example, Ortony, Clore, & Collins, 1988; Ortony, Clore, & Foss, 1987). My position on which states should or should not be considered emotions is in no sense fixed. In order to justify the limited choice of emotions I describe here, I offer a tentative classification using four main categories.

1. *Emotions resulting from harms, losses, and threats,* including anger, anxiety, fear, guilt, shame, sadness, envy, jealousy, and disgust. These are also referred to as negative emotions because the cognitive-motivational-relational process involved in their generation is based on thwarting.

2. *Emotions resulting from benefits,* defined as attaining a goal or making reasonable movement toward it, including happiness/joy, pride, gratitude, and love, either companionate or romantic. These emotions are generally considered positive because they derive from benefit. Though I think this kind of evaluation is somewhat oversimplified, I shall skip discussion of it here.

3. *Borderline cases,* such as hope, contentment, relief, compassion, and aesthetic emotions. Each of these feelings is problematic for different, sometimes complex reasons, and I refer the reader to a more complete treatment of this elsewhere (Lazarus, 1991c).

4. *Nonemotions,* which, though often emotional in Ortony, et al.'s (1988) sense, should not be regarded as emotion families. An emotion family consists of all the variants of the basic relational theme defining it; though each variant shares that theme with all the others, the variants also differ from each other in important ways. Thus, the emotion family of anger includes irritation, rage, anger with attack, anger with inhibited or denied attack, righteous anger, anxious anger, pouting, gloating, biding one's time for seeking vengeance, and so forth. Although these feelings differ in intensity, the focus action, level of distress, provocation or motivation, and coping processes involved, we assume that all share a common scenario of provocation and type of response to it.

Nonemotions fall into a number of subcategories: (a) complex states, including grief and depression; (b) ambiguous positive states, such as expansiveness, challenge, confidence, determination; (c) ambiguous negative states, such as frustration, disappointment, and meaninglessness; (d) mental confusion, such as bewilderment and confusion; (e) contentless excitement or arousal, such as upset, such as upset, distress, nervousness, tension, and agitation; and (f) pre-emotions, such as interest, curiosity, anticipation, alertness, surprise, and amazement.

The first two categories, consisting of negative and positive emotions, are relatively standard. The borderline cases are more controversial, and the nonemotions are the most controversial of all. For example, grief and depression are commonly treated as emotions, though I believe this categorization is incorrect (they are, of course, emotional); and I have sometimes treated challenge as an emotion, but I now believe that, like threat, it is best thought of as a mediating appraisal from which emotions such as hope, or the problematic states of enthusiasm and excitement, may be derived. Frustration is often treated as an emotion but, like challenge and threat, I regard it as an appraisal. A similar argument could be made for disappointment and meaninglessness. They may lead to anger, anxiety, or sadness, but they are not themselves emotions. Finally, although clearly emotional, upset, distress, and the like refer only to generalized arousal, without any clear relational content. In effect, terms like these single out one facet of a more complex emotional configuration and, in my view, not the most important facet, so that one doesn't know precisely what the person-environment relationship and appraisal pattern might be without reference to the whole configuration.

WHAT MUST A COGNITIVE-MOTIVATIONAL-RELATIONAL THEORY DO?

The key terms need to be defined before proceeding to the task of stating theoretical propositions. *Relational* refers to the metatheoretical assumption that emotions are always about person-environment relationships, not about environmental demands or intrapsychic needs and processes as such. For too long we have looked for the causal processes in emotion in the environment or within the person and underplayed ongoing and changing relationships. The two sets of variables must be conjoined in an adaptational encounter to create the personal harm, threat, or benefit on which the emotions are predicated.

Motivational refers to hierarchies of importance for goals that we bring to any encounter and to transactions in a particular situational context that activate these goals as stakes in the outcome of the encounter and generate new ones. The motivational principle in emotion is that emotions are reactions to the status of goals in everyday encounters and in our overall lives.

Cognitive refers to knowledge and to the appraisal of what is happening in an adaptational encounter (Lazarus & Smith, 1988; see also Lazarus, 1991a). These two kinds of cognition have seldom been distinguished. *Knowledge* consists of a set of beliefs, either situational or generalized across situations, about how the world works. We habitually think of knowledge as truth; however, psychologists realize that each person's truth is to some degree unique and is often private and that the relationship between subjective and objective truth (that is, agreed by consensus) is a complex philosophical and empirical issue.

Impersonal knowledge, however, is cold and is not sufficient to generate emotion. *Appraisal,* an evaluation of the significance of what is happening in terms of one's well-being, is essential to the generation of an emotion because it concerns one's personal stake in an adaptational encounter.

To create a self-consistent and researchable analysis of the emotions, a theory must do two things: First, it must offer general propositions about the emotion process by delineating the key variables and showing how they operate; second, it must offer specific propositions about each individual emotion. Such analysis amounts to stating how each emotion is generated and then influences subsequent actions and reactions and is tantamount to creating separate subtheories for each individual emotion, which must be consistent with the general propositions.

Space limitations preclude a discussion here of some of the central and often controversial issues about emotion, including questions of definition, emotions and nonemotions, acute emotions versus moods, emotions as categories versus dimensions, whether physiological changes should be a hallmark of emotion, and biological versus social science conceptualizations. I invite the reader to examine my recent treatments of these and other issues elsewhere (Lazarus, 1991a, 1991b, 1991c).

THE CONCEPTUAL HEART OF THE THEORY

Emotions are organized psychophysiological reactions to information and knowledge about the significance for personal well-being of relationships with the environment (most often, another person). The quality (e.g., anger versus anxiety, guilt, pride, etc.) and intensity (degree of involvement and physiological change) of emotions depend on subjective evaluations—which I call cognitive appraisals—of how we are doing with respect to our goal commitments in the short and long run and on the tendencies to act that are generated by these appraisals as part of the emotional reaction. Emotions are, in effect, cognitive-motivational-relational configurations whose status changes with changes in the person-environment relationship, as understood and evaluated (appraised) by the individual experiencing them.

The best way to portray the heart of the theory is to convert cognition, motivation, and person-environment relationships into personal meanings, which I refer to as core relational themes and patterns of appraisal (see Horowitz, 1989, and Lazarus, 1991c, for a discussion of other, similar uses of this term by Luborsky, 1984). The ultimate aim of the theory is to specify deterministically what emotion or emotions a person will experience in an adaptational encounter on the basis of the core relational theme (CRT) and the appraisal pattern. A central premise of this analysis is that the CRT and the appraisal pattern comprising it are distinctive for each individual emotion. The two are mutually interdependent, with core relational themes being molar syntheses and appraisal patterns being molecular analyses of the evaluations that combine into the CRT's.

Core Relational Themes

I believe that, regardless of cultural variations, certain relational themes are universal in human affairs and always result in a specific emotion when they occur. These themes are features of our biology, and history provides continuous evidence that each of these emotion scenarios is expressed in the emotion biologically linked to it. Although there is argument about detail, by the time we are adults all of us have experienced, or are capable of experiencing, each of these classic human relationships. The essence of the CRT for each of an illustrative sample of emotions can be summarized as follows:

Anger: A demeaning offense against me and mine.
Anxiety: Facing uncertain, existential threat.
Fright: An immediate, concrete, and overwhelming physical danger.
Guilt: Having transgressed a moral imperative.
Shame: Failing to live up to an ego-ideal.
Sadness: Having experienced an irrevocable loss.
Envy: Wanting what someone else has.
Jealousy: Resenting a third party for loss or threat to another's affection.
Disgust: Taking in or being too close to an indigestible object or idea (metaphorically speaking).
Happiness: Attaining a goal or making acceptable progress toward it.
Pride: Enhancement of one's self worth by taking credit for a valued object or accomplishment.
Relief: A distressing condition that has changed for the better or gone away.
Hope: Fearing the worst, but yearning for better.
Love: Desiring or participating in reciprocated affection.
Compassion: Being moved by another's suffering and wanting to help.

Although I view the core relational themes as biological givens in our species, society and its culture also play important roles both in setting the meanings crucial to these themes (via the process of appraisal) and in regulating the expression of emotion once it is generated. Levy (1973) has referred to the former as constitutive rules of emotion and the latter as regulative rules (see Ekman, 1977, on display rules and Hochschild, 1979, on feeling rules).

As Lutz and White (1986) have pointed out, cultures emphasize certain problems of living more than others, interpret these problems differently—for example, what is considered dangerous or a loss, how to think about the social management of violations of a social code (e.g., justifiable or unjustifiable anger, what is shameful, and so on), and how we are permitted to react to such experiences as a loss or an attack on our integrity. These sociocultural variations influence how an encounter in life is appraised—with the resulting generation of a particular emotion—as well as how the emotion produced by such an encounter is regulated. I propose, nevertheless, that the core relational themes of human emotion, once they have occurred, will always result in the emotion that is biologically scripted.

Appraisal Patterns

Core relational themes are useful syntheses of the essence of relationships between person and environment, but they are too molar to provide the necessary details of the emotion-generating cognitive-motivational-relational process. A more molecular analysis of the appraisal patterns contributing to each core relational theme is necessary to understand and predict that process. An appraisal consists potentially of six key decisional components, three primary and three secondary. The *primary appraisal* components have to do with the motivational aspects of an encounter.

1. *Goal relevance* concerns what, if anything, is at stake, which determines whether there is any potential for an emotion in the encounter. If nothing is at stake, there can be no emotion; if, however, a goal is engaged by the transaction—that is, if there is a personal stake in the encounter's outcome—its fate, whether positive or negative, will lead to an emotion, the intensity of which depends in large part on the importance or motivational strength of that goal.

2. *Goal congruence or incongruence* has to do with whether an encounter is deemed harmful (or threatening) to the goal (incongruence) or beneficial (congruence). This evaluation determines whether the emotion will be negative or positive. If there is incongruence, the emotion will be negative; if there is congruence, the emotion will be positive.

3. *Type of ego-involvement* refers to one or more of the six types or facets of ego-identity to which we are variously committed. Emotions often, but perhaps not always, engage some facet of ego-identity, though in a somewhat different way for each individual emotion. Ego-involvements, which refer to commitments, might be thought of as goals that fall within the rubric of what we usually mean by ego-identity. The types or facets are listed below without elaboration.

   a. self- and social esteem
   b. moral values
   c. ego-ideals
   d. meanings and ideas
   e. persons and their well-being
   f. life goals

The *secondary appraisal* components have to do with options for coping and expectations about what will happen.

4. *Blame* and *credit* depend on attributions (knowledge; see Lazarus & Smith, 1988) about who, if anyone, is accountable (responsible) for the harm or benefit and whether these persons could have controlled their harmful or beneficial actions. For example, if we blame ourselves, we feel guilt, shame, or anger at ourselves. If blame is directed externally to another, anger at that person is experienced. If we take credit for something that enhances our ego-identity, we experience pride; however, if a good thing happens for which we do not take credit, then we feel happy rather than proud (Hume, 1957).

5. *Coping potential* concerns whether and in what way we can influence the person-environment relationship for better or worse. I remind the reader sophisticated in appraisal theory that coping potential does not refer to the thoughts or acts of an actual coping process but an appraisal of conditions relevant to them.

6. *Future expectations* consist of changes in the person-environment relationship that we believe will take place—for example, whether or not things will work out favorably for whatever reasons.

This analysis of appraisal is cast as a decision tree, a series of discrete choices that proceed from the general to the particular—that is, whether an emotion will occur, whether it will be negative or positive, and so on. Ultimately, the range of possibilities is narrowed down to a particular emotion. I use a decision tree format not because I imagine that the mind works as a sequential series of questions and answers but because it is a didactic device to reveal the theoretical rationale for the role of appraisal in emotion. In other words, this format provides the discriminanda for each individual emotion.

I do not assume a fixed sequence in these appraisal decisions, as Scherer (1984) does in his list of "stimulus evaluation checks," nor do I believe that our minds operate in this sequential fashion. Quite the contrary, many evaluative decisions have been all but made much earlier, as a result of prior experience, and are automatically and without deliberation called forth by some contextual cue. Several components may also be evaluated at the same time, as when we grasp as a whole a familiar emotion scenario and react to it accordingly.

Action Tendencies and Physiological Activity

One of the hallmarks of emotion is that it is an organismic reaction, an engaged and embodied state in contrast to routine or automatized adaptations and impersonal or cold cognitions. If this were not so, then it would be difficult to distinguish emotions from nonemotions. In fact, Duffy (1941) argued that emotion is an unnecessary concept because it refers to activities that are not different from life itself, which concerns adapting to the demands, constraints, and opportunities of living.

However, emotions are different in important ways from many other adaptational activities because they are characterized by active psychobiological involvement in what is happening; with emotion, one has a stake in the outcome and the state is the opposite of cool detachment. One of the psychological mechanisms for controlling emotions is detachment or distancing, and a number of philosophies—including those of the Greek Stoics and the Buddhists—center on renunciation of the standard human goals, which make people vulnerable to emotional distress. The reader interested in a more in-depth treatment of the arguments about physiological activity and action tendencies in the emotions is invited to consult Lazarus (1991c).

The case for physiological activity as an essential criterion of emotion is made problematic—as Duffy pointed out—because many of the response characteristics of emotion, such as a physiologically aroused state, apply also in nonemotional contexts. For example, similar homeostatic adjustments are made to exercise, hunger, or heat and cold. Nevertheless, when an emotion is set in motion by the appraisal of harms or benefits in an adaptational encounter, the process can be treated as a special psychobiological system whose rules of operation are distinguishable from what happens in nonemotional contexts.

This criterion works well for some emotions, such as anger and fright, which involve physiological mobilization to cope with threat, but less well for other emotions, such as sadness, relief, and happiness. The problem with sadness is that it is, par excellence, an emotion of inactivity because it is associated with helplessness, which is contrary to the idea of mobilization. The problem with relief is that it is defined as a subsidence of tension when a threat has been overcome or proved false. Thus, in this case, too, mobilization does not apply; however, when there is reduction of tension there is parasympathetic activity (Kemper, 1987). In these cases, we do better to think of physiological change rather than mobilization or activation. The problem with happiness and, incidently, most mildly positive emotions, is that it is difficult, but not impossible, to specify any distinctive physiological activity. Psychophysiological research to confirm or reject physiological correlates does not exist for these emotions. This problem leaves unsettled the issue of whether physiological activity is a necessary condition of emotion.

Why should there by physiological activity in emotion? For anger and fright the best answer is mobilization for coping, but what about other emotions? A concept that might help us understand why emotions are embodied is *action tendency,* and some writers postulate a distinctive and innate one for each and every emotion (Frijda, 1986; Lazarus, 1991c). Action tendency helps rationalize the physiological activity considered to be a feature of every emotion. One speaks of action tendency, impulse, or readiness because the action is a disposition that is not necessarily manifest but may be inhibited or transformed.

For anger, the action tendency is presumed to be attack in order to demolish the threatening agent or gain vengeance to restore one's injured self-esteem. For fright (and anxiety), the action tendency is avoidance or escape. However, as we move to the emotions of sadness, relief, happiness, and hope, we have difficulty in specifying an action tendency, though reasonable speculations are possible. This difficulty has led to considerable argument about the proposition that each emotion has a distinctive action tendency (e.g., Ortony, Clore, & Collins, 1988).

Allow me to note also that an action tendency is presumably an innate, biological disposition to act in some preordained way, and though it can be inhibited by social regulation, or what Ekman (1977) calls display rules, the specific tendency is presumably rather rigid. This fixed response is in marked contrast with coping, which is far more deliberate, learned, psychological, complex, and sustained than action tendencies. As an action tendency the impulse to attack is thoughtless and must be restrained. As coping, however, it is quite different, as is illustrated by the fictional Count of Monte Cristo in the novel by Alexander Dumas. Once a victim, the hero gains wealth and power, and plotted the demise of his enemies in a skein of careful, disguised, subtle, and long-term steps, which drew on learned skills and a sophisticated understanding of the social world. Coping is the psychological analogue of action tendency, but it is subject to quite different rules.

Examples of Appraisal Patterns for Individual Emotions

The ground has now been laid for considering the distinctive patterns of appraisal for individual emotions. Some emotions, and especially those involving more subtle relational nuances within an emotion family—for example, gloating and pouting—are forms of anger and require five or six appraisal components to discriminate among them. However, considerable mileage can be attained for many common emotions by using only four appraisal components: goal relevance, goal congruence or incongruence, type of ego-involvement, and blame or credit. I use only these four to describe the appraisal patterns for a sample of emotions including anger, anxiety, guilt, shame, sadness, and pride (in order to include a positive emotion in the analysis).

Anger. Because the core relational theme of anger is a demeaning offense against me and mine, I propose that anger depends on the appraisal that the self-esteem in one's ego-identity is at stake in an encounter. Social esteem is also relevant, but I think that threats to it are, at bottom, threats to self-esteem. In an anger scenario, self-esteem (a type of ego-involvement) is injured or threatened, implying both goal relevance and goal incongruence, and the injury or threat is blamed on another. This process creates the core relational theme of an unfair slight or insult (using Aristotle's, 1941, language).

An appraisal of blame requires two attributions—first, that you or someone else is accountable (or responsible) for the injury or threat, and, second, that this person could have acted otherwise. This results in blame—accountability is not always blameworthy—and a construal that one has been demeaned, slighted, or taken for less than one wishes. (See Berkowitz, 1989, for a different account, in which injury to self-esteem is a modifying variable that increases the probability or intensity of anger rather than being fundamental.) In the 1940s and 1950s there was considerable debate about the role of arbitrariness and intent to harm as a factor in aggression (anger), but the issue was never fully resolved by research.

A typical scenario for anger might be the experience of being ignored by a clerk in a shop who is engaged in an interminable personal phone call. An alternative condition that is not conducive to anger might be when the clerk is trying to give the best possible service but also makes us wait because the store is filled with customers. In such a case, any anger we feel will be directed toward the store management, or toward ourselves for getting caught in this frustrating situation, or at other targets, but not at the clerk.

I suggest that anger arises when we are treated as less than we would wish, whether or not the intent is malevolent, but especially when it is. The nature of the perceived intention explains why retaliation and vengeance are so much a part of the anger that comes in response; we retaliate as a way of repairing a damaged self-esteem. Those with a vulnerable self-esteem more readily become angry than others because it is difficult for them to wave off the assault as unimportant.

I must make two important qualifications. First, the preceding analysis seems, incorrectly, to imply a totally self-centered process, as if we only become angry when we personally, not others, have been harmed. This implication overlooks the fact that we develop commitments to persons other than ourselves and even to ideas that we cherish. Thus, when others are harmed, our own ego-identity is also assaulted. We may see some innocent person harmed—say, a helpless child—this violates our basic values of fairness and justice, to which we have become committed as a feature of our ego-identity. We perceive the situation as if we or those we love are being offended. The realm of our ego-identity encompasses far more than our immediate well-being; in effect, our personal commitments extend far beyond our skin.

The second qualification is that my analysis deals with adult anger, which is not necessarily the same as infant anger, either in the way it is generated or in the nature of the emotional experience. I cannot deal here with the developmental aspects of the emotions, but there are good grounds for believing that infants get angry without having the capacity to make all the appraisals involved in adult anger, though they are capable of making many of the key appraisals by roughly four or five months of age (see Lazarus, 1991c, for a more complete analysis of this issue; also Stenberg & Campos, 1990). We need to know much more than we do about the appraisal capabilities of infants and young children. Moreover, adults may react on the basis of developmentally immature processes. Not all anger is the same, or is brought about in the same way, and we must try to integrate conceptually our observations of preverbal infants with those of postverbal children, adolescents, and adults.

As in the past, there will continue to be some diversity in the way theorists view the process of anger generation, its core relational themes, and its appraisal patterns. I hope this debate will lead to productive research on anger and other emotions as well. One could, for example, take my account of adult anger as only one scenario—although, perhaps, a most common one—because there are other kinds of anger with their own special rules and thus reject my proposal that this type of anger is prototypical for adults.

To assume alternative scenarios means that at some point we must decide whether the variations in the anger process fall within a single emotion family, representing a common psychobiological process, or should be distinguished as separate emotions. I treat pouting and gloating as forms of anger, but these states could instead be regarded as different emotions or as ways of coping with anger. In constructing subtheories of distinguishable categories of emotion, there will always be a tension between differentiating among and adding more categories on the one hand and the desire to reduce the categories to a minimum number on the other. Because the decision tends to be arbitrary, there is no right or wrong answer, only one that is more or less fruitful in portraying how the issue might best be conceived.

As I said previously, the action tendency in anger is attack, though as Averill (1983) observes, the episodes of anger reported by college students rarely involved actual attack. Anger is a troubling and ambivalent emotion in our society because of its socially destructive nature. It has been argued, for example, that anger's strong biological impulse toward aggression is no longer as adaptive as when the mechanism was required to overcome dangerous predators. Those who emphasize the illness potential for anger assume that it is maladaptive in the modern social world. Because the complex social structures of the modern industrial world favor cool, controlled, and deliberate ways of coping, the adaptational advantages of the innate mechanisms of anger may be considerably diminished and the disadvantages increased.

Anxiety. Because the core relational theme of anxiety is facing an existential threat, I—along with a number of others (e.g., Averill, 1988)—regard anxiety as the result of a threat to our being and to the essential meanings that comprise it. When the threat is of this sort, one doesn't know what will happen, when it will happen, and, therefore, what is to be done about it. Even when the threat is concretized and externalized—say, as a failure in an examination, a job interview, or some other performance—the concrete condition represents the more existential questions of who we are and what life meanings we hold. When one such threat has been dealt with, another always comes in its wake.

This pattern makes anxiety a special emotion and is one of the reasons why theories of psychopathology have so often centered on anxiety. Freudian, neo-Freudian, existentialist, and reinforcement learning theories all center on inappropriate ways of coping with anxiety as the basic cause of psychopathology. I should note, in passing, that—in contrast with anxiety—fright occurs in response to a concrete, sudden threat of harm to one's physical well-being. Though fright shares some features in common with anxiety (for example, the action tendency, some aspects of its subjective feel, and, even more fundamentally, the fact that the harm is in the future), as an emotion it is quite different from anxiety, both in the process of generation and in some of its consequences.

Meanings and ideas in which one is ego-involved are at stake in anxiety, and a threat to these creates goal incongruence. In contrast to anger, however, there is no blame. If the threat is blamed on something or someone, another person or oneself, then the emotion will not be anxiety but anger, guilt, shame, envy, jealousy, or disgust. In guilt the blame is on oneself and the type of ego-involvement is a moral imperative that has been transgressed. In shame the blame is also on oneself and the type of ego-involvement is living up to an ego-ideal that we believe we have failed. Among the negative emotions, only sadness shares with anxiety this quality of no blame. Thus, it is very difficult in both cases to mount a satisfactory action-centered coping process to ameliorate the loss. This lack of an object of blame also makes the biological action tendency of avoidance or escape unsatisfactory, because the source of the threat is existential and, therefore, inevitably ambiguous—we don't know what to avoid, or how.

Guilt. The core relational theme for guilt is self-blame for a moral transgression, though it may have occurred only in fantasy or imagination. The set of appraisal components that bring this theme involves goal relevance, in that a moral standard is at stake that in turn provides the type of ego-involvement distinctive of guilt. In addition, the transgression provides the goal incongruence. Blame is internal—that is, we accept the attribution not only that we are accountable for the transgression but also that it was in our power to have acted otherwise and that we should have.

A variety of analyses of the psychodynamics and development of guilt have been contrasted by Zahn-Waxler and Kochanska (1990) in a major treatment of this emotion. Dealing primarily with the social and developmental conditions of guilt, they note that guilt has been regarded theoretically as innate or learned, as functional or dysfunctional, and as a state or a trait; sometimes the focus has centered on affective, behavioral, or cognitive components. The authors identify three main emphases—psychoanalytic, one based on prosocial feelings and empathic concern, and a third based on children's gradual learning to perceive and understand the social significance of violations of standards of conduct. The three perspectives overlap because blaming oneself for a moral transgression is always involved in guilt.

We might speculate that the action tendency in guilt is to expiate, make amends, or atone for what one has done. Though it is also common for people to cope with guilt by externalizing the blame—for example, blaming the victim—to make it psychologically easier to bear, more commonly we berate ourselves for what we have done. Preoccupation with sin is a major component of the Judeo-Christian religious outlook. In Christianity, for example, the crucifixion is considered to be the way that Jesus took on the sins of humankind, beginning with the original sin of Adam and Eve.

Freud suggested a paradox of guilt: the most guilt-ridden people may actually be less blameworthy than most, because the feelings of guilt socialize them to act morally. For Freud, guilt was a neurotic obsession to be overcome in psychotherapy. In his later years,

Mowrer (1976) took the opposite stance by stating that guilt-ridden people have been transgressors against the moral law and that psychotherapy should explore their sins so that these people can learn to avoid them in the future. Guilt has been of great interest to psychoanalysts, who speak of unconscious needs for self-punishment as a factor in some psychopathologies.

Shame. Lewis (1971) has been critical of psychoanalysis for not distinguishing clearly enough between shame and guilt and for failing to recognize the importance of shame in psychopathology. She suggests, for example, that shame is a common emotional experience, but that the sufferer is apt to be unaware of its basis, which is the threat of rejection and abandonment during childhood.

The pattern of appraisal for shame must result in the core relational theme of failure to live up to an ego-ideal, which is underlying theme suggested by Lewis. The desire to live up to this ideal is the type of ego-involvement, which makes for goal relevance. Because one has failed to meet the ideal goal incongruence is created and blame for the failure is accepted as one's own.

One of the most interesting features of shame, in contrast to guilt, is its action tendency, which is presumably to hide evidence of one's failure. In our research on coping (Folkman, Lazarus, Dunkel-Schetter, DeLongis, & Gruen, 1986), we observed that when a person's stake in a stressful encounter is the well-being of another, it is common to seek social support. However, when the stake is preservation or enhancement of one's own ego-identity, social support is eschewed, presumably because self-centeredness engenders the potential for shame, which makes us want to hide.

Comparisons of research by Schachter (1959) and Sarnoff and Zimbardo (1961) suggests a similar psychodynamic. In the former, when subjects awaited a painful electric shock, they preferred to wait with another person who was to undergo the same treatment. In the latter, however, when subjects awaited an embarrassing task, such as sucking on baby nipples, they preferred to wait alone. These findings also support the contrast in the action tendencies between shame and guilt.

Sadness. Aside from some ambiguity about whether it is a mood or an acute emotion, sadness is unique among the negative emotions in being a reaction to an irrevocable loss. The loss creates goal incongruence, and what has been lost may be any of the six types of ego-involvement listed previously. As with anxiety, there is no blame in sadness. If we blame someone for our loss, then we are apt to experience anger, guilt, or shame, which are the emotions of an active coping struggle. Only when we have accepted that the loss is irrevocable do we have the essential secondary appraisal component for sadness—lack of coping potential.

Sadness is unique among the emotions in that it rarely, if ever, occurs at an early stage of a loss; instead, it comes at the end of a long struggle—the grieving process—to come to terms with the loss. When we have accepted that we are helpless to change the matter, we can be sad; when we are not ready to accept this, we experience numbness, denial, or other emotions such as anger, anxiety, guilt, or shame, all of which focus on trying to restore or ameliorate the threat or loss. I agree with Marris (1975) that the essence of loss consists of meanings in which we are invested. The loss is to one's ego-identity, which can be expressed in terms of self or social esteem, moral values, ego-ideals, other persons and their well-being, or life goals—the six meaning-centered facets or types of ego-involvement.

Pride. Pride is closely related to anger because it involves self-esteem, but rather than being a response to a belittlement, pride results when esteem has been enhanced. For similar reasons, it is also an opposite of shame. Pride occurs in an encounter in which our ego-identity is goal relevant or at stake, there is *goal congruence,* and the conditions of the encounter favor ego-enhancement because we take credit (Hume, 1957) for the positive value of an object or accomplishment. These factors express the core relational theme for pride.

Many cultures seem to deal with pride ambivalently. For example, the response to what might be called overweaning pride or the pride that comes before the fall is negative, but appropriate pride, whatever that is, receives a positive response. In Japan more than the United States, for example, there are strong social constraints on manifest pride, so that if we give personal compliments to Japanese people, they are likely to respond with a mild denial of the compliment, a sort of minimization. Such a personal compliment elevates the individual above the social norm, and this position is more alien to a Japanese than to an American. Whether this response reflects the person's actual state of mind or is merely an observance of social rules is not clear.

Furthermore, Japanese are more likely to take pride in strong effort rather than in ability and to feel shame in not making an effort; Americans, however, tend to be proud of ability and use lack of effort as an excuse for not having done well. Ambivalence about pride should not be surprising when we realize that ego-enhancement often occurs at another's expense, or that making too much of our positive qualities or good fortune may belittle others. Consequently, considerable social delicacy is required in the display of pride. Again, this case demonstrates the considerably enhanced power to grasp what is happening in the person-environment relationship and the struggle to adapt when we take into account the fifteen or so possible emotions and how they are brought about.

COPING AND EMOTION

The person-environment relationships leading to the emotions are always changing, just like emotions, which are usually context-dependent and therefore continually in flux. The changes in both are the result, in part, of the continuous flow of events in an adaptational transaction. Another reason for changes in person-environment relationships is that when encounters are harmful or threatening, coping processes are set in motion, that, if successful, eliminate or ameliorate the harmful condition along with the emotion it produced.

Even in beneficial relationships and the positive emotions they generate, coping may be required to bring about and sustain a positive condition or to ward off threats to it. When we are happy as a result of having attained a goal or moved closer to it, we cannot bask long in the pleasure; instead, we must shortly move on to other agendas that flow from a positive event (Lazarus, Kanner, & Folkman, 1980). Thus, upon achieving a doctorate, we are in a position to go from student to job-seeker, a transition that soon creates a new set of goals and the coping strategies needed to attain them. The struggles of living last until death, and each encounter is part of a continuous and usually directional flow.

Although the concept of coping has been applied mainly in the context of stress, it is no less important to the emotions, especially the goal-incongruent or negative ones, but also positive emotions. Coping is an essential feature of stress, but social scientists seem less clear about this role in the case of emotion. The extent to which coping has been underplayed in emotion theory and research weakens understanding and research on the emotion process.

Coping is best defined as efforts to manage demands that tax or exceed our resources, the latter phrase being a definition of stress. The many forms or strategies of coping need to be conceptualized and measured (Lazarus & Folkman, 1984, 1987; Folkman & Lazarus, 1988a), but I have long maintained that although coping has many functions (e.g., Cohen & Lazarus, 1979, 1983), two stand out as particularly important: one problem-focused coping and emotion-focused coping (see also Folkman & Lazarus, 1988a&b, 1990).

Coping that serves problem solving results in changes in the person-environment relationship through direct actions on the environment or through changing our own part in that relationship. If we can change our troubled relationships with the environment, we can control to some extent the conditions that are responsible for goal incongruence and the negative emotions that results from it as well as goal congruence and the positive emotions that result from it.

Emotion-focused coping produces subjective change (not actual change) in the person-environment relationship. These subjective changes are, in effect, reappraisals that we are not as much or in the same ways in jeopardy as previously, so that emotional distress is reduced or positive emotional states, such as relief and affection, are generated.

There are two basic processes through which subjective change can result from emotion-focused coping. In one, attention may be temporarily diverted from a troubling relationship, as when we try to sleep by avoiding thoughts about unresolved threats or when we engage in sports or recreation, which might distract us from distressing thoughts. Earlier I spoke of this process as a breather from stress. When we are not busy doing something that occupies our attention, it is very difficult to deploy our attention away from troubling concerns. Even after we manage to fall asleep, we may awaken during the night and find ourselves ruminating about what is troubling us.

In the other basic process, efforts are mounted to change the personal meaning of the person-environment relationship that has resulted in distressing emotions such as anger, anxiety, guilt, shame, envy, jealousy, and disgust. Standard ego-defensive maneuvers such as denial, reaction formation, intellectualization (or distancing) fall within this category. By changing the meaning of a relationship, the basis for the emotional distress is changed. Thus, if we can reinterpret another person's demeaning actions toward us as innocent naiveté or as a result of vulnerable self-esteem rather than malevolence, we need no longer be angry. And if we can come to believe that the failure to live up to an ego-ideal is the doing of another rather than ourselves, we will feel externally directed anger rather than shame. Anger is more palatable as an emotional state than shame because it relieves us of the blame and gives us the illusion that we can control things.

The bottom line of how coping influences emotion is always a change in appraisal. Whatever the method, to change an emotion one must change the appraisal, which is its proximate cause, whether the appraisal is realistic or merely an illusion. This last principle applies to both problem-focused and emotion-focused coping; the former alters the objective features of the person-environment relationship; the latter alters how that reality is evaluated with respect to its significance for personal well-being. Thus, by virtue of its effects on appraisal, coping is an important part of the emotion-generating process as well as a reaction to an emotion.

Emotions, or rather the cognitive and motivational factors that result in them, also influence coping, as I implied above. Laux and Weber (1991) have examined two aspects of this. First, they point out that the choice of a coping strategy may depend on the emotion that is being experienced. Thus, anger, which depends on an assault on one's self-esteem, will lead to a different pattern of coping than anxiety, which depends on an existential threat to meanings to which we are committed.

Second, depending on the interpersonal history and context of an anger-producing encounter, marital partners in a quarrel may have different intentions, which lead to different coping strategies. For example, if one or both partners' main concern in the quarrel is to repair wounded self-esteem, then overt anger may be escalated to exact punishment against the other, so that the injured party may defend himself or herself by responding with retaliatory anger. However, if the concern is with preserving the relationship, depending on beliefs and values about the importance of honesty, the coping strategy may be to conceal the affront and suppress the anger. My own work and that of others has mistakenly divorced coping from the broad goals and situational intentions that powers and directs it along with stress and distress. Not only does coping belong within the rubric of finding solutions but it also falls within the realm of motivation; this realization brings new insights into how coping strategies are influenced.

CONCLUSION

The explosion of interest in the emotions is a very important and desirable change of fashion in the social and biological sciences from an emphasis on a valuable but limited concept, stress, to an emphasis on a broader, richer, and clinically more useful concept, emotion. Everything that could be learned from stress in the understanding of human adaptation and dysfunction can also be learned from the study of the emotions—and more—without the sacrifice of any concepts and principles on which we had previously relied.

Humans, with their elaborate minds and social structures, are probably the most emotional creatures on earth. From the earliest times, writers of fiction and drama have understood this and celebrated the emotions as the essence of what makes us human. Because of the capacity of emotion to integrate cognition, motivation, and social relationships in organized adaptational response configurations, it is high time for psychology, among the social and biological sciences, to place emotion at the center stage of the analyses of mind and to lavish more attention on the topic wherever psychology is taught.

REFERENCES

ANTONOVSKY, A. *Health, stress, and coping.* San Francisco, CA: Jossey-Bass, 1979.

————. *Unraveling the mystery of health: How people manage stress and stay well.* San Francisco, CA: Jossey-Bass, 1987.

————. Pathways leading to successful coping and health. In M. Rosenbaum (ed.), *Learned resourcefulness: On coping skills, self-control, and adaptive behavior.* New York: Springer, 1990.

ARISTOTLE. Rhetoric. In R. McKeon (ed.), *The basic works of Aristotle.* New York: Random House, 1941.

AVERILL, J. R. Studies on anger and aggression: Implications for theories of emotion. *American Psychologist,* 1983, *38,* 1145–1160.

————. Disorders of emotion. *Journal of Social and Clinical Psychology,* 1988, *6,* 247–268.

BANDURA, A. Self-efficacy mechanism in human agency. *American Psychologist,* 1982, *44,* 1175–1184.

BERKOWITZ, L. Frustration-aggression hypothesis: Examination and reformulation. *Psychological Bulletin,* 1989, *106,* 59–73.

CANNON, W. B. *The wisdom of the body.* (2d ed.). New York: W. W. Simon, 1939.

COHEN, F., & LAZARUS, R. S. Coping with the stresses of illness. In G. C. Stone, F. Cohen, N. E. Adler, & Associates (eds.), *Health psychology: A handbook.* San Francisco: Jossey-Bass, 1979.

COHEN, F., & LAZARUS, R. S. Coping and adaptation in health and illness. In D. Mechanic (ed.), *Handbook of health, health care, and the health professions.* New York: The Free Press, 1983.

DUFFY, E. An explanation of "emotional" phenomena without the use of the concept of "emotion." *Journal of General Psychology,* 1941, *25,* 283–293.

EKMAN, P. Biological and cultural contributions to body and facial movement. In J. Blacking (ed.), *A.S.A. monograph 15, The anthropology of the body.* London: Academic Press, 1977.

EPSTEIN, S., & MEIER, P. Constructive thinking: A broad coping variable with specific components. *Journal of Personality and Social Psychology,* 1989, *57,* 332–350.

FOLKMAN, S., & LAZARUS, R. S. *Manual for the ways of coping questionnaire.* Palo Alto, CA: Consulting Psychologists Press, 1988.(a)

―――――. Coping as a mediator of emotion. *Journal of Personality and Social Psychology,* 1988, *54,* 466–475.(b)

―――――. Coping and emotion. In N. Stein, B. Leventhal, & T. Trabasso (eds.), *Psychological and biological approaches to emotion.* Hillsdale, NJ: Erlbaum, 1990.

FOLKMAN, S., LAZARUS, R. S., DUNKEL-SCHETTER, C., DeLONGIS, A., & GRUEN, R. The dynamics of a stressful encounter: Cognitive appraisal, coping, and encounter outcomes. *Journal of Personality and Social Psychology,* 1986, *50,* 992–1003.

FRIJDA, N. H. *The emotions.* Cambridge: Cambridge University Press, 1986.

GERGEN, K. J. The social constructionist movement in modern psychology. *American Psychologist,* 1985, *40,* 266–275.

GOLEMAN, D. *Vital lies, simple truths: The psychology of self-deception.* New York: Simon & Schuster, 1985.

HILGARD, E. R. The trilogy of mind: Cognition, affection, and conation. *Journal of the History of the Behavioral Sciences,* 1980, *16,* 107–117.

HINKLE, L. E., JR. The concept of "stress" in the biological and social sciences. *Science, Medicine & Man,* 1973, *1,* 31–48.

HOCHSCHILD, A. R. Emotion work, feeling rules, and social structure. *American Journal of Sociology,* 1979, *85,* 551–575.

HOROWITZ, M. J. *Introduction to psychodynamics.* New York: Basic Books, 1988.

HOROWITZ, M. J. Relationship schema formulation: Role relationship models and intrapsychic conflict. *Psychiatry,* 1989, *52,* 260–274.

HUME, D. *An inquiry concerning the principles of morals.* New York: Library of Liberal Arts, 1957.

KEMPER, T. D. How many emotions are there? Wedding the social and the autonomic components. *American Journal of Sociology,* 1987, *93,* 263–289.

LAUX, L., & WEBER, H. 1991 Presentation of self in coping with anger and anxiety: An intentional approach. *Anxiety Research,* 1991, *3,* 233–255.

LAZARUS, R. S. *Psychological stress and the coping process.* New York: McGraw-Hill, 1966.

―――――. The costs and benefits of denial. In S. Breznitz (ed.), *The denial of stress.* New York: International Universities Press, 1983.

―――――. Cognition and motivation in emotion. *American Psychologist,* 1991, *46,* 352–367.(a)

―――――. Progress on a cognitive-motivational-relational theory of emotion. *American Psychologist,* 1991, *46,* 819–834.

―――――. *Emotion and adaptation.* New York: Oxford University Press, 1991.(c)

LAZARUS, R. S. & FOLKMAN, S. *Stress, appraisal, and coping.* New York: Springer, 1984.

―――――. Transactional theory and research on emotions and coping. In L. Laux & G. Vossel (special eds.), Personality in biographical stress and coping research. *European Journal of Personality,* 1987, *1,* 141–169.

Lazarus, R. S., Kanner, A. D., & Folkman, S. Emotions: A cognitive-phenomenological analysis. In R. Plutchik & H. Kellerman (eds.), *Theories of emotion. vol. 1: Emotion: Theory, research and experience.* New York: Academic Press, 1980.

Lazarus, R. S., & Smith, C. A. Knowledge and appraisal in the cognition-emotion relationship. *Cognition and emotion,* 1988, *2,* 281–300.

Levy, R. I. *Tahitians: Mind and experience in the Society Islands.* Chicago: University of Chicago Press, 1973.

Lewis, H. B. *Shame and guilt in neurosis.* New York: International Universities Press, 1971.

Lindsley, D. B. Emotion. In S. S. Stevens (ed.), *Handbook of experimental psychology.* New York: Wiley, 1951.

Luborsky, L. *Principles of psychoanalytic psychotherapy.* New York: Basic Books, 1984.

Lutz, C., & White, G. M. The anthropology of emotions. *Annual Review of Anthropology,* 1986, *15,* 405–436.

Maddi, S. R., & Kobasa, S. C. *The hardy executive: Health under stress.* Pacific Grove, CA: Brooks/Cole, 1984.

Marris, P. *Loss and change.* Garden City, Anchor Books, 1975.

Mowrer, O. H. From the dynamics of conscience to contract psychology: Clinical theory and practice in transition. In G. Serban (ed.), *Psychopathology of human adaptation.* New York: Plenum, 1976.

Orr, E., & Westman, M. Does hardiness moderate stress, and how? A review. In M. Rosenbaum (ed.), *Learned resourcefulness: On coping skills, self-control, and adaptive behavior.* New York: Springer, 1990.

Ortony, A., Clore, G. L. & Collins, A. *The cognitive structure of emotions.* Cambridge: Cambridge University Press, 1988.

Ortony, A., Clore, G. L., & Foss, M. A. The referential structure of the affective lexicon. *Cognitive Science,* 1987, *11,* 341–364.

Peterson, C., Seligman, M. E. P., & Vaillant, G. E. Pessimistic explanatory style is a risk factor for physical illness: A thirty-five year longitudinal study. *Journal of Personality and Social Psychology,* 1988, *55,* 23–27.

Rosenbaum, M. *Learned resourcefulness: On coping skills, self-control, and adaptive behavior.* New York: Springer, 1990.

Sarnoff, I., & Zimbardo, P. Anxiety, fear, and social affiliation. *Journal of Abnormal and Social Psychology,* 1961, *62,* 356–363.

Schachter, S. *The psychology of affiliation.* Stanford, CA: Stanford University Press, 1959.

Scheier, M. F., & Carver, C. S. Dispositional optimism and physical well-being: The influence of generalized outcome expectancies on health. *Journal of Personality,* 1987, *55,* 169–210.

Scherer, K. R. On the nature and function of emotion: A component process approach. In K. R. Scherer & P. Ekman (eds.), *Approaches to emotion.* Hillsdale, NJ: Erlbaum, 1984.

Selye, H. *The stress of life.* New York: McGraw-Hill, 1956, 1976.

————. *Stress without distress.* Philadelphia: Lippincott, 1974.

Stenberg, C. R., & Campos, J. J. The development of anger expressions in infancy. In N. Stein, B. Leventhal, & T. Trabasso (eds.), *Psychological and biological approaches to emotion.* Hillsdale, NJ: Erlbaum, 1990.

Taylor, S. E. *Positive illusions: Creative self-deception and the healthy mind.* New York: Basic Books, 1989.

WOLFF, H. G. *Stress and disease.* Springfield, IL: Thomas, 1953.

YERKES, R. M., & DODSON, J. D. The relation of strength of stimulus to rapidity of habit-formation. *Journal of Comparative Neurology and Psychology,* 1908, *18,* 459–482.

ZAHN-WAXLER, C., & KOCHANSKA, G. The origins of guilt. In R. A. Thompson (ed.), *Nebraska Symposium on Motivation, 1988.* Lincoln, Nebraska: University of Nebraska Press, 1990.

4

Thought, Memory, and Learning: Effects of Emotional Stress

George Mandler

INTRODUCTORY CONCEPTS

A discussion of the effects of emotional stress on thought and memory needs a definition of *emotional stress* ("stress" in the remainder of this chapter). Unfortunately, definitions of stress introduced by major investigators of the *physiological* stress concept (such as Selye) are psychologically opaque. Selye defines stress as the results of any demand on the body, using "objective indicators such as bodily and chemical changes that appear after any demand" (Selye, 1982 p. 7). It is only when these changes are psychologically effective—i.e., act on receptors and influence thought and action—that they become relevant to the stress concept. More typical definitions of stress describe occasions for sympathetic nervous system arousal, as well as the noxious nature of the stress stimulus and the resultant attempts to remove it. Within the confines of this chapter I am concerned mainly with the relation between autonomic (sympathetic) arousal and performance. Such arousal, perceived and interacting with ongoing processes, is of primary *psychological* interest. It is the perceived (phenomenal) experience of stress that determines its effect on such other processes as thought and memory.[1] It is the perception of arousal as well as the preoccupation with the stressing occasion that interfere with continuous conscious processing (Mandler 1979, 1984).

In general, it has been useful to use a general measure of sympathetic nervous system activity as an index of the source of arousal (and experienced stress). Current knowledge about the effects of such arousal is strongly influenced by Easterbrook's (1959) hypothesis that increased arousal (emotion) reduces the number of cues utilized in a situation. The suggestion also reflected psychiatric concerns (Callaway & Dembo, 1958) and was often coupled with the notion that arousal (e.g., indexed by anxiety or panic) frequently produced

Preparation of this chapter was supported in part by a grant from the Spencer Foundation. Selected portions are taken from "Thought processes, consciousness and stress" in V. Hamilton and D. W. Warburton (eds.), *Human stress and cognition,* New York: Wiley, 1979; "Affect and learning: Causes and consequences of emotional interactions," in D. B. McLeod & V. M. Adams (eds.), *Affect and mathematical problem solving: A new perspective,* New York: Springer-Verlag, 1989; and "Memory, arousal and mood: A theoretical integration" in S.-A. Christianson (Ed.), *Handbook of emotion and memory,* Hillsdale, NJ: Lawrence Erlbaum Associates, 1992.

task-irrelevant behavior (Bachrach, 1970; Mandler & Sarason, 1952). In addition, research on work in dangerous environments added the important suggestion that tasks central to the current situation tend to improve in the presence of danger (arousal), whereas performance on peripheral tasks deteriorate (Baddeley, 1972).

There is a body of evidence that efficiency differs for the central and for the peripheral aspects of a stressful situation. Some of the evidence for the central/peripheral distinction comes from research showing that auditory noise may differentially affect central and peripheral aspects of performance (Hockey, 1970). Other supporting evidence was found in situations that simulate danger, where peripheral stimuli apparently receive less attention (Weltman, Smith, & Egstrom, 1971). Bacon (1974) was concerned with developing an independent criterion for the distinction. He noted that responsiveness to those aspects of the situation that initially attract "a lesser degree of attentional focus" is reduced. This distinction makes it possible to identify peripheral events in terms of initial attention. It appears, then, that arousal and noise generate similar effects, and it is useful to think of both of them as noise that interferes with conscious capacity.

Two mechanisms mediate the effect of arousal on attention. Autonomic arousal first narrows attention automatically by the direct action of the autonomic nervous system, and there is evidence that the autonomic nervous system acts as a signal to the organism that the world is different from what is expected (cf. Mandler, 1975). Secondly, autonomic arousal acts indirectly by occupying some of the limited capacity of attention-consciousness and thereby limiting the remaining available attentional capacity to those events or stimuli that have originally been perceived as central. Irrelevant mentation will, of course, produce similar interference, but I concentrate here on the effects of arousal as such.

The Functions of Consciousness and Schemas

I assume that current conscious contents are a function of activated (preconscious) structures/schemas on the one hand and the requirements of the task and situation on the other. Consciousness functions to provide a representation of currently important aspects of the external (and internal) world. It does so by using activated underlying representations (the preconscious) and intentions, task demands, needs, and other abstract schemas. In that fashion, consciousness makes sense of our current situation. In addition, the conscious contents are relatively limited representations with limited capacity that occur in a serial manner—we cannot be conscious of more than one limited scenario at any one time.

The most useful concept to represent what is available to conscious construction is the schema. The concept of the schema has served psychologists well for the last two-hundred years, and particularly for the past fifty years. A schema is a coherent and structured representation that organizes experience. Schemas are not carbon copies of experience, but generalized representations of experienced regularities. Schemas range from the very concrete, involving the categorization of perceptual experience, to the very abstract, representing general levels of meaning such as *love* or *justice*. Abstract schemas subsume more concrete schemas; the resulting structure is hierarchical. Schemas are built up in the course of interaction with the social and physical environment. They organize and interpret experience in that current encounters are defined and interpreted in terms of the schemas laid down by past cognate experiences. Currently active schemas define what we are likely to see, hear, and remember, and also determine what we are unlikely to hear or see. Thus, we note the time when looking at a clock in a public square, but we are unlikely to see (process) the precise form of the numerals. The activation of schemas proceeds automatically from concrete to general schemas (from the bottom up), and also from high-level schemas, which constrain perception and conception, to lower schemas (from the top down). Expectations include those elements of schemas activated by top-down processing that are not directly supported by input evidence.

A schema represents the unit of thought and perception; it is bounded and distinct. When co-occurrences in the world have been organized into a schema of the event or scene, they appear to evoke one another. However, organization of two or more events, other than some purely perceptual or procedural events, into a new schema requires active elaborative processing (see subsequently). Sheer contiguity is—under this view—not sufficient for subsequent evocation.

Of equal importance to the current discussion is a view of consciousness as a complement to an underlying representational system that is characterized by schemas represented by distributed features (cf. Rumelhart & McClelland, 1985). Such a system is relatively large (i.e., it represents the accumulated experiences of the individual), it is relatively fast in accessing information, and it operates in a parallel fashion (i.e., a large number of relevant features and schemas are accessed and activated at the same time). These characteristics would—without an additional buffer—make action and thought difficult, if not impossible. The individual would be overwhelmed by information rapidly emerging in parallel fashion, and action decisions in particular and decision processes in general would be swamped by the amount and speed of the information produced. Consciousness is the buffer that solves this problem. It is first of all serial (i.e., however well activated, only an organized—small—cluster of information is accessed in consciousness at any one time), it is relatively slow compared with spreading activation in the underlying system, and it is limited in capacity to a few items or events. It is the limited capacity of consciousness in particular that is of importance in the interaction between thought and emotion (for extensive discussions of these issues see Mandler 1984, 1985, 1988, 1992b).

Emotion

My theoretical approach to emotion has been extensively documented in the past fifteen years (Mandler, 1975, 1984, 1990). It is a constructivist theory that addresses the subjective experience of emotion, but it is not a theory of emotional behavior, which may or may not be accompanied or followed by positive or negative emotional experience. This contrast avoids a confusion that has been with us at least since Charles Darwin—a confusion that equates the observation of effectively categorized behavior with emotional experience. The theory views the construction of emotion as consisting of the concatenation of a cognitive evaluative schema with visceral arousal (which is perceived as emotional intensity). This conscious construction is a unitary experience, even though it may derive from separate and even independent schematic representations (Mandler, 1985; Marcel, 1983). Such a view of emotion only approximates the common sense meaning of the term. To ask "what is an emotion?" is not—in principle—answerable. The term is a natural language expression that has all the advantages (communicative and inclusive) and disadvantages (imprecise and vague) of the common language. However, for communicative purposes one needs to approximate the common meaning as a first step.

I have focused on two dimensions out of the many available from analyses of common language "emotions": the notion that emotions represent evaluative cognitions, and the assertion that emotions are hot—they imply a gut reaction, a visceral response. Evaluative cognitions of what is good or bad, pleasant or unpleasant, or noxious or desirable provide the quality of the emotional experience, and the visceral reactions generate its quantitative aspect. Given the many different possible evaluative states, one of the consequences of such a position is that it leads to the postulation of a potentially innumerable number of different emotional states. Of course, regularities in human thought and action produce general categories of these constructions that have family resemblances and overlap in the feature that is selected for analysis (whether it is the simple dichotomy of good and bad, or the appreciation of beauty, or the perception of evil). These families of occasions and meanings construct the categories of emotions found in the natural language (and psychology).

The source of the categories of emotion varies from case to case, and different emotional categories may be based on different experiential or environmental factors. Sometimes an emotional category is based on the similarity of external conditions (as in the case of some fears and environmental threats). Sometimes an emotional category may be based on a collection of similar behaviors (in the subjective feelings of fear related to avoidance and flight). Sometimes a common category arises from a class of incipient or intended actions (as in hostility and destructive action). Sometimes hormonal and physiological reactions provide a common basis (as in the case of lust), and sometimes purely cognitive evaluations constitute an emotional category (as in judgments of helplessness that eventuate in anxiety). Others, such as guilt and grief, depend on individual evaluations of having committed undesirable acts or trying to recover the presence or comfort of a lost person or object. All of these emotional states involve evaluative cognitions, and the features common to any particular category give rise to the appearance of discrete categories of emotions.

The problem of *cognitive evaluation* is common to all emotion theories. Even advocates of a small vocabulary of basic emotions need to have an analytic mechanism whereby the individual evaluates the current scene. For the basic emotion theorist, such evaluations could then be postulated to elicit prepackaged emotions. For all theories of emotion, the problem of evaluation involves the different external and internal sources that lead us to see some person or event as good or bad, evil or benign, or harmful or beneficent.

Evaluative cognitions provide the quality of an emotional experience, and visceral activity provides its intensity and peculiar "emotional" characteristic. Degree of autonomic (sympathetic) arousal can be mapped into the felt intensity of an emotion. However, affective judgments can obviously occur without visceral involvement. Saying that something is pretty, fine, awful, or even disgusting may be stated quite dispassionately. Thus, so-called affective or evaluative judgments are experienced as such, but under this interpretation they are not full-blown emotions. What we need to understand are the occasions when visceral activity (however slight) co-occurs with these affective judgments.

In the common understanding of emotion, the occurrence of some visceral or gut reaction is assumed. Emotions are said to occur when we feel aroused, agitated, when our "guts are in an uproar," etc. The reference is almost invariably to some sympathetic nervous system activity, such as increased heart rate, sweating, or gastrointestinal upheavals. The autonomic nervous system (ANS) has been systematically implicated in quasi-emotional activity ever since Walter Cannon (1929) delineated the workings of the sympathetic and parasympathetic systems in fight or flight reactions and recognized their function over and beyond the energy-expending and energy-conserving roles that keep the internal environment stable.

Discrepancies and Interruptions Produce Autonomic Arousal

A majority of occasions for visceral (sympathetic nervous system) arousal follow the occurrence of some perceptual or cognitive discrepancy or the interruption or blocking of some ongoing action. It should be remembered, though, that discrepancies are only a sufficient, not a necessary, condition for sympathetic arousal. Other sources of sympathetic nervous system arousal can and do play a role in emotional experience. Discrepancies and interruptions depend to a large extent on the organization of the mental representations of thought and action. Within the purview of schema theory, these discrepancies occur when the expectations generated by some schema are violated. This is the case whether the violating event is worse or better than the expected one so that visceral arousal occurs on both unhappy and joyful occasions. Most emotions follow such discrepancies, just because the discrepancy produces visceral arousal. And the combination of that arousal with an ongoing evaluative cognition is the subjective experience of an emotion. Interruption, discrepancies, blocks, frustrations, novelties, etc. are occasions for ANS activity (MacDowell & Mandler, 1989; Mandler, 1964).

The notion that the strange and the unusual have emotional consequences has appeared in various places in the psychological literature. In the context of attachment theory, Bowlby (1969) has discussed the problem of fear and its ontogeny in relation to the attachment to caregivers and the fear of strangers. Hebb (1946) has shown that fear occurs in response to perceptual discrepancies, and that the fear of the strange does not occur until familiarity and expectations have been developed.

A consideration of discrepancies and interruptions in daily life is useful in understanding what is usually considered stressful. In short, stress occurs on the occasions when the world is not as we expect it to be. If our life proceeds as expected, if home and work change little, we do not experience stress. If, however, a spouse behaves in unexpected ways, or if demands at work are new, discrepancies occur, sympathetic nervous system reactions are triggered, and stress is experienced. Examine the statement "I have been under a lot of stress lately," and you will find an individual who is faced with a lot of unexpected, surprising, and discrepant events.

The notion of discrepancy as the basis for much of the intensity of human emotions may at first sound out of place when one is dealing with the positive emotions. However, positive events are often unexpected, and, in addition, some reflection discloses that the complexity of human thought practically always produces ambivalences and alternative outcomes for positive as well as negative events. Fear of the loss of the loved one, anticipation of possible negative outcomes even for the most joyful occasions, and alternative constructions of negative outcomes illustrate the ambivalences that provide the discrepancies for most emotional occasions (see also Mandler, 1990).

Emotion and Consciousness

One of the functions of consciousness is to bring into awareness situations in which automatic actions fail or are disrupted. Claparède (1934) has called this the *law of awareness*.[2] But, as we have seen, these failures and disruptions also produce sympathetic nervous system arousal and emotional experiences. Since the construction of emotions requires conscious capacity, the experience of emotion pre-empts the limited capacity of consciousness. Limited capacity refers to the fact that conscious contents are highly restricted and limited at any one point in time. Whenever some particular construction pre-empts conscious capacity, then other processes that require such capacity will be impaired. The best example is found in stress and panic reactions, when emotional reactions prevent adequate problem-solving activities. Emotional experiences may inhibit the full utilization of our cognitive apparatus, thoughts may become stereotyped and canalized, and we tend to revert to simpler modes of problem solving. However, the effects of emotion are not necessarily intrusive and deleterious. In part, the effects will depend on other mental contents and processes that are activated by the emotional experience and that may become available for dealing with stressful situations. For example, stress tends to focus attention on the perceived central aspects of a situation, and such focusing may be useful. The relationship of emotions to discrepancies and autonomic nervous system recruitment also points to their adaptive function; emotions occur at important times in the life of the organism and may serve to prepare it for more effective thought and action when focused attention is needed.

THINKING AND REMEMBERING

In the present context, I use the terms *thought* and *thinking* to refer to problems and memories that are brought to consciousness for further mental processes to operate on them. The major mental mechanisms that are at work in simple thought and memory processes are briefly discussed in the following paragraphs.[3]

1. Underlying representations of objects and events are subject to two kinds of processes: Activation/integration and elaboration. Sheer presentation of previously experienced objects and events activates the relevant representations. The activation of these representations (best considered as schemas with distributed features) leads to further mutual activation of the constituent features and results automatically in the integration of the representation and its unitization. One of the consequences of activation is the phenomenal experience of familiarity. Activation occurs automatically—i.e., it does not involve or require conscious participation. Elaboration, on the other hand, probably requires deliberate (conscious) activity. Elaboration is the process whereby existing mental units (representations) are related to each other, and it makes possible retrieval and search processes.

2. Bringing to mind previously experienced and/or stored events (*recall* in the memory rubric) requires elaboration at time of presentation that makes possible later access by providing appropriate connections to and relations with other mental contents. These pathways established by elaboration make possible retrieval processes, which are often marked by waystations that appear in consciousness. Thinking and remembering are typically achieved by higher order structures/schemas that specify the gist or context of the information to be recalled and produce veridical information as well as the typical context-related errors in recall and problem solving.

3. The recognition of previously experienced objects or events may involve both activation and elaborative processes. The dual process approach of recognition (Mandler, 1980) distinguishes between two components of phenomenal recognition—the experience *that* an event has been encountered previously, and the identification of *what* the event is. These phenomena are in turn generated respectively by activation and elaboration. However, rudimentary recognition performance is possible with activation alone. Prior presentation of an item activates its representation, and the presentation of a copy of the item shortly thereafter further raises its activation. The result of such a highly activated representation is the phenomenal experience of familiarity. The effect is similar to, but not identical with,

some priming phenomena, in which activation of a representation makes it (or a related representation) more accessible.

THE INTERACTION OF THINKING AND EMOTION

This section addresses the most widely investigated interactions between thinking and emotion within the context of the approach to consciousness, thinking, and emotion discussed previously. One obvious point of departure is the distinction between the two components of emotional experience—arousal and evaluation. When discussing the relation between thought and stress, I am primarily concerned with stress as expressed in arousal.[4]

Thought and Arousal

An older tradition—exemplified by the Yerkes-Dodson law—typically addresses the arousal function as a problem of the relation between cognitive efficiency and stress. Yerkes and Dodson (1908) found *improvement* in the performance of easy tasks with increasing stress, but with difficult tasks they found an inverted U-shaped function of better performance with medium stress and worse performance with low or high stress. The distinction between easy and difficult tasks and the fact that the law was developed by the use of electric shock to implement stress is sometimes forgotten.

Two difficulties in applying the Yerkes-Dodson inverted U-shaped function to the stress and thinking literature are that (1) it is generally assumed that the task is difficult, i.e., that the inverted U-shaped function actually applies, and (2) frequently subjective judgments determine what is the functional stress level in any particular study. For example, Deffenbacher (1983) in a review of the literature on arousal and eyewitness testimony, concluded that ten studies suggested better eyewitness accuracy with high arousal, while another eleven studies produced lower accuracy of memory. Deffenbacher then reclassified stress levels in the various studies and concluded that most of the studies reviewed revealed the inverted U-shaped function.

We can attempt an explanation of the inverted U-shaped function of performance as a function of increasing arousal. I deal with the function in two parts: the increase in accuracy with arousal moving from low to moderate levels, and the subsequent decrease as arousal becomes severe. For low levels of arousal, the focus of attention (i.e., the current conscious content) is likely to be the main task at hand, and with moderate increases of arousal these central, important events will receive exclusive access to conscious capacity. The same pattern is likely to be true of easy tasks that do not in themselves produce significant stress and arousal. At the lowest level of arousal (often associated with very easy tasks or situations) there will be a low level of attention to the task and haphazard accuracy. With increasing, but low, levels of arousal, attention will focus on central aspects of the task and will produce increasing efficiency with moderate increases in arousal. When arousal attains high levels, it is likely to be because of a failure to solve the task or because external sources (e.g., arousal inducers such as shock) require additional attention to the sources of the disturbance. Under these circumstances, task-irrelevant behavior is likely to increase; attention to such behavior is by definition peripheral. In addition, the further limitation of conscious capacity makes very little of it available for attention to the central aspects, and other mental contents will intrude. As a result, memorial accuracy with respect to the central aspect of the situation suffers with increasing arousal. One example is found in conditions of panic, in which people often pursue failing solutions without being able to consider other possible responses (e.g., by rushing for the same exit in a fire, or failing to follow instructions not to open windows, etc.). In general, severe limitations of conscious capacity are likely to produce a situation in which concentration on the central aspect of the situation will be lost.

What is the experimental evidence for the inverted U-shaped function? I first address the effect of arousal/emotion on memory and then turn to some of the questions about central and peripheral memorial processing.

Apart from the clinical literature, which I do not cover, a direct demonstration of the effect of emotional reaction on memory was given by Loftus and Burns (1982), who showed that inserting a disturbing element into film produced retrograde loss of detailed information. A more detailed demonstration was given by Christianson and Nilsson (1984) who showed worse memory performance for verbal descriptors presented with mutilated faces than for those presented with neutral control faces. Christianson and Nilsson also collected physiological data (skin conductance and heart rate) that showed that the experimental subjects were sympathetically aroused. One can assume that autonomic interference as well as preoccupation with the mutilated faces interfered with the adequate elaboration (encoding) of the tested information. Christianson and Nilsson also showed anterograde recall decrements on items following the traumatic ones, a finding that suggests that elaboration was interfered with by the lingering effects of the emotional items. However, there was no anterograde *recognition* decrement for the neutral items following the emotional ones. It is interesting to contrast the recognition decrement for the target items with the lack of an effect on subsequent (anterograde) items. The recognition decrement of the target items could be due either to a lack of elaboration (demonstrated in recall) or to avoiding looking at the traumatic material at all (i.e., activation is absent). For the neutral items, the recall decrement on the one hand and the maintenance of recognition performance on the other hand indicates that activation of neutral items was not affected.

It does not seem clear whether arousal itself is an adequate condition for the restriction of conscious capacity and the impairment of memory. The theoretical approach outlined here does, of course, predict that positive emotional events will produce autonomic arousal just as negative ones do (MacDowell & Mandler, 1989) and that these should also have an interfering effect on memory (Christianson, 1986). As far as sheer arousal is concerned, Zillmann (1978) has conducted extensive studies showing that arousal from a prior (usually unrelated) event produced emotional reactions in a subsequent situation. He interpreted these findings of excitatory transfer in terms of an attribution model in which the prior arousal is attributed to a current affective situation in which emotional reactions are then observed. However, he noted that when the prior induction of arousal was "immediately apparent and unambiguous" subjects did not misattribute the excitation produced by the prior event. He concluded that whenever subjects are aware of a causal connection between the arousal and the prior event, they will not attribute the arousal to the current situation. In contrast, Christianson and Mjörndal (1985) found no difference in memorial performance between a group autonomically aroused with adrenaline and a control group given saline injections. In their experiment, it was likely that the subjects connected any perceived arousal with the injections (but see also Christianson, Nilsson, Mjörndal, Perris, & Tjellden, 1986, where only a few subjects attributed their arousal to the injections).

In addition, individual differences may also play a role in this effect. Overson (1989) gave subjects an addition task immediately following physical exercise (which raised heart rates by 70%). The subjects were told that the exercise should "help them think more clearly." A control group was given no exercise and informed that their performance and heart rate would be used to provide baseline data for other subjects. Under these conditions, Overson found no difference in accuracy, but, when compared with control subjects, there were slower performance rates for high-anxiety subjects and faster performance rates for low-anxiety subjects following exercise.

Assigning the arousal to the prior event (whether activity or injection) makes it possible for the individual either to ignore the subjective arousal or to maintain attention on the central aspect of the task. Emotional effects apparently require a belongingness between the arousal and the target material.

On the question of differential memory for central or peripheral aspects of emotional events, one needs first of all to disengage a research literature on memory of outstanding, unique, unusual events (such as flashbulb memories). These events are not typically related to situations where arousal (i.e., full emotions) usually occurs. Thus, if memory of particularly impressive events seems to be better than usual, one can assume that this recall is related to the special processing (e.g., attention, rehearsal, extensive elaboration) that they engender. The only study of which I am aware that tested and confirmed the notion that central aspects of *emotional* events are better remembered than peripheral ones is one by Christianson and Loftus (1987), who investigated both short-term and long-term memories for traumatic and nontraumatic slide presentations. Christianson and Loftus compared traumatic and nontraumatic versions of the same event and noted that the theme of the traumatic materials was better remembered after a period delay than the the theme of the nontraumatic material.

In a paper that claims to show negative evidence for the Easterbrook hypothesis, and specifically for the effects of arousal on constricting memory to central details, Heuer and Reisberg (1990) failed to produce any significant emotional arousal with their experimental slides. They showed better central as well as peripheral memory for their experimental group, but that group showed a decline in heart rate. They conclude that their "stimuli evoked the species of arousal associated with an orienting response, rather than the arousal associated with flight (including heart-rate acceleration)." If sympathetic nervous system arousal is responsible for the focusing effect, then these data are, of course, irrelevant to the hypothesis.

How does prior experience affect one's ability to handle arousal and stress? The effect of experience must be related to the proposition that autonomic arousal is linked to the interruption of ongoing behavior, plans, and expectations and that stress occurs when no available action or thought structures are available to handle the situation. Astronauts, for example, are trained to have response sequences, plans, and problem-solving strategies available for all imaginable emergencies (Mandler, 1967). An emergency then ceases to be one; it is another routine situation, by definition not unexpected—and not stressful. Similarly, novice parachute jumpers have a high pulse rate before a jump, which drops to a normal level upon landing, whereas the experienced jumper shows the reverse effect (Epstein & Fenz, 1965). Novice parachutists ruminate on possible outcomes, none of which they are able to handle, and on emergencies that they either imagine or remember and for which no action structures are available. At the end of the jump, this interruptive effect—interrupting thoughts about the successful completion of the jump—is eliminated because the original plan (to complete the jump successfully) has been achieved.

How does the mastery of threat and the effect of interpreted threat influence the efficiency of the performance of complex intellectual tasks? Here we come close to observing the outcomes of complex thought processes directly and at the same time addressing a topic of some practical importance. Specifically, we are concerned with the effect of perceived threat on the performance of test-like tasks.

The major research strategy has been to select individuals who report (on paper-and-pencil tests) high and low degrees of anxiety or concern about test situations (Mandler & Sarason, 1952). Subjects who score high on such a test tend to observe their own behavior and examine their failures, whereas individuals with low anxiety orient their behavior and cognitions toward the specific requirements of the task (Mandler, 1972).

Individuals with high levels of anxiety perform worse on intelligence tasks, but the absence of any further instructions is beneficial for the high-anxiety people. On the other hand, telling subjects that they failed is most helpful for individuals whose anxiety is low (Mandler & Sarason, 1953). Similarly, highly anxious subjects solve anagrams more efficiently than do individuals with low anxiety when the situation is nonthreatening—that is, when they are instructed that they are not expected to finish all the anagrams. When the subjects are told that the task is directly related to one's intelligence level and that they should finish easily if they were of average intelligence, the individuals whose anxiety is low perform significantly better than the highly anxious ones (Sarason, 1961).

We conclude that many people bring stress into a situation, just as the situation brings out their stress potential. Both a potentially threatened individual and a properly interpretable situation are needed to produce the stress reaction. That reaction presumably takes two forms: first, the individual ruminates—thinks—about the irrelevant aspects of the task, including his or her own state, performance, and reactions; and, second, the threat interpretation produces autonomic activity that is in itself attention demanding. Both of these sets of internal events then vie for the limited capacity and thereby reduce the conscious capacity available for thought processes that the task itself requires.

EMOTIONS IN PROBLEM SOLVING—DISCREPANCIES AND HUMAN ERROR

Any discrepancy in the course of problem solving represents a potential affective episode.[5] Such episodes must be seen within the context of a general flow of affective and mood-like changes. However, it is possible to identify specific kinds of discrepancies and interruptions that may occur in the course of problem solving. The major class of such events can be generally classed as errors, when the learner does something or thinks something that is different from the original intention or is different from what "ought to happen." I shall discuss errors as such shortly, but we must keep in mind that people frequently engage in actions that they believe to be the correct ones (i.e., they proceed as intended), but that are false, incorrect, illogical, etc. In the case of unintended errors, the discrepancy arises because of a mismatch between what is intended and what occurs; in the other case, the mismatch is between an expected outcome ("I thought what I did would solve the problem") and the real response ("It didn't work"). Most intended and unintended errors are coupled with a negative evaluation of the current situation. These errors usually result in negative affect (unhappiness, disgust, or despair in various degrees of intensity). The result is interference with ongoing cognitive processes, because of both the pre-emption of conscious capacity and the search for correction (looking for the source of the disruption). If this process is allowed to go unchecked—i.e., if the learner is continuously producing errors—the intensity of negative affect will increase. Such a sequence may eventually produce abandonment of the task as being too noxious to tolerate, panicky quasi-random attempts at a solution, and general disorganization.

The other general class of discrepancies are successes. These may be intended or unintended as well. The intended success is a step in the solution process that works; the unintended one is when a particular action or thought produces unexpected positive results ("I just tried that because I couldn't think of anything else and it worked"). In general, the smooth progression of some planned course of problem solving will produce little arousal. After all, if I go through some cookbook steps toward a solution, the expectation is that each step will be successful and no discrepancy occurs. It is when I am not sure of the successive steps that success may be slightly arousing. Thus, during the early stages of the learning process, when the learner is unsure, we expect—and, of course, find—more affective states and more interference with learning. The well-practiced solution runs off smoothly and by definition produces little affect. From a more global point of view, the final solution of a problem produces discrepancy if the learner was unsure of his or her ability—that is, joy, delight, or satisfaction result from the success.

Donald Norman analyzed action slips within the general context of schema theory (Norman, 1981). Well-learned action sequences (and, by implication, thought sequences) are specified by a high level schema—the intention—which then recruits lower level schemas that guide the various components of the developing sequence. These component schemas are presumably activated both by the original intention (and its descendants) and by appropriate conditions of the task as the sequence (the problem solving) develops—i.e., the thought sequence emerges interactively from both top-down and bottom-up sources. Norman discusses three categories of slips: errors in the formation of an intention, defective activation of component schemas, and defective triggering. In another paper, Norman makes the distinction between mistakes, which result from errors in the formation of an intention, and slips, which are errors in the execution of an intention (Norman, 1980).[6]

Errors: What Are They Good For?

The typical work on human error and slips pays hardly any attention to the affective consequences of errors. Norman, for example, is much concerned with problems of limited conscious capacity (he refers to it as short term memory—STM—capacity), but the possibility that affective consequences of errors demand and pre-empt such capacity is not seriously entertained (Norman, 1980). I am not concerned here with the causes or categorization of errors, but rather with their affective consequences. The affect that occurs when errors or mistakes are made is a conscious event; it preempts our limited conscious capacity and has several consequences. First of all, the perception of autonomic arousal, when severe, is by itself demanding enough to make it difficult to act effectively ("I am so upset, I can't think straight"). Second, the occurrence of strong negative affect produces an immediate attempt to remove the reason (the cause). That consequence may be useful when the removal of the offending event is more important than a continuation of the problem-solving activity. However, in the usual learning context, the latter may be more adaptive. Third, even a positive affective experience in the context of problem solving may be deleterious. The individual solves some subroutine and stops, in part to admire the achievement, in part to savor the affect. In the process, the current contents of consciousness are displaced and one loses one's place in the stream of problem solution.

Is it the case, then, that errors and mistakes should be avoided whenever possible and that tasks should be designed so that problem solutions can be learned without errors? I now come to the question of errorless learning: Can it happen and is it "good"? I shall return to the real world soon and discuss the inevitability of errors and mistakes and the advantages of having had prior experiences with them.

The concern with errorless learning started about twenty-five years ago when B. F. Skinner (1961) argued that learning should involve as few errors as possible and that it should be possible—for example, by making incremental steps small enough—to acquire skills and knowledge without the nuisance and debilitating effects of errors. Skinner provided little if any empirical evidence for his argument, but Terrace (1963, 1972) demonstrated an analogue of human errorless learning in animal discrimination training. The animal is required to distinguish between a positive stimulus ($S+$) and a negative stimulus ($S-$). The required response must be made when $S+$ is presented and must be omitted when $S-$ is presented. Terrace showed that by slowly bringing in the negative stimulus ($S-$) the animal (typically a pigeon) could learn to discriminate between a positive ($S+$) stimulus and the $S-$ without making many (or any) responses to $S-$. The major claim about errorless learning that concerns me here is that one of the byproducts of discrimination learning does not appear following errorless learning. That byproduct is emotional (and aggressive) behavior when $S-$ is presented. If a method could be found that eliminated the emotional consequences of negative stimuli (and their avoidance) it would have important consequences for theories of learning and teaching. However, that is not the case. Rilling and his students (Rilling, 1977) showed that most of the byproducts of discrimination learning, and in particular aggressive emotional behavior, also occur following errorless learning.[7]

I am not advocating that the animal learning literature is a highway toward understanding human cognitive processing. However, the only data available suggest that errorless learning does not produce an affect-free learning environment. If we assume, therefore, that at present there are no methods for producing painless learning, that the consequences of learning—no matter how painless—may still produce affective reactions, how do we accommodate to such a state of affairs?

My main argument should be obvious by now. I do not believe that it is possible for an individual to live a cocooned life in which no failures, no mistakes, and no slips are encountered. These mis-steps in life can be highly deleterious if totally unexpected; they are less interfering and less intense if their occurrence is a normal feature of life and therefore expected to occur at some time or another. The occurrence of affective reactions to learning experiences, arousal due to discrepancies during the learning process, and other "bad experiences," all build up expectancies, and are built up into experiential schemas. Events that are totally unexpected produce maximal arousal and affective reactions. If, however, we know that errors (and very specific errors) can occur in problem-solving situations, the errors are neither surprising nor are their consequences unexpected. The cocooned individual reacts extremely to novel situations. In short, I believe—at least in the problem-solving situation—that it is advantageous for an individual to be exposed to the "school of hard knocks." Again, a nice set of demonstrations is available in the animal (and human) experimental literature on the partial reinforcement effect. Briefly, if a response is consistently reinforced during learning, then extinction of that response (once reinforcement is absent) will be relatively rapid. However, if the initial reinforcement is only given on some percentage of the acquisition trials, then extinction of the response will be slow. It is the experience with unreinforced responses that makes them less effective during extinction.[8]

How, then, to design learning and teaching tasks? We need to analyze the task and the learner to ensure that the surprises, errors, and mis-steps during acquisition are relatively minor—i.e., that they can be mastered by some alternative route, by substitute actions, or by a restatement of the problem (one's intentions). At the same time, we do not want to avoid such affective incidents altogether because we want the learner to be prepared for them in the future. Thus, small incremental steps, specific instruction in subroutines, attention to possible difficulties, and instructions for the anticipation of difficulties all play a role in analyzing and constructing a task. We also need to take into account the individual's attitudes and beliefs about the problem, because they will interact with the expectations that will be developed and that might be confirmed or violated.

Affectless learning is not a possible goal either for a theory or the praxis of instruction. Common sense tells us that emotions and affective reactions are with us now and forever. And the usual measures of individual differences tell us, not surprisingly, the same thing. Tests of individual differences give us some indication of the person's affective preoccupations with tests, cognitive tasks, etc. These dispositions will interact with the emotional consequences of specific errors, failures, successes, and strategies. Thus, we would expect that an individual with a high level of anxiety or arousal with produce a more debilitating emotional reaction than will a more placid, unresponsive person. Both in the analysis of a task and in the design of learning, such factors could well be attended to and different (less demanding) acquisition paths could be designed for the more emotionally reactive learners. Apart from the inescapable fact that emotions and affect are an integral part of what we call human nature, what we recognize as the constitutive aspects of our humanity, one can argue that affectless learning would not be very useful.

NOTES

1. As we shall see subsequently, the reason is that the "phenomenal" aspect affects the limited capacity of consciousness.
2. For further discussions of this troubleshooting function of consciousness, see Mandler 1975, 1984.
3. I have previously presented an extended discussion of memory phenomena and their relation to the functions of consciousness (Mandler, 1989b).
4. The evaluative aspects of emotion are primarily relevant to effects of mood on thought and memory (Mandler, in press a).
5. For more extensive discussions of these issues, see Mandler 1989a.
6. Other important contributions to error theory are Reason's papers (e.g., 1977, 1979).
7. In my only excursion into animal experimentation, I demonstrated that the absence of reinforcement is a very powerful inducer of extreme emotional reactions, even when the animals are satiated—i.e., the lack of opportunity for engaging in well-learned behavior has marked emotional consequences. However, when substitute behaviors are made available to the animals, the emotional behavior can be suppressed (Mandler & Watson, 1966).
8. See my *Mind and Emotion* (1975) for a more detailed discussion of the affective consequences of partial reinforcement.

REFERENCES

Bachrach, A. J. Diving behavior. In *Human performance and scuba diving*. Chicago: Athletic Institute, 1970.

Bacon, S. J. Arousal and the range of cue utilization. *Journal of Experimental Psychology*, 1974, *102*, 81–87.

BADDELEY, A. D. Selective attention and performance in dangerous environments. *British Journal of Psychology,* 1972, *63,* 537–546.

BOWLBY, J. *Attachment* (Attachment and Loss, Vol. 1). London: Hogarth Press and Institute of Psychoanalysis, 1969.

CALLAWAY, E., III, & DEMBO, D. Narrowed attention: A psychological phenomenon that accompanies a certain physiological change. *AMA Archives of Neurology and Psychiatry,* 1958, *79,* 74–90.

CANNON, W. B. *Bodily changes in pain, hunger, fear and rage* (2d ed.). New York: Appleton-Century-Crofts, 1929.

CHRISTIANSON, S.-A. Effects of positive emotional events on memory. *Scandinavian Journal of Psychology,* 1986, *27,* 287–299.

CHRISTIANSON, S.-A., & LOFTUS, E. F. Memory for traumatic events. *Applied Cognitive Psychology,* 1987, *1,* 225–239.

CHRISTIANSON, S.-A. & MJÖRNDAL, T. Adrenalin, emotional arousal and memory. *Scandinavian Journal of Psychology,* 1985, *26,* 237–248.

CHRISTIANSON, S.-A., & NILSSON, L.-G. Functional amnesia as induced by psychological trauma. *Memory & Cognition,* 1984, *12,* 142–155.

CHRISTIANSON, S.-A., NILSSON, L.-G., MJÖRNDAL, T., PERRIS, C., & TJELLDEN, G. Psychological versus physiological determinants of emotional arousal and its relationship to laboratory induced amnesia. *Scandinavian Journal of Psychology,* 1986, *27,* 300–310.

CLAPARÈDE, E. *La genèse de l'hypotheses.* Geneva: Kundig, 1934.

DEFFENBACHER, K. A. The influence of arousal on reliability of testimony. In S. M. A. Lloyd-Bostock & R. B. Clifford (eds.), *Evaluating witness evidence: Recent psychological research and new perspectives.* Chichester, Eng.: Wiley, 1983.

EASTERBROOK, J. A. The effect of emotion on cue utilization and the organization of behavior. *Psychological Review,* 1959, *66,* 183–201.

EPSTEIN, S., & FENZ, W. D. Steepness of approach and avoidance gradients in humans as a function of experience: Theory and experiment. *Journal of Experimental Psychology,* 1965, *70,* 1–13.

HEBB, D. O. On the nature of fear. *Psychological Review,* 1946, *53,* 259–276.

HEUER, F., & REISBERG, D. Vivid memories of emotional events: The accuracy of remembered minutiae. *Memory & Cognition,* 1990, *18,* 496–506.

HOCKEY, G. R. J. Effect of loud noise on attentional selectivity. *Quarterly Journal of Experimental Psychology,* 1970, *22,* 28–36.

LOFTUS, E. F., & BURNS, T. E. Mental shock can produce retrograde amnesia. *Memory and Cognition,* 1982, *10,* 318–323.

MACDOWELL, K. A., & MANDLER, G. Constructions of emotion: Discrepancy, arousal, and mood. *Motivation and Emotion,* 1989, *13,* 105–124.

MANDLER, G. The interruption of behavior. In E. Levine (ed.), *Nebraska symposium on motivation: 1964.* Lincoln: University of Nebraska Press, 1964.

————. Invited commentary. In M. H. Appley & R. Trumbull (eds.), *Psychological stress.* New York: Appleton-Century-Crofts, 1967.

————. Helplessness: Theory and research in anxiety. In C. D. Spielberger (ed.), *Anxiety: Current trends in theory and research. Vol. II.* New York: Academic Press, 1972.

————. *Mind and emotion.* New York: Wiley, 1975.

————. Thought processes, consciousness, and stress. In V. Hamilton & D. M. Warburton (eds.), *Human stress and cognition: An information processing approach.* London: Wiley, 1979.

————. Recognizing: The judgment of previous occurrence. *Psychological Review,* 1980, *87,* 252–271.

————. *Mind and body: Psychology of emotion and stress.* New York: Norton, 1984.

————. *Cognitive psychology: An essay in cognitive science.* Hillsdale, NJ: Lawrence Erlbaum Associates, 1985.

————. Problems and directions in the study of consciousness. In M. Horowitz (ed.), *Psychodynamics and cognition.* Chicago: Chicago University Press, 1988.

————. Affect and learning: Causes and consequences of emotional interactions. In D. B. McLeod & V. M. Adams (eds.), *Affect and mathematical problem solving: A new perspective.* New York: Springer Verlag, 1989.(a)

————. Memory: Conscious and unconscious. In P. R. Solomon, G. R. Goethals, C. M. Kelley, & B. R. Stephens (eds.), *Memory: Interdisciplinary approaches.* New York: Springer-Verlag, 1989.(b)

————. A constructivist theory of emotion. In N. S. Stein, B. L. Leventhal, & T. Trabasso (eds.), *Psychological and biological approaches to emotion.* Hillsdale, NJ: Lawrence Erlbaum Associates, 1990.

————. Memory, arousal, and mood: A theoretical integration. In S.-A. Christianson (ed.), *Handbook of emotion and memory.* Hillsdale, NJ: Lawrence Erlbaum Associates, 1992.(a)

————. Toward a theory of consciousness. In H. G. Geissler, S. Link, & J. G. Townsend (eds.), *Cognition, information processing and psychophysics: Basic issues.* Hillsdale, NJ: Lawrence Erlbaum Associates, 1992.(b)

MANDLER, G., & SARASON, S. B. A study of anxiety and learning. *Journal of Abnormal and Social Psychology,* 1952, *47,* 166–173.

————. The effect of prior experience and subjective failure on the evocation of test anxiety. *Journal of Personality,* 1953, *21,* 336–341.

MANDLER, G., & WATSON, D. L. Anxiety and the interruption of behavior. In C. D. Spielberger (ed.), *Anxiety and behavior.* New York: Academic Press, 1966.

MARCEL, A. J. Conscious and unconscious perception: An approach to the relations between phenomenal experience and perceptual processes. *Cognitive Psychology,* 1983, *15,* 238–300.

NORMAN, D. A. *Errors in human performance* (report no. 8004). San Diego: Center for Human Information Processing, University of California, San Diego, 1980.

————. Categorization of action slips. *Psychological Review,* 1981, *88,* 1–15.

OVERSON, C. *Stress and anxiety in mathematical problem solving.* Unpublished doctoral dissertation, University of California, San Diego, 1989.

REASON, J. T. Skill and error in everyday life. In M. Howe (ed.), *Adult learning.* London: Wiley, 1977.

————. Actions not as planned. In G. Underwood & R. Stevens (eds.), *Aspects of consciousness.* London: Academic Press, 1979.

RILLING, M. Stimulus control and inhibitory processes. In W. K. Honig & J. E. R. Staddon (eds.), *Handbook of operant behavior.* Englewood Cliffs, NJ: Prentice-Hall, 1977.

RUMELHART, D. E., & McCLELLAND, J. L. *Parallel distributed processing: Explorations on the microstructure of cognition. Vol. 1: Foundations.* Cambridge, MA: MIT Press, 1985.

SARASON, I. G. The effects of anxiety and threat on the solution of a difficult task. *Journal of Abnormal and Social Psychology,* 1961, *62,* 165–168.

SELYE, H. History and present status of the stress concept. In L. Goldberger & S. Breznitz (eds.), *Handbook of stress: Theoretical and clinical aspects.* New York: The Free Press, 1982.

SKINNER, B. F. Why we need teaching machines. *Harvard Educational Review,* 1961, *31,* 377–398.

TERRACE, H. S. Discrimination learning with and without errors. *Journal of the Experimental Analysis of Behavior,* 1963, *6,* 1–27.

————. By-products of discrimination learning. In G. H. Bower (ed.), *The psychology of learning and motivation. Vol. 5.* New York: Academic Press, 1972.

WELTMAN, G., SMITH J. E., & EGSTROM, G. H. Perceptual narrowing during simulated pressure-chamber exposure. *Human Factors,* 1971, *13,* 99–107.

YERKES, R. M., & DODSON, J. D. The relation of strength of stimulus to rapidity of habit-formation. *Journal of Comparative and Neurological Psychology,* 1908, *18,* 459–482.

ZILMANN, D. Attribution and misattribution of excitatory reactions. In J. H. Harvey, W. Ickes & R. F. Kidd (eds.), *New directions in attribution research. Vol. 2.* Hillsdale, NJ: Lawrence Erlbaum Associates, 1978.

5

Decisionmaking under Stress

Irving L. Janis

DURING THE PAST THREE DECADES, *rational–choice models,* based on *game theory* and *subjective–expected utility theory,* have been dominant in the psychological research literature on decisionmaking. These models assume that decisionmakers deliberately choose their courses of action on a rational basis by taking account of the values and the probabilities of the consequences that would follow from selecting each of the available alternatives (e.g., Edwards, 1954; Miller & Star, 1967; Raiffa, 1968). Models of rational choice have led to the development of formal methods for decision analysis, which provide useful normative rules that specify how people should make sound decisions when they have to take risky actions (Wheeler & Janis, 1980). One central idea is that it is essential to make the best estimates of the probability that each of the expected consequences will occur; another is that the relative importance of each of the anticipated favorable and unfavorable consequences should be taken into account—their expected utility value from the decisionmaker's own standpoint.

Although valuable for prescriptive purposes, rational models run into considerable difficulty when they are proposed as *descriptive* theories that explain how people actually do make decisions (Broadhurst, 1976; Kahneman & Tversky, 1979; Lee, 1971; Rapoport & Wallsten, 1972; Simon, 1976; Slovic, Fishhoff, & Lichtenstein, 1977). One major reason that people deviate from a rational model pertains to the cognitive limitations of the human mind (Simon, 1976). People simply cannot understand and keep in mind all the relevant information needed for an optimal solution to the decisionmaking problems they face. Nor do they have at their command all the necessary knowledge about cause and effect relationships and all the baseline data essential for making accurate probability estimates of alternative outcomes. Another major reason that people do not consistently follow rational procedures has to do with the effects of emotions on the cognitive processes involved in decisionmaking. This is where stress enters the picture.

DETRIMENTAL EFFECTS OF STRESS

One source of stress arises from the decisionmakers' awareness of their own limited knowledge and problem-solving capabilities. This type of *cognitive stress,* as George (1974)

This chapter is based on more extensive discussions of the same topic in Janis (1983) and in Janis and Mann (1977).

labeled it, is well illustrated by something President Warren Harding told a friend when he was struggling with a major domestic problem.

> John, I can't make a damn thing out of this tax problem. I listen to one side and they seem right, and then God! I talk to the other side and they seem just as right, and there I am where I started. I know somewhere there is a book that would give me the truth, but hell, I couldn't read the book. I know somewhere there is an economist who knows the truth, but I don't know where to find him and haven't the sense to know him and trust him when I did find him. God, what a job! (George, 1974:187, quoted from Fenno, 1959:36)

Other sources of stress include fear of suffering from various losses that would occur no matter which alternative were chosen, worry about unknown things that could go wrong when vital consequences are at stake, concern about making a fool of oneself in the eyes of others, and losing self-esteem if the decision works out badly. Vital decisions often involve conflicting values, which convinces the decisionmaker that any choice he or she makes will require the sacrifice of ideals. As a result, the decisionmaker's anticipatory anxiety, shame, or guilt is increased, which adds to the level of stress (Janis & Mann, 1977).

When the level of stress is very high, the decisionmaker is likely to display *premature closure*—terminating the decisional dilemma without generating all the alternatives and without seeking or appraising the available information about the outcomes to be expected for the limited set of alternatives under consideration. A high level of stress reduces the decisionmaker's problem-solving capabilities, especially when dealing with the complicated cognitive tasks posed by decisions rendered difficult by numerous competing values. The person's attention and perceptions are somewhat impaired and there are various manifestations of cognitive rigidity. These cognitive deficiencies result in narrowing the range of perceived alternatives, overlooking long-term consequences, inefficient searching for information, erroneous assessing of expected outcomes, and using oversimplified decision rules that fail to take account of the full range of values implicated by the choice. George (1980) listed various cognitive crutches that policymakers are especially likely to rely on when they are beset by uncertainties and threats that generate stress: (1) using a minimally satisfactory criterion of choice—what Simon (1976) called "satisficing"—rather than using optimizing criteria; (2) confining the alternative choices to small incremental changes when gross alterations may be required; (3) deciding on the basis of what people in the organization seem to want without considering the main outcomes to be expected; (4) giving undue weight to historical analogies, and (5) relying on either a general formula based on ideological principles or an operational code as a guide to action without carrying out detailed analyses of the specific policy issues at hand.

Stress encroaches most profoundly on decisionmaking processes when the decisionmaker is in a dilemma about what to do about imminent threats of physical suffering, bodily injury, or death. Elstein and Bordage (1979) pointed out that at times of acute distress, one of the main assumptions of theories of rational choice is violated, namely, that preferences will remain sufficiently stable so that the person will regard any given outcome as having essentially the same utility shortly after making a decision as he or she did at the time the decision was made: "A patient in severe pain or grave distress may evaluate a variety of outcomes quite differently than when pain and distress are absent. Consequently, a set of utility estimates obtained under one condition may not apply when conditions are altered" (p. 363).

These and other changes arising from stress account for gross deviations from the decisionmaking behavior predicted by descriptive rational models for many vital decisions, such as those made by patients who need medical treatment or surgery. For example, the vast majority of patients with acute myocardial infarctions, according to Hackett and Cassem (1975), realize that they may be having a heart attack but delay calling a physician for four or five hours. "The decision making process," the authors asserted, "gets jammed by the patient's inability to admit that he is mortally sick" (p. 27). Similar maladaptive delay, which significantly increases a patient's chances of dying, has been observed among people suffering from symptoms of cancer (Blackwell, 1963; Kasl & Cobb, 1966). Few patients who postpone a medical examination are unaware of the danger. The majority have been found to be familiar with the warning signs of cancer, more so than patients who promptly seek medical aid (Goldsen, Gerhardt, & Handy, 1957; Kutner, Makover, & Oppenheim, 1958). The most plausible explanation for the delay seems to be that the patients fail to make a decision on a rational basis because they are trying to ward off anxiety by avoiding exposure to threat cues, such as distressing information from a physician.

The same criticisms also apply to the *health-belief model* developed by Hochbaum (1958), which incorporates essentially the same assumptions about rational choices as the subjective–expected utility model. Nevertheless, it is quite possible that for certain types of decisions pertaining to preventive measures, such as cutting down on smoking, made at a time when people are not emotionally aroused, a rational model may predict fairly well (Becker & Maiman, 1975; Kirscht & Rosenstock, 1979; Mausner & Platt, 1971). Ultimately, a comprehensive theory needs to be developed to predict and explain when choices will be made on a rational basis and when not.

A CONFLICT-THEORY ANALYSIS

Stress does not always have detrimental or maladaptive effects. On the contrary, anticipatory fear of excessive losses sometimes prevents premature closure. Such concerns can serve as incentives to carry out the adaptive "work of worrying," which leads to careful information search and appraisal (Janis, 1958, 1971; Janis & Mann, 1977). This brings us to another major problem that requires theoretical analysis and empirical research: under what conditions does stress have favorable versus unfavorable effects on the quality of decision-making? In other words, when is stress healthy and when not?

The *conflict-theory analysis* formulated by Janis and Mann (1977) attempted to answer this question, as well as the broader question posed earlier concerning the conditions under which people will use sound decisionmaking procedures to arrive at a rational choice. This analysis focused on different ways people deal with stress when they are making vital decisions, contrasting coping patterns that result in defective forms of problem–solving with a vigilant coping pattern, which generally meets the standards of rational decisionmaking. Janis and Mann began their analysis by specifying the main criteria that can be used to judge whether or not a person's decision is of high quality with regard to the problem-solving procedures that lead up to the act of commitment. The following seven criteria were extracted from the extensive literature on effective decisionmaking. The decisionmaker (1) thoroughly canvasses a wide range of alternative courses of action; (2) takes account of the full range of objectives to be fulfilled and the values implicated by the choice; (3) carefully weighs whatever he or she knows about the costs or drawbacks and the uncertain risks of negative consequences, as well as the positive consequences, that could flow from each alternative; (4) intensively searches for new information relevant for further evaluation of the alternatives; (5) conscientiously takes account of any new information or expert judgment to which he or she is exposed, even when the information or judgment does not support the course of action he or she initially preferred; (6) reexamines the positive and negative consequences of all known alternatives, including those originally regarded as unacceptable, before making a final choice; and (7) makes detailed provisions for implementing the chosen course of action, with special attention to contingency plans that might be required if various known risks were to materialize.

Failure to meet any of these seven criteria is assumed to be a defect in the decisionmaking process. The more such defects are present before the decisionmaker becomes committed, the greater the chance that he or she will undergo unanticipated setbacks and postdecisional regret, which favor reversal of the decision. Although systematic data are not yet available on this point, it seems plausible to assume that *high-quality decisions*—in the sense of satisfying these procedural criteria—have a better chance than others of attaining the decisionmaker's objectives and of being adhered to in the long run.

Janis and Mann (1977) postulated that stress engendered by decisional conflict frequently is a major determinant of failure to meet the criteria for high-quality decisionmaking. *Decisional conflict* refers to simultaneous tendencies within the individual to accept and to reject a given course of action. The most prominent symptoms of such conflicts are hesitation, vacillation, feelings of uncertainty, and signs of acute psychological stress (anxiety, shame, guilt, or other unpleasant affect) whenever the decision comes to the focus of attention. Such conflicts arise whenever the decisionmaker is concerned about the material and social losses he or she might suffer from whichever course of action is choosen—including the costs of failing to live up to prior commitments. The more severe the anticipated losses, the higher the level of stress. Stress is augmented when the person recognizes that his or her reputation and self-esteem as a competent decisionmaker are also at stake.

In assuming that the stress itself is frequently a major cause of errors in decisionmaking, Janis and Mann (1977) did not deny the influence of other common causes, such as ignorance, prejudice, and bureaucratic politics. They maintained, however, that many ill-conceived and poorly implemented decisions reflect the motivational consequences of decisional conflict, particularly attempts to ward off the stresses generated by agonizingly difficult choices.

In line with their initial assumptions, Janis and Mann (1977) postulated that there are five basic patterns of coping with the stresses generated when people have to make a vital choice. Each pattern is associated with a specific set of antecedent conditions and a characteristic level of stress. These patterns, listed below, were derived from an analysis of the research literature on psychological stress bearing on how people react to warnings that urge protective action to avert disasters, health hazards, or other serious threats.

1. *Unconflicted inertia.* The decisionmaker complacently decides to continue whatever he or she has been doing, ignoring information about associated risks.

2. *Unconflicted change.* The decisionmaker uncritically adopts whichever new course of action is most salient or most strongly recommended, without making contingency plans and without psychologically preparing for setbacks.

3. *Defensive avoidance.* The decisionmaker evades the conflict by procrastinating, by shifting responsibility to someone else, or by constructing wishful rationalizations that bolster the least objectionable alternative, minimizing the expected unfavorable consequences and remaining selectively inattentive to corrective information.

4. *Hypervigilance.* The decisionmaker, in a paniclike state, searches frantically for a way out of the dilemma, rapidly shifts back and forth between alternatives, and impulsively seizes upon a hastily contrived solution that seems to promise immediate relief. He or she

overlooks the full range of consequences of his or her choice because of emotional excitement, repetitive thinking, and cognitive constriction (manifested by reduction in immediate memory span and by simplistic ideas).

5. *Vigilance.* The decisionmaker searches painstakingly for relevant information, assimilates information in an unbiased manner, and appraises alternatives carefully before making a choice.

While the first two patterns occasionally are adaptive in saving time, effort, and emotional wear and tear, especially for routine or minor decisions, they often lead to defective decisions when the individual must make a choice that has serious personal or family consequences or profound implications for the organization he or she represents. Similarly, defensive avoidance and hypervigilance may be adaptive in certain extreme situations but generally reduce the decisionmaker's chances of averting serious losses. Consequently, all four are regarded as defective patterns of decisionmaking. The fifth pattern, vigilance, although occasionally maladaptive if danger is imminent and a split-second response is required, generally leads to decisions that meet the main criteria for rational or sound decisionmaking.

Janis and Mann (1977) postulated that people will weigh the benefits of a recommended course of action against the perceived costs of, or barriers to, taking that action, as is assumed by rational-choice models, *only when their coping pattern is vigilance.* When any of the four defective coping patterns is dominant, the decisionmaker will *fail* to carry out adequately the cognitive tasks that are essential for arriving at stable decisions. Then when they experience undesirable consequences, such as the usual unpleasant side effects of a standard medical treatment or unexpected demands for overtime work shortly after starting on a new job, they are likely to overreact. They suffer not just from the distressing setback but also from strong feelings of postdecisional regret, which may interfere with their ability to curtail the losses or to make a sound new decision that will enable them to recover rapidly from the setback. Postdecisional regret entails intense emotional arousal, such as anxiety and rage, which creates a high level of stress and could give rise to psychosomatic disorders (Janis, Defares, & Grossman, 1982).

What are the conditions that foster vigilance and how do they differ from those that underlie each of the four defective coping patterns? The answer to this question is presented in Figure 5–1, which is a schematic summary of the Janis and Mann (1977) conflict model of decisionmaking. This model specifies the psychological conditions responsible for the five coping patterns and the level of stress that accompanies them. The coping patterns are determined by the presence or absence of three conditions: (1) awareness of serious risks associated with whichever alternative is chosen (i.e., arousal of conflict), (2) hope of finding a better alternative, and (3) belief that there is adequate time in which to seek information and to deliberate before a decision is required. Although there may be marked individual differences in preference for one or another of the coping patterns, all five patterns are assumed to be in the repertoire of every person when he or she functions as a decisionmaker. In different circumstances the same person will use different coping patterns depending on which of the three crucial conditions are present or absent.

Janis and Mann (1977) did not claim that the five patterns occur *only* as a result of specified conditions. Rather, they argued that the patterns are linked dependably with the mediating psychological conditions specified in Figure 5–1—a claim that has numerous implications, including descriptive hypotheses about environmental circumstances that generate vigilance and prescriptive hypotheses about deliberate interventions that could be used to counteract the beliefs and perceptions responsible for defective coping patterns.

Antecedent Conditions   Mediating Processes   Consequences

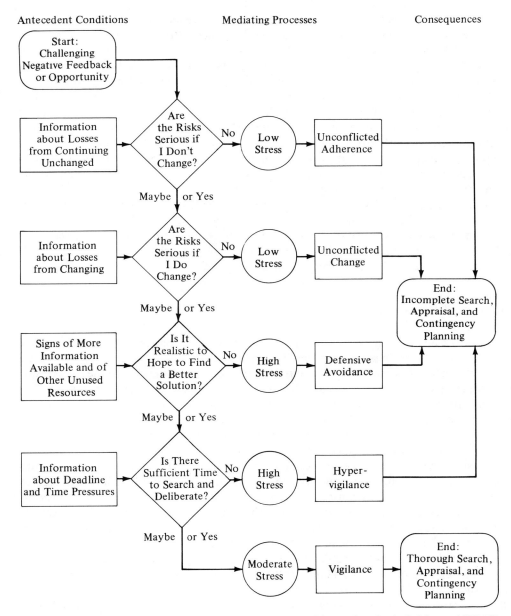

FIGURE 5-1. The conflict-theory model of decisionmaking *(after Janis & Mann, 1977:70).*

In their review of social–psychological studies bearing on premature closure, postdecisional regret, and a number of other aspects of decisional behavior, Janis and Mann (1977) called attention to scattered findings consistent with predictions about the behavioral consequences of vigilant versus nonvigilant coping patterns, from which they concluded that their theoretical analysis is plausible. They also described a few of their own experiments that were designed to test hypotheses derived from their conflict model. One such experiment by

Mann, Janis, and Chaplin (1969), for example, dealt with threats of the type encountered by many people who have to make decisions about taking medications or undergoing medical treatments that create nausea and other temporary side effects that are harmless but unpleasant. As predicted by the conflict-theory model, subjects who were led to believe that no additional information could be expected (which reduced their hope of finding a more adequate solution) tended to bolster the alternative they had originally preferred, which is a manifestation of defensive avoidance. Bolstering was evidenced by a spread in the relative attractiveness of the alternatives. In contrast, among subjects who were led to expect more information, there was virtually no tendency to bolster—another finding consistent with the conflict model, which specifies that vigilance will be the dominant coping pattern under such circumstances. The results indicated that bolstering occurs before overt commitment if the conditions that foster defensive avoidance are present.

None of the studies carried out so far can be regarded as crucial experiments that definitively test the conflict-theory model or enable one to decide that this model is better in general than other psychological theories of decisionmaking. In the present early stage of research on decisionmaking under stress, the conflict-theory model appears to have heuristic value in that it calls attention to neglected variables that affect decisionmaking behavior.

Effects of Warnings

Any theory of decisionmaking under stress should have something important to say about the effects of warnings about impending dangers. Throughout their lives, people are exposed to an unending stream of challenging warnings that call attention to the risks of suffering serious losses unless they decide to adopt a new course of protective action. The challenging information is sometimes conveyed by disturbing events, as when a heavy smoker develops a chronic cough. Fairly often, however, the challenging information that initiates the decisionmaking process is contained in impressive communications, such as a weather bureau's warning of an oncoming tornado or a physician's warning to stop smoking after a physical checkup has revealed precancerous cells in a patient's lungs. Just as with scare propaganda, authentic warnings that arouse intense emotional reactions can lead to resistance to change, misattributions, erroneous judgments, and defective decisions, sometimes as a result of panic or extreme reactions of defensive avoidance. What can be done to prevent such adverse reactions? Under what conditions are fear arousing warnings most likely to be effective in evoking decisions to take adaptive action?

Some tentative answers have come from social–psychological studies of the effects of warnings and emotional appeals (Janis, 1967, 1971; Leventhal, 1973; McGuire, 1969; Rogers & Mewborn, 1976). Dozens of controlled attitude change experiments have been carried out to determine whether acceptance of precautionary recommendations increases or decreases when strong fear appeals, as compared with milder ones, are used. One set of such experiments dealing with real-life threats of illness or other adverse consequences, indicated that there can be diminishing returns as the level of fear arousal is increased (Janis & Feshbach, 1953; Janis & Terwilliger, 1962; Rogers & Thistlethwaite, 1970). These experiments support the following conclusion, which is consistent with the Janis and Mann (1977) conflict model: when fear is strongly aroused by a communication but is not fully relieved by reassurances that build up hope of averting the danger, the recipients will display a pattern of defensive avoidance as manifested by tendencies to ignore, minimize, or deny the importance of the threat. On the other hand, another set of experiments dealing with similar threats showed that strong threat appeals can be more effective than milder ones. These experiments pointed to the facilitating effects of fear arousal (Insko, Arkoff, & Insko, 1965; Leventhal, Singer, & Jones, 1965).

Taken together, the two sets of results suggest that changes in feelings of vulnerability to a threat and subsequent adoption of a recommended course of action depend upon the relative strength of facilitating and interfering reactions, both of which are likely to be evoked whenever a warning by an authority arouses fear. If so, we cannot expect to discover any simple generalization applicable to warnings given by authoritative sources that will tell us whether strong fear arousing presentations that vividly depict the expected dangers or milder versions that merely allude to the threats will be more effective. Rather, we must expect the optimal level of fear arousal to vary for different types of threat, for different types of recommended action, and for different personalities.

Social–psychological investigators generally agree that the effectiveness of any fear-arousing communication urging people to take protective action depends partly upon three content variables that interact in complex ways (Hovland, Janis, & Kelley, 1953; McGuire, 1969; Rogers & Mewborn, 1976):

1. magnitude of the threat (if it were to materialize)
2. probability of the threat's materializing (if no protective action is taken)
3. probable effectiveness of the recommended protective action (if that action is taken)

These three components are among the key components of the subjective–expected utility model and the health-belief model, discussed earlier. According to these rational-choice models, people suffering from an illness can be expected to accept their physicians' recommendations if they believe that the probable consequences of doing what is recommended—despite all the costs in terms of money, time, effort, and discomfort—are preferable to the consequences of the untreated illness. But, as I have already stated, this model is expected to hold only in the presence of the conditions necessary for a vigilant pattern of coping. Some of the findings cited earlier on delay of treatment and other maladaptive responses among patients suffering from heart disease or cancer appear to bear out this assumption.

The crucial role of the third component—perceived efficacy of the recommended means for averting or minimizing the threat—is repeatedly borne out by social-psychological research on the effects of public health messages that contain fear-arousing warnings (Chu, 1966; Leventhal, 1973; Leventhal, Singer, & Jones, 1965; Rogers & Deckner, 1975; Rogers & Thistlethwaite, 1970). Rogers and Mewborn (1976), for example, found that assertions about the efficacy of recommended protective actions had a significant effect on college students' intentions to adopt the practices recommended in three different public health communications dealing with well-known hazards that produce preventable human suffering—lung cancer, automobile accident injuries, and venereal disease.

The findings just cited appear to be consistent with the following hypothesis derived from the conflict-theory model: when a warning message presents realistic information about the unfavorable consequences of alternative courses of action—such as consent forms that describe the risks and suffering that could arise from undergoing surgery or painful medical treatments—it is most likely to induce vigilance and to instigate sound decisionmaking procedures if it is accompanied by impressive information about the expected efficacy of the recommended course of action, which instills hope about dealing effectively with anticipated threats. Vigilance is likely to be replaced by unconflicted inertia, however, once people have been given warnings that turn out to be false alarms. Breznitz's (1967, 1976) laboratory experiments using the threat of electric shock indicated that when people are warned about an impending threat and then told that the danger has been postponed or canceled, they show a characteristic false-alarm reaction in response to subsequent warnings about the same danger; they tend to display much less fear and to ignore the new warnings.

Hypervigilance

The grossest errors in decisionmaking are to be expected whenever hypervigilance is the dominant stress reaction. The emotional state of panic or near panic that is at the core of the hypervigilant pattern might involve what Selye (1956) called the initial *alarm reaction* of the *general adaptation syndrome* evoked by powerful stressors. According to Selye, this stage, which is distinguished by a marked increase in sympathetic-adrenal activity, is followed by a *stage of physiological resistance* and then a final *stage of exhaustion or collapse.*

Fortunately, the paniclike state that characterizes hypervigilance seldom occurs in everyday life or even in extreme emergencies (Schultz, 1964). On those rare occasions when hypervigilance is elicited by warnings of, or actual confrontations with, danger, cognitive functioning is seriously impaired.

Many controlled psychological experiments have tested cognitive performance after exposure to threats, such as telling subjects that they are going to be given painful electric shocks. In general, it appears that minor threats have little or no effect but serious threats can evoke temporary impairment in cognitive functioning (Hamilton, 1975; Janis, 1971; Janis & Leventhal, 1968).

Excessive alertness to all signs of potential threat results in diffusion of attention. This is one of the main sources of cognitive inefficiency whenever someone becomes hypervigilant, and it probably accounts for some of the failures to meet the criteria for effective decisionmaking. Persons in a hypervigilant state are strongly motivated to engage in thorough search and appraisal. But as they try to carry out essential cognitive tasks, such as searching for reliable information about what seems to be a promising course of action (by consulting an expert) or trying to remember what happened when they tried to deal with similar threats in the past, they are constantly distracted and their train of thought gets derailed. Their attention shifts rapidly to all sorts of other threat cues, many of which are inauthentic or unimportant but nevertheless alarming. They are also likely to be distracted from essential cognitive tasks by obsessional ideas about all the things that could go wrong or about the worst possible outcomes. Because of their indiscriminate attentiveness to all sorts of threats, relevant and irrelevant, much of the time and energy available for working out a satisfactory decision about the best available course of protective action is wasted. Then when a deadline is at hand, they are likely to seize upon an ill-conceived solution that is useful mainly for mitigating whichever source of danger happens to be most salient at the moment but that may be a poor solution because it overlooks other threats that need to be taken into account. For example, in a state of near panic after hearing a horror story from an ill-informed and thoughtless visitor, a cancer patient in dire need of extensive surgery may suddenly decide not to have a recommended operation and leave the hospital.

An experiment by Sigall and Helmreich (1969) provided impressive evidence of the tendency for people in a state of high fear to fail to discriminate between credible and noncredible sources of a persuasive communication, which results in indiscriminate acceptance of the message. The failure to make such discriminatory evaluations and also the failure to adopt a critical stance in evaluating the authenticity, plausibility, and personal applicability of warning messages may be caused partly by the diffusion of attention and partly by the lowering of mental efficiency that occurs whenever a person is in a state of high emotional arousal.

Along with cognitive constriction there is a marked tendency toward stereotyped thinking in terms of oversimplified categories and reliance on simpleminded decision rules. In fire emergencies that occur in crowded theaters or restaurants, for example, where fear is very high and decision time is very short, people tend to follow the simple decision rule that the best way to escape is to do what everyone else is doing, i.e., to run to whichever exit the crowd is heading for. Other available escape routes are overlooked as everyone converges on the same exit, which soon becomes blocked; as a result, many people unnecessarily lose their lives (Schultz, 1964). But if someone who is perceived as a leader is present in panic-inducing situations, mass convergence into a bottleneck can be prevented by authoritative directives. In such instances, the simple decision rule to do whatever others are doing appears to be replaced by the equally simple rule to do whatever an authority figure tells one to do. Both decision rules may reflect a general increase in social dependence that occurs under conditions of high fear, which is manifested by overt efforts to avoid being separated from companions, strong preference for contact with authority figures who are capable of giving reassurances, and increased compliance (Janis, 1958, 1971; Schachter, 1959).

Other behavioral consequences of strong fear arousal have been investigated in field studies of natural disasters and in laboratory experiments. Closely related to the temporary loss of cognitive efficiency is the temporary loss of perceptual acuity, perceptual-motor coordination, and motor skills (Duffy, 1962). Clumsiness on manual tasks results partly from the muscular tenseness that occurs in states of fear arousal, which is manifested by the stiffening of muscles all over the body and by muscular tremors. Facial expressions also tend to become rigid, partly because of taut facial muscles (Ekman, Freisen, & Ellsworth, 1972; Izard, 1971).

Lazarus (1966, 1976) pointed out that coping with stress is essentially a matter of problem-solving under conditions wherein it is not clear what to do. Because problem-solving activities become grossly inefficient when people are in a state of hypervigilance, they are likely to fail to choose an adaptive course of action that will reduce the risks posed by the anticipated danger. Efforts to escape or to aggress against the perceived source of threat are likely to be misdirected and ineffectual.

When people suddenly realize that they may be entrapped in a danger situation, such as a rapidly approaching tornado, they tend to become so agitated that they fail to use whatever time is available to find the best available escape route and fail to notice obvious defects in the one they impulsively choose (see Fritz & Marks, 1954). Similar failures to make full use of their cognitive capabilities have been observed in the emergency decisionmaking of jittery people who display less extreme forms of hypervigilance, when confronted with community warnings about potential radiation hazards in a nearby atomic energy plant or with personal warnings from a physician about the possibility that a skin growth might be malignant. Many such people become obsessed with images of horrifying things that may happen to them and fall prey to informational overload as they indiscriminately pay attention to all sorts of warnings, advice, and rumors about the threat (Horowitz, 1976; Janis, 1971). Sometimes a person's impulsive action takes the form of unwarranted fight rather than flight.

The disruptive effects of a high level of stress in circumstances requiring immediate protective activity are illustrated by the thoughtless action taken by a law enforcement agent during the race riot in Detroit in 1967, as described in the Report of the National Advisory Commission on Civil

Disorders (1968, p. 98). A white National Guardsman believed that his own life was in immediate danger from snipers when he heard shots nearby after having been summoned by a nightwatchman to investigate looting. Instead of taking cover and watching to see what was going on, he promptly decided to shoot to kill when he caught sight of a black man holding a pistol. The victim turned out to be the nightwatchman, who had shot his pistol into the air to scare off the looters. (Janis & Mann, 1977:61)

During and immediately after tornadoes, earthquakes, explosions, conflagrations, air raids, or other major disasters, large numbers of survivors admit that they feel terrified and at the same time, they display marked signs of high physiological arousal (Janis, 1951, 1971; Rachman, 1978). Most disaster survivors recover rapidly, within a half hour after the danger has subsided, but in a minority of cases symptoms of jitteriness persist for days and sometimes weeks, along with excessive physiological arousal in response to noises and minor threats, which appear to be reactivations of the alarm reaction. When this occurs, the person repeatedly displays the characteristic symptoms of psychological trauma—trembling of the hands, preoccupation with possible recurrences of danger, and terrifying nightmares and intrusive daytime visions in which traumatic events are reexperienced (Horowitz, 1976; Janis, 1951). This persisting state of hypervigilance, which continues to interfere with effective decisionmaking, may alternate with feelings of numbness, denial of loss, efforts to ward off exposure to reminders of the disaster, and other manifestations of extreme defensive avoidance tendencies (Horowitz, 1976).

The readiness to become jittery, agitated, and preoccupied with frightening images in response to any threat of physical danger is thought to be related to a number of personality variables. Among the predisposing attributes frequently mentioned in the literature on personality research are chronic anxiety neurosis, low ego strength, low self-confidence, low problem-solving ability, and low capacity for developing or using a network of social supports (e.g., Jenkins, 1979). Empirical findings bearing on such variables, however, are not clear-cut and sometimes are mutually contradictory. Obviously, methodological refinements are needed in personality research in order to pin down the predisposing variables related to different ways of coping with threat (Cohen & Lazarus, 1979).

Somewhat more dependable evidence is available on situational variables that are thought to be determinants of ineffective coping. The evidence points to a number of primary and secondary causal factors that contribute to hypervigilant reactions.

Near-miss Experiences, Time Pressures, and Other Causal Factors

Considerable evidence of the traumatizing effects of exposure to danger stimuli has accumulated from case studies and surveys of people who have been injured or have undergone narrow escapes in accidents or disasters (Janis, 1971). Even among the most stable personalities, hypervigilance apparently occurs at least temporarily following direct involvement in a disaster. Why do some survivors fail to recover rapidly from emotional shock and display hypervigilant reactions for many weeks each time they are exposed to reminders of how close they came to being either badly hurt or killed? One of the critical determinants of sustained hypervigilance seems to be what MacCurdy (1943) labeled a *near-miss experience*. Studies of wartime and peacetime disasters have indicated that the most intense and prolonged symptoms of hypervigilance tend to develop among survivors who were in close proximity to actual danger and experienced a near miss, such as narrowly escaping serious injury when their home was destroyed, being pinned down by fàllen debris, losing relatives or friends, and seeing maimed bodies (Janis, 1951; Rachman, 1978; Wolfenstein, 1957). Survivors who had *remote-miss experiences*, on the other hand, showed a marked tendency toward increased tolerance of stress, manifested by decreased fear with successive exposure to the same type of danger, presumably as result of habituation or emotional adaptation.

Survey data on 544 combat flying officers (Grinker, Willerman, Bradley, & Fastarsky, 1946) indicated that fliers who had developed extreme fear and symptoms of traumatic neurosis during combat duty were much less likely to give affirmative answers to questions about feelings of personal invulnerability ("While others might be hurt or killed, it couldn't happen to me") than were fliers who had undergone similar tours of duty without developing severe fear or anxiety symptoms. Although such correlational findings cannot establish a causal sequence, they are consistent with the hypothesis that when people develop the characteristic pattern of hypervigilance following exposure to danger, the mediating psychological process is a change in attitude concerning personal vulnerability. This hypothesis appears to be plausible in light of impressionistic observations in peacetime disasters (Janis, 1962; Wolfenstein, 1957), but has not yet been tested systematically.

In the extensive research literature on human fear reactions, a number of other factors in addition to near-miss exposures have been described that apparently augment fear during disasters and that may hamper decisionmaking after frightening encounters with extreme danger. Among the factors most frequently implicated as antecedents of hypervigilant reactions are lack of contact with family members or other supportive persons, restrictions of activity, lack of perceived control over dangerous events, and lack of preparatory information about the stressful events to be expected and about what to do to build up one's coping skills (Cox, 1978; Epstein, 1973; Janis, 1971; Rodin & Janis, 1979; Monat & Lazarus, 1977; Rachman, 1978). Both field studies and laboratory experiments have indicated that these factors can increase the probability of sustained hypervigilance, although not in all circumstances. Considerable research is required to determine the conditions under which each of these factors has the expected detrimental effect as against a favorable effect or no effect at all.

Janis and Mann's (1977) analysis of emergency decisionmaking emphasized *time pressure* as one of the major determinants of hypervigilance when people are exposed to serious threats of physical injury or death. Disaster studies indicate that panic, the most extreme form of hypervigilance, tends to occur when people perceive that danger is imminent and that escape routes are rapidly closing off. That is to say, people facing danger are likely to become hypervigilant if they expect to be helpless to avoid being victimized unless they act very quickly. Under these conditions, the most extreme instances of cognitive impairment, poor judgment, and maladaptive impulsive decisions are likely to occur. There is even some evidence suggesting that when people are told that a disaster is expected to strike within a few minutes, their frantic escape attempts are so unrealistic that they increase rather than decrease the danger and that most poeple would be better off with no warning at all (Fritz & Marks, 1954).

In a series of laboratory experiments that confronted subjects with the threat of painful electric shocks, Kelley and his co-workers (1965) found that paniclike reactions resulting in entrapment were likely when subjects were under extreme time pressure. The findings indicated that when fear is aroused in a threat situation that allows only a short time for escape, people frantically take action without regard for the available opportunities that would enable them to escape successfully.

Janis and Mann (1977) postulated that the hypervigilant pattern is fostered by deadline pressures whenever people must take action to avert a threatened loss, whether it concerns their personal safety, career goals, social or financial status; or other important values. At a time when decisionmakers are in a state of acute decisional conflict because of the perceived risks entailed by whichever available course of action is chosen, the likelihood that they will become excessively preoccupied with the threatened losses and will display the other symptoms of hypervigilance increases if they receive information about an impending deadline that leads them to believe that they have insufficient time to search for a good solution. Under these pressing conditions, people become indiscriminately receptive to rumors about terrible things that might happen. They fail to take account of evidence indicating the improbability of exaggerated dangers, vacillate as they try to avoid each of the risky alternatives that could lead to catastrophe, and finally choose hastily whichever course of action appears at the moment to be least dangerous.

Some persons may be under constant time pressure as a result of either situational demands that create an overloaded daily schedule of urgent obligations or personality predispositions or both. Whatever the cause may be, such persons can be expected to become hypervigilant much more readily than others in response to warnings and approaching deadlines, which leads to ill-considered decisions that are frequently followed by postdecisional conflict and frustration. It is noteworthy that a chronic sense of time urgency has been found to be a major component of *type A personalities,* who are at high risk with regard to coronary heart disease (see Glass, 1977).

The combination of sudden, unexpected threat, with extreme time pressure to avert the danger, appears to be one of the conditions that most consistently fosters a state of hypervigilance, in which people are likely to commit themselves impulsively to courses of action that they soon will have cause to regret. This treacherous combination is most likely to occur, according to Janis and Mann (1977), when decisionmakers have failed to react vigilantly to earlier warnings about the threat. When reactions to initial warnings take the form of defensive avoidance rather than vigilance, people ignore the warnings, fail to search for relevant information, and do not adequately appraise the risks entailed by the alternative courses of action. They evade decisional conflict by shifting responsibility for the decision to someone else, by procrastinating, and/or by constructing wishful rationalizations that bolster the least objectionable alternative, which results in their minimizing the losses to be expected. As Figure 5–1 indicated, this defective coping pattern is most likely to occur when people in a state of high decisional conflict about the risks entailed by choosing any of the available alternatives have little hope of finding a satisfactory solution.

When defensive avoidance is the dominant pattern, decisionmakers remain inattentive to corrective information until they are confronted by a dramatic threat that catches them by surprise, which sets the stage for a hypervigilant reaction. The same thing is likely to happen if decisionmakers misunderstand or fail to grasp the significance of earlier warnings and, as a result, feel genuinely unconcerned about the risks or dangers that might lie ahead. This pattern of unconflicted inertia leaves decisionmakers just as unprepared for sudden bad news about threats of serious losses as does defensive avoidance. Unconflicted inertia and defensive avoidance in response to early warnings about a given threat can be regarded as psychological reactions that increase the probability of hypervigilance in response to a subsequent confrontation with the danger.

PREVENTION OF DEFECTIVE COPING PATTERNS

In recent years a variety of psychological techniques have been designed to prevent the onset of defective coping patterns in threatening situations or to minimize such reactions if they already exist. These include benign preexposure to the threatening situation, stress inoculation via preparatory communications, and controlled breathing and relaxation procedures designed to moderate physiological responses to emotion arousing situations. Studies of these techniques, although seldom sufficiently well controlled to provide definitive results, have suggested that each of them is at least partially successful for some people in some circumstances (Janis, Defares, & Grossman, 1982).

The conflict-theory analysis of decisionmaking (Fig. 5-1) leads us to expect that counseling can be an effective aid to making decisions under stressful conditions insofar as it counteracts the conditions underlying defective coping patterns and promotes the psychological conditions conducive to vigilance. A number of interventions have been developed for this purpose, including an awareness-of-rationalizations procedure, new forms of role-playing in structured psychodramas, and a balance-sheet procedure to induce awareness of the full range of consequences (Janis & Mann, 1977).

Perhaps the most promising type of intervention for fostering a vigilant approach to recurrent threats that are likely to be disruptive and demoralizing is *stress inoculation*. This technique is usually applied shortly after a decision has been made but before it is implemented. Inoculation for emotional stress involves exposing the decisionmaker to preparatory information that vividly describes what it will be like to experience the expected negative consequences of the chosen course of action. Preparatory information functions as a form of inoculation if it enables the person to increase his or her tolerance for postdecisional stress by developing effective reassurances and coping mechanisms (Janis, 1958, 1971; Meichenbaum, 1977; Meichenbaum & Turk, 1976). This type of intervention is called inoculation because it may be analogous to the process whereby antibodies are induced in response to injections of mildly virulent toxins.

The underlying principle is that accurate preparatory information about an impending crisis gives people the opportunity to anticipate the loss, to start working through their anxiety or grief, and to make plans that will enable them to cope more adequately. The psychological processes stimulated by preparatory information include correcting faulty beliefs, reconceptualizing the threat, and engaging in realistic self-persuasion about the value of protective action, as well as developing concepts and self–instructions that enable the person to deal more effectively with setbacks (Janis, 1971, 1982).

We would expect stress inoculation procedures to be effective for any decision that entails severe short-term losses before substantial long-term gains are attained. Most decisions concerning personal health problems belong in this category because they usually require the person to undergo painful treatments and deprivations before his or her physical well-being improves. Much of the evidence concerning the effectiveness of stress inoculation procedures has come from studies of such decisions—voluntary submission to abdominal surgery, painful medical treatments, and the like. Correlational results from Janis's (1958) studies of surgical patients indicated that those who received information about the unpleasant consequences beforehand were less likely to overreact emotionally to setbacks and adverse events during the postdecisional period. Supporting evidence has come from a number of controlled field experiments with people who decided to accept their physicians' recommendations to undergo surgery (Egbert, Battit, Welch, & Bartlett, 1964; Johnson, 1966; Schmidt, 1966; Schmitt & Wooldridge, 1973; Vernon & Bigelow, 1974). These studies indicated that when physicians or nurses gave preoperative information about the stresses of surgery and ways of coping with those stresses, adult patients showed less postoperative distress and sometimes better recovery. Positive results on the value of stress inoculation also were found in studies of childbirth (Breen, 1975; Levy & McGee, 1975) and of noxious medical examinations requiring patients to swallow tubes (Johnson & Leventhal, 1974).

Field experiments by Moran (1963) and by Wolfer and Visintainer (1975) with children on pediatric surgery wards yielded similar results.

A completely different area, that of work decisions, also has produced evidence that stress inoculation can dampen postdecisional conflict and minimize the tendency to reverse the decision when setbacks are encountered. New employees who are given realistic preparatory information at the time they are offered the job, or immediately after they accept the job, are more likely to stay with the organization (Gomersall & Myers, 1966; Macedonia, 1969; Wanous, 1973; Youngberg, 1963).

All these findings support the conclusion that many people will display higher stress tolerance in response to undesirable consequences if they have been given advance warnings about what to expect, together with sufficient reassurance, so that fear does not mount to an intolerably high level. There are exceptions, of course, such as neurotic personalities who are hypersensitive to any threat cues. But such considerations do not preclude the possibility that techniques of stress inoculation might be developed and used by decision counselors to help mitigate the impact of a wide variety of anticipated postdecisional setbacks, especially when the chosen course of action requires undergoing temporary losses in order to achieve long-term goals.

Meichenbaum's (1977) stress inoculation training program involves three main steps: (1) discussing the nature of stress reactions to provide clients with a conceptual framework and to motivate them to acquire new coping skills; (2) teaching and inducing rehearsal of coping skills—such as collecting information about what is likely to happen and arranging for ways to deal effectively with anxiety engendering events; and (3) encouraging the client to practice and apply the newly acquired coping skills to stressful conditions, by means of either role-playing in imagined stress situations or actual exposure to real-life stresses. This type of training has been found to be at least partially successful in increasing adherence to a number of stressful choices, including decisions to reenter phobic situations (Meichenbaum & Cameron, 1973) and to undergo pain (Turk, 1975). Some negative results, however, were reported by Girodo and Roehl (1976) for the decision to travel by plane by college women who were afraid of flying. After reviewing the positive and negative outcomes of studies employing stress inoculation training, Girodo (1977) suggested that the successful components are those that induce the person to reconceptualize the threat into nonthreatening terms and that all other self-statements serve merely as attention diversion mechanisms. Any such generalization, however, gives undue weight to a limited set of findings and is premature until we have well-replicated results from a variety of investigations that carefully test the effectiveness of each component of stress inoculation. It remains for the next phase of research to determine which components are the necessary and sufficient ingredients for promoting effective coping in stressful situations.

Related types of psychological intervention also need to be investigated, especially those that may help people to reconceptualize the stresses engendered by a stressful course of action, such as going through with a divorce, a drastic career change, or a surgical operation. For example, an effective coping device developed for use by counselors in hospitals and other medical settings by Langer, Janis, and Wolfer (1975) involves encouraging an optimistic reappraisal of anxiety provoking events to build up the clients' realistic hopes of dealing effectively with whatever suffering or setbacks might be encountered.

By inducing people to arrive at an accurate blueprint of the consequences that might be in store for them and of the coping resources at their disposal, decision counselors should be able to help clients build a basic attitude of self-confidence, maintain a vigilant approach throughout all the stages of decisionmaking, and develop realistic reassurances. This type of reassurance can have a dampening effect whenever a postdecisional setback occurs that otherwise might evoke a high degree of stress, resulting in defective coping reactions.

REFERENCES

BECKER, M. H., & MAIMAN, L. A. Sociobehavioral determinants of compliance with health and medical care recommendations. *Medical Care,* 1975, *13,* 10–24.

BLACKWELL, B. The literature of delay in seeking medical care for chronic illnesses. *Health Education Monographs,* 1963, *3*(16), 3–31.

BREEN, D. *The birth of a first child: Towards an understanding of femininity.* London: Tavistock, 1975.

BREZNITZ, S. Incubation of threat, duration of anticipation, and false alarm as determinants of fear reaction to an unavoidable frightening event. *Journal of Experimental Research in Personality,* 1967, *2,* 173–180.

————. False alarms: Their effects on fear and adjustment. In I. G. Sarason & C. D. Speilberger (eds.), *Stress and anxiety,* vol 3. New York: Wiley, 1976.

BROADHURST, A. Applications of the psychology of decisions. In M. P. Feldman & A. Broadhurst (eds.), *Theoretical and experimental bases of the behavior therapies.* New York: Wiley, 1976.

CHU, C. C. Fear arousal, efficacy, and imminency. *Journal of Personality and Social Psychology,* 1966, *4,* 517–524.

COHEN, F., & LAZARUS, R. S. Coping with the stresses of illness. In G. C. Stone, F. Cohen & N. E. Adler (eds.), *Health psychology.* San Francisco: Jossey-Bass, 1979.

COX, T. *Stress.* New York: Macmillan, 1978.

DUFFY, E. *Activation and behavior.* New York: McGraw-Hill, 1962.

EDWARDS, W. The theory of decision making. *Psychological Bulletin,* 1954, *51,* 380–417.

EGBERT, L., BATTIT, G., WELCH, C., & BARTLETT, M. Reduction of post-operative pain by encouragement and instruction. *New England Journal of Medicine,* 1964, *270,* 825–827.

EKMAN, P., FREISEN, W., & ELLSWORTH, P. *Emotion in the human face.* Oxford: Pergamon, 1972.

ELSTEIN, A. A., & BORDAGE, G. Psychology of clinical reasoning. In G. C. Stone, F. Cohen, & N. E. Adler (eds.), *Health psychology.* San Francisco: Jossey-Bass, 1979.

EPSTEIN, S. Expectancy and magnitude of reaction to a noxious UCS. *Psychophysiology,* 1973, *10,* 100–107.

FENNO, R. F. *The president's cabinet.* Cambridge: Harvard University Press, 1959.

FRITZ, C., & MARKS, E. The NORC studies of human behavior in disaster. *Journal of Social Issues,* 1954, *10,* 26–41.

GEORGE, A. Adaptation to stress in political decision making: The individual, small group, and organizational contexts. In G. V. Coelho, D. A. Hamburg, & J. E. Adams (eds.), *Coping and adaptation.* New York: Basic Books, 1974.

————. *Presidential decision making in foreign policy: The effective use of information and advice.* Boulder: Westview, 1980.

GIRODO, M. Self-talk: Mechanisms in anxiety and stress management. In C. D. Spielberger & I. G. Sarason (eds.), *Stress and anxiety,* vol. 4. New York: Wiley, 1977.

GIRODO, M., & ROEHL, J. Cognitive preparation and coping self-talk: Anxiety management during stress of flying. *Journal of Clinical Psychology,* 1978, *46,* 978–989.

GLASS, D. *Behavioral antecedents of coronary heart disease.* Hillsdale: Erlbaum, 1977.

GOLDSEN, R. K., GERHARDT, P. T., & HANDY, V. H. Some factors related to patient delay in seeking diagnosis for cancer symptoms. *Cancer,* 1957, *10,* 1–7.

GOMERSALL, E. R., & MYERS, M. S. Breakthrough in on-the-job training. *Harvard Business Review,* 1966, *44,* 62–72.

GRINKER, R. R., WILLERMAN, B., BRADLEY, A. D., & FASTARSKY, A. A study of psychological predisposition to the development of operational fatigue. *American Journal of Orthopsychiatry,* 1946, *16,* 191–214.

HACKETT, T. P., & CASSEM, N. H. Psychological management of the myocardial infarction patient. *Journal of Human Stress,* 1975, *1,* 25–38.

HAMILTON, V. Socialization, anxiety, and information processing: A capacity model of anxiety-induced performance. In I. G. Sarason & C. D. Spielberger (eds.), *Stress and anxiety,* vol. 2. New York: Wiley, 1975.

HOCHBAUM, G. *Public participation in medical screening programs: A sociopsychological study.* PHS publication no. 572. Bethesda: U.S. Public Health Service, 1958.

HOROWITZ, M. J. *Stress response syndromes.* New York: Aronson, 1976.

HOVLAND, C. I., JANIS, I. L., & KELLEY, H. H. *Communication and persuasion.* New Haven: Yale University Press, 1953.

INSKO, C. A., ARKOFF, A., & INSKO, U. M. Effects of high and low fear arousing communications upon opinions toward smoking. *Journal of Experimental Social Psychology,* 1965, *1,* 256–266.

IZARD, C. *The face of emotion.* New York: Appleton, 1971.

JANIS, I. L. *Air war and emotional stress.* New York: McGraw-Hill, 1951.

————. *Psychological stress,* New York: Wiley, 1958.

————. Psychological effects of warnings. In D. Chapman & G. Baker (eds.), *Man and society in disaster.* New York: Basic Books, 1962.

————. Effects of fear-arousal on attitude change. In L. Berkowitz (ed.), *Advances in experimental social psychology,* Vol. 3. New York: Academic, 1967.

————. *Stress and frustration.* New York: Harcourt, 1971.

————. The patient as decision maker. In D. Gentry (ed.), *Handbook of behavioral medicine.* New York: Guilford, 1983.

JANIS, I. L., DEFARES, P. B., & GROSSMAN, P. Hypervigilant reactions to threat. In H. Selye (ed.), *Selye's guide to stress research,* vol. 3. New York: Van Nostrand, 1982.

JANIS, I. L., & FESHBACH, S. Effects of fear-arousing communications. *Journal of Abnormal and Social Psychology,* 1953, *48,* 78–92.

JANIS, I. L., & LEVENTHAL, H. Human reactions to stress. In E. Borgatta & W. Lambert (eds.), *Handbook of personality theory and research.* Chicago: Rand McNally, 1968.

JANIS, I. L., & MANN, L. *Decision making: A psychological analysis of conflict, choice, and commitment.* New York: Free Press, 1977.

JANIS, I. L., & TERWILLIGER, R. An experimental study of psychological resistance to fear-arousing communications. *Journal of Abnormal and Social Psychology,* 1962, *65,* 403–410.

JENKINS, C. D. Psychosocial modifiers of response to stress. *Journal of Human Stress,* 1979, *5,* 3–15.

JOHNSON, J. E. *The influence of purposeful nurse-patient interaction on the patient's postoperative course.* ANA monograph series no. 2: Exploring medical-surgical nursing practice. New York: American Nurses' Association, 1966.

JOHNSON, J. E., & LEVENTHAL, H. Effects of accurate expectations and behavioral instructions on reactions during a noxious medical examination. *Journal of Personality and Social Psychology,* 1974, *29,* 710–718.

KAHNEMAN, D., & TVERSKY, A. Prospect theory: An analysis of decision under risk. *Econometrica,* 1979, *47,* 263–292.

KASL, S. V., & COBB, S. Health behavior, illness behavior, and sick role behavior. *Archives of Environmental Health,* 1966, *12,* 246–541.

KELLEY, H. H., CONDRY, J. C., JR., DAHLKE, A. E., & HILL, A. H. Collective behavior in a simulated panic situation. *Journal of Experimental Social Psychology,* 1965, *1,* 20–54.

KIRSCHT, J. P., & ROSENSTOCK, I. M. Patients' problems in following recommendations of health experts. In G. C. Stone, F. Cohen, & N. E. Adler (eds.), *Health psychology.* San Francisco: Jossey-Bass, 1979.

KUTNER, B., MAKOVER, H. B., & OPPENHEIM, A. Delay in the diagnosis and treatment of cancer: A critical analysis of the literature. *Journal of Chronic Diseases,* 1958, *7,* 95–120.

LANGER, E. J., JANIS, I., & WOLFER, J. Reduction of psychological stress in surgical patients. *Journal of Experimental Social Psychology,* 1975, *1,* 155–166.

LAZARUS, R. S.*Psychological stress and the coping process.* New York: McGraw-Hill, 1966.

————. *Patterns of adjustment.* New York: McGraw-Hill, 1976.

LEE, W. *Decision theory and human behavior.* New York: Wiley, 1971.

LEVENTHAL, H. Changing attitudes and habits to reduce risk factors in chronic disease. *American Journal of Cardiology,* 1973, *31,* 571–580.

LEVENTHAL, H., SINGER, R. E., & JONES, S. Effects of fear and specificity of recommendations. *Journal of Personality and Social Psychology,* 1965, *2,* 20–29.

LEVY, J. M., & MCGEE, R. K. Childbirth as crisis: A test of Janis' theory of communication and stress resolution. *Journal of Personality and Social Psychology,* 1975, *31,* 171–179.

MACCURDY, J. *The structure of morale.* New York: Macmillan, 1943.

MACEDONIA, R. M. Expectations-press and survival. Doctoral dissertation, New York University, 1969.

MANN, L., JANIS, I. L., & CHAPLIN, R. The effects of anticipation of forthcoming information on predecisional processes. *Journal of Personality and Social Psychology,* 1969, *11,* 10–16.

MAUSNER, B., & PLATT, E. S. *Smoking: A behavioral analysis.* Oxford: Pergamon, 1971.

MCGUIRE, W. J. The nature of attitudes and attitude change. In G. Lindzey & E. Aronson (eds.), *The handbook of social psychology,* vol. 3. Reading: Addison-Wesley, 1969.

MEICHENBAUM, D. *Cognitive-behavior modification: An integrative approach.* New York: Plenum, 1977.

MEICHENBAUM, D., & CAMERON, R. An examination of cognitive and contingency variables in anxiety relief procedures. Manuscript, University of Waterloo, Waterloo, Ontario, 1973.

MEICHENBAUM, D., & TURK, D. C. The cognitive-behavioral management of anxiety, anger, and pain. In P. O. Davidson (ed.), *The behavioral management of anxiety, depression, and pain.* New York: Brunner/Mazel, 1976.

MILLER, D. W., & STAR, M. K. *The structure of human decisions.* Englewood Cliffs: Prentice-Hall, 1967.

MONAT, A., & LAZARUS, R. S. (eds.). *Stress and coping: an anthology.* New York: Columbia University Press, 1977.

MORAN, P. A. An experimental study of pediatric admission. Master's thesis, Yale University School of Nursing, 1963.

RACHMAN, S. J. *Fear and courage.* San Francisco: Freeman, 1978.

RAIFFA, H. *Decision analysis.* Reading: Addison-Wesley, 1968.

RAPOPORT, A., & WALLSTEN, T. S. Individual decision behavior. In P. H. Mussen & M. R. Rosenzweig (eds.), *Annual review of psychology,* vol. 23. Palo Alto: Annual Reviews, 1972.

RODIN, J., & JANIS, I. L. The social power of health-care practitioners as agents of change. *Journal of Social Issues,* 1979, 35, 60–81.

ROGERS, R. W., & DECKNER, W. C. Effects of fear appeals and physiological arousal upon emotion, attitudes, and cigarette smoking. *Journal of Personality and Social Psychology,* 1975, *32,* 220–230.

ROGERS, R. W., & MEWBORN, C. R. Fear appeals and attitude change: Effects of a threat's noxiousness, probability of occurrence, and the efficacy of coping responses. *Journal of Personality and Social Psychology,* 1976, *34,* 54–61.

ROGERS, R. W., & THISTLETHWAITE, D. L. Effects of fear arousal and reassurance upon attitude change. *Journal of Personality and Social Psychology,* 1970, *15,* 227–233.

SCHACHTER, S. *The psychology of affiliation.* Stanford: Stanford University Press, 1959.

SCHMIDT, R. L. An exploratory study of nursing and patient readiness for surgery. Master's thesis, Yale University School of Nursing, 1966.

SCHMITT, F. E., & WOOLDRIDGE, P. J. Psychological preparation of surgical patients. *Nursing Research,* 1973, *22,* 108–116.

SCHULTZ, D. P. (ed.). *Panic and behavior: Discussion and readings.* New York: Random House, 1964.

SELYE, H. *The stress of life.* New York: McGraw-Hill, 1956.

SIGALL, H., & HELMREICH, R. Opinion change as a function of stress and communicator credibility. *Journal of Experimental Social Psychology,* 1969, *5,* 70–78.

SIMON, H. A. *Administrative behavior: A study of decision-making processes in administrative organization* (3d ed.). New York: Free Press, 1976.

SLOVIC, P., FISHHOFF, B., & LICHTENSTEIN, S. Behavioral decision theory. *Annual Review of Psychology,* 1977, *28,* 1–38.

TURK, D. T. Cognitive control of pain: A skills-training approach. Master's thesis, University of Waterloo, Waterloo, Ontario, 1975.

VERNON, D. T. A., & BIGELOW, D. A. The effect of information about a potentially stressful situation on responses to stress impact. *Journal of Personality and Social Psychology,* 1974, *29,* 50–59.

WANOUS, J. P. Effects of a realistic job preview on job acceptance, job attitudes, and job survival. *Journal of Applied Psychology,* 1973, *58,* 321–332.

WHEELER, D., & JANIS, I. L. *A practical guide for making decisions.* New York: Free Press, 1980.

WOLFENSTEIN, M. *Disaster: A psychological essay.* New York: Free Press, 1957.

WOLFER, J. A., & VISINTAINER, M. A. Pediatric surgical patients' and parents' stress responses and adjustment as a function of psychologic preparation and stress-point nursing care. *Nursing Research,* 1975, *24,* 244–255.

YOUNGBERG, C. F. An experimental study of job satisfaction and turnover in relation to job expectations and self-expectations. Doctoral dissertation, New York University, 1963.

PART III

BASIC BIOLOGICAL PROCESSES

6

Inquiries into Hardiness

Suzanne C. Ouellette

"AT THIS TIME, hardiness appears to be an intriguing concept requiring more research to adequately explain its relationship with health-related outcomes, especially under conditions of stress" (Manning, Williams, & Wolfe, 1988). So ends a report on the relationship between the personality construct of hardiness and a variety of work- and health-related outcomes. The publication date for this article is nearly a decade after the appearance of the first hardiness and health study; that initial study introduced and supported the idea that adults with three interrelated orientations toward self and world expressive of commitment, control, and challenge are less likely to fall physically ill under highly stressful life events than persons without these views (Kobasa, 1979).[1] What is notable about the Manning et al. quotation is not simply its forward-looking attitude. The majority of published articles on hardiness end optimistically with authors encouraging other researchers to continue to pursue the empirical properties of the personality construct. One's attention is captured by the Manning closing because it follows the report of some rather surprising hardiness results.

Contrary to their predictions and what had previously appeared in the literature, hardiness not only failed to function as a stress moderator—i.e., to reduce the negative effects of stress—but it appeared, instead, to enhance stress. Manning and colleagues observed in 7 of their 45 moderator regression analyses ($n = 468$ working adults) that as stress increases, people who score high on hardiness show a more rapid decline in positive outcomes or a sharper increase in negative outcomes than subjects scoring low on hardiness. This finding is in direct opposition to the longstanding hardiness moderator hypothesis. Also somewhat disconcerting, given the basic conceptualization of hardiness as relatively independent of the stressors it is said to buffer, Manning and colleagues reported that hardy individuals are less likely to report environmental demands. They find significant correlations (ranging from $-.13$ to $-.37$) between hardiness and all of the variables designated as stressors in the research. All that these investigators are able to preserve of their original formulation is proof of meaningful direct effects of hardiness on emotional and psychological factors important for personal well-being and work performance.

I wish to acknowledge the help of J. Brian Cassel and Paul Bartone with this chapter. Their comments on the manuscript and their continuing efforts to ensure that the assessment of hardiness is taken as seriously as its conceptualization are much appreciated.

In spite of their unanticipated results, Manning and colleagues do not recommend abandoning the ship. They emphasize their positive findings and recommend that other researchers persevere, possibly by supplementing traditional strategies with the use of different methods of measurement. Other researchers have taken their advice. In the two and a half years following the publication of the Manning, et al. piece, at least twenty-four new empirical papers and two review articles on hardiness have appeared in the literature. I dedicate this chapter to all of these brave sailors.

Taking seriously the purpose of a handbook, I submit this chapter as a responsive reference source for many of the current hardiness research issues. The published material on hardiness is now extensive. The initial work by Kobasa, Maddi, and their colleagues in Chicago provides retrospective (Kobasa, 1979, 1982) and prospective (Kobasa, Maddi, & Kahn, 1982) support for hardiness as a stress-resistance resource. It demonstrates how hardiness works with other resources like social support and exercise to protect physical as well as mental health (Kobasa, Maddi, Puccetti, & Zola, 1985; Ouellette Kobasa & Puccetti, 1983). These founding studies argue for the independence of hardiness from stressful life event occurrence (Kobasa, et al., 1982) as well as demographic factors such as age, education, religion, marital status, and job level (Kobasa, 1979; Kobasa, Maddi, & Courington, 1981; Kobasa, et al., 1982). Finally, the body of work first framed in Chicago generalizes the relevance of hardiness to health across a number of occupational groups, including business executives, lawyers, and army officers (Kobasa, 1982).

Later work by other investigators in different research settings takes varied forms. Summary comments necessarily take on a two-sided or "yes, but" nature. Some reports are explicitly offered as critiques of the original hardiness work and propose alternative approaches to personality and health (Funk & Houston, 1987; Hull, Van Treuren, & Virnelli, 1987). Other contributions essentially confirm or expand the original hardiness results in new contexts (Bartone, 1989; Bartone, Ursano, Wright, & Ingraham, 1989; Keane, Ducette, & Adler, 1985; Magnani, 1990; Westman, 1990).

Some studies effectively converge to offer empirical support for critical assumptions of the original hardiness formulation. These demonstrate specific process mechanisms such as those through which hardiness influences persons' appraisal of stress (Allred & Smith, 1989; Hull, Van Treuren, & Propsom, 1988; Rhodewalt & Agustsdottir, 1984; Rhodewalt & Zone, 1989; Roth, Wiebe, Fillingim, & Shay, 1989; Wiebe, 1991). Other contributions are sharply divergent and leave unresolved two important pieces of hardiness conceptualization: one involving gender differences (Holahan & Moss, 1985; Rhodewalt & Zone, 1989; Schmied & Lawler, 1986; Wiebe, 1991) and the other concerning psychophysiological arousal correlates of hardiness (Allred & Smith, 1989; Contrada, 1989).

Some recent studies maintain the founding notion that hardiness operates as a stress buffer as well as a direct influence on health. Westman (1990), for example, provides impressive longitudinal data on how the training performance of Israeli defense forces cadets is shaped both directly by hardiness and by hardiness in interaction with stress. The stress of army training is a significant predictor of performance only for those cadets low in hardiness. Other studies, however, fail to find a stress-hardiness interaction when they look for it (McCranie, Lambert, & Lambert, 1987; Roth, Wiebe, Fillingim & Shay, 1989; Topf, 1989a).

Some field reports draw conclusions provocatively supporting the external validity of hardiness while simultaneously raising serious internal and construct validity questions (Kuo & Tsai, 1986; Nakano, 1990; Topf, 1989b). Other studies take hardiness and college students into the laboratory and through experimental manipulations enhance internal and construct validity but leave real-world relevance unsubstantiated (Wiebe, 1991).

Most hardiness studies continue to rely strictly on self-report measures of outcomes or dependent variables. Two studies, however, provide intriguing objective measures of physical health (Okun, Zautra, & Robinson, 1988) and performance (Westman, 1990).

What is one to make of observations as complex as these? Borrowing from existential philosophy, in which hardiness has its origins, one might describe the available findings as constituting a dialectic awaiting synthesis. One also, however, needs to recognize that the synthesis is not immediately at hand. To make sense of this mixed bag of approaches and findings while simultaneously encouraging new directions in hardiness research, I have kept a particular reader foremost in my mind: the new investigator in the early stages of a project wanting to make use of hardiness. His or her questions, expressed through many telephone calls and letters over the last twelve years, have guided my choice of what to present here. In fact, a working subtitle through the first draft was "Everything you ever wanted to know about hardiness and were not afraid to ask." The most common questions, listed in their order of frequency, have included:

1. Has anyone looked at hardiness in a group of people like those I want to study (elderly individuals, nurses, etc.)?
2. How can I best measure hardiness? Should I use the 36-items, the third generation test, or is there a new scale?
3. Do I look only at the hardiness composite or enter three separate component scores in my analyses?
4. Is hardiness only to be studied in healthy people?
5. Does hardiness have implications for life issues other than physical health and illness?
6. Given that hardiness has to do with personality, can it be changed?
7. How do you think hardiness really works to make people more stress resistant?
8. If you had laboratories well equipped to measure and analyze physiological and biological factors, what biopsychosocial hardiness hypothesis would you test?
9. If I want to do a dissertation on personality and health, should I use hardiness or some other construct?
10. Would you expect to find hardiness effects in a non-American sample? What about socially disadvantaged groups?

In what follows, I consider three of the several inquiries into hardiness. I revisit the original formulation of the hardiness construct, comment upon what now exists in the literature, and point to what has usefully yet to be done.[2] In some instances, my responses may lead readers (as they have many telephone callers) to discover that their single questions are actually many questions that need to be confronted before their research can proceed. The second working subtitle for the chapter was "More than you ever wanted to know about hardiness." What I offer is less a summary of the existing work than some ways of thinking about what is there and not there.[3] Returning to the nautical metaphor, I intend to provide some charts of the waters that others have already sailed; but, more importantly, I suggest radar-like devices to help the investigator discover and navigate some new territory. And, if all goes well, there may be some readers who find reason in my review to hoist a spinnaker and soar in research on human health and basic personality processes.

HAS ANYONE LOOKED AT HARDINESS IN MY GROUP YET?

Ideally, the person posing this question will not be hoping for a simple "no." Investigators have substantially broadened the field of research subjects since the original hardiness studies on middle- and upper-level executives working for a public utility (Kobasa, 1979). Alongside the undergraduates who are ubiquitous as subjects of psychological research, one finds lawyers, army officers, clergy of many persuasions, bus drivers, printers, nurses, physicians, university employees, elementary and secondary school teachers, adolescents, the elderly, candidates in training for a number of occupations, immigrants to the United States, persons with chronic illnesses, and Japanese businessmen. All have been written about with regard to their hardiness.

It is critical to recognize that more is involved in this large and diversified body of work than just attempts to establish the empirical generality of hardiness across occupation, life stage, health, and culture. The motivation of many investigators, revealed typically in their introduction and discussion sections, is to use the hardiness notion to reveal something that has been previously overlooked in the group about which they are concerned. The need to correct the omissions figures importantly in what inspires them. Prominent among the omissions taken on by hardiness researchers are these three: attention to persons who do well under stress, active and positive assumptions about personality within the group, and appreciation of the seriousness of the stresses encountered by the group.

What Hardiness Reveals about Groups

Looking at Persons Doing Well under Stress.   In the original hardiness study (Kobasa, 1979), business executives were chosen as subjects because the case needed to be made strongly that not everyone falls sick under stress. I have described elsewhere (Kobasa, 1982; Ouellette Kobasa, 1990) that, at the time of the original work, the emphasis of researchers was almost strictly on demonstrating a causal link between the occurrence of stressful life events and the onset of illness. Little attention was paid to individual differences and to examples of persons encountering high stress situations and staying healthy. In this research climate, business executives took on the status of classic stress victims. In the popular media, executives were portrayed carrying bulging briefcases and running from one appointment to the next. By making the case that even among this highly besieged group there were thriving individuals, we intended to capture peoples' attention and direct it toward a less pessimistic and more useful view of stress.

A similar interest in telling the more optimistic side of a group's story is expressed in the research on immigrants' health by Kuo and Tsai (1986). These researchers were troubled because the majority of social science studies on the immigrant experience has sought almost exclusively to document the negative implications of leaving one's country of birth and moving to another. The literature is filled with references to cultural conflicts, social isolation, poor assimilation and integration, identity crises, loss of social status, racial discrimination, and the likelihood that all of these will lead to poor health and other forms of impairment in immigrants. Kuo and Tsai did not deny these negative realities, but they sought to go beyond them to reveal positive immigration outcomes and the factors responsible for successful adaptation. The hardiness construct, coupled with the literature on social networking, provides the basis for the generation of new immigration hypotheses. Its application provides support for what was already in the literature—immigration is very stressful and can have detrimental effects on well-being—and some new findings. They conclude that the aspects of hardiness they have measured in Asian immigrants minimize adaptation difficulties and predict lower depression as well as less worry about finances.

Studies of teachers and of persons with a chronic illness provide additional examples of using hardiness to show that individuals can do well in situations about which the consensus is to expect the worst. Holt, Fine, & Tollefson (1987) present their hardiness research as marking a "philosophical shift" from a reactive to a proactive view of elementary school teachers, school districts, and teacher training institutions; they suggest ways in which their hardiness and burnout results might be applied in interventions to promote active responses to stress. Pollock (1989) seeks to extend the hardiness work to apply to adults with chronic illness and to understand more about those who adapt well.

The Need for Positive Assumptions about Personality. Another statement about groups is found in the second of Kuo and Tsai's hardiness aims. They sought to compensate for what other immigration researchers have suggested about personality. They correctly concluded that prior work either ignored personality factors or speculatively portrayed immigrants in essentially negative terms such as "schizoid personalities," "adventurers," and "misfits in their own communities." Kuo and Tsai looked for a very different way of characterizing immigrants that would allow for the measurement of purposive action and would capture the personality characteristics that—in combination with social, historical, and political factors—explain immigrants' success. They find what they had sought in hardiness and in the existential theory of personality from which it is derived (Kobasa & Maddi, 1977).

> In contrast to personality theories that hold a passive view and reactive view of man, theories proposed by existential psychologists accentuate the strenuous traits of authentic living: competence, appropriate striving and productive orientation. For our purpose, we suggest use of the concept of hardiness to measure the quality of the immigrant's purposive actions: his/her ruggedness or assertiveness in attaining and manipulating external rewards, initiative, willingness to take risks, and ability to face uncertainty. (Kuo & Tsai, 1986:137)

A similar use of the hardiness notion is made by other investigators seeking to depict elderly and patient groups more fully than they have heretofore been depicted in the research literature. For Magnani (1990), hardiness serves as a vehicle for making the point that personality differences among elderly persons help explain why some age more successfully than others. She views hardiness assessment as giving the elderly a voice that professionals should hear to better direct their efforts at health promotion. Okun, Zautra, and Robinson (1988) argue that research on persons with chronic illnesses, particularly those living with rheumatoid arthritis, has for too long restricted itself to examined abnormal personality issues. They employ hardiness to address positive personality characteristics in women with rheumatoid arthritis and hypothesize and demonstrate relationships between hardiness and objective and perceived health status. Druss and Douglas (1988) offer case reports of three individuals who demonstrated unusually strong courage in the fact of congenital abnormality, illness, and death. For them, the hardiness concept is a way of going beyond the insufficient notion of healthy denial to consider other "dimensions of patients that enable them to feel well and function effectively confronting disabling illness" (p. 166).

Appreciation of the Seriousness of Stress. A third kind of statement about groups by hardiness researchers reveals the distinctive stress encountered by those they observe. With the first hardiness study, stress was identified as a critical construct.

To the social psychologist interested in personality, it offered a way of taking situational characteristics seriously. In the wake of the person-situation debate sparked by the publication of Mischel's (1968) *Personality and assessment . . .* researchers found themselves looking for occasions
in which they might observe individual predispositions for acting, thinking, and feeling in particular ways in transaction with the components of the environment. Stressful life events presented
themselves as important and measurable situation variables. (Kobasa, 1982:3)

The best current example of revealing a situation through a hardiness investigation is
provided by the Bartone, Ursano, Wright, and Ingraham (1989) study of U.S. Army Survival Assistance Officers. Their first research aims were to document the roles played by
these men and women as they responded to mass tragedies such as the 1985 army airline
crash in Newfoundland and to identify their major sources of stress. According to these
researchers, earlier work on disasters had focused almost exclusively on the immediate and
primary disaster victims and ignored workers who provided practical assistance and emotional support to bereaved family members. Because of the data suggesting that people
involved with disasters in such ways face serious health consequences, these authors thought
it imperative to learn more about the demands that assistance workers actually confront.

On their way to examining the link between disaster assistance stresses and well-being
and to identifying resistance resources that modulate stress reaction, Bartone, et al. reported on both the content analysis of responses to open-ended questions about stress and
a composite measure of exposure/stress they constructed. The latter reflects the duration
and intensity of assistance officers' contact with bereaved family members. The former
reveals four critical areas of stress involving (a) officers' unpreparedness for the profound
emotions actively expressed by surviving family members, (b) difficulties obtaining factual
information and maintaining lines of communication during the weeks immediately after
the disaster, (c) the lengthy body identification process, and (d) disengaging from the victim
and the family and returning to normal activities. All of these findings have important
prevention and treatment implications for organizations sponsoring disaster assistance activities (Williams, Solomon, & Bartone, 1988).

Suggestions for Future Hardiness Groups

Although some of the studies noted previously may be judged lacking on one or more
conceptual or methodological criteria, each of them has raised some important questions
about human behavior and offered observations about people worthy of further study. I
encourage new investigators to approach their subject groups with equal seriousness. Even
groups that do not appear very exotic deserve this kind of attention. It is unfortunate that
researchers working with college students—researchers who have most explicitly taken on
the improvement of the science of hardiness as their aim—have not taken the situation of
their group more seriously. There is much to be learned about such issues as the distinctive
kinds of stresses that students undergo. Missing from the literature reviewed is consideration of hardiness in college students as they face stresses like tuition increases, difficulties
in obtaining financial support for research, sexual harassment, and lack of jobs following
graduation.

As researchers take on the application of hardiness in new groups, it is critical that
they note the extent to which current hardiness conceptualization and measurement may
need to be altered to fit the group under study. This point has particular salience as one
considers applying hardiness in a life-span context other than adulthood. In developing the

concept of hardiness for adults (Kobasa, 1979), I drew from the depiction of that life stage in the adulthood developmental literature (Henry, 1968; Neugarten, 1974). Notions such as mid-life as a time when life goals are increasingly integrated across a widening diversity of situations were influential in my definition of the hardiness components and prediction of their relevance to health.

As one shifts attention away from adulthood and seeks to understand hardiness in later life or in adolescence, one may need to go back to the appropriate basic developmental literature. The distinctive psychological, social, and biological demands of a particular age group may require a significant recasting of hardiness, both as a concept and as something to be measured. Pollock makes a similar point as she considers the life-span implications of hardiness: "Is there more than a single pattern of hardiness depending on developmental processes?" (1989:62)

The value of this conceptual regrouping is well illustrated through a comparison of available hardiness studies on older adults with those on adolescents. Magnani (1990) effectively interpreted her findings of an association between hardiness and activity levels in 115 elderly adults (ranging in age from 60 to 90) by referring to Erikson's and Neugarten's theories of later life. Hadley (1990), responding to Magnani's work, further highlighted the salience of hardiness to older adults by using additional basic developmental literature. She took up the longstanding discussions and debates over disengagement and continuity in later life to provide both a broad conceptual framework for Magnani's work and a possible explanation for why Magnani found positive effects for control and commitment but not challenge among her subjects.

In contrast to the analysis of the elderly, we have essentially atheoretical hardiness work on adolescence. Although Hannah and Morrissey (1987) claimed that it is critical to develop an appropriate hardiness construct for adolescents, they did little more than simply transplant the notion and its measure from adult studies. They did a reliability check on the thirteen items that they selected to use but no formal construct validity work. Although they expressed interest in posing a developmental question about hardiness within the adolescent stage, they made the assumption that by age twelve one can observe what is recognized as adulthood hardiness.

To these and other researchers interested in hardiness in adolescence, I would advise beginning work with a more formal review of the basic literature on adolescence, including that from an existential perspective (Kobasa & Maddi, 1977; Maddi & Kobasa, 1984). In seeking to understand what adolescent personality processes precede hardiness as we know it in adulthood, researchers may find themselves working with constructs quite unlike commitment, challenge, and control as they have been defined to date. For example, Kobasa and Maddi draw on Kierkegaard to depict self-indulgence and rigid idealism, characteristics not at all constitutive of adulthood hardiness, as essential to the early life process that leads to mature and healthy psychological responses to stress in later life.

A final suggestion: There is clear need for new investigators to bring hardiness to bear on socially disadvantaged and more racially diversified groups. The majority of the research has been conducted on middle-class, white Americans. Would hardiness have a health-enhancing effect if individuals were confronting stressors such as poverty and discrimination? Would it matter if hardiness were the only stress-resistance resource that members of the group seemed to possess? Would having no financial resources or losing all critical support providers cancel the positive effects of personality? Might the hardiness notion help explain observed differences between blacks and whites in physiological responses to stress and morbidity rates? Are there critical experiences in early life that enable one to develop hardiness despite growing up in a highly stressful environment? Answers to these questions would have important social relevance as well as usefulness in expanding the conceptualization of hardiness.

Nurses and the Study of Hardiness: A Special Case

In categorizing and reviewing hardiness studies with regard to the groups involved, one particular group quickly stands out as deserving special comment. Nurses emerge as different from the rest on several counts. One is the simple magnitude of the work. I have identified seventeen published hardiness pieces in the nursing literature and by now there are likely to be many more given the number of master's papers and Ph.D. dissertations by nurses on hardiness. Of all the phone calls and letters I have received about hardiness in the last five years, more have come from nurses than any other single professional group.

Also unique is the object of nurses' study. Nurses have applied hardiness, as have most other investigators, in the study of the *other;* in the case of nurses, the other is typically the patient. However, nurses have also turned the research spotlight on themselves by using hardiness as a way of better understanding and potentially relieving burnout in their ranks. Finally, hardiness is explicitly discussed by nurses as contributing to the development of a general theory for nursing and securing nursing's place as a profession and a research science. Editorials as well as research articles about hardiness appear in the nursing literature:

> Once nurse scientists understand the effects of hardiness and how it promotes health and adaptation in both well individuals and those with health problems, the implications for nursing practice will be limitless. (Pollock, 1989:53)
>
> If hardiness can be taught, nurses may be the first to take advantage of such an educational experience, given their job requirement. Patients who are experiencing chronic illness may also be prime candidates for hardiness instruction as they learn to cope with the stress of their illness. . . . Even nurse educators and administrators might need to recognize that if they possess or could acquire the personality characteristic, hardiness, they too might be more committed to their work, feel more in control of their daily lives and be more challenged by their everyday experience. (Lambert & Lambert, 1987:95)

The hardiness research contributions provided by nurses are diversified. They include demonstrations of all of the following: links between hardiness components and burnout for nurses involved in various kinds of nursing care (Keane, Ducette, & Adler, 1985; Mc-Cranie, Lambert, & Lambert, 1987; Rich & Rich, 1987; Topf, 1989a); the effectiveness of hardiness as a resistance resource for the stress of noise in critical care units (Topf, 1989b); the relationship between hardiness and activity levels in the elderly (Magnani, 1990); the influence of hardiness upon student nurses' positive appraisal of their first medical-surgical experience (Pagana, 1990); and the salience of hardiness for the lives of persons with serious illness (Pollock, 1989; Pollock, Christian, & Sands, 1990; Pollack & Duffy, 1990).

Conceptual and methodological critiques of some of these studies are presented at later points in the chapter. Here, I simply offer some speculation on *why* nurses have devoted so much of their research time and energy to hardiness. Both in their studies of patients and themselves, nurses place a high premium on all of those group revelations reviewed previously: the presence of people who do well under stress, the importance of positive and active assumptions about personality, and the need to recognize the environmental demands or stressors placed upon people. For example, faced with increasing dehumanization within the high-tech modern medical setting, it is critical for nurses to ensure that the individual needs and differences of patients are recognized. In addition, I think that nurses' interest in hardiness needs to be understood in terms of longstanding struggles within the profession.[4] Drawing from a paper by Fox, Aiken, and Messikomer (1990) on the culture of the nursing, I suggest that the attention given to hardiness has much to do with nurses' attempts to explicate their distinctive identity as health care professionals.

Fox and her colleagues describe the nursing community as intent on revealing and legitimizing its own principles and practices of caring for patients. Hardiness may be a useful tool for this endeavor. Both in its general characterization as part of peoples' essential and strenuous search for meaning and in its more specific description as a composite of commitment, control, and challenge, hardiness may be well suited to nurses' "drive to distinguish their field from the profession of medicine by which it has been historically dominated, and to liberate nursing from some of the fettering aspects of its inherited definition as 'women's work'" (p. 121).

Consider, for example, how Fox and colleagues depict nurses' understanding of the current professional crisis, which is characterized by burnout, serious personnel shortages, turnover of staff, and decline in application to nursing schools. According to the authors, each element of the crisis is related to nurses' perception that they have lost control over their practice. But as Fox and colleagues explain, the loss of control nurses feel is particular: it is not simply a matter of lacking power over others but rather control "over their ability to care for patients in a manner consistent with their deeply held values" (p. 122). This view of control is easily linked with the hardiness definition that makes control part of a triad that also includes commitment and challenge (cf. Kobasa, 1982).

The salience of all three parts of the triad emerge as Fox and colleagues depict both the demands and opportunities offered to the nursing profession by AIDS. What nurses say they do best—namely, caring—is certainly called for by the epidemic. There is ample room for nurses to take responsibility and act on their belief that they can influence the course of some events in AIDS care—hardiness control. In carrying out their critical role, nurses find themselves drawing upon the entire range of physical, social, and spiritual interventions that they are uniquely trained to provide and are involving themselves fully in their work—hardiness commitment. Finally, AIDS in its extremes as a medical and social crisis calls nurses to go beyond that with which they are familiar. There are many occasions to exercise hardiness challenge in response to AIDS, as the epidemic makes unprecedented technological and psychosocial demands. Hardiness emerges as both fitting what nurses wish to see as the "cornerstone and quintessence of their profession" (Fox, et al., 1990:119) and the key to successfully delivering new forms of care.

HOW DO I MEASURE HARDINESS?

Much to the chagrin of many a phone caller and letter writer, I have not been able to recommend *the* final, perfect hardiness scale.[5] This news is very disappointing for the prospective hardiness investigator, especially one who has freshly reviewed the published studies and found several different hardiness scales, including some lacking any apparent connection with the original conceptualization or operationalization of hardiness. The new investigator understandably wants some reassurance after confronting a literature that once led one group of researchers to proclaim: "Unfortunately, there now exist nearly as many ways to measure hardiness and its subcomponents as there are people conducting research on the topic. Obviously, if progress is to be made in this area, this practice must stop" (Hull, Van Treuren, & Virnelli, 1987).

My message to future researchers is different. I appreciate the dilemma felt by the new investigator seeking a hardiness measure for use in a dissertation. The five-scale composite measure, or the shortened versions of it that most frequently appear in the literature (an important criterion for dissertation committees), has—as the following pages make clear— formidable problems. On the other hand, the newer scale written about encouragingly by Maddi (1990) and others as the "Personal Views Survey" or "third generation hardiness measure" has not as yet had much exposure. The ratio of appearance in the literature of the earlier scales to the third generation measure is now four to one. Many of the studies using the later version of hardiness measurement are still underway or only now being prepared for publication. The choice of this scale might strike some dissertation advisors as premature. The situation is further complicated by the fact that very impressive hardiness findings continue to emerge through the application of the five-scale composite measure. One excellent example of this is the impressive experimental work by Wiebe (1991) on the appraisal and arousal mechanisms of hardiness-based stress moderation. In addition, there are some signs on the research horizon that hardiness measurement may still be improved, with investigators continuing to make changes in the scale and claiming room for still more.

I encourage the new investigator to construe all of this activity in the literature as an ongoing endeavor to develop strong hardiness measures. My overall view is that we have made some significant psychometric gains in hardiness measurement, but we are still working. I invite new investigators to join in the continuing effort. Let me here offer some general points about how work on hardiness has so far progressed, where future efforts might be directed, and what pitfalls should be avoided.

Major Episodes in the Development of a Hardiness Test

The Most Popular Measure. The five-scale composite described in the original pro-spective test of hardiness (Kobasa, Maddi, & Kahn, 1982) and the thirty-six- and twenty-item abridged spinoffs (Allred & Smith, 1989; Rhodewalt & Agustsdottir, 1984; Rhodewalt & Zone, 1989) comprise the set of scales that has been used in most of the currently pub-lished studies. The original sources for these scales are the Alienation Test (Maddi, Kobasa, & Hoover, 1979), the California Life Goals Evaluation Schedules (Hahn, 1966), The Internal-External Locus of Control Scale (Rotter, Seeman, & Liverant, 1962), and the Per-sonality Research Form (Jackson, 1974). Their use by Kobasa and Maddi and members of their research group in Chicago as well as by other investigators has contributed some important extensions of the hardiness work. Adding to the work already cited from the original Chicago group, studies using these scales have shown the effects of hardiness on several outcome variables, including burnout (Keane, et al., 1985; McCrainie, et al., 1987; Pierce & Molloy, 1990; Rich & Rich, 1987), general well-being (Lambert, Lambert, Klipple, & Mewshaw, 1989; Manning, et al., 1988), levels of activity (Magnani, 1990), and work performance (Westman, 1990). In addition, studies using these scales have contributed to efforts to explicate the mechanisms underlying the stress, personality, and health relation-ships (Allred & Smith, 1989; Banks & Gannon, 1988; Contrada, 1989; Rhodewalt & Agusts-dottir, 1984; Rhodewalt & Zone, 1989; Roth, et al., 1989; Wiebe, 1991; Wiebe & McCal-lum, 1986).

These impressive findings should not, however, distract one from recognizing problems with these scales. Overall, there is a lack of balance between positive and negative items with most of the items worded negatively (Fund & Houston, 1987; Gentry & Kobasa, 1984). This preponderance of negative items opens the door to two concerns: subjects with acquiescent response styles might show lower hardiness scores than they would if there were an equal number of positively and negatively keyed items (cf. Parkes & Rendall, 1988) and the possible confounding of hardiness with neuroticism or maladjustment (cf. Maddi, 1990). Looking at component scores, one sees that items intended to tap the challenge dimension of hardiness have not consistently shown high internal reliability (Hull, Van Treuren, & Virnelli, 1987, with college students; Manning, Williams, & Wolfe, 1988, with working adults; Pierce & Molloy, 1990, with secondary school teachers). Challenge items have also been inconsistent in their correlations with control and commitment, not always correlating positively with these other dimensions of hardiness (Magnani, 1990; Pierce & Molloy, 1990). Finally, results from factor analyses sometimes indicate a single unitary factor of hardiness (Kobasa, Maddi, & Kahn, 1982; Manning, Williams, & Wolfe, 1988); sometimes, a three-component solution (Hull, Van Treuren, & Virnelli, 1987); and in yet other situations, neither of these configurations (Funk & Houston, 1987; Pierce & Molloy, 1990; Rich & Rich, 1987).

The Personal Views Survey. The Chicago group, beginning in the early 1980s, recognized many of these problems and attempted to correct for them. The locus of the effort was a study of Chicago bus drivers. Requiring a scale to administer to a blue collar group not as well educated as the business executives studied by his research group, Bartone (1984) led the effort to create a more psychometrically sound and generally applicable scale.[6] Items from the earlier measure with low item-scale correlations or highly skewed frequency distributions were eliminated; items from the Nowicki and Strickland (1973) locus of control measure were slightly modified and put in the place of items originally taken from the Rotter test (Rotter, Seeman, & Liverant, 1962); and, finally, new items were written—most designed to tape the challenge dimension of hardiness. The initial work with this scale was promising. Citing Bartone and working with other data sets available to the Chicago group and his Hardiness Institute, Maddi reports that fifty items from this effort constitute a "third generation Hardiness Test" (Maddi, 1987, 1990). He notes that this test, usually distributed to subjects as the Personal Views Survey, represents a better balance of positive and negative elements and produces a total score as well as three component scores with internal consistency and stability. Factor analyses reveal three related factors interpretable as commitment, challenge, and control. Also, according to Maddi, the third-generation scale correlates with earlier forms of hardiness measurement and provides replications of the predicted and meaningful stress, personality, and health findings that had been obtained with the earlier measures.

Additional support for this newer way of approaching hardiness measurement comes from five studies now in the literature. Parkes and Rendall (1988) conclude that in their United Kingdom sample ($n = 87$ postgraduate education students) the Personal Views Survey produces acceptable alpha values ranging from .68 to .89, positive intercorrelations between the hardiness components, no evidence of social desirability bias, and frequency statistics consistent with those obtained in the United States. Okun, Zautra, and Robinson (1988), using the scale with thirty-three women with rheumatoid arthritis, report strong internal reliability for the total and component scores, with alpha scores showing a range from .70 to .84, and generally adequate intercorrelations between components. They confirm their prediction of an association between hardiness and self-reported health status (perceived health relative to one's same age peers) as well as objective health (percentage of T-cells). As expected, they find no relationship between hardiness and functional limitation and pain intensity.

Campbell, Amerikaner, Swank, and Vincent (1989) and Pagana (1990) offer no additional basic psychometric information on the Personal Views Survey but report evidence for construct validity. The first group of investigators claim the relevance of the hardiness test for the assessment of healthy personality, finding in forty-two women both overlap and difference between constructs assessed by the Personal Views Survey and Maslow's notion of self-actualization as measured by the Personal Orientation Inventory (POI) (Knapp, Shostrom, & Knapp, 1978). Pagana reports a low but significant correlation between student nurses' ($n = 261$) hardiness scores and the extent to which they perceive their first clinical experience in a medical-surgical setting as challenging.

Bartone, et al. (1989) use a "slightly modified version" of the Personal Views Survey in their study of survival assistance officers. They limit their administration to the forty-five items identified through the bus driver study (described previously) as the best items— i.e., those showing high item-scale correlations for both bus driver ($n = 787$) and low-level business manager ($n = 190$) samples. These items also have the advantage of breaking into equal numbers of items for commitment, control, and challenge.

With an equal number of items contributing to the component scores, investigators are no longer required to transform raw component scores into standardized z scores before adding them to create a total sample-specific hardiness score (Kobasa, Maddi, & Kahn, 1982). Investigators can now assign raw values to their subjects and compare component and total hardiness scores across different samples. This change in hardiness measurement has been convincingly called for by a number of investigators (Roth, et al., 1989; Wiebe, 1991).

Bartone, et al. report that their forty-five items correlate $-.93$ with the older, longer, and most frequently used hardiness measure taken as a whole and $-.71$ when only nonredundant items are used.[7] With regard to the psychometric viability of this measure, investigators show internal reliability figures ranging from .62 to .82 for the component scores and at .85 for the total score. They also report a reconfirming of the three-factor model of hardiness found in the bus driver analysis through a principal components factor analyses (varimax rotation) on a group of 111 army officers. In addition, they provide evidence for the health-protective function of hardiness over time for disaster helpers.

Ongoing Work on Hardiness Measurement. Recalling Hull, et al.'s (1987) plea for an end to the proliferation of hardiness measures, I confess an inclination to rely on the positive indications from these studies and proclaim the Personal Views Survey or Bartone's slightly modified version as *it*. But taking seriously the work yet to be done that these investigators and my own recent work on hardiness have also brought to light, I can only say that the Personal Views Survey is closer to *it* than earlier versions.

Parkes and Rendall (1988) point to the wording and content of the items in the Personal Views Survey and express a continuing concern that the items are inappropriate for samples that are not employed, professional, or predominantly male.. The shadow of the original application of hardiness measurement to groups of middle-class, Midwestern, and male telephone company executives remains to darken the generality of the scale. Campbell, et al. (1989) offer a similar complaint. The nonworking women in their sample expressed difficulties with some items and explained how they handled them by "rephrasing" the items to refer to previous work experience or current volunteer activities. The investigators rightfully question the implications of their subjects' comments for scale validity among nonworking women and, possibly, women in general. As Parkes and Rendall note, however, this problem with wording and content could be fixed through minor additional revisions.

Parkes and Rendall also discuss the issue of balance between positively and negatively keyed items in the scale. Although the Personal Views Survey is an improvement over earlier scales on this count, the majority of items (39) continue to be negatively worded and to require reverse scoring. In addition, the negative items are unequally distributed across the three components. The problem with response bias remains that "individuals with acquiescent response tendencies will tend to show lower hardiness scores than they would do if keying of questionnaire items was balanced, and this tendency will affect different scales to different extents" (p. 788).

Parkes and Rendall go on to discuss the implications of the predominance of negative items for yet another lingering problem in hardiness assessment—the issue of a confounding of hardiness and neuroticism. Citing earlier demonstrations of the relationship between high neuroticism and both acquiescence and generalized beliefs about lack of control, the investigators label the imbalance a likely inflator of the overall negative correlation between hardiness and neuroticism. "Consistent with this view, in the present data, neuroticism was correlated $-.47$ ($p < 0.001$) with the total of the reverse-scored negative items, but was unrelated to the total of the 11 positive items ($r = -0.11$, N.S.). Furthermore, the higher the proportion of negative items on a particular component scale, the stronger the relationship between neuroticism and the scale concerned." (p. 788) Parkes and Rendall conclude by calling for additional attention to item balance and for controls for acquiescent response biases.

Bartone, in collaboration with several other investigators, has continued work with the forty-five hardiness items effectively used in the study of army disaster workers. Their efforts have led to a thirty-item version of the measure (Bartone, 1991). This shortened form addresses a number of problems noted previously. It has an equal number of items for each of the three components, with complete balance for positive and negative items within each component. In support of its psychometric standing, Bartone reports that the thirty items correlate $-.74$ with nonredundant items from the original hardiness scale and show adequate stability over three- (.58) and six-month (.57) periods, a generally consistent three factor or component structure, and sound internal reliability for the total scale (alpha ranging from .70 to .85, depending on the sample). Drawing on data collected from thirteen different military and college samples, Bartone also offers norms on his short hardiness scale—a response to the many other investigators who have called for such standards by which to evaluate their own samples. Bartone's groups vary in gender, marital status, race, and age; and range in size from 24 to 8,003 subjects. Finally, he offers evidence for convergent, discriminant, and predictive validity of the scale reporting correlations with optimism and several forms of mental and physical well-being.

The only unfortunate news that Bartone delivers has to do with the ten items assessing challenge. The scale's internal consistency across samples is questionable, with alpha values showing a low of .35 and a high of only .62. The addition of new challenge items having equal numbers of positive and negative items, and the removal of items from the Hahn security scale that potentially suggest political conservatism in nonmanagerial groups (cf. Maddi, 1990) have not completely succeeded. Difficulties in challenge measurement noted by users of the earlier hardiness test (Hull, Van Treuren, & Virnelli, 1987; Manning, Williams, & Wolfe, 1988; Pierce & Molloy, 1990) apparently remain. Bartone recommends, regardless of the successful identification of three dimensions through factor analysis, that investigators use only the total hardiness score.

Future Measurement Efforts

Taking into account all of the information now available as well as the typical history of paper and pencil self-report scales, one can make a strong case for using the Personal Views Survey, especially Bartone's shortened form. A weaker case can also be made for the earlier hardiness measure. Potentially useful suggestions for those making use of measures already available are to restrict one's study sample to those subjects scoring at the extremes of the hardiness distribution (cf. Rhodewalt & Zone, 1989; Wiebe, 1991) and to require that subjects meet criteria on at least two separate measures of hardiness (cf. Allred & Smith, 1989). But for the new investigator interested in strengthening hardiness measurement, there are also significant ways of contributing to a continuing effort. Two points at which one might jump in are considered here.

Measuring Component as Well as Composite Scores.   The original hardiness prediction was that individuals who scored highly on all three components—commitment, control, and challenge—would not get sick under stress. The constellation or dynamic interplay between the three was critical. It was assumed that the component scores would not serve to compensate for each other. For example, being very high on control and challenge would not make up for being very low on commitment when it comes to stress resistance. Instead, the presence of each component would be required to influence and temper that of the others. The cognitive flexibility associated with challenge would keep a person high in control from becoming too rigid. The openness to new experiences associated with challenge would protect someone high in commitment from becoming blindly dedicated to a single cause. On the other hand, someone high in control, commitment, and challenge would be more able to experiment and try out many roles in life, while at the same time remaining focused on fundamental sources of meaning, than would someone high in challenge but low in control or commitment.

In the initial hardiness study (Kobasa, 1979), a broad battery of measuring instruments was used. Some items were chosen because they seemed particularly well targeted to one of the components. Other sets of items were judged better suited to get at facets of all three. For example, some items were selected because while they tapped commitment they did so without violating any of the assumptions made about the psychological implications of control or challenge. Results of the discriminant function analysis showed that a number of scales differentiated between the high stress/high illness and high stress/low illness groups, and item review established that elements of all three components were present in the significant discriminators. Offering further support to the hardiness constellation notion, a principal components factor analysis of business executive hardiness data (Kobasa, Maddi, & Kahn, 1982) revealed a single hardiness factor.

In later work in the Chicago group, an interest grew in being able to test some of our ideas about patterns of hardiness components. To do this test, it seemed essential to have three related but distinct scales, each getting at a particular hardiness component. With these in hand, we thought we would then be able to identify subjects scoring high on challenge but low on control and commitment, high on commitment but low on control and challenge, etc.[8] The next round of factor analyses by our group and other investigators suggested we might be on to something, with three interrelated factors emerging (Maddi, 1990).

However, our optimism proved to be not completely warranted. Factor analyses by other investigators using the earlier forms of hardiness measurement showed item loadings and, to a lessor extent, the number of factors to be unstable (Funk & Huston, 1987; Hull,

Van Treuren, & Virnelli, 1987; Manning, Williams, & Wolfe, 1988; Pierce & Molloy, 1990; Rich & Rich, 1987). Bartone's most recent work (1991) shows the desired three factors, but one of these—challenge—has poor internal reliability.

As one looks across the several studies that have tried to contend with the three components, one point emerges very strongly. We are not doing as good a job as we might in measuring challenge. Witness the inconsistent loadings of challenge items, lack of relationship between challenge and the other two components, and low alpha values for challenge scales. Equally serious but also not surprising given the basic psychometric findings, one also sometimes sees low correlations between challenge and other personality as well as health variables. These correlations throw the construct validity into question.

Part of the problem is the one stated by Maddi (1990). In the earlier, or five-scale, composite measure and its shortened versions, many of the challenge items were drawn from the California Life Goals Evaluation Schedule (Hahn, 1966).

> With adults in managerial or professional roles, the items of this scale appear to tap socioeconomic insecurity and, as such, show an empirical covariation pattern permitting an interpretation of negatively measured challenge. But younger subjects still in college appear to respond to this scale in terms of political ideology, finding its items representative of conservatism. It is understandable, then, that for undergraduate subjects, the challenge component . . . might operate somewhat independently of the other two components. (Maddi, 1990:137).

In our studies in New York, which included physicians, nurses, social workers, and volunteers working in health settings, I find adult subjects reading items as Maddi suggests that college students do. It may be that the business executive, for whom agreement with items such as "A retired person should be free of all taxes" and "Government should guarantee jobs for all" represents low challenge, is the exceptional subject rather than the norm. Researchers, therefore, may want to avoid the Hahn items in most of the groups they consider for hardiness. Indeed, in the Personal Views Survey, all but three of the Hahn items have been removed.

There appears, however, to be more to the challenge problem. Bartone's (1991) recently reported that low internal reliability figures indicate that there is still more work to be done on measuring this component. Challenge items upon which one can depend are required before one can seriously grapple with substantive and methodological questions such as those raised by Okun, et al. (1988) on whether challenge—unlike commitment and control—is irrelevant for how patients cope with chronic illness or by Carver (1989) on how best to analyze data on multifaceted personality constructs.

To the new investigator eager to take up this challenge about challenge, I recommend a revisiting of its original definition.[9] Before writing or selecting new items, one should note the complexity of the description of the person high in challenge:

> Persons who feel positively about change are catalysts in their environment and are well practiced at responding to the unexpected. Because they value a life filled with interesting experiences, change seekers have well explored their environment and know where to turn for resources to aid them in coping with stress. They have a predisposition to be cognitively flexible, which allows them to integrate and effectively appraise the threat of new situations. Their basic motivation for endurance allows them to persist even when the new information is exceedingly incongruous . . . it should be clear that the [person high in challenge] is not engaging in irresponsible adventurousness. (Kobasa, 1979:4)

This passage refers to all of the following: ways of viewing self, values, behavior patterns, cognitive style, and motivation. It may be useful at this juncture to take this complexity seriously and consider the value of approaching challenge as several different constructs for measurement. It appears that in the past, investigators have taken the tack of putting a little bit of each of these in a single scale. It may be better to try another approach. We may need to work toward a single scale only after arriving at separate scales for each of the pieces of the challenge notion. Given the positive results that we do have about challenge and the fact that challenge is the element that best distinguishes hardiness from other personality variables now connected with stress and health (optimism, sense of coherence, generalized expectancy of control, type A), this and other kinds of continued measurement effort strike me as worthwhile.

Trying Other Approaches to Personality. In all the work on hardiness of which I am aware, investigators have relied strictly on self-report paper-and-pencil instruments for assessment. It may be time to try something new. In my most recent conversations with prospective hardiness researchers, I encourage them to supplement their use of a tool like the personal views survey with some other strategy. What other approach they choose, of course, depends on their research questions, the nature of their subject group, and the practical constraints of the research setting. Remaining within the conceptual framework defined by an existential theory of personality, however, one can make a case for all of the following as valid ways of measuring hardiness: interviews, performance measures, projective tests, ratings by familiar and objective observers, and analysis of diaries and other personal documents. The most provocative research may classify subjects as high or low on hardiness on the basis of not only scores on more than one self-report form but on two or more distinct measurement approaches to personality.

Pitfalls to Avoid in Measurement

The existing literature raises at least two concerns of which the new investigator should be aware about the choice of a hardiness assessment tool: the use of makeshift scales and theoretically inappropriate scales. The Kuo and Tsai (1986) study of immigrants was described earlier in this chapter as a provocative application of the hardiness notion to a group much deserving of better empirical study. These investigators offered one of the most theoretically elaborate justifications for the choice of hardiness and an existential orientation found to date in the literature. Unfortunately, however, the power of their introduction was not matched by that of their methods section. Following their detailed expectations for the place of hardiness in the immigrants' life experience, they presented *three* items through which to assess it. And although they explained that all three components of hardiness are relevant for immigrants' coping abilities, they used only three control items. Each had to be answered *yes* or *no,* and a subject's hardiness score was the total number of affirmative responses. Apart from showing a relationship between hardiness scores and immigrants' stated reasons for migrating (the higher the hardiness, the more likely that the immigrant left for further education, better work opportunities, a higher standard of living, or adventure rather than to join family or get married), the researchers offered no information on the reliability or validity or their approach to measuring hardiness.

One could counter my complaints by noting that these investigators did call for additional studies on the other hardiness components and that, although I may regret their short shrift of hardiness items, they did succeed in making the empirical points they set out to make. I recognize these points, but I also regret the loss in this study of important opportunities better to understand (a) the specific mechanisms underlying the relevance of personality for the consequences of immigration by Asian groups and (b) the relationship between hardiness and social network variables that might have been possible with a more developed measurement strategy. This study strikes me as a good example of the situation Bartone describes: "Unfortunately, progress in assessing hardiness has not kept pace with interest in the construct" (1991:1).

Even more troubling are the studies that have employed the hardiness conceptualization along with a scale for a construct that conceptually has very little to do with hardiness. Both Howard, Cunningham, and Rechnitzer (1986) and Nakano (1990) measure hardiness by a secondary dimension of the Sixteen Personality Factor Questionnaire (16PF) (Cattell, Eber, & Tatsuoka, 1970), dependence/independence. People scoring high on independence are said to be "independent, radical, and a law unto themselves . . . more imaginative, wrapped up in inner urgencies, and careless of practical matters . . . 'internally autonomous' and tend to be more radical, as opposed to conservative, of temperament" (Howard, et al., 1986:232). I hope that enough has been said about the nature of hardiness in this chapter for the reader to agree that there may be some areas of overlap between the two psychological concepts, but far from enough overlap to have the hardiness and dependence/independence constructs be interchangeable.

Nakano's final discussion of results strikes a tone of irony. He describes hardiness as especially relevant to the situation of the Japanese businessperson. Hardiness is portrayed as uniquely allowing for both self-discipline and attentiveness to others. In combing control, commitment, and challenge, hardiness is a resource well-suited to modern Japanese society. Nakano speculates that hardiness enables people to be both competitive and in harmony with others. Unfortunately, by using the dependence/independence dimension rather than a scale such as the personal views survey, Nakano misses tapping those aspects of hardiness highlighted in the intriguing theoretical sections of the paper. He thus lost a chance at an important cross-cultural consideration of hardiness in business groups.

A Final Word on Measurement

In avoiding these pitfalls and the perils of any other hardiness measurement one engages in, it is critical for the new investigator not to let empirical concerns overshadow conceptual requirements. In the effort to find more psychometrically convincing items, one should not lose sight of either the conceptual changes in or violations of the original hardiness framework one's efforts have wrought.

Pollock's work on adaptation to chronic illness in several patient groups (Pollock, 1989; Pollock, Christian, & Sands, 1990; Pollock & Duffy, 1990) is a good example of a significant change in hardiness theory. Taking the approach that greater specificity increases predictive power, Pollock developed a Health-Related Hardiness Scale that differs from earlier hardiness measures in its use only of health-related items. Her items, drawn either from the Multidimensional Health Locus of Control Scales or newly written, included: "Having regular contact with a physician is the best way for me to avoid illness," "If I get sick, it is my own behavior that determines how soon I will get well again," "Involvement in health support groups will decrease my change of developing health problems," and "I am interested in exploring new health care regimens."

In reviewing her scale, one has to ask what relevance it has to the original definition of personality hardiness as *a general orientation toward self and world* expressive of commitment, control, and challenge. Something other than taking hardiness out of the executive setting, with its focus on work stress, and bringing it to bear on persons living with chronic illness is going on in her work. The items making up Pollock's scale might more usefully be called a measure of patients' attitudes toward health or a measure of patients' engagement in health promotion. In Pollock's empirical work, as distinct from her theoretical endeavors and her comments on nursing as a profession, it is difficult to see what she gains by bracketing her work with studies on personality hardiness and stress. The point here is not that Pollock's questions should not be asked of patients; rather, using the hardiness label for these questions risks conceptual murkiness.

Another example of conceptually hazardous waters can be found in the current struggle over a confounding of hardiness with negative affectivity, neuroticism, or maladjustment (Allred & Smith, 1989; Funk & Houston, 1987; Hull, et al., 1987). Important theoretical points are at stake here. It would be a mistake to see this struggle as one that can simply be resolved empirically. One needs to do more than watch that the number of negative hardiness items matches that of positive items, control for acquiescence and other response sets, and check on how much the hardiness variable contributes to the regression equation after negative affectivity has been entered. One also should take seriously the implications of the models in which variables like hardiness are typically depicted. We need to extend the basic theory of stress and include within it a thorough conceptualization of personality.

The stress and stress-resistance model that has guided most of the hardiness research assumes a relationship between hardiness and strain: the higher one's hardiness, the less likely one is to report distress or strain. As Maddi (1990) points out, one has to expect some correlation between hardiness and negative affectivity. The scales that are said to measure strain are the very same scales that have negative affectivity, neuroticism, or maladjustment as their target. Maddi makes better precision in the theories of negative affectivity and similar constructs a prerequisite for resolving the current dilemma.

Similarly, Lazarus (1990) considers the resolution of the debate about confounding between proponents of negative affectivity and proponents of variables (like hassles and hardiness) to be dependent upon greater attention to theoretical issues by stress researchers. Lazarus characterizes the current state as one in which most researchers simply proclaim negative affectivity to be the pre-eminent or fundamental individual difference variable providing explanation for all observed connections between health and psychological factors. Constructs like hassles and hardiness are epiphenomenal. Understandably, Lazarus is not taken with this majority view.

The simplest and most provocative of his rebuttals presents the reasonable counterposition that the issue of hassles or hardiness plays the primary role. The link between negative affectivity and health is made secondary:

> The presumption by Ben-Porath and Tellegen, Costa and McCrae, and Watson is that negative affectivity (or neuroticism) is *the* basic factor in the claimed confounding. However, the argument could just as logically, and perhaps even more fruitfully, be turned around so that appraisal or coping styles are treated as key variables in the relationship between negative affectivity (or neuroticism) and subjective distress or complaints about dysfunction. (p. 44)

Again, it strikes me that only by going back to the conceptual drawing board will we resolve the current impasse in the research literature. Only by better defining our constructs and clarifying their place in a broader and more sensitive view of human psychology than is typically invoked in contemporary research will we usefully engage in debates and learn something new about behavior. We may need to go beyond the middle-level theorizing to which we have become so accustomed. It may be helpful to revisit the existing grand theories. Within both psychoanalytic and humanistic schemes, one finds distinctions that may be useful in making sense of the overlapping and distinctive roles of the many psychological variables now thought to be relevant to health and illness. These distinctions include those between biologically based and learned structures of personality, individually determined and socially shaped behaviors, and conscious processes and those outside of awareness (cf. Ouellette Kobasa 1990; Westen, 1990).

IS HARDINESS REALLY THE PERSONALITY CONSTRUCT TO STUDY?

Reflected throughout this chapter is a tension that characterizes much of contemporary social science—the struggle between empirical precision and broad-based conceptualization of human behavior. In several instances in hardiness research one has been sacrificed for the sake of the other. For example, in studies done on college students, experimental sophistication is impressive, but one is left wondering about external validity and to what extent and how what is carefully measured has relevance in the real world. On the other hand, there are studies done in the field in which the researchers were clearly struggling with some poignant human experiences but that leave one wishing that personality had been evaluated more carefully. I believe that the best hardiness research will come from embracing this tension and encouraging dialogue between what now appear to be two very different sides of the research fence.

The paragraph you have just read represents a statement I typically give to the prospective hardiness researcher who follows the questions and answers about what group to study and how best to measure hardiness with a third question: "Is hardiness really the personality construct to study?" Such researchers express continuing worry about the criticisms of hardiness in the literature and wonder whether one of the many other personality constructs now presented in the literature as predictive of health will provide a bigger, empirical punch (e.g., a more significant change in r square). I cannot promise such investigators that current instruments will bypass all of the problems that critics have noted or that hardiness will have predictive power stronger than optimism, sense of coherence, type A, or any of the other variables for which health effects have been found. After saying what I have already said about group choice and measurement, the best I can do is encourage researchers to consider *why* they are planning to do health and personality research and to evaluate existing approaches with regard to the basic motivations embedded within these approaches. It helps to remind the caller or letter writer of what I thought I was doing when I did a dissertation on hardiness.[10]

Bowers (1987) aptly characterizes most of the work on personality and health as outcome-driven—i.e., as a search to find the variable that most strongly relates to significant health outcomes (fewer symptoms, lower T-cell counts, fewer days in the hospital, etc.) My primary investment in hardiness research, however, places me in Bower's other, smaller research camp—the one devoted to an expansion of basic personality psychology.

My interest in hardiness, in its original formulation and now, is to use it as a vehicle for discovering and saying something important about peoples' general orientations in life. The question about stress and health that generated much research interest in the 1970s were for me an entry point for existential personality notions that had been long neglected in American psychology. These notions include the fundamental importance of having a sense of meaning or purpose in life, the value of a life lived strenuously, the power and responsibility of freedom, subjective experience as the primary reality, and the possibility of individuals significantly shaping society. In short, research on stress, personality, and health was primarily a way for me to ask some questions about human behavior that I thought and still think are important to ask. I encourage all ambivalent prospective hardiness researchers personally to review what they want to better understand and say about human nature before picking any measurement tools.

NOTES

1. Please note that Suzanne C. Ouellette, Suzanne C. Ouellette Kobasa, and Suzanne C. Kobasa are one and the same person. The first is the preferred name.
2. I have restricted the review to published articles and chapters. Not covered here because of space restrictions are the many doctoral dissertations in the behavioral sciences, nursing, and other fields on hardiness. Individuals have contributed some very important and unique work in completion of their requirements for degrees and I hope soon to see it in formal published form.
3. I refer the reader interested in reviews of the hardiness literature to two recent chapters (Maddi, 1990; Orr & Westman, 1990). Maddi summarizes all of the hardiness work stemming from the original Chicago-based studies, answers many of the critics of this work, and discusses stress intervention strategies based on hardiness and other psychological constructs. Orr and Westman review additional studies and organize them all through a framework defined both by what many researchers have identified as the most pressing concerns about hardiness and the components generally recognized as the critical pieces of stress and stress-resistance models.
4. Much of what is said here about hardiness also might be applied to the construct of sense of coherence developed by Antonovsky (1979, 1987). This is another construct of stress-resistance to which nurses frequently refer as they present and justify their research questions. What nurses appear to find compelling about hardiness involves the aspects in which it is most similar to coherence.
5. Others have provided more detail than there is room for here on the nature, problems, and promise of available hardiness scales. The reader concerned about measurement should also consult Bartone, Ursano, Wright, and Ingraham (1989); Funk and Houston (1987); Hull, Van Treuren, and Virnelli (1987); Maddi (1990), Orr and Westman (1990), and Parkes and Rendall (1988). These sources provide both specific points and overview statements on hardiness measurement. To obtain a copy of the third-generation hardiness test described in this chapter, contact the Hardiness Institute, 5 Revere Drive, Suite 200, Northbrook, IL 60062 for a machine-scorable hardiness measure or see the appendix of the Bartone, et al. article for their slightly altered version of the test that they distributed to U.S. Army personnel (as well as Bartone's shortened thirty-item test). In addition, the reader can contact Paul T. Bartone of the Neuropsychiatry Division, Walter Reed Army Institute of Research, Washington, D.C. 20307, for documentation of further developments in hardiness measurement.
6. The research group at The University of Chicago involved in the revision of hardiness measurement included Mike Atella, Paul Bartone, Kathy Beisel, Ed Donner, Suzanne Kobasa, Salvatore Maddi, Bill Merrick, Mark Puccetti, Mel Schneider, Hilla White, and Marc Zola.
7. For both of these correlations, the older hardiness test produces a "nonhardy," or lack of hardiness, score and the newer version, a positive hardiness indicator, thereby determining a negative correlation between the two scales. Bartone obtained these results using his group of 787 bus drivers as subjects.
8. It is important to add at this point that there never was any interest in discovering the "real hardiness component"—in parsimoniously concluding something like, stress-resistance is really all about commitment and researchers need not worry about control and challenge. In fact, from

the beginning of this enterprise, I have been awakened in the night by worries over my attempt to base a meaningful statement about personality on only a tripartite notion, let alone a single variable (cf. Ouellette Kobasa, 1985).

9. I am indebted to J. Brian Cassel for this suggestion.

10. As I was writing this chapter, I received a preprint of an article by Aaron Antonovsky (1991) that is to appear in an edited collection on personality and stress. Given the notions I was struggling to present here, I found his paper to be a true gift. Antonovsky well demonstrates the value of looking beyond the particular empirical findings that have been generated around constructs (in the case of this article, the constructs are self-efficacy, locus of control, hardiness, and sense of coherence) to consider seriously the basic theoretical and philosophical assumptions that generated the constructs. In reviewing hardiness work, he makes a strong case for the need for researchers to recognize its existential roots.

REFERENCES

ALLRED, K. D., & SMITH, T. W. The hardy personality: Cognitive and physiological responses to evaluative threat. *Journal of Personality and Social Psychology,* 1989, *56,* 257–266.

ANTONOVSKY, A. *Health, stress, and coping.* San Francisco: Jossey-Bass, 1979.

————. *Unraveling the mystery of health.* San Francisco: Jossey-Bass, 1987.

————. The structural sources of salutogenic strengths. In C. I. Cooper & R. Payne (eds.), *Personality and stress: Individual differences in the stress process.* New York: Wiley, 1991.

BANKS, J. K., & GANNON, L. R. The influence of *hardiness* on the relationship between stressors and psychosomatic symptomatology. *American Journal of Community Psychology,* 1988, *16,* 25–37.

BARTONE, P. T. *Stress and health in Chicago Transit Authority bus drivers.* Unpublished doctoral dissertation, Department of Behavioral Sciences, The University of Chicago, 1984.

————. Predictors of stress-related illness in city bus drivers. *Journal of Occupational Medicine,* 1989, *31,* 857–863.

————. *Development and validation of a short hardiness measure.* Poster presented at the Third Annual Convention of the American Psychological Society, Washington, D.C., 1991.

BARTONE, P. T., URSANO, R. J., WRIGHT, K. M., & INGRAHAM, L. H. The impact of a military air disaster on the health of assistance workers: A prospective study. *The Journal of Nervous and Mental Disease,* 1989, *177,* 317–328.

BOWERS, K. S. Toward a multidimensional view of personality and health. *Journal of Personality,* 1987, *55,* 343–350.

CAMPBELL, J. M., AMERIKANER, M., SWANK, P., & VINCENT, K. The relationship between the hardiness test and the personal orientation inventory. *Journal of Research in Personality,* 1989, *23,* 373–380.

CARVER, C. S. How should multifaceted personality constructs be tested? Issues illustrated by self-monitoring, attributional style, and *hardiness. Journal of Personality and Social Psychology,* 1989, *56,* 577–585.

CATTELL, R. B., EBER, H. W., & TATSUOKA, M. M. *Handbook for the sixteen personality factor questionnaire,* Champaign, IL: Institute for Personality and Ability Testing, 1970.

CONTRADA, R. J. Type A behavior, personality *hardiness,* and cardiovascular responses to stress. *Journal of Personality and Social Psychology,* 1989, *57,* 895–903.

DRUSS, R. G., & DOUGLAS, C. J. Adaptive responses to illness and disability. *General Hospital Psychiatry,* 1988, *10,* 163–168.

FOX, R. C., AIKEN, L. A., & MESSIKOMER, C. M. The culture of caring: AIDS and the nursing profession. *The Milbank Quarterly,* 1990, *68,* Supplement 2, 226–256.

Funk, S. C., & Houston, B. K. A critical analysis of the hardiness scales' validity and utility. *Journal of Personality and Social Psychology,* 1987, *53,* 572–578.

Ganellen, R. J., & Blaney, P. H. Hardiness and social support as moderators of the effects of life stress. *Journal of Personality and Social Psychology,* 1984, *47,* 156–163.

Gentry, W. D., & Kobasa, S. C. Social and psychological resources mediating stress-illness relationships in humans. In W. D. Gentry (ed.), *Handbook of behavioral medicine.* New York: Guilford, 1984.

Hadley, B. J. Response to "Hardiness, self-perceived health, and activity among independently functioning older adults." *Scholarly Inquiry for Nursing Practice: An International Journal,* 1990, *4,* 185–188.

Hahn, M. E. *California Life Goals Evaluation Schedules.* Palo Alto, CA: Western Psychological Services, 1966.

Hannah, T. E., & Morrissey, C. Correlates of psychological *hardiness* in Canadian adolescents. *Journal of Social Psychology,* 1987, *127,* 339–344.

Harris, R. B. Reviewing nursing stress according to a proposed coping-adaption framework. *Advances in Nursing Science,* 1989, *11,* 12–28.

Henry, W. E. Personality change in middle and old age. In E. D. Norbeck, D. Price-Williams, & W. M. McCord (eds.), *The study of personality: An interdisciplinary appraisal.* Chicago: Holt, Rinehart, & Winston, 1968.

Holahan, C. J., & Moos, R. H. Life stress and health: Personality, coping, and family support in stress resistance. *Journal of Personality and Social Psychology,* 1985, *49,* 739–747.

Holt, P., Fine, M. J., & Tollefson, N. Mediating stress: Survival of the hardy. *Psychology in the Schools,* 1987, *24,* 51–58.

Howard, J. H., Cunningham, D. A., & Rechnitzer, P. A. Personality *(hardiness)* as a moderator of job stress and coronary risk in type A individuals: A longitudinal study. *Journal of Behavioral Medicine,* 1986, *9,* 229–244.

Hull, J. G., Van Treuren, R. R., & Propsom, P. M. Attributional style and the components of *hardiness. Personality and Social Psychology Bulletin,* 1988, *14,* 505–513.

Hull, J. G., Van Treuren, R. R., & Virnelli, S. Hardiness and health: A critique and alternative approach. *Journal of Personality and Social Psychology,* 1987, *53,* 518–530.

Jackson, D. N. *Personality research form manual.* Goshen, NY: Research Psychologists Press, 1974.

Keane, A., Ducette, J. & Adler, D. Stress in ICU and non-ICU nurses. *Nursing Research,* 1985, *34,* 231–236.

Knapp, R., Shostrom, E. L., & Knapp, L. Assessment of the actualizing person. *Advances in psychological assessment.* Vol. 4. San Francisco: Jossey-Bass, 1978.

Kobasa, S. C. Stressful life events, personality, and health: An inquiry into hardiness. *Journal of Personality and Social Psychology,* 1979, *37,* 1–11.

————. The hardy personality: Toward a social psychology of stress and health. In G. Sanders & J. Suls (eds.), *Social psychology of health and illness.* Hillsdale, NJ: Erlbaum, 1982.

Kobasa, S. C., & Maddi, S. R. Existential personality theory. In R. J. Corsini (ed.), *Current personality theories.* Itasca, IL: F. E. Peacock, 1977.

Kobasa, S. C., & Maddi, S. R., & Courington, S. Personality and constitution as mediators in the stress-illness relationship. *Journal of Health and Social Behavior,* 1981, *22,* 368–378.

Kobasa, S. C., Maddi, S. R., & Kahn, S. Hardiness and health: A prospective study. *Journal of Personality and Social Psychology,* 1982, *42,* 168–177.

Kobasa, S. C., Maddi, S. R., Puccetti, M. C., & Zola, M. A. Effectiveness of hardiness, exercise, and social support as resources against illness. *Journal of Psychosomatic Research,* 1985, *29,* 525–533.

KUO, W. H., & TSAI, Y. Social networking, hardiness, and immigrant's mental health. *Journal of Health and Social Behavior,* 1986, *27,* 133–149.

LAMBERT, C. E., JR., & LAMBERT, V. A. Hardiness: Its development and relevance to nursing. *Image* 1987, *19,* 92–95.

LAMBERT, V. A., & LAMBERT, C. E., KLIPPLE, G. L., & MEWSHAW, E. A. Social support, hardiness, and psychological well-being in women with arthritis. *Image,* 1989, *21,* 128–131.

LAZARUS, R. S. Theory-based stress measurement: Author's response. *Psychological Inquiry,* 1, 41–51.

MADDI, S. R. Hardiness training at Illinois Bell Telephone. In J. P. Opatz (ed.), *Health promotion evaluation.* Stevens Point, WI: National Wellness Institute, 1987.

————. Issues and interventions in stress mastery. In H. S. Friedman (ed.), *Personality and disease.* New York: Wiley, 1990.

MADDI, S. R., & KOBASA, S. C. The hardy executive: Health under stress. Homewood, IL: Dow Jones-Irwin, 1984.

MADDI, S. R., KOBASA, S. C., & HOOVER, M. An alienation test. *Journal of Humanistic Psychology,* 1979, *19,* 73–76.

MAGNANI, L. E. Hardiness, self-perceived health, and activity among independently functioning older adults. *Scholarly Inquiry for Nursing Practice: An International Journal,* 1990, *4,* 171–184.

MANNING, M. R., WILLIAMS, R. F., & WOLFE, D. M. Hardiness and the relationship between stressors and outcomes. *Work & Stress,* 1988, *2,* 205–216.

McCRANIE, E. W., LAMBERT, V. A., & LAMBERT, C. E., JR. Work stress, hardiness, and burnout among hospital staff nurses. *Nursing Research,* 1987, *36,* 374–378.

MORRISSEY, C., & HANNAH, T. E. Measurement of psychological *hardiness* in adolescents. *Journal of Genetic Psychology,* 1987, *148,* 383–395.

NAKANO, K. *Hardiness,* type A behavior, and physical symptoms in a Japanese sample. *Journal of Nervous and Mental Disease,* 1990, *178,* 52–56.

NEUGARTEN, B. L. The middle years. In S. Arieti (ed.), *American handbook of psychiatry.* New York: Basic Books, 1974.

NOWICKI, S., & STRICKLAND, B. R. A locus of control scale for children. *Journal of Consulting and Clinical Psychology,* 1973, *40,* 148–154.

OKUN, M. A., ZAUTRA, A. J., & ROBINSON, S. E. *Hardiness* and health among women with rheumatoid arthritis. *Personality and Individual Differences,* 1988, *9,* 101–107.

ORR, E., & WESTMAN, M. Does hardiness moderate stress, and how?: A review. In M. Rosenbaum (ed.), *On coping skills, self-control, and adaptive behavior.* New York: Springer, 1990.

OUELLETTE KOBASA, S. C. Personality and health: Specifying and strengthening the conceptual links. In P. Shaver (ed.), *Review of Personality and Social Psychology,* 1985, *6,* 291–311.

————. Lessons from history: How to find the person in health psychology. In H. S. Friedman (ed.), *Personality and disease.* New York: Wiley, 1990.

OUELLETTE KOBASA, S. C., & PUCCETTI, M. C. Personality and social resources in stress resistance. *Journal of Personality and Social Psychology,* 1983, *45,* 839–850.

PAGANA, K. D. The relationship of hardiness and social support to student appraisal of stress in an initial clinical nursing situation. *Journal of Nursing Education,* 1990, *29,* 255–261.

PARKES, K. R., & RENDALL, D. The hardy personality and its relationship to extraversion and neuroticism. *Personality and Individual Differences,* 1988, *9,* 785–790.

PIERCE, C. M. B., & MOLLOY, G. N. Psychological and biographical differences between secondary school teachers experiencing high and low levels of burnout. *British Journal of Educational Psychology,* 1990, *60,* 37–51.

POLLOCK, S. E. The hardiness characteristic: A motivating factor in adaptation. *Advances in Nursing Science,* 1989, *11,* 53–62.

POLLOCK, S. E., CHRISTIAN, B. J., & SANDS, D. Responses to chronic illness: Analysis of psychological and physiological adaptation. *Nursing Research,* 1990, *39,* 300–304.

POLLOCK, S. E., & DUFFY, M. E. The health-related *hardiness* scale: Development and psychometric analysis. *Nursing Research,* 1990, *39,* 218–222.

RHODEWALT, F. & AGUSTSDOTTIR, S. On the relationship of *hardiness* to the type A behavior pattern: Perception of life events versus coping with life events. *Journal of Research in Personality,* 1984, *18,* 211–223.

RHODEWALT, F., & ZONE, J. B. Appraisal of life change, depression, and illness in hardy and non-hardy women. *Journal of Personality and Social Psychology,* 1989, *56,* 81–88.

RICH, V. L., & RICH, A. R. Personality hardiness and burnout in female staff nurses. *Image,* 1987, *19,* 63–66.

ROTH, D. L., WIEBE, D. J., & FILLINGIM, R. B., & SHAY, K. A. Life events, fitness, hardiness, and health: A simultaneous analysis of proposed stress-resistance effects. *Journal of Personality and Social Psychology,* 1989, *57,* 136–142.

ROTTER, J. B., SEEMAN, M., & LIVERANT, S. Internal vs. external locus of control of reinforcement: A major variable in behavior theory. In N. F. Washburne (ed.), *Decisions, values, and groups.* London: Pergamon, 1962.

SCHMIED, L. A., & LAWLER, K. A. Hardiness, type A behavior, and the stress-illness relation in working women. *Journal of Personality and Social Psychology,* 1986, *51,* 1218–1223.

STONES, M. J., STONES, L., & KOZMA, A. Indicators of elite status in persons over 60 years: A study of Elderhostelers. *Social Indicators Research,* 1987, *19,* 275–285.

TOPF, M. Personality hardiness, occupational stress, and burnout in critical care nurses. *Research in Nursing & Health,* 1989, *12,* 179–186.(a)

————. Sensitivity to noise, personality hardiness, and noise-induced stress in critical care nurses. *Environment and Behavior,* 1989, *21,* 717–733.(b)

WESTEN, D. Psychoanalytic approaches to personality. In L. A. Pervin (ed.), *Handbook of personality: Theory and research.* New York: Guilford, 1990.

WESTMAN, M. The relationship between stress and performance: The moderating effect of hardiness. *Human Performance,* 1990, *3,* 141–155.

WIEBE, D. J. Hardiness and stress moderation: A test of proposed mechanisms. *Journal of Personality and Social Psychology,* 1991, *60,* 89–99.

WIEBE, D. J., & MCCALLUM, D. M. Health practices and hardiness as mediators in the stress-illness relationship. *Health Psychology,* 1986, *5,* 425–438.

WILLIAMS, C. L., SOLOMON, S. D., & BARTONE, P. T. Primary prevention in aircraft disasters: Integrating research and practice. *American Psychologist,* 1988, *43,* 730–739.

7

Effects of Stress on the Neurochemistry and Morphology of the Brain: Counterregulation versus Damage

Bruce S. McEwen   Scott Mendelson

STRESS IS A TERM used for certain types of experiences, as well as the body's response to such experiences. The term generally refers to challenges, real or implied, to the homeostatic regulatory processes of the organism. Thus, heat and cold, as well as physical trauma, are direct assaults on homeostasis, whereas fear, joy, surprise, and other emotions represent internal states that threaten the internal stability of the body. Of particular interest have been the factors that determine whether the body's response to stress leads to adaptation or to maladaptation and disease. Both outcomes involve changes in brain and behavior arising from the ability of the brain to control body functions through neural and hormonal output.

It is important to note the difference between the stressor and the stress response. The stress response consists of a cascade of neural and hormonal events that have short- and long-lasting consequences both both brain and body. Although a common connotation of the word *stressor* is an environmental event that is likely to cause a negative outcome—e.g., a disease—a preferable view is that a stressor is an event that challenges homeostasis, with a disease outcome being looked upon as a failure of the normal process of adaptation to the stressor. Psychological stressors such as fear involve perceived threats to homeostasis and are likely to evoke psychosomatic reactions, such as gastric ulcers and immunosuppression. Such psychosomatic reactions involve changes in the neural and hormonal output, and may lead to adaptive responses or exacerbate disease processes.

Whether the emphasis is on adaptation or disease, it is essential to understand the processes in the brain that are activated by stressors, how these processes influence functions throughout the body, and how they are modified by the agents that participate in the process of adaptation. The brain not only controls many aspects of the stress response and is the source of psychological stress, but the brain itself is also an important target of the hormones of stress.

What is the relationship between adaptation to stress and pathophysiological responses to stress? A primary focus of research has been upon the adrenal steroids as agents that mediate both adaptation and damage as a result of stress. The original formulation of the notion of stress by Selye (Selye, 1973) asserted that the adrenal steroids play an important role in both processes: adaptation requires some adrenal steroids to be present, but too much adrenal steroid can lead to damage and disease. A subsequent reformulation of this biphasic action by Munck, Guyre, and Holbrook (1984) holds that the body has primary responses to stressors, such as inflammation, and that adrenal steroids counteract such primary responses and buffer the body against their overreaction. However, as noted by Selye, excess adrenal steroids can suppress the primary responses to such an extent that they no longer function adequately to exert their primary protective function.

Do such counterregulatory influences of adrenal steroids operate in the central nervous system? If so, how do they participate in the neurochemical and behavioral response to stress? Do they counterbalance the primary responses of neural systems to activation by stressors? This chapter examines the role of adrenal steroids in adaptation to stress as well as in the pathophysiology associated with failure to adapt to stressors.

STRESSORS AND ADAPTATION TO STRESS

The brain is a living organ that changes with environmental input and experience and that controls neural and hormonal outputs affecting the rest of the body. Neural inputs innervate all major organs of the body, including the heart, intestines, thymus, spleen, and lymph nodes. Neural activity influences body processes such as cardiovascular output, digestion, immune function, and metabolism. Hormone outputs emanate from the hypothalamus, which controls the pituitary gland via neural inputs to the posterior lobe and via blood-borne chemical messengers that activate the anterior lobe to release trophic hormones such as adrenocorticotrophin (ACTH).

As is the case with all inputs to the brain, stressors turn on the activity of nerve cells. Resulting patterns of neural activity, which are undoubtedly specific to each stressor, evoke responses in the rest of the body via the various neural and hormonal outputs. Neural activity is transmitted from neuron to neuron by the neurotransmitters released at synaptic endings. Besides activating electrical responses, neurotransmitters also trigger the formation of intracellular second messengers, such as cyclic adenosine monophosphate (Figure 7-1). Through such second messengers, neurotransmitters have an impact on neuronal function that lasts beyond the period of electrical activity that triggered their release. This

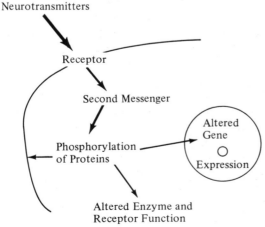

FIGURE 7-1. Role of phosphorylation of intracellular proteins in modifying enzyme and receptor function and gene expression. Phosphorylation is the final step that begins when a neurotransmitter or a peptide or protein hormone binds to a cell surface receptor and initiates formation of a second messenger, such as cycli 3′,5′ AMP, which, in turn, triggers the phosphorylation reaction.

is because second messengers like cyclic AMP promote the enzymatic phosphorylation of proteins within the cell. Such phosphorylation alters the function of the protein over many minutes until the protein is dephosphorylated by other enzymes. The phosphorylation of the enzyme tyrosine hydroxylase (TH) is one example. Phosphorylation of TH increases its catalytic efficiency in performing a key step in the formation of the catecholamine neurotransmitters, noradrenaline, epinephrine, and dopamine (Figure 7–1). Second messenger-stimulated phosphorylation also occurs on proteins that regulate genes in the cell nucleus, and resulting changes in gene expression can last for hours or days and lead to changes in levels of key enzymes and structural proteins in nerve cells. The induction of new TH formation by repeated stress is one example of the long-term adaptive response of the brain. This induction involves the operation of phosphorylated proteins that regulate genes (Figure 7–1).

Many stressors also activate the neurally mediated discharge of adrenaline from the adrenal medulla, as well as hormones from the hypothalamus that initiate the neuroendocrine cascade that culminates in glucocorticoid release from the adrenal cortex. (Figure 7–2). Thus, became virtually every organ and tissue is affected by stress hormones, the activity of neurons triggered by stressful experiences and by physical trauma, fear, or anger

FIGURE 7–2. Adrenal activity is activated by stress. The adrenal medulla receives direct neural input to trigger the release of adrenaline, whereas the adrenal cortex manufactures and releases glucocorticoids in response to ACTH from the pituitary, which is released in response to CRH and vasopressin from the hypothalamus. The release of glucocorticoids is a slower process than the release of adrenaline, in large part because of the cascade of events involving the neuroendocrine system. As a result, glucocorticoids are involved in the aftermath of the initial stress response and help to restore homeostatic balance that has been disrupted by stressors.

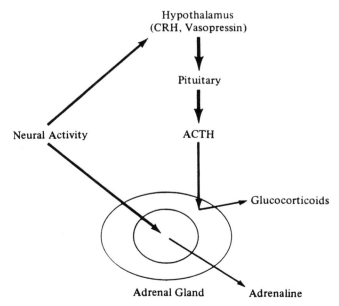

initiates hormone secretion that has effects throughout the body. The hypothalamic hormone that triggers the neuroendocrine cascade is called corticotrophin-releasing hormone (CRH), and it directly stimulates the pituitary to secrete ACTH. In response to certain stressors, the hypothalamus also releases vasopressin and oxytocin, which act synergistically with CRH on the pituitary to potentiate the secretion of ACTH. Various stressors differ in their ability to promote oxytocin and vasopressin release (Gibbs, 1986), but all stressors stimulate release of CRH. Other hormones are also affected by stressors, including prolactin and thyroid hormones; the metabolic hormones insulin, epinephrine, and glucagon; and the endogenous opiates, endorphin, and enkephalin.

However, in the study of adaptation to stress the adrenal steroids have been a primary focus of interest. Initial studies of adrenalectomized rats revealed that fear response in rats was enhanced in the absence of adrenal steroids (Weiss, McEwen, Silva, & Kalkut, 1970). Subsequent work has established that in rats the principal glucocorticoid, corticosterone, has anxiolytic effects when administered to adrenalectomized rats in conflict tests (File, Vellucci, & Wendlandt, 1979). Moreover, learned helplessness in rats is more frequent when the rats are bilaterally adrenalectomized (Edwards, Harkins, Wright, & Henn, 1990); this finding suggests that adrenal secretions antagonize the neurochemical responses that cause this behavioral state.

ADRENAL STEROIDS MODULATE NEURONAL STRUCTURE AND ACTIVITY

The brain is a dynamic and changing organ in which synapses, dendrites, and the neurochemicals of synaptic neurotransmission are continually being renewed and remodelled over the entire lifespan of an individual. Gene activity, controlled by environmental signals and mediated by circulating hormones, is fundamental to this plasticity (Figure 7–3). Our understanding of these relationships has arisen in part from studies that have identified and characterized receptor sites for adrenal, gonadal, and thyroid hormones in the brain. Together with ongoing advances in our understanding of how steroid and thyroid hormone receptors regulate gene expression, this information has stimulated a new area of investigation into how the brain changes in response to circulating hormones such as those that are secreted during stress.

Recent evidence indicates that steroids also act on some cells via membrane receptors that mediate rapid changes in ion flux and other aspects of cell surface activity (Figure 7–3). In some cases, the metabolism of the steroid by enzymes present in the brain as well as other tissues is required to generate the steroid derivative that acts on the membrane receptor (Simmonds, 1990). Thus, progesterone and desoxycorticosterone can be converted to 5alpha pregnane steroids, which are potent ligands for a site on the chloride channel of the GABAa-benzodiazepine receptor complex. These steroid metabolites activate chloride flux and exert anaesthetic and anxiolytic actions on the brain. We will see subsequently that these actions are part of the endocrine response to stress.

ADRENAL STEROID RECEPTORS AND THE BRAIN

In 1968, we reported that tritiated corticosterone (B) is taken up and selectively retained by the hippocampus in adrenalectomized (ADX) rats (McEwen, Weiss, & Schwartz, 1968). Later we demonstrated the same phenomenon by autoradiography in the hippocampus of

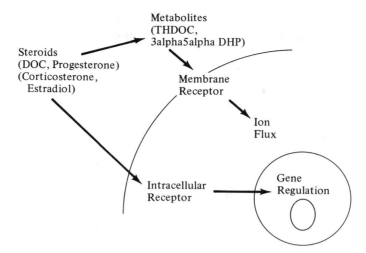

FIGURE 7–3. Steroids have two fundamentally different effects on cell function, either via cell membrane receptors that influence ion movements or via intracellular receptors that alter gene expression. Membrane activity of steroids can, but does not always, involve metabolism to steroid products that interact only with the membrane receptors and not with the known intracellular steroid receptors.

rats and rhesus monkeys (Gerlach & McEwen, 1972; Gerlach, McEwen, Pfaff, Moskovitz, Ferin, Carmel, & Zimmerman, 1976); this finding suggests that all mammals may have this property. Uptake and retention of ^{3}H B is related to the presence of cytosolic protein receptor sites in the hippocampus (reviewed in McEwen, DeKloet, & Rostene, 1986) and results in the labelling of receptors that can be extracted from isolated and purified cell nuclei (McEwen & Plapinger, 1970). Studies in a number of laboratories have characterized two receptor subtypes for glucocorticoids (GC), designated as type I, found mainly in hippocampus, and type II, found in hippocampus and other brain areas (reviewed in McEwen, DeKloet, & Rostene, 1986). Researchers have also begun to identify the role that these receptors play in mediating effects of the diurnal variation and stress elevation of GCs, including their role in the regulation of the pituitary-adrenal axis (reviewed in Sapolsky, Krey, & McEwen, 1986a). Other investigations have revealed tonic effects of GCs on the basic structure and composition of the brain, including the induction of enzymes and alterations in levels of structural components of glial cells and myelin (Meyer, 1985) but also including the death and survival of neurons, particularly in the hippocampus (Landfield, 1987; McEwen & Gould, 1990; Sapolsky, 1990).

Thus there is increasing evidence that a number of important structural and neurochemical features of the brain are altered by stress and by GCs and that we have only touched the surface of these interesting phenomena. Are there any generalizations that allow us to put these actions of adrenal steroids into perspective as far as their physiological role? In keeping with the work of Selye as modified by Munck et al. (1984), we have noted above that adrenal steroids have counterregulatory effects on many of the processes that are primary responses to stressors, such as inflammation and immunity. Similar counterregulatory effects of adrenal steroids operate in the brain. However, there are, in addition, damaging and destructive effects of adrenal steroids that appear to be an exception to the counterregulatory notion. A schematic overview of these relationships is presented in Figure 7–4. The following sections examine both the counterregulatory influences and the destructive effects of adrenal steroids, and their relationship to each other.

GLUCOCORTICOIDS AND ADAPTATION TO STRESS

One of the seeming paradoxes of the pituitary-adrenal axis is that its role in the response and adaptation to stress sometimes involves counterregulation of the body's other primary responses to the stressor. In this respect, it should be noted that adrenal steroids mediate the adaptation of noradrenaline-stimulated cAMP formation in cerebral cortex to repeated stressors (Figure 7–4). The first reports of this counterregulation established that in the cerebral cortex repeated stress suppresses the ability of noradrenaline to stimulate production of the second messenger, cAMP, via beta adrenergic receptors, and this effect appears to be mediated by glucocorticoids via their ability to suppress one of the alpha-1 adrenergic receptors that works synergistically to potentiate the beta adrenergic receptor (Stone, McEwen, Herrera, Carr, 1987). This suppressive effect, which would presumably decrease the efficacy of released noradrenaline, is opposite to the elevation of tyrosine hydroxylase activity, enzyme protein, and mRNA in the locus coeruleus that is produced by repeated stress (Musacchio, Julou, Kety, & Glowinski, 1969; Richard, Faucon-Biguet, Labatut, Rollet, Mallet, & Buda, 1988). Thus glucocorticoids help to keep the noradrenergic arousal system in check, and this type of adaptive mechanism may serve an antidepressant role, insofar as a hyperreactive and dysregulated noradrenergic system appears to be a hallmark of depression (Gold, Goodwin, & Chrousos, 1988a,b). Evidence in support of this notion includes the fact that imipramine treatment also suppresses the cAMP response to noradrenaline, although via a beta receptor mechanism, whereas the suppressive effect of adrenal steroids occurs upon an alpha adrenergic receptor that potentiates the beta adrenergic response (Stone, et al., 1987).

The findings on the glucocorticoid effect on the postsynaptic cAMP response to noradrenaline in cerebral cortex originated from studies which showed that adrenalectomy

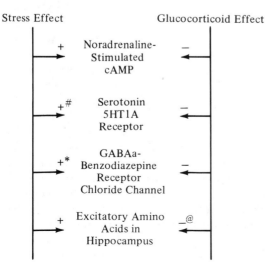

Stress Effect   Glucocorticoid Effect

+   Noradrenaline-Stimulated cAMP   –

+#   Serotonin 5HT1A Receptor   –

+*   GABAa-Benzodiazepine Receptor Chloride Channel   –

+   Excitatory Amino Acids in Hippocampus   –@

FIGURE 7–4. Counterregulation by glucocorticoids of the primary response to stressors, as described in the text. The symbol # denotes that adrenal steroids also facilitate the primary response, increased 5-HT turnover, in response to stress. The symbol * denotes that metabolites of desoxycorticosterone, such as 3alpha5 alpha tetrahydro DOC, activate the chloride channel of the GABAa-benzodiazepine receptor. The symbol @ denotes that glucocorticoid effects on excitatory amino acid actions on neurons can be counter regulatory as well as potentiating their damaging effects.

increased the cAMP response to noradrenaline and that this effect was reversed by corticosterone replacement; moreover, adrenal medulectomy had no effect, and hypophysectomy produced the same result as adrenalectomy (Mobley, Manier, & Sulser, 1983). Therefore, adrenal steroids are implicated and not adrenal epinephrine or pituitary ACTH.

As to the underlying mechanisms behind the suppressive effects of glucocorticoids, there is much work to be done. We have recently found that the calcium/calmodulin stimulation of adenylate cyclase in rat cerebral cortex is also negatively regulated by GCs in relation to repeated stress (Gannon, & McEwen, 1990). These effects are detected in the cerebral cortex but are not evident in the hippocampus, where, in fact, adrenal steroids appear to have a positive influence on the calcium-calmodulin adenylate cyclase response and may even participate in the positive regulation of this system during the diurnal cycle (Gannon, Brinton, Sakai, & McEwen, 1991). The suppressive effects of glucocorticoids in the cerebral cortex of rats repeatedly stressed over 21 days are mimicked by corticosterone injections but not by passive administration of corticosterone in the drinking water (Gannon, et al., 1990). This interesting observation raises the possibility that corticosterone may act synergistically with ongoing stress to produce its effects on this system.

BENZODIAZEPINE RECEPTORS AND STRESS

In contrast to the activating effects of noradrenaline on brain systems in response to stressors, the benzodiazepines (BZ) reduce stress responsiveness behaviorally and in terms of pituitary-adrenal function (Lahti & Barsuhn, 1974). Moreover, benzodiazepines suppress 5HT turnover in hippocampus (Nishikawa & Scatton, 1986) and thus may reduce anxiogenic stimulation by endogenous serotonin of 5HT1A receptors (see subsequently).

In keeping with the counterregulatory effects on other systems, adrenal steroids modulate the BZ system, but they do so biphasically. Recent evidence indicates that membrane-active endogenous metabolites of GCs formed in vivo during stress acutely activate the chloride channel of the GABAa-BZ receptor and promote activity of this complex (Havoundjian, Paul, & Shkolnick, 1986; Purdy, Morrow, Moore, & Paul, 1990; Schwartz, Wess, Labarca, Shkolnick, & Paul, 1987). These activating effects of adrenal steroids on the GABAa-benzodiazepine receptor system are analogous to an acute activating effect of adrenal steroids on the turnover of serotonin induced by stressors.

It should be noted that the acute effects of adrenal steroids on the GABAa-benzodiazepine system are anxiolytic and not arousing. The notion of counterregulation by adrenal steroids acting chronically would predict that even these anxiolytic actions of stress would be counteracted by adrenal actions in chronically stressed animals. Indeed, adrenal secretions chronically reduce the number of BZ receptor sites in hippocampus, striatum, and cerebral cortex (Acuna, Fernandez, Gomar, Aguila, & Castillo, 1990; De Souza, Goeders, & Kuhar, 1986) (Figure 7–4). Thus, adrenal suppression of BZ receptor number may be a feedback loop that keeps the acute effects of GC metabolites in check by limiting the number of available receptor sites that are part of the receptor complex through which steroid metabolites can act. This is only an hypothesis and requires further testing to show whether the benzodiazepine receptors that are chronically suppressed by the adrenals are part of the complex with GABAa receptors and respond to the acute activating effects of stress via the membrane active metabolites of desoxycorticosterone.

Developmental manipulations also affect levels of BZ receptors in the hippocampus. It has been reported that random prenatal stress, which increases emotional reactivity and fear in adulthood, decreases benzodiazepine binding (Fride, Dan, Gavish, & Weinstock, 1985), whereas postnatal handling, which decreases adult emotional reactivity, increases BZ binding in adult hippocampus (Aitken, Bodnoff, Suranyi-Cadotte, Quirion, & Meaney, 1987). Neither type of change has been mapped in the brain in relation to sites where GC modulation occurs in adulthood or where GCs modulate 5HT1A receptors.

SEROTONIN AND STRESS

The serotonin (5-HT) system is also implicated in the response to stress and in depressive illness (Kennet, Marcou, Dourish, & Curzon, 1987; van de Kar, 1989). The role of adrenal steroids in modulating the serotonergic response to stress is more complex than for noradrenaline and similar in some respects to the benzodiazepine system described previously. That is, adrenal steroids have the ability to promote 5-HT formation by activating tryptophan hydroxylase activity but may also suppress a stress-induced sensitivity to 5-HT. In counteracting enhanced 5-HT sensitivity, the actions of glucocorticoids fit into the counterregulatory actions described in Figure 7-4. However, the interactions between 5-HT, stress, and glucocorticoids are complex; because they have not previously been reviewed in any detail, we do so in the following sections of this chapter.

Stress Effects on 5-HT Turnover

Stress-induced increases in serotonergic activity in the brain occur independently of activation of the adrenal glands, but the maintenance of high levels of serotonergic activity during stress appears to require enhancement of 5-HT synthesis by corticosterone. Acute stress increases whole brain levels of tryptophan and 5-hydroxyindoleacetic acid (5-HIAA), the metabolite of 5-HT (Bliss, Ailion, & Zwanziger, 1968; Curzon & Green, 1969; Joseph & Kennet, 1983; Mueller, Twohy, Chen, Advis, & Meites, 1976). Repeated stress enhances increases in 5-HT turnover in response to subsequent acute stress (De Souza & Van Loon, 1986). In intact rats, acute stress has little effect on levels of 5-HT; however, in adrenalectomized rats, acute stress causes significant depletion of brain 5-HT (Curzon & Green, 1969). One explanation is that adrenal secretions potentiate the formation of serotonin. Indeed, it has been found that stress enhances the activity of tryptophan hydroxylase in the midbrain and forebrain, and that this effect of stress is blocked by adrenalectomy (Azmitia & McEwen, 1969, 1974). In unstressed rats, decreases in tryptophan hydroxylase activity observed after adrenalectomy are reversed by administration of corticosterone (Azmitia & McEwen, 1969, 1974). A variety of stress effects on 5-HT formation are potentiated by adrenal steroids: cold, ether, foot shock, alcohol, barbiturates, sound stress (Azmitia & McEwen, 1974; Neckers & Sze, 1975; Singh, Corley, Phan, & Boadle-Biber, 1990; Sze, Neckers & Towle, 1976; Yanai & Sze, 1983).

The mechanism by which stress increases tryptophan hydroxylase activity appears to be complex. These increases are blocked by adrenal steroid receptor antagonists such as Ru 38486, a finding that implicates the type II adrenal steroid receptor (Boadle-Biber, Corley, Graves, Phan, & Rosecrans, 1989). However, in the hippocampus decreases in 5-HT turnover brought on by adrenalectomy are reversed by corticosterone and not by dexamethasone, a finding that implicates the type I adrenal steroid receptor (DeKloet, Kovacs, Szabo, Telegdy, Bohus & Versteeg 1982). Curiously, aldosterone, an excellent agonist for the type

I receptor, blocks the ability of corticosterone to increase 5-HT turnover in the hippocampus of adrenalectomized rats (DeKloet, Versteeg & Kovacs, 1983). Corticosterone effects on tryptophan hydroxylase activity are also blocked by protein synthesis inhibitors, puromycin, and cycloheximide. However, the effects of adrenal steroids are evident concurrently in midbrain and forebrain regions, so that induction and transport of tryptophan hydroxylase would appear to be ruled out as factors (Azmitia & McEwen, 1974, 1976). More recent studies of this phenomenon have distinguished effects of stress with two time courses—namely, an acute effect that appears to involve phosphorylation of tryptophan hydroxylase and a long-term elevation of enzyme activity by repeated stress that does not involve enhanced phosphorylation (Singh, et al, 1990). Thus the possibility of a stress induction of tryptophan hydroxylase must still be considered.

Interestingly, the liver may also play a role in the actions of stress and glucocorticoids on the serotonin system. Single prolonged exposures to stress can result in decreases in whole brain levels of 5-HT and 5-HIAA (Corrodi, Fuxe, & Hokfelt, 1968; Curzon & Green, 1969, 1971; Nistico & Preziosi, 1969). These decreases could be due in part to an inability to sustain stress-induced increases in turnover of 5-HT. However, the apparent decreases in serotonergic activity that occur after several hours of severe stress have been found to coincide with the induction of liver tryptophan pyrrolase (Curzon, 1971). Tryptophan pyrrolase shunts tryptophan into the kynurenine pathway of metabolism, and activity of the enzyme makes less of the amino acid available in plasma for uptake and processing into 5-HT by the brain. Glucocorticoids are known to induce the enzyme (Knox & Auerbach, 1955), and administrations of corticosterone and other glucocorticoids have been found to decrease brain 5-HT in unstressed rats (Curzon & Green, 1968, 1971; De Schaepdryver, Preziosi, & Scapagnini, 1969; Scapagnini, Preziosi, & De Schaepdryver, 1969). It is worth noting, however, that after chronic exposure to glucocorticoids, reduced levels of brain 5-HT begin to normalize (Curzon, 1971), a result that may be related to the effects described in the previous paragraph.

Serotonin in the Hippocampus and the Effects of Stress

The hippocampus is an especially important area for the effects of stress and involvement of both glucocorticoids and the 5-HT system. The initial effect of stress in the hippocampus is to increase serotonergic activity (Joseph & Kennet, 1983; Morgan, Rudeen, & Pfeil, 1975). Chronic stress of low to moderate severity is often found to have little effect on levels of 5-HT or 5-HIAA in the hippocampus and many other areas of the brain (Kennet, Dickinson, & Curzon, 1985); Roth, Mefford, & Barchas, 1982). In some cases, slight increases in serotonergic activity have been observed in the hippocampus after chronic exposure to low or moderately severe stress (Adell, Garcia-Marquez, & Gelpi, 1989). However, when chronic stress is very severe, decreases in serotonergic activity can occur (Kitayama, et al., 1989). For example, after fourteen days of nearly constant immobilization, significant reductions in 5-HT-immunoreactivity are observed in the dorsal raphe and other serotonergic nuclei. Interestingly, in one study of activity-induced stress, animals that developed gastric ulcers had decreased levels of 5-HT and 5-HIAA in the hippocampus, whereas those that did not develop ulcers had increases in levels of these substances (Hellhammer, Hingtgen, Wade, Shea, & Aprison, 1983). Curiously, animals that display learned helplessness following subjection to repeated sessions of uncontrollable shock do not necessarily show decreases in serotonergic activity in the hippocampus or other areas of the brain (Hellhammer, et al., 1984; Weiss, Goodman, Losito, Corrigan, Charry, & Bailey, 1981). Indeed, quite paradoxically, pretreatment with the 5-HT synthesis inhibitor PCPA has been found to prevent the development of learned helplessness (Edwards, Johnson, Anderson, Turano, & Henn, 1986.

Stress Effects on 5-HT Receptors

There is evidence that some 5-HT receptors are up-regulated by stressful procedures. Initially, 5-HT receptors were categorized into two major subtypes, designated as 5-HT$_1$ and 5-HT$_2$ (Peroutka & Snyder, 1979). In subsequent studies it has been determined that the 5-HT$_1$ class of receptors consists of subtypes that, in the rat brain, have been designated as 5-HT$_{1A}$, 5-HT$_{1B}$ and 5-HT$_{1C}$ (Pazos, Hoyer, Palacios, 1984; Pedigo, Yamamura, & Nelson, 1981). Most recently, the 5-HT$_3$ subtype of 5-HT receptor also has been found to exist in rat brain (Kilpatrick, Jones, & Tyers, 1987). Interestingly, each subtype of 5-HT receptor is uniquely distributed in the brain, a finding that suggests complex and selective effects of 5-HT.

In two studies in which binding was evaluated in homogenates of brain tissue, stress induced by foot shock was found to have no effects on 5-HT$_{1A}$ receptors in the cortex or hippocampus of rats (Edwards, Harkins, Wright, & Henn, 1991; Ohi, Mikuni, & Takahashi, 1989). However, in a recent study we used quantitative autoradiography to evaluate the effects of acute and chronic restraint stress on subtypes of 5-HT receptors in specific areas of the dorsal hippocampus of male and female rats. We found that binding at 5-HT$_{1A}$ receptors increased in the oriens layer of CA4 24 hours after one 2-hour session of restraint and in the infrapyramidal portion of the dentate gyrus 24 hours after 1 and 5 daily restraint sessions (Mendelson & McEwen, 1991).

The mechanism by which the binding at 5-HT$_{1A}$ increases after restraint stress is unclear. It is conceivable that the increases in binding are due to up-regulation in the number of receptors in response to decreases in local release of 5-HT. However, chronic restraint stress has been reported to have no effect on levels of either 5-HT or 5-HIAA in the hippocampus (Kennet, et al., 1985). Furthermore, whereas significant increases in binding at 5-HT$_{1A}$ receptors were observed as early as one day after initiation of restraint, it has been reported to take at least one week for increases in binding at hippocampal 5-HT$_1$ receptors (of which the 5-HT$_{1A}$ subtype is predominant) to occur, even after profound depletion of local serotonin levels with 5,7-DHT (Nelson, Herbert, Bourgoin, Glowinski, & Hamon, 1978). Thus, we believe it unlikely that the increases in binding were due to decreases in serotonergic activity. However, it has recently been reported that administration of morphine or beta-endorphin magnifies, whereas the opiate antagonist naloxone blocks, the enhancement of sensitivity to 5-methoxy-N, N-dimethyltryptamine (5-MeODMT) that occurs after chronic application of restraint (Cancela, Volosin, & Molina, 1990). Thus, the increases in binding at 5-HT$_{1A}$ receptors that occur with restraint may be induced by some nonsteroidal, possibly opiate-mediated component of the stress response.

We found that restraint stress has no effect on 5-HT$_{1C}$ receptors in the hippocampus. Moreover, stress per se does not appear to affect binding to 5-HT$_{1B}$ receptors (Edwards, et al., 1991). However, animals that displayed learned helplessness 24 hours after being subjected to a session of uncontrollable shock were found on the following day to have higher numbers of 5-HT$_{1B}$ receptors than those observed in control animals in cortex, hippocampus, septum, and hypothalamus. Animals that did not show learned helplessness did not have higher numbers of these receptors. Reports on the effects of stress on 5-HT$_2$ receptors are somewhat inconsistent. Neither restraint- (Mendelson & McEwen, 1991) nor foot-shock-induced (Ohi, et al., 1989) stress has been found to affect binding at 5-HT$_2$ receptors in the hippocampus. In one study, a slight increase in binding at hippocampal 5-HT$_2$ receptors was observed 1 hour after an injection of saline, a finding that might indicate a stress-induced increase in binding (Paul, Duncan, Kuhn, Mueller, Hong, & Breese, 1990). However, in the same study, no increases in the density of those receptors were noted in other animals an hour after saline injection and immediately after 5 minutes of forced swimming. Foot shock also has no effect on 5-HT$_2$ receptors in cortex, and no change has been found in the density of cortical 5-HT$_2$ receptors either 23 hours after an initial experience or 10 minutes after a second subjection to forced swimming (Paul, et al., 1990). However, Torda, Murgas, Cechova, Kiss, and Saavedra (1990) found that 2 hours of immobilization increases binding at 5-HT$_2$ receptors in the rat cortex. This effect of stress is not blocked by 5, 7, DHT lesions of the serotonin system but is prevented by propranolol treatment; this finding indicates that it involves adrenergic innervation and beta adrenergic receptors. Interestingly, it is the cerebral cortex where stress-induced gluco-corticoid secretion counteracts noradrenaline-simulation of cAMP formation by reducing the alpha-adrenergic potentiation of a beta adrenergic response (see previously). Therefore, a glucocorticoid counterregulation of 5-HT$_2$ receptor sensitivity may occur by this mechanism rather than directly.

Modulation of 5-HT Receptor Subtypes by Adrenal Steroids

In keeping with the notion of counterregulation by adrenal steroids of some of the primary responses of the brain to stress, the adrenal steroids appear to modulate activity at serotonin (5-HT) receptors and to counteract at least some of the up-regulatory effects of stress described previously. The initial link of adrenal steroids to 5HT receptors was a study in quantitative autoradiography that demonstrated that the binding of [^{3}H]5-HT increased in the CA1 region of the hippocampus of male rats one week after adrenalectomy (ADX) (Biegon, Rainbow, & McEwen, 1985). In a subsequent autoradiographic study (De-Kloet, Sybersma, & Reul, 1986), increases in the binding of [^{3}H]5-HT were observed in the subiculum and dentate gyrus, although not in the CA fields, 1 hour after ADX. In those studies, the increases in the binding of [^{3}H]5-HT were reversed by administrations of corti-costerone sufficient to result in full occupancy of mineralocorticoid (MR), but not gluco-corticoid (GR), receptors. Thus, while those data suggest that activation of MR might decrease binding at hippocampal 5-HT$_1$ receptors, the possibility remains that activation of GR by high stress-induced levels of corticosterone could increase binding at the 5-HT$_{1A}$ subtype of receptor, as was observed in animals subjected to restraint stress. In yet another study, increases were found in the numbers of both 5-HT$_1$ and 5-HT$_2$ receptors in homogenates of hippocampus after adrenalectomy. Although the increase in the number of 5-HT$_2$ receptors after adrenalectomy was reversed by corticosterone replacement, it remains to be determined which kind of steroid receptor might mediate the effect.

In the initial evaluations of the effects of ADX and steroid replacement on 5-HT receptors, [^{3}H]5-HT was used as the radioligand. Because [^{3}H]5-HT labels the entire class of 5-HT$_1$ receptors, those studies provided no information on the effects ADX might have on the 5-HT$_{1A}$, 5-HT$_{1B}$, or 5-HT$_{1C}$ subtypes of receptors. Recently, however, we have determined that ADX results in increases in binding at 5-HT$_{1A}$ receptors in the CA2–4 regions and the dentate gyrus of the hippocampi of male rats (Mendelson & McEwen, 1990). Curiously, the increases in binding at 5-HT$_{1A}$ receptors that occurred after ADX were very similar in pattern to those observed after restraint stress (Mendelson & McEwen, 1991). Thus, it appears that, like the increases in serotonergic activity that occur in response to stressors, the increase in binding at 5-HT$_{1A}$ receptors may occur independently of adrenal activity. However, our most recent data indicate that sustained, high levels of corticosterone decrease binding at 5-HT$_{1A}$ receptors in the dentate gyrus (Mendelson & McEwen, 1992). We are presently trying to determine whether similar decreases in binding at 5-HT$_{1A}$ receptors occur in animals subjected to severe stress over long periods of time. It should also be noted that acute inhibitory effects of adrenal steroids on 5HT$_{1A}$ receptor-mediated inhibition have been shown to be likely mediators of a corticosterone-induced facilitation of neuronal excitation in the hippocampus (Joels & DeKloet, 1990).

In an initial study, we found no changes in the density of 5-HT$_{1B}$ receptors in the hippocampus after adrenalectomy (Mendelson & McEwen, 1990). More recently we have observed a slight but significant increase in 5-HT$_{1B}$ receptors in the infrapyramidal blade of the dentate gyrus of adrenalectomized rats, but in no other area of the hippocampus (Mendelson & McEwen, 1992). We also found that a high, sustained level of corticosterone reduced binding at 5-HT$_{1B}$ receptors in the infrapyramidal blade of the dentate gyrus, in comparison with untreated, adrenally intact control animals. Moreover, in animals treated with corticosterone, binding at 5-HT$_{1B}$ receptors was substantially lower than that observed in adrenalectomized animals in the infra- and suprapyramidal blades of the dentate gyrus and in the oriens and lacunosum moleculare layers of CA4. Thus it appears that prolonged activation of GR may reduce the number of 5-HT$_{1B}$ receptors in some areas of the hippocampus. Still, the 5-HT$_{1B}$ receptor appears to be less sensitive than 5-HT$_{1A}$ receptors to the effects of adrenal steroids.

Behavioral Implications of Counterregulation of 5-HT$_{1A}$ Receptors in the Hippocampus

It remains to be determined what the behavioral significance might be of the increases in binding at 5-HT$_{1A}$ receptors that occur in the hippocampus after restraint-induced stress. A predominance of evidence suggests that an overall increase in serotonergic activity has an anxiogenic effect in rats (Iversen, 1984; Johnston & File, 1986; Moser, et al, 1990). However, evidence is inconsistent with regard to whether activation of 5-HT$_{1A}$ receptors in the hippocampus would be anxiogenic. For example, whereas some authors have found the anxiolytic ipsapirone (Fernandes-Guasti & Lopez-Rubalcava, 1990) to be a weak partial agonist capable of blocking the effects of 5-HT at hippocampal 5-HT$_{1A}$ receptors (Bagdy, Calogero, Charanjit, Szemeredi, & Nurphy, 1989; Tricklebank, Forler, & Fozard, 1984), others have found the drug to be a full and relatively potent agonist in the hippocampus (O'Conner, Rowan, & Anwyl, 1990; Rowan & Anwyl, 1986). Nonetheless, it is interesting that high levels of corticosterone, which has been reported to have anxiolytic effects (File, et al., 1979), have been found to decrease sensitivity to the 5-HT$_{1A}$ agonist 5-MeODMT in unstressed rats (Dickinson, Kennet, & Curzon, 1985). Administration of the corticosterone synthesis inhibitor metyrapone has been found to hasten the increase in the sensitivity to 5-MeODMT that occurs after several daily periods of restraint stress (Kennet, Dickinson, & Curzon, 1985). Most recently, the administration of high doses of cortisol has been found to diminish the ability of 8-OH DPAT to stimulate the release of prolactin in intact rats (Bagdy, et al., 1989). Although speculative, it is reasonable to suggest that high levels of corticosterone may buffer anxiogenic effects of stress through an ability to diminish the effects of activity at certain 5-HT$_{1A}$ receptors.

New Insights into Neuroanatomy of 5-HT Innervation of the Hippocampus

Autoradiographic analyses of tissue labelled by uptake or anterograde transport of [^{3}H]5-HT have shown that the distribution of serotonergic axons and terminals is heterogenous across the hippocampus (Moore & Halaris, 1975; Oleskevich & Descarries, 1990). There is also evidence of at least two anatomically and, perhaps, functionally, distinct subsytems of serotonergic neurons innervating the hippocampus (Molliver, et al. 1990). One subsystem of neurons arises from the dorsal raphe in the brainstem. These neurons have fine axons with small, fusiform varicosities distributed along their length. The neurons of the second subsystem arise from the median raphe. These neurons have a beaded appearance, with large, spherical varicosities on their axons. The neurons from the median raphe appear to be predominant in the serotonergic innervation of the hippocampus. Indeed, whereas lesions of the median raphe reduce levels of 5-HT in the hippocampus by up to 80%, lesions of the dorsal raphe have frequently been found to have little, if any, effect (Jacobs, Wise, & Taylor, 1974; Lorens & Guldberg, 1974).

Serotonergic neurons from the median and dorsal raphe nuclei project to many of the same areas of the hippocampus; however, there are some differences in the distributions of their terminals. Of particular interest is the recent association of the beaded axons of median raphe neurons, but not those of the dorsal raphe, with inhibitory interneurons in the CA3 area and dentate gyrus (Tork, 1990). It is conceivable that in some areas of the hippocampus, neurons from the dorsal and median raphe nuclei might have opposite effects—i.e., neurons from the dorsal raphe might inhibit pyramidal cells, whereas those from the median raphe nuclei might disinhibit pyramidal cells through action at interneurons. The 5-HT$_{1A}$ receptors are densely distributed in layers of the hippocampus that contain both pyramidal cells and interneurons (Sloviter, & Nilaver, 1987). Although 5-HT$_{1A}$ receptors are known to exist on pyramidal cells (Andrade & Nicoll, 1987), it remains to be determined whether they also exist on interneurons. We are presently performing experiments designed to resolve this question. If this were the case, however, it would be interesting to consider the possibility that stress and/or adrenal steroids may have differential effects on the subpopulations of 5-HT$_{1A}$ receptors served by the dorsal and median raphe nuclei.

The possibility of subpopulations of 5-HT$_{1A}$ receptors playing differential roles in anxiety and stress is also suggested by our recent finding of a positive correlation between serum levels of CORT and binding at 5-HT$_{1A}$ receptors in CA1, but not other areas of the hippocampus (unpublished data). Although there has been conflicting data, there is evidence that the various regions of the hippocampus can have differential effects on serum corticosterone levels. In one study, electrical stimulation of CA1 resulted in further increases in high urethane-induced levels of corticosterone, whereas stimulation of CA3 and the dentate gyrus resulted in decreases in these corticosterone levels (Dunn & Orr, 1984). It is tempting to suggest that such regional differences might allow the organism to maintain an anxiolytic level of corticosterone during the initial stages of adaptation to a stressor.

Sex Differences in 5-HT in the Hippocampus

It is interesting to note that we also found sex differences in the density of 5-HT$_{1A}$ receptors in the hippocampus (Mendelson & McEwen, 1991a). In the oriens and lacunosum moleculare layers of CA1, levels of [^{3}H]8-OH DPAT binding were significantly higher in female rats than in male rats. Interestingly, neither estrogen nor estrogen plus progesterone treatment was found to affect the binding of [^{3}H]8-OH DPAT in the hippocampi of OVX rats. Thus, it seems unlikely that the sex differences observed in this study occurred simply as a function of the females being in a particular phase of the estrous cycle. Also consistent with earlier reports (Kant, Lenox, Bunnell, Mougey, Pennington, & Meyerhoff, 1983; Kitay, 1961) was our finding of sex differences in serum corticosterone levels. Levels of corticosterone in tail blood collected during restraint stress and in trunk blood collected after 3 minutes in an open field were significantly higher in females than in males. If corticosterone does act as an anxiolytic by dampening activity at 5-HT$_{1A}$ receptors, then females, with higher levels of corticosterone, should show more tolerance to aversive and stressful stimuli. This characteristic may be reflected in the higher level of activity shown by females in the open field. Females have also been found to acquire more slowly and extinguish more quickly passive-avoidance behavior (Heinsbroek, van Haaren, & van de Poll, 1988). Interestingly, sex differences in the acquisition of passive avoidance behavior can be eliminated by depletion of central 5-HT [Heinsbroek, Feenstra, Boon, van Haaren, & van de Poll, 1988].

Serotonin and Depression

The role played by hippocampal 5-HT$_{1A}$ receptors in depression is controversial. Long-term administrations of antidepressants, including tricyclics and the atypical antidepressant mianserin, have been found to enhance the 5-HT$_{1A}$-mediated inhibitory effects of 5-HT in the CA1 and CA3 areas of the hippocampus (Blier, de Montigny, & Tardif, 1984; de Montigny & Aghajanian, 1978). However, not all antidepressants enhance activity at hippocampal 5-HT$_{1A}$ receptors (Blier, et al., 1984), nor do all researchers find particular drugs to be effective (Beck & Halloran, 1989). In any case, our data suggest that it is unlikely that the apparent vulnerability of females in models of animal depression (Kennet, Chaouloff, Marcou, & Curzon, 1986) could be due to an inability to increase binding at hippocampal 5-H$_{1A}$ receptors in response to stress. Moreover, while the higher corticosterone levels of females might contribute to the sex difference in vulnerability over a long period of time, the present data indicate that corticosterone levels in female rats decrease significantly in a process of adaptation to a stressor and that these decreases seem to occur within a time course of adaptation similar to that observed in male rats. Still, it is tempting to suggest that the increases in 5-HT$_{1A}$ receptors observed after 1 or 5 days of restraint stress may reflect successful adaptation to stress. Our recent finding of reductions in the density of 5-HT$_{1A}$ receptors in the hippocampus after long-term exposure to high levels of corticosterone (Mendelson & McEwen, 1992) suggest the possibility of similar decreases in the density of these receptors after failure to adapt to prolonged and severe stress, with resultant vulnerability to depression. In future studies we wish to determine if there are sex differences in the effects of long-term exposure to high levels of corticosterone.

NEURONAL DEATH AND SURVIVAL

As we have noted, adrenal steroid effects on the brain involve not only the counterregulation of the effects of stress on the brain and other organs of the body, but also include the subsequent occurrence of damage and destruction of neurons. Death of hippocampal neurons was first reported after repeated GC or ACTH treatment in guinea pigs (aus der Muhlen & Ockenfels, 1969); it was later found in the aging rat hippocampus (Landfield, Baskin, & Pitter, 1981; Sapolsky, Krey, & McEwen, 1986b) and as a result of GC exacerbation of the effects of transient ischemia (Sapolsky & Pulsinelli, 1985) and exogenous kainic acid administration (Sapolsky, 1986). Repeated GC treatment of young rats causes premature loss of hippocampal neurons, particularly in the CA3 field of hippocampus (Sapolsky, Krey, & McEwen, 1985), and this effect is preceded by loss of neuronal branching.

Parodoxically, adrenalectomy (ADX) causes loss of neurons in the dentate gyrus (Sloviter, et al., 1989). We have found that this loss begins within 3 days, but that it can be prevented by low doses of B (principal glucocorticoid in the rat), aldosterone (mineralocorticoid), or even the synthetic GC, dexamethasone. This loss of neurons, which does not occur in cerebellar granule cells or in pyramidal neurons of CA1-3 of the hippocampus, may indicate a positive, trophic effect of adrenal steroids on the dentate gyrus (Gould, Woolley, & McEwen, 1990; Woolley, Gould, & McEwen, 1990). It may also be causally related to what happens with excess GC in CA3 because of the mossy fiber projection from the dentate gyrus to CA3 (Woolley, Gould & McEwen, 1990). The implications and underlying mechanisms of these relationships remain to be explored. Moreover, the ability of stress to produce altered hippocampal morphology, and even cell death, remains to be investigated. One report has found that chronic social stress in vervet monkeys results in CA3 neuronal death in the hippocampus of subordinate males who were so severely debilitated that they died of stress-related diseases (Uno, Ross, Else, Suleman, & Sapolsky, 1989).

HIPPOCAMPAL INVOLVEMENT IN PITUITARY-ADRENAL AXIS REGULATION

An important feature of hippocampal neuronal destruction is that it compromises the ability of the hippocampus to act in the shut-off of the pituitary-adrenal stress response (Sapolsky, Krey, McEwen et al., 1986a). Indeed, aging rats show prolongation of stress responses after stress is over (Sapolsky, et al., 1986a), and human Alzheimer patients with documented hippocampal damage based on a CT scan show cortisol hypersecretion after a glucose tolerance test (DeLeon, et al., 1988). A variety of lesion experiments have shown that pituitary-adrenal hyperfunction is a typical result of hippocampal damage, whereas stimulation of sites within the hippocampus can give rise to either stimulation or inhibition of pituitary-adrenal function (for a review, see Sapolsky, Krey & McEwen et al., 1986b).

The net effect of hippocampal damage is to increase pituitary-adrenal activity, and the actions of elevated glucocorticoid secretion, which cause further damage to the hippocampus, have led to the notion of a positive feedback loop leading to the progressive destruction of the hippocampus. This has been called the *glucocorticoid cascade hypothesis* and is one possible mechanism by which the wear and tear of stress during daily life could lead to aging of the hippocampus (Sapolsky, Krey & McEwen et al., 1986b).

How are the negative influences of the hippocampus on pituitary-adrenal function able to reach the paraventricular hypothalamus, from which emanates the CRH and vasopressin that govern ACTH secretion? The hippocampus projects to the paraventricular nuclei at least in part via the bed nuclei of the stria terminalis (Herman, et. al., 1989b), and disruption of this output results in elevated levels of CRHmRNA in parvocellular PVN neurons (Herman, et al., 1989a). Previously, it was shown that ADX also increases the co-expression of AVP by CRH-containing neurons (Sawchenko, Swanson, & Vale, 1984; Whitnall, Mezey, & Gainer, 1985). Repeated stress of various types enhances the level of CRHmRNA in parvocellular PVN (22) and also causes the increased expression of vasopressin immunoreactivity (Barrett, Silverman, & Hou-Yu, 1989) and vasopressin mRNA in parvo- and magnocellular PVN (Herman, et al., 1989a). The role of the hippocampus in these stress effects remains to be explored as well as the time course and nature of the stress conditions that give rise to elevated AVP and CRH expression.

GLUCOCORTICOIDS AND THE EFFECTS OF EAA

Adrenal steroid involvement in the death of neurons in the hippocampus appears to be primarily the potentiation of the destructive effects of excitatory amino acids via calcium ion mobilization on the pyramidal neurons of Ammons horn. In these actions, the ability of glucocorticoids to inhibit glucose transport in the hippocampus and thus reduce energy supplies is thought to be a key step. Depriving hippocampal neurons of energy when they are excited by excitatory amino acids and have calcium mobilized within their cytoplasm can retard the removal of those ions to storage sites. Free calcium can then activate proteolytic enzymes and lead to free radical generation, lipid peroxidation, and then cell damage and death.

In addition, we hypothesize that glucocorticoids may stimulate the functional activity of dentate granule neurons, whose survival they also protect, and that the enhanced activity of the mossy fiber system innervating CA3 pyramidal neurons may make them especially vulnerable to destructive actions of glucocorticoids.

Besides these actions of glucocorticoids to promote neuronal damage and destruction, other effects of glucocorticoids may counteract such damaging effects (McEwen & Gould, 1990). These effects include the induction of glutamine synthetase, an enzyme that generates a storage form of glutamate; the suppression of the generation of quinolinic acid, an endogenous excitotoxin; and the suppression of the number of binding sites for excitatory amino acids in the hippocampal formation. Although these effects of glucocorticoids have been demonstrated, there is not ability at this time to assess where and how they may retard the damaging effects that glucocorticoids also produce.

WHAT ARE THE CONDITIONS FOR PROTECTION AND DESTRUCTION?

Given the paradox of adrenal involvement in both destruction and protection in relation to stress, a key question is what is the dividing line between them. When do protection and adaptation fail so that destruction begins? A key factor may be the involvement of other agents in addition to GCs in both protection and destruction. That is, GCs are permissive in their actions as far as increasing the activity of the 5-HT system (Azmitia & McEwen, 1974), and they appear to be permissive in relation to suppressing the noradrenaline- and calcium/calmodulin-stimulated cAMP responses. On the other hand, destructive effects of

GCs on hippocampal neurons (Figure 7-4) may involve potentiation of the negative effects of excitatory amino acids via NMDA receptors (McEwen & Gould, 1990) and may occur because GCs inhibit glucose uptake in the hippocampus and thus can retard the production of energy needed for buffering calcium ions mobilized by NMDA agonists (Horner, Packan, & Sapolsky, 1990; McEwen & Gould, 1990). In other words, not only the presence of GCs but also the activity of other neurochemical systems is important in determining the final outcome. Because neurotransmitters are released by neural activity, the types of stressful experiences that the animal or person has, the ways they are perceived by the stressed individual, and the behavioral response, must also be considered.

CONTROL OF STRESS

Controllability of stress is recognized to be an important factor in the severity of its consequences for gastric ulcers and NA activity of the locus coeruleus system (Weiss, et al., 1981). The behavior known as learned helplessness, used sometimes as an animal model of depressive illness, frequently results from exposure of rats to stresses that they cannot control (Sherman & Petty, 1980), and is altered by hippocampal damage (Elmes, Jarrard, & Swart, 1975; Leshner & Segal, 1979). Very little is known about the neurochemical and morphological consequences of repeated exposure of rats to a stress that they cannot control as opposed to a stress that they can control. The prolongation of NA activity in uncontrollable stress (Tsuda & Tanaka, 1985) would suggest that the controllable versus uncontrollable distinction might result in a different neurochemical mileau in which the permissive actions of GCs might have different consequences.

DEVELOPMENTAL INFLUENCES ON THE REACTIVITY TO STRESS

Besides the proximal behavioral contributions to the permissive actions of GCs secreted in stress, there is also the important issue of developmental determinants of the responsiveness to stress. The procedure referred to as *handling* of newborn rats, which involves separating them from their mothers for 15 minutes per day during the first 14 postnatal days of life, results in animals whose pituitary-adrenal axis shows less reactivity to stress and novelty (Hess, Denenberg, Zarrow, & Pfeifer, 1969; Levine, 1962; Meaney, Aitken, & Sapolsky, 1987). In contrast, random prenatal stress of the pregnant mother results in offspring that are hyper-reactive to stressors and novel situations (Fride, Dan, Feldon, Halevy, & Weinstock, 1986). One key aspect of the effects of neonatal handling appears to be an enhancement of type II (GC) receptors in the hippocampus (Meaney, Aitken, Bodnoff, Iny, Tatarewicz, & Sapolsky, 1985). Since the hippocampus appears to be involved in shut-off by GCs of the stress response (Sapolsky, Krey & McEwen et al., 1986a), having more receptors in the hippocampus may lead to more efficient termination of the stress response (Meaney, Aiken, Viau, Sharma, & Sarrieau, 1989). More efficient shut-off of the stress response would limit the lifetime exposure to GCs and might lead to slower hippocampal neuronal loss with age. This response was observed in neonatally handled rats (Meaney, Aitken, Berkel, Bhatnager, & Sapolsky, 1988). Meaney suggests that handling produces its effects by transient hypothermia, which elevates thyroid hormone levels, and has found that neonatal hyperthyroidism elevates hippocampal type II receptors, as does handling (Meaney, Aiken, Viau, Sharma, & Sarrieau, 1989). However, other hormones, such as growth hormone, are known to be perturbed in newborn rats by stress and handling (Kuhn, Butler, Schanberg, 1978), and the role of thyroid hormone and growth hormone in the development of the hippocampus deserves further exploration. Nothing is known yet about the consequences of elevating pituitary-adrenal reactivity by random prenatal stress in terms of hippocampal neuronal survival with age and stress or other aspects of stress responsiveness of neurochemical systems.

CONCLUSIONS

Stress is a likely factor in precipitating depressive illness (Anisman & Zacharko, 1982) as well as in increasing vulnerability to tumors and infections by suppressing immune function via the modulation of neural and hormonal outputs that affect the immune system (Dunn, 1988). As stated and developed throughout this review, our working hypothesis is that depressive illness represents a failure of normal adaptive mechanisms to operate and that adrenal steroids, particularly GCs, play a role in the adaptation to stress, as is shown in Figure 7-4 for three neurochemical systems. In this limited sense, GCs are the body's antidepressant—or at least one of them. We feel that by understanding the normal adaptive mechanisms to stress in terms of biochemical and morphological changes in the brain we may be better prepared to recognize what goes wrong under conditions in which adaptation fails and the animal becomes "depressed"—as in an uncontrollable stress situation when learned helplessness appears. Besides relevance to depressive illness, the effects of adrenal steroids on the survival and destruction of neurons, particularly in the hippocampus, raise the possibility that the course of Alzheimer's disease and other neural degenerative diseases may be accelerated by stress and GCs (Sapolsky, Krey & McEwen, 1986b). Better understanding of the beneficial, as well as the destructive, aspects of GC actions on neuronal survival may aid in developing treatment strategies to slow the rate of progress of the disease (Sapolsky & McEwen, 1986). The successful application of the CT scan in the early diagnosis of hippocampal shrinkage before Alzheimer's disease is diagnosed (de Leon, George, Stylopoulos, Smith, & Miller, 1989), together with the abnormal elevations of cortisol seen in patients with hippocampal shrinkage (de Leon, et al., 1988), are findings that were stimulated by work on adrenal steroid effects in the hippocampus. In addition, knowing that GCs accelerate neuronal destruction has stimulated attempts to improve treatment of head trauma and stroke by modifying the GC molecule to avoid the damage-potentiating effects and keep the ability to protect against a presumed final step of the damage cascade—namely, lipid peroxidation-induced damage of the membrane (Hall, McCall, Chase, Yonkers, & Braughler, 1987).

REFERENCES

Acuna, D., Fernandez, B., Gomar, M. Aguila, C., & Castillo, J. Influence of the pituitary-adrenal axis on benzodiazepine receptor binding to rat cerebral cortex. *Neuroendocrinology,* 1990 *51,* 97–103.

Adell, A., Garcia-Marquez, C., & Gelpi, A. Chronic administration of clomipramine prevents the increase in serotonin and noradrenaline induced by chronic stress. *Psychopharmacology,* 1989, *99,* 22–26.

AITKEN, D., BODNOFF, S., SURANYI-CADOTTE, B., QUIRION, R., & MEANEY, M. The benzodiazepine receptor and habituation. *Abstracts of the Society of Neuroscience,* 1987, *13,* 127.8.

ANDRADE, R., & NICOLL, R. Pharmacologically distinct actions of serotonin on single pyramidal neurones of the rat hippocampus recorded in vitro. *Journal of Physiology,* 1987, *394,* 99–124.

ANISMAN, H., & ZACHARKO, R. Depression: The predisposing influence of stress. *Behavioural Brain Science,* 1982, *5,* 89–137.

AUS DER MUHLEN, K., & OCKENFELS, H. Morphologische veranderungen im diencephalon und telencephalon: Storungen des regelkreises adenohypophysenebennierenrinde. *Z. Zellforsch. Mikrosck. Anat.,* 1969, *93,* 126–141.

AZMITIA, E., & McEWEN, B. S. Corticosterone regulation of tryptophan hydroxylase in rat midbrain. *Science,* 1969, *166,* 1274–1276.

――――. Adrenocortical influence on rat brain tryptophan hydroxylase activity. *Brain Research,* 1974, *78,* 291–302.

――――. Early response of rat brain tryptophan hydroxylase activity to cycloheximide, puromycin and corticosterone. *Journal of Neurochemistry,* 1976, *27,* 773–778.

BAGDY, G., CALOGERO, A., CHARANJIT, S., SZEMEREDI, K., & NURPHY, D. Long-term cortisol treatment impairs behavioral and neuroendocrine responses to 5-HT$_1$ agonists in the rat. *Neuroendocrinology,* 1989, *50,* 241–247.

BARRETT, J., SILVERMAN, A., & HOU-YU, A. Chronic behavioral stress increases CRF immunoreactivity and CRP/VP co-localization. *Abstracts of the Society of Neuroscience,* 1989, *15,* 58.5.

BECK, S., & HALLORAN, P. Imipramine alters adrenergic, but not serotonergic mediated responses in rat hippocampal pyramidal cells. *Brain Research,* 1989, *504,* 72–81.

BIEGON, A., RAINBOW, T., & McEWEN, B. S. Corticosterone modulation of neurotransmitter receptors in rat hippocampus: A quantitative autoradiographic study. *Brain Research,* 1985, *332,* 309–314.

BLIER, P., DE MONTIGNY, C., & TARDIF, D. Effects of two antidepressant drugs mainserin and indalpine on the serotonergic system: Single cell studies in the rat. *Psychopharmacology,* 1984, *84,* 242–249.

BLISS, E., AILION, J., & ZWANZIGER, J. Metabolism of norepinephrine, serotonin and dopamine in rat brain with stress. *Journal of Pharmacology and Experimental Therapeutics,* 1968, *164,* 122–134.

BOADLE-BIBER, M., CORLEY, K., GRAVES, L., PHAN, T.-H., & ROSECRANS, J. Increase in the activity of tryptophan hydroxylase from cortex and midbrain of male Fischer 344 rats in response to acute or repeated sound stress. *Brain Research,* 1989, *482,* 306–316.

CANCELA, L., VOLOSIN, M., & MOLINA, V. Opioid involvement in the adaptive change of 5-HT1 receptors induced by chronic restraint. *European Journal of Pharmacology,* 1990, *176,* 313–319.

CORRODI, H., FUXE, K., & HOKFELT, T. The effect of immobilization stress on the activity of central monoamine neurons. *Life Sciences,* 1968, *7,* 107–112.

CURZON, G. Effects of adrenal hormones and stress on brain serotonin. *American Journal of Clinical Nutrition,* 1971, *24,* 830–834.

CURZON, G., & GREEN, A. Effect of hydrocortisone on rat brain 5-hydroxytryptamine, *Life Science,* 1968, *7,* 657–663.

――――. Effects of immobilization on rat liver tryptophan pyrrolase and brain 5-hydroxytryptamine metabolism. *British Journal of Pharmacology,* 1969, *37,* 689–697.

――――. Regional and subcellular changes in the concentration of 5-hydroxytryptamine and 5-hydroxyindoleacetic acid in the rat brain caused by hydrocortisone, DL-methyltryptophan, L-kynurenine and immobilization. *British Journal of Pharmacology,* 1971, *43,* 39–52.(a)

DeKLOET, E. R., KOVACS, G., SZABO, G., TELEGDY, G., BOHUS, B., & VERSTEEG, D. Decreased serotonin turnover in the dorsal hippocampus of rat brain shortly after adrenalectomy: Selective normalization after corticosterone substitution. *Brain Research,* 1982, *239,* 659–663.

DEKLOET, E. R., SYBERSMA, H., & REUL, H. Selective control by corticosterone of serotonin1 receptor capacity in raphe-hippocampal system. *Neuroendocrinology,* 1986, *42,* 513–521.

DEKLOET, E. R., VERSTEEG, D., & KOVACS, G. Aldosterone blocks the response to corticosterone in the raphe-hippocampal serotonin system. *Brain Research,* 1983, *264,* 323–327.

DE LEON, M., GEORGE, A., STYLOPOULOS, L., SMITH, G., & MILLER, D. Early marker for Alzheimer's disease: the atrophic hippocampus. *Lancet,* 1989, 672–673.

DE LEON, M., McRAE, T., TSAI, J., GEORGE, A., MARCUS, D., FREEDMAN, M., WOLF, A., & McEWEN, B. S. Abnormal cortisol response in Alzeheimer's disease linked to hippocampal atrophy. *Lancet,* 1988, 391–392.

DE MONTIGNY, C., & AGHAJANIAN, G. Tricyclic antidepressants: Long-term treatment increases responsivity of rat forebrain neurons to serotonin. *Science,* 1978, *202,* 1303–1306.

DE SCHAEPDRYVER, A., PREZIOSI, P., & SCAPAGNINI, U. Brain monoamines and stimulation or inhibition of ACTH. *Archives Internationales de Pharmacodynamie et de Therapie,* 1969, *180,* 11–18.

DE SOUZA, E., GOEDERS, N., & KUHAR, M. Benzodiazepine receptors in rat brain are altered by adrenalectomy. *Brain Research,* 1986, *381,* 176–181.

DE SOUZA, E., & VAN LOON, G. Brain serotonin and catecholamine responses to repeated stress in rats. *Brain Research,* 1986, *367,* 77–86.

DICKINSON, S., KENNET, G., & CURZON, G. Reduced 5-hydroxytryptamine-dependent behavior in rats following chronic corticosterone treatment. *Brain Research,* 1985, *345,* 10–18.

DUNN, A. Nervous system–immune system interactions: An overview. *Journal of Receptor Research,* 1988, *8,* 589–607.

DUNN, J., & ORR, S. Differential plasma corticosterone responses to hippocampal stimulation. *Experimental Brain Research,* 1984, *54,* 1–6.

EDWARDS, E., HARKINS, K., WRIGHT, G., & HENN, F. Effects of bilateral adrenalectomy on the induction of learned helplessness behavior. *Neuropsychopharmacology,* 1990, *3,* 109–114.

————. (1991). 5-HT$_{1B}$ receptors in an animal model of depression. *Neuropharmacology,* 1991, *30,* 101–105.

EDWARDS, E., JOHNSON, J., ANDERSON, D., TURANO, P., & HENN, F. Neurochemical and behavioral consequences of mild, uncontrollable shock: Effects of PCPA. *Pharmacology Biochemistry and Behavior,* 1986, *25,* 414–421.

ELMES, D., JARRARD, L., & SWART, P. Helplessness in hippocampectomized rats: Response perservation? *Physiological Psychology,* 1975, *3,* 51–55.

FERNANDEZ-GUASTI, A., & LOPEZ-RUBALCAVA, C. Evidence for the involvement of the 5-HT$_{1A}$ receptor in the anxiolytic action of indorenate and ipsapirone. *Psychopharmacology,* 1990, *101,* 354–358.

FILE, S., VELLUCCI, S., & WENDLANDT, S. Corticosterone—an anxiogenic or an anxiolytic agent? *Journal of Pharmacy of Pharmacology,* 1979, *31,* 300–305.

FRIDE, E., DAN, Y., FELDON, J., HALEVY, G., & WEINSTOCK, M. Effects of prenatal stress on vulnerability to stress in prepubertal and adult rats. *Physiology and Behavior,* 1986, *37,* 681–687.

FRIDE, E., DAN, Y., GAVISH, M., & WEINSTOCK, M. Prenatal stress impairs maternal behavior in a conflict situation and reduces hippocampal benzodiazepine receptors. *Life Sciences,* 1985, *36,* 2103–2109.

GANNON, M., BRINTON, R., SAKAI, R., & McEWEN, B. S. Diurnal differences and adrenal involvement in calmodulin stimulation of hippocampal adenylate cyclase activity. *Journal of Neuroendocrinology,* 1991, *3,* 37–43.

GANNON, M., & McEWEN, B. S. Calmodulin involvement in stress- and corticosterone-induced down-regulation of cyclic AMP-generating systems in brain. *Journal of Neurochemistry,* 1990, *55,* 276–284.

GERLACH, J., & McEWEN, B. S. Rat brain binds adrenal steroid hormone: Radioautography of hippocampus with corticosterone. *Science,* 1972, *175,* 1133–1136.

GERLACH, J., McEWEN, B. S., PFAFF, D., MOSKOVITZ, S., FERIN, M., CARMEL, P., & ZIMMERMAN, E. Cells in regions of rhesus monkey brain and pituitary retain radioactive estradiol, corticosterone and cortisol differently. *Brain Research,* 1976, *103,* 603–612.

GIBBS, D. Vasopressin and oxytocin: Hypothalamic modulators of the stress response: A review. *Psychoneuroendocrinology,* 1986, *11,* 131–140.

GOLD, P., GOODWIN, F., & CHROUSOS, G. Clinical and biochemical manifestations of depression. Part 1. *New England Journal of Medicine,* 1988, *319,* 348–353.(a)

―――――. Clinical and biochemical manifestations of depression. Part 2. *New England Journal of Medicine,* 1988, *319,* 413–420.(b)

GOULD, E., WOOLLEY, C., & McEWEN, B. S. Short-term glucocorticoid manipulations affect neuronal morphology and survival in the adult dentate gyrus. *Neuroscience,* 1990, *37,* 367–375.

HALL, E., McCALL, H., CHASE, R., YONKERS, P., & BRAUGHLER, M. A nonglucocorticoid steroid analog of methylprednisolone duplicates its high-dose pharmacology in models of central nervous system trauma and neuronal membrane damage. *Journal of Pharmacology and Experimental Therapeutics,* 1987, *242,* 137–142.

HAVOUNDJIAN, H., PAUL, S., & SHKOLNICK, P. Rapid, stress-induced modification of the benzodiazepine receptor-coupled chloride ionophore. *Brain Research,* 1986, *375,* 401–406.

HEINSBROEK, R., FEENSTRA, M., BOON, P., VAN HAAREN, F., & VAN DE POLL, N. Sex differences in passive avoidance depend on the integrity of the central serotonergic system. *Pharmacology Biochemistry and Behavior,* 1988, *31,* 499–503.

HEINSBROEK, R., VAN HAAREN, F., & VAN DE POLL, N. Sex differences in passive avoidance behavior of rats: Sex-dependent susceptibility to shock-induced behavioral depression. *Physiology and Behavior,* 1988, *43,* 201–206.

HELLHAMMER, D., HINGTGEN, J., WADE, S., SHEA, P., & APRISON, M. Serotonergic changes in specific areas of rat brain associated with activity-stress gastric lesions. *Psychosomatic Medicine,* 1983, *45,* 115–122.

HELLHAMMER, D., REA, M., BELL, M., BELKIEN, L., & LUDWIG, M. Learned helplessness: Effects on brain monoamines and the pituitary-gonadal axis. *Pharmacology Biochemistry and Behavior,* 1984, *21,* 481–485.

HERMAN, J., SCHAFER, M., SLADEK, C., DAY, R., YOUNG, E., AKIL, H., & WATSON, S. Chronic electroconvulsive shock treatment elicits up-regulation of CRF and AVP mRNA in select populations of neuroendocrinets neurons. *Brain Research,* 1988, *501,* 235–246.(a)

HERMAN, J., SCHAFER, M., YOUNG, E., THOMPSON, R., DOUGLASS, J., AKIL, H., & WATSON, S. Evidence for hippocampal regulation of neuroendocrine neurons of hypothalamo-pituitary-adrenocortical axis. *Journal of Neuroscience,* 1989, *9,* 3072–3082.(b)

HESS, J., DENENBERG, V., ZARROW, M., & PFEIFER, W. Modification of the corticosterone response curve as a function of handling in infancy. *Physiology and Behavior,* 1969, *4,* 109–111.

HORNER, H., PACKAN, D., & SAPOLSKY, R. Glucocorticoids inhibit glucose transport in hippocampal neurons and glia. *Neuroendocrinology,* 1990, *52,* 57–64.

IVERSEN, S. 5-HT and anxiety. *Neuropharmacology,* 1984, *23,* 1553–1560.

JACOBS, B., WISE, W., & TAYLOR, K. Differential behavioral and neurochemical effects following lesions of the dorsal or median raphe. *Brain Research,* 1974, *79,* 353–361.

JOELS, M., & DeKLOET, R. Mineralocorticoid receptor-mediated changes in membrane-properties of rat CA1 pyramidal neurons in vitro. *Proceedings of the National Academy of Sciences,* 1990, *87,* 4495–4498.

JOHNSTON, A., & FILE, S. Promises and pitfalls. *Pharmacology, Biochemistry and Behavior,* 1986, *24,* 1467–1470.

JOSEPH, M., & KENNET, G. Stress-induced release of 5-HT in the hippocampus and its dependence on increased tryptophan availability: An in vivo electrochemical study. *Brain Research,* 1983, *270,* 251–257.

KANT, G., LENOX, R., BUNNELL, B., MOUGEY, E., PENNINGTON, L., & MEYERHOFF, J. Comparison of stress response in male and female rats: Pituitary cyclic AMP and plasma prolactin, growth hormone and corticosterone. *Psychoneuroendocrinology,* 1983, *8,* 421–428.

KENNET, G., CHAOULOFF, F., MARCOU, M., & CURZON, G. Female rats are more vulnerable than males in an animal model of depression: The possible role of serotonin. *Brain Research,* 1986, *382,* 416–421.

KENNET, G., DICKINSON, S., & CURZON, G. Central serotonergic responses and behavioural adaptation to repeated immobilization: The effect of the corticosterone synthesis inhibitor metyrapone. *European Journal of Pharmacology,* 1985, *119,* 143–152.

KENNET, G., MARCOU, M., DOURISH, C., & CURZON, G. Single administration of 5-HT$_{1A}$ agonists decreases 5-HT$_{1A}$ presynaptic, but not postsynaptic receptor-mediated responses: Relationship to antidepressant-like action. *European Journal of Pharmacology,* 1987, *138,* 53–60.

KILPATRICK, G., JONES, B., & TYERS, M. Identification and distribution of 5-HT3 receptors in rat brain using radioligand binding. *Nature,* 1987, *330,* 746–748.

KITAY, J. Sex differences in adrenal cortical secretion in the rat. *Endocrinology,* 1961, *68,* 818–824.

KITAYAMA, I., CINTRA, A., JANSON, A., FUXE, K., AGNATI, L., ENEROTH, P., ARONSSON, M., HARF-STRAND, A., STEINBUSH, H., VISSER, T., GOLDSTEIN, M., VALE, W., & GUSTAFSSON, J. Chronic immobilization stress: Evidence for decreases of 5-hydroxy-tryptamine immunoreactivity and for increases of glucocorticoid receptor immunoreactivity in various brain regions of the male rat. *Journal of Neural Transmission,* 1989, *77,* 93–130.

KNOX, W., & AUERBACH, V. The hormonal control of tryptophan peroxidase in the rat. *Journal of Biological Chemistry,* 1955, *214,* 307–313.

KUHN, C., BUTLER, S., & SCHANBERG, S. Selective depression of serum growth hormone during maternal deprivation in rat pups. *Science,* 1978, *201,* 1034–1036.

LAHTI, R., & BARSUHN, C. The effect of minor tranquilizers on stress-induced increases in rat plasms corticosteroids. *Psychopharmacologia,* 1974, *35,* 215–220.

LANDFIELD, P. Modulation of brain aging correlates by long-term alterations of adrenal steroids and neurally-active peptides. *Progress in Brain Research,* 1987, *72,* 279–300.

LANDFIELD, P., BASKIN, R., & PITTER, T. Brain-aging correlates: Retardation by hormonal-pharmacological treatments. *Science,* 1981, *214,* 581–584.

LESHNER, A., & SEGAL, M. Fornix transection blocks "learned helplessness" in rats. *Behavioral Neural Biology,* 1979, *26,* 497–501.

LEVINE, S. Plasma-free corticosteroid response to electric shock in rats stimulated in infancy. *Science,* 1962, *135,* 795–796.

LORENS, S., & GULDBERG, H. Regional 5-hydroxytryptamine following selective midbrain raphe lesions in the rat. *Brain Research,* 1974, *78,* 45–56.

MCEWEN, B. S., DEKLOET, E. R., & ROSTENE, W. Adrenal steroid receptors and actions in the nervous system. *Physiology Review,* 1986, *66,* 1121–1188.

MCEWEN, B. S., & GOULD, E. Adrenal steroid influences on the survival of hippocampal neurons. *Biochemical Pharmacology,* 1990, *40,* 2393–2402.

MCEWEN, B. S., & PLAPINGER, L. Association of corticosterone-1,2 3H with macromolecules extracted from brain cell nuclei. *Nature,* 1970, *226,* 263–264.

MCEWEN, B. S., WEISS, J., & SCHWARTZ, L. Selective retention of corticosterone by limbic structures in rat brain. *Nature,* 1968, *220,* 911–912.

MEANEY, M., AITKEN, D., BERKEL, H., BHATNAGER, S., & SAPOLSKY, R. Effect of neonatal handling on age-related impairments associated with the hippocampus. *Science,* 1988, *239,* 766–768.

MEANEY, M., AITKEN, D., BODNOFF, S., INY, L., TATAREWICZ, J., & SAPOLSKY, R. Early, postnatal handling alters glucocorticoid receptor concentrations in selected brain regions. *Behavioral Neuroscience,* 1985, *99,* 765–770.

MEANEY, M., AITKEN, D., & SAPOLSKY, R. Thyroid hormones influence the development of hippocampal glucocorticoid receptors in the rat: A mechanism for the effects of postnatal handling on the development of the adrenocortical stress response. Neuroendocrinology, 1987, *45,* 278–285.

MEANEY, M., AIKEN, D., VIAU, V., SHARMA, S., & SARRIEAU, A. Neonatal handling alters adrenocortical negative feedback sensitivity and hippocampal type II glucocorticoid receptor binding in the rat. *Neuroendocrinology,* 1989, *50,* 597–604.

MENDELSON, S., & MCEWEN, B. S. Adrenalectomy increases the density of 5-HT$_{1A}$ receptors in rat hippocampus. *Neuroendocrinology Letters,* 1990, *12,* 353.

―――――. Autoradiographic analyses of the effects of restraint-induced stress on 5-HT$_{1A}$, 5-HT$_{1C}$ and 5-HT$_2$ receptors in the dorsal hippocampus of male and female rats. *Neuroendocrinology,* 1991, *54,* 454–461.

―――――. Autoradiographic analyses of the effects of adrenalectomy and corticosterone on 5-HT$_{1A}$ and 5-HT$_{1B}$ receptors in the dorsal hippocampus and cortex of the rat. *Neuroendocrinology,* 1992, *55,* 444–450.

MEYER, J. Biochemical effects of corticosteroids on neural tissues. *Physiology Review,* 1985, *65,* 946–1020.

MOBLEY, P., MANIER, D., & SULSER, F. Norepinephrine-sensitive adenylate cyclase system in rat brain: Role of adrenal corticosteroids. *Journal of Pharmacology and Experimental Therapeutics,* 1983, *226,* 71–77.

MOLLIVER, M., BERGER, U., MAMOUNAS, L., MOLLIVER, D., O'HEARN, E., & WILSON, M. Neurotoxicity of MDMA and related compounds: Anatomic studies. *Annals of the New York Academy of Science,* 1990, *600,* 640–664.

MOORE, R., & HALARIS, A. Hippocampal innervation by serotonin neurons of the midbrain raphe in the rat. *Journal of Comparative Neurology,* 1975, *164,* 171–184.

MORGAN, W., RUDEEN, K., & PFEIL, K. Effect of immobilization stress on serotonin content and turnover in regions of the rat brain. *Life Sciences,* 1975, *17,* 143–150.

MOSER, P., TRICKLEBANK, M., MIDDLEMISS, D., MIR, A., HIBERT, M., & FOZARD, J. Characterization of MDL 73005EF as a 5-HT1a selective ligand and its effects in animal models of anxiety: Comparison with buspirone, 8-OH-DPAT and diazepam. *British Journal of Pharmacology,* 1990, *99,* 343–349.

MUELLER, G. B., TWOHY, C., CHEN, H., ADVIS, J., & MEITES, J. Effects of 1-tryptophan and restraint stress on hypothalamic and brain serotonin turnover and pituitary TSH and prolactin release in rats. *Life Sciences,* 1976, *18,* 715–724.

MUNCK, A., GUYRE, P., & HOLBROOK, N. Physiological functions of glucocorticoids in stress and their relation to pharmacological actions. *Endocrinology Review,* 1984, *5,* 25–44.

MUSACCHIO, J., JULOU, L., KETY, S., & GLOWINSKI, J. Increase in rat brain tyrosine hydroxylase activity produced by electroconvulsive shock. *Proceedings of the National Academy of Science,* 1969, *63,* 1117–1119.

NECKERS, L., & SZE, P. Regulation of 5-hydroxytryptamine metabolism in mouse brain by adrenal glucocorticoids. *Brain Research*, 1975, *93*, 123–132.

NELSON, D., HERBERT, A., BOURGOIN, S., GLOWINSKI, J., & HAMON, M. Characteristics of central 5-HT receptors and their adaptive changes following intracerebral 5,7-dihydroxytryptamine administration in the rat. *Molecular Pharmacology*, 1978, *14*, 983–995.

NISHIKAWA, T., & SCATTON, B. Neuroanatomical site of the inhibitory influence of anxyiolytic drugs on central serotonergic transmission. *Brain Research*, 1986, *371*, 123–132.

NISTICO, G., & PREZIOSI, P. Brain and liver tryptophan pathways and adrenocortical activity during restraint stress. *Pharmacology Research Communications*, 1969, *1*, 363–368.

O'CONNER, J., ROWAN, M., & ANWYL, R. Actions of 5-HT$_1$ ligands on excitatory synaptic transmission in the hippocampaus of alert rats. *British Journal of Pharmacology*, 1990, *101*, 171–177.

O'HEARN, E., BATTAGLIA, G., SOUZA, E., KUHAR, M., & MOLLIVER, M. Methylenedioxyamphetamine (MDA) and methylenedioxymethamphetamine (MDMA) cause selective ablation of serotonergic axon terminals in forebrain: Immunohistochemical evidence for neurotoxicity. *Journal of Neuroscience*, 1988, *88*, 2788–2803.

OHI, K., MIKUNI, M., & TAKAHASHI, K. Stress adaptation and hypersensitivity in 5-HT neuronal systems after repeated foot shock. *Pharmacology Biochemistry and Behavior*, 1989, *34*, 603–608.

OLESKEVICH, S., & DESCARRIES, L. Quantified distribution of the serotonin innervation in adult rat hippocampus. *Neuroscience*, 1990, *34*, 19–33.

PAUL, I., DUNCAN, G., KUHN, C., MUELLER, R., HONG, J., & BREESE, G. Neural adaptation in imipramine-treated rats processed in forced swim test: Assessment of time course, handling, rat strain and amine uptake. *Journal of Pharmacology and Experimental Therapeutics*, 1990, *252*, 997–1005.

PAZOS, A., HOYER, D., & PALACIOS, J. The binding of serotonergic ligands to the porcine choroid plexus: Characterization of a new type of serotonin recognition site. *European Journal of Pharmacology*, 1984, *106*, 539–546.

PEDIGO, N., YAMAMURA, H., & NELSON, D. Discrimination of multiple hydroxytryptamine binding sites by the neuroleptic brain. *Journal of Neurochemistry*, 1981, *36*, 220–226.

PEROUTKA, S., & SNYDER, S. Multiple serotonin receptors: Differential binding of (3H) 5-hydroxytryptamine, (3H) lysergic acid diethylamide and (3H) spiroperidol. *Molecular Pharmacology*, 1979, *16*, 687–699.

PURDY, R., MORROW, A., MOORE, P., & PAUL, S. Formation of anxiolytic steroids following acute stress. *Journal of Cellular Biochemistry Abstract*, 1990, 14F CP209-p. 45.

RICHARD, F., FAUCON-BIGUET, N., LABATUT, R., ROLLET, D., MALLET, J., & BUDA, M. Modulation of tyrosine hydroxylase gene expression in rat brain and adrenals by exposure to cold. *Journal of Neuroscience Research*, 1988, *20*, 32–37.

ROTH, K., MEFFORD, I., & BARCHAS, J. Epinephrine, norepinephrine, dopamine and serotonin: Differential effects of acute and chronic stress on regional brain amines. *Brain Research*, 1982, *239*, 417–424.

ROWAN, M., & ANWYL, R. Neurophysiological effects of buspirone and ipsapirone in the hippocampus: Comparison with 5-hydroxytryptamine. *European Journal of Pharmacology*, 1986, *132*, 93–96.

SAPOLSKY, R. Glucocorticoid toxicity in the hippocampus: Temporal aspects of synergy with kainic acid. *Neuroendocrinology*, 1986, *43*, 440–444.

——————. Glucocorticoid hippocampal damage and the glutamatergic synapse. *Progress in Brain Research*, 1990, *86*, 13–23.

SAPOLSKY, R., KREY, L., & McEWEN, B. S. Prolonged glucocorticoid exposure reduces hippocampal neuron number: Implications for aging. *Journal of Neuroscience*, 1985, *5*, 1222–1227.

—————. Stress glucocorticoids and their role in degenerative changes in the aging hippocampus. In T. Crook, R. Bartus, S. Ferris, & S. Gershon (eds.), *Treatment development strategies for Alzheimer's disease.* Madison, CT: Mark Powley, 1986.(a)

—————. The neuroendocrinology of stress and aging: The glucocorticoid cascade hypothesis. *Endocrinology Review,* 1986, *7,* 284-301.(b)

SAPOLSKY, R., & PULSINELLI, W. Glucocorticoids potentiate ischemic injury to neurons: Therapeutic implications. *Science,* 1985, *229,* 1397-1399.

SAWCHENKO, P., SWANSON, L., & VALE, W. Co-expression of CRF- and vasopressin-immunoreactivity in parvocellular neurosecretory neurons of adrenalectomized rats. *Proceedings of the National Academy of Science,* 1984, *81,* 1883-1887.

SCAPAGNINI, U., PREZIOSI, P., & DE SCHAEPDRYVER, A. Influence of restraint stress, corticosterone and betamethasone on brain amine levels. *Pharmacology Research Communications,* 1969, *1,* 63-69.

SCHWARTZ, R., WESS, M., LABARCA, R., SHKOLNICK, P., & PAUL, S. Acute stress enhances the activity of the GABA receptor-gated chloride ion channel in brain. *Brain Research,* 1987, *411,* 151-155.

SELYE, H. The evolution of the stress concept. *American Scientist,* 1973, *61,* 692-699.

SHERMAN, A., & PETTY, F. Neurochemical basis of the action of antidepressants on learned helplessness. *Behavioral and Neural Biology,* 1980, *30,* 119-134.

SINGH, V., CORLEY, K., PHAN, T.-H. & BOADLE-BIBER, M. Increases in the activity of tryptophan hydroxylase from rat cortex and midbrain in response to acute or repeated sound stress are blocked by adrenalectomy and restored by dexamethasone treatment. *Brain Research,* 1990, *516,* 66-76.

SIMMONDS, M. *Steroids and neuronal activity.* John Wiley and Sons, London 1990.

SLOVITER, R., & NILAVER, G. Immunocytochemical localization of GABA-, cholecystokini-, vasoactive intestinal polypetide, and somatostatin-like immunoreactivity in the area dentata and hippocampus of the rat. *Journal of Comparative Neurology,* 1987, *256,* 42-60.

SLOVITER, R., VALIQUETTE, G., ABRAMS, G., RONK, E., SOLLAS, A., PAUL, L., & NEUBORT, S. Selective loss of hippocampal granule cells in the mature rat brain after adrenalectomy. *Science,* 1989, 243, 535-538.

STONE, E., MCEWEN, B. S., HERRERA, A., & CARR, K. Regulation of α and β components of noradrenergic cyclic AMP response in cortical slices. *European Journal of Pharmacology,* 1987, *141,* 347-356.

SZE, P., NECKERS, L., & TOWLE, A. Glucocorticoids as a regulatory factor for brain tryptophan hydroxylase. *Journal of Neurochemistry,* 1976, *26,* 169-173.

TORDA, T., MURGAS, K., CECHOVA, E., KISS, A., & SAAVEDRA, J. Adrenergic regulation of [3H]ketanserin binding sites during immobilization stress in the rat frontal cortex. *Brain Research,* 1990, *527,* 198-203.

TORK, I. Anatomy of the serotonergic system. *Annals of the New York Academy of Science,* 1990, *600,* 9-35.

TRICKLEBANK, M., FORLER, C., & FOZARD, J. The involvement of subtypes of 5-HT 1 receptor and of catecholaminergic systems in the behavioural response to 8-hydroxy-2 (di-n-propylaminotetralin in the rat. *European Journal of Pharmacology,* 1984, *106,* 271-282.

TSUDA, A., & TANAKA, M. Differential changes in noradrenaline turnover in specific regions of rat brain produced by controllable and uncontrollable shocks. *Behavioral Neuroscience,* 1985, *99,* 802-817.

UNO, H., ROSS, T., ELSE, J., SULEMAN, M., & SAPOLSKY, R. Hippocampal damage associated with prolonged and fatal stress in primates. *Journal of Neuroscience,* 1989, *9,* 1705-1711.

VAN DE KAR, L. Neuroendocrine aspects of the serotonergic hypothesis of depression. *Neuroscience and Biobehavioral Reviews,* 1989, *13,* 237–246.

WEISS, J., GOODMAN, P., LOSITO, B., CORRIGAN, S., CHARRY, J., & BAILEY, W. Behavioral depression produced by an uncontrollable stressor: Relationship to norepinephrine, dopamine and serotonin levels in various regions of rat brain. *Brain Research Review,* 1981, *3,* 167–205.

WEISS, J., MCEWEN, B. S., SILVA, M., & KALKUT, M. Pituitary-adrenal alterations and fear responding. *American Journal of Physiology,* 1970, *218,* 864–868.

WHITNALL, M., MEZEY, E., & GAINER, H. Co-localization of corticotropin-releasing factor and vasopressin in median eminence neurosecretory vesicles. *Nature,* 1985, *248,* 250.

WOOLLEY, C., GOULD, E., & MCEWEN, B. S. Exposure to excess glucocorticoids alters dendritic morphology of adult hippocampal pyramidal neurons. *Brain Research,* 1990, *531,* 225–231.

YANAI, J., & SZE, P. Adrenal glucocorticoids as required factor in barbiturate-induced changes in functional tolerance and brainstem tryptophan hydroxylase. *Brain Research,* 1983, *269,* 297–302.

Stress, the Immune System, and Health and Illness

Marvin Stein   Andrew H. Miller

IN THE FIRST EDITION of the *Handbook of Stress,* published in 1982, it was noted that the newly developing field of psychoneuroimmunology may provide information about the mechanisms involved in stress effects on health and illness. Several paragraphs reviewed the increasing interest in the brain, behavior, and the immune system. Since that time, there has been an explosive growth in neurobiological and immunological research. The investigation of the relationship among the brain, behavior, and the immune system has undergone a parallel period of rapid expansion, with compelling evidence for central nervous system (CNS) and behavioral interactions with the immune system. Among the behavioral influences, stress effects on the immune system in animals and humans have received considerable attention. The early studies of stress and immune function focused on the effects of stress on immune-related disorders, such as infections and neoplastic disorders.

STRESS AND IMMUNE-RELATED DISORDERS

Stress and Infection

A range of psychosocial factors have been shown to modify host resistance to infection. In the 1960s in an extensive series of studies, Rasmussen and colleagues (Jensen & Rasmussen, 1963; Johnsson, Lavender, Hullin, & Rasmussen, 1963; Rasmussen, 1969; Rasmussen, Marsh, & Brill, 1957) utilized avoidance learning procedures as an experimental model of psychosocial stress. They demonstrated that repeatedly exposing mice to a shock-avoidance procedure resulted in increased susceptibility to herpes simplex virus (Rasmussen, et al., 1957), poliomyelitis virus (Johnsson & Rasmussen, Jr., 1965), Coxsakie B virus (Johnson, 1963) and polyoma virus infection (Rasmussen, 1969). Rasmussen, et al. (1957) found that physical restraint also increased the susceptibility of mice to herpes simplex virus, and high intensity sound altered the susceptibility to vesicular stomatitis virus (Jensen, & Rasmussen, 1963). In contrast to the stress effects on mice, avoidance stress

This research was supported in part by National Institute of Mental Health Research Scientist Award MH00680 (Dr. A. H. Miller) and research grant RO1MH47674. The authors thank Abrar Husain for his help in preparing the manuscript.

in monkeys increased host resistance to poliomyetis virus (Marsh, Lavender, Chang, & Rasmussen, 1963). These differences between mice and monkeys in stress-related susceptibility to infection may be related to species differences or to differences in avoidance paradigms utilized.

Social factors, such as the effect of differential housing, also have an effect upon host resistance. Ader and co-workers (Friedman, Glasgrow, & Ader, 1969) in a series of studies in the 1960s demonstrated that the susceptibility to both viral and parasitic infections was influenced by whether the animals were housed individually or in groups. More recent studies of psychosocial effects on infections in animals have been reviewed in detail elsewhere (Rabin, Cohen, Ganguli, Lysle, & Cunnick, 1989; Riley, 1981).

The role of stress in infectious diseases in humans has also attracted considerable attention. For example, the influence of stress and other psychological factors—e.g., personality and coping—have been considered in relation to herpesvirus infections and bacterial infections (Cohen & Williamson, 1991). Glaser and colleagues (Glaser, et al., 1987) found that first-year medical students reported more infectious illnesses, primarily upper respiratory infections, during high-stress examination periods than during low-stress pre-examination periods. A review of the role of stress in both viral and bacterial infectious diseases in man suggests that stress effects may be involved in illness behavior, but the evidence is not conclusive for an association between stress and infection (Cohen & Williamson, 1991). A recent prospective study, however, has shown that psychological stress is associated with an increased risk of the common cold, and the risk is related to increased rates of infection and not to an increased frequency of symptoms following infection (Cohen, Tyrell, & Smith, 1991). These studies highlight the complexity and potential confounds in the investigation of stress effects and infection in humans.

Stress and Tumors

Considerable experimental evidence indicates that stress plays a role in the development, course, and outcome of tumors in animals. For example, brief daily handling and mild electric shock administration early in life modify the rate of tumor development and survival of rats injected with Walker 256 sarcoma (Ader & Friedman, 1965). Justice (1985), in a recent extensive review of the literature of stress effects on tumors in laboratory animals, has pointed out that the time of the stress application and the type of tumor—i.e., viral or nonviral tumors—are critical determinants in studying stress and tumors in animals. Justice's review delineates many of the confounds and flaws in this area of study as well as the difficulty in interpreting the findings and understanding the mechanisms that may be involved.

There has been a longstanding interest in the relationship between stress and cancer in humans. The findings have in general been controversial, and a number of reviews have considered the problems inherent in such research (Cassileth, Lusk, Miller, Brown, & Miller, 1985; Fox, 1978; Sklar & Anisman, 1981). There is some evidence that the psychological response to nonmetastatic cancers may influence survival (Greer, 1991). The findings with metastatic cancer, however, are equivocal and further emphasize the need to consider the type of cancer in relation to psychosocial factors such as stress. More research concerned with stress and cancer in humans is needed and should include prospective studies involving large numbers of subjects, utilizing valid psychological measures, and taking into account the biological mechanisms that may be involved.

STRESS AND THE IMMUNE SYSTEM

Overall, the evidence indicates that stress has an effect in animals on infections and tumor resistance, as well as other immune-related disorders, such as autoimmune diseases (Rabin et al., 1989). In humans, the findings are strongly suggestive, but not definitive. Stress effects on the immune response are believed to underlie the influence of stress on infections and tumors, and there is a growing body of research concerned with stress and the immune system. Prior to considering stress effects and the immune system, it is important to have a general understanding of the various components of the immune response and the methods utilized to measure and evaluate immune function.

The Immune System

The immune system is responsible for the maintenance of the integrity of the organism in relation to foreign substances such as bacteria, viruses, and neoplasia. The basic cellular unit of the immune system is the lymphocyte, and T and B lymphocytes play a major role in immunity. Several subsets of T lymphocytes have been described and include helper T cells, suppressor T cells, and cytotoxic T lymphocytes. In addition to T and B lymphocytes, other cell types are involved in immune processes and include monocytes, macrophages, mast cells, and neutrophils.

In the development of an immunological response, antigens (substance recognized as foreign) are engulfed and processed by macrophages and then presented to lymphocytes. Each lymphocyte is committed to recognize a specific target antigen that binds to its cell-surface receptor and, thereby, stimulates the cell. When an antigen binds to the surface of a specific lymphocyte, cell division and differentiation occur, which result in a permanent increase in the number of circulating lymphocytes with that particular antigen-binding specificity. This clonal expansion results in a more rapid and extensive secondary reaction upon re-exposure to the antigen. Following activation by signals from macrophages and helper T cells, sensitized B cells proliferate and differentiate into plasma cells that synthesize antigen-specific antibodies or immunoglobulins.

The primary protective function of the B cell is against infections by viruses and bacteria, especially encapsulated bacteria—e.g., pneumococci and streptococci. At times however, B cell antibody responses can be pathological, such as in anaphylaxis or asthma and, occasionally, in response to the organism's own tissues (antibodies to sell or autoantibodies) as in autoimmune disorders such as systemic lupus, erythematosus, and rheumatoid arthritis. Antibodies present in bodily fluids including blood, saliva, and cerebrospinal fluid can be measured to determine whether an individual has been exposed to a particular infectious agent or whether there are autoantibodies.

In contrast to the B cell, whose role is primarily secretory, the T cell participates in the immune response. Effector T lymphocytes mediate delayed-type hypersensitivity, such as the response observed in chemical contact sensitivity or in the tuberculin reaction. T cells are also involved in cytotoxicity reactions; cytotoxic lymphocytes, also known as killer T cells, are a subset of effector T cells. They recognize, bind, and lyse target cells bearing the inducing foreign antigen. T cells are involved in protection against viral, fungal, and intracellular bacterial infection; transplantation reactions; and immune surveillance against neoplasia.

Subsets of the T cells, helper T cells and suppressor T cells, have important regulatory functions that serve to control the initiation and termination of both T and B cell effector responses. A shift in the number or function of these cell types may result in either impaired or exaggerated immune responses with consequent pathological effects.

It has been demonstrated that exposure to antigen is not sufficient to stimulate T cell division. Macrophages or other accessory cells are required for T cell activation and produce a lymphocyte-activating factor, known as interleukin-1 (IL-1). IL-1 does not directly stimulate T cell division but induces helper T cells to produce a T cell growth factor, interleukin-2 (IL-2), and to express cell-surface receptors for IL-2. IL-2 then stimulates T cells to proliferate. The immune system thus operates by means of highly specific responses that incorporate an amplifying component involving a complex interplay of nonspecific chemical signals for growth and differentiation. These regulatory functions may have both protective and pathological effects on the organism.

In addition to T and B lymphocytes, a subpopulation of lymphocytes that spontaneously recognize and selectively kill some virally infected cells and cancer cells has recently been described. These cells are known as natural killer (NK) cells, since they mediate a cytotoxic reaction without the need for prior sensitization.

Various techniques and assays are available that permit detailed evaluation and investigation of the immune system in relation to the brain and behavior. Cells of the immune system can be identified by surface markers with antigenic properties. The unique surface markers for the various cell types can be detected in vitro by specific monoclonal antibodies and the number of specific cells thereby enumerated. Monoclonal antibodies are available to assess the total number of T and B lymphocytes, as well as helper T cells and suppressor T cells. Cell markers are also available for NK cells. The quantification of cell types provides information about the composition of lymphocyte subpopulations in the peripheral blood but not about lymphocyte function and other aspects of the immune response, including immunoregulatory processes.

A range of functional measures is available that can be employed in psychoneuroimmunologic research. Many studies investigating stress and the immune system have used in vitro assays of immune function.

Lymphocyte stimulation is an in vitro technique that is commonly used to assess the in vivo function and interaction of lymphocytes participating in the immune response. In the procedure, sensitized lymphocytes involved in the immune response are cultured and activated with specific antigens or nonsensitized cells are activated with nonspecific stimulants, known as mitogens. A number of plant lectins and other substances have been utilized as mitogens. Phytohemagglutinin (PHA) and concanavalin A (Con A) are predominantly T cell mitogens, and pokeweed mitogen (PWM) stimulates primarily T-dependent B lymphocytes.

When lymphocytes are stimulated, there is an increase in DNA synthesis that eventually results in cell division and proliferation. The measurement of DNA synthesis is made by labeling stimulated cultures with a radioactive nucleoside precursor such as tritiated thymidine, which is incorporated into newly synthesized DNA. The determination of the amounts of precursor incorporated provides a measure of DNA synthesis and is employed as the standard measure of lymphocyte responsiveness.

In addition to evaluating cellular immunoregulatory mechanisms, it is possible to assess interleukins and their receptors by utilizing lymphocyte stimulation techniques and monoclonal antibodies. The availability of procedures to assess immunoregulatory processes at a cellular and chemical level provides a means to further understand brain and behavior in relation to immune function.

Natural killer cell activity is assayed in vitro by the incorporation of ^{51}Cr into specific tumor cell lines and evaluating the lysis of the tumor cells by the release of the radioisotope following the addition of NK cells.

Many of the measures described previously are influenced by day-to-day variations, diurnal rhythms, sex, age, and a range of nonimmunological factors, such as medication effects. Special attention and controls for confounding influences must, therefore, be carefully considered in studies of the effects of brain and behavior on the immune system. These considerations are noted in the various sections in this chapter.

Stress and Humoral and Cell-Mediated Immune Responses

A variety of stressors have been found to alter measures of both humoral and cell-mediated immune responses. Early studies indicated that avoidance learning procedures decrease the susceptibility of mice to passive anaphylaxis (Rasmussen, Spencer, & Marsh, 1959) and that the production of specific antibodies could be suppressed in a variety of species by stressful stimuli such as electric shock, noise, light, movement, or housing conditions (Hill, Greer, & Felsenfeld, 1967; Hirata-Hibi, 1967; Solomon, 1969; Vessey, 1964). While acute exposure to a stressor typically suppresses humoral immune responses, repeated exposure to a stressor can result in an apparent adaptation of the immune response and, in some cases, to an enhanced response (Hirata-Hibi, 1967; Solomon, 1969). Several reviews discuss stress influences on humoral immune responses in animals and humans (Rabin, et al., 1989; Stein, Schleifer, & Keller, 1985).

Considerable attention has been given to the effects of stress on cellular aspects of the immune system. Among the early studies, it was observed that while short-term exposure to sound stress suppressed the lymphocyte proliferative response to murine splenic lymphocytes to the mitogen Con A, extended exposure led to an enhanced proliferative response (Monjan & Collector, 1977). This provocative study, however, is somewhat limited because of its small sample size and needs to be replicated.

Separation experiences in primates have been investigated in relation to the immune system, and decreased lymphocyte responses to the T cell mitogens, PHA and Con A, were found following peer separation for two weeks in pigtailed monkeys raised together from early infancy (Reite, Harbeck, & Hoffman, 1981). Mitogen responses returned to baseline within several weeks after reunion.

A number of investigators have utilized electric shock as a stressor in studies of stress and the immune system. For example, Keller and colleagues (Keller, Weiss, Schleifer, Miller, & Stein, 1981) demonstrated a relationship between the nature and intensity of an acute stressor and the degree of suppression of cellular measures of the immune system. A graded series of stressors, including restraint in an appartus, low-level electric tail shock and high-level tail shock, produced a progressively greater suppression of both the number of circulating lymphocytes and PHA-induced stimulation of peripheral blood lymphocytes. There was no stressor effect, however, in the response of splenic lymphocytes to PHA. More recently, Lysle and co-workers (Lysle, Lyte, Fowler, & Rabin, 1987) found that the magnitude of suppression of the mitogen response to electric shock is related to the number of shocks. It is of interest that these investigators observed a marked reduction in the response to mitogenic stimulation of both peripheral blood and splenic lymphocytes.

Stress-induced suppression of mitogen-stimulated lymphocyte proliferation may also be related to the psychological state of the animal. An intriguing study (Laudenslager,

Ryan, Drugen, Hyson, & Maier, 1983) suggested that coping may be an important variable in stress effects on the immune system. PHA and Con A stimulation of lymphocytes was suppressed in rats exposed to inescapable, uncontrollable electric shock for 80 minutes, followed by several minutes of tail shock 24 hours later. However, animals receiving the same total amount of shock using a yoked paradigm, but able to terminate the stressor, did not have decreased lymphocyte activity compared with nonstressed controls. These findings are consistent with the hypothesis that the ability to cope with a stressor may mitigate against some of its noxious effects. However, the effect of stressor controllability on mitogen-induced lymphocyte responses has not been replicated (Maier & Laudenslager, 1988).

Weiss and co-workers (Weiss, Sundar, Becker, & Cierpial, 1989) have shown that shock influences not only mitogen lymphocyte responses but a number of other key components of the immune response. In rats exposed to 19 hours of intermittent tail shock, there was a suppression of both the proliferative response to PHA and NK cell activity as compared to home-cage controls. The production of IL-2 and interferon was also reduced in the shocked animals.

Recent studies have shown the effect of a fear-producing environment (Lysle, Cunnick, Fowler, & rabin, 1988), and housing, as well as gender (Rabin, et al., 1989) on cellular immune measures, such as mitogen responses and NK cell activity. Further information can be found in several recent reviews of stress effects on cellular immune responses in animals (Keller, Schleifer, & Demetrikopoulos, 1991; Rabin, et al., 1989).

Life Stress and the Immune System

The effects of life stress in humans on measures of the immune system have attracted considerable attention. Kiecolt-Glaser and Glaser (1991) have investigated the association of a range of stressful life events with the immune response. This research group initially focused their attention on academic stress among medical students as a commonplace stressful situation. They found a decrease in NK cell activity during the final examination period as compared to a pre-examination baseline. The examination stress was also associated with changes in the number of T cells, mitogen responses, interferon production, and antibody titers to latent herpesviruses. Kiecolt-Glaser and Glaser (1991) have also studied the effect of chronic life stressors, such as caretaking of Alzheimer's patients, on immune measures. These interesting and important studies of life stress and immune function in humans have been reviewed in detail elsewhere (Kiecolt-Glaser and Glaser, 1991).

Conjugal bereavement is among the most potentially stressful of commonly occurring life events and has been associated with increased medical morbidity and mortality. The most compelling data regarding bereavement and health is derived from epidemiologic studies (Helsing, Szklo, & Comstock, 1981). A link between bereavement and altered measures of the immune system was suggested by Bartrop and co-workers (Bartrop, Lazarus, Luckherst, & Kiloh, 1977) who found that bereaved individuals had lower mitogen-stimulated lymphocyte proliferative responses compared to controls.

Schleifer and colleagues (Schleifer, Keller, Camerino, Thornton, & Stein, 1983) investigated the effects of bereavement on immune measures in a prospective longitudinal study of spouses of women with advanced breast carcinoma. Lymphocyte stimulation was measured in men before and after the deaths of their wives. Lymphocyte stimulation responses to PHA, Con A, and PWM were significantly lower during the first two months following bereavement compared with prebereavement responses. The number of peripheral blood lymphocytes and the percentage and absolute number of T and B cells during the prebereavement period, however, were not significantly different from those in the postbereavement period. Follow-up during the remainder of the postbereavement year revealed that lymphocyte stimulation responses had returned to prebereavement levels for the majority, but not all of the subjects. Moreover, prebereavement mitogen responses did not differ from those of age- and sex-matched controls. These findings demonstrate that suppression of mitogen-induced lymphocyte stimulation is a direct consequence of the bereavement event and that a pre-existing suppressed immune state did not account for the depressed lymphocyte response in the bereaved. Furthermore, the long-term stress of the spouse's illness did not appear to result in habituation of the lymphocyte's response to stress following bereavement. The long-term stress may, in fact, have sensitized the subject to the effects of bereavement.

The processes linking the experience of bereavement to effects on lymphocyte activity are complex. Changes in nutrition, activity levels, exercise, sleep, and drug use, which are often found in the widowed, could influence lymphocyte function. The subjects in the above research, however, did not report major or persistent changes in diet, activity, or the usage of medication, alcohol, tobacco, or other drugs. Moreover, no significant changes in weight were noted. Further study is required to determine if subtle changes in these variables are related to the effects of bereavement on lymphocyte function.

It is important to emphasize that the immune findings associated with bereavement do not adequately explain the epidemiologic findings of increased morbidity and mortality following the stressor. The causes of death following bereavement are primarily associated with the cardiovascular system and not the immune system (Osterweiss, Solomon, & Green, 1984). It remains to be determined whether stress-induced immune changes, such as decreased mitogen responses, are related to the onset or course of physical illness following life stress.

The functional measures of the immune system used in many of the stress studies only assess in vitro correlates of immune system activity, so it has not been established that the levels of mitogen-induced lymphocyte stimulation or NK cell activity are related to in vivo immune responses, as might be expected in response to infections or tumors. Some evidence suggests a relationship between NK activity and in vivo viral infections (Herberman, 1986). However, no studies have demonstrated concomitantly in the same individual stress-related alterations in NK cell activity, mitogen responses, or in any immune measures and changes in health and illness; casual inferences are thereby limited. Altered in vitro peripheral blood lymphocyte responses may indicate that biologically important systemic events are occurring that may have a variety of consequences for the organism. Whether biologically important systemic effects include clinically relevant changes in the ability to respond to infections or other in vivo challenges affecting health outcome remains to be determined. For example, a great deal of attention has been directed to the notion that stress may influence immunocompetence in human immunodeficiency virus stress (HIV) seropositive individual and may thereby serve as a co-factor in the progression of HIV infection to clinically acquired immunodeficiency syndrome (AIDS). Rabkin and colleagues (Rabkin, Williams, Remien, Goetz, Kertzner, & Gorman, 1991) explored the relationship of psychosocial factors and numbers of T cell subsets among HIV-seropositive adults. They found no relationship between life stress and counts of helper T (CD4) lymphocytes, suppressor T (CD8) cells, or helper/suppressor T cell ratios in a cohort of 124 HIV-seropositive homosexual men. Furthermore, the stress measures were not related to more advanced illness over time. Perry

(1990), in a study of 116 HIV-seropositive adults, also did not find any significant effect of a range of psychosocial variables, including measures of stress, on the total number of helper T cells at entry into the study or over time. However, it may well be that the virulence of HIV confounds psychosocial effects on immune measures. For example, a decreased number of helper T cells in HIV-seropositive populations is a manifestation of disease progression rather than a determinant of disease (Polk, Fox, Brookmeyer, Kanchanaraksa, Kaslow, Visscher, Rinaldo, & Phair, 1987); therefore, the number of helper T lymphocytes may not be the most appropriate or meaningful immune measure to study psychosocial effects on the immune system in HIV-positive individuals. Nevertheless, both of these reports (Perry, 1990; Rabkin, et al., 1991) raise questions about the relationship between stress and measures of the immune system and health and illness, and suggest that psychosocial factors, such as stress, may not have a measurable or substantial effect on the immune system in relation to severe immunologic disorders, such as AIDS. As in the preceding reports, future studies concerned with stress influences on immunocompetence require clinically relevant and specific immune measures and/or the use of a disease end point.

Several recent animal studies have begun to address the issue of direct evidence of a causal relationship among stress, immune alterations, and disease states. An intriguing study by Ben-Eliyahu and co-workers (Ben-Eliyahu, Yirmiya, Liebeskind, Taylor, & Gale, 1991) found that rats exposed to an acute swimming stress had decreased NK activity against a mammary tumor in vitro and showed an increase in tumor lung metastases when injected with the same tumor. Bonneau and colleagues (Bonneau, Sheridan, Feng, & Glaser, 1991) have shown that restraint stress in mice suppressed measures of the cellular immune response to a specific herpes simplex viral infection. These immune alterations may have contributed to the increased herpes simplex virus local infection observed in these animals following the restraint stress.

These recent animal studies support the hypothesis that stress effects on tumors and infection are associated with suppression of the immune system. Further research is required to determine the mechanisms that may be involved. Human studies at this time, in addition to the complexity of the problem, often introduce multiple confounds in terms of the stressor, measures of the immune system, and disease end points that limit interpretation of the findings. There is a need for well-designed studies that include sound research conceptualizations and the appropriate methods to answer the questions being asked. Animal models may provide further understanding of the effect of stress on the immune system and the consequences for immune-related disorders and, thereby, enhance the development of the much-needed and required human research.

Mediation of Stress Effects on the Immune System

Over the past decade many studies have considered the pathways by which stress may influence immune responses. For many years the immune system was considered an autonomous, self-regulatory network of cells and cell products that maintained immunological homeostasis. There is increasing evidence of reciprocal interactions between the CNS and the immune system (Ader, Felten, & Cohen, 1991), including the effects of lesions of the hypothalamus on immune responses; the presence of receptors on lymphocytes for hormones and neurotransmitters; the influence of hormones, neurotransmitters, and peptides on immune function; and neuroanatomic and neurochemical evidence of direct innervation of lymphoid tissue. Recently, a series of observations (Berkenbosch, Van Oers, del Rey,

Tilders, & Besedovsky, 1987; Bernton, Beach, Holaday, Smallridge, & Fein, 1987; Sapolsky, Rivier, Yamamoto, Plotsky, & Vale, 1987) indicate that the relationship of the CNS and neuroendocrine system with the immune system is not unidirectional and that immune processes can modulate CNS function and neuroendocrine activity.

The primary biological components of the stress response are the hypothalamic-pituitary-adrenal (HPA) axis and the autonomic nervous system (ANS). Either or both of these stress pathways may influence immune responses. The endocrine system is highly responsive to life experiences and psychological state and has a significant influence, although complicated, on the immune system. The most widely studied hormones are those of the HPA axis. A wide range of stressful experiences is capable of inducing the release of corticosteroids (Rose, 1984), the final produce of the HPA activation. Corticosteroids have extensive and complex effects on immune responses. Of particular interest is the demonstration that glucocorticosteroids can suppress mitogen-induced lymphocyte stimulation (Cupps & Fauci, 1982) and induce a redistribution of T cells and T helper cells from the circulating blood pool to the bone marrow (Clayman, 1972; Cupps, Edgar, Thomas, & Fauci, 1984). Several reports have demonstrated that the recirculating lymphocyte traffic in humans is sensitive to endogenous corticosteroids and varies in relation to endogenous cortisol levels (Abo, Kawate, Itko, & Kumagai, 1981; Tavadia, Fleming, Hume, & Simpson, 1975; Thompson, McMahon, & Mugent, 1980).

Secretion of corticosteroids has long been considered to be the primary endocrine mechanism of stress-induced modulation of immunity and related disease processes (Riley, 1981; Selye, 1976). The regulation of immune function in response to stress, however, may not be limited to corticosteroids, As noted earlier, Keller and colleagues (Keller, et al., 1981) demonstrated that unpredictable and unavoidable electric tail shock in rats suppressed measures of the immune system, as determined by the number of circulating lymphocytes and PHA-induced lymphocyte proliferation in the peripheral blood. In an effort to determine if the adrenal is required for these stress-induced alterations in immune parameters in the rat, these investigators studied the effect of tail shock in animals adrenalectomized two weeks prior to stress exposure (Keller, Weiss, Schleifer, Miller, & Stein, 1983). The previously noted stress-induced lymphopenia was no longer apparent in adrenalectomized animals; however, despite the absence of adrenal hormones, isolated lymphocytes from the peripheral blood of stressed, adrenalectomized rats, like nonoperated controls, continued to exhibit a significant decrease in PHA-induced lymphocyte proliferation. These findings demonstrate that stress-induced lymphopenia in the rat occurs in association with stress-induced secretion of corticosteroids and can be prevented by adrenalectomy. However, stress-induced adrenal secretion of corticosteroids is not required for stress-related suppression of peripheral blood lymphocyte stimulation by the T cell mitogen PHA in the rat. The suppression of T cell proliferation may be due to an adrenal-independent stress-induced depletion of functional subpopulations of T cells or a selective redistribution of T cells in lymphoid tissues. Nevertheless, a variety of other hormonal, neurosecretory, and immunologic mechanisms may be involved in the adrenal-independent stress-induced modulation of T cell function.

The findings of adrenal-dependent stress-induced lymphopenia and of adrenal-independent effects on lymphocyte stimulation indicate that stress-induced modulation of the immune system is a complex phenomenon involving several, if not multiple, mechanisms. Changes in thyroid hormones, growth hormones, and sex steroids have been associated with exposure to stressors, and all have been reported to modulate immune function (Ader, Felten, & Cohen, 1991). Further, it has been shown that the hypothalamus, which plays a central role in neuroendocrine function, modulates both humoral and cell-mediated immunity (Cross, Brooks, Roszman, & Markesbery, 1982; Stein, Keller, & Schleifer, 1981). These findings suggest that a range of neuroendocrine processes may be involved in stress-induced alterations of the immune system.

Since a variety of hormones under pituitary control have been associated with immunoregulatory processes, Keller and co-workers (Keller, Schleifer, Liotta, Bond, Farhoody, & Stein, 1988) investigated the role of the pituitary in mediating stress-induced alterations of immunity. They studied the effects of tail shock on immune function in hypophysectomized rats. Plasma ACTH and corticosterone were increased in the stressed groups with intact pituitaries but were below detectable levels in the stressed, hypophysectomized animals. In both the nonoperated and sham-hypophysectomized rats there was a stress-induced decrease in the number of lymphocytes in the peripheral blood as well as a stress-related decrease in the number of T lymphocytes and T helper cells. Because the number of T suppressor cells and B lymphocytes was not altered by the stressful conditions, stress-induced lymphopenia in the rat is selective for T cells and for specifically T helper cells. In the hypophysectomized animals, however, no stress-related changes were found in the absolute number of lymphocytes or lymphocyte subsets. These results demonstrate that the stress-induced lymphopenia is pituitary-dependent, consistent with the observation that the number of circulating immunocompetent cells in response to a stressor is regulated by the HPA axis. The mechanism of this stress-related decrease in peripheral blood lymphocytes is unknown but may be related to vascular margination or migration of cells into the interstitial compartment, the lymphatics, or lymph nodes.

In contrast to the effects of hypophysectomy on lymphocytopenia, hypophysectomy did not reverse the effects of stress on PHA-induced lymphocyte proliferation. These findings demonstrate that factors not of pituitary origin mediate the stress-induced suppression of peripheral blood lymphocyte proliferation. In addition to the hypothalamic-pituitary axis, as noted, the ANS is another major stress-activated system, and stress-induced modulation of lymphocyte function may be related to ANS-associated neurotransmitter alterations. Utilizing a stressor similar to that employed in the hypophysectomy study, Weiss and Simson (1986) found a marked depletion of norepinephrine in various regions of the rat brain, including the hypothalamus and locus ceruleus. It may well be that the findings of a pituitary-independent stress-induced suppression of peripheral blood lymphocyte proliferation is related to ANS involvement via central and peripheral catecholamine systems, which have been shown to regulate immune processes. For example, intracerebraventicular administration of corticotropin-releasing factor (CRF) leads to activation of the autonomic nervous system and suppression of splenic NK cell activity (Irwin, Hauger, Brown, & Britton, 1988). This effect of CRF on NK activity was reversed by ANS blockade using chlorisondamine (Irwin, et al., 1988).

Another interesting and major finding in these studies was that the magnitude of the stress-induced suppression of lymphocyte function in hypophysectomized animals was significantly greater than in control animals with intact pituitaries. These findings demonstrate that pituitary processes may be involved in countering stress-induced immunosuppressive mechanisms. The specific pituitary-dependent mitigating or compensating processes are not known, but probably involve multiple hormones with immuno-enhancing properties, including growth hormone and prolactin (Bernton, Bryant, & Holaday, 1991; Kelley, 1991). These findings suggest that a regulatory network of hormonal and nonhormonal systems is involved in the maintenance of immunologic capacity following exposure to stressors. The restraining influence of the pituitary on stress responses may be of relevance to the understanding of homeostatic maintenance of critical body functions.

It is of note that in all of the stress research with rats conducted by Keller and colleagues (Keller, et al., 1981; Keller, et al., 1983; Keller, et al, 1988), including the hypophysectomy study, in contrast to the findings with peripheral blood lymphocytes, there were no stress effects on splenic lymphocyte stimulation by PHA. The lack of a stress effect on the stimulation of splenic lymphocytes in contrast to peripheral blood lymphocytes may reflect differences in the various compartments of the immune system, each with its own microenvironment and subject to specific modulators and regulators.

Cunnick and co-workers (Cunnick, Lysle, Kuscinski, & Rabin, 1990) have found that mild foot shock in rats suppressed both splenic and peripheral blood lymphocyte responses to T cell mitogens. Adrenalectomy prevented the shock-induced suppression of the mitogenic response of the peripheral blood lymphocytes but did not modify the suppression of splenic lymphocytes. These investigators found that beta-adrenergic receptor antagonists attenuated the stress-induced suppression of splenic lymphocytes but did not alter the suppression of the peripheral blood lymphocyte mitogen response. These findings suggest that specific and distinct mechanisms are involved in the stress-induced suppression of lymphocyte responses to mitogens in the peripheral blood and spleen. Catecholamines and the ANS appear to play a large role in the splenic mitogen response, and adrenal steroids are responsible for the suppression of peripheral blood lymphocyte responses to mitogens.

As a means of further understanding the relationship between adrenal steroid hormones and lymphocyte function, attention has been directed to the study of adrenal steroid receptors in immune cells and tissues. Two separate high-affinity receptors for glucocorticoids have been characterized (Reul & DeKloet, 1985), and both type I (also referred to as mineralocorticoid receptors) and type II (also referred to glucocorticoid receptors) adrenal steroid receptors have been demonstrated in human peripheral blood lymphocytes (Armanini, Strasser, & Weber, 1985; Armanini, Witzgall, Strasser, & Weber, 1985). Few studies have evaluated the relative presence of type I and type II receptor binding in other immune compartments. Miller and colleagues (Miller, Spencer, Stein, & McEwen, 1990) have found that type I and type II receptors are differentially expressed in the spleen and thymus. Both type I and type II receptor bindings has been found in the spleen, whereas only type II binding was detected in the thymus. This differential expression of receptors may confer on these tissues different sensitivity or responsivity to glucocorticoids and, thereby, explain why one immune compartment or cell type may respond differently following stress compared to another.

Spencer and associates (Spencer, Miller, Kang, Stein, & McEwen, 1991) have also noted that the occupation and activation of adrenal steroid receptors in various immune tissues differs following stress. After one hour of restraint stress, for example, type II receptors in the thymus were significantly occupied and activated, whereas type I but not type II receptors in the spleen exhibited evidence of receptor activation. Furthermore, while no stress-induced receptor activation was found in peripheral blood in the morning, when resting levels of endogenous glucocorticoids are low, one hour of restraint led to significant activation of peripheral blood adrenal steroid receptors in the evening, when resting levels of endogenous glucocorticoids are high. These findings demonstrate that there is not only differential expression but also that there is a considerable degree of heterogeneity in the activation of receptor subtypes in immune tissue following stress. Miller and his co-workers (Miller, Spencer, Trestman, Kim, McEwen, & Stein, 1991) have recently shown that receptor activation highly correlated with decreases in immune function and that evidence of receptor activation, therefore, may be critical for determining when and in which tissues adrenal steroid stress effects modulate the immune response.

SUMMARY

This review has emphasized that the psychological and biological effects of stress on the immune system are multifaceted, including complex neuroendocrine and neurotransmitter interactions. Research concerned with the brain, behavior, and the immune system should include the pursuit of more basic knowledge about brain-neuroendocrine and neurotransmitter-immune interactions. The availability of such basic information may lend itself to further understanding of the relationship among stress, the immune system, and health and illness.

Future research in the area of stress, the brain, and the immune system offers an exciting opportunity to increase our knowledge in neurobiology and immunology and to provide a foundation for clinically relevant studies.

REFERENCES

ABO, T., KAWATE, T., ITKO, K., & KUMAGAI, K. Studies on the bioperiodicity of the immune response. I: Circadian rhythms of human T, B, and K cell traffic in the peripheral blood. *Journal of Immunology,* 1981, *126,* 1360–1363.

ADER, R., FELTEN, D. L., & COHEN, N. (eds.) *Psychoneuroimmunology,* (2d ed.). San Diego: Academic Press, 1991.

ADER, R., & FRIEDMAN, S. B. Differential early experiences and susceptibility to transplanted tumors in the rat. *Journal of Comparative Physiology,* 1965, *59,* 361–364.

ARMANINI, D., STRASSER, T., & WEBER, P. C. Characterization of aldosterone binding sites in circulating human mononuclear leukocytes. *American Journal of Physiology,* 1985, *248,* (Endocrinology Metabolism 11), E388–E390.

ARMANINI, D., WITZGALL, H., STRASSER, T., & WEBER, P. C. Mineralocorticoid and glucocorticoid receptors in circulating leukocytes of patients with primary hyperaldosteronism. *Cardiology,* 1985, *72,* 99–101.

BARTROP, R. W., LAZARUS, L., LUCKHERST, E., & KILOH, L. H. Depressed lymphocyte function after bereavement. *Lancet,* 1977, *1,* 834–836.

BEN-ELIYAHU, S., YIRMIYA, R., LIEBESKIND, J. C., TAYLOR, A. N., & GALE, R. P. Stress increases metastatic spread of mammary tumor in rats: Evidence for mediation by the immune system. *Brain, Behavior, and Immunity,* 1991, *5,* 193–205.

BERKENBOSCH, F., VAN OERS, J., DEL REY, A., TILDERS, F., & BESEDOVSKY, H. Corticotropin-releasing factor-producing neurons in the rat activated by interleukin-1. *Science* 1987, *238,* 524–226.

BERNTON, E. W., BEACH, J. E., HOLADAY, J. W., SMALLRIDGE, R. C., & FEIN, H. G. Release of multiple hormones by a direct action of interleukin-1 on pituitary cells. *Science,* 1987, *238,* 519–521.

BERNTON, E. W., BRYANT, H. U., & HOLADAY, J. W. Prolactin and immune function. In R. Ader, D. L. Felten, & N. Cohen (eds.), *Psychoneuroimmunology* (2d ed.). San Diego: Academic Press, 1991.

BONNEAU, R. H., SHERIDAN, J. F., FENG, N., & GLASER, R. Stress-induced suppression of herpes simplex virus (HSV)-specific cytotoxic T lymphocyte and natural killer cell activity and enhancement of acute pathogenesis following local HSV infection. *Brain, Behavior, and Immunity,* 1991, *5,* 170–192.

CASSILETH, B. R., LUSK, E. J., MILLER, D. S., BROWN, L. L., & MILLER, C. Psychosocial correlates of survival in advanced malignant disease? *New England Journal of Medicine,* 1985, *312,* 1551–1555.

CLAYMAN, H. N. Corticosteroids and lymphoid cells. *New England Journal of Medicine,* 1972, *287,* 388–397.

COHEN, S., TYRELL, A. J., & SMITH, A. P. Psychological stress and susceptibility to the common cold. *New England Journal of Medicine,* 1991, *325,* 606–612.

COHEN, S., & WILLIAMSON, G. M. Stress and infectious disease in humans. *Psychological Bulletin,* 1991, *109,* 5–23.

CROSS, R. J., BROOKS, W. H., ROSZMAN, H. L., & MARKESBERY, R. Hypothalamic-immune interactions. *Journal of Neurological Science,* 1982, *53,* 557–566.

CUNNICK, J. E., LYSLE, D. T., KUCINSKI, B. J., & RABIN, B. S. Evidence that shock-induced immune suppression is mediated by adrenal hormones and peripheral B adrenergic receptors. *Pharmacology, Biochemistry, and Behavior,* 1990, *36,* 645–651.

CUPPS, T. R., EDGAR, L. C., THOMAS, C. A., & FAUCI, A. S. Multiple mechanisms of B cell immunoregulation in man after the administration of in vivo corticosteroids. *Journal of Immunology,* 1984, *132,* 170–175.

CUPPS, T. R., & FAUCI, A. S. Corticosteroid-mediated immunoregulation in man. *Immunological Reviews,* 1982, *65,* 134–155.

FOX, B. H. Premorbid psychological factors as related to cancer incidence. *Journal of Behavioral Medicine,* 1978, *1,* 45–133.

FRIEDMAN, S. B., GLASGOW, L. A., & ADER, R. Psychosocial factors modifying host resistance to experimental infections. *Annals of the New York Academy of Science,* 1969, *164,* 381–392.

GLASER, R., RICE, J., SHERIDAN, J., FERTEL, R., STOUT, J., SPEICHER, C. E., PINSKY, D., KOTUR, M., POST, A., BECK, M., & KIECOLT-GLASER, J. K. Stress-related immune suppression: Health implications. *Brain, Behavior, and Immunity,* 1987, *1,* 7–20.

GLASER, S. Psychological response to cancer and survival. *Psychological Medicine,* 1991, *21,* 43–49.

GREER, S. Psychological response to cancer and survival. *Psychological Medicine,* 1991, *21,* 43–49.

HELSING, K. J., SZKLO, M., & COMSTOCK, G. W. Factors associated with mortality after widowhood. *American Journal of Public Health,* 1981, *71,* 802–809.

HERBERMAN, R. B. *Natural killer cells. Annual Review of Medicine,* 1986, *37,* 347–352.

HILL, C. W., GREER, W. E., & FELSENFELD, O. Psychological stress, early response to foreign protein, and blood cortisol in vervets. *Psychosomatic Medicine,* 1967, *29,* 279–283.

HIRATA-HIBI, M. Plasma cell reaction and thymic germinal centers after a chronic form of electric shock. *Journal of the Reticuloendothelial Society,* 1967, *4,* 370–389.

IRWIN, M., HAUGER, R. L., BROWN, M., & BRITTON, K. T. CRF activates autonomic nervous system and reduces natural killer cell cytotoxicity. *American Journal of Physiology,* 1988, *255,* R744–R747.

JENSEN, M. M., RASMUSSEN, A. F., JR. Stress and susceptibility to viral infection. Sound stress and susceptibility to vesicular stomatitis virus. *Journal of Immunology,* 1963, *90,* 21–23.

JOHNSSON, T., LAVENDER, J. F., HULLIN, E., & RASMUSSEN, A. F., JR. The influence of avoidance-learning stress on resistance to coxackie B virus in mice. *Journal of Immunology,* 1963, *91,* 569–575.

JOHNSSON, T., & RASMUSSEN, A. F., JR. Emotional stress and susceptibility to poliomyelitis virus infection in mice. *archiv fur des Gesamte Virusforschung,* 1965, *18,* 390.

JUSTICE, A. Review of the effects of stress on cancer in laboratory animals: Importance of time stress application and type of tumor. *Psychological Bulletin,* 1985, *98,* 108–138.

KELLER, S. E., SCHLEIFER, S. J., & DEMETRIKPOULOS, M. K. Stress-induced changes in immune function in animals: Hypothalamo-pituitary-adrenal influences. In R. Ader, D. L. Felten, & N. Cohen (eds.), *Psychoneuroimmunology* (2d ed.). San Diego: Academic Press, 1991.

KELLER, S. E., SCHLEIFER, S. J., LIOTTA, A. S., BOND, R. N., FARHOODY, N., & STEIN, M. Stress-induced alterations of immunity in hypophysectomized rats. *Proceedings of the National Academy of Science,* 1988, *85,* 577–566.

KELLER, S., WEISS, J. M., SCHLEIFER, S. J., MILLER, N. E., & STEIN, M. Suppression of immunity by stress: Effects of a graded series of stressors on lymphocyte stimulation in the rat. *Science,* 1981, *213,* 1397–1400.

————. Stress-induced suppression of immunity in adrenalectomized rats. *Science,* 1983, *221,* 1301–1304.

KELLEY, K. W. Growth hormone in immunobiology. In R. Ader, D. L. Felten, & N. Cohen (eds.), *Psychoneuroimmunology* (2d ed.). San Diego: Academic Press, 1991.

KIECOLT-GLASER, J. K., & GLASER, R. Stress and immune function in humans. In R. Ader, D. L. Felten, & N. Cohen (eds.), *Psychoneuroimmunology* (2d ed.). San Diego, CA: Academic Press, 1991.

LAUDENSLAGER, M. L., RYAN, S. M., DRUGEN, R. L., HYSON, R. L., & MAIER, S. F. Coping and immunosuppression: Inescapable but not escapable shock suppresses lymphocyte proliferation. *Science,* 1983, *221,* 568–570.

LYSLE, D. T., CUNNICK, J. E., FOWLER, H., & RABIN, B. S. Pavlovian conditioning of shock-induced suppression of lymphocyte reactivity: Acquisition, extinction, and preexposure effects. *Life Sciences,* 1988, *42,* 2185–2194.

LYSLE, D. T., LYTE, M., FOWLER, H., & RABIN, B. S. Shock-induced modulation of lymphocyte reactivity: Suppression, habituation, and recovery. *Life Sciences,* 1987, *41,* 1805–1814.

MAIER, S. F., & LAUDENSLAGER, M. L. Inescapable shock, shock controllability, and mitogen stimulated lymphocyte proliferation. *Brain, Behavior, and Immunity,* 1988, *2,* 87–91.

MARSH, J. T., LAVENDER, J. F., CHANG, S., & RASMUSSEN, A. F., JR. Poliomyelitis in monkeys: Decreased susceptibility after avoidance stress. *Science,* 1963, *140,* 1414–1415.

MILLER, A. H., SPENCER, R. L., STEIN, M., & MCEWEN, B. Adrenal steroid receptor binding in spleen and thymus after stress or dexamethasone. *American Journal of Physiology,* 1990, *259,* (Endocrinology Metabolism 22), E405–E412.

MILLER, A. H. SPENCER, R. L., TRESTMAN, R. L., KIM, C., MCEWEN, B., & STEIN, M. Adrenal steroid receptor activation in vivo and immune function. *American Journal of Physiology,* 1991, *261* (Endocrinology Metabolism 24), E126–E131.

MONJAN, A. A., & COLLECTOR, M. I. Stress-induced modulation of the immune response. *Science,* 1977, *196,* 307–308.

OSTERWEISS, M., SOLOMON, F., & GREEN, M. (eds.). *Bereavement: Reactions, consequences, and care.* Washington, DC: National Academy Press, 1984.

PERRY, S. W., III. Psychosocial variables and CD4 cells in HIV + adults. In *new research programs and abstracts of the 143rd annual meeting of the American Psychiatric Association.* New York: American Psychiatric Association, 1990.

POLK, B. F., FOX, R., BROOKMEYER, R., KANCHANARAKSA, S., KASLOW, R., VISSCHER, B., RINALDO, C., & PHAIR, J. Predictors of the acquired immunodeficiency syndrome developing in a cohort of seropositive homosexual men. *New England Journal of Medicine,* 1987, *316,* 61–66.

RABIN, B. S., COHEN, S., GANGULI, R., LYSLE, D. T., & CUNNICK, J. E. Bidirectional interaction between the central nervous system and the immune system. *Critical Reviews in Immunology,* 1989, *9,* 279–312.

RABKIN, J. G., WILLIAMS, J. B. W., REMIEN, R. H., GOETZ, R. KERTZNER, R., & GORMAN, G. M. Depression, distress, lymphocyte subsets, and human immunodeficiency virus symptoms on two occasions in HIV-positive homosexual men. *Archives of General Psychiatry,* 1991, *48,* 111–119.

RASMUSSEN, A. F., JR. Emotions and immunity. *Annals of the New York Academy of Science,* 1969, *164,* 458–461.

RASMUSSEN, A. F., JR., MARSH, J. T., & BRILL, N. Q. Increased susceptibility to herpes simplex in mice subjected to avoidance-learning stress or restraint. *Proceedings of the Society of Experimental Biological Medicine,* 1957, *96,* 183–189.

RASMUSSEN, A. F., JR., SPENCER, E. T., & MARSH, J. T. Decrease in susceptibility of mice to passive anaphylaxis following avoidance learning stress. *Proceedings of the Society of Experimental Biology Medicine,* 1959, *100,* 878–879.

REITE, M., HARBECK, R., & HOFFMAN, A. Altered cellular immune response following peer separation. *Life Sciences,* 1981, *29,* 1133–1135.

REUL, J. M., & DEKLOET, E. R. Two receptor systems for corticosterone in rat brain: Microdistribution and differential occupation. *Endocrinology,* 1985, *117,* 2505–2511.

RILEY, V. Psychoneuroendocrine influences on immunocompetence and neoplasia. *Science,* 1981, *212,* 1100–1109.

ROSE, R. M. Overview of endocrinology in stress. In G. M., Brown, S. H. Koslow, & S. Reichlin (eds.), *Neuroendocrinology and psychiatric disorder.* New York: Raven Press, 1984.

SAPOLSKY, R., RIVIER, C., YAMAMOTO, G., PLOTSKY, P., & VALE, W. Corticotropin-releasing-factor-producing neurons in the rat activated by interleukin-1. *Science,* 1987, *238,* 522–524.

SCHLEIFER, S. J., KELLER, S. E., CAMERINO, M., THORNTON, J. C., & STEIN, M. Suppression of lymphocyte stimulation following bereavement. *Journal of the American Medical Association,* 1983, *250,* 374–377.

SELYE, H. *Stress in health and disease.* Boston: Butterworth, 1976.

SKLAR, L. S., & ANISMAN, H. Stress and cancer. *Psychological Bulletin,* 1981, *89,* 369–406.

SOLOMON, G. F. Stress and antibody response in rats. *International Archives of Allergy,* 1969, *35,* 97–104.

SPENCER, R. L., MILLER, A. H., KANG, S. S., STEIN, M., & MCEWEN, B. S. Diurnal comparisons of adrenal steroid receptor activation in brain, pituitary, and immune tissue. *Abstracts, Society for Neuroscience,* 21st Annual Meeting, New Orleans, 1991, *17,* 829.

STEIN, M., KELLER, S., SCHLEIFER, S. The hypothalamus and the immune response. In H. Weiner, M. A. Hofer, & A. J. Stunhard (eds.), *Brain, behavior, and bodily disease.* New York: Raven Press, 1981.

STEIN, M., SCHLEIFER, S. J., & KELLER, S. E. Brain, behavior and immune processes. In R. Michels & J. O. Cavenar, Jr. (eds.), *Psychiatry,* Vol. 2. Philadelphia: J. B. Lipincott, 1985.

TAVADIA, H. B., FLEMING, K. A., HUME, R. D., & SIMPSON, H. W. Circadian rhythmicity of human plasma cortisol and PHA-induced lymphocyte transformation. *Clinical and Experimental Immunology,* 1975, *22,* 190.

THOMSON, S. P., MCMAHON, L. J., & MUGENT, C. A. Endogenous cortisol: A regulator of lymphocytes in peripheral blood. *Clinical Immunology and Immunopathology,* 1980, *17,* 506.

VESSEY, S. H. Effects of grouping on levels of circulating antibodies in mice. *Proceedings of the Society of Experimental Biology Medicines,* 1964, *115,* 252–255.

WEISS, J. M., & SIMSON, P. G. Antidepressants and receptor function. *Ciba Foundation Symposium,* 1986, *123,* 191–215.

WEISS, J. M., SUNDAR, S. K., BECKER, K. J., & CIERPIAL, M. A. Behavioral and neural influences on cellular immune responses: Effects of stress and interleukin-1. *J. Clinical Psychiatry,* 1989, *50* (suppl.), 43–53.

9

Psychophysiological Assessment of Stress

Edward S. Katkin   Susan Dermit   Susan K. F. Wine

IT IS ALMOST IMPOSSIBLE to survey the literature on stress without encountering some reference to autonomic responses, whether as dependent variables or merely as observable byproducts of stress induction or stress responding. "In fact," Appley and Trumbull (1967) stated many years ago, "the most widely accepted types of operational definitions of the existence of stress are physiological indices" (p. 6). These authors also noted the somewhat chaotic use of physiological measures of stress: "Unfortunately, one investigator relies on the GSR, a second on blood volume changes, a third on pulse rate or heart rate, a fourth on muscle action potential, and so on" (Appley & Trumbull, 1967:6).

We wish that we could report that the chaos has been reduced twenty-five years later. On the contrary, the intervening years have seen a continuation of the widespread use of all the old techniques as well as the proliferation of a wide variety of new approaches to psychophysiological assessment (see Cacioppo & Tassinary, 1990).

In this chapter we briefly present a description of the primary psychophysiological methods and their proper utilization for the assessment of autonomic stress responses. We also review some of the ways in which cardiovascular psychophysiology has been applied to the study of behavioral medicine. During the past decade *behavioral medicine,* or *health psychology,* has grown at an unusually rapid rate, and a primary element of its growth and development has been the focusing of attention on the effects of stress on psychophysiological response patterns that may constitute risk factors for disease (see, for instance, Manuck & Krantz, 1986; Wright, Contrada, & Glass, 1985).

SOME CONCEPTUAL ISSUES

It will come as no surprise to any reader of this volume that the concept of stress refers to many different phenomena. *Stress* may refer to environmental stimuli that impinge on the organism; such stress may be chronic (e.g., poverty), transitory (e.g., noise), or highly idiosyncratic (e.g., a bad relationship with a significant other). Stress is also used to de-

The preparation of this chapter was supported in part by a grant from the American Heart Association to Richard Friedman and Edward S. Katkin and by Biomedical Research Support grants awarded to Edward S. Katkin and Susan Dermit by the National Institute of Mental Health, on behalf of the State University of New York at Stony Brook.

scribe responses of the organism (e.g., high blood pressure). We will focus primarily on the response side of the stress equation. That is, in any discussion of the utility of psychophysiological assessment in the study of stress, the focus must be on the measurable physiological response of the organism. For this reason, psychophysiological research has focused on the environment only to the extent that certain situations elicit observable changes in physiology. Should a putative stress situation fail to elicit a physiological response, then for the psychophysiologist the stimulus is not an "effective stressor." This is not to say that the stressful situation did not elicit a stressful experience, nor does it suggest that the person may not report the results of this stress experience. Indeed, there may be instances in which a subject reports feeling stressed but shows no obvious physiological sign of sympathetic arousal (the de facto sign of stress). In such cases, psychophysiological analysis offers little constructive contribution to the understanding of the phenomenology of stress.

Conversely, there may be instances in which a person shows clear patterns of physiological reactivity to an eliciting stimulus but shows no behavioral signs of distress and reports no subjective stress. This situation is not at all unusual, for example, among patients with essential hypertension, a disorder often referred to as the silent killer because its presence goes undetected. How should the psychophysiologist interpret such dysjunctions among behavior, subjective experience, and physiological response? Is it reasonable to assume that psychophysiological responses alone define a stress response? Or is the proper definition of stress, in the final analysis, a phenomenological one?

The point that we would like to emphasize is that psychophysiological assessment is not always necessary for the proper evaluation of stress. There are, however, certain instances in which stress may be properly understood as a pathophysiological response pattern. One of the most pertinent areas for psychophysiological assessment of stress is in the measurement of those physiological responses presumed to be associated with risk for physical disease. This utility of psychophysiological assessment is predicated upon two assumptions: (1) that psychological stress may have adverse effects on physical well-being (i.e., a restatement of the familiar psychosomatic hypothesis), and (2) that the linkage between psychological stress and physical illness is mediated by pathophysiological responses. This point has been articulated by Goldband, Katkin, and Morell (1979) and by Wright, et al. (1985), among others.

Later in this discussion we review some models and summarize some data that bear on the relationships among stress, psychophysiological reactivity, and disease. First, however, we review the methods and techniques that are employed in psychophysiological assessment.

METHODS AND TECHNIQUES

Psychophysiology is a relatively new field, born of the common interest of psychologists, physicians, and biomedical engineers in the analysis of mind-body interactions through the measurement of bioelectric signals. As such, the field represents a heterogeneity of interests, and to a large extent it is defined by its methods. Psychophysiology, a subdiscipline of the broader interdisciplinary field of behavioral neuroscience, is distinguished by its use of surface recordings of bioelectric activity rather than invasive procedures for the study of nervous system responses.

Although the sympathetic and parasympathetic divisions of the autonomic nervous system comprise all the nerves that innervate the smooth muscles of the viscera, the endocrine glands, the heart, and the blood vessels, psychophysiological attention has focused primarily on cardiovascular measures and on the measurement of palmar sweat gland secretions. Sweat gland secretions are typically assessed by measuring changes in the electrical conductivity of the skin, which are known generically as electrodermal activity. Indeed, some have argued that the origin of the discipline of psychophysiology can be "traced to the discoveries of electrical properties of the skin in the nineteenth century by Féré (1888) and Tarchanoff (1890)" (Katkin & Hastrup, 1982:387).

Electrodermal Responses

Skin conductance measurement has become a central feature of psychophysiological assessment for both theoretical and pragmatic reasons. The theoretical basis of its popularity as a stress index lies both in the fact that the innervation of the sweat glands is exclusively sympathetic and that these glands are remarkably responsive to environmental stimuli known to evoke anxiety (Szpiler & Epstein, 1976) and/or stress reactions (Katkin, 1965, 1966). The practical reasons for its popularity are that the measure is simple to quantify and inexpensive to implement. The exact relationship between psychological phenomena and electrodermal responses (EDRs) is still not entirely understood, and controversy remains concerning the psychological meaning of the EDR. For a detailed and exhaustive review of both theoretical and technical aspects of electrodermal recording, the reader should consult Fowles (1986).

Throughout most of the early years of psychophysiological research, electrodermal activity was referred to as the GSR (galvanic skin response) or the PGR (psychogalvanic reflex). These terms, however, are generic and do not describe adequately whether the response in question is an index of skin potential (endosomatic) or skin resistance (exosomatic); nor do these older terms indicate if the measurement reflects tonic or phasic response components. An endosomatic assessment is obtained when one measures the electrical *potential* (volts) between two points on the skin surface; this is the technique originally developed by Tarchanoff (1890). Exosomatic measurement, on the other hand, assesses the *resistance* (ohms) of the skin to the imposition of an externally applied current, or its mathematical reciprocal, the *conductance* (siemens) of the skin to an externally applied current; this is the technique originally developed by Féré (1888).

Regardless of whether the investigator is interested in measuring skin potential, skin resistance, or skin conductance, a choice must be made about three additional parameters of each: level, elicited response, and spontaneous response. *Level* refers to the average amount of resistance, conductance, or potential observed during some predetermined time period. An *elicited response* is a transitory change in level that is associated with a specific stimulus. A *spontaneous electrodermal response* is a transitory change in level, usually of small magnitude, that occurs in the absence of any known specific stimulus. Levels are usually measured by sampling regularly, perhaps once per second, over some predetermined interval and then computing a mean of the sample. Elicited responses are measured as amplitude of response from the point of stimulus onset to the point of maximum change, which occurs within 3 to 5 seconds of stimulus presentation. Spontaneous responses are usually counted over some predetermined time interval and reported as frequency per time; the amplitude of spontaneous responses is considered irrelevant. In order to facilitate communication among different laboratories a standard nomenclature for electrodermal activity for (EDA) research has been developed. Table 9-1 contains the appropriate acronyms for the various electrodermal indexes.

A great many technical considerations are necessary for the proper measurement of EDA, including electrode size and composition, contact medium, electrode placement sites, and electronic circuity. Recommended standards for the measurement of electrodermal activity have been established by the Society for Psychophysiological Research (Fowles, et al., 1981); researchers who plan to utilize electrodermal measures should acquaint themselves with these standards.

Cardiovascular Activity

Electrocardiography. The electrocardiogram is a measure of the electrical activity associated with the contraction of cardiac muscle. Unlike EDA, the heart is innervated by both sympathetic and parasympathetic fibers, and its rate of firing during periods of normal activity is primarily under the regulation of the vagus nerve, a parasympathetic cholinergic cranial nerve whose primary action is to slow the heart rate. The heart is also innervated by sympathetic adrenergic fibers, whose primary purpose is to increase the heart's rate and contractile force is emergency situations. These primary functions of sympathetic and parasympathetic innervation represent a gross oversimplification of what is an unusually complex self-regulatory system. Heart rate may be increased, for instance, by inhibition of vagal activity, with or without concomitant sympathetic arousal; thus heart rate changes cannot be interpreted simply as reflections of sympathetically mediated stress responses.

Although it is well known that psychological stress may elicit changes in cardiac rate, it must be understood that the major function of the heart is to pump blood to the brain and the muscles, thereby providing necessary oxygen for metabolism. Thus, as Obrist (1981) has argued eloquently, cardiac changes in response to "psychological stress" are best interpreted in the context of the homeostatic regulatory function that is served by the cardiovascular system.

Figure 9-1 depicts an idealized cardiac cycle—that is, the electrical events associated with one heart beat. The cycle begins with a neural impulse at the sino-atrial node of the right atrium, represented by point 0 on the time line of Figure 9-1. The impulse then travels across the atria, which contract about 60 milliseconds (msec) after innervation. This atrial contraction is represented by the P-wave of the EKG. The impulse is then conducted further by a combination of specialized cardiac conduction cells and neural cells and arrives at the

TABLE 9-1
Common Abbreviations Used
in Electrodermal Research

SCL	Skin Conductance Level
SCR	Skin Conductance Response
SSCR	Spontaneous Skin Conductance Response
SRL	Skin Resistance Level
SRR	Skin Resistance Response
SSRR	Spontaneous Skin Resistance Response
SPL	Skin Potential Level
SPR	Skin Potential Response
SSPR	Spontaneous Skin Potential Response

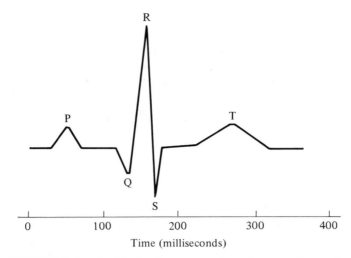

Time (milliseconds)

FIGURE 9-1. An idealized representation of one cardiac cycle. Point 0 on the time line represents innervation at the sino-atrial node.

atrio-ventricular node about 125 msec after the initial sino-atrial innervation. The activation of the atrio-ventricular node is represented in the EKG by the Q-wave. Immediately after the impulse reaches the atrio-ventricular node and the bundle of His, a large voltage spoke is initiated. This spike, the R-wave in Figure 9-1, represents the innervation of the ventricles and actually precedes the ventricular muscle contraction by about 50 msec. At the end of the R-wave, as can be seen in Figure 9-1, the voltage rebounds to a level slightly higher (by convention, the upward direction is negative and the downward direction is positive voltage) than it was at the onset of the R-wave. This is followed by the S-wave, a rapid but slight rise up to baseline level. When the ventricles contract (systole), the pressure inside them increases rapidly, and when the pressure inside the left ventricle exceeds the pressure in the aorta, the aortic valve is forced open and blood flows into the aorta and reaches its peak pressure at the time represented by the T-wave. The time between the T-wave and the next P-wave is quiescent and is known as the diastole.

For measurements of heart rate (HR), the investigator typically records the time between R-waves to yield a measure of interbeat interval (IBI). It can be seen readily that $60,000/IBI_{(msec)}$ equals HR in beats per minute (bpm). Clinical evaluation of cardiac function often focuses on the segment between S and T, known as the S-T segment. If the cardiac muscle is not receiving sufficient blood supply because of atherosclerotic disease, the lack will be reflected in S-T segment depression, in which the voltage level between S and T does not show the characteristic change noted in, Figure 9-1.

Until recently, attempts to assess cardiodynamic factors more complex than HR required either invasive catheterization or extremely expensive echocardiographic or Doppler sound measurement techniques. During the past decade, however, substantial advances have been made in the assessment of systolic time intervals, myocardial contractile force, and stroke volume from surface bioelectrical measurements of thoracic impedance.

Impedance Cardiography. The impedance cardiograph is employed to measure the impedance of the thorax to a high frequency (100 Khz) low level (4 milliamp) alternating current going from the neck to the abdomen through band electrodes wrapped around the torso. The thorax is a volume conductor, so its impedance is affected by changes in its total volume. These volume changes are mainly caused by the inflation and deflation of the lungs and the beating of the heart. If respiratory contributions to impedance change are removed, then the remaining variance in impedance change can be attributed to blood volume changes. A number of statistical and methodological algorithms are available to accomplish this goal (see Kelsey & Guethlein, 1990; Sherwood, et al., 1990).

Changes in impedance (Z), and especially changes in the first derivative of impedance change over time (dZ/dt), can be recorded continuously using an instrument based on that described by Kubicek, et al. (1974). A detailed description of this technique can be obtained from Sherwood, et al. (1990) and additional useful information can be obtained from Wilson, Lovallo, and Pincomb (1989). The value of impedance cardiography lies in the fact that it not only yields measures of blood volume changes but that specific parts of the dZ/dt wave indicate with great accuracy the opening and closing of the aortic valve. Together with simultaneous information from the EKG, impedance cardiography allows accurate measurement of systolic time intervals, including the pre-ejection period (PEP), which is the time between the depolarization of the ventricle and the opening of the aortic valve; and the left ventricular ejection time (LVET), which is the time between opening and closing of the aortic valve. Kubicek, et al. (1974) have demonstrated that by using the values of maximum dZ/dt (dZ/dt_{max}), basal impedance (Z_0), LVET, and the distance between the recording electrode bands (D), a reasonable estimate of cardiac stroke volume (SV) can be ascertained from the formula:

$$SV = \text{rho } (D/Z_0)^2 \text{ (LVET) } (dZ/dt_{max})$$

in which rho represents blood resistivity. It is common practice to substitute a constant for rho in instances where the resistivity is not expected to show transitory changes.

The theoretical significance of these measures is based upon the assumption that systolic time intervals are influenced primarily by sympathetic nervous system activity. Further, Heather (1969) has demonstrated that the dZ/dt_{max} divided by the time interval between the EKG Q-wave and the time of dZ/dt_{max} is a valid index of myocardial contractility. Thus impedance cardiography is useful in measuring the contractile force of the heart, a sympathetically mediated response that may have significant utility in evaluating pathophysiological responses to psychological stress (see Dermit, 1990). Impedance-derived estimates also allow the calculation of cardiac output (CO) by the simple formula, CO = HR × SV. As Wilson, et al. (1989) have noted, if blood pressure is also assessed, then total peripheral resistance (TPR) can be estimated by dividing mean arterial blood pressure by CO and multiplying by 0.8. This allows for an interpretation of blood pressure changes as a function of both myocardial and vascular contributions.

Blood Pressure. The blood circulates throughout the arterial tree in pulses of rising and falling pressure, initiated by the contraction of the ventricles. Thus the pressure within the arteries varies during each cardiac cycle, from a maximum (systole) associated with the ventricular contraction to a minimum (diastole) achieved between heartbeats. The arterial walls are elastic, and after systole they recoil and force the blood further through the capillaries (Berne & Levy, 1977). As the blood travels further from the heart, the pressure drops; thus pressure in the major arteries is much higher than in the smaller ones, and pressure in the veins, which transport the blood back to the right atrium, is low.

The level of blood pressure is determined by the interaction between CO and TPR. Given that CO is the product of HR and SV, it may be seen that a blood pressure increase may result from an increase in either HR, SV, or TPR. To complicate matters further, all of these variables are affected by sympathetic arousal, and HR also may be elevated by inhibition of the parasympathetic vagus nerve; thus a change in blood pressure cannot be readily ascribed to sympathetic or parasympathetic influence without further information. Despite these difficulties of interpretation, blood pressure measurement continues to be of interest to stress researchers because of their belief that psychological stress elevates pressure, especially among individuals who may have a familial predisposition to essential hypertension (Falkner, Onesti, Angelakos, Fernandes, & Langman, 1979; Obrist, 1981).

The most accurate way to read blood pressure is to insert a catheter into an artery and connect it to a pressure transducer, but because this technique is painful and risky, it is reserved for acutely ill hospitalized patients. More commonly blood pressure is estimated indirectly using a sphygmomanometer; a cuff is wrapped around the upper arm and inflated until the brachial artery is occluded. A microphone placed under the cuff cannot detect any sound of pulsation when the cuff has occluded the artery. As the cuff is deflated slowly, the microphone detects a high-frequency pulse sound at the time that the cuff pressure equals the maximum intra-arterial pressure during systole. This sound is the Korotkoff sound, and the observed cuff pressure at its onset indicates the systolic blood pressure. As the cuff deflates further, the Korotkoff sounds continue to be heard until the cuff pressure drops below the minimum intra-arterial pressure during diastole—the diastolic pressure— at which point the Korotkoff sounds disappear.

A complete cycle of inflation and deflation of the cuff can take as long as 60 seconds, even when the inflation and the sound detection is under electronic control. Thus research applications requiring the assessment of rapid blood pressure changes in response to stress are difficult to achieve with this technology. For these reasons considerable effort has been devoted to the development of new noninvasive algorithms for the continuous assessment of blood pressure by using cuffs that are only partially inflated and held at a constant pressure. As a result, a number of devices for continuous, noninvasive detection of blood pressure have been developed that enable stress researchers to assess blood pressure changes on each beat of the heart. Some of these techniques have been described in a compendium on cardiovascular research techniques edited by Orlebeke, Mulder, and Van Doornen (1985).

PSYCHOPHYSIOLOGICAL ASSESSMENT AND BEHAVIORAL MEDICINE

We have suggested in this chapter that it is both sensible and worthwhile to employ psychophysiological methods to index those physiological responses that may be involved in the etiology of physical disorders. Although psychophysiological methods have bee applied to a wide range of disorders, they have been particularly valuable for assessing variables thought to be associated with coronary heart disease (CHD) and hypertension. While it is generally believed that job stress and other pressing social stresses are critical in the etiology of CHD, the preponderance of the literature evaluating the relationship between stress and CHD or hypertension has focused on measuring reactivity to stressful laboratory tasks. Stress-evoked reactivity of the cardiovascular system has generated much enthusiasm among researchers largely because of the hypothesized role of stress-induced cardiovascular hyper-reactivity in the development of disease.

The tendency of some individuals to respond consistently to stressful events with marked cardiovascular changes has been proposed frequently as a factor contributing to the pathogenesis of coronary heart disease (see Manuck & Krantz, 1986). Yet adequate empirical investigations of the cumulative effects of excessive myocardial responses to repeated of chronic real-life stressors are very difficult to conduct. Within a laboratory setting, it is possible to evoke large acute cardiovascular changes in response to short-term exposure to a controlled stressor. Assuming that these in vitro responses to laboratory stress tasks represent reasonable estimates of in vivo responses to stress, and assuming that responses to acute events reflect processes underlying the etiology of chronic diseases, measures of experimentally elicited myocardial reactivity may be useful indicators of coronary risk.

Individual differences in physiological reactivity to psychological stress have been well established (Kasprowicz, Manuck, Malkoff, & Krantz, 1990; Krantz & Manuck, 1984; Matthews, et al., 1986). Some individuals (reactors) respond to stressful stimuli with greater autonomic arousal than others (nonreactors). Furthermore, the tendency to react to stressful events with marked arousal seems to be a stable, "trait-like" characteristic (Burns, Ferguson, Fernquist, & Katkin, 1992; Kasprowicz, et al., 1990; Manuck & Garland, 1980). Promising evidence exists to support the association between sympathetic reactivity and pathogenesis of cardiovascular disease. Furthermore, biologically plausible pathways linking reactivity to cardiovascular disease have been proposed (Krantz & Manuck, 1984).

A Model of Stress and Essential Hypertension

One of the most influential models of the mechanism linking psychological stress to cardiovascular disease is the *overperfusion* model of Obrist (1981) and his colleagues. Obrist has reported that some individuals exhibit a characteristic beta-adrenergic "hyperreactivity" pattern reflected in elevated heart rate and pressor and neuroendocrine changes in response to stress. He has hypothesized that this exaggerated sympathetic beta-adrenergic activation is related to the pathogenesis of hypertension. The key feature of this model stipulates that heightened cardiovascular reactivity in excess of the metabolic demand of the stressful situation results in greater perfusion of peripheral tissue than is required for homeostasis. This overperfusion of the tissue sets off a chain of automatic beta-adrenergic sympathetic regulatory adjustments that result in elevated blood pressure, thereby increasing the individual's risk for disease. For example, Obrist (1981) found HR accelerations and adrenergically mediated increases in myocardial contractility in response to a reaction time shock avoidance task that were metabolically unwarranted by the physical demands (as assessed by oxygen consumption) of the stressful situation. This pattern of results, demonstrating substantial increases in sympathetically driven heart rate unaccompanied by corresponding increases in oxygen consumption during a reaction time shock avoidance task, has been found with both animals (Langer, Obrist, & McCubbin, 1979) and humans (Langer, et al., 1985). This pattern of tissue overperfusion in response to psychological stress contrasts with the response to exercise stress, in which an orderly correspondence between heart rate and oxygen consumption is observed.

It has been suggested (Langer, et al., 1979; Obrist, 1981) that overperfusion contributes to disease because reflex peripheral vasoconstriction is elicited to compensate for the excess perfusion. This reflex vasoconstriction results in increased peripheral resistance and thus in increased blood pressure. It is further assumed that if this process is repeated or prolonged it will result eventually in chronically increased blood pressure. Thus, according to this model, repeated elicitations of exaggerated responses to stress, over time, can lead to disease. Whether overperfusion is etiologically relevant to the pathogenesis of cardiovascular disease and, if so, whether autoregulation is the operative mechanism remain controversial. Convincing prospective longitudinal studies have not been conducted, and such studies are necessary before substantial claims can be made.

Individual Differences in Hyper-reactivity to Stress. Research investigating the relationship between stress and hypertension has focused on measures of reactivity to psychological stress among patients with established hypertension or borderline hypertension as compared with healthy control subjects. Findings of high reactivity in borderline hypertensives coupled with research demonstrating higher reactivity in normotensive males who have a family history of hypertension than in those who do not (Light, 1981) suggest that reactivity may be a preclinical marker for hypertension.

Light, Koepke, Obrist, and Willis (1983) also have found that subjects who were borderline hypertensive or normotensive but had at least one hypertensive parent showed significantly greater retention of urinary sodium and fluid in response to a competitive reaction time task than did normotensives without a family history. Furthermore, Light, et al. (1983) observed a direct relationship between the degree of sodium retention and the magnitude of HR reactivity to the task, a finding that suggests a common sympathetic mediation for these two responses. Further evidence that reactivity is mediated by beta-adrenergic sympathetic reactivity comes from the observation that the ingestion of drugs (e.g., propranolol) that block beta-adrenergic receptors eliminates or reduces the high level of cardiovascular reactivity to stress (Light, 1981), and that drugs that enhance beta-adrenergic activity (e.g., chloralose) augment cardiovascular reactivity to stress (Kaplan, Manuck, Williams, & Strawn, in press).

In a study of hemodynamic responses to a mental arithmetic task, Schulte and Neus (1983) found that blood pressure increased to a greater degree and remained elevated for a longer period of time following termination of stress in borderline hypertensives and mild hypertensives as compared to normotensives. Furthermore, their results for HR and CO paralleled those for blood pressure. Schulte and Neus (1983) attributed the observed hemodynamic pattern to stronger sympathetic stimulation in subjects demonstrating early hypertension.

Family History of Hypertension and Hyper-reactivity. It has been suggested that heart rate reactivity in response to stressful tasks in healthy individuals may predict the development of hypertension later in life. Light and Obrist (1980), for instance, found a greater incidence of parental hypertension among normotensive high cardiovascular reactors as compared to low reactors. Hastrup, Light, and Obrist (1982) reported a greater incidence of hypertension in parents of young normotensive subjects who showed high cardiovascular reactivity to stress than in parents of young normotensive low reactors. Anderson, Mahoney, Lauer, and Clarke (1987) found also that normotensive adolescents with a hypertensive parent exhibited greater increases in forearm blood flow during a mental arithmetic stress task than those with normotensive parents. In a study of stress-induced pressor responses in normotensive adolescents, Ewart, Harris, Zeger, and Russell (1986) found that adolescents with a family history of hypertension were most reliably distinguished from subjects without a family history by a "persistently diminished" pulse pressure in response to a video game stress task. In this study, a pattern of cardiovascular reactivity with increased peripheral resistance and decreased cardiac output was manifested by normotensives who had a family history of hypertension.

Insufficient data exist to demonstrate whether high reactors are indeed at greater risk of disease. Although more long-term prospective studies are necessary to link observations of myocardial hyper-reactivity to acute psychological stress to later development of disease, a few prospective studies have supported the hypothesized association. In a prospective study of adolescent borderline hypertensives, Falkner, Onesti, and Hamstra (1981) found that the degree of SBP reactivity to a mental arithmetic task was predictive of hypertension 5 years later. More recent work by Light (1991) indicates that subjects who exhibited high HR reactivity in early adulthood were found to have increased blood pressure at a 10–15-year follow-up.

Stress and Coronary Heart Disease

Atherosclerosis. The relationship between reactivity to psychological stress and coronary heart disease is usually investigated by comparing cardiac patients with controls. The results of these case-control studies have indicated greater physiologic reactivity to stress in post infarct patients or patients with angina than in healthy subjects. However, difficulties inherent in controlling for degree of cardiac damage and medication usage in this type of population precludes definitive conclusions (Krantz & Raisen, 1988).

Cardiovascular reactivity may be associated with any of several factors that could be connected to the development of atherosclerosis, such as increased serum catecholamines, which are thought to facilitate arterial plaque accumulation, and increased shearing force on the lining of vessels and changes in pulsatile flow, both of which may result in damage to endothelial cells of the blood vessels. The balance between sympathetic and parasympathetic influences also may influence the occurrence of fatal arrhythmias in response to stress (Cinciripini, 1986). Further investigations aimed at clarifying potentially pathogenic mechanisms need to be carried out.

An important determination to be made is whether responsivity to psychological stress provides any incremental information over and above that obtained from traditional physical stress testing, such as treadmill tests. Blascovich and Katkin (in press) investigated the relative ability of psychological and physical stress tests to predict coronary artery disease in patients undergoing coronary angiography. Using coronary artery occlusion as their criterion variable, they found that psychophysiological assessments of HR, SBP, and DBP reactivity to a deadline choice reaction time task yielded significant and substantial predictive power over and above that provided by traditional clinical predictors that were based on response to exercise stress (ST segment depression, premature ventricular contractions, pain).

Ischemia. Recent work has linked psychological stress to myocardial ischemia as well as to atherosclerotic disease, although the pathogenic mechanisms involved are unclear. In general, the results of such studies indicate that ischemia induced by mental stress is seen in those subjects who also show ischemia in response to physical stress (Rozanski, et al., 1988). For example, Specchia, et al. (1984) exposed 122 patients with suspected or known heart disease to both mental arithmetic (MA) and exercise stress. They found that some patients responded with ST segment depression, a clinical marker for ischemia, to the exercise test but not to the MA task, but that all patients who exhibited ST segment depression in response to MA also exhibited abnormal responses to a physical exercise test. In other words, those who exhibited ST segment abnormalities to the MA test represent a potentially important subset of those subjects who respond abnormally to that exercise test. Higher indexes of myocardial oxygen consumption in response to the mental arithmetic task, as well as a shorter exercise duration, were observed in those patients who responded with ST segment depression to both the physical and mental stress. Patients who did not show ST segment depression in response to either task were found to have significantly lower prevalence of coronary artery disease than other patients. This suggests that a combination of both physical and mental stress testing may be a more powerful approach to the identification of patients at risk for heart disease than exercise testing alone.

Ambulatory EKG monitoring of patients with coronary artery disease has revealed frequently occurring transient episodes of silent ischemia, which is otherwise asymptomatic, in response to mental stress. A recently developed and highly promising technique to investigate left ventricular function in response to psychological stress is ambulatory radionuclide monitoring (Kayden, in press). Evidence suggests that this technique may be more sensitive than ambulatory ECG monitoring in detecting transient episodes of silent myocardial ischemia in patients with coronary artery disease and offers promise as a psychophysiological tool. In a recent study of LaVeau, et al. (1989), left ventricular ejection fraction (LVEF) was evaluated in patients with coronary artery disease in response to mental stress and exercise. Left ventricular ejection fraction, which is correlated with stroke volume, is a measure of the proportion of blood in the ventricle that is ejected on each contraction. If the heart muscle is diseased or damaged, then the ejection fraction is reduced because the muscle cannot pump efficiently. It was found that in response to psychological stressors LVEF decreased in patients with coronary artery disease who exhibited decreases in response to exercise. In contrast, among healthy patients the mental stress elicited either an increase or no change in LVEF.

STRESS TASK SELECTION

We argued earlier that for purposes of psychophysiological research the primary definitional focus of "stress" resides in the response side rather than the stimulus side of the stimulus-response equation. Nevertheless, it is obvious that the experimental evaluation of stress responses requires careful selection of appropriate tasks. Several laboratory and naturalistic stressors have been employed to evoke reactivity, including reaction time tasks, mental arithmetic, personally relevant public speaking tasks, cold pressor, stress interviews, cognitive problems such as the Stroop color-word test, shock or threat of shock, video games, mirror tracing, and even piloting a helicopter.

The choice of tasks is determined by a number of factors. First is the task's efficacy in eliciting the expected physiological response; second is its ease of administration. Mental arithmetic is a commonly used laboratory stressor because it can be administered easily in a standardized manner and has been found reliably to elicit cardiovascular changes (Brod, Fencl, Hejl, & Jirka, 1959; Krantz, Manuck, & Wing, 1986). In a typical MA task, a subject is asked to subtract serially from a three or four digit number by sevens or some other odd number, and to do so rapidly and accurately. Sometimes the subject is urged on or harassed during performance of this difficult task. Carroll, Turner, and Hellawell (1986) have refined the technique by providing a mechanism by which its demands are adjusted for level of difficulty for each subject.

A third, and important, consideration in the choice of laboratory stress task is the physiological system to be stimulated. Different stressors evoke different physiological response patterns. For example, tasks that require active coping have been found to be more potent elicitors of metabolically excessive sympathetic influences on the myocardium than tasks that require passive coping (Obrist, 1981; Obrist, et al., 1978; Sherwood, Allen,

Obrist, & Langer, 1986). The distinction between *active* and *passive* coping has been defined by Obrist and his colleagues analogically as the difference between instrumental avoidance conditioning and classical aversive conditioning. In instrumental avoidance conditioning, the organism can learn to avoid the delivery of a noxious stimulus by instrumental responding (i.e., active coping with the environment). In classical aversive conditioning, however, a neutral stimulus precedes a noxious stimulus at all times, and the organism has no ability to change the contingency. The result is that the organism has no overt coping response available. In a series of elegant investigations in both human and infra-human subjects, Obrist has demonstrated that active coping tasks elicit homeostatically inappropriate over-perfusion whereas passive coping tasks do not. Thus it has become customary in cardiovascular stress research to use tasks that are presumed to engage the subject's active coping mechanisms. Typical laboratory stressors such as the cold pressor (immersion of the arm in ice) or painful electric shock are not considered to be elicitors of active coping if the subject is unable to take instrumental action to avoid or escape from them..

An example of the importance of these considerations may be seen in the work of Lovallo, et al. (1985), who studied the effects of both active and passive coping in response to unpredictable noise and shock. Their dependent measures included HR, BP, systolic time intervals, CO, TPR, blood assays of free fatty acids and catecholamines, as well as self-report of mood. In all conditions, exposure to stress produced significant cardiovascular and neuroendocrine changes indicative of sympathetic arousal. The greatest changes, however, were obtained in the condition in which subjects could actively avoid noxious stimulation. Similar findings have been reported by Weiss (1972), who found that pathophysiological response to stress in rats was related to their efforts to control their stimulus environment.

CONCLUSION

We have focused our attention primarily on the application of psychophysiological techniques to cardiovascular behavioral medicine mostly because the greatest technical advances have been made and the largest database has been accumulated in this area. However, both the methodological and conceptual framework for psychophysiological research on stress is likely to expand significantly in the near future. Current developments in the field of psychoneuroimmunology, for instance, suggest that the normal immune response of the organism may be compromised by psychosocial stress (Glaser, et al., 1985). Further, recent evidence suggests that sympathetic nervous system activation is related to the extent of immune compromise (Manuck, Cohen, Rabin, Muldoon, & Bachen, 1991; Stone, et al., 1991; Valdimarsdottir, et al., 1991). To date, there have been no definitive studies that directly implicate stress-related immune suppression in disease, but it is a clear working hypothesis that if stress reduces the efficiency of the immune system then it may contribute to increased probability of disease.

In summary, the past decade has witnessed a major shift in the focus of psychophysiological research on stress away from traditional studies of psychological *dis*tress and toward the effects of stress on physical illness. This transition has resulted, in our estimation, in a most appropriate allocation of psychophysiological research resources and represents the best avenue by which psychophysiological research methods can contribute to the evaluation of stress-related behavior.

REFERENCES

Anderson, E. A., Mahoney, L. T., Lauer, R. M., & Clarke, W. R. Enhanced forearm blood flow during mental stress in children of hypertensive parents. *Hypertension*, 1987, *10,* 544–549.

Appley, M. H., & Trumbull, R. On the concept of psychological stress. In M. H. Appley & R. Trumbull (eds.), *Psychological stress.* New York: Appleton-Century-Crofts, 1967.

Berne, R. M., & Levy, M. N. *Cardiovascular physiology.* St. Louis, MO: C. V. Mosby, 1977.

Blascovich, J., & Katkin, E. S. Psychological stress testing for coronary heart disease. In J. Blascovich & E. S. Katkin (eds.), *Cardiovascular reactivity and disease: The evidence* Washington, DC: American Psychological Association, in press.

Brod, J., Fencl, V., Hejl, Z., & Jirka, J. Circulatory changes underlying blood pressure elevation during acute emotional stress (mental arithmetic) in normotensive and hypertensive subjects. *Clinical Science,* 1959, *18,* 269–279.

Burns, J. W., Ferguson, M. L., Fernquist, S. K., & Katkin, E. S. Test-retest reliability of inotropic and chronotropic measures of cardiac reactivity. International Journal of *Psychophysiology,* 1992, *12,* 165–168.

Cacioppo, J. T., & Tassinary, L. G. (eds.), *Principles of psychophysiology: Physical, social, and inferential elements.* Cambridge, Eng.: Cambridge University Press, 1990.

Carroll, D., Turner, J. R., & Hellawell, J. C. Heart rate and oxygen consumption during active psychological challenge: The effects of level of difficulty. *Psychophysiology,* 1986, *23,* 174–181.

Cinciripini, P. M. Cognitive stress and cardiovascular reactivity: I. Relationship to hypertension. *American Heart Journal,* 1986, *112,* 1044–1050.

Dermit, S. Behavior and cardiovascular reactivity under operant schedule demands: An empirical approach to coronary proneness. Unpublished doctoral dissertation, Department of Psychology, State University of New York at Stony Brook, 1990.

Ewart, C. K., Harris, W. L., Zeger, S., & Russell, G. A. Diminished pulse pressure under mental stress characterizes normotensive adolescents with parental high blood pressure. *Psychosomatic medicine,* 1986, *48,* 489–501.

Falkner, B., Onesti, G., Angelakos, E. T., Fernandes, M., & Langman, C. Cardiovascular response to mental stress in normal adolescents with hypertensive parents. *Hypertension,* 1979, *1,* 23–30.

Falkner, B., Onesti, G., & Hamstra, B. Stress response characteristics of adolescents with high genetic risk for essential hypertension: A five year follow-up. *Clinical and Experimental Hypertension,* 1981, *3,* 583.

Féré, C. Note sur des modifications de la résistance électrique sous l'influence des excitations sensorielles et des émotions. *Comptes Rendus des Séances de la Société de Biologie,* 1988, *5,* 217–219.

Fowles, D. C. The eccrine system and electrodermal activity. In M. G. H. Coles, E. Donchin, & S. W. Porges (eds.), *Psychophysiology: Systems, processes, and applications.* New York: Guilford Press, 1986.

Fowles, D. C., Christie, M. J., Edelberg, R., Grings, W. W., Lykken, D. T., & Venables, P. H. Publication recommendations for electrodermal measurements. *Psychophysiology,* 1981, *18,* 232–239.

Glaser, R., Kiecolt-Glaser, J. K., Stout, J. C., Tarr, K. L., Speicher, C. E., & Holliday, J. E. Stress-related impairments in cellular immunity. *Psychiatric Research,* 1985, *16,* 233–239.

Goldband, S., Katkin, E. S., & Morell, M. A. Personality and cardiovascular disorder: Steps toward demystification. In I. G. Sarason & C. D. Spielberger (eds.), *Stress and anxiety.* Vol. 6. Washington DC: Hemisphere Publishing, 1979.

HASTRUP, J. L., LIGHT, K. C., & OBRIST, P. A. Parental hypertension and cardiovascular response to stress. *Psychophysiology,* 1982, *19,* 615–622.

HEATHER, L. W. A comparison of cardiac output values by the impedance cardiograph and dye dilution techniques in cardiac patients. In W. G. Kubicek, D. A. Witsoe, R. P. Patterson, & A. H. L. From (eds.), *Development and evaluation of an impedance cardiographic system to measure cardiac output and other cardiac parameters.* (NASA-CR-101965). Houston, TX: National Aeronautics and Space Administration, 1969.

KAPLAN, J. R., MANUCK, S. B., WILLIAMS, J. K., & STRAWN, W. Psychosocial influences on atherosclerosis: Evidence for effects and mechanisms in nonhuman primates. In J. Blascovich & E. S. Katkin (eds.), *Cardiovascular reactivity disease: The evidence.* Washington, DC: American Psychological Association, in press.

KASPROWICZ, A. L., MANUCK, S. B., MALKOFF, S. B., & KRANTZ, D. S. Individual differences in behaviorally evoked cardiovascular response: Temporal stability and hemodynamic patterning. *Psychophysiology,* 1990, *27,* 605–620.

KATKIN, E. S. Relationship between manifest anxiety and two indices of autonomic response to stress. *Journal and Personality and Social Psychology,* 1965, *2,* 324–333.

————. The relationship between a measure of transitory anxiety and spontaneous autonomic activity. *Journal of Abnormal Psychology,* 1966, *71,* 142–146.

KATKIN, E. S., & HASTRUP, J. L. Psychophysiological methods in clinical research. In P. C. Kendall & J. N. Butcher (eds.), *The Handbook of research methods in clinical psychology.* New York: Wiley, 1982.

KAYDEN, D. Radionuclide methodology. In J. Blascovich & E. S. Katkin (eds.), *Cardiovascular reactivity disease: The evidence.* Washington, DC: American Psychological Association, in press.

KELSEY, R. M., & GUETHLEIN, W. G. An evaluation of the ensemble averaged impedance cardiogram. *Psychophysiology,* 1990, *27,* 24–33.

KRANTZ, D. S., & MANUCK, S. B. Acute psychophysiologic reactivity and risk of cardiovascular disease: A review and methodologic critique. *Psychological Bulletin,* 1984, *96,* 435–464.

KRANTZ, D. S., MANUCK, S. B., & WING, R. Physiological stressors and task variables as elicitors of reactivity. In K. A. Matthews, S. M. Weiss, T. Detre, T. M. Dembroski, B. Falkner, S. B. Manuck, & R. B. Williams, Jr. (eds.), *Handbook of stress, reactivity, and cardiovascular disease.* New York: Wiley, 1986.

KRANTZ, D. S., & RAISEN, S. E. Environmental stress, reactivity and ischaemic heart disease. *British Journal of Medical Psychology,* 1988, *61,* 3–16.

KUBICEK, W. G., KOTTKE, F. J., RAMOS, M. V., PATTERSON, R. P., WITSOE, D. A., LABREE, J. W., REMOLE, W., LAYMAN, T. E., SCHWENING, H., & GARAMELLA, J. T. The Minnesota impedance cardiograph—theory and applications. *Biomedical Engineering,* 1974, *9,* 410–416.

LANGER, A. W., McCUBBIN, J. A., STONEY, C. M., HUTCHESON, J. S., CHARLTON, J. D., & OBRIST, P. A. Cardiopulmonary adjustments during exercise and an aversive reaction time task: Effects of beta-adrenoceptor blockade. *Psychophysiology,* 1985, *22,* 59–68.

LANGER, A. W., OBRIST, P. A., & McCUBBIN, J. A. Hemodynamic and metabolic adjustments during exercise and shock avoidance in dogs. *American Journal of Physiology: Heart and Circulatory Physiology,* 1979, *5,* H225-H230.

LaVEAU, P. L., ROZANSKI, A., KRANTZ, D. S., CORNELL, C. E., CATTANACH, L., ZARET, B. L., & WACKERS, S. J. Transient left ventricular dysfunction during provocative mental stress in patients with coronary artery disease. *American Heart Journal,* 1989, *118,* 1–8.

LIGHT, K. C. Cardiovascular responses to effortful active coping: Implications for the role of stress in hypertension development. *Psychophysiology,* 1981, *18,* 216–225.

————. Reactivity and hypertension. Paper presented at the American Psychological Association

Conference on the Evidence: Cardiovascular Reactivity to Psychological Stress and Cardiovascular Disease, Buffalo, NY, 1991.

LIGHT, K. C., KOEPKE, J. P., OBRIST, P. A., & WILLIS, P. W. Psychological stress induces sodium and fluid retention in men at high risk for hypertension. *Science,* 1983, *220,* 429–431.

LIGHT, K. C., & OBRIST, P. A. Cardiovascular response to stress: Effects of opportunity to avoid shock experience and performance feedback. *Psychophysiology,* 1980, *17,* 243–252.

LOVALLO, W. R., WILSON, M. F., PINCOMB, G. A., EDWARDS, G. L., TOMPKINS, P., & BRACKETT, D. J. Activation patterns to aversive stimulation in man: Passive exposure versus effort to control. *Psychophysiology,* 1985, *22,* 283–291.

MANUCK, S. B., COHEN, S., RABIN, B. S., MULDOON, M. F., & BACHEN, E. A. Individual differences in cellular immune response to stress. *Psychological Science,* 1991, *2,* 111–115.

MANUCK, S. B., & GARLAND, F. N. Stability in individual differences in cardiovascular reactivity: A 13 month follow-up. *Physiology and Behavior,* 1980, *21,* 621–624.

MANUCK, S. B., & KRANTZ, D. S. Psychophysiological reactivity in coronary heart disease and essential hypertension. In K. A. Matthews, S. M. Weiss, T. Detre, T. M. Dembroski, B. Falkner, S. B. Manuck, & R. B. Williams, Jr. (eds.), *Handbook of stress, reactivity, and cardiovascular disease.* New York: Wiley, 1986.

MATTHEWS, K. A., WEISS, S. M., DETRE, T., DEMBROSKI, T. M., FALKNER, B., MANUCK, S. B., & WILLIAMS, R. B. Jr. (eds.), *Handbook of stress, reactivity, and cardiovascular disease.* New York: Wiley, 1986.

OBRIST P. A. *Cardiovascular psychophysiology: A perspective.* New York: Plenum Press, 1981.

OBRIST, P. A., GAEBELEIN, C. J., TELLER, E. S., LANGER, A. W., GRIGNOLO, A., LIGHT, K. C., & MCCUBBIN, J. A. The relationship among heart rate carotid dp/dt and blood pressure in humans as a function of the type of stress. *Psychophysiology,* 1978, *15,* 102–115.

ORLEBEKE, J. F., MULDER, G., & VAN DOORNEN, L. J. P. (eds.), *Psychophysiology of cardiovascular control: Models, methods, and data.* New York: Plenum, 1985.

ROZANSKI, A., BAIREY, N., KRANTZ, D. S., FRIEDMAN, J., RESSER, K. J., MORELL, M., HILTON-CHALFEN, S., HESTRIN, L., BIETENDORF, J., & BERMAN, D. S. Mental stress and the induction of silent myocardial ischemia in patients with coronary artery disease. *New England Journal of Medicine,* 1988, *318,* 1005–1012.

SCHULTE, W., & NEUS, H. Hemodynamics during emotional stress in borderline and mild hypertension. *European Heart Journal,* 1983, *4,* 803–809.

SHERWOOD, A., ALLEN, M. T., FAHRENBERG, J., KELSEY, R. M., LOVALLO, W. R., & VAN DOORNEN, L. J. P. Methodological guidelines for impedance cardiography. *Psychophysiology,* 1990, *27,* 1–23.

SHERWOOD, A., ALLEN, M. T., OBRIST, P. A., & LANGER, A. W. Evaluation of beta-adrenergic influences on cardiovascular and metabolic adjustments to physical and psychological stress. *Psychophysiology,* 1986, *23,* 89–104.

SPECCHIA, G., DE SERVI, S., FALCONE, C., GAVAZZI, A., ANGOLI, L., BRAMUCCI, E., ARDISSINO, D., & MUSSINI, A. Mental arithmetic stress testing in patients with coronary artery disease. *American Heart Journal,* 1984, *108,* 56–63.

STONE, A., VALDIMARSDOTTIR, H., KATKIN, E., BURNS, J., COX, D., NEALE, J., & BOVBJERG, D. Stress-induced autonomic reactions are associated with altered mitogen responses. Presented at the meetings of the American Psychosomatic Association, Santa Fe, CA, 1991.

SZPILER, J. A., & EPSTEIN, S. Availability of an avoidance response as related to autonomic arousal. *Journal of Abnormal Psychology,* 1976, *85,* 73–82.

TARCHANOFF, J. Über die Galvanischen Erscheinungen an der Haut des Menschen bei reizung der Sinnesorgane und bei verscheidenen Formen der psychische Tätigkeit. *Pflüger's Archiv Psychologischen,* 1890, *46,* 46–55.

VALDIMARSDOTTIR, H., STONE, A., BURNS, J., KATKIN, E., COX, D., LEE, S., FINE, J., INGLE, D., & BOVBJERG, D. Experimental induction of psychological distress and reduced mitogen responses. Presented at the meetings of the Society of Behavioral Medicine, Washington, DC, 1991.

WEISS, J. M. Psychological factors in stress and disease. *Scientific American,* 1972, *226,* 104–113.

WILSON, M. F., LOVALLO, W. R., & PINCOMB, G. A. Noninvasive measurements of cardiac functions. In N. Schneiderman, S. M. Weiss, & P. G. Kaufmann (eds.), *Handbook of research methods in cardiovascular behavioral medicine.* New York: Plenum, 1989.

WRIGHT, R. A., CONTRADA, R. J., & GLASS, D. C. Psychophysiological correlates of type A behavior. In E. S. Katkin & S. B. Manuck (eds.), *Advances in behavioral medicine.* Greenwich, CT: JAI Press, 1985.

PART IV

MEASUREMENT OF STRESS AND COPING

10

The Assessment of Stressful Life Events

Thomas W. Miller

THE CLINICAL ASSESSMENT of the impact of stressful events has been the focus of several recent clinical investigations (Miller, 1989a). The diagnosis and understanding of stressful life events and their impact on the human organism require clinical measures to aid our growing comprehension of the etiology, onset, and progression of the psychopathology that can emerge when an organism experiences the broad spectrum of these events.

At the forefront of our understanding are multiple independent assessment techniques, which are capable of providing diagnostic information about patients. Numerous researchers have utilized varying systematic approaches in the development, standardization, and utilization of these techniques. This chapter reviews some of the more prominent scales used in assessing stressful life events.

MULTIAXIAL ASSESSMENT OF LIFE STRESS

The comprehensive assessment of stressful life events involves meeting a number of basic goals, including (1) the identification of experiences and symptoms, (2) a consideration of the presence of co-existing psychological disorders, and (3) the attainment of specificity with respect to the most recent diagnostic and statistical evaluation criteria of the American Psychiatric Association and other international organizations that classify disorders. Approaches often include structured clinical interviews, psychometric assessment, and behavioral assessment strategies. Some—but by no means all—of the multiaxial measures currently used to assess stressful life events are described in the following sections.

STRESSFUL LIFE EVENTS SCALES

Social Readjustment Rating Scale

In 1964, Holmes and Rahe (1967) devised the Social Readjustment Rating Questionnaire (SRRQ) to obtain numerical estimates of the average degree of life change and readjustment that subjects assign to changes in their lives. The life changes studied involved modifications of sleeping, eating, social, recreational, personal, and interpersonal habits that required or indicated varying degrees of adjustment. Holmes and Rahe subsequently revised the original scale to become the Social Readjustment Rating Scale (SRRS), which assigned magnitudes to each of 42 life change items according to the amount, severity, and duration of adjustment each requires. The scaling instrument was found concordant among various segments of the U.S. population and between American citizens and people of other cultures.

Holmes and Rahe then devised the Schedule of Recent Experience (SRE), a self-administered paper-and-pencil survey that listed life changes by year of occurrence. The current version of the SRE, the recent life changes questionnaire (RLCQ), retains the essence of the 42 original life change questions of the SRE, but the wording of questions has been altered for clarity and to allow for clarity and to allow for specific options of response. Instructions were placed at the end of the RLCQ so that subjects could self-scale their own subjective life change scores for each change they had recently experienced. Patients obtained at least three different life change scores for analyses with various illness criteria. First, subjects obtained a 6-month life change unit (LCU) score for the 42 SRE items. Second, they scored a sum of all recent life changes indicated in a 6-month time period. This method was called unit scaling and proved to be particularly useful with subjects between 18 and 25 years of age, a group that usually experiences few high LCU life changes. (The investigator is recommended to use the LCU scoring system when dealing with samples of older subjects who may have experienced more life changes such as marriage, childbirth, divorce, business readjustment, illnesses of family members, death in the family, and so on). Finally, a subjective life change unit (SLCU) score was obtained that yielded a 6-month SLCU total for the original 42 SRE life change questions; SLCU scores were then subtracted from the standard LCU scores for those 42 questions.

Coddington (1972) modified the SRRQ to assess stressful life events in childhood. Using the method in the SRRQ, he constructed a different list of experiences for each of the following groups: preschool age, elementary school age, junior high school age, and senior high school age. The 250 people who did the rating included teachers, pediatricians, and mental health workers. Inter-rater agreement was high, with rank order correlations of $r \leq .90$.

Ruben, Gunderson, and Arthur (1971) assessed the predictive validity of the SRE. A stepwise multiple regression analysis was used with favorable results to predict the onset of emotional disturbance for navy personnel. In another study, Rahe, Mahan, and Arthur (1970) demonstrated a linear relationship between the mean illness rate of shipboard personnel and the magnitude of life change.

Skinner and Lei (1980) conducted a factor analysis using an interactive principal factor model with a least squares estimate. The results suggest that a relatively homogeneous subset of life events can be identified among the SRE items. The six factors isolated by Skinner and Lei are: (1) personal and social activities, (2) work changes, (3) marital problems, (4) residence changes, (5) family issues, and (6) school changes. The clinical population used by Skinner and Lei consisted of 353 individuals who voluntarily sought help for alcohol and/or substance abuse.

Skinner and Lei found an internal consistency reliability estimate of $r = .80$ for the SRE with this clinical population. Often, the 43 life events are scaled by social readjustment weights (the SRRs) to yield a weighted total score in life change units (LCU). However, Skinner and Lei found overlap between the SRE and LCU scores, a correlation of $r = .97$. Also, the reliability estimate, $r = .72$ for the LCU scores, was lower than the SRE. Reliability and validity studies with SRE show variable results. Three reliability estimates of the

SRE that used college students as subjects and allowed only a week between test and retest had high correlations, between $r = .87$ and $r = .90$ (Hawkins, 1957; Rahe, 1974). Rahe (1989) and Rahe, Floistad, and Bergan (1974) reported that when the interval between test and retest was extended to 6 to 9 months, resident physicians obtained correlations around $r = .70$, and the U.S. Navy enlisted men obtained a correlation of $r = .55$.

The potential user of the most recent version of the SRE should consider a number of issues before applying the instrument to clinical and/or research use. The SRE instructions are limited and nonspecific and the lack of carefully worked out pretested instructions is a concern when working with people who are experiencing stressful life events. Furthermore, social desirability and response sets must be assessed, because this issue is not addressed satisfactorily. The SRE could also be enhanced if it employed measures similar to the Likert scale for items. The degree of severity must be assessed for individual items for valid comparability; validity and reliability data might better be presented in tables rather than in the text of articles. Disappointingly little information is available on the application of the SRE to both clinical and normal samples. Until more information is available, the SRE has limited application in clinical settings. While the SRE has done much to identify the importance of assessing stressful life events, it has not kept pace with more recent measures. The SRE requires more sophisticated measurement techniques; however, it stands as an interesting and promising clinical and research tool.

Hassles Scale

The Hassles Scale (Kanner, Coyne, Schaefer, & Lazarus, 1981) consists of 117 hassles involving work, health, family, friends, environment, practical considerations, and chance occurrences. Examples of hassles include misplacing and losing things, declining physical abilities, not enough time for family, concerns about owing money, and pollution. An earlier version of the scale was used in a study of Kaiser Permanente patients with high life events scores. Subjects were encouraged to suggest hassles they had experienced that were not included in the original scale, and a number of these suggestions were incorporated in the current scale.

The Hassles Scale yields three summary scores: (1) frequency, a simple count of the number of items checked, which could range from 0 to 117; (2) cumulated severity, the sum of the 3-point severity ratings, which ranges from 0 to 351 (3 × 117); and (3) intensity, the cumulated severity divided by the frequency, which ranges from 0 to 3. The latter score is an index of how strongly or intensely the average hassle is experienced, regardless of the number (frequency) of hassles checked. The correlations between frequency and cumulated severity are extremely high ($r \leq 0.95$).

The Uplifts Scale is constructed in a fashion similar to that of the Hassles Scale. The Uplifts Scale consists of a list of 135 uplifts that was generated using the content areas of the Hassles Scale as guidelines. Examples of uplifts include relaxing, spending time with family, using skills well at work, praying, and nature.

Results with the Hassles Scale support the hypothesis that hassles are more strongly associated with adaptational outcomes than are life events. The variance in symptoms that can be accounted for by life events can also be accounted for by hassles. Thus, major life events had little effect independent of daily hassles.

The results further suggest that hassles contribute to symptoms independent of major life events; a substantial relationship remained with hassles even after the effect due to life events had been removed. Moreover, the remaining relationship between hassles and psychological symptoms was generally greater than between life events and symptoms.

Questionnaire on Resources and Stress for Families with Chronically Ill or Handicapped Members

The Questionnaire on Resources and Stress (QRS) (Holroyd, 1988) measures stress in families who are caring for ill or disabled members. It assesses the impact of an illness or handicap on the respondent and on other family members and provides information about a variety of problem areas for the respondent, the family, and the disabled family member. Clinical cases used in the development of the QRS included developmental disabilities, psychiatric problems, renal disease, cystic fibrosis, neuromuscular disease, and cerebral palsy.

The QRS consists of 285 self-administered true-false items in 15 subtests, each designed to provide a maximum amount of information about family stress: poor health/mood, excess time demands, negative attitude, overprotection/dependency, lack of social support, overcommitment/martyrdom, pessimism, lack of family integration, limits on family opportunity, financial problems, physical incapacitation, lack of activities, occupational limitations, social obtrusiveness, and difficult personality characteristics.

The QRS was normed on parents of 107 normal children and parents of 329 clinical cases, including children with developmental disabilities, psychiatric problems, and medical illnesses. Results are reported in standard scores, and the overall internal consistency reliability for the 285 items is .96. An extensive rationale for content, criteria, construct, and discriminant validity is available in the test manual.

Psychiatric Epidemiological Research Interview—Life Events Scale

The Psychiatric Epidemiological Research Interview—Life Events Scale (PERI—LES) was developed by Dohrenwend, Krasnoff, Askenasy, and Dohrenwend in 1978 (Dohrenwend & Dohrenwend, 1978) to measure such life events as divorce, loss of job, and other more minor events. A number of these life events have been shown to correlate with the onset of medical and psychiatric illness. PERI—LES was constructed as part of a New York City study designed to develop methods for psychiatric epidemiological research in community populations. During the study, a sample of life events characteristic of New York City was drawn from the experience of the local population. The list of 102 events was constructed from previous lists, the researcher's own experiences, and the events reported in to Washington Heights studies. Subjective events were excluded from the list because, theoretically and practically, they were included in the description of events in their list.

The Dohrenwend group accorded much research effort to assessing the applicability of their scale, and that research suggested that ratings obtained on the PERI—LES yield significant group differences. More of those differences were due to ethnic background than social class or sex variation. However, the PERI—LES has technical weaknesses. First, there is no reliability data on the frequency of occurrence of individual life events; and, second, the samples that judges used in assessing the ratings of life events were too small to assure that group differences were reliable.

The strength of this scale is its potential methodological rigor. Researchers should be able to create improved revisions of their scale that will provide clinical researchers with more valid and reliable estimates of assessing stressful life events. Multiple measures that incorporate lists of stressful life events such as the Dohrenwend group generated must be assessed from a number of perspectives. Estimates of psychological constructs can aid in understanding the interplay of multiple factors as the individual perceives and responds to stressful life events.

Universal- and Group-specific Life Events Scales

The Veterans Administration/University of California, Los Angeles, Life Change and Illness Research Project has developed Universal- and Group-specific Life Change Scales (Hough, 1980), which include weights for their five scales. These scales include standardized weights derived from latent trait analysis of the qualities of scale items.

Hough (1980) and his colleagues developed the scales of life change events to be applied to culturally heterogenous populations. The scales were compiled from a random sampling of adults, ages 21–60, from El Paso, Texas, and from a multilevel clustered sampling of similar adults from Ciudad Juarez, Mexico. Respondents were asked to rate the seriousness of 95 stressful life events. The specific 95 were chosen after a review of events used in previous life events scales. Assessment criteria included interviewer reports on the respondent's ability to do the task, completeness of the responses, the rating of undesirable versus desirable events, the correlation of the individual's scores with his or her group's average, and case-specific criteria. Several scales were constructed on the basis of latent trait analysis. Scale I, the Universal Scale, contains 51 events seen essentially alike by the ethnic groups studied.

There is a scale of life events for each ethnic group as well. These scales contain the Universal Scale items and items scaled for each ethnic group. Items in the scales met two criteria: small mean square error and agreement among groups on the change value assigned to an item. The 51 items in the Universal Scale are those for which response patterns fit the latent trait model and over which there was little disagreement among the ethnic groups sampled. The same criteria were applied within each of the ethnic groups to obtain the group-specific scale items. Statistical analyses suggest that the scales have a ratio quality. Hough and colleagues found ethnic differences similar to the Dohrenwend group. The use of the Hough scales has added a dimension to this early phase of assessing stressful life events and confirmed the importance of distinguishing between universal- and group-specific change variables.

New Haven Life Events Measure

The New Haven group (Paykel, Prusoff, & Uhlenhuth, 1971) employed a checklist format of 60 items to ascertain events that occurred within six months prior to the onset of illness. Events were assessed by activity area—including work, family, and change in health—and by whether these life event changes represented entrances to or exits from a person's social field. A third rating determined whether these events were socially desirable or undesirable. Weights accommodated degrees of desirability to the average person for comparability purposes. The weighted scores were added to estimate the life event stress experienced by the subject. Brown's research group (Brown & Birley, 1968) explored criteria for which life events should be regarded as most and least stressful. Identified criteria included changes in life circumstances or role, subject experiences, health changes, and the personality and influence of relatives and members of the immediate living environment—a key factor. Circumstances and critical life events were documented, with date, context, and verification by significant others in the subject's environment. In the second stage, the research team rated the severity of life events experienced by the subject and compared the findings with the perceived threats that these events might have to the average person. The subject's reaction to the life event was not weighted in the rating. Brown and colleagues were attempting to reduce or eliminate the bias that confused previous studies. Should the identification and scaling of events be accomplished with satisfactory reliability, then researchers have succeeded in eliminating a key bias and have strengthened the process of life events scaling by accommodating the variability of circumstances and events that comprise our daily life experiences.

TRAUMA SCALES FOR VICTIMS OF TORTURE

Allodi Trauma Scale

The Allodi Trauma Scale (Allodi, 1985) is a semi-structured interview schedule developed to document traumatization caused by torture. The 41 items of this questionnaire assesses traumatic experiences associated with political persecution, imprisonment, and disappearance and death of individuals and families. It includes 7 parts: (1) nonviolent persecution, (2) arrest history, (3) physical torture, (4) deprivation during imprisonment, (5) sensory manipulation, (6) psychological torture and ill treatment, and (7) violence to family members. The instrument yields a subtotal for each section, as well as a total score measuring the victim's total trauma/torture experience.

Harvard Trauma Questionnaire

The Harvard Trauma Questionnaire (HTQ) (Mollica, Wyshak, de Marneffe, Khuon & Lavelle 1987) is designed to empirically measure the trauma events and trauma syndromes of individuals who have survived torture and mass violence. The HTQ is available in three Indochinese languages as well as English after the successful validation of the Hopkins Symptom Checklist 25 for anxiety and depression. The HTQ has three sections. The first section covers 17 specific trauma events that are historically accurate for assessing the Indochinese refugee experience. Events range from starvation to the killing of family members. The second section consists of an open-ended question that asks the respondent to describe the most terrifying events that have happened to him or her. The third section elicits 30 symptoms related to torture/trauma experience. Sixteen of these symptoms are derived from the DSM-III-R criteria for post-traumatic stress disorder (PTSD). Initial validation of the HTQ has revealed inter-rater reliability of .93. Preliminary analysis suggests that highly symptomatic respondents have the best test–retest concordance.

Impact of Events Scale

The Impact of Events Scale (Zilberg, Weiss, & Horowitz, 1982) is a 15-item scale measuring two core phenomena of traumatizing stress: (1) ideational and affective re-experiencing of the traumatic events, and (2) defensive avoidance and/or denial of trauma-related memories and emotions. Zilberg et al. report that inter-scale correlations at .42 indicate that these dimensions assess separate but related phenomena. Several studies have demonstrated excellent discriminant validity for the Impact of Events Scale in distinguishing patients with PTSD symptoms from traumatized asymptomatic control subjects in military and nonmilitary populations. Mean scores for veterans of combat have been reported to be 25.6 for the intrusion subscale and 27.7 for the avoidance subscale.

MEASURES OF POST-TRAUMATIC STRESS DISORDER

Structured Clinical Interview for DSM-III-R

The Structured Clinical Interview for DSM-III-R (SCID-R) (Spitzer & Williams, 1987) for post-traumatic stress disorder is an instrument that provides operational criteria for assessing the 17 symptoms of post-traumatic stress disorder within the categories of re-experiencing, numbing avoidance, and physiological arousal. The SCID-R instructs the clinician to ask specific questions, the answers to which determine whether a patient satisfies the diagnostic criteria for major Axis I disorders. For the patient, the number of symptoms positively endorsed is added to arrive at an index of PTSD symptom severity.

Vietnam Experiences Questionnaire

The Vietnam Experiences Questionnaire (VEQ) (Miller & Buchbinder, 1982) is a 70-item measure that has been factor-analyzed into six distinct scale descriptions. Scales include: (1) disturbance in interpersonal relationships, (2) sleep disturbance, (3) hyper-sensitivity, (4) psychotic-like symptomatology, (5) perceived capacity for violence, and (6) motivational disturbances. The VEQ assesses the impact of stressful life events utilizing symptoms associated with post-traumatic stress disorder as well as items similar to the critical items of the Minnesota Multiphasic Personality Inventory (MMPI). Kuder Richardson-20 reliabilities for the six subscales of the VEQ are: (1) disturbances in interpersonal relationships ($r = .68$), sleep disturbance ($r = .75$), hypersensitivity to sound ($r = .74$), psychotic-like symptomatology ($r = .79$), perceived capacity for violence ($r = .91$), and motivational disturbances ($r = .75$). While the VEQ was developed primarily for use with veterans from the Vietnam War, its applicability to other populations who have been traumatized through combat or war-type experiences is recognized.

The Boston Clinical Interview for Post-traumatic Stress Disorder

The Boston Clinical Interview for Post-traumatic Stress Disorder (Gerardi & Wolfe, 1989) is a 122-item structured clinical interview that first includes demographic information and background, a family diagram, and pre-military history. The interview then addresses such factors as home life and school situation, legal problems prior to the military service, involvement in substance abuse, and stressful experiences or significant losses prior to military experience. A third section deals with the military history by carefully evaluating specific stressful life events and patterns of coping. The fourth section of this instrument looks at post-military experience and adjustment, including post-military stressful experiences or significant losses. The fifth section addresses family and social relationships and is followed by a sixth section addressing history of psychiatric treatment, including prescription medications taken and hospitalizations. A medical history section and a section addressing veterans' perceptions of which problem areas need treatment and clinicians' observations are included in this measure.

Clinician-Administered Post-traumatic Stress Disorder Scale

The Clinician-Administered Post-traumatic Stress Disorder Scale (CAPS) (Blake, Weathers, & Nagy, et al., 1990) is a structured clinical interview designed to assess the 17 symptoms of post-traumatic stress disorder outlined in DSM-III-R. In addition, it also assesses 8 associated features. The CAPS provides a means of evaluating the frequency and intensity of the dimensions of each symptom, the impact of the symptoms on patients' social and occupational functioning, the overall severity of the symptom complex, the patient's global improvement since baseline, and the validity of the ratings obtained. The time frame for each symptom measured is one month. A frequency rating of 1 or greater and an intensity rating of 2 or greater reflects significant problems with a particular symptom and should be considered a symptom endorsement.

Mississippi Scale for Combat-Related Post-traumatic Stress Disorder

The Mississippi Scale for Combat-Related Post-traumatic Stress Disorder (M-PTSD) (Keane, Caddell, & Taylor, 1988) is a 35-item Likert scale questionnaire originally developed to assess DSM-III symptoms and various associated features in Vietnam veterans who have been exposed to combat. The Mississippi scale has high internal consistency (alpha = 0.94). A score above 106 has been shown to have high sensitivity (93%) and specificity (89%) in discriminating combat veterans with PTSD from noncombat psychiatric patients and nonpatient veteran populations. Subsequent validation studies of the Mississippi scale have found similarly high levels of sensitivity and specificity in discriminating patients with PTSD from various control subjects without PTSD. The factor structure for this instrument is stable, and the six factors could be labeled as re-experiencing the traumatic experiences, affective interpersonal problems, depression, memory/concentration problems, aggression, and sleep disturbance.

The Civilian Mississippi Scale

The Civilian Mississippi (Keane, et al., 1988) is a 39-item inventory based on the Mississippi Scale for Combat-Related PTSD but adapted to civilian experiences independent of combat or war. Its applicability and utilization include natural disasters and other types of traumatizing experience. The factor structure for this instrument attempts to measure symptomatology consistent with traumatic stress, including sleep disturbance, memory and concentration difficulties, depression, interpersonal problems, affective disturbance, and the re-experiencing of the traumatic event.

The Mississippi Scale—Hostage Version

The Mississippi Scale—Hostage Version (Keane, et al., 1988) is also a 39-item inventory adapted from the original Mississippi Scale for Combat-Related PTSD. This scale assesses DSM-III-R criteria, including symptoms and associated features of victims of hostage-takers. Like the Civilian Mississippi, the hostage version is adapted specifically for the assessment of post-hostage adaptation and focuses on difficulties in memory and concentration, aggression, sleep disturbance, interpersonal difficulties, and re-experiencing the trauma.

The Mississippi Scale for Persian Gulf War Zone Personnel

The Mississippi Scale for Persian Gulf War Zone Personnel (Keane, Wolfe & Gerardi, 1991) is a 38-item measure adapted from the Mississippi Scale for Combat-Related PTSD. The scale is designed to assess the impact of involvement in the Persian Gulf War as related to symptomatology consistent with DSM-III-R criteria for post-traumatic stress disorder. Validation studies of the original Mississippi Scale for Combat-Related PTSD, normed on Vietnam veterans, showed high levels of sensitivity and specificity in discriminating patients with PTSD from various non-PTSD control subjects. Factors measured on the Mississippi Scale for Persian Gulf War Zone Personnel include the six factors labeled re-experiencing the trauma, affective and interpersonal problems, depression, memory/concentration difficulties, aggression, and Sleep Disturbance. The scoring procedures for this measure are consistent with those for the Mississippi PTSD Scale and the other versions of this scale.

Vietnam Era Stress Inventory

The Vietnam Era Stress Inventory (Wilson & Krauss, 1984) is a 44-item inventory developed for use with patients who have had specific exposure to war conflict. Forty items of the inventory have demonstrated, through factor analysis, to identify dimensions of injury or death and exposure to ecological stresses. Reliability analysis has demonstrated high internal consistency for the total scale (alpha = 0.94) and corrected correlations between items and total score average $r = .50$.

PTSD Subscales of the Minnesota Multiphasic Personality Inventory and Minnesota Multiphasic Personality Inventory-2

The MMPI and MMPI-2 (Hathaway & McKinley, 1967) are two of the most standardized measures utilized for the assessment of psychopathology. The MMPI and MMPI-2 PTSD subscales have been used extensively in the study of traumatization and stress. The PTSD subscale of the MMPI consists of 49 items from the MMPI that have been found to discriminate psychiatric patients with mixed diagnoses, but not PTSD, from patients with a PTSD diagnosis. A minimum subscale score of 30 has been used as a criterion indicating the presence of PTSD. Correct classification of PTSD and non-PTSD patients has ranged from 66% to 82% in a variety of studies.

SCALES FOR RELATED PSYCHOPATHOLOGY

State-Trait Anxiety Inventory

The State-Trait Anxiety Inventory (STAI) (Spielberger, Gorsuch, & Lusbene, 1970), used to assess anxiety in two modes, both state and trait, has been used extensively in the evaluation of anxiety and stress. PTSD subjects reported significantly more state and trait anxiety than did normal controls on the STAI and there was a trend toward some directions in PTSD patients compared to diagnostically heterogeneous psychiatric controls.

Beck Depression Scale

A substantially used screening device, the Beck Depression Scale (Beck, Ward, Mendelson, Urock, & Erbaus, 1961) has been utilized primarily for assessing depression and depressive symptoms, but it also has been applied to the study of stress because it is helpful in distinguishing the incidence of traumatizing stress from that of other groups, including nonpsychotic psychiatric controls. Much of the symptomatology associated with traumatizing stress is related, both theoretically and descriptively, to psychiatric depression. Fairbank, et al. (1983) applied the Beck Depression Scale to assess depression associated with PTSD and found that PTSD subjects reported significantly more depression than both normal and psychiatric controls; when measured on other scales, such as the Zung, these subjects showed greater depression than normal controls. Depression scores for PTSD groups were greater than those of psychiatric controls. The Beck Depression Inventory addresses both cognitive and behavioral features thought to be associated with major depression and is considered to be an important diagnostic screening measure in the study of post-traumatic stress.

Millon Clinical Multiaxial Inventory

The Millon Clinical Multiaxial Inventory (MCMI) (Millon, 1982) is a 175-item inventory specifically designed to assess the DSM-III categories of personality disorders and clinical syndromes. Many of these categories are associated with traumatizing or stressful experience and address the etiology and onset potential of the patient for symptoms consistent with traumatizing stress and anxiety. Theory-derived constructs are quantitatively measured to suggest diagnoses and psychodynamics, as well as testable hypotheses about patient history and current behavior. The clinical interpretive report includes a profile and provides a detailed narrative explanation of the psychodynamic relationships between the patient's personality patterns of behavior and feelings and the accurate clinical symptoms exhibited.

DISCUSSION

A growing body of evidence suggests that specific environmental factors can have traumatic and long-lasting psychological consequences. Diagnostic assessment of such traumatizing experiences, however, is addressed through three basic organizational forms of assessment. These three areas are: (1) structured clinical interviews, (2) psychological testing, and (3) psychophysiological evaluations. Miller, Komenchenko, & Krasniansky (1992) thoroughly have defined and summarized the development of both unstructured and semistructured clinical interviews when examining trauma-related disorders. These interviews often were organized with a chronological perspective in mind and surveyed a developmental history as well as situational-specific traumatic factors.

The development of the structured clinical interview for diagnosis of the DSM-III-R— as well as the Jackson Structured Clinical Interview—has helped to organize relevant and important material necessary to assess and diagnosis patients. These interviews have brought to light such factors as current status, which includes relevant background demographics, current living conditions, and educational, vocational, and social situations; factors leading up to treatment, which include important antecedent events and their consequences; and the formation of symptom clusters, with specific attention to the presence of clinical features that reflect cardinal symptoms of traumatizing stress.

A growing body of multiple independent assessment techniques is available to provide helpful diagnostic information about patients with stress-related disorders and traumatization. Such instruments yield information ranging from background factors to specific response measures. The advantages of such instruments include: (1) greater validity and reliability of diagnosis, (2) a greater understanding of patient adaptability and psychopathology through multiaxial models, and (3) multiple sources that provide the necessary ingredients for a convergence of the data obtained. Numerous areas remain in need of systematic research and development, including those dealing with the following considerations:

1. It is important to understand the individual's personality within the context of life events. Biological and intellectual variables limit adaptation.
2. Life events are mediated by several variables, including psychological, social, biological, and physical characteristics of individuals and their interfaces with their environments.
3. Cultural factors are an important influence on the individual's perception of life stress and adaptation. In the development of life events scales, It is essential to consider social and cross-cultural differences in impact of life stress events.
4. The processing and impact of traumatization from man-made versus natural traumas, physical versus psychological traumas, and traumas associated with domestic violence must be clearly differentiated.
5. Age and gender are important ingredients in understanding different adaptation processes, and assessment measures to effectively differentiate for age and gender must be developed.
6. Clustering of life events affects adjustment. For example, individuals adapt well to life events, such as retirement, departure of a last child from home, widowhood, or illness, unless two or more such events occur simultaneously.
7. Beyond the structured clinical interview, better measures to assess variables that affect life events, such as socioeconomic status and interpersonal support systems, must be developed.

Miller and Basoglu (1992) have argued that the assessment of life stress events must include more research studies addressing: (1) how life events contribute to the etiology and onset of illness, (2) the full range of psychological components that contribute to adjusted personality, and (3) the range of effects each stressful life event produces on different types of people. In addition to these areas, biosocial approaches to understanding stressful life events and the individual differences among human beings must be explored. Within the context of each of these charges is the essential need to have instruments that validly and reliably measure this important area of psychopathology. The scientific community must appreciate the efforts made so far to identify and analyze the impact of life stress on psychological and physical adjustment and must continue to support further efforts to refine and understand the impact of stressful life events on our lives.

REFERENCES

ALLODI, F. Physical and psychiatric effects of torture: Canadian study. In E. Stover E. O. Nightingale (eds.), *The breaking of bodies and minds: Torture, psychiatric abuses and the health professions.* New York: W.H. Freeman, 1985.

AMERICAN PSYCHIATRIC ASSOCIATION *Diagnostic and Statistical Manual of Mental Disorders* (3d ed., rev.) Washington, DC: A Psychiatric Association, 1987.

BECK, A. T., WARD, C. H., MENDELSON, M., MOCK, J., & ERBAUG, J. An inventory for measuring depression. *Archives of General Psychiatry,* 1961, *12,* 63-70.

BLAKE, W., WEATHERS, P., & NAGY, R. *Clinician-administered PTSD scale (CAPS).* Boston: National Center for PTSD, Behavioral Sciences Division, 1990.

BROWN, G. W., & BIRLEY, J. L. Crisis and life changes and the onset of schizophrenia. *Journal of Health and Social Behavior,* 1968, *9,* 203-214.

CODDINGTON, R. D. The significance of life events as etiological factors in the diseases of children. Part 1: A survey of professional workers. *Journal of Psychosomatic Research,* 1972, *16,* 7-18.

DEROGATIS, L. R., LIPMAN, R. S., & COVI, L. SCL-90: An outpatient psychiatric rating scale—preliminary report. *Psychopharmacology Bulletin,* 1973, *9,* 13-25.

DOHRENWEND, B. S., & DOHRENWEND, B. P. Some issues in research on stressful life events. *Journal of Nervous and Mental Disorders,* 1978, *153,* 207-234.

FAIRBANK, T. A., & KEANE, T. M. Flooding for combat-related stress disorders: Assessment of anxiety reduction across traumatic memories. *Behavior Therapy,* 1982, *13,* 499-510.

GERARDI, R. & WOLFE, J. *Boston clinical interview for PTSD.* Boston: National Center for PTSD, Behavioral Science Division, 1989.

HATHAWAY, S. R., & MCKINLEY, J. C. *Minnesota Multiphasic Personality Inventory: Manual for administration and scoring.* New York: Psychological Corporation, 1967.

HAWKINS, N. G. Evidence of psychosocial factors in the development of pulmonary tuberculosis. *American Review of Tubercular and Pulmonary Diseases,* 1957, *75,* 768-780.

HOLMES, T. H., & RAHE, R. H. The Social Readjustment Rating Scale. *Journal of Psychosomatic Research,* 1967, *11,* 213-218.

HOLROYD, J. Questionnaire on resources and stress. *Manual for QRS,* New York: Consulting Psychologists Press Inc.

HOUGH, R. L. *Universal- and Group-specific Life Change Scales.* Life Change and Illness Research Project, University of California, Los Angeles (unpublished manuscript).

KANNER, A. D., COYNE, J. C., SCHAEFER, C., & LAZARUS, R. S. Comparison of two modes of stress measurement: Daily hassles and uplifts versus major life events. *Journal of Behavioral Medicine,* 1981, *4,* 1-39.

KEANE, T. M., CADDELL, J. M., & TAYLOR, K. L. Mississippi Scale for combat-related post-traumatic stress disorder: Three studies in reliability and validity. *Journal of Consulting and Clinical Psychology,* 1988, *56,* 85-90.

KEANE, T. M., MALLORY, P. F., & FAIRBANK, J. A. Empirical development of an MMPI subscale for the assessment of combat-related post-traumatic stress disorder. *Journal of Consulting and Clinical Psychology,* 1984, *52,* 881–891.

KEANE, T. M., WOLFE, J., & GERARDI, R. *Mississippi Scale for Persian Gulf War Zone Personnel.* Boston: National Center for PTSD, Behavioral Science Division, 1991.

MILLER, T. W. Advances in understanding the impact of stressful life events on health. *Hospital and Community Psychiatry,* 1988, *39,* 615–622.

————. (ed.). *Stressful life events.* New York: International Universities press, 1989.(a)

————. Conceptual and theoretical problems in measuring life stress. In T. W. Miller (ed.), *Stressful life events.* Madison, CT: International Universities Press, 1989.(b)

MILLER, T. W., & BASOGLU, M. Post traumatic stress disorder: The impact of life stress events on adjustment, *Integrative Psychiatry,* 1992, *44,* 209–217.

MILLER, T. W., & BUCHBINDER, J. Vietnam Experiences Questionnaire (VEQ), an experimental measure for assessing stress in veterans. Lexington, KY: Department of Psychiatry, College of Medicine, University of Kentucky, 1982.

MILLER, T. W., KOMENCHENKO, A., & KRASNIANSKY, A. Assessment of life stress events: The etiology and measurement of traumatic stress disorder. *The International Journal of Social Psychiatry,* 1992, *38,* 672–676.

MILLON, T. *Millon Clinical Multiaxial Inventory Manual* (2d ed.). Minneapolis, MN: National Computer Systems, 1982.

MOLLICA, R. F., WYSHAK, G., DE MARNEFFE, D., KHUON, F., & LAVELLE, J. Indochinese versions of the Hopkins Symptom Checklist-25: A screening instrument for the psychiatric care of refugees. *American Journal of Psychiatry,* 1987, *144,* 497–500.

PAYKEL, E. S., PRUSOFF, B. A., & UHLENHUTH, E. H. Scaling of life events. *Archives of General Psychiatry,* 1971, *25,* 340–347.

RAHE, R. H. A model for life changes and illness research. Cross-cultural data from the Norwegian Navy. *Archives of General Psychiatry,* 1974, *31,* 172–177.

————. Recent life change stress and psychological depression. In T. W. Miller (ed.), *Stressful life events.* Madison, CT: International Universities Press Inc, 1989, pp. 5–11.

RAHE, R. H., FLOISTAD, R. L., & BERGAN, C. A model for life changes and illness research. Cross-cultural data from the Norwegian Navy. *Archives of General Psychiatry,* 1874, *31,* 172–177.

RAHE, R. H., MAHAN, W. J., & ARTHUR, R. J. Prediction of near-future health change from subjects' preceding life changes. *Journal of Psychosomatic Research,* 1970, *13,* 401–405.

RUBEN, R. T., GUNDERSON, E. K. E., & ARTHUR, R. J. Life stress and illness patterns in the U.S. Navy, IV: Environmental and demographic variations in relation to illness onset in a battleship's crew. *Journal of Psychosomatic Research,* 1971, *15,* 221–227.

SKINNER, H. A., & LEI, H. The multidimensional assessment of stressful life events. *Journal of Nervous and Mental Disorders,* 1980, *168,* 535–541.

SPIELBERGER, C. D., GORSUCH, R. L., & LUSBENE, R. E. *Manual for the State-Trait Anxiety Inventory (Self-Evaluation Questionnaire).* Palo Alto, CA: Consultant Psychologists Press, 1970.

SPITZER, R. J., & WILLIAMS, J. B. W. *Structured Clinical Interview for DSM-III (SCID 3/15/83).* New York: Biometrics Research Department, New York State Psychiatric Institute, 1987.

WILSON, J., & KRAUSE, N. *Vietnam Era Stress Inventory (VESI).* New York: unpublished manuscript, 1984.

ZILBERG, N. J., WEISS, D. S. & HOROWITZ, M. J. Impact of Events Scale: A cross-validation study and some empirical evidence supporting a conceptual model of stress response syndromes. *Journal of Consulting and Clinical Psychology,* 1982, *50,* 407–414.

11

The Structured Event Probe and Narrative Rating Method for Measuring Stressful Life Events

Bruce P. Dohrenwend   **Karen G. Raphael**   **Sharon Schwartz**
Ann Stueve   **Andrew Skodol**

AS BARBARA DOHRENWEND AND HER COLLEAGUES pointed out in their chapter in the previous edition of this book (B.S. Dohrenwend, Krasnoff, Askenasy, & Dohrenwend, 1982), clinical interest in stressful life events can be traced back to the 1930s, when Adolf Meyer and his colleagues advocated the use of the life chart in medical diagnosis. The events to be recorded in the life chart were described as follows: "the changes of habitat; of school entrance, graduations or changes, or failures; the various 'jobs'; the dates of possible important births and deaths in the family; and other *fundamentally important environmental incidents*" (Meyer, 1951:53, italics added).

For investigators such as Holmes and Rahe (1967), who were most immediately influenced by Meyer in developing more explicit measures of life events for research purposes, the importance of events was conceptualized in terms of the amount of change and readjustment that the events were likely to bring about. Similarly, Barbara Dohrenwend and her colleagues defined stressful life events as "objective occurrences of sufficient magnitude to bring about changes in the usual activities of most individuals who experience them" (B.S. Dohrenwend, et al., 1982:336). As interest in research on life events and their effects increased, a number of very different definitions of stressful events were put forth that relied on the meaning of the events to the particular individuals who experience them rather than the changes they required as the core dimension for assessing the importance of events (e.g., Brown & Harris, 1978; Cohen, Kamark, & Mermelstein, 1983; Kanner, Coyne, Schaefer, & Lazarus, 1981; Rahe, 1981). For some investigators (e.g., Lazarus & DeLongis, 1983), even events requiring little or no change for most persons could have large personal meaning and hence important implications for the role of stress in health outcomes. This latter ap-

The work leading to SEPRATE has been supported by research grants MH36208, DE05989, MH30710, Clinical Research Center Grant MH30906, Research Scientist Award KO5MH14663 from the U.S. National Institute of Mental Health, the National Institutes of Health, the U.S. National Science Foundation Grant DAR-80-08463, the National Alliance for Research on Schizophrenia and Depression, and the Ann P. Lederer Research Institute. We would like to acknowledge the critical contributions of Bruce G. Link, Rochelle Kern, Patrick E. Shrout, and Jeffrey Markowitz to the development and analysis of the rating procedure and the strong influence of the late Barbara Snell Dohrenwend on the theoretical formulation underlying the approach and the design of the initial research out of which it has grown.

proach involves a major shift, with more emphasis on the role of the person than on the role of the environment in stressful person-environment interactions.

Over the past twenty-five years, stressful life events, conceptualized and measured in different ways, have been shown to be related to a wide variety of physical and mental disorders (e.g., Brown & Harris, 1989; B. S. Dohrenwend & Dohrenwend, 1974, 1983; Lazarus & DeLongis, 1983). There is controversy, however, about the magnitude and interpretation of these relationships. Many reviewers have concluded that life events show only a small relationship with adverse health outcomes (e.g., Cohen & Wills, 1985; Rabkin & Struening, 1976). Others have pointed to problems in interpretation of some reports of substantial relationships because the measures of life events have been confounded with the measures of physical and mental health outcomes (e.g., B. S. Dohrenwend, Dohrenwend, Dodson, & Shrout, 1984; Schroeder & Costa, 1984). For example, the widely used checklist measure of events developed by Holmes and Rahe (1967) includes as events "changes in sleeping habits" and "sexual difficulties," phenomena that could be symptoms of physical or mental disorders. More problems involve questions about the types of specific events people think of when presented with event categories (B. S. Dohrenwend, et al., 1982) and whether the sources of some events, such as divorce and loss of job, are a function of a person's personality and behavior or environmental adversity (e.g., B. P. Dohrenwend, 1974; Rutter, 1986). Such ambiguities in the measures used lead to confusion about the meaning of relationships between life events and health outcomes and consequently about their implications for preventive or ameliorative actions.

This chapter reports steps we have taken to address these problems as they arise in the context of a particular theoretical orientation to studying the role of life stress processes in adverse health outcomes. We first consider previous approaches to measuring life events to illustrate further the nature of the problem. We next describe the theoretical approach that places life events in the context of a broader set of personal and situational variables that are likely to be important in stress processes affecting health. We then discuss the development of a method of measuring life events within this framework. While more needs to be done to establish the reliability and validity of this approach, we feel that the work is far enough along to present the method publicly.

PREVIOUS APPROACHES TO MEASURING LIFE EVENTS

The earliest, best known, and most widely used approach to measuring life events is that developed by Holmes and Rahe (1967), mentioned earlier. They devised a list of event categories such as "marriage," "birth of a child," "divorce," and "death of spouse" on the basis of a study of types of events reported by more than 5,000 medical patients to have occurred close to the time of disease onset. To provide an objective measure of the relative magnitude of the event categories on their list, Holmes and Rahe asked volunteer raters to assign scores to each event category in terms of the amount of readjustment they thought would be required by events in each category. Since then, a host of life event lists using this or similar scoring procedures has been developed, including the Psychiatric Epidemiology Research Interview (PERI) Life Events Scale (B. S. Dohrenwend, Krasnoff, Askenasy, & Dohrenwend, 1982). The measures resulting from this general checklist approach are convenient to use, with simple instructions and formats that facilitate comparable administration across studies. However, studies using such checklists tend to find relationships of low magnitude between events and health problems (e.g., Rabkin & Struening, 1976).

Most of the existing studies of life events and health outcomes have assessed stressful events using one or another of these event category checklist approaches. One of the reasons for their low correlations with health outcomes may be the large amount of measurement error inherent in checklists. The difficulty stems from what we call the problem of *intracategory variability;* that is, the kinds of events included in a given category vary greatly. One indication of the problem can be found in the great variability in raters' estimates of the amount of change and readjustment required by events in each event category (B. S. Dohrenwend, et al., 1982). Such variability suggests that the raters were thinking of very different types of occurrences when assigning magnitude scores to checklist items. Indeed, as we showed in a previous study, the actual events reported by respondents within particular checklist categories were highly variable. We asked respondents who checked a particular item on the list to describe the actual event and the resulting changes (B. P. Dohrenwend, Link, Kern, Shrout, & Markowitz, 1990; Raphael, Cloitre, & Dohrenwend, 1991). When we examined the respondents' descriptions of what actually occurred, we found that the amount of change attributed to events within checklist categories was often as great as changes between categories. For example, some ''deaths of close friends'' turned out to involve long-absent, childhood friends to whom the respondents were no longer close; ''serious'' illness and injury events ranged from episodes of flu and sprained arms to serious heart attacks.

Some investigators have tried to deal with the problem of intracategory variability by using respondents' own assessments of the magnitude of events (e.g., Cohen, Kamark, & Mermelstein, 1983; Rahe, 1983). This approach is based on a different conception of what is important about events, and it involves a change from objective to subjective scoring. While such scoring is likely to improve the association between the events and the outcome, it is also likely to confound the measurement of stress, the independent variable, with the measurement of health outcomes, the dependent variables, especially if these outcomes include subjective distress and psychiatric disorder (e.g., Grant, Gerst, & Yager, 1976; Schless, Schwartz, Goetz, & Mendels, 1974; Theorell, 1974).

The dominant alternative approach in life event measurement to both objectively scored and subjectively scored checklists has been developed by George Brown and colleagues (1974, 1981; Brown & Harris, 1978). This approach is designed to deal with both the problem of intracategory variability in objective scoring of checklist categories and the problem of confounding in subjective scoring. Semistructured interviews are conducted to elicit a detailed description of each life event. Raters then evaluate the likely meaning of an event for an individual by assessing its place within the respondent's personal history and current situation—what Brown and Harris (1978) refer to as ''the person's biographically determined circumstances'' (p. 90). The measures and ratings are explicitly normative—i.e., what most persons in this particular biographical set of circumstances would experience—so that the life event measure is not confounded with distress-laden health outcomes in retrospective studies. Brown and his colleagues have demonstrated the reliability of their ratings and have trained others to replicate them (Tennant, Smith, Bebbington, & Hurry, 1979). Brown and his colleagues report strong relationships between life events thus measured and a variety of mental and physical health outcomes (Brown & Harris, 1989).

Criticism of Brown's method has focused on the most important measure it has produced—contextual threat. While his sternest critics agree that, in general, his approach is preferable to the events checklist method (Tennant, Bebbington, & Hurry, 1981:387), they point to the following central problem:

> Brown and Harris' recent work (1978) combines events with other antecedent variables. . . . The contextual rating of an event is based on social data which also serve as 'independent' antecedent

variables. Thus, employment status, the number of children at home and the nature of the relationship with spouse of lover are used to define the degree of threat and to serve as vulnerability factors. This procedure would tend to produce an association between life events and other antecedent variables which would not be empirical and thus overestimate the causal role of life events in illness. (Tennant, Bebbington, & Hurry, 1981:380).

Thus, Brown's approach implicitly collapses situational and personal variables that may be important risk factors into the single life event measure of contextual threat. The resulting ambiguity is an obstacle to understanding the relationship between life events and disorders as distinct from other aspects of the stress process (such as personal characteristics and on going situations). The reason is that there is no way to tell which of the components of information that go into the global threat rating account for a particular association.

THE STRUCTURED EVENT PROBE AND NARRATIVE RATING METHOD

We have also been developing a new approach to measuring life events that attempts to address these serious problems with previous widely used methods. Since our approach derives from our conceptualization of the nature of life stress processes in relation to adverse health outcomes, we first discuss our theoretical framework and then turn to the method.

Theoretical Framework

We conceive of life stress processes as consisting of three main structural components (B.S. Dohrenwend & Dohrenwend, 1981). The first is the stimulus component of life events, ranging from extreme situations such as man-made or natural disasters to more usual events such as marriage, the birth of a child, divorce, and job loss.

The second component is the ongoing social situation that existed before the occurrence of the life event(s) and that is likely to both affect and be affected by the occurrence of the life event(s). The ongoing situation includes such factors as the individual's occupational circumstances, domestic arrangements, and social network.

The third component consists of the personal characteristics or disposition of the individual exposed to the life event. Such characteristics may also affect and/or be affected by the occurrence of life event(s). These characteristics involve such factors as the individual's genetic vulnerabilities, past experiences with episodes of physical illnesses, psychiatric disorders, other major life events, and personality characteristics that are likely to be related to his or her ability to cope with the events and changing situation.

Figure 11-1 portrays how these components may be related to one another as they affect adaptation and health (B. P. Dohrenwend & Dohrenwend, 1980:187). We believe that relations among these components of the life stress process hold the strongest clues as to whether, to what extent, and how environmental stress induces adverse health changes. Standard, well-validated measures are not easy to secure for any of these components and all of them require conceptual and methodological development. We focus here on life events, the trigger component that sets changes in the other two components or their relations to each other in motion.

Based on analyses of stress experiments with animals and the literature on extreme

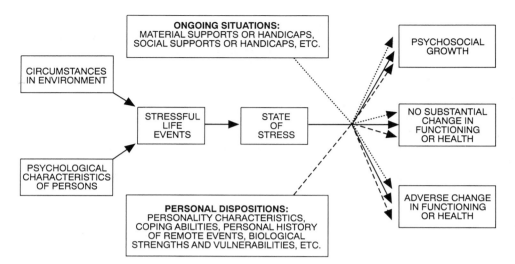

FIGURE 11-1. Components of the life stress process *(adapted from B. P. Dohrenwend & Dohrenwend, 1980).*

situations faced by humans (especially prolonged exposure to combat, prisoner of war experiences, and incarceration in concentration camps), we have extracted what we believe are the most important objective stress-inducing properties of a life event: (1) the event's negative valence (undesirable rather than desirable; representing loss rather than gain); (2) its fatefulness—that is, the extent to which the occurrence of a negative event is outside the control of the individual (the less control over the occurrence, the more stressful) and independent of his or her behavior; (3) the extent to which the event is life-threatening; (4) the magnitude of change in usual activities that is likely to be brought about for an average person experiencing the event; and (5) whether the change is likely to be physically exhausting (B. P. Dohrenwend, 1979; B. P. Dohrenwend & Dohrenwend, 1969; B. P. Dohrenwend & Dohrenwend, 1980; B. S. Dohrenwend & B. P. Dohrenwend, 1983).

Note that in setting forth these objective characteristics of events we are not suggesting that meaning in general and subjective appraisals in particular are unimportant. These elements are central to investigating the nature of coping with objective events and are likely to be affected both by the objective nature of the events and the ongoing situation and the personality characteristics of respondents. They are likely to be related, for example, to the actual (as opposed to normative) amount of negative change experienced, to actual physical exhaustion, and ultimately, to individual differences in health outcome. Meaning and subjective appraisal provide important information about the processes by which the objective components of life stress are related to one another in determining health outcomes.

Introduction to the Interview and Rating Procedure

Our Structured Event Probe and Narrative Rating, or SEPRATE, method of life events measurement attempts to reduce the problem of intracategory variability in assessing important characteristics of the events without confounding the events with health outcomes and without compromising the separate and distinct measurement of each of the above components of life stress processes. In common with Brown and Harris's approach, event narratives are used to increase precision, but distinct from that approach, consideration of stressful characteristics of the ongoing situation and the nature of personal dispositions are excluded in ratings of stress-inducing event characteristics. Moreover, magnitude is conceived of as normative change rather than contextual threat.

SEPRATE entails both interview (see Appendix 11–1) and rating (see Appendix 11–2) components. The interview includes an events checklist and probes to obtain detailed information on the number, dates, and types of events experienced by each respondent. Emphasis is placed on obtaining a descriptive narrative about what led to the occurrence of each event and what took place when the event occurred. The interviewer is instructed to use different probes for different checklist events. For example, if a respondent indicates on the checklist that he or she "broke up with a friend," the interviewer than asks: "Can you tell me what led up to it?" "How was it decided/was it your decision/did you want it?" "Has it ever happened before (with that friend)?" If a respondent reports on the checklist that he or she "returned to work after not working for a long time," the interviewer asks: "What was the cause? Could you tell me about it?" "What were you doing before?" "How long as it been since this took place?" "How was it decided?" "Was it your decision?" "Did you want it?" Our explicit inclusion of structured probes is intended to systematize the types and amounts of information collected in the event narratives and, thereby, reduce variability caused by interviewer skills.

Event descriptions are then abstracted from the interview material and rated by two or more judges (other than the persons who conducted the interview) on the dimensions of theoretical interest, as shown in Appendix 11–2. Some of the ratings are *normative ratings*—that is, judges are asked to rate how "most people" (or the "average person") would experience or respond to the situation as presented in the event description. By rating how much change in usual activities most people would experience following the event described, we avoid confounding this measure of the objective magnitude with the coping ability of the respondent, which could affect the change he or she undergoes. Other ratings are particular to the respondent. For example, in rating a respondent's likely influence on or control over the event's occurrence, we need to consider details of what the respondent and others did that led up to or triggered the event because it is the origin or source of the event that is at issue.

In making these ratings, judges are kept blind to information about other components in the life stress process by carefully stripping such information from the event descriptions to be rated. For example, material indicating respondents' social and personal characteristics (e.g., socioeconomic status, ethnic background), outcome status (e.g., case or control), and emotional response to (as opposed to actions leading up to) the event are removed from event descriptions insofar as possible. In addition, judges are admonished to ignore any remaining material pertaining to respondents' actual responses to the event that may indicate poor (or good) coping. In this way, we attempt to avoid the problem of confounding antecedent and other concurrent psychosocial factors and consequent health outcome variables with measures of life event characteristics.

Respondents' subjective appraisals of events are also separately elicited and quantified during the interview (see Appendix 11–1). By and large, the questions about respondent appraisals tap the same dimensions as those rated by judges. Respondent appraisals, however, are not revealed to judges and are analyzed separately.

Two Studies Involved in Developing and Investigating the SEPRATE Method

Some variant of this general method of life events measurement, and the conceptualization on which it is based, was used in (and evolved from) two substantive studies of the relationship between stress and adverse health outcomes. The two studies differ in some of the questions addressed, in the nature of some of the health outcomes investigated,and in details of the method used. Each has at its core, however, a focus on the three sets of life stress variables described previously and portrayed in Figure 11–1 (recent life events, the ongoing situation, and personal dispositions), and each uses a variant of the general method described above.

The first is a case/control study in New York City of 98 patients with recent episodes of major depression, 65 patients with recent episodes of nonaffective psychotic disorders, and 404 controls sampled from the general population (hereafter, the New York Risk Factor Study). Both cases and controls were drawn from populations with diverse socioeconomic and ethnic backgrounds, including substantial proportions of blacks and Hispanics as well as non-Hispanic whites (B. P. Dohrenwend, Shrout, Link, Martin, & Skodol, 1986; Shrout, Link, Dohrenwend, Skodol, Stueve, & Mirotznik, 1989).

The second study was also a case/control study, with both longitudinal and retrospective components. It examined 151 white female patients suffering from a myofascial pain disorder and 139 controls (hereafter, the Pain Study) (Marbach, Lennon, & Dohrenwend, 1988).

The New York Risk Factor Study is the earlier. As such, its procedure was less developed. In this study, respondents were first given an event checklist, and then asked to describe what happened at the time selected negative events had occurred. The initial purpose of asking for more detail about each event was mainly to help the cases recall the dates of the events so that the temporal relation between event occurrences and the onset of psychotic or depressive episodes could be clearly established. Over 2,500 events were probed in this fashion. When the event descriptions were reviewed, the extent to which intracategory variability plagues the checklist approach became evident (B. P. Dohrenwend, Link, Kern, Shrout, & Markowitz, 1990). Very diverse event descriptions were included in the same, supposedly homogeneous, categories on the life events checklist, which was developed in earlier research (B. S. Dohrenwend, Krasnoff, Askenasy, & Dohrenwend, 1982). Such measurement error would decrease the magnitude of the relationship between events and outcomes. This discovery led to investigation of the intracategory variability problem and to development and initial testing of the SEPRATE method described previously. Using the descriptive information about each event, a reliable rating procedure was developed to measure the important event characteristics of valence, independence, fatefulness, magnitude of change, and life-threatening quality (B. P. Dohrenwend, Link, et al., 1990). It was subsequently possible to show that the resulting approach increased measurement precision. In this investigation, supposedly fateful and disruptive checklist events such as "laid-off" and "death of close friend" were re-evaluated on the basis of the narratives provided by the respondents about what actually occurred. The odds ratios for the re-rated fateful events proved to be almost twice as high as the odds ratios for the checklist measure in this case/control study of depression (Shrout, Link, Dohrenwend, Skodol, Stueve, & Mirotznik, 1989). The problems and questions that arose in making the ratings were also used to improve our method for eliciting information from respondents about the nature of the events.

These improved interview and rating procedures were incorporated into the Pain Study. In this investigation, ten monthly telephone interviews using an events checklist were combined with a retrospective interview at the end of the study using the SEPRATE technique. Relevant portions of this detailed, final interview about life events and related variables are included in the Appendixes. Note especially the set of nineteen probes that are keyed to each event category as well as the detailed probes about changes respondents experienced following events (see Appendix 11–1).

The design of the Pain Study permitted examination of two sets of issues regarding life events measurements. First, it was possible to investigate some aspects of the construct validity of our approach to rating life event characteristics. Specifically, we were able to investigate how the normative change ratings made by judges (blind to respondent appraisals) related to the amount of change reported by each respondent. Unlike controls, pain cases' subjective ratings of negative changes following events significantly exceeded the normative ratings of negative change assigned by the SEPRATE judges. This finding suggests maladaptive coping with the event on the part of the pain cases (Lennon, Dohrenwend, Zautra, & Marbach, 1990).

Second, the longitudinal component of the Pain Study made it possible to investigate further the limitations of the more usual checklist approaches and to compare these approaches with the SEPRATE method (Raphael, Cloitre, & Dohrenwend, 1991). Reports of life events for the preceding month at each of ten monthly interviews (hereafter concurrent reports) were compared to reports for the same ten-month period recalled at its end (hereafter retrospective reports). Analyses revealed problems of inaccuracy inherent in checklists and their inconsistent use by respondents that exacerbate problems of event recall. For example, nearly half the time that an event was reported retrospectively but not concurrently, and more than ten percent of the time that an event was reported concurrently but not retrospectively, it was evident that respondents were referring to the same event in a different event category. In addition, we found that the fall-off in number of events reported as the referenced time period increased was not related to the checklist-based magnitude of change scores, but was related to magnitude scores based on our newer SEPRATE method. In other words, large magnitude events were recalled over a longer period of time than smaller magnitude events only when the definition of magnitude was based on SEPRATE ratings. Given the reasonable assumption that larger events should be recalled more accurately than smaller ones, these findings indicate greater validity of ratings based on the structured probe method than those based on normative checklist methods.

NEXT STEPS

While some tests bearing on the reliability and construct validity of the SEPRATE method have already been conducted and mentioned in the proceeding section, more should be done. For example, interviewers used in the two studies described previously have had graduate degrees or have been studying for graduate degrees in the health professions. We have not investigated systematically the ability of different types of interviewers with different levels of formal education to elicit adequately detailed event narratives from the same respondents. We believe that the best training for an interviewer is not only to conduct supervised interviews with respondents but also to make the required ratings of narratives provided by other interviewers. In this way, the prospective interviewer can see where and how adequate information has been provided, or has failed to be provided, by a fellow interviewer. However, we have not tested this supposition to verify that interviewers who are also trained as raters elicit the most adequate event narratives.

Tests in the New York Risk Factor Study suggest that inter-rater reliability was good among the developers of the method (Shrout, et al., 1989). However, the SEPRATE approach to life event measurement has been, to the best of our knowledge, used almost exclusively by the researchers at Columbia University who have developed the method. Reliability still needs to be established with different raters in other studies, and tests of validity need to be conducted for types of disorders other than depression and with types of events other than fateful ones. It will be especially important to secure accounts from at least one other informant to cross-check and supplement the reports of the respondents. It will also be important to investigate the effects of rater characteristics. Can raters reliably assess events experienced by groups whose sociocultural backgrounds are vastly different from their own?

We have focused on a limited set of event characteristics to be rated. While we think these characteristics are basic, it is likely that other investigators will want to add other ratings, which will probably vary with the different theoretical and subject interests of the researchers. Meanwhile, to increase the usefulness of the method in its present form, we have tried to make the approach more explicit in the attached appendixes. SEPRATE's use by others, as well as ourselves, should improve substantive research and speed its development.

REFERENCES

BROWN, G. W. Meaning, measurement, and stressful life events. In B. S. Dohrenwend & B. P. Dohrenwend (eds.), *Stressful life events: Their nature and effects.* New York: Wiley, 1974.

————. Life events, psychiatric disorder and physical illness. *Journal of Psychosomatic Research,* 1981, *25,* 461–473.

BROWN, G. W., & HARRIS, T. *Social origins of depression: A study of psychiatric disorder in women.* New York: Free Press, 1978.

————. (eds.). *Life events and illness.* New York: Guilford, 1989.

COHEN, S., KAMARK, T., & MERMELSTEIN, A global measure of perceived stress. *Journal of Health and Social Behavior,* 1983, *24,* 385–396.

COHEN, S., & WILLS, T. A. Stress, social support, and the buffering hypothesis. *Psychological Bulletin,* 1985, *98,* 310–357.

DOHRENWEND, B. P. Problems in defining and sampling the relevant population of stressful life events. In B. S. Dohrenwend & B. P. Dohrenwend (eds.), *Stressful life events: Their nature and effects.* New York: Wiley, 1974.

————. Stressful life events and psychopathology: Some issues of theory and methods. In J. Barrett, R. M. Ross, & G. L. Klerman (eds.), *Stress and mental disorder.* New York: Raven, 1979.

DOHRENWEND, B. P., & DOHRENWEND, B. S. *Social status and psychological disorder: A casual inquiry.* New York: Wiley, 1969.

————. Psychiatric disorders and susceptibility to stress: Reactions to stress of varying magnitudes and varying origins. In L. N. Robins and J. K. Wing (eds.), *The Social consequences of psychiatric illness.* New York: Bruner/Mazel, 1980.

DOHRENWEND, B. P., LINK, B. G., KERN, R., SHROUT, P. E., & MARKOWITZ, J. Measuring life events: The problem of variability within event categories. *Stress Medicine,* 1990, *6,* 179–187.

DOHRENWEND, B. P., & SHROUT, P. E. Hassles in the conceptualization and measurement of life stress variables. *American Psychologist,* 1985, *40,* 780–785.

DOHRENWEND, B. P., SHROUT, P. E., LINK, B. G., MARTIN, J. L. & SKODOL, A. E. Overview and initial results from a risk factor study of depression and schizophrenia. In J. E. Barrett (ed.),. *Mental disorders in the community: Progress and Challenge.* New York: Guilford Press, 1986.

DOHRENWEND, B. S., & DOHRENWEND, B. P. *Stressful life events: Their nature and effects.* New York: Wiley, 1974.

————. Life stress and illness: Formulation of the issues. In B. S. Dohrenwend & B. P. Dohrenwend (eds.), *Stressful life events and their contexts.* New York: Prodist, 1981. Reprinted New Brunswick, NJ: Rutgers University Press, 1983.

DOHRENWEND, B. S., DOHRENWEND, B. P., DODSON, M., & SHROUT, P. E. Symptoms, hassles, social supports, and life events: The problem of confounded measures. *Journal of Abnormal Psychology,* 1984, *93,* 222–230.

DOHRENWEND, B. S., KRASNOFF, L., ASKENASY, A. R., & DOHRENWEND, B. P. The Psychiatric Epidemiology Research Interview life events scale. In L. Goldberger & S. Bresnitz (eds.), *Handbook of stress: Theoretical and clinical aspects.* New York: Free Press, 1982.

GRANT, I., GERST, M., & YAGER, J. Scaling of life events by psychiatric patients and normals. *Journal of Psychosomatic Research,* 1976, *20,* 141–149.

HOLMES, T. H., & RAHE, R. H. The social readjustment rating scale. *Journal of Psychosomatic Research,* 1967, *11,* 213–218.

KANNER, A. D., COYNE, J. L., SCHAEFER, C., & LAZARUS, R. S. Comparison of two models of stress measurement: Daily hassles and uplifts versus major life events. *Journal of Behavioral Medicine,* 1981, *4,* 1–39.

LAZARUS, R. S., & DELONGIS, A. Psychological stress and coping in aging. *American Psychologist,* 1983, *38,* 245–254.

LAZARUS, R. S., DELONGIS, A., FOLKMAN, S., & GRUEN, R. Stress and adaptional outcomes: The problems of confounded measures. *American Psychologist,* 1985, *40,* 770–779.

LENNON, M. C., DOHRENWEND, B. P., ZAUTRA, A. Z., & MARBACH, J. J. Coping and adaptation to facial pain in contrast to other stressful life events. *Journal of personality and Social Psychology,* 1990, *59,* 1040–1050.

MARBACH, J. J., LENNON, J. C., & DOHRENWEND, B. P. Candidate risk factors for temporomandibular pain and dysfunction syndrome: Psychosocial, health behavior, physical illness, and injury. *Pain,* 1988, *34,* 139–151.

MEYER, A. The life chart and the obligation of specifying positive data in psychopathological diagnosis. In E. G. Winters (ed.), *The collected papers of Adolf Meyer. Vol. 3: Medical teaching.* Baltimore, MD: Johns Hopkins, 1951.

RABKIN, J. G., & STRUENING, E. L. Life events, stress, and illness. *Science,* 1976, *194,* 1013–1020.

RAHE, R. H. Developments in life change measurement: Subjective life change unit scaling. In B. S. Dohrenwend & B. P. Dohrenwend (eds.), *Stressful life events and their contexts.* New York: Prodist, 1981. (Reprinted, New Brunswick, NJ: Rutgers University Press, 1983.

RAPHAEL, E. G., CLOITRE, M., & DOHRENWEND, B. P. Problems of recall and misclassification with checklist methods of measuring stressful life events. *Health Psychology,* 1991, *10,* 62–74.

RUTTER, M. Meyerian psychobiology, personality development, and the role of life experiences. *American Journal of Psychiatry,* 1986, *143,* 1077–1087.

SCHLESS, A. P., SCHWARTZ, L., GOETZ, C., & MENDELS, J. How depressives view the significance of life events. *British Journal of Psychiatry,* 1974, *125,* 406–410.

SCHROEDER, D. H., & COSTA, P. T. Influence of life event stress on physical illness: Substantive effects or methodological flaws? *Journal of Personality and Social Psychology,* 1984, *46,* 853–863.

SHROUT, P. E., LINK, B. G., DOHRENWEND, B. P., SKODOL, A. E., STUEVE, A., & MIROTZNIK, J. Characterizing life events as risk factors for depression: The role of fateful loss events. *Journal of Abnormal Psychology,* 1989, *98,* 460–467.

TENNANT, C., BEBBINGTON, P., & HURRY, J. The role of life events in depressive illness: Is there a substantial causal relation? *Psychological Medicine,* 1981, *11,* 379–389.

TENNANT, C., SMITH, A., BEBBINGTON, P., & HURRY, J. The contextual threat of life events: The concept and its reliability. *Psychological Medicine,* 1979, *9,* 525–528.

THEORELL, T. Life events before and after the onset of a premature myocardial infarction. In B. S. Dohrenwend & B. P. Dohrenwend (eds.), *Stressful life events: Their nature and effects.* New York: Wiley, 1974.

Now I'll ask you about experiences that people have.

Some of these things happen to most people at one time or another, while some of these things happen to only a few people.

I'll ask you about experiences that you have had since (_____).
MONTH/YEAR

The first questions are about *schooling*.

CARD —Please use card _____ to help with the choices.

1. Since _____ did either of these things happen to you?
MONTH/YEAR

(*CIRCLE PROPER CODE...FOR EACH "YES" CIRCLED DO FOLLOW UP PROBE WHEN ALL LIFE EVENTS ARE COMPLETED.*)

	YES	
	R	No
A. Started school or a training program after not going to school for a long time	1	9
B. Graduated from school or training program	1	9
C. Was unable to enter school or training program	1	9
D. Was unable to stay in school or training program	1	9

Were there any other things about school that happened to you since _____ that we haven't talked about yet or that you just remembered?

Here are some things about work.

2. Since _____, did either of these things happen *to you* or *to your (Spouse/Mate).*
MONTH/YEAR
By spouse/mate we mean anyone with whom you lived during the past year whether or not you're presently living with them.

	YES R	YES Spouse or Mate	No
A. Started work for the first time	1	2	9
B. Returned to work after not working for a long time	1	2	9
C. Changed jobs for a better one	1	2	9
D. Changed jobs for a worse one	1	2	9
E. Had trouble with a boss	1	2	9
F. Did not get an expected wage or salary increase	1	2	9
G. Demoted at work	1	2	9
H. Took a cut in wage or salary without a demotion	1	2	9
I. Found out that was not going to be promoted at work	1	2	9
J. Promoted	1	2	9
K. Got a substantial increase in wage or salary without a promotion	1	2	9
L. Had significant or important success in work	1	2	9
M. Laid off	1	2	9
N. Fired	1	2	9
Q. Quit job	1	2	9
P. Started a business or profession	1	2	9
Q. Expanded business or professional practice	1	2	9

		YES	YES Spouse or Mate	No
		R		
R.	Suffered a business loss or failure	1	2	9
S.	Sharply reduced work load	1	2	9
T.	Retired	1	2	9
U.	Stopped working, not retirement, for an extended period	1	2	9

Were there any other things about work that happened *to you* or *to your (Spouse/Mate)* since _____ that we haven't talked about yet or that you just remembered?

Here are some things about *love* and *marriage*.

3. Since _____ , did either of these things happen *to you* or *to (any of) your*
   MONTH/YEAR
   child(ren)?

		Yes	Yes Child(ren)	No
		R		
A.	Became engaged	1	3	9
B.	Engagement was broken	1	3	9
C.	Married	1	3	9
D.	Started a love affair	1	3	9
E.	Relations with spouse/mate changed for the worse, without separation or divorce	1	3	9
F.	Married couple separated	1	3	9
G.	Divorce	1	3	9
H.	Relations with spouse/mate changed for the better	1	3	9
I.	R—Engaged in marital infidelity	1	3	9
J.	Spouse/mate engaged in marital infidelity	1	3	9
K.	Spouse/mate died	1	3	9
L.	Married couple got together again after separation	1	3	9
M.	Ended a love affair	1	3	9

Were there any other things involving love and marriage that happened *to you* or *to (any of) your* *child(ren)* since _____ that we haven't talked about yet or that you just remembered?

Here are some events related to having *children*.

4. Since _____ , did any of these things happen *to you, to your (spouse/mate),*
   MONTH/YEAR
   (or *to (any of) your child(ren))*?

		YES	YES Spouse or Mate	YES Child(ren)	No
		R			
A.	Birth of a first child	1	X	3	9
B.	Became pregnant	1	2	3	9
C.	Birth of a child after the first	1	X	3	9
D.	Abortion	1	2	3	9
E.	Miscarriage or still birth	1	2	3	9
F.	Found out that cannot have children	1	2	3	9
G.	Child died	1	X	3	9
H.	Adopted a child	1	X	3	9
I.	Started menopause	1	2	X	9

Were there any other things related to *having children* that happened *to you, to your (spouse/mate),* or *to (any of) your child(ren)* since _____ that we haven't talked about yet or that you just remembered?

Here are some events relating to *family matters.*

5. Since _____, did any of these things happen to you?
   MONTH/YEAR

	YES R	N No
A. New person moved into the household	1	9
B. Person moved out of the household	1	9
C. Family member other than spouse or child died	1	9

Were there any other things related to *family matters* that happened *to you* since _____ _____ that we haven't talked about yet or that you just remembered?

Here are some events related to *where you live.*

6. Since _____, did any of these things happen *to you*?
   MONTH/YEAR

	YES R	No
A. Moved to a better residence or neighborhood	1	9
B. Moved to a worse residence or neighborhood	1	9
C. Built a home or had a home built	1	9
D. Lost a home through fire, flood or other disaster	1	9

Were there any other things related to where you live that happened *to you* since _____ _____ that we haven't talked about yet or that you just remembered?

Here are some things about crime and legal matters.

7. Since _____, did any of these things happen *to you* or *to a member of your*
   MONTH/YEAR
   family or *to another person who is important to you*?

	YES R	YES Spouse or Mate	YES Child(ren)	YES Important Other(s)	No
A. Physically assaulted or attacked	1	2	3	4	9
B. Robbed	1	2	3	4	9
C. Burglarized	1	2	3	4	9
D. Involved in a lawsuit	1	2	3	4	9
E. Accused of something for which a person could be sent to jail	1	2	3	4	9
F. Arrested	1	2	3	4	9
G. Went to jail	1	2	3	4	9
H. Got involved in a court case	1	2	3	4	9
I. Convicted or found guilty of a crime	1	2	3	4	9
J. Acquitted or found innocent of a crime	1	2	3	4	9
K. Released from jail	1	2	3	4	9
L. Didn't get out of jail when expected to	1	2	3	4	9

Were there any other things related to *crime and legal matters* that happened *to you, to a member of your family* or *to another person who is important to you* since _____ that we haven't talked about yet or that you just remembered?

Here are some things about money and financial matters.

8. Since _____, did any of these things happen *to you* or *to your (spouse/mate)*?
   MONTH/YEAR

	YES R	YES Spouse or Mate	No
A. Took out a mortgage..	1	X	9
B. Started buying a car, furniture or other large purchase on the installment plan..	1	2	9
C. Repossession of a car, furniture or other items bought on installment plan	1	2	9
D. Suffered a financial loss or loss of property not related to work.............	1	2	9
E. Went on welfare..	1	X	9
F. Went off welfare	1	X	9
G. Had a financial improvement not related to work	1	2	9

Were there any other things related to *money and financial matters* that happened *to you* or *to your (spouse/mate)* since _____ that we haven't talked about yet or that you just remembered?

Here are some events relating to *social life and recreation*.

9. Since our last interview, that is _____, did any of these things happen *to you?*
   MONTH/YEAR

	YES R	NO No
A. Broke up with a friend	1	9
B. Close friend died	1	9

Were there any other things related to social life and recreation that happened to you since _____ that we haven't talked about yet or that you just remembered?

Now some miscellaneous questions.

10. Since our last interview, that is _____, did any of these things happen *to you,* or *to a member of your family,* or *to another person who is important to you?*
    MONTH/YEAR

	YES R	YES Spouse or Mate	YES Child(ren)	YES Important Other(s)	No
A. Entered the armed services	1	2	3	4	9
B. Left the armed services	1	2	3	4	9
C. Took a trip other than a vacation trip..........	1	2	3	4	9

Lastly, here are some questions about *health.*

11. Since _____, did any of these thing happen *to you, to a member of your family,* or *to another person who is important to you?*
    MONTH/YEAR

	YES R	YES Spouse or Mate	YES Child(ren)	YES Important Other(s)	No
A. Physical health improved	1	2	3	4	9
B. Serious physical illness started or got worse ...	1	2	3	4	9
C. Serious injury occurred or got worse	1	2	3	4	9
D. Unable to get treatment for a serious illness or injury..	1	2	3	4	9
E. Serious mental or emotional illness started or got worse..	1	2	3	4	9

Were there any other things related to *health* that happened *to you, to a member of your family,* or *to another person who is important to you* since _____ that we haven't talked about yet or that you just remembered?

12. Did anything else important happen since _____ that I haven't asked you about?
MONTH/YEAR

Yes (*ASK A*) 1
No... 2

A. What was that? (*RECORD VERBATIM AND PROBE AS OFTEN AS NEC-ESSARY WITH: Did anything else important happen? RE-CODE/CORRECT CHECKLIST AS NECESSARY.*)

INSTRUCTIONS FOR FILLING OUT LIFE-EVENTS GRID

*FILL IN PARTS OF THE LIFE EVENTS GRID [APPENDIX 1a] AS DESCRIBED BELOW.

A. TO WHOM EVENT OCCURRED.
B. EVENT ID #. (*LIFE EVENT QUESTION AND ITEM*)
C. EVENT

PROCEED TO LIFE EVENTS TIME GRID IN ORDER TO OBTAIN THE FOLLOWING INFOR-MATION FROM "R".

A. THE MONTH IN WHICH EACH REPORTED EVENT OCCURRED.
B. ORDERING OF ANY EVENTS WHICH OCCURRED IN THE SAME MONTH.

ORDER LIFE EVENTS TO BE PROBED STARTING WITH MOST REMOTE REGARDLESS OF TO WHOM IT OCCURRED, AND ENDING WITH MOST RECENT EVENT. ALL EVENTS ARE INTENSIVELY PROBED. THE PROBES THAT FOLLOW ARE LINKED TO EACH EVENT CATEGORY. THEY ARE INTENDED TO ENCOURAGE THE R TO SUPPLY A NARRATIVE OF THE EVENT THAT IS SUFFICIENTLY RICH IN FACTUAL DETAIL TO EVALUATE THE EVENT'S DESIRABILITY, THE LIKELY MAGNITUDE AND OF CHANGE IN USUAL ACTIVI-TIES ENGENDERED BY THE EVENT, THE EVENT'S FATEFULNESS, ETC. THE PROBES ARE INTENDED TO BE SUGGESTED PROBES AND SHOULD NEITHER BE CONSIDERED MINIMAL OR MAXIMAL QUESTIONS TO BE ASKED. DEPENDING ON THE SPECIFIC CIR-CUMSTANCES OF THE EVENT, ADDITIONAL QUESTIONS MAY BE NECESSARY; SOME-TIMES, A RESPONDENT WILL SUPPLY ALL THE NECESSARY INFORMATION IN RE-SPONSE TO THE FIRST PROBE "COULD YOU TELL ME ABOUT IT?"

*WE HAVE RESPONDENTS COMPLETE ANY SELF-ADMINISTERED QUESTIONNAIRES WHILE THE INTERVIEWER COMPLETES THE LIFE-EVENTS GRID.

INTRODUCTION TO PROBING: (TO BE READ TO RESPONDENT)

Now we are going to go over all of the events you mentioned. We would like you to recall what actually happened.

Please tell me first as much as you can about the facts of what happened. Later, I'll be asking you about your reaction to and evaluation of what happened. Again, I'd like you to avoid telling me right now about your feelings, and to just stick to the facts surrounding the event's occurrence. Let's start with _____.
 [EVENT]

PROBES TO ELICIT LIFE EVENT NARRATIVES

EVENT NAME _____   EVENT I.D. _____

EVENT DATE _____   TO WHOM EVENT OCCURRED (CF) _____

(RECORD ALL RESPONSES VERBATIM)	RESPONDENT AND SPOUSE/MATE	OTHERS
1. What was the reason/cause of (*EVENT*)? Could you tell me about it? *(FOR ILLNESS/INJURY Q'S PROBE FOR SYMPTOMS)*	1. 1A 2A,2B,2C,2F,2G,2H,2I,2J,2K 2M,2N,2A,2T,2U 3A,3B,3I,3K 4A,4B,4C,4E,4F,4G 5A,5B,5C 6A,7L,8D,9B 10A,10B,10C 11A,11B 12B,12C 13	3A,3B,3I,3K 4A,4B,4C,4E,4F,4G 7L 10A,10B,10C 12B,12C
2. Can you tell me what led up to (*EVENT*)?	2. 1A 2C,2D,2E,2M,2N,20,2P,2Q 3B,3C,3F,3G,3I,3L,3M 4D,4H 6B,6C 8A,8B 9A,9B 12B,12C,12D 13	3B,3C,3F,3G,3I,3L,3M 4D,4H
3. What happened?	3. 1B 2E,2L,2R 3D,3E,3H,3J 4I 6D 7A,7B,7C,7D,7E,7F,7G, 7H,7I,7K 8C,8E,8F,8G 12A,12D,12E	3D,3E,3H,3J 4I 7A,7B,7C,7D,7E,7F, 7G,7H,7I,7K 12A,12B,12C,12D,12E
4. How often did you speak the year before he/she died?	4. 3K 4G	3K 46

(RECORD ALL RESPONSES VERBATIM)	RESPONDENT AND SPOUSE/MATE	OTHERS
5. What were you doing before?	5. 1A 2A,2B,2P	DO NOT ASK
6. How long has it been since (*R's ACTIVITIES BEFORE*) this event took place?	6. 2B	DO NOT ASK
7. Did (*YOU*) plan (*EVENT*)? YES....... (*ASK 7A*)....... X NO............................. Y	7. 2T,2U 4A,4B,4C	DO NOT ASK
7A. How was it decided?		
8. Did you play any part in this decision (*OF EVENT*)? YES....... (*ASK 8A*)....... X NO............................. Y	8. DO NOT ASK	3A,3B,3C,3F,3G,3L,3M 4D,4H 10A,10B,10C
8A. What part?		
9. How was it decided? Was it your decision? Did you want it?	9. 1A 2A,2B,2C,2D,2E,2F, 2H,2J,2K,2M,2N,2O, 2P,2Q,2S 3A,3B,3C,3F,3G,3M,3L, 4D,4H 5A,5B 6A,6B,6C 8A,F,8G,8H 9A 10C	DO NOT ASK
10. Was (*NEW EVENT*) better or worse than old situation?	10. 1A 2C,2D,2M,2N,2O,2P,2U 5B	DO NOT ASK
11. Has this happened to others at work?	11. 2E,2F,2H,2I,2K,2M,2N	DO NOT ASK
12. Did you (*HE/SHE*) recover fully? YES ....1 NO..........(*ASK 1*)..........2	12. 12B,12C,12D,12E	12B,12C,12D,12E
1. How are you (HE/SHE) still affected?		
13. To what from what?	13. 2C,2D,2G,2J	DO NOT ASK
14. Has (*EVENT*) ever happened before? YES .(ASK 14A) ....X NO ....Y	14. 2C,2D,2E,2I,2J,2L, 2M,2N,2O,2R,2U 3E,3F,3L 4E 6A,6B,6D	3E,3F,3L 4E 7A,7B,7C,7D,7E 7F,7G,7H,7I,7J 12B,12C,12D,12E

(RECORD ALL RESPONSES VERBATIM)	RESPONDENT AND SPOUSE/MATE	OTHERS
	7A,7B,7C,7D,7E,7F,7G,7H, 7I,7J 8C,8E,8F,8G 9A (specific to that friend) 11A,11B 12B,12C,12D,12E	
15. When do you plan to be married?	15. 3A	DO NOT ASK
16. Who moved out?	16. 3F,3G 5B	3F,3G
17. Who moved in?	17. 5A	DO NOT ASK
18. What kind of discharge was it?	18. 10B	10B
19. Was this event life-threatening?	19. 12A,12B,12C,12D	12A,12B,12C,12D

YES 1
NO.............................. 2
MAYBE 3

QUESTIONS ABOUT RESPONDENT'S SUBJECTIVE APPRAISALS OF EACH EVENT

20. Think about the actual [EVENT]. Before [EVENT], how sure were you that [EVENT] would happen [that you would (EVENT)]? Would you say you were....

absolutely sure..................................... 4
very sure 3
fairly sure... 2
not very sure 1
or, that [EVENT] was completely
unexpected, (you [EVENT] completely
on the spur of the moment)? 0

21. Which of the following terms best describe how you saw [EVENT] at the time it occurred? Would you say you saw it as....

(READ CHOICES 1-6 FOR
EVENTS LIKELY TO BE
GOOD AND 6-1 FOR EVENTS
LIKELY TO BE BAD)

Very good 1
fairly good 2
both good and bad 3
neither good nor bad...... 4
fairly bad.................... 5
very bad?.................... 6

22. To what extent could you have prevented [EVENT]/(made [EVENT] happen)? Would you say its occurrence was....

completely under your control 1
mostly under your control...................................... 2
that you shared control about equally with others 3
that it was mostly under the control of others 4
or, that it was completely out of your control?.......... 5

CHANGES FOLLOWING EVENT

EVENT ID _____ EVENT DATE _____ CF _____

	Column A	Column B
23. As a result of [EVENT] what kinds of changes have you experienced which lasted for more than a week after [EVENT]. By change we mean new things you did or old things you did not do because of [EVENT].		*(FOR EACH "YES" ASK:)* Would you say that [CHANGE] was:

		Mainly good	Mainly bad	About equally good and bad
Has there been a change in.....				
A. Duties or responsibilities at work?	Yes – 1 No – 2 NA – 3	1	2	3
B. Amount or type of work?	Yes – 1 No – 2 NA – 3	1	2	3
C. Relationships with people at work?	Yes – 1 No – 2 NA – 3	1	2	3
D. Financial or money matters?	Yes – 1 No – 2 NA – 3	1	2	3
E. Buying or shopping activities?	Yes – 1 No – 2 NA – 3	1	2	3
F. Relationships with spouse or mate?	Yes – 1 No – 2 NA – 3	1	2	3
Has there been a change, which lasted more than a than a week. . .				
G. Relationships with children?	Yes – 1 No – 2 NA – 3	1	2	3
H. Relationships with other family members?	Yes – 1 No – 2 NA – 3	1	2	3
I. Family routine?	Yes – 1 No – 2 NA – 3	1	2	3
J. Living space at home?	Yes – 1 No – 2 NA – 3	1	2	3
K. Amount or type of housework?	Yes – 1 No – 2 NA – 3	1	2	3
L. Friends - Made new ones or lost old?	Yes – 1 No – 2 NA – 3	1	2	3

EVENT ID _____ EVENT DATE _____ CF _____

23. (Continued)

	Column A	Column B
		(FOR EACH "YES" ASK:) Would you say that [CHANGE] was:

Has there been a change that lasted for more than a week in. . .

				Mainly good	Mainly bad	About equally good and bad
M. Relationships with friends?	Yes	–	1	1	2	3
	No	–	2			
	NA	–	3			
N. Recreation or sport activities?	Yes	–	1	1	2	3
	No	–	2			
	NA	–	3			
O. How much you study or read?	Yes	–	1	1	2	3
	No	–	2			
	NA	–	3			
P. Physical health?	Yes	–	1	1	2	3
	No	–	2			
	NA	–	3			
Q. Sleeping patterns?	Yes	–	1	1	2	3
	No	–	2			
	NA	–	3			
R. Eating patterns?	Yes	–	1	1	2	3
	No	–	2			
	NA	–	3			

Has there been a change, which lasted more than a than a week
. . .

				Mainly good	Mainly bad	About equally good and bad
S. Way of communication with people?	Yes	–	1	1	2	3
	No	–	2			
	NA	–	3			
T. Sexual activity?	Yes	–	1	1	2	3
	No	–	2			
	NA	–	3			
U. Religious involvement?	Yes	–	1	1	2	3
	No	–	2			
	NA	–	3			
V. Political involvement?	Yes	–	1	1	2	3
	No	–	2			
	NA	–	3			
W. Attention to personal or family security?	Yes	–	1	1	2	3
	No	–	2			
	NA	–	3			

EVENT ID _____ EVENT DATE _____ CF _____

24. X. Were there any other changes that I have not asked you about, which lasted for more than a week after [*EVENT*]? That is, new things you did or old things you did not do because of [*EVENT*]?

YES ....(*ASK C D*) 1
NO............(GO TO Q.25)............2

COLUMN C	*COLUMN D*

What were these changes?
(RECORD ONE CHANGE PER BOX BE-
LOW; THEN ASK FOR EACH BEHAVIORAL
CHANGE.)

(FOR EACH "YES" ASK): Would you say that [CHANGE] was:

	Mainly good	*Mainly bad*	*About equally good and bad*
CHANGE 1	1	2	3
CHANGE 2	1	2	3
CHANGE 3	1	2	3
CHANGE 4	1	2	3

(IF NO CHANGES REPORTED IN RESPONSE TO ALL 24 ITEMS IN CHANGE CHECKLIST, CIRCLE I AND SKIP TO Q. 27; OTHERWISE CIRCLE 2 AND GO TO Q.25.)

NO CHANGES..*(SKIP TO Q. 27)*..1
CHANGES *(GO TO Q.25)* 2

25. Of all the changes that you told me about, were any life threatening?

YES ....(*ASK A B*) 1
NO.................(GO TO Q.26)..................2

A. Which one(s) was/were life threatening? *(RECORD VERBATIM)*

B. How is/was your life in danger as a result of [*CHANGE*]? *(RECORD VERBATIM)*

26. Now let me ask you to rate the amount of change that lasted for more than a week after [*EVENT*]. Would you say that [*ALL CHANGES*] amounted to....

Card H		

An extremely large amount of change...............................1
A large amount of change 2
CARD H A moderate amount of change..........................3
A little change 4

(ASK Q. 27 ONLY ONCE-AFTER THE LAST EVENT HAS BEEN PROBED.)

27. Since [*BASELINE DATE*] were you ever exhausted for a week or more; that is, so tired that you had great difficulty performing your usual activities for a week or more?

YES..........(ASK A, B, AND C)..........1
NO 2

A. When was this? *(RECORD VERBATIM)*

B. How did it interrupt you usual activities? *(RECORD VERBATIM)*

C. Was this exhaustion related to any of the events (and changes) we have been talking about?

EVENT ID ———— EVENT DATE ———— CF ————

YES..*(ASK D, E, AND F)*..1
NO.................................. 2

   D. Which events? *(RECORD VERBATIM)*

   E. Which changes? *(RECORD VERBATIM)*

   F. What happened? *(RECORD VERBATIM)*

Step 1: Preparation of event-narratives by editors for coder/judges

(a) Identify each event with:
(1) The respondent ID number
(2) The event ID number (each event for a given respondent should be assigned a unique ID number)
(3) The event category code as it appears in the checklist
(4) The central figure of the event, i.e. the person to whom the event occurred
(5) The date of the event

(b) Type the respondent's narrative description of each event verbatim

(c) Put the narrative descriptions in chronological order of occurrence, from most remote to most recent. Remove events that occurred before or after the time period under investigation.

(d) Edit the event narratives to consist of the objectives facts of what occurred.
(1) Remove evidence of the respondent's status in the outcome or exposure variable under study.
(2) Remove respondent expressions of emotion or other psychological reactions to the objective facts
(3) Remove references to respondents's ethnic background and socioeconomic background and/or other potential risk factors of central research interest.

Step 2: After reviewing the entire sequence of event narratives, coder/judges rate each event on the following basic characteristics of *origin, desirability, magnitude,* whether *physically exhausting* and whether *life threatening.*

In making these ratings, there are some general principles the rater/judges should keep in mind:

1. *BECOME FAMILIAR WITH ALL THE INFORMATION GIVEN ABOUT EACH RESPONDENT BEFORE MAKING ANY JUDGMENTS.* This means reading through all of the material and thinking about it. Formulate, as fully as possible, an answer to the question, "What is going on for this individual?" Then go back and do the ratings for each reported life event in chronological order.

2. Pay close attention to the objective facts reported by the respondent. However, what is reported will usually include some "distortion." For example, respondents may need to deny or exaggerate painful experiences or want to present a "self" that fulfills an ideal image. Try to stay close to descriptions of what happened and *AVOID RELYING ON THE RESPONDENT'S EVALUATION OR INTERPRETATION OF THOSE FACTS.* We do ask respondents for their assessment of their life events and code that information elsewhere.

3. The extent to which raters agree with each other will be assessed. It is *EXTREMELY IMPORTANT THAT RATERS DO NOT DISCUSS THE MATERIAL WHILE DOING THE RATING WITH OTHER CODERS.* We will be using statistical procedures to assess the extent to which coders "agree". For these procedures to be valid, the ratings must be made independently of each other. Joint discussions violate this condition. It is also important that raters write down any responses, problems, concerns, etc. you have on the coding sheet itself. There will be meetings for comparing ratings and discussing reasons for differences among coders.

A. *Fatefulness.* The major distinction to be made here is whether event occurs in a person's life more because of his or her state, behavior or actions or because of circumstances in his or her environment. To make this determination, the rater must consider (a) the *prelude* to the occurrence of the event and (b) what happened at the time of the *immediate occurrence* of the event. For example, in an event like "being fired", the prelude might consist of repeatedly being late to work and not getting ones's job done;

the immediate occurrence might be being told by your boss that you are fired. The ratings in this example would be as follows:

	Prelude	*Occurrence*
0 – Completely determined by external circumstances		X
1 – Mostly determined by external circumstances		
2 – Equally determined by R's behavior and external circumstances		
3 – Mostly determined by R's behavior	X	
4 – Completely determined by R's behavior		

B. *Desirability.* This is the narrative rating that addresses the questions: Would most people (the average person) who experience this event find it, at the time of its occurrence, desirable or undesirable? The categories to be rated are:
1. Mainly desirable at time of occurrence
2. Mainly undesirable at time of occurrence
3. About equally desirable and undesirable at time of occurrence.

For most events, this rating will be clear-cut. For some, however, it may be difficult. Raters should pay close attention to the context in which the event occurs (referring if necessary to other events being rated) and ignore statements of the respondent's reaction. This is a rating of how desirable most people, placed in the described situation, would find the event when it occurred.

C. *Magnitude.* Magnitude is measured in terms of the amount of change in usual activities lasting at least a week that most people (*the average person*) would undergo as a consequence of the event. Usual activities are those that characterize family relations, work, and non-work-related social and leisure activities. Change consists of new things done and/or things no longer done in these domains of activity. These ratings are made in the following graded categories; note that changes, however large, lasting less than a week are scored "5".
1. An extremely large amount of change lasting week or more. (e.g., Woman pregnant with her first child, experiences sudden death of her husband)
2. A large amount of change lasting a week or more. (e.g., Man's wife gave birth to a stillborn child that would have been their first and that both wanted)
3. A moderate amount of change lasting a week or more. (e.g., A woman's husband suffered a bad break of his arm and was unable to work, and had to stay home for a month)
4. A little change lasting a week or more. (e.g., A man completed one job and started another that required application of the same skills)
5. No change lasting a week or more. (e.g., A woman's husband's uncle who they rarely saw or kept in touch with died)

D. *Severity* (illness and injury events only). Illness and injury for events occurring to the respondent are rated for *severity* and *lethality* by physicians and/or other medically knowledgeable judges using the Wyler index of severity and the Hinkle index of lethality as guides (Wyler, Masuda, & Holmes, 1968; Hinkle, Redmont, Plummer, & Wolff, 1960).

E. *Likelihood of inducing exhaustion*: This rating assesses whether the event and/or changes stemming from the event would lead to physical exhaustion for most people (the average person). The ratings are as follows:
1. Event only leads to exhaustion
2. Change only leads to exhaustion
3. Both changes and events lead to exhaustion
4. Neither change nor event lead to exhaustion

F. *Life Threatening*: This rating addresses whether the event and/or changes stemming from the event would be life threatening for most people (the average person). Medically knowledgeable raters may be required for illness and injury events (see C). The rating categories are as follows:

1. Event only is life threatening
2. Change only is life threatening
3. Both event and changes are life threatening
4. Neither event nor changes are life threatening

Step 3: Additional rating depending on theoretical interests of investigators and subject matter of investigation.

A. Our suggestions
   1. Linkages or interdependencies among events (i.e., loose links: a distal event is sequentially related to the proximal event, but the distal event is a necessary but not sufficient condition for occurrence of the proximal event; close links: events where one event directly implies the occurence of the other event, such as "finishing school" implying "starting school".
   2. Anticipatability (this is reported by respondents in the section on subjective appraisals by respondent. It is difficult to rate objectively.
   3. Altruism (does event involve provision of help by respondent to others?).
   4. Positive vs. negative impact on developmental stages.
   5. Positive vs. negative impact on socioeconomic security and achievement
   6. Positive vs. negative impact on domestic relations.

Step 4: The quality of the data and/or raters confidence in their ratings should be scored for all event ratings central to the investigation, using the following categories:

Quality of data for assessing (*dimensions*), (e.g., magnitude)
1. Data very adequate
2. Fairly adequate
3. Inadequate

Raters confidence in his/her scoring of (*dimension*):
1. Very confident
2. Somewhat confident
3. Not very confident

Step 5: As a check on possible confounding of rating with the outcome or exposure under study, raters should indicate their best estimate of the respondent's status on the variable of interest, e.g., 1 = case, 2 = control; 1 = exposed to risk factor, 2 = not exposed.

REFERENCES

HINKLE, L. E., REDMONT, R., PLUMMER, N., & WOLFF, H. G. An examination of the relation between symptoms, disability, and serious illness, in two homogeneous groups of men and women. *American Journal of Public Health*, 1960, *50*, 1327–1336.

WYLER, A. R., MASUDA, M., & HOLMES, T. H. Seriousness of illness rating scale. *Journal of Psychosomatic Research*, 1968, *11*, 363–374.

12

Self-report Measures of Stress

Leonard R. Derogatis   Helen L. Coons

As mentioned in the first edition of the *Handbook of Stress,* the inauguration of formalized self-report measurement is typically attributed to Galton (1883), while application of the method of self-report to the study of emotional integration was first implemented by Woodworth (1918). Woodworth's Personal Data Sheet, developed as a screening test for psychiatric disorder in World War I, serves as the prototype for all subsequent self-report measures of psychological distress. Although *stress* and *distress* are not equivalent constructs, the measurement of psychological distress has direct relevance for stress assessment because of the pervasive tendency for measures of *distress* to be employed as prima facie evidence of stress (see Coyne & Downey, 1991).

In this review of self-report stress measures, we forego a reexamination of the fundamental characteristics of the self-report modality. The basic features of self-report measurement are well-known to most readers, and for those who wish to reassess them, the first edition of this chapter (Derogatis, 1982) provides an overview. Instead, we would like to proceed directly to the relationship between stress theory and stress measurement and attempt to highlight both the direction and the guidance that the theory provides, as well as the constraints and limitations it imposes on the operations of measurement. As was true of the chapter in the earlier edition of this book, the present review is not intended as a comprehensive review of stress measurement. This limitation is particularly necessary in light of the recent observation by Vingerhoets and Marcelissen (1988) that the number of published reports on stress in behavioral science journals tripled between 1976 and 1985. Simply enumerating the psychological test instruments that have been developed to operationalize stress represents an encyclopedic task. Readers interested in comprehensive reviews of such instruments are referred to Conoley and Kramer (1989); Ciarlo, Brown, Edwards, Kiresuk, and Newman (1986); or Corcoran and Fischer (1987). Here we selectively focus on those methods that possess a productive history in stress research, with more attention to recent developments that exhibit promise.

THEORIES OF STRESS AND THE STRUCTURE OF MEASUREMENT

Science is such that the nature of the theories proposed frequently dictates operational definitions and through these specifies, or at least imposes a structure upon, the nature of measurement. Stress research is no exception in this regard. However, because of the com-

200

plex and sometimes contradictory array of stress theories, stress measurement has developed via a multitude of operational formats. Self-report is, nevertheless, the primary modality for stress measurement, because so many prominent stress theories emphasize intrapsychic cognitive processes (e.g., appraisal, coping) and/or emotional states (e.g., anxiety, depression) as being central to the definition of stress. In spite of the fervent desire of most investigators in the area to have more objective measures of stress, fundamental biological markers (e.g., neurotransmitters, corticosteroids, neuropeptides) lack sufficient specificity. Alternately, phenomenological methods (e.g., clinician ratings, consensual judgments of stimulus values) either introduce an alternative source of bias or fail to evaluate the personal valences that stressors may have for each individual under study. This being the case, self-report, with all of its criticisms of subjectivity, is and will remain a cardinal method of stress assessment.

Classically, theories of stress have been partitioned into three types: stimulus-oriented theories, response-oriented theories, and interactional, or transactional, theories (Lazarus, 1966). More recently, additional models have been developed that represent hybrids of previous models (e.g., Henry & Stephens, 1977) as well as a number of new theoretical approaches (e.g., Hobfoll, 1989). In spite of energetic theory development during the recent decade, few contemporary stress measures were developed through a strategies determined by stress constructs. Most have been adapted as stress measures because the construct(s) they operationalize were judged to represent, *a posteriori,* acceptable definitions of stress. In this chapter, we address the three traditionally defined classes of theories as well as newer theoretical developments before turning directly to specific stress measures.

Stimulus-oriented theories view stress as a potential residing within the stimulus provided by the organism's environment. According to this approach, those aspects of the environment that increase demands upon or disorganize the individual impose stress upon him or her. Cox (1978) points out that stimulus theorists frequently use an engineering analogy, which possesses surface appeal although it often is too simplistic a model for human stress phenomena. The engineering model essentially posits that each individual has an innate capacity to withstand environmental stressors (i.e., resiliency); when the cumulative stress experienced is greater than the individual's tolerance, he or she undergoes deterioration in function—the reaction to stress. Such approaches focus measurement efforts on the characteristics of the individual's environment (e.g., life events, time demands, external and internal noxious conditions) and attempt to utilize instruments that will accurately reflect cumulative environmental stress.

Certain stimulus-based theorists (e.g., Elliot & Eisdorfer, 1982) distinguish among different classes of stimulus stressors and their relative capacities to induce stress. These particular theorists distinguish between: (1) *acute, time-limited stressors,* such as confronting an aggressive dog on the street or awaiting the results of a medical laboratory test; (2) *stressor sequences,* such as unemployment or death of a family member; (3) *chronic intermittent stressors,* like final examinations for students, periodontal surgery, or learning to drive a car; and (4) *chronic stressors,* such as a hostile supervisor on the job, a chronic and debilitating medical illness, financial strains, or an unremitting sexual dysfunction. These theorists take a normative approach to defining events and occurrences as stressful; if the event typically leads to psychological distress, behavioral disruption, or deterioration in performance then it is characterized as a stressor. Similarly, Vingerhoets and Marcelissen (1988) distinguish seven additional classes of stressors beyond those categorized as traditional life events—among them, *daily hassles.*

With regard to daily hassles, Lazarus and his colleagues (DeLongis, Coyne, Dakof,

Folkman, & Lazarus, 1982; Lazarus & DeLongis, 1983) have taken the lead in identifying the stress-inducing potential of relatively mundane, chronic daily events. These investigators have shown that daily hassles not only parallel major life events in their potential to engender stress, but have an even stronger relationship than traditional life events measures in predicting physical health status (DeLongis, et al., 1982; Kanner, Coyne, Schaefer, & Lazarus, 1981). *Response-oriented theories* define stress in a different light. According to this approach, the response of the individual or organism to the events of the environment defines the presence of stress. In particular, the pattern and amplitude of responses have been used as operational measures of stress. Response definitions may be neurobiological (e.g., levels of monoamines, neuropeptides, corticosteroids), physiological (e.g., galvanic skin response, blood pressure, muscle tension), or psychological (e.g., negative affect states, degree of symptomatic distress).

Response-oriented theories of stress find their modern beginnings in the work of Cannon (1929, 1932), who essentially investigated the responses of organisms to extreme variations in the physical environment. A response-oriented definition was also adopted by Selye (1950, 1970) and elucidated in his theory of the *general adaptation syndrome*. More recent theories arising from this position tend to be more interactional (e.g., Henry & Stephens, 1977; Kagen & Levi, 1974); however, they continue to define stress in terms of response variables and hold that this response pattern is a precursor to, or instrumental in, the development of functional derangement and diseases. When defined in psychological terms, response-oriented models tend to focus assessment on measures of disorganized or maladaptive functioning. Psychological symptom inventories, affect and mood scales, and instruments reflecting general psychological adjustment have been utilized explicitly or implicitly to define stress by these theorists. At the biological level, exciting contemporary research is elucidating the pivotal functions of the neuropeptides as mediators between psychological and physiological functions in stress states (Blalock, 1989; Daruna & Morgan, 1990); however, such operations are beyond the purview of self-report.

Interactional theories are held by the third major group of stress theorists—those who emphasize the characteristics of the organism as major mediating mechanisms between the stimulus characteristics of the environment and the responses they invoke. Interactionist theorists are critical of unelaborated stimulus and response theories because both of these orientations dismiss the important variable of the person in the stress equation and, with it, the extensive number of major mediating characteristics that form the basis for individual differences. Many theorists with this orientation go a step further in insisting that theirs is actually a *transactional* approach: not only does the individual mediate the impact of environmental stimulus upon responses, but, in addition, the perceptual, cognitive, and physiological characteristics of the individual affect and become a significant component of the environment (Cox & MacKay, 1976; Lazarus, 1976, 1981). These theorists describe a dynamic, cybernetic system in which reciprocal interactions occur between the individual's cognitive, perceptual, and emotional functions, on the one hand, and the characteristics of the external environment on the other. Feedback pathways allow for constant interplay among the components of the system and result in a dynamic equilibrium.

During the initial phases of their development, transactional theories did not provide a strong impetus for new developments in stress measurement, in large part because of the inherent difficulties of measurement in a constantly changing system. Transactionalists hold that the perceptual, cognitive, and emotional mediating processes of the individual actively affect the *demand characteristics* of the environment, thus resulting in a system that is constantly changing. For these theorists, the ongoing, active relationship between the person's adaptive mechanisms (i.e., coping) and the stimulus properties of the environment is central to the definition of stress. Such a definition implies that reliable measurement of the stimulus field, the response pattern, and/or the stable mediating traits of the individual is insufficient to capture the essence of the phenomenon, since the dynamic relationship among them is constantly altering component values. The conundrum may be more apparent than real, however, in that all measurement, even of dynamic systems, must have a stable time referent. More recently, investigators with transactional approaches have showed a greater interest in developing innovative measurement methods, techniques more consistent with what Lazarus (1981) has identified as "ipsative-normative research designs."

Several contemporary interactional theories of adjustment to stressful events share the conceptual notion that an individual's private beliefs about the event play a central role in the coping process. Lazarus's model is perhaps the best known example of a transactional theory that emphasizes primary and secondary cognitive appraisal of the stressor (Folkman & Lazarus, 1988a; Lazarus & Folkman, 1984). Taylor's (1983) theory of cognitive adaption to threatening events attempts to explain adjustment with three themes or factors including: "a search for meaning in the experience, an attempt to regain mastery over the event in particular, and over one's life more generally, and an effort to restore self-esteem through self-enhancing valuations" (p. 1161). These constructs, as well as the concept of selective evaluation, have been used to understand women's reactions to breast cancer (Taylor, Lichtman, & Wood, 1984) and victimization (Taylor, Wood, & Lichtman, 1983).

Leventhal's common sense theory of illness representations attempts to explain individual reactions to health threats (Leventhal, Leventhal, & Schaeffer, in press; Leventhal, Nerenz, & Steele, 1984; Nerenz & Leventhal, 1983). Private beliefs or representations about an illness and its treatment may include six attributes: the disease symptom, its label, its cause, its duration or timeline, its consequence, and its controllability or cure (Leventhal & Diefenbach, in press). Thoughts about the illness guide coping behavior aimed at both objective and emotional reactions. Individuals monitor or appraise the outcome of their coping efforts, which in turn affect their perceptions of the health threat and the emotional response to it (Leventhal, Leventhal, & Schaeffer, in press).

These interactional theories provide frameworks to understand how individuals cope with stress in general and health threats in particular. In contrast, the Double ABCX Model of Family Adaption to Stress advanced by McCubbin and his colleagues (Lavee, McCubbin, & Patterson, 1985; McCubbin & Patterson, 1983; Patterson & McCubbin, 1983a) has been developed to account for variability in responses to threatening situations within and across families. The theory has guided research on family reactions to chronic physical conditions—cerebral palsy, cystic fibrosis, and cancer—natural disasters, war separation and reunion, and crisis proneness (Koch, 1985; McCubbin, Cauble, & Patterson, 1982; McCubbin & Patterson, 1982, 1983; Patterson & McCubbin, 1983b). The Double ABCX model attempts to explain adjustment during and following a stressful event with multiple, interacting, individual, family, and social factors. Adaption is reciprocal in the family system insofar as reactions to a threatening event for specific individuals are affected by the responses of other relatives in the family unit. The Double ABCX model also views adaptation as a continuum and thus may be used to account for the range of reactions common among individuals and families coping with stressful events. This interactional family model has led to the development of self-report measures that assess family levels of stress. Some of these instruments are reviewed in the later section on interactional measures.

SELF-REPORT MEASURES OF STRESS

Stimulus-oriented Measures

As mentioned previously, stimulus-oriented stress research focuses on the intrinsic potential for stress in the environment. Logically then, measurement derived from such a position would address the significant characteristics of the environment that impinge upon the individual and would include methods that differentially assign weights or quantify the stress value of environmental stimuli. Although numerous aspects of the environment can be demonstrated to be stress-inducing (see Weitz, 1970), few approaches have given rise to a consistent psychological measurement strategy. An exception to this trend is life events research. This body of research is the primary focus of our review of stimulus-oriented measures.

It is worthwhile to note at the outset that research on the impact of life events is not a mid-century innovation, although most tend to date it to the past few decades. As Rahe (1978) accurately observed, Adolph Meyer, the first Henry Phipps Professor of Psychiatry at Johns Hopkins, made life events a central part of his theoretical model and attempted to relate such events to the medical status of individuals through his "life chart" method (Meyer, 1951).

Modern research on life events can be dated to the publication of the first version of the *Schedule of Recent Experience* (SRE) (Hawkins, Davies, & Holmes, 1957), or more precisely to its revision (Rahe, Meyer, Smith, Kjaer, & Holmes, 1964). The original SRE contained forty-two items and was conceived as a life events incidence measure. Although many minor alterations have occurred through the years (Rahe, 1978), the forty-two original items have remained by and large intact. Rahe (1974) subsequently integrated thirteen "productive new life change questions" with the original set and added instructions for subjective life changing scaling. According to Rahe, the Recent Life Changes Questionnaire (RLCQ) was designed for prospective research on life change and illness.

A source of confusion in this area of stress research stems from the fact that a parallel program of studies has been conducted by these same investigators on *life change scaling*. The initial study in this series was designed to measure the magnitude of adjustment associated with each of the 42 events (Holmes & Rahe, 1967). The investigators utilized direct magnitude estimation, a psychological scaling technique, to arrive at mean life change scores for the forty-two events. The instrument developed was termed the Social Readjustment Rating Questionnaire (SRRQ), and the mean values derived from this scaling exercise became labeled *life change units* (LCUS) (Rahe, McKeen, & Arthur, 1967). When the life events included in these studies are ranked-ordered by mean LCU score, the resulting scale is termed the Social Readjustment Rating Scale (SRRS) (Holmes, 1979).

Despite the limitations intrinsic to a stimulus-oriented definition of stress, life events scales have served as sensitive, predictively valid measures of the construct. These measures tend to be less affected by response biases and memory distortions than are many others, and through the definition of stress as a cumulative phenomenon they facilitate the summation of differential event weights (including unit weights) to achieve a total stress score. These scores then may be used in nomothetic or ipsative designs (i.e., studies that contrast the subject's status with his or her own previous status rather than with normative values derived from a group) to evaluate the relationships of stress to disease, job performance, psychiatric symptoms, or many other variables.

A large number of empirical studies have demonstrated correlations between life events and various indexes of health status. Rahe (1968) demonstrated an affiliation between life stress and deterioration of health. Rahe and Lind (1971) subsequently found a relationship between life events and sudden cardiac death, the mechanisms for which were thoughtfully reviewed by Engel (1971). Edwards (1971) also observed a link between life events and myocardial infarction, as did Theorell and Rahe (1971). Gorsuch and Key (1974) demonstrated a relationship between life stress and complications with pregnancy and birth. Furthermore, both Clive and Chosey (1972) and Marx, Garrity, and Bowers (1975) confirmed an association between life events and health. The general conclusion of these studies seems to be that life events reduce resistance to disease in a nonspecific fashion, so that the individual's general susceptibility to illness is increased by the cumulative, adverse effects of life stress.

Consistent associations have also been reported between life events and psychiatric symptomatology. Paykel and his colleagues (1969) observed a significant relationship between life stress and the presence of depressive disorder, a connection confirmed by Markush and Fayero (1974), Ilfeld (1977), and Warheit (1979). Meyers and his associates (Meyers, Lindenthal, & Pepper, 1971, 1972) and Dekker and Webb (1974) also demonstrated a clear association between life events and the prevalence of psychiatric disorders, as did Uhlenhuth and Paykel (1973) with psychiatric severity. Barrett (1979) published a comprehensive review of the relationship between psychiatric disorder and life stress, as have Dohrenwend and Dohrenwend (1974) and Rabkin and Struening (1976). More recently, a number of theorists have raised questions concerning the possibility of a serious confounding of the relationships between life events and psychological symptoms (Cooper, 1988; Dohrenwend, Dohrenwend, Dodson, & Shrout, 1984). They point to evidence suggesting that life events stress measures are significantly confounded with symptoms of psychological distress, so that the affiliation between life events and psychiatric disorders is artificially inflated. However, Lazarus, DeLongis, Folkman, and Gruen (1985) present both data and counterarguments concerning the criticism of confounded measures in stress research.

The issue of potential confounding is not the only criticism leveled at life events measures. General conceptual and methodological critiques of the approach have raised additional serious questions. To begin with, the original assumptions concerning life events stress held that the desirability of events was irrelevant to their potential to produce stress; the cumulative impact of life change associated with the events was identified as the etiologic agent (Holmes & Rahe, 1967). Subsequent research has argued strongly against this position. Brown (1974) seriously challenged the idea that profoundly negative events are no more stressful than positive events. Furthermore, Vinokur and Selzer (1975) demonstrated convincingly that stress-related measures of affect and symptoms correlated selectively with negative, as opposed to positive, life events. Subsequently, Zeiss (1980) demonstrated a high correlation between LCU scores and aversiveness of events, and Bryne and White (1980) showed that life events as discriminators of patients with myocardial infarction have little power unless the patients' subjective interpretations of the events are considered. To increase the predictive power of life change assessment, Horowitz and his colleagues (Horowitz, Wilner, & Alvarez, 1979) developed a life events scale that measures the subjective impact of the events.

Another problem with life stress measures concerns the differential weighing schemes for events. The LCU scores computed from the differential weights of the SRRS are widely used in life stress studies, as are other differential weighting systems. Evidence is accumulating that differential weighing of life events may be predictively irrelevant. Grant, Sweetwood, Gerst, and Yager (1978) contrasted four different weighting schemes (including SRE unit weights) and found no appreciable enhancement of event-symptom correlations associated with the differential weighing. Similarly, predicting the outcome from psychometric theory, Lei and Skinner (1980) demonstrated a correlation of .97 between SRE unit weights and differential weights developed from the SRRS. Further, they showed that the SRRS approach results in a reduction of internal consistency reliability. These investigators also showed high SRE-SRRS correlations (i.e., .93–98) when life events scores were dimensionalized into six subdomains via factor analysis.

In addition to these problems, the issue of dimensionality has represented a persistent dilemma for life stress instruments (Miller, Bentz, Aponte, & Brogan, 1974; Rahe, Pugh, Erickson, Gunderson, & Rubin, 1971). Typically, life events instruments have represented life stress as undimensional, with events contributing to an overall stress score. If there are distinct dimensions or domains to life events stress, then a single overall score can easily obscure significant relationships between such specific dimensions and important outcome variables as disease, psychiatric disorder, or job performance. Exemplifying this difficulty, Skinner and Lei (1980) determined six life event dimensions through factor-analysis in a sample of 353 alcohol and drug abuse patients. They demonstrated, as one would expect, that internal consistency reliability estimates for these scales, equal in length to the SRE, were significantly higher than that for the unidimensional SRE. More importantly, they were able to show somewhat higher correlations for specific dimensions with important health and demographic variables.

More general critiques of life events research have also been forthcoming. Cleary (1980) cited ten methodological problems that have plagued this area of research, Thoits (1983) evaluated work relating life events to psychological health, and Schroeder and Costa (1984) critically reviewed research relating life events to physical well-being. Although the general operating assumption underlying life events research has been that the environment and the individual are independent entities, there is increasing evidence that certain persons actively instigate higher levels of life events via their behavior and adaptive styles (Monroe, 1989). Following in this line of investigation, McGuffin, Katz, and Bebbington (1988) recently observed that first-degree relatives of depressed probands reported significantly more life events than control relatives. Similarly, Black and colleagues (Black, Bell, Hulbert, & Nasrallah, 1988) reported that the co-morbidity of an axis II personality disorder coupled with a major affective disorder significantly increases the level of major life events, as well as being associated with poorer response to treatment.

Fifteen years ago, Goldberg and Comstock (1976) reviewed prospective studies of the relationship between life events and subsequent illness and cautioned that there was little hard evidence of predictive power in these investigations. Today we still very much perceive the need for more prospective studies in life events stress research (Hobfoll, 1989; Monroe, 1989); however, it does not appear that they are being done, at least not with the scientific rigor required. Andrews and Tennant (1978) somewhat portentously noted that when initial hopes concerning a concept or agent's etiological significance are not fulfilled in the psychological and medical sciences, we frequently observe a period of preoccupation with methodology; this methodological preoccupation sometimes simply represents an attempt to solve with enhanced precision what is basically a problem of irrelevance.

Before ending our discussion on life events measurement, we should make explicit that numerous other scales beyond the SRE and the SRRS measure life stress. Just to enumerate a few, Sarason, Johnson, and Siegal (1979) published the Life Experiences Survey (LES), while Horowitz, Schaefer, Hiroto, Wilner, and Levin (1977) have proposed several innovative life stress measures. Linn (1985) has recently developed the Global Assessment of Recent Stress (GARS). We should also note that one of the pervasive criticisms of life events measurement—that the events that comprise the scales are irrelevant for many subgroups of society—is beginning to be addressed. Both Blake, Fry, and Pesjack (1984) and Green berg (1990) have developed effective life events scales for college-aged populations, and Dise-Lewis (1988) has developed a similar instrument for middle-school-aged children.

Ultimately, one's conclusions concerning the adequacy of the life events approach to stress measurement are determined by one's measurement objectives. If the desired goal is to achieve group measurement of the stress potential inherent in the environment, and the group of interest is comprised of young to middle-aged adults, then the normative taxonomy of events stress is sufficient to accomplish the task handily. If, alternatively, one's purpose is to achieve precise individual measurement and prediction, then these measures do not appear to possess sufficient predictive validity. Compromised reliabilities coupled with person-specific mediating variables (Johnson & Sarason, 1979; Krantz & Glass, 1984) so transform the ultimate effects of environmental stressors from one individual to the next that life events share insufficient unique variance with criterion variables to enable effective prediction.

Response-oriented Measures

Although obvious from the previously mentioned work of Cannon (1932) and Selye (1950) that response-oriented measurement has theoretical underpinnings in stress theory, the majority of measuring instruments arise from clinical research in psychopathology. Cognitive dysfunctions, disorganized interpersonal/social relationships, and symptomatic distress-longstanding hallmarks of psychiatric disorders—have come to be adopted by investigators in this area as prima facie evidence of the presence of stress.

By modest estimate, hundreds of self-report measures have been developed to address to the various domains of psychopathology, mood and affect, psychological adjustment, social competence, etc., that could conceivably meet the basic requirements of a response-oriented definition of stress. As before, we do not attempt to provide a comprehensive review or evaluation of this broad area but, rather, focus upon a few instruments that we consider to be exemplary of these various classes of response-oriented measurement. For more thorough reviews, the reader may consult Ciarlo, Brown, Edwards, Kiresuk, and Newman (1986); Comrey, Backer, and Glaser (1973); Hargreaves, Attkisson, Siegal, and McIntyre (1975); Lamping (1985); Monroe (1989); Piotrowski and Lubin (1990); and Waskow and Parloff (1975).

The classes of self-report instruments that have been utilized most prominently as presumptive measures of stress are *psychological symptom inventories* and *scales that reflect mood and affect*. This observation is borne out vividly in a recent review by Piotrowski and Lubin (1990), which revealed that seven out of ten of the most frequently used scales in health psychology are instruments of this type. Traditionally, most of these instruments have been multidimensional, reflecting the multiple symptom complexes and myriad dysphoric emotions typically invoked to define stress. However, specific syndromes, particularly those that have become synonymous with definitions of stress (e.g., anxiety), have fostered dedicated unidimensional instruments as well.

Multidimensional Psychological Symptom Inventories. The MMPI, the *Minnesota Multiphasic Personality Inventory,* is one of the best-known psychological tests (Hathaway & McKinley, 1940). An enormous amount of research has been done using the instrument in an extremely diverse range of clinical situations and with a broad spectrum of samples. The MMPI has been pivotal in the development of personality research over a forty-year period and has provided enormous heuristic as well as scientific value (Dahlstrom & Welsh, 1960; Dahlstrom, Welsh, & Dahlstrom, 1972). In spite of its broad appeal, the MMPI is not without problems (Butcher, 1972). The 566 items of the scale make it extremely lengthy, and since it measures both state and trait characteristics, it is somewhat difficult for stress researchers to separate emotional responses (to stress) from some of the cognitive character- istics that mediate them. In a series of reviews of psychotherapy change measures (Waskow & Parloff, 1975), of the four reviews on self-report scales, Dahlstrom (1975) recommended the MMPI highly, Gleser (1975) was critical of the MMPI, and Imber (1975) and Cartwright (1975) did not mention it in their reviews.

Although often criticized as an operational definition of stress, the MMPI continues to be used as an outcome measure in stress studies, in large part because of the immense research literature on the scale. Examples of such studies include a report by Miyabo, Asato, and Mizushima (1979) detailing a relationship between cortisol and growth hormone levels and MMPI scores in neurotic patients, as well as a study by Bieliauskas (1980), which failed to find a relationship between 17-hydroxycortisteriod (17-OHCS) level and K-scale scores on a shortened version of the MMPI. Keegan, Sinha, Merriman, and Shipley (1979) observed only marginal differences between type A and type B cardiac patients on the MMPI, in spite of significant differences between groups in terms of medical conditions and interpersonal and social indexes. Pancheri and associates (1978) found the MMPI to discriminate clearly between improved and nonimproved patients who had suffered a severe myocardial infarction, and Davis and Wedseth (1978) concluded the scale was sensitive to stress among male college students. More recently, Stanwyck and Anson (1986) used the MMPI in a cluster-analytic study to support the idea of a generic disease-prone personality, and the Centers for Disease Control Vietnam Experience Study (1988) reported on an inves- tigation with the scale of over 4,000 Vietnam veterans. It should also be noted that the subset of items of the MMPI known as the Cook-Medley Hostility Scale (Cook & Medley, 1954) has been used repeatedly to successfully predict stress-related cardiovascular morbid- ity and mortality (Greenglass & Julkunen, 1989; Williams & Barefoot, 1988).

The revised MMPI (the MMPI-2) has been made available only recently, and conse- quently it does not have the track record of the original scale. The MMPI-2 and manual were published in 1989 following a restandardization project involving, 1,138 men and 1,462 women with diverse demographic backgrounds from different geographic regions of the United States (Butcher, 1990; Butcher, Dahlstrom, Graham, Tellegen, & Kaemmer, 1989). Restandardization was conducted to correct problems with outdated items, sexist language, or poorly written questions. The MMPI-2 contains 567 items; 82 of the original items were rewritten and 68 were subsequently retained in the updated version. Research designed to evaluate the psychometric properties of the MMPI-2 has examined the stability of the rewritten items as well as profiled the compatibility of scores, with cross-administra- tion of the MMPI (Ben-Porath & Butcher, 1989a, 1989b; and code-types Graham, Tim- brook, Ben-Porath & Butcher, 1991; Munley, 1991). At present, however, few studies have used the MMPI-2 with clinical populations in either the psychiatric or medical setting (see Egeland, Farrell Erickson, Butcher & Ben Porath, 1991; Gass, 1991; Hjemboe & Butcher, 1991; Lees-Haley, 1991; Litz, et. al., 1991; Weed, Butcher, McKenna & Ben-Porath, 1991).

The *SCL-90-R* is a multidimensional self-report symptom inventory designed to assess symptomatic psychological distress. A prototypical version of the scale was developed in 1973 (Derogatis, Lipman, & Covi, 1973), and the final version of the instrument was published two years later (Derogatis, 1975b). An introductory paper by Derogatis, Rickels, and Rock (1976) was followed by the publication of the administration and scoring manual (Derogatis, 1977). Subsequently, a second edition of the manual has been published (Derogatis, 1983), and a third edition is due in 1992. The SCL-90-R is related most closely to the Hopkins Symptom Checklist (HSCL) (Derogatis, Lipman, Rickels, Uhlenhuth, & Covi 1974 a,b); however, certain items may be traced back to Woodworth's original self-report inventory (1918).

The SCL-90-R reflects psychological distress in terms of nine primary symptom dimensions and three global indexes of distress. Somatization (SOM), obsessive-compulsive (OBS), interpersonal sensitivity (INT), depression (DEP), anxiety (ANX), hostility (HOS), phobic anxiety (PHOB), paranoid ideation (PAR), and psychoticism (PSY) are the primary symptom constructs. Three global indexes represent summary measures of psychological disorder that, although correlated, have been shown to display distinct aspects of psychopathology (Derogatis, Yevzeroff, & Wittelsberger, 1975). Specifically, the general severity index (GSI) combines information on numbers of symptoms and intensity of distress; the positive symptom total (PST) reflects only numbers of symptoms; the positive symptom distress index (PSDI) is a pure intensity measure, adjusted for numbers of symptoms present.

Currently, four formal published norms are associated with the SCL-90-R, including those developed with psychiatric outpatients, psychiatric inpatients, nonpatient normal adults, and nonpatient normal adolescents. During 1991–1992 it is anticipated that geriatric norms, the initial set of change norms, and several specialty norms (e.g., cancer patients) will be published. In each case, separate (gender-keyed) norms are available for men and women. Each norm represents the raw score distributions of the nine symptom dimensions and three globals in terms of area T-scores. Beyond formal norms, profile data are available for numerous specific clinical groups on the SCL-90-R. An added feature of the SCL-90-R is that it is available in twenty-six languages.

The SCL-90-R has demonstrated high levels of both test-retest and internal consistency reliability (Derogatis, 1977; Edwards, Yarvis, Mueller, Zingale, & Wagman, 1978), and validation has been approached in a programmatic fashion. Derogatis, Rickels, and Rock (1976) demonstrated very high convergent and discriminant validity for the SCL-90-R in comparison with the MMPI in a sample of symptomatic volunteers, while Boleoucky and Horvath (1974) provided a similar demonstration using the Middlesex Hospital Questionnaire (MHQ) (Crown & Crisp, 1966) in a sample of nonpatient normals. In a large factor-analytic study, Derogatis and Cleary (1977a) confirmed the nine-dimension clinical-rational structure of the instrument, and thereby contributed to its construct validity. In addition, in a subsequent report Derogatis and Cleary (1977b) revealed factorial invariance of the scale's nine primary symptom dimensions across gender.

In the almost two decades since its introduction, the SCL-90-R has become somewhat of a standard in the multidimensional measurement of psychological distress. This status is clearly reflected by the fact that numerous recently developed instruments have utilized the "90" in both concurrent and construct validation studies. For example, the Modified Somatic Perception Questionnaire (MSPQ) (Main, 1983), the Pain Disability Index (Tait, Pollard, Margolis, & Duckro, 1987), the Toronto Alexithymia Scale (Taylor, et al., 1988), and the Perinatal Grief Scale (Toedter, Alhadeff, & Lasker, 1988) all utilized the SCL-90-R in such a fashion.

The SCL-90-R has proven very sensitive to change in a broad variety of clinical and medical contexts. Research on depression has shown the 90 to be particularly discriminating regarding the presence of clinical depression and its response to treatment. In a study focused on the distinctions between primary and secondary depression, the SCL-90-R proved to be very effective in demonstrating differential severity of symptoms between the two groups (Weissman, et al., 1977). In a second investigation by this research team, the instrument demonstrated its capacity to accurately detect depression in five psychiatric populations and a community sample (Weissman, Sholomskas, Pottenger, Prusoff, & Locke, 1977.) More recently, Keller and Lavori (1989) utilized the SCL-90-R to evaluate the adequacy of depressive treatments, while Cassano and colleagues (Cassano, et al., 1989) employed the scale to help characterize the phenomenology of major depressions. The 90 also has been used in a number of prospective longitudinal studies—e.g., the Depressive Disorders of Childhood reports by Kovacs, Gatsonis, Paulauskas, and Richards (1989) and the well-known Zurich Study conducted by Angst and his associates (see Angst & Dobler-Mikola, 1984).

The SCL-90-R has also proven sensitive to psychological distress arising from sexual disorders (Derogatis, Meyer, & Gallant, 1977; Derogatis, Meyer, & King, 1981); from conditions associated with sleep disturbance (Kales, et al., 1980); from chronic pain (Hendler, Derogatis, Avella, & Long, 1977); from headache (Harper & Steger, 1978); and from cancer (Craig & Abeloff, 1974; Derogatis, Abeloff, & McBeth, 1976). Recently, a bibliography of approximately 500 published studies with the SCL-90-R, arising from 70 areas of health care and medicine, has been made available (Derogatis, 1990).

Use of the SCL-90-R specifically in stress research has been reported by Carrington and her associates (Carrington, et al., 1980); they showed the instrument to be highly sensitive to differences in the efficacies of various meditation interventions in reducing stress. Horowitz, Wilner, Kaltreider, and Alvarez (1980) carefully profiled the DSM-III post-traumatic stress disorders in terms of the SCL-90-R. In addition, Horowitz, et al. (1981) also demonstrated high discriminative sensitivity for the instrument concerning the stress inherent in parental death. The SCL-90-R was also used in a series of studies documenting stress arising from the Three Mile Island disaster (Baum, Gatchel, & Schaeffer, 1983; Bromet, Schulberg, Dunn, & Parkinson, 1987; Hartsough & Savitsky, 1984; Schaeffer & Baum, 1984), and in several life events stress studies (Dohrenwend, Dohrenwend, Dodson, & Shrout, 1984; Roth & Holmes, 1987).

An important additional characteristic of the SCL-90-R is that it does not exist solely as a distinct psychological test but, rather, is one component in a matched series of test instruments. A brief form of the scale, the Brief Symptom Inventory (BSI) (Derogatis & Spencer, 1982), measures the same nine symptom dimensions and three global indexes as the 90 and correlated very highly with it in a psychiatric population (Derogatis, 1977, 1983). In addition, two matched clinical observer's scales have been developed to measure the same nine symptom constructs (Derogatis, 1977, 1983). The two observer's scales differ primarily in the level of knowledge of psychopathology required to use them. These instruments greatly expand the nature of the research that may be done with the SCL-90-R and enormously facilitate doctor-patient comparisons (Abramowitz & Herrera, 1981; Derogatis, Abeloff, & McBeth, 1976; Derogatis, & Abeloff, Freeland, 1979).

Undimensional Psychological Symptom Measures. A cursory review of the domain of unidimensional symptom scales indicates that it is vast indeed. Limiting her focus to anxiety measures, DeBonis (1974) documented twenty-seven distinct inventories in use. Addressing the task more recently, both Finney (1985) and Uhlenhuth (1985) identified similar numbers of scales. Our selection of exemplary unidimensional symptom scales from this large array was dictated by two principles: first, since anxiety and depression are the negative affect states and symptom complexes most often deemed isomorphic with stress, these constructs should be the primary measurement target; second, the instrument must possess an established record of predictive validity across a broad range of clinical research contexts. With these two notions in mind, we selected three instruments to discuss: the Beck Depression Inventory, the State-Trait Anxiety Inventory, and the Center for Epidemiological Studies Depression Scale. Obviously, many other measures fulfill these criteria.

The BDI, the *Beck Depression Inventory,* is a unidimensional symptom inventory focused on the measurement of depression. In his introductory paper, Beck (Beck, Ward, Mendelson, Mock, & Erbaugh, 1961) described the BDI as "an instrument designed to measure the behavioral manifestations of depression" (p. 53). Additionally, Beck and Beamesderfer (1974) described the BDI as "an inventory for measuring the depth of depression" (p. 154). The BDI arose from a dissatisfaction with the vagaries of clinical judgment, which reflect both the idiosyncracies of individual practitioners and the inherent weaknesses in the nosological system. The use of a self-report inventory was perceived as a more objective approach and one that enabled the power of psychometrics to be brought to bear on the problem of measuring depression.

The BDI rests upon twenty-one "symptom-attitude categories," which were clinically derived by Beck and his colleagues and judged to be characteristic of their patients and specific for depression. Each category represents a characteristic manifestation of depression (e.g., pessimism, self-dislike, fatigability), which the patient rates using a series of four-point ordinal scales. Individual category scores are summed to produce a total BDI score. Beck indicated that the particular form of the BDI was dictated by his observations that: (1) severity of depression and numbers of symptoms are correlated, (2) intensity of distress and severity of depression are correlated, and (3) frequency of depressive symptoms has a stepwise distribution through the continuum from nondepressed to severely depressed (Beck & Beamesderfer, 1974).

Beck and Beamesderfer (1974) reported internal consistency reliability for the scale of .86 but for some reason skirted the issue of test-retest reliability; they argued in a less-than-compelling fashion that memory could bias findings over the short term and that natural fluctuations in the condition would reduce coefficients over any appreciable duration. Concurrent validity studies, with clinician ratings and other self-report measures, are numerous for the BDI, and a series of studies related to construct validation are well documented (Beck & Beamesderfer, 1974). In 1972, a thirteen-item version of the BDI was introduced (Beck & Beck, 1972). Reynolds and Gould (1981) demonstrated good reliability for the scale with internal consistency coefficients of .83 for the short form, .85 for the long form, and a correlation of .93 between the two.

Although the BDI is unidimensional in the sense that it measures a single construct, a number of factor-analytic studies have isolated several distinct factors consistently from patient cohorts. These factors appear to represent the physiological-vegetative aspects of depression, hopelessness-despair, guilt–self-abasement, and fatigue-inhibition. Nonetheless, multidimensional scoring or interpretation of the BDI has never become a major interpretive aspect of the instrument.

In response to the question of cut-off scores for "caseness" with the BDI, Beck and Beamesderfer (1974) indicated that it is extremely difficult to identify a single score by which to make such assignments. They note, essentially presaging the current excitement over Receiver Operating Characteristic (ROC) analysis (Derogatis, DellaPietra, & Kilroy, 1990), that the relevance of any score depends upon the cohort being predicted from, the selectivity and specificity associated with various cut-offs in that sample, and the utility functions involved in determining the cost of false negatives and false positives in the particular context in question. However, as Reynolds and Gould (1981) observed, there are significant gender differences on the BDI (particularly the short form) and this fact should be taken into account when using cut-off scores.

The BDI is broadly used to measure the stress and distress associated with psychological disorders (Beck & Beamesderfer, 1974). In addition, it has been shown to be sensitive to the stress associated with medical illnesses among in-patient (Schwab, Bialow, Brown, & Holzer, 1967) and out-patient cohorts (Nielsen & Williams, 1980). The scale is often used as a measure of depression in life events studies (e.g., Johnson & Sarason, 1978) and has been shown to be applicable to adolescents with psychological disorders (Strober, Green, & Carlson, 1981). The BDI has also been utilized with numerous specific medical illness groups (Craven, Rodin, & Littlefield, 1988), and recently Whitaker and his colleagues (1990) used the BDI to screen for depression in a cohort of 5,108 community adolescents.

The STAI, the *State-Trait Anxiety Inventory,* is a self-report symptom-mood inventory designed to provide an operational distinction between anxiety as an enduring personality characteristic—*trait anxiety*—and anxiety as a transient emotional experience—*state anxiety*. Spielberger and his colleagues (Spielberger, Gorsuch, & Lushene, 1970) developed the STAI with the notion of creating two distinct scales with high internal consistency that would provide valid measurement of these separate but related components of anxiety as postulated by state-trait anxiety theorists (Cattell, 1960, 1966; Spielberger, 1966, 1972).

The STAI is comprised of two sets of twenty statements concerning how an individual feels. Respondents are instructed to endorse one set concerning how they feel at the particular moment (*A-state*), while they respond to the second set of items in terms of how they feel generally (*A-trait*). A children's version of the instrument, the STAIC (Spielberger, 1973) and a Spanish edition of the adult scale (Spielberger, Gonzalez-Reigosa, & Martinez-Urrutia, 1971) are available.

Smith and Lay (1974) compiled an annotated bibliography of research done with the STAI through 1972 and documented sensitivity for the instrument in a wide variety of stress contexts. Stress conditions ranged from surgery (Delong, 1971; Florell, 1971), through dental treatment (Lamb & Plant, 1972), to public speaking (Lamb, 1970). Kendall and his associates (Kendall, Finch, Auerbach, Hooke, & Mikulka, 1976) completed a study of the STAI focused on the factor structure of the instrument. They discovered a unitary trait anxiety factor but observed two distinct dimensions of state anxiety. Relationships between high and low trait anxiety and levels of the two state anxiety measures under self-esteem and physical threat conditions were evaluated; equivocal support was observed for the relationship predicted from theory.

Frequent examples of the use of the STAI in stress-related research may be found in the literature. Johnson and Sarason (1978) utilized the instrument in life events studies, while Sarason, Johnson, and Siegal (1979) demonstrated a significant correlation between negative, but not positive, life change scores and the STAI. Arena, Blanchard, and Andrasik (1984) used the STAI to demonstrate the role of affect in chronic headache syndromes. Because of its brevity, ease of use, and its distinction between current emotional states versus characteristic affective postures, the STAI continues to be an attractive instrument in stress research.

Although not formally thought of as a stress measure, the *Center for Epidemiologic Studies Depression Scale* (CES-D) has frequently been used in such a capacity. The CES-D was originally developed by Radloff (1977), as a brief unidimensional depression scale comprised of twenty items. The CES-D assesses mood and level of overall functioning during the most recent seven-day period. Subsequent to its introduction, four basic dimensions (i.e., depressed affect, positive affect, interpersonal problems, and somatic problems) have been isolated.

The CES-D has been utilized effectively as a screening device with community cohorts (Comstock & Helsing, 1976; Frerichs, Areshensel, & Clark, 1981; Radloff & Locke, 1985), and has been used as a screening device in clinic populations (Roberts, Rhoades, & Vernon, 1990). Recently, Shrout and Yager (1989) demonstrated that a highly shortened version of the scale remained capable of valid prediction.

Affect and Mood Scales. In addition to response-oriented measures based upon psychological symptoms, affect and mood scales constitute a second class of measures that have been employed to operationalize stress. Intrinsically, moods and affects tend to be viewed as more transient than symptomatic signs of stress. However, characteristic (i.e., trait as opposed to state) expressions of affect routinely have been shown to have substantial predictive validity relative to stress-related phenomena. In addition, affect measures have repeatedly shown themselves to be the first instruments to reveal impending therapeutic change; furthermore, they are extremely cost-efficient and cost-beneficial. Typically, these instruments are collections of adjectives that depict various mood states, often selected on the basis of factor-analytic studies. Although a large number of mood scales exist, we have selected three to discuss here: the Profile of Mood States (POMS), because of its proven sensitivity in many clinical research contexts, and the Affects Balance Scale (ABS) and the Positive and Negative Affect Schedule (PANAS) because their approach to the measurement of affect features both positive and negative affect states.

The POMS, the *Profile of Mood States,* is a sixty-five-item adjective checklist that reflects measurement in terms of six primary mood states derived through repeated factor analyses (McNair, Lorr, & Droppleman, 1971). The mood dimensions are labeled tension-anxiety, depression-dejection, confusion, anger-hostility, vigor, and fatigue. Each item of the POMS is scaled on a five-point scale from not at all to extremely; the measurement context is "the past week including today." The scale takes approximately ten to fifteen minutes to complete, and language levels have been assessed to keep word difficulty at a minimum.

Reported internal consistency coefficients for the POMS range from .74 to .92, with test-retest coefficients of .61–.69 based on a one-month interval (McNair & Lorr, 1964). Repeated factor analyses of the instrument have confirmed its basic factor structure (Lorr, McNair, & Weinstein, 1963; McNair & Lorr, 1964), and separate male and female norms are available based upon a large sample evaluated at a university health center.

The POMS is well conceived and well constructed and has proven itself to be a sensitive response-oriented measure of stress in a wide variety of contexts. It has shown predictive validity in a broad spectrum of clinical change studies involving both psychotherapy (Imber, 1975) and psychopharmacology (McNair, 1974). In a fascinating study, Haskell, Pugatch, and McNair (1969) demonstrated independent predictive variance associated with symptoms, as measured by the Hopkins Symptom Checklist, and affective status, as measured by the POMS. In more recent studies, the POMS has also been used to assess the stress associated with pain (Shacham, Reinhardt, Raubertas, & Cleeland, 1983), breast cancer (Taylor, Lichtman, & Wood, 1984) and affective postures during smoking cessation (Hall, Rugg, Tunstall, & Jones, 1984).

The *Affects Balance Scale* (ABS) is a forty-item adjective checklist that incorporates both positive and negative affect. A review of the majority of adjective mood scales reveals that most dimensions of these scales focus upon negative affect states. When used as measures of current emotional status, general well-being, or treatment-induced change, these instruments are limited to operational definitions based almost entirely upon levels of dysphoric affects. Many investigators who have functioned in the clinical role have observed that current emotional status, as well as prognosis, is often determined in at least equal measure by the positive affect status of the individual. This posture is consistent with the belief espoused by the World Health Organization (1960) that health is more than merely an absence of physical or psychological pathology, but includes a comprehensive state of physical and psychosocial well-being.

One of the first investigators to formally equate the distinction between health and impairment and positive and negatives affects was Bradburn (1969), who devised a 10-item scale termed the Affect Balance Scale. Subsequently, studies of the health correlates of positive and negative affectivity have increased dramatically. As examples, Mechanic & Hansell (1987) demonstrated a significant relationship between perceived psychological well-being and academic performance, perceived health, and participation in athletics among 1,000 high school students. In a similar fashion, Clark & Watson (1988) observed that high levels of positive affects were strongly related to levels of social interaction and physical activity and inversely related to health complaints among young adults. In a laboratory measurement paradigm, James (1986) showed direct relationships between anxiety scores and blood pressure, while a measure of happiness was inversely related to blood pressure. Similarly, Wetzler & Orsano (1988) demonstrated a significant association between positive affects, overall sense of well-being, and seven major physical health practices (e.g., alcohol consumption, exercise, smoking) in a cohort of over 6,600 air force personnel.

Consistent with these observations, although unaware of Bradburn's work, Derogatis (1975) developed an adjective mood scale, also termed the Affect Balance Scale, comprised of four positive affect dimensions (joy, contentment, vigor, and affection), and four negative dimensions (anxiety, depression, guilt, and hostility). The ABS is a 40-item adjective instrument that scales mood adjectives on a 5-point scale from not at all (0) to extremely (4), and takes approximately 5 minutes to complete. Summations across the 8 affect dimensions lead to positive and negative affect totals, and an overall difference score between these two provides an affect balance index. Derogatis (1982) completed a factor analysis of the ABS based upon 417 psychiatric out-patients and confirmed all four negative affect dimensions and three of the four positive affect constructs. A higher-order factor analysis of the correlations among the primary factors resulted in two distinct dimensions, one reflecting positive, the other negative, affects.

A number of studies have examined the predictive validity of the ABS. Derogatis, Meyer, and Vasquez (1978) showed the ABS to be highly sensitive to the dysphoric affect of men with gender dysphoria, an affect posture distinct from that of women with gender dysphoria (Derogatis, Meyer, & Boland, 1981). Negative affect states associated with both male and female sexual dysfunction have also been explicitly documented with the ABS (Derogatis & Meyer, 1979). Among medical cohorts, Fontana, Marcus, Dowds, and Hughes (1980) evaluated the psychological well-being of the physically ill with the instrument, and the DCCT Research Group (1988) evaluated the psychometric aspects of the scale as a measure of the quality of life of diabetics. Derogatis & Georgopolous (1986) observed that reduced positive affects scores on the ABS significantly separated diabetics with substantial peripheral neuropathy from those free of this complication, while negative affects scores did not.

In the area of neoplastic diseases, Derogatis, Abeloff, and Melisaratos (1979) showed that ABS affect profiles significantly discriminated long-term from short-term survivors with metastatic breast cancer. In addition, Levy, Lee, Bagley, and Lippman (1988) and Northouse (1988) found the ABS to be sensitive to the emotional profiles of women with breast cancer. In addition, Holland and her colleagues (1990) have demonstrated the ABS to be sensitive to the therapeutic effects of alprazolam in reactive anxiety states among cancer patients.

Hoehn-Saric and his colleagues have utilized the ABS in an integrated series of studies on anxiety disorders and their treatment. An initial report characterizing such patients in general (Hoehn-Saric, 1981) was followed by a second report focused specifically on the affect profiles of chronically anxious patients (Hoehn-Saric, 1983). A study focused on the social adjustment of these patients was also published concurrently (Sangal, Coyle, & Hoehn-Saric, 1983). Furthermore, the group has utilized the ABS in several therapeutic drug trials, which documented its sensitivity to pharmacotherapeutic efficacy in this group of patients (Hoehn-Saric, McLeod, & Zimmerli, 1988; Hoehn-Saric, Merchant, Kaiser, & Smith, 1981).

In studies of stress in nonclinical populations, Derogatis, Falkner, Kareken, and Graber (1990) demonstrated significant relationships between positive affects scores on the ABS and blood pressure among inner-city black adolescents, and Wolf, Elston, and Kissling (1989) used the ABS to relate hassles and life events to well-being in freshman medical students.

The PANAS, the *Positive and Negative Affect Schedule,* is a recently developed mood scale also designed to express the idea that both positive and negative effects must be measured to achieve a valid estimate of general well-being. The PANAS was developed by Watson and his colleagues (Watson, Clark, & Tellegen, 1988), who have conducted a highly systematic series of investigations in this area. These investigators conceptualize positive and negative affects as two fundamental, essentially orthogonal constructs that comprise the cardinal dimensions of emotional experience. They further discriminate state and trait versions of the constructs (Watson & Tellegen, 1985). At the trait level, positive and negative effectivity are described as corresponding to the personality dimensions of extraversion and neuroticism, respectively. Trait NA (negative affect) is described as a broadly based, persistent tendency to experience life events in the context of dysphoric emotional coloring that progressively extends to negatively influence cognitive style and self-concept. Trait PA (positive affect) is characterized as a persistent inclination to respond to the environment with an active, enabling posture that reflects a general sense of competence and mastery. Watson and his associates have used the PANAS to demonstrate significant relationships between positive affects and social activity and exercise (Watson, 1988). In addition, they have further shown positive affectivity to be a reliable discriminator between depressive states (where it is substantially diminished) and anxiety disorders (where it remains relatively unaffected) (Watson, Clark, & Carey, 1988).

Interaction-oriented Measures

As was noted previously, interactional theorists posit that cognitive, perceptual, personality, and other characteristics of the individual mediate responses to stress. Enduring traits, coping strategies, psychodynamic mechanisms of defense, and many other person variables enter into interactional postulations concerning stress. In this section we examine some of the instruments that have been developed from individual and family interactionist models. By comparison, these stress measures are relatively new, since the transactional, or process-oriented, position is more recent in stress research.

The JAS, the *Jenkins Activity Survey,* is a self-report screening instrument developed by Jenkins and his colleagues (Jenkins, Rosenman, & Friedman, 1967; Jenkins, Zyzanski, & Rosenman, 1976, 1976) to measure a specific pattern of behavior thought to have a high association with proneness to coronary disease. This behavioral complex has come to be known as the *type A* behavior pattern. The scale actually represents an attempt to develop a more rigorous, objective operational definition of a pattern of behavior originally described via an interview known as the Stress Interview (SI) (Friedman & Rosenman, 1959).

The JAS has been demonstrated to have convergent validity (70–73% agreement) with structured interviews designed to measure the same behavior complex (Jenkins & Zyzanski, 1980) and has shown substantial predictive validity concerning the prevalence of coronary heart disease (Jenkins, 1971, 1976; Jenkins, Rosenman, & Zyzanski, 1974). Furthermore, Glass (1977) has made a substantial contribution to the construct validity of the type A behavior pattern using the JAS in a fascinating series of studies.

The JAS consists of 52 items scaled in terms of multiple-point descriptors. Jenkins and Zyzanski (1980) indicated that the instrument is comprised of four scales, only one of which is the type A scale. The type A scale was derived through discriminant function analysis, and the remaining three scales were developed through a factor analysis of the items that discriminated type A behavior from other patterns (i.e., type B). These scales are described as orthogonal to each other but correlated with type A. The corresponding factors have been labeled speed and impatience, job involvement, and hard-driving-competitive.

The JAS has been used extensively in stress research (at least, that aspect related to coronary heart disease), and has been translated into numerous languages, including Dutch, Polish, Russian, and Swedish (Jenkins & Zyzanski, 1980). Excellent reviews of research done with the scale have been provided by Glass (1977), Goldband, Katkin, and Morell (1979), Jenkins (1971, 1976), and Jenkins and Zyzanski (1980), with an interesting editorial on the subject published by Marmot (1980).

Research with the JAS initially indicated an increased risk of coronary artery disease when both type A behavior and social insecurity were present (Jenkins, Zyzanski, Ryan, Flessas, & Tannenbaum, 1977). However, a therapeutic exercise program disproportionately reduced physiologic coronary risk factors in type A subjects (Blumenthal, Williams, Williams, & Wallace, 1980). Another report showed hostility and the type A behavior pattern to be independently predictive of atherosclerosis (Williams, et al., 1980), and Nielson and Dobson (1980) found that the type A behavior pattern was virtually uncorrelated with a series of measures of trait anxiety among college students.

More recently, the JAS has been called into question as a faithful representation of the constructs measured by the SI interview. Matthews, Krantz, Dembrowski, and MacDougal (1982) reported a correlation of only .30 between the two measures, indicating slightly less than 10% shared variance between the two definitions of type A. Additionally, Matthews (1988) recently completed a meta-analysis demonstrating that type A behavior is significantly associated with coronary heart disease when data is drawn from studies that used the SI interview, but reveals an insignificant relationship when studies using the JAS are used as a basis for data.

In spite of these cautions, the JAS has proven to be an extremely productive research instrument and has facilitated a large body of research on the relationship between physical disease and psychosocial factors. Although limited to a specific area of stress focus (i.e., coronary heart disease), the JAS represents a measurement benchmark that will probably remain quite useful.

The DSP, the *Derogatis Stress Profile,* is an interactional stress instrument that was introduced when the first edition of this handbook was published. The DSP is somewhat unique because it is one of the very few stress instruments whose constructs were derived directly from stress theory. It also reflects stimulus, response, and interactional elements. The DSP is a seventy-seven-item test, with eleven underlying dimensions and two global scores. One global measure represents a summation of scores over the eleven primary dimensions, while the second is an analogue measure of the individual's subjectively perceived current level of stress. The test takes ten to fifteen minutes to complete and is readily hand-scored.

Three of the eleven DSP scales measure stimulus elements arising from the job environment, the home environment, and the health environment. These scales are termed vocational satisfaction, domestic satisfaction, and health posture, respectively. Five dimensions measure characteristic personal attributes and coping mechanisms that have been shown to have significant mediating effects on stress. These are labeled time pressure, which is self-defining; driven behavior, which reflects the compulsive need to be constantly involved in behavior deemed constructive; attitude posture, which reflects the achievement ethic; relaxation potential, which measures the potential for healthy diversions; and role definition, which is designed to measure the role-determined expectancy of bearing sole responsibility for the resolution of life demands. The three remaining dimensions reflect the primary response-oriented measures of stress via the emotion-symptom constructs of aggression-hostility, tension-anxiety, and depression. The two former measures gain fundamental support as valid measures of stress through Cannon's (1929) original postulation of the neuroendocrine mechanisms of the fight-flight response. Depression finds support as a valid measure of stress via Selye's (1970) work with the general adaptation syndrome and subsequent explication by a number of theorists (Horowitz, 1979; McLean, 1976).

The DSP was conceived to be a truly interactional measure of stress. The three stimulus scales provide an indication of the level of environmental stress the individual is subjected to; the five mediating behavior scales may be thought of as capable of magnifying or reducing the impact of stressors; finally, the three response measures indicate the level of conscious emotional distress the individual is experiencing as a result of stressor-mediator interaction. Each scale has an equal opportunity to contribute to overall interactional stress score.

A comprehensive monograph on the DSP, describing both psychometric properties and validation studies, was recently published (Derogatis, 1987), and a number of studies have found the scale to possess high predictive validity. Greenberg, Kazak, and Meadows (1989) used the DSP to document stress levels of parents whose children survived cancer, while Lewandowski, et al. (1987) compared the DSP profiles of cardiac patients to medical staff's perception of their adjustment. Lundeen and his colleagues, (Lundeen, Sturdevant, & George, 1987; Lundeen, George, & Sturdevant, 1988) employed the DSP in a number of studies to document the role of stress in temporomandibular joint disorders. In addition, they used the scale to verify stress levels in a dental student population (Sturdevant, George, & Lundeen, 1989). Richardson and McGrath (1989) also used the DSP to measure stress levels in a study of cognitive behavior therapy for the treatment of migraine headaches, while Solis (1990) recently examined stress among Marine Corps officers using the DSP.

Although interactional theories of stress have guided the development of relatively few self-report measures, several additional creative efforts have been forthcoming. Lazarus and his colleagues developed the *Ways of Coping Checklist* (WCCL) (Folkman & Lazarus, 1980) as well as its revision (Folkman & Lazarus, 1985) to identify strategies individuals use to deal with the demands of a stressful event. On the revised version, respondents rate (on a four-point Likert scale) the extent to which they used sixty-six cognitive or behavioral coping strategies. The scale may be used to examine coping strategies for a particular stressful event identified by the respondent or for a specific stressor specified by the investigator. Factor analysis of the revised WCCL identified two forms of problem-focused coping (a confrontative or interpersonal approach and planful problem-solving), and six forms of emotion-focused coping (distancing, escape-avoidance, accepting responsibility or blame, exercising self-control over the expression of feelings, seeking social support, and positive reappraisal (Folkman & Lazarus, 1988 a, b; Folkman, Lazarus, Dunkel-Schetter, DeLongis, & Gruen, 1986; Folkman, Lazarus, Gruen, & DeLongis, 1986). This easily administered self-report measure has been used with diverse populations such as married adults across the life span, the elderly, college students, and individuals coping with physical illness.

Several promising interactional self-report measures have come out of the family stress research program conducted by McCubbin and his colleagues. Two scales were explicitly guided by the Double ABCX Model of Family Adaptation to Stress mentioned earlier in the chapter. McCubbin, Patterson, and Wilson (1981) developed the *Family Inventory of Life Events and Changes* (FILE) to assess family reactions to the accumulation of demands associated with normative and nonnormative stressful events and changes. Factor analysis of the seventy-one items identified nine scales: (1) intrafamily strains, (2) marital strains, (3) pregnancy and childbearing strains, (4) finance and business strains, (5) work-family transitions and strains, (6) illness and family care strains, (7) losses, (8) transitions in and out, and (9) family legal violations. In spite of these subscales, the authors recommend that the total score be used. Norms are based on responses from 980 couples across the family life cycle. Patterson and McCubbin (1983a) found that the build-up of family life changes was related to the pulmonary function of children with cystic fibrosis.

McCubbin, Larsen, and Olson (1981) also developed a self-report measure of family coping strategies based on the coping dimensions of the Double ABCX Model of Family Adaptation to Stress. The *Family Crisis Oriented Personal Evaluation Scales* (F-COPES) is a thirty-item inventory designed to evaluate the cognitive and behavioral coping strategies families use when faced with stressful events. Coping behavior is assessed irrespective of whether the stressor is within the family system or outside but affects individuals as well as the family unit. The items then assess the extent to which families use different coping attitudes and behaviors to deal with stressors. Factor analysis identified five scales: (1) acquiring social support, (2) reframing, (3) seeking social support, (4) mobilizing family to acquire and accept help, and (5) passive appraisal.

McCubbin, et al. (1983) also developed a self-report inventory to examine the coping strategies used by parents who have a chronically ill child. The CHIP, *Coping Health Inventory for Parents,* was designed to describe parental coping patterns and to identify those strategies useful in maintaining both the family environment and health of the child. In a study of one hundred families coping with a child with cystic fibrosis, factor analysis of the forty-five items identified three parental coping dimensions: (1) maintaining family integration, cooperation, and an optimistic definition of the situation; (2) maintaining social support, self-esteem, and psychological stability; and (3) understanding the medical situation through communication with other parents and consultation with the medical staff. This family assessment device provides useful information about parental coping strategies that may affect on their own as well as their ill child's psychological and medical status.

The family systems approach to stress research is a promising area that has received limited attention compared to the individual orientation. Nevertheless, this area has much to offer insofar as the focus of measurement may be the individual, family, marital dyad, and/or family unit. Individuals within the family system may differ in their perceptions of the stressor as well as in their coping strategies (Coons, 1990; McCubbin, et al., 1980). Relatively little is known, however, about how these discrepancies affect adaptation to the event at the individual, marital, or family system level.

CONCLUSION

Approximately ten years after completing the chapter for the first edition of the *Handbook of Stress,* it seems to us that reviewing self-report measures of stress during the final decade of the twentieth century remains analogous to the task of European navigators of the fifteenth century in charting a direct westward route to India. There clearly have been some productive attempts at operationalizing stress via self-report during this period. Unfortunately, the construct is intrinsically diffuse and unwieldy, and thus renders any operational definition incomplete, at best. In the final analysis, just as a more accurate appreciation of the world's geography and the invention of the airplane have vitiated the need for a direct western sea route, so, too, our ever-increasing knowledge of the fundamental neurobiological and neurochemical mechanisms underlying stress phenomena may soon substantially diminish our reliance on an imprecise construct such as stress.

It may be, as Hinkle (1979) contended, that the construct is so embellished with excess meaning that it can no longer serve a useful scientific purpose relative to the pathogenesis of disease or psychopathology. It is also possible that stress will ultimately turn out to be a *transitional* construct that has served to bridge the progression in science from one state of knowledge to the next. In terms of Thomas Kuhn's (1970) theory of scientific revolutions, thinking concerning the diverse aggregation of phenomena arrayed under the rubric of "stress" may be on the verge of a paradigm shift. The enormous recent progress made in the fields of neurochemistry, neurobiology, and the neurosciences in general may well lead to a new scientific paradigm that redefines the hierarchy of scientific problems in this field. Should a new paradigm emerge, it almost certainly will not foster diffuse constructs such as stress, but, rather, it will enable scientific investigation to progress in terms of more precise constructs and more tangible, quantifiable entities. New paradigms may arise from contemporary research in psychoneuroimmunology (O'Leary, 1990), affectivity (Watson & Pennebaker, 1989), neuroendocrinology (Pert, 1986), or any number of other areas of research that consider the complex relationships between developmental, psychosocial, and biological sciences.

Whatever the source, to the extent that human cognitions, perceptions, emotions, and behaviors are requisite elements of any new model, self-report measurement will continue to serve as an important mechanism for developing operational constructs. In spite of concerns about scale imperfections, test-taking sets, and individual biases, ultimately the experiencing individual possesses the most unique, and potentially veridical, appreciation of human stress.

REFERENCES

ABRAMOWITZ, S. I., & HERRERA, H. R. On controlling for patient psychopathology in naturalistic studies of sex bias: A methodological demonstration. *Journal of Consulting and Clinical Psychology,* 1981, *49,* 597–603.

ANDREWS, G., & TENNANT, C. Life event stress and psychiatric illness. *Psychological Medicine,* 1978, *8,* 545–549.

ANGST, J., & DOBLER-MIKOLA, A. The Zurich study: The continuum from normal to pathological depressive mood swings. *European Archives of Psychiatric Neurological Science.,* 1984, *234,* 21–29.

APPELS, A. Psychological prodromata of myocardial infarction and sudden death. *Psychotherapy and Psychosomatics,* 1980, *34,* 187–195.

APPELS, A., POOLS, J., & LUBSEN, T. Psychische prodromen van het hartinfaret. *Nederlands Tijdschrift Psychologie,* 1979, *34,* 213–223.

ARENA, J. G., BLANCHARD, E. B., & ANDRASIK, F. The role of affect in the etiology of chronic headache. *Journal of Psychosomatic Research,* 1984, *28,* 79–86.

BARRETT, J. E. (ed.). *Stress and mental disorder.* New York: Raven, 1979.

BECK, A. T., & BEAMESDERFER, A. Assessment of depression: The depression inventory. In P. Pichot (ed.), *Modern problems in pharmacopsychiatry.* Vol 7. Basel: Karger, 1974.

BECK, A. T., & BECK, R. W. Screening depressed patients in family practice: A rapid technic. *Post Graduate Medicine,* 1972, *52,* 81–85.

BECK, A. T., WARD, C., MENDELSON, M., MOCK, J., & ERBAUGH, J. An inventory for measuring depression. *Archives of General Psychiatry,* 1961, *4,* 53–63.

BAUM, A., GATCHEL, R. J., & SCHAEFFER, M. A. Emotional, behavioral, and physiological effects of chronic stress at Three Mile Island. *Journal of Consulting and Clinical Psychology,* 1983, *51*(4), 565–572.

BEN-PORATH, Y. S., & BUTCHER, J. N. Psychometric stability of rewritten MMPI items. *Journal of Personality Assessment,* 1989, *53,* 645–653. (a)

————. The comparability of MMPI and MMPI-2 scales and profiles. *Psychological Assessment: A Journal of Consulting and Clinical Psychology,* 1989, *1,* 345–347. (b)

BIELIAUSKAS, L. Life events, 17-OHCS measures, and psychological defensiveness in relation to aid seeking. *Journal of Human Stress,* 1980, *6,* 28–36.

BLACK, D. W., BELL, S., HULBERT, J., & NASRALLAH, A. The importance of axis II disorders in patients with major depression: A controlled study. *Journal of Affective Disorders,* 1988, *14,* 115–122.

BLAKE, P., FRY, R., & PESJACK, M. *Self-assessment and behavior change manual.* New York: Random House, 1984.

BLALOCK, J. E. A molecular basis for bidirectional communication between the immune and neuroendocrine systems. *Physiological Reviews,* 1989, *69,* 1–32.

BLUMENTHAL, J. A., WILLIAMS, R. S., WILLIAMS, R. B., & WALLACE, A. G. Effects of exercise on the type A (coronary prone) behavior pattern. *Psychosomatic Medicine,* 1980, *42,* 289–296.

BOLEOUCKY, Z., & HORVATH, M. (1974) SCL-90 rating scale: First experience with the Czech version in healthy male scientific workers. *Activitas Nervosa Superior* (Praha), 1974, *16,* 115–116.

BRADBURN, N. M. *The structure of psychological well-being.* Chicago: Aldine, 1969.

BROMET, E. J., SCHULBERG, H. C., DUNN, L. O., PARKINSON, D. K.: Mental health effects of the Three Mile Island Nuclear Reactor restart. *American Journal of Psychiatry,* 1987, *144,* 1074.

BROWN, G. W. Meaning, measurement and stress of life events. In D. S. Dohrenwend & D. P. Dohrenwend (eds.), *Stressful life events: Their nature and effects.* New York: Wiley, 1974.

BUROS, O. K. *The tenth mental measurement yearbook.* Highland Park, NJ: Gryphon Press, 1989.

BUTCHER, J. N. (ed). *Objective personality assessment: Changing perspectives. New York: Academic, 1972.*

BUTCHER, J. N. *The MMPI-2 in psychological treatment.* New York: Oxford University Press, 1990.

BUTCHER, J. N., DAHLSTROM, W. G., GRAHAM, J. R., TELLEGEN, A., & KAEMMER, B. *Manual for* the restandardized *Minnesota Multiphasic Personality Inventory: MMPI-2.* Minneapolis: University of Minnesota Press, 1989.

BYRNE, D. G., & WHITE, H. M. Life events and myocardial infarction revisited: The role of measures of individual impact. *Psychosomatic Medicine,* 1980, *42,* 1-10.

CANNON, W. B. *Bodily changes in fear, hunger, pain, and rage: An account of recent researches into the function of emotional excitement* (2d ed.). New York: Appleton, 1929.

————. *The wisdom of the body* (2d ed.). New York: Norton, 1932.

CARRINGTON, P., COLLINS, G. H., BENSON, H., ROBISON, H., WOOD, L. W., LEHRER, P. M. WOOLFOLK, R. L., & COLE, J. The use of meditation-relaxation techniques for the management of stress in working population. *Journal of Occupational Medicine,* 1980, *22,* 221-231.

CARTWRIGHT, D. S. Patient self-report measures. In I. E. Waskow & M. B. Parloff (eds.), *Psychotherapy change measures.* Rockville, MD: National Institute of Mental health, 1975.

CASSANO, G. B., AKISKAL, L., MUSETTI, G., PERUGI, SORIANI, A., & MIGNANI. Psychopathology, temperament, and past course in primary major depressions. *Psychopathology,* 1989, *22*(2), 278-288.

CATTELL, R. B. The dimensional (unitary-component) measurement of anxiety, excitement, effort stress, and other mood reaction patterns. In L. Uhr & J. G. Miller (eds.), *Drugs and behavior.* New York: Wiley, 1960.

————. Anxiety and motivation: Theory and crucial experiments. In C. D. Spielberger (ed.), *Anxiety and behavior.* New York: Academic, 1966.

CENTERS FOR DISEASE CONTROL VIETNAM EXPERIENCE STUDY. Health status of Vietnam veterans: Psychosocial characteristics. *Journal of the American Medical Association,* 1988, *259,* 2701-2707.

CIARLO, J. A., BROWN, T. R., EDWARDS, D. W., KIRESUK, T. J., & NEWMAN, F. L. *Assessing mental health treatment outcome measurement techniques.* Rockville, MD: U.S. Department of Health and Human Service, PHS, ADAMHA, 1986.

CLARK, L. A., & WATSON D. Mood and the Mundane: Relations between daily life events and self-reported mood. *Journal of Abnormal and Social Psychology.* 1988, *54,* 296-308.

CLEARY, P. J. A checklist for life event research. *Journal of Psychosomatic Research, 24,* 1980, 199-207.

CLIVE, D., & CHOSY, J. A prospective study of life changes and subsequent health changes. *Archives of General Psychiatry,* 1972, *27,* 51-53.

COMREY, A. L., BACKER, T. E., & GLASER, E. M. *A sourcebook for mental health measures.* Los Angeles: Human Interaction Research Institute, 1973.

COMSTOCK, G. W., & HELSING, K. J. Symptoms of depression in two communities *Psychological Medicine,* 1976, *6,* 551-564.

CONOLEY, J. C., & KRAMER, J. J. (eds.). *The tenth mental measurements yearbook.* Lincoln: University of Nebraska Press, 1989.

COOK, W. W., & MEDLEY, D. M. Proposed Hostility pharisaic virtue scales for the MMPI. *Journal of Applied Psychology,* 1954, *38,* 414-418.

COONS, H. L. *Psychosocial aspects of chemotherapy for women with breast cancer and their partners.* Unpublished doctoral dissertation, Temple University, Philadelphia, 1990.

COOPER, C. L. Editorial: Research in stress, coping, and health: Theoretical and methodological issues. *Psychological Medicine,* 1988, *18,* 15-20.

CORCORAN, K., & FISCHER, J. *Measures for clinical practice: A sourcebook.* New York: Free Press, 1987.

COX, T. *Stress.* Baltimore, MD: University Park Press, 1978.

COX, T., & MACKAY, C. J. *A psychological model of occupational stress.* Paper presented to the Medical Research Council meeting on mental health in industry, London, 1976.

COYNE, J. C., & DOWNEY, G. Social factors and psychopathology: Stress, social support and coping processes. *Annual Review of Psychology,* 1991, *42,* 401–425.

CRAIG, T. J., & ABELOFF, M. D. Psychiatric symptomatology among hospitalized cancer patients. *American Journal of Psychiatry,* 1974, *131,* 1323–1327.

CRAVEN, J. L., RODIN, G. M., & LITTLEFIELD, C. The Beck Depression Inventory as a screening device for major depression in renal dialysis patients. *International Journal of Psychiatry in Medicine,* 1988, *18,* 365–374.

CROWN, S., & CRISP, A. H. A short clinical diagnostic self-rating scale for psychoneurotic patients: The Middlesex Hospital Questionnaire (MHQ). *British Journal of Psychiatry,* 1966, *112,* 917–923.

DAHLSTROM, W. G. Recommendations for patient measures in evaluating psychotherapy: Test batteries and inventories. In I. E. Waskow, & M. B. Parloff (eds.), *Psychotherapy change measures.* Rockville, MD: National Institute of Mental Health, 1975.

DAHLSTROM, W. G. & WELSH, G. S. *MMPI Handbook: A guide to use in clinical practice and research.* Minneapolis, University of Minnesota Press, 1960.

DAHLSTROM, W. G., WELSH, G. S., & DAHLSTROM, L. E. *An MMPI handbook: Clinical interpretation Minneapolis.* Vol 1. Minneapolis: University of Minnesota Press, 1972.

DARUNA, J. H., & MORGAN, J. E. Psychosocial effects on immune function: Neuroendocrine pathways. *Psychosomatics,* 1990, *31,* 4–12.

DAVIS, D. A., WEDSETH, J. C. A Minnesota Multiphasic Personality Inventory indicator of psychological distress in male students. *Journal of Counseling Psychology,* 1978, *25,* 469–472.

DCCT RESEARCH GROUP. Reliability and validity of a diabetes quality of life measures for the diabetes control and complications trail. *Diabetes Care,* 1988, *11,* 725–732.

DEBONIS, M. Content analysis of 27 anxiety inventories and rating scales. In P. Pichot (ed.), *Modern problems in pharmacopsychiatry.* Vol. 7. Basel: Karger, 1974.

DEKKER, D. J., & WEBB, J. T. Relationships of the social readjustment rating scale to psychiatric patient status, anxiety, and social desirability. *Journal of Psychosomatic Research,* 1974, *18,* 125–130.

DELONG, R. D. Individual differences in patterns of anxiety arousal, stress-relevant information, and recovery from surgery. *Dissertation Abstracts International,* 1971, *32,* 554.

DELONGIS. A., COYNE, J. C., DAKOF, G., FOLKMAN, S., & LAZARUS, R. A. Relationship of daily hassles uplifts and major life events to health status. *Health Psychology,* 1982, *1,* 119–136.

DEROGATIS, L. R. *The Affects Balance Scale.* Baltimore: Clinical Psychometric Research, 1975. (a)

————. *The SCL-90-R.* Baltimore: Clinical Psychometric Research, 1975. (b)

————. *SCL-90-R administration, scoring & procedures manual.* Vol. 1. Baltimore: Clinical Psychometric Research, 1977.

————. *The Derogatis Stress Profile (DSP).* Baltimore: Clinical Psychometric Research, 1980.

————. Self-report measures of stress. In L. Goldberger & S. Brenznitz (eds.), *Handbook of stress.* New York: Free Press, 1982.

————. *SCL-90-R: Administration, scoring & procedures manual-II* (2d ed.). Baltimore: Clinical Psychometric Research, 1983.

————. The Derogatis, Stress Profile (DSP): Quantification of psychological stress. In G. Fava and T. Wise (eds.), *Advances in psychosomatic medicine.* Basel: Karger, 1987.

————. *SCL-90-R: A bibliography of research reports.* Baltimore: Clinical Psychometric Research, 1990.

DEROGATIS, L. R., ABELOFF, M. D., & FREELAND, C. *Doctor versus patient perception of psychologi-*

cal distress among cancer patients. Paper presented to the annual meeting of the American Society of Clinical Oncology, New Orleans, 1979.

DEROGATIS, L. R., ABELOFF, M. D., & MCBETH, C. D. Cancer patients and their physicians in the perception of psychological symptoms. *Psychosomatics,* 1976, *17,* 197–201.

DEROGATIS, L. R., ABELOFF, M. D., & MELISARATOS, N. Psychological coping mechanisms and survival time in metastic breast cancer. *Journal of the American Medical Association,* 1979, *242,* 1504–1508.

DEROGATIS, L. R., & CLEARY, P. Confirmation of the dimensional structure of the SCL-90: A study in construct validation. *Journal of Clinical Psychology,* 1977, *33,* 981–989. (a)

————. Factorial invariance across gender for the primary symptom dimensions of the SCL-90. *British Journal of Social and Clinical Psychology,* 1977, *16,* 347–356. (b)

DEROGATIS, L. R., DELLAPIETRA, L., & KILROY, V. Screening for psychiatric disorder in medical populations. In M. Fava, G. Rosenbaum, & R. Birnbaum (eds.), *Research designs and methods in psychiatry.* St. Louis, MO: Mosby, 1990.

DEROGATIS, L. R., FALKNER, B., KAREKEN, D. A. & GRABER, C. Psychosocial features and elevated blood pressure in adolescents. *11th Annual Meeting of the Society of Behavioral Medicine,* Chicago IL, April 19–20, 1990.

DEROGATIS, L. R., & GEORGOPOLOUS, A. Psychological factors predictive of glycemic control in diabetics on insulin pump therapy. *48th Annual Meeting of the American Diabetes Association,* Anaheim, CA, June 22–24, 1986.

DEROGATIS, L. R., LIPMAN, R. S., & COVI, L. SCL-90: An outpatient psychiatric rating scale: Preliminary report. *Psychopharmacology Bulletin,* 1973, *9,* 13–27.

DEROGATIS, L. R., LIPMAN, R. S., RICKELS, K., UHLENHUTH, E. H., & COVI, L. The Hopkins Symptom Checklist (HSCL): A self-report symptom inventory. *Behavioral Science,* 1974, *19,* 1–15. (a)

————. The Hopkins Symptom Checklist (HSCL): A measure of primary symptom dimensions. In P. Pichot (ed.), *Psychological measurements in psychopharmacology.* Basel: Karger, 1974. (b)

DEROGATIS, L. R., & MEYER, J. K. A psychological profile of the sexual dysfunctions. *Archives of Sexual Behavior,* 1979, *8,* 201–223.

DEROGATIS, L. R., MEYER, J. K., & BOLAND, P. A psychological profile of the transsexual. Part II: The female. *Journal of Nervous and Mental Disease,* 1981, *169,* 157–168.

DEROGATIS, L. R., MEYER, J. K., & GALLANT, B. W. Distinctions between male and female invested partners in sexual disorders. *American Journal of Psychiatry,* 1977, *134,* 385–390.

DEROGATIS, L. R., MEYER, J. K., & KING, K. M. Psychopathology in individuals with sexual dysfunction. *American Journal of Psychiatry,* 1981, *138,* 757–763.

DEROGATIS, L. R., MEYER, J. K., & VASQUEZ, N. A psychological profile of the transsexual. Part I: The male. *Journal of Nervous and Mental Disease,* 1978, *166,* 234–254.

DEROGATIS, L. R., RICKELS, K., & ROCK, A. The SCL-90 and the MMPI: A step in the validation of a new self-report scale. *British Journal of Psychiatry,* 1976, *128,* 280–289.

DEROGATIS, L. R., & SPENCER, P. M. *The Brief Symptom Inventory: Administration, scoring & procedures manual—I.* Baltimore: Clinical Psychometric Research, 1982.

DEROGATIS, L. R., & WISE, T. N. *Anxiety and depressive disorders in the medical patient.* Washington, DC: American Psychiatric Press, 1989.

DEROGATIS, L. R., YEVZEROFF, H., & WITTELSBERGER, B. Social class, psychological disorder, and the nature of the psychopathologic indicator. *Journal of Consulting and Clinical Psychology,* 1975, *43,* 183–191.

DISE-LEWIS, J. E. The life events and coping inventory: An assessment of stress in children. *Psychosomatic Medicine,* 1988, *50,* 484–489.

Dohrenwend, B. S., Dohrenwend, B. P. (eds.). *Stressful life events: Their nature and effects.* New York: Wiley, 1974.

Dohrenwend, B. S., Dohrenwend, B. P., Dodson, M., & Shrout, P. E. Symptoms, hassles, social supports, and life events: Problem of confounded measures. *Journal of Abnormal Psychology,* 1984, *93,* 222–230.

Edwards, D. W., Yarvis, R. M., Mueller, D. P., Zingale, H. C., & Wagman, W. J. Test-taking and the stability of adjustment scales. *Evaluation Quarterly,* 1978, *2,* 275–291.

Edwards, M. K. *Life crises and myocardial infarction.* Unpublished master's thesis, University of Washington, Seattle, 1971.

Egeland, B., Farrell Erickson, M., Butcher, J. N., & Ben-Porath, Y. S. MMPI-2 profiles of women at risk for child abuse. *Journal of Personality Assessment,* 1991, *57,* 254–263.

Elliot, G. R., & Eisdorfer, C. *Stress and human health.* New York: Springer, 1982.

Engel, G. L. Sudden and rapid death during psychological stress: Folklore or folk wisdom? *Annuals of Internal Medicine,* 1971, *74,* 771–782.

Finney, J. Anxiety: its measurement by objective personality tests. In A. H. Tuma & J. Master (eds.), *Anxiety and the anxiety disorders.* Hillsdale, NJ: Lawrence Erlbaum, 1985.

Fiske, D. W. *Measuring the concepts of personality.* Chicago: Aldine, 1971.

Florell, J. L. Crisis intervention in orthopedic surgery. *Dissertation Abstracts International,* 1971, *32,* 633.

Folkman, S., & Lazarus, R. S. An analysis of coping in a middle-aged community sample. *Journal of Health and Social Behavior,* 1980, *21,* 219–239.

Folkman, S., & Lazarus, R. S. If it changes it must be a process: A study of emotions and coping. *Journal of Personality and Social Psychology,* 1985, *48,* 150–170.

Folkman, S., & Lazarus, R. R. Coping as a mediator of emotion. *Journal of Personality and Social Psychology,* 1988, *54,* 466–475. (a)

————. The relationship between coping and emotion: Implication for theory and research. *Social Science and Medicine,* 1988, *26,* 309–317. (b)

Folkman, S., Lazarus, R. R., Dunkel-Schetter, C., DeLongis, A., & Gruen, R. The dynamics of a stressful encounter: Cognitive appraisal, coping, and encounter outcomes. *Journal of Personality and Social Psychology,* 1986, *50,* 992–1003.

Folkman, S., Lazarus, R. R., Gruen, R. J., & DeLongis, A. Appraisal, coping, health status, and psychological symptoms. *Journal of Personality and Social Psychology,* 1986, *50,* 571–579.

Fontana, A. F., Marcus, J. L., Dowds, B. N., & Hughes, L. A. Psychological impairment and psychological health in the psychological well-being of the physically ill. *Psychosomatic Medicine,* 1980, *42,* 279–288.

Fowler, R. D. Automation and the computer. In J. N. Butcher (ed.), *MMPI: Research developments and clinical applications.* New York: McGraw-Hill, 1969.

Frerichs, R. R., Areshensel, C. S., & Clark, V. A. Prevalence of depression in Los Angeles County. *American Journal of Epidemiology,* 1981, *113,* 691–699.

Friedman, M., & Rosenman, R. H. Association of specific overt behavior pattern with blood and cardiovascular findings. *Journal of the American Medical Association,* 1959, *169,* 1286–1296.

Galton, F. *Inquiries into human faculty and its development.* New York: Macmillan, 1983.

Gass, C. S. MMPI-2 interpretation and closed head injury: A correction factor. *Psychological Assessment: A Journal of Consulting and Clinical Psychology,* 1991, *3,* 27–31.

Glass, D. C. Stress, behavior patterns and coronary disease. *American Scientist,* 1977, *65,* 177–187.

Gleser, G. C. Evaluation of psychotherapy outcome by psychological tests. In I. E. Waskow & M. B., Parloff (eds.), *Psychotherapy change measures.* Rockville, MD: National Institute of Mental Health, 1975.

GLUECK, B. C., & STROEBEL, C. F. The computer and the clinical decision process. *American Journal of Psychiatry,* 1969, *125* (suppl.), 2–7.

GOLDBAND, S., KATKIN, E. S., & MORELL, M. A. Personality and cardiovascular disorder: Steps toward demystification. In I. G. Sarason & C. D. Spielberger (eds.), *Stress and anxiety.* Vol. 6. New York: Wiley, 1979.

GOLDBERG, E. L., & COMSTOCK, G. W. Life events and subsequent illness. *American Journal of Epidemiology,* 1976, *104,* 146–158.

GORSUCH, R. L., & KEY, M. K. Abnormalities of pregnancy as a function of anxiety and life stress. *Psychosomatic Medicine,* 1974, *36,* 352.

GRAHAM, J. R., TIMBROOK, R. E., BEN-PORATH, Y. S. & BUTCHER, J. N. Code-types congruence between MMPI and MMPI-2: Separating fact from artifact. *Journal of Personality Assessment,* 1991, *57,* 205–215.

GRANT, L., SWEETWOOD, H., GERST, M. S., & YAGER, J. Scaling procedures in life events research, *Journal of Psychosomatic Research,* 1978, *22,* 525–530.

GREENBERG, H. S., KAZAK, A. E., & MEADOWS, A. T. Psychologic functioning in 8-to-16 year old cancer survivors and their parents. *Journal of Pediatrics,* 1989, *114,* 488–493.

GREENBERG, J. S. *Comprehensive stress management.* Dubuque, IA: William. C. Brown, 1990.

GREENGLASS, E. R., & JULKUNEN, J. Construct validity and sex differences in Cook-Medley hostility. *Personality and Individual Differences,* 1989, *10,* 209–218.

HALL, S. M., RUGG, D., TUNSTALL, C., & JONES, R. T. Preventing relapse to cigarette smoking by behavioral skill training. *Journal of Consulting and Clinical Psychology,* 1984, *52,* 372–382.

HARGREAVES, W. A., ATTKISSON, C. C., SIEGAL, L. M., & McINTYRE, M. H. *Resource material for community mental health program evaluation, part 4.* Rockville, MD: National Institute of Mental Health, 1975.

HARPER, R. G., & STEGER, J. C. Psychological correlates of frontalis EMG and pain in tension headache. *Headache Journal,* 1978, *18,* 215–218.

HARTSOUGH, D. M. AND SAVITSKY, J. C. Three Mile Island—Psychology and environmental policy at a crossroads. *American Psychologist,* 1984, *39*(10), 1113–1122.

HASKELL, D., PUGATCH, D., & McNAIR, D. M. Time-limited psychotherapy for whom? *Archives of General Psychiatry,* 1969, *21,* 546–552.

HATHAWAY, S. R., & McKINLEY, J. C. A multiphasic personality schedule (Minnesota). Part I: Construction of the schedule. *Journal of Psychology,* 1940, *10,* 249–254.

HAWKINS, N. C., DAVIES, R., & HOLMES, T. H. Evidence of psychosocial factors in the development of pulmonary tuberculosis. *American Review of Tuberculosis and Pulmonary Disorders,* 1957, *75,* 768–780.

HENDLER, N., DEROGATIS, L. R., AVELLA, J., & LONG, D. EMG biofeedback in patients with chronic pain. *Disease of the Nervous System,* 1977, *38,* 505–509.

HENRY, J. P., & STEPHENS, P. M. *Stress, health and the social environment: A sociobiologic approach to medicine.* New York: Springer, 1977.

HINKLE, L. E. Commentary: On stress and cardiovascular disease. *Cardiovascular Medicine,* 1979, *26,* 192–202.

HJEMBOE, S., & BUTCHER, J. N. Couples in marital distress: A study of personality factors as measured by the MMPI-2. *Journal of Personality Assessment, 57,* 1991, 216–237.

HOBFOLL, S. E. Conservation of resources: A new attempt at conceptualizing stress. *American Psychologist,* 1989, *44,* 513–524.

————. Affective profiles of chronically anxious patients. *Journal of Clinical Psychiatry,* 1983, *5,* 43–56.

HOEHN-SARIC, R. Characteristics of chronic anxiety patients. In D. F. Klein & J. Rabkin (eds.), *Anxiety: New research and changing concepts.* New York: Raven Press, 1981.

HOEHN-SARIC, R., MCLEOD, D. R., ZIMMERLI, W. D. Differential effects of alprazolam and imipramine in generalized anxiety disorder: Somatic versus psychic symptoms. *Journal of Psychiatry,* 1988, *49,* 293–301.

HOEHN-SARIC, R., MERCHANT, A., KAISER, M., & SMITH, V. Effects of clonidine in anxiety disorders. *Archives of General Psychiatry,* 1981, *Nov.,* 1278–1282.

HOLLAND, J. C., MORROW, G. R., SCHMALE, A., DEROGATIS, L. R., STEFANEK, M., BERENSON, S., BREITBART, W., & FELDSTEIN, M. Randomized clinical trial of alprazolam versus progressive relaxation in cancer patients with anxiety and depressive symptoms. *Journal of Clinical Oncology,* 1991, *9,* 1004–1011.

HOLMES, T. H. Development and application of a quantitative measure of life change magnitude. In J. E. Barrett (ed.), *Stress and mental disorder.* New York: Raven, 1979.

HOLMES, T. H., & RAHE, R. H. The Social Readjustment Rating Scale. *Journal of Psychosomatic Research,* 1967, *11,* 213–218.

HOROWITZ, M., SCHAEFER, C., HIROTO, D., WILNER, N., & LEVIN, B. Life event questionnaires for measuring presumptive stress. *Psychosomatic Medicine,* 1977, *39,* 413–431.

HOROWITZ, M. J. Depressive disorders in response to loss. In I. G. Sarason & C. D. Spielberger (eds.), *Stress and anxiety.* Vol. 6. New York: Wiley, 1979.

HOROWITZ, M. J., KRUPNICK, J., KALTREIDER, N., WILNER, N., LEONG, A., & MARMER, C. Initial psychological response to parental death. *Archives of General Psychiatry,* 1981, *38,* 316–323.

HOROWITZ, M. J., WILNER, N., & ALVAREZ, W. Impact of event scale: A measure of subjective stress. *Psychosomatic Medicine,* 1979, *41,* 209–218.

HOROWITZ, M. J., WILNER, N., KALTREIDER, N., & ALVAREZ, W. Signs and symptoms of posttraumatic stress disorder. *Archives of General Psychiatry,* 1980, *37,* 85–92.

ILFELD, F. W., JR. Current social stressors and symptoms of depression. *American Journal of Psychiatry,* 1977, *134,* 161–166.

IMBER, S. D. Patient direct self-report techniques. In I. E. Waskow & M. B. Parloff (eds.), *Psychotherapy change measures.* Rockville, MD: National Institute of Mental Health, 1975.

JAMES, G. D., YEE, L. S., HARSHFIELD, G. A., BLANK, S. G., & PICKERING, T. G. The influence of happiness, anger, and anxiety on the blood pressure of borderline hypertensives. *Psychosomatic Medicine.* 1986, *48,* 502–508.

JENKINS, C. D. Psychologic and social precursors of coronary disease. *New England Journal of Medicine,* 1971, *284,* 244–317.

————. Recent evidence supporting psychologic and social risk factors for coronary disease. *New England Journal of Medicine,* 1976, *294,* 987–994, 1033–1038.

JENKINS, C. D., & ROSENMAN, R. H., & FRIEDMAN, M. Development of an objective psychological test for the determination of the coronary-prone behavior pattern in employed men. *Journal of Chronic Diseases,* 1967, *20,* 371–379.

JENKINS, C. D., ROSENMAN, R. H., & ZYZANSKI, S. J. Prediction of clinical coronary-prone behavior pattern. *New England Journal of Medicine,* 1974, *290,* 1271–1275.

JENKINS, C. D., & ZYZANSKI, S. J. Behavioral risk factors and coronary heart disease. *Psychotherapy and Psychosomatics,* 1980, *34,* 149–177.

JENKINS, C. D., ZYZANSKI, S. J., & ROSENMAN, R. H. Risk of new myocardial infarction in middle-aged men with manifest coronary heart disease. *Circulation,* 1976, *53,* 342–347.

JENKINS, C. D., ZYZANSKI, S. J., RYAN, T. J., FLESSAS, A., & TANNENBAUM, S. I. Social insecurity and coronary-prone type A responses as identifiers of severe atherosclerosis. *Journal of Consulting and Clinical Psychology,* 1977, *45,* 1060–1067.

JOHNSON, J. H., & SARASON, I. G. Life stress, depression, and anxiety: Internal-external control as a moderator variable. *Journal of Psychosomatic Research,* 1978, *22,* 205–208.

————. Moderator variables in life stress research. In I. G. Sarason & C. D. Spielberger (eds.), *Stress and anxiety.* Vol. 6. New York: Wiley, 1979.

KAGAN, A. R., & LEVI, L. Health and environment—psychosocial stimuli: A review. *Social Science & Medicine,* 1974, *8,* 225–291.

KALES, J. D., KALES, A., SOLDATOS, C. R., CALDWELL, A. B., CHARNEY, D. S., & MARTIN, E. Night terrors: Clinical characteristics and personality patterns. *Archives of General Psychiatry,* 1980, *37,* 1406–1410.

KANNER, A. D., COYNE, J. C., SCHAEFER, C., & LAZARUS, R. Comparisons of two modes of stress measurement: Daily hassles & uplifts versus major life events. *Journal of Behavioral Medicine,* 1981, *4,* 1–39.

KEEGAN, D. L., SINHA, B. N., MERRIMAN, J. E., & SHIPLEY, C. Type A behavior pattern. *Canadian Journal of Psychiatry,* 1979, *24,* 724–730.

KELLER, M. B., & LAVORI, P. W. The adequacy of treating depression. *Journal of Nervous and Mental Disease.* 1988, *176,*(8), 471–474.

KENDALL, P. C., FINCH, A. J., JR., AUERBACH, S. M., HOOKE, J. F., & MILKULKA, P. J. The state-trait anxiety inventory: A systematic evaluation. *Journal of Consulting and Clinical Psychology,* 1976, *44,* 406–412.

KOCH, A. A strategy for prevention: Role flexibility and affective reactivity as factors in family coping. *Family Systems Medicine,* 1985, *3,* 70–81.

KOVACS, M., GATSONIS, C., PAULAUSKAS, S. L., & RICHARDS, C. Depressive disorders in childhood: IV. A longitudinal study of comorbidity with and risk for anxiety disorders. *Archives of General Psychiatry,* 1989, *46,* 776.

KRANTZ, D. S., & GLASS, D. C. Personality, behavior patterns and physical illness: Conceptual and methological issues. In W. D. Gentry (ed.), *The handbook of behavioral medicine.* New York: Guilford, 1984.

KUHN, T. S. *The structure of scientific revolutions: International Encyclopedia of Unified Science* (2d ed.). Chicago: University of Chicago Press, 1970.

LAMB, D. H. The effects of public speaking on self-report physiological and behavioral measures of anxiety. *Dissertation Abstracts International,* 1970, *31,* 2284.

LAMB, D. H., & PLANT, R. Patient anxiety in the dentist's office. *Journal of Dental Research,* 1972, *51,* 986–989.

LAMPING, D. L. Assessment in health psychology. *Canadian Psychology,* 1985, *26,* 121–139.

LAVEE, Y., MCCUBBIN, H. I., & PATTERSON, J. M. The Double ABCX Model of Family Stress and Adaptation: An empirical test by analysis of structural equations with latent variables. *Journal of Marriage and the Family,* 1985, *47,* 811–825.

LAZARUS, R. S. *Psychological stress and the coping process.* New York: McGraw-Hill, 1966.

————. *Patterns of adjustment.* New York: McGraw-Hill, 1976.

————. The stress and coping paradigm. In C. Eisdorfer, D. Cohen, A. Kleinman, & P. Maxim (eds.), *Models for clinical psychopathology.* New York: Spectrum, 1981.

LAZARUS, R. A., & DELONGIS, A. Psychological stress and coping in aging. *American Psychologist,* 1983, *38,* 245–254.

LAZARUS, R. S., DELONGIS, A., FOLKMAN, S. & GRUEN, R. Stress and adaptational outcomes: The problem of confounded measures. *American Psychologist,* 1985, *40,* 770–779.

LAZARUS, R. S., & FOLKMAN, S. *Stress, appraisal, and Coping.* New York: Springer, 1984.

LEES-HALEY, P. R. Ego strength denial on the MMPI-2 as a clue to simulation of personal injury in vocational neuropsychological and emotional distress evaluations. *Perceptual and Motor Skills,* *72,* 1991, 815–819.

LEHRER, P. M., WOOLFOLK, R. L., & COLE, J. The use of meditation-relaxation techniques for the management of stress in a working population. *Journal of Occupational Medicine,* 1980, *22,* 221–231.

LEI, H., & SKINNER, H. A. A psychometric study of life events and social readjustment. *Journal of Psychosomatic Research,* 1980, *24,* 57–66.

LEVENTHAL, H., & DIEFENBACH, M. The active side of illness cognition. In J. A. Skelton & R. T. Croyle (eds.), *Mental representation in health and illness.* New York: Springer-Verlag, in press.

LEVENTHAL, H., LEVENTHAL, E. A., & SCHAEFFER, P. M. Vigilant coping and health behavior. In M. Ory & R. Abeles (eds.), *Aging, health, and behavior.* Baltimore: Johns Hopkins, in press.

LEVENTHAL, H., NERENZ, D. R., & STEELE, D. J. Illness representations and coping with health threats. In A. Baum & J. Singer (eds.), *A handbook of psychology and health.* Vol. 4. Hillsdale, NJ: Erlbaum, 1984.

LEVY, S. M., LEE, J., BAGLEY, C., & LIPPMAN, M. Survival hazards analysis in first recurrent breast cancer patients; Seven-year follow-up. *Psychosomatic Medicine,* 1988, *50,* 520.

LEWANDOWSKI, A., BYL, N., FRANKLIN, B., GORDON, S., TIMMIS, G. C., & BEAUMONT, W. Relationship of the Derogatis Stress Profile (DSP) to staff perception of adjustment and prognosis of cardiac patients: Implications for rehabilitation. *Journal of Cardiopulmonary Rehabilitation,* 1987, *VII,* 502.

LINN, M. W. A Global Assessment of Recent Stress (GARS) scale. *International Journal of Psychiatry in Medicine,* 1985, *15,* 47–59.

LITZ, B., PENK, W. E., WALSH, S., HYER, S., HYER, L., BLAKE, D. D., MARX, B., KEANE, T. M., & BITMAN, D. Similarities and differences between MMPI and MMPI-2 applications to the assessment of posttraumatic stress disorder. *Journal of Personality Assessment, 57,* 1991, 238–253.

LORR, M., MCNAIR, D. M., & WEINSTEIN, G. J. Early effects of chlordiazepoxide (Librium) used with psychotherapy. *Journal of Psychiatric Research,* 1963, *1,* 257–270.

LUNDEEN, T. F., & GEORGE, J. M., & STURDEVANT, J. R. Stress in patients with pain in the muscles of mastication and the temporomandibular joints. *Journal of Oral Rehabilitation,* 1988, *15,* 631–637.

LUNDEEN, T. F., STURDEVANT, J. R., GEORGE, J. M. Stress as a factor in muscle and temporomandibular joint pain. *Journal of Oral Rehabilitation,* 1987, *14,* 447–456.

MAIN, C. J. The Modified Somatic Perception Questionnaire (MSPQ). *Journal of Psychosomatic Research,* 1983, *27,*(6), 503–514.

MARKUSH, R. E., & FAYERO, R. V. Epidemiologic assessment of stressful life-events, depressed mood, and psychophysiological symptoms: A preliminary report. In B. S. Dohrenwend & B. P. Dohrenwend (eds.), *Stressful life events: Their nature and effects.* New York: Wiley, 1974.

MARMOT, M. Type A behavior and ischemic heart disease. *Psychological Medicine,* 1980, *10,* 603–606.

MARX, M. B., GARRITY, T. F., & BOWERS, F. R. The influence of recent life experience on the health of college freshman. *Journal of Psychosomatic Research,* 1975, *19,* 87.

MATTHEWS, K. A. CHD and type A behavior: Update on an alternative to the Booth-Kewley and Friedman Quantitative Review. *Psychological Bulletin,* 1988, *104,* 373–380.

MATTHEWS, K. A., KRANTZ, D. S., DEMBROWSKI, T. M., & MACDOUGAL, J. M. Unique and common variance in structured interview and Jenkins activity survey measures of type A behavior pattern. *Journal of Personality and Social Psychology,* 1982, *42,* 303–313.

McCubbin, H. I., Cauble, A. E., & Patterson, J. M., (eds.) *Family stress, coping and social support*. Springfield, IL: Charles C. Thomas, 1982.

McCubbin, H. I., Joy, C. B., Cauble, A. E., Comeau, J. K., Patterson, J. M., & Needle, R. H. Family stress and coping: A decade review. *Journal of Marriage and the Family*, 1980, *42*, 855–871.

McCubbin, H. I., Larsen, A., & Olson, D. H. *Family Crisis Oriented Personal Evaluation Scales (F-COPES)*. St. Paul, MN: Family Social Science, 1981.

McCubbin, H. I., McCubbin, M. A., Patterson, J. M., Cauble, A. E., Wilson, L. R., & Warwick, W. CHIP-Coping Health Inventory for Parents: An assessment of parental coping patterns in the care of the chronically ill child. *Journal of Marriage and the Family*, 1983, *45*, 359–370.

McCubbin, H. I., & Patterson, J. M. Family adaptation to crises. In H. I. McCubbin, A. E. Cauble, & J. M. Patterson (eds.), *Family stress, coping, and social support*. Springfield, IL: Charles C. Thomas, 1982.

————. The family stress process: The Double ABCX Model of Adjustment and Adaptation; *Marriage and Family Review*, 1983, *6*, 7–35.

McCubbin, H. I., Patterson, J. M., & Wilson, L. *The Family Inventory of Life Events and Changes (FILE)*. St. Paul, MN: Family Social Science, 1981.

McGuffin, P., Katz, R., & Bebbington, P. E. The Camberwell Collaborative Depression Study: II. Depression and adversity in the relatives of depressed probands. *British Journal of Psychiatry*, 1988, *152*, 775–782.

McLean, P. D. Depression as a specific response to stress. In I. G. Sarason & C. D. Spielberger (eds.), *Stress and anxiety*. Vol. 3. New York: Wiley, 1976.

McNair, D. M. Self-evaluations of antidepressants. *Psychopharmacologia*, 1974, *37*, 281–302.

McNair, D. M., & Lorr, M. An analysis of mood in neurotics. *Journal of Abnormal and Social Psychology*, 1964, *69*, 620–627.

McNair, D. M., Lorr, M., & Droppleman, L. F. *Profile of mood states*. San Diego, CA: Educational and Industrial Testing Service, 1971.

Mechanic, D., & Hansell, S. Adolescent competence, psychological well-being and self-assessed health. *Journal of Health and Social Behavior*, 1987, *28*, 364–374.

Meehl, P. E., & Dahlstrom, W. G. Objective configural rules for discriminating psychotic from neurotic MMPI profiles. *Journal of Clinical and Consulting Psychology*, 1960, *21*, 375–387.

Meyer, A. The life chart and the obligation of specifying positive data in psychopathological diagnosis. In E. Winters (ed.), *The collected papers of Adolph Meyer*. Vol. 3. Baltimore: Johns Hopkins Press, 1951.

Miller, F. T., Bentz, W. K., Aponte, J. R., & Brogan, D. R. Perception of life crisis events. In B. S. Dohrenwend & B. P. Dohrenwend (eds.), *Stressful life events: Their nature and effects*. New York: Wiley, 1974.

Miyabo, S., Asato, T., & Mizushima, N. Psychological correlates of stress-induced cortisol and growth hormone releases in neurotic patients. *Psychosomatic Medicine*, 1979, *41*, 515–523.

Monroe, S. M. Stress and social support: Assessment issues. In N. Schneiderman, S. M., Weiss, & P. G. Kaufmann (eds.), *Handbook of research methods in cardiovascular behavioral medicine*. New York: Plenum Press, 1989.

Munley, P. H. A comparison of MMPI-2 and MMPI T-scores for men and women. *Journal of Clinical Psychology*, 47, 1991, 87–91.

Myers, J. K., Lindenthal, J. J., & Pepper, M. P. Life events and psychiatric impairment. *Journal of Nervous and Mental Disorders*, 1971, *152*, 149–157.

—————. Life events and mental status: A longitudinal study. *Journal of Health and Social Behavior,* 1972, *13,* 398–406.

Nerenz, D. R., & Leventhal, H. Self-regulation theory in chronic illness. In T. G. Burish & L. Bradley (eds.), *Coping with chronic disease: Research and applications.* New York: Academic Press, 1983.

Nielsen, W. R., & Dobson, K. S. The coronary-prone behavior pattern and trait anxiety: Evidence for discriminant validity. *Journal of Consulting and Clinical Psychology,* 1980, *48,* 546–547.

Nielson, A. C., III, & Williams, T. A. Depression in ambulatory medical patients. *Archives of General Psychiatry,* 1980, *37,* 999–1004.

Norman, W. T. On estimating psychological relationships: Social desirability and self report. *Psychological Bulletin,* 1967, *67,* 273–293.

—————. Psychometric considerations for a revision of the MMPI. In J. N. Butcher (ed.), *Objective personality assessment: Changing perspectives.* New York: Academic, 1972.

Northouse, L. L. Social support in patients and husbands adjustment to breast cancer. *Nursing Research,* 1987, *37,* 91–95.

Northouse, L. L., & Swain, A. Adjustment of patients and husbands to the initial impact of breast cancer. *Nurses Research,* 1987, *36,* 221.

O'Leary, A. Stress, emotion and human immune function. *Psychological Bulletin,* 1990, *108,* 363–382.

Pancheri, P., Bellaterra, M., Matteoli, S., Cristofari, M., Polizzi, C., & Puletti, M. Infarct as a stress agent: Life history and personality characteristics in improved versus non-improved patients after severe heart attack. *Journal of Human Stress,* 1978, *5,* 16–22.

Patterson, J. M., & McCubbin, H. I. The impact of family life events and changes on the health of a chronically ill child. *Family Relations,* 1983, *32,* 255–264. (a)

—————. Chronic illness: Family stress and coping. In C. R. Figley & H. I. McCubbin (eds.), *Stress and the family: Coping with catastrophe.* Vol. 2. New York: Brunner-Mazel, 1983. (b)

Paykel, E. S., Myers, J. K., Dienett, M. N., Klerman, G. L., Lindenthal, J. J., & Pepper, M. P. Life events and depression: A controlled study. *Archives of General Psychiatry,* 1969, *21,* 753–760.

Pert, C. B. The wisdom of the receptors: Neuropeptides, the emotions and bodymind. *Advances: Institute for Advancement of Health,* 1986, *3,* 8–16.

Piotrowski, C., & Lubin, B. Assessment practices of health psychologist: Survey of APA division 38 Clinicians. *Professional Psychology,* 1990, *21,* 99–106.

Plumin, R. The role of inheritance in behavior. *Science,* 1990, *248,* 183–188.

Rabkin, J. G., & Struening, E. L. Life events, stress, and illness. *Science,* 1976, *194,* 1013.

Radloff, L. S. The CES-D Scale: A self-report depression scale for research in the general population. *Applied Psychological Measurement,* 1977, 1, 385–401.

Radloff, L. S., & Locke, B. Z. The Community Mental Health Assessment Survey and the CES-D Scale. In M. M. Weissman, J. K. Meyers, C. G. Ross (eds.), *Community Surveys of Psychiatric Disorder.* New Brunswick, Rutgers University Press, 1985.

Rahe, R. H. Life change measurement as a predictor of illness. *Proceedings of the Royal Society of Medicine,* 1968, *61,* 1124–1126.

—————. The pathway between subjects' recent life changes and their near future illness reports: Representative results and methodological issues. In B. S. Dohrenwend & B. P. Dohrenwend (eds.), *Stressful life events: Their nature and effects.* New York: Wiley, 1974.

—————. Life change measurement clarification. *Psychosomatic Medicine,* 1978, *40,* 95–98.

Rahe, R. H., & Lind, E. Psychosocial factors and sudden cardiac death: A pilot study. *Journal of Psychosomatic Research,* 1971, *15,* 19.

RAHE, R. H., MCKEEN, J. D., & ARTHUR, R. J. A longitudinal study of life change and illness patterns. *Journal of Psychosomatic Research,* 1967, *10,* 355.

RAHE, R. H., MEYER, M., SMITH, M., KJAER, G., & HOLMES, T. H. Social stress and illness onset. *Journal of Psychosomatic Research,* 1964, *8,* 35–44.

RAHE, R. H., & PUGH, W. M., ERICKSON, J., GUNDERSON, E. K. E., & RUBIN, R. T. Cluster analyses of life changes. Part I: Consistency of clusters across large navy samples. *Archives of General Psychiatry,* 1971, *25,* 330.

REYNOLDS, W. M., & GOULD, J. W. A psychometric investigation of the standard and short form Beck Depression Inventory. *Journal of Consulting and Clinical Psychology,* 1981, *49,* 306–307.

RICHARDSON, G. M., & MCGRATH, P. J. Cognitive-behavioral therapy for Migraine headaches: A minimal-therapist-contact approach versus a clinic-based approach. *Headache,* 1989, *29,* 352–357.

ROBERTS, R. E., RHOADES, H. M. & VERNON, S. W. Using the CES-D Scale to Screen for Depression and Anxiety Effects of Language and Ethnic Status. *Psychological Research,* 1990, *31,* 69–83.

ROGENTINE, D. S., VANKAMMEN, D. P., FOX, B. H., DOCHERTY, J. P., ROSENBLATT, J. E., BOYD, S. L., & BUNNEY, W. E. Psychological factors in the prognosis of malignant melanoma: A prospective study, *Psychosomatic Medicine,* 1979, *41,* 647–655.

RORER, L. G. The great response-style myth. *Psychological Bulletin,* 1965, *63,* 129–156.

ROTH, D. L., & HOLMES, D. S. Influence of aerobic exercise training and relaxation training on physical and psychologic health following stressful life events. *Psychosomatic Medicine,* 1987, *49,* 355–365.

SANGAL, R., COYLE, G., & HOEHN-SARIC, R. Chronic anxiety and social adjustment. *Comprehensive Psychiatry,* 1983, *24,* 75–78.

SARASON, I. G., JOHNSON, J. H., & SIEGAL, J. M. Assessing the impact of life changes. In I. G. Sarason & C. D. Spielberger (eds.), *Stress and anxiety.* Vol. 6. New York: Wiley, 1979.

SCHAEFFER, M. A., & BAUM, A. Adrenal cortical response to stress at Three Mile Island. *Psychosomatic Medicine,* 1984, *46*(3), 227–237.

SCHROEDER, D. H., & COSTA, P. T. Influence of life event stress on physical illness: Substantive effects or methodologic flaws. *Journal of Personality and Social Psychology,* 1984, *46,* 853–863.

SCHWAB, J. J., BIALOW, M., BROWN, J. M., & HOLZER, C. E. Diagnosing depression in medical inpatients. *Annals of Internal Medicine,* 1967, *67,* 695–707.

SELYE, H. *The physiology and pathology of exposure to stress.* Montreal: Acta, 1950.

————. The evolution of the stress concept. *American Journal of Cardiology,* 1970, *26,* 289–299.

SHACHAM, S., REINHARDT, L. C., RAUBERTAS, R. F., & CLEELAND, C. S. Emotional states and pain: Intraindividual and interindividual measures of association. *Journal of Behavioral Medicine,* 1983, *6,* 405–409.

SHROUT, P. E., & YAGER, T. J. Reliability and validity of screening scales: Effect of reducing scale length. *Journal of clinical Epidemiology,* 1989, *42,* 69–78.

SKINNER, H. A., & LEI, H. Differential weights in life change research: Useful or irrelevant? *Psychosomatic Medicine,* 1980, *42,* 367–370.

SMITH, R. C., & LAY, C. D. State and trait anxiety: An annotated bibliography. *Psychological Reports,* 1974, *34,* 519–594.

SOLIS, C. Psychological stress in Marine Corps officers. *Military Medicine,* 1990, *156,* 223–227.

SPIELBERGER, C. D. Theory and research on anxiety. In C. D. Spielberger (ed.), *Anxiety and behavior.* New York: Academic, 1966.

————. Anxiety as an emotional state. In C. D. Spielberger (ed.), *Anxiety: Current trends in theory and research.* Vol. 1. New York: Academic, 1972.

————. *Preliminary test manual for the State-Trait Anxiety Inventory for Children ("How I feel Questionnaire")*. Palo Alto, CA: Consulting Psychologists Press, 1973.

Spielberger, C. D., Gonzalez-Reigosa, F., & Martinez-Urrutia, A. Development of the Spanish edition of the State-Trait Anxiety Inventory. *Interamerican Journal of Psychology*, 1971, *5*, 3–4.

Spielberger, C. D., Gorsuch, R. C., & Lushene, R. E. *Manual for the State-Trait Anxiety Inventory*. Palo Alto, CA: Consulting Psychologists Press, 1970.

Stanwyck, D., & Anson, C. Is personality related to illness: Cluster profiles of aggregated data. *Advances: Institute for the Advancement of Health*, 1986, *3*, 4–15.

Strober, M., Green, J., & Carlson, G. Utility of the Beck Depression Inventory with psychiatrically hospitalized adolescents. *Journal of Consulting and Clinical Psychology*, *49*, 1981, 482–483.

Sturdevant, J., George, J. M., & Lundeen, T. F. An interactional view of dental students' stress. *Journal of Dental Education*, 1989, *51*, 246–249.

Tait, R. C., Pollard, C. A., Margolis, R. B., & Duckro, P. N. The Pain Disability Index: Psychometric and validity data. *Archives in Physical Medicine Rehabilitation*, 1987, *68*, 438.

Taylor, S. E. Adjustment to threatening events: A theory of cognitive adaptation. *American Psychologist*, 1983, *38*, 1161–1173.

Taylor, S. E., Lichtman, R. R., & Wood, J. V. Attributions, beliefs about control, and adjustment to breast cancer. *Journal of Personality and Social Psychology*, 1984, *46*, 489–502.

Taylor, S. E., Wood, J. V., & Lichtman, R. R. It could be worse: Selective evaluation as a response to victimization. *Journal of Social Issues*, 1983, *39*, 19–40.

Taylor, G. J., Bagby, R. M., Doody, K. F., Keefe, P., Parker, J. D. A., & Ryan, D. P. Criterion validity of the Toronto Alexithymia Scale. *Psychosomatic Medicine*, 1988, *50*(5), 500–509.

Toedter, L. J., Alhadeff, J. M., & Lasker, J. N. The Perinatal Grief Scale development and initial validation. *American Journal of Orthopsychiatry*, 1988, *58*(3), 435–449.

Theorell, T., & Rahe, R. H. Psychosocial factors and myocardial infarction. Part I: An inpatient study in Sweden. *Journal of Psychosomatic Research*, 1971, *15*, 25–31.

Thoits, P. A. Life events and psychological distress. In H. B. Kaplan (ed.), *Psychological Stress: Trends in theory and research*. New York: Academic Press, 1983.

Uhlenhuth, E. H. The measurement of anxiety. In A. H. Tuma & J. Maser (eds.), *Anxiety and the anxiety disorders*. Hillsdale, NJ: Lawrence Erlbaum, 1985.

Uhlenhuth, E. H., & Paykel, E. S. Symptom intensity and life events. *Archives of General Psychiatry*, 1973, *28*, 473–477.

Van Doornen, L. J. P. The coronary risk personality: Psychological and physiological aspects. *Psychotherapy and Psychosomatics*, 1980, *34*, 204–215.

Van Dul, H., & Nagelkerke, N. Statistical discrimination of male myocardial infarction patients and healthy males by means of a psychological test and a tracing of basic dimensions of the infarction personality. *Psychotherapy and Psychosomatics*, 1980, *34*, 196–203.

Verhagen, F., Nass, C., Appels, A., Van Bastelier, A., & Winnbust, J. Cross-validation of the A/B typology in the Netherlands. *Psychotherapy and Psychosomatics*, 1980, *34*, 178–186.

Vingerhoets, A. J., & Marcelissen, F. H. Stress research: Its present status and issues for future developments. *Social Sciences in Medicine*, 1988, *26*, 279–291.

Vinokur, A., & Selzer, M. L. Desirable versus undesirable life events: Their relationship to stress and mental distress. *Journal of Personality and Social Psychology*, 1975, *32*, 329.

Warheit, G. J. Life events, coping stress, and depressive symptomatology. *American Journal of Psychiatry*, 1979, *136*, 502–507.

WASKOW, I. E., & PARLOFF, M. B. (eds.). *Psychotherapy change measures.* Rockville, MD: National Institute of Mental Health, 1975.

WATSON, D. Intraindividual and interindividual analyses of positive and negative affect: Their relation to health complaints, perceived stress, and daily activities. *Journal of Personality and Social Psychology,* 1988, *54,* 1020–1030.

WATSON, D., CLARK, L. A., & CAREY, G. Positive and negative affectivity and their relation to anxiety and depressive disorders. *Journal of Abnormal Psychology,* 1988, *97,* 346–353.

WATSON, D., CLARK, L. A., & TELLEGEN, A. Development and validation of brief measures of positive and negative affect: The PANAS Scales. *Journal of Personality and Social Psychology,* 1988, *54,* 1063–1070.

WATSON, D., & PENNEBAKER, D. W. Health complaints, stress and distress: Exploring the center race of negative affectivity. *Psychological Review,* 1989, *96,* 234–254.

WATSON, D., & TELLEGEN, A. Toward a consensual structure of mood. *Psychological Bulletin,* 1985, *98,* 219–235.

WEED, N. C., BUTCHER, J. N., MCKENNA, T., & BEN-PORATH, Y. S. New measures for assessing alcohol and drug abuse with the MMPI-2: The APS and AAS. *Journal of Personality Assessment, 58,* 1992, 389–404.

WEISSMAN, M. M., POTTENGER, M., KLEBER, H., RUBEN, H. L., WILLIAMS, D., & THOMPSON, W. D. Symptom patterns in primary and secondary depression: A comparison of primary depressives with depressed opiate addicts, alcoholics, and schizophrenics. *Archives of General Psychiatry,* 1977, *34,* 854–862.

WEISSMAN, M. M., SHOLOMSKAS, D., POTTENGER, M., PRUSOFF, B. A., & LOCKE, B. Z. Assessing depressive symptoms in five psychiatric populations: A validation study. *American Journal Epidemiology,* 1977, *106,* 203–214.

WEITZ, J. Psychological research needs on the problems of human stress. In J. E. McGarth (ed.), *Social and psychological factors in stress.* New York: Holt, 1970.

WETZLER, H. P., & ORSANO, R. J. A positive association between physical health practices and psychological well-being. *Journal of Nervous and Mental Disease,* 1988, *129,* 280–283.

WHITAKER, A., JOHNSON, J., SHAFFER, D., RAPPORT, J. L., KALIKOO, K., WALSH, B. T., DAVIES, M., BRAIMAN, S., & DOLINSKY, A. Uncommon trouble in young people: Prevalence estimates of selected psychiatric disorders in a nonreferred adolescent population. *Archives of General Psychiatry,* 1990, *47,* 487–496.

WIGGINS, J. S. Convergences among stylistic response measures from objective personality tests. *Education Psychological Measurement,* 1964, *24,* 551–562.

WILDE, G. J. S. Trait description and measurement by personality questionnaires. In R. B. Cattell (ed.), *Handbook of modern personality theory.* Chicago: Aldine, 1972.

WILLIAMS, R. B., & BAREFOOT, J. C. Coronary-prone behavior: The emerging role of the hostility complex. In B. K. Houston & C. R. Snyder (eds.), *Type A behavior pattern. Research, theory, and intervention.* New York: Wiley, 1988.

WILLIAMS, R. B., HANEY, T. L., LEE, K. L., KANG, Y., BLUMENTHAL, J. A., & WHALEN, R. E. Type A behavior, hostility, and coronary atherosclerosis. *Psychosomatic Medicine,* 1980, *42,* 538–549.

WORLD HEALTH ORGANIZATION. *WHO constitution.* Geneva: World Health Organization, 1960.

WOLF, T. H., ELSTON, R. C., & KISSLING, G. E. Relationship of hassles, uplifts, and life events to psychological well-being of freshman medical students. *Behavioral Medicine,* 1989, (*Spring*), 37–45.

WOODWORTH, R. S. *Personal data sheet.* Chicago: Stoelting, 1918.

ZEISS, A. M. Aversiveness versus change in the assessment of life stress. *Journal of Psychosomatic Research,* 1980, *24,* 15–19.

13

Coping Resources and Processes: Current Concepts and Measures

Rudolf H. Moos   Jeanne A. Schaefer

IN THE PAST TWO DECADES, we have gained a better understanding of the role of coping resources in the stress process and of the specific processes people use to manage stressful life circumstances. In this chapter, we build on two earlier reviews of this area (Moos, 1974; Moos & Billings, 1982) and focus on how four theoretical perspectives have contributed to current concepts and measures of coping. We use ideas from this literature to formulate a conceptual framework that focuses on the coping resources and processes that influence how people resolve and adapt to stressful life circumstances. We then use the framework to guide a review of recent developments in the assessment of coping and to examine research on the determinants and consequences of coping processes.

In general, we use the term coping *resources* to refer to the relatively stable personal and social factors that influence how individuals try to manage life crises and transitions. Coping *processes* refer to the cognitive and behavioral efforts individuals employ in specific stressful circumstances.

THEORETICAL ANTECEDENTS OF COPING CONCEPTS

Four related perspectives have shaped current approaches to understanding coping: evolutionary theory and behavioral adaptation, psychoanalytic concepts and ideas about personal growth, life cycle theories of human development, and case studies of the process of managing life crises and transitions.

Evolutionary Theory and Behavioral Adaptation

Charles Darwin's theory of evolution examined the process of adaptation to the environment. The two central elements in Darwinian theory are variation in the reproduction and inheritance of living organisms and natural selection for the survival of the fittest. The

Part of this manuscript was adapted from Moos and Billings (1982). Preparation of the manuscript was supported by Department of Veterans Affairs Medical and Health Services Research and Development Service research funds and by NIAAA Grants AA02863 and AA06699.

internal factor of variation is seen as positive and creative; it produces the diversity needed for progress. The external factor of natural selection eliminates the harmful or less useful variations and enables those that are beneficial to develop and reproduce. Living organisms exist in the "web of life" in which they "struggle for existence" in a specific environment.

Darwin's ideas shaped the formation of ecology, which is the study of the connections between organisms or groups of organisms and their environment. Evolutionary thought and human ecology have focused primarily on communal adaptation. Human beings cannot adapt to their environment alone; they are interdependent and must make collective efforts to survive. Human ecology posits that the formation of social bonds is an essential aspect of effective transaction with the environment. Communal adaptation is an outgrowth of individual adaptation and of specific coping strategies that serve to contribute to group survival and promote human community.

This orientation led to an emphasis on behavioral problem-solving activities that enhance individual and species survival. The behaviorist tradition initially considered the functional aspects of goal-directed behavior, but more recent approaches have highlighted the role of cognition in effective adaptation. Cognitive behaviorism is concerned with an individual's appraisal of the self and the meaning of an event as well as with behavioral problem-solving skills. A sense of self-efficacy is thought to be an essential coping resource. Successful coping promotes expectations of self-efficacy, which lead to more vigorous and persistent efforts to master new tasks (Bandura, 1989).

Psychoanalytic Concepts and Personal Growth

Sigmund Freud's psychoanalytic perspective set the stage for an intrapsychic and cognitive counterpoint to the evolutionary emphasis on behavioral factors. Freud attributed behavior to the drive to reduce tension by satisfying sexual and aggressive instincts. He believed that ego processes served to resolve conflicts between an individual's impulses and the constraints of external reality. In essence, ego processes reduce tension by enabling the individual to express sexual and aggressive impulses indirectly without recognizing their true intent. Ego processes are cognitive mechanisms (though their expression may involve behavioral components) whose main functions are defensive (to distort reality) and emotion-focused (to reduce tension).

The neo-Freudian ego psychologists objected to these ideas. They posited a "conflict-free ego sphere" with autonomous energy that fueled reality-oriented processes such as attention and perception. Moreover, they thought that the exercise of ego functions such as cognition and memory was rewarding in its own right. Although there is a strong drive to reduce excessive tension, many people search for novelty and excitement and try to master their environment. They possess such aspects of competence motivation as curiosity and an exploratory drive, a need for new and varied stimulation ("stimulus hunger"), and a sense of agency and of being in control of their lives.

These ideas formed the basis for a new set of growth or fulfillment theories. For example, Carl Rogers believed that people try to actualize or develop their capacities in ways that serve to maintain life and promote growth (Rogers, 1961). Abraham Maslow distinguished between deficiency and growth motivation. Deficiency motivation reflects a drive to survive and aims to decrease tension arising from such needs as hunger and thirst. In contrast, growth motivation reflects an orientation toward self-actualization and entails the urge to enrich one's experience and expand one's horizons. According to Maslow, mature, healthy persons perceive reality accurately, are solution-centered and spontaneous, and have a strong social interest, a genuine desire to help others, and a broad perspective on life (Maslow, 1968).

Developmental Life Cycle Theories

Psychoanalytic theorists posited that life events in infancy strongly affect or even determine adult personality. But information about the growth of ego functions and normal patterns of maturation shows that early life events do not necessarily foreshadow an individual's character or pattern of reaction to crises and transitions. In addition to highlighting the processes of defense and coping, psychoanalysis and ego psychology thus provided the basis for developmental approaches that consider the gradual acquisition of personal coping resources over the life span.

Erik Erikson (1963) described eight life stages, each of which encompasses a new challenge or "crisis" that must be negotiated successfully in order for an individual to cope adequately with the next stage. Personal coping resources (such as the formation of trust and ego integrity) accrued during the adolescent and young adult years are integrated into the self-concept and shape the process of coping in adulthood and old age. Adequate resolution of the issues that occur at one stage in the life cycle leaves a legacy of coping resources that can help to resolve subsequent crises.

Stage models such as Erikson's often are depicted as a spiral staircase; failure to attain one landing implies failure to attain the next. In contemporary life, however, adulthood is not usually composed of an invariant sequence of stages that occur at specific chronological ages. Most people do expect certain life events to occur at particular times, and they develop a mental clock stipulating whether they are on time. But our idea of social timing has changed dramatically over the past two decades. The rhythm of the life cycle is much more fluid as more men and women are divorcing and remarrying, children are reared in blended families, and more middle-aged people go back to college or begin a new family. The increasing flexibility of adulthood has highlighted the transitions of middle and old age and how individuals cope with them.

Coping with Life Crises and Transitions

In-depth studies of the process of adaptation to life crises and transitions have sparked renewed interest in human competence and coping. Some of the most compelling accounts are of the harrowing conditions in prisoner-of-war and concentration camps. Camp inmates experienced brutal and degrading living conditions, forced labor, malnutrition, disease, and the ever-present threat of imminent death. But even under these conditions many people managed to salvage some control over their fate. Some prisoners of war resisted their interrogators, developed underground communication networks, and tried to remain loyal to their idealized self-image. Some concentration camp inmates endured so they could later bear witness or seek revenge.

Other work in this area has focused on more prevalent stressors, such as parental and sibling death, migration and relocation, disasters such as floods and tornadoes, and being the victim of rape, kidnapping, or terrorism (Moos, 1986). Similar studies have examined how individuals adapt to serious physical illness or injury and face life-threatening surgery and other painful medical procedures (Moos, 1984). In general, these studies highlight the adaptive aspects of individual and group coping; they show that most people cope reasonably effectively with life transitions and crises. Such findings are consistent with evolutionary theory and our knowledge about life cycle development and personal growth.

Taken together, the four perspectives outlined in the preceding sections identify the major sets of factors that should be included in a conceptual framework of the process of stress and coping.

AN INTEGRATED CONCEPTUAL FRAMEWORK

We conceptualize research on stress and coping using the model shown in Figure 13–1. The environmental system (Panel 1) is composed of ongoing life stressors and social resources in important life domains, such as physical health, finances, and relationships with family members and friends. The personal system (Panel 2) includes an individual's sociodemographic characteristics; such personal coping resources as self-confidence, ego development, and problem-solving skills; personal commitments and aspirations; and prior crisis and coping experiences. The model posits that life crises or transitions (Panel 3) and the environmental and personal factors that foreshadow them (Panels 1 and 2) shape cognitive appraisal and coping responses (Panel 4) and their influence on health and well-being (Panel 5).

The bi-directional paths indicate that these processes are transactional and show that reciprocal feedback can occur at each stage. Personal coping resources affect ongoing life stressors and transitions, as well as the appraisal and coping processes people use to manage

FIGURE 13–1. A conceptual model of the stress and coping process.

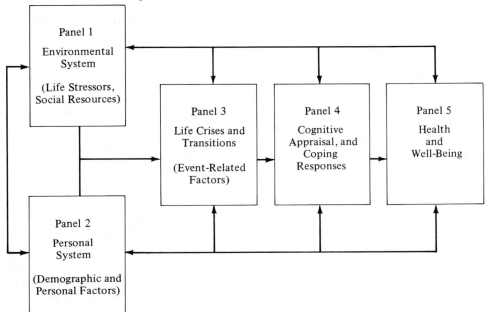

them. These processes influence health and well-being, which, in turn, may alter factors in both the personal and environmental systems.

The concepts of cognitive appraisal and coping processes emphasize people's active *selection* among specific consequences to which they attend and their *choice* among alternative coping processes in light of their appraisal of the consequences. Appraisal and coping processes influence the stressors to which individuals are exposed, their reaction to the threats and challenges these stressors offer, and how stressors change both short- and long-term adaptation. Thus, the framework acknowledges that people are active agents and may shape the outcomes of life stressors as well as be shaped by them.

In the sections that follow, we describe some major sets of personal resources and coping processes and use the framework to consider how personal and social resources influence the selection of coping processes and how coping processes alter the outcomes of life stressors and affect adaptation.

PERSONAL COPING RESOURCES

As noted earlier, personal coping resources are a complex set of personality, attitudinal, and cognitive factors that provide part of the psychological context for coping. Personal resources are relatively stable dispositional characteristics that affect the selection of appraisal and coping processes and, in turn, may be altered by the cumulative outcomes of these processes. Selecting from many factors in this domain, we briefly review some measures of ego development; self-efficacy, optimism, and sense of coherence; cognitive styles; defense and coping styles; and problem-solving abilities.

Ego Development

Loevinger (1976) conceptualized ego development as the "master trait," encompassing an individual's frame of reference and the processes through which new experiences are integrated into a coherent whole. The ego progressively unfolds to achieve a more differentiated perception of the self and the social world. Each step represents a qualitatively different stage of structural organization. Although the sequence of developmental stages is invariant, individuals differ in the final stage they attain. Loevinger assumed that the measurement of ego development requires a projective technique that permits individuals to reveal their own "unbiased" frame of experience.

Loevinger's Sentence Completion Test of Ego Development (SCT) measures an individual's impulse controls, interpersonal style, conscious preoccupations, and cognitive style by responses to thirty-six sentence stems (such as "Raising a family _____" and "When they avoided me _____"). Each response is matched to one of nine stages of ego development, varying from impulsive and self-protective to individualist, autonomous, and integrated. Browning (1987) provided age-specific norms for a twelve-item version of the SCT based on a national random sample of adolescent and young adult men and women.

Because ego development is a broad concept, no single behavioral criterion can be used to validate the SCT. Existing findings generally support the theory and measure. Ego development has been related to complex patterns of behavior such as help-giving, empathy, and independence, as well as to global measures of social attitudes, maturity, and moral development (Browning, 1987). Higher levels of ego development are associated with more varied and effective coping styles. In addition, the SCT can help therapists match patients with specific treatment modalities. Dill and Noam (1990) found that patients at higher stages of ego development prefer insight-oriented treatment; those at lower stages prefer social interventions.

Self-efficacy, Optimism, and Sense of Coherence

Personality researchers have sought to measure aspects of the self-concept that function as personal resources in handling adverse events. We comment briefly here on indexes of self-efficacy, dispositional optimism, and sense of coherence.

Self-efficacy. In general, persons with higher levels of self-efficacy tend to approach challenging situations in an active and persistent style, whereas those with lower levels are less active or tend to avoid such situations. Bandura's (1989) theory has led to the development of indexes of self-efficacy in specific content domains, such as physical, social, and academic skills; computer skills; counseling skills; infant care; coping with marital separation; and so on. Some of these indexes predict important criteria. For example, higher scores on the Situational Confidence Questionnaire (SCQ), a measure of how well alcoholic patients believe they can cope with potential relapse-inducing situations, are related to better treatment outcome (Solomon & Annis, 1990).

Dispositional Optimism. Scheier and Carver (1985, 1987) define dispositional optimism as a general expectancy for positive outcomes, especially in difficult or ambiguous situations. Dispositional optimism is measured by the Life Orientation Scale, which is composed of twelve items such as "In unusual times, I usually expect the best" and "I hardly ever expect things to go my way." Optimism is associated with better physical and psychological adaptation to stressful life circumstances, perhaps because optimists are more likely to rely on problem-focused coping and less likely to use avoidance processes such as venting their feelings and disengagement. Thus, compared with pessimists, optimists rely more on coping processes that are likely to foster favorable outcome expectancies, more persistent coping, and better outcomes (Scheier, Weintraub, & Carver, 1986). For example, optimism has been associated with successful completion of aftercare following treatment for alcoholism (Strack, Carver, & Blaney, 1987).

Sense of Coherence. Antonovsky (1987) has developed a twenty-seven-item scale to measure the sense of coherence, which he sees as a relatively stable and enduring orientation that consists of three components: (1) comprehensibility, or how much an individual sees the world as structured and predictable; (2) manageability, or how much individuals believe that they have adequate personal and social resources to meet environmental demands; and (3) meaningfulness, or the feeling that it is worthwhile to try to cope actively with stressful circumstances. People who have a high sense of coherence are likely to try to impose structure on situations, to accept challenge and identify personal and social resources that facilitate the coping process, and to actively consider alternative coping options. Thus, a sense of coherence may have positive consequences for health and well-being.

Cognitive Styles

Our "cognitive glasses"—habitual patterns of perception and information processing—have formative effects on learning and adaptive processes. Field orientation and information processing are two of the broadest and most extensively studied cognitive styles.

Field Dependence and Independence. Field-dependent individuals' perceptions of a complex stimulus are strongly influenced by the surrounding context, whereas field-independent individuals experience complex stimuli as separate and unaffected by the context. Field-dependent persons are more attuned to their social environment and hence are perceived as warmer and friendlier. They are attracted to social situations, have better social skills, and tend to be more emotionally expressive. In contrast, field-independent persons have a more well-defined identity and are more autonomous and sensitive to their internal needs. People are highly consistent in field orientation; women tend to be somewhat more field dependent than men.

The adaptive value of each cognitive orientation depends on the nature of the situation. Field-independent persons tend to be more analytic and structured and are likely to be more successful in dealing with situations that require logical analysis and self-reliance. Field-dependent individuals may use their social skills to solve interpersonal problems more effectively. However, highly field-dependent persons may look to their immediate environment for apparent solutions to life problems, as suggested by the finding that people who misuse alcohol are more field dependent than are normal drinkers or abstainers (for reviews, see Witkin & Goodenough, 1977, 1981).

Information-processing Styles. A more specific cognitive style involves the extent to which a person seeks information under threat. The Monitor-Blunter Style Scale (Miller, 1987, in press) assesses the tendency to seek or avoid information (high versus low monitoring) and to be focused versus nonfocused (low versus high blunting). Respondents are asked to imagine four stress-evoking scenes and answer eight items about what they would do in each situation. In one study, people who generally sought information and were more focused were more aroused and anxious and tried to find out more about the nature of a physically aversive event; in contrast, people who tended to avoid information and to be nonfocused were able to distract themselves and to relax (Miller, 1987).

These coping styles may have important implications for health. Miller, Brody, and Summerton (1988) found that, compared with low monitors, high monitors came to physicians with less severe medical problems even though they reported comparable levels of distress and dysfunction. Moreover, high monitors requested more tests, information, and counseling during their visit but wanted a less active role in their own care. Finally, high monitors reported less improvement in physical and psychological problems after their visit. Thus, people's information processing styles may be related to their use of health care and the outcome of that care.

Defense and Coping Styles

Some investigators assume that people have relatively stable preferences for particular defense and coping styles to handle different life situations. For example, Vaillant (1977) proposed a hierarchy of three levels of ego defenses in which immature defenses include projection and unrealistic fantasy, neurotic defenses include repression and reaction formation, and mature defenses include suppression and realistic anticipation. Reliance on more mature defenses, as rated from life history interviews, is associated with less psychopathology and better adaptation. In addition, as individuals mature, they shift toward more adaptive defensive styles (Vaillant 1977, 1986). We consider two measures of such defense and coping styles here (for an additional set of measures, see Haan, 1977).

Defense Style Questionnaire. Bond and his colleagues (Bond, Gardner, Christian, & Sigel, 1983; Bond, et al., 1989) developed the Defense Style Questionnaire to assess individuals' characteristic styles of dealing with conflict. Respondents rate a series of items, such as "I act like a child when I am frustrated," and "People tend to mistreat me," on nine-point scales ranging from strongly disagree to strongly agree. These items assess four main defensive styles: (1) maladaptive action styles, such as acting out and withdrawal; (2) styles reflecting image distortion, such as omnipotence and primitive idealization; (3) styles associated with self-sacrifice, such as reaction formation and pseudo-altruism; and (4) adaptive or mature styles, such as suppression and humor. People who relied more on mature styles tended to have more ego strength and higher scores on Loevinger's scale of ego development; in contrast, higher scores on the first thee styles were associated with less ego strength and less mature ego development (Bond, et al., 1983).

Vaillant, Bond, and Vaillant (1986) examined the associations between ego defense mechanisms and psychological health among middle-aged men who were followed prospectively for forty years. Clinical assessments of the maturity of the men's defenses according to Vaillant's hierarchy were predictably associated with independent outcome criteria. Importantly, the maturity of defenses was more closely associated with adult mental health among men who had more problems during childhood. The Defense Style Questionnaire was given to a subsample of these men six to eight years after the interview and identified essentially the same styles of defense that had been identified earlier by clinical assessment.

Defense Mechanisms Inventory. The Defense Mechanisms Inventory (DMI) assesses the relative reliance on five groups of defenses. The DMI consists of ten brief vignettes, two in each of five conflict areas (such as authority, independence, and competition), followed by questions about the respondent's actual behavior, fantasy behavior, thoughts, and feelings in the situations described. Each question provides five choices typifying the defenses of projection, intellectualization (labelled principalization), reversal (responding positively or neutrally to a person or object that typically evokes a negative reaction), turning against object (expressing hostility outward), and turning against self (expressing hostility inward). Respondents choose the alternatives that are most and least representative of how they would react.

The DMI subscales are predictably related to standard personality scales such as the Minnesota Multiphasic Personality Inventory and the Sixteen Personality Factors Questionnaire. People who turn their hostility outward or use projection tend to score higher on indexes of aggression, suspiciousness, and physical symptoms, and lower on emotional stability. People who turn their hostility inward are likely to experience more anxiety and depression and to show greater declines in estimates of their own ability after a failure experience. In contrast, the defense mechanisms of intellectualization and reversal are associated with less anxiety and depression, fewer physical symptoms and less psychopathology, higher self-esteem and emotional stability, and better overall adjustment (for overview of these findings and other studies using the DMI, see Cramer, 1988; and Ihilevich & Gleser, 1986).

Studies with the DMI have shown that persons who are field independent are likely to express anger and hostility directly toward others; persons who are field dependent tend to express such feelings indirectly. Field-dependent persons are more likely to use global defenses such as expressing hostility toward the self and reversal, whereas field-independent persons prefer differentiated defenses such as projection and expressing hostility toward a person or object (Ihilevich & Gleser, 1986).

Problem-solving Abilities

Social learning approaches have emphasized the importance of effective problem-solving behavior for successful adaptation. To quantify such behavior, Cornelius and Caspi (1987) developed the Everyday Problem-Solving Inventory (EPSI), which assesses cognitive and behavioral problem solving in situations adults may actually encounter in specific areas of their daily lives, such as at home or work or among family or friends. Performance on the EPSI was positively associated with performance on a traditional ability test. More important, performance on the EPSI increased with age, whereas performance on a traditional problem-solving measure declined after middle age. Measures such as the EPSI can be used to assess the effectiveness of interventions aimed at enhancing problem-solving skills.

Heppner's (1988) Problem Solving Inventory assesses self-confidence in problem-solving abilities, an approach versus avoidant problem-solving style, and the perception of personal control in handling problems. The inventory focuses on individuals' overall perceptions of their problem-solving skills rather than on problem solving in a specific situation. In general, people who have more self-confidence, perceived control, and an approach problem-solving style are more persistent and assertive, more likely to expect success, less anxious and depressed, and have fewer health problems and physical symptoms (Heppner, 1988) Moreover, individuals who see themselves as more effective problem solvers seem to be less prone to depression when they experience a high level of stressors. The question of whether such individuals rely more on approach than avoidance coping processes in specific stressful situations remains unresolved.

APPRAISAL AND COPING PROCESSES

We have focused on Panel 2 of our conceptual model (Figure 13–1) and reviewed some concepts and measures of personal coping resources. To understand the more specific ways in which people manage stressful life circumstances, however, we need to consider appraisal and coping processes—that is, the cognitive and behavioral efforts individuals use to construe and manage specific stressful episodes. These processes are shown in Panel 4 of the conceptual framework in Figure 13–1.

Appraisal Processes

Appraisal and coping processes are closely interrelated. According to Lazarus and Folkman (1984), primary appraisal involves people's judgments about what is at stake in a stressful encounter, while secondary appraisal involves their beliefs about the viable options for coping. In general, appraisals have been measured with one-item indexes that assess individuals' immediate reactions (threat, challenge, harm, or benefit) to the situation and the extent to which it can be changed or must be accepted. Because of space limitations, we do not review these measures here.

Peacock and Wong (1990) have developed a Stress Appraisal Measure that assesses three aspects of primary appraisal (threat, challenge, and centrality) and three aspects of secondary appraisal (controllable by self, controllable by others, and uncontrollable). Initial findings show that the dimensions are only moderately interrelated and are linked to the overall stressfulness of the situation in expected ways. Moreover, individuals who appraised an examination situation as more threatening, central, and uncontrollable reported more psychological symptoms and depressed mood.

Coping Processes

Although no single method for categorizing coping processes has yet emerged, most researchers have used one of two main conceptual approaches to classify coping processes. One approach emphasizes the *focus* of coping: a person's orientation and activity in response to a stressor. An individual can approach the problem and make active efforts to resolve it and/or try to avoid the problem and focus mainly on managing the emotions associated with it. A second approach emphasizes the *method* of coping people employ— that is, whether a response entails primarily cognitive or behavioral efforts.

We have combined these two approaches to develop a more integrated conceptualization of coping processes. We consider an individual's orientation toward a stressor and separate coping into approach and avoidance domains. Each of these two domains is divided into categories that reflect cognitive or behavioral coping. Accordingly, we propose four basic types of coping processes: approach-cognitive, approach-behavioral, avoidance-cognitive, and avoidance-behavioral.

Cognitive approach coping includes logical analysis and positive reappraisal. These coping processes encompass paying attention to one aspect of the situation at a time, drawing on past experiences, mentally rehearsing alternative actions and their probable consequences, and accepting the reality of a situation but restructuring it to find something favorable. *Behavioral approach coping* includes seeking guidance and support and taking concrete action to deal directly with a situation or its aftermath.

Cognitive avoidance coping comprises responses aimed at denying or minimizing the seriousness of a crisis or its consequences, as well as accepting a situation as it is and deciding that the basic circumstances cannot be altered. *Behavioral avoidance coping* covers seeking alternate rewards—that is, trying to replace the losses involved in certain crises by becoming involved in new activities and creating alternate sources of satisfaction. It also includes openly venting one's feelings of anger and despair and behavior that may temporarily reduce tension, such as acting impulsively, going on an eating binge, and taking tranquilizers or other medications.

Researchers have developed some new measures of these types of coping processes (Cohen, 1987). We briefly describe five such measures here. The first three measures focus on coping episodes. The other two measures focus on coping dispositions, but they assess dimensions that are conceptually comparable to those assessed by the episodic measures, and they can be used to tap coping responses in specific situations.

Coping Responses Inventory. The Coping Responses Inventory (CRI) is composed of eight subscales that assess the four types of coping processes just described (Table 13–1). After constructing several preliminary versions and subscales, we applied a seventy-two-item version of the CRI to more than 1,800 late-middle-aged and older adults. Respondents were asked to identify a recent stressful episode and rate on four-point scales their reliance on each of the seventy-two coping responses. We used both conceptual and empirical criteria to develop the current forty-eight-item adult form of the CRI (Moos, 1992; Moos, Brennan, Fondacaro, & Moos, 1990). We also developed a version of the CRI that focuses on how health care staff cope with work-related stressors (Schaefer & Moos, 1991)

TABLE 13-1
Dimensions Assessed by Selected Measures of Coping Processes

Measure	Approach		Avoidance	
	Cognitive	*Behavioral*	*Cognitive*	*Behavioral*
Coping Responses Inventory	Logical analysis	Seek guidance and support	Cognitive avoidance	Seeking alternative rewards
	Positive reappraisal	Problem solving	Resigned acceptance	Emotional discharge
Ways of Coping Questionnaire	Positive reappraisal	Seeking support	Distancing	Escape-avoidance
	Accepting responsibility	Problem solving	—	—
	Self-control	Confrontation	—	—
Life Situations Inventory	—	Problem solving*	Resignation	Avoidance
Multidimensional Coping Inventory	—	Seeking support	Disengagement	—
		Active coping and planning*	Acceptance	—
Coping Inventory for Stressful Situations	—	Task-oriented	Avoidance-oriented	Emotion-oriented

*Includes aspects of cognitive approach processes.

and a youth form to assess coping processes among youth aged twelve to eighteen (Ebata & Moos, 1991; Moos, 1990).

Ways of Coping Questionnaire. The revised Ways of Coping Questionnaire (WOC) asks individuals to identify a specific stressful situation and rate on four-point scales their reliance on sixty-six specific coping responses. As shown in Table 13-1, six of the eight subscales assess approach coping and two assess avoidance coping. Folkman and her colleagues (1986) identified some associations between the appraisal of a stressor and reliance on these coping responses. When faced with a threat to self-esteem, for example, people tend to use more confrontive and self-control coping and to accept more responsibility. When people appraise situations as changeable, they tend to rely more on approach coping, specifically accepting responsibility, positive reappraisal, confrontation, and problem solving. In contrast, when people confront stressors that must be accepted, they rely more on distancing and escape-avoidance. More generally, the WOC has been used to examine the personal and situational concomitants of coping and to link coping processes to adjustment (Folkman & Lazarus, 1988).

Medical Coping Modes Questionnaire and Life Situations Inventory. Feifel and his colleagues (1987b) formulated a nineteen-item Medical Coping Modes Questionnaire (MCMQ) that assesses three forms of coping with medical illness: confrontation, avoidance, and acceptance-resignation. Patients with life-threatening illnesses relied more on confrontation than on avoidance or acceptance-resignation. These patients also were more likely to use confrontation (including seeking information from physicians and friends, asking for advice, and cognitive redefinition) than were patients with a non-life-threatening disability. Among life-threatened patients, those who relied less on avoidance or accept-ance-resignation tended to cope more effectively (Feifel, Strack, & Nagy, 1987a).

Feifel and Strack (1989) also developed the Life Situations Inventory (LSI), which as-sesses problem solving, avoidance, and resignation processes. They used the LSI to have middle-aged and older men describe their coping responses to five conflict situations: decision-making, defeat in a competitive circumstance, frustration, authority conflict, and peer disagreement. However, some of the specific coping items differ from those used on comparable dimensions in the MCMQ.

Multidimensional Coping Inventory. Carver, Scheier, and Weintraub (1989) devel-oped a dispositional measure of coping by asking individuals what they usually did in stress-ful circumstances. A second-order analysis identified four factors that reflected active cop-ing, seeking support, denial and disengagement, and acceptance and reinterpretation (see Table 13–1). There were some associations between appraisal and coping. People who saw stressful situations as changeable reported more active coping, seeking instrumental sup-port, and suppression of competing activities. When people rated events as more important, they sought more support, but also relied more on expressing their emotions and denial.

In one study, participants were asked to describe how they dealt with a specific stressful event. The psychometric characteristics of the coping subscales in this situational format were comparable to those obtained using the dispositional format. However, there were only low to moderate correlations between the situational and the dispositional coping in-dexes. Such findings imply that dispositional indexes provide only limited information about the coping processes people use in specific stressful contexts.

Coping Inventory for Stressful Situations. Endler and Parker's (1990; 1991) Coping Inventory for Stressful Situations (initially called the Multidimensional Coping Inventory) assesses task-oriented, emotion-oriented, and avoidance-oriented coping styles. Respon-dents are asked to rate forty-eight coping activities on five-point scales in terms of how much they engage in the activities when they encounter a difficult, stressful, or upsetting situation. Initial evidence indicates that the inventory has acceptable construct validity (ex-pected associations with the Ways of Coping Questionnaire) and moderate criterion valid-ity. For example, the inventory subscales (especially emotion-oriented coping) are corre-lated in expected ways with criterion measures of depression and anxiety.

THE DETERMINANTS OF COPING PROCESSES

Our model of the stress and coping process (Figure 13–1) posits that aspects of the personal system (such as demographic and other personal factors), the environmental system (such as life stressors and social resources), characteristics of the focal life crisis or transition (such as its type and severity), and an individual's appraisal of the situation provide a context for the selection and effectiveness of coping responses. Earlier, we described some findings on the associations between appraisal and coping processes. In this section, we focus briefly on how personal factors influence the selection of coping responses (associa-tions between Panels 2 and 4 in the model) and how family and work resources provide a social context for coping (associations between variables in Panels 1 and 4). Because of space limitations, we do not consider the links between stressor characteristics and coping responses.

Demographic and Personality Factors

Gender and Age. Some investigators have identified gender differences in coping. McCrae (1989) found that women are more likely than men to use avoidance coping processes such as hostile reaction, distraction, passivity, and wishful thinking (see also Endler & Parker 1990). However, compared with men, we found that women reported more reliance on both approach and avoidance coping (Moos, 1992). In part, these findings may reflect the fact that women confront more severe objective or appraised stressors, which are associated with more avoidance and sometimes with more approach coping.

There also are some associations between age and coping preferences. Folkman and her colleagues (1987) found that older adults are more likely to rely on cognitive approach (positive reappraisal) and avoidance (distancing and escape-avoidance) coping and less likely to utilize behavioral approach processes such as seeking social support, problem solving, and confrontation. Similarly, other investigators have found that older adults are less likely to rely on hostile reaction and emotional expression and are less likely to vent frustration on other people (Costa, Zonderman, & McCrae, 1991; Felton & Revenson, 1987; McCrae, 1989).

According to Feifel and Strack (1989), older men prefer resignation to avoidance, whereas middle-aged men do not. Older men may have a shrinking sense of time and thus may want to resolve conflicts and attain closure on important life issues. However, because older men are more likely to focus on health concerns and middle-aged men to focus on work problems, some of these age differences may be due to differences in focal stressors.

Personality Factors. In general, personal coping resources such as self-efficacy (Fleishman, 1984) and an internal locus of control (Parkes, 1984) are associated with more reliance on approach coping. For example, we found that self-confident persons rely more on approach coping and less on avoidance coping. Easy-going people also are less inclined to use avoidance coping. In a one-year follow-up, we found that self-confidence predicted an increase in approach coping and a decline in avoidance coping (Holahan & Moos, 1987a).

Other investigators have identified conceptually similar associations between personality variables and coping. For example, Feifel, Strack, and Nagy (1987a) noted that men who are more competitive and extroverted tend to rely more on confrontation and less on acceptance-resignation. Men who are more impulsive rely more on avoidance and acceptance, whereas self-confident men are less likely to rely on these coping processes. Carver and his colleagues (1989) found that individuals high on optimism, control, and self-esteem are more likely to rely on active coping and planning. Less desirable personal qualities are associated with more dysfunctional coping tendencies. Finally, several researchers have noted that neuroticism is associated with more avoidance coping (Bolger, 1990; Costa & McCrae, 1990; Endler & Parker, 1990).

The Social Context of Coping

A number of studies have focused on how people's family and work resources (Panel 1 in the model) can influence adaptation by facilitating the use of more active coping processes (Panel 4).

Family Resources and Coping. Consistent with the idea that social support can promote effective coping, people who enjoy more social resources, especially from family and friends, seem to rely more heavily on approach processes. For example, Feifel, Strack, and Nagy (1987a) found that men who have more social support rely more on confrontation and less on acceptance-resignation in coping with a serious medical illness. Similarly, late-life problem drinkers who have better relationships with their spouses and friends are more likely to rely on positive reappraisal and seeking support and less likely to use cognitive avoidance and emotional discharge (Moos, Brennan, et al., 1990). Moreover, in a longitudinal study, high family support predicted an increase in approach coping and a decline in avoidance coping over time (Holahan & Moos, 1987a).

Manne and Zautra (1989) obtained comparable findings among a group of women with rheumatoid arthritis. When the husband is supportive, his wife is more likely to rely on cognitive restructuring and seeking information, which were associated with better psychological adjustment. However, when the husband tends to be critical of his wife, she engages in more wishful thinking, which was related to poorer adjustment. Thus, social support is beneficial and criticism harmful because of their influence on the partner's coping processes.

Work Resources and Coping. Kohn and Schooler (1983) have noted that occupational experiences can affect a person's value system and coping strategies. In essence, occupational conditions conducive to self-direction in one's work—such as high autonomy, innovation, and support—are associated with valuing self-direction and the use of active coping processes. People's jobs affect their perceptions and values by confronting them with demands that must be met; coping processes used to handle problems at work then are generalized to manage other situations.

Consistent with these ideas, we found that men in more involving and supportive work settings are more likely to seek information and support. Moreover, men who experience increases in work support seek more information and support over time (Fondacaro & Moos, 1987). Similarly, Parkes (1986) found that student nurses use more approach coping responses in major stressful episodes when work support is high—that is, when the availability of supportive supervisors enables the students to cope directly with serious work problems. When there is little support from supervisors, students also rely on approach coping processes, but only to manage minor stressful episodes.

The Interplay of Personal and Social Factors

In general, coping processes are affected by both personal and situational factors; they reflect individual preferences and are responsive to changing environmental circumstances. The relative importance of personal and social factors is likely to vary among different individuals and situations. For example, personal factors may be especially important determinants of coping among some groups of psychiatric patients who lack the ability to vary their coping appropriately according to the situation (Holahan & Moos, 1987a). Conversely, some powerful situations may elicit common coping processes among diverse individuals. Proximal factors such as the type (acute versus chronic, life domain in which the stressor occurs) and severity of stressors should be examined in any study of the determinants of coping processes (Mattlin, Wethington, & Kessler, 1990).

One way to focus on these issues is to examine the same individuals' coping preferences in different situations. For example, Feifel and Strack (1989) found that middle-aged men relied more on problem solving than on avoidance or resignation in managing peer disagreement, frustration, and defeat in a competitive situation. Compared with older men, however, middle-aged men relied more on avoidance coping in situations involving authority conflict and decisionmaking. Feifel and Strack (1989) speculate that older men's more established sense of identity permits them to be more forthright in authority conflict and decisionmaking situations. Consistent with our perspective, these findings indicate that both personal factors (age) and the type of stressor influence the choice of specific coping responses.

COPING PROCESSES, STRESSOR OUTCOMES, AND ADAPTATION

There is growing interest in the associations between coping processes, stressor outcomes, and proximal and distal indexes of adaptation (that is, between variables in Panels 4 and 5 of the model).

Coping and the Outcome of Psychiatric and Substance Abuse Disorders

Some investigators have focused on patients' coping processes and their associations with the outcome of treatment, especially for depressed and alcoholic patients and for individuals who are trying to quite smoking.

Coping Processes and Depression. We have examined the relationship between coping processes and the short-term (one-year) and medium-term (four-year) outcome of treatment for depression. At the one-year follow-up, more reliance on problem solving and less on information seeking and emotional discharge were related to better outcome. These results are consistent with prior findings linking problem-focused coping with less severe depression, and rumination, indecisiveness, and emotional discharge coping with more severe depression (Billings & Moos, 1985). Similarly, Parker, Brown, and Bignault (1986) found that depressed patients who relied more on self-consolation and distraction at baseline showed poorer treatment outcome twenty weeks later.

At the four-year follow-up, patients who relied more on problem solving and less on emotional discharge coping were less depressed and more self-confident. Moreover, patients who relied less on emotional discharge processes at the one-year follow-up reported less depression and fewer physical symptoms at four years (Swindle, Cronkite, & Moos, 1989). In this respect, Gaston and her colleagues (1988) noted that depressed patients who rely more heavily on avoidance processes find it harder to form a positive relationship with a therapist in short-term psychotherapy.

Coping Processes and Alcohol Abuse. There is growing interest in the role of coping processes in problem drinking and substance abuse. Perri (1985) identified coping strategies used by people who succeeded in self-management of a drinking problem. Abstainers and nonproblem drinkers use a greater variety of coping methods; in particular, behavioral processes such as stimulus control (spending less time with heavy-drinking friends, removing alcoholic beverages from their home), changing their daily routine, developing alternative pursuits (such as new hobbies and physical exercise), and seeking advice and support.

We obtained comparable findings on the relationship between coping processes and the outcome of treatment for alcohol abuse. Reliance on cognitive approach coping was associated with better treatment outcome, especially at a two-year follow-up; the use of avoidance coping was associated with worse outcome at both two-year and ten-year follow-ups. In longitudinal analyses, we found that cognitive approach coping at two years predicted less alcohol consumption, physical symptoms, and depression at ten years. More avoidance coping at two years predicted more depression at ten years. Thus, even though coping processes are somewhat situation-specific, they may capture an aspect of stable personal tendencies that is associated with long-term functioning (Moos, Finney, & Cronkite, 1990).

Coping Processes and Smoking. Cognitive and behavioral coping skills have been associated with maintenance of smoking cessation. Shiffman (1985) found that both cognitive and behavioral approach responses are effective in averting relapse; the combination of both types is better than either one alone. Cognitive approach coping is especially important in that it is used independently of situational stressors. Behavioral approach coping is more responsive to contextual factors such as alcohol consumption, which diminish its use, and depression, which lessen its effectiveness. Cognitive coping strategies can be used flexibly in many circumstances; they are less under situational control and thus not as likely to be disrupted by increased life stressors or reduced social support.

Coping Processes and General Indexes of Functioning and Adaptation

A substantial number of studies have examined the associations between coping processes and general indexes of adaptation. We can draw some overall conclusions about the relative efficacy of coping processes; however, the outcome of specific coping strategies may vary depending on personal and contextual factors, reliance on other coping responses, and the match between stressor characteristics, appraisal, and coping.

Most generally, people who rely more on approach coping (especially behavioral processes) tend to adapt better to life stressors and experience fewer psychological symptoms, whereas those who rely on avoidance coping (especially fantasy and emotional discharge) adapt less well. Cognitive coping methods such as positive reappraisal are associated with better marital and occupational adjustment and with higher scores on mental health criteria such as happiness and productivity. When used together, seeking information and problem solving are generally helpful in managing both acute and chronic stressors. These types of associations between coping processes and adaptation have been identified in varied groups, including healthy adults, medical patients with diverse disorders, family caregivers, and so on. (For example, see Aldwin & Revenson, 1987; Costa & McCrae 1990; Revenson & Felton, 1989; Suls & Fletcher, 1985; Taylor & Brown, 1988).

A consistent body of research points to reliance on avoidance coping processes (primarily emotional discharge) as an important risk factor that predicts distress among both adults and their children. For example, in a series of studies, we found that more reliance on emotional discharge was associated with more depression and other indexes of dysfunction (Moos, 1988). In one study, more use of avoidance coping was associated with more concurrent distress and with more distress one year later, even after prior distress was controlled (Holahan & Moos, 1987b). Moreover, children of mothers who relied more heavily on avoidance coping experienced more dysfunction.

Maladaptive Aspects of Approach Coping. Although it is an approach coping process, seeking information and support has been associated with more depression among both depressed patients and adults who are late-life problem drinkers. In part, this association may occur because more severe stressors elicit more support seeking and are related to poorer outcomes. Alternatively, seeking support may prolong problem resolution. Seemingly supportive family members and friends may avoid open communication about a stressor, minimize or trivialize a person's problems and thereby discourage efforts to alleviate them, or criticize how the person is handling the situation (Dakof & Taylor, 1990). Moreover, seeking support is not the same as receiving it; distressed individuals may request help from those who cannot or will not assist them. In general, information and support are not sufficient to manage a stressor. When this coping strategy is used in the context of rumination and an inability to take direct action, it is likely to lead to a negative outcome.

Adaptive Aspects of Avoidance Coping. There is considerable evidence that cognitive avoidance or inattention may be an effective way to cope with some short-term stressors, such as noise, pain, blood donation, and some uncomfortable medical diagnostic procedures (Suls & Fletcher, 1985). More important, cognitive avoidance or denial is predictive of better medical outcome during acute hospitalization for coronary heart disease (Levenson, Mishra, Hamer, & Hastillo, 1989; Levine, et al., 1987). In the long run, however, the attenuated experience of pain and distress characteristic of repressive coping may be associated with reduced immunocompetence and less resistance to disease (Jamner, Schwartz, & Leigh, 1988).

Another exception to the general rule that avoidance processes are maladaptive is that seeking alternative rewards may be associated with more well-being and less distress. Seeking alternative rewards is an avoidance coping strategy because it does not involve direct attempts to change a stressor. In contrast to other avoidance processes, however, it involves active engagement with the environment and with other people. In the aftermath of unchangeable stressors, or in the process of recovery from psychiatric and substance abuse disorders, seeking alternative rewards may be beneficial because it affords diversions and new sources of satisfaction.

Configurational and Ipsative Analyses of Coping Processes. A few investigators have emphasized the importance of examining the relative reliance on specific coping processes. For example, Mattlin and his colleagues (1990) found that behavioral approach coping is adaptive in handling a short-term problem; avoidance strategies are maladaptive, but so is active cognitive and reappraisal coping. The authors speculated that cognitive approach coping may be maladaptive when it is not used as part of a pattern of versatile coping—that is, continually thinking about a situation may be detrimental unless it is followed by subsequent action. Similarly, positive reappraisal may promote adjustment primarily when it facilitates problem-focused coping.

These issues can be examined by developing separate indexes of versatile or flexible coping (Mattlin, et al., 1990) or by considering relative coping scores (percentage of coping efforts) as distinct from the more usual raw scores (frequency of efforts). Vitaliano and his colleagues (1987) have shown that relative scores may be more closely associated with outcome indexes such as depression. Taken together, these findings highlight the importance of a configurational approach toward understanding the association between coping processes and adaptation.

CONCEPTUAL ISSUES AND PRACTICAL APPLICATIONS

We have described some important sets of personal coping resources and coping processes and their associations with treatment outcomes and individual adaptation. We focus here on three issues: matching coping processes with stressor characteristics and appraisal, coping and personal growth, and applications to treatment and prevention.

Matching Coping Processes with Stressor Characteristics and Appraisal

A new line of research is examining the match or goodness of fit between specific coping processes, stressor characteristics, and appraisal. For example, approach coping processes should be most effective in situations that are appraised as changeable and controllable. Avoidance coping processes should be most effective in situations that cannot be altered. In this respect, an individual's coping style needs to fit the situation; individuals who are flexible in their choice of coping should show better adaptation (Miller, 1990).

Vitaliano and his coworkers (1990) found some support for these ideas. When a stressor was appraised as changeable, problem-focused coping was associated with less depression and emotion-focused coping was related to more depression. These associations did not occur or were much weaker when stressors were seen as not changeable. The authors speculate that involvement in palliative or cathartic activities may divert energy from problem solving and engender feelings of guilt and failure in situations in which constructive action can be taken.

In a study of youth, Compas, Malcarne, and Fondacaro (1988) also found some support for the idea that outcome is better when coping efforts match appraisals. Youth thought that academic stressors were more controllable than social stressors and they generated more problem-focused coping strategies to manage academic stressors. Youth who generated more problem-focused strategies when they believed they had control over the stressor had fewer behavior problems, as did youth who generated fewer problem-focused strategies when they believed they lacked control.

Coping and Personal Growth

The difficult aspects of life crises cannot be denied. People in crises typically experience intense emotional pain, psychological turbulence, and loss. Yet, many people are remarkably resilient in the face of adversity. Individuals often emerge from a crisis with new coping skills, closer relationships with family and friends, broader priorities, and a richer appreciation of life. People have described positive changes as outcomes of encounters with a wide variety of stressors, including divorce, bereavement, chronic illness, and childhood adversity. Accordingly, investigators need to consider the possibility of a new and better level of adaptation that reflects personal growth rather than a return to the status quo (for a review of these issues, see Schaefer & Moos, in press).

In research that illustrates the potential growth-enhancing effect of encountering and successfully overcoming stressful life circumstances, Haan (1977) found that women who had experienced family changes during adolescence were more empathic as adults. Men who had experienced changes in the early adult years were more tolerant of ambiguity and showed more empathy during middle age. Haan concluded that effective coping is facilitated by accommodation and instrumental approaches to problems, as well as by periods of assimilation. Moreover, moral development among youth may be fostered by ego processes that permit stress to be experienced and resolved rather than simply negated.

Our conceptual framework is consistent with the idea that stressors can provide an opportunity for personal growth. When we examined this issue empirically, we found that more than half of the individuals who experienced two or more stressful events during a twelve-month interval either remained stable or improved in functioning. In fact, thirty percent of individuals whose functioning improved experienced two or more stressors, and more than half of this group experienced three or more stressors. Individuals whose functioning improved after experiencing a high level of stressors showed an increase in personal and social resources, perhaps due to positive feedback from effective coping with stressors (Holahan & Moos, 1990).

We need to learn more about the type and level of adaptive challenge that can promote resilience. More controllable stressors may facilitate growth more readily than less controllable ones. Alternatively, life stressors may foster enhanced resilience only when they encompass demands sufficient to enable individuals to learn new coping skills. We also need more research on the different processes and outcomes that may result from acute and chronic adaptive challenges. Intense, effortful coping following an acute crisis may promote outcomes such as improved problem-solving skills and more reliance on family and friends. In contrast, the cumulative experience of trial-and-error coping with prolonged adaptive demands may result in outcomes such as wisdom, tolerance, and increased empathy.

Applications to Treatment and Prevention

The stress and coping framework shown in Figure 13-1 encompasses the major sets of factors involved in planning and evaluating intervention programs. According to Albee (1982), interventions can be directed toward the presumed noxious agent (stressful life circumstances) or toward one or more of the factors that strengthen individual resistance, such as personal coping resources and processes. These ideas have implications for assessment and diagnosis and for intervention programs that focus on enhancing coping skills.

Assessment procedures can contribute to better treatment outcome by enhancing treatment planning. In this vein, measures of personal coping resources, such as self-efficacy and problem-solving styles, can help to increase individuals' awareness of their coping abilities, predict individuals' responses to specific intervention procedures or styles of communication, and plan and evaluate treatment programs. Situation-specific indexes of self-efficacy can be used to identify the contexts that may be related to relapse in substance abuse and other disorders. Finally, knowledge about preferred information processing styles may help health care staff decide how best to inform patients about their medical diagnoses and potentially effective interventions.

Measures of defense and coping processes can be used in similar ways. They can help to describe a person's current coping strategies, monitor stability and change related to treatment, examine how new life events affect a person's ways of coping, and identify how coping processes change an individual's life situation and functioning. To illustrate such applications, we have described the Coping Responses Inventory profiles of adults with drinking problems and of youth with mood and conduct disorders (Moos, 1988, 1990). Such information can be used in clinical case descriptions to help clinicians understand how their clients manage specific stressful circumstances, identify coping factors associated with symptom remission and relapse, and plan intervention programs that target clients' precise coping deficits.

Most coping skills training programs emphasize behavioral problem-solving strategies; however, cognitive strategies may be just as effective in promoting well-being and preventing relapse. In fact, cognitive coping processes can be used in all kinds of circumstances, including those in which behavioral options are unavailable. They can also serve to facilitate behavioral coping. These ideas are consistent with the secondary prevention program formulated by Sanchez-Craig and her colleagues (1987), who noted that recovering problem drinkers relied on cognitive coping at least as much as on behavioral coping. In fact, clients used cognitive strategies, such as self-reinforcement and reappraisal, in almost all of the situations in which they tried to cope with a strong urge to drink.

CONCLUSION

The conceptual framework and assessment procedures we have described can help to guide and integrate research in stress and coping theory and to plan and evaluate intervention programs. Researchers can use the framework and procedures to examine how coping with life crises can lead to positive outcomes and to identify the personal and contextual determinants of reliance on specific coping processes. In addition, the framework can guide formulation of a more in-depth understanding of stress and coping processes and of how they moderate the influence of acute and chronic stressors on health and well-being. We have seen modest progress toward these goals in the past twenty years; growing interest in these issues and enhanced conceptual and methodological awareness should contribute to significant new knowledge in these areas in the next two decades.

REFERENCES

ALBEE, G. W. Preventing psychopathology and promoting human potential. *American Psychologist,* 1982, *37,* 1043–1050.

ALDWIN, C. M., & REVENSON, T. A. Does coping help? A reexamination of the relation between coping and mental health. *Journal of Personality and Social Psychology,* 1987, *53,* 337–348.

ANTONOVSKY, A. *Unraveling the mystery of health: How people manage stress and stay well.* San Francisco: Jossey-Bass, 1987.

BANDURA, A. Self-regulation of motivation and action through internal standards and goal systems. In L. A. Pervin (ed.), *Goal concepts in personality and social psychology.* Hillsdale, NJ: Erlbaum, 1989.

BILLINGS, A., & MOOS, R. Life stressors and social resources affect posttreatment outcomes among depressed patients. *Journal of Abnormal Psychology,* 1985, *94,* 140–153.

BOLGER, N. Coping as a personality process: A prospective study. *Journal of Personality and Social Psychology,* 1990, *59,* 525–537.

BOND, M., GARDNER, S. T., CHRISTIAN, J., & SIGEL, J. Empirical study of self-rated defense styles. *Archives of General Psychiatry,* 1983, *40,* 333–338.

BOND, M., PERRY, C., GAUTIER, M., GOLDENBERG, M., OPPENHEIMER, J., & SIMAND, J. Validating the self-report of defense styles. *Journal of Personality Disorders,* 1989, *3,* 101–112.

BROWNING, D. Ego development, authoritarianism, and social status: An investigation of the incremental validity of Loevinger's Sentence Completion Test (Short Form). *Journal of Personality and Social Psychology,* 1987, *53,* 113–118.

CARVER, C. S., SCHEIER, M. F., & WEINTRAUB, J. K. Assessing coping strategies: A theoretically-based approach. *Journal of Personality and Social Psychology,* 1989, *56,* 267–283.

COHEN, F. Measurement of coping. In S. V. Kasl & C. L. Cooper (eds.), *Stress and health: Issues in research methodology.* New York: Wiley, 1987.

COMPAS, B. E., MALCARNE, V., & FONDACARO, K. Coping with stressful events in older children and young adolescents. *Journal of Consulting and Clinical Psychology,* 1988, *56,* 405–411.

CORNELIUS, S., & CASPI, A. Everyday problem solving in adulthood and old age. *Psychology and Aging,* 1987, *2,* 144–153.

COSTA, P. T., & McCRAE, R. R. Personality, stress, and coping: Some lessons from a decade of research. In K. S. Markides & C. L. Cooper (eds.), *Aging, stress, social support, and health.* New York: Wiley, 1990.

COSTA, P. T., ZONDERMAN, A. B., & McCRAE, R. R. Personality, defense, coping, and adaptation in older adulthood. In E. M. Cummings, A. L. Greene, & K. K. Karraker (eds.), *Life span developmental psychology: Perspectives on stress and coping.* Hillsdale, NJ: Erlbaum, 1991.

CRAMER, P. The Defense Mechanisms Inventory: A review of research and discussion of the scales. *Journal of Personality Assessment,* 1988, *52,* 142–164.

DAKOF, G. A., & TAYLOR, S. E. Victims' perceptions of social support: What is helpful from whom? *Journal of Personality and Social Psychology,* 1990, *58,* 80–89.

DILL, D., & NOAM, G. Ego development and treatment requests. *Psychiatry,* 1990, *53,* 85–91.

EBATA, A., & MOOS, R. Coping and adjustment in distressed and healthy adolescents. *Journal of Applied Developmental Psychology,* 1991, *12,* 33–54.

ENDLER, N. S., & PARKER, J. D. A. Multidimensional assessment of coping: A critical evaluation. *Journal of Personality and Social Psychology,* 1990, *58,* 844–854.

————. *Coping Inventory for Stressful Situations: Manual.* Toronto: Multi-Health Systems, 1991.

ERIKSON, E. H. *Childhood and society* (2d ed.). New York: Norton, 1963.

FEIFEL, H., & STRACK, S. Coping with conflict situations: Middle-aged and elderly men. *Psychology and Aging,* 1989, *4,* 26–33.

FEIFEL, H., STRACK, S., & NAGY, V. T. Coping strategies and associated features of medically ill patients. *Psychosomatic Medicine,* 1987, *49,* 616–625. (a)

————. Degree of life-threat and differential use of coping modes. *Journal of Psychosomatic Research,* 1987, *31,* 91–99. (b)

FELTON, B., & REVENSON, T. A. Age differences in coping with chronic illness. *Psychology and Aging,* 1987, *2,* 164–170.

FLEISHMAN, J. A. Personality characteristics and coping patterns. *Journal of Health and Social Behavior,* 1984, *25,* 229–244.

FOLKMAN, S., & LAZARUS, R. S. *Manual for The Ways of Coping Questionnaire.* Palo Alto, CA: Consulting Psychologists Press, 1988.

FOLKMAN, S., LAZARUS, R. S., DUNKEL-SCHETTER, C., DeLONGIS, A., & GRUEN, R. J. Dynamics of a stressful encounter: Cognitive appraisal, coping, and encounter outcomes. *Journal of Personality and Social Psychology,* 1986, *50,* 992–1003.

FOLKMAN, S., LAZARUS, R. S., PIMLEY, S., & NOVACEK, J. Age differences in stress and coping processes. *Psychology and Aging,* 1987, *2,* 171–184.

FONDACARO, M., & MOOS, R. Social support and coping: A longitudinal analysis. *American Journal of Community Psychology,* 1987, *15,* 653–673.

GASTON, L., MARMAR, C. R., THOMPSON, L. W., & GALLAHER, D. Relation of patient pretreatment characteristics to the therapeutic alliance in diverse psychotherapies. *Journal of Consulting and Clinical Psychology,* 1988, *56,* 483–489.

HAAN, N. *Coping and defending: Processes of self-environment organization.* New York: Academic Press, 1977.

HEPPNER, P. P. *The Problem Solving Inventory manual.* Palo Alto, CA: Consulting Psychologists Press, 1988.

HOLAHAN, C. J., & MOOS, R. Personal and contextual determinants of coping strategies. *Journal of Personality and Social Psychology,* 1987, *52,* 946–955. (a)

————. Risk, resistance, and psychological distress: A longitudinal analysis with adults and children. *Journal of Abnormal Psychology,* 1987, *96,* 3–13. (b)

HOLAHAN, C. J., & MOOS, R. Life stressors, resistance factors, and improved psychological functioning: An extension of the stress-resistance paradigm. *Journal of Personality and Social Psychology,* 1990, *58,* 909–917.

IHILEVICH, D., & GLESER, G. *Defense mechanisms: Their classification, correlates, and measurement with the Defense Mechanisms Inventory.* Owosso, MI: DMI Associates, 1986.

JAMNER, L. D., SCHWARTZ, G. E., & LEIGH, H. The relationship between repressive and defensive coping styles and monocyte, eosinophile, and serum glucose levels: Support for the opioid peptide hypothesis of repression. *Psychosomatic Medicine,* 1988, *50,* 567–575.

KOHN, M. L., & SCHOOLER, C. *Work and personality: An inquiry into the impact of social stratification.* Norwood, NJ: Ablex Publishing, 1983.

LAZARUS, R., & FOLKMAN, S. *Stress, appraisal, and coping.* New York: Springer, 1984.

LEVENSON, J. L., MISHRA, A., HAMER, R. M., & HASTILLO, A. Denial and medical outcome in unstable angina. *Psychosomatic Medicine,* 1989, *51,* 27–35.

LEVINE, J., WARRENBURG, S., KERNS, R., SCHWARTZ, G., DELANEY, R., FONTANA, A., GRADMAN, A., SMITH, S., ALLEN, S., & CASCIONE, R. The role of denial in recovery from coronary heart disease. *Psychosomatic Medicine,* 1987, *49,* 109–117.

LOEVINGER, J. *Ego development: Conceptions and theories.* San Francisco: Jossey-Bass, 1976.

MANNE, S. L., & ZAUTRA, A. J. Spouse criticism and support: Their association with coping and psychological adjustment among women with rheumatoid arthritis. *Journal of Personality and Social Psychology,* 1989, *56,* 608–617.

MASLOW, A. H. *Toward a psychology of being* (2d ed.). Princeton, NJ: Van Nostrand, 1968.

MATTLIN, J. A., WETHINGTON, E., & KESSLER, R. C. Situational determinants of coping and coping effectiveness. *Journal of Health and Social Behavior,* 1990, *31,* 103–122.

MCCRAE, R. R. Age differences and changes in the use of coping mechanisms. *Journals of Gerontology,* 1989, *44,* P161–P169.

MILLER, S. M. Monitoring and blunting: Validation of a questionnaire to assess styles of information seeking under threat. *Journal of Personality and Social Psychology,* 1987, *52,* 345–353.

————. To see or not to see: Cognitive informational styles in the coping process. In M. Rosenbaum (ed.), *Learned resourcefulness: On coping skills, self-regulation, and adaptive behavior.* New York: Springer Press, 1990.

MILLER, S. M., BRODY, D. S., & SUMMERTON, J. Styles of coping with threat: Implications for health. *Journal of Personality and Social Psychology,* 1988, *54,* 142–148.

MOOS, R. Psychological techniques in the assessment of adaptive behavior. In G. V. Coelho, D. A. Hamburg, & J. E. Adams (eds.), *Coping and adaptation.* New York: Basic Books, 1974.

————. (ed.). *Coping with physical illness: New perspectives.* New York: Plenum, 1984.

————. (ed.). *Coping with life crises: An integrated approach.* New York: Plenum, 1986.

————. *Coping Responses Inventory manual.* Palo Alto, CA: Center for Health Care Evaluation, Department of Veterans Affairs and Stanford University Medical Centers, 1992.

————. *Coping Responses Inventory Youth Form preliminary manual.* Palo Alto, CA: Center for Health Care Evaluation, Department of Veterans Affairs and Stanford University Medical Centers, 1990.

MOOS, R., & BILLINGS, A. Conceptualizing and measuring coping resources and processes. In L. Goldberger & S. Breznitz (eds.), *Handbook of stress: Theoretical and clinical aspects.* New York: Free Press, 1982.

MOOS, R., BRENNAN, P., FONDACARO, M., & MOOS, B. Approach and avoidance coping responses among older problem and nonproblem drinkers. *Psychology and Aging,* 1990, *5,* 31–40.

MOOS, R., FINNEY, J., & CRONKITE, R. *Alcoholism treatment: Context, process, and outcome.* New York: Oxford University Press, 1990.

PARKER, G., BROWN, L., & BLIGNAULT, I. Coping behaviors as predictors of the course of clinical depression. *Archives of General Psychiatry,* 1986, *43,* 561–565.

PARKES, K. R. Laws of control, cognitive appraisal, and coping in stressful situations. *Journal of Personality and Social Psychology,* 1984, *46,* 655–668.

PARKES, K. R. Coping in stressful episodes: The role of individual differences, environmental factors, and situational characteristics. *Journal of Personality and Social Psychology,* 1986, *51,* 1277–1292.

PEACOCK, E. J., & WONG, P. T. P. The Stress Appraisal Measure (SAM): A multidimensional approach to cognitive appraisal. *Stress Medicine,* 1990, *6,* 227–236.

PERRI, M. G. Self-change strategies for the control of smoking, obesity, and problem drinking. In S. Shiffman & T. A. Wills (eds.), *Coping and substance use.* New York: Academic Press, 1985.

REVENSON, T. A., & FELTON, B. J. Disability and coping as predictors of psychological adjustment to rheumatoid arthritis. *Journal of Consulting and Clinical Psychology,* 1989, *57,* 344–348.

ROGERS, C. R. *On becoming a person: A therapist's view of psychotherapy.* Boston: Houghton Mifflin, 1961.

SANCHEZ-CRAIG, M., WILKINSON, D. A., & WALKER, K. Theory and methods for secondary prevention of alcohol problems: A cognitively based approach. In W. M. Cox (ed.), *Treatment and prevention of alcohol problems: A resource manual.* New York: Academic Press, 1987.

SCHAEFER, J., & MOOS, R. *Work stressors and coping among long-term care staff.* Palo Alto, CA: Center for Health Care Evaluation, Department of Veterans Affairs Medical Centers, 1991.

————. Life crises and personal growth. In B. N. Carpenter (ed.), *Personal coping: Theory, research, and applications.* New York: Praeger, in press.

SCHEIER, M. F., & CARVER, C. S. Optimism, coping, and health: Assessment and implications of generalized outcome expectancies. *Health Psychology,* 1985, *4,* 219–247.

————. Dispositional optimism and physical well-being: The influence of generalized outcome expectancies on health. *Journal of Personality,* 1987, *55,* 169–210.

SCHEIER, M. F., WEINTRAUB, J. K., & CARVER, C. S. Coping with stress: Divergent strategies of optimists and pessimists. *Journal of Personality and Social Psychology,* 1986, *51,* 1257–1264.

SHIFFMAN, S. Coping with temptations to smoke. In S. Shiffman & T. A. Wills (eds.), *Coping and substance use.* New York: Academic Press, 1985.

SOLOMON, K. E., & ANNIS, H. M. Outcome and efficacy expectancy in the prediction of posttreatment drinking behavior. *British Journal of Addiction,* 1990, *85,* 659–665.

STRACK, S., CARVER, C. S., & BLANEY, P. H. Predicting successful completion of an aftercare program following treatment for alcoholism: The role of dispositional optimism. *Journal of Personality and Social Psychology,* 1987, *53,* 579–584.

SULS, J., & FLETCHER, B. The relative efficacy of avoidant and nonavoidant coping strategies: A meta-analysis. *Health Psychology,* 1985, *4,* 249–288.

SWINDLE, R., CRONKITE, R., & MOOS, R. Life stressors, social resources, coping, and the 4-year course of unipolar depression. *Journal of Abnormal Psychology,* 1989, *48,* 468–477.

TAYLOR, S. E., & BROWN, J. D. Illusion and well-being: A social psychological perspective on mental health. *Psychological Bulletin,* 1988, *103,* 193–210.

VAILLANT, G. E. *Adaptation to life.* Boston: Little, Brown, 1977.

————. (ed.). *Empirical studies of ego mechanisms of defense.* Washington, DC: American Psychiatric Press, 1986.

VAILLANT, G. E., BOND, M., & VAILLANT, C. O. An empirically validated hierarchy of defense mechanisms. *Archives of General Psychiatry,* 1986, *43,* 786–794.

VITALIANO, P. P., MAIURO, R. D., RUSSO, J., & BECKER, J. Raw versus relative scores in the assessment of coping strategies. *Journal of Behavioral Medicine,* 1987, *10,* 1–8.

VITALIANO, P. P., DEWOLFE, D. J., MAIURO, R. D., RUSSO, J., & KATON, W. Appraised changeability of a stressor as a modifier of the relationship between coping and depression: A test of the hypothesis of fit. *Journal of Personality and Social Psychology,* 1990, *59,* 582–592.

WITKIN, H. A., & GOODENOUGH, D. R. Field dependence and interpersonal behavior. *Psychological Bulletin,* 1977, *84,* 661–689.

————. *Cognitive styles: Essence and origins.* New York: International Universities Press, 1981.

14

The Assessment of Coping, Defense, and Stress

Norma Haan

BEFORE ASSESSING, INVESTIGATORS NEED DEFINITIONS of what they want to assess. Investigators of coping, defense, and stress are handicapped by a lack of consensus on the meaning of these terms. The concept of stress is used and understood by laypersons, but its scientific study has proven difficult. Plainly, *stress* is whatever stresses people, but its essential properties are not clear. Is stress whatever upsets people (Paykel, Prusoff, & Uhlenhuth, 1971) or is it whatever requires them to adjust (Holmes & Rahe, 1967)? To discuss assessment of the concepts of coping, defense, and stress, then, I shall first indicate how I understand these words. My definitions draw on common sense, hoping that its modest consensual definitions will make it possible to discuss, without too much equivocation, the issues and means of assessing coping, defending, and stress. I shall agrue, that we must start with common sense to resolve the "crisis in stress research" (Rose & Levin, 1979).

PRELIMINARY DEFINITIONS

Stress

We commonly understand that stress ensues when situations are "bad" from a personal point of view, for example, the cancelation of an eagerly anticipated "good" event. Despite our seemingly contradictory recognition that stress is in the eye of the beholder, we well understand the commonsense meaning of stress in our everyday lives. We know when we and others are stressed. Of course, we may have special, deeper understandings of another person's plight if we have experienced the same stress. Acknowledgment that stress has common, shared human meanings is the underlying justification for the methodology used in life events research. As Holmes and Rahe (1967) showed, when people make impersonal social judgments about the stressfulness of events—all other matters of living being held equal—their agreements are rather good, whatever the criticisms about the items in different lists or the psychometric errors committed.

No one disagrees that traumatic events like losing a loved one, experiencing the Holocaust, being a POW, or serving as one of Milgram's subjects are stressful, but mild or moderate stresses occasion argument. Many are probably stressful in the eye of the beholder, constructed for reasons of personal history or cultural background. For example, women admit more readily than men to being stressed, and Hinkle's (1974) studies suggest that Hungarian refugees were more stressed than Chinese refugees by the necessity of immigration, apparently for reasons of cultural facilitation and vulnerability. Socioeconomic disadvantage is a well-understood stress. Common sense suggests other sources of individual differences: if persons have experienced numerous, intense, or prolonged episodes of stress, their resistance will be reduced. But as yet we have little researched based understanding of personal vulnerabilities.

The experience of stress, moreover, does not inevitably lead, in commonsense terms, to personal deterioration. Although we expect deterioraton, we contrarily expect that stress benefits people, making them more tender, humble, and hardy. Both gains and losses have been identified in longitudinal studies (Haan, 1977). When subgroups divided on the basis of incidence of hospitalizations and illnesses were compared, the more frequently ill were seen at later dates as typically more empathic and tolerant of ambiguity, although less able smoothly to regulate their affect. Moreover, people like stress in some ways. Stimulation by some difficulty keeps us interacting, and to experience stress and survive gives us knowledge of ourselves. To rust out is seen, at least in this culture, as even less desirable than to burn out. Once the stress has passed, we relish telling our stories of war, surgery, and divorce. We imply that we have proven ourselves and are better and wiser for our experience. Many research designs do not include provisions for assessing personal gains and thus the unstated supposition that stress is invariably decremental in effect is reified. Common sense is far wiser about the wear and tear of life; the ubiquitous hope is to manage stress and survive.

Our culture's idolization of success seems to evoke the idea—particularly in researchers of the behaviorist persuasion—that the strong person is invulnerable to stress. In this perspective, he or she simply does not become aroused. In fact, an assumption of research using scales like Holmes-Rahe's (1967) is that it is better not to have anything happen to one, not even marriage or pregnancy. Dubos (1959) has countered this position. Being human, he wrote, means having the capacity to experience stress. Invulnerability to stress may be a massive defensive maneuver. At root, these are contrasting value judgments about the best way to live.

In sum, stress is either a bad event or a good event that did not come about; its meanings are commonly understood even though some people's histories may be especially vulnerable to certain kinds of stress. Contrasting values about the best way to live—invulnerability or reactivity—permeate stress research. Finally, stress does not invariably lead to deterioration. It may facilitate growth by tempering arrogance and by enhancing our tenderness toward ourselves and others.

Coping and Defending

Coping and defense are no less controversial concepts than is stress. *Coping* is described as either a subcategory of defense (Cohen & Lazarus 1979) or a reaction that appears only in extremis (White, 1974). More often, its meanings are concretized as particular strategies appropriate for the special situation under study, like adjusting to college life (Coelho, Hamburg, & Murphey, 1963). Alternatively, I (Haan, 1977) have argued that coping is commonly understood to be a good way to handle problems; moreover, coping can be distinguished from defense. In *Webster's Third Unabridged Dictionary* coping means "to maintain a contest or combat, usually on equal terms or even with success . . . or to face, encounter . . . or overcome problems and difficulties." Concurring with clinical usage, *Webster's* supplies the following ideas about defense: "defendents' denial, answer, or plea opposing the truth of prosecutor's claims . . . fortification, justification . . . manner of self-protection." Thus, in common parlance, coping is not an action evoked solely by trauma, nor is coping a defense. Instead, it is an attempt to overcome difficulties on equal terms; it is an encounter wherein people reach out and within themselves for resources to come to terms with difficulties. *Defense* is unyielding fortification. Notice that a self-protective maneuver, undertaken with awareness, could be a sensible coping response in a situation of dangerous oppressiveness. Whether an action is coping or not can be decided only within context. Thus, coping does not insure a successful outcome because not all situations permit just or reasonable solutions.

The features that set coping and defense apart from one another are plain, so a question arises as to why some researchers shy away from explicit recognizing their differences, particularly when the differentiation clarifies conceptualizations and differentiates research designs. The positivists' mandate that social scientists be value-neutral probably accounts for this reluctance because coping does represent the value based conclusion of common sense that there are good and better, and bad and worse ways of handling stress.

The definitive and essentially epistemological argument that social science has only pretensions of being value-neutral cannot be taken up here. The basic point is that social-psychological knowledge is a human construction and it does not have the same objective reality that physical constructs do. Bernstein (1976), for instance, analyzed social science's confusion in this regard and suggested that our pretensions to value neutrality lie at the root of our frequent crises, which are then set aside by the claim that social science is still in its infancy. The solution most observers propose is that social science should admit its value basis and then proceed with analyses relying on the common value (Haan, 1977; Haan, Bellah, Rabinow, & Sullivan, 1981; Habermas, 1971, 1981).

Our lack of objective targets can be seen in stress research. We "know" what kind of experiences are stressful because we are in commonsense agreement that people are stressed when they have stress experiences. If we were to admit openly that our knowledge of stress arises from common, shared understandings and not from objective reality, the insight would be liberating. We could then use what we already know in our everyday lives: stress is handled in "richer and poorer, effective and less effective ways" (Frenkel-Brunswik, 1954).

In any event, we are not more value-neutral for focusing exclusively on the defensive, destructive ways in which stress is handled and its detrimental results of personal decrement. In fact, the concept of defense is also value-based; it rests on the assumption that negating, distorting, and obscuring both self-knowledge and contextual knowledge is not as good as knowing the "truth." Furthermore, we are not entitled as scientists to obscure or circumvent certain classes of human actions (Frenkel-Brunswick, 1954), nor do we have license to revise the common meanings of words. The conceptual position of attempting to achieve in the social sciences the value-neutral stance of physical science turns us away from life and distorts our use of garden-variety values.

ACHIEVING GENERALITY IN STRESS REASEARCH

For stress researchers to obtain a general understanding of the conditions and effects of stress, identification of stressors, coping, and defensive reactions that transcend situationally specific stresses and personal processes is needed. Otherwise research will generate small facts but no insights. No listing of so-called objective, situationally specific stress stimuli is likely to be satisfactory because stress is the result of a situation's having a certain meaning.

Fortunately, such meanings may have some common properties that could help us construct a taxonomy of stress situations.

Both common sense and research (McGrath, 1970) suggest that people's *assimilation* of undesirable circumstances is more difficult (1) when they have not anticipated a bad event or their hopes for good news have been dashed, (2) when the onset is out of their control, (3) when the conditions of their situation are ambiguous, (4) when they think that they will be stressed, (5) when the situation resembles other poorly resolved events, (6) when they are already stressed by other matters, and (7) when their efforts to secure pertinent information are defeated. *Accommodations* to stress are more difficult (1) when one has little or no possibility of diminishing the stress—its outcome is beyond one's control (Seligmann, 1975), (2) when the stress is intense, (3) when stressful experiences closely follow one on another, and (4) when one has had no previous experience with the particular kind of stress. Moreover, researchers have recently recognized what common sense already taught: lack of social or institutional supports exacerbates stress reactions, whereas such support facilitates effective reactions.

If this taxonomy of properties has face validity, then it might be useful for researchers to begin classifying stress situations not only according to their content—like bereavement—but also according to their stress properties. For instance, controversy has centered on the positive events included in the original Holmes-Rahe (1967) list, which could be differentiated by such a taxonomy. By and large, their life course events, like the birth of a baby, are to be expected; however, when a life event occurs off schedule, such as having a baby at age 15 or age 45 (Neugarten, 1979), its meaning changes. It is not expected and it becomes an adventitious stressful event.

A concomitant of the growing awareness that stress can be defined only in a circular fashion is the theme that stress involves interaction between events and people. Thus, *interaction*—not only personal responses to stress stimuli—must be assessed if we are to understand stress and stressed people. Temporal sequences need to be measured by assessing and reassessing *both* situations and people. The relevant personal aspects in this context are the processes people use to interact. Therefore, most stress researchers, unlike traditional personologists, have turned to the study of person's processes. Traits will not do because they denote the perseveration of the same response over time.

Surely in interacting, people would prefer to cope if they could. However, most often in stress situations we not only cope but also defend and frequently *fragment,* however briefly, in a sequence or in some desperate, random combination of all three modes. Following methodological convention, we tend to type people, in the manner of early personality theorists, as all or forever good or bad, as either copers or defenders. But in their attempts to unravel a stressful event, the same people—even psychotics—cope, defend, and fragment, so measures of all three reaction modes are needed.

Coping, defending, and fragmenting are general approaches, not specific processes. People have more specific ways of dealng with stress that are represented in their hierarchies of preferred ego processes. For instance, a professor faced with an emotional interpersonal problem may rely first on logical analysis, not on empathy, or he or she may intellectualize in an attempt to resolve the difficulty. But again, preferred, specific processes are readily abandoned in a situation if they do not work. People's intelligence in reacting appropriately to the features of different situations and their virtuosity in inventing new ways of interacting have been the bane of traditional personologists. These capabilities generated the controversy over cross-situational consistency in personality. In sum, then, coping and defense cannot be understood outside the context of the situational stress, and stress is not known apart from the ways people interact with it. To elucidate the interaction between people and stress, research designs need to include the features reviewed in the next section.

ASSESSMENT PROVISIONS IN RESEARCH DESIGN

Time Frame

Assimilating and accommodating to stress necessarily take place over time. Thus, designs need a time frame of a length appropriate to the problem under investigation. Hosack's (1968) study should alert us to the possibility of reaching erroneous conclusions when data are collected at a single point in time. She found that mothers whose first child was malformed and who later coped with the baby's condition by health professionals' standards of appropriate care were intelligently upset at the baby's birth, in contrast to defensive mothers, who were seemingly more tranquil both early and later. If Hosack's model of successfully handling stress had been the characterologically nonaroused person, she might have been content with a single data collection immediately following the baby's birth. But then she would have concluded that the defensive mothers had handled the stress of the baby's condition in the most effective way. To cope with stress, it must be admitted, but to admit stress has to be upsetting, at least in the beginning.

Transcending Specific Situations

In order for social scientists to achieve general understanding of the meanings that stress has for people (so useful recommendations about public policy can eventually be made), coping, defense, and stress need to be operationalized in general, not situationally bound terms. In other words, the variables need to be sufficiently abstract to transcend specific contexts and particular kinds of maneuvers. As suggested earlier, stressful situations could be classified according to commonly understood properties, like anticipated or not, controlled or not. Likewise, the person's processes of handling stress need to be generalized, as many investigators already recognize.

Capturing a Wide Array of Processes

Because attempts to resolve stressful events involve sequences of interactions as persons make more or less apt responses in an attempt to preserve their own integrity, an array of processes usually appears. Consequently, the net for assessing process variables needs to be thrown wide. Moreover, as Bem and Funder (1978) observed, not all people use all processes. If for reasons of methodological simplicity and rigor, the design permits only one or two processes to be assessed or collapses discrete processes into global notions like overall coping, the analysis of some person-stress interactions will be incomplete or wrong.

Repeated Assessments

Focus on interactions means not only that the person's processes need to be assessed at different points during the process of resolution but also that stressful situations need to be assessed and reassessed at different points.

Effective and Ineffective Ways of Handling Stress and Its Outcomes

Provisions need to be made for evaluating effective processes and personal gains, as well as ineffective processes and personal losses, in relation to the stress experience. Thus, both coping, as a value based representation of the more effective and richer ways of processing stress, and defensiveness, as the less effective and narrower way, must be assessed. We need to know what kinds of stress, handled with what kinds of processes in the context of what kinds of exogenous support, eventually have humanizing and actualizing, as well as detrimental, effects.

Supports of All Kinds

The effects of stress can be exacerbated or tempered by varying the person's social supports (Brown, 1978; Cobb, 1976), or, more comprehensively, "resistance resources" (Antonovsky, 1979). However, social support is only one environmental resource for alleviating stress; economic, financial, or political power also expands response options (Pearlin & Schooler, 1978). Moreover, social support must go beyond tender care to include help in sorting out the implications of one's experience, discarding one's exaggerations and distortions, and consensually validating the reality of one's reactions and the situation. Crisis intervention clinics and self-help groups now formally provide such support for the process of working through stress. Crisis clinics base their operation on the accumulated wisdom that stressed people adopt, usually by six weeks, truly equilibrated or false, rigid solutions because prolonged and unremitting stress is intolerable.

Studies of social support have tended to be only correlative in design. Research distinguishing the mechanisms and effects of the different kinds of support—social, material, and cognitive-clarifying—is much needed.

Naturalistic Study

Although psychologists earlier studied artificially aroused stress in laboratories, many workers now prefer naturalistic study. The meanings of stress experienced in the laboratory turned out to be unpredictably constructed by subjects (Haan, 1969; Lazarus, Opton, Tomita, & Kodama, 1966; Maguire, Maclean, & Aitken, 1973). However, the study of naturalistic events is not an easy road to truth. First, the variety of stress events is enormous. Second, investigators must know the subjects' status prior to the stress in order to isolate the effects of stress. Third, all manner of events other than the target stress may be experienced by subjects during the investigation. Still, the advantages of studying real-life interactions undoubtedly outweigh the disadvantages. Researchers who conduct naturalistic investigations will have to tolerate error variance and prediction failure (Bem & Funder, 1978).

MEASUREMENT OF COPING AND DEFENDING

In this section, measurement of stress is not directly taken up because other chapters in this volume cover the topic well. However, the reverberations between people and events means that the measurement of people cannot be divorced from the evaluation of situations.

The two main ways of measuring coping and defending are (1) observations by professionals or intimates of stressed persons and (2) self-reports of behaviors or responses to test items. The distinction between observations and self-reports may not be as important in advancing stress research as is the scheduling of measurements; assessments need to be made within the situation of stress or outside it, the latter to include ratings done before, after, or during but still removed from the target event.

An ideal design would include measurements of coping and defending made before stress—to evaluate input status; within the situation—to assess actual reactions; and afterward—to assess enduring effects. Naturalistic situations almost never permit premeasurements because the investigator usually comes upon the scene when the stress is under way. Moreover, premeasurements of large samples at risk for experiencing a particular stress—like a coronary attack—are prohibitively expensive.

An alternative is to attempt to trigger a stressful experience in a naturalistic way. However, these designs also have difficulties. Paramount is the ethical hazard of investigators' deliberately invoking stress. If they first give fully informed consent, subjects will react to the stressful situation in unnatural ways. Plainly, Milgram's (1974) subjects would not have been troubled had they known that the electric shock they were asked to administer was bogus. In an ongoing project, my colleagues and I inform subjects (at first adolescent but subsequently young adult friendship groups) that we are studying morality. We tell subjects that they will be given moral problems to solve as groups and that, as a result, they are likely to become angry with their friends and argue. Our forewarning probably accounts for one general result, although our subjects do become angry and stressed: stressful problems result in significantly lower levels of coping than do nonstressful problems, but not in markedly higher levels of defensiveness, as we unthinkingly hypothesized. Thus, informed consent may allow subjects to cope instead of defend.

Despite the difficulties, within-situation measurement of coping and defending may have the greatest payoff for stress research for several reasons. First, the controversy over cross-situational consistency of personality is evidence in itself that theories of personality based solely on persons' predispositions do not tell us enough about how people act in stressful circumstances. Second, the lengthy inferential reach required to connect actions taken in stress situations with predispositions is obviated by within-situation measurement; instead, the actual reaction needs to be measured. Finally, studies including within-situation measurement are rare so that we know little about how people actually interact with stress. Of course, within-situation measurement is not an end in itself: societies need to predict in order to construct policies that might prevent breakdowns and decompensations.

Measures Taken Outside the Stress Situation

I have limited the subsequent presentation to measurements of processes and I evaluate them substantively and conceptually instead of psychometrically. Readers will want firsthand information about the psychometric status of measures. How much unreliability an investigator will tolerate with complex variables is a personal decision that may put validity at risk whenever reliability is too high or too low.

Human virtuosity in selecting and sequencing processes in accordance with specific situations means that an array of measures, not just one or two, should be used; otherwise, the reactive processes of some persons will slip through the assessment net. Paper and pencil measures do not directly represent the objective reality of persons' processes, or even their traits, but instead their processes of test taking—that is, only what they are willing to have the investigator know. I suggest, however, that interactions with investigators are not markedly different from interactions with others in the person's life.

An early study by Miller and Swanson (1960) illustrates the need for flexibility in measurement. Their observational assessment included only defense mechanisms, which they aroused by various stimuli. However, a number of subjects did not become defensive. Because these investigators had no conceptual provisions for handling nondefensive behavior—which may have been coping behavior—they eliminated these subjects from their analyses. They may have thereby excluded from scrutiny an important segment of the range of human reaction.

The use of paper and pencil measures brings up the issue of social desirability, which in the process oriented view becomes a defense in itself, not an extraneous intrusion that can be corrected with the expectancy that the "real truth" about the individual's personality will be revealed. For example, I (Haan, 1977) found that defensive denial scores were positively associated with the Minnesota Multiphasic Personality Inventory (MMPI's) lie, K, and social desirability scales at the .001 level (correlations ranged from .44 to .52) and with the California Psychological Inventory (CPI's) good impression and commonality scores at the .001 and the .05 level, respectively (correlations were .34 and .21) in samples of 85 men and 90 women. The MMPI F-scale was positively associated with defensive doubt and defensive regression at the .001 level (r's of .41 and .39, respectively). According to this view, stress researchers should not want to correct scores for test taking attitudes.

Locus of Control. Although the Locus of Control instrument was not constructed to represent a process, it seems to do so. *Internal control* attributes agency to oneself, a coping procedure, whereas *external control* gives agency to others or to fate (presumably a defensive expectation that leads to helplessness) (Seligmann, 1975). Both aspects of control are likely to occur in situations of stress.

To discuss this instrument at length is not possible here. However, investigators using the Locus of Control in stress research need to take its several substantive limitations into account. First, people cannot realistically attribute responsibility to themselves for many stressful events, although they may habitually think that they determine their own fate. In fact, an almost invariant property of a stressful situation is that people are not able to control its onset or outcome. Dohrenwend (1973) illustrated this point well when she showed that women and blacks experience more stressful life events than do white males, an understandable finding in view of their lower status. Women and blacks are also known to have lower internal control scores than do white males. This limitation may not always be an important drawback if assessment is done before or after stress or even during mild stress that does not color all the interpretations that persons make of themselves and their lives. Thus, the problem is to separate specific reactions to stress from habitual expectations but, of course, this problem accompanies any measure made outside the stress situation.

Second, internal locus of control is a global measurement of general coping and investigators may want greater differentiation among coping processes. Furthermore, external control seems to include several ways of defending, e.g., displacement and projection. Kuypers (1972) found, as evidence, that persons higher on internal locus of control were also higher than externals on all 10 of Haan's coping processes, significantly higher on 6 of these, and lower on 9 of the 10 defensive processes but significantly lower on only 1. In sum, differentiation of the coping behaviors used by internals cannot be attained with this measure and some kinds of defensive behavior may not be assessed for externals.

Cognitive Controls. During the late 1950s and early 1960s, a series of publications described certain cognitive styles as typical of persons who preferred certain defenses, and it was reasonably shown that these cognitive styles, regarded as ways of organizing information, accounted for individual variations in adaptive behavior (see Gardner, Holzman, Klein, Linton, & Spence, 1959). For example, Gardner, Holtzman, Klein, Linlon, & Spence, (1959) showed that *cognitive leveling* was associated with repressive tendencies and that *cognitive scanning* was related to isolating tendencies. Leveling (or sharpening) referred to persons' tendency to mute (or maximize) differences in their experience, whereas scanning refers to their tendency to cast about for different solutions. Witkin and his associates (Witkin, Dyk, Faterson, Goodenough, & Karp, 1962) took part in this early work and developed the concept of field independence-dependence, which seems near in meaning to locus of control. *Field independents* have agency; *field dependents* allow the field to organize them. Moos (1974) reviewed recent research on cognitive styles and general adaptation, not stress and coping per se, but investigators who consider using cognitive controls and styles would be rewarded by reading his account. In the original work by the Gardner and Witkin teams, a variety of interesting quasi-experimental measures were developed to measure the cognitive controls of leveling, sharpening, tolerance for unrealistic experiences, focusing, constricted-flexible, and field independence-dependence. Additional measures indexed the styles persons use in reacting to Rorschach blots. Sharpening of differences, as opposed to leveling, and field independence, as opposed to field dependence, were regarded as good styles— coping styles I would say—, although the investigators did not admit the value bias underlying their procedures.

MMPI Scales. Scanning the appendix of the *MMPI Handbook,* volume 2, (Dahlstrom, Welsh, & Dahlstrom, 1960), which lists specially developed scales, indicates that measurement of processes in stress research need not start from scratch. The titles of the following special scales suggest that they measure the kinds of processes likely to occur with some frequency in stress situations (I do not credit their authors; I am merely mentioning possibilities): facilitation-inhibition, conflict resolution, sensitivity, perceptual distortion, rigidity, use of the will to set and hold goals, blaming self, feeling sorry for self, punishing self, self-rejection distress, concern for health, acting out, ego control, neurotic overcontrol, neurotic undercontrol, acting out hostility, resisting being told what to do, blaming others, criticism of others, demandingness, and possibly Barron's (1953) ego strength, which may measure character more than it does processes.

In 1965, I published a study that I had done on developing preliminary coping and defensive scales based on MMPI items. The scales included intellectualizing, doubt, denial, projection, regression, displacement, repression, and primitive defense, Joffe and Naditch (1977) subsequently used larger samples and more sophisticated statistical techniques, primarily on CPI items but also on MMPI items, to develop coping and defensive scales based on my ego model (Haan, 1977). Their scales are discussed in the next section. In reviewing the validity of my original scales, Morrissey (1977) suggested that their usefulness was uneven, but investigators will find his careful review helpful.

CPI Scales. Most of the standard CPI scales developed by Gough (1957) do not appear on their face to measure processes. Gough had wanted to measure folk concepts about personalities, but the line of demarcation between process and personality is sometimes thin. Several of his scales do seem to measure coping processes, namely, tolerance, good impression, achievement conformance, achievement independence, intellectual efficiency, psychological mindedness, and flexibility. In addition, Gough (1976, 1977) developed a modernity scale that measures the extent to which people favor social change and experimentation and indicates whether they are optimistic about the future and their capacity to cope with new experiences. Persons with high and low scores on modernity should handle stress differently.

Joffe and Naditch (1977) constructed a set of CPI and MMPI based coping and defending scales. As mentioned earlier, their scales undoubtedly are an excellent replacement for my preliminary coping and defending scales (Hahn, 1965). Scales that Joffe and Naditch regarded as "probably acceptable by existing standards," which were replicated for both sexes, were the coping scales of intellectuality, logical analysis, tolerance of ambiguity, regression in the service of the ego, and total coping, along with the defense scales of intellectualizing, doubt, and regression. "Less acceptable" scales for both sexes, which did not meet all criteria of validation, reliability, or discriminant validity, were sublimation and substitution (coping) and rationalization (defending). Another set of scales met either the strict or the relaxed criteria for one or the other of the sexes: for men, expressiveness (coping) and projection, isolation, primitive defense, and total defense (defending); for women, denial, displacement, projection, structured defense, and primitive defense (defending). Joffe and Naditch (1977) also developed several MMPI based ego scales for projection and regression (defense) and concentration and suppression (coping). (The recency of these scales' development means that only two published studies so far have tested their validity in separate samples of stressed persons, blind males and Marine recruits being discharged for nonperformance [Joffe & Bast, 1978; Vickers, & Hervig, 1981].)

Coping as Measured by Shanan. Shanan (1973) developed an articulated and dynamic definition of coping and proposed methods of its assessment by means of a sentence completion test and the Thematic Apperception Test (TAT). The distinctive features of this definition of coping are (1) the availability of free cathetic energy for directing attention to difficulty and identifying complexity, (2) the articulation of transactions between field and self, (3) the tendency to confront or avoid complexity and conflict, and (4) the optimal balance between demands of reality and self. Measurements are accomplished as follows: *energy:* the number of stems completed on a sentence completion test and the total number of all words and verbs indicating activity used in TAT stories; *transaction between field and self:* the number of sentence completion responses that refer to other persons and objects, as opposed to the self and the number of complex situations describing conflict in TAT stories, along with the number of time dimensions and ambiguous endings; *dealing with complexity and conflict:* the number of sentence completions that indicate tendencies to give up as opposed to persevere and, within the TAT stories, the same tendencies in the actions of characters. Shanan did not state how optimal balances between the demands of reality and self are to be measured. His conceptualization and convincing operationalizations of coping are interesting and relevant to stress research and he did report several validating studies. However, his methods may be too time-consuming for many investigators.

The Defense Mechanism Inventory. Gleser and Ihilevich (1969) developed an objective instrument for the measurement of five clusters of defenses: turning against the object, projection, principalization (splitting affect from content and repressing content), turning against the self, and reversal (responding positively or neutrally to a frustrating object). They defined these mechanisms in the classical way as processes whereby the "ego attacks, distorts, or become selectively unaware of certain aspects of the internal or external world" (p. 52). The instrument includes 10 stories; after reading each story, the person responds to questons that refer to actual behavior, impulsive behavior, thoughts, or feelings. Five alternative answers for each question correspond to each of the five defense clusters. The respondent indicates the alternatives that are most and least representative of what he or she would be likely to do. Gleser and Sacks (1973) used this inventory, with results that confirmed hypotheses, to assess defense reactions in undergraduates prior to their being told that their performance was deficient on a test of scholastic ability. Vickers, and Hervig (1981) investigated the relationship of the inventory's scores with clinical ratings of defense in a group of men who were presumably stressed because they were being discharged from the Marine Corps prior to completing their basic training. Here the results were disappointing as compared to those with the Joffe-Naditch (1977) scales. Nevertheless, the original validation studies and the conceptual framework for this instrument suggest that it may be useful in stressful research.

Persons' Self-Described Coping and Defending. Another recently developed method of assessing coping by self-report is illustrated by the work of Pearlin and Schooler (1978), Folkman and Lazarus (1980), and Billings and Moos (1981). All these studies used nonsymptomatic community samples. Subjects were asked to report how they usually coped with noxious events or with specific experiences. At the same time, subjects also reported their stresses, strains, and negative life events. The investigators developed these instruments by surveying the literature, testing pilot samples, and/or relying on their own theories or common sense. This method differs from those discussed previously because it is based on the presumption that people *can* directly describe their coping strategies with the aid of a checklist or questionnaire. This assumption needs to be supported by comparisons of such self-reports with clinical observations.

Folkman and Lazarus included only coping items in their inventory, whereas the other two investigations had mixtures of coping and defense. From the standpoint of the present distinction between coping and defending, a question must be raised as to whether people can describe their defenses inasmuch as these are customarily thought to operate at the preconscious level. People should be able to describe their coping efforts because a hallmark of coping is conscious choice. Our accrued understanding from psychotherapeutic situations, which is the context par excellence for observing processes in action, is that people do not ordinarily recognize their defenses. In fact, the purpose of psychotherapy is to facilitate clients' recognition of their defenses so that they can choose how to act—in other words, how to cope. If this reasoning is correct, this self-report method should elicit more coping than defense responses.

Folkman and Lazarus (1980) and Billings and Moos (1981) used a rather similar classification of coping, the division between *problem-focused* and *emotion-focused coping*. However, this separation does not seem to be conceptually clear. Stress situations that can be resolved by problem-focused coping must also involve emotions and vice versa. As it turns out, in 98% of the stress incidents reported by Folkman and Lazarus, both kinds of coping were used despite modest correlations of about .45 between the two measures. But differences were still discernible: people used more problem-focused coping in situations in which they thought "something could be done" and more emotion-focused coping when they thought they could only accept the situation. This result seems to tell us exactly what we would expect.

The Folkman-Lazarus (1980) checklist, called Ways of Coping, contains 64 items—24 for problem-focused coping and 40 for emotion-focused coping. Examination of these items indicates that almost all could represent coping as it is defined in this chapter. In fact, Folkman and Lazarus came close to endorsing such a definition: "Coping is defined as the cognitive and behavioral efforts made to master, tolerate, or reduce external and internal demands and conflicts among them" (p. 223). However, whether or not items are coping or defending depends on the situation and the respondent's level of awareness. Endorsing the idea of coping is a clear loss if the price is to discard defense, a time-honored and well-understood means of handling stress. To its credit, the Billings-Moos (1981) instrument of 19 items includes both coping and defense items (e.g., "Sometimes took it out on other people when I felt angry or depressed," "Tried to step back from the situation and be more objective").

A final problem of conceptual clarity needs to be mentioned. These instruments include a conglomeration of coping (or defense) processes, a characteristic that reduces differentiation; at the same time, the processes included may be insufficiently abstract to permit the eventual generalizations that stress research needs. In fact, Folkman and Lazarus (1980) expressed concerned that "it may be that to identify coping styles that transcend situational contexts, we must look at another level of abstraction" (p. 229).

The Pearlin-Schooler (1978) study of 2300 persons took a sociological approach and thus used variables like household economics and "limited societal opportunity structures." Psychologists tend to overlook their subjects' objective resources, which generate response options, and then implicitly assign the better coping of their objectively advantaged subjects to intrinsically better character. However, all data in this study came from self-reports and the distinction between coping and defense is not made. Subjects were asked to make fine distinctions among stresses, strains, coping resources, and coping responses. For example, in the content area of spouse, strain was operationalized as nonacceptance by spouse; stress, as being unhappy, bothered, frustrated, tense, bored, discontented, and so forth with the spouse; coping resources, as self-denigration, mastery, and self-esteem; and coping responses, as self-reliance versus advice seeking, controlled reflective versus emotional discharge, selective ignoring versus paying attention.

Measurements Made Inside the Stress Situation

To show how people interact with stressful experiences, measurements made within the stress situation are needed. However premeasurements are also required if effects of the stress itself are to be separated from effects related to prior status. Within-measurements of naturalistic situations will almost always be based on observations because there are ethical questions involved in asking stressed persons to make self-reports like answering yes or no to items on a personality inventory for the purpose of psychologists' research. A different interpersonal exchange obtains when professionals extract measures of coping and defending from interviews that have the purpose of helping persons with their feelings and problems. For this reason, transcribed interviews conducted in crisis intervention clinics seem an excellent data base for obtaining measurements of stress.

The full force of the conceptual difficulties in systematizing the ways people cope and defend is felt when the multifaceted, real-life reactions of stressed persons are confronted. Here the means of assessment must almost always be ratings in some form. A common approach is to take the content of a specific stress situation and deduce the likely dimensions. For example, Silber and his associates (Silber, Coelho, Murphey, Hamburg, Pearlin, & Rosenberg, 1961), in their study of competent adolescents coping with the problem of college entrance, organized their observations according to such headings as the use of environmental resources in learning about colleges, application strategies, assessment of the potential self-college fit, and parents' roles in students' choice of college.

In order to generalize the most common processes people use in dealing with all kinds of stress, various schemes of either coping or coping and defending have been offered. Cohen and Lazarus (1979) suggested that the four main modes of coping are information seeking, which has a self-evident meaning; direct actions, for which the authors gave the examples of running away, arguing, or "in short, doing something about the problem"; inhibition of action, which they briefly stated is "a mode of coping"; and intrapsychic processes, for which the examples of the defenses of denial, avoidance, and the like were given. This scheme well illustrates the conceptual problems that develop when coping is regarded as defense. Not only are all intrapsychic coping processes classified as defenses, but also intrapsychic processes are apparently thought to be conceptually different from cognitive processes and unrelated to action. Taking action and inhibiting action probably are the two extremes of the same dimension. Too much information seeking may be an obsession and the prudence of acting or not acting depends on the nature of the situation. However, Cohen and Lazarus remained true to their own position; they did not posit a good way to handle stress.

Moos and Tsu (1977) offered an integrated and comprehensive scheme specifically to describe coping within the context of physical illness; however, most of their dimensions have generality. They identified six separate processes: denying or minimizing the seriousness of the crisis; seeking relevant information; requesting reassurance; learning specific illness related procedures; setting concrete, limited goals; rehearsing alternative outcomes; and finding a general purpose or meaning in the event.

Finally, the multidimensional scheme of coping, defending, and fragmentation that I (Haan, 1977) proposed is most easily understood by recounting its development. Each of the 10 coping and 10 fragmenting processes was constructed to represent the same general processes involved in 10 classical defense mechanisms; however, the coping and fragmenting items have different properties from those of their defense counterparts. For example, within the same generic ego process of interpersonal sensitivity, projection is the defense, empathy is the coping counterpart, and delusions are the fragmented manifestation.

In this model (Haan, 1977), five properties identify coping: open consideration of options; orientation to the realities and future implications of the situation and to the implications of one's possible reactions; differentiated thinking that integrates rational, conscious considerations and preconscious elements; flexible and inventive creation of response options; and governance of disturbing affects and tempered affective expression. In a few words, coping rests on the value of accuracy in assimilating the critical elements of one's situation and one's reactions and accuracy in acting and accommodating, after consideration of the various possible transactions that might be undertaken and their future consequences.

In contrast, the common and classical meanings of defense involve negation of choice; slanting the present situation in terms of the past; disregarding future implications and the consequences of one's action; distorted and undifferentiated cognitive considerations; separation of thought from concomitant feelings; expectancies that disturbing feelings can be magically removed; and impulse gratification by subterfuge. Intersubjective and intrasubjective inaccuracies typify defensive strategies.

Still another set of properties describes the fragmented processes of persons we ordinarily think of as psychotic (or those of normal people for brief moments). Here the processes are repetitive, ritualistic, and automated; assumptions about reality and the future are privatistically based and nonresponsive to the requirements of the present situation; affect determines reactions; and unmodulated gratification of impulse occurs.

My colleague (Kroeber, 1963) and I hoped that the resulting trios of coping, defensive, fragmenting process was near to being a comprehensive map of the main ego processes that encompassed cognitive, affective, intraceptive, and attention focusing functions. Moreover, we reasoned that the values underlying coping—and defense, too, for that matter—might be at some distance from our personal values. A main difficulty of the model seems to be that it is too abstract from a nonclinical investigator's point of view.

Assessment of the relevant variables in most of these schemes to represent coping and for defense usually must be done by ratings; sometimes, unobtrusive measures can be used. For instance, information seeking (coping) by a physically ill patient could be evaluated by nurses on the ward. Although some investigators are discomfited by so-called soft measures, like ratings, others take the position that human reactions and interactions are so complex that they can be captured only by equally flexible and complex human minds. Until we have a consensual taxonomy of human processing of stress, most researchers will undoubtedly develop rating systems of within-situation stress reactions that express their own theoretical preferences. For instance, my 60-item Q-Sort of Ego Processes (Haan, 1977) includes three items for the 10 coping and 10 defensive processes; I did not include fragmenting processes because I work mostly with normal subjects, who do not fragment frequently.

CONCLUSION

A rosy picture of the art of assessing coping, defending, and stress could not be painted in this chapter. We lack consensus about the meanings of these terms and about the likely connections among them. Undoubtedly, if we had consensus, measures would be quickly developed. I suggested that our difficulties emanate from our continued pretension that stress research is a science that concerns objective realities. Not only is stress the construction of the stressed, but also we know by common sense that there are both good (accurate, logical, socially sensitive, and informed) and bad (distorted, decompensated, and socially destructive) ways of handling stress. But this admission would invalidate the social scientist's claims of value neutrality.

The parent of stress research is the long worked but chaotic field of personology, which aims to conceptualize and understand the whole person. The basic parameters of stress research are much clearer: we are interested in the effects of environments that lead people to feel trapped, helpless, and oppressed and we seek to understand how people handle these experiences. The long-term goal is plainly a humane one—knowledge of how societies might organize themselves to avoid the unnecessary stresses that people experience and to buffer the inevitable stresses that citizens must suffer. In a way, interest in psychometric assessment at this time is premature because our debates have not yet resolved the basic questions of definition: what is stress, coping, and defending? But then social science never proceeds in an orderly way.

REFERENCES

ANTONOVSKY, A. *Health, stress, and coping.* San Francisco: Jossey-Bass, 1979.

BARRON, F. An ego-strength scale which predicts response to psychotherapy. *Journal of Consulting Psychology,* 1953, *17,* 327–333.

BEM, D., & FUNDER, D. Predicting more of the people more of the time: Assessing the personality of situations. *Psychological Review,* 1978, *85,* 485–501.

BERNSTEIN, R. *The restructuring of social and political theory.* New York: Harcourt, 1976.

BILLINGS, A., & MOOS, R. The role of coping responses and social resources in attenuating the stress of life events. *Journal of Behavioral Medicine,* 1981.

BROWN, G., & HARRIS, T. *The social origins of depression.* New York: Free Press, 1978.

COBB, S. Social support as a moderator of life stress. *Psychosomatic Medicine,* 1976, *38,* 300–314.

COELHO, G. V., HAMBURG, D. A., & MURPHEY, E. B. Coping strategies in a new learning environment. *Archives of General Psychiatry,* 1963, *9,* 433–443.

COHEN, F., & LAZARUS, R. S. Coping with the stresses of illnesses. In G. C. Stone, F. Cohen, & N. E. Adler (eds.), *Health psychology.* San Francisco: Jossey-Bass, 1979.

DAHLSTROM, W., WELSH, G., & DAHLSTROM, L. *An MMPI handbook* (rev. ed.), vol. 2. Minneapolis: University of Minnesota Press, 1975.

DOHRENWEND, B. S. Social status and stressful life events. *Journal of Personality and Social Psychology,* 1973, *28,* 225–235.

DUBOS, R. *Mirage of health.* New York: Harper, 1959.

FOLKMAN, S., & LAZARUS, R. An analysis of coping in a middle-aged community sample. *Journal of Health and Social Behavior,* 1980, *21,* 219–239.

FRENKEL-BRUNSWIK, E. Social research and the problem of values. *Journal of Abnormal and Social Psychology,* 1954, *49,* 466–471.

GARDNER, R. W., HOLZMAN, P. S., KLEIN, G. S., LINTON, H. P., & SPENCE, D. P. Cognitive control: A study of individual consistencies in cognitive behavior. *Psychological Issues,* 1959, *1,* 1–186, whole issue.

GLESER, G., & IHILEVICH, D. An objective instrument for measuring defense mechanisms. *Journal of Consulting and Clinical Psychology,* 1969, *33,* 51–60.

GLESER, G., & SACKS, M. Ego defenses and reaction to stress: A validation study of the Defense Mechanism Inventory. *Journal of Consulting and Clinical Psychology,* 1973, *40,* 181–187.

GOUGH, H. *Manual for the California Psychological Inventory.* Palo Alto: Consulting Psychologists, 1957.

————. A measure of individual modernity. *Journal of Personality Assessment,* 1976, *40,* 3–9.

————. Further validation of a measure of individual modernity. *Journal of Personality Assessment,* 1977, *41,* 49–57.

HAAN, N. Coping and defense mechanisms related to personality inventories. *Journal of Consulting Psychology,* 1965, *29,* 373–378.

————. A tripartite model of ego functioning, values, and clinical and research applications. *Journal of Nervous and Mental Disease,* 1969, *148,* 14–30.

————. Two moralities in action contexts. *Journal of Personality and Social Psychology,* 1978, *36,* 286–305.

————(ed.). *Coping and defending: Processes of self-environment organization.* New York: Academic, 1977.

HABERMAS, J. *Knowledge and human interests,* trans. J. J. Shapiro. Boston: Beacon, 1971.

HINKLE, L. E. The effect of exposure to cultural change, social change, and changes in interpersonal relationships on health. In B. S. Dohrenwend & B. P. Dohrenwend (eds.), *Stressful life events.* New York: Wiley, 1974.

HOLMES, T. H. & RAHE, R. H. The social adjustment rating scale. *Journal of Psychosomatic Research,* 1967, *11,* 213–218.

HOSACK, A. A comparison of crises: Mother's early experiences with normal and abnormal first-born infants. Doctoral dissertation, Harvard University School of Public Health, 1968.

JOFFE, P. E., & BAST, B. E. Coping and defense in relation to accommodation among a sample of blind men. *Journal of Nervous and Mental Disease,* 1978, *166,* 537–552.

JOFFE, P. E., & NADITCH, M. Paper and pencil measures of coping and defense processes. In N. Haan (eds.), *Coping and defending: Processes of self-environment organization.* New York: Academic, 1977.

Kroeber, T. C. The coping functions of the ego mechanisms. In R. White (ed.), *The study of lives.* New York: Atherton, 1963.

Kuypers, J. A. Internal-external locus of control, ego functioning, and personality characteristics in old age. *Gerontologist,* 1972, *12,* 168–173.

Lazarus, R. S., Opton, E., Tomita, M., & Kodama, M. A cross-cultural study of stress-reaction patterns in Japan. *Journal of Personality and Social Psychology,* 1966, *4,* 622–633.

Maguire, G., Maclean, A., & Aitken, R. Adaptation on repeated exposure to film-induced stress. *Biological Psychology,* 1973, *1,* 43–51.

McGrath, J. *Social and psychological factors in stress.* New York: Holt, 1970.

Milgram, S. *Obedience to authority.* New York: Harper & Row, 1974.

Miller, D., & Swanson, G. E. *Inner conflict and defense.* New York: Holt, 1960.

Mischel, W. *Personality and assessment.* New York: Wiley, 1968.

Moos, R. Psychological techniques in the assessment of adaptive behavior. In G. Coelho, D. Hamburg, & J. Adams (eds.), *Coping and adaptation.* New York: Basic Books, 1974.

Moos, R., & Tsu, V. The crisis of physical illness: An overview. In R. H. Moos (ed.), *Coping with physical illness.* New York: Plenum, 1977.

Morrissey, R. The Haan model of ego functioning: An assessment of empirical research. In N. Haan (ed.), *Coping and defending: Processes of self-environment organization.* New York: Academic, 1977.

Neugarten, B. L. Time, age, and the life cycle. *American Journal of Psychiatry,* 1979, *136,* 887–894.

Paykel, E. S., Prusoff, B. A., & Uhlenhuth, E. H. Scaling of life events. *Archives of General Psychiatry,* 1971, *25,* 340–347.

Pearlin, L., & Schooler, C. The structure of coping. *Journal of Health and Social Behavior,* 1978, *19,* 2–21.

Rose, R., & Levin, M. The crisis in stress research. *Journal of Human Stress,* 1979, *5,* whole issue.

Seligman, M. E. P. *Helplessness.* San Francisco: Freeman, 1975.

Shanan, J. Coping behavior in assessment for complex tasks. *Proceedings of the 17th International Congress of Applied Psychology,* 1973, *1,* 313–321.

Silber, E., Coelho, G., Murphey, D., Hamburg, D., Pearlin, L., & Rosenberg, M. Competent adolescents coping with college decisions. *Archives of General Psychiatry,* 1961, *5,* 517–527.

Vickers, R., & Hervig, L. Comparison of three psychological defense questionnaires as predictors of clinical ratings of defense. *Journal of Personality Assessment,* 1981, 45, *6,* 630–638.

White, R. Strategies of adaptation: An attempt at systematic decription. In G. Coelho, D. Hamburg, & J. Adams (eds.), *Coping and adaptation.* New York: Basic Books, 1974.

Witkin, H. H., Dyk, R. B., Faterson, H. F., Goodenough, D. R., & Karp, S. H. *Psychological differentiation: Studies of development.* New York: Wiley, 1962.

15

Paraverbal Correlates of Stress: Implications for Stress Identification and Management

Aron Wolfe Siegman

THE RESEARCH REVIEWED IN THIS CHAPTER is part of a longstanding attempt on the part of psychologists to find objective, quantifiable correlates of stress. In the past, this search focused primarily on physiological measures, but more recently it has come to encompass a broader range of behaviors, especially expressive vocal (paraverbal) and nonverbal behaviors.[1] The interest in the latter two is motivated by the expectation that paraverbal and nonverbal behaviors, unlike physiological behavior, can provide nonobtrusive indexes of stress. From a practical point of view, such nonobtrusive indexes are critical in situations that preclude the cooperation necessary for physiological measurements—as is the case, for example, when negotiating with terrorists. However, even when such cooperation can be obtained, the obtrusiveness, if not the outright intrusiveness, of physiological measures can be a source of serious confounding. The very presence of monitoring devices can be stressful and anxiety arousing. Furthermore, they inevitably betray the investigator's purpose and may give rise to various countermeasures on the part of the subject. For example, in criminal investigations, subjects may deliberately make themselves anxious during the investigation so as to minimize the difference between control and critical questions. This is not to say that similar maneuvers cannot be attempted even in the absence of obtrusive instruments, but this manipulation is more difficult to accomplish when one does not know what aspect of one's behavior is being monitored and when. Therefore, the search for nonobtrusive paraverbal and nonverbal correlates of stress is a matter of practical importance.

STRESS AND ANXIETY

The earlier version of this chapter (Siegman, 1982) finessed the issue of the relationship between stress and anxiety by taking the position that they are overlapping constructs and without specifying the distinctions between them. In fact, throughout the earlier chapter, the two terms were used almost interchangeably. While it still may be foolhardy to take on

The preparation and some of the research for this chapter were supported by a grant from the National Heart, Lung, and Blood Institute (HL-36027).

this challenge, I believe that it is necessary to do so in order to understand the nature of the relationship between stress and nonverbal and paraverbal behavior.

The early research on stress, especially Hans Selye's work (1982), focused on the autonomic nervous system (ANS) and adrenocortical correlates of physical stressors. Selye (1982:14) acknowledges, however, that strong emotions also call forth the stress response. In fact, he considers emotions as the most frequent activators of the stress response. He merely argues that they are not the only source of stress. From this point of view, then, anxiety and other strong emotions represent one source of stress, albeit a major one.

An alternative approach is to view emotions as part of the stress response. Lazarus and associates (Lazarus, 1966; Lazarus & Folkman, 1982) have argued that psychological stress requires a prior judgment that environmental and/or internal demands tax or exceed the individual's resources for managing them. This judgment and the individual's efforts to manage the situation are conceptualized in terms of two interacting processes: appraisal and coping. In this context, it is important to note that many modern theorists view emotions in a very similar way—i.e., as responses to the perception of existential threat. Depending on the circumstances, one responds with fear-flight, or with anger-fright, or with depression and resignation. From this perspective, then, the negative emotions are part of the coping dimension of the stress response. Of course, the two points of view are not mutually exclusive, and emotions can be and probably are both a source of stress and part of the coping response to stress.

If intense emotional experiences are the major source of psychological stress, as has been argued by Selye (1982:14), and if the negative emotions are coping responses to stress, then we have a basis for expecting a relationship between stress and nonverbal and paraverbal behavior. An extensive literature now exists on the nonverbal and paraverbal correlates of affective experiences, especially for the negative affects such as fear-anxiety, sadness-depression and anger. Contemporary students of emotions (e.g., Buck, 1987; Leventhal, 1986; Plutchik, 1986) believe that the expressive behaviors that are associated with the different emotions, such as the loud and rapid voice that is associated with anger, are not mere secondary consequences of emotions, but represent an integral dimension of emotional experiences, conceptually on par with their physiological and cognitive dimensions. This point of view has its roots in the writings of Charles Darwin (1955), who believed that the various expressive behaviors that are associated with emotions have a biological basis, that they serve communicative functions, and that they have clear-cut survival values. In a somewhat similar vein, Lange and James (1967) argued that the expressive and physiological changes that occur during emotional behavior trigger the subjective feeling of emotion, not the other way around. We do not run because we are scared; we are scared because we run. A contemporary version of this theory, articulated by Tompkins (1962) and Ekman (1972) proposes that emotions start in the face, and that feedback from facial expressions to the brain starts a process that brings about autonomic, hormonal, and behavioral changes as well as the subjective emotional experience. Of course, facial expressions are not the sole manifestations of emotions. Studies conducted in our laboratory and elsewhere have shown that emotions also have specific vocal correlates: a loud and rapid voice with anger, a soft and slow voice with sadness-depression, and a rapid and high-pitched voice with fear-anxiety (Siegman, 1985, 1987a, 1987b, 1992), and that, by attenuating or exacerbating these vocal expressions, we can change the very nature of the emotional experience, including its physiological manifestations (Siegman, Anderson, & Berger, 1990; Siegman, 1991, 1992, in press). Since the different affective states are associated with unique patterns of paraverbal behavior, for example, anger with loud, rapid, and interruptive speech, and sadness with the very opposite speech pattern, the nonverbal and paraverbal correlates of stress are likely to vary as a function of the affective state, or states, that are involved in the stress experience.[2]

The recent Type A literature provides yet another basis for the expectation that stress is likely to have a variety of nonverbal and paraverbal manifestations. The Type A behavior pattern (TABP) can be measured by a paper-and-pencil test such as the Jenkins Activity Survey (JAS) (Jenkins 1979) or by a Structured Interview (SI) (Rosenman, 1978), preferably the latter.[3] In the SI, the questions focus on traits and behaviors that constitute the conceptual definition of the TABP (namely, competitive, hard driving, impatient, time pressured, aggressive, and hostile) and they are asked in a professionally objective, sometimes rapid-fire style with occasional interruptions of the interviewee. The SI, then, can also be viewed as a structured stress interview. It should be noted that the SI-derived Type A/B designation is based primarily on the interviewee's speech style, not on the content of the interviewee's responses. While not all interviewees perceive the SI as a stressful situation, those who do (the Type As) respond to the questions with short latencies, loud and rapid accelerated speech, and with frequent interruptions of the interviewer (Rosenman, 1978). Type As also exhibit specific facial expressions (Chesney, Ekman, Friesen, Black, & Hecker, 1990) and other nonverbal behaviors (e.g., fist clenching) during the SI (Friedman & Powell, 1984). It would seem, then, that for those individuals for whom the SI is a stressful experience, it is associated with a wide array of nonverbal and paraverbal behaviors.

The focus in this chapter is on expressive vocal correlates of affective arousal, rather than on purely nonverbal correlates, in part because this has been the focus of my research, but also because more research exists on the vocal channel than on the nonverbal channels of communication. This abundance of research on the vocal channel may very well reflect its exquisite sensitivity to affective states and to changes in such states, but undoubtedly it also reflects the relative ease with which vocal parameters lend themselves to quantification.

Furthermore, the primary focus of this chapter is on the paraverbal correlates of stress-related anxiety. The reason for the emphasis on anxiety as opposed to the other negative emotions is that whatever the conceptual distinctions between stress and anxiety may be, the situations that have been used to study the effects of anxiety—such as public speaking in audience-phobic individuals, lying, parachute jumping, anticipation of electric shock, and even discussions of anxiety-arousing topics—are also the kind of situations that are used to study the effects of stress. The conceptual distinctions between stress and anxiety notwithstanding, their operational definitions tend to overlap considerably. Moreover, anxiety, defined as apprehension about future outcome, may very well be the most typical emotional response in stressful situations. Nevertheless, frustration-produced anger or helplessness-produced depression also occur in response to stressful experiences. Consequently, despite the focus of this chapter on the paraverbal correlates of anxiety, there will also be a brief review of the expressive vocal correlates of anger and sadness-depression.

ANXIETY AROUSAL AND SPEECH

Siegman and Pope (1965a, 1972; Pope, Blass, Siegman, & Raher, 1970) investigated the effects of anxiety arousal on speech within the context of the clinical interview. Differential anxiety levels were aroused in interviewees by means of topic manipulation. Interviewees were selected so that questions focusing on their family relations would be more anxiety arousing than questions focusing on their school experiences. A post-interview questionnaire revealed that this manipulation was effective, although even the family questions proved to be only mildly stressful and anxiety arousing. Siegman and Pope looked at the effects of anxiety arousal on disruptions in the interviewee's speech, on interviewee's productivity levels, and on the temporal pacing of speech. Speech disruption was measured by Mahl's (1956) Speech Disturbance Ratio (SDR), which includes categories such as incomplete sentences, sentence corrections, repetitions, stutters, and tongue-slips. The interviewer's anxiety-arousing questions were found to be associated with higher SDR scores than were the neutral questions. With one notable exception (Boomer & Goodrich, 1961), this association between anxiety arousal and speech disruption has been documented by many of the early investigators (e.g., Cook, 1969; Feldstein, Brenner, & Jaffe, 1963; for a comprehensive review see Rochester, 1973). In the Siegman and Pope study (1965, 1972; Pope, et al., 1970), the interviewees' responses to the anxiety-arousing questions, in contrast to their responses to the neutral ones, were also associated with a faster speech rate, a faster articulation rate, and fewer long silent pauses—that is, with a more accelerated pacing of speech (including fewer filled pauses, when "ah" and "ehm" are used). Speech rate was obtained by dividing number of words by response time, which included silent pauses. Articulation rate was obtained by dividing number of words by response time minus the duration of silent pauses. Speech rate, then, was a function of the articulation rate and the duration of the silent pauses of the speaker. Finally, interviewees gave more productive, or longer, responses to the anxiety-arousing than to the neutral questions. Siegman and Pope (1972) suggested that these findings can be readily explained in terms of a drive conceptualization of anxiety arousal (see Taylor, 1951; Taylor & Spence, 1952).

One methodological problem with the Siegman and Pope (1965, 1972) study, and with other investigations in which anxiety arousal is achieved by topic manipulation, is that different topics have been shown to be associated with different productivity levels and speech rates (Siegman & Reynolds, 1983a, 1984). Nevertheless, other studies have found that experimentally produced anxiety is associated with an accelerated speech rate, independent of topical focus. For example, in a series of word association studies by Kanfer (1958a, b), subjects were administered intermittent shocks, which were preceded by an auditory warning signal. Subjects showed an increase in post-tone speech rate (in anticipation of the shock) and a decrease in post-shock speech rate, suggesting that anxiety arousal had an accelerating effect on speech rate.

The flurry of research activity on paraverbal and nonverbal behavior during the late 1950s, the 1960s, and the early 1970s was followed by a period of quiescence. Nevertheless, two very recent studies confirm the earlier findings that stress and anxiety arousal have an accelerating effect on speech. In one study (Siegman, 1991, 1992), thirty-six male students at Ben-Gurion University, Israel, were required to describe recent events that caused them to become fearful and anxious, as well as recent neutral events. The study included an experimental manipulation of speech rate. The participants described one third of the events using their normal, or habitual, speech rate. In describing another third of the events, they spoke as quickly as possible, and in describing yet another third of the events, they spoke as slowly as possible.

After each speech rate condition, the participants rated themselves on a number of anxiety and fear-related adjectives. Blood pressure (BP) and heart rate (HR) measurements were obtained throughout the fear-anxiety arousing and the neutral descriptions. Talking quickly about fear and anxiety-arousing events was associated with significantly higher fear-anxiety self-ratings and with significantly higher BP and HR levels than talking normally or slowly about them (Figure 15-4, p. 291). The fear and anxiety-arousing descrip-

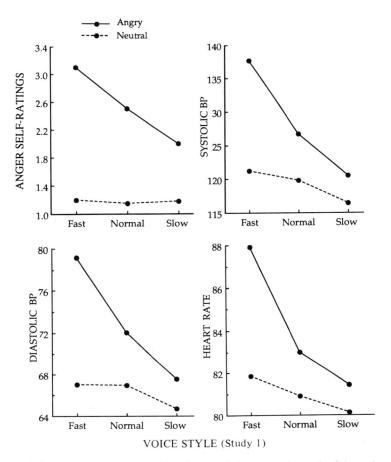

FIGURE 15-1. Anger self-ratings and CV arousal as a function of loud, normal, and soft speech in angry and neutral communications in study 1.

tions were associated with significantly higher diastolic BP and HR levels than the neutral descriptions, but only in the fast speech condition (Figure 15-4). These findings are consistent with the hypothesis that fear and anxiety arousal are associated with rapid accelerated speech rather than with slow speech. The other recent study (Harrigan, 1991) was similar to the 1965a Siegman and Pope study, except that the author used monologues rather than interviews. Descriptions of an anxiety-arousing event, in contrast to a happy event, were associated with significantly higher speech rates and fewer silent pauses than the descriptions of the happy event. As far as the hypothesized accelerating effect of anxiety arousal on speech is concerned, we now have replications across populations, laboratories, cultures, and even decades.

Additional support for the link between stress and a time-pressured speech style comes from the Type A literature. In a study conducted in our laboratory, we looked at expressive vocal behavior as a function of the Type A/B behavior pattern (as assessed by the JAS) during stressful and nonstressful conversations.[4] During the stressful conversations or dialogues, the participants' conversational partners (confederates of the experimenter) behaved in a cold manner, challenged the subjects' responses (for example, "Why do you say that?" "I don't see your point." "I disagree."), and occasionally interrupted the subjects in the midst of their statements. During the control conversations, the confederates were warm and friendly and refrained from stress-producing behaviors. The Type A behavior pattern was associated with shorter latencies ($r(43) = -.30$), a faster speech rate ($r(43) = -.34$), and shorter duration of vocalizations ($r = -.32, p < .05$).

It is important to note that, compared to Type Bs, Type As respond to stressful interviews and to other challenging and stressful tasks with heightened catecholamine levels (Williams, 1989)—i.e., with the physiological manifestation of stress. In fact, recent evidence (Williams, Suarez, Kuhn, Zimmerman, & Schonberg, 1991) suggests that as Type As grow older they develop chronically elevated catecholamine levels. Furthermore, the administration of beta blockers, which attenuates the physiological symptoms of the stress response, results in an attenuation of the Type A speech style (Krantz & Durell, 1983; Schneider, Freidrich, Neus, & Rudell, 1982). Stress, then, expresses itself not only in terms of the classical physiological stress responses but also in terms of a specific stressful speech style.

Despite the variety of data that appear to support the link between stress-produced anxiety arousal and an accelerated speech pattern, this relationship is by no means simple. To the contrary, it can be modified by a variety of factors.

THE MODERATING EFFECT OF ANXIETY LEVEL AND TASK COMPLEXITY

In discussing the energizing-facilitating effect of arousal on behavior, a number of authors have argued that this effect is likely to reach an asymptote with increasing levels of arousal and eventually will reverse itself (Duffy, 1962; Fiske & Maddi, 1961; Hebb, 1955). Consequently, even if mild and moderate levels of anxiety arousal tend to accelerate speech, very high levels of anxiety arousal should be associated with a slower speech rate and longer silent pauses. Although this hypothesis, usually referred to as the *inverted U-curve hypothesis,* seems reasonable enough both from a theoretical and a common sense point of view, it is difficult to test empirically. It is difficult to calibrate levels of anxiety arousal and to identify in advance precisely which anxiety levels will produce a facilitating effect and which will produce the reverse. Failures to obtain the hypothesized asymptote or reversal can always be attributed, post hoc, to insufficient arousal.

Perhaps the most clear-cut evidence in favor of the inverted U-curve hypothesis comes from a study by Fenz and Epstein (1962), which, incidentally, is one of the few studies on the effects of naturally occurring anxiety, rather than experimentally manipulated anxiety, on speech. Fenz and Epstein obtained stories in response to TAT-like (thematic apperception test) cards from a group of novice parachutists on their day of jumping and from a control group of nonparachutists. The parachutists also served as their own controls by responding to the cards on a nonjumping day. Subjects always responded to three kinds of cards: neutral (no relevance to parachute jumping), low relevance, and high relevance. The reaction time (RT) data clearly suggest that anxiety arousal has an activating effect on response latency. Conditions that can be assumed to have aroused mild to moderate anxiety were associated with a decrease in RT. On the other hand, the one condition that probably aroused very high anxiety levels—namely, the high relevance cards on the day of jumping— was associated with a steep increase in RT. Pauses in the parachutists' stories on the day of jumping also showed an activation effect, with lower pause ratios in the low relevance than in the neutral cards and higher pause ratios in the high relevance than in the low relevance cards. There were no significant differences in the control group. Subjects' verbal rate data followed a similar pattern, but these differences were not significant. By and large, the results of the Fenz and Epstein study support the inverted U-curve hypothesis as far as anxiety and temporal indexes of speech are concerned.

The results of another study, however, appear to be inconsistent with the inverted U-curve hypothesis (Pope, Blass, Siegman, & Raher, 1970). In this study, six hospitalized psychiatric patients spoke into a tape recorder each morning for their entire hospitalization, describing for about ten minutes any of their experiences during the preceding day. The patients were also rated each day by a team of trained nurses on a number of manifest anxiety scales. Speech samples recorded during each patient's eight most anxious and eight least anxious days were compared. It should be noted that all the patients had psychosomatic diagnoses and that they all occasionally manifested extreme anxiety, as well as stretches of calm and relaxed behavior. The results were based on a within-subjects comparison (high anxiety versus low anxiety days) and were not confounded by subjects' psychiatric diagnoses. Speech samples recorded during high anxious days, in contrast to speech samples recorded during low anxious days, were associated with faster speech rates, lower pause ratios, and faster articulation rates, but only the differences for speech rate and pause ratio were significant (this study did not yield RT scores). These findings suggest that even high anxiety arousal—it seems reasonable to assume that during their high anxiety days these patients were extremely anxious—can be associated with a relatively fast speech rate because of a reduction in silent pauses.

Perhaps the conflicting findings can be reconciled if we consider the different tasks that were involved in the two studies. From a drive theory point of view, the effect of arousal on behavior is in part a function of the nature of the task. For example, it has been shown that the same level of anxiety arousal that facilitates simple learning tasks (tasks in which the predominant response tendency is the correct one) will interfere with complex learning tasks (tasks that elicit competing response tendencies) (Siegman, 1957; Taylor & Spence, 1952). By the same token, the effects of anxiety arousal and stress on the temporal pacing of speech should also be a function of the nature of the speaking task. The same arousal level that accelerates highly habituated speech sequences, or relatively automatic speech, such as is involved in discussing a familiar topic, is likely to slow down speech that requires planning and decisionmaking, such as is involved in making up stories in response to TAT cards. This finding could account for the fact that even fairly high anxiety levels accelerated patients' speech when they were asked to talk about anything that occurred to them (Pope, Blass, Siegman, & Raher, 1970) but had the opposite effect on subjects in the Fenz and Epstein (1962) study, who were asked to make up creative stories about ambiguous TAT-like cards.

More direct empirical support for the hypothesized mediating role of task complexity comes from a study in which subjects were asked to give truthful responses to a series of routine questions and to make up imaginative responses to a set of similar questions (Siegman & Reynolds, 1981b). In post-experimental ratings, subjects indicated that the make-believe task was considerably more difficult than the control condition. As hypothesized, subjects' anxiety scores, obtained from Eysenck's (1959) neuroticism scale, correlated negatively with their RT scores in the control condition and positively in the make-believe condition.

Thus, there is considerable evidence that anxiety arousal is associated with an accelerated speech style—specifically, with short reaction times, relatively fast articulation rates, and few and/or short silent pauses—provided the speech task does not involve complex decisionmaking. However, at least two research areas suggest that under certain circumstances stress-induced anxiety arousal can be associated with slow rather than fast speech— specifically, with long response latencies, slow articulation rates, and long silent pauses. Moreover, under such circumstances the stress-induced anxiety arousal may not be associated with an increase in speech disruptions. These two research areas involve the effects of stage fright and deception on speech. We will now take a closer look at this research and its implications for understanding the effects of anxiety arousal on speech.

AUDIENCE ANXIETY AND SPEECH

Public speaking is a stressful situation for many people. Considering the effects of situational anxiety on speech (summarized earlier in this chapter), one would expect public speaking, in contrast to dyadic conversation, to have several distinguishing paralinguistic or paraverbal features. First, one would expect public speaking, to the extent that it is anxiety arousing, to be associated with speech disruptions as measured by Mahl's (1956) SDR. Second, public speaking should be associated with an accelerated speech tempo if the speaking task is simple and with a reduced speech tempo if the speaking task is complex. Findings are reviewed separately for each of the speech variables.

Speech Disturbances

A number of investigators have looked at the effect of public speaking anxiety, or audience anxiety as it is referred to in the literature, on speech disturbances. Unfortunately, some studies combined the speech disturbance categories with silent pauses (*ah*'s) and filled pauses into a single dysfluency index (e.g., Levin, Baldwin, Gallwey, & Paivio, 1960), which makes evaluation of results difficult. Of several investigators who looked specifically at the impact of audience anxiety on either the SDR or on its separate components, none obtained the expected disruptive effect (Geer, 1966; Levin & Silverman, 1965; Paivio, 1965; Reynolds & Paivio, 1968). Considering the evidence that situational anxiety tends to be associated with an increase in the SDR, this absence is puzzling. Before attempting to provide an explanation for this finding, I first present data on the effects of audience anxiety on the temporal pausing of speech.

Temporal Measures

A number of investigators have looked at the effects of audience anxiety on the temporal patterning of speech. By and large, the evidence suggests that audience anxiety slows down the speaker's pace. However, most studies that have investigated this relationship used complex tasks, such as making up stories in response to TAT cards and interpreting cartoons, rather than the highly habituated speech that is found in most dyadic conversation. However, even the few studies that used relatively simple speaking tasks found that audience anxiety had a slowing down effect on speech. For example, Reynolds and Paivio (1968) looked at the effects of audience anxiety on speech in a group of college students whose task was to define a series of abstract and concrete nouns, the latter certainly being a simple task. The experimental manipulation had no significant independent effect on either of the two temporal indexes: response latency and pause ratio. However, as far as the silent pauses were concerned, there was a significant interaction between subjects' scores on an inventory designed to measure audience sensitivity (ASI) and the experimental manipulation. While high ASI scorers showed an increase in silent pauses from the control to the public speaking condition, low ASI scorers showed a decrease. Moreover, in the control condition, the high scorers had lower pause rates than did the low scorers. A similar interaction between subjects' ASI scores and public versus private speaking was reported by Paivio (1965) in relation to speech rate. If one makes the assumption that the public speaking situation produced mild anxiety arousal in the low ASI scorers and fairly high anxiety in the high ASI scorers, then the results of these two studies are consistent with the inverted U-curve hypothesis—namely, that mild anxiety arousal accelerates speech, whereas strong arousal has the reverse effect.

The Reynolds and Paivio (1968) findings thus suggest that a relatively high level of audience anxiety can be associated with slow speech even if the task is relatively simple. This finding, of course, is contrary to that obtained by Pope and associates (1970) with psychiatric patients. The difference may lie in the circumstances surrounding the anxiety-arousing conditions of the two studies. It is not at all obvious that the patients in the study by Pope and associates were aware of their anxiety arousal. Moreover, even if they were, there is no particular reason why they should have been motivated to conceal it. By way of contrast, people with high audience anxiety are likely to be aware that they become very anxious when having to address an audience. Moreover, when placed in such a situation, they do not want the audience to be aware of their discomfort, and they are likely to engage in measures designed to cover up their anxiety arousal. Knowing that when they become anxious they tend to speak too quickly, they are likely to make an effort to speak slowly. However, as is frequently the case with such attempts, they may overshoot their mark, resulting in a slower pace than normal. Alternatively, people high in audience anxiety may deliberately adopt a markedly slow pace, knowing from experience that by doing so they can avoid the speech disruptions that are normally associated with anxiety arousal. Whatever the explanation, the puzzling absence of speech disruptions in speakers with high audience anxiety may very well be related to the relatively slow pace of their speech.

In other words, the effects of anxiety arousal on the temporal pacing of speech is a function not only of task complexity but also of the speaker's motivation to conceal his or her anxiety arousal. Should the speaker be so motivated, then anxiety arousal may not have the expected accelerating effect on speech, even if the task involves simple speech sequences. In fact, when the speaker is so motivated, anxiety arousal may be associated with deliberate and slow speech. Of course, unnaturally slow speech can be no less a telltale sign of anxiety arousal than is a fast speech rate. Implicit in what has been said thus far is the assumption that, should they so desire, speakers can regulate the pacing of their speech at will, or at least they can slow down the rate. The results of a study by Siegman and Reynolds (1983b) (discussed in detail subsequently) and a previous study by Sloan (1976) indicate that this assumption is valid, at least for some, if not all, individuals. Furthermore, this assumption is not necessarily at variance with yet another assumption that the vocal channel is relatively "leaky"—i.e., it is likely to betray the true feelings that the speaker is trying to conceal. Leakage is a function not only of controllability but also of awareness. Speakers may be relatively unaware of naturally occurring changes in their speech rate yet may be able to regulate their speech rate when instructed to do so by others or by themselves.

TELLING LIES

Recently there has been a surge of research activity on the nonverbal and paraverbal correlates of deceptive communications, with some studies focusing on the veridical nonverbal and paraverbal correlates of deceptive messages and other studies focusing on the nonverbal and paraverbal cues that listeners use in detecting lies. On the assumption that for normal people lying is a stressful experience that causes the liar to feel anxious about being caught, this research has obvious implications for the central concern of this chapter: the effects of stress and anxiety arousal on paraverbal behavior.

The findings were summarized in a comprehensive review by Zuckerman, DePaulo, and Rosenthal (1981) and were later updated in a subsequent review article by Zuckerman and Driver (1985). Their conclusions on the effects of deception on paraverbal variables are based on the results obtained in eleven to seventeen independent studies; the precise number of studies depends on the variable being investigated, except for pitch, for which there were only four independent studies. Compared to truthful communications, deceptive ones are relatively short, high pitched, contain many speech disruptions, as indexed by Mahl's SDR (1956), and many hesitations (*ah*'s, etc), with the latter being more strongly and more significantly associated with lying than any other nonverbal or paraverbal measure except pupil dilation. As far as the temporal aspect of speech is concerned, however, no clear-cut pattern seems to emerge from the various studies. It is possible, however, that for a variety of reasons many of these deception studies cannot provide us with critical information about the effects of anxiety arousal on nonverbal and paraverbal behavior. First, in almost all these studies, the subjects are instructed by the experimenter to give truthful responses to some questions and to lie in response to others. To the extent that subjects were instructed by their experimenter to lie, they should have little reason to be anxious about lying, or so it would seem on first glance. In justifying the relevance of these laboratory studies to lying in the real world, where it can be a source of considerable anxiety arousal, it has been argued that, if lying has been conditioned to anxiety in the past, deception in the lab is likely to be at least minimally anxiety arousing even when sanctioned by the experimenter. Also, in order to increase subjects' anxiety level, some experimenters tell their subjects that the ability to deceive is associated with intelligence and professional success. Even so, the relevance of such laboratory paradigms to natural lying that involves considerable anxiety arousal is dubious at best. A second problem is that in many of the deception studies the participants are required to spontaneously make up a fictitious response. The making up of such fictitious responses is cognitively more demanding than simply telling the truth, which may explain why in some deception studies lying was associated with slower speech than the truthful responses. In fact, when Zuckerman and Driver (1985) grouped the deception studies into those in which subjects had no opportunity to plan and rehearse their deceptive communications and those in which the subjects were given an opportunity for preplanning, they found a significant negative correlation between lying and speech rate in the former set of studies, whereas there was a significant positive correlation between the two in the latter. However, the results of a study conducted in our laboratory (Reynolds, 1981) strongly suggest that spontaneous lying is associated with long response latencies, relatively frequent and long pauses, and a relatively slow speech rate, even when the participants have reason to be fairly anxious about their lying. It is suggested that the subjects in that study found themselves in a conflict over whether to respond truthfully or to lie, and that this approach-avoidance conflict reversed the otherwise positive association between anxiety arousal and speech. Furthermore, what was said earlier within the context of audience anxiety—namely, that individuals who suffer from such anxieties frequently try to cover up their anxiety symptoms and in so doing they may overshoot the mark—may be of relevance in deceitful communications as well. People are likely to want to cover up the nonverbal and paraverbal manifestations of their deceitfulness and in so doing overshoot the mark. Of course, from a lie detection point of view, it does not matter whether the individual speaks more quickly or more slowly than usual—as long as the deviation is an indication that the person is lying.

Yet another finding that was obtained within the context of deceptive communications is of relevance to the broader issue of whether it is possible to control expressive nonverbal and paraverbal behavior. It has been claimed that whereas verbal behavior is a product of cognitive activity, expressive nonverbal and paraverbal behaviors represent a direct expression of affective experience and are relatively free from cognitive control (Zajonc, 1980). Recent evidence, however, suggests that such behavior is far from being a pure expression of affect, uncontaminated by cognitive processes. For example, as part of the aforementioned deception study, Siegman and Reynolds (1983b) investigated the relationship between personality variables and lying skills, with the latter operationally defined as the ability to control one's temporal pacing of speech so that it would be nearly the same when lying as when telling the truth. Three separate indexes measured the participants' lying skills, based respectively on their reaction times, silent pauses, and speech rates when lying as compared to their truthful responses. The lower the discrepancy, the better one's lying skill. Of particular interest was the relationship between Snyder's Self-Monitoring Scale (SMS) (Snyder, 1974) and lying skills, because this scale was designed to measure, at least in part, the ability to control, or to regulate, one's expressive self-presentation behavior. Whereas subjects' overall SMS scores correlated significantly with only one out of the three indexes measuring lying skills, their scores on two SMS subscales—Extraversion and Acting skills—correlated significantly with all three indexes designed to measure lying skills. Specifically, the extroverts and subjects with good acting skills were more successful liars than the introverts and the individuals with poor acting skills. These findings, which have been replicated in a subsequent study (Siegman & Reynolds, 1984), indicate that people can and do regulate their expressive behavior and that this ability involves specific social skills.

TRAIT ANXIETY AND PARAVERBAL BEHAVIOR

The distinction between state anxiety and trait anxiety (Spielberger, 1966) is now widely accepted. State anxiety refers to a person's momentary or situational anxiety, which varies over time and across settings. Trait anxiety, on the other hand, refers to a person's more stable, characteristic overall anxiety level. The discussion thus far has dealt with the effects of state anxiety on speech, but what about the effects of trait anxiety? One might reasonably expect that the effects of trait anxiety on speech would parallel the effects of state anxiety, as described earlier. The available empirical evidence, however, provides only partial support for this expectation. Contrary to expectation, there is no evidence for a positive correlation between measures of trait anxiety, such as the Taylor's (1953) Manifest Anxiety Scale (MAS), and Mahl's SDR (Siegman, 1987a). On the other hand, trait anxiety apparently has an accelerating effect on speech. In a review article, Murray (1971) cited six studies that correlated measures of trait anxiety with response latency. All six correlations were negative; three, significantly so. Similarly, Siegman and Pope (1965b) obtained a significant positive correlation between the Taylor MAS and articulation rate. Other investigators, however, reported significant positive correlations between trait anxiety and indexes of silent pausing (Helfrich & Dahme, 1974). It is possible, of course, that trait anxiety is associated with short response latencies, and even with a fast articulation rate, and at the same time with intermittent, long silent pauses.

In an attempt to reconcile these apparently paradoxical findings, I have suggested elsewhere (Siegman, 1987a) that chronically anxious individuals may compensate for their quick response times and their fast articulation rates by resorting to more frequent long silent pauses in order to insure fluent speech, free from speech disruptions. Scherer (1979), on the other hand, approaches these paradoxical findings from a social-psychological perspective. There is considerable evidence that listeners are attracted and attribute positive personality traits to individuals who speak with a relatively fast articulation rate and without unduly long silent pauses (Brown, 1980; Feldstein & Crown, 1979; Siegman & Reynolds, 1982a). High MAS scorers tend to be socially insecure and anxious individuals, with a heightened sensitivity to social evaluation. Scherer suggests that such individuals are likely to accelerate their speech rate to make a positive impression on listeners. At the same time, their concerns about self-presentation have sensitized them to signals of listener reaction, which they monitor closely. Unexpected listener signals such as a frown of doubt or disapproval should severely interfere with their ongoing thought and speech processes and cause them to make long silent pauses to reorient and restructure the content and manner of their responses. The results of a study conducted in our laboratory (Siegman & Reynolds, 1982b) confirm Scherer's assumption that socially insecure individuals show relatively long within-response silent pauses in dyadic interactions.

Perhaps the paradoxical findings on the relationship between the Taylor MAS and various temporal indexes are related to that scale's multifactorial composition. Some of the items seem to involve social inadequacy and insecurity, but others seem to index autonomic nervous system arousal. While the latter is likely to have an accelerating effect on speech, the former may have a slowing down effect on speech. Researchers interested in the relationship between trait anxiety, as assessed by the MAS, and the temporal patterning of speech may be well advised to look at the effects of each of these dimensions on a broad variety of temporal indexes. Whatever the explanation for the contradictory findings, it is clear from this discussion that trait anxiety is one individual difference variable that can moderate the effect of stress-produced anxiety on paraverbal behavior. Yet another source of individual differences in response to stress-induced anxiety is the Type A/Type B behavior pattern. This variance is probably because situations that are perceived as stressful by Type As are not perceived as such by Type Bs (Smith, 1989). Finally, recent research indicates that extroversion and acting skills are two potent sources of variance in people's ability to regulate their expressive vocal behavior (Siegman & Reynolds, 1981b, 1982b, 1983b).

OTHER PARAVERBAL CORRELATES
OF STRESS AND ANXIETY AROUSAL

Thus far, our discussion of the effects of stress and anxiety arousal on paraverbal behavior has focused on speech disruptions and the temporal pacing of speech, primarily because these variables have been looked at in a variety of anxiety-arousing situations (e.g., topic anxiety, fear of electric shock, public speaking anxiety, anxiety linked to lying, and parachutists' fear of falling), so that the results, to the extent to which they show consistent trends, possess a measure of ecological and construct validity. However, investigators have also looked at a number of other paraverbal indexes, at least one of which (pitch) is a strong candidate for being yet another marker of anxiety arousal.

The increase in muscle tone and the deepening of respiration and dilation of the bronchi under stress (Gray, 1971) would lead one to expect higher intensity and higher fundamental frequency in the speech signal caused by increased subglottal pressure and higher medial compression and tension of the vocal folds, as well as a shift of the energy concentration in the spectrum to higher frequencies. Some of the most realistic studies of the effects of stress on the speech signal have involved air-to-ground communications in flights made under dangerous conditions. Most studies have reported an increase in fundamental frequency (F_o), or pitch, with increasing danger (for a recent review of the literature, see Scherer, 1981). In their review of the deception literature, Zuckerman, DePaulo, and Rosenthal (1981) also found lying to be associated with an increase in pitch. However, in a laboratory study on the effects of task-induced stress on the acoustic signal, Hecker, Stevens, von Bismarck, and Williams (1968) reported that while some subjects always produced a higher fundamental frequency when under stress, others always produced a lower fundamental frequency. Similar individual differences were reported by Friedhoff, Alpert, and Kurtzberg (1964), who studied the effect of stress (in a lying situation) on loudness.

In part, such differences may reflect different emotional responses to the identical stress-producing stimulus: some individuals may respond with anger, others with anxiety, and yet others with shame or various combinations thereof. Furthermore, facing the same emotional reaction, different individuals resort to different coping strategies. For example, consider two individuals who respond to the same stressful situation with anxiety; one may openly express such symptoms, while the other, as pointed out earlier, may suppress all such symptoms or overcompensate for them. Whatever the explanation, individual variations in response to stress complicate matters enormously for anyone trying to develop a theoretical model of the effects of stress behavior. However, from a practical point of view, as long as we know an individual's baseline response, significant deviations therefrom, whether above or below baseline, can be viewed as indications of stress.

Some years ago, there was considerable interest in a stress measuring device, the Psychological Stress Evaluator (PSE), which according to its developers measures the absence of microtremors in the voice (Holden, 1975). Microtremors are supposed to be present under normal conditions but ostensibly disappear under stress. The PSE has been used most extensively as a lie detection instrument. In reviewing this literature, Scherer (1981) concluded that "the justification for these claims cannot be properly established, since important methodological details are either not reported or remain unclear" (p. 175). Furthermore, even if it were possible to detect stress with the PSE, it is not at all clear what is being measured (Podlesny & Raskin, 1977); indeed, the very existence of voice tremors is considered problematic (Shipp & McGlone, 1973).

ANGER AND PARAVERBAL BEHAVIOR

As pointed out earlier, the physiological and paraverbal manifestations of stress are, at least in part, consequences of stress-produced emotions. We have reviewed the paraverbal correlates of anxiety. Another emotion not infrequently related to stress is frustration-produced anger. Scherer (1981), who reviewed the early studies on the vocal manifestations of anger, concludes that anger is associated with a high pitched, loud voice and with a fast speech tempo. However, most of the studies reviewed by Scherer (1981) used simulated anger. The results of such studies are at best suggestive, because they may reflect people's theatrical stereotypes of how people talk when angry rather than the veridical correlates of anger. The handful of exceptions are not very helpful either because their findings are based on subjective judgments rather than on careful objective measurements, and/or involve single subjects. However, the results of several studies that have been conducted since in our laboratory and that are not subject to the preceding strictures confirm Scherer's conclusions, at least as far as the temporal pacing of speech and loudness are concerned.

In an early study, Crown, Feldstein, and Siegman (1979) found that subjects who were being thwarted and frustrated in their teaching task spoke with significantly shorter pauses than the controls. Our next and most recent study (Siegman, Anderson, & Berger, 1990) on this topic involved the experimental manipulation of speech rate and loudness and its effects on the experience of anger and its cardiovascular manifestations. In this study, 36 participants—18 female and 18 male undergraduates at Ben-Gurion University, Israel—described 9 recent experiences that caused them to become very angry. One third of the events were described in the participants' normal voice, another third in a loud and rapid manner, and yet another third in a soft and slow speech style. The speech rate manipulation had a highly significant effect on the participants' feelings of anger and their physiological manifestations (systolic BP, diastolic BP, and HR). The participants felt most angry and showed the highest levels of cardiovascular arousal when they discussed the anger-arousing events speaking loudly and quickly, and felt least angry and showed the lowest levels of cardiovascular arousal when they discussed these events speaking softly and slowly (Figure 15-1, p. 278). The participants' average increase in cardiovascular reactivity (CVR) from the normal speech to the loud, fast speech condition was 18 mm Hg for systolic BP, 12 mm Hg for diastolic BP, and 7 BPM for HR. For some individuals, the average increase was as much as 20 mm Hg for systolic BP and 25 mm Hg for diastolic BP. The average drop in CVR from the normal speech to the soft, slow speech condition was 6 mm Hg for systolic BP and 5 mm Hg for diastolic BP. These findings have since been replicated in a subsequent study with 48 participants (Siegman, 1991, 1992) (Figure 15-2, p. 288).

It should be noted that in both experiments (Siegman, 1991; Siegman, Anderson, & Berger, 1990) the participants described events that caused them to be angry in the past, but, even so, these recollections were associated with significant increases in BP. One can only speculate about the magnitude of the BP elevations at the time the anger-arousing events actually occurred.

It should be noted that the findings of these two experiments are consistent with results obtained in previous correlational studies that only the expression of anger, not its mere experience, is associated with heightened levels of cardiovascular reactivity (Siegman, 1989a, 1989b, in press; Siegman & Anderson, 1990; Siegman, Anderson, Herbst, Boyle, & Wilkinson, 1992). Moreover, it should be noted that the same distinction between the expression versus the experience of anger also holds true for coronary heart disease (CHD), with only the expression of anger being a significant risk factor for CHD (Helmig, Houston, & Vavak, 1991a; Mendes de Leon, 1992; Siegman, in press; Siegman, Dembroski, & Ringel, 1987). Our next study dealt with the vocal correlates of trait anger-hostility. In this study (Siegman, 1985), 85 undergraduates, 43 males and 42 females, were administered a student version of the Structured Interview (SI) (Dembroski & MacDougall, 1983). Clinical judgments were used to assign each participant a score reflecting the participant's potential for expressing anger-hostility as well as an anger-inhibition score (usually referred to as anger-i in the literature). Additionally, the participants' responses were scored by means of AVTA—an automated computerized scoring system (Jaffe & Feldstein, 1970)—for the

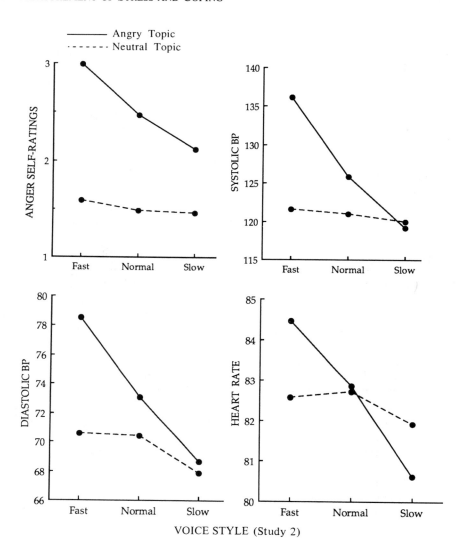

FIGURE 15–2. Anger self-ratings and CV arousal as a function of loud, normal, and soft speech in angry and neutral communications in study 2.

following paraverbal variables: response latency, or RT, speech rate, average (silent) pause duration, loudness, frequency of simultaneous speech, and average duration of vocalizations. In males, significant positive correlations obtained between the participants' potential for expressing anger-hostility scores and the following paraverbal variables: speech rate ($r = .35$, $p < .05$), loudness ($r - .37$, $p < .05$), average duration of vocalization ($r = .30$, $p = .05$), and frequency of interruptions ($r = .40$, $p < .05$). The findings on speech rate and loudness are, of course, precisely what one would expect on the basis of previous experimental findings with state anger. It should be noted that for the female participants there was only one significant correlation—namely, between their potential for expressing anger-hostility and loudness scores ($r = .31$). Given our cultural norms, which expect

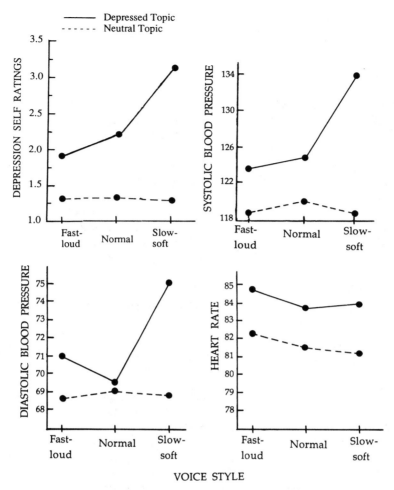

FIGURE 15–3. Sadness-depression self-ratings and CV arousal as a function of loud, normal, and soft speech in sad-depressed and neutral communications.

women to control and not to express their anger, it is not particularly surprising that the expressive vocal correlates of anger-hostility were less pronounced in females than in males.

By and large, the speech style associated with the participants' anger-inhibition scores was in the opposite direction from that associated with the expression of anger-hostility scores.

In this connection, it should be noted that two of the expressive vocal correlates of expressed-anger—loudness and frequent interruptions of one's interlocutor—have also been identified as significant predictors of the severity of coronary heart disease (CHD) (Siegman, Feldstein, Tomasso, Ringel, & Lating 1987). These findings are consistent with the position espoused by this author (Siegman, in press, Siegman, Dembroski, & Ringel, 1987) and others (Dembroski, MacDougall, Costa, & Grandits, 1989) that the *expression* of anger is the "toxic" element in the multifactorial TABP construct as far as risk for CHD is concerned.

COPING WITH ANGER

Early psychoanalytic writings about the negative consequences of anger repression (e.g., Alexander, 1939) led many professionals and lay people to conclude that it is best to express anger. The idea that the expression of anger has cathartic effects gave rise, during the 1960s, to the encounter group movement, which encouraged the full-blown expression of anger. However, as pointed out previously, our findings indicate that such a full-blown expression of anger, rather than having a therapeutic effect, is a risk factor for CHD. Of course, this finding does not imply that one should keep one's anger in or that one should repress angry feelings. There is evidence that the repression of emotions is related to a variety of immune-related diseases (e.g., Esterling, Antoni, Kumar, & Schneiderman, 1990; Pennebaker, 1989). However, a number of years ago Robert Holt (1970) distinguished between the constructive and the destructive expression of anger. In the latter case, anger is expressed "in an entirely or primarily nonverbal way, for example, by physical attack . . . or with an overwhelming emphasis on the expressive rather than the semantic use of words" (1970:9). By way of contrast, in the constructive expression of anger, "I communicate fully and clearly how I see what happened and how it affected me, so as to get you to see why I feel the way I do. . . . The clearing of the air that can occur . . . refers to cognitive clarification or restructuring" (1970:9). In a recent review, Pennebaker (1989) cites a number of studies that provide empirical support for Holt's (1970) distinction between the two types of emotional expression. These studies show that whereas the full-blown expression of negative emotions has harmful physical consequences, the cognitive clarification and integration of negative emotional experiences has beneficial health consequences. Similarly, our findings show that the "nonangry" discussion of anger-arousing experiences does not produce the kind of cardiovascular upheaval that occurs when these experiences are communicated in an angry voice. This approach to coping with anger—i.e., not to stew in it, repress it, or express it in anger, but to communicate and discuss it—is the approach that is now advocated by the various self-assertion training groups. As pointed out by Holt (1970), Freud never advocated the promiscuous expression of anger and other negative emotions; instead, he advocated insight into one's emotions and bringing them under conscious control. Claims to the contrary represent, according to Holt, a misunderstanding of Freud's position.

SADNESS-DEPRESSION AND PARAVERBAL BEHAVIOR

In contrast to anger, which is associated with loud and fast speech, there is convincing evidence that sadness-depression is associated with the opposite speech style: slow and soft speech (Scherer, 1979, 1981; Siegman, 1985). Changes in speech rate seem to be the best prognosticator of mood changes in clinical depression, even better than psychiatrists' impressions (Siegman, 1985, 1987a, 1987b). We wanted to find out, therefore, whether a reduction in speech rate and loudness when speaking about sad and depressing events would be associated with a corresponding increase in feelings of sadness-depression and, conversely, whether an increase in speech rate and loudness level would be associated with a corresponding decrease in feelings of sadness-depression and cardiovascular (CV) arousal.

There is evidence to suggest that sadness-depression is associated with heightened CV responses (Ekman, Levenson, & Friesen, 1983; Schwartz, 1986).

Twenty-four undergraduates at Ben-Gurion University, 12 males and 12 females, participated in this study. They went through the same procedure as did the participants in the earlier anger studies, except that in the present study (Siegman, 1992) they discussed sad and depressing events instead of the anger-arousing events that they had discussed in the previous study. Also, in the new study, they rated themselves on sadness-relevant rather than anger-relevant adjectives. BP and HR measurements were obtained throughout the descriptions of the depressing and the neutral events.

The participants felt most sad and depressed when they spoke slowly and softly—i.e., with an appropriately sad voice—less so when they spoke in their normal voice, and least depressed when they spoke with a vigorous voice—i.e., loud and fast. Our findings also showed that discussing sad and depressing events in a mood-congruent voice—i.e., in a slow and soft voice—was associated with significantly higher systolic BP and diastolic BP arousal than discussing the same events in a normal voice (8 mm Hg for systolic BP and 6 mm Hg for diastolic BP) or when discussing the same events in a mood-incongruent voice—i.e., in a loud and fast voice—(10 mm Hg for systolic BP and 4 mm Hg for diastolic BP) (Figure 15-3, p. 289).

FIGURE 15-4. Fear-anxiety self-ratings and CV arousal as a function of loud, normal, and soft speech in fearful-anxious and neutral communications.

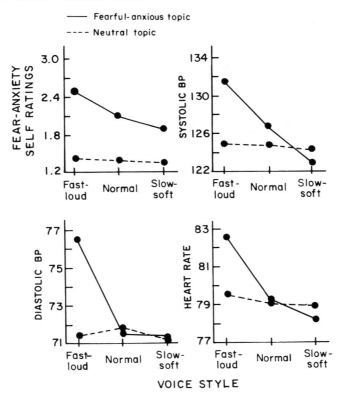

Taken together, the findings of the previous two experiments on the angry voice and the later study on the sad-depressed voice provide strong support for the position that the expressive dimension of affective states is an integral part of the emotional experience. By eliminating or attenuating the expressive dimension, we can change the very nature of the emotional experience, including its physiological manifestations.

IMPLICATIONS FOR STRESS MANAGEMENT

Our experiments with angry, anxious, and sad voices indicate that people can control their negative emotions by modifying their expressive vocal behavior. Speaking slowly and softly when angry or anxious will attenuate these emotions and their physiological manifestations. Conversely, speaking loudly and forcefully when sad and depressed will significantly attenuate this emotion and its physiological manifestations. Speaking in a mood-incongruent voice can cancel the negative emotions and their physiological manifestations. In order to understand this phenomenon, we need to appreciate the nature of emotions.

Beyond the multidimensional nature of emotions—i.e., their cognitive, physiological, and expressive nonverbal and paraverbal manifestations—it is also important to realize that there is feedback between these different dimensions; that they interact with each other in a dynamic, reciprocal fashion (Figure 15–5). Thus, people who are angry experience an increase in BP, HR, cortisol, epinephrine, etc. They also raise their voice, accelerate their speech rate, and interrupt their partner. However, the heightened levels of BP, HR, and catecholamines will further intensify the speaker's angry voice and subjective feelings of anger. Similarly, an angry voice will further intensify physiological arousal and subjective feelings of anger. This accounts for the escalating nature of emotions: anger turns into rage, fear into panic, and sadness into despair. But emotions have yet another characteristic: they are contagious. With the best intentions to remain calm, it is very difficult to interact with

FIGURE 15–5. Schematic representation of the reciprocal interactions of anger, expressive vocal behavior, and CVR.

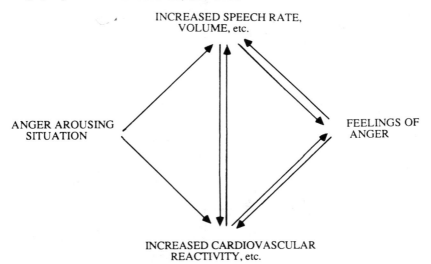

an angry person without becoming angry oneself. Here, too, nonverbal and paraverbal behavior plays a significant role. There is considerable evidence that participants in dyadic interactions match each other's paraverbal behavior, including each other's loudness level and speech rate, even if these interactions are neutral (Feldstein & Welkowitz, 1987). Thus, when an angry person raises his or her voice and accelerates his or her speech rate, so will that person's partner. This response is likely to raise the partner's blood pressure and feelings of anger. This phenomenon accounts not only for the contagion effect, but also contributes to the spiraling nature of emotions, because the listener's reactions will in turn affect the speaker, and so on. The other side of this coin is that by intervening at any level, we can reverse this vicious cycle. By modifying our paraverbal behavior, we can short circuit the escalating nature of emotional interactions.

It should be noted that this phenomenon is not restricted to the artificial context of the laboratory: it works in real-world situations as well. We have used our procedure with patients in the ICC unit of the Soroka Hospital, in Beer Sheba, Israel, who were instructed to speak more slowly and softly, and we found that this discipline helped reduce their feelings of stress and levels of cardiovascular arousal. Moreover, we now have reports from many healthy individuals who have followed our instructions and found that reducing speech rate and loudness is effective in controlling stress-related emotions. Our experience indicates that, while accelerating or decelerating speech rate and loudness is a rather simple procedure, it has powerful implications for the control of emotions. A study (Siegman, 1992) that was conducted during the Gulf War, when Scud missiles were still directed against civilian centers in Israel, provides a dramatic illustration of the calming effects of slow and soft speech. Twelve female undergraduates at Ben-Gurion University, Israel, described fear- and anxiety-arousing events (mostly concerning the Scuds), using three speech styles: fast-loud, normal, slow-soft. The participants obtained exceedingly high BP and HR levels even when they talked about these events in a normal voice. However, even under these high levels of emotional arousal, slow and soft speech had a calming effect which reduced the participants' systolic BP and HR levels to normal. Although their diastolic BP levels remained somewhat elevated, they too were no longer in the dangerous range when the participants spoke slowly and softly. Clearly, the paraverbal correlates of emotions are important not only for the identification of stress but also for its management. In fact, one of the most interesting developments since the earlier version of this chapter (Siegman, 1982) concerns people's ability to modify their negative emotions, as well as their physiological manifestations, by the control of expressive vocal behavior. These findings have important implications for stress management and the avoidance of stress-related illnesses.

NOTES

1. Some authors use the term *nonverbal* in a very broad sense that includes the vocal parameters of speech such as pitch, tempo, and loudness. Others, in what is probably a more precise usage, restrict the term to gestural and other "purely" nonverbal parameters of speech and use terms such as nonlinguistic, paralinguistic, extralinguistic, or paraverbal to refer to the vocal parameters of speech. In this chapter, I use the latter term to designate the vocal parameters of speech.
2. While in the laboratory it is possible to elicit a particular emotion relatively unconfounded by other emotions, in the real world they are typically confounded (Siegman, 1991, 1992).
3. Despite the evidence that the JAS is a valid measure of the TABP's central features, its epidemio-

logical validity (i.e., its ability to predict coronary heart disease endpoints) has never been clearly demonstrated. It should be noted that according to the most recent evidence, the SI-derived global Type-A scores too are not very good predictors of CAD (coronary artery disease) or CHD (Dembroski & Czajkowski, 1989). Instead, the evidence points to the expression of anger and hostility—one of the components of the TABP—as a serious risk factor for CAD and CHD in both men and women (Dembroski, MacDougall, Costa, & Grandits, 1989; Siegman, in press; Siegman, Dembroski, & Ringel, 1987; Siegman, Lating, Johnston, & Boyle, 1992). Of course, the failure of the TABP to predict CAD and CHD does not undermine its potential importance as a personality variable of relevance in a variety of social-psychological situations.

4. In this study, the JAS, rather than the SI, was used as a measure of the TABP because we did not want our measure of the TABP to be confounded with speech style, which would have been the case if we had used the SI. Moreover, as pointed out in the previous note, the JAS is more closely related to the conceptual definition of the TABP than is the SI.

REFERENCES

ALEXANDER, F. G. Emotional factors in essential hypertension: Presentation of a tentative hypothesis. *Psychoanalytic Medicine,* 1939, *1,* 175–179.

APPLEY, M. H., & TRUMBULL, R. *Psychological stress.* New York: Appleton, 1967.

BLUMENTHAL, J. A., WILLIAMS, R., KONG, Y., SCHANBERG, S. M., & THOMSON, L. W. Type A behavior pattern and angiographically documented coronary disease. *Circulation,* 1978, *58,* 634–635.

BOOMER, D. S., & GOODRICH, D. W. Speech disturbance and judged anxiety. *Journal of Consulting Psychology,* 1961, *25,* 160–164.

BROWN, B. L. Effects of speech rate on personality attributions and competency evaluations. In H. Giles, W. P. Robinson, & P. M. Smith (eds.), *Language: Social psychological perspectives.* New York: Pergamon Press, 1980.

BUCK, R. The psychology of emotion. In J. E. Ledoux & W. Hirst (eds.), *Mind and brain.* Cambridge: Cambridge University Press, 1987.

CHESNEY, M. A., EKMAN, P., FRIESEN, W. V., BLACK, G. W., & HECKER, M. H. L. Type-A behavior pattern: Facial behavior and speech components. *Psychosomatic Medicine,* 1990, *53,* 307–319.

COOK, M. Anxiety, speech disturbances, and speech rate. *British Journal of Social and Clinical Psychology,* 1969, *8,* 13–21.

CROWN, C. L., FELDSTEIN, S., & SIEGMAN, A. W. *Speech sounds and silences in nonsimulated expressions of anger.* Paper presented at the Eastern Psychological Association, Philadelphia, PA, 1979.

DARWIN, C. R. *The expression of emotions in man and animals.* New York: Philosophical Library, 1955. (Originally published 1896.)

DEMBROSKI, T. M., & CZAJKOWSKI, S. M. 1989. Historical and current developments in coronary-prone behavior. In A. W. Siegman & T. M. Dembroski (eds.), *In search of coronary-prone behavior: Beyond Type-A.* Hillsdale, NJ: Lawrence Erlbaum, 1989.

DEMBROSKI, T. M., & MacDOUGALL, J. M. Behavioral and psycho-physiological perspectives on coronary-prone behavior. In T. M. Dembroski, T. H. Schmidt, & G. Blumchen (eds.), *Biobehavioral bases of coronary heart disease.* New York: Karger, 1983.

DEMBROSKI, T. M., MacDOUGALL, J. M., COSTA, P. T., JR., & GRANDITS, G. A. Components of hostility as predictors of sudden death and myocardial infarction in the Multiple Risk Factor Intervention Trial. Psychosomatic Medicine, 1989, *51,* 514–522.

DUFFY, E. *Activation and behavior.* New York: Wiley, 1962.

EKMAN, P. Universals and cultural differences in facial expression of emotion. In J. K. Cole (ed.), *Nebraska Symposium on Motivation.* Lincoln: University of Nebraska Press, 1972.

EKMAN, P., & FRIESEN, W. V. Nonverbal behavior and psychopathology. In R. J. Friedman & M. M. Katz (eds.), *The psychology of depression: Contemporary theory and research.* Washington, DC: U.S. Government Printing Office, 1972.

EKMAN, P., LEVENSON, R. W., & FRIESEN, W. V. Autonomic nervous system activity distinguishes among emotions. *Science,* 1983, *221,* 1208-1210.

ESTERLING, B. A., ANTONI, M. H., KUMAR, M., & SCHNEIDERMAN, N. Emotional repression, stress disclosure responses, and Epstein•Barr viral capsid antigen titers. *Psychosomatic Medicine,* 1990, *52,* 397-410.

EYSENCK, H. J. *Manual of the Maudsley Personality Inventory.* London: London Press, 1959.

FELDSTEIN, S., BRENNER, M. S., & JAFFE, J. The effect of subject sex, verbal interaction, and topical focus on speech disruption. *Language and Speech,* 1963, *6,* 505-509.

FELDSTEIN, S., & CROWN, C. L. *Interpersonal perception in dyads as a function of race, gender, and conversational time patterns.* Paper presented at the annual meeting of the Eastern Psychological Association, Philadelphia, PA, 1979.

FELDSTEIN, S., & WELKOWITZ, J. A chronography of conversation: In defense of an objective approach. In A. W. Siegman & S. Feldstein (eds.), *Nonverbal behavior and communication.* Hillsdale, NJ: Lawrence Erlbaum, 1987.

FENZ, W. D. J., & EPSTEIN, S. Measurement of approach-avoidance conflict along a stimulus dimension by a thematic apperception test. *Journal of Personality,* 1962, *30,* 613-632.

FISKE, D. W., & MADDI, S. R. (eds.). *Functions of varied experience.* Homewood, IL: Dorsey, 1961.

FRIEDHOFF, A. J., ALPERT, M., & KURTZBERG, R. L. An electro-acoustic analysis of the effects of stress on voice. *Journal of Neuropsychiatry,* 1964, *5,* 266-272.

FRIEDMAN, M., & POWELL, L. H. The diagnosis and quantitative assessment of Type A behavior: Introduction and description of the videotaped structured interview. *Integrative Psychiatry,* 1984, *2,* 123-129.

FRIEDMAN, M., & ROSENMAN, R. H. Association of specified overt behavior pattern with blood and cardiovascular findings. *Journal of the American Medical Association,* 1959, *169,* 1286-1296.

GEER, J. H. Effects of fear arousal upon task performance and verbal behavior. *Journal of Abnormal Psychology,* 1966, *71,* 119-123.

GRAY, J. A. *The psychology of fear and stress.* New York: McGraw-Hill, 1971.

HARRIGAN, J. A. *Sounds of anxiety in monologues without visible audience.* Unpublished manuscript, Department of Psychology, California State University, Fullerton, CA, 1991.

HEBB, D. O. Drives and the CNS (conceptual nervous system). *Psychological Review,* 1955, *62,* 243-254.

HECKER, M. H. L., STEVENS, K. N., VON BISMARCK, G., & WILLIAMS, C. E. Manifestations of task-induced stress in the acoustical speech signal. *Journal of the Acoustical Society of America,* 1968, *44,* 993-1001.

HELFRICH, H., & DAHME, G. Sind Verzogerungsphanomene bein spontanen Sprechen Indikatoren personlichkeitsspezifischer Angstverarbeitung. *Zeitschrift fur Sozialpsychologie,* 1974, *5,* 55-65.

HELMIG, L., HOUSTON, B. K., VAVAK, C. R., & MULLIN, J. *Hostility-related variables, self-schemata, and CHD.* Annual meetings of the Society of Behavioral Medicine, Washington, DC, March 1991.

HOLDEN, C. Lie detectors; PSE gains audience despite critics' doubt. *Science,* 1975, *190,* 359-362.

HOLT, R. On the interpersonal and intrapersonal consequences of expressing or not expressing anger. *Journal of Consulting and Clinical Psychology,* 1970, *35,* 8-12.

HOWLAND, E. W., & SIEGMAN, A. W. Toward the automated measurement of the Type-A behavior pattern. *Journal of Behavioral Medicine,* 1982, *5,* 37–54.

JAFFE, J., & FELDSTEIN, S. *Rhythms of dialogue.* New York: Academic, 1970.

JENKINS, C. D. *Jenkins Activity Survey.* New York: Psychological Corporation, 1979.

KANFER, F. H. Effect of a warning signal preceding a noxious stimulus on verbal rate and heart rate. *Journal of Experimental Psychology,* 1958, *55,* 78–80. (a)

————. Supplementary report: Stability of a verbal rate change in experimental anxiety. *Journal of Experimental Psychology,* 1958, *56,* 182. (b)

KRANTZ, D. S., & DUREL, L. A. Psychobiological substrates of the Type A behavior pattern. *Health Psychology,* 1983, *2,* 393–411.

LANGE, C. G., & JAMES, W. *The emotions.* New York: Hafner, 1967. (Originally published 1922.)

LAZARUS, R. S. *Psychological stress and the coping process.* New York: McGraw-Hill, 1966.

LAZARUS, R. S., & FOLKMAN, S. Coping and adaptation. In W. D. Gentry (ed.), *The handbook of behavioral medicine.* New York: Guilford, 1982.

LEVENTHAL, H. A. Perceptual motor theory of emotion. In K. Scherer & P. Ekman (eds.), *Approaches to emotion.* Hillsdale, NJ: Lawrence Erlbaum, 1986.

LEVIN, H., BALDWIN, A. L., GALLWEY, M., & PAIVIO, A. Audience stress, personality, and speech. *Journal of Abnormal and Social Psychology,* 1960, *61,* 469–473.

LEVIN, H., & SILVERMAN, I. Hesitation phenomena in children's speech. *Language and Speech,* 1965, *8,* 67–85.

MAHL, G. F. Disturbances and silences in the patient's speech in psychotherapy. *Journal of Verbal Learning and Verbal Behavior,* 1956, *53,* 1–15.

MENDES DE LEON, C. F. Anger and impatience/irritability of patients of low socioeconomic status with acute coronary heart disease. *Journal of Behavioral Medicine,* 1992, *15,* 273–289.

MURRAY, D. C. Talk, silence, and anxiety. *Psychological Bulletin,* 1971, *75,* 244–260.

OVERALL, J. E., & GORHAM, E. R. The Brief Psychiatric Rating Scale. *Psychological Reports,* 1962, *10,* 799–812.

PAIVIO, A. Personality and audience influence. In B. A. Mahr (ed.), *Progress in experimental personality research.* Vol 2. New York: Academic, 1965.

PENNEBAKER, J. W. Confession, inhibition and disease. *Advances in Experimental Social Psychology,* 1989, *22,* 211–244.

PLUTCHIK, R. Emotions: A general psychoevolutionary theory. In J. D. Maser (ed.), *Approaches to emotion.* Hillsdale, NJ: Lawrence Erlbaum, 1986.

PODLESNY, J. A., & RASKIN, D. C. Physiological measures and the detection of deception. *Psychological Bulletin,* 1977, *84,* 782–799.

POPE, B., BLASS, T., SIEGMAN, A. W., & RAHER, J. Anxiety and depression in speech. *Journal of Consulting and Clinical Psychology,* 1970, *35,* 128–133.

REYNOLDS, M. *Vocal correlates of unfeigned deceit.* Master's thesis, University of Maryland Baltimore County, 1981.

REYNOLDS, M., & PAIVIO, A. Cognitive and emotional determinants of speech. *Canadian Journal of Psychology,* 1968, *22,* 164–175.

ROCHESTER, S. R. The significance of pauses in spontaneous speech. *Journal of Psycholinguistic Research,* 1973, *2,* 51–81.

ROSENMAN, R. H. The interview method of assessment of the coronary-prone behavior pattern. In T. Dembroski, S. Weiss, J. Shields, S. Haynes, & M. Feinleib (eds.), *Coronary-prone behavior.* New York: Springer, 1978.

SCHERER, K. Personality markers in speech. In K. R. Scherer & H. Giles (eds.), *Social markers in speech*. New York: Cambridge University Press, 1979.

————. Vocal indicators of stress. In J. K. Darby (ed.), *Speech evaluation in psychiatry*. New York: Grune and Stratton, 1981.

SCHERWITZ L., BERTON, B. S., & LEVENTHAL, H. Type A assessment and interaction in the behavior pattern interview. *Psychosomatic Medicine*, 1977, *39*, 299–240.

SCHNEIDER, R., FREIDRICH, G., NEUS, J., & RUDDEL, J. Effect of beta-blockers on Type A coronary-prone behavior. *Psychosomatic Medicine*, 1982, *44*, 129–130.

SCHUCKER, B., & JACOBS, D. R. Assessment of behavioral risk for coronary disease by voice characteristics. *Psychosomatic Medicine*, 1977, *39*, 219–228.

SCHWARTZ, G. E. Emotion and psychophysiological organization: A systems approach. In M. G. H. Coles, E. Donchin, & S. W. Porges (eds.), *Psychophysiology: Systems, processes and applications*. New York: Guilford Press, 1986.

SELYE, H. History and present status of the stress concept. In L. Goldberger & S. Breznitz (eds.), *Handbook of stress: Theoretical and clinical aspects*. New York: Free Press, 1982.

SHIPP, T., & MCGLONE, R. E. Physiologic correlates of acoustic correlates of psychological stress. *Journal of the Acoustical Society of America*, 1973, *53*, 63.

SIEGMAN, A. W. *Some relationships of anxiety and introversion-extraversion to serial learning*. Unpublished doctoral dissertation, Columbia University, 1957.

————. Cognition and hesitation in speech. In A. W. Siegman & S. Feldstein (eds.), *Of time and speech: Temporal speech patterns in interpersonal contexts*. Hillsdale, NJ: Lawrence Erlbaum, 1979.

SIEGMAN, A. W. Nonverbal Correlates of Anxiety and Stress. In L. Goldberger & S. Breznitz (eds.), *Handbook of Stress: Theoretical and Clinical Aspects*, 1982.

————. Expressive correlates of affective states and traits. In A. W. Siegman & S. Feldstein (eds.), *Nonverbal behavior: A multi-channel perspective*. Hillsdale, NJ: Lawrence Erlbaum, 1985.

————. The telltale voice: Nonverbal messages of verbal communication. In A. W. Siegman & S. Feldstein (eds.), *Nonverbal behavior and communication* (2d ed.). Hillsdale, NJ: Lawrence Erlbaum, 1987. (a)

————. The pacing of speech in depression. In J. D. Maser (ed.), *Depression and expressive behavior*. Hillsdale, NJ: Lawrence Erlbaum, 1987. (b)

SIEGMAN, A. W. In search of coronary-prone behavior. In R. W. Wilner (ed.), *The individual, communication, and society: Essays in memory of Gregory Bateson*. Cambridge/New York: Cambridge University Press, 1989a.

SIEGMAN, A. W. The role of hostility neuroticism, and speech style in coronary artery disease. In A. W. Siegman & T. M. Dembroski (eds.), *In search of coronary-prone behavior: Beyond Type A*. Hillsdale, N.J.: Lawrence Erlbaum, 1989b.

————. *The biological context of human communication: Cardiovascular correlates of emotional and neutral communications:* Symposium paper presented at the fourth International Conference on Language and Social Psychology, Santa Barbara, CA, August 1991.

SIEGMAN, A. W., & ANDERSON, R. W., JR. Dimensions of hostility and cardiovascular reactivity: The role of challenge. *Psychosomatic Medicine*, 1990, *52*, 235–236.

————. On the cardiovascular consequences of expressing and regressing anger. In A. W. Siegman & T. W. Smith (eds.), *Anger, hostility and the heart*. Hillsdale, NJ: Lawrence Erlbaum, in press.

SIEGMAN, A. W., ANDERSON, R. W., JR., & BERGER, T. The angry voice: Its effects on the experience of anger and cardiovascular reactivity. *Psychosomatic Medicine*, 1990, *52*, 631–643.

SIEGMAN, A. W., ANDERSON, R. W., JR., HERBST, J., BOYLE, S., & WILKINSON, J. Dimensions of anger-hostility and CVR in provoked and angered men. *Journal of Behavioral Medicine,* 15, 257–272, 1992.

SIEGMAN, A. W., & BOYLE, S. *The expression of anger and cardiovascular reactivity in men and women: An experimental investigation.* Paper presented at fiftieth annual meeting of the American Psychosomatic Society, New York City, April 1992.

SIEGMAN, A. W., DEMBROSKI, T. M., & RINGEL, N. Components of hostility and the severity of coronary artery disease. *Psychosomatic Medicine,* 1987, *45,* 539–549.

SIEGMAN, A. W., FELDSTEIN, S., TOMASSO, C. T., RINGEL, N., & LATING, J. Expressive behavior and the severity of coronary artery disease. *Psychosomatic Medicine,* 1987, *49,* 545–561.

SIEGMAN, A. W., LATING, J., JOHNSTON, G. S., & BOYLE, S. *Structured Interview derived hostility scores and thallium stress test results in men and women.* Paper presented at the fiftieth annual meetings of the American Psychosomatic Society, New York City, April 1992.

SIEGMAN, A. W., & POPE, B. Effects of question specificity and anxiety producing messages on verbal fluency in the initial interview. *Journal of Personality and Social Psychology,* 1965, *4,* 188–192. (a)

————. Personality variables associated with productivity and verbal fluency in the initial interview. *Proceedings of the American Psychological Association,* 1965, *20,* 273–274. (b)

————. The effects of ambiguity and anxiety on interviewee verbal behavior. In A. W. Siegman & B. Pope (eds.), *Studies in dyadic communication.* New York: Pergamon Press, 1972.

SIEGMAN, A. W., & REYNOLDS, M. *The effects of rapport and topical intimacy on interviewee productivity and verbal fluency.* Manuscript, University of Maryland Baltimore County, 1981. (a)

————. *Self-monitoring and speech style.* Paper presented to the annual meeting of the Eastern Psychological Association, New York City, 1981. (b)

————. *Speaking without seeing: Intimacy and verbal behavior in the initial interview.* Manuscript, University of Maryland Baltimore County, 1981. (c)

————. Interviewer-interviewee nonverbal communications: An interactional approach. In M. Davies (ed.), *Interaction rhythms: Periodicity in communicative behavior.* New York: Human Sciences Press, 1982. (a)

————. *The validity of Snyder's Self-Monitoring Scale as a measure of expressive self-control.* Paper presented to the annual meeting of the Eastern Psychological Association, Baltimore, MD, 1982. (b)

————. Effects of mutual invisibility and topical intimacy on verbal fluency in dyadic communication. *Journal of Psycholinguistic Research,* 1983, *12,* 443–5. (a)

————. Self-monitoring and speech in feigned and unfeigned lying. *Journal of Personality and Social Psychology,* 1983, *45,* 1325–1333. (b)

————. Speaking without seeing, or the effect of interviewer absence on interviewee disclosure time. *Journal of Psycholinguistic Research,* 1983, *12,* 595–602. (c)

————. The facilitating effects of interviewer rapport and the paralinguistics of intimate communications. *Journal of Clinical and Social Psychology,* 1984, *2,* 89–96. (a)

————. *Personality and speech in truthful and deceptive communications.* Unpublished manuscript, University of Maryland Baltimore County, 1984. (b)

SLOAN, B. *Nonverbal patterns of speech as a function of introversion and extraversion.* Master's thesis, University of Maryland Baltimore County, 1976.

SMITH, T. W. Interactions, transactions, and the Type A pattern: Additional avenues in the search for coronary-prone behavior. In A. W. Siegman & T. M. Dembroski (eds.), *In search of coronary-prone behavior: Beyond Type-A.* Hillsdale, NJ: Lawrence Erlbaum, 1989.

SNYDER, M. Self-monitoring of expressive behavior. *Journal of Personality and Social Psychology,* 1974, *30,* 526–537.

SPIELBERGER, C. D. The effects of anxiety on complex learning and academic achievement. In C. D. Spielberger (ed.), *Anxiety and behavior*. New York: Academic, 1966.

SUAREZ, E. C., WILLIAMS, R. B., JR., KUHN, C. M., ZIMMERMAN, E. H., & SCHANBERG, S. M. Biobehavioral basis of coronary-prone behavior in middle-aged men. Part II: Serum cholesterol, the type A behavior pattern, and hostility as interactive modulators of physiological reactivity. *Psychosomatic Medicine*, 1991, *53*, 528–537.

TAYLOR, J. A. The relationship of anxiety to the conditioned eyelid response. *Journal of Experimental Psychology*, 1951, *41*, 81–92.

TAYLOR, J. A., & SPENCE, K. W. The relationship of anxiety level to performance in serial learning. *Journal of Experimental Psychology*, 1952, *44*, 61–64.

TAYLOR, Y. A. A personality scale of manifest anxiety. *Journal of Abnormal and Social Psychology*, 1953, *48*, 285–290.

TOMKINS, S. S. *Affect, imagery, consciousness: I. The positive affects*. New York: Springer-Verlag, 1962.

WILLIAMS, R. B. Biological mechanisms mediating the relationship between behavior and coronary heart disease. In A. W. Siegman & T. M. Dembrowski (eds.), *In search of coronary-prone behavior: Beyond Type A*. Hillsdale, NJ: Lawrence Erlbaum Associates, 1989.

WILLIAMS, R. B., JR., SUAREZ, E. C., KUHN, C. M. ZIMMERMAN, E. A., & SCHANBERG, S. M. Biobehavioral basis of coronary-prone behavior in middle-aged men. Part I: Evidence for chronic SNS activation in Type As. *Psychosomatic Medicine*, 1991, *53*, 517–527.

ZAJONC, R. B. Feeling and thinking: Preferences need no inferences. *American Psychologist*, 1980, *35*, 151–175.

ZUCKERMAN, M., & DRIVER, R. E. Telling lies: Verbal and nonverbal correlates of deception. In A. W. Siegman & S. Feldstein (eds.), *Multichannel interpretations of nonverbal behavior*. Hillsdale, NJ: Lawrence Erlbaum, 1985.

ZUCKERMAN, M., DEPAULO, B. M., & ROSENTHAL, R. Verbal and nonverbal communication in deception. In L. Berkowitz (ed.), *Advances in experimental social psychology*, Vol. 14, New York: Academic Press, 1981.

PART V

COMMON STRESSORS

A. Environmental and Social Sources

16

The Social Contexts of Stress

Leonard I. Pearlin

THIS CHAPTER IS CONCERNED PRIMARILY with identifying social conditions that stand as sources of stress. In surveying the literature, one discovers rather quickly that an appreciable part of what we know about the social origins of stress has not come necessarily from work focused on stress. Indeed, prior to the 1960s there was relatively little research directed to any of the naturalistic cause of stress, social or other. There are probably many reasons for this lack. One is certainly that interest in how stress is aroused has been distinctly subordinate to interest in the consequences of stress for organismic functioning. To this day, most stress research is concerned with the response of the various organs and systems of the body to stress, not with the antecedents of the stress.

Researchers who are interested mainly in the effects of stress clearly do not have to depend on its spontaneous or naturalistic occurrence in order to carry out their studies. On the contrary, research into the biological and biochemical functioning of the organism can be conducted much more effectively when the stress is experimentally aroused and controlled in the laboratory. Moreover, the laboratory researcher often decides that animals are better suited than human subjects to his research purposes. The importance of laboratory based work to our understanding of the organismic manifestations of stress hardly needs acknowledgment. But as important as this kind of research is, we are not likely to acquire knowledge about social sources of stress from it.

While the tilt of current research is still prominently in the direction of the consequences of stress, a growing concern with its naturalistic origins can be discerned. In part, this development is linked to the emergence of questions and issues that cannot be dealt with by laboratory based research. In particular, there is a growing interest in the epidemiology of diseases thought to result from stress. The incidence of hypertension, cardiovascular ailments, and depression, to take but a few examples, varies with such factors as race, sex, marital status, and income. This kind of socioeconomic variation of disease indicates that the stresses that presumably dispose people toward these ailments are somehow anchored to the conditions that people confront as they occupy their various positions and statuses in the society. From a public health perspective, it becomes mandatory to identify these conditions, for the eventual control of diseases caused by stress depends on understanding the social etiology of the stress. And, of course, these goals can be accomplished only by moving research out of the laboratory.

The naturalistic sources of stress also have received some attention in several other fields. One is the study of rather cataclysmic events that occasionally befall large collectivities. Studies of disasters and of their effects on populations (e.g., Erikson, 1976) are but one step away, theoretically, from studies of other, less eruptive, naturalistic sources. Another area of research that has stimulated interest in the social origins of stress. Students struggling to satisfy the requirements for the Ph.D. (Mechanic, 1972) and air traffic controllers (Rose, Hurst, & Kreger, 1978), who labor with the constant awareness of the grim consequences of error, are examples of such groups. Next, large-scale studies of the well-being of people living in the community and engaged in ordinary life pursuits have contributed importantly to the interest in stressful conditions of social life (Gurin, Veroff & Feld, 1960; Srole, Langer, Michael, Opler, & Rennie, 1962). Later I shall discuss some of this research in greater detail.

It should be noted, finally, that current social perspectives of the stress process have been reinforced by a sensitivity to the fact that different people experiencing similar life conditions are not necessarily affected in the same manner; i.e., some may be stressed by these conditions and others not. In attempting to account for these differences, researchers have been intensively examining people's access to and use of support systems, along with their coping repertoires. The nature of supports and their distribution along lines of social demarcation have been widely documented (e.g., Brown, 1978). What may be less readily recognized, however, is that individuals' coping repertoires are also appreciably social. That is, the manner in which people attempt to avoid or remedy painful situations, the perceptual and cognitive behaviors they use to reduce threat, and their techniques for managing tensions are largely learned from the groups to which they belong. Although constellations of coping responses may be distinctive for individuals, coping dispositions to a considerable extent are acquired from the social milieu (Pearlin, 1980b; Pearlin & Schooler, 1978).

The history of research into stress, then, is characterized by preoccupation with bodily functioning, a concern that is not dependent on knowledge of the naturalistic sources of stress. This orientation has begun to change as a result of several conditions: greater awareness of the social epidemiology of ailments having a stress etiology; efforts to understand the consequences of disasters; concern with at-risk groups in the society; studies of people in their community settings; and greater attention to the soical influences underlying the mediators of stress, coping, and supports. These developments portend a rapid and rich growth in the future. At present, however, the boundaries of our knowledge about the social causes of stress are somewhat narrow and not always clearly discernible. In describing what is currently known—or assumed—about the social underpinnings of stress, I shall not attempt a detailed canvassing of the diffuse and uneven literature. Instead, I shall seek to convey an understanding of the scope and diversity of the origins of stress. This is a strategy that depends more on the selective presentation of work that will help to exemplify major lines of inquiry than on an exhaustive cataloguing of the literature. The first step toward this task is a brief specification of the concept of stress itself.

STRESS: A CONCEPTUAL GLIMPSE

Almost all stress researchers experience some confusion and despair about the field. Indeed, there is some doubt that the concept of stress is worth preserving. Pearlin, Lieberman, Menaghan & Mullan (1981) suggested that it is not the core meaning of the concept that is confusing, for there is general agreement that *stress* refers to a *response of the organism to a noxious or threatening condition*. The doubt and disagreement arise with regard to where and how to identify this response. Is stress, for example, to be recognized by the functioning of an organ or a system of organs, by biochemical or physiological alterations, by changes in emotional states, or by the presence of disease entities? Is it manifested in short-run reactions of the organism or in long-run dysfunctions? Are people aware of the stress they harbor to the extent that they can report it, or must its presence be determined by independent assays? Is stress a global, encompassing state, or is it confined to situations in which it is aroused? The real problem in understanding stress is not that there are no answers to these questions, but that the answer to each of them is yes. That is, manifestations of stress are found at every level of organismic functioning, from the microbiological to the emotional; stress can be both a short-run response and a pattern that emerges slowly over time; individuals may be keenly aware that they are host to stress, although stress may also be present at a level below consciousness; finally, stress responses can be highly contained and situationally bounded, but they also can develop into a prevailing state that persists through time and extends through space.

It is in the very nature of stress that it can be so many things, and we should not try to reduce the multidimensionality of this phenomenon by arbitrarily declaring that stress is only one thing or another. It is much more productive, I believe, to recognize the diffuse character of the stress phenomenon and to bend our efforts to understanding how its multiple manifestations are interconnected. But it is not likely that this shift will occur quickly, for research into the various ways in which stress can be manifested is closely organized around disciplines, and disciplinary lines are not easily breached. The social scientist is not likely to study the production of steroids, and the endocrinologist is equally unlikely to study the production of depression. Firmly and actively engaged in his chosen research, each investigator is convinced that the manifestations of stress that he is examining represent "real" stress.

My own conviction is that it is prudent to retain the concept of stress despite its problems and shortcomings. It is not unusual in science for the same concept to acquire diverse meaning and to recruit the interest of many disciplines. The confusion that inevitably results is forgivable and should not inhibit continued work at multiple levels.

I turn now to a consideration of what is central to this chapter: social contributions to the arousal of stress.

SOCIAL CONTRIBUTIONS TO PERSONAL STRESS

It is not an easy matter to assemble what is known about stressful social conditions. One major reason for this difficulty is that the sources of stress extend from the most immediate contexts of people's lives to the outermost boundaries of societies and cultures. A detailed treatment of social stressors touches, at one end, on the microenvironments of individuals and, at the other, on large-scale social organization. A second difficulty stems from a somewhat paradoxical source to which I have already alluded: some of the early writing that is highly relevant to social stress paid little attention to social stress. Scholarly work of this type was aimed more often at such matters as social disorganization, deviance, conflict, and racism than at stress per se. Thus, important intellectual roots of the field are planted quite outside the edges of the field.

The vastness and uneven quality of the literature, coupled with the theoretical range of relevant work, require that I be highly selective (and somewhat arbitrary) in the research that I bring into discussion and that I impose some sort of schema to find order in an unruly field. The schema is a simple one. It begins with the broadest sources of stress, those that are thought to reside in the very nature of societies and their cultures; it then narrows to an examination of those stressful conditions that reside within institutional contexts, such as stratification systems, work roles, and family; and, finally, it funnels in still further to examine sources of stress from the perspective of individual experience. Needless to say, the conditions that exist at these different levels are not insulated from one another. Nevertheless, each level can be treated as a separate context out of which stress may grow.

Society as Stressor

The social science literature reveals an established interest in certain overarching features of society that have the potential to arouse stress. Two general themes run through this literature. One calls attention to the faulty integration among systems of cultural values, beliefs, precepts, goals, and aspirations. The second theme also deals with cultural and structural malintegration but emphasizes rapid social change as the inevitable forerunner of such malintegration. I shall first illustrate these themes and then examine the assumptions on which they rest.

Several classical studies viewed society and culture as a reservoir of personal stress and maladjustment. Anthropologists, in particular, have been very sensitive to discrepancies between the real and the ideal, the differences between the principles and beliefs to which a society claims adherence and those that are reflected in the actions of members of the society. To the extent that individuals internalize both the idealized values and the discrepant norms regulating actions, they would presumably be host to inner conflict detrimental to their well-being. Perhaps the most comprehensive study reflecting this perspective was done not by an anthropologist but by a Swedish economist and observer of the United States (Myrdal, Steiner, & Rose, 1944). Myrdal and his collaborators argued that the deep commitment of the nation to an egalitarian ethos contrasted sharply with discriminatory practices directed against blacks. The resulting dilemma, they observed, was deeply imprinted on the character of Americans, residing there as an impediment to be struggled with.

Other scholars have pointed to conflicts that do not involve the uncongeniality of the real and the ideal but result, instead, from discrepancies between the behaviors to which people are socialized as children and those to which they are expected to conform as adults. The well-known work of Benedict (1938) is an outstanding case in point. She observed that boys are taught to be obedient and responsive to the will and directions of their elders and to be sexually neutral. By contrast, adult males are expected to be independent, autonomous, and sexually aggressive. To the extent that these incompatible elements have been incorporated into a man's personality, his inner conflicts presumably will reflect those existing in the society at large.

A third perspective on society as a stressor has influenced sociological orientations to stress more than any other approach has done. This view, embodied in Merton's important essay on "Social Structure and Anomie" (1957), is similar to those outlined above in that Merton, too, was concerned with cultural values, particularly those that emphasize achievement and success. But unlike the others, he was interested less in how continuous or discontinuous these values are with other values than in how the valuation of success fits with the structure of opportunities. Briefly, Merton suggested that the system of values stimulates motivations toward the attainment of monetary and honorific success among more people than could possibly be accommodated by the opportunity structure. Consequently, many of us who internalize the culturally prized success goals are doomed to failure. Failure, in turn, leads on to a variety of possible adaptive and maladaptive modes. For Merton, society stands as a stressor not by presenting uncongenial values but by stimulating values that conflict with the structures in which they are to be acted upon. This is a landmark theory of how people participating in the mainstream systems of social life can be caught between the goals and values to which they have been socialized and the constraints of the structures in which they must act.

The various types of societal conflict and stress that I have sketched may exist during periods of relative stability. It is a fairly common view, however, that stressful conditions are especially likely to arise out of rapid social change. That is, under conditions of profound change the kinds of social conditions I described above are apt to surface at an accelerated pace. When social institutions and the norms and belief systems that support them go through rapid alterations, it grows increasingly likely that people will come to hold mutually anatagonistic values, that their early socialization will not be appropriate to the demands of current realities, or that there will be no opportunity structures or institutional contexts that can accommodate the goals and aspirations that have been internalized. In addition, of course, large-scale change can carry with it other problems; people may be physically uprooted, experience a weakening or destruction or social ties, or have an alien culture imposed on or incorporated into their native culture. And, when the social change entails increased industrialization and urbanization, people must obviously shift away from earlier economic activities; established kinship arrangements are often disrupted; and, usually, informal perparation for occupational life gives way to formal and specialized training. It is understandable that profound social change has been of interest to students of stress.

But what are the mechanisms by which social change undermines the will-being of people? Whether one looks at the intensification of value conflicts or at the erosion of established forms of social organization, one assumes a direct, causal tie between upheavals in our external world and those in our inner world. However, the stress that people experience may not be a simple and direct consequence of culture conflict and social disorganization. In this vein, Marris (1974) elucidated a number of indirect pathways through which the deleterious effects of change come about. He pointed out that change can leave people with a sense of loss of control over their own destinies; it can undermine people's ability to predict their futures; it can erode the precepts by which people interpret and derive meaning from experience; and it may engender a profound feeling of loss of the past, leaving people in a bereavementlike state. The adverse effects of change, therefore, do not stem from an inherent proclivity for stability. Such effects may result, instead, from a host of losses produced by the change.

I have suggested that the uncertainties and contradictions that arise in societies, especially during periods of extensive change, can act as precursors of stress. This emphasis, however, should not be interpreted to mean that societal disorganization and change inevitably translate into personal stress. Some conditions can neutralize the effects of the kinds of broad social forces that I have been discussing. And, although relatively little research has been directed at these conditions, it is possible to suggest a few of them. One such condition involves the separation of roles in time and space. Although we are many things—workers, parents, children, religious followers, political participants, and so on—fortunately, we are not all of them simultaneously. To the extent that internalized values are organized around the roles that people play, the spatial and temporal segregation of roles may enable people to avoid direct confrontations among incompatible values. A man can be both a shady businessman and a pious worshiper. And as long as he does not conduct his business in church, he is likely to escape the severe personal dilemma that would otherwise result from his conflicting commitments.

With regard to elements of childhood socialization that are not appropriate to current realities—the kind of discontinuity of which Benedict wrote—there again may be less personal conflict than might be assumed on logical grounds. When we recognize that socialization is a continuous process, occurring not only in childhood but extending over the life span, then we can understand that many of the things we learn early in life go through gradual transformations. Learning to be obedient as young children, for example, does not preclude learning to be assertive as adults; the socialization that occurs later can preempt that which occurred earlier. Consequently, if we compare only early training with later requirements, many discontinuities will appear, but if we take into account all the intervening training that takes place, the process of preparing people for adult roles will appear more continuous. Finally, and more generally, we need to understand how the violation of cherished norms may be supported by other, equally cherished, norms. As Williams (1970) noted, every society provides institutionalized evasions of institutionalized norms. To the extent that our evasions are as acceptable as the norms from which we are departing, whatever conflicts result are probably neither severe nor durable. Clearly, we must be very cautious in judging the stressfulness of societal forces solely on the basis of what appears to be logically reasonable. Societies are both sources of stress and sources of mechanisms by which people avoid stress.

Social Organizations as Stressors

Any society, if it is to survive, must organize its activities and structure the relationships among its collectivities. Social organization varies considerably in scope: it is very extensive, encompassing entire populations, and it is also more limited, involving, for example, elites or members of special communities. In this section I shall be concerned with the more overarching forms of social organization, attempting to convey how formal properties themselves may come to constitute sources of stress. For this purpose I shall first discuss selected aspects of systems of stratification and then turn to a consideration of a few institutionalized features of occupation and family.

In recent years there has been some rather tantalizing research into the stressful consequences of people's locations in stratified economies. Enough evidence has been accumulated to assure us that psychological distress increases linearly with a decrease in income level (e.g., Pearlin & Radabaugh, 1976). Furthermore, a variety of indicators of stress show that economic fluctuations have powerful aftereffects on the psychological functioning of populations (Brenner 1973; Catalano & Dooley, 1977). The struggles and uncertainties of people in lower economic echelons of the society are sources of stress whose importance has not been appreciated fully. If one attempts to trace personal stress back to its societal roots, one it likely to be led eventually to the economic organization of societies.

Societies are stratified along status and power dimensions, as well as along economic lines. The very multidimensional nature of stratification has itself been recognized as a social source of stress. The central point of the substantial literature concerned with this issue is that the consistency of one's standing in the various stratification orders may be as important to stress as is one's position within any one of them. To use an example with which young academics will be familiar, one may enjoy a relatively high occupational status along with an incommensurately low income. This kind of discrepency produces stress presumably because inconsistent statuses produce inconsistent elements of identity. At any rate, a number of studies have found a disproportionate concentration of stress symptoms among people whose standing on one dimension of stratification is higher than their standing on others (e.g., Hornung, 1977; Jackson, 1967). Such symptoms are especially likely to appear, according to Hornung (1978), when the inconsistency is accompanied by aspirations for social advancement. Thus, a woman who has a high income from a low-status occupation may be indifferent to the inconsistency if she is indifferent to status; the same inconsistent circumstances are likely to be more stressful if the person is a status striver.

Occupational settings and their organization represent more closely delineated contexts for stress than do extensive systems of social and economic stratification. This does not mean that their relationships to stress are more simple. On the contrary, overviews of work in this area have revealed that the formal features of occupational settings and their relationships to stress are highly complex (e.g., Gross, 1970). In identifying some of these features, I shall report primarily from the work of Katz and Kahn (1978).

As these workers noted, there are many approaches to identifying those formal aspects of occupational settings that have stressful consequences for their members. One such approach focuses on the various subsystems of occupations. Production is an example of a basic subsystem. The inherent task of production, Katz and Kahn (1978) pointed out, is the enhancement of proficiency, a goal that triggers a number of interlocking conditions leading to stress. Briefly, the achievement of proficiency often depends on increased specialization of work. This aspect of work, in turn, is conducive to overload, monotony, and the absence of variety, all of them seedbeds of stress. There are four additional subsystems: the production supportive, which regulates transactions between the organization and its environment; the maintenance subsystem, which regulates and manages the reward structure; an adaptive structure, which guides changes within the organization in response to changing external conditions; and, finally, the managerial system, which monitors and directs activities. Each subsystem can be viewed as operating in response to its own unique set of imperatives and as being capable of generating its own set of stressful conditions.

Katz and Kahn's (1978) perspectives are interesting and informative in their own right but they are notable also in that they attempt to account for stress strictly in terms of the organizational features of occupational contexts. That is, they identify the sources of occupational stress as inherent in the universal properties of formal organization. Within this conceptual framework, occupational stress can be considered not as something that now and then besets unfortunate workers but as a normal consequence of laboring in organized work settings. From this prespective, the absence, not the presence, of occupational stress is anomalous.

Inevitably, this scanning of institutional sources of stress must come to rest on the family. As in the case of occupation, I wish to identify a few institutionalized aspects of family life that potentially result in stress, a focus that is quite different from that which centers on the individual experiences of family members. Once more, I find it necessary to add the caveat that within these pages it is possible at best to skim a few of the more salient issues. For inclusive reviews, the reader needs to consult other sources (Croog, 1970; Mc-Cubbin, Joy, Canble, Comeau, Patterson, & Needle, 1980).

The family has multiple functions in the stress process. First, within the constellation of social institutions, the family can be seen as the one in which life strains that are engendered elsewhere can be expressed and acted upon most easily. For example, the distress that the alienated worker feels after an unpleasant encounter with his boss may be displaced in an overly punitive reaction to his child's transgressions; one may lose a job, but not family membership, by displaying outrage. Similarly, a child who suffers humiliation on the playground may engage in some puzzling rebelliousness at the dinner table. More than a target for displaced stress, the family is also a source of solace and sympathy when people suffer defeat in the outside world. The family stands in most contemporary societies as the welcoming haven where we can be refreshed and reassured. For many people, home may not be simply the preferred place to turn in times of distress but the only place in which one has access to acceptance and support.

However, even while it soothes and supports, the family also may inflict emotional pain and punishment. Several institutional and structural features of the contemporary family help make it a potential source of stress, as well as a source of succor. First, such factors as urbanization, geographic movement, and class mobility increase the likelihood that marital partners will come from significantly different social and economic backgrounds. An appreciable proportion of marriages, for example, involve partners whose fathers' occupational statuses are unequal. Status inequality by itself seems to be unrelated to marital stress (Pearlin, 1975); however, when the partner who "marries down" also holds values that bespeak a desire for status aggrandizement, marriages of unequal partners then become fertile ground for stress. Whether or not marriage is a source of stress, therefore, depends in part on both the background characteristics that spouses bring to the marriage and the manner in which these characteristics combine with values and aspirations.

One should not infer from this description that the course of marriage is dictated only by what is brought to the marriage at its inception. We know that socialization takes place across the entire life span; consequently, marriage itself is a context for learning and socialization. The relevance of this point for stress is that socialization will not be identical for the marital partners; they probably will change at different rates and in different directions. The inevitable strains produced by these differences can challenge severely the adaptational capacities of the partners. In addition to marital changes that inexorably stem from adult socialization, other equally inexorable changes come with adult role transitions. I refer, of course, to the family cycle and all of the role losses and role gains that it entails—from marrying, through childrearing, and ultimately ending in the death of a spouse. At this time there is an incomplete understanding of the conditions under which life cycle transitions are apt to lead to individual and marital stress. In general, however, it appears that the movement into and out of roles and statuses may result in less marital stress than has been assumed (Menaghan, 1980; Pearlin, 1980a).

The stresses generated within the family context involve parent-child relations, as well as marital relations. Problems with children spring out of a variety of social conditions. For example, one may point to the prolonged period of training required by industrialized societies, to the concomitant extended dependence, and to the parent-child conflict that can be fed by these conditions. Social change also may play a part in this conflict. The ultimate functions of the socialization of children are found not in childhood, but in adulthood. That is, training and rearing practices are directed toward the social roles that children will assume when they are adults, not toward the perfection of childhood behaviors. Parents typically evaluate the current behavior of their children in terms of its consistency with that they perceive as the requirements of their children's future roles. However, parental conceptions of what is good and worth striving after often are different from their children's conceptions. During periods of widespread change and upheaval, these intergenerational differences probably become intensified. Parents are then apt to arrive at the alarming conclusion that their children's course of development diverges from cherished goals. A distressing state, indeed.

Among the rich array of family based stresses are those that exist between adult children and their aged parents. The very people who are contending with the needs of their minor children may be contending at the be same time with the needs of their parents. As longevity is increased, this becomes a fairly common circumstance, one that is winning growing attention from researchers (Lieberman, 1978; Troll, 1971). Some of the strains and problems that can arise from the relations between aged parents and their adult children are self-evident. When there is debilitating illness or a decline in physical self-sufficiency, or when parents' economic resources are not adequate to their needs, a turnabout in the parent-child relationship may occur. Adult children at first may assume more of a peer relationship with their parents but, as problems continue, go on to assume a larger degree of responsibility for the latter's material, legal, and emotional well-being. The turnabout clearly has the potential for arousing stress; the adult child may find it a drain on energy, on emotions, and on resources; the aged parent, on the other hand, may find that this new dependence violates his desire for autonomy and self-direction. The internal conflicts of each party easily can develop into a conflict between the parties.

In sum, I have dealt in this section with ways in which people's actions and relationships are organized, looking specifically at the hierarchical ordering of people in stratification systems; the structuring of work and work tasks; and the network of family relations and their changes across the life course. I have sought to call attention to an important issue: people who are engaged in the mainstream institutional life of the society can be stressed as a sheer result of the organizational arrangements of these institutions and the changes that normally occur within them. From a social perspective, stress is not the consequence of bad luck, unfortunate encounters, or unique circumstances. It is, instead, the consequence of engagement in social institutions whose very structures and functioning can engender and sustain patterns of conflict, confusion, and distress.

STRESSFUL EXPERIENCES

Thus far, I have tried to indicate how the properties of societies and their institutions can evoke stress. Eventually, however, the researcher needs to ask how institutional conditions are incorporated into individual experience. Individual experience, of course, is ultimately inseparable from the larger social circumstances that I have been discussing. Nevertheless, in order to understand how these circumstances penetrate the lives of people, we must shift our focus from a societal and institutional to an individual level.

My own research into stress and coping is pitched largely at this level, and I shall be drawing on this research for much of the discussion here. Essentially, I distinguish two broad classes of experience, that which is eventful and that which is repeated or continuous. Both types of experience are likely to arise within the institutional settings of the society. That is, to a large extent, experience is organized around the roles and statuses we have as workers, spouses, parents, children, friends, and neighbors. This is not to say that people are never overtaken by events or confronted by continuing problems outside these roles. Anyone who has been the victim of a mugger or who daily sits in slow moving commuter traffic can attest to the ubiquitous nature of stressful experience. Nevertheless, because so much behavior is organized around major social roles, it is here that one is able to discover patterns of stressful experience.

Eventful experiences and their consequences for stress have been the focus of considerable research, much of it stimulated by the development of the Social Readjustment Rating Scale (Holmes & Rahe, 1967). This research has been subjected to a good deal critical scrutiny (e.g., Dohrenwend & Pearlin, 1981), which need not be recapitulated here. What I would like to emphasize about life events studies is that they increasingly regard the stressful impact of events as depending more on the quality of the events than solely on the magnitude of the changes they entail. The voluntary or involuntary character of events is one quality that has been addressed. Another quality, perhaps the most commonly considered, concerns the desirability of events. A third distinction, one that we have found useful (Pearlin & Lieberman, 1979), is between scheduled and unscheduled events. I shall explicate briefly the nature of this distinction.

Scheduled events are those that have, in advance, a high probability of occurrence. We may not know precisely when they will emerge, but we have a fair degree of certainty that they will emerge. Events of this type derive their scheduled character from being an inherent part of the life cycle; that is, they are found in those family and career transitions that represent the junctures between life stages (Lowenthal, Thurnher, Chiriboga, & Associates, 1975). Transitions typically involve the separation from one role or status and/or entrance into another. Marriage, having children, the movement of children toward their own eventual launching from the parental home, grandparenthood, retirement, and death of a spouse are scheduled transitional events.

On the face of the far-reaching life changes that are involved in many scheduled events, one could reasonably expect them to be stressful. Certainly, some transitional events entail a rather profound reorganization of life. Yet, our own work generally has indicated that there is no notable association between experiencing this kind of life event and manifesting symptoms of stress (Pearlin & Lieberman, 1979). It would be premature to discount scheduled events as antecedents of stress, but it is tempting to speculate that the very forecastable nature of scheduled events helps to minimize what would otherwise be their considerable stressful impact. Because these events can be foreseen long before their occurrence, they may be preceded by a great deal of anticipatory coping. By the time we actually assume a new role, we may already have considerable understanding of its demands. If transitional events are not clearly related to stress, therefore, it may be because of the coping that was initiated years before the person actually confronted the transition.

It is a different story with *unscheduled events*. Although events of this type do not always descend upon us without prior warning, they are not built into our set of expectations, as in the case of scheduled events. Divorce, injury and illness, job disruption, premature death, and ruptured friendships are examples of unscheduled events. In contrast to those that are scheduled, these events are notably associated with stress (Pearlin & Lieberman, 1979). One may wonder, too, whether they also differ from scheduled events in their sensitivity to different kinds of coping and social support interventions. I suspect that unscheduled crises, more than events having a long and explicit prelude, are likely to mobilize social supports and short-run coping responses. Obviously, these are questions that at this point in time are easier to raise than to answer.

Despite the unanswered questions, it is possible to underscore some promising gains being made by current research into the effects of eventful experience. First, it is obvious from my discussion of life events that there is a movement away from a concern with eventful change per se and a commensurately greater concern with identifying the quality of those events that are likely to exert a stressful impact. As far as emotional stress is concerned, eventful experiences are not equally provocative. Those that are voluntary, desired, or scheduled have no apparent emotional consequences; involuntary, undesired, and unscheduled events do.

Another area in which there are hints of progress involves the possibility that different kinds of eventful experience may call out different adaptive modes. As I noted previously, successful adjustment to scheduled or transitional experiences may rely on anticipatory coping and preparation to a considerable extent, while successful adjustment to eruptive events may depend more on the ability of people both to mobilize quickly an array of coping responses and to utilize various support measures. Future research into stress and coping can be expected to look more closely for a fit between types of eventful experience and types of mediators people can invoke to meet such contingencies.

Finally, research probably will be increasingly sensitive to the links between the emergence of particular events in the lives of people and life course processes. Life events are amenable to a number of conceptual classifications, but one of the particularly useful features of the scheduled-unscheduled distinction is that it helps to clarify how many events are systematically distributed along the life span. In general, research into eventful experiences as antecedents of stress will benefit by viewing the events within the organization of people's lives through time, not by treating them as temporally happenstance occurrences. We need to know how the stressful events one experiences as a young person become the contingencies for the events one will experience as an older person.

The second major type of stressful experience, it will be recalled, is that which is *repeated* or *chronic*. Efforts to identify the persistent experiences that are built into the fabric of daily life have been overshadowed somewhat in recent years by the burgeoning interest in life events. This disparity cannot be explained by the relative stressfulness of events and chronic strains. On the contrary, it appears that the latter exert a more powerful stressful impact than the former. Thus, we have been able to identify persistent elements of marital relations, of parent-child relations, and of occupational experience that bear a close association with various indicators of stress (Pearlin & Lieberman, 1979). If one were interested only in the more potent sources of stress, one would devote more attention to chronic stress and far less to life events.

However, we have learned that the parts played by life events and by chronic strains as sources of stress are understood most clearly by observing them together rather than by regarding them as separate and unrelated antecedents (Pearlin, Lieberman, Menaghan, & Mullan, 1981). Concretely, events—especially undesired, unscheduled events—arouse stress indirectly by changing adversely the conditions of life with which people must live. Let us take as an example the involuntary disruption of work. This is an event that has a moderately strong statistical relationship to symptoms of stress, but the relationship is explained largely by the effect of the event on the economic resources of people. That is, the life event contributes to stress through its negative effect on economic circumstances, an ongoing feature of one's world. If these two causes of stress were looked at separately, we would fail to see how they come together in a unitary process. Indeed, the challenge of future research is to understand how the antecedents of stress, its mediators, and its symptoms converge to constitute the stress process.

CONCLUSION

Perhaps the most salient message to be taken from this chapter is that the array of social sources of personal stress is highly diverse and ranges from the very distal to the very proximal. These sources may be seen as including some of the central features of society itself: its value systems, the stratified ordering of its populations, the organization of its institutions, and the rapidity and extent of changes in these elements.

Sources of stress also can be identified in the direct experiences of individuals. Both eventful experience, involving undesirable, unscheduled or involuntary change, and continuing experience, involving persistent problems within social roles, can be powerful conditions for stress. Although the empirical demonstration of the stressful consequences of some of these sources is far from convincing, overall we can be quite certain that stress is indeed often rooted in the social contexts in which individuals are engaged.

There is little reason to rest with the present state of our knowledge about the social origins of stress. First, as I noted, some of this knowledge is more putative than convincingly documented. But beyond the obvious need to be less assertive and more empirical in drawing out the connections between social life and stress, there is other work to be done. I would emphasize in particular the need to move away from attempts to identify separate sources of stress to the specification of the process leading to stress. Some start has been made in this direction in our own research, which shows the confluence of life events, chronic strains, and self-concept in producing stress. What is not sufficiently known is how life events and role strains themselves stem from broad-scale social and institutional organization and their changes. Not all personal stress can be traced to social contexts, of course, and not all problems in these contexts necessarily result in stress. However, if we are to understand personal problems as an expression of social problems, then we also must understand the processes by which features of our social system become transformed into features of the emotional interiors of individuals.

REFERENCES

BENEDICT, R. Continuities and incontinuities in cultural conditioning. *Psychiatry,* 1938, *2,* 161–170.

BRENNER, M. H. *Mental illness and the economy.* Cambridge: Harvard University Press, 1973.

BROWN, B. Social and psychological correlates of help-seeking behavior among urban adults. *American Journal of Community Psychology,* 1978, *6,* 425–439.

CATALANO, R., & DOOLEY, D. Economic predictors of depressed mood and stressful life events in a metropolitan community. *Journal of Health and Social Behavior,* 1977, *18,* 292–307.

CROOG, S. H. The family as a source of stress. In S. Levine & N. A. Scotch (eds.), *Social stress.* Chicago: Aldine, 1970.

DOHRENWEND, B., & PEARLIN, L. I. *Report of the panel on life events.* Washington, D.C.: Institute of Medicine, 1981.

ERIKSON, K. T. *Everything in its path: Destruction of community in the Buffalo Creek flood.* New York: Simon & Schuster, 1976.

GROSS, E. Work, organization, and stress. In S. Levine & N. A. Scotch (eds.), *Social stress*. Chicago: Aldine, 1970.

GURIN, G., VEROFF, J., & FELD, S. *Americans view their mental Health*. New York: Basic Books, 1960.

HOLMES, T. H., & RAHE, R. H. The Social Readjustment Rating Scale. *Journal of Psychosomatic Research*, 1967, *11*, 213–218.

HORNUNG, C. A. Social status, status inconsistency, and psychological stress. *American Sociological Review*, 1977, *42*, 623–628.

————. Status inconsistency, importance of getting ahead, and psychological stress. In A. Rappaport (ed.), *Avoiding social catastrophes and maximizing social opportunities*. Washington, D.C.: Society for General Systems Research, 1978.

JACKSON, E. H. Status consistency and symptoms of stress. *American Sociological Review*, 1967, *27*, 469–480.

KATZ, D., & KAHN, R. *The social psychology of organizations* (2d ed.). New York: Wiley, 1978.

LIEBERMAN, G. Children of the elderly as natural helpers: Some demographic differences. *American Journal of Community Psychology*, 1978, *6*, 489–498.

LOWENTHAL, F. F., THURNHER, M., CHIRIBOGA, D., & ASSOCIATES. *Four stages of life: A comparative study of women and men facing transitions*. San Francisco: Jossey-Bass, 1975.

MARRIS, P. *Loss and change*. London: Routledge & Kegan Paul, 1974.

MCCUBBIN, H. I., JOY, C. B., CANBLE, A. E., COMEAU, J. K., PATTERSON, J. M., & NEEDLE, R. H. Family stress and coping: A decade review. *Journal of Marriage and the Family*, 1980, *42*, 855–871.

MECHANIC, D. *Students under stress*. New York: Free Press, 1972.

MENAGHAN, E. Assessing the impact of family transitions on marital experience: Problems and prospects. Doctoral dissertation, University of Chicago, 1980.

MERTON, R. K. Social structure and anomie. In R. K. Merton (ed.), *Social theory and social structure* (2d ed.). New York: Free Press, 1957.

MYRDAL, G., STEINER, R., & ROSE A. *An American dilemma*, vol 1. New York: Harper, 1944.

PEARLIN, L. I. Status inequality and stress in marriage. *American Sociological Review*, 1975, *40*, 344–357.

————. The life cycle and life strains. In H. M. Blalock, Jr. (ed.), *Sociological theory and research: A critical approach*. New York: Free Press, 1980.

————. Life-strains and psychological distress among adults. In N. J. Smelser & E. H. Erikson (eds.), *Themes of love and work in adulthood*. Cambridge: Harvard University Press, 1980.

PEARLIN, L. I., & LIEBERMAN, M. A. Social sources of emotional distress. In R. Simmons (ed.), *Research in community and mental health*, vol. 1. Greenwich: JAI, 1979.

PEARLIN, L. I., LIEBERMAN, M. A., MENAGHAN, E. G., & MULLAN, J. T. The stress process. *Journal of Health and Social Behavior*, 1981, *22*, 337–356.

PEARLIN, L. I., & RADABAUGH, C. Economic strains and the coping functions of alcohol. *American Journal of Sociology*, 1976, *82*, 652–663.

PEARLIN, L. I., & SCHOOLER, C. The structure of coping. *Journal of Health and Social Behavior*, 1978, *19*, 2–21.

ROSE, R. M., HURST, M. W., & KREGER, B. E. Predictors of hypertension in air traffic controllers: A prospective study. *Psychosomatic Medicine*, 1978, *40*, 86.

SROLE, L., LANGNER, T. S., MICHAEL, S. T., OPLER, M. K., & RENNIE, T. A. C. *Mental health in the metropolis*. New York: McGraw-Hill, 1962.

TROLL, L. The family in later life: A decade review. *Journal of Marriage and Family Living*, 1971, *33*, 263–290.

WILLIAMS, R. M., JR. *American Society* (3d ed.). New York: Knopf, 1970.

17

Stress as a Consequence of the Urban Physical Environment

Eric Graig

SINCE THE FIRST EDITION OF THIS HANDBOOK, the focus of research into environmental stress has shifted. Early work, which established links between features of the physical environment and stress, has given way to concern about the processes through which stress reactions are mediated by physical, social, and personal variables. Put differently, environmental stress research has become increasingly contextual in orientation. This chapter focuses on stress as a consequence of one particular context: the urban physical environment. I discuss a number of features that characterize urban living—urban press, air pollution, commuting, crime, office work, and the built environment—and their role in producing stress reactions. Space considerations have precluded more than a cursory mention of competing theoretical models of stress. More detailed consideration, however, is given to congruence and contextual approaches because they seem particularly relevant to the task at hand. Those desiring a more complete theoretical treatment are referred to recent reviews by Evans and Cohen (1987) and Cohen. Evans, Stokols, and Krantz (1986).

CONTEXTUAL AND CONGRUENCE APPROACHES TO ENVIRONMENTAL STRESS

Traditional theories have tended to define stress in terms of adaptation to noxious physical stimuli. According to such approaches, stressful situations are those that exceed an individual's ability to cope (Cohen, et al., 1986; Evans, 1982). More recently, consideration of the personal evaluation of potential stressors has entered this definition (Evans & Cohen, 1987; Fleming, Baum, & Singer, 1984), so that stress reactions are now said to arise when an individual makes an appraisal that his or her coping abilities are threatened. In other words, psychological stress is based upon the perception and interpretation of an event and an evaluation of one's ability to cope with it. This evaluation process is said to have three parts: primary appraisal (determination of the threat and appraisal of potential harm), secondary appraisal (evaluation of coping resources within the individual and the environ-

This chapter is based on an article of the same title in the previous edition of this handbook by Robert Kaminoff and Hal Proshansky. When Dr. Proshansky was asked to update this work he asked for my help in my role as his graduate assistant. Sadly, only a few weeks later he died. His original work with Bob Kaminoff remain very much a part of this chapter although, as its author, I take full responsibility for any errors and omissions.

ment), and reappraisal (repetition of the above two as the stressor changes over time). Coping may be directed toward the physical manifestations of the stressor (instrumental coping) or toward the individual's perceptions or feeling about it (palliative coping). The coping strategy employed will depend upon factors in the situation and the individual.

Implicit in a coping approach is the idea that individuals have certain goals to fulfill—goals which require a particular set of environmental conditions. The question asked by the threat-coping model is, how are these goals blocked. Attentional models focus on the narrowing of attention that takes places in the presence of excessive stimulation. According to this approach, the individual focuses attention on the task at hand and ignores inputs that are not immediately relevant to performance (Broadbent, 1971). A number of empirical findings (Nagar & Panady, 1987) seem to support such a theory. Information processing models have also been developed. These hold that stressors cause people to adopt strategies designed to filter or deflect sources of stimulation not necessary for the task at hand. As more cognitive capacity is allocated to monitor the stressor however, capacity available for task performance is reduced and performance suffers. The level of threat posed by the stressor determines the degree of cognitive capacity allowed to monitor it and hence the degree to which task performance is compromised. Under such conditions, the individual may adapt by allocating capacity according to the most central aspects of the task at hand (Cohen, et al., 1986).

Contextual and congruence models of stress are both based on the premise that stress may arise when individual goals are blocked. These models differ from appraisal models in that they attempt to focus on the ecological environment as a totality rather than just the interactions between physical stimuli, one or more mediator variables, and stress outcomes. Cohen and his colleagues (1986) state that a fundamental idea underlying contextual approaches is embeddedness. According to this concept, psychological phenomena are viewed in relation to the spatial, temporal, and sociocultural milieu in which they exist. To raise a question about a particular phenomena—in this case psychological stress—is at the same time to ask about each part of this milieu and the relationships between them (see also Bronfenbrenner, 1979). For example, a contextual model of crowding in a recreational setting would have to consider not only issues such as density and control, but also factors such as the origin of the individual's goals in the setting and his or her knowledge of it. Contextual studies are also interested in the ways in which different life domains influence and are influenced by stress. Stokols and Novaco (1981), for instance, suggest that factors in the home and the work environment may influence commuting stress. Another area that context-based studies may address concerns the potential for *recursive stress reactions*. This term refers to processes in which "stress begets stress." One example of such a process concerns stress that results from difficulties in way-finding. If problems in navigating through a city lead to anxiety, then that reaction may in turn increase difficulties in way-finding and lead to increasingly higher levels of stress. Contextual theories allow for open-ended processes because they are not constrained by the action-reaction epistemology of other models. Put more generally, contextual research allows for the possibility of multiple outcomes that may feed back into the very processes from which they result.

One further concept that can be tied to the contextual approach also needs to be addressed. Even as environments help give rise to particular goal structures, they may constrain the fulfillment of goals. Where this occurs, the fit or congruence between person and environment is minimal and stress results. (It is interesting here to note that under such a conceptualization the environment is also subject to stress according to the same process.) The idea is that the environment is the supplier of resources (floor space, quiet, safety) that individuals require in order to realize their projects. If a particular environment fails to supply these resources, stress results because goals are blocked. The person enters into this equation because he or she determines the goals (of course, as noted previously, these goals are deeply embedded in context) and brings to the situation particular attributes (also part of the total environment) that are relevant to their realization.

AMBIENT STRESSORS

Campbell (1983) provides a framework from which to approach the empirical study of environmental stress. Her approach is valuable because it does an excellent job of clarifying the issues around environmental stress and of laying out some of the distinctions between it and other types of stress. Campbell's work develops a model of ambient stress that refers to chronic conditions in the ecological environment not readily resolvable through individual action. In contrast, daily hassles are usually amenable to solution and do not persist over time. For example, noise from a neighbor's party would be considered a daily hassle, but one can ask the neighbor to lower the stereo or call the police; in any case, the party will eventually be over. Noise from highway traffic, on the other hand, because of its chronicity and the fact that there is no effective individual response, would be considered an ambient stressor. Perhaps the best way to think of ambient stressors is an noxious stimulators existing in the background. From the individual's point of view, such stressors may almost be thought of as inherent features of the physical environment.

Ambient stressors possess a negative tone but do not threaten immediate harm. Because they are also usually out of the control of the individual (collective action may be effective in controlling them), coping with such stressors is usually palliative and based on their reappraisal as benign. Alternatively, ambient stressors may be reevaluated in terms of their beneficial aspects. For example, a factory that produces air pollution may be viewed as a necessary because of the jobs it provides. Ambient stressors may effect several dimensions of well-being, including motivation, emotions, attention, and health. They may also interact with other stressors. In a survey study of the effects of major life events and daily hassles (which does not distinguish daily hassles and ambient stressors), DeLongis, Coyne, Dakoff, Folkman, and Lazarus (1982) found the latter to be more strongly associated with somatic health. While the study looked at a wide range of daily hassles and not only those related to environmental stress, the results do suggest that low intensity stressors can affect physiological well-being.

URBAN PRESS

Previous reviews of the urban environmental stress literature have tended to address the issues of crowding and noise separately. However, in most urban contexts such a separation—perhaps traceable to early laboratory work—misses the essential quality of urban life. More than either crowding or noise alone, urban dwellers experience a flow of stimuli related to the physical, social, visual, and aural aspects of their environment. Attempts to break up this flow, which I refer to as urban press, remove a basic feature of urban life from its context. Crowding for example, which can be manipulated so readily in the laboratory, takes on a totally different dimension when it occurs in the extremely heterogenous setting of a city street or housing complex. There are high levels of intermittent and ambient noise to contend with, concerns about personal safety, travel impedance, and way-finding difficulties that create situations well beyond the accepted definitions of crowding, although they may be referred to under that term. The point here relates to what was said earlier about contextual approaches to urban stress. Noise and crowding, even though they are mediated through social and personal processes, remain essentially physical phenomena. Urban press on the other hand, because it includes a range of physical and social elements, is fundamentally rooted in context.

Fleming, Baum, and Weiss (1987) went a long way toward adopting an urban press perspective in a study of perceived control and crowding stress. Their research compared stress on city blocks characterized by the presence of small stores with blocks of similar residential density that did not have stores. Interestingly, even though both groups exhibited similar levels of residential density, residents on the streets with stores perceived higher levels of crowding and showed higher levels of stress. While the streets with stores did have higher levels of density because of an increase in the number of shoppers, the presence of stores on a street probably did much more than just add density. Commercial establishments contribute additional visual stimuli, more noise, more vehicular traffic, an increase in pedestrian activity, and an increase in social interaction and social diversity. Interestingly, Fleming's subjects reported more unwanted and undesirable social activity with neighbors and strangers and indicated that they often intentionally avoided people in order to minimize this interaction. While Fleming and his colleagues attribute the differences in stress to this last observation, an environmental press model would have to consider some of the effects of stores mentioned previously.

Crowding

Crowding stress occurs when the individual experiences undesired social interaction (Cohen, 1985) or when the availability of resources necessary for goal attainment is restricted (Epstein, 1982). While crowding is usually discussed in terms of density factors such as interpersonal distance, total area size, seating arrangements, and the shape of the space are other important physical dimensions (Suedfeld, 1985).

Crowding has been shown to have adverse physiological, behavioral, and social consequences (Epstein, 1982; Weiss & Baum, 1987). Recent evidence has accumulated documenting the effects of crowding on the sympathetic nervous system (Epstein, 1982), cardiac reactivity (Fleming, Baum, Davidson, & Rectanus, 1987), urinary catecholamine levels (Schaeffer, Baum, Paulus, & Gaes, 1988), cognitive task performance and affect (Nagar & Panady, 1987), helplessness (Baum & Gatchel, 1981), and mental health.

A number of different models have been developed to conceptualize these effects. For example, personal space, defined as the area individuals maintain around themselves into which others cannot intrude without arousal (Hayduk, 1983), may be implicated in crowding responses. Vine (1982) has noted that personal space preferences are predictive of reactions to crowding and suggests that this relationship may be rooted in aversion to touch, which, at least in Western contexts, represents a significant taboo. A multidimensional scaling model developed by Schultz-Gambard, Feierabend and Hommel (1988) found that crowding was most often associated with familiar secondary environments in which respondents were voluntary participants. Crowded situations were characterized by excessive stimulation, minimized interaction distances, behavioral constraint, and scarce resources. The two dimensions that emerged as most salient in their multidimensional scaling model were concerned with goal blocking and negative affect.

Epstein (1982) places emphasis on the goal-blocking effects of crowding, which become more threatening as the salience of the task increases. He notes that since crowding is a group phenomenon, group characteristics will be important in mediating the stress responses. The maximal reaction will occur when the goal is particularly important, the threat to its attainment severe, and the group unresponsive. Folkman (1984), while noting the importance of features of the situation, also emphasizes the role of individual appraisal in responses to crowding.

The ways in which group and individual factors come to together to mediate crowding at the community level is explored by Sally Engle Merry (1987). Her work emphasizes the role played by social, cultural, institutional, and physical environmental factors in determining and enforcing rules about the use of a community's physical environment. In an excellent series of studies, she explores the ways in which neighborhood residents manage conflicts over territory. Relying on ethnographic data and the close analysis of a number of neighborhood disputes, Merry was able to observe the ways in which conflicts were mediated by personality, social position, and previous experience in the neighborhood. In one of these cases, an elderly man filed a complaint against his neighbors, a young couple, for playing their stereo too loudly. The man claimed that the sound of the stereo reverberated against his walls and created a booming sound that exacerbated a wide range of health problems. The young couple, who had recently purchased the house in what was a rapidly gentrifying area, denied playing the stereo too loudly and stated that they thought the man should have been pleased that they were working to fix up their house. The close proximity of the two houses created the conditions for the conflict, but differences in age, the gap between old-timers and newcomers, and personality factors—the elderly man's vulnerability and the young couple's aloofness—exacerbated the conflict. Such a case goes a long way toward establishing that physical design features (in this case proximity) are mediated through social processes that—certainly in the case of this neighborhood—are constantly evolving.

Westover (1989) develops a model of crowding perception in recreational settings that, like Merry's, is fundamentally contextual. Westover's approach captures the dynamic interplay of person-environment characteristics that feed into perceptions of crowding. Her work lays out a systems model in which characteristics of both the site (both permanent and temporal) and the individual (sociodemographics, motivations, past experiences, and knowledge) create an image of the environment that, played through the individual's goals for the site, leads to a perception of crowdedness. While not specifically concerned with urban settings, Westoever's model embraces a fully contextual approach to crowding that provides workers interested in urban dimensions a conceptualization with which to begin.

A number of studies have looked at the individual's ability to adapt to crowded conditions. Nagar & Panady (1987) found that subjects exposed to crowding in their residential environment exhibited better task performance and more positive affect in a laboratory situation than those with no crowding experience. On the other hand, Ruback, Carr, and Hopper (1986) observed that prison inmates from urban environments exhibited more crowding-related symptoms than those from rural environments. Similarly, Loo and Ong (1984) explored attitudes to crowding among residents of San Francisco's Chinatown and found no evidence that Chinese adapt to crowded conditions any better than the general public.

Baum and Gatchel (1981) explored the ways in which crowding effects develop over time. In a longitudinal study that compared student residents of dormitories characterized by a double-loaded corridor design with those living in a clustered design, the authors found that the former were less satisfied with their living arrangements, reported more problems with other students in the dorm, experienced more social withdrawal, had fewer friends, and were initially more competitive in a prisoner's dilemma game but exhibited increasing signs of signs of helplessness over time. Interestingly, residents in the long corridor design first attributed their problems to themselves; as the study progressed, however, they tended to blame factors in the environment. Moreover, the degree to which they blamed environmental factors predicted the degree to which they chose the withdrawal option (indicative of helplessness) in the prisoner's dilemma game.

Noise

Noise is defined unpleasant, bothersome sound that interferes with important activities or is believed to be physiologically harmful. While noise stress is partly function of loudness, at levels typically encountered in an urban setting other factors may be more important in creating stress effects. For example, conversation, because it is meaningful, has been shown to be particularly problematic for office workers, even though its absolute level is low. Along these same lines, noises that are novel, intermittent, or unpredictable tend to have the greatest impact on performance.

Effects of chronic exposure to noise include elevated urinary catecholamine levels, increased electrodermal activity, and higher blood pressure. Noise has also been linked to stress-related disorders such as ulcers and allergies (Weiss & Baum, 1987). In addition to these physiological effects, the literature describes a number of effects on cognitive task performance and social behavior. Complex tasks seem the most affected by noise, visual tasks and those requiring dexterity and coordinated movement, on the other hand, are not affected.

Nagar and Panady (1987) studied the combined effects of density and noise on cognitive task performance and affect using a 2×3 factorial design. As predicted, both crowding and noise led to a deterioration in task performance on complex but not on simple tasks. Density and noise also generated negative feelings in the subjects. Most interesting, however, were the observed interaction affects. Under low noise levels subjects in the low density situation did better on the complex task than those in the high density situation. However, under high noise levels their performance fell off substantially and approached that of the high density subjects who, significantly, did not exhibit much of a drop under high noise. The authors interpret this finding as evidence that once a particular level of arousal is reached, increases in arousal have no effect. Social effects of noise exposure include decreased helping behavior (Moser, 1988), decreased levels of informal social interaction (Cohen & Weinstein, 1982), reduced empathy (Sauser, Arauz, & Chambers, 1978), and increased sensitivity to crowding in men (Bell & Barnard, 1984).

A number of factors have been shown to mediate noise exposure. Topf (1989), for example, found that critical care nurses with a high degree of commitment to their role were less affected by noise than other nurses. Meanings associated with particular noises are also significant. Annoyance, for example, is more likely to result when people view the noise as serving no purpose or when it originates from a negatively valanced source. A study by Sorensen (cited in Cohen & Weinstein, 1982) observed that complaints about military aircraft noise decreased when local residents were given propaganda about the importance of a strong air defence system.

Two longitudinal studies looked at adaptation to noise over time and found no evidence of habituation. In a study of the effects of aircraft noise, Cohen and his colleagues (1986) found that distractibility, attitudes toward noise, and performance deficits persisted over time. Similarly, Weinstein (1982) found no evidence that persons exposed to noise from a new highway adapt to it over time. Subjects in his survey study reported the same level of annoyance at the noise and the same tendency to focus on it just after the highway opened and several months later when they were surveyed again.

Air Pollution

While evidence of the physiological effects of air pollution continues to mount, research into its psychological dimensions remains sparse (Evans & Cohen, 1987). Studies have shown that, while people may consider air pollution a problem if queried directly about it, they usually do not place it near the top of a list of general community problems. Even when asked about local health problems, few people mention air pollution explicitly. Public response to air pollution varies according to the nature of the pollution, its color and odor, the degree to which it causes eye irritation and respiratory problems, and the amount of damage it may do to property (Evans & Jacobs, 1982).

Much of the evidence about the psychological impacts of air pollution concerns the effects of carbon monoxide. In a number of studies, subjects exposed to elevated levels of this gas exhibited decreased performance on tasks requiring alert vigilance and also on those that were very boring. Mental health effects were also noted in two studies cited by Evans, Jacobs, Dooley, and Catalano (1987). Strahileritz and colleagues found a positive correlation between ambient levels of nitrogen dioxide and carbon monoxide and psychiatric admissions. Briere and colleagues found the same correlation in a study that looked at the overall pollution index and psychiatric admissions. More recently, Evans and his colleagues (1987) found that residents exposed to air pollution who had recently experienced a stressful life event exhibited poorer mental health than those who were just exposed to the pollution.

A recent study by Bullinger (1989) compared the psychological state, mental functioning, and physiological arousal of two groups of German women living in areas with different levels of air pollution. For two months, daily assessments of mood, stress, air quality, and annoyance reactions were obtained along with recordings of several air pollutants common to the region. Reaction time, ability to concentrate, urinary cortisol and catecholamine levels, blood pressure, and assessments of health status were obtained each week. At the end of the study, pollution levels at both sites were found to be relatively low. Even so, the group in the higher pollution area experienced a decreased ability to concentrate and impairment on the reaction time test. No physiological changes were noted. Interestingly, women in the polluted location spontaneously mentioned air pollution as a problem in their community and reported more distress because of it. Complaints centered around the perceptible features of the pollution, including odor and dust. In addition, the women attributed respiratory problems, tiredness, and impaired performance to exposure. Unfortunately there have been few similar studies with which to make comparisons.

Some studies have investigated the influence of air pollution on social interaction. For example, in laboratory studies, unpleasant odors have been shown to affect mood states and the evaluation of photographs and paintings. Another study found that subjects experiencing a moderate degree of unpleasant odor tended to administer more electrical shocks to confederates than either those experiencing very low odor or very high odor. A field study by Cunningham (cited in Evans & Jacobs, 1982), found that air pollution influenced helping behavior. In addition, the number of calls to the emergency operator tend to increase under polluted conditions. Little is known about how air pollution affects the daily lives of those exposed to it. One study by Rivlin (cited in Evans & Jacobs, 1982), for example, saw no decrease in the use of urban parks on high pollution days, whereas another study, by a different author, found a weak but significant negative relationship between ambient carbon monoxide levels and the use of outdoor recreation facilities.

Given the harmful effects known to result from physical exertion in polluted environments and the fact that outdoor recreational activities are essentially voluntary, the uncertain relationship between pollution and outdoor recreation suggests that perceptions of air pollution are mediated by other processes. Publicity about pollution and attitudes toward its source (e.g., if the polluter is a major employer in the community) probably play a role, as does adaptation. Evans, Jacobs, and Frager (1982) report on a study that looked at this last possibility. Their research into responses to pollution in Los Angeles found that long-term residents were less sensitive to photochemical smog, mentioned it less frequently as a community problem, suffered fewer respiratory problems, and felt themselves less vulnerable to it than recent immigrants to the city. New arrivals were also more likely to adopt instrumental coping strategies rather than palliative ones. These findings lend support to the notion that people adapt to air pollution, although why this is so remains an open question. Perhaps they view pollution as part of the ambient environment and, as such, perceive it to be outside of their control (cf., Campbell, 1983).

THE URBAN BUILT ENVIRONMENT

Way-finding and Spatial Orientation

Given their scale, heterogeneity, and complexity, cities present particular challenges to an individual's ability to move through them. The physical patterns that order the visual environment and make it imagible are usually different from city to city, often vary from neighborhood to neighborhood, and change over time. Even long-term residents of a city can become disoriented in an unfamiliar setting. Way-finding and spatial orientation refer to the behaviors and cognitive strategies individuals employ in navigating through the built environment. According to Lynch (1960), people tend to organize urban space according to the paths they follow through it, the nodes where these paths cross, the edges that define socially or physically distinct areas, and the memorable landmarks around which each of these elements is organized. Cities in which these features are clearly distinctive encourage effective way-finding by allowing residents and visitors to create accurate cognitive representations of their physical layout (Zimring, 1982).

To the extent that movement through a city is impeded because its layout is not readily legible, stress may result because personal goals are blocked (not to mention the anxiety that often accompanies being lost). It is interesting to note here the recursive interaction of environmental legibility and stress. While illegible environments may induce stress, stress makes reading an environment more difficult. Unfortunately research to date has treated stress as an outcome variable and has not looked at the ways in which it is implicated in its own manifestation.

Social Interaction

In four decades of work, ecological psychology (Barker, 1968; Schoggen, 1989; Wicker, 1987) has developed the idea that settings shape individual behavior and social interaction. If, as Altman (cited in Zimring, 1982) and others suggest, social relationships are a requirement of healthy functioning, then it is possible to establish another link between stress and the physical environment by way of interaction. Through social interaction individuals come to develop a sense of self (Mead, 1977), a feeling of affiliation with others, and the knowledge necessary for living in a meaningful world (Blumer, 1969). If the physical environment interferes with these processes, self-assessment and attachment to others is reduced and role identity becomes ambiguous. The need for social involvement, of course, varies from person to person and over time. Well designed environments take this into account by allowing individuals to control the level and the form of their interaction (Zimring, 1982). Bectel (cited in Zimring, 1982), for example, has suggested that informal social contacts may be encouraged in institutionalized settings by locating facilities such as lounges and lobbies in places where people naturally come in contact with one another. Such placement gives users an excuse for social interaction but does not require that they make a commitment to it.

COMMUTING

Stokols and Novaco's (1981) review of the literature on commuting notes several dimensions of the commuting experience that may lead to stress reactions. Automobile commuters are routinely exposed to traffic congestion (and its attendant effects on goal blocking), air pollution, noise, and heat. Users of public transportation are subject to stress effects arising from crowding (in particular as it relates to violations of personal space), noise, travel delays, and threats of victimization. Each of these elements has been implicated in stress reactions. For example, under conditions of traffic congestion, drivers have been shown to experience elevated blood pressure and urinary catecholamine levels, chest pains, cardiac arrhythmia, and changes in galvanic skin response characteristic of tension. Another study looking at the effects of noise and heat on subjects in a driving simulator found physiological, affective, and performance changes indicative of stress.

While there has been little research examining the effects of public transportation and stress, one study suggests several interesting areas for further work. Singer, Lundberg, and Frankenhauser (!978) looked at perceived crowding and urinary adrenaline and noradrenaline levels in two groups of Swedish commuters. Those in the first group boarded the Nynashamn-Stockholm train at its first stop and traveled for a total of 79 minutes. The second group boarded the same train at an intermediary stop and experienced a 43-minute trip. A comparison between the two groups yielded several interesting trends. First, both groups were able to consistently gauge the level of crowding on the train and both noted that it became more intense toward the end of the trip. Second, both groups displayed elevated levels of urinary adrenaline and noradrenaline. Most significant, however, was the finding that those experiencing the shorter commute had the biggest increases. Singer and his colleagues suggest that this is due to the decreased opportunity for environmental control this group experienced. Those who entered early could position themselves comfortably and arrange their personal effects as it suited them. The passengers who boarded later had fewer choices available, as seats were already taken and territories delimited. This study points out the importance of environmental control in general and, in particular, the ways in which it relates to commuting stress. Stokols and Novaco (1981), however, point out that the study fails to partial out variables that may covary with commuting distance, such as differences in residence.

Stokols and his colleagues (Stokols, Novaco, Stokols, & Campbell, 1978) studied the physiological, affective, and performance effects of automobile commuting on a group of one hundred commuters. Traffic congestion was defined in terms of travel impedance, which consisted of measures of distance and travel time. The authors' impedance construct was validated by their respondents, who exhibited higher levels of physiological arousal, performance decrements, and negative affect, although personality factors mediated these results. Novaco, Stokols, Campbell, and Stokols (1979), reporting on the same data, noted that subjects characterized by internal locus of control experienced higher stress levels than externals, although their task performance remained superior. This finding was attributed to the difficulty the internals had when experiencing situations they could not change.

Similar results were obtained by Schaeffer, Street, Singer, and Baum (1988). Their study, however, also attempted to explore the ways in which personal control mediates reactions to commuting stress. Results indicated that drivers who participated in a car pool, and thus had less control over the interior environment of the car, exhibited higher levels of stress than solo drivers. Curiously, drivers who had some choice over which route to take to work displayed higher levels of stress than those with no choice. The authors attribute this response to concern over the possibility of selecting the wrong route.

CRIME AND ENVIRONMENT

While crime rates have risen dramatically in recent years, individual crime victimization remains a relatively uncommon event. However, concern about crime has become such a prominent feature of urban life that many researchers have begun to conceptualize it separately from crime itself. The anxiety many people feel walking down a deserted street or contemplating a night ride on the subway is stressful in itself, but fear of victimization has a variety of other negative effects on quality of life. For example, fear of crime can limit individual mobility in the city. Such a restriction serves to hinder the realization of individual goals and to limit participation in the social and economic activities that make urban living worthwhile. For example, in a recent study (Graig, 1990), residents of a New York City neighborhood stated that fear of crime had led them to reduce the informal evening social interaction that helped integrate the community in the past. Several approaches have been taken to explain this concern about victimization.

Under conditions of uncertainty, individuals have been shown to rely on rules of thumb for evaluating the risks they encounter in everyday life (Tversky & Kahneman, 1974). Fear of crime may arise from a number of factors, including past victimization, vulnerability, and the presence of social and physical incivilities such as graffiti, vacant buildings, litter, or the presence of street people. Rohe and Burby (1988) tested which of these factors was most significant to a sample of housing project residents. While their research lends qualified support to all three models, the incivilities approach was found to possess the greatest predictive power. Riger (1985) adds to this appraisal model the idea that fear is also rooted in expectations about the victimization experience. She also points out that appraisal varies over time, even if environmental conditions are held constant. A particularly violent crime or crime spree may lead individuals to view an unchanged physical environment differently.

Similarly, appraisals of neighborhood safety are dependent upon personal factors such as past history of victimization, vulnerability, familiarity with the environment, and knowledge of behaviors likely to lessen the chances of victimization.

Taylor (1987) states that residents read incivilities as indications of the breakdown in social control in a neighborhood; they stand as testimony to the collapse of the social order and to a pervasive normlessness that may be stressful in itself. Criminals also rely on such cues in selecting locations for their activities (D'Alessio & Stolzenberg, 1990). Explanation of these effects can be found in work by Rapoport (cited in Taylor, 1982), who argues that territorial markers in the physical environment communicate nonverbal messages to both insiders and outsiders about control in the neighborhood. Markers may include features such as fencing and well-kept streets, although certain forms of street activity (a block party, for example) may serve a similar function. If changes occur in a neighborhood that affect the presence or legibility of these markers, they cease to function as indicators of ownership and territoriality and the physical environment instead broadcasts a mesage of decay. This in turn exacerbates the problem by causing further abandonment and deterioration.

Newman's (1973) work on the concept of defensible space addresses the role that design can play in reducing criminal activity. Several of the strategies he proposes are also likely to reduce fear. According to Newman, environments that are easy to monitor and that establish natural territorial markers (and hence personal identification) are less likely to the target of criminal activity than environments lacking these features. Although there have been a number of criticisms of Newman's work, many of his recommendations have been found to reduce criminal behavior in a variety of settings. For example, Sommer (1987) found that college residence halls designed with defensible space in mind were found to have substantially lower rates of crime and vandalism than those with poor defensible space. In another study, Brown and Altman (cited in Taylor, 1987) compared burglarized and nonburglarized homes in a suburban setting and observed that the nonburglarized homes possessed more territorial markers.

This research brings up a larger question about the stress that results from the interpretation of physical conditions. Unlike a noisy neighborhood, there is nothing inherently stressful about a dilapidated one. Noise, though it is partially mediated by social and personality processes, is by definition essentially physical. It touches the individual directly. Physical incivilities, on the other hand, do not produce stress in the same way. Their effect is wholly through the action of an interpretive process. Stress reactions that arise from incivilities are entirely social constructions based on a reading of the physical environment by knowledgable individuals. This statement is not to suggest that such readings are necessarily inaccurate but simply that they are interpretations that may or may not be verifiable. The point here is that the environment is implicated in stress reactions not only to the extent that it is a source of unwanted stimulation but also because it is a source of meanings that may, in and of themselves, be stressful.

OFFICE ENVIRONMENTS

The importance of office environments is often neglected in research on urban life. Kleeman (1988) notes that office workers are vulnerable to a number of different work-related health problems, including musculoskeletal problems, vision problems, and the possible effects of ionizing radiation. In addition to these hazards, office workers may be affected by the electromagnetic fields emanating from video display terminals, indoor air pollution, and the effects of the office microclimate. For example, Wineman (1982a, 1982b) notes that inadequate ventilation can lead to depletions in oxygen level, which in turn can cause headaches, fatigue, and an inability to concentrate. Three recent reviews of this literature (Sundstrom, 1987; Wineman, 1982a, 1982b) and a survey study by Klitzman and Stellman (1989) outline some of the factors that may be related to performance, satisfaction, and psychological stress in office settings. These parameters include aspects of the visual, aural, and interpersonal environments.

Lighting is implicated in the stress process to the degree that it affects accuracy and productivity in office tasks. Inappropriate lighting levels may make work more difficult and interfere with its completion. In addition to lighting level, quality of light may also be important. Office workers have been shown to prefer natural light, although in urban settings this type of illumination is the most difficult to provide. In addition to offering natural light, offices with views to the outside may decrease crowding stress. Office sound levels also play a role in task performance and productivity. More important than absolute sound level is the source of the sound. For example, conversation, because it is meaningful to others, it the most frequently mentioned source of annoyance by office workers. For this reason, a certain level of background noise may be desirable to mask out more distracting sounds. Office productivity is also influenced by the physical flow of work through the environment. If the design makes it difficult to bring people and other inputs to a task together, individual and group goals may become blocked and cause stress reactions.

Visual privacy is another aspect of the office that may affect stress. A lack of visual privacy may be stressful to the extent that it causes individuals to allocate resources toward maintaining appearances, which in turn leaves less attention available for task performance. Goffman's (1959) notion of front and back regions provides an interesting way to view this question. According to Goffman, all social presentations require a certain degree subterfuge or stage management. In order for actors to prepare these subterfuges, they require "back regions" out of the view of their audience. It seems probable that monitoring of such regions and the normally hidden preparatory activities that take place within them could bring about a stress reaction. Not surprisingly, Block and Stokes (1989) found that office workers prefer private offices to open-plan designs, especially when working on complex tasks.

Offices, of course, are designed not only to maximize productivity but also to communicate a variety of symbolic messages to workers and the general public. The relationship between symbolism in the urban environment and stress reactions is considered elsewhere in this chapter.

ENVIRONMENTAL MEANING

Thus far, this review has looked at some of the ways in which the urban environment may create *physical* situations which are stressful to human beings. Another aspect of urban stress that the literature has not explicitly addressed concerns the urban environment's role as a transmitter of meaningful symbolic messages that may, separate from any physical effects, lead to stress reactions. Physical features play a role in mediating social relationships in a neighborhood and affect the collective identify of those who live in it (Graig, 1990; Taylor, 1982). To the extent that the environment establishes a detrimental identity, stress may result.

The notion that environments are readily interpretable has been established by a number of studies. Sadalla, Vershure, and Burroughs (1987), for example, found that people are able to infer a homeowner's self-concept from the way that person has arranged the physical environment of the home. Similarly, Nasar (1989) found that lay people interpret architectural symbols in remarkably similar ways. Both studies suggest that architecture is read almost like a language by lay people, who use it to understand and to communicate meaning.

Shumaker and Reizenstein (1982) developed a conceptualization of the hospital that pays close attention to the role of symbolism in mediating stress reactions. They state that design communicates messages to patients about their relative position in the setting and the degree to which their needs are viewed as important. Both messages may influence the degree to which patients become involved in their treatment as well as its outcome. Of particular interest is the notion that aspects of design can contribute to patients' feelings of efficacy in the environment. Messages about the relative power of different users in an environment are communicated through the allocation of space, the quality of space, and the way it is maintained. For example, hospitals that provide a large lounge area for nurses but fail to provide one for patients communicate a message about the relative importance of the two groups.

Such effects, of course, are not limited to hospital environments. Wineman (1982a) states that the amount and the location of space granted to particular users in an office indicates their status in the organization. One does not have to speculate very far to extend these conclusions to larger-scale environments such as residences or even whole neighborhoods. Once again the idea is that the urban physical environment is not merely physical but also meaningful. To the extent that human beings may be stressed by the meanings they encounter, it will be fruitful to study the messages urban physical environments transmit, the ways in which those messages are interpreted, and the stresses that may arise from them. To date few researchers have considered this question explicitly from the standpoint of stress.

CONCLUSION

Environmental stress research has, in the last decade, shifted attention away from the simple enumeration of stress sources, toward an examination of person and environment factors which mediate the stress response. Increasingly, this research has moved out of the laboratory and into field settings where stressors can be studied as they actually exist and interact. Most research however, remains focused on sources of physically measurable stress—noise, crowding, air pollution—and typically considers such sources in isolation from one another. There are of course, substantial methodological problems to overcome in moving stress research in a different direction, particularly where researchers are interested in the interaction of stressors in naturally occurring environments. The concept of urban press, introduced earlier, represents one attempt to at least conceptualize this interaction.

Stress which results from the meaningful aspects of the urban physical and social environment has also received scant attention. The question of meaning enters into research on urban stress in two ways. First, the appraisal of noxious physical stimuli (e.g., noise, mal odor) and the resources available to cope with them are based, at least in part, upon inferences about the likely effects of those stimuli. These inferences are based on knowledge about the total environment which in turn is based on the meanings which are ascribed to different objects in that environment. Second, and perhaps more interesting, is stress that results from an individual's "reading" of the environment. As I have noted, such stress may be related to fear of crime, fear of strangers, or simply fear of being lost in an unfamiliar section of town. The urban physical and social environment may also encode messages about social position which give rise to (or ameliorate) feelings of helplessness and their attendant stress reactions. Again, although these types of questions are difficult to address in empirical research they are no less real than physical stressors such as noise.

As the study of stress begins to move outside the laboratory, these sorts of questions will become more readily apparent to researchers confronted with real world settings. It is important, however, that we begin addressing them conceptually and theoretically even as we grapple with them empirically.

REFERENCES

BARKER, R. *Ecological psychology: Concepts and methods for studying the environment of human behavior.* Stanford, CA: Stanford University Press, 1968.

BAUM, A., & GATCHEL, R. Cognitive determinants of reaction to uncontrollable events. *Journal of Personality and Social Psychology,* 1981, *40,* 1078–1089.

BELL, P., & BARNARD, W. Effects of heat and noise and sex of subject on a projective measure of personal space permeability. *Perceptual and Motor Skills,* 1984, *59,* 442.

BLOCK, L., & STOKES, G. Performance and satisfaction in private versus non-private work settings. *Environment and Behavior,* 1989, *21,* 277–297.

BLUMER, H. *Symbolic interactionism.* Englewood Cliffs, NJ: Prentice-Hall, 1969.

BROADBENT, D. *Decision and stress.* New York: Academic Press, 1971.

BRONFENBRENNER, U. *The ecology of human development: Experiments by nature and design.* Cambridge, MA: Harvard University Press, 1979.

BULLINGER, M. Psychological effects of air pollution on healthy residents: A time series approach. *Journal of Environmental Psychology,* 1989, *9,* 103–118.

CAMPBELL, J. Ambient stressors. *Environment and Behavior,* 1983, *15,* 355–380.

COHEN, S. Cognitive processes as determinants of environmental stress. Social issue: Stress and anxiety. *Issues in Mental Health Nursing,* 1985, *7,* 65–81.

COHEN, S., EVANS, G., STOKOLS, D., & KRANTZ, D *Behavior, health, and environmental stress.* New York: Plenum Press, 1986.

COHEN, S., & WEINSTEIN, N. Nonauditory effects of noise on behavior and health. In G. Evans (ed.), *Environmental stress.* New York: Cambridge University Press, 1982.

D'ALESSIO, S., & STOLZENBERG, L. A crime of convenience: The environment and convenience store robbery. *Environment and Behavior,* 1990, *22,* 255–271.

DELONGIS, A., COYNE, J., DAKOF, G., FOLKMAN, S., & LAZARUS, R. Relationship of daily hassles, uplifts, and major life events to health status. *Health Psychology,* 1982, *1,* 119–136.

EPSTEIN, Y. Crowding stress and human behavior. In G. Evans (ed.), *Environmental stress.* New York: Cambridge University Press, 1982.

EVANS, G. General introduction. In G. Evans (ed.), *Environmental stress.* New York: Cambridge University Press, 1982.

EVANS, G., & COHEN, S. Environmental stress. In D. Stokols & I. Altman (eds.), *The handbook of environmental psychology.* New York: Wiley, 1987.

EVANS, G., & JACOBS, S. Air pollution and human behavior. In G. Evans. (ed.), *Environmental stress*. New York: Cambridge University Press, 1982.

EVANS, G., JACOBS, S., DOOLEY, D., & CATALANO, R. The interaction of stressful life events and chronic strains on community mental health. *American Journal of Community Psychology*, 1987, *15*, 23-34.

EVANS, G., JACOBS, S., & FRAGER, N. Behavioral responses to air pollution. In A. Baum & J. Singer (eds.), *Environment and health*. Hillsdale, NJ: Lawrence Erlbaum, 1982.

FLEMING, I., BAUM, A., DAVIDSON, L., & RECTANUS, E. Chronic stress as a factor in physiologic reactivity to challenge. *Health Psychology*, 1987, *6*, 221-237.

FLEMING, R., BAUM, A., & SINGER, J. Towards an integrative approach to the study of stress. *Journal of Personality and Social Psychology*, 1984, *46*, 939-949.

FLEMING, I., BAUM, A., & WEISS, L. Social density and perceived control as mediators of crowding stress in high-density residential neighborhoods. *Journal of Personality and Social Psychology*, 1987, *52*, 889-906.

FOLKMAN, S. Personal control and stress and coping process: A theoretical analysis. *Journal of Personality and Social Psychology*, 1984, *46*, 839-852.

GOFFMAN, E. *The presentation of self in everyday life*. New York: Anchor Books, 1959.

GRAIG, E. *Social interaction, social reproduction and the making of place in an urban religious grotto*. Master's thesis, the Graduate School and University Center of The City University of New York, 1990.

HAYDUK, L. Personal space: Where we now stand. *Psychological Bulletin*, 1983, *94*, 293-335.

KLEEMAN, W. The politics of office design. *Environment and Behavior*, 1988, *20*, 537-549.

KLITZMAN, S., & STELLMAN, J. The impact of the physical environment on the psychological well-being of office workers. *Social Science and Medicine*, 1989, *29*, 733-742.

LOO, C., & ONG, P. Crowding perception, attitudes, and consequences among the Chinese. *Environment and Behavior*, 1984, *16*, 55-87.

LYNCH, K. *The image of the city*. Cambridge, MA: MIT Press, 1960.

MEAD, G. H. *On social psychology*. Chicago: University of Chicago Press, 1977.

MERRY, S. E. Crowding, conflict and neighborhood regulation. In I. Altman & A. Wandersman (eds.), *Neighborhood and community environments*. New York: Plenum Press, 1987.

MOSER, G. Urban stress and helping behavior: Effects of environmental overload and noise on behavior. *Journal of Environmental Psychology*, 1988, *8*, 287-298.

NAGAR, D., & PANADY, J. Affect and performance on cognitive task as a function of crowding and noise. *Journal of Applied Social Psychology*, 1987, *17*, 147-157.

NASAR, J. Symbolic meanings of house styles. *Environment and Behavior*, 1989, *21*, 235-257.

NEWMAN, O. *Defensible space*. New York: Macmillan, 1973.

NOVACO, R., STOKOLS, D., CAMPBELL, D., & STOKOLS, J. Transportation, stress and community psychology. *American Journal of Community Psychology*, 1979, *7*, 361-380.

RIGER, S. Crime as an environmental stressor. *Journal of Community Psychology*, 1985, *13*, 270-280.

ROHE, W., & BURBY, R. Fear of crime in public housing. *Environment and Behavior*, 1988, *20*, 700-720.

RUBACK, B., CARR, T., & HOPPER, C. Perceived control in prison: Its relation to reported crowding, stress, and symptoms. *Journal of Applied Social Psychology*, 1986, *16*, 375-386.

SADALLA, E., VERSHURE, B., & BURROUGHS, J. Identity symbolism in housing. *Environment and Behavior*, 1987, *19*, 569-587.

SAUSER, W., ARAUZ, C., & CHAMBERS, R. Exploring the relationship between level of office noise and salary recommendations: A preliminary research note. *Journal of Management,* 1978, *4,* 57–63.

SCHAEFFER, M., BAUM, A., PAULUS, P., & GAES, G. Architecturally mediated effects of social density in prison. *Environment and Behavior,* 1988, *20,* 3–19.

SCHAEFFER, M., STREET, S., SINGER, J., & BAUM, A. Effects of control on the stress reactions of commuters. *Journal of Applied Social Psychology,* 1988, *18,* 944–957.

SCHOGGEN, P. *Behavior settings: A revision and extension of Roger Barker's ecological psychology.* Stanford, CA: Stanford University Press, 1989.

SHULTZ-GAMBARD, J., FEIERABEND, C., & HOMMEL, B The experience of crowding in real life environments: An action oriented approach. In D. Canter, J. C. Jesuino, L. Soczka, & G. Stephenson (eds.), *Environmental social psychology.* Dordrecht, Neth.: Kluwer Academic Publishers, 1988.

SHUMAKER, S., & REIZENSTEIN, J. Environmental factors affecting in patient stress in an acute care hospital. In G. Evans. (ed.), *Environmental stress.* New York: Cambridge University Press, 1982.

SINGER, J., LUNDBERG, U., & FRANKENHAEUSER, M. Stress on the train: A study of urban commuting. In A. Baum, J. Singer, & S. Valins (eds.), *Advances in environmental psychology.* Hillsdale, NJ: Lawrence Erlbaum, 1978.

SOMMER, R. Crime and vandalism in university residence halls: A confirmation of defensible space theory. *Journal of Environmental Psychology,* 1987, *7,* 1–12.

STOKOLS, D., & NOVACO, R. Transportation and well-being: An ecological perspective. *Human Behavior and Environment Advances in Theory and Research,* 1981, *5,* 85–130.

STOKOLS, D., NOVACO, R., STOKOLS, J., & CAMPBELL, J. Traffic congestion, type A behavior and stress. *Journal of Applied Psychology,* 1978, *63,* 467–480.

SUEDFELD, P. Stressful levels of environmental stimulation. Special issue: Stress and anxiety. *Issues in Mental Health Nursing,* 1985, *7,* 83–104.

SUNDSTROM, Work and office environments. In D. Stokols & I. Altman (eds.), *Handbook of environmental psychology.* New York: Wiley, 1987.

TAYLOR, R. Neighborhood physical environment and stress. In G. Evans (ed.), *Environmental stress.* New York: Cambridge University Press, 1982.

————. Toward an environmental psychology of disorder: Delinquency, crime, and fear of crime. In D. Stokols & I. Altman (eds.), *The handbook of environmental psychology.* New York: Wiley, 1987.

TOPF, M. Sensitivity to noise, personal hardiness and noise induced stress in critical care nurses. *Environment and Behavior,* 1989, *21,* 717–733.

TVERSKY, A., & KAHNEMAN, D. Judgements under uncertainty: Heuristics and biases. *Science,* 1974, 1985, 1124–1131.

VINE, I. Crowding and stress: A personal space approach. *Current Psychological Reviews,* 1982, *2,* 1–18.

WEINSTEIN, N. Community noise problems: Evidence against adaptation. *Journal of Environmental Psychology,* 1982, *2,* 87–97.

WEISS, L., & BAUM, A. Physiological aspects of environment-behavior relationships. In E. Zube & G. Morre, *Advances in environmental Psychology,* Vol. 1. New York: Plenum Press, 1987.

WESTOVER, T. Perceived crowding in recreation settings: An environment-behavior model. *Environment and Behavior,* 1989, *21,* 258–276.

WICKER, A. Behavior setting reconsidered: Temporal stages, resources, internal dynamics, context. In D. Stokols & I. Altman (eds.), *Handbook of environmental psychology.* New York: Wiley, 1987.

WINEMAN, J. *The office environment as a source of stress. In G. Evans (ed.), Environmental stress.* New York: Cambridge University Press, 1982. (a)

————. Office design and evaluation. *Environment and Behavior,* 1982, *14,* 271–298.

ZIMRING, C. The built environment as a source of psychological stress: Impacts of buildings and cities on satisfaction and behavior. In G. Evans (ed.), *Environmental stress.* New York: Cambridge University Press, 1982.

18

Sensory Deprivation and Overload

Leo Goldberger

SENSORY DEPRIVATION and sensory overload are topics that appear to have found a permanent place in the literature as environmental sources of stress, that is, as external, physical stressors. This chapter presents a succinct and largely retrospective overview of sensory deprivation and, to a lesser extent, sensory overload research and highlights the substantive yield of knowledge in an area that has been characterized by a morass of misinformation, exaggeration, and confounding of variables. It should be noted at the outset that my focus will be the identification of effects, whether stressful or not, attributable primarily to either sensory restriction or excessive stimulation. Such obviously stressful situations as imprisonment, solitary confinement, being cast adrift, or experiencing urban noise and overcrowding—in which sensory deprivation or sensory overload per se are aspects or components but certainly not the most salient determinants—will be ignored in this overview. Experimentally induced sensory deprivation and sensory overload may indeed be experienced by many subjects as stressful, but these laboratory situations may also be experienced as tolerable and even pleasurable. The wide range of responses largely reflects mediation by cultural and individual differences (see Suedfeld, 1980, for a discussion of nonstressful response to sensory deprivation).

SENSORY DEPRIVATION

Even before the publication of the first findings on the "effects of decreased variation in the sensory environment" (Bexton, Heron, & Scott, 1954), word had spread about experiments at McGill University (conceived of by Hebb and his students) in which college student subjects, kept isolated and deprived of perceptual experiences, experienced vivid hallucinations, body image disturbances, and thought disorders. The first published report captured the imagination of psychiatric and psychological researchers, who quickly put together their own experimental setups (soundproofed rooms, respirators, or water tanks) to probe this area themselves. These early investigators—Lilly, Vernon, Solomon, Azima, Goldberger and Holt, Silverman, Cohen, Ruff, Freedman, and a handful of others—were essentially exploring the range and limits of this new experimental technique. Soon both the specialized journals and the popular press were filled with discussions of perceptual isolation and sensory or stimulus deprivation; reviews of anecdotal data appeared (C. Brownfield, 1965); and in 1958 the first symposium was organized bringing together the initial group of investigators (Solomon, Kubzansky, Leiderman, Mendelson, & Wexler, 1961). A new field had been born.

The widespread fascination with sensory deprivation in part reflected to the original tie-in with "brainwashing"—a timely subject in the early 1950s. This interest also had relevance to another popular concern, the Mercury space program, which included sensory deprivation among the stress procedures used to screen potential astronauts. But perhaps even more fundamental was the fact that on the face of it, here was a manipulation that made a *real difference*. To be able to induce major behavioral and physiological changes by psychological means was indeed worthy of attention. To induce a phenomenon experimentally is to get close to understanding its cause. Such was the promise held out by early research on sensory deprivation.

The field reached its peak in the 1960s, during which period increasingly more sophisticated and ingeniously controlled studies were being conducted, notably by Zubek, Zuckerman, Suedfeld, and Myers—all among the contributors to perhaps the most authoritative volume in the area, edited by Zubek (1969), which critically reviewed and summed up the field and included a bibliography of some 1300 items.

Methods

Sensory deprivation is the generic term for a variety of complex experimental conditions (frequently quite stressful) aimed at drastically reducing the level and variability of a person's normal stimulation from, and commerce with, his environment for a relatively prolonged period of time.

The original aim of sensory deprivation research was to determine the effects on human functioning of a drastic curtailment of sensory stimulation. The approach paralleled that used in animal experiments: human beings were placed in laboratory settings of three basic types: bed confinement in a sound attenuated or soundproofed room, confinement in a tank type respirator, or suspension in a water tank. The salient experimental variable was presumed to be a reduction of environmental stimulation—in either the variety or the amount of sensory input (as it turns out, the oft made conceptual distinction between perceptual isolation and sensory deprivation proper has only little empirical significance).

Typically, subjects were used either in short-term studies, as in the water immersion studies (up to 8 hours), or in long-term experiments, in which a 72-hour stretch was fairly characteristic, though in some cases as much as a week was used. The basic experimental paradigm called for baseline testing on a variety of psychological and physiological measures, with periodic testing during the study (usually via intercommunication arrangements) and a posttesting session. Subjects in the long-term studies generally were able to go to the toilet and to feed themselves, thus making any social contact unnecessary, except via the intercommunication system for emergency purposes, for periodic, self-regulated, subjective reports on thoughts and feelings, and for testing. The standardized, 242-item Isolation Symptom Questionnaire (Myers & Zubek, 1969) was increasingly used.

The original research aim met with obstacles from a variety of methodological sources, so that interpretation of findings was difficult. It was nearly impossible to control for each of the many potentially relevant parameters inherent in the complex of conditions. Among the variables found to affect and confound the interpretation of experimental results were type of confinement, instructions, duration, restriction of movement, expectations, and the everpresent variable of personality. And because each laboratory used its own experimental setup and its own procedures for assessing effects, comparability of data suffered. Effects originally ascribed to sensory reduction might in fact have been caused by any number of other variables, singly or in combination. Moreover, experience taught most investigators that another very troublesome obstacle to unambiguous findings lay in the fact that a subject undergoing sensory deprivation is in a totally altered life situation, which affects his defenses, fantasies, motivations, and cognitive and interpersonal stratagems.

Findings

In view of both the inherent methodological problems and the procedural differences marking the sensory deprivation field, it is surprising that any enduring, replicable, and meaningful findings emerged. But the bulk of the evidence gathered since the McGill report (Bexton, Heron, & Scott, 1954) does support the original claims, albeit with some qualifications necessitated by the additional specification of the variables responsible for the effects. To summarize briefly, it is still valid to assert that sensory deprivation induces an altered state of consciousness that is characterized

1. *neurologically* by a progressive slowing in mean alpha frequency and by the appearance of marked delta—and, in long-term studies, also of excessive theta—wave activity, especially in the temporal lobes;
2. *autonomically* by a decrease in skin resistance (i.e., increased arousal), though by no other consistent autonomic differences (e.g., in heart rate, respiration, temperature, blood pressure, metabolic rate);
3. *biochemically* by no consistent findings in urinary levels of oxycorticoids and catecholamines (except for subjects in the respirator setup), but by certain individual differences between "stayers" and "quitters" in pre-isolation levels of adrenaline and serum uric acid, as well as in urine excreted during deprivation. The evidence suggests, however, that the *major sources of stress* inhere in the *confinement, social isolation,* and *physical immobility* aspects of the total experimental situation rather than in sensory restriction per se;
4. *psychologically* by boredom, apathy, and a state of motivational loss, which in the realm of thought processes takes the form of mind wandering, reverie, and fantasy activity interspersed with periods of sleep and attendant hypnogogic and hypnopomic phenomena. Subjective reports of attention and concentration deficits and of impairment in the maintenance of logical, directed thinking receive support from objective cognitive test findings, with deficits revealed only on tasks requiring complex, self-directed efforts. Rote learning, simple digit-span performance, and memory for meaningful material, however, tend to be facilitated!

Most investigators have strongly cautioned against linking the phenomena subsumed under the generic label "hallucinatory activity"—vividly projected images, varying in content, complexity, and origin, rendered primarily in the visual mode and occurring most frequently during high to medium arousal—to hallucinations observed in the psychoses. Rather, these phenomena appear more akin to those found in certain drug induced hallucinatory states, albeit not as vivid, colorful, or persistent (Goldberger & Holt, 1958; Zubek, 1969).

Certain sensory effects, such as lowered thresholds and increased acuity, are a consistent concomitant of sensory deprivation, which is in keeping with the general sensitivity to minimal and residual stimulation and the stimulus hunger that subjects characteristically show.

Another consistent finding in relation to stress has been that about one-third of all subjects in sensory deprivation experiments quit before the official termination of the experimental run—no matter how long the scheduled duration. Individual differences have loomed large in regard not only to endurance to sensory deprivation but also to most other effect measures, but they have not been readily reducible to personality variables. In large part, this reflects the multidimensional nature of the total experimental situation. With systematic fractionation, each situational parameter or dimension would be found to have a special linkage to a set of personality characteristics. Effects such as anxiety and anger, for example, are clearly attributable to the extraneous and most stressful aspects of the situation, such as confinement, enforced passivity, and social isolation, and could be expected to relate to personality variables quite different from those linked to tolerance for the curtailment of external stimulation. Nevertheless, such personal characteristics as overall ego strength, tolerance for primary-process ideation, field dependence-independence, and sensation seeking needs have been consistently identified as meaningful individual difference correlates (Goldberger, 1961; Goldberger & Holt, 1961; Zuckerman, 1974).

Theoretical Formulations

The theoretical context of sensory deprivation studies has naturally varied in accordance with the special interest and focus of the investigator. Though the various theoretical constructs employed are by no means incompatible with one another, they derive from three different levels of behavior analysis: neurophysiological, psychoanalytic, and psychological.

The neurophysiological perspective was introduced by Hebb (1955), who saw in these experiments a way of clarifying sensory-cortical interaction. Within this formulation, repetitive, homogeneous, or drastically reduced stimulation is seen as causing the diffuse projection system of the *reticular formation*—the neurological system deemed essential for arousal and organized cortical activity—to become habituated. When this occurs, cortical functioning becomes disorganized and synchronous firing of cells takes place. The sensory deprivation effects are thus interpreted as a reflection of a general *habituation syndrome*.

From the psychoanalytic viewpoint, an intimate relationship between mode of thought and the presence or absence of reality contact is postulated (Rapaport, 1958). With diminished reality contact (as in sensory deprivation or sleep), a shift from the *secondary-process* (logical, realistic) to the *primary-process* (drive organized, developmentally primitive) mode takes place.

In the main, the psychological theories have involved a broad cognitive perspective in which constructs derived from information processing theory play a central role, along with a general social-psychological approach in which the key concepts revolve around the role of the subject's expectations and the demand characteristics of the situation. A narrower and more specialized conception posits a specific drive for sensory variation, termed *sensoristatis* (Schultz, 1965), and suggests that each person has an optimal level of arousal that is determined by a number of confluent factors, including constitution, age, learning, recent level of stimulation, task demands, and diurnal cycling.

Applications

One cannot help but be impressed by the many-sidedness of the sensory deprivation field. The range of topics, ideas, and foci in the literature is staggering. Though it is easy to criticize so-called method oriented research, it must be remembered that methods do legitimately open doors to the investigation of a variety of problems other than the ones to which they are first applied. Sensory deprivation is a powerful technique—a life-sized, temporally extended, projective test that calls for a real adaptive response rather than simply a test response. For many researchers this avenue of study has led not only to stress (i.e., Zuckerman, 1964) but also to personality, ego autonomy, response to unstructured situations (Goldberger, 1961), suggestibility, sensitivity to internal cues, stimulus seeking behavior, temporal orientation (see Zubek, 1965), clinical problems (e.g., the effects of post–eye surgery patching (Ziskind, 1965), and therapeutic application (Cooper, Adams, & Cohen, 1964). It has permitted exploration of the social psychology of the psychological experiment (Orne & Scheibe, 1964). It has brought within the sphere of the laboratory analogues of a number of real-life problems—space flight, work under arctic weather conditions, small-group confinement, monotony in assembly line jobs, long-distance truck driving, and geographic or social isolation in natural settings (Rasmussen, 1973). And it has required behavioral researchers at least to acknowledge such cognitive or phenomenological notions as purpose, meaning, doing, structure, and states of consciousness, along with such poorly understood phenomena as boredom, encapsulation, and sense of isolation.

SENSORY OVERLOAD

The concept of *sensory overload* (sensory overstimulation) designates a situation in which the organism is bombarded by higher than normal levels of sensory stimulation, usually in more than one sensory modality. It is the obverse of sensory deprivation (sensory underload) and is similarly classed as a potential stressor.

Considering the implications of sensory overload research for the comon experience of overstimulation in today's technologically advanced society, it is surprising that there has been only a handful of experimental studies on the effects of overload, in contrast to the large number of sensory deprivation studies (Zubek, 1969). Would-be investigators may be discouraged by the operational specification of stimulation as excessive and the frequently added definitional requirement that the stimulation be sudden and unpredictable, not to mention the methodological problems inherent in separating the attributes of diversity, instability, novelty, complexity, and meaningfulness of stimulation.

Despite the meager data base, references abound to the maladaptive effects of sensory overload, running the gamut of psychopathology from schizophrenic and organiclike symptoms to phenomena associated with so-called psychedelic states. Perhaps the most dramatic view of the consequences now broadly attributed to overstimulation is afforded by Toffler's (1970) *Future Shock,* in which the additional notions of *information overload* and *decision stress* are treated as sharing essential characteristics with sensory overload. Information overload, a concept introduced in 1959 by Miller (1964), is intimately connected with sensory overload: sensory input is usually also the conveyor of symbolic meaning (i.e., information). Nonetheless, the two concepts may be conceptually and operationally distinguished. Lipowsky (1975) placed still other areas within the orbit of sensory overload, such as field studies of urban life and experimental studies on the effects of crowding, population density, and noise. Lipowsky argued that sensory and informational overloads are vitally important concepts that have far-reaching implications for the psychological and physical well-being of man. A number of authors, among them McReynolds (1960) and Silverman (1972), have also seen sensory overload as a relevant construct for the understanding of schizophrenia. Finally, Spitz (1964), in discussing experiments by Calhoun (1962) that showed the deleterious effects of crowding and overstimulation on rats, extrapolated to clinical observations on infants who suffered emotional overload associated with the "wrong kind of mothering," "undisciplined parental behavior," and other excessive stimulation; he suggested the relevance of sensory overload to developmental disorders.

Theoretical Formulations

The scientific interest in sensory overload may be traced to Lindsley's (1961) proposal that the conditions of sensory overload, sensory underload, and sensory distortion have a common neurophysiological mechanism, namely, the ascending reticular formation. Lindsley viewed the ascending reticular formation as a barometer for both sensory input and sensory output; a homeostatic regulator of input-output relations that is subject to an adaptation level. Any deviation from the established level upsets the balance of the regulating system, resulting in a variety of disturbances. Specifically addressing the condition of overstimulation of two or more sense modalities (especially if there is a sudden and intense input from afferent and corticofugal sources), Lindsley noted that "blocking of the reticular formation may occur and behavioral immobilization and general confusion may result" (p. 176).

A number of related conceptions and theoretical elaborations have been introduced that have a bearing on sensory overload. Hebb (1955) proposed a homeostatic theory that views the organism as acting so as to produce an optimal level of excitation. Berlyne (1960) ascribed drive inducing properties to deviations from an optimum influx of arousal potential. Malmo (1959) and many others have written extensively about the notion of a general activation level, which in turn has been related to external sensory input and the inverted U-curve formulation: under conditions of excessive sensory input, a correspondingly high activation level will ensue, resulting in impaired performance across a variety of tasks. Mention should also be made of concepts that emphasize the organism's limited capacity to deal with a massive sensory influx: Freud's "protective barrier against stimulation" (Freud, 1922) (frequently viewed as a developmental precursor of the classic defense mechanisms); Pavlov's (1955) "protective inhibition" concept; and the "filter theory of attention," associated with Broadbent's (1958, 1971) work. Aside from speculating about defective filter mechanisms, or a "thin stimulus barrier" (Bergman & Escalona, 1969), some investigators have invoked various conceptions of cognitive control and stylistic or protective strategies as heuristic explanations for observed individual differences in habitual sensitivity and response to extreme stimulation (see for example, Silverman's [1964] work on scanning; Haer's [1971] on field dependence; and Petrie's [1967] on the augmenting-reducing dimension).

Experimental Studies

The experimental studies that have been conducted on sensory overload (Gottschalk, Haer, & Bates, 1972; Haer, 1970, 1971; Ludwig, 1971, 1972, 1973), including a series of experiments at Tohuku University in Japan and a few other investigations (see Lipowsky, 1975), have all been of short duration, averaging some 2.5 hours, in contrast to the fairly long runs characteristic of deprivation studies. This fact may in itself be a reflection of the greater aversiveness of the sensory overload condition. Most of the studies have aimed quite specifically at inducing an altered state of consciousness (or psychedelic state) by whatever psychological means seemed most promising and potent. This aim is apparent in the techniques used and, because of the obvious demand characteristics in Orne's (1962) sense, may have exerted a strong influence on subjects' responses.

Essentially, the procedure involves confining a subject in a so-called sensory overload chamber—a total sensory environment like a geodesic dome (10 feet in diameter)—in which the subject is surrounded by and immersed in visual and auditory input. Typically, the subject reclines comfortably on a carpeted floor; a 16mm movie projector displays films of various kinds (abstract, colored designs); electronic music or cacophonous sounds blare from all directions; and intense and changing colored illumination is provided. The experimental paradigm usually calls for the stimulation to be varied and random in presentation and maintained at high levels of intensity (experimental situations that are close analogues to 1960s discotheques featuring rock music and psychedelic light shows). In the studies by Ludwig (1971, 1973), which, within certain limits, allowed the subject to regulate the level and type of input by employing a fixed-ratio button-pressing method, the stimulation was totally devoid of symbolic meaning. By contrast, in the studies by Haer (1970, 1971) and by Gottschalk, Haer, and Bates (1972), emotionally arousing thematic contents were injected into the visual stimulation, although the themes appeared in quick succession and in random order.

Findings have varied somewhat from study to study as a function of the stimuli and the mode of presentation; nevertheless, the evidence suggests that overstimulation tends to be more aversive than understimulation. Subjects in the former condition show heightened arousal: they report vivid imagery (and occasionally also hallucinatory and delusional processes), body image distortion, temporal disorientation, and intellectual-cognitive impairment. Significant individual differences have also been noted. The findings are no more than preliminary and suggestive, however, subject to qualification as more systematic work is performed on the much needed specification of the separate variables and their effects. What, for example, are the effects attributable solely to the factors of confinement, enforced passivity and the demand characteristics? What are the specific contributions to the overall stress of such *cognitive* variables as predictability of and perceived control over stimulation? Taking a clue from Glass and Singer's (1972) research on noise, it may well be these cognitive mediators, along with such factors as the meaning of the stimulation—excessive or not—for the person and his ongoing activity, that determine stress response to sensory overload. (See also Kaminoff and Proshansky, Chapter 23, this volume).

REFERENCES

BERGMAN, P., & ESCALONA, S. K. Unusual sensitivities in very young children. *Psychoanalytic Study of the Child,* 1949, *4,* 333–352

BEXTON, W. H., HERON, B., & SCOTT, T. H. Effects of decreased variation in the sensory environment. *Canadian Journal of Psychology,* 1954, *8,* 70–76.

BROADBENT, D. E. *Decision and stress.* New York: Academic, 1971.

Brownfield, C. A. *Isolation: Clinical and experimental approaches.* New York: Random House, 1965.

Calhoun, J. Population density and social pathology. *Scientific American,* 1962, *206,* 139–148.

Cooper, G. D., Adams, H. B., & Cohen, L. D. Personality changes after sensory deprivation. *Journal of Nervous and Mental Disease,* 1965, *140,* 103–118.

Freud, S. *Beyond the pleasure principle.* London. Hogarth, 1922.

Glass, D. C., & Singer, J. E. *Urban stress.* New York: Academic, 1972.

Goldberger, L. Reactions to perceptual isolation and Rorschach manifestations of the primary process. *Journal of Projective Techniques,* 1961, *25,* 287–302.

Goldberger. L., & Holt, R. R. Experimental interference with reality contact (perceptual isolation): Method and group results. *Journal of Nervous and Mental Disease.* 1958, *127,* 99–112.

Goldberger, L., & Holt, R. R. *A comparison of isolation effects and their personality correlates in two divergent samples.* WADC technical report no. 61–417, contract AF33(616)–6103. Wright-Patterson Air Force Base, 1961.

Gottschalk, L. A., Haer, J. L., & Bates, D. E. Effects of sensory overload on psychological state. *Archives of General Psychiatry,* 1972, *27,* 451–456.

Haer, J. L. Field dependency in relation to altered states of consciousness produced by sensory overload. *Perceptual and Motor Skills,* 1971, *33,* 192–194.

Hebb, D. O. Drives and the CNS (central nervous system). *Psychological Review,* 1955, *62,* 243–254.

Lindsley, D. Common factors in sensory deprivation, sensory distortion, and sensory overload. In P. Solomon, P. E. Kubzansky, P. H. Leiderman, J. H. Mendelson, & D. Wexler, (eds.), *Sensory deprivation.* Cambridge: Harvard University Press, 1961.

Lipowsky, Z. J. Sensory and information inputs overload: Behavioral effects. *Comprehensive Psychiatry,* 1975, *16,* 199–221.

Ludwig, A. M., & Stark, L. H. Schizophrenia, sensory deprivation, and sensory overload. *Journal of Nervous and Mental Disease,* 1973, *157,* 210–216.

McReynolds, P. Anxiety, perception, and schizophrenia. In D. Jackson (ed.), *The etiology of schizophrenia.* New York: Basic Books, 1960.

Miller, J. G. Psychological aspects of communication overloads. In R. W. Waggoner & D. J. Carek (eds.), *International psychiatry clinics: Communication in clinical practice.* Boston: Little, Brown, 1964.

Orne, M. On the social psychology of the psychological experiment: With particular reference to the demand characteristics and their implications. *American Psychologist,* 1962, *17,* 776–783.

Orne, M. T., & Scheibe, K. E. The contribution of non-deprivation factors in the production of sensory deprivation effects: The psychology of the panic button. *Journal of Abnormal and Social Psychology,* 1964, *68,* 3–12.

Pavlov, I. P. *Selected Works.* Moscow: Foreign Languages Publishing House, 1955.

Rapaport, D. The theory of ego-autonomy: A generalization. *Bulletin of the Menninger Clinic,* 1958, *22,* 13–35.

Rasmussen, J. (ed.). *Man in isolation and confinement.* Chicago: Aldine, 1973.

Schultz, D. P. *Sensory restriction: Effects on behavior.* New York: Academic, 1965.

Silverman, J. Scanning-control mechanism and "cognitive filtering" in paranoid and nonparanoid schizophrenia. *Journal of Consulting Psychology,* 1964, *28,* 385–393.

Solomon, P., Kubzansky, P. E., Leiderman, P. H., Mendelson, J., & Wexler, D. (eds.). *Sensory deprivation.* Cambridge: Harvard University Press, 1961.

Spitz, R. The derailment of dialogue: Stimulus overload, action cycles, and the completion gradient. *Journal of the American Psychoanalytic Association,* 1964, *12,* 752–775.

SUEDFELD, P. *Restricted environmental stimulation: Research and clinical application.* New York: Wiley Interscience, 1980.

TOFFLER, A. *Future shock.* New York: Random House, 1970.

ZUBEK, J. P. (ed.). *Sensory deprivation: Fifteen years of research.* New York: Appleton, 1969.

ZUCKERMAN, M. The sensation-seeking motive. In B. Maher (ed.), *Progress in experimental personality research,* vol. 7. New York: Academic, 1974.

ZUCKERMAN, M. Perceptual isolation as a stress situation. A review. *Archive General Psychiatry,* 1964, *11,* 225–276.

ZISKIND, E. An explanation of mental symptoms found in acute sensory deprivation experiments: Researches 1958–1963. *American Journal of Psychiatry,* 1965, *121,* 939–946.

19

Occupational Stress

Robert R. Holt

WORK HAS ALWAYS BEEN considered at best a mixed blessing, if not an absolute curse. The lack of any need to work was the chief attraction of the Garden of Eden, and when Adam was expelled God proclaimed: "In the sweat of thy face shalt thou eat bread." For centuries, it was taken for granted that work is hard, that it is only rarely its own reward, or gratifying in itself, but that it is undertaken in the first instance for extrinsic benefits—those of survival first, then comforts, pleasures, luxuries, and higher cultural rewards. Among the latter was the moral benefit of keeping out of mischief: Satan finds work for idle hands. Or, as Voltaire put it in *Candide,* perhaps reversing historical order, "Work keeps at bay three great evils: boredom, vice, and need."

The industrial revolution, which so transformed Western civilization in a few decades around the turn of the nineteenth century, profoundly changed the nature and organization of work. The factory was a new social invention, a special workplace for large numbers of people away from their homes, in which power machinery greatly multiplied workers' productivity and also exposed them to both obvious and subtle dangers. The new industrial processes made possible a great and widespread increase in the standard of living, but subjected factory workers to amputations, burns, and other accidental traumas. Both travelers and workers on the newly invented forms of mechanical transportation (railways, automobiles, airplanes) now risked accidents more severe and frequent than the era of the stagecoach ever knew, and the condition of traumatic neurosis had to be named and treated. More recently, whole populations are being exposed to pathogenic chemicals and ionizing radiation by industry.

A less obvious consequence of the new organization of work was that the producer of goods lost the autonomy he had had under the guild system and became a part of a hierarchical organization in which he was expected to do what he was told, often without understanding the function or value of the task assigned because of the great growth in the division of labor. The machine had its own pace; man was expected to keep up with it. The clock came to dominate most aspects of the worker's life, adding a new kind of pressure, time urgency. Perhaps we shall one day look on much of the stress of modern life as a previously unrecognized externality of our mechanized means of production (Mumford, 1967, 1970).

Preparation of this chapter was supported by a U.S. Public Health Service research career award (5-K06-MH-12455) from the National Institute of Mental Health.

These properties of industrial work created not only danger and stress but also a great imbalance of power between the entrepreneur, who had the capital to start an enterprise, and the people he hired. The trade union was invented as an attempt to regain some of the workers' lost power. From the beginning, the union movement sought to gain control over the unwanted and threatening side effects of work, diminishing if not abolishing these dangers. Pressure on employers from unions and later from government reinforced the weaker influence of enlightened humanitarianism and has made work safer in many respects than it was a few generations ago, although new dangers are constantly being discovered and the need for vigilance is eternal.

Though the fact is seldom mentioned, it should be apparent that the field of occupational stress (OS) easily becomes embroiled in social controversy, labor-management struggles, and even politics (witness the attacks of the 1980 political campaigns on the Occupational Safety and Health Administration). A psychologist may naively believe that proposed research on OS is just a disinterested search for truth but soon find himself under pressure to produce results that will support one or the other side in a union organizing drive centered on job hazards or in a management campaign against federal regulation. Therefore, research funded by either management or unions falls under inevitable suspicion.

Marx introduced one of the first general critiques of work that went beyond the traditional recognition that labor is fatiguing and dirtying, with sometimes unpleasant physiological side effects. Work for the vast majority under capitalism, said Marx, is alienated, deprived of its true meaning and significance and thus of its proper intrinsic value. Only since the rise of the mental health movement, however, has society become generally aware of a new class of deleterious aspects of work, defined by their largely psychological effects or, in some cases, by their psychological and sociological repercussions. Just as publicity about physical dangers brought abrupt reforms in the organization and conduct of various kinds of work that have made it possible to accomplish the same useful purposes without the harmful impacts, so now we are seeing an era of change or proposed change in the social and psychological circumstances of work to accomplish the same benefit.

Thus, OS is not a new phenomenon, but it is a relatively new concept and field of study. Perhaps the two essential ingredients necessary for OS to come into being as a subdiscipline were the founding of the field of psychosomatic medicine by Dunbar and others and the pioneering work of Selye on stress and the *general adaptation syndrome* as a fresh conceptualization of the nature of' much illness. New hypotheses appeared about diseases of previously puzzling or unknown etiology, like peptic ulcer and essential hypertension, and perhaps not coincidentally these conditions began greatly increasing in observed numbers. Surveys by the Life Extension Institute (of New York City), covering 40,000 health examinations annually, indicated that between 1958 and 1972 stress diseases seemed to become "epidemic" (Chase, 1972).

Another important historical event, helping to crystallize OS as a new field of research, was the passage of the Occupational Safety and Health Act of 1970, creating the Occupational Safety and Health Administration (OSHA), in the Department of Labor, and the National Institute of Occupational Safety and Health (NIOSH), in the Department of Health, Education, and Welfare the following year. The former was charged with setting and enforcing standards of industrial health and safety, the latter with conducting and funding the research necessary to undergird these standards. From its beginning, NIOSH was directed to include psychological, behavioral, and motivational factors in the investigations it sponsored and carried out (Cohen & Margolis, 1973).

Papers on OS often begin with the remark that the concept of stress is unclear and variously defined. The chief source of confusion is whether to conceive of stress as a situational factor (the distressing circumstances external to the person) or a reaction (the disturbance of a person's normal state, viewed either physiologically or psychologically). Selye (1956) preferred the second definition, calling the external initiators of an organismic stress reaction *stressors*. Ironically, hardly anyone follows this usage. Indeed, stress is almost never used as a technical concept but just as a general term of negative evaluation for a state of upset or its precipitant. McGrath (1976) and some other writers try to use the word "stress" nonevaluatively, as more or less equivalent to activation, but that convention makes cross-study comparisons difficult. I shall follow the general practice of not trying to define stress more precisely than as a pointer to the dark side of work.

Put in commonsense terms, the basic proposition of the whole field of OS might be expressed thus: some aspects of many kinds of work have bad effects on most people under certain circumstances. The expansion and specification of that simple statement have already busied a few generations of good minds, and plenty of work remains to be done. By a process sometimes called a response definition of the stimulus, the field of occupational stress then becomes the study of those aspects of work that either have or threaten to have bad effects. The prevalent research paradigm is *stress* (independent variable) → *undesirable consequences* (dependent variable) under certain *parametric conditions* (moderator variable), which are not always included. This chapter investigates each domain in turn.

TYPES OF OCCUPATIONAL STRESS

As an initial orientation to OS, let us look at Table 19–1, which displays the main independent variables of OS research. The table has two principal parts, depending on whether stress is defined objectively or subjectively. This is not the same distinction as Selye's (1956) differentiation of stressor from stress; operationally, it is a matter of whether the researcher (or another outsider) defines what is stressful or the person being stressed does so.

TABLE 19–1
Types of Stress Measured in OS Research (Independent Variables)

Objectively defined
　Physical properties of the working environment
　　Physical hazards, chronic dangers (Althouse & Hurrell, 1977)[a]
　　Pollution, less immediate dangers (House, 1972)
　　Extremes of heat, cold, humidity, pressure, etc. (Biersner and associates, 1971)
　　Noise (Glass & Singer, 1972)
　　Bad man-machine design (Swain & Guttmann, 1980)

　Time variables
　　Change in time zone or length of workday (McFarland, 1974)
　　Nonstandard working hours (shift work) (Rentos & Shepard, 1976)
　　Deadlines (Pearse, 1977)
　　Time pressure (Schmidt, 1978)

　Social and organizational properties of work and its setting[b]
　　Machine pacing (Murphy & Hurrell, 1980)
　　Organizational or administrative irrationality, red tape (Cummings & De Cotiis, 1973)
　　Work load, overload (Caplan, 1972)

Objectively defined (cont.)
    Responsibility load (Cobb, 1973)
    Monotony (Quinn, 1975)
    Participation
    Availability of intrinsic rewards (House, 1972)
    Availability of extrinsic rewards (pay scale, prestige) (House, 1972)
    Piecework versus hourly pay
    Poor labor-management relations (Colligan & Murphy, 1979)
  Changes in job
    Loss of job (unemployment) (Cobb & Kasl, 1977; Jahoda, 1979)
    Demotion (Kasl & French, 1962)
    Qualitative changes in job (Lederer, 1973)
    Overpromotion (Brook, 1973)
    Transfer of job locus (Renshaw, 1976)
    Change in shift pattern (Theorell, 1974)
    Null changes (nonevents) (Jolly, 1979)

Subjectively defined
  Role related
    Role ambiguity versus clarity (Kahn, 1973)
    Role conflict (Kahn, 1973)
    Role strain (MacKinnon, 1978)
    Degree of control over work processes (Frankenhaeuser & Gardell, 1976)
    Responsibility for people (Caplan and associates, 1975)
    Responsibility for things (Cobb, 1973)
    Participation (Caplan and associates, 1975)
    Feedback and communication problems (Moch, Bartunek, & Brass, 1979)
  Miscellaneous
    Job complexity, qualitative load (Caplan et al., 1975)
    Quantitative overload or underload (Kahn, 1973)
    Relationship to supervisor (Theorell, 1974)
    Inadequate support from, or performance by, supervisors (Pearse, 1977)
    Relationship to, or isolation from, co-workers (Theorell, 1974)
    Conflict with, or inadequate performance by, subordinates (Pearse, 1977)
    Conflict with, or pressure from, customers and/or community (Kroes and associates, 1974)
    Ambiguity about future, job insecurity (Caplan et al., 1975)
    Monotony (Quinn, 1975)
    Inequality of pay (Caplan et al., 1975)
    Underutilization of abilities (Caplan et al., 1975)
    Quantity-quality conflict (Kahn, 1973)
  Person-environment (job) fit
    Role ambiguity (Caplan et al., 1975)
    Responsibility for people (Caplan et al., 1975)
    Responsibility for things (French, 1973)
    Quantitative work load (Caplan et al., 1975)
    Job complexity (Caplan et al., 1975), qualitative work load (French, 1973)
    Degree of control over work processes (Harrison, 1976)
    Participation (French, 1973; Singer, 1975)
    Opportunity for advancement (French, 1973)
  Off-job stress
    Disturbed life pattern of miscellaneous stresses (Neves, 1969)
    Stressful life events (Dohrenwend & Dohrenwend, 1974)
    Demands of husband and children on working women (Waldron, 1978)

---

[a]References in this table and in Tables 19–2 and 19–3 are purely illustrative. They cite sources in which the variables listed are described and defined and are not intended in any way to be comprehensive.
[b]These items are inferred, for the most part, not measured.

Objectively Defined Stress

The objective stress of noise occupies a special place among occupational hazards. Though very high levels directly cause damage to the middle and the inner ear, with consequent impairment of hearing, less severe noise is treated as a psychological stress because, though distressing, it does not cause physical damage. A good many studies have focused directly on the irritation, tension, fatigue, and impaired efficiency of workers exposed to annoying noise (e.g., Cohen, 1980; Glass & Singer, 1972), but perhaps because it does not seem psychological enough noise is often neglected as a complicating factor in studies of other kinds of OS. Ferguson (1973), however, found that telegraphers showing signs of neurosis differentially complained of noise in the workplace and held negative attitudes toward the job and supervision.

In general, noise resembles many other physical stressors in that normal environments, which most people find comfortable and conducive to work, contain moderate levels. Outside a range of stimuli to which people adapt without effort or attention, either too little or too much light, temperature, humidity, barometric pressure, etc., is obtrusive and involves some adaptive strain, while extreme values damage tissues. Certain other aspects of the physical environment (e.g., exposure to electromagnetic fields, microwaves, or ionizing radiation) seem to have no optima above zero, but since they are difficult or impossible to sense directly their potential as psychological stressors is largely unknown. In general, people are so adaptable that they can learn to work for long periods, even all their lives, under conditions most of us would find intolerable—e.g., in arctic cold, aboard submarines, or in humid jungles.

Among other physical properties of the working environment, its dangerousness—the exposure of workers to possible loss of life or limb—would seem to be an important source of psychological stress. Quite aside from the physiological impact of bruises or broken bones, chronic exposure to such dangers (even when they are successfully avoided) should tend to arouse the general adaptation syndrome (Selye, 1956), with detectable results on mental or physical health. A study of 486 coal miners found, however, that they did not *report* more stress than did 452 workers in jobs of similar status level, although they did experience significantly more "affective strains"—anxiety, depression, irritation, and somatic complaints (Althouse & Hurrell, 1977). Here is a first indication that subjective and objective measures of stress may give different results, and it is not always evident which will have the greater effect on health.

Several types of OS are hardly definable in any other than an objective way. One such stressor is nonstandard hours of work, or shift work. The phenomenon is widespread in the United States, with about one in every four workers having something other than usual daytime hours (Smith, Colligan, & Hurrell, 1980); the proportion of manufacturing workers on evening shifts is as high as 43% in Detroit (Owen, 1976). For various reasons, notably the reduced cost of off-peak energy, the numbers of workers affected will probably continue to rise rapidly, so this may be expected to become a more prominent source of OS.[1]

The basic research findings to date may be summarized in the following scheme: evening or night work causes disturbed circadian rhythms (of sleep, body temperature, gastrointestinal function, etc.) (A) and disturbed rhythms of social living (B); A in turn causes bad moods, poor sleep, and digestive compalints (C), while B causes malfunctioning in social roles and disruption of the family (D); C and D interact to bring about individual and social pathology. The problems are a good deal more complex than this scheme suggests. There are diverse shift schedules; and there are great differences in stability, with scheduled rotations effected daily, weekly, less frequently, or not at all. Consequently, it is difficult to compare research findings.

Another complicating aspect of research on the health effects of shift work is that people who cannot tolerate it drop out. It has been estimated that as many as 20% of workers cannot adapt to shift work (Bruusgard, 1975). Hence, the statistics that are gathered, being limited to those who can adapt, tell us little about the intrinsic relation between this particular kind of stress and illnesses or other strains. There should be little surprise, therefore, that many surveys of studies that simply compared morbidity rates in shift and nonshift workers (e.g., Taylor, 1973) found little evidence of deleterious effects except for complaints most obviously related to disturbed circadian rhythms—difficulties in sleeping and complaints about digestive and eliminative functions (Axelsson & Lundberg, 1975; Levine, 1976; Tasto & Colligan, 1978). In one study, however, which compared workers who stayed with shift work for three years and those who dropped out after six months, those who stayed showed *more* of the same troubles all had initially reported—disturbed sleep and GI functioning, anxiety, etc. (Meers, Maasen, & Verhaegen, 1978). In a large and more sophisticated study conducted under NIOSH auspices, Tasto and Colligan (1978) studied 1200 nurses and 1200 food processors. In both occupations, those who were on rotating shifts had more serious illnesses and more accidents than did those on steady shifts. Shift work (especially evening and rotating shifts) seems to have a negative impact on the domestic lives of workers, especially their sexual activity and parental responsibilities (Mott, Mann, McLoughlin, & Warwick, 1965; Tasto & Colligan, 1978).

Machine pacing has been much studied ever since Kornhauser's (1965) classic study of assembly line workers in the automobile industry. As Murphy and Hurrell (1980) pointed out, machine pacing is much more complex than one might at first think; the degree of the worker's control, the rigidity of pacing, the amount of rest time, etc., vary widely. These are easily manipulated variables, however, so the problem lends itself to experimental study. The only well-established finding from such research so far is that as the pressure of externally imposed work demand increases, heart rate goes up (Amaria, 1974; Ettema & Zielhuis, 1971; Johansson & Lindstrom, 1975). Though these experiments generally lacked ecological validity, the finding was supported by a field study of Swedish sawmill workers, which documented a higher incidence of caridovascular and other psychosomatic disorders among machine-paced than among nonpaced workers (Frankenhaueser & Gardell, 1976). Machine pacing produced elevated levels of excreted adrenaline and noradrenaline, often cited as cardiac risk factors (see also Froberg, Karlsson, Levi, Lidberg, & Seeman, 1970). As Kornhauser (1965) reported, machine-paced workers also complain more of monotony and general mental strain (Frankenhaueser & Gardell, 1976). Caplan and associates (Caplan, Cobb, French, Harrison, & Pinneau, 1975) found that of the 23 occupations they studied, assemblers and relief men on a machine-paced assembly line reported the most boredom and dissatisfaction wih their work; machine tenders also were very high on these measures. These three kinds of workers rated themselves most anxious, depressed, and irritated as well, and somatic complaints were most frequent among assemblers and relief men; assemblers made most visits to dispensaries. All in all, these two groups of machine-paced workers had the highest stress and strain of the workers studied (over 2000 subjects). Using the same measures of strain, Wilkes, Slammerjohn, and Lalich (n.d.) reported that machine-paced poultry inspectors scored only slightly lower on dissatisfaction with job and workload, boredom, and somatic complaints. None of these studies was either prospective or longitudinal, but several studies along such lines are under way (under NIOSH auspices).

Most social and organizational properties of work listed in Table 25–1, when not measured by workers' reports, are inferred or generally observed properties of jobs, cited in interpretations of findings. For example, seeking to explain the well-replicated findings that general practitioners have significantly more coronary heart disease than do other physicians (Morris, Heady, & Barley, 1952; Russek, 1960), and that foremen have peptic ulcers much more often than do the men they supervise (Doll & Jones, 1951; Vertin, 1954), Cobb (1973) hypothesized that the additional responsibility for persons is pivotal.

It is no historical accident that unemployment, the focus of pioneering psychological studies during the Great Depression, was relatively neglected as a source of OS until the end of the 1970s. One important study followed 162 blue-collar workers from the initial announcement that two plants were closing through the period of unemployment until they were relocated, repeatedly collecting physiological and psychological data (Cobb & Kasl, 1977; Kasl, Gore, & Cobb, 1975). As compared both to control workers and to themselves upon reemployment, the unemployed men had higher blood pressure (especially diastolic) during the periods of anticipation and joblessness. Results with other blood consituents (e.g., uric acid, cholesterol) were less clear-cut. Other recent research concentrated on mental health outcomes (Dooley & Catalano, 1980; Theorell, Lind, & Floderus, 1975). As Jahoda (1979) commented, the recent work found the same types of impact as did studies 40–50 years earlier: deterioration of family relationships, more depression and irrational self-doubt, lower self-esteem (also reported by Cobb & Kasl, 1972), and higher incidence of psychiatric disorders.

Subjectively Defined Aspects of Stress

With the emergence of internally consistent measures, workers' own reports about many aspects of OS have proven highly useful (the Institute of Social Research, at the University of Michigan, played a major part in developing such measures). It has long been known that little participation in decisionmaking, ambiguity about job security, and poor use of skills and abilities are correlated with such strains as job related tension and job dissatisfaction (Argyris, 1964; Likert, 1961; Quinn, Seashore, Kahn, Mangione, Campbell, Slaines & McCullough, 1971). Nonparticipation was correlated especially strongly with eight strain measures, including depressed mood, escapist drinking, and overall physical health, reported by 1500 workers in 12 occupations (Quinn & Shepard, 1974). Hamner and Tosi (1974) and Caplan and associates (1975) reported significant associations between job conflict and anxiety. Similarly, Hite (1976) found job challenge (a mixture of utilization of abilities, degree of control over work processes, etc.) to be positively related to job self-esteem and negatively to the Zung (1965) measure of depression. Singer (1975) reported that among 1148 male governmental employees, underutilization of abilities and insufficient participation on the job accounted for more variance in psychological and somatic symptoms than did nonoccupational life stresses. These two variables were among the most strongly correlated with job dissatisfaction (r's of .42 and .36, respectively) and boredom (r's .59 and .31) in a sample of 310 men in 23 occupations (Caplan et al., 1975), along with ambiguity about job future ($r = .39$ with job dissatisfaction, .36 with boredom, and .24 with depression). Compare the findings of Margolis, Kroes, and Quinn (1974) from another large national sample of U.S. workers: nonparticipation was correlated .34 with job dissatisfaction and .21 with depressed mood.

One of the oldest subjectively defined OS variables is *role ambiguity*, the opposite of clarity about what one is supposed to do on a job, its purpose, responsibilities, etc. Kahn, Wolfe, Quinn, Snoek, and Rosenthal (1964) reported substantial correlations of ambiguity with strain variables (measured by self-report in a national survey of 1500 respondents), some of which have been replicated: job satisfaction ($r = -.32$), job related tension (.51), and self-confidence ($-.27$). Among 205 NASA engineers, scientists, and administrators, French and Caplan (1970) found that role ambiguity was correlated with job satisfaction ($r = -.42$) and with feelings of job related threat to well-being (.40). Kahn (1973), studying 150 aerospace engineers and administrators, found role ambiguity to be associated with job satisfaction ($r = -.4$), job related threat (.5), self-esteem (.2), and a four-item measure of somatic symptoms of depression (.5). In a national sample of 1496 workers, Margolis, Kroes, and Quinn (1974) found significant but much lower correlations: job satisfaction ($-.13$) and self-esteem ($-.16$). Here, incidentally, is an example of a frequently noticeable trend: correlations that are strong in one occupation (or a cluster of closely related jobs) may become attenuated when sought in a vocationally heterogeneous sample.

The next step in the development of subjective measures was taken by French (1973) and his co-workers at the Institute of Social Research (ISR) (French, Rodgers, & Cobb 1974).[2] It became increasingly evident that psychological stress variables are like their physical counterparts in that the optimum is usually a middle, not an extreme, value. Hence, to find what is least stressful for any one person, one should ask him what level of, say, quantitative or qualitative work load he prefers and relate the response to the demand made upon him by his workrole, by supervisors, or by other apsects of the work environment. The resulting relational scores measure *person-environment (P-E) fit.*

Harrison (1976), using a representative subsample of 318 men from the Caplan et al. (1975) survey, demonstrated that while neither the worker's report of the actual complexity of his job nor the level he wanted was significantly related to depression, the P-E fit measure had a highly reliable curvilinear relation: when the fit was exact, depression was minimal. In a Canadian study, Coburn (1975) similarly reported a curvilinear effect on mental health of P-E fit with respect to job complexity. Harrison (1976) also was able to show that the absolute amount of misfit significantly improved the multiple correlations of the component P and E scores on job complexity with each of the six strains (job dissatisfaction, boredom, somatic complaints, anxiety, depression, and irritation). Further multiple regression analyses were carried out in which all 34 of the study's measures of stress were entered as predictors of the various strains; the great majority of the consistent independent predictors of overall job dissatisfaction and boredom were fit measures. Another important finding from this survey was that in every occupation studied, approximately equal numbers of men were dissatisfied because of either too much or too little job complexity or work load (see also London & Klimoski, 1975). Harrison (1976) noted the implication that proposals for job enrichment will improve fit for many workers but make it *worse* for others.

Although I found no clearly replicated results on the effects of off-the-job stress, a good theoretical case can be made that stressful events in the nonoccupational part of a worker's life can lower his threshold of resistance to OS or cause sensitization to certain classes of OS, thus contributing to an eventual pathological outcome (e.g., Cooper & Marshall, 1976).

The relative utility of objectively and subjectively defined stress measures is a more complex issue than might at first be supposed and surely is not a question to be decided in terms of ideological preference for one or the other type across the board. Some subjective indicators of stress take the form of direct questions (e.g., "Is your job stressful? Does anything about your work upset you, make you tense, or cause you any other difficulty?"). Such an approach runs up against the need of many persons (perhaps men in particular, and especially those in lower status, blue-collar jobs) to maintain a public posture of toughness or machismo. Such a hypothesis would help account for the anomalous fact that men in more objectively rigorous, physically demanding, and dangerous jobs often deny any stress yet exhibit the highest rates of stress diseases. Compare, for example, Cherry's (1978) report that in a representative sample of 1415 workers, the following proportions reported "nervous debility and strain": professionals, 54%; intermediate nonmanual (white-collar) workers, 57%; skilled nonmanuals, 44%; semiskilled nonmanuals, 50%; skilled manual (blue-collar) workers, 31%; semiskilled manuals, 15%; and unskilled manual laborers, 10%. Yet Smith, Colligan, and Hurrell (1980) found that unskilled laborers had by far the highest rates of stress diseases, both physical and mental, and that the top 12 occupations in terms of combined indexes included no professionals but did include mine operatives; college professors appeared among the 13 occupations with the fewest stress diseases.

The remarkable adaptability of human beings sometimes works to their detriment. Faced with the choice between a boring, dangerous, or otherwise stressful job and unemployment, most people will choose to work and will find a way to reduce the dissonance.[3] Some people are characterological complainers, while others take pride in never complaining, and there is no reason to suppose that these types are randomly distributed across occupations.

DEPENDENT VARIABLES IN OS RESEARCH

Table 19–2 lists the most important recurrent variables treated as effects or products of OS. With some misgivings, I have followed the prevalent practice of classifying these variables as strains or illnesses, but the distinction is arbitrary. What one author treats as a strain (a relatively minor side effect of working at an occupation), another takes as evidence of impaired health. To a degree, this lack of agreement represents the confused state of symptomatology and the controversial status of the concept of disease, especially outside the realm of physical and physiological medicine. Even more, however, it points to a necessary clash between methodological approaches. The traditional atomistic-analytic conception of scientific research makes investigators look for linear effects between stress and strain—causal variables and effect variables, each conceived of as continuously distributed and treatable in

TABLE 19–2
Types of Effects Measured in OS Research (Dependent Variables)

Strains
   Physiological
      Pulse rate, blood pressure (Caplan et al., 1975)
      Erythrocyte sedimentation rate, protein-bound iodine, serum iron (Froberg et al., 1970)
      Serum cholesterol, high- and low-density lipoproteins (Chadwick, 1980)
      Serum cortisol, thyroid hormones, serum glucose, serum uric acid (Caplan et al., 1975)
      Catecholamine excretion (Frankenhaeuser & Gardell, 1976)
      Electrocardiogram (Shirom et al., 1973)
      Lung function tests (House et al., 1979)
      Disrupted sleep, bowel function, or eating habits (Mott, 1976)
      Somatic complaints (Caplan et al., 1975)

Strains (cont.)
  Psychological
    Job dissatisfaction (Caplan et al., 1975)
    Boredom, anxiety, depression, irritation (Caplan et al., 1975)
    Self-esteem: occupational (House, 1972) or general (Beehr, 1976)
    Alienation from, or confidence in, organization (Kahn, 1973)
    Tension, experienced conflict (Kahn, 1973)
    Fatigue (Beehr et al., 1976)
    Satisfaction with life (Iris & Barrett, 1972)
    Sexual maladjustment (Mott, 1976)
  Behavioral and social
    Authoritarian punitiveness (Fodor, 1976)
    Strikes (Belbin & Stammers, 1972)
    Early retirement, changing jobs (Jacobson, 1972; Powell, 1973)
    Burnout (Daley, 1979)
    Rate of smoking, caffeine intake (Caplan et al., 1975)
    Use of drugs or alcohol on the job (Mangione & Quinn, 1975)
    Counterproductive behaviors (spreading rumors; doing inferior work on purpose; stealing from employer; damaging property, equipment, or product on purpose; damaging property accidentally but not reporting) (Mangione & Quinn, 1975)
    Absenteeism (Akerstedt, 1976)
    Disrupted performance of social role as spouse and parent (Mott, 1976)
    Disrupted performance of social role as citizen (Gardell, 1976)
    Interference with friendships, socializing, dating (Mott, 1976)
Illnesses and mortality
  Somatic-physiological (including psychosomatic)
    Heart disease (Glass, 1977)
    Hypertension (Cobb & Rose, 1973)
    Cerebral accident (stroke) (*Work in America,* 1973)
    Peptic ulcer (Cobb & Rose, 1973; House et al., 1979)
    Arthritis (Cobb, 1971)
    Headache (Kimball, 1979)
    Respiratory illness (bronchitis, asthma, cough, phlegm) (Caplan et al., 1975)
    Dermatitis, other skin afflictions (House et al., 1979)
    Diabetes melitus (Cobb & Rose, 1973)
    General, diffuse sickness (Mechanic, 1974)
    Total rate of illness (Hinkle, 1974; Rahe et al., 1972)
    Frequency of visits to doctor or dispensary (Caplan et al., 1975)
    Mortality rates (Colligan et al., 1977)
  Psychological
    Mental health versus mental illness (Gavin, 1975)
    Visits to community mental health center (Colligan et al., 1977)
    Depression (Ilfeld, 1977)
    Alcoholism, drug abuse (Lederer, 1973)
    Neurotic symptoms reported on questionnaire (House et al., 1979)
    Neurosis, character disorder, etc., diagnosed clinically (Ferguson, 1973)
    Mass psychogenic illness (Colligan & Murphy, 1979)
  Behavioral and social
    Violence (*Work in America,* 1973)
    Other antisocial acting out (e.g., white-collar crime) (*Work in America,* 1973)
    Delinquency of worker's children (*Work in America,* 1973)
    Impaired interpersonal relations (*Work in America,* 1973)
    Accidents and errors, with harm to self (Theorell, 1974)
    Accidents and errors, with harm to others (Colquhoun, 1976)
    Suicide (Karcher, 1978)

isolation even though the scientist recognizes that reality is more complex and that it will be necessary to put the pieces back together. By contrast, the clinical disciplines have been forced to recognize the intrinsically patterned and discontinuous nature of the troubles for which people consult practitioners.

Consider, for example, blood pressure, serum cholesterol, and serum uric acid, elevated levels of which are associated with coronary heart disease. Neither these nor any of the other physiological variables Caplan and associates (1975) managed with great difficulty and expense to measure on 390 men in eight occupations was related to any of their questionnaire measures of stress or strain. In an ongoing study of coronary heart disease among 400 managers and supervisors in an aerospace corporation, such so-called risk factors as uric acid, blood glucose, dopamine-beta-hydroxylase, and cholesterol were found to be related to one another and to cardiovascular status (pulse rate, blood pressure, etc.) but *not* to coronary heart disease (Chadwick, 1980). They were also unrelated to the only good predictor of heart attacks, *personality types A and B* (see below, p. 354, and Chapter 25). Chadwick (1980) therefore rejected the simple formula that stress causes strain causes heart disease and called for a consideration of "second order things: the person-environment fit and nonlinear interactions" (p. 28).

On the other hand, a researcher may accept as a fact of life the self-defined nature of illness and take as his dependent variable either the frequency of visits to dispensaries, physicians, or other medical facilities or the record of days lost on account of illness as the bottom line with which employers have to cope. Yet good data on these patterns are hard to get: even though a company has a dispensary, some employees may prefer to seek medical help elsewhere, and taking time off for illness is notoriously easy to abuse in some settings. Some people continue to work with clinically detectable, fully developed illnesses, while others stay home at every sniffle. This very difference may be related to stress, however. In one study of angina, when subjects were equated for the amount of reported chest pain and the condition of their coronary arteries was directly checked, those who had higher independently measured levels of stressful life events had more nearly *normal* arterial status than those who registered lower levels of stress (Chadwick, 1980). Apparently, feeling under pressure made the former group experience a milder degree of coronary pathology as acutely painful. Even when an illness can be objectively diagnosed with ease, to find all cases in a given population may require subjecting all members to a medical examination—an expensive and difficult undertaking.[4]

Let us consider next the evidence that the psychological strains listed in Table 19–2 are relevant to health and disease. A classical 15-year study of aging examined genetic inheritance, medical status, and use of tobacco in 268 volunteers and found that the best predictor of longevity was work satisfaction ($r = .26$) (Palmore, 1969). Among males who were most likely to be working full-time, the correlation was highest (.38). In three separate samples of 12, 16, and 36 occupational groups, Sales and House (1971) found negative relationships between average level of job satisfaction and mortality rates for heart disease, but not for any other morbidity measure. Those correlations existed across groups, not individuals. In a representative sample of 228 men from one community, House (1972) found no correlation between job satisfaction and several cardiac risk factors such as cholesterol and blood pressure; but when he analyzed the data by occupations, a negative correlation appeared in several white-collar groups. Occupational self-esteem has been found to be negatively related to cardiac risk factors (House, 1972; Kasl & Cobb, 1970) and to dispensary visits (Kasl & French, 1962). These results should be viewed with caution not only because of the negative findings on self-esteem and cardiac risk reported by Caplan (1972) and by French, Tupper, and Mueller (1965), and the lack of a clear association between job satisfaction and cardiac risk (Caplan and associates, 1975), but also because the alleged risk factors are often unrelated to morbidity in prospective research (Chadwick, 1980).

The central finding of Kornhauser's (1965) justly celebrated study of Detroit automobile workers was a positive relationship (not expressed as a correlation coefficient) between job satisfaction and mental health. Gechman and Wiener (1975) reported a similar finding, but Ronan, Cobb, Garrett, Lazarri, Mosser, and Racine (1974) found no correlation after having attempted to replicate Kornhauser's study, using his measures, over a fairly wide occupational distribution. Once again, because relationships may not generalize beyond the specific occupational groups in which they were originally found does not mean that they are of no interest. On the whole, job satisfaction is evidently highly relevant to OS and its pathogenic effects. For reviews of the extensive literature on the measurement and correlates of job satisfaction, see Katzell, Yankelovich, Fein, Oornati, and Nash (1975) and Locke (1976).

Fatigue has long been studied by industrial psychologists and is occasionally mentioned in OS research (e.g., Cameron, 1971), but I found no direct evidence linking it to illness. In a comprehensive review of research on OS in secretaries, Dainoff (1979) reported that the best-established findings were that sustained work with cathode-ray tube displays led to ocular fatigue and related complaints, and that keyboard operators complained of muscular distress. In both instances, correctable flaws in design and operator training apparently played large roles and the effects seemed to be reversible.

A few observers have noted the neglect of what are classified in Table 19–2 as behavioral strains—notably the "counterproductive behaviors" studied by Mangione and Quinn (1975) in a national sample of 1327 wage and salary workers: deliberately trying to make trouble or to harm the employer by spreading rumors; doing work badly or incorrectly; deliberately damaging property, equipment, or products; failing to report accidental damage; and stealing from the employer (Spector, 1975; *Work in America*, 1973). Especially in men over 30, counterproductive acts were related to job dissatisfaction.[5] These touchy topics *can* be investigated, but white-collar crime of all kinds, including bribery, cheating, and the interface between legitimate business and organized crime, remains as little touched by scientific study as by the criminal justice system.

Psychiatrists classify alcoholism and drug abuse among the character disorders, hence as diseases rather than strains. In a large survey, Margolis, Kroes, and Quinn (1974) found "escapist drinking" to be significantly associated with job stress. It is, of course, extremely difficult to prove cause. Persons like long-distance truckers, who must remain alert on a dangerous but soporific, monotonous job, are at risk of taking amphetamines (Harris & Mackie, 1972) and at times abuse such a seemingly innocuous drug as caffeine with serious (albeit usually reversible) effects on their health.

We come now to diseases in the narrower sense as dependent variables. A considerable variety of pathologies have been said to be caused or exacerbated by OS: cardiovascular diseases, mental illnesses of several kinds (including suicide), asthma and other respiratory illnesses such as bronchitis, thyroid disorders, skin diseases, arthritis of various types, obesity (also considered a strain), tuberculosis, migraine, peptic ulcers, ulcerative colitis, and diabetes (Cooper & Marshall, 1978; Kroes, 1976; Selye, 1976). Backing up such medical opinions or beliefs by hard evidence is a difficult matter. The simplest type of research, comparing morbidity rates across occupational groups or social statuses, leaves a great deal to be desired: the criterion groups differ in many respects other than inferred (or measured average) levels of stress, and the direction of casual influence is ambiguous. It could easily be that people who have a disease or a predisposition to it seek out certain kinds of jobs or are selected into them. Schizophrenics are found in disproportionately large numbers in the least skilled jobs with lowest status, for example, partly because many of them are unable to work at more demanding tasks.

A great deal of attention has focused on cardiovascular diseases, especially coronary heart disease (CHD), which has become in modern times the principal cause of death in the United States. The origins of CHD are unclear and multiple, and OS has been clearly implicated (for earlier reviews see Cooper & Marshall, 1976; House, 1974; Jenkins, 1976). Evidence continues to accumulate of a significant positive association between various aspects of OS and heart disease—House, McMichael, Wells, Kaplan, and Landerman (1979) found links between eight measures of perceived stress and angina, hypertension, and other risk factors and Falger (1979) noted associations between work overload and myocardial infarction—but negative findings also have been reported (Haynes and associates, 1978).[6] The one well-established, frequently replicated finding links cardiovascular disease and the Type A behavior pattern: "excessive drive, aggressiveness, ambition, involvement in competitive activities, frequent vocational deadlines, and enhanced sense of time urgency" (Jenkins, Rosenman, & Friedman, 1968). (For a detailed review of Types A and B, see Chapter 25.)

If heart disease of several kinds is so closely related to OS, what about other cardiovascular disorders? The two principal possibilities are hypertension (high blood pressure) and cerebral vascular accident (stroke). Hardly any research has been done on the latter, perhaps because even though stroke is a frequent cause of death, it tends to occur at a late age, often after retirement. Here is one of the most difficult problems in occupational medicine: the pathogenesis of a number of major killers, notably including cancer, is a long, slow process. It not only complicates the legal process of demonstrating responsibility—for example, of an employer for subjecting workers to low levels of such radioactive carcinogens as radon, or such chemical carcinogens as benzene, or byssinosis-producing cotton dust—when years elapse between the exposure and the insidious onset of the disease; it also impedes research. Quite possibly, OS will someday be shown to have a presently undetected pathogenic influence on various diseases of delayed onset. As to hypertension, however, there has been a fair amount of research, but the only well-established finding links it to the Type A personality. Investigative designs tend to be more naive in blood pressure studies than they are in cardiac research. The state of knowledge about both hypertension and CHD will doubtless advance considerably a few years hence, when some large, sophisticated prospective studies have been completed and reported (Chadwick, 1980; Haynes and associates, 1980; Rose, Jenkins, & Hurst, 1978). At the benign end of the dependent variable, however, there is one well-established finding: scientists have significantly lower systolic blood pressure than do other occupational groups tested, e.g., administrators and air traffic controllers (Caplan, 1972; Caplan and associates, 1975).

Though in the popular conception peptic ulcer has long been the prototypical OS disease, medical opinion about the evidence has been divided: Susser (1967) concluded from a survey of research that there is a definite link; Weiner (1977), that none had been proved. It is to be expected, therefore, that more recent results should be fragmentary. In a group of blue-collar workers in a rubber factory, House and colleagues (1979) found a significant association between reported OS—particularly stressful relations with others—and ulcer, despite controls for seven possibly confounding variables. Air traffic controllers were found to have unusually high rates of peptic ulcer (Cobb & Rose, 1973), but in another study using self-report only they did not differ from other occupational groups (Caplan and associates, 1975). Doubtless, stable results must wait on more complex approaches. For example, Mendeloff and Dunn (1971) reported that young women who work and have family responsibilities have more ulcers than those with only one type of responsibility; Kahn and French (1970) found that rates of peptic ulcer rise as self-esteem declines.

Many of the people who show up in doctors' offices or clinics refuse to settle into diagnostic pigeonholes, "being bothered by all sorts of ailments, feeling weak all over, having undefined pains, lacking energy, feeling tense and nervous, feeling depressed, drowsiness, nervous stomach, having personal worries, being nervous, feeling blue, and having headaches" (Mechanic, 1974:90). A high proportion of the people who seek medical help do so for what seems to be poor general organismic functioning, not for specific organic diseases, yet most research has concentrated on the latter. Patients of the former kind are looked on as a nuisance, almost as an embarrassment; they are suspected of hypochondria or malingering, as if these patterns were not themselves forms of pathology worthy of study and correction. Though there is a dearth of information on days lost from work because of unclassifiable illness, Hinkle (1974) suggested that the number may be high and that the phenomenon is suitable for, and fully deserving of, much more intensive investigation.

One approach that has the merit of not excluding unclassifiable illnesses is having the worker rate his own general state of health or well-being. A few studies reported relations between OS variables and such measures, usually in specific occupations (Coburn, 1978; Rahe, Ganderson, Pugh, Rubin, & Arthur, 1972; Tung & Koch, 1980).

Faced with the choice between being considered a "mental patient" or being regarded as someone with a somatic illness, most people consciously or unconsciously choose the latter, socially more acceptable patient role. Small wonder, therefore, that there is a great deal of OS literature in which the dependent variables are bodily diseases or their precursors and very little in which specific neuroses, psychoses, or other established psychodiagnostic categories play that role. The only replicated result I found concerns depression: a couple of large epidemiological studies found that while life events as a whole seemed to play a small role in this etiology, OS was significantly associated with depression for married men (Holzer, Warheit, & Kuldau, 1978; Ilfeld, 1977).

A survey by occupation of all first admissions to 22 of the 27 community mental health centers in the state of Tennessee from January 1972 through June 1974 bypassed the diagnostic issues and showed striking differences among occupations (Colligan, Smith, & Hurrell, 1977). Occupations were ranked in terms of admission rate per 1000 employees, thus holding constant differences in the numbers of persons employed in different vocations, and these rates were compared with expected frequencies based on population norms. The group with by far the highest rate was health technology technicians, and five others of the top 20 in the list are relatively low-status health care occupations. Doubtless, these workers experience much pressure and authoritarian treatment to which they cannot respond directly, but they also should be better informed about mental health facilities and more inclined to seek help than are many other persons. The same artifactual influence may apply to registered nurses and social workers, also in the top 27. (After reviewing the literature on psychiatric illness in physicians, Murray [1974] found that they, their wives, and paramedics stand out in being prone to drug addiction and suicide. Since these persons have easy access to drugs, it is uncertain whether OS plays a role in the high morbidity rates.)

Waiters and waitresses had the second highest rate in the Tennessee study (Colligan, Smith, & Hurrell, 1977), and a fair number of other personal service occupations had high ranks, suggesting that the interpersonal strains in serving the public in subordinate, nonprofessional capacities may have an etiological role in stress related disorders. Telephone operators ranked seventeenth on clinic admission rates; a Russian study likewise found that 280 female intercity operators had a higher frequency of "nervous disorders and neurotic reactions" than did control workers (Ryzhkova, Lanskiy, Nevskaya, & Simonova, 1978).

Men in high-status, more intrinsically interesting occupations yield paradoxical findings: more job satisfaction but also more depression (Quinn & Shepard, 1974) or more "nervous strain" (Cherry, 1978). It is difficult to tell whether holders of high-level jobs report more "mental symptoms" because of OS, or because they are sophisticated enough to be more introspective and more willing to admit, or seek help for, conditions like depressed mood; or some interaction of the foregoing.

Incidentally, much of the OS literature deals with the special problems of specific occupations. Space does not permit a summary of findings. For specific reviews see Cooper (1980) on dentists, Davidson and Veno (1980) on policemen, and Marshall (1980) on nurses. A good deal of work recently has concentrated on human service occupations under the catchphrase "staff burnout" (e.g., Cherniss, 1980).

Outbreaks of mass psychogenic illness in work settings apparently have become more frequent in recent years. Colligan and Murphy (1979) concluded from a review of 16 published and unpublished studies that groups of workers reported physical symptoms (usually including headache, dizziness, and/or nausea) without ascertainable physical basis, often after experiencing an unusual odor. Affected workers were predominantly women who had been subject to considerable OS: boredom, production pressure, poor labor-management relations and communications, and a noisy, unpleasant working environment.

Accidents on the job have long been a subject of research, much of it an inconclusive attempt to identify accident proneness. There are no definitive demonstrations that industrial accidents are caused by OS, but enough positive indications from adequately complex research to warrant further careful study of accidents as the resultant of stressful conditions impinging on dissatisfied persons (perhaps with some degree of internally distracting anxiety or depression, or other nonspecific predisposition). Such research is urgently needed because, as Colquhoun (1976) pointed out, "even though an actual accident may be a rare event in any particular factory or plant, in more and more cases nowadays, such an accident could be disastrous"—not only to workers but to large sectors of the public. Since the accident at Three Mile Island, attention is beginning to be focused on human factors in workers at nuclear reactors (e.g., Swain & Guttmann, 1980), but it is distressing to report that to date there has been no published research on OS in control room operators and the Nuclear Regulatory Commission knows of no such work in progress in the United States. Compare, by contrast, the dozens of OS studies on air traffic controllers (reviewed by Crump, 1979).

It has long been known that mortality rates differ strikingly across occupations (e.g., Cobb & Rose, 1973; Sales & House, 1971), reminding us of the vital significance of OS. Research using death in general or a special form, such as suicide, as the dependent variable is usually of a large-scale, statistical kind. Studies of suicide rates by occupation and other demographic classifications, in the sociological tradition of Durkheim (Bsuglass & Duffy, 1978; Karcher, 1978; Reinhart, 1978), have found that such stresslike or strainlike inferred variables of the work setting as weakness of social organization and anomie are significantly associated with self-destructive acts or attempts.

MODERATOR VARIABLES AND INTERACTION EFFECTS

An important and fairly recent development in OS, toward more sophisticated and adequate research designs, is the explicit introduction of moderating (sometimes called *conditioning*) variables. Instead of merely attempting to connect stress with strain, investigators pursue the hypothesis that a given stress has deleterious effects on health only under specified parametric conditions. Table 19–3 lists some moderator variables that have been investigated in OS research.

So far, there seem to be very few replicated findings of this kind. Quinn (1972) and Cohen (1976) found symptoms of poorer mental health in stressed and dissatisfied workers who felt locked into jobs. Results of great plausibility and convincingness have been

TABLE 19–3
Moderating Variables Used in OS Research

Physiological
   Use of alcohol, drugs, caffeine (Cobb, 1974)
   Disruption of diet (Halberg & Nelson, 1976), low fat diet (Russek, 1973)
   Exposure to dust and chemical pollution (House et al., 1979)
   Exposure to microwave radiation (Becker, 1979)

Characteristics of individuals
   Age (House, 1972; Mangione & Quinn, 1975)
   Sex (Ramos, 1975)
   Ethnicity (Ramos, 1975)
   Nationality (Orth-Gomer, 1979)
   Stage of life (Kellam, 1974)
   Number of life changes (Cobb, 1974)
   Lark versus owl (capacity for wakefulness) (Ostberg, 1973)
   Work addiction (Theorell, 1974)
   Work values (Crain, 1974)
   Attachment to organization (Porter & Dubin, 1975)
   Neurotic anxiety (Kahn, 1973)
   Depressive tendencies (Mott, 1976)
   Schizoid or introvert lack of sociability (Mott, 1976)
   Neuroticism (Gulian, 1974)
   Self-esteem (London & Klimoski, 1975)
   Strength of higher order needs (Beehr et al., 1976)
   Flexibility-rigidity (Kahn, 1973)
   Effectiveness of defenses (Cobb, 1974)
   Resistance resources (Antonovsky, 1974)
   Type A (versus Type B) behavior pattern (Caplan, 1972)
   Machiavellianism (Gemmill & Heisler, 1972)
   Need for clarity at work (Miles & Petty, 1975)

Situational
   Size of work unit (Schriesheim & Murphy, 1976)
   Group cohesiveness (Beehr, 1976)
   Autonomy on job (Beehr, 1976), opportunity for formal control (Gemmill & Heisler, 1972)
   Social support from co-workers (Caplan et al., 1975)
   Social support from supervisors (Caplan et al., 1975)
   Job enrichment (Abdel-Halim, 1978)

Organizational
   Tall versus flat organizational structure (Ivancevich & Donnelly, 1975)
   Model I versus Model II (Argyris, 1973)
   Organizational climate (James & Jones, 1974)
   Structural dimensions of organization (James & Jones, 1976)

Sociological
   Social support from home (spouse, relatives, friends) (Caplan et al., 1975)
   Other interpersonal ties and involvements (Antonovsky, 1974)
   Community involvement (Antonovsky, 1974)

reported: House and colleagues (1979) found that perceived stress was positively related to the incidence of respiratory and dermatological symptoms only in rubber workers who had been exposed to possibly noxious fumes, and may yet be replicated.

Social support as a moderator, or buffer, of stress effects has received a good deal of attention during recent years, especially by the investigative team at ISR (e.g., Caplan and associates, 1975; Cobb, 1976). According to Pinneau (1976): "Men with high support from either supervisor or co-workers generally reported low role conflict, low role ambiguity, and low future ambiguity, high participation, and good utilization of their skills" (p. 35). Interestingly, in light of the psychoanalytic expectation, depression was the strain measure most frequently correlated with support. Depression, anxiety, and irritation were affected by support both at home and on the job; most other strains were related only to support in the occupational setting—effects that remained significant across 16 occupational groups when the simultaneous and complicating effects of other stresses were controlled by multiple regression analyses (Pinneau, 1976). There was, however, no clear evidence of any buffering effect, no diminution of the pathological effect of a stress, when support was present, and Pinneau added that his scrutiny of previous research failed to find any either. The buffering hypothesis remains attractive, however, and deserves to be examined further, using the person-environment fit approach, especially in experimental attempts to modify strains. Social support should be most ameliorative when the amount available fits the amount wanted.

TRENDS IN OS THEORIES AND RESEARCH

The field of OS seems to have gone through four phases of development.

The first phase was marked by efforts to find simple cause and effect relationships, largely of this type: stress → illness or death. Both cause and effect tended to be objectively defined (that is, in terms of the researcher's judgment, not that of the affected persons). The few such correlations found were usually low; understanding of the mediating process was meager or wholly lacking. The work was methodologically naive, and the variables used were defined traditionally, uncritically accepted from sources outside the research field. I include here, also, clinical reports based on unsystematic and usually small samples.

The second phase was marked by increasing differentiation of independent and dependent variables and of the cause-effect chain. The latter often was expressed in terms of explicit theories; for example, environmental stressors → perceived stress → strain → illness. Interactions were not sought and only occasionally found. Investigators were more willing to make deliberate use of subjectively defined variables, or at least were clear which variables were objectively and which were subjectively defined. With better defined and psychometrically developed measures and with the strategy of looking for effects in subsamples (e.g., by sex, by age group, or by general classes of occupations like white- versus blue-collar), investigators sometimes reported larger effect sizes.

The third phase was signaled by the emergence of theories and designs in which interactions and moderator variables played an explicit role. Investigators recognized that low or negligible zero-order correlations between a kind of stress and an effect variable often meant that there were dissimilar or even opposite relationships in different parts of the original sample, which canceled each other out. This phase saw an increase in the sophistication of measurement, research designs, and statistical analyses necessary to detect such interactions and not just linear but curvilinear relationships.

Finally, in the currently emerging phase, prospective (longitudinal) designs have become more prominent; there is a new emphasis on amelioration in controlled studies of therapeutic programs derived from and testing theories of pathogenesis; awareness of the complexity of the phenomena has resulted in multidisciplinary research and movement away from linear conceptions of cause and effect toward explanatory models influenced by systems theories, incorporating various feedback loops.

Many of the problems of OS research are not unique to this field but are local manifestations of endemic defects in research in the human sciences. For obvious reasons, simple research designs are easier to carry out than more complex ones and are tried first. Unhappily, when we are dealing with such important human concerns as work and health, which are interrelated as parts of highly intricate, nested, and overlapping systems, we can expect a kind of Gresham's law to prevail: since oversimplified approaches are cheaper, quicker, and easier to explore than adequate ones, the products of inadequate investigations naturally tend to dominate the literature.

Apparently, certain basic truths need to be emphasized over and over again: people's feelings about their work are highly overdetermined and almost always mixed (ambivalent), hence not easily ascertained by a few blunt, direct questions with precoded answers; work takes place in a multilayered social and cultural context in which many important and often conflicting values intersect; workers are also members of families, and of social, religious, recreational, political, educational, and other institutions, from which they derive a mixture of costs and benefits, of stress and support, interacting with their work lives in highly variable ways depending on the person, the occupation, and other factors; health and illness are extraordinarily complex states that resist reduction to sociological, psychological, or biological terms alone. Nevertheless, a shrewd or lucky investigator can still uncover important links with relatively simple and manageable designs and samples of practicable size. Despite the complexities of occupational stress, some effects are big enough to be detectable with crude instruments and are nearly enough universal so that sophisticated sampling is not always necessary.

NOTES

1. *Ergonomics,* 1978, *21* (10), was devoted entirely to shift work.
2. A similar conception was set forth by Argyris (1957, 1964) in his "personality and organization theory."
3. Sheppard and Herrick (1972) found that workers on a dull, routine job reported the largest amount of dissatisfaction when they started working at it; after three to five years, they began to say that they were satisfied. Note, however, Korman's (1971) finding that people doing repetitive work were satisfied with it when they had poor self-acceptance, but those who did accept themselves expressed dissatisfaction with the same job.
4. Omitting from a study people who actually have an illness but do not define themselves as sick distorts findings, for true positives may get incorrectly classified as false negatives.
5. Ominously, a number of instances of sabotage at nuclear electrical facilities have occurred (Mullen, Davidson, & Jones, 1980), and such acts by disgruntled workers may be on the rise (Emshwiller, 1980).
6. One reason for failure to replicate is suggested by Byrne and White's (1980) finding that 120 myocardial infarct patients did not report more life events of a stressful kind than did 40 less severely ill heart patients but did rate the same events as more emotionally distressing.

REFERENCES

ABEL-HALIM, A. Employee affective responses to organizational stress: Moderating effects of job characteristics. *Personnel Psychology,* 1978, *31,* 561–579.

AKERSTEDT, T. Shift work and health: Interdisciplinary aspects. In P. G. Rentos & R. D. Shepard (eds.) *Shift work and health.* Washington, D.C.: U.S. Government Printing Office, 1976.

ALTHOUSE, R., & HURRELL, J. *An analysis of job stress in coal mining.* DHEW (NIOSH) publication no. 77-217. Washington, D.C.: U.S. Government Printing Office, 1977.

AMARIA, P. J. Effects of paced and unpaced work situations. In C. H. Gudnason & E. N. Corlett (eds.), *Development of production systems.* London: Taylor & Francis, 1974.

ANTONOVSKY, A. Conceptual and methodological problems in the study of resistance resources and stressful life events. In B. S. Dohrenwend & B. P. Dohrenwend (eds.), *Stressful life events: Their nature and effects.* New York: Wiley, 1974.

ARGYRIS, C. *Personality and organization.* New York: Harper, 1957.

————. *Integrating the individual and the organization.* New York: Wiley, 1964.

————. Personality and organization theory revisited. *Administrative Science Quarterly,* 1973, *18,* 141–167.

AXELSSON, R., & LUNDBERG, U. *Working environment of operating personnel in a nuclear power plant: A pilot study.* Report No. TA 875-R1, Bromma, Sweden, 1975.

BECKER, R. O. Brain pollution. *Psychology Today,* 1979, *9*(12), 124.

BEEHR, T. A. Perceived situational moderators of the relationship between subjective role ambiguity and role strain. *Journal of Applied Psychology,* 1976, *61,* 35–40.

BEEHR, T. A., WALSH, J. T., & TABER, T. D. Relationship of stress to individually and organizationally valued states: Higher order needs as a moderator. *Journal of Applied Psychology,* 1976, *61,* 41–47.

BELBIN, R. M., & STAMMERS, D. Pacing stress, human adaptation, and training in car production. *Applied Erogonomics,* 1972, *3,* 142–146.

BIERSNER, R. J., GUNDERSON, E. K., RYMAN, D. H., & RAHE, R. H. *Correlations of physical fitness, perceived health status, and dispensary visits with performance in stressful training.* USN Medical Neuropsychiatric Research Unit technical report no. 71-30. U.S. Navy, 1971.

BROOK, A. Mental stress at work. *Practitioner,* 1973, *210,* 500–506.

BRUUSGARD, A. Shift work as an occupational health problem. *Studia Laboris et Salutis* (Stockholm), 1975, *4,* 9–14.

BSUGLASS, D., & DUFFY, J. C. The ecological pattern of suicide and parasuicide in Edinburgh. *Social Science and Medicine,* 1978, *12,* 241–253.

BYRNE, D. G., & WHITE, H. M. Life events and myocardial infarction revisited: the role of measures of individual impact. *Psychosomatic Medicine,* 1980, *42,* 1–10.

CAMERON, C. Fatigue problems in modern industry. *Ergonomics,* 1971, *14,* 713–720.

CAPLAN, R. D. Organizational stress and individual strain: A social psychological study of risk factors in coronary heart disease among administrators, engineers, and scientists. *Dissertation Abstracts International,* 1972, *32*(11B), 6706B.

CAPLAN, R. D., COBB, S., FRENCH, J. R. P., JR., HARRISON, R. V., & PINNEAU, S. R., JR. *Job demands and worker health: Main effects and occupational differences.* DHEW (NIOSH) publication no. 75-160. Washington, D.C.: U.S. Government Printing Office, 1975.

CHADWICK, J. F. Psychological job stress and coronary heart disease: A current NIOSH project. In R. M. Schwartz (ed.), *New developments in occupational stress.* Cincinnati: National Institute for Occupational Safety and Health, 1980.

CHASE, D. J. Sources of mental stress and how to avoid them. *Supervisory Management*, 1972, *17*, 33–36.

CHERNISS, C. *Staff burnout: Job stress in the human services*. Beverly Hills: Sage, 1980.

CHERRY, N. Stress, anxiety, and work: A longitudinal study. *Journal of Occupational Psychology*, 1978, *51*, 259–270.

COBB, S. *The frequency of the rheumatic diseases*. Cambridge: Harvard University Press, 1971.

————. Role responsibility: The differentiation of a concept. *Occupational Mental Health*, 1973, *3*, 10–14.

————. A model for life events and their consequences. In B. S. Dohrenwend & B. P. Dohrenwend (eds.) *Stressful life events: Their nature and effects*. New York: Wiley, 1974.

————. Social support as a moderator of life stress. *Psychosomatic Medicine*, 1976, *38*, 300–314.

COBB, S., & KASL, S. V. Some medical aspects of unemployment. In G. M. Shatto (ed.), *Employment of the middle-aged: Papers from industrial gerontology seminars*. Springfield: Thomas, 1972.

————. *Termination: The consequences of job loss*. Cincinnati: National Institute for Occupational Safety and Health, 1977.

COBB, S., & ROSE, R. M. Psychosomatic disease in air traffic controllers: Hypertension, diabetes, and peptic ulcer. *Journal of the American Medical Association*, 1973, *224*, 489–492.

COBURN, D. Job-worker incongruence: Consequences for health. *Journal of Health and Social Behavior*, 1975, *16*, 198–212.

————. Work and general psychological and physical well-being. *International Journal of Health Services*, 1978, *8*, 415–435.

COHEN, A., & MARGOLIS, B. Initial psychological research related to the Occupational Safety and Health Act of 1970. *American Psychologist*, 1973, *28*, 600–606.

COHEN, J. German and American workers: A comparative view of worker distress. *International Journal of Mental Health*, 1976, *5*, 138–147.

COHEN, S. Aftereffects of stress on human performance and social behavior: A review of research and theory. *Psychological Bulletin*, 1980, *88*, 82–108.

COLLIGAN, M. J., & MURPHY, L. R. Mass psychogenic illness in organizations: An overview. *Journal of Occupational Psychology*, 1979, *52*, 77–90.

COLLIGAN, M. J., SMITH, M. J., & HURRELL, J. J. Occupational incidence rates of mental health disorders. *Journal of Human Stress*, 1977, *3*, 34–39.

COLQUHOUN, W. P. Accidents, injuries, and shift work. In P. G. Rentos & R. D. Shepard (eds.), *Shift work and health*. Washington, D.C.: U.S. Government Printing Office, 1976.

COOPER, C. L. Dentists under pressure: A social psychological study. In C. L. Cooper & J. Marshall (eds.), *White collar and professional stress*. New York: Wiley, 1980.

COOPER, C. L., & MARSHALL, J. Occupational sources of stress: A review of the literature relating to coronary heart disease and mental ill health. *Journal of Occupational Psychology*, 1976, *49*, 11–28.

————. Sources of managerial and white collar stress. In C. L. Cooper & R. Payne (eds.), *Stress at work*. New York: Wiley, 1978.

————. (eds.). *White collar and professional stress*. New York: Wiley, 1980.

CRAIN, R. D. The effect of work values on the relationship between job characteristics and job satisfaction. *Dissertation Abstracts International*, 1974, *34*(11B), 5729B.

CRUMP, J. H. Review of stress in air traffic control: Its measurement and effects. *Aviation, Space, and Environmental Medicine*, 1979, *50*, 243–248.

CUMMINGS, L. L., & DeCOTIIS, T. A. Organizational correlates of perceived stress in a professional organization. *Public Personnel Management*, 1973, *2*, 275–282.

Dainoff, M. J. *Occupational stress factors in secretarial/clerical workers: Annotated research bibliography and analytic review.* Cincinnati: National Institute for Occupational Safety and Health, 1979.

Daley, M. R. Burnout: Smoldering problem in protective services. *Social Work,* 1979, *24,* 375–379.

Davidson, M. J., & Veno, A. Stress and the policeman. In C. L. Cooper & J. Marshall (eds.), *White collar and professional stress.* New York: Wiley, 1980.

Dohrenwend, B. S., & Dohrenwend, B. P. (eds.). *Stressful life events: Their nature and effects.* New York: Wiley, 1974.

Doll, R., & Jones, A. F. *Occupational factors in the aetiology of gastric and duodenal ulcers.* Medical Research Council special report no. 276. London: HMSO, 1951.

Dooley, D., & Catalano, R. Economic change as a cause of behavioral disorder. *Psychological Bulletin,* 1980, *87,* 450–468.

Emshwiller, J. R. Sabotage by insiders: How serious is the threat to atomic facilities? *Wall Street Journal,* 3 September 1980, pp. 1,20.

Ettema, J. H., & Zielhuis, R. L. Psychological parameters of mental load. *Ergonomics,* 1971, *14,* 137–144.

Falger, P. R. Changes in work load as a potential risk constellation for myocardial infarction: A concise review. *Gedrag: Tijdschrift voor Psychologie* (Tilburg, Netherlands), 1979, *7,* 96–114.

Ferguson, D. A study of occupational stress and health. *Ergonomics,* 1973, *16,* 649–664.

Fodor, E. M. Group stress, authoritarian style of control, and use of power. *Journal of Applied Psychology,* 1976, *61,* 313–318.

Frankenhaeuser, M., & Gardell, B. Underload and overload in working life: Outline of a multidisciplinary approach. *Journal of Human Stress,* 1976, *2,* 35–46.

French, J. R. P., Jr. Person-role fit. *Occupational Mental Health,* 1973, *3,* 15–20; also in A. McLean (ed.), *Occupational stress.* Springfield: Thomas, 1974.

French, J. R. P., Jr., & Caplan, R. D. Psychosocial factors in coronary heart disease. *Industrial Medicine,* 1970, *39,* 383–397.

French, J. R. P., Jr., Rodgers, W. L., & Cobb, S. Adjustment as person-environment fit. In G. Coelho, D. Hamburg & J. Adams (eds.), *Coping and adaptation.* New York: Basic Books, 1974.

French, J. R. P., Jr., Tupper, C. J., & Mueller, E. F. *Work load of university professors.* Ann Arbor: Institute for Social Research, 1965.

Froberg, J., Karlsson, C.-G., Levi, L., Lidberg, L., & Seeman, K. Conditions of work: Psychological and endocrine stress reactions. *Archives of Environmental Health,* 1970, *21,* 789–797.

Gardell, B. Reactions at work and their influence on nonwork activities: An analysis of a sociopolitical problem in affluent societies. *Human Relations,* 1976, *29,* 885–904.

Gavin, J. F. Employee perceptions of the work environment and mental health: A suggestive study. *Journal of Vocational Behavior,* 1975, *6,* 217–234.

Gechman, A. S., & Wiener, Y. Job involvement and satisfaction as related to mental health and personal time devoted to work. *Journal of Applied Psychology,* 1975, *60,* 521–523.

Gemmill, R., & Heisler, W. J. Machiavellianism as a factor in managerial job strain, job satisfaction, and upward mobility. *Academy of Management Journal,* 1972, *15,* 51–62.

Glass, D. C. Stress, behavior patterns, and coronary disease. *American Scientist,* 1977, *65,* 177–187.

Glass, D. C., & Singer, J. E. *Urban stress: Experiments on noise and social stressors.* New York: Academic, 1972.

Gulian, E. Fatigue and neuroticism: A differential approach. *Revista de Psihologie* (Bucharest), 1974, *20,* 15–30.

Halberg, F., & Nelson, W. Some aspects of chronobiology relating to the optimization of shift work. In P. G. Rentos & R. D. Shepard (eds.), *Shift work and health.* Washington, D.C.: U.S. Government Printing Office, 1976.

HAMNER, W. C., & TOSI, H. Relationship of role conflict and role ambiguity to job involvement measures. *Journal of Applied Psychology,* 1974, *59,* 497–499.

HARRIS, W., & MACKIE, R. R. *A study of the relationship among fatigue, hours of service, and safety of operations of truck and bus drivers.* Washington, D.C.: U.S. Department of Transportation, 1972.

HARRISON, R. V. Job stress as person-environment misfit. Paper presented to the annual meeting of the American Psychological Association, Washington, D.C. 1976.

HAYNES, S. G., FEINLEIB, M., & KANNEL, W. B. The relationship of psychosocial factors to coronary heart disease in the Framingham Study. Parts I and II. *American Journal of Epidemiology,* 1978, *107,* 362–402.

————. The relationship of psychosocial factors to coronary heart disease in the Framingham Study. Part III: Eight-year incidence of coronary heart disease. *American Journal of Epidemiology,* 1980, *111,* 37–58.

HINKLE, L. E., JR. The effect of exposure to culture change, social change, and changes in the interpersonal relationships on health. In B. S. Dohrenwend & B. P. Dohrenwend (eds.), *Stressful life events: Their nature and effects.* New York: Wiley, 1974.

HITE, A. L. Some characteristics of work roles and their relationships to self-esteem and depression. *Dissertation Abstracts International,* 1976, *36*(7B), 3609B.

HOLZER, C. E., III, WARHEIT, G. J., & KULDAU, J. M. *Life stress and continuity of depressive symptoms.* New York: American Psychiatric Association, 1978.

HOUSE, J. S. The relationship of intrinsic and extrinsic work motivations to occupational stress and coronary heart disease risk. *Dissertation Abstracts International,* 1972, *33*(5A). 2514A.

————. Occupational stress and coronary heart disease: A review and theoretical integration. *Journal of Health and Social Behavior,* 1974, *15,* 12–27.

HOUSE, J. S., MCMICHAEL, A. J., WELLS, J. A., KAPLAN, B. H., & LANDERMAN, L. R. Occupational stress and health among factory workers. *Journal of Health and Social Behavior,* 1979, *20,* 139–160.

ILFELD, F. W., JR. Current social stressors and symptoms of depression. *American Journal of Psychiatry,* 1977, *134,* 161–166.

IRIS, B., & BARRETT, G. V. Some relations between job and life satisfactions and job importance. *Journal of Applied Psychology,* 1972, *56,* 301–304.

IVANCEVICH, J. M., & DONNELLY, J. H. Relation of organizational structure to job satisfaction, anxiety-stress, and performance. *Administrative Science Quarterly,* 1975, *20,* 272–280.

JACOBSON, D. Fatigue-producing factors in industrial work and preretirement attitudes. *Occupational Psychology,* 1972, *46,* 193–200.

JAHODA, M. The impact of unemployment in the 1930s and the 1970s. *Bulletin of the British Psychological Society,* 1979, *32,* 309–314.

JAMES, L. R., & JONES, A. P. Organizational climate: A review of theory and research. *Psychological Bulletin,* 1974, *81,* 1096–1112.

————. Organizational structure: A review of structural dimensions and their conceptual relationships with individual attitudes and behavior. *Organizational Behavior and Human Performance,* 1976, *16,* 74–113.

JENKINS, C. D. Recent evidence supporting psychologic and social risk factors for coronary disease. *New England Journal of Medicine,* 1976, *294,* (Part I), 987–994; (Part 2), 1033–1038.

JENKINS, C. D., ROSENMAN, R. H., & FRIEDMAN, M. Replicability of rating the coronary-prone behavior pattern. *British Journal of Preventive and Social Medicine,* 1968, *22,* 16–22.

JOHANSSON, G., & LINDSTROM, B. *Paced and unpaced work under salary and piece-rate conditions.* University of Stockholm, Department of Psychology report no. 359. 1975.

JOLLY, J. A. Job change: Its relationship to role stresses and stress symptoms according to personality and environment. *Dissertation Abstracts International,* 1979, *40*(5), 2418B.

KAHN, R. L. Conflict, ambiguity, and overload: Three elements in job stress. *Occupational Mental Health,* 1973, *3,* 2–9.

KAHN, R. L., & FRENCH, J. R. P., JR. Stress and conflict: Two themes in the study of stress. In J. E. McGrath (ed.), *Social and psychological factors in stress.* New York: Holt, 1970.

KAHN, R. L., WOLFE, D. M., QUINN, R. P., SNOEK, J. D., & ROSENTHAL, R. A. *Organizational stress: Studies in role conflict and ambiguity.* New York: Wiley, 1964.

KARCHER, C. J. Normative integration of the industrial setting. *Dissertation Abstracts International,* 1978, *38*(7A), 4384A.

KASL, S. V., & COBB, S. Blood pressure changes in men undergoing job loss: A preliminary report. *Psychosomatic Medicine,* 1970, *32,* 19–38.

KASL, S. V., & FRENCH, J. R. P., JR. The effects of occupational status on physical and mental health. *Journal of Social Issues,* 1962, *18,* 67–89.

KASL, S. V., GORE, S., & COBB, S. The experience of losing a job: Reported change in health, symptoms, and illness behavior. *Psychosomatic Medicine,* 1975, *37,* 106–122.

KATZELL, R. A., YANKELOVICH, D., FEIN, M., OORNATI, O. A., & NASH, A. *Work, productivity, and job satisfaction.* New York: Psychological Corporation, 1975.

KELLAM, S. G. Stressful life events and illness: A research area in need of conceptual development. In B. S. Dohrenwend & B. P. Dohrenwend (eds.) *Stressful life events: Their nature and effects.* New York: Wiley, 1974.

KIMBALL, W. H. Psychological correlates of tension headaches. *Dissertation Abstracts International,* 1979, *39*(10B), 5073B.

KORMAN, A. *Industrial and organizational psychology.* Englewood Cliffs: Prentice-Hall, 1971.

KORNHAUSER, A. *Mental health of the industrial worker.* New York: Wiley, 1965.

KROES, W. H. *Society's victim, the policemen: An analysis of job stress in policing.* Springfield: Thomas, 1976.

KROES, W., HURRELL, J., & MARGOLIS, B. Job stress in police administrators. *Journal of Police Science and Administration,* 1974, *2,* 381–387.

LEDERER, L. G. Psychologic and psychopathologic aspects of behavior during airline pilot transition training. *Revue de Médicine Aeronautique et Spatiale* (Paris), 1973, *12,* 299–300.

LEVINE, H. Health and work shifts. In P. G. Rentos & R. D. Shepard (eds.), *Shift work and health.* Washington, D.C.: U. S. Government Printing Office, 1976.

LIKERT, R. *New patterns of management.* New York: McGraw-Hill, 1961.

LOCKE, E. A. The nature and causes of job satisfaction. In M. D. Dunnette (ed.), *Handbook of industrial and organizational psychology.* Chicago: Rand-McNally, 1976.

LONDON, M. & KLIMOSKI, R. J. Self-esteem and job complexity as moderators of performance and satisfaction. *Journal of Vocational Behavior,* 1975, *6,* 293–304.

MACKINNON, N. J. Role strain: An assessment of a measure and its invariance of factor structure across studies. *Journal of Applied Psychology,* 1978, *63,* 321–328.

MANGIONE, T. W., & QUINN, R. P. Job satisfaction, counterproductive behavior, and drug use at work. *Journal of Applied Psychology,* 1975, *60,* 114–116.

MARGOLIS, B. L., KROES, W. H., & QUINN, R. P. Job stress: An unlisted occupational hazard. *Journal of Occupational Medicine,* 1974, *16,* 659–661.

MARSHALL, J. Stress amongst nurses. In C. L. Cooper & J. Marshall (eds.), *White collar and professional stress.* New York: Wiley, 1980.

McFARLAND, R. A. Influence of changing time zones on air crews and passengers. *Aerospace Medicine,* 1974, *45,* 648–658.

McGRATH, J. E. Stress and behavior in organizations. In M. D. Dunnette (ed.), *Handbook of industrail and organizational psychology.* Chicago: Rand McNally, 1976.

MECHANIC, D. Discussion of research programs on relations between stressful life events and episodes of physical illness. In B. S. Dohrenwend & B. P. Dohrenwend (eds.), *Stressful life events: Their nature and effects.* New York: Wiley, 1974.

MEERS, A., MAASEN, A., & VERHAEGEN, P. Subjective health after six months and four years of shift work. *Ergonomics,* 1978, *21,* 857–859.

MENDELOFF, A., & DUNN, J. P. *Digestive diseases.* Cambridge: Harvard University Press, 1971.

MILES, R. H., & PETTY, M. M. Relationships between role clarity, need for clarity, and job tension and satisfaction for supervisory and nonsupervisory roles. *Academy of Management Journal,* 1975, *18,* 877–883.

MOCH, M. K., BARTUNEK, J., & BRASS, D. J. Structure, task characteristics, and experienced role stress in organizations employing complex technology. *Organizational Behavior and Human Performance,* 1979, *24,* 258–268.

MORRIS, J. N., HEADY, J. A., & BARLEY, R. G. Coronary heart disease in medical practitioners. *British Medical Journal,* 1952, (4757), 503–520.

MOTT, P. E. Social and psychological adjustment to shift work. In P. G. Rentos & R. D. Shepard (eds.), *Shift work and health.* Washington, D.C.: U.S. Government Printing Office, 1976.

MOTT, P. E., MANN, F. C., McLOUGHLIN, Q., & WARWICK, D. P. *Shift work: The social psychological consequences.* Ann Arbor: University of Michigan Press, 1965.

MULLEN, S. A., DAVIDSON, J. J., & JONES, H. B., JR. *Potential threat to licensed nuclear activities from insiders.* Washington, D.C.: U.S. Nuclear Regulatory Commission, 1980.

MUMFORD, L. *The myth of the machine.* Vol. 1: *Technics and human development.* New York: Harcourt, 1967.

————. *The myth of the machine.* Vol. 2: *The pentagon of power.* New York: Harcourt, 1970.

MURPHY, L. R., & HURRELL, J. J., JR. Machine pacing and occupational stress. In R. M. Schwartz (ed.), *New developments in occupational stress.* Cincinnati: National Institute for Occupational Safety and Health, 1980.

MURRAY, R. M. Psychiatric illness in doctors. *Lancet* (London), 1974, *151,* 1211–1213.

NEVES, I. F. Social adaptation and accidents on the job. *Revista Interamericaa de Psicología,* 1969, *3,* 139–162.

ORTH-GOMER, K. Ischemic heart disease and psychological stress in Stockholm and New York. *Journal of Psychosomatic Research,* 1979, *23,* 165–173.

OSTBERG, O. Interindividual differences in circadian fatigue patterns of shift workers. *British Journal of Industrial Medicine,* 1973, *30,* 341–351.

OWEN, J. D. The economics of shift work and absenteeism. In P. G. Rentos & R. D. Shepard (eds.), *Shift work and health.* Washington, D.C.: U.S. Government Printing Office, 1976.

PALMORE, E. B. Predicting longevity: A follow-up controlling for age. *Gerontologist,* 1969, *9,* 247–250.

PEARSE, R. *What managers think about their managerial careers.* New York: American Management Association, 1977.

PINNEAU, S. R. Effects of social support on occupational stresses and strains. Paper presented to the annual meeting of the American Psychological Association, Washington, D.C., 1976.

PORTER, L. W., & DUBIN, R. *The organization and the person: Final report of the Individual Occupational Linkages Project.* Washington, D.C.: U.S. Office of Naval Research, 1975.

POWELL, M. Age and occupational change among coal-miners. *Occupational Psychology,* 1973, *47,* 37–49.

QUINN, R. P. *Locking-in as a moderator of the relationship between job satisfaction and worker health.* Ann Arbor: University of Michigan, Survey Research Center, 1972.

————. What makes jobs monotonous and boring? Paper presented to the annual meeting of the American Psychological Association, Chicago, 1975.

Quinn, R. P., Seashore, S. Kahn, R., Mangione, T., Campbell, D., Staines, G., & McCullough, M. *Survey of working conditions: Final report on univariate and bivariate tables.* Washington, D.C.: U.S. Government Printing Office, 1971.

Quinn, R., & Shepard, L. *The 1972-73 quality of employment survey.* Ann Arbor: University of Michigan, Survey Research Center, 1974.

Rahe, R. H., Gunderson, E. K. E., Pugh, W., Rubin, R. T., & Arthur, R. J. Illness prediction studies: Use of psychosocial and occupational characteristics as predictors. *Archives of Environmental Health,* 1972, *25,* 192-197.

Ramos, A. A. The relationship of sex and ethnic background to job-related stress of research and development professionals. *Dissertation Abstracts International,* 1975, *36*(3)A, 1862A.

Reinhart, G. R., IV. Social structure and self-destructive behavior. *Dissertation Abstracts International,* 1978, *38*(7A), 4390A.

Renshaw, R. An exploration of the dynamics of the overlapping worlds of work and family. *Family Process,* 1976, *15,* 143-165.

Rentos, P. G., & Shepard, R. D. (eds.). *Shift work and health: A symposium.* DHEW (NIOSH) Publication no. 76-203. Washington, D.C.: U.S. Government Printing Office, 1976.

Ronan, W. W., Cobb, J. M., Garrett, T. L., Lazarri, J. D., Mosser, D. R., & Racine, A. E. Occupational level and mental health: A note. *Journal of Vocational Behavior,* 1974, *5,* 157-160.

Rose, R. M., Jenkins, C. D., & Hurst, N. W. Health change in air traffic controllers: A prospective study. *Psychosomatic Medicine,* 1978, *40,* 142-165.

Russek, H. I. Emotional stress and coronary heart disease in American physicians. *American Journal of Medical Sciences,* 1960, *240,* 711-721.

————. Emotional stress as a cause of coronary heart disease. *Journal of the American College Health Association,* 1973, *22,* 120-123.

Ryzhkova, M. N., Lanskiy, V. P., Nevskaya, Y. M., & Simonova, T. A. Metodicheskiye voprosi psikholigiyenicheskikh issledovaniy v professiyakh nervonapryazhen-nogo truda. [Methodical questions of psychohygienic research on professions entailing stressful work.] *Gigyena Truda i Professional'nyye Zabolevaniya* (Moscow), 1978, *8,* 24-27.

Sales, S. M., & House, J. Job dissatisfaction as a possible risk factor in coronary heart disease. *Journal of Chronic Diseases,* 1971, *23,* 861-873.

Schmidt, W. H. Basic causes of organizational stress: Causes and problems. In R. M. Schwartz (ed.), *Occupational stress: Proceedings of the conference on occupational stress.* Washington, D.C.: U.S. Government Printing Office, 1978.

Schriesheim, C. A., & Murphy, C. J. Relationships between leader behavior and subordinate satisfaction and performance: A test of some situational moderators. *Journal of Applied Psychology,* 1976, *61,* 634-641.

Selye, H. *The stress of life.* New York: McGraw-Hill, 1956.

————. *Stress in health and disease.* London: Butterworths, 1976.

Sheppard, H. L., & Herrick, N. Q. *Where have all the robots gone? Worker dissatisfaction in the '70s.* New York: Free Press, 1972.

Shirom, A., Eden, D., Silberwasser, S., & Kellerman, J. J. Job stress and risk factors in coronary heart disease among five occupational categories in kibbutzim. *Social Science and Medicine,* 1973, *7,* 875-892.

Singer, J. N. Job strain as a function of job and life stresses. *Dissertation Abstracts International,* 1975, *36*(6B), 3109B.

Smith, M., Colligan, M., & Hurrell, J. Three incidents of industrial mass psychogenic illness. *Journal of Occupational Medicine,* 1978, *20,* 399-400.

Smith, M. J., Colligan, M. J., & Hurrell, J. J., Jr. A review of psychological stress research carried out by NIOSH, 1971 to 1976. In R. M. Schwartz (ed.), *New developments in occupational stress.* Cincinnati: National Insititue for Occupational Safety and Health, 1980.

SPECTOR, P. E. Relationships of organizational frustration with reported behavioral reactions of employees. *Journal of Applied Psychology,* 1975, *60,* 635–637.

SUSSER, M. Causes of peptic ulcer: A selective epidemiological review. *Journal of Chronic Diseases,* 1967, *20,* 435–456.

SWAIN, A. D., & GUTTMANN, H. E. *Handbook of human reliability analysis with emphasis on nuclear power plant applications.* Washington, D.C.: U.S. Nuclear Regulatory Commission, 1980.

TASTO, D., & COLLIGAN, M. *Health consequences of shiftwork.* DHEW (NIOSH) publication no. 78-154. Washington, D.C.: U.S. Government Printing Office, 1978.

TAYLOR, P. J. The effects of shift work on worker health. *Industrial Medicine and Surgery,* 1973, *42,* 13–19.

THEORELL, T. Life events before and after the onset of a premature myocardial infarction. In B. S. Dohrenwend & B. P. Dohrenwend (eds.), *Stressful life events: Their nature and effects.* New York: Wiley, 1974.

THEORELL, T., LIND, E., & FLODERUS, B. The relationship of disturbing life-changes and emotions to the early development of myocardial infarctions and other serious illnesses. *International Journal of Epidemiology,* 1975, *4,* 281–293.

TUNG, R. L., & KOCH, J. L. School administrators: Sources of stress and ways of coping with it. In C. L. Cooper & J. Marshall (eds.), *White collar and professional stress.* New York: Wiley, 1980.

VERTIN, P. G. *Bedrijfsgeneeskundige Aspecten van het Ulcus Pepticum.* Eindhoven: Hermes, 1954.

WALDRON, J. The coronary-prone behavior pattern, blood pressure, employment, and socio-economic status in women. *Journal of Psychosomatic Research,* 1978, *22,* 79–87.

WEINER, H. *Psychobiology and human disease.* New York: Elsevier, 1977.

WILKES, B., STAMMERJOHN, L., & LALICH, N. *Job demands and worker health in machine-paced poultry inspection.* NIOSH final project report can. no. 0-9277766. Washington, D.C.: U.S. Government Printing Office, n.d.

Work in America: Report of a special task force to the Secretary of Health, Education, and Welfare. Cambridge: MIT Press, 1973.

ZUNG, W. W. A self-rating depression scale. *Archives of General Psychiatry,* 1965, *12,* 63–70.

20

The Effects of Workload and the Social Environment at Work on Health

Rena L. Repetti

WORK CAN BE HAZARDOUS to your health. In addition to injuries, the National Institute for Occupational Safety and Health (1986, 1988) lists cardiovascular disease, lung disease, cancer, disorders of reproduction, neurotoxic disorders, hearing loss, dermatologic conditions, and psychological disorders among the leading work-related health problems. Along with accidents and exposure to hazardous agents, psychosocial stressors contribute to an unhealthy work environment. Unfortunately, progress in the study of psychosocial stressors in the workplace has been impeded by a failure in many investigations to differentiate among different types of stressors. This shortcoming has been addressed in recent years by increasing efforts to identify specific psychosocial conditions at work that may affect the health of individual workers. Two of the most fruitful areas of investigation have been studies that focus on the health consequences of work overload and a poor social environment at work (Repetti, Matthews, & Waldron, 1989). This chapter reviews the empirical evidence that has been amassed to date regarding the physical and mental health outcomes associated with these two particular job stressors and suggests some promising avenues for future research.

THE EFFECTS OF PSYCHOLOGICAL WORKLOAD ON HEALTH

The term psychological workload, which refers to mental exertion, is distinguished in the occupational stress literature from physical workload or physical exertion, such as heavy lifting. Psychological workload may be defined by a combination of (a) the number of demands placed on the individual, (b) the degree of alertness or arousal required to carry out tasks at work, and (c) the pace of work or time pressure under which the tasks must be completed. A growing body of research addresses the health consequences of jobs that require workers to over-exert themselves in order to meet task and scheduling demands. However, no single study has measured all of the different aspects of psychological workload. Instead, most investigators have asked workers to evaluate either their overall workload or some aspect of workload, such as the number of demands or the amount of time spent at work. A few have used objective measures, such as the number of telephone calls and radio transmissions handled by police radio dispatchers or, for air traffic controllers, air traffic volume and visibility conditions at the airport. The differing measurement strategies that have been used in this literature may account for some of the inconsistent findings that are reported below.

The Direct Effects of Psychological Workload on Long-term Health Outcomes

Mental Health Outcomes. The available empirical evidence is consistent with the idea that when employed persons are exposed to chronically high levels of psychological workload, their mental health suffers. A one-year longitudinal study of over 300 married, male, power plant employees provides the strongest evidence that perceived workload is associated with the development of psychological problems. After controlling for age, higher levels of self-reported job demands were associated with an increase in symptoms of psychological distress and with an increased risk of affective disorder (Bromet, Dew, Parkinson, & Schulberg, 1988). Two cross-sectional questionnaire studies reported a significant association between self-reported demands at work and symptoms of depression. Both studies included appropriate demographic controls, such as age and marital status, before testing for the effects of workload. One of the studies was based on a very large sample ($n = 8,700$) of white collar workers in Sweden (Karasek, Gardell, & Lindell, 1987); the other was based on data from 289 mostly female hospital and nursing home employees in the United States (Landsbergis, 1988). In contrast to these findings, two large surveys of employed men failed to find statistically significant correlations between respondents' descriptions of job demands and symptoms of depression (Karasek, Triantis, & Chaudhry, 1982; LaRocco, House, & French, 1980).

Several other studies, which did not control for demographic factors, have reported significant cross-sectional relations between perceived workload and other indexes of mental health. A French study of over 1,500 female hospital workers found that two measures of perceived workload, mental load and strain due to scheduling demands, were associated with indicators of psychological distress, including the use of medications (such as antidepressants and sedatives), fatigue, and high scores on the General Health Questionnaire (Estryn-Behar, et al., 1990). In two student surveys, perceived overload was again linked to self-reports of psychological strain (Osipow & Davis, 1988; Parkes, 1990).

Because the studies cited above all rely on individuals' subjective assessments of the level of pressures and demands that they experience at work or school, it is likely that the cross-sectional correlations are at least partly inflated by respondent biases. In addition, evidence suggests that some portion of the covariance in the cross-sectional studies can be explained by the effect that psychological distress has on perceptions of conditions at work. In an intensive study of air traffic controllers (ATCs), Rose and his colleagues found that ATCs with a chronic depressive disorder and those with a chronic anxiety disorder tended to perceive much higher workloads than that indicated by objective measures (Rose, Jenkins, & Hurst, 1978). Objective measures of workload allow researchers to more convincingly evaluate the effects that actual demands at work have on mental health, as opposed to the effects of individual appraisals of workload. In the study of ATCs, those with high levels of anxiety and those with high levels of depression had greater objective workloads (Rose, Jenkins, & Hurst, 1978). Unfortunately, no other published studies of long-term mental health outcomes have included objective indicators of workload.

Physical Health Outcomes. Three types of physical health outcomes have been examined in studies of occupational workload: general symptoms or health complaints, indicators of coronary heart disease (CHD) or risk factors associated with CHD, and mortality. Few longitudinal studies examine the main effects of workload on physical health. However, there are consistent reports of cross-sectional associations between perceived psychological workload and health complaints. Three cross-sectional studies that included appropriate demographic controls found perceived job demands linked to physical/psychosomatic complaints and problems with sleep (Landsbergis, 1988) and to a variety of symptoms such as stomach problems, headaches, and dizziness (Barnett, Davidson, & Marshall, 1991; Karasek, et al., 1987). Other studies, without controlling for demographic characteristics, have reported similar results. For example, in a survey of over 3,000 employed persons in three different industries, perceived overload at work was associated with more minor health complaints, such as headaches and fatigue (Steffy, Jones, & Noe, 1990). In contrast, one study of office workers failed to find a significant main effect of occupational demands on a symptom scale that included both affective and somatic disturbances (Sauter, 1989).

In general the data suggest a link between perceived workload and poor health, as indicated by self-reported physical symptoms. However, these findings must be evaluated in light of Watson and Pennebaker's (1989) argument that health complaint scales assess two factors, one that is related to objective health status and another that is more subjective and psychological. Therefore, the results involving health complaints may be subject to the same third variable problem present in studies of mental health outcomes. An individual psychological/perceptual variable may at least partly account for the observed association between subjective workload and symptoms.

A number of investigations have focused on coronary heart disease as a potential long-term health outcome associated with chronic work overload. These studies, which generally include better assessments of health end points, provide only limited support for a main effect of workload on CHD. Supportive evidence comes from two early studies of Swedish populations. Theorell and Floderus-Myrhed (1977) analyzed questionnaire data from over 5,000 Swedish building construction workers and related them to information from various health registers maintained in Sweden. The results indicated that reports of high levels of perceived workload were associated with an increased age-adjusted risk of myocardial infarction. Karasek and his colleagues (1981) found that, in a random sample of the Swedish male workforce, reports of high job demands were associated both with the development of signs and symptoms of CHD and with increased risk of cardiovascular or cerebrovascular death over the ensuing six years, after controlling for risk factors like age and smoking habits.

Although these results are impressive, they have not been replicated in subsequent studies. The Tecumseh Community Health Study examined the cross-sectional association between self-reported hours worked per week and several health indexes, after controlling for age and education. Among the over 1,000 employed men and over 750 employed women, work hours were not related to a diagnosis of suspect or probable CHD (defined as a probable history of myocardial infarction, angina, or electrocardiographic evidence) (House, Strecher, Metzner, & Robbins, 1986). In a study of Swedish men who survived a myocardial infarction, there was no association between retrospectively reported psychological demands at work and degree of atherosclerosis based on coronary angiograms and there was no difference in job demands between the patient group and a matched control group (Theorell, Hamsten, de Faire, Orth-Gomer, & Perski, 1987). Finally, Landsbergis (1988) did not find a significant cross-sectional link between perceived job demands and a validated self-report measure of CHD symptoms.

Recent studies have also failed to support an association between workload and two important CHD risk factors: elevated blood pressures and high serum cholesterol levels. Analysis of the Minnesota Heart Survey data from over 2,500 currently employed persons in the United States indicated that, after controlling for age, sex, education, and other relevant occupational and personality variables, neither of two indicators of workload, the number of hours worked per week and the frequency of deadlines at work, were significantly associated with two clinical risk factors for CHD: total serum cholesterol and systolic blood pressure (Sorensen et al., 1985). In the Tecumseh Community Health Study, work hours were not related to a diagnosis of probable hypertension (defined as either elevated blood pressure levels or subjects' reports of the use of "blood pressure medicine") (House, Strecher, Metzner, & Robbins, 1986). Pieper, LaCroix, and Karasek (1989) reported the results of a meta-analysis of 5 other epidemiological investigations conducted in the United States representing a total of over 12,000 men. There was no evidence that psychological demands at work were related to blood pressure or to cholesterol levels. Finally, in the Swedish study of men who survived a myocardial infarction, there was no association between demands at work and lipoprotein (cholesterol and triglyceride) concentrations (Theorell, Hamsten, de Faire, Orth-Gomer, & Perski, 1987).

Given these findings, it is not surprising that workload does not appear to be related to rates of all-cause mortality. In the Tecumseh Community Health Study, work hours were not associated with mortality over a 10-year period (House et al., 1986). There was also no association between perceived job demands and mortality rates 22 years later in a study of male employees of a Swedish pulp and paper company (Astrand, Hanson, & Isacsson, 1989).

Health Behaviors.   Risky health behaviors, such as cigarette smoking, have also been examined as possible outcomes associated with occupational overload. Significant findings in this area might indicate that certain behavioral responses to overload mediate the effects of job demands on poor health. Data from some U.S. samples suggest that employed persons who work more hours also smoke more. Increased work hours were linked to more cigarette smoking for both men and women in the Minnesota Heart Survey (Sorensen et al., 1985). In the Tecumseh Community Health Study, the number of hours worked per week was also associated with increased smoking among employed women but not among employed men (House et al., 1986).

With the exception of the number of hours spent at work, no other indicators of workload have been linked to smoking. A meta-analysis of findings from four U.S. epidemiological investigations indicated that the level of demands associated with an occupation is not related to the amount of smoking among people employed in that occupation (Pieper, LaCroix, & Karasek, 1989). Individuals' perceptions of workload also were not associated with smoking in a large survey of Swedish white collar workers (Karasek et al., 1987) nor in a Swedish study of myocardial infarction survivors (Theorell et al., 1987). However, in one small sample study, which averaged data collected over 14 days from U.S. navy officers, high levels of perceived workload were linked to increased smoking (Conway, Vickers, Ward, & Rahe, 1981).

Findings from the Minnesota Heart Survey indicate that people who spend more hours at work may engage in less physical exercise (Sorensen, et al., 1985). However, data from several studies are consistent in suggesting that work overload is not associated with greater consumption of alcohol (Bromet et al., 1988; Conway et al., 1981; House et al., 1986; Theorell et al., 1987).

Conclusion.   The available empirical evidence indicates that greater demands at work are associated with both minor physical and mental health complaints. However, because almost all of the studies used cross-sectional designs and respondents' perceptions of workload, the findings do not permit a causal ordering of the variables. The promising results of these initial studies warrent a progression to prospective longitudinal designs and assessments of both objective and subjective workload. This second stage of research will allow investigators to begin to distinguish among three different types of effects: (a) the health effects of objective workloads that are determined by environmental conditions, (b) the health effects of individually perceived workloads that are determined by a combination of environmental conditions and individual psychological processes, and (c) the effects of distress on perceptions of workload.

There is mixed support for a main effect of workload on risk for coronary heart disease and, except for an association between work hours and smoking, there is almost no evidence that workload alone is linked to known CHD risk factors. The research discussed next suggests that the effects of work overload may only be linked to CHD when combined with little control or autonomy at work.

The Demand-Control Model

Robert Karasek and a number of Swedish investigators have argued that the effects of job demands are best understood by taking into account the worker's level of control or autonomy at work (Karasek & Theorell, 1990). They argue that a high level of control offers the worker an opportunity to cope with occupational stressors like work overload. Control therefore functions as a stress-moderating factor with risk-reducing consequences. According to the model, the joint effects of demands and control predict stress-related illness such that the most adverse outcomes are associated with jobs that combine high levels of demands with low levels of control. Such "high strain" jobs include machine paced operatives and service workers. Although control is usually conceptualized as the worker's authority to make decisions on the job and the extent to which the worker's skills are used on the job, in practice it has been operationalized in many different ways. For example, monotony at work is sometimes used as an indicator of low control. The demand-control model has been tested with both mental and physical health outcomes.

Mental Health Outcomes. There is some evidence that the combination of job demands and control predicts general symptoms of psychological distress; however, the effect that workload has on depression does not appear to be influenced by job control. Two studies that reported significant main effects for workload also tested the interaction between workload and job decision latitude. In the one-year longitudinal study of power plant employees there was a significant interaction between job demands and decision latitude associated with increased symptoms of psychological distress, but decision latitude did not moderate the association between job demands and risk of affective disorder (Bromet, et al., 1988). In addition, the cross-sectional study of hospital and nursing home employees also failed to find more depressive symptoms among employees who described high strain jobs (Landsbergis, 1988).

Physical Health Outcomes. Two cross-sectional tests of the demand-control model with general symptom scales has also produced mixed results. Although the model has not received support when evaluated with conventional multiplicative interaction terms (demands × control), there is some support from tests that compare the symptom reports of employees who describe high strain jobs to the symptoms reported by those in all other jobs (Landsbergis, 1988; Sauter, 1989).

Most investigations of the demand-control model consider coronary heart disease and

CHD risk factors as outcomes. Alfredsson, Spetz, and Theorell (1985) analyzed data from several Swedish national registers representing over 958,000 people and found that hospitalization rates for myocardial infarctions were higher among both men and women in jobs independently categorized as "hectic and monotonous" (e.g., telephone operator, waitress), and among men in jobs categorized as "hectic with few possibilities to learn new things" (e.g., painters, postmen). Because the job and health variables were assessed by independent sources, respondent biases could not have played a role in this finding. This general finding has been replicated in several studies that measured individuals' perceptions of the level of demands and control that they experience at work. In a case-control study of a random sample of the Swedish male workforce, the risk of cardiovascular or cerebrovascular death over a six-year period was significantly increased for men who at the beginning of the study described their jobs as combining high demands with little control over their allocation of time (Karasek et al., 1981). Landsbergis (1988) reported a significant cross-sectional association between CHD symptoms and an interaction of perceived job demands with decision latitude. One analysis of data from the Framingham Heart Study used an unconventional measure of control at work, reports of clarity of supervision from the immediate supervisor. After controlling for standard risk factors, such as age, systolic blood pressure, serum cholesterol, and smoking, it was found that employed women who described their jobs as combining high demands with low supervision clarity were at an increased risk for coronary events involving angina pectoris. However, the demand-control model was not supported using data from employed men (LaCroix & Haynes, 1987). In the Swedish study of male survivors of a myocardial infarction, the ratio of demands to control at work differentiated between patients and matched controls in one out of three tests only when a single-item measure of the opportunity to learn new things at work was used as the measure of control. In addition, the monotony of work alone significantly discriminated the two groups (Theorell et al., 1987).

In contrast to the general support that the demand-control model has received in studies of CHD, it has received little support in studies of CHD risk factors. Using a procedure in which job characteristics were independently assigned on the basis of occupational codes, the Pieper, et al. (1989) meta-analysis of five epidemiological investigations of U.S. men failed to find an association between CHD risk factors, such as cholesterol level and blood pressures, and a combination of demands and decision latitude at work. Interestingly, the meta-analysis did reveal evidence that job decision latitude alone has a main effect on at least two risk factors associated with CHD, systolic blood pressure, and smoking. In a cross-sectional study that included controls for age and sex, the ratio between self-reported job demands and control (decision latitude and skill discretion) was not related to heart rate measured over a twenty-four hour period (Unden, Orth-Gomer, & Elofsson, 1991). Theorell and his colleagues (1987) similarly failed to find a reliable pattern of correlations between the ratio of demands to control and CHD clinical risk factors among the survivors of a myocardial infarction. However, some support for the demand-control model was found in a study that identified cases of hypertension on the basis of casual and ambulatory monitoring of blood pressures at work. After controlling for many potentially confounding factors (such as age, education, smoking status, type A behavior, and physical activity level of the job), men with elevated diastolic blood pressures at work were more likely to be employed in jobs that they rated as having high strain characteristics (Schnall et al., 1990).

The demand-control model has also been tested with all-cause mortality as an outcome. The study of male employees of a Swedish pulp and paper company failed to predict mortality from a combination of questionnaire measures of demands and job decision latitude taken twenty-two years earlier. However, the control variable alone was a significant risk factor. Higher mortality rates were observed among workers below the median for job decision latitude (Astrand et al., 1989).

Conclusion. Current research strongly supports the demand-control model with regard to CHD events and symptoms. The moderating role of control at work may explain why there has not been consistent evidence of direct effects of workload on CHD. As Karasek and his colleagues have argued, it may be only those people whose jobs combine high load with low control that are at an increased risk. Surprisingly, data on clinical risk factors associated with CHD, such as cholesterol levels and blood pressures, have not conformed to the demand-control model of job stress. However, some evidence indicates that low levels of control at work alone may have a direct effect on CHD risk factors, CHD, and mortality.

In contrast to the CHD data, there is evidence for a main effect of workload on mental and physical health complaints, and there is not consistent evidence to indicate that these effects are moderated by levels of control at work. The concept of control or autonomy at work may be critical to understanding the impact of workload on CHD; however, it may not play a role in the link between workload and other health problems.

The Short-term Effects of Workload

In all of the studies discussed so far, the question of how workload affects health has been framed in terms of the long-term consequences of chronically stressful conditions at work. However a few investigations have focused on short-term psychological and physiological changes that accompany daily variability in workload. An understanding of these short-term outcomes should lead to the development of better process models linking workload with health. Short-term changes are probably most clearly observed through within-subject designs, which remove the effects of stable individual differences. Unless otherwise noted, the studies summarized below examine how daily variability in workload is linked to concomitant short-term changes in the same individual's psychological and physiological functioning.

Mood. Empirical evidence suggests that increased workload may have a short-term effect on mood. Three studies have examined the same-day association between perceived workload and mood on a within-subjects basis. All three found that employed persons reported more distressed mood states on days when they described a relatively high load at work (Bolger, DeLongis, Kessler, & Schilling, 1989; Repetti, 1991a; Stone, 1987). Repetti's (1991a) study also included two objective measures of daily workload. She found that air traffic controllers (ATCs) reported more negative moods on days when there was a greater volume of air traffic as indicated by FAA records. A study of police radio dispatchers examined the short-term effect of workload on tension and anxiety in a between-subjects analysis (i.e., each dispatcher was studied on only one shift). There was a significant between-subjects association between perceived workload and tense-anxious mood at the end of the shift, but not between an objective indicator of workload and mood (Kirmeyer & Dougherty, 1988).

Arousal. Another acute response to a short-term increase in workload may be heightened physiological arousal. The Air Traffic Controller Health Change Study (Rose et al., 1978) showed that systolic blood pressure increased on objectively defined high workload days. This effect was magnified for the hypertensive ATCs. There is also evidence of increased blood pressure and heart rate during the more demanding periods of a paramedic's workday, such as while at the scene of an emergency or at the hospital (Jamner, Shapiro, Goldstein, & Hug, 1991). In addition some Swedish research suggests that excessive overtime is associated with increased adrenaline excretion and elevated heart rate both during the day at work and in the evenings at home (Frankenhaeuser, 1981; Lundberg & Palm, 1989).

Health Complaints. Repetti (1991a) found that a high level of perceived workload was associated with a same-day increase in ATCs' health complaints, such as headaches and stomach pains. This effect was sustained after controlling for the individual's mood on each day, which eliminated a potential third variable account for the association between subjective perceptions of workload and daily symptoms. However, there were not significant associations between two measures of objective workload (air traffic volume and visibility) and daily health complaints in Repetti's study. In contrast to the mood findings, it may be that an awareness of physical discomfort occurs only when an individual appraises that day's workload as highly demanding.

Short-term Behavioral Responses. Other research indicates that employed persons engage in more unhealthy behaviors that can further increase arousal, such as cigarette smoking and coffee drinking, on days when workload is perceived to be high (Conway, et al., 1981). Although some short-term behavioral responses may mediate the adverse impact of work overload on health, the individual may also use coping behaviors that help to reduce negative outcomes. For example, evidence suggests that female smokers use cigarettes to help control negative affect (Chesney, 1991). Results from Repetti's (1989, 1991b) air traffic controller study indicated that social withdrawal may be one short-term behavioral response to increased workload. Repetti (in press) has suggested that some short-term outcomes associated with stress, such as negative affect and increased arousal, may be alleviated by a period of withdrawal immediately following the stressful encounter. If, in the short run, social withdrawal facilitates mood repair and accelerates recovery from physiological arousal it may, in the long run, help to reduce the health risks associated with chronic overload at work.

Conclusion. Although more studies are needed to understand the short-term impact of workload on health-related outcomes, the available evidence suggests that increases in load have immediate effects on mood, arousal, and behavior. Daily repetitions of negative affect and increased arousal may underlie some of the deleterious health outcomes associated with chronic work overload. For example, it has been suggested that a sustained physiological arousal following exposure to a stressor can result in systemic damage both directly (e.g., ulcers) and indirectly (e.g., by depressing the effectiveness of the immune response) (Lazarus & Folkman, 1984). Further investigation of physiological, emotional, and behavioral responses to short-term increases in workload is needed. A more accurate understanding of these acute reactions can suggest pathogenic mechanisms connecting chronic work overload with long-term health outcomes.

THE EFFECTS OF THE SOCIAL ENVIRONMENT OF WORK ON HEALTH

The Direct Effects of the Social Environment on Mental Health

A fairly large research literature addresses the cross-sectional association between the quality of the social environment at work and individual psychological distress. The underlying assumption is that supportive, nonconflictual social relations at work can directly enhance health by meeting basic human needs for affiliation, approval, and a sense of belonging. Because most employed people spend about half of their waking hours at work, it seems reasonable to expect that co-workers and supervisors may play an important role in the satisfaction of these needs. However, it is important to keep in mind that, in addition to the effect that interpersonal relations at work have on mental health, an individual's psychological functioning certainly has an impact on the quality of his or her personal relationships and on perceptions of relationships. Unfortunately, because there are no longitudinal investigations, the question of causal priority cannot be clearly resolved from most of these studies.

Supervisor Relations. A large number of questionnaire/interview studies have examined the cross-sectional association between respondents' descriptions of the quality of their relationships with supervisors (usually a measure of supervisor support) and symptoms of depression or depressed mood. With few exceptions (e.g., Jayaratne & Chess, 1984), almost all have reported significant correlations between these two variables. Depending on the occupational groups included in the study and the sample size, the published zero-order correlation coefficients between measures of poor supervisor relations and depression have ranged from $r = .16$ to $r = .52$, with most falling in the .30 range (Beehr, King, & King, 1990; Karasek, Triantis, & Chaudhry, 1982; LaRocco, House, & French, 1980; Repetti, 1987; Winnubst, Marcelissen, & Kleber, 1982). Findings from studies that included controls for other risk factors and possible third variables indicated that this is a robust cross-sectional association. Reports of poor relationships with supervisors, such as low levels of support and high levels of conflict, usually remain significantly associated with self-reported symptoms of depression in analyses that control for one or several important variables (such as age, sex, marital status, other types of job stressors, and other aspects of the social environment at work) (Beehr, King, & King, 1990; Golding, 1989; Karasek, Gardell, & Lindell, 1987; Karasek, Triantis, & Chaudhry, 1982; Repetti, 1987).

Other mental health outcomes also appear to be associated with poor supervisor relations. Consistent with the depression findings, most studies that have included measures of anxiety or low self-esteem have reported significant cross-sectional associations, with a wide range in the published correlation coefficients (r's ranging from .15 to .47) (LaRocco, House, & French, 1980; Repetti, 1987; Winnubst, Marcelissen, & Kleber, 1982). Kirmeyer and Dougherty (1988) measured tense-anxious mood among police radio dispatchers at the end of a shift and found that it was negatively correlated with measures of supervisor support. However, interpreting this finding is somewhat problemmatic because the measure of supervisor support was taken weeks after the mood rating. In addition, the association was not significant after controlling for the dispatchers' workload on the day that mood was rated.

Co-worker Relations. Although there is evidence of a link between the quality of relationships with co-workers and mental health, the results are not as strong, nor as consistent, as the findings for supervisors. Some studies have found significant cross-sectional associations between ratings of low co-worker support and self-reported symptoms of depression, with zero-order correlation coefficients ranging from $r = .12$ to .38 (Karasek et al., 1982; LaRocco et al., 1980; Revicki & May, 1985; Winnubst et al., 1982), and some have not (Golding, 1989; Jayaratne & Chess, 1984; Repetti, 1987). Perceptions of low co-worker support have been more consistently associated with anxiety, with a narrow range of published correlation coefficients ($r = .20$ to .24) (LaRocco et al., 1980; Repetti, 1987; Winnubst et al., 1982). However, not all studies have found co-worker support to be significantly associated with anxiety (Jayaratne & Chess, 1984), and there have been reports of insignificant correlations with self-esteem (Repetti, 1987) and with a measure of neurosis (House & Wells, 1978).

The Common Social Environment. Repetti (1987) has suggested that the effects of the individual social environment at work, or the individual's personal set of relationships at work, should be differentiated from the common social environment, or the social climate that is shared by all employees who work in the same setting. In theory, a single individual's personal characteristics play a very important role in determining his or her own individual social environment but play a much weaker role in shaping the common social environment at work. It is accordingly easier to study the mental health effects of the common social environment than the effects of the individual social environment because the common environment is less confounded with individual personality type variables. The Relationship Dimension of the Work Environment Scale (WES) (Insel & Moos, 1974) assesses individuals' perceptions of the overall social climate at work, in particular levels of involvement (the extent to which employees are concerned and committed to their job), peer cohesion (how friendly and supportive employees are to each other), and supervisor support. In a random sample of employed men in the San Francisco Bay area, Billings and Moos (1982) found that respondents' scores on these three scales were moderately correlated with three self-report indexes of mental health, depression, anxiety, and self-confidence (r's ranging from .13 to .29), and with health complaints (r's ranging from .13 to .23). Among women, however, the only statistically significant correlation was between depression and peer cohesion.

Repetti (1987) developed a measure of the perceived social climate at work that assesses the tendency for relations in a work group to be cohesive, friendly, and respectful and that contains many items from the WES. Female bank workers' scores on this scale were significantly correlated with their self-reported levels of depression, anxiety, and self-esteem (r's ranging from .26 to .52). In addition to measuring an individual's perception of the common social environment, Repetti (1987) also computed consensual scores by averaging the ratings of the common social environment made by each respondent's co-workers. This aggregate rating of the bank branch's social climate, which did not include the respondent's own rating, was significantly correlated with individual self-reported depression ($r = -.26$) and anxiety ($r = -.20$). These findings demonstrate that the association between social relations at work and mental health is not due solely to individual respondent bias. In addition, Repetti (1987) pointed out that groups of employees with poor mental health would have had to be initially assigned to the same bank branch in order for psychological distress to have been a major determinant of the group climate. Seemingly more plausible are mechanisms though which the common social environment influenced mental health.

Short-term Effects of the Social Environment. Few studies have examined the short-term impact that daily fluctuations in the social environment at work have on psychological functioning. The limited available evidence indicates that reports of more negative social interactions at work are associated with a short-term increase in negative mood and a short-term decrease in positive mood (Repetti, 1991a; Stone, 1987).

Conclusion. There does appear to be an association between individual mental health and both the individual and the common social environment at work. Within the individual social environment, there is a moderate association between long-term mental health outcomes and the quality of relationships with supervisors, particularly with regard to levels of supervisor support. Unfortunately, the almost exclusive use of cross-sectional designs and individuals' own descriptions of their relationships with supervisors makes it impossible to conclude that supervisor support directly affects mental health. For example, it is possible that distressed workers have more problems with supervisors because their mental health interferes with their performance at work, or they may regard their supervisors as nonsupportive because they have a greater need for support.

The findings for co-worker support are less consistent and may indicate either that there is no reliable association with mental health or that the link is weak. There is not yet any evidence to account for the overall stronger effects of supervisors compared to co-workers. The imbalance of power in the supervisor-subordinate relationship suggests one possible explanation. Workers may feel more threatened and vulnerable in their relationships with supervisors because they are less able to control those interactions. In addition, an employee's reaction to conflicts with a supervisor might be compounded by worries about job evaluations, chances for promotion, and possibly even the loss of the job.

The Direct Effects of the Social Environment on Physical Health

Because social contacts and social structure affect basic physiological processes and behaviors that are central to health maintenance, investigators have also explored the possibility that social factors at work have a direct impact on physical well-being.

Supervisor Relations. Several studies have reported weak but statitically significant cross-sectional associations between perceptions of supervisor support and health complaints, with correlation coefficients ranging from $r = -.05$ to $r = -.27$ (Buunk & Verhoeven, 1991; Greenberger, Goldberg, Hamill, O'Neil, & Payne, 1989; House & Wells, 1978; Jayaratne & Chess, 1984; LaRocco, et al., 1980; Winnubst, et al., 1982). In the Air Traffic Controller Health Change Study, controllers who perceived their supervisors as more considerate had fewer illnesses than those who perceived their supervisors as having less consideration for employees (Rose et al., 1978). Karasek et al. (1987) found that, for both men and women, reports of conflicts with a supervisor were associated with increased risk of a variety of physical illness symptoms, such as stomach problems and headache, after controlling for age and marital status. However, supervisor support sometimes does not emerge as a significant correlate of health symptoms when other job characteristics are controlled in the analysis (Barnett, Davidson, & Marshall, 1991; Greenberger et al., 1989).

There is consistent evidence for an association between having a conflictual, nonsupportive relationship with a work supervisor and being at an increased risk for CHD symptoms and events. An early study of Israeli male civil service employees over age 40 found that the risk for development of angina pectoris was higher among those men who, five years earlier, had reported more "problems with superiors" at work (Medalie et al., 1973). In the Framingham Heart Study the 10-year incidence of CHD was almost twice as high among female clerical workers as among other employed women. And, among the married female clerical workers, having a nonsupportive boss was an added risk factor for developing CHD, even after controlling for other standard risk factors, such as age, blood pressure, serum cholesterol, and smoking (Haynes, Eaker, & Feinleib, 1984). Health complaints specifically related to CHD have shown weak but significant correlations with ratings of supervisor support ($r = -.04$ and $-.08$) (House & Wells, 1978; Winnubst et al., 1982). Self-reported "heart problems" have also been associated with supervisor conflicts (Karasek et al., 1987).

Studies of a possible link between supervisor relations and CHD risk factors do not present as clear a picture. In their study of male blue collar workers, Matthews, Cottington, Talbott, Kuller, and Siegel (1987) found that men who reported having a nonsupportive foreman also had significantly elevated diastolic blood pressures, independent of major risk factors for hypertension (age, alcohol consumption, smoking, family history, and body mass). However, this finding was only marginally significant when other job characteristics (e.g., uncertain job future) were included in the analysis. And, in a mostly male Dutch sample, supervisor support was not significantly correlated with any of three measured clinical risk factors for CHD: systolic blood pressure, diastolic blood pressure, and cholesterol levels (Winnubst et al., 1982).

There is also mixed evidence regarding the association between cigarette smoking and supervisor relations. In a Swedish study, reports of conflict with a supervisor were linked to more smoking among men and to less smoking among women (Karasek et al., 1987). In the Dutch study mentioned previously there was no relation between a measure of perceived supervisor support and smoking (Winnubst et al., 1982).

Co-worker Relations.   Low to moderate negative correlations, ranging from $-.12$ to $-.35$, have been reported between perceptions of co-worker support and health complaints (Greenberger et al., 1989; Jayaratne & Chess, 1984; LaRocco et al., 1980; Winnubst et al., 1982). However, this association has not been found in every study (Buunk & Verhoeven, 1991; House & Wells, 1978). In Hibbard and Pope's (1985) analysis, co-worker support was linked to perceived health status among women who were 40 years and older, but not among women under 40. In both age groups, though, women who felt more integrated with and supported by co-workers spent fewer days in the hospital over the course of an average year.

In the Israeli study of civil service employees, the risk for development of angina pectoris over a five-year period was higher among men who reported more "problems with co-workers" (Medalie et al., 1973). However, CHD-type health complaints have shown weak (Winnubst et al., 1982) or non-significant (House & Wells, 1978) associations with co-worker support. There are also inconsistent findings for CHD risk factors. In the Matthews, et al. (1987) study of male blue collar workers, perceptions of co-worker support were significantly associated with diastolic blood pressure after controlling for major risk factors for hypertension. However, this effect was no longer significant after controls for other job characteristics were added to the analysis. The Dutch study failed to find a significant correlation between co-worker support and three clinical risk factors (Winnubst et al., 1982).

Short-term Effects of the Social Environment.   Repetti (1991a) found, in a marginally significant finding, that air traffic controllers complained of more physical symptoms on days that they described as having been marred by more negative social interactions at work. However, the effect of social interaction was no longer significant when daily workload was controlled in the analysis.

Conclusion.   People who describe their relationships with supervisors and co-workers as conflictual and nonsupportive appear to be at a slightly increased risk for a variety of minor physical symptoms and illnesses. Unfortunately, most of these findings are subject to the same third variable and reverse causality explanations as the findings regarding mental health outcomes. For example, some research suggests that negative mood and negative affectivity may contaminate the association between ratings of interpersonal relations at work and health complaints (Brett, Brief, Burke, George, & Webster, 1990; Repetti, 1991a). Interestingly, the same studies indicate that perceptions of workload are not as affected by negative affect. In addition, findings from some of the studies reviewed here indicate that the link between interpersonal relationships at work and health may sometimes be explained by other job characteristics, such as salary, job future, and workload. Investigators can avoid such a misspecification by including several different occupational variables in studies of the social environment at work.

The research reviewed here also suggests that a poor relationship with a work supervisor may be a risk factor for coronary heart disease in particular. Surprisingly, despite its link to CHD, it has not been clearly demonstrated that supervisor support plays a role in the development of risk factors typically associated with CHD.

The Buffering Effect of Social Support at Work

Many investigations of social support focus on its potential to mitigate or buffer the effects of stress. One proposal in this literature is that social support, for example, may function by changing the individual's appraisal of the stressor or by preventing damaging behavioral or biological responses to stress. According to this perspective, supportive relationships at work should have their greatest (or only) impact on health among those who are exposed to at least moderate levels of stress. Similarly, occupational stressors should have their greatest (or only) impact among those who have the least amount of support.

Mental Health Outcomes. Some cross-sectional studies either have failed to find any reliable evidence that the effects of various occupational role stressors on mental health outcomes are moderated by social support from co-workers and supervisors (Beehr et al., 1990; Jayaratne & Chess, 1984; Winnubst et al., 1982) or have found only weak evidence (House & Wells, 1978). LaRocco et al. (1980) found that co-worker support buffered the effects of several job stressors (e.g., role conflict) on depression and/or anxiety, but found little evidence for supervisor support as a buffer. However, in another analysis of questionnaire data, Karasek and his colleagues (1982) reported an overall tendency for the association between depression and a composite measure of job demands and job control to be stronger among men who reported poor relationships with either co-workers or supervisors. Finally, when support from a supervisor was considered in the study of police radio dispatchers, it was found that high levels of perceived and objective workload on a shift were followed by a more distressed mood after work only among those dispatchers who perceived relatively little support (Kirmeyer & Dougherty, 1988).

Some evidence suggests that supervisor support may have an impact on depression only in the context of a negative general climate at work. Repetti (1987) found in her study of bank tellers that there was a strong association between ratings of supervisor support and depression scores among women who worked in bank branches with a negative overall climate (as described by co-workers). There was a non-significant association for women who worked in bank branches with a positive climate.

Physical Health Outcomes. The results from cross-sectional questionnaire studies that have included measures of health complaints also provide only limited evidence for the moderating role of social support at work. On the one hand, House and Wells' (1978) data indicated that supervisor support, but not co-worker support, buffered the effects of job stressors on several different physical symptoms in a sample of white male workers in a manufacturing plant. On the other hand, the LaRocco et al. (1980) study, which used very similar measures and included men employed in a variety of occupations, indicated the reverse: co-worker support, but not supervisor support, appeared to buffer the effects of job stressors on a composite measure of somatic complaints. To account for the conflicting results, LaRocco and his colleagues suggested that the nature of tasks at work and the degree of interdependence among workers may determine which sources of support are more salient. However, two studies failed to replicate either set of results. There was no evidence that support from either co-workers or supervisors moderated an association between perceived occupational stressors and somatic complaints in a heterogeneous group of employed people in the Netherlands (Winnubst et al., 1982) nor in a sample of U.S. social workers (Jayaratne & Chess, 1984). The Dutch study also included measures of CHD-related outcomes. Here, too, there was no reliable pattern to indicate that social support at work buffered the effects of job stressors.

Conclusions. The results of studies that have examined whether social support from co-workers and supervisors reduces the deleterious impact of occupational stressors on health are inconclusive. It is possible that, although poor relationships with co-workers and supervisors may act as stressors with a direct impact on health, supportive relationships at work may not be able to counteract the effects of other occupational stressors. This would be somewhat surprising given the evidence that social support from family and friends moderates the health effects of a variety of different types of stressors (Cohen & Wills, 1985). Perhaps the correlation between a lack of support and other psychosocial stressors at work impedes our ability to observe a buffering effect.

SUMMARY AND SUGGESTIONS FOR FUTURE RESEARCH

The research reviewed here is consistent with the opening sentence of the chapter. It looks like work can, indeed, be hazardous to your health. In particular, the stress associated with the two occupational conditions discussed here, workload and the social environment, appears to play some role in the development of mental and physical health problems. Three of the conceptual models discussed in this chapter, the direct effects models for work overload and for social stressors and the demand-control model, received consistent support for at least some health outcomes. More mental health problems are reported by employed people who perceive a high workload and by those who describe their supervisors as nonsupportive. More physical health problems are reported by people who perceive a high workload and by those who describe poor relationships with either supervisors or coworkers. In addition, having a poor relationship with a supervisor or a job that combines high demands with little control may increase a worker's risk for coronary heart disease. However, there is surprisingly little evidence of increased rates of known CHD risk factors among the same two groups of workers. This latter pattern of findings is problemmatic because there have not been suggestions of alternative pathways to account for the observed disease outcome.

The literature reviewed here suggests several directions for future research. Although the conceptual models that are currently available have helped investigators to determine whether certain occupational conditions play any role in health, they do not explain *how* those occupational experiences may influence health. Greater effort should therefore be devoted to the study of pathogenic processes that link occupational stressors to health. A better understanding of acute responses to short-term increases in stressors may suggest psychophysiological mechanisms that over time lead to the development of mental and physical health problems. Of course, physiological and psychological differences between individuals are probably associated with differences in vulnerability to occupational stressors. It is therefore important to include individual variables, such as differences in physiological reactivity, appraisal and coping styles, and social support outside of work in process models.

As has been pointed out here and by many others (e.g., Frese, 1985; Mackay & Cooper, 1987) there are reasonable alternative interpretations of results from cross-sectional correlational studies that were intended to test whether occupational stressors cause health problems. These designs should be replaced by prospective longitudinal designs that control for initial health status and that include measures of several different occupational conditions. Two important goals for longitudinal studies are to determine (a) which occupational stressors are associated with which health problems and (b) how those occupational conditions influence health.

Finally, occupational stressors should be conceptualized and measured both (a) as individual subjective perceptions and (b) as objective conditions existing outside of the person. Evidence suggests that environmental conditions and the phenomenological experience of those conditions are two distinct components of stress (Lazarus, 1990; Lobel & Dunkel-Schetter, 1990). Investigators should therefore analyze the effects of specific external occupational conditions separately from the effects of individual appraisals of and vulnerabilities to those conditions. The extent to which each of these two types of occupational stressors influences health is not only of obvious theoretical importance, but it also has practical implications. For example, knowledge about objective job characteristics that increase health risks can lead to the development of sensible stress-reducing interventions in the workplace.

REFERENCES

ALFREDSSON, L., SPETZ, C. L., & THEORELL, T. Type of occupation and near-future hospitalization for myocardial infarction and some other diagnoses. *International Journal of Epidemiology,* 1985, *14,* 378–388.

ASTRAND, N. E., HANSON, B. S., & ISACSSON, S. O. Job demands, job decision latitude, job support, and social network factors as predictors of mortality in a Swedish pulp and paper company. *British Journal of Industrial Medicine,* 1989, *46,* 334–340.

BARNETT, R. C., DAVIDSON, H., & MARSHALL, N. L. Physical symptoms and the interplay of work and family roles. *Health Psychology,* 1991, *10,* 94–101.

BEEHR, T. A., KING, L. A., & KING, D. W. Social support and occupational stress: Talking to supervisors. *Journal of Vocational Behavior,* 1990, *36,* 61–81.

BILLINGS, A. G., & MOOS, R. H. Work stress and the stress-buffering roles of work and family resources. *Journal of Occupational Behavior,* 1982, *3,* 215–232.

BOLGER, N., DELONGIS, A., KESSLER, R. C., & SCHILLING, E. A. Effects of daily stress on negative mood. *Journal of Personality and Social Psychology,* 1989, *56,* 808–818.

BRETT, J. F., BRIEF, A. P., BURKE, M. J., GEORGE, J. M., & WEBSTER, J. Negative affectivity and the reporting of stressful life events. *Health Psychology,* 1990, *9,* 57–68.

BROMET, E. J., DEW, M. A., PARKINSON, D. K., & SCHULBERG, H. C. Predictive effects of occupational and marital stress on the mental health of a male workforce. *Journal of Organizational Behavior,* 1988, *9,* 1–13.

BUUNK, B. P., & VERHOEVEN, K. Companionship and support at work: A microanalysis of the stress-reducing features of social interaction. *Basic and Applied Social Psychology,* 1991, *12,* 243–258.

CHESNEY, M. A. Women, work-related stress, and smoking. In M. Frankenhaeuser, U. Lundberg, & M. A. Chesney (eds.) *Women, work, and health.* New York: Plenum Press, 1991.

COHEN, S., & WILLS, T. A. Stress, social support, and the buffering hypothesis. *Psychological Bulletin,* 1985, *98,* 310–357.

CONWAY, T. L., VICKERS, R. R., JR., WARD, H. W., & RAHE, R. H. Occupational stress and variation in cigarette, coffee, and alcohol consumption. *Journal of Health and Social Behavior,* 1981, *22,* 155-165.

DIGNAM, J. T., & WEST, S. G. Social support in the workplace: Tests of six theoretical models. *American Journal of Community Psychology,* 1988, *16,* 701-724.

ESTRYN-BEHAR, M., KAMINSKI, M., PEIGNE, E., BONNET, N., VAICHERE, E., GOZLAN, C., AZOULAY, S., & GIORGI, M. Stress at work and mental health status among female hospital workers. *British Journal of Industrial Medicine,* 1990, *47,* 20-28.

FRANKENHAEUSER, M. Coping with stress at work. *International Journal of Health Services,* 1981, *11,* 491-510.

FRESE, M. Stress at work and psychosomatic complaints: A causal interpretation. *Journal of Applied Psychology,* 1985, *70,* 314-328.

GOLDING, J. M. Role occupancy and role-specific stress and social support as predictors of depression. *Basic and Applied Social Psychology,* 1989, *10,* 173-195.

GREENBERGER, E., GOLDBERG, W. A., HAMILL, S., O'NEIL, R., & PAYNE, C. K. (1989). Contributions of a supportive work environment to parents' well-being and orientation to work. *American Journal of Community Psychology,* 1989, *17,* 755-783.

HAYNES, S. G., EAKER, E. D., & FEINLEIB, M. The effect of employment, family, and job stress on coronary heart disease. In E. B. Gold (ed.), *The changing risk of disease in women: An epidemiologic approach.* Lexington, MA: D. C. Heath, 1984.

HIBBARD, J. H., & POPE, C. R. Employment status, employment characteristics and women's health. *Women and Health,* 1985, *10,* 59-77.

HOUSE, J. S., STRECHER, V., METZNER, H. L. & ROBBINS, C. A. Occupational stress and health among men and women in the Tecumseh community health study. *Journal of Health and Social Behavior,* 1986, *27,* 62-77.

HOUSE, J. S., & WELLS, J. A. Occupational stress, social support, and health. In A. McLean, G. Black, & M. Collogan (eds.), *Reducing occupational stress: Proceedings of a conference (publication number 78-140).* Washington, DC: U.S. Government Printing Office, 1978.

INSEL, P. M., & MOOS, R. H. *Work Environment Scale-Form R.* Palo Alto, CA: Consulting Psychologists Press, 1974.

JAMNER L. D., SHAPIRO, D., GOLDSTEIN, I. B., & HUG, R. Ambulatory blood pressure and heart rate in paramedics: Effects of cynical hostility and defensiveness. *Psychosomatic Medicine, 53,* 1991, 393-406.

JAYARATNE, S., & CHESS, W. A. The effects of emotional support on perceived job stress and strain. *The Journal of Applied Behavioral Science,* 1984, *20,* 141-153.

KARASEK, R., BAKER, D., MARXER, F., AHLBOM, A., & THEORELL, T. Job decision latitude, job demands, and cardiovascular disease: A prospective study of Swedish men. *American Journal of Public Health,* 1981, *71,* 694-704.

KARASEK, R., GARDELL, B, & LINDELL, J. Work and non-work correlates of illness and behaviour in male and female Swedish white collar workers. *Journal of Occupational Behaviour,* 1987, *8,* 187-207.

KARASEK, R., & THEORELL, T. *Healthy work: Stress, productivity and the reconstruction of working life.* New York: Basic Books, 1990.

KARASEK, R. A., TRIANTIS, K. P., & CHAUDHRY, S. S. Coworker and supervisor support as moderators of associations between task characteristics and mental strain. *Journal of Occupational Behaviour,* 1982, *3,* 181-200.

KIRMEYER, S. L., & DOUGHERTY, T. W. Work load, tension, and coping: Moderating effects of supervisor support. *Personnel Psychology,* 1988, *41,* 125-139.

LaCroix, A. Z., & Haynes, S. G. Gender differences in the health effects of workplace roles. In R. C. Barnett, L. Biener, & G. K. Baruch (eds.), *Gender and stress.* New York: Free Press, 1987.

Landsbergis, P. A. Occupational stress among health care workers: A test of the job demands-control model. *Journal of Organizational Behavior,* 1988, *9,* 217–239.

LaRocco, J. M., House, J. S., French, J. R. P. Social support, occupational stress, and health. *Journal of Health and Social Behavior,* 1980, *21,* 202–218.

Lazarus R. S. Theory-based stress measurement. *Psychological Inquiry,* 1990, *90,* 3–13.

Lazarus, R. S., & Folkman, S. Coping and adaptation. In W. D. Gentry (ed.), *Handbook of behavioral medicine.* New York: Guilford Press, 1984.

Lobel, M., & Dunkel-Schetter, C. Conceptualizing stress to study effects on health: Environmental, perceptual, and emotional components. *Anxiety Research,* 1990, *3,* 213–230.

Lundberg, U., & Palm, K. Workload and catecholamine excretion in parents of preschool children. *Work and Stress,* 1989, *3,* 255–260.

Mackay, C. J., & Cooper, C. L. Occupational stress and health: Some current issues. In C. L. Cooper & I. T. Robertson (eds.), *International review of industrial and organizational psychology.* New York: John Wiley & Sons, 1987.

Matthews, K. A., Cottington, E. M., Talbott, E., Kuller, L. H., & Siegel, J. M. Stressful work conditions and diastolic blood pressure among blue collar factory workers. *American Journal of Epidemiology,* 1987, *126,* 280–291.

Medalie, J. H., Snyder, M., Groen, J. J., Neufeld, H. N., Goldbourt, U., & Riss, E. Angina pectoris among 10,000 men. *The American Journal of Medicine,* 1973, *55,* 583–594.

National Institute for Occupational Safety and Health. *Proposed national strategies for the prevention of leading work-related diseases and injuries: Part 1.* Published by the Association of Schools of Public Health, Washington, D.C.

————. *Proposed national strategies for the prevention of leading work-related diseases and injuries: Part 2.* Published by the Association of Schools of Public Health, Washington, D.C.

Osipow, S. H., & Davis, A. S. The relationship of coping resources to occupational stress and strain. *Journal of Vocational Behavior,* 1988, *32,* 1–15.

Parkes, K. R. Coping, negative affectivity, and the work environment: Additive and interactive predictors of mental health. *Journal of Applied Psychology,* 1990, *75,* 399–409.

Pieper, C., LaCroix, A. Z., & Karasek, R. A. The relation of psychological dimensions of work with coronary heart disease risk factors: A meta-analysis of five United States data bases. *American Journal of Epidemiology,* 1989, *129,* 483–494.

Repetti, R. L. Individual and common components of the social environment at work and psychological well-being. *Journal of Personality and Social Psychology,* 1987, *52,* 710–720.

————. Effects of daily workload on subsequent behavior during marital interaction: The roles of social withdrawal and spouse support. *Journal of Personality and Social Psychology,* 1989, *57,* 651–659.

————. Short-term effects of occupational stressors on daily mood and health complaints. In press—*Health Psychology* 1991. (a)

————. Short-term and long-term processes linking perceived job stressors to father-child interaction. Manuscript under review. no change yet in status 1991. (b)

————. Social withdrawal as a short-term coping response to daily stressors. In H. S. Friedman (ed.), *Hostility, coping and health.* Washington, DC: American Psychological Association, 1992 (pp. 151–165).

Repetti, R. L., Matthews, K. A., & Waldron, I. Employment and women's health: Effects of paid employment on women's mental and physical health. *American Psychologist,* 1989, *44,* 1394–1401.

REVICKI, D. A., & MAY, H. J. Occupational stress, social support, and depression. *Health Psychology,* 1985, *4,* 61–77.

ROSE, R. M., JENKINS, C. D., & HURST, M. V. *Air traffic controller health change study* (FAA report no. AM–78-39). Washington, DC: Federal Aviation Administration, 1978.

SAUTER, S. L. Moderating effects of job control on health complaints in office work. In S. L. Sauter, J. J. Hurrell, Jr., & C. L. Cooper (eds.), *Job control and worker health.* New York: John Wiley & Sons, 1989.

SCHNALL, P. L., PIEPER, C., SCHWARTZ, J. E., KARASEK, R. A., SCHLUSSEL, Y., DEVEREUX, R. B., GANAU, A., ALDERMAN, M., WARREN, K., & PICKERING, T. G. The relationship between "job strain," workplace diastolic blood pressure, and left ventricular mass index. *Journal of American Medical Association,* 1990, *263,* 1929–1935.

SORENSON, G., PIRIE, P., FOLSOM, A., LUEPKER, R., JACOBS, D., & GILLUM, R. Sex differences in the relationship between work and health: The Minnesota heart survey. *Journal of Health and Social Behavior,* 1985, *26,* 379–394.

STEFFY, B. D., JONES, J. W., & NOE, A. W. The impact of health habits and life-style on the stressor-strain relationship: An evaluation of three industries. *Journal of Occupational Psychology,* 1990, *63,* 217–229.

STONE, A. A. Event content in a daily survey is differentially associated with concurrent mood. *Journal of Personality and Social Psychology,* 1987, *52,* 56–58.

THEORELL, T., & FLODERUS-MYRHED, B. "Workload" and risk of myocardial infarction—a prospective psychosocial analysis. *International Journal of Epidemiology,* 1977, *6,* 17–21.

THEORELL, T., HAMSTEN, A., DE FAIRE, U., ORTH-GOMER, K., & PERSKI, A. Psychosocial work conditions before myocardial infarction in young men. *International Journal of Cardiology,* 1987, *15,* 33–46.

UNDEN, A., ORTH-GOMER, K., & ELOFSSON, S. Cardiovascular effects of social support in the work place: Twenty-four-hour ECG monitoring of men and women. *Psychosomatic Medicine,* 1991, *53,* 50–60.

WATSON, D., & PENNEBAKER, J. W. Health complaints, stress, and distress: Exploring the central role of negative affectivity. *Psychological Review,* 1989, *96,* 234–254.

WINNUBST, J. A. M., MARCELISSEN, F. H. G., & KLEBER, R. J. Effects of social support in the stressor-strain relationship: A Dutch sample. *Social Science Medicine,* 1982, *16,* 475–482.

21

Burnout

Ayala M. Pines

BURNOUT WAS INTRODUCED to the scientific literature in the early 1970s by the New York clinical psychologist Herbert J. Freudenberger (1974) and the University of California social psychologist Christina Maslach (1976). The evocative image of the term made it a hot topic in the media and newspapers, magazines, television, and radio helped popularize the topic. Fortunately, serious research was also carried out. A 1991 literature search of the *Psychological Abstracts* revealed over one thousand research articles and close to one hundred books on burnout.

DEFINITIONS

Definitions of burnout vary slightly, but three of the most frequently quoted definitions are given here. According to Herbert J. Freudenberger burnout is "a state of fatigue or frustration brought about by devotion to a cause, way of life, or relationship that failed to produce the expected reward" (Freudenberger, 1980:13). According to Christina Maslach, "burnout is a syndrome of emotional exhaustion, depersonalization, and reduced personal accomplishment that can occur among individuals who do 'people work' of some kind" (Maslach, 1982a:3). According to Ayala Pines and Elliot Aronson, burnout is "a state of physical, emotional and mental exhaustion caused by long term involvement in emotionally demanding situations" (Pines & Aronson, 1988:9).

While the definitions of burnout vary, they all describe the end result of a process in which highly motivated and committed individuals lose their spirit. Individuals who enter a profession (e.g., nursing or counseling) with a cynical attitude are unlikely to burn out; but those with a strong desire to give of themselves and who feel helpful, excited, and idealistic are susceptible to the most severe burnout.

BURNOUT AND STRESS

Stress happens to more people and in more situations than burnout. Everyone can experience stress, but burnout can only be experienced by people who entered their careers with high ideals, motivation, and commitment. You cannot burn out unless you were "on fire" initially. A person without such initial motivation can experience job stress, alienation, or depression—but not burnout. Those who have never expected anything from their work except a paycheck can still be vulnerable to stress.

Unlike stress, which can occur in almost every type of work, burnout occurs most often among those who work with people and results from the emotional stress that arises during the interaction with them. Nevertheless, stress as such does not cause burnout. People are able to flourish in stressful and demanding jobs if they feel that their work is significant and appreciated.

THE COST OF BURNOUT

Burnout occurs frequently and to a wide range of highly motivated individuals. It has been identified as a problem in the work of such professionals as: physicians (Hosmer Mawardi, 1983; Pines, 1981), nurses (McConnell, 1982; Pines & Kanner, 1982; Schaufeli & Janczur, 1990), organizational consultants (Pines, 1992a), managers (Etzion, Kafry, & Pines, 1982; Hallsten, 1990), police officers (Jones, 1985; Maslach & Jackson, 1979; Pines & Silbert, 1985), teachers (Maslach & Pines, 1977; Sakharov & Farber, 1983), lawyers (Maslach & Jackson, 1978), social workers (Jayaratne & Chess, 1983; Pines & Kafry, 1978), mental health workers (Pines & Maslach, 1980), and psychotherapists (Farber, 1983a).

Burnout is an extremely painful experience for the individual and a very costly phenomenon for the organization. For the individual, burnout is accompanied by an array of physical, emotional, and attitudinal symptoms. The physical symptoms include physical depletion, chronic fatigue, frequent and prolonged colds, headaches, sleep problems (insomnia, nightmares, excessive sleeping), ulcers, gastrointestinal disorders, sudden losses or gains in weight, flare-ups of pre-existing medical disorders (e.g., diabetes, high blood pressure, asthma), injuries from high-risk behavior, muscular pain (particularly in the lower back and neck), increased premenstrual syndrome, and increased consumption of cafffeine, tobacco, alcohol, over-the-counter medications, and prescription and illicit drugs. The emotional symptoms of burnout include feelings of depression, failure, helplessness, hopelessness, and disillusionment and loss of the emotional meaning of work. People feel trapped, angry, and frustrated, and fear they may be "going crazy."

The attitudinal symptoms include negative and cynical attitudes toward work, service recepients, colleagues, supervisors, and the organization as a whole. These negative attitudes cause professionals to feel isolated from co-workers and clients and increase conflicts among staff members and between the staff and the administration. Feelings of isolation on the job can lead to over-reliance on the spouse for acknowledgment and support and can cause the negative effects of burnout to spill over into the marriage (Pines, 1988).

Signs of burnout within the work environment include low morale, absenteeism (especially sick leave), tardiness, a decrease in average length of stay on the job, high job turnover, increased accidents on the job, and poor performance. Workers and management way express mutual disrespect and distrust. Workers may arrive late at work, leave early, and fail to show up for important meetings and appointments. Managers may spend more and more time away from the organization and otherwise reduce the amount of time spent in direct contact with their staff. There may be an increase in employee theft (Jones, 1981). Most importantly there will be a decrease in the quality of services delivered to the people who need them most (Maslach & Pines, 1979).

While a particular individual or organization may not exhibit all of these symptoms, they have been found to be associated with burnout (Carroll & White, 1982; Freudenberger, 1980; Maslach, 1982a; Pines & Aronson, 1988).

THE MEASUREMENT OF BURNOUT

There are two primary measures of burnout. The Maslach Burnout Inventory (MBI) (Maslach & Jackson, 1981) and the Burnout Measure (BM) (Pines & Aronson, 1988). The MBI is designed to measure burnout of human service professionals and is currently the most widely used index of burnout in studies with individuals who do "people work." The BM is easier to administer and score than the MBI and can be used to study other professionals as well. The BM is the most widely used index of burnout in workshop settings where participants measure their own levels of burnout.

The MBI measures three aspects of burnout:

1. emotional exhaustion (e.g., "I feel emotionally drained from my work." "Working with people all day is really a strain for me.") A frequency of several times a month or more indicates high burnout.
2. depersonalization (e.g., "I've become callous toward people since I took this job." "I worry that the job is hardening me emotionally.") A frequency of once a month or more indicates high burnout.
3. reduced personal accomplishment (e.g., "In my work, I deal with emotional problems very calmly." "I feel I'm positively influencing other people's lives through my work.") A frequency of *less than once a week* indicates high burnout.

These three dimensions were not deduced theoretically before the test construction of the MBI; they were labeled after factor analysis of empirical data from human service samples.

The BM is measured by a 21-item questionnaire. The items are theoretically derived from the three aspects of burnout: physical exhaustion (e.g., feeling tired or rundown), emotional exhaustion (e.g., feeling depressed, trapped, or hopeless), and mental exhaustion (e.g., feeling worthless, disillusioned, or resentful toward people). The items are presented in random order and are each evaluated on a 7-point frequency scale (1 = never, 4 = sometimes, 7 = always). A score of 4 indicates burnout.

Factor analysis suggests that the BM is a unidimensional measure (Corcoran, 1986; Justice, Gold, & Klein, 1981). The BM is highly correlated with the emotional exhaustion subscale of the MBI (e.g., Enzmann & Kleiber, 1990; Hallsten, 1990; Marek & Noworol, 1990; Schaufeli & Peeters, 1990). Both measures have been used with very large samples and with professionals from different countries.

BURNOUT AMONG NURSES

Three different studies investigated burnout among nurses using the BM. One study involved 200 Polish and 183 Dutch nurses (Schaufeli & Janczur, 1990). The second study involved 352 American and 169 Israeli nurses (Pines & Kanner, 1982). The third study involved 43 German nurses (Kleiber & Enzmann, 1990). The mean burnout scores of the five samples of nurses were:

Polish nurses = 3.3
American nurses = 3.2
German nurses = 3.1
Israeli nurses = 3.0
Dutch nurses = 2.8

Questionnaires and interviews with nurses in the five countries help explain both the similarities and the differences in their working conditions that help explain the character of their reported burnout.

There are certain similarities in the work of nurses wherever they are. A nurse who worked both in Israel and the United States and who was familiar with nursing in the former Soviet Union explained:

> There is a mutual goal in your work as a nurse, no matter where you work, and that is to take care of the patient. Nursing is a job in which you are always under pressure. You are dealing with life and death issues on a daily basis. You can't come to work and say: I slept only five hours tonight and I'm tired. You have to be in full alert at all times. You work under incredible pressure with very little rewards. The salary is in no proportion to the investment in learning and training and the responsibility and stress of the job. Nurses work days, nights, holidays, and are on call when they don't work—with almost no compensation.

Despite the physical and emotional demands of the work, and despite the inadequate monitary rewards, certain aspects of the work are emotionally rewarding. These experiences tell nurses that their work is important and has a significant impact on people's lives. "The greatest reward is when a seriously injured patient is saved, or a seriously sick person goes through a series of operations and is saved." (Unpublished manuscript, Pines, 1991) Nurses who identified with the romantic image of the nurse as an "angel of mercy" and who entered nursing in order to help people in pain derive a sense of existential significance from their work when a patient is saved or healed.

Another positive and rewarding aspect of nursing work is the relationship among the nurses:

> When there is a crisis situation everyone lends a hand. It's a team work. When you have an emergency, you know that some other nurse will volunteer to help. You just know that there's no other choice. You can't tell a patient in an operation—I'm sorry, but the nurse who was supposed to take part in your operation is sick. This mutual support creates a feeling of a family—and it's the same wherever nurses work.

Despite these satisfying aspects of nursing, other aspects of the work are universally recognized as stressful:

> All nurses are faced not only with the physical demand of the patients, but also with the heave demands for pity, sympathy, and compassion . . . and daily are forced to carry out tasks which are by ordinary standards disgusting, distasteful, and frightening. (Gentry, Foster, & Froehling, 1972:293)
>
> Sights of blood, vomitus and excreta, exposed genitalia, mutilated wasting bodies, and unconscious and helpless people assault the sensibilities. Unceasingly, the . . . nurse must face these affect-laden stimuli with all the distress and conflict that they engender. As part of her daily routine, the nurse must reassure and comfort the man who is dying of cancer, she must change the dressing of a decomposing gangrenous limb; she must calm the awaking disturbed "overdosed" patient; she must bathe the genitalia of the helpless and comatose; she must wipe away

the bloody stool of the gastrointestinal bleeder; she must comfort the anguished young wife who knows her husband is dying. It is hard to imagine any other situation that involves such intimacy with the frightening, repulsive, and forbidden. (Hay & Oaken, 1985:108)

These kinds of emotional and physical stresses, when combined with the absence of adequate rewards, result in nurses' burnout (McConnell, 1982). In one of the samples of nurses, burnout was found to be related to both the presence of negative conditions and the absence of positive conditions (Pines & Kanner, 1982). Burnout correlated positively with such variables as pressure on the job ($r = .53$, $p < .01$), reponsibility for patients ($r = .48$, $p < .01$), conflict between work and family ($r = .43$, $p < .01$), and stressful work environment ($r = .37$, $p < .01$). Burnout correlated negatively with such factors as feeling successful ($r = -.49$, $p < .01$), quality of personal relations at work ($r = -.44$, $p < .01$), and tangible rewards ($r = -.32$, $p < .05$).

In addition to the universal aspects of nursing work, cultural differences help explain the differences in levels of burnout among the five samples of nurses.

The Polish nurses reported the highest level of burnout; the Dutch nurses reported the lowest level. Several differences between these Eastern and Western European samples can help explain the variance in their burnout (Schaufeli & Janczur, 1990). Dutch nurses receive an intensive four-year theoretical and practical training, and nursing is recognized as an independent profession requiring a license to practice. In Poland, many nurses receive only a two-year on-the-job training in a hospital, and both their theoretical and practical schooling is poor and inadequate. In addition, nursing is not considered an independent profession in Poland (there is no nursing license or certificate), so that the status of nurses is low. Moreover, Dutch hospitals are far better equipped than those in Poland. Dutch nurses work in small teams and on specialized wards. They work up to 38 hours a week, but many work part time. In Poland, nurses work in large groups, up to 42 hours a week, and part-time jobs are rare.

Although Dutch nurses, like nurses almost everywhere, are not paid very well (about $1,500 a month), Polish nurses' wages are much lower (about $60 a month) and are considered extremely low even in Poland. Life outside work is much harder in Poland as well. Many young Polish nurses leave their jobs within one or two years because of the poor conditions and low status of their work.

The difference between the Israeli and American nurses can be explained by the greater sense of social unity and mutual fate in Israel. The cohesion that characterizes Israeli society may be one source of the good social relationships, the high level of emotional reciprocity, and the sharing of stresses reported by Israeli workers (Etzion & Pines, 1986). The nurse who worked both in Israel and in the United States describes the difference:

In Israel relationships among nurses and between nurses and doctors are closer and less hierarchical. Everyone is part of the team. Everyone knows everyone else's family. If you have a personal problem, the whole team will get together to help you—with no money and no waiting in line. In the US nurses work conditions are better. They get paid better, and get better continuous education, but when you have a problem, you can't stop a doctor in the corridor and ask him to look at your arm, you have to go to his office, so he can get paid for your visit.

Despite the cultural differences, the highly demanding daily work of nurses is basically the same everywhere. In addition, nursing attracts people who have similar goals and expectations when they enter the profession. While the working conditions of the nurses in the five countries are very different and are reflected in the nurses' different levels of burnout, the underlying process leading to their burnout is very similar.

THE UNDERLYING CAUSE OF BURNOUT

Years of studying burnout among nurses, physicians, dentists, teachers, psychologists, counselors, social workers, managers, secretaries, organizational consultants, police officers, and lawyers lead me to believe that the cause of burnout lies in our need to believe that our lives are meaningful and that the things we do are useful, important, even heroic (Pines 1990, 1992b). As Ernest Becker argues in *The Denial of Death* (1973), all of us have a need to feel heroic and significant and to believe that we matter in the larger, cosmic scheme of things. In previous eras, religion filled this purpose; however, for many people today, religion is no longer adequate. For people who have rejected the religious answer to the existential quest, one of the frequently chosen alternatives is work. Thus the stakes in work have become very high. People who choose this path are trying to derive from their work a sense of meaning for their entire life. When they think they have failed, they burn out.

Failure in the existential quest for meaning is the root cause of burnout and explains why burnout tends to afflict people who enter their professions with high motivation and idealism. Thus, burnout is a particular hazard in occupations in which professionals relate to their work as a "calling." And, as noted earlier, this factor also marks the difference between burnout and stress. This existential perspective can be applied to virtually all of the descriptions of the process of burnout that have appeared in the scientific literature. Here I examine two examples:

According to Christina Maslach (1982a), "A pattern of emotional overload and subsequent emotional exhaustion is at the heart of the burnout syndrome. A person gets overly involved emotionally, overextends him - or herself, and feels overwhelmed by the emotional demands imposed by other people. The response to this situation is emotional exhaustion. People feel drained and used up" (p. 3). Such people get "overly involved emotionally" because they want to have impact on people and want their work to be significant. The emotional demands imposed by other people are no problem as long as it is possible to satisfy them. They become a cause of burnout only when they are overwhelming, when it is not possible to respond to them adequately. In such situations, these demands contribute to a feeling of failure. For the person who looks for existential significance in work, such a failure is devastating and, as Christina Maslach rightly points out, a primary cause of burnout.

Herbert J. Freudenberger (1982) describes people who are "prone to burning out." "Initially, they enter the job market full of good intentions—idealistic, hopeful and somewhat naive. They give it their all and more, in order to attain the hoped-for good sense of self" (p. 179). The "good sense of self" Freudenberger refers to is people's belief that their work matters and that, consequently, they matter. Because the ideals and hopes of burnout-prone people center on having work achievements that provide existential significance, they "give it their all" and then burn out when they think they have failed.

In all other descriptions of the burnout process in the scientific literature, the underlying dynamic is similar. This existential perspective is presented graphically in Figure 21–1 (Pines, 1990, 1992b).

Highly motivated individuals enter their work with high goals (for themselves) and

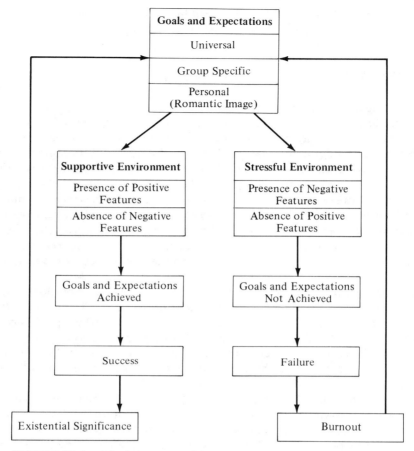

FIGURE 21–1. The burnout model.

expectations (of what the work will provide). Some of these expectations are universal (e.g., do something significant, have impact, be successful); some are profession-specific. In the human services, for example, expectations include working with people and helping those in trouble. Others expectations are personal, perhaps based on an internalized romantic image of the work that is modeled after an important person or an event. When combined, these expectations serve as the basis for how the work is intended to give one's life a sense of meaning.

In a supportive environment (which maximizes positive features, such as support and challenge, and minimizes negative features, such as bureaucratic hassles and administrative interference), highly motivated individuals can reach their goals and fulfill their expectations. Success provides a sense of existential significance that, in turn, increases the original motivation for the work. When the same highly motivated people enter a stressful work environment (which maximizes negative and minimizes positive features), they can't get the resources or authority they need to achieve their goals. The result is failure. For individuals who expect a sense of significance from work, failure is a powerful cause of burnout.

AN EXPERIENTIAL DEMONSTRATION
OF THE EXISTENTIAL PERSPECTIVE

An experiential exercise I include in virtually every burnout workshop I lead (Pines & Aronson, 1988; Pines, 1992c) is inspired by and demonstrates the existential perspective on burnout. In preparation for the exercise, I ask the workshop participants to write down their goals and expectations when they started their careers and the stresses that currently contribute most to their burnout. In the next stage of the exercise, I divide the participants into groups of four. The people in each group are asked to share their goals and expectations with each other and to discover which of those were shared by all four of them. This information is presented by a spokesperson of the group to the rest of the participants and written on a board.

Whenever the workshop involves more than three groups, the first three presentations usually cover all the items; the remaining groups mostly repeat what is already on the board. These shared goals and expectations reflect the profession-specific motivations of the participants. The following goals and expectations, for example, were mentioned by a group of middle managers:

> improve performance of the group
> achieve something significant
> be successful
> grow professionally
> contribute to the success of the organization
> change the organization's environment
> meet challenge
> achieve personal growth
> be supported
> be adequately rewarded

Next, participants are asked to return to their groups to share with each other the causes of their burnout and to discover the stresses they have in common. The shared stresses are once again presented by a spokesperson and written on the board. The middle managers mentioned the following burnout-causing stresses:

> lack of resources in people and time to get the job done
> no control over the situation
> inability to make organization perform according to expectations
> unwanted organizational changes
> organizational policies
> lack of support from top management
> top management interference
> unmotivated workers
> unrealistic expectations
> lack of recognition

In the third stage of the exercise, participants are asked to look at the two lists on the board and to note any relationships between them.

What becomes very obvious is that the stresses can be stated as frustrated goals and expectations. If we examine the two lists produced by the middle managers, each one of the stresses mentioned reflects a failure to achieve some goal or expectation. The lack of human resources and time needed to get the job done is stressful for highly motivated managers because they expected to be successful, and the lack of adequate resources prevents them from achieving their goals. Similarly, having little control and being blocked by top management are stressful because they prevent the middle managers from doing things the way they feel they should be done. The inability to make the organization perform according to their expectations is stressful because it makes it difficult for them to contribute to the success of the organization. Unwanted organizational changes are stressful because they make it plain to the managers that they are unable to change the organization's environment the way they wanted to. Organizational policies frustrate the expectation of having a challenging job in which it is possible to succeed. Lack of support from top management is frustrating for workers who expected to be supported in their efforts. Unmotivated workers are frustrating for managers who expected to improve the performance of the group under their supervision. Unrealistic expectations, which can only lead to failure, are very stressful for workers who expected to be successful and achieve personal and professional growth in their work. Lack of recognition is stressful for workers who expected to be recognized for accomplishing something significant.

As noted earlier, when the group is from one field of work (e.g., nurses, teachers, social workers, police officers), the shared goals and expectations reveal the participants' profession-specific motivations for entering their career. For nurses, motivations almost always include expecting to ease the pain of sick people; for social workers, helping people in trouble; for teachers, educating and enlightening. For all highly motivated professionals there is an added universal goal and expectation to be successful and appreciated. Both the profession-specific and the universal goals and expectations reflect the sense of existential significance that work was expected to provide.

As the exercise demonstrates, the most stressful aspects of work can almost always be stated as frustrated goals and expectations. For nurses, whose goal was to ease the pain of sick people, the most frequently mentioned stresses are those aspects of hospital work that make it difficult to ease the pain of their patients effectively. For teachers, whose goal was to educate and enlighten, the most frequently mentioned stresses are the discipline and budget problems that make it difficult for them to educate. For social workers, the most stressful factors are the bureaucratic aspects of the work that interfere with their efficient delivery of services. Comparison between goals and stresses demonstrates that the most stressful, burnout-causing aspects of work are those that prevent highly motivated individuals from getting a sense of existential significance from their work.

This important conclusion has far-reaching implications for strategies to cope with burnout because it implies that effective coping strategies need to focus not on stresses but on people's goals and expectations. Ultimately, in order to prevent burnout, professionals need to discover new ways to achieve their goals and expectations and thus get a sense of meaning from their work.

Making the goals versus stresses comparison is the first—and essential—step in coping with burnout. We must recognize that the aspects of the work that we find most stressful are a result of something in us: our hopes, ideals, goals, and expectations. While it may be easier to blame the organization, the service recipients, or the boss, recognition of the fact that we choose (by our goals and expectations) the stresses that will cause our burnout can free us to cope with them more creatively and positively.

Another experiential exercise that demonstrates the existential perspective of the burnout process concerns the "best and worst clients" scenario (Pines, 1992c). Participants in the exercise are asked to think about their two favorite clients (or employees or service recipients), the two they most enjoy working with, appreciate, and trust, and then to make a list of the characteristics these two people have in common. These characteristics are likely to include such qualities as intelligence, positive energy, appreciation, ability to learn and grow, willingness to improve, and openness to change.

When participants share their lists, they discover that their best clients' qualities are not unique. Rather, there are common characteristics that describe the "universal best client." By a similar process they also discover the common characteristics of the "universal worst client."

When asked to compare the two lists to see if the best and worst clients share any dimensions, participants always discover such dimensions. If the best client is intelligent, the worse client is dull-witted; if the best client is positive, the worst client is negative; if the best client is appreciative, the worst client is critical; if the best client is able to grow, the worst client resists change; if the best client is open, the worse client is closed minded.

After establishing these dimensions, the next question is: Do you see any relationship between the shared dimensions of the best and worst clients and your own goals and expectations? A moment's reflection usually makes it clear that there is an obvious connection. The best clients are those who enable the participants to achieve their goals and who acknowledge their professional success. The worst clients prevent the participants from achieving their goals and contribute to their feelings of failure. In other words, the most important dimension is the dimension of our personal efficacy. (See also Cherniss, 1990.) We perceive and evaluate the people we work with according to the degree to which they fulfill our need to get a sense of significance from our work.

COPING WITH BURNOUT

The existential view of burnout assumes that the root cause of burnout lies in our need to believe that our lives are meaningful (Frankl, 1963), that the things we do in our work are useful and important. Thus, as noted earlier, effective coping strategies need to help people achieve a sense of meaning in their work.

Coping refers to efforts to master conditions of harm, threat, or challenge when an automatic response is not readily available (Monat & Lazarus, 1985). Coping itself does not imply success in overcoming the stressful situation, only the effort. Coping is the link between stress and adaptation. Coping can take place on the level of the individual, the work group, or the organization.

Coping with Burnout on the Individual Level

People deal with burnout in different ways (Pines & Aronson, 1988). Some burned-out workers leave their professions, but quitting a career after long years of training is almost always a painful experience associated with a deep sense of failure. The loss is also costly for the organization and for society as a whole.

Other people leave their particular job as a result of burnout, but stay in the same profession or in the same organization. Typically, these people find the same problems in their new job. After burning out in a series of jobs they often develop a chronic sense of helplessness, hopelessness, and failure.

Still others climb the administrative ladder as a way of escaping the emotional demands of the job in which they have burned out. Caseworkers who burn out in their work with clients at times decide to go back to school for a higher degree that enables them to become administrators, far removed from direct contact with clients. While this may seem like a reasonable solution, few things are as burnout-producing as a burned out worker who is supervising others.

There are also those who never quit, even when they are totally burned out. These people are usually motivated by a need for security, and when a job offers them tenure and acceptable retirement benefits they frequently choose to stay—as "dead wood."

Another way of coping with burnout is to turn it into a trigger for personal growth. The crisis of burnout can make idealistic workers aware of problems, spur them to examine the demands imposed on them, and provide an opportunity for evaluating their life priorities, their strengths and weaknesses, and the scope for expanding their skills and abilities. This process can lay the foundation for building a support system and improving their coping strategies.

A study of the relationship between burnout and coping identified four categories of coping (Pines & Kafry, 1981):

1. active = direct (e.g., changing the source of stress, confronting the person who causes stress)
2. inactive = direct (e.g., ignoring the source of stress, leaving the stressful situation)
3. active = indirect (e.g., talking about the stress to a supportive other, getting involved in other activities)
4. inactive = indirect (e.g., drinking alcohol, taking drugs)

The study, which involved two samples, one of 147 subjects and the other of 84, revealed that the active strategies were most effective in coping with burnout. The most ineffective was the inactive = indirect strategy. Active strategies alleviate burnout because they help change the situation, the individual, or both. In many cases, a positive change increases the likelihood that highly motivated workers will find a sense of meaning in their work.

In order to cope with burnout successfully, an individual needs to do four things: 1. Become aware of the problem. This step involves the simple recognition of the problem as well as the realization that it is largely a result of a stressful situation that prevents goal achievement rather than of one's own inadequacy. 2. Take responsibility for doing something about the problem. Often, people have more control over their work environment than they realize. Taking responsibility for change reduces the debilitating effects of helplessness. 3. Achieve a degree of cognitive clarity. Develop the ability to discriminate what can be changed in the work environment from what cannot. This understanding allows workers to channel their efforts in the directions in which there is the greatest likelihood of significant progress. Not only is the change beneficial, but being able to effect change reduces hopelessness and helplessness and, consequently, burnout. 4. Develop new tools for coping, and improve the range and quality of old tools (see Pines & Aronson, 1988, ch. 7).

Coping with Burnout on the Work Group Level

The goals that people set for themselves are influenced by the norms of the groups to which they belong and wish to belong. The individual is usually a member of many overlapping social groups: a nuclear family, an extended family, a work group, a professional group, or a political party. While these groups have different degrees of influence on different individuals, and while their influence varies at different times, belonging to a group always involves certain demands. There are certain expectations of a father, a wife, a business partner, and a co-worker. If we violate these expectations we are likely to be criticized or ridiculed. In extreme cases we may be divorced, fired, or punished by law. In addition to demands, each of the groups we belong to also provides certain rewards.

Given the fundamental importance of the elaborate network of social groups surrounding each one of us, with their concomitant benefits and demands, it is not surprising that conflicting demands from different groups (for example, work and family), or the inability to respond to an important group's demands, are a major cause of burnout. On the other hand, the efficient and creative use of social support is among the most effective ways of coping with burnout (Pines, 1983; Pines & Aronson, 1988).

It is important for people to examine carefully the demands various groups place on them to ascertain the extent to which these demands are essential, current, legitimate, and reasonable. It is especially important to clarify any ambiguity between a real demand and one's own self-demand, which may arise from unrealistic expectations and thus lead to failure.

In addition to making demands, groups are a source of some of our most important rewards. One of these rewards is social support. An extensive literature documents the protective effect of social support as a mediator of stress (e.g., Caplan, 1974; Cobb, 1976; Lieberman, 1982). The creative use of social support also serves as a buffer against burnout (Pines, 1983; Westman & Etzion, 1990; Winnubst, 1990).

Social support serves a multitude of functions. In my work with Elliot Aronson, we identified six basic functions:

1. listening (active listening, without giving advice or making judgment)
2. technical support and appreciation (from a person who is an expert in the field and whose honesty can be trusted)
3. technical challenge (from a person who is good enough at the job to be able to identify what could be improved and who can provide the challenge for our benefit and not at our expense)
4. emotional challenge (from a person who can help us think rationally when we are too emotionally involved in a situation)
5. emotional support (from a person who is on our side, no matter what)
6. shared social reality (from a person who sees things the way we do and has similar values and priorities)

A work group that fulfills at least three of these functions (technical support, technical challenge, and shared social reality) helps reduce job stress and protects from burnout (see Pines & Aronson, 1988, ch. 8).

Unfortunately, most people, especially when under stress, do not make the effort to avail themselves of the important support that a work group can offer. By realizing that social support involves different functions we can think of social support not in a global sense but as a number of separate functions that can be fulfilled by different people in our environment.

How does one establish a social support group at work? One way to start is to ask for support, challenge, and reality checks from appropriate colleagues and to offer support and challenge when it seems appropriate. Anyone may be instrumental in changing an unsupportive work environment to a supportive one. If two or three people take the lead by offering appreciation, challenge, and shared reality to those around them, others recognize that such behavior feels good and it tends to be contagious.

While different people have different needs for support, and while different people can and should serve different support functions for each other, social support is an important buffer against burnout. Fortunately, social support is also very cost effective. A supportive work group does not depend on a complicated bureaucratic structure for its development and maintenance, and the cost to establish it is minimal—all that is required is the decision by a group of co-workers to get together regularly at a particular time and place. Usually, once the initial effort is made to establish such meetings, very little effort is needed to keep them going.

Coping with Burnout on the Organizational Level

Organizations that are similar in function, structure, size, and resources still can have very different levels of worker burnout (Cox, 1990; Golembiewski, 1982; Pines, 1982; Winnubst, 1990). Levels of burnout depend upon such factors as work relationships, availability of social support, degree of autonomy, manageability of the workload, bureaucratic and administrative interference, and the work environment.

The variables that play a role in either promoting or preventing burnout can be grouped into psychological, physical, social, and organizational features (Pines, 1982). The psychological features include aspects that affect workers' emotional well-being (such as the sense of meaning and opportunities for personal growth) as well as aspects that affect them cognitively (such as variety, overload, and underload). The physical features include fixed aspects (such as adequacy of space, crowding, and noise) and the flexibility to change the environment according to workers' needs and tastes. The social features include all the people coming in direct contact with the individual, including service recipients (their number and the severity of their problems), co-workers (the quality of relations with them and their capacity to provide "time out," support, challenge, and shared social reality), supervisors and administrators (the nature of their feedback and whether they offer support, challenge, and shared social reality). The organizational features include bureaucratic hassles (such as red tape and paper work), administrative rules and regulations, and role conflict.

To help their workers cope with burnout, organizations not only need to minimize stressful work features (such as overload, paper work, red tape, and role conflict), but they need to maximize positive work features (such as autonomy, variety, support, challenge, and opportunity for personal growth) (Kanner, Kafry, & Pines, 1978).

COPING WITH BURNOUT: AN EXISTENTIAL PERSPECTIVE

Coping with burnout is most effective when done simultaneously on the level of the individual, the work group, and the organization. The focus in all three cases must be on the sense of significance that the worker is looking for and that the work should provide. On the individual level, turning burnout into a trigger for personal growth is possible only if idealistic workers are able to achieve a sense of significance from their work. On the group level, only if the work group helps its members achieve their goals and feel that their work is important and makes a difference can it buffer them against burnout. Therefore, it is essential that group support meetings should not only focus on problems and stresses, but participants should share their goals, expectations, and hopes and explore together the best ways to overcome the obstacles to achieving them. For organizations, too, the best way to avoid employee burnout is to focus on the ways to help highly motivated workers to achieve their goals. In a sense, what is best for the individual is also best for the organization. Only if workers can achieve a sense of significance in their work is a burnout-free organization possible.

BURNOUT: PAST, PRESENT AND FUTURE

Soon after the concept's introduction, over fifteen years ago, and despite a general agreement on its presenting symptoms, there was a debate among scholars on the exact definition of burnout (e.g., Farber, 1983b; Maslach, 1982b; Paine, 1982). Since that time, together with the accumulation of data from a large number of empirical studies on burnout in different professional groups, there has been growing agreement among scholars about both the definition of burnout and the best methods to measure it (e.g., Enzmann & Kleiber, 1990; Hallsten, 1990; Schaufeli & Peeters, 1990). Cross-cultural studies have documented the existence of burnout in countries outside the United States (e.g., Etzion & Pines, 1986; Kleiber & Enzmann, 1990; Schaufeli & Janczur, 1990; Westman & Etzion, 1990).

More recently, attention has been directed to the need for a theory of burnout (e.g., Burisch, 1990). Some scholars have attempted to place burnout in the context of existing theoretical formulations, such as theories of stress (Cox, 1990), organizational theories (Hallsten, 1990), and even psychoanalytic theory (Garden, 1990). Others focus on the unique dynamic of the burnout process. Cary Cherniss, for example, focuses on the role of professional self-efficacy in the etiology of burnout (Cherniss, 1990). Matthias Burisch focuses on the loss of autonomy as the salient factor (Burisch, 1990). In this chapter, I have focused on the role played by a perceived failure in the existential quest for meaning.

In the future, we are likely to see more cross-cultural studies of burnout, more longitudinal studies (in which individuals are followed from their entry into a career until their burnout), more controlled studies (in which control groups are used), and a greater agreement on the theoretical underpinnings of burnout that can help integrate the vast amount of empirical data that has accumulated.

REFERENCES

BECKER, E. *The denial of death.* New York: Free Press, 1973.

BURISCH, M. *In search of theory—stop looking for the burnout virus.* Paper presented at the first European Network of organizational Psychologists conference on professional burnout. Cracow, Poland, September 24–27, 1990.

CAPLAN, G. *Support systems and community mental health.* New York: Behavioral Publications, 1974.

CARROL, J. F. X., & WHITE, W. L. Theory building. Integrating individual and environmental factors within an ecological framework. In W. S. Paine (ed.), *Job stress and burnout.* Beverly Hills, CA: Sage, 1982.

CHERNISS, C. *Professional burnout in human service organizations.* New York: Praeger, 1980.

————. *The role of self-efficacy in the etiology of burnout.* Paper presented at the first European

Network of Organizational Psychologists conference on professional burnout. Cracow, Poland, September 24–27, 1990.

Cherniss, C., & Krantz, D. L. The ideological community as an antidote to burnout in the human services. In B. Farber (ed.), *Stress and burnout in the human service professions*. New York: Pergamon Press, 1983.

Cobb, S. Social support as a moderator of life stress. *Psychosomatic Medicine,* 1976, *5,* 300–314.

Corcoran, K. J. Measuring burnout: A reliability and convergent validity study. *Journal of Social Behavior and Personality,* 1986, *1,* 107–112.

Cox, T. *Stress, burnout and organizational health.* Paper presented at the first European Network of Organizational Psychologists conference on professional burnout. Cracow, Poland, September 24–27, 1990.

Enzmann, D., & Kleiber, D. *Construct validity and work related factors in burnout.* Paper presented at the first European Network of Organizational Psychologists conference on professional burnout. Cracow, Poland, September 24–27, 1990.

Etzion, D., Kafry, D., & Pines, A. Tedium among managers: a cross cultural American-Israeli comparison. *Journal of Psychology and Judaism,* 1982, *1,* 30–41.

Etzion, D., & Pines, A. Sex and culture as factors explaining burnout among human service professionals. *Journal of Cross Cultural Psychology,* 1986, *17,* 191–209.

Farber, B. A. Dysfunctional aspects of the psychotherapeutic role. In B. A. Farber (ed.), *Stress and burnout in the human service professions*. New York: Pergamon Press, 1983. (a)

————. A Critical perspective on burnout. In B. Farber (ed.), *Stress and burnout in the human service professions*. New York: Pergamon Press, 1983. (b)

Frankl, V. *Man's search for meaning.* Boston: Beacon Press, 1963.

Freudenberger, H. J. Staff burnout. *Journal of Social Issues,* 1974, *30,* 159–165.

————. *Burn-out: The high cost of high achievement.* Garden City, NY: Doubleday, 1980.

————. Counseling and dynamics: Treating the end-stage person. In W. S. Paine (ed.), *Job stress and burnout.* Beverly Hills, CA: Sage, 1982.

Garden, A. M. *A Jungian view—does burnout have a purpose?* Paper presented at the first European Network of Organizational Psychologists conference on professional burnout. Cracow, Poland, September 24–27, 1990.

Gentry, W. D., Foster, S. B., & Froehling, S. Psychological response to situational stress in intensive care and maintenance care nursing. *Heart and Lung,* 1972, *1,* 793–796.

Golembiewski, R. T. Organizational development (OD) interventions: Changing interactions, structures, and policies. In W. S. Paine (ed.), *Job stress and burnout.* Beverly Hills, CA: Sage, 1982.

Hallsten, L. *From burnout to burning out: Some issues and a model.* Paper presented at the first European Network of Organizational Psychologists conference on professional burnout. Cracow, Poland, September 24–27, 1990.

Hay, D., & Oaken, D. The psychological stress of intensive care unit nursing. In A. Monat & R. S. Lazarus (eds.), *Stress and coping.* New York: Columbia University Press, 1985.

Hosmer Mawardi, B. Aspects of the impaired physician. In B. A. Farber (ed.), *Stress and burnout in the human service professions.* New York: Pergamon Press, 1983.

Jayaratne, S., & Chess, W. A. Job satisfaction and burnout in social work. In B. A. Farber, (ed.), *Stress and burnout in the human service professions.* New York: Pergamon Press, 1983.

Jones, J. W. Staff burnout and employee counterproductivity. In J. W. Jones (ed.), *The burnout syndrome.* Park Ridge, IL: London House Press, 1981.

————. (ed.). *Burnout in policing.* Park Ridge, IL: London House Press, 1985.

Justice, B., Gold, R. S., & Klein, J. P. Life events and burnout. *Journal of Psychology,* 1981, *108,* 219–226.

KANNER, A., KAFRY, D., & PINES, A. Conspicuous in its absence: The lack of positive conditions as a source of stress. *Journal of Human Stress,* 1978, 4, 33–39.

KLEIBER, D., & ENZMANN, D. 1978, *Complexity and closeness to everyday life of the work in the human services as determinants of burnout.* Paper presented at the first European Network of Organizational Psychologists conference on professional burnout. Cracow, Poland, September 24–27, 1990.

LIEBERMAN, M. A. The effect of social supports on responses to stress. In L. Goldberger & S. Breznitz (eds.), *Handbook of stress.* New York: Free Press, 1982.

MAREK, T., & NOWOROL, C. *Burnout: A psychophysiological approach.* Paper presented at the first European Network of Organizational Psychologists conference on professional burnout. Cracow, Poland, September 24–27, 1990.

MASLACH, C. Burned out. *Human Behavior,* 1976, 5, 16–22.

————. *Burnout—The cost of caring.* Englewood Cliffs, NJ: Prentice-Hall, 1982. (a)

————. Understanding burnout: Definitional issues in analyzing a complex phenomenon. In W. S. Paine (ed.), *Job stress and burnout.* Beverly Hills, CA: Sage, 1982. (b)

MASLACH, C., & JACKSON, S. E. Lawyer burn-out. *Barrister,* 1978, 5, 51–54.

————. Burned-out cops and their families. *Psychology Today,* 1979, 12, 59–62.

————. The measurement of experienced burnout. *Journal of Occupational Behavior,* 1981, 2, 99–113.

MASLACH, C., & PINES, A. The "burnout" syndrome in day care settings. *Child Care Quarterly,* 1977, 6, 100–113.

————. Burnout, the loss of human caring. In A. Pines & C. Maslach (eds.), *Experiencing social psychology.* New York: Random House, 1979.

McCONNELL, E. A. (ed). *Burnout in the nursing profession.* St. Louis, MO: C. Mosbey, 1982.

MONAT, A., & LAZARUS, R. S. *Stress and coping.* New York: Columbia University Press, 1985.

PAINE, W. S. Overview: Burnout stress syndromes and the 1980s. In W. S. Paine (ed.), *Job stress and burnout.* Beverly Hills, CA: Sage, 1982.

PINES, A. Burnout: A current problem in pediatrics. *Current Issues in Pediatrics,* May issue 1981, 3–32.

————. Changing organizations: Is a work environment without burnout an impossible goal? In W. S. Paine (ed.), *Job stress and burnout.* Beverly Hills, CA: Sage, 1982.

————. On burnout and the buffering effects of social support. In B. Farber (ed.), *Stress and burnout in the human service professions.* New York: Pergamon Press, 1983.

————. *Keeping the spark alive. Preventing burnout in love and marriage.* New York: St. Martin's Press, 1988.

————. *Burnout—an existential perspective.* Paper presented at the first European Network of Organizational Psychologists conference on professional burnout. Cracow, Poland, September 24–27, 1990.

————. Burnout in organizational consultation. In R. Golembiewski (ed.), *Handbook of organizational consultation.* New York: Marcel Dekker, 1992. (a)

————. Burnout—an existential perspective. In W. Schaufeli, T. Marek, & C. Maslach (eds.), *Professional burnout: developments in theory and research.* New York: Hemisphere Press, 1992. (b)

————. A burnout workshop: Design and rationale. In R. T. Golembiewski (ed.), *Handbook of Organizational Consultation.* New York: Marcel Dekker, 1992. (c)

PINES, A., & ARONSON, E. *Career burnout: Causes and cures* (2d ed.). New York: Free Press, 1988.

PINES, A., & KAFRY, D. Occupational tedium in social service professionals. *Social Work,* 1978, 23, 499–507.

————. Coping with burnout. In J. Jones (ed.), *The burnout syndrome*. Parkridge, IL.: London House Press, 1981.

PINES, A. & KANNER, A. Nurses' burnout: Lack of positive conditions and presence of negative conditions as two independent sources of stress. *Journal of Psychosocial Nursing,* 1982, 8, 30–35.

PINES, A., & MASLACH, C. Characteristics of staff burnout in mental health settings. *Hospital and Community Psychiatry,* 1978, 29, 233–237.

PINES, A., & MASLACH, C. Combatting staff burnout in child care center: A case study. *Child Care Quarterly,* 1980, 9, 5–16.

PINES, A., & SILBERT, M. Police officer's burnout. In J. Jones (ed.), *Burnout in policing*. Park Ridge, IL: London House Press, 1985.

REPPUCI, N. D. Social psychology of institutional change: General principles of intervention. *American Journal of Community Psychology,*, 1973, *1,* 330–341.

SAKHAROV, M., & FARBER, B. A. A critical study of burnout in teachers. In B. A. Farber (ed.), *Stress and burnout in the human service professions*. New York: Pergamon Press, 1983.

SCHAUFELI, W. B., & JANCZUR, B. *Burnout among nurses. A Polish-Dutch comparison.* Paper presented at the first European Network of Organizational Psychologists conference on professional burnout. Cracow, Poland, September 24–27, 1990.

SCHAUFELI, W. B., & PEETERS, M. C. W. *The measurement of burnout.* Paper presented at the first European Network of Organizational Psychologists conference on professional burnout. Cracow, Poland, September 24–27, 1990.

WESTMAN, M., & ETZION, D. *Job stress and burnout: The moderating effect of social support and sense of control.* Paper presented at the first European Network of Organizational Psychologists conference on professional burnout. Cracow, Poland, September 24–27, 1990.

WINNUBST, J. A. M. *Burnout, social support, and organizational structure.* Paper presented at the first European Network of Organizational Psychologists conference on professional burnout. Cracow, Poland, September 24–27, 1990.

B. Sociocultural and Developmental Sources

22

Psychological Stress and Coping in Old Age

Paul T. Costa, Jr.   Robert R. McCrae

ONE OF THE RECURRING ISSUES in the study of stress and coping is the proper level of analysis. Should we approach it as a universal phenomenon, like Selye's (1956) general adaptation syndrome? As a set of enduring individual differences, like Haan's (1977) styles of coping and defense? As an array of general strategies for dealing with particular stressors, like Folkman and Lazarus's (1980) ways of coping? Or must we treat each stressful situation as a discrete problem that requires its own unique solutions? Research over the past decade suggests that, in terms of general processes, older individuals resemble adults of all ages; age is not a powerful determinant of perceived stress, preferred ways of coping, or adaptational outcomes. But older individuals do face a distinctive set of stressors, and some of the most concretely useful research focuses on solutions to these problems.

A NOTE ON MEASUREMENT

There are formidable problems in the measurement of most elements of the stress and coping process. When an individual is asked to recall a stressful event, describe what he or she did in response, and report the resulting disease or distress, the possibilities for distortions due to failures of memory and subjective biases are enormous (e.g., Schroeder & Costa, 1984). The measurement of coping is hampered by the fact that there is no recognized taxonomy of ways of coping that a coping inventory should assess. Further complications occur when research questions concern age-specific stress and coping. There are no fully satisfactory solutions to these problems yet; nevertheless, some instruments and approaches are better than others.

For the measurement of life stress, the most common approach has been the use of life event checklists derived from the work of Holmes and Rahe (1967), sometimes adapted for use with older populations (e.g., McCrae, 1982). This approach has been widely criticized (Schroeder & Costa, 1984); certainly users should be familiar with the criticisms and eliminate from the instruments items that are particularly susceptible to confounding and bias. At a more molecular level, Lazarus and his colleagues have advocated an examination of daily hassles. The revised version of an instrument to measure hassles and uplifts (DeLongis, Folkman, & Lazarus, 1988) is superior to the original, but still has many problems (Costa & McCrae, 1990). Vitaliano, Young, and Russo (1991) provide a review of measures of caregiver burden, one of the major stressors of old age.

With respect to measures of coping, the most widely used instrument is the Ways of Coping (Folkman & Lazarus, 1980), which was initially developed to assess coping in a middle-aged community sample. The major limitation of this instrument is that there is no generally accepted way to score its items. A promising alternative is provided by the scales of Carver, Scheier, and Weintraub (1989), which can be administered to measure either general coping styles or specific coping behaviors.

Many of the difficulties in the measurement of stress and coping processes are due to the pervasive influence of the personality disposition of neuroticism, which affects the perception of stress, ways of coping, and adaptational outcomes such as well-being and somatic complaints (McCrae, 1990). Researchers and clinicians would be well advised to include measures of this and other personality traits in their assessments. The Revised NEO Personality Inventory (Costa & McCrae, 1992) provides measures of neuroticism and other major dimensions of personality that have been used with adults across the full age range. Many other personality instruments, such as the Eysenck Personality Questionnaire (Eysenck & Eysenck, 1975), also provide valid measures of neuroticism.

AGE DIFFERENCES IN STRESS AND COPING

Until recently relatively little attention was paid to possible age differences in coping, defense, and adaptation to stress. There were, however, a number of popular stereotypes and some clinical observations that depicted older individuals as increasingly vulnerable to stress. It was probably in response to these perceptions that the National Institute on Aging created the intramural research Section on Stress and Coping in 1978. Research conducted here and elsewhere, however, has shown that most older individuals handle stress as well— or as poorly—as other adults and that other characteristics, such as social supports and personality traits, may be more relevant to predicting stress outcomes.

Is Old Age a Particularly Stressful Period?

It is commonly assumed that older individuals face the most difficult time of life. Health declines, disabilities increase, youthful physical attractiveness fades. Friends are lost to death and loss of spouse is common, especially for women. Retirement and relocation bring major life changes that can pose significant problems. Some older people face financial hardship, some are neglected by their children, some feel alienated by social change (Fiske, 1982). Many face the social stigmatization that comes with the devalued status of old age in some cultures. And all other people face the prospect of dementia, institutionalization, and death.

Without minimizing the seriousness of these stressors, it is well to put them in perspective. Most of them are not universal. Although health problems are increasingly common with age, most individuals over the age of 65 are not incapacitated. Fewer than five percent require institutionalization (Moritz & Ostfeld, 1990); with recent improvements in geriatric medicine and changes in lifestyle, most older men and women lead active and satisfying lives (Rowe, 1990). Most individuals adjust well and rapidly to retirement (Vinick & Ekerdt, 1989) and thoroughly enjoy the leisure it affords. In the United States and most of the developed world, programs like Social Security and Medicare have dramatically reduced the extent of poverty among the elderly. Despite stereotypes of neglected parents and grandparents, strong bonds and frequent contact between generations is the rule (Costa & McCrae, 1983; Troll, Miller, & Atchley, 1979). Far from feeling alienated, older Americans are actively involved in shaping their society. As every politician knows, this age group votes heavily in both local and national elections. Even social stereotypes are not uniformly bad. The elderly are often revered as sources of wisdom, and distinguished men and women are showered with awards in old age.

The depiction of old age as a period of particular stress also fails to consider that all periods of life involve stressors of some kind. Adolescents must make like choices on the basis of little experience; young adults must deal with the pressures of beginning a family and starting a career; middle-aged adults face financial obligations ranging from college tuition to nursing services for their parents. Death of a spouse is unusual for young men and women, but death of a parent or grandparent is not. Most older people lead relatively uneventful and, in that sense, stress-free lives.

It is true that death is inevitable, but the approach of death is not as traumatic as it might seem. Only a small portion of older individuals have a strong fear of death, and these tend to be chronically fearful people (Kastenbaum & Costa, 1977). Many consider death a release from the problems of this world and an opportunity to rejoin those who have gone before. Perhaps most importantly, death in old age is expectable, and individuals learn to accept it.

Can Old People Cope?

Even if old age is not a particularly stressful period of life, it may be that the limited capacities of older individuals to adjust make it a difficult time. Pfeiffer (1977) argued that older individuals regress to the use of primitive and ineffective defenses: "unmodified anxiety, depression-withdrawal, projection, somatization, and denial are the preponderant mechanisms used in this age group" (p. 651). Stereotypically, old people are rigid and inflexible; even minor stressors may exceed their capacity to adapt.

These assertions may be correct for the minority of older individuals with serious cognitive impairments, but they do not apply to healthy older men and women. Consider the case of bereavement. Most life event researchers consider death of a spouse to be the among the most stressful of events (Holmes & Rahe, 1967), and widowed individuals typically show some excess mortality, especially within the first six months after the death of the spouse (Stroebe & Stroebe, 1987). But among the great majority who survive, the predominant picture is one of psychological resilience (McCrae & Costa, 1988). In a ten-year follow-up of a national sample, long-term widowed and long-term married individuals were compared with more recently widowed individuals. At follow-up, the three groups showed little or no difference in terms of social network size, self-rated health, activities of daily living, general well-being, depression, or the personality variables of extraversion and openness to experience. It appears that the great majority of bereaved individuals are able to work through the grief process and return to their typical levels of psychological functioning; this was true for older (65 to 74) as well as younger (25 to 64) men and women.

It is often thought that depression is common among the elderly, and it is tempting to explain this by reference to greater stress or poorer coping. In fact, however, depression is weakly related to age (Costa, McCrae, & Locke, 1990), and surveys of psychological well-being show that older individuals are just as happy and satisfied with life as are younger individuals (Costa & McCrae, 1984). Even the widespread idea that age is associated with increased somatization is largely myth: The medical complaints that older people make are usually a reflection of actual medical problems (Costa & McCrae, 1985).

Do Older People Cope Differently?

It is possible that there are age differences in the ways in which people cope, even if there are no differences in the ultimate outcomes. This question has received considerable recent attention, as stress and coping researchers have explored the correlates of newly developed measures of coping (Felton & Revenson, 1987; Irion & Blanchard-Fields, 1987; Lazarus & DeLongis, 1983). There are many different ways to solve problems and reduce distress, ranging from seeking help and taking direct action to positive thinking and humor. In a pair of cross-sectional studies, McCrae (1982) examined 28 such coping mechanisms in three age groups. He found no consistent age differences in the use of 26 of the mechanisms, but reported that middle-aged and older men and women were somewhat less likely than young adults to use hostile reactions and escapist fantasy.

A seven-year longitudinal follow-up to this study used repeated measures and cross-sequential analyses to examine changes in the use of coping mechanisms (McCrae, 1989); none of the mechanisms showed consistent evidence of change with age. This analysis confirmed the conclusions of Felton and Revenson (1987), who stated that the influence of aging on the coping process was "limited in scope and modest in strength" (p. 168).

McCrae's (1989) study, however, also showed modest longitudinal consistency in individual differences in the use of coping mechanisms. Individuals prone to use, say, expression of feelings or wishful thinking or faith in dealing with a stressor in 1980 were likely to use the same mechanism for dealing with another stressor in 1987. This finding suggests that there is merit to the older notion of coping and defense styles (Haan, 1977), ways in which individuals characteristically respond to a variety of different losses, threats, and challenges.

Costa, Zonderman, and McCrae (1991) examined associations between age and defense mechanism scales from the Defense Mechanism Inventory (DMI; Ihilevich & Gleser, 1986; $n = 182$), the Defense Style Questionnaire (DSQ; Bond, Gardner, Christian, & Sigal, 1983; $n = 292$), and Haan's (1965) scoring of the MMPI ($n = 477$). Subjects were volunteer participants in the Baltimore Longitudinal Study of Aging (Shock, et al., 1984) and their spouses and ranged in age from 20 to 92. Age was positively correlated with DMI principalization and reversal, MMPI repression, denial, and intellectualization, and DSQ self-sacrificing defenses; it was negatively correlated with DMI turning against object and projection, and DSQ maladaptive action pattern. Age was not significantly related to DMI turning against self, MMPI regression, displacement, projection, and doubt, or DSQ image-distorting and adaptive scales. These correlations present a relatively consistent picture of older people as being more willing to meet adversity cheerfully and less prone to vent frustrations on others. However, most of the significant correlations were quite small (median absolute value .21), and they may represent generational differences rather than developmental changes in the choice of defenses used. Longitudinal studies are needed here.

Should We Study Stress and Aging?

We have argued that old age is not necessarily a stressful period, that older men and women have the same psychological resilience that younger adults have, and that age is a very weak determinant of ways of coping and defending. Does this mean that stress and coping should not be a topic of interest to gerontologists? Not at all. The more we can learn about the causes and consequences of stress and the most effective ways different individuals can deal with different kinds of problems, the better equipped we are to help older men and women.

We know that the types of coping mechanisms individuals characteristically choose are, in part, reflections of their enduring personality traits. For example, people who are high in openness to experience—that is, who are imaginative, creative, empathic, exploring, curious, and liberal—often resort to humor as a way of coping with stress. Those who are low in openness—down-to-earth, conventional, practical, and traditional—rely on faith (McCrae & Costa, 1986). Both humor and faith appear to be relatively mature and effective ways to deal with stress, but they appeal to very different kinds of people. Counselors trying to help a widow deal with her grief or a cancer patient deal with his anxiety may be more effective if they know the personality traits of their clients and the associations between personality and coping (McCrae & Costa, 1991).

In the same way, basic knowledge about the situational determinants of coping (McCrae, 1984), the temporal course of adaptation (Folkman & Lazarus, 1985), the underlying dynamic processes (Horowitz, 1988), the role of social supports (Holahan & Moos, 1986), and the long-term consequences of particular styles of coping and defense (Vaillant, 1977) should be of value in developing interventions to assist aging men and women faced with stressful events or conditions. Old people are, first and foremost, people (Keith, 1982), and principles derived from the study of stress and coping in any group of adults is likely to be generalizable to this population.

COPING WITH THE STRESSORS OF OLD AGE

Older people do differ from younger adults in the specific stressful situations and conditions they are likely to encounter. Few 30-year-olds face cataract surgery, forced retirement, or loss of the ability to drive. Developing effective advice on how to deal with such problems forms the applied side of stress and coping research, and this research has a distinctively gerontological focus and flavor. A recent issue of *The Gerontologist,* a journal that has traditionally been concerned with applied science (Kane, 1991), included articles on activities appropriate for Alzheimer's disease patients (Teri & Logsdon, 1991), police protection for the elderly (Zevitz & Gurnack, 1991), and home medical and housekeeping assistance (Thorslund, Norstrom, & Wernberg, 1991). Popular books have provided information, advice, and reassurance on such topics as urinary incontinence (Burgio, Pearce, & Lucco, 1990) and living with an Alzheimer's disease patient (Mace & Rabins, 1991).

Perhaps no topic has received more attention than coping with the burden of Alzheimer's disease in a parent or spouse. A recent bibliography listed seventy-one publications on family relations and caregiving in Alzheimer's disease between 1974 and 1988 (Costa, Whitfield, & Stewart, 1989), and many more have appeared since then. Pearlin, Mullan, Semple, and Skaff (1990) provided an analysis of caregiving in terms of primary stress (directly related to the severity of the patient's illness) and secondary stress (associated problems such as family conflicts and limitations in social contacts). Vitaliano, Young, and Russo (1991) reviewed instruments for measuring caregiver burden. Williamson and Schulz (1991) reported that caregivers who felt close to the patient before the illness were less burdened by caregiving. Whitlatch, Zarit, and von Eye (1991) evaluated interventions for caregivers and found that an individual and family counseling program benefited caregivers, whereas a mutual support group program did not.

It is beyond the scope of a *Handbook on Stress* chapter to examine in detail the specifics of these applied programs, except insofar as they illustrate general principles about stress and coping. The general principle they illustrate most clearly is the specificity of what Folkman and Lazarus (1980) called "problem-focused coping." A retirement planning program, for example, may provide information on finances, taxes and the law, health insurance, consumer rights, and leisure and volunteer opportunities (Rowen & Wilks, 1987). The details of such programs are unique to the topics they address. They fall within the scope of science insofar as they systematically assess the problems, develop educational programs and other interventions, and evaluate the results. With respect to evaluation, the message is again one of specificity: Global measures of morale or well-being are generally inappropriate criteria for evaluating interventions; specific, program-relevant responses should be used instead (Carp, 1977; Rosow, 1977).

At the opposite extreme from such concretely problem-focused research is the search for general techniques of stress management that can be applied in any and all situations, such as relaxation, meditation, or imagery. When age has been examined, it appears that such techniques work as well for the elderly as for younger individuals (Puder, 1988).

But it should be noted that the need for such emotion-focused approaches is a matter of individual differences and has little to do with age. Not all individuals facing retirement need to learn progressive relaxation or meditation skills; most can handle whatever stress the experience produces by themselves. Stress management techniques may benefit some older men and women, and it would be desirable to have programs available to those who require them, but we should not assume that the elderly have a special need for this kind of assistance.

Which of the elderly are most likely to need help in dealing with distress? Probably those who are highest in the personality dimension of neuroticism, a life-long propensity to experience negative affect (McCrae & Costa, 1990; Watson & Clark, 1984). As Maas and Kuypers (1974) noted, "old age does not usher in or introduce decremental psychological processes. Rather, old age may demonstrate, in perhaps exacerbated forms, problems that have long-term antecedents" (p. 203). Older individuals are as susceptible to problems of emotional adjustment as are younger adults (Zonderman, Stone, & Costa, 1989)—but not more so. As we move from the specific to the general, from problem focused to emotion focused, the relevance of age disappears.

CONCLUSION

The field of stress and coping is a sometimes awkward hybrid of person and environment, problem and emotion. As Goldberger and Breznitz (1982) noted in the introduction to the first edition of this handbook, the field's current prominence may be due to an environmentalist bias that prefers to see the source of human difficulties in easily manipulated external factors rather than in enduring individual characteristics. As research accumulates and the early optimism about the potential benefits of studying coping fades (Aldwin & Revenson,

1987; Costa & McCrae, 1989), it may be time to consider a reformulation of the enterprise of coping research.

On one level, coping is a matter of solving problems, often by anticipation and planning that prevents their occurrence. By its nature, this problem-focused coping must be tailored to the specifics of the problem, and older individuals face a distinctive set of difficulties that merit individual study. It is perhaps less glamorous to enumerate environmental features that can reduce falls (Tideiksaar, 1988) than to propound models of intrapsychic conflict or develop taxonomies of coping strategies, but it is a legitimate and important application of the study of stress and coping to the problems of the elderly.

On another level, coping is a matter of dealing with disturbing emotions. These result to some extent from events and circumstances in the environment, but they are also intimately related to the personality characteristics of the individual (Ben-Porath & Tellegen, 1990). Techniques for helping individuals deal with anxiety, grief, and resentment are the stock-in-trade of the psychotherapeutic professions, and research on emotion-focused coping is ipso facto research on psychotherapeutic processes. Acknowledging these links could faciliate progress in this area.

In this second branch of the field, age is essentially irrelevant: Older men and women— at least those who are cognitively intact—show the same range of personality characteristics, the same emotional processes, the same ways of coping, the same response to therapy (Schlossberg, 1990) that younger adults do. Basic research on personality structure, emotional adjustment, and psychotherapeutic interventions in adults of all ages will find direct applications in the older population.

REFERENCES

ALDWIN, C. M., & REVENSON, T. A. Does coping help? A reexamination of the relation between coping and mental health. *Journal of Personality and Social Psychology,* 1987, *53,* 337–348.

BEN-PORATH, Y. S., & TELLEGEN, A. A place for traits in stress research. *Psychological Inquiry,* 1990, *1,* 14–40.

BOND, M., GARDNER, S. T., CHRISTIAN, J., & SIGAL, J. J. Empirical study of self-rated defense styles. *Archives of General Psychiatry,* 1983, *40,* 333–338.

BURGIO, K. L., PEARCE, K. L., & LUCCO, A. J. *Staying dry: A practical guide to bladder control.* Baltimore, MD: Johns Hopkins University Press, 1990.

CARP, F. M. Morale: What questions are we asked of whom? In C. N. Nydegger (ed), *Measuring morale: A guide to effective assessment.* Washington, DC: Gerontological Society, 1977.

CARVER, C. S., SCHEIER, M. F., & WEINTRAUB, J. K. Assessing coping strategies: A theoretically based approach. *Journal of Personality and Social Psychology,* 1989, *56,* 267–283.

COSTA, P. T., JR., & McCRAE, R. R. Contributions of personality research to an understanding of stress and aging. *Marriage and Family Review,* 1983, *6,* 157–173.

————. Personality as a lifelong determinant of well-being. In C. Malatesta & C. Izard (eds.), *Affective processes in adult development and aging.* Beverly Hills, CA: Sage, 1984.

————. Hypochondriasis, neuroticism, and aging: When are somatic complaints unfounded? *American Psychologist,* 1985, *40,* 19–28.

————. Personality, stress, and coping: Some lessons from a decade of research. In K. S. Markides & C. L. Cooper (eds.), *Aging, stress, social support and health.* New York: Wiley, 1989.

————. Personality: Another "hidden factor" in stress research. *Psychological Inquiry,* 1990, *1,* 22–24.

————. *Revised NEO Personality Inventory (NEO-PIR) and NEO Five-Factor Inventory (NEO-FFI) professional manual.* Odessa, FL: Psychological Assessment Resources, 1992.

COSTA, P. T., JR., MCCRAE, R. R., & LOCKE, B. Z. Personality factors. In J. Cornoni-Huntley, R. Huntley, & J. J. Feldman (eds.), *Health status and well-being of the elderly: National Health and Nutrition Examination I-Epidemiologic Followup Study.* New York: Oxford University Press, 1990.

COSTA, P. T., JR., WHITFIELD, J. R., & STEWART, D. (eds.). *Alzheimer's disease: Abstracts of the psychological and behavioral literature.* Washington, DC: American Psychological Association, 1989.

COSTA, P. T., JR., ZONDERMAN, A. B., & MCCRAE, R. R. Personality, stress, and coping in older adulthood. In E. M. Cummings, A. L. Greene, & K. H. Karraker (eds.), *Life-span developmental psychology: Perspectives on stress and coping.* Hillsdale, NJ: Lawrence Erlbaum, 1991.

DELONGIS, A., FOLKMAN, S., & LAZARUS, R. S. The impact of daily stress on health and mood: Psychological and social resources as mediators. *Journal of Personality and Social Psychology,* 1988, *54,* 486–495.

EYSENCK, H. J., & EYSENCK, S. B. G. *Manual of the Eysenck Personality Questionnaire.* San Diego, CA: EdITS, 1975.

FELTON, B. J., & REVENSON, T. A. Age differences in coping with chronic illness. *Psychology and Aging,* 1987, *2,* 164–170.

FISKE, M. Challenge and defeat: Stability and change in adulthood. In L. Goldberger & S. Breznitz (eds.), *Handbook of stress: Theoretical and clinical aspects.* New York: Free Press, 1982.

FOLKMAN, S., & LAZARUS, R. S. An analysis of coping in a middle-aged community sample. *Journal of Health and Social Behavior,* 1980, *21,* 219–239.

————. If it changes it must be a process: Study of emotion and coping during three stages of a college examination. *Journal of Personality and Social Psychology,* 1985, *48,* 150–170.

GOLDBERGER, L., & BREZNITZ, S. Stress research at a crossroads. In L. Goldberger & S. Breznitz (eds.), *Handbook of stress: Theoretical and clinical aspects.* New York: Free Press, 1982.

HAAN, N. Coping and defense mechanisms related to personality inventories. *Journal of Consulting Psychology,* 1965, *29,* 373–378.

————. *Coping and defending.* New York: Academic Press, 1977.

HOLAHAN, C. J., & MOOS, R. H. Personality, coping, and family resources in stress resistance: A longitudinal analysis. *Journal or Personality and Social Psychology,* 1986, *51,* 389–395.

HOLMES, T. H., & RAHE, R. H. The social readjustment rating scale. *Journal of Psychosomatic Research,* 1967, *11,* 213–218.

HOROWITZ, M. J. *Introduction to psychodynamics: A new synthesis.* New York: Basic Books, 1988.

IHILEVICH, D., & GLESER, G. C. *Defense mechanisms: Their classification, correlates, and measurement with the Defense Mechanism Inventory.* Owosso, MI: DMI Associates, 1986.

IRION, J. C., & BLANCHARD-FIELDS, F. A cross-sectional comparison of adaptive coping in adulthood. *Journal of Gerontology,* 1987, *42,* 502–504.

KANE, R. A. Aging of *The Gerontologist:* Continuity and change. *The Gerontologist,* 1991, *31,* 6–7.

KASTENBAUM, R., & COSTA, P. T., JR. Psychological perspectives on death. *Annual Review of Psychology,* 1977, *28,* 225–249.

KEITH, J. *Old people as people: Social and cultural influences on aging and old age.* Boston: Little, Brown, 1982.

LAZARUS, R. S., & DELONGIS, A. Psychological stress and coping in aging. *American Psychologist,* 1983, *38,* 245–254.

MAAS, H. S., & KUYPERS, J. A. *From thirty to seventy.* San Francisco: Jossey-Bass, 1974.

MACE, N. L., & RABINS, P. V. *The 36-hour day: A family guide to caring for persons with Alzheimer's disease, related dementing illnesses, and memory loss in later life* (rev. ed.). Baltimore, MD: Johns Hopkins University Press, 1991.

MCCRAE, R. R. Age differences in the use of coping mechanisms. *Journal of Gerontology,* 1982, *37,* 454–460.

—————. Situational determinants of coping responses: Loss, threat, and challenge. *Journal of Personality and Social Psychology,* 1984, *46,* 919–928.

—————. Age differences and changes in the use of coping mechanisms. *Journal of Gerontology: Psychological Sciences,* 1989, *44,* 161–169.

—————. Controlling neuroticism in the measurement of stress. *Stress Medicine,* 1990, *6,* 237–241.

MCCRAE, R. R., & COSTA, P. T., JR. Personality, coping, and coping effectiveness in an adult sample. *Journal of Personality,* 1986, *54,* 385–405.

—————. Psychological resilience among widowed men and women: A 10-year followup of a national survey. *Journal of Social Issues,* 1988, *44,* 129–142.

—————. *Personality in adulthood.* New York: Guilford, 1990.

—————. The NEO Personality Inventory: Using the five-factor model in counseling. *Journal of Counseling and Development,* 1991, *69,* 367–372.

MORITZ, D. J., & OSTFELD, A. M. The epidemiology and demography of aging. In Hazzard, W. R., Andres, R., Bierman, E. L., & Blass, J. P. (eds.), *Principles of geriatric medicine and gerontology* (2d ed.). New York: McGraw-Hill, 1990.

PEARLIN, L. I., MULLAN, J. T., SEMPLE, S. J., & SKAFF, M. M. Caregiving and the stress process: An overview of concepts and their measures. *The Gerontologist,* 1990, *30,* 583–594.

PFEIFFER, E. Psychopathology and social pathology. In J. E. Birren & K. W. Schaie (eds.), *Handbook of the psychology of aging.* New York: Van Nostrand Reinhold, 1977.

PUDER, R. S. Age analysis of cognitive-behavioral group therapy for chronic pain patients. *Psychology and Aging,* 1988, *3,* 204–207.

ROSOW, I. Morale: Concept and measurement. In C. N. Nydegger (ed.), *Measuring morale: A guide to effective assessment.* Washington, DC: The Gerontological Society, 1977.

ROWE, J. W. Toward successful aging: Limitation of the morbidity associated with "normal: aging. In W. R. Hazzard, R. Andres, E. L. Bierman, & J. P. Blass (eds.), *Principles of geriatric medicine and gerontology* (2d ed.) New York: McGraw-Hill, 1990.

ROWEN, R. B., & WILKS, C. S. Pre-retirement planning, a quality of life issue for retirement. *Employee Assistance Quarterly,* 1987, *2,* 45–56.

SCHLOSSBERG, N. K. Training counselors to work with older adults. *Generations,* 1990 (winter), 7–10.

SCHROEDER, D. H., & COSTA, P. T., JR. Influence of life event stress on physical illness: Substantive effects or methodological flaws? *Journal of Personality and Social Psychology,* 1984, *46,* 853–863.

SELYE, H. *The stress of life.* New York: McGraw-Hill, 1956.

SHOCK, N. W., GREULICH, R. C., ANDRES, R., ARENBERG, D., COSTA, P. T., JR., LAKATTA, E. G., & TOBIN, J. D. *Normal human aging: The Baltimore longitudinal study of aging* (NIH publication no. 84-2450). Bethesda, MD: National Institutes of Health, 1984.

STROEBE, W., & STROEBE, M. S. *Bereavement and health.* New York: Cambridge University Press, 1987.

TERI, L., & LOGSDON, R. G. Identifying pleasant activities for Alzheimer's disease patients: The Pleasant Events Schedule—AD. *The Gerontologist,* 1991, *31,* 124–127.

THORSLUND, M., NORSTROM, T., & WERNBERG, K. The utilization of home help in Sweden: A multivariate analysis. *The Gerontologist,* 1991, *31,* 116–119.

TIDEIKSAAR, R. *Falling in old age: Its prevention and treatment.* New York: Springer, 1988.

TROLL, L. E., MILLER, S. J., & ATCHLEY, R. C. *Families in later life.* Belmont, CA: Wadsworth, 1979.

VAILLANT, G. E. *Adaptation to life.* Boston: Little, Brown, 1977.

VINICK, B. H., & EKERDT, D. J. Retirement and the family. *Generations,* 1989, *13,* 53–56.

VITALIANO, P. P., YOUNG, H. M., & RUSSO, J. Burden: A review of measures used among caregivers of individuals with dementia. *The Gerontologist,* 1991, *31,* 67–75.

WATSON, D., & CLARK, L. A. Negative affectivity: The disposition to experience aversive emotional states. *Psychological Bulletin,* 1984, *96,* 465–490.

WHITLATCH, C. J., ZARIT, S. H., & VON EYE, A. Efficacy of interventions with caregivers: A re-analysis. *The Gerontologist,* 1991, *31,* 9–14.

WILLIAMSON, G. M., & SCHULZ, R. Relationship orientation, quality of prior relationship, and distress among caregivers of Alzheimer's patients. *Psychology and Aging,* 1991, *5,* 502–509.

ZEVITZ, R. G., & GURNACK, A. M. Factors related to elderly crime victims' satisfaction with police service: The impact of Milwaukee's "Gray Squad." *The Gerontologist,* 1991, *31,* 92–101.

ZONDERMAN, A. B., STONE, S. V., & COSTA, P. T., JR. *Age and neuroticism as risk factors for the incidence of diagnoses of psychotic and neurotic disorders.* Paper presented at the Annual Convention of the American Psychological Association. New Orleans, August 1989.

23

Challenge and Defeat: Stability and Change in Adulthood

Marjorie Fiske

CONSENSUS ON THEORIES AND METHODOLOGIES appropriate to the study of stress, coping, and adaptation is rare. Even more controversial is the complex and relatively new field of psychosocial change in adulthood, an area rich in literature of uneven merit. The objectives of this chapter on stress from a life course perspective must therefore be selective. My goal is to summarize evidence for continuity versus change both in the emotional and cognitive experience of what is stressful and in the buffers that help people deal with stress as they grow from young adulthood toward old age. In keeping with the flood of technological and social innovations, which affect all social strata, a recurrent theme will be social change as stress.

For centuries, theories of adult change were embedded in the humanities. Later, the biological sciences took up this subject. Empirical social and behavioral research on life course change appeared in Europe quite early in the nineteenth century and, as Reinert (1979) noted, Hall's works on adolescence (1904) and senescence (1922) were among the first reflections of interest in this country. Hall's contributions were followed by an early textbook of Hollingworth's (1927), a volume set firmly in a life span framework (Baltes, 1979). From then until the 1960s, interest in adult change was slight; the current multidisciplinary flourish spans little more than a decade. Some of this upsurge can be attributed to intriguing results from studies of children that were continued as the subjects grew to middle age and beyond. Such studies, especially those that include in-depth life histories, as well as structured tests, are at present the method of choice.

One-time surveys covering a broad age range and repeated with different samples frequently suggest life course change in attitudes, beliefs, and behavior, and many life course researchers have found results stimulating enough to pursue longitudinally. For example, some quite consistent differences among age cohorts and between the sexes in regard to stressful conditions in adult life have been reported. National surveys conducted by the University of Michigan's Institute for Social Research found that, among young adults, single women had much higher scores than did single men on indicators of psychological stress, but among young marrieds with no children, women ranked much lower on the stress index than did men. Widowed women in comparison with widowers (Campbell, Converse, & Rogers, 1976) also reported fewer stress symptoms. Among the divorced, on the other hand, in a 1957 survey by the institute, women were far more likely than men to report stress symptoms, and there was little change in this respect when the same questions were repeated with another sample about 20 years later (Institute for Social Research, 1979). A recent cross-sectional study of divorce (which has since become a longitudinal research program) also reported more distress among women than among men but only in the turbulent predecision period; once divorce proceedings had been initiated, men ranked higher on stress indicators (Chiriboga & Cutler, 1977). This sample ranged in age from 20 to 70, and among both men and women the youngest (in their twenties) were the least distressed, while those 50 and older were the most so.

The Michigan surveys cited earlier also reflect stresses linked to intervening social change. It appears that, in general, the lot of the young has deteriorated, while that of the old has improved. In 1957, about a third of the respondents reported that they worried always or a lot, with those 65 and older worrying the most. In a 1976 study, this life course trend was reversed: the oldest reported the least worry, while among people 21–39 nearly half ranked high on the worry scale, up from 30% in 1957 (Institute for Social Research, 1979). This pattern may not necessarily be susceptible to a straightforward interpretation, a possibility I consider later in discussing a longitudinal mental health study that identified the sociohistorical periods in which cohorts grew up and aged as at least as important in affecting life course change as was age per se.

The most comprehensive recent work on successive cross-sectional national surveys was done by Yankelovich (1981). This study, too, suggested differences across the stages of life in stressors and in stress responses. While in the 1960s mainly the young reported that they were searching for new meanings and for self-fulfillment, Yankelovich found such searching at present to be "an out-pouring of popular sentiment . . . an authentic grass roots phenomenon, involving as many as four-fifths of *all* adult Americans" (p. 39; italics supplied). Along with this search for change, and perhaps accounting for its feverish nature, come nostalgia and "a hungering for community" now lost. The one-fifth who maintained traditional values through to the 1980s (mainly rural dwellers—less privileged and somewhat older than the other respondents), whom Yankelovich called "weak formers," derived a sense of comfort from continuity. The four-fifths majority, though reporting symptoms of stress such as worry and anxiety, were not sufficiently distressed to return to old rules.

STRESS, COPING, AND MENTAL HEALTH

The extent to which cross-sectional studies, even if they repeat the same questions over time, may promote fallacies about life course change becomes apparent in both prestructured, quantitative and in-depth, longitudinal research. Let us consider the 20-year follow-up of the Midtown Manhattan Study, originally undertaken in 1955 (Srole, 1978; Srole, Langer, Michael, Opler, & Rennie, 1962). At the outset, the age range of the sample was 20–59; results pointed to a significant decline in mental health and adaptive modes with advancing age. If there is a general age linked deterioration, one would expect, with the youngest subjects now middle-aged and the oldest near 80, an even greater age linked impairment to prevail 20 years later. This was not the case.

Considered as simply another cross-sectional survey, the follow-up might seem to confirm the findings of the original study (Srole, et al., 1962). When, for example, the follow-up respondents were divided by age, the proportion severely impaired increased in successive age groups. The fallacy of such a conclusion can be demonstrated by comparing birthdate cohorts with themselves 20 years earlier. In such a comparison, age linked deterioration *decreases* (albeit not significantly) among all cohorts except the very youngest (20–29 at the baseline). The concept of the cohort, in fact, is the key to unraveling the paradox posed by these findings. Compared with people the same age in 1954, those aged 40–59 in 1974 had significantly fewer symptoms of mental impairment. Moreover, in each age cohort divided by sex, among men there was no significant difference in mental impairment rate between those who were 40–59 in 1954 and those who were the same age in 1974. On the other hand, among women, who in 1954 had nearly twice as many maladaptive symptoms as did their male cohort peers, there was a dramatic improvement, putting them by 1974 on a par with men of the same age. The link between psychological symptoms and self-appraisals of poor physical health being well established, it is not surprising that women improved in this sphere. In other words, subgroup analysis within a longitudinal framework shows that an age linked decline in coping and adaptation that appeared to hold true for women up to age 60 in 1954 was not found 20 years later. Here we see, across birthdate cohorts, evidence for consistency (among men) and change (among women) over a period that encompassed the latest version of a women's movement.

Subgroup qualitative analysis characterized Vaillant's (1977) follow-up study, at ages 47–52, of nearly 100 of the 268 elite-college men who initially participated in the Grant Study. The rich biographical material from baseline and intervening contacts enabled the author to trace unanticipated adaptive modes and levels of mental health at middle age. The Grant men were selected, by standards of the late 1930s and early 1940s, as outstanding in qualities and attributes considered predictive of high achievement and good adaptation in later life, yet several proved to be "perpetual boys" in the intervening quarter century. Others, from less privileged backgrounds and with fewer inner and outer resources while in college, became successful, mature, and loving adults. Throughout, Vaillant's work provides many clues as to why and how some of the Grant men developed strong and flexible adaptive modes, while others remained sophomoric; his in-depth case studies offer tentative answers to perplexing questions about change in the adult life course that cannot be illustrated in this short chapter.

While most people in all periods of life manage to sustain a bearable balance between change and stability, the extremes are worth noting. At one end are static people, who use socially or biographically inappropriate adaptive modes, such as Vaillant's (1977) perpetual boys or Yankelovich's (1981) weak formers, patterns recently evidenced by the so-called moral majority. At the other extreme are the top segment of Yankelovich's "strong formers", highly reminiscent of Lifton's (1976) "protean man."

In summing up the meaning of his own studies on the impact of several forms of change, or lack thereof, among people in a variety of life stages and cultures, Marris (1975) concluded that the human need for a degree of predictability (stability, continuity) is fundamental and universal. This need coexists with the equally fundamental need for innovation (change). His and other studies, in a variety of disciplines, have suggested that although there may be stressful exacerbation of the need for continuity as the individual grows older, the often positive changes of young adulthood and of the prime of life that bring with them a sense of discontinuity and loss of a real or imagined past may also produce stress.

FINDINGS FROM THE HUMAN DEVELOPMENT AND AGING PROGRAM

Longitudinal research conducted by the Human Development and Aging Program at the University of California, San Francisco, over nearly a quarter of a century has from the outset adopted a flexible paradigm of stress and adaptation. One of the principal objectives of this model has been to assess change and continuity in several domains. The current transitions study [1] grew directly out of 10 years of large-scale panel studies of normal and abnormal aging. This earlier research, begun in 1958, soon led to two conclusions: a stress adaptation paradigm is a very suitable model for reducing masses of data about older people who range in age from 60 to the late nineties (Lowenthal, Berkman, & Associates, 1967); moreover, to understand both stability and changeability in stress proneness, adaptive processes, and supportive resources, one needs to know much more about people in earlier periods of adulthood and about their childhood and adolescence as well. In the transitions study, the data on the latter are retrospective, based on in-depth life histories.

Having been the senior investigator in boths sets of studies, I cannot resist a rather sweeping generalization about changes in coping with aging; namely, there has been, among the middle and lower echelons of our society, a marked deterioration in the adaptive processes of late middle-aged and older people. The nature of this change might be summed up as retreatism, escapism, or a search for numbing, in pill form or otherwise. This trend has created a condition serious for both individual and society, for in their effort to protect themselves from the tensions and pressures of postindustrial technological culture, older people create a new form of stress for themselves, one unfortunately overlooked by most researchers: the passive stress of ennui. In reading the life histories of older people in the current studies, I felt nostalgic for the gusty personalities of the early 1960s. While these two longitudinal investigations are, of course, not strictly comparable, the reader may find support for this generalization in the remainder of the chapter.

Relative Deprivation and Stress Preoccupation in Adulthood

As Elder (1974, 1979) reported, severe deprivation in childhood or adolescence—his study looked at the Great Depression and its impact on family life and family structure—is about as likely to have good consequences in adulthood as poor. The often devastating effects of the depression on the child's family may provide a benchmark against which future familial and economic problems pale, in much the same way that experiencing the death of a close other when young may provide the individual with the reassuring knowledge that he or she can cope with the inevitable personal losses of middle and old age. Many people in Elder's (1979) middle-aged cohorts, like those in our study of transitions (Lowenthal, Thurnher, Chiriboga, & Associates, 1975), seemed to apply to their personal life course the sociological construct of *relative deprivation,* originally applied by scholars to self-assessments in relation to current reference groups. The individual, in other words, uses the former self as a referent other. But before exploring this relativity further, I should briefly note the difference between *exposure* to and preoccupation with, presumed stress in the life course.

Earlier work by the Human Development and Aging Program indicated that stress exposure, as well as stress preoccupation, varies enormously and changes over relatively short intervals (Lowenthal, Berkman and Associates, 1967). Furthermore, people who have been exposed to many stresses seem to differ from those who have experienced few. They are, for example, more complex, in both their inner and outer lives. While they have many inner and outer resources, at the same time they have more personal and social handicaps and deficiencies. Such people have broader perspectives, on both themselves and society, than do the lightly stressed and they are more growth oriented, insightful, and competent. In other words, they represent the kind of people who seek out a challenging lifestyle, which is bound to be stressful on occasion.

Persons who have experienced little stress, on the other hand, have more limited perspectives on themselves and the rest of the world; they also have fewer psychological and social handicaps and fewer inner and outer resources. Unlike people who have had a great many stressful experiences, they have long since adopted lifestyles that protect them from stress. When we divide these two groups into those who are and who are not very pre-occupied with whatever stresses they are or were exposed to, we have a typology of four kinds of people, as Table 23-1 illustrates.

The *overwhelmed,* beset by many ostensibly stressful situations, dwell on them at length in discussing the ups and downs of their present and past; many, in fact, seem still to be liv-ing them through, even though their difficult experiences may have occurred in the remote past. The *challenged,* similarly besieged by many presumptive stresses or a few severe ones, are, in contrast, not excessively preoccupied with them. In recounting their life histories, they simply report, and perhaps briefly describe, such events and circumstances and then quickly move on to other topics that interest them more. The *self-defeating,* although they recount few stressful experiences, weight their life reviews heavily with themes of loss and deprivation, which they, like the overwhelmed, seem to be reliving with much of the original turmoil. On the other hand, the *lucky,* who also have had few or mild stresses, rarely discuss them, and loss is not a theme in their life stories. A few may report that they feel myster-iously protected or that luck has been on their side. While the more prosaic simply say, "I've been lucky, I guess," others speak of fate, the stars, or God, feeling that some mystical or magical force is protecting them. (In this context, it is perhaps important to recall that, ac-cording to recent surveys, a third of the people in the United States consider themselves to be born-again Christians [Vidal, 1978]; the proportions who report ESP experiences, consult astrologers, regularly read their horoscopes, or visit palm readers and other fortune-tellers regularly are equally impressive.)

In baseline assessments, about three-fifths of the subjects participating in the transi-tions study had expectable reactions to the situations judged stressful by the researchers who had developed the life events schedule used in the investigation. Slightly more than half the people who had experienced little stress were of the *lucky* type; Holmes and Rahe (1967) a slight majority of those who had experienced a great deal of stress were overwhelmed, that is, they have been highly stressed by normative standards, and dwell upon it at length. But this leaves a great many "deviants": about two-fifths of those who had experienced a great many of the presumed stresses fell into the challenged category; finally, among those ex-posed to very little stress, some 40% spoke as though their lives were an unending series of problems, i.e., they were self-defeating in orientation. Middle-aged men were far more likely to be challenged by considerable stress than were younger men, while both young and older lightly stressed men tended to consider themselves lucky. Severely stressed young women

TABLE 23-1
Stress Typology

	Preoccupation with stress	
Presumed stress	*Considerable*	*Little*
Frequent and/or severe	Overwhelmed	Challenged
Infrequent and/or mild	Self-defeating	Lucky

were more challenged than were middle-aged women (the ratio was three to one). Lightly stressed young women, unlike young men, reacted more negatively to little stress, whereas lightly stressed middle-aged women, like the middle-aged and the young men, tended to be in the lucky group. In situations of considerable stress, then, while many men rise to the occasion and are challenged, women seem to lose their stress tolerance: the great majority of the more severely stressed middle and late middle-aged women were overwhelmed. Details on operationalizing the preoccupation dimension of the typology appear in Lowenthal and Chiriboga (1973) (baseline) and Chiriboga (1977) (follow-up).

Subsequently, using data from several follow-up assessments of the sample, which represented four age groups ranging from high school seniors to people very close to retirement (see Lowenthal et al., 1975, on the sample's makeup), we were able to trace many changes. We found, for example, that middle-aged parents, now for the most part post–empty nest, reported the greatest increase in both positive and negative life events, while the now mainly retired oldest people reported more negative and fewer positive ones. The two younger groups reported fewer negative stressful events than did the two older, but, to our surprise, the young did not report as great an increase in positive changes as did the middle-aged. There were notable differences between these sexes at each life stage, too, and there also was evidence of change in stress preoccupation over a 10-year period (Chiriboga & Cutler, 1980). For example, newlyweds, who at the baseline had been highly preoccupied with positive life events, were now much less euphoric. By contrast, negatively preoccupied high school seniors had, by their late twenties, come to resemble those who had been newlywed at the baseline.

Aware of the pervasive assumption that the stresses of deprivation in childhood continue to have an impact on adaptive modes and stress levels in adulthood, we selected, as a simple indicator of life stress up to age 15, the loss or absence of one or both parents. What we found at the baseline was that in the two younger groups both men and women who had suffered such loss were less well adapted than were those who had not (Lowenthal & Chiriboga, 1975). Among the middle and late middle-aged, however, only women showed the effects of such deprivation. Subsequent follow-ups that used preoccupation with negative life events or circumstances as a criterion supported the original findings: middle-aged and older men (now averaging 66) who had lost one or both parents in childhood had further declined in stress preoccupation, while older women similarly deprived showed no change. At the 10-year follow-up in 1980, these sex differences were also maintained. Interestingly, there was also a trend toward less stress preoccupation among the younger men (now averaging 32), suggesting that for them the impact of childhood deprivation was wearing off.

Longitudinal findings also provide support for the thesis developed in our original stress typology (Lowenthal & Chiriboga, 1973) that people who are challenged by stress tend to adopt lifestyles that keep them challenged (Chiriboga & Cutler, 1980). The converse hypothesis that self-protectiveness (stress avoidance) increases with age in the lower-middle-income groups is indirectly supported, for we found an upswing in stress preoccupation as our two older groups reached their sixties and early seventies.

Change in Stress Mediators

Theory and empirical evidence from a number of disciplines suggest that there is more consistency in intrapersonal mediating resources than there is in outer supports, perceptions of what is stressful, preoccupation with stress, and adaptive processes. Thus far, two such resources have been identified that are especially significant throughout much of adulthood. Their nature is no cause for surprise—except, perhaps, among people who are skeptical about Freud's (possibly apocryphal) love and work thesis. Freud presumably referred to these capacities as criteria for adaptation and maturity. Their possible role as buffers of stress is reported by several contributing authors to the recently published book *Themes of Work and Love in Adulthood* (Smelser & Erikson, 1980). For purposes of this chapter, *love* is empirically examined in terms of the individual's beliefs about his or her own closest relationships, using the respondent's definitions of closeness, intimacy, mutuality, or having a confidant. *Work* is more broadly defined and includes commitments such as competence, mastery, and creativity.

While much research has been reported on social supports and networks at various life stages, particularly later life (for a review see Lowenthal & Robinson, 1976), most respondents attach more importance to their closest relationships, thus posing a far more difficult task for the researcher. The Human Development and Aging Program became interested in this sphere, as in many others, through its work on aging, conducted in the late 1950s and 1960s. The significance of a confidant surfaced serendipitously (Lowenthal & Haven, 1968), and in-depth exploration of self-defined intimate relationships became part of the design for the ensuing transitions study. The importance of intimacy was subsequently verified in conjunction with the stress typology. The contrast between challenged and overwhelmed men makes the point well. Of the four stress types, the challenged, who tend to be complex in several spheres of their lives, had the highest ratings of mutuality and emotional involvement among middle and late middle-aged men, while the overwhelmed men ranked lowest. Among middle-aged and older women, on the other hand, few were in the challenged category to being with, and many were self-defeating. Like women in most studies, female subjects in the transitions study reported higher levels of mutuality and close relationships, both intrafamilial and extrafamilial, but for them these capacities did not serve as buffers against stress.

Pauline and Robert Sears follow-up of Terman's sample of gifted children at age 62 provokes speculation about the notable differences between them and our considerably less privileged groups, in this instance the women. One hunch that proved to be well founded was that for many of this elite sample, both work and love were stress mediators (Sears, 1977). The sizable proportion of Terman's female subjects who had combined career with family were more satisfied with their family relationships and with life in general than were women who had devoted themselves to family and volunteer activities. Indeed, at the most recent follow-up, many of the latter expressed regret that they had not embarked on careers as younger women (Sears & Barbee, 1977). This suggests that a "balance model" (Lowenthal & Chiriboga, 1975) is helpful in understanding not only stressors (both positive and negative) and adaptation but also mediators. For example, we know that the stress-satisfaction axis can tilt from one side to the other at very short intervals. Having deep commitments in, say, two domains of life provides opportunity for sequential distancing and perspective. A mother's problems with her rebellious adolescent daughter may temporarily recede in the demands and engrossment of the work setting, and she may return home with a different mental and emotional set toward this particular stress from the set she manifested in the morning. By contrast, the woman who stays home or who does very routine paid work, as do about half the women in the transitions study, is likely to remain embroiled.

It is tempting to formulate a firm hypothesis that two or more strong commitments strengthen stress resistance in adulthood. Such hypothesis would find support in an important longitudinal project (Maas & Kuypers, 1974). Maas (1981), in response to my conjecture (Fiske, 1980b), reported that the working-class, family committed women in that study were aging more unhappily than were upper-middle-class women who, in addition to strong family concerns, were deeply involved in organizations outside the home. While the hypothesis was confirmed for younger subjects in the transitions study as they approached early middle age, among older men and women, strength and balance of commitments was no longer associated with stress resistance. Quite the contrary, among them the more complex people were aging most unhappily. This finding was somewhat more true of women than men; the explanation probably lies in the fact that their lower-class status added to the strong sex bias that continues to be found in blue-collar groups especially, poses barriers to fulfilling commitments that are not encountered by the more privileged.

Findings and hypotheses such as these convinced us that a commitment paradigm would be more helpful than the prevailing self-actualizing, growth oriented models and theories in elucidating patterns of behavior in adulthood. To this end, we constructed a model centered on the patterning, or configuration, sometimes hierarchical, of the fundamental concerns the individual harbors at a given time. This inner gestalt is drawn upon, consciously or not, to allot priority to one kind of choice or activity in preference to another. Thus far, the commitment framework embraces four domains (Fiske, 1980b, c): (1) curiosity, mastery, and creativity; (2) commitment to other people, including intimate relationships; (3) concerns that transcend self-in-present networks, including support and nurture of values such as integrity of the self, close others, and society at large; and (4) self-orientation or self-protectiveness, which may be either an age linked concern or a lifelong narcissism, pathological or otherwise (both forms would be expected to be associated with stress preoccupation).

A Commitment Paradigm

Among the more clear-cut patterns that have been traced is one of diversity, manifest among people who are about equally committed to a few of the first three domains. At the other extreme are people who put all their commitment eggs into one basket. Thus far, in tracing change in commitment structure through two follow-up assessments of our middle-aged and older groups, we have found at least as much change as continuity. Though most people in each stage had lived through the same type of normative life course transition in the intervening years, there was a great deal of variation in the ways in which their configurations were rearranged, as Figures 23–1 and 23–2 illustrate.

When we first talked with Mrs. M. R., she had been divorced for a few years. She held a responsible secretarial job, was studying for a professional degree, and was highly committed both to meeting the needs of her son, a high school senior who lived with her, and to attaining her work goals. Disillusioned by a difficult marriage and a later unhappy love affair, she was very protective of herself, in the hope of achieving a more satisfying life. At the 5-year follow-up she was 47, had nearly completed her education, and had been offered an interesting and prestigious new job. She no longer felt responsible for her son, who, happily married, was pursuing his own goals. As Figure 23–1 shows, both her interpersonal and mastery commitments had become strengthened, and she was no longer wrapped in a self-protective cocoon. We have not yet plotted her chart for the 10-year follow-up, but we do know that she is now thoroughly enjoying grandparenthood.

Mr. F. C., a former navy career man, presented a very different configuration (see

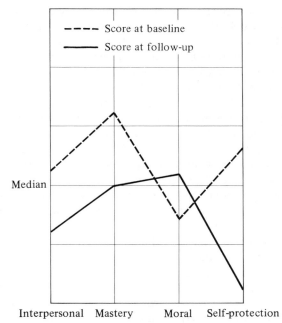

FIGURE 23–1.   Commitment scores: Mrs. M. R.

FIGURE 23–2.   Commitment scores: Mr. F. C.

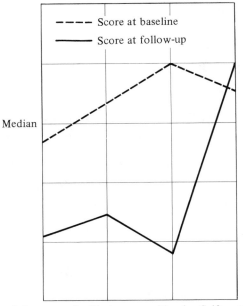

Figure 23–2). He had a modest business of his own when he was first contacted. A true child of the Great Depression, Mr. F. C. was concerned most with financial security, and at that time he was achieving this goal to his own satisfaction. Five years later, he had bought a new business and had become even more affluent. Despite this success and the resolution of difficulties in his relationship with one of his daughters, he had become much more cynical and was very bored. Mr. F. C. had all along found his marriage to be "not the greatest." During the interval, he had been hard hit by the realization that his life was quite empty despite considerable security and material comfort. At 50, he regretted not having had a professional career, found his work "not worthwhile," and admitted that "the money doesn't mean a goddamn thing. . . . I'm just not a happy person." His decline in all commitments except to himself was the most drastic in his cohort of middle-aged men. The recent follow-up (not yet charted) found Mr. F. C. to be by his own account more affluent, still very bored, but quite happy. Since he also now considers his marriage somewhat better than most and describes his relationship with one of his daughters as "a dream," we suspect that his chart will show an increase in interpersonal commitment.

Another way to examine commitment change is to place each individual within the context of his or her life stage group and to examine change in each domain separately. Figures 23–3 and 23–4 show, respectively, change in commitment to mastery among the initially late middle-aged women (then in their late fifties) and among somewhat younger men, first confronting an empty next (then in their late forties). As we can see in Figure 23–3, the late middle-aged women were more likely to have increased their self-expressive (mastery) commitments than to have reduced or relinquished them, several subjects to a very significant extent.

By contrast, only two empty nest men had increased their mastery commitments to any

FIGURE 23–3. Change in commitment to mastery: preretired females.

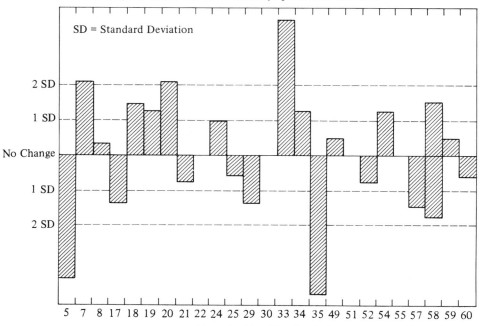

Subjects by Identification Number

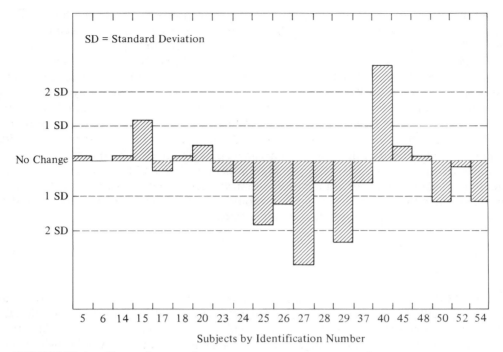

FIGURE 23-4. Change in commitment to mastery: empty nest males.

significant extent, and the graph for the entire male cohort is heavily weighted on the decline side. (Mr. F. C., number 27, had the steepest drop over the five-year period.)

Among most employed middle-aged men, commitments to competence and the accompanying satisfaction of effectance (White, 1965) can no longer be fulfilled in the work arena. When occupational peaking occurs, usually in the late thirties or early forties, men find themselves facing two decades or more of lack of challenge, if not sheer boredom in and hatred of their jobs. To these negative stresses, they themselves often add anxiety about retirement, even though this stage is far in the future. At the time of the five-year follow-up, inflation was already beginning to lean heavily upon our male respondents although the majority had selected their jobs in the first place with a keen eye for the security that pension plans and other benefits provide. Some were becoming anxious about another problem as well: how, in the immediate future, as well as during retirement could they retain, if not bolster, their self-esteem? That this worry may not be fully conscious is suggested in the change in projective materials, gathered at the time when their increasing interpersonal needs began to emerge (Thurnher, 1975).

This apparently age linked change is in the Jungian (Jung, 1933) tradition (as is the increase in mastery needs among women) and has been reported in other studies (Gutmann, 1969; Neugarten & Gutmann, 1968). The same trend appeared among the highly educated, self-assessing, often very successful men studied by Vaillant (1977) and by Sears (1977). These more privileged men, at both middle and late middle age, had come to value interpersonal relationships as much as, if not more than, their work, to which most had long been strongly committed. This change may be explained by reference to Erikson's (1950) concept of *generativity* as the main function of the later stages of life. In contrast, among men in the transitions study, the primary need appeared to be nurturance from and ego bolstering by others, especially their wives, at a time when women of the same age were seeking opportunities for autonomy and self-expression and lowering their commitments to the interpersonal sphere. Many of these women suffered bitter and painful inner conflict, for they realistically feared that if they became engrossed in any tasks or interests other than those that contributed to the husband's needs, their marriages might fail. Our five-year follow-up of the empty nest women demonstrated that some of them had compromised and in the process become more assertive and bossy at home—no way to nurture the already fragile egos of their husbands. Other women, however, did find opportunities for self-expression outside the home; about a third of this group got divorced (a few of these subsequently remarried). We have found no evidence of such sharply conflicting needs and trajectories between the sexes in more highly educated segments of American society, but among the people we have been studying in the transitions project such conflicts not only create new stress but undermine any buffering effect that personal commitments might have.

CONCLUSION

Since the Middle Ages, at least in Western societies, the self-conscious task of many young people, especially but not only university students, has been to acquire and to question the heritage bequeathed by their elders. Their teachers and leaders rarely felt threatened in their own beliefs and values because change in societal values and norms proceeded slowly. In this century, after World War I, elders seem to have become less secure. Since World War II, and especially in the past two decades, there has been both a resurgence of youthful questioning and an accelerated change in its content and consequences. After the short-lived retreatism of those who were young in the 1950s, the renewed opposition and activism among the youth of the 1960s was challenging to themselves and to some of their parents and teachers. Now, while there are no hippies or flower children in the Haight, and there are once again ambitious young people in the universities, most middle- and lower-middle-class parents find their offspring's style of living incomprehensible and distressing.

The choices and behaviors suitable for fulfilling any of the three substantive commitments (mastery, interpersonal, or moral-societal) require appropriate arenas, usually within social contexts. While access is fairly open through early middle age, by late middle age, except for the privileged and/or very talented, the avenues become severely restricted. Among average Americans, the pace of social and technological change exacerbates the stress of such roadblocks and their commitments come to seem obsolete. While they might agree with Erikson's conviction that generativity should be a major commitment after middle age, they cannot readily conceive of anything important that they might have to offer succeeding generations.

Some say that the best one can do is teach the young to be flexible and to bow with whatever winds of change may blow. Others suspect that the pace of technological change is now so rapid that the gap in values and knowledge between youngest and oldest adults may soon be unbridgeable, with each looking to the other like a creature from another world, a stressful circumstance for both. Late middle-aged parents, many of whom have living parents and parents-in-law, may soon become the most highly stressed of all, as they lose the sense of generational continuity with the young and become caretakers of the very old.

NOTE

1. This longitudinal study began in 1968. At the baseline the sample consisted of 216 men and women facing one of four normative adult transitions: departure from parental home, newly married, youngest child about to leave home, and people within a year or two of retirement. They lived in a homogeneous section of a metropolitan area and were (by design) primarily caucasian, blue- and white-collar workers. They have now been interviewed *in depth* and assessed by a variety of structured instruments five times. The most recent contact was in 1980.

REFERENCES

BALTES, P. B. Life-span developmental psychology: Some converging observations on history and theory. In P. B. Baltes & O. G. Brim, Jr. (eds.), *Life-span development and behavior,* vol. 2. New York: Academic, 1979.

CAMPBELL, A., CONVERSE, P. E., & RODGERS, W. L. *The quality of American life: Perceptions, evaluations, and satisfactions.* New York: Russell Sage, 1976.

CHIRIBOGA, D. A. Life event weighting systems: A comparative analysis. *Journal of Psychosomatic Research,* 1977, *21,* 415–422.

CHIRIBOGA, D. A., & CUTLER, L. Stress responses among divorcing men and women. *Journal of Divorce,* 1977, *1,* 95–106.

————. Stress and adaptation: A life span study. In L. Poon (ed.), *Aging in the 1980s: Selected contemporary issues in the psychology of aging.* Washington, D.C.: American Psychological Association, 1980.

ELDER, G. H., JR. *Children of the Great Depression.* Chicago: University of Chicago Press, 1974.

————. Historical change in life patterns and personality. In P. B. Baltes & O. G. Brim, Jr. (eds.), *Life-span development and behavior,* vol. 2. New York: Academic, 1979.

ERIKSON, E. H. Childhood and society. New York: Norton, 1950.

FISKE, M. Changing hierarchies of commitment in adulthood. In N. J. Smelser & E. H. Erikson (eds.), *Themes of work and love in adulthood.* Cambridge: Harvard University Press, 1980. (a)

————. The interplay of social and personal change in adulthood. Paper presented to the annual meeting of the Gerontological Society of America, San Diego, 1980. (b)

————. Tasks and crises of the second half of life: The interrelationship of commitment, coping, and adaptation. In J. E. Birren & R. B. Sloane (eds.), *Handbook of mental health and aging.* Englewood Cliffs: Prentice-Hall, 1980. (c)

GUTMANN, D. *The country of old men: Cross-cultural studies in the psychology of later life.* University of Michigan–Wayne State University, occasional paper no. 5. 1969. Institute of Gerontology.

HOLLINGWORTH, H. L. *Mental growth and decline: A survey of developmental psychology.* New York: Appleton, 1927.

HOLMES, T. H. & RAHE, R. H. The social readjustment rating scale. *Journal of Psychosomatic Research,* 1967, *11,* 213–218.

Institute for Social Research. Americans seek self-development, suffer anxiety from changing roles. *IRS Newsletter* (Ann Arbor), 1979, *7,* 4–5.

JUNG, C. G. The stages of life. In C. G. Jung, Modern man in search of a soul. New York: Harcourt, Brace, 1933.

LIFTON, R. J. *The life of self.* New York: Simon & Schuster, 1976.

LOWENTHAL, M. F., BERKMAN, P. L., & ASSOCIATES. *Aging and mental disorder.* San Francisco: Jossey-Bass, 1967.

LOWENTHAL, M. F., & CHIRIBOGA, D. Social stress and adaptation: Toward a life course perspective. In C. Eisdorfer & M. P. Lawton (eds.), *The psychology of adult development and aging.* Washington, D.C.: American Psychological Association, 1973.

————. Responses to stress. In M. F. Lowenthal, M. Thurnher, D. Chiriboga, & Associates, *Four stages of life: A comparative study of women and men facing transitions.* San Francisco: Jossey-Bass, 1975.

LOWENTHAL, M. F., & HAVEN, C. Interaction and adaptation: Intimacy as a critical variable. *American Sociological Review,* 1968, *33,* 20–30.

LOWENTHAL, M. F., & ROBINSON, B. Social networks and isolation. In R. Binstock & E. Shanas (eds.), *Handbook of aging and the social sciences.* New York: Van Nostrand, 1976.

LOWENTHAL, M. F., THURNHER, M., CHIRIBOGA, D., & ASSOCIATES. *Four stages of life: A comparative study of women and men facing transitions.* San Francisco: Jossey-Bass, 1975.

MAAS, H. S. Personal communication, 2 February 1981.

MAAS, H. S., & KUYPERS, J. A. *From thirty to seventy.* San Francisco: Jossey-Bass, 1974.

MARRIS, P. *Loss and change.* New York: Doubleday Anchor, 1975.

NEUGARTEN, B. L., & GUTMANN, D. L. Age-sex roles and personality in middle age: A thematic apperception study. In B. L. Neugarten (ed.), *Middle age and aging.* Chicago: University of Chicago Press, 1968.

REINERT, G. Prolegomenon to a history of life-span developmental psychology. In P. B. Baltes & O. G. Brim, Jr. (eds.), *Life-span development and behavior,* vol. 2. New York: Academic, 1979.

SEARS, P. S., & BARBEE, A. H. Career and life satisfaction among Terman's gifted women. In J. Stanley, W. George, & C. Solano (eds.), *The gifted and the creative: A fifty year perspective.* Baltimore: Johns Hopkins Press, 1977.

SEARS, R. Sources of life satisfactions of the Terman gifted men. *American Psychologist,* 1977, *32,* 119–128.

SMELSER, N. J., & ERIKSON, E. H. (eds.). *Themes of work and love in adulthood.* Cambridge: Harvard University Press, 1980.

SROLE, L. The Midtown Manhattan Study: Longitudinal focus on aging, genders, and life transitions. Paper presented to the annual meeting of the Gerontological Society, Dallas, 1978.

SCROLE, S., LANGNER, T. S., MICHAEL, S. T., OPLER, M. K., & RENNIE, T. A. C. *Mental health in the metropolis: The Midtown Manhattan Study.* New York: McGraw-Hill, 1962.

THURNHER, M. Continuities and discontinuities in value orientation. In M. F. Lowenthal, M. Thurnher, D. Chiriboga, & Associates, *Four stages of life: A comparative study of women and men facing transitions.* San Francisco: Jossey-Bass, 1975.

VAILLANT, G. Adaptation to life. Boston: Little, Brown, 1977.

VIDAL, G. Burt and Labelle and Jimmy and God. *New York Review of Books,* 29 June 1978, p. 21.

WHITE, R. W. *Lives in progress* (3d ed.). New York: Holt, 1975.

YANKELOVICH, D. *New rules in American life.* New York: Random House, 1981.

24

Multiple Roles, Gender, and Psychological Distress

Rosalind C. Barnett

RECENT SHIFTS IN WORK AND FAMILY PATTERNS are changing the ways women and men define marital and parental roles, with concomitant effects on psychological distress. Wives' expectations for sharing and cooperation from their husbands are increasing, especially among employed women. Employment may offer married women opportunities to gain control that are not available in their nonworkplace roles. Income allows women to exert influence in their marital relationship and to buy services, thereby reducing some of their household responsibilities. As wives become less dependent, these roles may become less stressful. However, at least in the short term, some new stresses seem apparent. As employed women redefine their participation in child rearing so that it is more equal to that of their husbands, marital tensions seem likely to surface. These tensions may be felt more acutely by women, who have historically been more vulnerable to marital dissatisfaction. Alternatively, they may be more troubling for men, who may feel threatened by their wives' economic independence. In the long term, one can hope that these changes will result in a greater sense of equity for both husbands and wives.

This chapter examines the literature pertaining to the relationships between multiple roles, gender, and psychological distress. Research into these relationships is taking new directions in the wake of numerous studies showing positive effects of multiple role involvement on women's and men's physical and mental well-being (Barnett & Baruch, 1985; Crosby, 1984; Thoits, 1983; Verbrugge, 1983). Concern about the negative effects on women of involvement in multiple roles is abating because of increasing evidence that for women as well as men, the more roles one occupies, the greater the chances of being physically healthier, more satisfied with life, and less depressed. Nevertheless, echoes still resound of past warnings that multiple role involvement could take a heavy toll, especially on women. The initial focus in the research literature on number of roles and role occupancy is now widening to include consideration of the quality of experience in roles (e.g., see Aneshensel & Pearlin, 1987). Indeed, many studies suggest that role quality is a more significant predictor of stress and well-being than is role occupancy per se.

Studies further show that some roles and role combinations may be less beneficial than others. Moreover, the relationship between roles and distress may be different for men and

This chapter is based on a chapter originally published in R. C. Barnett, L. Biener, & G. K. Baruch (eds.), *Gender and Stress.* New York: Free Press, 1987.

427

for women (Barnett & Baruch, 1985; Baruch & Barnett, 1986a; Dytell, Pardine, & Napoli, 1985; Kandel, Davies, & Raveis, 1985; Verbrugge, 1982).

To examine how gender influences the relation between involvement in social roles and stress-related outcomes, I first discuss the hypotheses linking multiple role involvement to stress outcomes. Then I focus on specific roles—especially the major ones of spouse, parent, and paid worker—and consider both role occupancy and role quality. I also discuss the specific dimensions of roles that seem crucial to determining whether a particular role has beneficial or detrimental effects on the occupant's level of distress. The discussion of the effects of role-related experiences focuses both on stress indicators, such as depression and anxiety, and on well-being indicators, such as happiness, satisfaction, and self-esteem.

MULTIPLE ROLES AND STRESS

Two questions are central to the relationship between the number of roles one occupies and the experience of stress. Does role multiplicity augur well or poorly for psychological distress? Are there gender differences in the effects of multiple roles? Although many studies suggest that involvement in multiple roles may be beneficial, not all roles have equally positive effects. Further, the effects of the same role combinations may be different for men and for women; many researchers argue, for example, that the combination of paid worker and spouse roles has more beneficial effects for men than for women (Cleary & Mechanic, 1983; Gove & Tudor, 1973). This section reviews the evidence about the effects of multiple role involvement on well-being for women and men.

Research on multiple roles and their effects has focused largely on within-sex differences among women; men have received scant attention (Gove & Zeiss, 1987). Thus, only recently have researchers addressed the issue of gender differences in these effects.

The Scarcity Hypothesis

Many studies explore the relationship between the number of roles women occupy and particular role combinations by using such measures as self-reported happiness or depression. Underlying many of these studies is the expectation that roles drain energy; hence, the more roles a woman occupies the less energy she will have, the more conflict she will experience, and the more negatively her well-being will be affected.

This hypothesis, called the scarcity hypothesis, was first put forth by Goode (1960) and extended by Coser (1974), Slater (1963), and others. It rests on two premises: (1) that individuals have a limited amount of energy, and (2) that social organizations are greedy and demand all of an individual's allegiance. According to the scarcity model, people do not have enough energy to fulfill their role obligations; thus, role strain is normal and compromises are required. Therefore, the more roles one accumulates, the greater the probability of exhausting one's supply of time and energy and of confronting conflicting obligations; role strain and psychological distress are the result.

This hypothesis was developed to account for men's behavior in formal workplace organizations. When applied to women, the assumption is that family roles are greedy and require total allegiance and energy. If women with family roles taken on the role of paid employee, a role that exposes them to the heavy demands of the organization, they are assumed to be debilitated.

The Expansion Hypothesis

In the mid-1970s a competing hypothesis about human energy, the expansion hypothesis, emerged. It focuses on the net positive gains to be had from multiple roles. The major theorists of this revisionist position (Marks, 1977; Sieber, 1974), emphasize the privileges rather than the obligations that accrue to incumbents of multiple roles. They argue that such rewards as self-esteem, recognition, prestige, and financial remuneration more than offset the costs of adding on roles. Through role bargaining, that is delegating or eliminating onerous role obligations, men could reduce, to a manageable and presumably attractive set, the many demands on them associated with operating in two arenas. Thus, for men, multiple role involvement was hypothesized to enhance well-being. Early support for this view came from the work of Gove and Tudor (1973), who suggested that men experience fewer symptoms of psychiatric dysfunction than do women because they are committed simultaneously to work and family roles.

More recent research supports the expansion hypothesis for women as well as men (Crosby, 1984; Thoits, 1983; Verbrugge, 1982). Thoits (1983) reports a positive association between the number of roles a person (woman or man) occupies and psychological well-being. In an analysis of women's physical health, Verbrugge (1982) concludes that multiple role involvement is associated with better health. In sum, the expansion hypothesis is well supported; "the more roles, the better" (Gove & Zeiss, 1987; Thoits, 1983).

ASSUMPTIONS ABOUT CORE ROLES

Beyond the issue of number of roles per se, however, is the more intriguing question of how particular roles, role combinations, and role quality affect stress. In contrast to other stress-related research areas, most of the literature on the negative effects of multiple role involvement, such as role strain and role conflict, has centered on women. How can we account for this phenomenon?

Theoretical formulations regarding men's lives assume the centrality of the paid employee role and relegate nonworkplace roles to positions of minor importance. Because the roles of husband and father are viewed as subordinate to the employee role and traditionally have involved few obligations, issues of conflict and strain have rarely been addressed. Theories of women's lives, in contrast, have assumed both the primacy of and major commitment to nonworkplace roles. Involvement in the paid employee role, which also requires commitment, is assumed to entail strain and conflict. Therefore, with the rapid entrance into the paid labor force of women already occupying their primary roles—i.e., married women with children—researchers sought to examine the presumed deleterious effects of women's multiple role involvement. Thus, assumptions about core roles have generated strikingly different expectations about the effects of role occupancy for men and women.

Men's Core Role

The centrality of paid work in theories of men's lives (Erikson, 1959; Levinson, Darrow, Klein, Levinson, & McKee, 1978; Vaillant, 1977) is reflected in the descriptors Levinson, et al. use to identify the "Seasons of a Man's Life": entering the adult world, settling down, becoming one's own man (BOOM). The markers Levinson, et al. use to distinguish one "season" from another, and to assess success at each stage, are tied most strongly to events in the workplace. For example, a man's judgment regarding his relative success or failure in meeting the goals he set for himself during the BOOM stage depends on whether "he has achieved the desired position on his 'ladder';" whether he has been "affirmed within his occupational and social world;" and whether he is "becoming a senior member of that world with all the rewards and responsibilities seniority brings" (p. 191).

Further, we read that failure to achieve occupation goals results in a sense of personal failure.

> When a man experiences a developmental crisis in the late thirties, it stems from the overwhelm-ing feeling that he cannot accomplish the tasks of Becoming One's Own Man: he cannot advance sufficiently on his chosen ladder; cannot gain the affirmation, independence and seniority he wants; cannot be his own man in the terms defined by his current life structure. (Levinson et al., 1978:191)

According to later writers, this "myth of monism" (Long & Porter, 1984) presents a sorely impoverished view of men, even for the upwardly mobile, white middle-class men on whom it was based (see, e.g., Farrell & Rosenberg, 1981; Lamb, Pleck, Charnov, & Levine, 1985). Nevertheless, this view has had profound impact on theory and research. Indeed, most of the landmark studies on stress that focus on men (e.g., Rosenman, et al., 1975) do not even report the marital or parental status of their subjects, an omission that testifies to the pervasiveness of this one-dimensional view of men. In addition, this view has several consequences that impair the accuracy and comprehensiveness of our knowledge about the relationship between social roles and the experience of stress in men's lives: (a) an overem-phasis on the sources of strain in men's workplace role; (b) a neglect of rewarding aspects of their workplace role; and (c) a dearth of research on the relationship between men's nonworkplace roles and their well-being and stress. There is little discussion, moreover, of how men's work and family roles interact to affect men's experience of distress, (see Farrell & Rosenberg, 1981, for an exception). As yet, therefore, we have no answers to such ques-tions as: How does the quality of experience in the role of husband and/or father affect men's health? Do married or nonmarried men experience more stress at the workplace? Do men's experiences as parents influence the effects of workplace stress on physical and men-tal health outcomes?

Women's Core Roles

For women, family roles have been assumed to be the core roles. Indeed, in Erikson's seminal work, *Identity: Youth and Crisis* (1968), marriage and motherhood were considered crucial to the completion of a woman's identity. Young women often ask whether they can "have an identity" before they know whom they will marry and for whom they will make a home: "something in the young woman's identity must keep itself open for the peculiar-ities of the man to be joined and of the children to be brought up" (p. 283).

Success in the roles of wife and mother has been considered a prerequisite for women's psychological well-being. Indeed, the roles of wife and mother, although in reality quite separate and at times in conflict, are linked together as if one. Women's family roles typi-cally have been seen as natural and as crucial for women's well-being; until recently, women who did not occupy at least one or even both of these roles were assumed to be immature, unfeminine, incomplete, selfish, unnatural, deviant (Rossi, 1984; Teicholtz, 1978). Thus, it has been assumed that for women, the wife and mother roles are less stressful than the role of paid worker (Barnett & Baruch, 1985).

This view of women is being challenged by research exploring the impact of marriage and motherhood on women's well-being. Evidence is accumulating that women who have never married as well as those who are no longer married—i.e., divorced, separated, and widowed women—are not doomed to a life without an identity. Indeed, several studies suggest that unmarried women fare at least as well as their married counterparts on many indexes of psychological well-being (Baruch & Barnett, 1986a; Birnbaum, 1975; Gigy, 1980; Sears & Barbee, 1977).

Such recent research raises the question of whether the data support the "core role" assumptions. I believe this chapter demonstrates that the core role assumption is invalid; men's family roles and women's job roles are central for their psychological well-being. In order to establish this claim, it is helpful to examine evidence on this point separately for men's roles and women's roles.

MEN'S ROLES

Men's Family Roles

In contrast to the core role assumptions, the consensus from the research literature is that "the majority of men are more psychologically involved in their families than in their jobs" (Pleck, 1985:135); their psychological well-being is more dependent on their family roles than on their work roles. The core role model that depicts men's lives as dominated by their workplace role is too simplistic. Although this view captures the essence of the Protestant work ethic, it fails to relate to the actual experiences and values of most men's lives. The model needs to be replaced by one that reflects the multidimensionality of men's lives that is emerging from recent research.

Several studies suggest that men's family roles are central to men's psychological well-being and have both significant direct and indirect effects. Farrell and Rosenberg (1981), in their major study of 500 randomly selected men, report that they were surprised to discover the powerful impact of family relations on the experiences of men at midlife.

> Our contact with the families demonstrated the ways in which a man's experience of midlife is very much dependent on the culture and structure of his family. The changing relationships to wife and children act as precipitants for development in men. . . . This interlocking of individual and family developmental processes is a critical element in men's experience of midlife (p. vii).

The surprised voiced by the researchers may be due to their middle-class bias, which is also evident in the samples on which many of the theory-building studies were based (Levinson et al., 1978; Vailliant, 1977). When two-earner working-class and lower-middle-class families with preschool children were interviewed, the authors concluded that "men in contemporary industrial culture seek their primary emotional, personal, and spiritual gratification in their family setting" (Lein et al., 1974:118). Using a national probability sample, the authors of *The Inner American* (Veroff, Douvan, & Kulka, 1981) report similar findings. Male respondents who held all three roles of spouse, parent, and paid worker rated family roles as more critical than occupational roles. The one exception was older men, who chose self-actualization or security as their critical value in life over such alternatives as sense of belonging or being well-respected.

Pleck (1985) reviewed the literature on the consequences of husbands' psychological involvement in work and family roles and conducted new analyses of data from two national surveys completed in the late 1970s. He found that husbands experience their family roles as far more psychologically significant than their paid work role and that these non-workplace roles had greater positive impact on men's psychological well-being. Commenting on the discrepancy between the assumptions in the literature and these data, he says, "What is perhaps most surprising is that the view that most men are obsessed by their work and oblivious to their families has persisted so long in spite of the fact that the available data have almost always disconfirmed it" (p. 134).

Pleck notes, however, that a minority of men are more involved with their work than with their families. These men tend to be found among those who are highly educated and/or of high occupational status. Thus studies based on samples of such men (see, for example, Erikson, 1959; Valliant, 1977) "generally find somewhat higher work involvement and somewhat lower family involvement than is found in more representative samples. However, in even these highly educated samples, men who are more involved in their work than in their family are still in the minority" (Pleck, 1985:134–135). Similarly, Farrell and Rosenberg (1981) note that models such as the one proposed by Levinson, et al. "apply to a subset of men—most likely a creative and intellectual elite who achieve many of our cultural ideals of success" (p. 23). These authors go on to say that Levinson, et al.'s data "speak more to our cultural image of 'success' and 'self-actualization' than to either the reality of most people's lives or to universal psychological processes" (p. 23).

Several recent studies support Pleck's conclusion: family roles do play a great role in men's psychological economy. This body of evidence challenges the core role belief that the job role is the primary source of men's stress (Barnett, Marshall, & Pleck, 1992; Bolger, DeLongis, Kessler, & Wethington, 1990). In a study of 300 employed married men, Barnett and Marshall (in press, a) found that job role quality was not a significant predictor of men's physical health when the quality of their family roles was controlled. Surprisingly, Bolger, et al. (1990) found that men's experience of distress was more closely associated with their family roles than was true for women. These findings suggest strongly that family-based stressors and stress mitigators constitute significant unmeasured variance in many studies of the stress-illness relationship in men.

More specifically, there is considerable evidence that the marital role is central to men's mental and physical health. Several studies of psychological health indicate that men benefit more than women from being married (Cleary & Mechanic, 1983; Gove, 1972, 1973, 1978). With respect to physical health, too, there are indications that men benefit more from the role of spouse than do women. Whereas disease morbidity and mortality rates tend to be lowest among the married, they are lower among married men than married women. Similarly, compared to the nonmarried, married persons have the lowest rates of contact with physicians, hospital stays, and visits to psychiatric hospitals and out-patient clinics (Cleary, 1987). Furthermore, married men have lower contact rates than married women. These findings suggest that marriage is more protective for men than for women (Belle, 1982; Cleary, 1987).

Such findings suggests that loss of the marriage role will be more devastating for men than for women. Evidence supporting this view comes from studies of gender differences in the experience of both divorce and widowhood. In one longitudinal study, men were found to have a more difficult time coping with marital separation and divorce than did women (Wallerstein & Kelly, 1980). Widowers suffer more than widows, as reflected in such distress indicators as depression, psychiatric disorders, physical illness, mortality, and suicide (Stroebe & Stroebe, 1983).

Whereas the role of spouse seems to have largely beneficial, health-promoting effects for men, evidence concerning the role of father is less consistent. The role of father traditionally has been low in demands and high in control. Fathers' participation in childrearing in our culture has been quite minimal, and mothers have rarely expected or demanded much involvement. Yet, at least in principle, fathers have wielded ultimate authority; they could control their children's behavior in ways not possible for mothers. Viewing the traditional father role in Karasek's terms (see subsequently), we see that the combination of low demands and high control places it in the low-strain category. However, pressure for men to become more deeply involved in day-to-day parenting while maintaining their traditional provider role is likely to increase stress by increasing demands and reducing control.

Recent evidence suggests that although fatherhood per se is unrelated to men's experiences of distress, the quality of fathers' relationships with their children is significant (Barnett, Marshall, & Singer, 1992). Fathers who had positive relationships with their children reported low distress; those who had troubled relationships reported high distress. The contribution of father role quality to distress was significant, even after controlling for both job-role and marital-role quality. Thus, father-child relationships constitute an independent source of psychological reward when they are positive and an independent source of stress when they are negative.

Men's Workplace Roles

Interestingly, the role of paid employee is treated as both stressful in itself and as stress-reducing or buffering when combined with family roles. Research is now directed toward specifying which aspects of the workplace role are beneficial and which deleterious. It is taken as a given that "work is the sector of life most productive of stress for middle-aged men" (Weiss, 1990:17). However, surprisingly little research has been done to determine which aspects of the work role contribute to men's psychological well-being. The considerable literature on job conditions has focused almost exclusively on the relationship of such conditions as autonomy and challenge to job satisfaction and to stress, but not to well-being (House, Strecher, Metzner, & Robbins, 1986; Quinn et al., 1973; Quinn, Walsh, & Hahn, 1977). Within the stress research field, attention has been paid primarily to work as a source of stress. Indeed, the operating assumption is that the workplace is a jungle that exposes men to such dangers as time pressure, competition, and noxious stimuli.

By inference, if conditions opposite to those associated with stress are present, the job is assumed to contribute to men's sense of well-being. For example, the work of Robert Karasek and others (see subsequently) suggests that lack of control over both resources and pacing at work contributes to stress. Thus, the presence of control over these aspects of one's job is assumed to contribute to one's sense of well-being. This formulation is an intriguing first step toward understanding more completely the impact on men—and women—of the paid employee role.

Given that the role of paid employee can have a positive effect on men's well-being (Gore & Mangione, 1983; Pleck, 1985), we can better understand the impact of this role by examining both its rewarding and the problematic aspects. Awareness that roles have these two aspects and that each can function differently with respect to well-being outcomes is not new (Blood & Wolfe, 1960; Bradburn & Caplovitz, 1965). Similarly the notion that subjective experience in a role is a predictor of well-being has a long history (Aneshensel & Pearlin, 1987; Barnett & Baruch, 1985). In the later section on gender differences in stress spillover between roles, we discuss the relationship between rewarding and problematic role attributes.

Contagion and Spillover Between Men's Family and Workplace Roles

As more and more men and women combine work and nonworkplace roles, an understanding of role-stress contagion and spillover is crucial to the study of stress and well-being. Contagion refers to the relationship between distress experienced in one role and distress experienced in a second role. In contrast, spillover refers to the joint effects of subjective experiences in two roles on a third variable, usually a mental health indicator. For example, the relationship between stress at work and men's distress may differ for men who have positive relationships with their wives or children compared to those who do not. Although most often referring to the interaction effects of quality of experience in roles, the spillover concept can be applied to role occupancy. To illustrate, the association between workplace stressors and men's psychological distress may differ for men who do or do not also occupy family roles.

The almost universal assumption in the contagion literature is that work is men's primary source of stress; therefore, questions are framed about the contagion of workplace stress to other domains of men's lives (Crouter, Perry-Jenkins, Huston, & Crawford, 1989; Small & Riley, 1990; Pearlin & McCall, 1990; Weiss, 1990; as well as reviews of this literature, Staines, 1980). (Evidence presented later indicates that, at least for younger men, this assumption does not hold.) For example, in a study of 130 male bank executives, Small and Riley (1990) found that reports of work stress were associated equally strongly with men's experience of distress in four roles: parent-child, marital, leisure, and household responsibilities.

Until recently, men's family roles have been relatively stress free (Weiss, 1990); thus, home-to-work contagion has not been given serious attention by researchers (See Bolger, DeLongis, Kessler, & Wetherington, 1989 and Crouter, 1984 for exceptions.) Central to the traditional role of husband is being a good economic provider. Historically, success in that arena has satisfied both the demands of the paid worker role and those of the husband and father roles. In theory, husbands in general and good providers in particular could fulfill their family role obligations without having to meet any additional demands within the home. Weiss (1985) found that men do define their work role as fulfilling their family roles. In short, although work and family demands may compete for men's time, they are not experienced as competitive. Succeeding at his job enables a man to discharge his family responsibilities; having a family makes work meaningful. As a result, men are not often likely to experience inter-role conflict when, for example, they have to stay late at work and thereby lose some of their family time. As is discussed later, there is evidence that this synergy may be experienced more by older and more traditional men than by younger and less traditional men.

Indeed, men may experience role synergy where women experience role conflict. By virtue of their status as sole economic provider, husbands traditionally have had considerable authority over their wives, their children, and their households. By role bargaining within the home, employed men—especially those employed in prestigious, well-paying jobs—can trade off to their wives distasteful aspects of the parenting role as a means of managing conflicts between the demands of the workplace and of the home. Thus, the busy executive who is called away on a business trip gets his wife to go to the Boy Scout meeting in his place. Because his trip is seen as in the service of supporting the family, he is free of conflict and she takes over and forgives him.

It is illuminating to view the husband role as an occupation and to apply to it Karasek's model of job roles. Karasek and his colleagues (1982) have been examining job conditions associated with impaired health. Although their work was based on all male samples and was limited to the workplace, their concepts may, I believe, be applicable to males and females in their nonworkplace roles. These researchers tried to specify the particular attributes of an occupation that arouse stress-related hormones which then set in motion various disease processes, especially those affecting the cardiovascular system and the immune system. According to their research, the most stressful set of job conditions combines a low level of decision latitude and a high level of demand—that is, having low control over the pacing of one's tasks and the allocation of resources, as well as having tasks that are psychologically demanding, characterized by time pressures, deadlines, large workloads, and heavy emotional strains.

This "high-strain" combination is related to elevated risk for such negative health outcomes as coronary heart disease and ulcers. Presumably the high level of demands creates arousal, and the inability to exert control leads to frustration. To illustrate, a surgeon and a nurse may face similar levels of psychological demands, but they differ greatly in their power to control how they deal with these demands and, thus, presumably in the stressfulness of their occupational role. According to this formulation, the nurse would experience more distress than the surgeon.

The traditional husband role, which typically combines high control and low demands (a "low-strain" combination), suggests little stress and, therefore, little contagion from home to work, for good providers at least. Recent studies challenge this view of men's work and family roles. In a study of 166 married couples, the data on contagion were totally at odds with theoretical predictions (Bolder et al., 1989). Men experienced far more home-to-work stress contagion than did women! Basing their findings on data from daily diaries, the researchers found that "the inability of men to prevent this kind of contagion is pervasive" (p. 179). In contrast, evidence of work-to-home contagion was less consistent and less powerful.

There is a suggestion in the literature that men in contemporary two-earner couples in which women have financial power may be experiencing more family stress than men in traditional marriages (Bolder et al., 1989). However, in an earlier study, Kessler & McRae (1982) reported no evidence that "increased wife's earnings damages the well-being of husbands" (p. 223). The speculation is that among men in today's two-earner couples, wives' greater financial power increases the stress associated with marital conflict (Wethington, 1990). Without the sense of security associated with their economic domination, husbands are vulnerable to feelings of distress if their relationships with their wives are troubled. These data suggest that, as the obligations of the roles of husband and father become differentiated from those of successful economic provider, the role synergy men have enjoyed is being replaced by more complicated processes, including role conflict.

A related finding from the spillover literature indicates that among men in two-earner couples (Barnett & Marshall, in press, c), marital concerns compounded the negative mental health effects on men's distress of a poor job. More generally, when a man's relationship with his wife or children is troubled, it exacerbates the negative mental health effect of a problem job on psychological distress. When his marriage and family relationships are positive, they buffer a man from the negative mental health effects of a difficult job. Interestingly, there was no evidence of spillover from work to home. That is, problems at work did not exacerbate the relationship between marital-role or parent-role quality and distress.

WOMEN'S ROLES

Women's Family Roles

In contrast to the belief that women's occupancy of family roles is critical to their psychological well-being, the evidence is that women's mental and physical health does not depend on occupying the role of wife or mother (Bart, 1972; Baruch & Barnett, 1986a; Bernard, 1972; Brown, Feldberg, Fox, & Kohen, 1976). With respect to the role of wife, some studies show that wives do not have a psychological health advantage over unmarried women. In a sample of gifted women, highest life satisfaction was reported by women who were single and employed (Sears & Barbee, 1977). Another study found never-married and divorced women to be as high on some indexes of well-being—e.g., self-esteem—as married women (Baruch & Barnett, 1986a). However, some studies do show well-being advantages for married women (Verbrugge, 1983). The inconsistent results from these studies are due in part to differences in the outcome variables. When psychological well-being is assessed by indexes measuring happiness, marital status turns out to be predictive (Baruch & Barnett, 1986a; Campbell, Converse, & Rodgers, 1976; Depner, 1979); however, when self-esteem or life satisfaction are the measures of well-being, marital status has little impact (Baruch & Barnett, 1986a; Gigy, 1980).

Evidence suggests that whatever mental health advantage married women enjoy compared to single women is due to their higher income rather than to the presence of a spouse per se. When per capita income was controlled, employed single women were at no greater risk for psychological distress than were employed partnered women (Barnett & Marshall, 1991).

Evidence about the role of mother is more consistent: motherhood is rarely associated with psychological well-being and is often associated with psychological distress. Findings from recent studies, for example, indicate that being in the role of mother did not predict any of three well-being indicators—self-esteem, pleasure, or low levels of depressive symptomatology (Baruch & Barnett, 1986a). With respect to physical health, mothers compared to nonmothers have a small advantage (Verbrugge, 1984). This health advantage, however, is dependent on the ages and number of children. Having preschoolers or numerous children is associated with health problems. The "health debit" seems largest for employed single mothers (Verbrugge, 1984). Here, too, income may affect these findings. In a recent study, employed single mothers were at no greater risk for mental or physical health problems when per capita income was controlled (Barnett, Davidson, & Marshall, 1991; Barnett & Marshall, 1991). Thus, whether motherhood has a positive or negative effect on health depends on the children's characteristics, the mother's marital status, and the available financial resources.

Indeed, some studies suggest that the role of mother may be women's primary source of stress (Barnett & Baruch, 1985; Veroff, et al., 1981), whether alone or in combination with work and marital roles. Compared to other groups of women, those with children—particularly children six years of age and younger—are at greater risk for depression, and the risk increases with the number of young children at home (Pearlin, 1975; Radloff, 1975). Moreover, in a recent study of women's three major social roles, only occupancy of the role of mother, not of wife or paid worker, was related to the experience of role strain—i.e., role overload and role conflict (Barnett & Baruch, 1985). Gore and Mangione (1983) also found that after controlling for marital and employment status, women with children, reported higher levels of psychophysiological complaints: troubled breathing, poor appetite, and difficulty in sleeping.

These findings suggest that burdensome demands are associated with women's family roles (Aneshensel & Pearlin, 1987). Focusing on role occupancy by itself masks the fact that, although the roles of wife and of mother can be very rewarding for some women, for others they can be very troublesome (Baruch & Barnett, 1986a). Central to the traditional roles of wife and mother is the obligation to be available to meet the needs of the family, to be ready to respond whenever someone calls. In addition, wives and mothers are held, and hold themselves, responsible for the well-being of their role-partners—their husbands and their children. In the traditional view, if a woman's husband is unhappy, it is assumed to be due to her failings; if her children have problems, she is assumed to be responsible. This assumption of responsibility is particularly strong in the role of mother. In spite of the reality that one has relatively little control over the welfare and happiness of another person, mothers are prone to self-blame whenever their children show signs of distress. The combination of little control, relentless demands, and great responsibility exposes wives and mothers to many frustrations and failures and, applying Karasek's model, may account in part for the stressfulness of these roles.

Compounding this picture and adding to the stressfulness of women's family roles is the cultural expectation that women should perform these roles naturally and with no negative consequences. To admit to stress is tantamount to admitting to failure as a woman. This picture contrasts sharply with that of men, who are seen as legitimately experiencing stress in their primary role as breadwinner and as needing support, especially from their wives.

In sum, it appears that women's nonworkplace roles, especially the role of mother, are both low in control and high in demand; that is, these are high-strain roles, which are particularly problematic with respect to stress-related outcomes. Moreover, it is unlikely that these roles will become less stressful in the foreseeable future. Clearly the core role assumption that occupying these two roles is a prerequisite for women's psychological well-being is not supported.

Women's Workplace Roles

When women's role as paid employee is considered, it is almost always in the context of women's nonworkplace roles. Because the role of paid employee is assumed to be added on and, thus, to cause conflict, burden, and strain, women who occupy both family and workplace roles are automatically thought to be stressed. Yet it appears that the role of paid employee is associated with significant physical and mental health benefits for women. In contrast to women who occupy only the roles of wife and mother, those who also occupy the role of paid employee experience a significant health advantage (Thoits, 1983; Verbrugge, 1983).

Recent evidence indicates that the role of paid employees is both a direct and an indirect source of well-being (Barnett & Baruch, 1985). Using such indexes as self-reports of physical symptoms (Coleman, Antonucci, & Adelmann, 1987; Verbrugge, 1983; Waldron & Herold, 1984) and well-being indexes (Baruch & Barnett, 1986a; Merikangas, 1985), many studies show significant mental and physical health differences that favor employed versus unemployed women. Moreover, despite the belief that the more high-powered a woman's career, the more danger to her well-being, the advantage is greater for women in higher-status occupations (Verbrugge, 1984). However, being employed is beneficial even to women in low-status jobs (Belle, 1982; Ferree, 1976). Despite the growing consensus that the employee role is not typically as stressful for women as it has been assumed to be, scant attention has been paid to the beneficial effects of women's workplace roles.

In an attempt to identify aspects of work that have beneficial effects on women's health, we factor analyzed two scales, one assessing aspects of jobs that are experienced as rewarding, the other, aspects of jobs that are experienced as "of concern" (Barnett & Marshall, 1991). The subjects in this study were 403 women employed in two health care professions, social work and licensed practical nursing. Six job reward and five job concern factors were identified and confirmed, but only a subset were related to the health indicators (Barnett, Davidson, & Marshall, 1991; Barnett & Marshall, 1991). Of these, only one job reward factor, helping others at work, and one job concern factor, overload at work, were associated consistently with all three health outcomes—subjective well-being, psychological distress, and physical health symptoms. Employed women who reported high rewards from helping others reported low levels of health problems; women who reported high concerns about overload reported high levels of health problems. In addition to its direct effect on health outcomes, the helping others at work factor moderated the relationship between overload and all three health indicators. Women who reported high concerns about overload at work reported high mental and physical distress unless they had high rewards from helping others. Thus, at least for women health care providers, rewards from helping others at work—i.e., from being needed by others and from having a significant impact on others—mitigated the stress-enhancing effects of overload. While acknowledging the importance to women's health of rewards from helping others at work, it is important to note that these rewards have not been assessed in studies of the stress-illness relationship in men. Our currently on-going study of men and women in two-earner couples will allow us to examine the contribution of helping others at work to men's mental and physical health states.

In addition to cross-sectional findings, longitudinal studies indicate that changes over time in the quality of a woman's job is a significant predictor of changes over time in her level of psychological distress (Barnett, Marshall, & Singer, 1992). If her experiences at work improve, so does her mental health; if they deteriorate, so does her mental health. These effects were especially pronounced among women who did not occupy family roles. When considering the accumulated evidence about the core role assumptions for men and women, it seems clear that they have not been confirmed. In sum, it is ironic that the roles that appear to be most predictive for women's and men's well-being are ignored in the core role models—for men the role of husband, for women, the role of paid employee.

Contagion and Spillover Between Women's Family and Workplace Roles

In contrast to the assumption that, at least historically, men's work and family roles were synergistic, there has been no assumption of a natural congruence between a woman's roles as wife and mother and her role as a paid worker. Even now, little recognition exists of the many important ways in which women function as economic providers in relation to their children and husbands. This is but one reason why women traditionally have not been able to role bargain successfully with their husbands and with their children.

Other reasons include the fact that women's occupational roles are typically lower than men's in prestige, power, and income. Because of their relative disadvantage, women have less leverage for eliminating and delegating family role tasks, so that role bargaining with their husbands is unlikely (Long & Porter, 1984). Moreover, the weight of social sanctions for slighting wifely and maternal duties and the low probability that women can trade off to their husbands or children burdensome aspects of the wife and mother roles reduce the likelihood for successful negotiation between their workplace and nonworkplace roles. It thus appears that women have fewer options than do men to achieve control over competing role demands.

In spite of this disadvantage, it appears that for women the work role buffers the relationship between family role stress and distress indicators. Barnett and Baruch (1985) found that self-reports of role overload (having too many demands) and role conflict (having conflicting demands) were significantly related to self-reported symptoms of anxiety only among women who were not employed. In other word, nonemployed wives and mothers experience more anxiety when they are feeling stressed in their family roles than do wives and mothers who are employed.

More specifically, the stress a woman experiences as a mother may be mitigated by her occupancy of the paid worker role. Gove and his associates (Gove, 1972; Gove & Tudor, 1973) report that married nonemployed women with children report higher levels of depressive symptoms than their employed counterparts. Perhaps because of a greater sense of control, employed mothers appear less impaired by the stresses of childrearing than are housewives. Another interpretation comes from a recent longitudinal study (Wethington & Kessler, 1989) reporting that becoming a parent was not associated with increased depression, unless women also decreased their labor force participation. Wethington and Kessler speculate that full-time employment buffers women from the stress associated with the maternal role.

Few studies have attempted to study spillover among women's three major roles—wife, mother, and employee. The well-known Framingham Heart Study (Haynes & Feinleib, 1982) provides evidence of the interactive effects of women's employment, marital, and parental roles on their risk for coronary heart disease (CHD). By looking at the family role occupancy of employed women in this longitudinal study, the authors found clerical workers who were married to blue-collar husbands, or who had more than two children, or both, to be at high risk. Perhaps when a woman has children, is in a paid job that is high in demands and low in control, and is married to a blue-collar, presumably traditional husband, she is at particularly high risk for CHD.

Recent studies of spillover have included assessment of the quality of women's roles, and have asked two new questions: (1) is the relationship between the quality of experience in one role and psychological distress moderated by occupancy of another role?; and (2) Is the relationship between the quality of experience and distress in one role moderated by the quality of experience in another role?

Although it may seem a counterintuitive opinion, there is general agreement that women who experience job-role stress are at no greater risk for depression if they are also mothers or wives (Barnett & Marshall, 1991). Similarly, Bolger et al. (1990) reported that the impact of job stress on mood was not greater among women with children at home than among those without children. In fact, employed women with children reported less job stress (i.e., arguments at work) than employed women without children (Bolger et al., 1990) and occupying the role of mother buffered women from the effects of job role quality (Barnett & Marshall, 1991). A recent longitudinal study confirmed these findings; there was virtually no association between changes in job stress and changes in psychological distress among married women and women with children, however, there were significant effects among women without family roles (Barnett, Marshall, & Singer, 1992). Taken together, these studies are open to several interpretations. Chief among them are that employed women who are also mothers derive resources from their multiple roles which allow them to resist mental health problems, or that these women invest themselves less in their jobs, hence they are less reactive to the quality of their jobs and they have less exposure to arguments.

Is the effect on mental health of a bad job worse if the woman's marital or parental role is also troubled? The general answer is no: women appear to compartmentalize their affective experiences to a much greater degree than has previously been assumed (Barnett & Marshall, in press b; Bolger et al., 1990). This independence suggests that women are not so preoccupied with their family roles that problems with their husbands or children affect their functioning in their job role, placing them at an elevated risk for psychological distress. In other words, the relationship between job role quality and distress does not vary depending upon whether the employed mother has rewarding or distressing relationships with her children or husband. If a job is troubling, distress is high; however, it is not higher if the woman's marriage is problematic or her relationships with her children are disturbing. There is one important exception: A positive work experience can have a protective effect on women who are dissatisfied with the maternal role. Employed mothers who are concerned about their relationships with their children report high levels of psychological distress unless they have rewarding jobs (Barnett & Marshall, 1991). More specifically, having a challenging job offsets the distress associated with concerns over disaffection with children (Barnett, Marshall, & Sayer, in press).

GENDER DIFFERENCES

Contagion and Spillover Between Roles

It appears, contrary to popular ideas, that women compartmentalize their affective experiences with their partners more effectively than do men. Among married men, affective experiences with their spouses are not readily contained resulting in home-to-work contagion and spillover.

Only a few studies have addressed the question of gender differences in contagion and spillover effects. It appears that home-to-work contagion is more prevalent among men than among women. More specifically, arguments with their spouses the night before were associated with problems at work the next day among husbands but not wives (Wethington, 1990). It appears that married men are more vulnerable than married women to the effects of marital conflict.

Women suffer less and benefit more than men from spillover effects (Barnett & Marshall, in press b; Barnett & Marshall, in press c; Barnett, Marshall, & Sayer, in press). More specifically, women were better able than men to compartmentalize their marital troubles. Marital problems exacerbated the effects of a bad job on psychological distress among men but not women (Barnett & Marshall, in press c). In contrast, rewards at the job moderated the association between troubled relationships with children and distress among mothers but not among fathers (Barnett & Marshall, in press b). In particular, mothers who felt disaffected from their children reported high distress unless they were in challenging jobs (Barnett, Marshall, & Sayer, in press).

Crossover Between Spouses

Early studies showed that a husband's experiences in the workplace can lead to stress being experienced by the wife at home. Such effects are referred to as *crossover.* A wife's experience as a mother, for example, is affected by her husband's performance of the paternal role. The mothers in a study of 160 couples, especially those who were employed, were less satisfied in their marriages when they did more child care relative to their husbands (Barnett & Baruch, 1987). At the same time, however, wives of more participant fathers were more likely to criticize themselves, especially if employed, and to report that their work was interfering with their family responsibilities. Thus, for these women, the quality of their experience as wife had a direct effect on the quality of their experience as mother and vice versa, and the role behavior of the spouse had an impact on that relationship. Fathers' experiences are similarly conditioned by their wives' role behavior. The less employed mothers interacted with their children relative to the fathers, the more dissatisfied the fathers were with the wives' employment patterns and with the rewards they were getting in the marriage (Baruch & Barnett, 1986b). For both married men and women, the spouse's performance of the parental role has a strong influence on their experience of the marital role.

Beyond these direct effects, one partner's behavior can affect the relationship between an outside stressor and the partner's level of distress. To illustrate, Kessler and McRae (1982) found that the health advantage to married women of being employed was negated if their husbands did not participate in child care. Apparently well-being is enhanced when mothers are employed only if they perceive that their husbands are doing their fair share of child care.

Interestingly, wives' behaviors have been viewed by researchers as potentially moderating the relationship between the husbands' work stress and negative health outcome. The parallel study of husbands' behaviors as moderators of the relationship between wives' work stress and negative health outcomes has not been done. The focus on men's work role reflects the belief that "work is the sector of life most productive of stress for middle-aged men" (Weiss, 1990). The general finding is that wives' supportive behaviors allow men to cope better with their stress and, in so doing, reduce the likelihood of marital conflict and mental health problems for the men.

Several recent studies throw additional light on the processes by which wives' behavior ameliorates the relationship between husband's work stress and disruptive marital behaviors. A supportive wife facilitates her husband's recovery from a hard day at work by permitting him to withdraw, thereby allowing him to "avoid certain types of social stimuli at home that would further increase levels of emotional and psychological arousal" (Repetti, 1989:658). A similar buffering process was found by Bolger et al. (1989), who observed that women "increase their work effort at home in response to their spouse[s] having a hectic day at work," thus shielding them from "excessive accumulation of role demands" (p. 181). There is no evidence that husbands provide such a buffer for their wives after a hard day at work (Pearlin & McCall, 1990). Indeed there is evidence that after work male employees "unwind" physiologically, whereas female employees, especially female managers, do not (Frankenhaeuser et al., 1989). Speculatively, women are thrust into home situations requiring their attention and do not have the space to recuperate. Thus, although there may be crossover between work and home for both men and women, the effects on health indicators or marital behavior indicators are moderated in the case of men by their wives' behavior.

In sum, evidence is accumulating that challenges many long-held views about multiple roles, gender, and psychological distress. A new picture is emerging. Studies of full-time employed men and women in dual-earner couples indicate more similarity than difference in the relationship between role stressors and psychological distress. Men's distress is as affected by their relationship with their partners and children as is women's. Women's distress is as affected by the quality of their job experiences as is men's. It appears that as the pattern of men's and women's lives converge, what had been thought of as gender differences in the stress-illness relationship may disappear. Earlier findings of differences may have been due to differences in the external patterns of men's and women's lives, not to inherent sex or gender differences. Theories that are insensitive to these new social realities need to be abandoned.

REFERENCES

ANESHENSEL, C. S., & PEARLIN, L. I. Structural contexts of sex differences in stress. In R. C. Barnett, L. Biener, & G. K. Baruch (eds.), *Gender and stress.* New York: Free Press, 1987.

BARNETT, R. C., & BARUCH, G. K. Women's involvement in multiple roles and psychological distress. *Journal of Personality and Social Psychology,* 1985, *49,* 135–145.

————. Determinants of fathers' participation in family work. *Journal of Marriage and the Family,* 1987, *49,* 29–40.

BARNETT, R. C., DAVIDSON, H., & MARSHALL, N. L. Physical symptoms and the interplay of work and family roles. *Health Psychology,* 1991, *10,* 94–101.

BARNETT, R. C., & MARSHALL, N. L. Men, family-role quality, job-role quality, and physical health. *Health Psychology,* in press (a).

————. Worker and mother roles, spillover effects, and psychological distress. *Women and Health,* in press b.

BARNETT, R. C., & MARSHALL, N. L. Men's job and partner roles: Spillover effects and psychological distress. *Sex Roles,* in press (c).

BARNETT, R. C., MARSHALL, N. L., & PLECK, J. H. Adult son-parent relationships and their associations with sons' psychological distress. *Journal of Family Issues,* in press (b).

BARNETT, R. C., MARSHALL, N. L., & SAYER, A. Positive spillover effects from job to home: A closer look. *Women and Health,* in press.

BARNETT, R. C., MARSHALL, N. L., & SINGER, J. D. Job experiences over time, multiple roles, and women's mental health: A longitudinal study. *Journal of Personality and Social Psychology,* 1992, *64,* 634–644.

BART, P. Depression in middle-aged women. In J. M. Bardwick (ed.), *Readings on the psychology of women.* New York: Harper and Row, 1972.

BARUCH, G. K., & BARNETT, R. C. Role quality, multiple role involvement, and psychological well-being in midlife women. *Journal of Personality and Social Psychology,* 1986, *51,* 578–585.(a)

————. Consequences of fathers' participation in family work: Parents' role-strain and well-being. *Journal of Personality and Social Psychology,* 1986, *51,* 983–992.(b)

BELLE, D. (ed.). *Lives in stress: Women and depression.* Beverly Hills, CA: Sage, 1982.

BERNARD, J. *The future of marriage.* New York: World-Times, 1972.

BIRNBAUM, J. L. Life patterns, personality style and self-esteem in gifted family oriented and career committed women. In M. Mednick, S. Tangri, & L. W. Hoffman (eds.), *Women and achievement: Social and motivational analysis.* New York: Hemisphere-Halstead, 1975.

BLOOD, R. O., & WOLFE, D. M. *Husbands and wives.* Glencoe, IL: Free Press, 1960.

BOLGER, N., DELONGIS, A., KESSLER, R. C., & WETHINGTON, E. The contagion of stress across multiple roles. *Journal of Marriage and the Family,* 1989, *51,* 175–183.

————. The microstructure of daily role-related stress in married couples. In J. Eckenrode & S. Gore (eds.), *Stress between work and family.* New York: Plenum, 1990.

BRADBURN, N. M., & CAPLOVITZ, D. *Reports on happiness.* Chicago: Aldine, 1965.

BROWN, C. A., FELDBERG, R., FOX, E. M., & KOHEN, J. Divorce: Chance of a new lifetime. *Journal of Social Issues,* 1976, *32,* 119–133.

CAMPBELL, A., CONVERSE, P. E., & RODGERS, W. L. *The quality of American life.* New York: Sage, 1976.

CLEARY, P. D. Gender differences in stress-related disorders. In R. C. Barnett, L. Biener, & G. K. Baruch (eds.), *Gender and stress.* New York: Free Press, 1987.

CLEARY, P. D., & MECHANIC, D. Sex differences in psychological distress among married people. *Journal of Health and Social Behavior,* 1983, *24,* 111–121.

COLEMAN, L., ANTONUCCI, T., & ADELMANN, P. Role involvement, gender and well-being. In F. Crosby (ed.), *Spouse, parent, worker: One gender and multiple roles.* New Haven, CT: Yale University Press, 1987.

COSER, L. (with R. COSER). *Greedy institutions.* New York: Free Press, 1974.

CROSBY, F. Job satisfaction and domestic life. In M. D. Lee & R. N. Kanungo (eds.), *Management of work and personal life.* New York: Praeger, 1984.

CROUTER, A. C. Spillover from family to work: The neglected side of the work-family interface. *Human Relations,* 1984, *37,* 425–442.

CROUTER, A. C., PERRY-JENKINS, M., HUSTON, T. L., & CRAWFORD, D. W. The influence of work-induced psychological states on behavior at home. *Basic and Applied Psychology,* 1989, *10,* 273–292.

DEPNER, C. *The parental role and psychological well-being.* Paper presented at the meeting of the American Psychological Association, New York, 1979.

DYTELL, R. S., PARDINE, P., & NAPOLI, A. *Importance of occupational and nonoccupational stress among professional men and women.* Paper presented at the Eastern Psychological Association, Boston, 1985.

ERIKSON, E. Identity and the life cycle. *Psychological Issues,* 1959, *1,* 1–171, whole issue.

————. *Identity: Youth and crisis.* New York: Norton, 1968.

FARRELL, M. P., & ROSENBERG, S. D. *Men at midlife.* Dover, MA: Auburn, 1981.

FERREE, M. The confused American housewife. *Psychology Today,* 1976, *10,* 76–80.

FRANKENHAEUSER, M., LUNDBERG, U., FREDRIKSON, M., MELIN, B., TUOMISTO, M., MYRSTEN, A., BERGMAN-LOSMAN, B., HEDMAN, M., & WALLIN, L. Stress on and off the job as related to sex and occupational status in white-collar workers. *Journal of Organizational Behavior,* 1989, *10,* 321–346.

GIGY, L. L. Self-concept of single women. *Psychology of Women Quarterly,* 1980, *5,* 321–340.

GOODE, W. A theory of strain. *American Sociological Review,* 1960, *25,* 483–496.

GORE, S., & MANGIONE, T. W. Social roles, sex roles and psychological distress: Additive and interactive models of sex differences. *Journal of Health and Social Behavior,* 1983, *24,* 300–312.

GOVE, W. Sex, marital status, and mental illness. *Social Forces,* 1972, *51,* 34–55.

————. Sex, marital status, and mobility. *American Journal of Sociology,* 1973, *79,* 45–67.

————. Sex differences in mental illness among adult men and women: An examination of four questions raised regarding whether or not women actually have higher rates. *Social Science and Medicine,* 1978, *12,* 187–198.

GOVE, W. R., & TUDOR, J. Adult sex roles and mental illness. *American Journal of Sociology,* 1973, *78,* 812–835.

GOVE, W. R., & ZEISS, C. Multiple roles and happiness. In F. Crosby (ed.), *Spouse, Parent, Worker: On Gender and Multiple Roles.* New Haven, CT: Yale University Press, 1987.

HAYNES, S. G., & FEINLEIB, M. Women, work, and coronary heart disease: Results from the Framingham 10-year follow-up study. In P. Berman & E. Ramey (eds.), *Women: A developmental perspective* (NIH publication no. 82-2298). Washington, DC: U.S. Government Printing Office, 1982.

HOUSE, J. S., STRECHER, V., & METZNER, H. L., & ROBBINS, C. A. Occupational stress and health among men and women in the Tecumseh community health study. *Journal of Health and Social Behavior,* 1986, *27,* 62–77.

KANDEL, D. B., DAVIES, M., & RAVEIS, V. H. The stressfulness of daily social roles for women: Marital, occupational and household roles. *Journal of Health and Social Behavior,* 1985, *26,* 64–78.

KARASEK, R. A., SCHWARTZ, J., THEORELL, T., PIEPER, C., RUSSELL, B. S., & MICHELA, J. *Final Report: Job characteristics, occupations and coronary heart disease.* New York: Columbia University, Department of Industrial Engineering and Operations Research, 1982.

KESSLER, R. C., & MCRAE, J. A., JR. The effect of wives' employment on the mental health of married men and women. *American Sociological Review,* 1982, *47,* 217–227.

LAMB, M. E., PLECK, J. H., CHARNOV, E. L., & LEVINE, J. A. Paternal behavior in humans. *American Zoologist,* 1985, *25,* 883–894.

LEIN, L. DURHAM, M., PRATT, M., SCHUDSON, M., THOMAS, R., & WEISS, H. *Final report: Work and family life.* Cambridge, MA: Center for the Study of Public Policy, 1974.

LEVINSON, D. J., DARROW, C. N., KLEIN, E. B., LEVINSON, M. H., & MCKEE, B. *The seasons of a man's life.* New York: Ballantine, 1978.

LONG, J., & PORTER, K. L. In G. K. Baruch & J. Brooks-Gunn (eds.), *Women in midlife.* New York: Plenum, 1984.

MARSHALL, N. L., BARNETT, R. C., & SAYER, A. *Development of the job role quality scales: An application of confirmatory factor analysis.* (Working paper no. 207). Wellesley, MA: Wellesley College Center for Research on Women, 1990.

MARKS, S. R. Multiple roles and role strain: Some notes on human energy, time and commitment. *American Sociological Review,* 1977, *41,* 921–936.

MERIKANGAS, K. *Sex differences in depression.* Paper presented at Murray Center (Radcliffe College) Conference: Mental Health in Social Context. Cambridge, MA, 1985.

PEARLIN, L. I. Sex roles and depression. In N. Datan (ed.), *Lifespan developmental psychology: Normative life crises.* New York: Academic Press, 1975.

PEARLIN, L. I., & MCCALL, M. E. Occupational stress and marital support: A description of micro-processes. In J. Eckenrode & S. Gore (eds.), *Stress between work and family.* New York: Plenum, 1990.

PLECK, J. H. *Working wives/working husbands.* Beverly Hills, CA: Sage, 1985.

QUINN, R. P., MANGIONE, T. W., BARNOWE, J. T., SEASHORE, S. E., COBB, W., JR., CAMPBELL, D. B., FINE, B. D., HERRICK, N. Q., GUPTA, N., LEVITIN, T. E., STAINES, G. L., CROWLEY, J. E., BOUXSEIN, S., & BRADFORD, A. J. *The 1969-1970 survey of working conditions: Chronicles of an unfinished enterprise.* Ann Arbor: Survey Research Center, University of Michigan, 1973.

QUINN, R. P., WALSH, J. T., & HAHN, D. L. K. *The 1972-1973 quality of employment survey: Continuing chronicles of an unfinished enterprise.* Ann Arbor: Survey Research Center, University of Michigan, 1977.

RADLOFF, L. Sex differences in depression: The effects of occupation and marital status. *Sex Roles,* 1975, *1,* 249–265.

REPETTI, R. L. The effects of daily workload on subsequent behavior during marital interaction: The roles of social withdrawal and spouse support. *Journal of Personality and Social Psychology,* 1989, *57,* 651–659.

ROSENMAN, R. H., BRAND, R. J., JENKINS, C. D., FRIEDMAN, M., STRAUS, R., & WURM, M. Coronary heart disease in the Western Collaborative Group Study: Final follow-up experience of $8\frac{1}{2}$ years. *Journal of the American Medical Association,* 1975, *233,* 872–877.

ROSSI, A. Gender and parenthood. *American Sociological Review,* 1984, *49,* 1–19.

SEARS, P. S., & BARBEE, A. H. Career and life satisfaction among Terman's gifted women. In J. Stanley, W. George, & C. Solano (eds.), *The gifted and the creative: Fifty-year perspective.* Baltimore, MD: Johns Hopkins University Press, 1977.

SIEBER, S. Toward a theory of role accumulation. *American Sociological Review,* 1974, *39,* 567–578.

SLATER, P. On social regression. *American Sociological Review,* 1963, *28,* 339–364.

SMALL, S. A., & RILEY, D. Toward a multidimensional assessment of work spillover into family life. *Journal of Marriage and the Family,* 1990, *52,* 51–56.

STAINES, G. L. Spillover versus compensation: A review of the literature on the relationship between work and nonwork. *Human Relations,* 1980, *33,* 111–129.

STROEBE, M. S., & STROEBE W. Who suffers more? Sex differences in health risks of the widowed. *Psychological Bulletin,* 1983, *93,* 279–301.

TEICHOLTZ, J. G. *Psychological correlates of voluntary childlessness in married women.* Paper presented at the Eastern Psychological Association, Washington, DC, 1978.

THOITS, P. Multiple identities and psychological well-being. *American Sociological Review,* 1983, *48,* 174–187.

VAILLANT, G. E. *Adaption to life.* Boston: Little, Brown, 1977.

VERBRUGGE, L. M. Women's social roles and health. In P. Berman & E. Ramey (eds.), *Women: A developmental perspective* (Publication no. 82-2298). Washington, DC: U.S. Government Printing Office, 1982.

————. *Pressures, satisfactions, and the link to physical health of young women.* Paper presented at meeting of the American Psychological Association, Anaheim, CA, 1983.

————. *Women, work, and health.* Paper presented at the symposium Health Prospects for American Women at the meeting of the American Association for the Advancement of Science. New York, May 1984.

VEROFF, J., DOUVAN, E., & KULKA, R. A. *The inner American.* New York: Basic Books, 1981.

WALDRON, I., & HEROLD, J. *Employment, attitudes toward employment and women's health.* Paper presented at Society of Behavioral Medicine, Philadelphia, 1984.

WALLERSTEIN, J., & KELLY, J. *Surviving the breakup.* New York: Basic Books, 1980.

WEISS, R. S. Men and the family. *Family Process,* 1985, *242,* 49–58.

————. Bringing work stress home. In J. Eckenrode & S. Gore (eds.), *Stress between work and family.* New York: Plenum, 1990.

WETHINGTON, E. *Employment, family role stress, and mental health: A longitudinal study.* Paper presented at the 98th annual convention of the American Psychological Association. Boston, August, 1990.

WETHINGTON, E., & KESSLER, R. C. Employment, parental responsibility, and psychological distress: A longitudinal study of married women. *Journal of Family Issues,* 1989, *10,* 527–546.

PART **VI**

COMMON PSYCHIATRIC AND SOMATIC CONDITIONS

25

Relationships of the Type A Behavior Pattern with Coronary Heart Disease

Ray H. Rosenman

THE CONCEPT OF RISK FACTORS for coronary heart disease (CHD) is well established by the consistent findings of many prospective studies. However, these statistical, epidemiological relationships do not distinguish between predictive associations and causality and, in the latter instances, do not clarify pathogenetic mechanisms. They also do not fully explain gender differences, marked historical changes of CHD rates (White, 1974), wide geographic differences in CHD prevalence, or the striking differences of CHD incidence that occur in prospective studies in different populations at similar levels of the risk factors.

Even when taken together in multivariate fashion, they account for less than half of the numerical CHD incidence in prospective studies (Gordon & Verter, 1969; Rosenman, Brand, Sholtz, & Friedman, 1976) and do not explain a much higher rate that occurs in males in the United States compared to across Europe (Keys et al., 1972). The CHD incidence in males in the Framingham Heart Study, for example, is two or more times higher than occurs in men in similar prospective studies in Yugoslavia (Kozarevic et al., 1976), Hawaii and Puerto Rico (Gordon, Garcia-Palmieri, Kagan, Kannel, & Schiffman, 1974), or Paris (Ducimetiere, Cambien, Richard, Rakotovao, & Claude, 1980). It is therefore important to emphasize that the classical risk factors provide relative but not absolute levels of risk and do not account for individual specificity of risk.

The risk factor associations also do not clarify whether they are related to coronary artery disease (CAD) or to clinical complications, including myocardial infarction and sudden cardiac death. For example, although plasma cholesterol and lipoprotein distributions are correlated with the presence of CAD, their levels do not predict its extent or severity in angiographic studies (Kramer et al., 1983; Vlietstra et al., 1980). Moreover, in subjects without angiographic CAD, the distribution of plasma cholesterol is not different from that found in the general population (Vlietstra et al., 1980). There are a number of studies of large groups of patients undergoing repeat angiography over periods of many years, but without surgical interventions, and in which angiograms were interpreted by independent experts, with a priori defined criteria for CAD progression. They consistently find that plasma cholesterol and lipoprotein levels are not related to the rate of CAD progression (Bruschke, Wijers, Kolsters, & Landmann, 1981; Kramer et al., 1983).

This discrepancy is perhaps even more striking for cigarette smoking. Its well-known association with CHD morbidity and mortality is largely due to adverse effects in patients with underlying CAD. Although strongly related to incidence of myocardial infarction and sudden cardiac death in populations with high rates of CHD, smoking is poorly related to CAD per se. This is consistent with the rapid decline of acute coronary events that is associated with cessation of smoking, regardless of the duration of the habit (Kannel & Higgins, 1990). Thus, an antecedent history of smoking is not well related to severity of CAD at necropsy (Feinleib, Kannel, Tedeschi, Landau, & Garrison, 1979; Garcia-Palmieri et al., 1977; Solberg & Strong, 1983) and, in prospective studies, is therefore not found to be related to the incidence of angina pectoris that occurs without myocardial infarction (Haynes & Feinleib, 1982; Rosenman, Brand, Sholtz, & Friedman, 1976). The incidence of such angina is due to progression of CAD, but a history of antecedent smoking is little, if at all, related to angiographic CAD severity or to the rate or extent of progression of CAD (Kramer et al., 1983; Vlietstra et al., 1980, 1983).

These considerations do not denigrate the concept of risk factors, but do clearly indicate that other factors modulate their relationships with CHD, and that supposition might explain why only certain individuals develop CHD in association with, for example, hypertension, hypercholesteremia, or smoking. Thus, it is an individual with risk factors who suffers CHD, but at highly variable levels of such factors. Moreover, a significant percentage of patients do not have elevated levels of risk factors, nor did they have habitual patterns of diet or physical activity that differed from those who remain free of the disease in prospective studies or from the surrounding population of healthy individuals. Jenkins (1988) noted that, although pathogenetic mechanisms for CAD and CHD are primarily biological, psychosocial factors comprise the contributing causes, and these are primarily behavioral.

PSYCHOSOCIAL FACTORS AND CORONARY HEART DISEASE

Considerable evidence links CHD incidence with urbanization, population densification, and industrialization (Marmot, 1982) and thus suggests that associations between risk factors and CHD incidence are strongly mediated by the ambient situation in which an individual lives and works, as well as by other psychosocial factors that characterize different individuals. This evidence has led to a search for possibly relevant psychosocial factors, among which are marital status, level of education, social class and status, social and geographic mobility and status incongruity, social network and coping support, occupational factors (including work under- and overload), life events, changes, satisfactions and dissatisfactions, emotional and occupational deprivation and loss, personality, anxiety, neuroticism, hostility/anger dimensions and other emotions, and various behaviors.

Jenkins (1976) concluded from his review of such variables that certain psychosocial factors do put individuals at higher risk, but that many of these variables are not well documented for any causal relationship with CHD. He found the most consistent evidence for certain behavioral traits. The possible role of psychosocial factors in cardiovascular reactivity, and in the pathogenesis of CAD and CHD, has since been repeatedly reviewed (Manuck & Krantz, 1986), with the most consistent evidence again found for a relationship between certain behaviors and individual specificity of risk associated with the classical risk factors. Prominent among these is the type A behavior pattern (TABP).

THE TYPE A BEHAVIOR PATTERN CONCEPT

Such considerations led to conceptualization of the TABP in the 1950s (Rosenman, 1986), along with direct observation of the behaviors of CHD patients of both sexes (Friedman & Rosenman, 1959; Rosenman & Friedman, 1961). It was later found that a relationship of several type A behaviors with CHD had long ago been recognized by Von Dusch (1868), who observed that loud vocal stylistics were a characteristic of CHD patients, and by Osler (1892), who strongly implicated hard-driving behavior when he wrote that "I believe that the high pressure at which men live, and the habit of working the machine to its maximum capacity are responsible for [arterial degeneration] rather than excesses in eating and drinking." Osler described his typical angina patient as "not the delicate, neurotic person . . . but the robust, the vigorous in mind and body, the keen and ambitious man, the indicator of whose engine is always set at full speed ahead." Some decades later, the strongly aggressive tendencies of patients with CHD had been observed by the Menningers (1936), their hard-driving and goal-directed lives by Dunbar (1943), Arlow (1945), Gildea (1949), and Gertler and White (1954), and their ambitiousness and compulsive striving to achieve goals that incorporated power and prestige by Kemple (1945). These observers gave remarkably consistent descriptions, but failed to consider an interaction of the individual with the environmental milieu. However, Stewart (1950) believed that new stress was responsible for the twentieth-century increased incidence of CHD in England. The concept of TABP recognized the interaction of an individual with the environment, and its prevalence is correlated with industrialization and Western culture (Helman, 1987; Rosenman, 1986).

TABP was originally defined as an action-emotion complex that individuals use to confront their environmental milieus and challenges. The complex involves behavioral dispositions such as aggressiveness, competitiveness, and impatience; specific behaviors such as muscle tenseness, alertness, rapid and emphatic vocal stylistics, and accelerated pace of activities; and emotional responses such as irritation, covert hostility, and above-average potential for anger (Rosenman, 1986). A large number of studies have given TABP strong construct validation, with rather consistent findings that type A individuals are more aggressive, competitive, alert, impatient, time-conscious, impatient and fast-paced, hostile, orderly, well-organized, self-confident, self-controlled, deeply involved with vocation and less able to relax away from work, not easily distracted from task performance and preferring to work alone when challenged, and striving to control their environment (Friedman & Booth-Kewley, 1988; Glass, 1977; Rosenman, Rahe, Borhani, & Feinleib, 1976).

It was originally considered that TABP does not equate with stress nor with neuroticism in the latter's usual psychological construct, since it is neither a stressor nor a distressed situation (Rosenman, Swan, & Carmelli, 1988a). This assumption has since been questioned (Byrne & Rosenman, 1986a; Suls & Wan, 1989), and it has been shown that the TABP and encounters with stressful life events are not entirely independent (Byrne & Rosenman, 1986b; Suls, 1990). A recent meta-analysis of the literature also found that TABP is positively correlated with psychological disorders (Suls & Wan, 1989). Moreover, the underlying basis for an enhanced and sometimes inappropriate type A sense of competitiveness may be a deep-seated and covert anxiety that is associated with insecurity and fear of failure and that is different from neuroticism in the latter's usual construct (Rosenman, 1990; Strube, 1987; Suls, 1990). This suggestion is highly relevant, since enhanced behavioral competitiveness probably has the seminal importance for such other type A behaviors as aggressive drive, accelerated pace of activities, and potential for hostility/anger dimensions, while the latter are merely the overt manifestations of TABP (Rosenman, 1990).

Individuals who generally do not exhibit most type A behaviors are called type B. However, type Bs are not only characterized by the relative absence of type a behaviors— being less aggressive, and more relaxed and easy-going—but they have a different style of coping with their environments that does not often lead to impatient and fast-paced type A behaviors or to inappropriate competitive and hostile/angry responses.

TABP: DEMOGRAPHIC, ANTECEDENT, ASSESSMENT, AND INTERVENTION ISSUES

TABP prevalence is higher in industrialized areas than in more relaxed ones, in males than females, in white than in black populations, in white than in blue collar workers, and is less prevalent in youth not in occupational milieus, and shows some correlations with levels of education, social class, occupational status, and career advancement and achievement (Rosenman & Chesney, 1980). However, earlier differential relationships of TABP prevalence may be undergoing changes, with increasing prevalence in gainfully employed females and male blue collar workers.

The initial finding of little genetic variance for global TABP, albeit modest genetic variance for some type A behaviors (Rosenman, Rahe, et al., 1976), has been confirmed in later studies (Carmelli et al., 1988).

TABP is partly a learned behavior that reflects parental attitudes, behaviors, and performance standards for offspring (Matthews & Saal, 1978), with an expected familial similarity between parent and child. There may be higher TABP prevalence in children of parents with higher levels of education and occupational status (Matthews & Saal, 1978) and in children in urban rather than in rural areas. Although there may be childhood origins (Matthews, 1978), cultural factors and interactions with the environment play a dominant role in the pattern's development and emergence (Cohen, 1978). TABP has been found to have highly significant stability over time (Carmelli, Rosenman, & Chesney, 1987).

A structured interview (SI) was developed for assessment of TABP in the Western Collaborative Group Study (Rosenman et al., 1964). The SI was designed to provide a suitable challenge setting in which to assess an individual's response style and behaviors during the interview (Rosenman, 1978). The details of this methodology are described elsewhere (Rosenman, 1978, 1986). Since the SI requires training in its administration and assessment, there has been a search to find a self-report psychometric method for assessment (Byrne, Rosenman, Schiller, & Chesney, 1985; Rosenman, 1986). Although strong construct validation for TABP is provided by correlations with various psychometric measures, particularly with the Adjective Check List of Gough and Heilbrun and the Activity Scale of the Thurstone Temperament Schedule (Rosenman, Rahe, et al., 1976; Swan, Carmelli, & Rosenman, 1990), inherent bias and other errors of self-appraisal markedly limit the ability of self-report questionnaires to substitute for the SI (Carmelli, Swan, & Rosenman, 1990).

Another assessment approach was the attempt to develop questionnaires that more or less duplicate the SI. These include the Jenkins Activity Survey (Jenkins, Zyzanski, & Rosenman, 1979), the Bortner Scale (Bortner, 1969), and the Framingham Type A Scale (Haynes, Levine, & Scotch, 1978). These self-report measures exhibit only modest correlations among themselves and with the SI because they assess different behavioral characteristics and are largely concerned with individual perception of attitudes, attributes, and activities (Byrne et al., 1985). In addition to content-dependent items, the important psychological differences among self-report measures (Smith, Houston, & Zurawski, 1983) limit their generalizability across diverse cultures and populations. This constraint is emphasized by the lack of correlation between the content of answers and observed behaviors during the SI (Hecker, Chesney, Black, & Rosenman, 1981; Scherwitz, Berton, & Leventhal, 1977). Moreover, self-reports do not capture the stylistics and psychomotor behaviors that are essential to the construct and assessment of TABP (Byrne et al., 1985; Rosenman, 1978; Rosenman et al., 1988a) and are particularly unsuitable for assessment of TABP in individuals.

Trained observers capture the actual type A behaviors in the SI and, since this is a challenge type of interview, it extends the breadth and scope of assessment to far more closely fit the construct that portrays TABP as a set of overt behaviors that particularly occur in association with and in response to relevant situational stressors (Byrne et al., 1985; Rosenman, Swan, & Carmelli, 1988a). The SI also is far less likely to be influenced by occupational and other characteristics than are self-report measures of attitudes and values. Finally, the SI has been found to have much stronger predictive relationships with CAD and CHD compared to self-report measures (Booth-Kewley & Friedman, 1987).

In trained hands, the SI provides assessments with remarkably high inter-rater agreement (Rosenman et al., 1988a). Although the stability among self-report measures is also significant, it is greater than between the self-reports and the SI. There has been an attempt to quantitatively score the behaviors during a videotaped SI (Friedman & Powell, 1984) in order to provide a continuous scale. However, this method has not been well validated by other investigators. It purports to observe and score the behaviors that are exhibited independent of interviewer challenges, but the challenging and provocative circumstances of life in general, and of the SI in particular, elicit the TABP (Byrne et al., 1985; Rosenman, 1978). The methods developed to assess TABP in children and adolescents are discussed elsewhere (Rosenman et al., 1988a).

Issues concerned with pharmacological and behavioral interventions on TABP are discussed elsewhere (Levenkron & Moore, 1988; Price, 1988; Rosenman, 1983; Rosenman & Friedman, 1977; Roskies, 1987).

TYPE A BEHAVIOR PATTERN AND CORONARY HEART DISEASE

TABP was found to be related to the prevalence of CHD in both male (Friedman & Rosenman, 1959) and female subjects (Rosenman & Friedman, 1961), and this was confirmed in other populations (Kornitzer, Kittel, & De Backer, 1981; Rosenman & Chesney, 1980). The prospective relationship of TABP to CHD was then assessed in the Western Collaborative Group Study (WCGS), which is a study of 3,154 initially well males who were employed in 10 participating California companies and were aged 39 to 59 years at intake in 1960–1961. The methodology and intake findings have been described elsewhere (Rosenman et al., 1964). In the WCGS, TABP was found to be independently associated with a significantly higher incidence of initial CHD during 8.5 years of follow-up (Rosenman, Brand, et al., 1976).

This association was also found in large prospective studies in Belgium (De Backer, Kornitzer, & Kittel, 1983), in the French-Belgium Collaborative Group study (1982), and in the Framingham Heart Study (Eaker, Abbott, & Kannel, 1989; Haynes & Feinleib, 1982). Several later studies did not find TABP predictively related to CHD incidence (Cohen & Reed, 1985; Dembroski, MacDougall, Costa, & Grandits, 1989; Shekelle et al., 1985). However, the Honolulu study (Cohen & Reed, 1985) assessed TABP with a self-report questionnaire, now recognized to be inadequate for the purpose (Byrne et al., 1985), and negative findings in the analysis by Dembroski et al. (1989) are contradictory. Thus, their SI assessments found type A behavioral hostility, but not global type A, to be predictively related to CHD incidence. The validity of the assessments of global TABP in this study must therefore be questioned, because the measure used for scoring behavioral hostility in the SI (Dembroski, MacDougall, Shields, Pettito, & Lushene, 1978) is strongly based on this component being a cardinal manifestation of global TABP (Rosenman, 1985, 1990; Rosenman, Swan, & Carmelli, 1988a).

The relationship between TABP and primary CHD was reviewed (Matthews & Haynes, 1986), and Haynes and Matthews (1988) pointed out that the later negative studies were performed in years in which a decline of CHD mortality had occurred and in which there was widespread use of protective beta-adrenergic blockers for treatment of hypertension and CHD. These two researchers also observed that many negative studies had small sample sizes, bias in distribution of type A and B subjects, drift in SI assessments (Scherwitz, Graham, Grandits, Buehler, & Billings, 1986), age-related temporal changes of TABP in the direction of type B (Howard, Cunningham, & Rechnitzer, 1976), and low CHD rates in association with classical risk factors. Meta-analysis has been used in reviewing the literature to assess the role of TABP and other psychosocial variables with CHD. These studies found the strongest association for TABP particularly in cross-sectional population studies, rather than in intervention studies (Booth-Kewley & Friedman, 1987; Matthews, 1988). This difference is important, since intervention studies are flawed by selection bias and other problems (Rosenman, 1990).

Volunteers for CHD risk screening programs are thus biased by health consciousness (Edye, Mandryk, Frommer, Healey, & Ferguson, 1989; Gill et al., 1989) and are more often the "worried well," who have risk factors and no disease (Criqui, Austin, & Barrett-Connor, 1979). Dropouts may more often be smokers and in blue collar occupations (Oldridge et al., 1982), and CHD incidence is much higher in dropouts than in those remaining in intervention studies (Bruce, Frederick, Bruce, & Fisher, 1976). Moreover, results of such studies are applicable only to those who participated and are not representative of other populations (Werko, 1976). The problem of prospective intervention studies is particularly well shown by the low rate of CHD that occurs in association with the classical risk factors in such studies, as exemplified in the control subjects in the Multiple Risk Factor Trial Research Group's (1982) Intervention Trial.

A number of studies have found that TABP is predictively related to recurring coronary events and outcome from an initial myocardial infarction (Brackett & Powell, 1988; Jenkins, Zyzanski, & Rosenman, 1976; Jenkins, Zyzanski, Rosenman, & Cleveland, 1971; Rosenman, Friedman, Jenkins, Straus, & Kositchek, 1967). Conversely, other studies have not found TABP to be predictive of such outcomes (Case, Heller, Case, & Moss, 1985; De Leo et al., 1986; Dimsdale, Gilbert, Hutter, Hackett, & Block, 1981; Eaker & Castelli, 1988; Friedman et al., 1986; Ragland & Brand, 1988; Shekelle, Gale, & Norusis, 1985). Some of the negative studies used measures known to assess TABP poorly (Byrne et al., 1985). The study by Case et al. (1985) was strongly criticized for this flaw (Abbott, Peters, & Vogel, 1985), because the self-report measure was given to many acutely ill patients soon after an acute myocardial infarction and because a higher mortality occurred in those who did not complete the questionnaire (Oakes, 1985). The study purportedly found that TABP was not a postinfarction survival risk factor, while finding that the amount of myocardial damage was the predominant survival factor. This study was also criticized because type As with more damage and associated problems would under-rate their TABP on a self-report (Halperin & Littman, 1985). Moreover, it was pointed out (Pickering, 1985a) that the risk factors for postinfarction survival are different from those for first infarction, since they consist of factors that reflect the amount of myocardial damage and ischemia and not the primary risk factors for first infarction, as was found by the Multicenter Postinfarction Research Group (1983). In fact, Case et al. (1985) did not find the primary risk factors to predict survival.

During the past few years, an extensive 27-year follow-up was done in all participants in the WCGS (Rosenman et al., 1964). It has been found that, after multivariate adjustment for other risk factors, the intake assessment of TABP remained a significant and independent predictor of the prevalence of myocardial infarction in the long-term survivors in this prospective study (Rosenman et al., submitted for publication).

The relationship between TABP and CAD also has been assessed. A number of studies have found TABP to be independently related to the severity of CAD (Blumenthal, Williams, Kong, Schanberg, & Thompson, 1978; Derby & Pearson, 1989; Frank, Heller, Kornfeld, Sporn, & Weiss, 1978; Friedman, Rosenman, Straus, Wurm, & Kositchek, 1968; Krantz, Sanmarco, Selvester, & Matthews, 1979; Williams, Haney, & Lee, 1980; Williams et al., 1988; Zyzanski, Jenkins, Ryan, Flessas, & Everist, 1976). Conversely, TABP was not predictive of CAD in other studies (Dembroski et al., 1985; Dimsdale et al., 1978, 1979; Kornitzer et al., 1982; MacDougall, Dembroski, Dimsdale, & Hackett, 1985; Scherwitz et al., 1983). The studies by Dembroski et al. (1985) and MacDougall et al. (1985) again appear to be contradictory, because they found type A behavioral hostility, but not global type A, to be related to severity of CAD—a conflict because such behavioral hostility is a major facet of TABP (Rosenman, 1985; Rosenman et al., 1988a).

It has been pointed out that angiography studies cannot properly evaluate the role of behavioral risk factors for CHD because of selection bias in patients referred for evaluation (Derby & Pearson, 1989; Pearson, Gordis, Achuff, Bulkley, & Kwiterovich, 1982), lack of normal control subjects, use of different methodologies, poor correlation of CAD with all risk factors (Bruschke et al., 1981; Kramer et al., 1983), small sample sizes, and lack of appropriate end points (Booth-Kewley & Friedman, 1987; Haynes & Matthews, 1988; Pickering, 1985b). Moreover, subjects suspected of having CAD, but not confirmed at angiography, have higher prevalence of risk factors than do those without suspected CAD (Pearson et al., 1982). The problem of small sample size is exemplified by the final analysis of 2,289 patients referred for diagnostic angiography at Duke University (Williams et al., 1988). In this large population, a relationship of TABP to severity of CAD was confirmed, particularly at younger ages. The authors emphasized that prior negative studies were flawed by small sample sizes and age spans, and by use of inadequate self-report assessments of TABP. Such flaws are illustrated by one negative study (Helmer, Ragland, & Syme, 1990), in which a small number of subjects was studied, the interpretation of angiograms was not validated, and a simplistic, untested method was used purportedly to assess hostility.

Overall, it would appear that TABP is an independent risk factor for CAD, particularly at younger ages, and for the incidence of initial myocardial infarction and less so for the outcome and mortality from primary coronary events. However, some studies have related TABP far more to fatal CHD events than to CHD morbidity (Appels & Mulder, 1985) and suggest that it may be particularly related to precipitation of initial CHD events (Matthews, 1988).

HOSTILITY/ANGER DIMENSIONS AND CORONARY HEART DISEASE

A higher CHD incidence is strongly associated with urbanization and population density in the industrialized Western world, and this environment provides a stimulus for the enhanced competitiveness that underlies TABP in susceptible individuals (Rosenman, 1990). However, this competitiveness may be partly inappropriate because it is not an evolutionary development. Montagu (1976) thus points out that the drive for preservation of species and self leads to a type of competitiveness and aggression that is common to animals and humans and that is biologically adaptive, life-serving, and phylogenetically programmed, while many other forms of aggression are biologically maladaptive and arise mainly out of the human experience, since they are only found in humans. Montagu also emphasizes that the principal factor operating in animal evolution is cooperation, rather than the divisiveness, inappropriate aggression, competitiveness, and hostility that characterize the human experience and that are exemplified by coronary-prone facets of TABP (Rosenman, 1985).

Megargee (1985) noted that medical researchers who attempt to relate dimensions of anger, hostility, or aggression to cardiovascular disease may operationally define different constructs by using a confusing array of dissimilar techniques in their studies and often by using them interchangeably, without appropriate differentiation. However, he and other psychologists point out that there is considerable ambiguity and inconsistency with regard to how these constructs are defined, separated, or overlap and that there is even less agreement on how they are measured (Megargee, 1985; Spielberger et al., 1985; Treiber et al., 1989).

For example, hostility in the SI refers to a potential for hostility (Costa, McCrae, & Dembroski, 1989) that reflects an antagonistic interpersonal style rather than intrapsychic affect (Dembroski & Costa, 1987; Suls, 1990; Suls & Wan, 1989). This potential is strongly correlated with high expression of hostile or angry behaviors, but not with feelings of resentment, guilt, or mistrust (Musante, MacDougall, Dembroski, & Costa, 1989; Siegman, 1989; Siegman, Dembroski, & Ringel, 1987). These personality dimensions are independent (Costa et al., 1989), and type As, with high potential for hostility, do not often exhibit the neurotic hostility that is highly related to anxiety, characterized by feelings of annoyance, resentment, or rage (Suls & Wan, 1989). The importance of their differentiation is exemplified by the finding that severity of coronary artery disease may be positively correlated with the expression of hostility, but negatively with feelings of hostility (Siegman, 1989).

TABP has diverse behavioral components that include an enhanced potential for hostility (Rosenman, 1978, 1990), and it is now popular to focus on this component (Dembroski & Costa, 1987; Diamond, 1982; Williams, Barefoot, & Shekelle, 1985). An initial impetus was given by the finding that type A behavioral hostility, assessed from the SI (Rosenman, 1978), was significantly related to intake prevalence of silent myocardial infarction in the WCGS (Jenkins, Rosenman, & Friedman, 1966). Psychometric hostility items and scales are found to discriminate type A/B behaviors (Rosenman, Rahe, et al., 1976). Bortner later compared WCGS intake interviews of subjects who developed CHD during follow-up with paired control subjects who remained free of CHD, and his blind analysis found competitive drive, impatience, and potential for hostility to be the most important predictive, coronary-prone type A behaviors (Matthews, Glass, Rosenman, & Bortner, 1977).

A recent, different method of component scoring of the intake SIs in the WCGS confirmed a relationship of competitiveness and hostility to the CHD incidence that occurred during the first 8.5 years of follow-up (Hecker, Chesney, Black, & Frautschi, 1988). The role of such type A behavioral hostility as a risk factor for CAD and CHD has also been confirmed in studies that use another method of scoring the type A hostility component in the SI (Dembroski & Costa, 1987; Dembroski et al., 1989).

The hostility concept has been popularized by follow-up studies of subjects who were generally given the MMPI for other purposes, often when the subjects were students. Type A behavioral hostility is correlated with higher cardiovascular reactivity (Contrada & Krantz, 1988; Dembroski et al., 1978), and higher scores on the Cook and Medley Ho Scale (1954) of the MMPI may also be correlated with heightened reactivity (Hardy & Smith, 1988), but mainly for systolic pressor responses (Diamond et al., 1984; Steptoe, Melville, & Ross, 1984).

However, many studies have not found relationships between Ho Scale scores and cardiovascular reactivity (Houston, 1986; Manuck, Proietti, Rader, & Polefrone, 1985; Sallis, Johnson, Trevorrow, Kaplan, & Hovell, 1987; Smith & Frohm, 1985) except when subjects were harassed during testing (Suarez, Williams, & McRae, 1988). Although higher scores were associated with higher blood pressure reactivity and more anger response to tasks in another study, anger per se was not associated with reactivity (Weidner, Friend, Figarrotto, & Mendell, 1989). Reactivity studies have long been popular, but are unlikely to explain the pathogenesis of either CAD or CHD.

The Ho Scale was believed to be predictively related to the CHD incidence in a 25-year follow-up of 255 physicians who took the MMPI as students (Barefoot, Dahlstrom, & Williams, 1983) and in a 10-year follow-up of 1,877 men (Shekelle, Gale, Ostfeld, & Paul, 1983). However, in the first instance (Barefoot et al., 1983), the CHD incidence was not linearly related to Ho scores above the cutoff point, below which scores were not related to CHD. In the second instance (Shekelle et al., 1983), Ho Scale scores were not linearly related. Although the lowest CHD rates occurred in those with lowest scores and highest rates in those with middle range scores, the CHD rates were intermediate in those in the higher score quintiles.

Moreover, a relationship of Ho Scale scores was not found with incidence of CHD or with mortality from CHD or other causes in a 33-year follow-up of 1,399 university students (Hearn, Murray, & Luepke, 1989), in a 3-year follow-up of a large population of healthy, middle-aged Finnish men (Koskenvuo, Kaprio, & Rose, 1988), in a 25-year follow-up of 478 medical students (McCranie, Watkins, Brandsma, & Sisson, 1986), in a large Japanese study (Matsushima, Doba, Hinohara, Williams, & Shinoda, 1983) or in other studies (Leon, Murray, Finn, Bailey, & Castelli, 1988). In the Finnish study, Ho scores were related to CHD morbidity and mortality only in subjects with intake hypertension and CHD, thus being related only to the precipitation of acute coronary events in subjects with antecedent CAD.

Angiographic severity of CAD was found to be related to type A behavioral hostility (Dembroski et al., 1985; Siegman et al., 1987; Williams et al., 1980, 1988) and to Ho scores by its proponents (Williams et al., 1980, 1988). However, most other investigators have not found Ho scores to be related to CAD severity (Helmer et al., 1990; Matsushima et al., 1983; Tennant, Langeluddecke, Fulcher, & Wilby, 1987), whether or not subjects had CHD (Matsushima et al., 1983).

The serious problems with anger/hostility constructs (Megargee, 1985; Spielberger et al., 1985; Treiber et al., 1989) may particularly be relevant to the Cook and Medley Ho Scale (Sallis et al., 1987). Early correlations of this scale with behavioral hostility were made in teachers, adults convicted of violent crimes, and suicidal out-patients, and do not generalize to the normal population (Swan, Carmelli, & Rosenman, 1990). Some correlations have been found for the Ho Scale with anger (Blumenthal, Barefoot, Burg, & Williams, 1987; Costa, Zonderman, McCrae, & Williams, 1986; Hardy & Smith, 1988; Smith, Allred, & Frohm, 1988), social supports (Barefoot et al., 1983), social maladjustment (Blumenthal et al., 1987), psychosocial and physical distress (Watkins, Fisher, Southard, & Ward, 1988), ineffective coping style (Blumenthal et al., 1987), cynicism (Hardy & Smith, 1988), and mistrust (Costa, Zonderman, McCrae, & Williams, 1986; Hardy & Smith, 1988; Smith & Allred, 1989), and the term, *cynical mistrust* was coined to describe what is assessed by the Ho Scale (Smith et al. 1988).

The Ho Scale measures neuroticism and general psychopathology (Costa et al., 1986; Megargee, 1985; Smith & Allred, 1989; Swan et al., 1990) but is not found to be a reliable measure of hostility (Barefoot et al., 1983; Megargee, 1985; Shipman, 1965) or overtly aggressive behavior (Smith et al., 1988), and it is negatively correlated with MMPI and other psychometric measures of hostility and paranoia (Megargee, 1985; Rosenman et al., 1988b; Swan et al., 1990). Megargee (1985) authoritatively states that "Most distressing is the failure of Ho to measure hostility. All in all, the evidence for the construct validity of the Ho Scale is minimal. Thirty years after its derivation it is difficult to say with any confidence what Ho measures."

Type A behavioral hostility is not associated with psychopathology (Rosenman, Rahe, et al., 1976; Swan et al., 1990) and is not significantly related to the Ho Scale, with which it shares only a small part of its variance (Dembroski et al., 1985; Swan et al., 1990). There also is no significant association between type A behavioral hostility and Ho (Dembroski et al., 1985; Swan et al., 1990; Williams et al., 1980), whereas TABP is correlated with psychometric measures of tolerance, vigor, self-confidence, achievement via independence, and dominance (Rosenman, Rahe, et al., 1976; Swan et al., 1990). The psychological characteristic with the strongest association with Ho is the MMPI scale that measures social desirability, and high Ho scores characterize neurotic persons with attributes related to psychopathology (Megargee, 1985; Swan et al., 1990).

TABP is not a predictor of general illness (Suls & Sanders, 1988; Woods & Burns, 1984) nor of all cause mortality (Yakubovich, Ragland, Brand, & Syme, 1988). Studies in which Ho "predicted" CAD or CHD infer that this scale shows a causal relationship of hostility (Barefoot et al., 1983; Shekelle et al., 1983). However, Ho Scale scores were similarly related to cancer and to all-cause mortality in the two studies that purportedly found it to be related to CHD mortality. Aside from the fact that the Ho Scale was not found to predict either incidence of CHD or severity of CAD in most studies, the negative studies also found no relationship of the Ho Scale to all-cause mortality (Hearn et al., 1989; Leon et al., 1988; McCranie et al., 1986).

In studies by proponents of Ho (Barefoot et al., 1983; Shekelle et al., 1983), it would clearly appear that the Ho Scale only spuriously predicts CHD (Rosenman, 1990). Because it similarly predicts mortality from cancer, CHD, and all causes, a predictive relationship with CHD is not causal. The leading causes of death are CHD and cancer, hence a scale that predicts all-cause mortality does not actually predict or have a specific causal relationship with CHD mortality.

These findings strongly suggest that the Ho Scale is a measure of psychopathology that, in turn, is associated with an increased all-cause mortality. At best, the psychopathology measured by the Ho Scale may be related to the precipitation of fatal coronary events in persons with underlying CAD, as found in the Finnish Study (Koskenvuo et al., 1988), and may be consistent with the relationship of other measures of "suspiciousness" to cardiovascular mortality (Barefoot et al., 1987). An increased mortality from all causes may be related to low level of social support (Barefoot et al., 1987; Berkman & Syme, 1979), psychological distress (Appels, Mulder, & Hoppener, 1989; Menotti et al., 1983; Ruberman, Weinblatt, Goldberg, & Chaudbary, 1984; Somervell et al., 1989), and anger variables (Julius, Harburg, Cottington, & Johnson, 1986), although the number of life events during a year may be inversely related to total mortality that occurs in the following year (Hollis, Connett, Stevens, & Greenlick, 1990).

The variables associated with increased all-cause mortality are among those reflected by Ho Scale scores (Swan et al., 1990). Moreover, although Ho is strongly correlated with neurosis and psychopathology, little data show an association of psychopathology with increased CHD incidence. Conversely, the anxiety and neuroticism that are measured by the Ho Scale are not causally related either to CAD or CHD (Costa, 1986; Lantinga et al., 1988). It would appear that proponents of the Ho Scale have improperly used it to support their belief in hostility as the toxic behavior that relates TABP to CHD. In fact, the proponents continue to assume that Ho measures hostility (Williams, 1987), even though their own studies show that this is not the case (Barefoot et al., 1983).

In contrast to an ill-defined hostility construct, an enhanced and inappropriate type A competitiveness strongly looms as the toxic factor in TABP (Booth-Kewley & Friedman, 1987) because it appears to have seminal importance for type A aggressive drive, accelerated pace of activities, impatience, and hostility/anger dimensions (Rosenman, 1990). The importance of this factor is reflected by the higher incidence of CHD that occurred during follow-up in the WCGS in married type A men who had competitive relationships with their spouses (Carmelli, Swan, & Rosenman, 1985; Swan, Carmelli, & Rosenman, 1986). However, it is very unlikely that intercorrelated emotional and behavioral aspects of a human being can ever satisfactorily be subdivided into single component parts such as "hostility" (Rosenman, 1990).

CAUSAL RELATIONSHIPS OF TYPE A BEHAVIOR PATTERN AND CORONARY HEART DISEASE

The relationships of TABP with CHD raise issues of possible pathogenetic mechanisms. TABP's risk for CHD may be associated with inappropriate or low coping skills (Glass, 1977; Helman, 1987; Vickers, Hervig, Rahe, & Rosenman, 1981) or a depressive response that is termed "vital exhaustion" (Appels et al., 1989; Falger, 1989).

One pathway may be an influence of TABP on other risk factors. However, the relationship of TABP to CHD incidence appears to be largely independent of its associations with the classical risk factors (Rosenman, Brand, et al., 1976). The autonomic nervous system is strongly involved in responses to emotions, stress, and cigarette smoking and in cardiovascular reactivity, hypertension, regulation of serum lipids, coronary atherogenesis, and the clinical complications of CAD.

Sympathetic neural activity plays an under-rated role in regulating serum cholesterol (Howes, Krum, & Louis, 1987; Rosenman, 1989) and, therefore, in the variability that occurs in response to emotional arousal (Dimsdale & Herd, 1982; Friedman, Rosenman, & Carroll, 1958; Groen, Tjiong, Kamminger, & Willebrands, 1962; Grundy & Griffin, 1959; Jenkins, Hames, Zyzanski, Rosenman, & Friedman, 1969; O'Donnell et al., 1987). Compared to type Bs, type A persons of both sexes tend to have higher serum cholesterol levels (Rosenman & Friedman, 1974), particularly those who are also high on hostility dimensions (Weidner, Sexton McLelland, Connor, & Matarazzo, 1987), and correlations of anger dimensions with serum cholesterol have been found (Lundberg, Hedman, Melin, & Frankenhaeuser, 1989).

There is considerable evidence of an important role of the sympathetic nervous system in hypertension. Borderline hypertensives tend to have an elevated cardiac output and, relative to this, their peripheral vascular resistance is inappropriately normal. The cardiac output remains essentially unchanged across the spectrum of established mild to severe hypertension, and age-related increases of sympathetic neural activity and of peripheral vascular resistance may underlie the hemodynamic transition from borderline to established hypertension. Older established hypertensives thus tend to have lower cardiac output, heart rate, and stroke volume and higher renal and total peripheral vascular resistance (Egan & Schmouder, 1988; Messerli et al., 1983).

In the person who develops hypertension with high cardiac output, later increased peripheral resistance is a secondary result of hypertension, rather than its primary cause, and structural vascular wall changes may be largely responsible for the hemodynamic shift (Folkow, 1990; Julius, 1988a). It is possible that repetitive heightened pressor elevations in stress responses or delay in return to baseline might enhance structural damage in resistance vessels and thereby contribute to the hemodynamic transition from borderline to sustained hypertension (Bevan & Tsuru, 1981; Folkow, 1990).

Various anger/hostility dimensions have been related to increased variability of the blood pressure during ambulatory monitoring in the natural environment (Harshfield, Pickering, Yee, & Marion, 1985), and type As with higher potential for hostility/anger dimensions (Rosenman, 1985) may have heightened blood pressure variability that also contributes to structural vascular wall changes that relate to CAD.

Since heightened noradrenergic responses are often exhibited by type As during competitive, cognitive challenges in the laboratory setting (Friedman, Byers, Diamant, & Rosenman, 1975) as well as in the natural environment (Friedman, St. George, Byers, & Rosenman, 1960), a relationship of TABP with hypertension might a priori be suspected. A large number of studies have measured cardiovascular reactivity in type A and B subjects (Glass & Contrada, 1984; Houston, 1983; Manuck & Krantz, 1986; Rosenman & Chesney, 1980). In general, during exposure to a wide variety of stressors in the laboratory setting, differences in catecholamine and cardiovascular responses have often been found in type A and B subjects (Manuck & Krantz, 1986), the largest occurring when subjects are challenged to perform more difficult tasks in a competitive manner under time pressure (Rosenman, 1987; Ward et al., 1986). However, the pattern and the lack of consistency of these differences in many studies strongly suggest that type A and B persons do not have any intrinsic differences of reactivity, but only that highly competitive type As may have a heightened perception of relevant stressors that are found to be challenging. That perception, in turn, induces a more active coping style that is known to increase noradrenergic responses (Light, 1981).

Regardless of this coping style and their greater potential for hostility/anger dimensions, neither type As in general nor those with heightened cardiovascular reactivity exhibit either higher resting blood pressure levels or prevalence of sustained hypertension compared to type Bs (Rosenman, 1987, 1991).

Thromboxane A2 is a platelet aggregating agent and vasoconstrictor that plays an important role in unstable angina, thrombus formation, acute myocardial infarction, and sudden cardiac death (Freiherr, 1988). The local stimulus for platelet deposition is a breach of endothelium and, when a crack, rupture, or ulceration occurs in an atherosclerotic plaque, increased platelet accumulation may lead to vasoconstriction, thrombosis (Lam, Chesebro, & Steele, 1987), and myocardial infarction (Gertz, Uretsky, Wainberg, Navot, & Gottsman, 1981).

The endothelium is involved in determining the state of vascular smooth muscle contractility (Furchgott, 1983), and local mechanisms involved in endothelial dysfunction or denudation are activated when brain centers increase noradrenergic outflow during mental arousal, exposure to cold, and physical exercise (Crea et al., 1985). In subjects with CAD, anger may stimulate noradrenergic activity that triggers a fissure or rupture of an atherosclerotic plaque, which is the primary cause of acute transmural myocardial infarction and which also plays an important role in crescendo angina and sudden cardiac death (Davies

& Thomas, 1985). Anger also can trigger silent myocardial ischemia (Rozanski et al., 1988) and increase cigarette consumption with additive effects, and there is a high proportion of smokers in patients with vasospastic angina (Maseri et al., 1978). Compared to type B subjects, type As have a higher prevalence of smoking (Jenkins, Zyzanski, & Rosenman, 1973).

Smoking stimulates central noradrenergic activity, and its effects are caused by peripheral release of norepinephrine. Smoking induces coronary vasoconstriction in patients with CAD or variant angina (Winniford, Wheelan, & Kremers, 1986) and sometimes even in asymptomatic subjects without CAD (Brodsky, Sato, Iseri, Wolf, & Allen, 1987) because of a noradrenergically mediated increase in vascular resistance (Winniford et al., 1986) that acutely alters the ability of coronary vasculature to regulate blood flow in accordance with myocardial metabolic oxygen needs (Martin et al., 1984). Thus, smoking reduces coronary reserve and increases the potential for myocardial ischemia and cardiac arrhythmias. Smoking increases platelet aggregability and potentiates platelet responses to other aggregating agents (Nowak, Murray, Oates, & Fitzgerald, 1987) and, thereby, plays a potential role in thrombosis (Meade, 1987).

Proliferation of smooth muscle and deposition of cholesterol and calcium produce a focal atherosclerotic injury that propagates itself and enhances local sensitivity to vasoconstrictor mediators in a pattern that may help to explain the progression of CAD (Bove, 1986). Endothelial dysfunction or denudation that results from hemodynamic injury and metabolic effects can elicit a sequence of responses in the vessel wall that leads to progression of the atherosclerotic plaque (Nyrop & Zweifler, 1988; Ross, 1986; Selwyn & Ganz, 1988). Platelets and smooth muscle cells have many similarities, which include catecholamine receptors (Nyrop & Zweifler, 1988). Platelets that adhere to subendothelial tissues in areas of endothelial cell desquamation release a mitogenic factor that stimulates proliferation of intimal smooth muscle and collagen organization of platelet-fibrin thrombi (Fuster, Chesebro, Frye, & Elveback, 1981) that are both involved in atherogenesis. Endothelial injury and smooth muscle proliferation are thus important for coronary atherogenesis (Lown & DeSilva, 1980). Plasma fibrinogen also is assuming increased importance in CHD (Wilhelmsen, Svardsudd & Korsan-Bengsten, 1984) and is increasing by smoking (Meade, Brozovic, & Chakrabarti, 1986).

The rate of progression and severity of coronary atherogenesis are strongly related to silent myocardial ischemia (Lown & DeSilva, 1980; Moise et al., 1983); this finding at least partly explains the episodic nature of the disease's progression (Selwyn et al., 1985). The sympathetic nervous system plays an important role in platelet function and aggregation, and its activity may be enhanced in type A subjects (Simpson et al., 1974). Among subjects with CAD, type As also may experience more frequent occurrence of silent myocardial ischemia, at least during exercise (Siegel et al., 1989).

TABP may variously be related by such mechanisms to CAD progression and to the precipitation of acute coronary events in subjects with CAD. Considerable evidence indicates that sudden cardiac death from ventricular fibrillation can be triggered by behavioral and autonomic neural factors (Brackett & Powell, 1988; Brodsky et al., 1987; Lown, 1987; Reich, DeSilva, Lown, & Murawski, 1981; Skinner, 1985). Psychological stressors and augmented noradrenergic traffic to the myocardium can induce ventricular arrhythmias, lower the fibrillatory threshold, and, in ischemic myocardium, precipitate ventricular fibrillation (Brodsky et al., 1987; Lown, 1987; Skinner, 1985). Psychological stress is thus related to sudden arrhythmic death (Brackett & Powell, 1988; Brodsky et al., 1987; Reich et al., 1981). Type As have increased sympathetic neural responses to environmental stress (Dembroski et al., 1978; Glass & Contrada, 1984; Rosenman, 1989) and, in those with CHD, there is reported to be increased ventricular ectopy (Jennings & Follansbee, 1984) and sudden cardiac death (Brackett & Powell, 1988). Moreover, psychological stress can trigger noradrenergically induced coronary vasoconstriction and silent myocardial ischemia in patients with CAD (Rozanski et al., 1988), even in the absence of CAD (Brodsky et al., 1987).

Although the mechanisms that relate TABP to CAD and to CHD have not been clarified, there is good reason to suspect an important role of heightened noradrenergic activity. Type As often exhibit this type of activity in daily life (DeQuattro, 1989; Friedman, St. George, Byers, & Rosenman, 1960; Kahn et al., 1987; Schneider et al., 1987; Simpson et al., 1974) and particularly during competitive situations (Dembroski et al., 1978; DeQuattro, Loo, & Foti, 1985; Rosenman & Friedman, 1974). It is possible that increased sympathetic nervous system activity may be a final common pathway that causally relates most nutritional, environmental, and pathophysiological risk factors to the development and progression of CAD (Rosenman, 1989; Young & Landsberg, 1977a, 1977b).

THE POSSIBLE ROLE OF CARDIOVASCULAR REACTIVITY

There are many reasons why cardiovascular reactivity does not play a causal role in the pathogenesis of hypertension (Rosenman, 1991; Rosenman & Ward, 1988). Moreover, reactivity studies have played a very limited role in providing evidence for the importance of behavioral factors in hypertension (Pickering & Gerin, 1990). The specificity of heightened cardiovascular responses in hypertensives to mental stressors may be found in a subset of borderline hypertensives, but Julius (1987) believes that this finding is improperly interpreted to mean that behaviorally induced blood pressure reactivity is the mechanism by which sustained hypertension develops. Among many reasons for this conclusion is the fact that blood pressure regulation in hypertension is normal (Julius, 1988b) and that basal and reactive blood pressure responses have largely independent central regulatory mechanisms (Reis & LeDoux, 1987).

Nevertheless, prominent among psychophysiologists is the belief that an important aspect of TABP may reside in its association with heightened cardiovascular reactivity (Dembroski et al., 1978; Williams et al., 1982) and that the latter is causally related to CAD as well as to hypertension (Manuck & Krantz, 1986; Steptoe et al., 1984). However, although both the mean blood pressure level and its variability in the natural environment are related to cardiovascular structural damage and target organ damage in hypertensives (Kannel, Sorlie, & Gordon, 1980; Palatini et al., 1985; Parati, Pomidossi, Albini, Malaspina, & Mancia, 1987; Sokolow, Werdegar, Kain, & Hinman, 1966), cardiovascular reactivity has not been found to have any relationship to the severity of CAD (Krantz et al., 1981; Schiffer, Hartley, Schuman, & Abelmann, 1976). As with hypertension, reactive pressor responses do not appear to be causally related to CAD or significantly to its complications. Indeed, the concept of cardiovascular reactivity appears to require a change in favor of viewing pressor responses as physiological and homeostatically normal (Rosenman & Ward, 1988).

REFERENCES

ABOTT, A. V., & VOGEL, M. Letter to editor. *New England Journal of Medicine,* 1985, *312,* 451.

APPELS, A., & MULDER, P. Type A behavior and myocardial infarction: A 9.5 year follow-up of a small cohort. *International Journal of Cardiology,* 1985, *8,* 465–470.

APPELS, A., & MULDER, P., & HOPPENER, P. A prospective study about vital exhaustion as a precursor of myocardial infarction and other serious diseases. *Nederlands Tijdschrift voor de Psychologie,* 1989, *44,* 122–128.

ARLOW, J. A. Identification of mechanisms in coronary occlusion. *Psychosomatic Medicine,* 1945, *7,* 195–207.

BAREFOOT, J. C., DAHLSTROM, G., & WILLIAMS, R. B. Hostility, CHD incidence, and total mortality: A 25-year follow-up study of 255 physicians. *Psychosomatic Medicine,* 1983, *45,* 59–63.

BAREFOOT, J. C., SIEGLER, I. C., NOWLIN, J. B., PETERSON, B. L., HANEY, T. L., & WILLIAMS, R. B., JR. Suspiciousness, health and mortality: A follow-up study of 500 older adults. *Psychosomatic Medicine,* 1987, *49,* 450–457.

BERKMAN, L. F., & SYME, S L. Social networks, host resistance, and mortality: a nine year follow-up study of Alameda County residents. *American Journal of Epidemiology,* 1979, *109,* 186–204.

BEVAN, R. D., & TSURU, H. Long-term influence of the sympathetic nervous system on arterial structure and reactivity: Possible factor in hypertension. In F. Abboud, H. Fozzaro, J. D. Gilmore, & J. Reid (eds.), *Disturbances in neurogenic control of the circulation.* Bethesda, MD: American Physiology Society, 1981.

BLUMENTHAL, J. A., BAREFOOT, J., BURG, M. M., & WILLIAMS, R. B., JR. Psychological correlates of hostility among patients undergoing coronary angiography. *British Journal of Medical Psychology,* 1987, *60,* 349–355.

BLUMENTHAL, J. A., WILLIAMS, R. B., KONG, Y., SCHANBERG, S., & THOMPSON, L. Type A behavior and angiographically documented coronary disease. *Circulation,* 1978, *58,* 634–639.

BOOTH-KEWLEY, S., & FRIEDMAN, H. S. Psychological predictors of heart disease: A quantitative review. *Psychological Bulletin,* 1987, *101,* 343–362.

BORTNER, R. W. A short rating scale as a potential measure of pattern A behavior. *Journal of Chronic Diseases,* 1969, *22,* 87–91.

BOVE, A. A. Coronary spasm-etiology and diagnosis. *American College of Cardiology, Learning Center Highlights,* 1986, *2,* 1–5.

BRACKETT, C. D., & POWELL, L. H. Psychosocial and physiological predictors of sudden cardiac death after healing of acute myocardial infarction. *American Journal of Cardiology,* 1988, *61,* 979–983.

BRODSKY, M. A., SATO, D. A., ISERI, L. T., WOLF, L., & ALLEN, B. J. Ventricular tachyarrhythmia associated with psychological stress: The role of the sympathetic nervous system. *Journal of the American Medical Association,* 1987, *257,* 2064–2067.

BRUCE, E. M., FREDERICK, R., BRUCE, R. A., & FISHER, L. D. Comparison of active participants and dropouts in CAPRI cardiopulmonary rehabilitation programs. *American Journal of Cardiology,* 1976, *37,* 53–62.

BRUSCHKE, A. V. G., WIJERS, T. S., KOLSTERS, W., & LANDMANN, J. The anatomic evolution of coronary artery disease demonstrated by coronary arteriography in 256 nonoperated patients. *Circulation,* 1981, *63,* 527–536.

BYRNE, D. G., & ROSENMAN, R. H. Type A behaviour and the experience of affective discomfort. *Journal of Psychosomatic Research,* 1986, *30,* 663–672.(a)

————. The type A behaviour pattern as a precursor to stressful life events: A confluence of coronary risks. *British Journal of Medical Psychology,* 1986, *59,* 75–82.(b)

BYRNE, D. G., ROSENMAN, R. H., SCHILLER, E., & CHESNEY, M. A. Consistency and variation among instruments purporting to measure the type A behavior pattern. *Psychosomatic Medicine,* 1985, *47,* 242–261.

CARMELLI, D., ROSENMAN, R. H., & CHESNEY, M. A. Stability of the type A structured interview and related questionnaires in a 10-year follow-up of an adult cohort of twins. *Journal of Behavioral Medicine,* 1987, *10,* 513–525.

CARMELLI, D., ROSENMAN, R. H., CHESNEY, M. A., FABSITZ, R., LEE, M., & BORHANI, N. O. Genetic heritability and shared environmental influences of type A measures in the NHLBI Twin Study. *American Journal of Epidemiology,* 1988, *127,* 1041–1052.

CARMELLI, D., SWAN, G. E., & ROSENMAN, R. H. The relationship between wives' social and psychologic status and their husband's coronary heart disease. *American Journal of Epidemiology,* 1985, *122,* 90–100.

————. Self-ratings and perceptions of type A traits in adult twins. In M. Strube (ed.), *Type A behavior.* (Special issue). *Journal of Social Behavior and Personality,* 1990, *5,* 263–275.

CASE, R. B., HELLER, S., CASE, N. B., & MOSS, A. J. Multicenter Post-Infarction Research Group. Type A behavior and survival after acute myocardial infarction. *New England Journal of Medicine,* 1985, *312,* 734–741.

CHIERCHIA, S. The role of alpha-adrenergic receptors in the pathogenesis of coronary spasm. *Clinical Cardiology,* 1983, *6,* 496–500.

COHEN, J. B. The influence of culture on coronary-prone behavior. In T. Dembroski, S. Weiss, J. Shields, S. Haynes, & M. Feinleib (eds.), *Coronary-prone behavior.* New York: Springer/Verlag, 1978.

COHEN, J. B., & REED, D. Type A behavior and coronary heart disease among Japanese men living in Hawaii. *Journal of Behavioral Medicine,* 1985, *8,* 343–52.

COOK, W., & MEDLEY, D. Proposed hostility and pharisaic-virtue scales for the MMPI. *Journal of Applied Psychology,* 1954, *38,* 414–418.

CONTRADA, R. J., & KRANTZ, D. S. Stress, reactivity, and type A behavior: Current status and future directions. *Annals of Behavioral Medicine,* 1988, *10,* 64–70.

COSTA, P. T. Is neuroticism a risk factor for CAD? Is type A a measure of neuroticism? In T. Schmidt, T. Dembroski, & G. Blumchen, (eds.), *Biological and Psychological Factors in Cardiovascular Disease.* New York: Springer/Verlag, 1986.

COSTA, P. T., MCCRAE, R. R., & DEMBROSKI, T. M. Agreeableness versus antagonism: Explication of a potential risk factor for CHD. In A. Siegman & T. Dembroski (eds.), *In search of coronary-prone behavior: Beyond type A.* Hillsdale, NJ: Lawrence Erlbaum, 1989.

COSTA, P. T., ZONDERMAN, A. B., MCCRAE, R. R., & WILLIAMS, R. B., JR. Cynicism and paranoid alienation in the Cook and Medley Ho Scale. *Psychosomatic Medicine,* 1986, *48,* 283–285.

CREA, F., DAVIES, G., CHIERCHIA, S., ROMEO, F., BUGIARDINI, R., KASKI, J. C., FREEDMAN, B., & MASERI, A. Different susceptibility to myocardial ischemia provoked by hyperventilation and cold pressor test in exertional and variant angina pectoris. *American Journal of Cardiology,* 1985, *56,* 18–22.

CRIQUI, M. H., AUSTIN, M., & BARRETT-CONNOR, E. The effect of nonresponse on risk ratios in a cardiovascular disease study. *Journal of Chronic Diseases,* 1979, *32,* 633–638.

DAVIES M. J., & THOMAS, A. C. Plaque fissuring—the cause of acute myocardial infarction, sudden ischemic death, and crescendo angina. *British Heart Journal,* 1985, *53,* 353–373.

DE BACKER, G., KORNITZER, M., & KITTEL, F. Behavior, stress, and psychological traits as risk factors. *Preventive Medicine,* 1983, *12,* 32–36.

DE LEO, D., CARACCIOLO, S., BERTO, F., MAURO, P., MAGNI, G., & MIRAGLIA, G. Type A behavior pattern and mortality after recurrent myocardial infarction: Preliminary results from a follow-up study of five years. *Psychotherapy Psychosomatics,* 1986, *46,* 653–665.

DEMBROSKI, T. M., & COSTA, P. T. Coronary-prone behavior: Components of the type A pattern and hostility. *Journal of Personality,* 1987, *55,* 211–236.

DEMBROSKI, T. M., MACDOUGALL, J. M., COSTA, P. T., & GRANDITS, G. A. Components of hostility as predictors of sudden death and myocardial infarction in the Multiple Risk Factor Intervention Trial. *Psychosomatic Medicine,* 1989, *51,* 514–522.

DEMBROSKI, T. M., MACDOUGALL, J. M., SHIELDS, J. L., PETTITO, J., & LUSHENE, R. Components of the type A coronary-prone behavior pattern and cardiovascular responses to psychomotor performance challenge. *Journal of Behavioral Medicine,* 1978, *1,* 159–176.

DEMBROSKI, T. M., MACDOUGALL, J. M., WILLIAMS, R. B., JR., HANEY, T., & BLUMENTHAL, J. A. Components of type A hostility, and anger-in: Relationship to angiographic findings. *Psychosomatic Medicine,* 1985, *47,* 219–233.

DEQUATTRO, V. Primary hypertension, neural tone, and behavior: Role in pressor responses. In J. Izzo & R. Rosenman (eds.), *Hypertension. The Noradrenergic Factor. American Journal of Hypertension,* 1989 (suppl.), *2,* 345S–352S.

DEQUATTRO, V., LOO, R., & FOTI, A. Sympathoadrenal responses to stress: The linking of type A behavior pattern to ischemic heart disease. *Clinical and Experimental Hypertension,* 1985, A7 (*4*), 469–481.

DERBY, C. A., & PEARSON, T. A. Type A behavior: Associated with coronary disease or with arteriography. *Circulation,* 1989 (suppl.), *80,* II–613.

DIAMOND, E. L. The role of anger and hostility in essential hypertension and coronary heart disease. *Psychological Bulletin,* 1982, *92,* 410–413.

DIAMOND, E. L., SCHNEIDERMAN, N., SCHWARTZ, D., SMITH, J. C., VORP, R., & DECARLO PASIN, R. Harassment, hostility, and type A as determinants of cardiovascular reactivity during competition. *Journal of Behavioral Medicine,* 1984, *7,* 171–179.

DIMSDALE, J. E., GILBERT, J., HUTTER, A. M., HACKETT, T. P., & BLOCK, P. C. Predicting cardiac morbidity based on risk factors and coronary angiographic findings. *American Journal of Cardiology, 47,* 1981, 73–76.

DIMSDALE, J. E., HACKETT, T. P., HUTTER, A. M., BLOCK, P. C., & CATANZO, D. M. Type A personality and extent of coronary atherosclerosis. *American Journal of Cardiology,* 1978, *42,* 583–586.

————. Type A behavior and angiographic findings. *Journal of Psychosomatic Research,* 1979, *23,* 273–276.

DIMSDALE, J. E., & HERD, A. Variability of plasma lipids in response to emotional arousal. *Psychosomatic Medicine,* 1982, *44,* 413–430.

DUCIMETIERE, P., CAMBIEN, F., RICHARD, J. L., RAKOTOVAO, R., & CLAUDE, J. R. Coronary heart disease in middle-aged Frenchmen. *Lancet,* 1980, *1,* 1346–1349.

DUNBAR, H. F. *Psychosomatic diagnosis.* New York: Hoeber, 1943.

EAKER, A. D., ABBOTT, R. D., & KANNEL, W. B. Frequency of uncomplicated angina pectoris in type A compared with type B persons (the Framingham Study). *The American Journal of Cardiology,* 1989, *63,* 1042–1045.

EAKER, E. D., & CASTELLI, W. P. Type A behavior and mortality from coronary disease in the Framingham Study. *New England Journal of Medicine,* 1988, *319,* 1480–1481.

EDYE, B. E., MANDRYK, J. A., FROMMER, M. S., HEALEY, S., & FERGUSON, D. Evaluation of a worksite program for the modification of cardiovascular risk factors. *Medical Journal of Australia,* 1989, *150,*574–581.

EGAN, B., & SCHMOUDER, R. The importance of hemodynamic considerations in essential hypertension. *American Heart Journal,* 1988, *116,* 594–599.

FALGER, P. R. J. Interactions of stressful life changes, cognitive factors, and vital exhaustion in myocardial infarction patients: A life-span developmental study. In C. Spielberger, I. Sarason, & J. Strelau (eds.), *Stress and anxiety.* Washington, DC: Hemisphere, 1989.

FEINLEIB, M., KANNEL, W. B., TEDESCHI, C. G., LANDAU, T. K., & GARRISON, R. J. The relation of antemortem characteristics to cardiovascular findings at necropsy. The Framingham Study. *Atherosclerosis,* 1979, *34,* 145–157.

Folkow, B. "Structural factor" in primary and secondary hypertension. *Hypertension,* 1990, *16,* 89–101.

Frank, K. A., Heller, S. S., Kornfeld, D. S., Sporn, A. A., & Weiss, M. D. Type A behavior pattern and coronary atherosclerosis. *Journal of the American Medical Association,* 1978, *240,* 761–763.

Freiherr, G. Insights on thromboxane A2. *Cardiovascular Reviews and Reports,* 1988, *4,* 70–72.

French-Belgian Collaborative Group. Ischemic heart disease and psychological patterns. Prevalence and incidence studies in Belgium and France. In H. Denolin (ed.), *Psychological problems before and after myocardial infarction.* Basel: Karger, 1982.

Friedman, H. S., & Booth-Kewley, S. Validity of the type A construct: A reprise. *Psychological Bulletin,* 1988, *104,* 381–384.

Friedman, M., Byers, S. O., Diamant, J., & Rosenman, R. H. Plasma catecholamine response of coronary-prone subjects (type A) to a specific challenge. *Metabolism,* 1975, *4,* 205–210.

Friedman. M., & Powell, L. H. The diagnosis and quantitative assessment of type A behavior; Introduction and description of the Videotaped Structured Interview. *Integrative Psychiatry,* 1984, *2,* 123–136.

Friedman, M., & Rosenman, R. H. Association of specific overt behavior pattern with blood and cardiovascular findings. *Journal of the American Medical Association,* 1959, *169,* 1286–1296.

Friedman, M., Rosenman, R. H., & Carroll, V. Changes in the serum cholesterol and blood-clotting time in men subjected to cyclic variation of occupational stress. *Circulation,* 1958, *17,* 852–861.

Friedman, M., Rosenman, R., Straus, K., Wurm, M., & Kositchek, R. The relationship of behavior pattern A to the state of coronary vasculature. *American Journal of Medicine,* 1968, *44,* 525–537.

Friedman, M., St. George, S., Byers, S. O., & Rosenman, R. H. Excretion of catecholamines, 17-ketosteroids, 17-hydroxycorticoids, and 5-hydroxyindole in men exhibiting a particular behavior pattern (A) associated with high incidence of clinical coronary artery disease. *Journal of Clinical Investigation,* 1960, *39,* 758–764.

Friedman, M., Thoresen, C. E., Gill, J. J., Ulmer, D., Powell, L. H., Price, V. A., Brown, B., Thompson, L., Rabin, D. D., Breall, W. S., Bourg, E., Levy, R., & Dixon, T. Alteration of type A behavior and its effect on cardiac recurrences in post-myocardial infarction patients: Summary results of the Recurrent Coronary Prevention Project. *American Heart Journal,* 1986, *11,* 653–665.

Furchgott, R. F. Role of endothelium in responses of vascular smooth muscle. *Circulation Research,* 1983, *53,* 557–573.

Fuster, V., Chesebro, J. H., Frye, R. L., & Elveback, L. R. Platelet survival and the development of coronary artery disease in the young adult: Effects of cigarette smoking, strong family history and medical therapy. *Circulation,* 1981, *63,* 546–551.

Garcia-Palmieri, M. R., Castillo, M. I., Oalmann, M. C., Sorlie, P. D., & Costas, A. M. The relation of antemortem factors to atherosclerosis at necropsy. In G. Schettler, Y. Goto, Y. Hata, & G. Close (eds.), *Atherosclerosis.* Vol IV. New York: Springer-Verlag, 1977.

Gertler, M., & White, P. D. *Coronary disease in young adults: A multidisciplinary study.* Cambridge: Harvard University Press, 1954.

Gertz, S. D., Uretsky, G., Wainberg, R. S., Navot, N., & Gottsman, M. S. Endothelial cell damage and thrombus formation after partial arterial constriction: Relevance to the role of coronary artery spasm in the pathogenesis of myocardial infarction. *Circulation,* 1981, *63,* 476–486.

Gildea, E. Special features of personality which are common to psychosomatic disorders. *Psychosomatic Medicine,* 1949, *11,* 273–277.

Gill, T. P., Wahlqvist, M. L., Dennis, P. M., Balazs, N. D., Strauss, B. J. G., & Matthews,

P. G. Risk factors for coronary heart disease in a self-referred population compared with a general population. *Medical Journal of Australia,* 1989, *151,* 515–518.

GLASS, D. C. *Behavior patterns, stress and coronary disease,* Hillsdale, NJ: Lawrence Erlbaum, 1977.

GLASS, D. C., & CONTRADA, R. J. Type A behavior and catecholamines: A critical review. In M. Ziegler, & C. Lake (eds.), *Norepinephrine: Clinical aspects.* Baltimore, MD: Williams and Wilkins, 1984.

GORDON, T., GARCIA-PALMIERI, M. R., KAGAN, A., KANNEL, W. B., & SCHIFFMAN, J. Differences in coronary heart disease in Framingham, Honolulu, and Puerto Rico, *Journal of Chronic Diseases,* 1974, *27,* 329–337.

GORDON, T., & VERTER, J. Serum cholesterol, systolic blood pressure, and Framingham relative weight as discriminators of cardiovascular disease. In W. Kannel, & T. Gordon (eds.), *The Framingham Study: An epidemiological investigation of cardiovascular disease.* Washington, DC: U.S. Government Printing Office, 1969.

GROEN, J. J., TJIONG, B., KAMMINGER, C. E., WILLEBRANDS, A. F. The influence of nutrition, individuality and some other factors, including various forms of stress on the serum cholesterol; an experiment of nine months duration. *Voeding,* 1962, *13,* 556–573.

GRUNDY, S. M., & GRIFFIN, A. Relationship of periodic mental stress to serum lipoprotein and cholesterol levels. *Journal of the American Medical Association,* 1959, *171,* 1793–1796.

HALPERIN, P. J., & LITTMAN, A. B. Letter to editor. *New England Journal of Medicine,* 1985, *312,* 450.

HARDY, J. D., & SMITH, T. W. Cynical hostility and vulnerability to disease: Social support, life stress, and physiological response to conflict. *Health Psychology,* 1988, *7,* 447–459.

HARSHFIELD, G. A., PICKERING, T. G., YEE, L. S., & MARION, R. M. Does blood pressure predict reactivity under natural conditions? *Psychophysiology,* 1985, *22,* 594.

HARTZ, A. J., BARBORIAK, P. N., ANDERSON, A. J., HOFFMAN, R. G., & BARBORIAK, J. J. Smoking, coronary artery occlusion, and nonfatal myocardial infarction. *Journal of the American Medical Association,* 1981, *246,* 851–853.

HAYNES, S. G., & FEINLEIB, M. Type A behavior and the incidence of coronary heart disease in the Framingham Heart Study. In. H. Denolin (ed.), *Psychological problems before and after myocardial infarction. Advances in Cardiology.* Vol. 29. Basel: Karger, 1982.

HAYNES, S. G., LEVINE, S., & SCOTCH, N. The relationship of psychosocial factors to coronary heart disease in the Framingham Study: I. Methods and risk factors. *American Journal of Epidemiology,* 1978, *107,* 362–381.

HAYNES, S. G., & MATTHEWS, K. A. Review and methodologic critique of recent studies on type A behavior and cardiovascular disease. *Annals of Behavioral Medicine,* 1988, *10,* 47–59.

HEARN, M. D., MURRAY, D. M., & LUEPKE, R. V. Hostility, coronary heart disease, and total mortality: A 33-year follow-up study of university students. *Journal of Behavioral Medicine,* 1989, *12,* 105–121.

HECKER, M. H. L., CHESNEY, M. A., BLACK, G. W., & FRAUTSCHI, N. Coronary-prone behaviors in the Western Collaborative Group Study. *Psychosomatic Medicine,* 1988, *50,* 153–164.

HECKER, M. H. L., CHESNEY, M. A., BLACK, G. W., & ROSENMAN, R. H. Speech analysis of type A behavior. In J. Darby (ed.), *Speech evaluation in medicine.* New York: Grune and Stratton, 1981.

HELMAN, C. G. Heart disease and the cultural construction of time: Type A behavior pattern as a Western culture-bound syndrome. *Social Science and Medicine,* 1987, *25,* 969–979.

HELMER, D. C., RAGLAND, D. R., & SYME, S. L. Hostility and coronary artery disease. *American Journal of Epidemiology,* 1990, *123,* 112–122.

HOLLIS, J. F., CONNETT, J. E., STEVENS, V. J., & GREENLICK, M. R. Stressful life events, type A behavior, and the prediction of cardiovascular and total mortality over six years. *Journal of Behavioral Medicine,* 1990, *13,* 263–280.

HOUSTON, B. K. Psychophysiological responsivity and the type A behavior pattern. *Journal of Research Personality,* 1983, *17,* 22–39.

————. Psychological variables and cardiovascular and neuroendocrine reactivity. In K. Matthews, S. Weiss, T. Detre, T. Dembroski, B. Falkner, B. Manuck, & R. Williams (eds.), *Handbook of stress, reactivity, and cardiovascular disease.* New York: Wiley, 1986.

HOWARD, J. H., CUNNINGHAM, D. A., & RECHNITZER, P. A. Health patterns associated with type A behavior: A managerial population. *Journal of Human Stress,* 1976, *2,* 24–28.

HOWES, L. G., KRUM, H., LOUIS, W. J. Plasma cholesterol levels are dependent on sympathetic activity. *Journal of Hypertension,* 1987 (suppl. 5), *5,* S361–S363.

JENKINS, C. D. Recent evidence supporting psychologic and social risk factors for coronary disease. *New England Journal of Medicine,* 1976, *294,* 987–1038.

————. Epidemiology of cardiovascular diseases. *Journal of Consulting and Clinical Psychology,* 1988, *56,* 324–332.

JENKINS, C. D., HAMES, C. G., ZYZANSKI, S. J., ROSENMAN, R. H., & FRIEDMAN, M. Psychological traits and serum lipids. Part I. Findings from the California Psychological Inventory. *Psychosomatic Medicine,* 1969, *31,* 115–128.

JENKINS, C. D., & ROSENMAN, R. H., & FRIEDMAN, M. Components of the coronary-prone behavior pattern: Their relation to silent myocardial infarction and blood lipids. *Journal of Chronic Diseases,* 1966, *19,* 599–606.

JENKINS, C. D., ZYZANSKI, S. J., & ROSENMAN, R. H. Biologic, psychologic and social characteristics of men with different smoking habits. *Health Service Reports,* 1973, *88,* 834–843.

————. Risk of new myocardial infarction in middle-aged men with manifest coronary heart disease. *Circulation,* 1976, *53,* 342–347.

————. *The Jenkins Activity Survey.* New York: Psychological Corporation, 1979.

JENKINS, C. D., ZYZANSKI, S. J., ROSENMAN, R. H., & CLEVELAND, G. L. Association of coronary-prone behavior scores with recurrence of coronary heart disease. *Journal of Chronic Diseases,* 1971, *24,* 601–611.

JENNINGS, J. R., & FOLLANSBEE, W. P. Type A and ectopy in patients with coronary artery disease and controls. *Journal of Psychosomatic Research,* 1984, *28,* 449–454.

JULIUS, M., HARBURG, E., COTTINGTON, E. M., & JOHNSON, E. H. Anger-coping types, blood pressure, and all-cause mortality: A follow-up in Tecumseh, Michigan (1971–1983). *American Journal of Epidemiology,* 1986, *124,* 220–233.

JULIUS, S. Hemodynamic, pharmacologic and epidemiologic evidence for behavioral factors in human hypertension. In S. Julius & D. R. Bassett (eds.), *Handbook of hypertension. Vol. 9: Behavioral factors in hypertension.* Amsterdam: Elsevier, 1987.

————. Transition from high cardiac output to elevated vascular resistance in hypertension. *American Heart Journal,* 1988, *116,* 600–606.(a)

————. The blood pressure seeking properties of the central nervous system. *Journal of Hypertension,* 1988, *6,* 177–185.(b)

JULIUS, S., WEDER, A. B. & HINDERLITER, A. L. Does behaviorally induced blood pressure variability lead to hypertension? In K. A. Matthews, S. M. Weiss, T. Detre, T. M. Dembroski, B. Falkner, B. S. Manuck & R. B. Williams (eds.), *Handbook of stress, reactivity, and cardiovascular disease.* New York: Wiley, 1986.

KAHN, J. P., GULLY, R. J., COOPER, T. B., PERUMAL, S., THOMAS, T. M., & KLEIN, D. F. Correlation of type A behavior with adrenergic density: Implications for coronary artery disease pathogenesis. *Lancet,* 1987, *2,* 937–939.

KANNEL, W. B., & HIGGINS, M. Smoking and hypertension as predictors of cardiovascular risk in population studies. *Journal of Hypertension,* 1990 (suppl. 5), *8,* S3–S8.

KANNEL, W. B., SORLIE, P., & GORDON, T. Labile hypertension: A faulty concept? The Framingham Study. *Circulation,* 1980, *61,* 1183–1187.

KEMPLE, C. Rorschach method and psychosomatic diagnosis: Personality traits of patients with rheumatic disease, hypertension, cardiovascular disease, coronary occlusion, and fracture. *Psychosomatic Medicine,* 1945, *7,* 85–89.

KEYS, A., ARAVANIS, C., BLACKBURN, H., VANBUCHEM, F. S. P., BUZINA, R., DJORDJENIC, B. D., FIDANZA, F., KARVONEN, M. J., MENOTTI, A., PUDDU, V., & TAYLOR, H. L. Probability of middle-aged men developing coronary heart disease in 5 years. *Circulation,* 1972, *45,* 815–872.

KORNITZER, M., KITTEL, F., & DE BACKER, G. The Belgian Heart Disease Prevention Project: Type A behavior pattern and the prevalence of coronary heart disease. *Psychosomatic Medicine,* 1981, *43,* 133–145.

KORNITZER, M., MAGOTTEAU, V., DEGRE, V., KITTEL, F., STRUYVEN, J., & VAN THIEL, E. Angiographic findings and the type A behavior pattern assessed by means of the Bortner Scale. *Journal of Behavioral Medicine,* 1982, *5,* 313–319.

KOSKENVUO, M., KAPRIO, J., ROSE, R. J. Hostility as a risk factor for mortality and ischemic heart disease in men. *Psychosomatic Medicine,* 1988, *50,* 330–340.

KOZAREVIC, D., PIRE, B., RAVIC, Z., DAWBER, T. R., GORDON, T., & ZUKEL, W. J. The Yugoslavia cardiovascular study. II. Factors in the incidence of coronary heart disease. *Journal of Chronic Diseases,* 1976, *29,* 405–414.

KRAMER, J. R., KITAZUME, H., PROUDFIT, W. L., MATSUDA, Y., WILLIAMS, G. W., & SONES, F. M., JR. Progression and regression of coronary atherosclerosis: Relation to risk factors. *American Heart Journal,* 1983, *105,* 134–139.

KRANTZ, D. S., SANMARCO, M. I., SELVESTER, R. H., & MATTHEWS, K. A. Psychological correlates of progression of atherosclerosis in men. *Psychosomatic Medicine,* 1979, *41,* 467–475.

KRANTZ, D. S., SCHAEFFER, M. A., DAVIA, J. E., DEMBROSKI, T. M., MACDOUGALL, J. M., & SHAFFER, R. T. Extent of coronary atherosclerosis, type A behavior and cardiovascular responses to social interaction. *Psychology,* 1981, *18,* 654–664.

LAM, J. Y., CHESEBRO, J. H., & STEELE, P. M. Is vasospasm related to platelet deposition? Relationship in a porcine preparation of arterial injury in vivo. *Circulation,* 1987 (suppl. 1), *75,* 243–249.

LANTINGA, L. J., SPRAFKIN, R. P., McCROSKERY, H. H., BAKER, M. T., WARNER, R. A., & HILL, N. E. One-year psychosocial follow-up of patients with chest pain and angiographically normal coronary arteries. *American Journal of Cardiology,* 1988, *62,* 209–213.

LEON, G. R., MURRAY, D., FINN, S. E., BAILEY, P. & CASTELLI, W. P. Type A behavior and mortality from coronary disease in the Framingham Study. *New England Journal of Medicine,* 1988, *319,* 1480–1481.

LEVENKRON, J. C., & MOORE, G. The Type A behavior pattern: Issues for intervention research. *Annals of Behavioral Medicine,* 1988, *10,* 78–832.

LIGHT, K. C. Cardiovascular responses to effortful active coping: Implications for the role of stress in hypertension development. *Psychophysiology,* 1981, *18,* 216–225.

LOWN, B. Sudden cardiac death: Biobehavioral perspective. *Circulation,* 1987 (suppl. 1), *76,* I-186–I-196.

LOWN, B., & DeSILVA, R. A. Is coronary arterial spasm a risk factor for coronary atherosclerosis? *American Journal of Cardiology,* 1980, *45,* 901–903.

LUNDBERG, U., HEDMAN, M., MELIN, B., & FRANKENHAEUSER, M. Type A behavior in healthy males and females as related to physiological reactivity and blood lipids. *Psychosomatic Medicine,* 1989, *51,* 113–122.

MACDOUGALL, J. M., DEMBROSKI, T. M., DIMSDALE, J. E., & HACKETT, T. P. Components of type A hostility and anger-in: Further relationship to angiographic findings, *Health Psychology*, 1985, *4*, 137–152.

MANUCK, S. B., & KRANTZ, D. S. Psychophysiologic reactivity in coronary heart disease and essential hypertension. In K. Matthews, S. Weiss, T. Detre, T. Dembroski, B. Falkner, S. Manuck, & R. Williams (eds.), *Handbook of stress, reactivity and cardiovascular Disease*. New York: Wiley, 1986.

MANUCK, S. B., PROIETTI, J. M., RADER, S. J., & POLEFRONE, J. M. Parental hypertension, affect and cardiovascular response to cognitive challenge. *Psychosomatic Medicine*, 1985, *47*, 189–200.

MARMOT, M. Socioeconomic and cultural factors in ischemic heart disease. In H. Denolin (ed.), *Psychological problems before and after myocardial infarction*. Basel: Karger, 1982.

MARTIN, J. L., WILSON, J. R., FERRARO, N., LASKEY, W. K., KLEAVELAND, J. P., & HIRSCHFELD, J. W. Acute coronary vasoconstrictive effects of smoking in coronary heart disease. *American Journal of Cardiology*, 1984, *54*, 56–60.

MASERI, A., SEVERI, S., DE NES, M., L'ABBAYE, S., CHIERCHIA, S., MARZILLI, M., BALLESTRA, A. M., PARODI, O., BIAGINI, A., & DISTANTE, A. "Variant" angina: One aspect of a continuous spectrum of vasospastic myocardial ischemia. Pathogenetic mechanisms, estimated incidence and clinical and coronary arteriographic findings in 138 patients. *American Journal of Cardiology*, 1978, *42*, 1019–1035.

MATSUSHIMA, T., DOBA, N., HINOHARA, S., WILLIAMS, R. B., JR., & SHINODA, T. Studies on type A behavior pattern and hostility in Japanese male subjects with special reference to CHD. *Shin-shin-Igaku*, 1983, *213*, 321–328.

MATTHEWS, K. A. Assessment and development antecedents of the coronary-prone behavior pattern in children. In T. Dembroski, S. Weiss, J. Shields, S. Haynes, & M. Feinleib (eds.), *Coronary-prone behavior*. New York: Springer, 1978.

————. Coronary heart disease and type A behaviors: Update on and alternative to the Booth-Kewley and Friedman (1987) quantitative review. *Psychological Bulletin*, 1988, *104*, 373–380.

MATTHEWS, K. A., GLASS, D. C., ROSENMAN, R. H., & BORTNER, R. W. Competitive drive, pattern A, and coronary heart disease: A further analysis of some data from the Western Collaborative Group Study. *Journal of Chronic Diseases*, 1977, *30*, 489–498.

MATTHEWS, K. A., & HAYNES, S. G. Type A behavior and coronary disease risk. *American Journal of Epidemiology*, 1986, *123*, 923–960.

MATTHEWS, K. A., & SAAL, F. E. The relationship of the type A coronary-prone behavior pattern to achievement, power, and affiliation motives. *Psychosomatic Medicine*, 1978, *40*, 631–636.

MCCRANIE, E. W., WATKINS, L. O., BRANDSMA, J. M., & SISSON, B. D. Hostility, coronary heart disease (CHD) incidence, and total mortality: Lack of association in a 25-year follow-up study of 478 physicians. *Journal of Behavioral Medicine*, 1986, *9*, 119–125.

MEADE, T. W. Effects of changes in smoking and other characteristics on clotting factors and the risk of ischemic heart disease. *Lancet*, 1987, *2*, 986–988.

MEADE, T. W., BROZOVIC, M., & CHAKRABARTI, R. R. Haemostatic function and ischemic heart disease: Principal results of the Northwick Park Heart Study, *Lancet*, 1986, *2*, 533–537.

MEGARGEE, E. I. The dynamics of aggression and their application to cardiovascular disorders. In M. Chesney & R. Rosenman (eds.), *Anger and hostility in cardiovascular and behavioral disorders*. Washington, DC: Hemisphere, 1985.

MENNINGER, K. A., & MENNINGER, W. C. Psychoanalytic observations in cardiac disorders. *American Heart Journal*, 1936, *11*, 10–26.

MENOTTI, A., CONTI, S., DIMA, F., GIAMPAOLI, S., GIULI, B., RUMI, A., SECARECCI, F., & SIGNORETTI, P. Prediction of all causes of death as a function of some factors commonly measured in cardiovascular population surveys. *Preventive Medicine*, 1983, *12*, 318–325.

MESSERLI, F. H., SUNDGAARD-RIISE, K., VENTURA, H. O., DUNN, F. G., GLADE, L. B., & FROHLICH, E. D. Essential hypertension in the elderly: Hemodynamics, intravascular volume, plasma renin activity, and circulating catecholamine levels. *Lancet,* 1983, *2,* 983–986.

MOISE, A., THEROUX, P., TAEYMANS, Y., DESCOINGS, B., LESPERANCE, J., WATERS, D. D., PELLE-TIER, G. B., & BOURASSA, M. G., et al. Unstable angina and progression of coronary atherosclerosis. *New England Journal of Medicine,* 1983, *309,* 685–689.

MONTAGU, A. *The Nature of Human Aggression.* New York: Oxford University Press, 1976.

MULTICENTER POSTINFARCTION RESEARCH GROUP. Risk stratification and survival after myocardial infarction. *New England Journal of Medicine,* 1983, *309,* 331–336.

MULTIPLE RISK FACTOR TRIAL RESEARCH GROUP. Multiple risk factor Intervention Trial: Risk factor changes and mortality results. *Journal of the American Medical Association,* 1982, *248,* 1465–1477.

MUSANTE, L., MacDOUGALL, J. M., DEMBROSKI, T. M., & COSTA, P. T. Potential for hostility and dimensions of anger. *Health Psychology,* 1989, *8,* 343–354.

NOWAK, J., MURRAY, J. L., OATES, J. A., & FITZGERALD, G. A. Biochemical evidence of a chronic abnormality in platelet and vascular function in healthy individuals who smoke cigarettes. *Circulation,* 1987, *76,* 6–14.

NYROP, M., & ZWEIFLER, A. J. Platelet aggregation in hypertension and the effects of antihypertensive treatment. Editorial review. *Journal of Hypertension,* 1988, *6,* 263–269.

OAKES, T. W. Letter to editor. *New England Journal of Medicine,* 1985, *312,* 452.

O'DONNELL, L., O'MEAR, N., OWENS, D., JOHNSON, A., COLLINS, P., & TOMKIN, G. Plasma catecholamines and lipoproteins in chronic psychological stress. *Journal of the Royal Society of Medicine,* 1987, *80,* 339–334.

OLDRIDGE, N. B., DONNER, A. P., BUCK, C. W., JONES, N. L., ANDREW, G. M., PARKER, J. O., CUNNINGHAM, D. A., KAVANAGH, T., RECHNITZER, P. A., & SUTTON, J. R. Predictors of dropout from cardiac exercise rehabilitation—Ontario Exercise-Heart Collaborative Study. *American Journal of Cardiology,* 1982, *51,* 70–74.

OSLER, W. The Lumleian lectures on angina pectoris. *Lancet,* 1982, *1,* 829–844.

PALATINI, P., MORMINO, P., DI MARCO, A., LIBARDONI, M., MOS, L., MUNARI, L., PESSINA, A. C., & DAL PALU, C. Ambulatory blood pressure versus casual pressure for the evaluation of target organ damage in hypertension: complications of hypertension. *Journal of Hypertension,* 1985 (suppl. 3), *3,* S417–S425.

PARATI, G., POMIDOSSI, G., ALBINI, F., MALASPINA, D., & MANCIA, G. Relationship of 24-hour blood pressure mean and variability to severity of target-organ damage in hypertension. *Journal of Hypertension,* 1987, *5,* 93–98.

PEARSON, T., GORDIS, L., ACHUFF, S., BULKLEY, B., & KWITEROVICH, P. Selection bias in persons undergoing angiography. *American Journal of Epidemiology,* 1982, *116,* 568.

PICKERING, T. G. Letter to editor. *New England Journal of Medicine,* 1985, *312,* 451.(a)

————. Should studies of patients undergoing coronary angiography be used to evaluate the role of behavioral risk factors for coronary heart disease? *Journal of Behavioral Medicine,* 1985, *8,* 203–213.

PICKERING, T. G., & GERIN, W. Cardiovascular reactivity in the laboratory and the role of behavioral factors in hypertension: A critical review. *Annals of Behavioral Medicine,* 1990, *12,* 3–16.

PRICE, V. A. Research and clinical issues in treating type A behavior. In B. Houston & C. Snyder (eds.), *Type A behavior pattern: Research, theory and intervention.* New York: Wiley/Interscience, 1988.

RAGLAND, D. R., & BRAND, R. J. Type A behavior and mortality from coronary heart disease. *New England Journal of Medicine,* 1988, *318,* 65–69.

REICH, P., DeSILVA, R. A., LOWN, B., & MURAWSKI, J. Acute psychological disturbances preceding life-threatening ventricular arrhythmias. *Journal of the American Medical Association,* 1981, *246,* 233–235.

REIS, D. J., & LeDOUX, J. E. Some central neural mechanims governing resting and behaviorally coupled control of blood pressure. *Circulation,* 1987 (suppl.), *76,* S1–S9.

ROSENMAN, R. H. The interview method of assessment of the coronary-prone behavior pattern. In T. Dembroski, S. Weiss, J. Shields, S. Haynes, & M. Feinleib (eds.), *Coronary-prone behavior.* New York: Springer-Verlag, 1978.

—————. Coronary-prone behavior pattern and coronary heart disease: Implications for the use of beta-blockers for primary prevention. In R. Rosenman (ed.), *Psychosomatic risk factors and coronary heart disease; indications for specific preventive therapy.* Bern: Huber, 1983.

—————. Health consequences of anger and implications for treatment. In M. Chesney & R. Rosenman (eds.), *Anger and hostility in cardiovascular and behavioral disorders.* New York: Hemisphere, 1985.

—————. Current and past history of type A behavior pattern. In T. Schmidt, T. Dembroski, & G. Blumchen (eds.), *Biological and psychological factors in cardiovascular disease.* Heidelberg: Springer-Verlag, 1986.

—————. Type A behavior and hypertension. In S. Julius & D. Bassett (eds.), *Handbook of hypertension. Vol. 9: Behavioral factors in hypertension.* Amsterdam: Elsevier, 1987.

—————. Results of the multicenter antihypertensive treatment trials. Therapeutic implications and the role of the sympathetic nervous system. In J. Izzo & R. Rosenman (eds.), *Hypertension: the noradrenergic factor. American Journal of Hypertension,* 1989 (suppl., pt. 2), *2,* 313S–338S.

—————. Type A behavior pattern: A personal overview. In M. Strube (ed.), *Type A behavior.* (Special Issue). *Journal of Social Behavior and Personality,* 1990, *5,* 1–24.

—————. Type A behavior pattern and cardiovascular reactivity: Is there a relationship with hypertension? In E. Johnson, W. Gentry, & S. Julius (eds.), *Personality, elevated blood pressure, and essential hypertension.* Washington, DC: Hemisphere, 1992.

ROSENMAN, R. H., BRAND, R. J., SHOLTZ, R. I., & FRIEDMAN, M. Multivariate prediction of coronary heart disease during 8.5 year follow-up in the Western Collaborative Group Study. *American Journal of Cardiology,* 1976, *37,* 903–910.

ROSENMAN, R. H., & CHESNEY, M. A. The relationship of type A behavior pattern to coronary heart disease. *Activitas Nervosa Superior,* 1980, *2,* 1–45.

ROSENMAN, R. H., & FRIEDMAN, M. Association of specific behavior pattern in women with blood and cardiovascular findings. *Circulation,* 1961, *24,* 1173–1184.

—————. Neurogenic factors in pathogenesis of coronary heart disease. *Medical Clinics of North America,* 1974, *58,* 269–279.

—————. Modifying type A behavior pattern, *Journal of Psychosomatic Research,* 1977, *21,* 323–331.

ROSENMAN, R. H., FRIEDMAN, M., JENKINS, C. D., STRAUS, R. M., & KOSITCHEK, R. Recurring and fatal myocardial infarction in the Western Collaborative Group Study. *American Journal of Cardiology,* 1967, *19,* 771–775.

ROSENMAN, R. H., FRIEDMAN, M., STRAUS, R., WURM, M., KOSITCHEK, R., HAHN, W., & WERTHESSEN, N. T. A predictive study of coronary heart disease: The Western Collaborative Group Study. *Journal of the American Medical Association,* 1964, *189,* 15–22.

ROSENMAN, R. H., RAHE, R. H., BORHANI, N. O., & FEINLEIB, M. Heritability of personality and behavior. *Acta Genetica Medicae et Gemellologiae,* 1976, *25,* 221–224.

ROSENMAN, R. H., SWAN, G. E., & CARMELLI, D. Definition, assessment, and evolution of the type A behavior pattern. In B. Houston & C. Snyder (eds.), *Type A behavior pattern: Research, theory and intervention.* New York: Wiley/Interscience, 1988.(a)

————. Some recent findings relative to the relationship of type A behavior pattern to coronary heart disease. In S. Maes, C. Spielberger, P. Defares, & I. Sarason (eds.), *Topics in health psychology*. Chichester, Eng: Wiley, 1988.(b)

ROSENMAN, R. H., & WARD, M. W. The changing concept of cardiovascular reactivity. *Stress Medicine,* 1988, *4,* 241–251.

ROSKIES, E. *Stress management for the healthy type A: Theory and practice.* New York: Guilford Press, 1987.

ROSS, R. The pathogenesis of atherosclerosis—an update. *New England Journal of Medicine,* 1986, *314,* 488–495.

ROZANSKI, A., BAIREY, C. N., KRANTZ, D. S., FRIEDMAN, J., RESSER, K. J., MORREL, M., MILTON-CHAFEN, S., HESTRIN, L., BIENTENDORF, J., & BERMAN, D. S. Mental stress and the induction of silent myocardial ischemia in patients with coronary artery disease. *New England Journal of Medicine,* 1988, *318,* 1005–1012.

RUBERMAN, W., WEINBLATT, E., GOLDBERG, J. D., & CHAUDBARY, B. S. Psychosocial influences on mortality after myocardial infarction. *New England Journal of Medicine,* 1984, *311,* 522–529.

SALLIS, J. F., JOHNSON, C. C., TREVORROW, R., KAPLAN, R. M., & HOVELL, M. F. The relationship between cynical hostility and blood pressure reactivity. *Journal of Psychosomatic Research,* 1987, *31,* 111–116.

SCHERWITZ, L., BERTON, K., & LEVENTHAL, H. Type A assessment and interaction in the behavior pattern interview. *Psychosomatic Medicine,* 1977, *39,* 229–240.

SCHERWITZ, L., GRAHAM, L. E., GRANDITS, G., BUEHLER, J., & BILLINGS, J. Self-involvement and coronary heart disease incidence in the Multiple Risk Factor Intervention Trial. *Psychosomatic Medicine,* 1986, *48,* 187–199.

SCHERWITZ, L., McKELVAIN, R., LAMAN, C., PATTERSON, J., DUTTON, L., YUSIM S., LESTER, J., KRAFT, J., ROCHELEE, F., & LEACHMAN, R. Type A behavior, self-involvement, and coronary atherosclerosis. *Psychosomatic Medicine,* 1983, *45,* 47–57.

SCHIFFER, F., HARTLEY, L. H., SCHUMAN, C. L., & ABELMANN, W. H., The quiz electrocardiogram: A new diagnostic and research technique for evaluating the relation between emotional stress and ischemic heart disease. *American Journal of Cardiology,* 1976, *37,* 41–47.

SCHNEIDER, R. H., JULIUS, S., MOSS, G. E., DIELMAN, T. E., ZWEIFLER, A. F., & KARUNAS, R. New markers for type A behavior: Pupil size and platelet epinephrine. *Psychosomatic Medicine,* 1987, *49,* 579–590.

SELWYN, A. P., & GANZ, P. Myocardial ischemia in coronary disease. *New England Journal of Medicine,* 1988, *318,* 1058–1060.

SELWYN, A. P., SHEA, M. J., DEANFIELD, J. E., WILSON, R. A. deLANDSHEERE, C. M., & JONES, T. Clinical problems in coronary disease are caused by a wide variety of ischemic episodes that affect patients out of hospital. *American Journal of Medicine,* 1985 (suppl. 3A), *79,* 12–17.

SHEKELLE, R. B., GALE, M., & NORUSIS, M. Type A score (Jenkins Activity Survey) and risk of recurrent coronary heart disease in the aspirin myocardial infarction study. *American Journal of Cardiology,* 1985, *56,* 221–225.

SHEKELLE, R. B., GALE, M., OSTFELD, A. M., & PAUL, O. Hostility, risk of coronary heart disease, and mortality. *Psychosomatic Medicine,* 1983, *45,* 109–114.

SHEKELLE, R. B., HULLEY, S. B., NEATON, J. D., BILLINGS, H., BORHANI, N. O., GERACE, T. A., JACOBS, D. R., LASSER, N. L., MITTLEMARK, M. B., & STAMLER, J. The MRFIT Behavior Pattern Study. II. Type A behavior and incidence of coronary heart disease. *American Journal of Epidemiology,* 1985, *122,* 559–570.

SHIPMAN, W. G. The validity of MMPI hostility scales. *Journal of Clinical Psychology,* 1965, *21,* 186–190.

SIEGEL, W. C., MARK, D. B., HLATKY, M. A., HARRELL, F. E., PRYOR, D. B., BAREFOOT, J. C., &

WILLIAMS, R. B. Clinical correlates and prognostic significance of type A behavior and silent myocardial ischemia on the treadmill. *American Journal of Cardiology,* 1989, *64,* 1280–1283.

SIEGMAN, A. W. The role of hostility, neuroticism, and speech style in coronary artery disease. In A. Siegman & T. Dembroski (eds.), *In search of coronary-prone behavior: Beyond Type A.* Hillsdale, NJ: Lawrence Erlbaum, 1989.

SIEGMAN, A. W., DEMBROSKI, T. M., & RINGEL, N. Components of hostility and severity of coronary artery disease. *Psychosomatic Medicine,* 1987, *49,* 127–135.

SIMPSON, M. T., OLEWINE, D. A., JENKINS, D. A., RAMSEY, F. J., ZYZANSKI, S. J., THOMAS, G., & JAMES, C. G. Exercise-induced catecholamine and platelet aggregation in the coronary-prone behavior pattern. *Psychosomatic Medicine,* 1974, *36,* 476–487.

SKINNER, J. E. Psychosocial stress and sudden cardiac death: Brain mechanisms. In R. Beamish, P. Singal, & N. Dhalla (eds.), *Stress and heart disease.* Boston: Martinus Nijhoff, 1985.

SMITH, T. W., & ALLRED, K. D. Blood-pressure responses during social interaction in high- and low-cynically hostile males. *Journal of Behavioral Medicine,* 1989, *12,* 135–143.

SMITH, T. W., ALLRED, K. D., & FROHM, K. D. Components of the Cook-Medley Ho Scale. In *Proceedings of 9th Annual Society of Behavioral Medicine.* Boston, MA, 1988.

SMITH, T. W., & FROHM, K. D. What's so unhealthy about hostility? Construct validity and psychosocial correlates of the Cook and Medley Ho Scale. *Health Psychology,* 1985, *4,* 503–520.

SMITH, T. W., HOUSTON, B. K., & ZURAWSKI, R. M. The Framingham Type A Scale and anxiety irrational beliefs, and self-control. *Journal of Human Stress,* 1983, *3,* 32–37.

SOKOLOW, M., WERDEGAR, D., KAIN, H. K., & HINMAN, A. T. Relationship between level of blood pressure measured casually and by portable recorders and severity of complications in essential hypertension. *Circulation,* 1966, *34,* 297–298.

SOLBERG, L. A., & STRONG, J. P. Risk factors and atherosclerotic lesions. A review of autopsy studies. *Atherosclerosis,* 1983, *3,* 187–198.

SOMERVELL, P. D., KAPLAN, B. H., HEISS, G. H., TYROLER, H. A., KLEINBAUM, D. C., & OBRIST, P. A. Psychologic distress as a predictor of mortality. *American Journal of Epidemiology,* 1989, *130,* 1013–1023.

SPIELBERGER, C. D., JOHNSON, E. H., RUSSELL, S. F., CRANE, R. J., JACOBS, G. A., & WORDEN, T. I. The experience and expression of anger: Construction and validation of an anger expression scale. In M. Chesney & R. Rosenman (eds.), *Anger and hostility in cardiovascular and behavioral disorders.* Washington, DC: Hemisphere, 1985.

STEPTOE, A., MELVILLE, D., & ROSS, A. Behavioral response demands, cardiovascular reactivity, and essential hypertension. *Psychosomatic Medicine,* 1984, *46,* 33–48.

STEWART, I. M. G. Coronary disease and modern stress. *Lancet,* 1950, *2,* 867–878.

STRUBE, M. J. A self-appraisal model of the type A behavior pattern. In R. Hogan & W. Jones (eds.), *Perspectives in personality theory.* Vol. 2. Greenwich, CT: JAI Press, 1987.

SUAREZ, E. C., WILLIAMS, R. B., & MCRAE, A. R. High scores on the Cook and Medley Hostility Scale predict increased cardiovascular responses to harassment. *Psychosomatic Medicine,* 1988, *50,* 192.

SULS, J. Type A behavior pattern: The role of anxiety, self-awareness, and denial. In D. Byrne & R. Rosenman (eds.), *Anxiety and the heart.* Washington, DC: Hemisphere, 1990.

SULS, J., & SANDERS, G. S. Type A behavior as a general risk factor for physical disorder. *Journal of Behavioral Medicine,* 1988, *11,* 201–209.

SULS, J., & WAN, C. K. The relationship between type A behavior pattern and chronic emotional distress: A meta-analysis. Journal of Personality and Social Psychology, 1989, *57,* 503–512.

SWAN, G. E., CARMELLI, D., & ROSENMAN, R. H. Spouse-pair similarity on the California Psychological Inventory with reference to husband's coronary heart disease. *Psychosomatic Medicine,* 1986, *48,* 172–186.

————. Cook and Medley hostility and the type A behavior pattern: Psychological correlates of two coronary prone behaviors. In M. Strube (ed.), *Type A behavior.* (Special issue). *Journal of Social Behavior and Personality,* 1990, *5,* 89–106.

TENNANT, C. C., LANGELUDDECKE, P. M., FULCHER, G., & WILBY, J. Anger and other psychological factors in coronary atherosclerosis. *Psychological Medicine,* 1987, *17,* 425–431.

TREIBER, F. A., MUSANTE, L., RILEY, W., MABE, P. A., CARR, T., LEVY, M., & STRONG, W. B. The relationship between hostility and blood pressure in children. *Annals of Behavioral Medicine,* 1989, *Winter,* 173–178.

VICKERS, R. R., HERVIG, L. K., RAHE, R. H., & ROSENMAN, R. H. Type A behavior pattern and coping and defense. *Psychosomatic Medicine,* 1981, *43,* 381–396.

VLIETSTRA, R. E., FRYE, R. L., KRONMAL, R. A., SIM, D. A., PHIL, M., TRISTANI, F. E., & KILLIP, T., and participants in the Coronary Artery Surgery Study. Risk factors and angiographic coronary artery disease: A report from the coronary artery surgery study (CASS). *Circulation,* 1980, *62,* 251–261.

VLIETSTRA, R. E., KRONMAL, R. A., FRYE, R. L., SETH, A. K., TRISTANI, F. E., & KILLIP, T. Factors affecting the extent and severity of coronary artery disease in patients enrolled in coronary artery surgery. *Atherosclerosis,* 1983, *2,* 208–215.

VON DUSCH, T. *Lehrbuch der Herz Krankheiten.* Leipzig: Verlag von Wilhelm Engelman, 1868.

WARD, M. M., CHESNEY, M. S., SWAN, G. E., BLACK, G. W., PARKER, S. D., & ROSENMAN, R. H. Cardiovascular responses in type A and B men to a series of stressors. *Journal of Behavioral Medicine,* 1986, *9,* 43–49.

WATKINS, F. L., FISHER, E. B., SOUTHARD, D. R., & WARD, C. H. Comparison of hostility and type A behavior as cardiovascular disease risk factors within a worksite screening program. In *Proceedings of 9th Annual Society of Behavioral Medicine.* Boston, MA, 1988.

WEIDNER, G., FRIEND, R., FIGARROTTO, T. J., & MENDELL, N. R. Hostility and cardiovascular reactivity to stress in women and men. *Psychosomatic Medicine,* 1989, *51,* 36–45.

WEIDNER, G., SEXTON, G., McCLELLAND, R., CONNOR, S. L., & MATARAZZO, J. D. The role of type A behavior and hostility in an elevation of plasma lipids in adult women and men. *Psychosomatic Medicine,* 1987, *49,* 136–145.

WERKO, L. Risk factors and coronary heart disease—facts or fancy? *American Heart Journal,* 1976, *91,* 87–98.

WHITE, P. D. The historical background of angina pectoris. *Modern Concepts of Cardiovascular Disease,* 1974, *43,* 109–112.

WILHELMSEN, L., SVARDSUDD, K., KORSAN-BENGTSEN, K., LARSON, B., WELIN, L., & TIBBLIN, G. Fibrinogen as a risk factor for stroke and myocardial infarction. *New England Journal of Medicine,* 1984, *311,* 501–505.

WILLIAMS, R. B., JR. Refining the type A hypothesis: Emergence of the hostility complex. *American Journal of Cardiology,* 1987, *60,* 27J–32J.

WILLIAMS, R. B., JR., BAREFOOT, J. C., HANEY, T. L., HARRELL, F. E., BLUMENTHAL, J. A., & PRYOR, D. B. Type A behavior and angiographically documented coronary atherosclerosis in a sample of 2,289 patients. *Psychosomatic Medicine,* 1988, *50,* 139–152.

WILLIAMS, R. B., JR., BAREFOOT, J. C., & SHEKELLE, R. B. The health consequences of hostility. In M. Chesney & R. Rosenman (eds.), *Anger and behavior in cardiovascular and behavioral disorders.* Washington, DC: Hemisphere, 1985.

WILLIAMS, R. B., JR., HANEY, T. L., & LEE, K. L. Type A behavior, hostility, and coronary atherosclerosis. *Psychosomatic Medicine,* 1980, *42,* 539–549.

WILLIAMS, R. B., JR., LANE, J. D., KUHN, C., MELOSH, W., WHITE, A., & SCHANBERG, S. Type A behavior and elevated physiologic and neuroendocrine response to cognitive tasks. *Science*, 1982, *281*, 483–486.

WINNIFORD, M. D., WHEELAN, K. R., & KREMERS, M. S. Smoking-induced coronary vasoconstriction in patients with atherosclerotic coronary artery disease: Evidence for adrenergically-mediated alterations in coronary artery tone. *Circulation*, 1986, *73*, 662–667.

WOODS, P. J., & BURNS, J. Type A behavior and illness in general. *Journal of Behavioral Medicine*, 1984, *7*, 411–414.

YAKUBOVICH, I. S., RAGLAND, D. R., BRAND, R. J., & SYME, S. L. Type A behavior pattern and health status after 22 years of follow-up in the Western Collaborative Group Study. *American Journal of Epidemiology*, 1988, *128*, 579–588.

YOUNG, J. B., & LANDSBERG, L. Catecholamines and intermediary metabolism. *Clinical Endocrinology and Metabolism*, 1977, *6*, 599–631.(a)

————. Catecholamines and the regulation of hormone secretion. *Clinical Endocrinology and Metabolism*, 1977, *6*, 657–695.(b)

ZYZANSKI, S. J., JENKINS, C. D., RYAN, T. J., FLESSAS, A., & EVERIST, M. Psychological correlates of coronary angiographic findings. *Archives of Internal Medicine*, 1976, *136*, 1234–1237.

26

Stress and Psychiatric Disorders

Judith Godwin Rabkin

ALTHOUGH THE ETIOLOGY OF THE PSYCHIATRIC DISORDERS has constituted a hotly controversial issue throughout the history of psychiatry, and questions about the relative influence of genetic and socioenvironmental factors have never been consensually resolved, few today would entirely exclude from consideration either one realm or the other. It is generally assumed that to varying degrees, depending on the particular syndrome, both biology and experience contribute to the risk of becoming ill, and genetic factors are being increasingly acknowledged as well. Under the label "experience" is usually included not only lifelong exposure and patterns but also the idea of a particular experience or event that is either etiologically or temporally associated with illness onset. In view of this nearly universal conceptualization of stress as a relevant consideration in illness onset, it is all the more surprising that the large majority of studies of stress and psychiatric disorder have failed to demonstrate a clinically significant association, although small, statistically significant relationships repeatedly have been found.

Many who have studied and worked in this field for any length of time believe that a substantial proportion of the research is sufficiently flawed in conceptualization and design so as to preclude identification of clear-cut relationships even if they do exist. Certainly, most of these problems are not specific to the study of stress and psychiatric disorders, and note is taken of them elsewhere in this volume. Both in order fairly to appraise the quality and validity of previous research and to improve the design of future work, I review in some detail those issues of concept and design particularly germane to the study of psychiatric disorders. After brief consideration of the officially recognized stress syndromes, I summarize the cumulative findings for the three major classes of functional disorder: anxiety disorders, schizophrenia, and depressive disorders. The extent and quality of study of these disorders vary considerably. Least has been done with anxiety disorders, and fewer than 20 controlled studies have explored the association between stress and schizophrenia, although some solid work has been published. In contrast, dozens of investigators have considered aspects of the relationship between stress and depressive disorder. Volume is related to level of sophistication of the issues addressed; thus, studies range from simple explorations of proportions of patients who report precipitating events to comparatively refined analyses of the role of concurrent personal and social variables in mediating the effects of exposure to stressors.

In the following discussion, the terms "life events" and "stressors" are used interchangeably. Both refer to discrete changes in life conditions that are consensually recognized as entailing some degree of distress, challenge, and/or hazard by the individual and members of his/her social group.

METHODOLOGICAL CONSIDERATIONS

As in the field of psychotherapy research, the study of stress and illness seems to have generated as much commentary as original research. Numerous reviewers have identified and described potential and actual sources of error in instruments and methods (e.g., Brown, 1974; Dohrenwend & Dohrenwend, 1978; Rabkin & Struening, 1976a). Perhaps partly as a result of such critical assessment, the quality of life events research is improving, although numerous issues remain unresolved. In this chapter, I will briefly note those particularly relevent to the study of psychiatric disorders.

Choice of Stress Model

A remarkable number of studies are minimally informative because of naive or inappropriate conceptions of stress and illness, indifference to the issue of psychiatric diagnosis, or some combination of these defects. With rare exceptions, investigators develop a model of stress and illness that is applied to all forms of psychiatric disorder, ignoring the possibility that different conceptualizations might be appropriate for psychiatric disorders with different historical antecedents and prodromal stages.

At least three major models of stress and illness have evolved in relation to the study of psychiatric disorders. Dohrenwend and Dohrenwend [1981] delineated seven models, but several of these are related to each other. In the simplest and historically earliest approach, the *innocent victim model,* the prospective patient by chance is exposed to stressful environmental events or circumstances that cause illness. This conception of illness and stress scarcely applies to most medical or psychiatric conditions as they are understood today, although it is valid with respect to rare and catastrophic situations such as prisoner of war or concentration camp internment. In such extreme conditions, the probability of both immediate and delayed illness is significantly increased for perfectly healthy people (Ursano, Boydstun & Wheatley, 1981). In sufficiently adverse circumstances, then, it is not a matter of *whether* but of *when* disorders will be manifested. In the current psychiatric nomenclature of *DSM-III* (1980), such reactions to unusual traumatic events are classified separately as post–traumatic stress disorder. In most other circumstances, however, this model is inadequate.

A model more generally relevant to the study of psychiatric disorder is called the *vulnerability hypothesis* (Dohrenwend & Dohrenwend, 1981). According to this model, chance exposure to stressors triggers illness onset in already vulnerable people. The source of vulnerability may vary according to the disorder or the investigator's point of view and may include childhood experiences, family relationships, or genetic predisposition. In addition, the resources available to the person, such as social supports, fiscal backing, or personal coping skills, are considered mediating factors that determine the impact of the stressor on the person and therefore affect the probability of his/her becoming ill. This is perhaps the most popular current model.

A third construction is structural, interactive, and probably most appropriate for at least some types of psychiatric illness. The *interactive model* is similar to the proneness, or vulnerability, hypothesis of Dohrenwend and Dohrenwend (1981). It suggests that because of preexisting deficiencies in coping and interpersonal skills, people who later become clinically ill either are unable to forestall the occurrence of undesirable life events or by their behavior actively provoke them while at the same time they lack the ability to make good events happen. Their long-standing limitations not only influence the number and quality of the life events they encounter but also determine the availability and extent of mediating factors such as access to social and family supports. This interactive conception seems more relevant to some illness types (e.g., schizophrenia) than others (e.g., panic disorder).

In short, it seems advisable to select the stress model most nearly related to the clinical condition under study in order to maximize the likelihood of finding meaningful associations between stress and illness.

Illness Definition: Clinical Diagnosis

Comparatively little attention has been devoted to the systematic diagnosis of psychiatric disorders in most stress research, a regrettable state of affairs that has detracted from the value of many studies. Many investigators have been content either to identify the presence or absence of disorder (or *casedness*) based on global ratings or interviews that are either structured or not, or else to classify research subjects in terms of number of symptoms reported. In the latter case they use various checklists, which may or may not be factor-analysed to identify symptom clusters and which cumulatively often measure demoralization rather than the presence of any particular psychiatric disorder (Dohrenwend, 1979). In such studies, the type of symptom is often not specified, or else respondents with different symptom clusters are combined to facilitate data analysis. This approach used to characterize studies of stress and medical conditions in which, for example, patients with skin problems and coronary heart disease were together classified as suffering from chronic disorders (Rabkin & Struening, 1976). While this failure to disaggregate groups is seldom seen now in studies of medical disorders, it remains all too common in studies of psychiatric disorders.

In addition to the application of systematic diagnostic criteria for psychiatric disorders, such as the Research Diagnostic Criteria of Spitzer, Endicott, and Robins (1978) or the *DSM-III* (1980) categories, the medical condition and current medication regimens of study participants warrant assessment, since both may contribute to cognitive and behavioral deviations that may be mistaken for signs of psychiatric disorder. Concurrent medical conditions may or may not be related to the stressors being studied, but in any case they should not be confused with manifestations of psychiatric disorder. Finally, it would be useful to distinguish between the presence of psychiatric disorder as such and the seeking of treatment for psychiatric problems. Since we know that at least as many people with psychiatric disorders remain untreated as receive treatment, and since there is no reason to assume that treated cases are a representative sample of all cases, this distinction may contribute to an understanding of the relation between stressors and illness as such.

Event Definitions

Originally, life events researchers used scales consisting of 40 or more items, such as marriage, birth of child, fired at work (Holmes & Rahe, 1967). The respondent's total score consisted of the sum (sometimes weighted) of items reported to have occurred during the preceding six months or year. However, many questions have been raised about the meaning of such a score, combining as it does so many disparate events. Although not routinely done, it would be useful for events to be differentiated in terms of whether they are anticipated or unanticipated, familiar or novel, desirable or undesirable, sudden or gradual, discrete or temporally prolonged, subjectively perceived as stressful by the patient or not so perceived, and fateful (outside one's control) or nonfateful. Is it possible for a respondent to experience a given event? Does the absence of an anticipated or desired event such as marriage represent a stressful experience? Does it matter whether the event constitutes a "role entrance" rather than a "role exit"? How close in timing must an event be to illness onset to be considered contributory? What is the difference between a life event and a condition or problem in living? When does an event, such as the chronic illness of a relative, stop being counted as an event? Should rare events be excluded because of reliability problems? Such unresolved questions generally concern the nature of the domain of life events to be sampled and represent problems in content validity and methods of measurement.

In addition to the formal characteristics of the items to be included, their content warrants consideration. Certain kinds of stressors would seem more likely to be linked with a particular disorder—e.g., losses and depressive disorders, frightening experiences and simple phobias. Some evidence, to be reviewed later, suggests that such relationships are more difficult to establish than may have been anticipated. Nevertheless, focused questions of this nature would seem more fruitful, either to demonstrate or to disprove theories of etiology, than a purely quantitative approach to the study of stress and psychiatric disorder.

Timing Definitions

Most chronic diseases (e.g., coronary heart disease, cancer) have a preliminary, subclinical phase that entails gradual organic and/or behavioral alterations, but few medical illnesses are defined in terms of the presence of a distinctive prodromal phase, as are some psychiatric disorders such as schizophrenia. Other psychiatric conditions cannot be diagnosed unless they have lasted a specified period of time (e.g., manic disorder). Historically, identification of a prodromal phase as a criterion for diagnosis has been more popular among European than among American psychiatrists, but in the past decade the concept has become more widely emphasized in this country as well. In *DSM-III* (1980), identification of a continuous phase of illness of at least six months' duration has become an essential prerequisite for the diagnosis of schizophrenia. This six-month phase may consist of prior acute illness or manifestation of a prodromal phase, which is defined in terms of behavioral changes such as impaired routine daily functioning, social withdrawal, diminished effectiveness at school or work, irritability, lack of drive, and personality changes (p. 189). In contrast to these relatively insidious alterations, onset of the active phase of schizophrenia is defined in terms of flagrant psychotic symptomatology: hallucinations, delusions, and disturbed thought processes.

In documenting the occurrence of life events preceding schizophrenic onset, the investigator cannot ignore changes in the prodromal phase even when onset is defined in terms of the acute phase, as is the usual research procedure. There is also the probability that a substantial proportion of patients do not suddenly become acutely ill but drift into illness without a clear-cut onset. How, then, is one to identify the occurrence and the impact of life events or the temporal sequence of event and behavioral change? In this context, it seems essential to differentiate between *fateful events*—those that are clearly unrelated to the patient's behavior—and *nonfateful events*—those that he/she may have instigated by personal action or inaction, such as divorce, loss of a job, or changes in social relationships or in financial status. While this strategy increases the plausibility of causal inferences, it does reduce considerably the number of life events apt to befall a person in a restricted time period, thus making it difficult to demonstrate differences between groups.

Another unresolved issue of timing concerns the optimal interval between event and illness selected for study, which can also be thought of as the distinction between measuring *incidence* (new cases) and *prevalence* (cases counted at a given point in time) of morbidity. Most investigators have studied the six months or year preceding illness in retrospective studies. Brown and Harris (1978) found the three-week interval immediately preceding illness onset to be the critical period differentiating patients from normal controls in terms of number of life events experienced. On the other hand, in a prospective study of former Vietnam prisoners of war, Ursano and colleagues (1981) found a relationship between severity of stress and proportion of men with psychiatric diagnoses five years later, although this distinction was not apparent at the time of repatriation. Among those who had experienced maximal stress, the proportion with psychiatric morbidity increased during this five-year interval, while there was a decline among those whose experience had been comparatively less harsh. While the documented effects of POW internment may not be generalizable to other classes of stressor, it seems likely that the distinction between transient and long-term disorders is useful.

Problems of Retrospective Design

The difficulties incurred by use of retrospective designs in the study of life events and illness have been observed in many contexts, but they seem particularly intrusive in the investigation of psychiatric disorders. These difficulties fall into three general areas: errors of recall that can attributed either to ordinary forgetting or to the condition of being ill; retrospective falsification to justify illness; and differences between the evidence generated by the study of cases and findings from prospective research or cohorts.

Several groups of investigators have demonstrated that people forget events, with greater forgetting associated with longer periods of recall (e.g., Jenkins, Hurst, & Rose, 1979). Even events as presumably memorable as hospitalization for medical conditions are increasingly underreported with the passage of time, so that in one survey 40% of respondents failed to report such an event one year later (Lilienfeld, 1976). Yager, Grant, Sweetwood, and Gerst (1981) compared reports by male psychiatric patients, male nonpatients, and their partners, for three separate two-month periods, of events experienced by the index person. For all groups, perfect agreement was obtained for only one-third of events reported by at least one member of the pair. All patients had chronic, rather than acute, illnesses so that illness status evidently did not play a role in recall.

When patients are interviewed during or at the end of acute illness episodes, the illness itself is likely to modify recall. In acute onset schizophrenia, for example, the patient's thinking, judgment, perception, language, and communication are profoundly affected, so that recall, identification, and interpretation of prior life events must operate through a "screen of pathology." More generally, patients who recently have become ill often seek to justify their illness, to make sense of it in terms of recent experiences or events that might have contributed to the condition. A dramatic example of "retrospective contamination" was offered by Brown (1974), who cited a study published before the genetic etiology of Down's syndrome was established: mothers of Down's syndrome children reported more "shocks" early in pregnancy than did mothers of normal controls.

One of the problems with retrospective studies is not inherent in the method, namely, misinterpretation of results. Retrospective studies can show what proportion of those in a given illness or control group experience stress:

$$\text{rate} = \frac{\% \text{ experiencing stressor(s)}}{\text{number ill}}$$

This equation provides a measure of association but no direct insight into etiology. In contrast, prospective studies indicate what proportion of those who experience stressors become ill:

$$\text{rate} = \frac{\% \text{ ill}}{\text{number experiencing stressors}}$$

When results from retrospective studies are used to address etiological questions, problems then arise.

Despite the drawbacks associated with retrospective design, studies of stress and illness lend themselves to this approach. Events, after all, can be reported only after they have occurred, so that at least some data must be gathered retrospectively. The choices are three: to study those who have a particular characteristic (e.g., illness) in order to assess frequency of events; to study those who have experienced an event (e.g., bereavement, flood) and to follow them to see how many and who among them become ill; or to follow a randomly selected community cohort over a period of time to see who experiences stressors and who becomes ill. In the order presented, the three strategies become progressively more costly and sophisticated in their contributions to etiological insights. Most studies of stress and psychiatric disorder have used the first strategy, that of studying life events experienced and reported by different patient groups.

Sample Selection

In retrospective studies of life events, the selection of patients can strongly influence findings. The issue can be illustrated by considering the options possible in choosing a sample of schizophrenic patients. Because the investigator is concerned about pinpointing the timing of both events and illness onset, patients with good premorbid adjustment tend to be selectively included; reports by patients who have never done well at work, in school, or with other people are more difficult to interpret. Consequently, patients with acute onset and noticeable change in level of functioning are typically selected for study in order to facilitate dating of events. However, in the clinical tradition, acute onset is associated with a constellation of other variables, including presence of a precipitating event. If one then selects patients with acute onset and good premorbid functioning, is one increasing the probability of identifying recent precipitating events? Is the interviewer more persistent in efforts to define such an event? Is the patient more willing or able to report events? Such artifacts of data collection may account for an apparent association between the occurrence of a stressful life event and schizophrenic onset even if no association actually exists. Equivalent issues apply to the study of other syndromes.

Precipitant versus Hazard (Subjective versus Objective Stress)

A distinction infrequently drawn but undoubtedly meaningful in the study of life events and illness concerns the difference between *precipitant* and *hazard* (Beck & Worthen, 1972). In addition to seeking a stimulus, or precipitant, leading to an illness episode reported by either patient or relative, Beck and Worthen (1972) emphasized the utility of determining the degree of hazard signified by such an event according to other members of the same social group, as well as the correspondence between the hazard and the behavioral response.

It is commonly believed that people who become schizophrenic are exceptionally sensitive to perceived or actual threats to self-esteem and that psychotic episodes may follow situations not ordinarily regarded as objectively stressful or hazardous. As noted in a psychiatric textbook, "Those who have worked extensively with schizophrenics know that these patients . . . are very easily hurt by . . . behavior that, in most cases, would hardly be noticed by a person of normal sensitivity or, if noticed, certainly would not lead to traumatic experiences" (Lehmann, 1975: 891).

In life event studies, the distinction between precipitant and hazard is seldom observed, an omission that may lead to either conceptual or practical difficulties. When patients are asked about, or records searched for, life events immediately preceding a given illness episode, failure to make this distinction can generate misleading information.

Comment

No study of life events, stress, or psychopathology is entirely free of the foregoing problems of research method. However, more recent studies have taken many of these pitfalls into account. By seeking to identify consistent findings across studies, the methodological weaknesses of each individual study are minimized.

STRESS SYNDROMES

Included in the current psychiatric nosology of *DSM-III* (1980) are two syndromes specifically identified as a sequelae of "a recognizable stressor that would be expected to evoke significant symptoms of distress in most people" (pp. 200, 236). They are brief reactive psychosis and the post–traumatic stress disorder. The two are distinguished from each other by criteria regarding interval between precipitant and illness onset, by illness duration, and by type of symptoms. *Brief reactive psychosis* has a sudden onset immediately following exposure to stress, lasts at least a few hours but no more than two weeks, and has a clinical picture including emotional turmoil and at least one gross psychotic symptom. *Post–traumatic stress disorder* is classified as an anxiety disorder. In contrast to brief reactive psychosis, this condition may occur months or years after the precipitating event, and the disorder may last indefinitely. In addition, there is a distinctive clinical picture, including recurrent dreams or daytime flashbacks in which the trauma is reexperienced; emotional numbing; and one or more of several other symptoms, such as survival guilt, insomnia, or impaired concentration, not present before exposure to stress.

In both disorders, the precipitant is conceptualized as "outside the range of usual human experience," thus excluding the life events customarily studied in the stress literature. There is, however, a separate body of research on extreme situations, including man-made and natural disasters such as concentration camp internment, military combat, and floods and fires. This literature illustrates the reciprocal relationship between stressors, on the one hand, and social and individual characteristics, on the other. The more severe the stressor, the less significant are such characteristics in determining the likelihood and nature of response. When conditions are sufficiently harsh, breakdown is virtually universal (Horowitz, 1976), and individual variations are reflected only in the length of time before the reaction occurs and perhaps in recovery time. In contrast, when the stress is milder, social supports and individual characteristics can contribute to an understanding of why some people become ill and others do not.

Although it is suggested in *DSM-III* that "unstable" individuals are more likely to develop psychiatric disorders in response to stress than are others, and psychiatrists generally believe that stressful events within the realm of ordinary living cannot "cause madness in a person previously of sound mind" (Hudgens, 1974: 120), the empirical evidence is extremely limited. One is seldom in a position to have antecedent psychiatric assessments for survivors of major traumatic events, so that measures of change are not usually available. However, one recent study of six repatriated Vietnam prisoners of war who for various reasons had received extensive psychiatric assessments before their capture did address this issue (Ursano, 1981). Three men were found to be in superb psychological condition; three others had some sort of psychophysiological problem not severe enough to interfere with their military careers. No relationship was found between health status before and after internment, disproving the notion, as Singer (1981) pointed out in discussing this paper, that severe traumas "drive people out of their minds" or that those who develop psychiatric disorders after stress exposure "were covert or masked neurotics all the while" (p. 345).

The diagnostic criteria provided by *DSM-III* should facilitate the study of stress response syndromes, so that we learn more about the interaction among predisposing personal characteristics, social conditions, and response to stress.

STRESS AND ANXIETY DISORDERS

Defining Anxiety Disorders

Far-reaching changes in the diagnosis and classification of anxiety disorders have been introduced in the past decade by the Feighner Criteria (Feighner, 1972), the Research Diagnostic Criteria (Spitzer et al. 1978), and, most decisively, by *DSM-III* (1980). In the first two editions of the American Psychiatric Association's *Diagnostic and Statistical Manual* (1952, 1968), anxiety was presented as the chief characteristic of all neurotic disorders, and two subtypes, anxiety neurosis and phobic neurosis, were identified. In addition, transient situational disturbances, classified separately, referred to "acute reaction(s) to overwhelming environmental stress" in "individuals without any apparent underlying mental disorders" (1968: 48).

The authors of *DSM-III* reorganized, redefined, and provided operational criteria for anxiety disorders, which are now grouped into two major and nine minor classes. Phobic disorders include agoraphobia with or without panic attacks, as well as social and simple phobias. Anxiety states include panic disorder, generalized anxiety disorder, obsessive-compulsive disorder, post–traumatic stress disorder, and a residual category of atypical anxiety disorder. This new nosology permits more precision and specificity in sample composition, which should facilitate research on the role of stress in each of these syndromes.

Research findings in this area are very limited, perhaps to some extent because of the shifting diagnostic conceptualizations. Few controlled studies have been conducted, and much of the available evidence, such as it is, has come from clinical reports. Investigators have not progressed beyond the basic question of whether a relationship exists between life events and illness onset. Since more work has been done regarding stress and phobic disorders than other anxiety syndromes, these data will be reviewed to exemplify what is known to date about stress and anxiety disorders. For a comprehensive review of this literature, see Rabkin & Klein (1980).

Problems of Method

A major problem specific to the study of phobic disorders is the relative unavailability of new cases. Patients characteristically have been ill for years when they are identified for study or treatment, and, in fact, the most severely functionally disabled often seek medical help for varying periods of time before eventual referral to a psychiatrist (Klein, 1980). Treatment studies often report that the average illness duration of these patients is 8–10 years (Zitrin, Woerner, & Klein, 1981). Thus, it is difficult accurately to assess circumstances associated with illness onset no matter how carefully thought out are other design aspects.

Research Evidence

Despite long-standing recognition of the syndrome of phobic disorders and widespread assumptions by clinicians of the etiological role of stress in phobias, only in recent years have investigators begun to compile evidence concerning the presence and nature of such precipitants. Studies can be grouped into two categories: those in which the investigator assumes that each illness has a precipitant and the task is simply to identify it and those in which the investigator first asks whether or not illness onset is preceded by an identifiable stressor.

Studies in the first category usually consist of tabular presentations of events preceding illness onset for patients seen in various psychiatric treatment settings. Characteristically, neither definitions of stress nor diagnostic procedures are presented. Weekes's (1978) report is typical:

> For the majority of 528 agoraphobic men and women in my survey, the precipitating cause of their agoraphobia was stress . . . either sudden stress . . . or prolonged . . . stress created by some difficult life situation. . . . only 5% could offer no cause. (P. 358)

A more specific listing of 10 types of stressful factors was reported by Sim and Houghton (1966). They found that the most common precipitants of phobic disorder in their sample of 191 patients with agoraphobia and other phobias were bereavement and "sudden shock."

In studies such as these, absence of control groups, together with lack of precision in definition of terms concerning both stress and diagnosis, renders findings virtually uninterpretable. Furthermore, the question itself is of dubious validity since we know that nearly any illness or behavior change will be identified with a precipitant if the patient is asked to produce one. In general, then, this category of research is not a promising source of insight into the etiology of phobic disorders.

The second group of studies addresses the question of whether or not stressful events precede onset of phobic disorders. While these research designs represent an advance over the approach taken in the preceding category, systematic measurement of stressors continues to be weak or absent.

One of the better studies in this area—and one of the few to use a control group—was conducted by Buglass, Clarke, and Kreetman (1977). They studied 30 agoraphobic housewives and 30 controls enrolled in a general medical clinic. Their patients all experienced at least moderate functional impairment, which was found to vary markedly during illness course. In only 7 patients (23% of the sample) could discrete precipitating events be identified, and only 2 of these (7%) reported a particular fearful experience occurring away from home. The authors concluded that their data showed "no evidence that a specific stimulus commonly initiates the phobia" (p. 84). Turning to a consideration of personality style, in order to verify the widespread assumption of dependence in the pre-illness history of phobic patients, they found no differences between patients and controls in indexes of developmental signs of dependence (e.g., history of separation anxiety, problems of school adjustment, or unusual conformity).

In several other studies, about two-thirds of phobic patients reported a precipitating stressor, although the researchers themselves did not always agree with the patients' assessments (Roberts, 1964; Shafar, 1976; Woerner, 1980). Among patients with phobic disorders, those with agoraphobia appear to be least likely to report a specific illness precipitant, although far more work remains to be done before firm conclusions can be drawn.

Comment

Despite both clinical and lay expectations that phobic disorders are triggered, if not caused, by a particular stressor, investigators have not found a strong association. The available evidence is limited in terms of both design and definitional clarity. Base rates and control groups are scarcely evident, and even in studies that do differentiate phobic disorder from other anxiety disorders, the samples are often heterogeneous and time elapsed since illness onset is characteristically measured in years. Although initial results are not as encouraging as one might have anticipated, well-designed studies remain to be conducted so that it is premature to conclude that stress plays no significant role in the genesis of phobic disorders.

STRESS AND SCHIZOPHRENIA

Investigators working in this area have so far focused on determining whether patients with schizophrenia experience more or less stress before illness onset or subsequent exacerbations than do either patients with other psychiatric disorders or community controls. Studies are included in this review if their samples consisted of schizophrenic patients diagnosed according to specified criteria and considered as a distinct diagnostic group, if a comparison group was employed, and if data sources and time periods surveyed were reported by the investigators. For a detailed review, see Rabkin (1980).

As a general rule, investigators of stressful environmental conditions have been cautious in attributing an etiological role to such conditions and tend instead to emphasize their influence on the timing of the illness episode. This is most certainly the case in studies of stress and schizophrenia, in which life events are regarded as precipitating the onset of acute schizophrenic illness. Accordingly, the hypotheses presented in the studies reviewed here focus on the precipitating role of stressful events in already vulnerable people. Specifically, investigators have looked at whether schizophrenics, compared either to normal comparison groups or to other psychiatric subgroups, report events that are more severe, more frequent, of a singular nature, or in a specific category.

In order to facilitate comparison of findings, I have classified studies into three groups: comparison of life events reported by schizophrenics and other psychiatric patients; comparison of reports by schizophrenics and normals; and comparison of events reported by schizophrenic patients with and without subsequent relapses and comparison of events reported by chronic schizophrenic patients in the community and by controls.

Schizophrenics and Other Psychiatric Patients

The cumulative findings of studies in this area provide the following answers about the relationship between stressful life events and psychiatric syndromes. First, there is no evidence that events reported by schizophrenics are more frequent than those reported by other diagnostic groups preceding illness onset. Moreover, the one study that evaluated magnitude of stress associated with events found that events reported by schizophrenic patients were less objectively hazardous or "troublesome" than those reported by depressives (Beck & Worthen, 1972). Finally no investigator has gathered evidence to indicate that the events reported by schizophrenic patients either are of a singular nature or fall into categories different from those associated with other psychiatric patients.

Given the discrepancies in design and the unevenness of methodological rigor of these studies, one cannot justifiably conclude that they have disproved the possibility of an association between stressful life events and schizophrenia onset; rather, they have failed to provide positive evidence for such a link. At least three variables need further attention in order to clarify and to permit comparison of findings: magnitude of objective hazard associated with reported events, their fatefulness (i.e., independence of the patient's behavior), and the unit of time in which they occurred.

Schizophrenics and Normals

Studies in this group have compared events reported by schizophrenic patients and by normal samples drawn from the general population. Considered together, results do not point to any decisive agreement regarding the size of effect of stressful life events in precipitating illness. Brown and colleagues (Brown & Birley, 1968; Brown & Harris, 1978; Brown, Harris, & Peto, 1973), suggested that life events are significant factors that influence the timing, if not the probability, of illness. Jacob and Myers (1976) were more conservative in their evaluation of the role of recent life events, and Serban (1975) was least convinced about their influence. The only evidence of a positive effect is Brown and Birley's (1968) finding that more life events are reported by schizophrenics in the three weeks immediately preceding illness both in comparison to normals during the same period of time and in comparison to their own reports for earlier time periods. This single finding requires replication and further analysis before its significance can be assessed. In addition, the question of cumulative factors requires clarification. Serban's (1975) point that the so-called precipitating factors related to illness onset would not in themselves have such an effect in the absence of an inflated stress level was also noted by Brown and Birley (1968) and warrants additional study.

Schizophrenics with and without Relapses

Longitudinal studies have compared events reported by schizophrenic patients with and without subsequent relapses, as well as events reported by chronic schizophrenic patients in the community and normal controls (Birley & Brown, 1970; Leff, Hirsch, Gaind, Rhode & Stevens, 1973; Michaux, Gansereit, McCabe & Kurland, 1967; Schwartz (1975) & Myers, 1977). Overall, these investigators found reports of more events to be associated with relapse, although in each study some patients who did not report events also relapsed. Among chronic schizophrenics in the community, report of more events was related to greater psychiatric impairment. From these imperfect and preliminary studies, one may conclude that in schizophrenia, life events contribute an incremental component to the stress level of discharged patients, which is, in many cases, associated with subsequent rehospitalization.

Comment

Notwithstanding pervasive methodological problems and lack of equivalence in study designs, the weight of the evidence currently available suggests that schizophrenics do not report significantly more life events preceding illness onset than do other psychiatric patients or normal respondents, nor are the events they report of a singular nature or qualitatively unlike those reported by others. However, the few studies of life events and the probability of relapse suggests that relapsing schizophrenics report more events than do those who continue in remission. Cumulatively, these results tentatively indicate that life events contribute incrementally to an already inflated stress level and so influence the timing, if not the probability, of illness episodes. Whether or not the size of their effect is clinically meaningful remains to be demonstrated.

STRESS AND DEPRESSIVE DISORDERS

In the field of stress research, more investigators have studied depression than all other psychiatric disorders combined. As a result, the research is considerably more advanced, having progressed beyond efforts to demonstrate an association between stress and illness, which characterizes work with other syndromes. The number of studies and the range of issues addressed preclude a systematic review here. Instead, I will consider some of the major questions that have been raised, together with the available evidence.

Does the Occurrence of Stress Differentiate Depressed Patients from Others?

Depressed and Other Patients. In the studies cited in the section on stress and schizophrenia, several investigators reported that depressed patients report more life events than do schizophrenic patients, although a minority failed to find such a difference. In addition, Barrett (1979) found that depressed symptomatic volunteers reported more events in particular categories than did people with anxiety disorders. The cumulative evidence suggests that depressed patients do report more events in the period preceding the start of an illness episode.

Depressed Patients and the General Population. Depressed patients also report more life events than do normal controls, especially immediately before illness onset (Brown, Harris, & Peto, 1973; Lloyd, 1980; Paykel, 1979). As noted earlier, Brown and his colleagues (1973) found that the three-week period directly preceding illness was the critical juncture, distinguishing depressed patients from controls.

While these differences are neither large nor consistently reported, the available evidence suggests an association between increased frequency of life events and onset of depressive illness, in comparison both to other patient groups and to the general population. Overall, it seems justifiable to conclude that life events do play a role in the genesis of depressive disorders.

How Important Are Stressors in the Onset of Depression?

While an association has been established, its effect is small. The correlations between stressful life events and illness onset found in most studies are usually below .30, at best accounting for less than 10% of the variance in illness (Dohrenwend & Dohrenwend, 1981; Rabkin & Struening, 1976). While life events alter the risk for depression (Paykel, 1979), the difference in practical terms is unimpressive. Hudgens (1974) noted that most people do not become mentally ill even when terrible things happen to them, as evidenced by a recent report that less than one-quarter of repatriated Vietnam prisoners of war had diagnosable psychiatric disorders upon release (Ursano et al., 1981). Milder stressors experienced in ordinary living are even less likely to induce illness. Paykel (1974) estimated, for example, that less than 10% of role exits are followed by clinical depression, and Clayton (1979) found that one year after bereavement, only 16% of her sample were clinically depressed.

In addition to the fact that most people who experience losses, role exits, and other events presumably associated with depression do not in fact become ill, many who become depressed have not experienced a precipitating event of this or any other kind. In other words, as Holmes (1979), put it, some of the high-risk people remain well and one-third of the low-risk people get sick. Evidently, while often present, precipitating stress is neither necessary nor sufficient to account for depressive onset, and simply noting the presence or absence of stressful events contributes little to our ability to predict and control their pathological effects.

Is the Presence of Precipitating Stress Useful in Identifying Depressive Subtypes?

Clinicians have long recognized that there are different kinds of depressive disorders, although there is notably less agreement about how best to classify subtypes. One of the earliest and most widely accepted schemes distinguished between *reactive* and *endogenous* depressions, defined, respectively, by the presence or the absence of a stressor. Several other classification systems currently under study also include a distinction between categories that seem parallel; for example, Winokur's (1978) classification of familial pure depressive disorder versus depressive spectrum disorder, which is based entirely on family history of psychiatric disorder, and Klein's (1980) four-part conceptualization, which includes endogenomorphic depression, chronic dysphoria, atypical depression, and disappointment reaction, based on clinical symptoms and clinical history.

Investigators have not found life events to differentiate between subtypes in any of these classifications. Paykel (1979) reviewed his own data and found a correlation of .15 between symptom type and frequency of stress; patients with endogenous depression reported less life stress than did patients with nonendogenous depression. The size of this relationship was, however, far too small to have any practical meaning, accounting for less than 3% of the variance in illness subtype. Paykel concluded, "The so-called endogenous symptom pattern certainly does occur as a group of symptoms which cluster together, but the label is unfortunate: absence of stress is not a prominent feature" (p. 78). Others have also made this observation (e.g., Leff, Roach, & Bunney, 1970; Schless & Mendels, 1977).

Winokur (1979) also failed to find systematic differences in frequency of life events and patients with *depressive spectrum disorder* (diagnosed by a family history of antisocial personality and/or alcoholism) compared to patients with *familial pure depressive disorder* (family history of depression only). He suggested that instead of simple counts of events, the patient's response to their occurrence should be assessed. Similarly, Klein's (1980) endogenomorphic subtype could not be distinguished by the absence of precipitants, which were found in all groups. Barrett (1979) did find that patients with chronic depression reported fewer fateful events than did those with major or intermittent depression (using categories from the Research Diagnostic Criteria [Spitzer et al., 1978], but he was not studying new cases and his small samples and multiple comparisons render such findings tentative at best. Overall, depressive subtypes are not differentiated by frequency of stressful precipitants in the classification systems so far studied.

Does the Type of Event Matter?

A number of investigators have demonstrated that losses and exits from social roles cluster before depressive onset, as do undesirable events in general, although role entrances and desirable events do not show this clustering. This specificity is, however, weak: such events also cluster before the onset of other disorders, both psychiatric and medical. Furthermore, they seem to account for only about 25% of precipitating events among depressed patients. Altogether, there is some reason to suggest that event specificity is not as great as we might wish on theoretical grounds. These null findings do not mean that content of stressors is irrelevant but, rather, that no consistent and strong associations yet have been identified.

Do Childhood Losses Serve as Predisposing
Factors in Adult Depressive Disorders?

In the same month, Crook and Eliot (1980) and Lloyd (1980) reviewed this literature in prestigious journals and arrived at discordant conclusions. Crook and Eliot (1980) examined more than 20 controlled studies published in the past two decades concerning the relationship between parental death during childhood and adult depression. They concluded that "parental death during childhood has not been established as a factor of etiological significance in adult depression or any subtype of adult depression studied to date" (p. 252). They noted further that studies reporting such an association were, without exception, methodologically flawed, while those showing no differences in parental loss among adult depressives and normal controls were reasonably well designed. Lloyd (1980), on the other hand, reviewed the same body of literature and concluded that death of a parent in childhood "generally increases depressive risk by a factor of about 2 or 3. In addition, early loss events also seem to be related to the severity of the subsequent depression and to attempted suicide" (p. 529). The argument, analyses, and evidence presented by Crook and Eliot are more persuasive to me and are supported by more recent data published by Tennant, Smith, Bebbington, and Hurry (1981), who studied community residents and patients from the same neighborhood. They found no relationship between parental death in childhood and adult psychiatric impairment of any kind, either among untreated community residents or among patients. At present, the issue remains unresolved, although the explanatory power of this variable seems less promising now that a substantial number of studies have failed to establish its utility.

Do Mediating Variables Influence Illness
Risk after Exposure to Stressors?

The literature on the buffering effects of personal and social variables on the likelihood of becoming ill has been reviewed extensively elsewhere (Dohrenwend & Dohrenwend, 1977; Rabkin & Struening, 1976b). It seems clear that exposure to stressors alone is almost never a sufficient explanation for illness in ordinary human experience, just as genetic studies have shown that biological vulnerability alone does not produce psychiatric disorder. Other factors that require consideration include characteristics of the stressful situation, individual biological and psychological attributes, and social supports available to the individual at risk.

Characteristics of the stressor presumed to mediate its impact include such dimensions as its magnitude, duration, novelty, and predictability. Relevant personality variables include coping skills, personality style, age at exposure, biological vulnerabilities, and response thresholds. Social factors include availability of benevolent and supportive relatives and friends, access to helping resources, social influence and social class, community attitudes, and prevailing group morale.

Consideration of such mediating factors in relation to stress exposure leads to a multifactorial model of illness that includes a temporal sequence. It seems probable that such an approach ultimately will facilitate our understanding of who becomes ill in what circumstances.

Comment

Several factors undoubtedly contribute to the inconsistencies in reported findings and the weakness of observed associations. First is the problem of diagnostic heterogeneity within depressed samples, both in terms of symptom cluster and in terms of length of illness. In many studies it is not clear whether subjects have depressive symptoms or a diagnosable mood disorder. When the latter is established, the distinction between unipolar and bipolar illness is seldom noted. In addition, few investigators have distinguished between onset of illness (first episode) and illness recurrence (other than first episode). There is some reason to believe that life events may influence illness course (later episodes) even if their etiological role in initial onset is unclear, as suggested in the literature on schizophrenia.

In this and other contexts, it is becoming increasingly apparent that a simple count of reported stressful precipitants is not fruitful. Improved strategies include adoption of a multifactorial model taking into account the effects of historical and concurrent burdens and buffers. Another interesting approach is to test hypotheses regarding the role of particular combinations of events within specified periods of time. This strategy is exemplified by Dohrenwend and Dohrenwend's (1979) *pathogenic triad*. They postulated that depression is more likely to occur following the advent within a short period of time of fateful loss events (e.g., death of spouse), events that exhaust the individual physically (e.g., major medical illness), and disruption of social supports (e.g., geographical move). The combined impact of such events would be associated with a greater incidence of psychopathology in previously healthy people than would be observed either in the absence of such events or in their separate occurrence or in their association with other categories. While the utility of this approach remains to be tested, it is innovative and promising.

A dimension of vulnerability that has been insufficiently studied in this area concerns biological vulnerability. As van Praag (1979) pointed out, it is quite possible that certain biogenic amine deficiencies may be a predisposing rather than a causal factor in depressive illness. Buchsbaum, Coursey, and Murphy (1976) suggested that low platelet monoamine oxidase activity in apparently normal people may serve as a biological marker for increased vulnerability to psychiatric disorder in the presence of stressful conditions. A family history of psychiatric disorder (schizophrenia, affective disorder) may be another useful index of heightened vulnerability. Integration of biological risk factors with social and personal mediating variables may increase the prospects of predicting who is more likely to become ill in response to exposure to stress.

In summary, it has been demonstrated sufficiently often that some relationship exists between life events and depressive disorders, accounting for a small portion of the variance associated with illness onset. The next steps in this field should entail examination of the circumstances in which and for whom such events are enhanced or minimized.

REFERENCES

AMERICAN PSYCHIATRIC ASSOCIATION. *Diagnostic and statistical manual of mental disorders.* Washington, D.C.: American Psychiatric Association, 1952.

————. *Diagnostic and statistical manual of mental disorders* (2d ed.). Washington, D.C.: American Psychiatric Association, 1968

————. *Diagnostic and statistical manual of mental disorders* (3d ed.). Washington, D.C.: American Psychiatric Association, 1980.

Barrett, J. E. The relationship of life events to the onset of neurotic disorders. In J. E. Barrett (ed.), *Stress and mental disorder.* New York: Raven, 1979.

BECK, J., & WORTHEN, K. Precipitating stress, crisis theory, and hospitalization in schizophrenia and depression. *Archives of General Psychiatry,* 1972, *26,* 123–129.

BIRLEY, J. L., & BROWN, G. Crises and life changes preceding the onset or relapse of acute schizophrenia. *British Journal of Psychiatry,* 1970, *116,* 327–333.

BROWN, G. Meaning, measurement, and stress of life events. In B. S. Dohrenwend & B. P. Dohrenwend (eds.), *Stressful life events.* New York: Wiley, 1974.

BROWN, G., & BIRLEY, J. Crises and life changes and the onset of schizophrenia. *Journal of Health and Social Behavior,* 1968, *9,* 203–214.

BROWN, G. W., & HARRIS, T. *Social origins of depression: A study of psychiatric disorder in women.* London: Tavistock, 1978.

BROWN, G., HARRIS, T., & PETO, J. Life events and psychiatric disorders. Part II: Nature of causal link. *Psychological Medicine,* 1973, *3,* 159–176.

BUCHSBAUM, M. S., COURSEY, R., & MURPHY, D. L. The biochemical high-risk paradigm: Behavior and familial correlates of low platelet monoamine oxidase activity. *Science,* 1976, *194,* 339–341.

BUGLASS, D., CLARKE, J., & KREITMAN, N. A study of agoraphobic housewives. *Psychological Medicine,* 1977, *7,* 73–86.

CLAYTON, P., & DARVISH, H. Course of depressive symptoms following the stress of bereavement. In J. E. Barrett (ed.), *Stress and mental disorder.* New York: Raven, 1979.

CROOK, T., & ELIOT, J. Parental death during childhood and adult depression: A critical review of the literature. *Psychological Bulletin,* 1980, *87,* 252–259.

DOHRENWEND, B. P. Problems in defining and sampling the relevant population of stressful life events. In B. S. Dohrenwend & B. P. Dohrenwend (eds.), *Stressful life events.* New York: Wiley, 1974.

————. Stressful life events and psychopathology: Some issues of theory and method. In J. E. Barrett (ed.), *Stress and mental disorder.* New York: Raven, 1979.

DOHRENWEND, B. P., & DOHRENWEND, B. S. The conceptualization and measurement of stressful life events: An overview of the issues. In J. Strauss, H. Babigian, & M. Roff (eds.), *The origins and course of psychopathology.* New York: Plenum, 1977.

DOHRENWEND, B. S., & DOHRENWEND, B. P. Some issues in research on stressful life events. *Journal of Nervous and Mental Disease,* 1978, *166,* 7–15.

————. Life stress and illness: Formulation of the issues. In B. S. Dohrenwend & B. P. Dohrenwend (eds.), *Stressful life events and their contexts.* New York: Watson, 1981.

FEIGHNER, J., ROBINS, E., GUZE, S., WOODRUFF, R., WINOKUR, G., & MUNOZ, R. Diagnostic criteria for use in psychiatric research. *Archives of General Psychiatry,* 1972, *26,* 57–63.

HOLMES, T. General discussion. In J. E. Barrett (ed.), *Stress and mental illness.* New York: Raven, 1979.

HOLMES, T. & RAHE, R. The Social readjustment rating scale. *Journal of Psychosomatic Research,* 1967, *11,* 213–218.

HOROWITZ, M. *Stress response syndromes.* New York: Aronson, 1976.

HUDGENS, R. Personal catastrophe and depression. In B. S. Dohrenwend & B. P. Dohrenwend (eds.), *Stressful life events.* New York: Wiley, 1974.

JACOBS, S., & MYERS, J. Recent life events and acute schizophrenic psychosis: A controlled study. *Journal of Nervous and Mental Disease,* 1976, *162,* 75–87.

JENKINS, C. D., HURST, M. W., & ROSE, R. M. Life changes: Do people really remember? *Archives of General Psychiatry,* 1979, *36,* 379–384.

KLEIN, D. F. Anxiety reconceptualized. *Comprehensive Psychiatry,* 1980, *21,* 411–427.

Klein, D. F., Gittelman R., Quitkin, F., & Rifkin A. *Diagnosis and drug treatment of psychiatric disorders*. Baltimore: Williams and Wilkins, 1980.

Leff, J., Hirsch, S., Gaind, R., Rhode, P., & Stevens, B. Life events and maintenance therapy in schizophrenic relapse. *British Journal of Psychiatry*, 1973, *123*, 659–660.

Leff, M., Roatch, J., & Bunney, W. Environmental factors preceding onset of severe depressions. *Psychiatry*, 1970, *33*, 293–311.

Lehmann, H. Schizophrenia: Clinical features. In A. Freedman, H. Kaplan, & B. Sadock (eds.), *Comprehensive textbook of psychiatry* (2d ed.), vol. 1. Baltimore: Williams & Wilkins, 1975.

Lilienfeld, A. *Foundations of epidemiology*. New York: Oxford University Press, 1976.

Lloyd, C. Life events and depressive disorder reviewed (in two parts). *Achives of General Psychiatry*, 1980, *37*, 529–548.

Michaux, W., Gansereit, K., McCabe, O., & Kurland, A. The psychopathology and measurement of environmental stress. *Community Mental Health Journal*, 1967, *3*, 358–371.

Paykel, E. Life stress and psychiatric disorder: Applications of the clinical approach. In B. S. Dohrenwend & B. P. Dohrenwend (eds.), *Stressful life events*. New York: Wiley, 1974.

————. Causal relationships between clinical depression and life events. In J. E. Barrett (ed.), *Stress and mental disorder*. New York: Raven, 1979.

Rabkin, J. G. Stressful life events and schizophrenia: A review of the research literature. *Psychological Bulletin*, 1980, *87*, 408–425.

Rabkin, J. G., & Klein, D. F. Stress and phobic disorder: Review of empirical findings and research recommendations. Paper prepared for the Stress and Illness Panel of the Steering Committee for Research on Stress in Health and Disease, National Academy of Sciences, Washington, D.C.: 1980.

Rabkin, J. G., & Struening, E. L. Life events, stress, and illness. *Science*, 1976, *194*, 1013–1020. (a)

————. Social change, stress, and illness: A selective literature review. *Psychoanalysis and Contemporary Science*, 1976, *5*, 573–624. (b)

Roberts, A. Housebound housewives: A follow-up study of a phobic anxiety state. *British Journal of Psychiatry*, 1964, 110, 191–197.

Schless, A., & Mendels, J. Life stress and psychopathology. *Psychiatry Digest*, 1977, 25–35.

Schwartz, C., & Myers, J. K. Life events and schizophrenia: II. Impact of life events on symptom configuration. *Archives of General Psychiatry*, 1977, *34*, 1242–1245.

Serban, G. Stress in normals and schizophrenics. *British Journal of Psychiatry*, 1975, *126*, 397–407.

Shafar, S. Aspects of phobic illness: A study of 90 personal cases. *British Journal of Medical Psychology*, 1976, *49*, 221–236.

Sim, M., & Houghton, H. Phobic anxiety and its treatment. *Journal of Nervous and Mental Disease*, 1966, *143*, 484–491.

Singer, M. T. Viet Nam prisoners of war, stress, and personality resiliency. *American Journal of Psychiatry*, 1981, 138, 345–346.

Spitzer, R., Endicott, J., & Robins, E. *Research Diagnostic Criteria*. New York City: New York State Psychiatric Institute, 1978.

Tennant, C., Smith, A., Bebbington, P., & Hurry, J. Parental loss in childhood. *Archives of General Psychiatry*, 1981, *38*, 309–314.

Ursano, R. The Viet Nam era prisoner of war: Precaptivity personality and the development of psychiatric illness. *American Journal of Psychiatry*, 1981, *138*, 315–318.

Ursano, R., Boydstun, J., & Wheatley, R. Psychiatric illness in U.S. Air Force Viet Nam prisoners of war: A five-year follow-up. *American Journal of Psychiatry*, 1981, *138*, 310–314.

VAN PRAAG, H. M. Psychopsychiatry: Can psychosocial factors cause psychiatric disorders? *Comprehensive Psychiatry,* 1979, *20,* 215–225.

WEEKES, C. Simple, effective treatment of agoraphobia. *American Journal of Psychotherapy,* 1978, *32,* 357–369.

WINOKUR, G. General discussion. In J. E. Barrett (ed.), *Stress and mental disorder.* New York: Raven, 1979.

WINOKUR, G., BEHAR, D., VANVALKENBURG, C., & LOWRY, M. Is a familial definition of depression both feasible and valid? *Journal of Nervous & Mental Disease,* 1978, *166,* 764–768.

WOERNER, M. Unpublished data, Long Island Jewish Hillside Medical Center, 1980.

YAGER, J., GRANT, I., SWEETWOOD, H., & GERST, M. Life event reports by psychiatric patients, nonpatients, and their partners. *Archives of General Psychiatry,* 1981, *38,* 343–347.

ZITRIN, C., WOERNER, M., & KLEIN, D. F. Differentiation of panic anxiety from anticipatory anxiety and avoidance behavior. In D. F. Klein & J. G. Rabkin (eds.), *Anxiety: New research and changing concepts.* New York, Raven, 1981.

27

Stress and Psychosomatic Disorders

Francis Creed

THE LINK BETWEEN MEASURABLE ENVIRONMENTAL STRESS and the onset of symptoms is crucial to the study of psychosomatic mechanisms. However, the research requires a reliable and objective measure of environmental stress, and the first part of this chapter explains why self-administered questionnaires are inadequate for this purpose. The next requirement is a clearly defined disorder in terms of a recognized and datable onset, together with a clear understanding of whether demonstrable organic etiological factors are present or absent. Finally the role of psychiatric disorder, a common sequel to both stressful life events and severe physical illness, must be understood.

The chapter is primarily concerned with research using the Life Events and Difficulties Schedule (LEDS) (Brown & Harris, 1978) because this measure of environmental stress is the most reliable. It reviews research in gastroenterological disorders as the field most thoroughly researched and in which a relatively complete picture has emerged. Once the framework of research findings is established, other conditions are considered so far as they have been studied reliably.

CONCEPTS OF PSYCHOSOMATIC DISORDERS

The concept of specific psychosomatic disorders has been rejected in favor of a broader approach that includes the concurrent study of biological, psychological, and social variables in health and disease (World Health Organization, 1964). This chapter is confined to the study of onset of diseases and uses three paradigms that can be separated for experimental purposes.

The first paradigm is the comparison of *organic* and *nonorganic* (functional) disorders. In the medical clinics nonorganic disorders are very common, forming as many as 40% of all patients (Harvey, Mauad, & Brown, 1987; Hopkins, Menken, & DeFriese, 1989; Kroenke & Mangelsdorff, 1989; Perkin, 1989; Thompson, 1989:52). These disorders are sometimes considered to be "psychosomatic" on the basis that there is no organic disease and that there is a high prevalence of psychiatric disorder in this group of patients (Creed, Mayou, & Hopkins, 1991). An alternative approach is to study whether the somatic symptoms develop in relation to life stress.

The second paradigm is that in which the presentation and prognosis of the organic condition may be complicated by a coexisting psychiatric disorder. The latter may precede or follow the onset of the organic disorder (Moffic & Paykel, 1975), but the relationship with life events is helpful in unravelling the relationship.

Our third concern is the role of environmental stress alongside recognized organic etiological variables in the multifactorial causation of physical disease. This field of research is exciting and developing rapidly, but its theories have been developed in advance of reliable experimental data.

MEASUREMENT OF LIFE EVENTS

The problems of obtaining a reliable measure of life events has been the subject of many reviews (Brown, 1989; Brown & Harris, 1978; Dohrenwend, Levav, & Shrout, et al., 1987; Paykel, 1983). Dohrenwend and colleagues (1987) stated that there were very few case and control life event studies that "meet even minimal criteria for adequacy," including use of appropriate controls, assessing which events and circumstances occur independently of the subjects' prior mental state and behavior, and attempting to date the occurrence of events in relation to episodes of illness.

This statement arises because 90% of studies have used self-administered questionnaires, which are unreliable; some have been shown to have a test-retest reliability of as low as 0.2 (Cohen & Wills, 1985). A reliable retrospective interview method (with an interrater reliability of 75–92%) has only been used in a minority of studies in the psychosomatic field. Such interviews are lengthy and expensive in research time, but their advantages are numerous and will be briefly reviewed.

Accurate Recall

Unless numerous prompts are used, events distant from the time of interview are less likely to be recalled than recent ones, so that there is a fall-off of reported events with increasing time from the interview (Brown & Harris, 1978; Paykel, 1983; Wittchen, Essau, Hecht, Teder, & Pfister, 1989). Self-administered questionnaires make no specific attempt to prompt respondents or check the accuracy of the replies (Jenkins, Hurst, & Rose, 1979; Klein & Rubovits, 1987) and may have an unacceptable fall-off rate of about 5% per month. Interview methods with trained interviewers can achieve a fall-off rate of less than 1% per month (Brown & Harris, 1982; Paykel, 1983; Wittchen et al., 1989). For severely threatening events the figure may be as low as 2.9% per year with the LEDS (Neilson, Brown, & Marmot, 1989).

Definition of Events

Self-administered questionnaires include such items as: "Over the last six months, have you experienced concern over the health or behavior of a family member (major illness, accidents, etc.)?" This wording leaves the patient to decide who is a family member and what illnesses should be considered major, and it also makes no attempt to fix the exact date of the event. By contrast, the LEDS defines at the outset exactly which relatives and other individuals are to be included and the exact nature of life events; for these reasons a research interviewer must be trained in the use of the LEDS (Brown & Harris, 1982).

Without such exact definitions, subjects in the experimental group may unwittingly distort the events they recall. In an early study concerning stress and pregnancy, mothers who had given birth to a Down's Syndrome child reported that they had experienced more "emotional shocks" during pregnancy than mothers of normal children (Stott, 1958). This finding reflected their attempt to understand what had happened and their search for a reason for their abnormal child. This phenomenon, known as "effort after meaning," applies to all ill subjects and must be prevented from causing bias in any study comparing ill patients with a healthy control group.

Scoring Events

Once an event has been established, it must be scored in some way. The Schedule of Recent Experience (SRE) used the concept of "life change units," derived empirically by using the death of a spouse as 100 life change units and marriage as 50 (Holmes & Rahe, 1967). This system assumes that the life stress from different events is additive, but this method could produce anomalous results. Brown and Harris (1978:107) calculated that a young man who had recently been awarded a scholarship at Oxford could gain a total score of 79 life change units (with the end of formal schooling equalling 26, outstanding personal achievements at 28, a vacation at 13, and Christmas at 12). The total of 79 would be greater than that of a man whose wife has left him, who would receive a score of 65.

The LEDS scores events on a 4-point scale of threat or unpleasantness and applies this rating to both immediate and longer-term threat. Thus involvement in an accident might carry high short-term threat (grade 1 for one or two days) but if there were no lasting consequences, the long-term threat would be minimal (grade 4 for the ensuing weeks). The latter would be higher if there were serious injury or financial consequences extending over weeks or months. Other events, such as bereavement, diagnosis of cancer in a close relative, marital separation, or a court appearance when charged with a serious crime, carry high threat both at the time of discovery (short term) and one week later (long term). Events that carry high long-term threat are known as "severe events" and have been shown repeatedly to be associated with the onset of depression (Brown & Harris, 1989b, p. 55). The role of such events in the etiology of physical disorders is considered subsequently.

The LEDS is especially careful to avoid bias caused by the respondents' mental states. The interviewer relays the objective circumstances of the event to a group of experienced researchers without stating whether the subject was in the experimental or control group and without relaying the subject's emotional reaction to the event. The members of the group then make a consensus rating, taking into account the circumstances of that individual at that time. Thus, a car theft would be rated as severely threatening for the individual who depends on the car to go to work and to keep in touch with friends and family and who has no insurance and no possibility of replacing the car. The theft would be rated as much less threatening for an individual who has a company car that is immediately replaced. This is in contrast to the SRE, which assigns a standard rating for a particular type of event.

Exact Dating of Events and Illness Onset

It is not sufficiently appreciated that the life events research method is only applicable to illnesses with a clearly datable onset. Only under these circumstances can the researcher be sure that events prior to the onset are being considered in the etiology of the illness.

Thus, studies relating life events and back pain must first establish the date of onset of the back pain and must only consider events prior to that date (Craufurd, Creed, & Jayson, 1990). Some published studies have considered events prior to the clinical attendance, with the risk of including events such as "being off work" or "reduction of social contacts," which may have occurred after the back pain commenced (Leavitt, Garron, & Bieliauskas, 1979). Such events are likely to be the result of the back pain rather than its cause.

Independence of Events

Another way of coping with this problem is only analyzing events that are classified as totally independent of any developing illness. Examples of such events would be a factory closure, death of a spouse, a hurricane, or a child's automobile accident. Such events contrast with the person's loss of a job, involvement in an accident, or marital separation, in which the person's own actions or attitudes, possibly affected by incipient illness, might play a part in bringing about the event.

Life event results, using the LEDS, are generally expressed as the proportion of subjects who had experienced a severely threatening event during the preceding 38 weeks. This time period is important in the etiology of depression; it is long enough to include severe events, such as bereavement, that may affect the individual for some months afterward, but no so long that distorted data might result from poor recall.

Measurement of Life Events in Physical Disorders

There are a number of methodological advantages to measuring life events before the onset of physical illness compared to psychiatric illness, because a sudden, datable onset of symptoms often occurs—e.g., myocardial infarction, appendicitis, or cerebrovascular accident. Such onsets are more precisely defined than the onsets of depressive or psychotic illness. Comparison subjects may be available who have experienced similar symptoms, but who belong to a different diagnostic group (e.g., abdominal pain leading to appendectomy subdivides into acute appendicitis and normal appendix), so life events can be measured by an interviewer blind to the eventual diagnosis. It is also possible to interview the patients within a few days or weeks of the onset of illness, if medical treatment has been sought rapidly.

THE RELATIONSHIP BETWEEN THE ONSET OF NONORGANIC ABDOMINAL PAIN AND LIFE STRESS

Two studies of gastrointestinal disorder illustrate how life stress can relate to abdominal pain. The first study chose patients undergoing appendectomy who could be interviewed shortly after the onset of their abdominal pain but before the pathology (appendicitis or a normal appendix) had been ascertained (Creed, 1981). This timing meant that the patient, interviewer, and event raters were all blind to the eventual diagnosis. There was a striking difference between the groups: 60% of patients whose appendix was categorized as "not acutely inflamed" had experienced a severely threatening life event in the 38 weeks prior to the onset of their abdominal pain compared to 25% of those with appendicitis and 20%

of the healthy comparison group ($p < 0.01$). These figures are remarkably similar to those for depressed subjects (68%) and healthy comparison subjects (20%) in other studies using the same instrument (Brown & Harris, 1978:103; Brown & Harris, 1989b:55).

A number of checks on these data were possible (Creed 1985). Firstly, the appendectomy patients were followed up one year after the operation and during the post-operative year the rate of life events fell to that of the community comparison group. Secondly, it was possible to interview a number of siblings of the appendectomy patients regarding their experience of life events during the year prior to the index subjects appendectomy—these siblings formed a further healthy comparison group. They had experienced significantly fewer life events than the appendectomy patients over the same period preceding the operation. Lastly, the results were checked using data obtained in the original community study of women by using the LEDS (Brown & Harris, 1978). Data were extracted for women in the same age group as the appendectomy groups; 25% had experienced a severe event over the preceding 38 weeks, a figure very similar to the 27% and 20% of the appendicitis and matched community comparison subjects, respectively.

The experiment was repeated in selected patients presenting to a gastroenterology clinic who had a datable onset of abdominal pain during the six months prior to clinic attendance (Craig & Brown, 1984). Once again the patients could be interviewed before the diagnosis was ascertained—either organic causes (e.g., peptic ulcer) or no specific pathology: irritable bowel syndrome or functional dyspepsia. The results were remarkably similar to the appendectomy study—57% of the functional abdominal pain group had experienced a severe event compared to 23% of those with an organic diagnosis and 15% of the matched community comparison groups (Craig, 1989:240).

These strikingly similar results were compared to data collected in a third study using the same instrument—patients admitted to hospital following deliberate self-harm (Creed, Craig, & Farmer, 1988). Of these patients, 78% had experienced a severe life event during the 38 weeks prior to the self-harm.

Depression might account for the excess of severe life events in the functional abdominal pain groups, but this turned out not to be the case. Two-thirds of the patients with functional abdominal pain had experienced a severe event over previous weeks, whether or not they had psychiatric disorder (Creed et al., 1988).

It is tempting at this stage to speculate how environmental stress might be linked to functional abdominal pain, but several more aspects of these data should be considered. First, are removal of a "not acutely inflamed" appendix (mean age, 22 years) and irritable bowel syndrome/functional dyspepsia (mean age, 35 years) different disorders or part of the same disorder? Many of the normal appendix group developed clear IBS one year later. Others have reported that 30–50% of patients attending the gastrointestinal clinic with IBS have had a normal appendix removed previously (Chaudhury & Truelove, 1962; Keeling & Fielding, 1975; Lane, 1973) and many IBS patients report that the original onset was in their late teens or early twenties (Harvey, Mauad, & Brown, 1987; Waller & Misiewicz, 1969). It appears that the similarity of life event results might be accounted for by studying the same disorder at two points in time—at the original onset and at a later recurrence.

There are good data indicating that functional abdominal complaints are common in the community (Thompson, 1989:51), and our results might explain why these patients seek treatment rather than develop their original symptoms. This suggestion that life events lead to treatment-seeking rather than illness onset might explain attendance at the gastroenterology clinic but is less likely to explain why a patient who is admitted as an emergency case presents with acute abdominal pain suggesting appendicitis. Separate study of the onset of back pain and referral is possible and indicates the importance of separating the two points in time (Craufurd et al., 1990).

It is also necessary to check that other studies in different settings produce similar results. Vassilas (1990), using a modified version of the LEDS, found a significant excess of threatening events in patients with a normal appendix but abdominal pain and in self-poisoning patients compared to a community comparison group. Canton, Santonastaso, and Fraccon (1984) used another life events measure but also found that patients having a normal appendix removed had experienced life events very similar to a group of depressed patients attending a psychiatrist. Ford, Miller, Eastwood, and Eastwood (1987), using the LEDS in the gastroenterology clinic, found that the weighted life event scores for the IBS patients were twice that of the events experienced by patients with organic disease.

The most frequent type of severe event in the case of the functional abdominal pain involved a major disruption of close relationships: a marital separation, a family member leaving home, or the breakup of a serious romantic relationship. Such events occurred in the functional abdominal pain groups approximately 5 times as often as the organic illness and healthy comparison groups, and nearly as often as those in the overdose group (Creed et al., 1988). Vassilas (1990) found that the characteristics of the events prior to removal of a normal appendix involved threat, antisocial acts, and uncertainty of outcome.

It seems, therefore, that these studies have identified a group of patients who develop abdominal pain when exposed to a serious environmental stress. This finding appears to conform with the traditional psychosomatic paradigm. Because experimental stress affects colonic motility (Almy, 1985; Chaudhury & Truelove, 1962; Wangel & Deller, 1964), severe life events may lead to painful contractions of the colon in those who are constitutionally predisposed to respond in this way (14–20% of the population, Thompson, 1989). In addition, where psychiatric symptoms are present, depression or anxiety may also contribute to altered colonic motility (Latimer, Sarna, Campbell, et al., 1981) as well as to a lowered pain threshold.

If this conclusion were final it would simply endorse the traditional psychosomatic concept of mind affecting body, which has been discarded in favor of a more holistic approach (Lipowski, 1982). It is preferable to include in the model both physical and psychological factors. Chaudhury and Truelove (1962) did so in their original description of the irritable colon syndrome; a history of dysentery, and psychological problems. The former was associated with a good prognosis, recognized psychological problems were associated with a poor prognosis, and patients who had both etiological factors had an intermediate prognosis. Recent studies of patients with nonorganic abdominal pain confirm that concurrent psychiatric disorder predicts a poor prognosis (Creed, 1981; McDonald & Bouchier, 1980), but no recent study has concurrently measured psychological and physical etiological factors.

LIFE EVENTS AND PHYSICAL ILLNESS INVOLVING TISSUE DAMAGE

The results of the gastroenterology work so far have focused on events that are severely threatening in the long term: the events associated with the onset of depression (Brown & Harris, 1989b:55). Consideration of life events threatening in the short-term produced different results. Organic and nonorganic groups were similar, and both had experienced significantly more threatening life events than the community comparison group (Creed et al.,

1988). In other words, the onset of organic illness is associated with this type of stress, though the difference from community subjects is less striking than that for nonorganic conditions.

This finding can be understood in terms of the multifactorial causation of disease. A mathematical model of appendicitis requires a constitutional predisposition to develop the illness, plus two randomly occurring factors in the environment coming together at the same time (Ashley, 1967; Creed, 1989). One of the latter two might be related to the stressful event—for example, reduced immune function. Examples of the type of event associated with onset of organic gastrointestinal disease were enforced changes at work, housing crises, contact with the police, and loss of close interpersonal ties—i.e., different events from those associated with onset of nonorganic abdominal pain.

This difference is similar to that between events preceding depression and schizophrenia. Brown & Harris (1978) reported that minor events might "trigger" schizophrenia in a predisposed and vulnerable individual, whereas severe events are required to bring on depression, in which life stress is considered a key etiological factor. (For fuller discussion and reasoning see Brown & Harris, 1978:122.) Similarly, Jacobs, Prusoff, and Paykel (1974) found that events distinguishing depression from schizophrenia were serious arguments with nonresident family members, fiances, or girlfriends or boyfriends. These circumstances correspond to the severe events observed before onset of functional abdominal pain.

Goal-Frustrating Events

In the case of peptic ulcer, a specific type of experience was associated with its onset—the so-called "goal-frustrating" life event, in which an important life goal is frustrated by the occurrence of the stressor. Such experiences were more common in the peptic ulcer group than the nonorganic group (54% and 24%, respectively, and 9% in the community comparison group) (Craig & Brown, 1984). Examples of goal-frustrating events include a man's repeated attempt to sue the builder of his faulty house that was thwarted by repeated failure at court, a woman's well-established plan to separate from her husband and move in with her lover, who disappeared shortly before the move. It is debatable whether personality factors play a role in such events (Craig, 1989).

This association of goal frustration with peptic ulcer has now been replicated in an Australian study (Ellard, Beaurepaire, Jones, Piper, & Tennant, 1990). The concept of goal frustration arose from traditional psychosomatic literature (Craig, 1989), but it may not be specific to peptic ulcer (see the subsequent discussion).

CONCURRENT ORGANIC AND PSYCHIATRIC DISORDER

In an early study designed to circumnavigate the possible bias caused by treatment seeking, Murphy and Brown (1980) sought recent onset of physical illness in the community and found that this was not generally associated with severe events; the exception was the group who also had concurrent psychiatric illness. In this group, the psychiatric disorder occurred a few weeks after the severe life event and the organic disease several weeks later. The authors proposed a model in which life event stress led to depression, which might affect some physiological functioning and lead to organic disease. However, this model only explained the onset of physical illness in a minority of patients. There was some evidence in Craig's goal frustration work that the same sequence occurred in the majority of cases where psychiatric disorder and organic disease were both present (Craig, 1989).

Thus a consensus is emerging in studies using the LEDS that severely threatening events are associated with the onset of functional disorders such as nonorganic abdominal pain and menorrhagia (Harris, 1989). Severe events are also associated with the onset of organic disorders (where tissue damage is involved) only when there is concurrent psychiatric disorder. For the onset of organic disorders in the absence of depression, life events with lesser degrees of threat appear to be associated with onset in a more subtle way; life events play a smaller part in etiology, along with other agents such as vascular, infective, and dietary ones. In line with this concept, it is interesting that psychological treatments are much more effective in the irritable bowel syndrome than in peptic ulcer (Svedlund, 1983:46; Sjodin, 1983:47) and that life events affecting the course of the former are more likely to be divorce and separation in IBS compared to peptic ulcer patients.

RECENT LIFE EVENT STUDIES

Having established a fairly consistent pattern of life events prior to onset of organic and functional gastrointestinal disorder, it is appropriate to consider whether other LEDS studies support this pattern.

Myocardial Infarction

Early studies indicated a positive relationship between stress and myocardial infarction, but one study suggested the link was with bereavement, a severely threatening event (Parkes, Benjamin, & Fitzgerald, 1969). The other study, using an early version of the LEDS, indicated a significant, but not very prominent link with nonsevere events (Connolly, 1976). Siegrist, Dittman, Rittner, and Weber (1982) found an excess of "critical negative life events" among a large series of first myocardial infarction (MI) patients, but the effect was modest (31% MI versus 14% in controls) compared to studies of depression or functional somatic complaints.

The most recent LEDS study (Neilson, Brown & Marmot, 1989) indicated that during the year before MI, 22% of patients had experienced a severe event compared to 25% of controls. This lack of a difference in terms of severely threatening events is very similar to that mentioned previously concerning organic gastrointestinal disease. The proportions for goal-frustration were, however, significantly different (31% of MI patients versus 6% of controls) and indicate, perhaps, that this type of event is not specific to peptic ulcer. The same study also found a considerable excess (40% versus 15%) of work, housing, and financial difficulties extending over a 10-year period prior to MI.

The authors focused their attention on work-related stress, as this appeared to be prominent in both goal-frustrating events and long-term difficulties (the two were related). A combined index of work-related difficulties (long hours, little vacation time, and other stresses) discriminated best between MI and controls: 53% versus 14%, respectively, had experienced such a difficulty during 7 or more of the 10 years under study. The question remains whether these work difficulties were brought on by the subjects' type A behavior.

In fact, three quarters of the subjects high on the workload stress index also had high scores on the Bortner questionnaire.

Smoking and alcohol consumption were each twice as common among MI patients than controls. Neither of these variables was associated with workload stress, however, and it appeared that smoking, alcohol, and work stress were all making independent etiological contributions (Neilson et al., 1989:335).

Stroke

The Oxford stroke study (House, Dennis, Mogridge, Hawton, & Warlow, 1990) involved 113 patients, who were interviewed first regarding the year prior to the stroke and reinterviewed one year later. Individuals in matched control group were interviewed in an identical fashion. Physical health problems affecting the subject were excluded. The proportion of subjects experiencing a severe event was 24% of stroke patients in the year prior to stroke and 8% in the subsequent year; the corresponding figure for controls was 12%.

The authors examined other risk factors and found only one difference: patients with previously treated hypertension were twice as common among those without a preceding severe life event. Since the higher rate of stressful life events extended back over 6 months prior to the stroke, the authors speculated that the stressful event might accelerate the arteriosclerotic process, possibly by increased blood pressure or by increasing blood viscosity or coaguability. Penrose (1972) proposed a similar hypothesis to explain the link between life events and subarachnoid haemorrhage only in those patients without a berry aneurysm.

Back Pain and Arthritis

In order to study the life events preceding back pain, Craufurd, Creed, and Jayson (1990) had to seek patients with a recent onset of back pain. They were independently classified by the rheumatologists as having a definite organic cause or nonspecific pain. Only life events independent of the back pain were considered.

A significant excess of life events threatening in the short term was found for those who had a nonspecific cause for their back pain compared to the organic back pain group (58% and 31%, respectively, $p < 0.05$). There was a similar trend for severe events, though the difference failed to reach statistical significance: 35% of the nonspecific group and 15% of the organic group reported a severe event during the preceding 38-week period. The latter is in line with results for other organic conditions (see Table 27–1).

Results in rheumatoid arthritis are conflicting. Baker and Brewerton (1981) found an excess of stressful life events prior to onset, but their results were not repeated in the larger more recent study: 18% of recent onset cases had experienced a severe event during the preceding 6 months (Conway, 1992). This finding is in line with results in other organic diseases.

It is of interest that both these studies reported a low prevalence of psychiatric disorder: 6% in back pain and 5% in rheumatoid arthritis. These figures are in distinct contrast to studies including chronically ill back pain and arthritic patients, and they reflect the selective study of patients with a recent onset of the illness—a requirement for accurate measurement of events prior to onset.

TABLE 27-1
Percentage of Subjects Experiencing a Severely Threatening Event in 38 Weeks before Onset or Interview

Medical Condition	Functional	Organic	Comparison
Appendectomy	62	25	19
Abdominal pain	57	23	15
Myocardial infarction		22	14
Multiple sclerosis		77	35
Stroke		24	12
Physical disease in community		30	17
Back pain—organic	35	15	
Mennorrhagia	56		29
Secondary amenorrhoea	28		

Functional Dysphonia and Menorrhagia

Two other studies of functional disorders have been performed. One (Andrews & House, 1989) concerned women with functional dysphonia, where no tissue damage was involved, yet severe events were not related to onset. Events of lesser degrees of threat were associated with onset if they belonged to a class of event known as "conflict over speaking out." In these situations, the woman felt torn between conflicting obligations (e.g., work versus caring for an elderly relative) but could not speak out for fear of the consequences.

Results in menorrhagia, on the other hand, were similar to those with functional abdominal pain; 56% of menorrhagia patients, 28% of secondary amenorrhea, and 29% of community comparison subjects had experienced a severe event over the year prior to onset (Harris, 1989).

Multiple Sclerosis

The results presented so far have largely conformed to a pattern in which the onset of organic disease is not associated with severe life events. The exception is multiple sclerosis (MS) (Grant, Mcdonald, Patterson, & Trimble, 1989). In this study, patients were interviewed several years after the onset of the MS, which may have been difficult to date. Among the MS patients, 62% had experienced a severe event during the 6 months prior to onset compared to 15% of the control group ($p < 0.001$). This significant difference remained for those who did and did not know their diagnosis and if those with a first onset and exacerbation were considered separately. Relationship and housing problems showed the clearest difference between patients and controls.

There is a possibility that the patients in this study wrongly associated the onset of MS with severe life events because of difficulties in recalling exact dates such a long time previously. If the results are repeated, however, different mechanisms may be involved in the onset of MS compared to myocardial infarction, stroke, peptic ulcer, and, possibly, rheumatoid arthritis. Stressful life events might be related to a change in the immunological status of MS patients, but the exact date of the immunological changes (as opposed to the onset of symptoms) cannot be determined in the light of present knowledge.

The explanation provided by the authors of the MS paper is reminiscent of that quoted above for appendicitis. They suggest that at least two factors play an important role in determining vulnerability to MS: a susceptible host and exposure during youth to some environmental agent that occurs in temperate and northern climates. The role of the severe life event would be to "precipitate" an episode of MS, possibly by reducing immune tolerance (Irwin, Patterson, Smith, Caldwell, Brown, Gillin, & Grant 1990). This study did not assess depression at the time of onset of MS, presumably because of the retrospective nature of the study. This factor could have been important, however, because so many of the patients had experienced a severe event and depression is associated with reduced immune tolerance (Irwin et al., 1990). It is still not clear whether depression or experience of a severe life event is more closely linked to alteration of immune response and hormonal abnormalities (Irwin et al., 1990; Schleifer, Keller, Bond, Cohen, & Stein, 1989; Spurrell & Creed, 1992).

One recent study has shown a most impressive relationship between stress and infection (Cohen, Tyrell, & Smith, 1991). This study is unique because it is a truly prospective life events study that controlled for many possible confounding variables and demonstrated a dose-response relationship between psychological stress index and rate of infection. Unfortunately, the psychological stress index included both stressful life events, scored on a questionnaire, perception of stress, and items indicating negative affect. Consequently, the individual contributions of life events and depression could not be separated.

This study controlled for many variables. Each person was given a standardized dose of virus or saline and housed in a controlled environment. Analysis controlled for possible confounding variables such as age, sex, education, allergic status, weight, the season, number of subjects housed together in the unit, the infection status of subjects sharing the same housing, and virus-specific antibody status prior to nasal drops. A number of variables that might explain the stress-infection association were then considered: smoking, alcohol, exercise, diet, quality of sleep, white cell counts, total immunoglobulin levels, and the personality variables of low self-esteem, personal control, and degree of extroversion or introversion (EPI). Even with these variables controlled for, the relationship between psychological stress index and infection remained significant. The authors demonstrated the dose-response effect with five different viruses and argued that this suggests the biological generality of the effect.

INTERACTION BETWEEN LIFE STRESS AND OTHER VARIABLES

Establishing that stressful life events cause illness requires several conditions to be met (Cook, 1986; Day, 1989; Maes, Vingerhoets, & Van Heck, 1987). The evidence presented in this chapter has indicated a statistical correlation between life events and onset of disorder, and, particularly for the conditions that have a point onset we can be confident that events lead to illness, rather than the other way around. To a limited extent, the results have been repeated across different populations at different times, but, with the exception of the last study, the role of intervening variables and of a dose-response relationship have not been properly considered. This area of research now needs a more coherent framework of evidence linking the effect of stress on physiological variables and pathological processes.

The data reviewed in this chapter indicate that severely threatening events are associated with the onset of functional (or traditional psychosomatic disorders), organic illness accompanied by psychiatric disorder, and, possibly, multiple sclerosis. On the other hand, events that are threatening only for a short time are associated with organic illness, which develops without psychiatric disorder. Stress over a period of years might also be important in the genesis of heart disease (Nielson et al., 1989) and this stress, together with goal-frustrating events, might be related to underlying personality.

Concurrent measurement of life events, using the LEDS, and biological variables is possible and may indicate specificity of relationships that bears further study (Dolan, Calloway, Fonagy, De Souza, & Wakeling, 1985; Mutale, Creed, Maresh, & Hunt, 1991). Such work is central to clarification of psychosomatic relationships and will be a very fruitful field of investigation in the future, provided that theories are constructed only as sound empirical data become available.

REFERENCES

ALMY, T. P. Experimental studies on the irritable colon. *American Journal of Medicine,* 1951, *10,* 60–67.

ANDREWS, H., HOUSE, A. Functional dysphonia. In G. W. Brown & T. O. Harris (eds.), *Life events and illness.* New York: Guilford Press, 1989.

ASHLEY, D. J. B. Observations on the epidemiology of appendicitis. *Gut,* 1967, *8,* 533–538.

BAKER, G. H. B., BREWERTON, D. A. Rheumatoid arthritis: A psychiatric assessment. *British Medical Journal,* 1981, *282,* 2014.

BROWN, G. W. Life events and measurements. In G. W. Grown & T. O. Harris (eds.), *Life events and illness.* New York: Guilford Press, 1989.

BROWN, G. W., & HARRIS, T. O. *Social origins of depression: A study of psychiatric disorder in women.* London: Tavistock, 1978.

————. Fall-off in the reporting life events. *Social Psychiatry,* 1982, *17,* 23–28.

————. Depression. In G. W. Brown & T. O. Harris (eds.), *Life events and illness.* New York: Guilford Press, 1989.

CANTON, G., SANTONASTASO, P., & FRACCON, I. G. Life events, abnormal illness behaviour and appendectomy. *General Hospital Psychiatry,* 1984, *6,* 191–195.

CHAUDHURY, N. A., & TRUELOVE, S. C. The irritable colon syndrome. *Quarterly Journal of Medicine,* 1962, *31,* 307–322.

COHEN, S., TYRELL, D. A. J., & SMITH, A. P. Psychological stress and susceptibility to the common cold. *New England Journal of Medicine,* 1991, *325,* 606–612.

COHEN, S., & WILLS, T. A. Stress, social support and the buffering hypothesis. *Psychological Bulletin,* 1985, *98,* 310–357.

CONNOLLY, J. Life events before myocardial infarction. *Journal of Human Stress,* 1976, *2,* 3–17.

CONWAY, S. *Life events and rheumatoid arthritis.* M. Sc. thesis, University of Manchester, England, 1992.

COOKE, D. J. Inferring causality in life event research. *Stress Medicine,* 1986, *2,* 141–152.

CRAIG, T. J. K. Abdominal pain. In G. W. Brown & T. O. Harris (eds.), *Life events and illness.* New York: Guilford Press, 1989.

CRAIG, T. J. K., & BROWN, G. W. Goal frustrating aspects of life event stress in the etiology of gastrointestinal disorder. *Journal Psychosomatic Research,* 1984, *28,* 411–421.

CRAUFURD, D. I. O., CREED, F., & JAYSON, M. D. Life events and psychological disturbance in patients with low-back pain. *Spine,* 1990, *15,* 490–494.

CREED, F. Life events and appendicectomy. *Lancet,* 1981, *1,* 1381–1385.

————. *Psychosocial variables and appendicitis.* M.D. thesis, University of Cambridge, England, 1985.

————. Appendectomy. In G. W. Brown & T. O. Harris (eds.), *Life events and illness.* New York: Guilford Press, 1989.

CREED, F., CRAIG, T., & FARMER, R. Functional abdominal pain, psychiatric illness, and life events. *Gut,* 1988, *29,* 235–242.

CREED, F. H., MAYOU, R., HOPKINS, A. (eds.), *Medical out-patients without organic disease.* London: Royal Colleges of Physicians and Psychiatrists, 1991.

DAY, R. Schizophrenia. In G. W. Brown & T. O. Harris (eds.), *Life events and illness.* New York: Guilford Press, 1989.

DOHRENWEND, B. P., LEVAY, I., SHROUT, P. E., et al. Life stress and psychopathology: progress on research begun with Barbara Snell Dohrenwend. *American Journal of Community Psychology,* 1987, *15,* 677–715.

DOLAN, R. J., CALLOWAY, S. P., FONAGY, P., DE SOUZA, F. V. A., & WAKELING, A. Life events, depression and hypothalamic-pituitary-adrenal axis function. *British Journal of Psychiatry,* 1985, *147,* 429–433.

ELLARD, K., BEAUREPAIRE, J., JONES, M., PIPER, D., TENNANT, C. Acute chronic stress in duodenal ulcer disease. *Gastroenterology,* 1990, *99,* 1628–1632.

FORD, M. J., MILLER, R. McC., EASTWOOD, J., & EASTWOOD, E. A. Life events, psychiatric illness and the irritable bowel syndrome. *Gut,* 1987, *28,* 160–165.

GRANT, I., McDONALD, W. I., PATTERSON, T., & TRIMBLE, M. R. Multiple sclerosis. In G. W. Brown & T. O. Harris (eds.), *Life events and illness.* New York: Guilford Press, 1989.

GUTHRIE, E., CREED, F., DAWSON, D., & TOMENSON, B. A controlled trial of psychological treatment for the irritable bowel syndrome. *Gastroenterology,* 1991, *100,* 450–457.

HARRIS, T. O. Disorders of menstruation. In G. W. Brown & T. O. Harris (eds.), *Life events and illness.* New York: Guilford Press, 1989.

HARVEY, R. F., MAUAD E. C., & BROWN, A. M. Prognosis in the irritable bowel syndrome. A 5 year prospective study. *Lancet,* 1987, *1,,* 963–965.

HOLMES, K. M., SALTER, R. H., COLE, T. P., & GIRDWOOD, T. G. A profile of District Hospital gastroenterology. *Journal of Royal College of Physicians of London,* 1987, *21,* 111–114.

HOLMES, T. H., & RAHE, R. H. The social readjustment rating scale. *Journal of Psychosomatic Research,* 1967, *11,* 213–218.

HOPKINS, A., MENKEN, M., & DeFRIESE, G. A record of patient encounters in neurological practice in the United Kingdom. *Journal of Neurology, Neurosurgery and Psychiatry,* 1989, *52,* 436–438.

HOUSE, A., DENNIS, M., MOGRIDGE, L., HAWTON, K., & WARLOW, C. Life events and difficulties preceding stroke. *Journal of Neurology, Neurosurgery and Psychiatry,* 1990, *53,* 1024–1028.

IRWIN, M., PATTERSON, T., SMITH, T. L., CALDWELL, C., BROWN, S. A., GILLAN, J. C., GRANT, I. Reduction of immune function in life stress and depression. *Biological Psychiatry,* 1990, *27,* 22–30.

JACOBS, S., PRUSOFF, B., & PAYKEL, G. Recent life events in schizophrenia and depression. *Psychological Medicine,* 1974, *4,* 444–453.

JENKINS, C. D., HURST, M. W., & ROSE, R. M. Life changes: do people really remember? *Archives of General Psychiatry,* 1979, *36,* 379–384.

KEELING, P. W. N., & FIELDING, J. F. The irritable bowel syndrome: a review of 50 consecutive cases. *Journal of Irish College of Physicians and Surgeons,* 1975, *4,* 91–94.

KLEIN, D. N., & RUBOVITS, D. R. Reliability of subjects' reports on stressful life events inventories— longitudinal studies. *Journal of Behavioural Medicine,* 1987, *10,* 501–512.

KROENKE, K., & MANGELSDORFF, D. Common symptoms in ambulatory care: incidence, evaluation, therapy and outcome. *American Journal of Medicine,* 1989, *86,* 262–266.

LANE, D. The irritable colon and right iliac fossa pain. *Medical Journal of Australia,* 1973, *1,* 66–67.

LATIMER, P., SARNA, S., CAMPBELL, D., et al. Colonic motor and myoelectric activity: A comparative study of normal subjects, psychoneurotic patients with irritable bowel syndrome. *Gastroenterology,* 1981, *80,* 893–901.

LEAVITT, F., GARRON, D. C., & BIELIAUSKAS, A. Stressing life events and the experience of low back pain. *Journal of Psychosomatic Research,* 1979, *23,* 49–55.

LIPOWSKI, Z. J. Modern meaning of the terms "psychosomatic" and "liaison psychiatry." In F. Creed & J. M. Pfeffer (eds.), *Medicine and psychiatry: A practical approach.* London: Pitman, 1982.

MAES, S., VINGERHOETS, A., & VAN HECK, G. The study of stress and disease: Some developments and requirements. *Social Science Medicine,* 1987, *25,* 567–578.

McDONALD, A. J., & BOUCHIER, P. A. D. Non-organic gastro-intestinal illness: A medical and psychiatric study. *British Journal of Psychiatry,* 1980, *136,* 1276–1283.

MOFFIC, H. S., & PAYKEL, E. S. Depression in medical in-patients. *British Journal of Psychiatry,* 1975, *126,* 346–353.

MURPHY, E., & BROWN, G. W. Life events, psychiatric disturbance and physical illness. *British Journal of Psychiatry,* 1980, *136,* 326–338.

MUTALE, T., CREED, F. H., MARESH, M., & HUNT, L. Life events and low birthweight—analysis of infants preterm and small for gestational age. *British Journal of Obstetrics and Gynaecology,* 1991, *98,* 166–172.

NEILSON, E., BROWN, G. W., & MARMOT, M. Myocardial infarction. In G. W. Brown & T. O. Harris (eds.), *Life events and illness.* New York: Guilford Press, 1989.

PARKES, C. M., BENJAMIN, B., & FITZGERALD, R. G. Broken heart: A statistical survey of increased mortality among widowers. *British Medical Journal,* 1969, *1,* 740–743.

PAYKEL, E. S. Methodological aspects of life events research. *Journal of Psychosomatic Research,* 1983, *27,* 341–352.

PENROSE, R. J. J. Life events before subarachnoid haemorrhage. *Journal of Psychosomatic Research,* 1972, *16,* 329–333.

PERKIN, G. D. An analysis of 7836 successive new outpatient referrals. *Journal of Neurology, Neurosurgery and Psychiatry,* 1989, *52,* 447–448.

SCHLEIFER, S. J., KELLER, S. E., BOND, R. N., COHEN, J., & STEIN, M. Major depressive disorder and immunity: Role of age, sex, severity and hospitalization. *Archives of General Psychiatry,* 1989, *46,* 81–87.

SIEGRIST, J., DITTMAN, K. H., RITTNER, K., & WEBER, I. The social context of active distress in patients with early myocardial infarction. *Social Science and Medicine,* 1982, *16,* 443–454.

SPURRELL, M. T., CREED, F. H. Lympocyte response in depressed patients and subjects anticipating bereavement. *British Journal of Psychiatry,* 1992 (in press).

STOTT, D. H. Some psychosomatic aspects of causality in reproduction. *Journal of Psychosomatic Research,* 1958, *3,* 42–55.

————. Sjodin, I. Psychotherapy in peptic ulcer disease. *Acta Psychiatrica Scandinavica,* 1983, suppl. 306, *67,* 9–90.

SVEDLUND, J. Psychotherapy in the irritable bowel syndrome. *Acta Psychiatrica Scandinavica,* 1983, suppl. 306, *67,* 7–86.

THOMPSON, W. G. *Gut reactions: Understanding symptoms of the digestive tract.* New York: Plenum Press, 1989.

VASSILAS, C. A. Differentiating life stresses prior to admission to hospital for appendicectomy and suicide. *Journal of Psychosomatic Research,* 1990, *34,* 699–707.

WALLER, S. L., & MISIEWICZ, J. J. Prognosis in the irritable bowel syndrome. *Lancet,* 1969, *2,* 753–756.

WANGEL, A. E., & DELLER, D. J. Intestinal motility in man. III. Mechanism of constipation and diarrhoea with particular reference to irritable colon syndrome. *Gastroenterology,* 1964, *48,* 69–84.

WING, J. J., COOPER, J. E., & SARTORIUS, N. *The measurement and classification of psychiatric symptoms: An instruction manual for the Present State Examination and CATEGO Programme.* London: Cambridge University Press, 1974.

WITTCHEN, H. U., ESSAU, C. A., HECHT, H., TEDER, W., & PFISTER, H. Reliability of life event assessments: Test-retest reliability and fall-off effects of the Munich Interview for the assessment of life events and conditions. *Journal of Affective Disorders,* 1989, *16,* 77–92.

WORLD HEALTH ORGANIZATION. *Psychosomatic disorders.* Thirteenth report of the WHO Expert Committee on Mental Health. Geneva: World Health Organization, 1964.

28

Coping with Chronic Illness

Shelley E. Taylor   Lisa G. Aspinwall

AT ANY GIVEN TIME, 50% of the U.S. population has a chronic condition that requires medical management. These conditions range from relatively mild ones, such as partial hearing losses, to severe and life-threatening disorders such as coronary artery disease, cancer, and diabetes. Arthritis in its various forms afflicts approximately 37 million Americans (Lawrence, et al., 1989); 5 million Americans have had cancer (American Cancer Society, 1989); diabetes affects 11 million people (American Diabetes Association, 1986); more than 2 million people have sustained a stroke (American Heart Association, 1988); and almost 5 million people have had a history of heart attack and/or chest pain (American Heart Association, 1988). Nearly 29 million people have hypertension (United States Bureau of the Census, 1989), and estimates of the prevalence of high blood pressure run as high as 60 million (American Heart Association, 1988).

Given these figures, virtually every American will eventually develop at least one chronic disability or disease that may ultimately be the cause of death. What distinguishes these disorders from the major causes of death and disability in previous centuries is their chronic nature. Whereas influenza, pneumonia, and other acute conditions were the major causes of death until the early 1900s, individuals now may live with a chronic condition for fifteen years or longer. Consequently, the quality of life experienced by those with chronic illnesses and the ways in which they cope with the stressors raised by these illnesses have become increasingly important, not only to medical personnel who work with the chronically ill but also to psychologists and others attempting to understand how people cope with stress more generally.

In this chapter, we will first discuss criteria for coping effectively with stress based on the large and growing literature on quality of life among the chronically ill. We will then consider in detail some of the most common and problematic issues the chronically ill face, such as coping with anxiety and depression; managing restrictions on work and social life, and coping with threats to self-esteem and self-concept. Finally, we consider the coping strategies or resources that have been identified as adaptive or maladaptive for coping with the stress of chronic illness.

Preparation of this manuscript was supported by two grants from the National Institute of Mental Health (MH 42918, MH 42152) and a Research Scientist Development Award (MH 00311) to the first author. The second author was supported by a National Science Foundation Fellowship.

QUALITY OF LIFE

Until relatively recently, quality of life among the chronically ill was not considered an issue of importance. For many years, it was measured solely in terms of length of survival and signs of presence or absence of disease, with little consideration of the psychosocial consequences of illness and treatment (Aaronson, Calais de Silva, et al., 1986; Aaronson, van Dam, Polak, & Zittoun, 1986). Indeed, a recent examination of the research literature on quality of life revealed that psychological assessments of quality of life are outnumbered by medical citations more than 10 to 1 (Taylor & Aspinwall, 1990). However, medical criteria are poorly related to psychosocial assessments of quality of life. In one notable study of hypertension (Jachuck, Brierley, Jachuck, & Wilcox, 1982), although 100% of the physicians reported their patients' quality of life had improved following hypertensive medication, only have the patients agreed, and virtually none of the relatives did. Thus, quality of life can be a very subjective experience not directly dependent upon successful medical management.

In recent years, the measurement of quality of life has shifted from objective medical indicators to a consideration of psychological, social, and economic factors. Agreement on the need to assess subjective quality of life, however, has not produced agreement on how to do so. Relatively few reliable and valid measures of quality of life enjoy wide use. One such measure, the Sickness Impact Profile (SIP; Bergner, Bobbitt, Carter, & Gilson, 1981), assesses physical, psychosocial, and other (sleep, eating, work, recreation) functioning. The SIP appears to be responsive to changes in chronic diseases and treatments. The Activities of Daily Living measure (ADL; Katz, Ford, Moscovitz, Jackson, & Jaffee, 1983) yields scores for bathing, dressing, toileting, mobility, continence, and feeding. Yet these measures may be more responsive to gross changes and deteriorations in adjustment to chronic illness than to the more subtle problems, such as intermittent depression or specific physical difficulties that more commonly occur. Recently, quality of life measures that do provide this more fine-grained portrait have evolved, such as the Cancer Inventory of Problem Situations (CIPS; Schag, Heinrich, Aadland, & Ganz, 1990) for cancer patients.

The issue of quality of life will continue to be important with respect to coping with chronic illness for several reasons. First, in order to understand what coping methods are used and how effective those coping methods are, one needs an accurate assessment of the problems raised by chronic illness. This picture has, until recently, been entirely lacking and still needs to be more concretely addressed for many of the most prevalent chronic diseases. Second, the development of more fine-grained measures of quality of life will enable researchers to identify the impact of treatments on quality of life. For example, certain cancer treatments with disappointing survival rates may have side effects that are more harmful than the disease itself (Aaronson, Calais de Silva, et al., 1986). Third, quality of life measures can enable health policymakers to compare the impact of different chronic diseases and different treatments on health care costs and to assess cost effectiveness of different interventions in the context of quality of life information (Kaplan, 1985; Lubeck & Yelin, 1988).

Given the absence of detailed information for establishing quality of life indicators for different groups of chronically ill patients, researchers must currently fall back on the use of the criteria traditionally associated with successful coping with stressful events of all kinds. A primary criterion of coping success has been biochemical functioning. Coping efforts are generally judged to be successful if they reduce arousal and its indicators, such as blood rate, pulse rate, and skin conductivity. A second criterion of successful coping is whether and how quickly people can return to their prestress activities. To the extent that people's coping efforts enable them to resume usual activities, coping may be judged to be successful. With respect to chronic illness, however, there are implicit biases in this latter criterion. The criterion implies that the person's prior living situation was in some sense ideal, and this is not always true. In fact, substantial life change following a stressful event may be a sign of successful rather than unsuccessful coping. Moreover, diseases and treatments may impose restrictions on the resumption of usual activities that have nothing to do with coping; that is, a person who is unable to resume prior activities may not necessarily be coping poorly. Finally and most commonly, researchers judge coping according to its effectiveness in reducing psychological distress. When anxiety or depression is reduced, coping responses are judged to be successful.

CHRONIC ILLNESS: THE NATURE OF THE STRESSOR

As in acute diseases, there is a temporary first phase in chronic illness when all life activities are disrupted. Patients are often in a state of crisis marked by physical, social, and psychological disequilibrium (Moos, 1977). They find that habitual ways of coping with problems do not work, at least temporarily; therefore, they may experience intense feelings of disorganization, anxiety, fear, and other emotions (Taylor & Aspinwall, 1990). Eventually, the crisis phase of chronic illness passes, and patients begin to develop a sense of how the chronic illness will alter their lives. Thus, chronic disease carries the need to make specific changes in physical, vocational, or social activities. In addition, those experiencing chronic illnesses must integrate the patient role into their lives psychologically if they are to adapt successfully to their disorders.

Physical Problems and Rehabilitation

Physical problems requiring rehabilitation may arise as the result of illness, may emerge from treatments, or both. Physical problems produced by the disease include physical pain, such as the chest pain experienced by heart patients or the discomfort associated with advancing cancer; breathlessness, associated with respiratory disorders; metabolic changes, associated with diabetes and cancer; and motor difficulties, produced by spinal cord injuries. Cognitive impairments may occur, such as the language, memory, and learning deficits associated with stroke. Such physical consequences may place severe restrictions on the patient's activities.

Treatment of primary symptoms may also produce difficulties in physical functioning. Cancer patients who are receiving chemotherapy, for example, often suffer from nausea, vomiting, hair loss, skin discoloration, and other unattractive and uncomfortable bodily changes. Radiation therapy patients must cope with the burning of the skin, gastrointestinal problems, and other temporary disturbances (Nail, King, & Johnson, 1986). Chemotherapy can produce changes in taste acuity and taste aversions, sometimes leading to anorexia (Grunberg, 1985). Medications for hypertension can produce a variety of unpleasant side effects, including drowsiness, weight gain, and impotence. Sexual dysfunction as a result of treatment may occur for those with hypertension, myocardial infarction, and cancer (e.g., Andersen, Anderson, & deProsse, 1989a, 1989b). Restrictions on the activities of patients who have had a heart attack include dietary changes, elimination of smoking, and exercise requirements.

Life stress is an important factor in physical management of chronic disease. Stress has been heavily implicated in the downward course of diabetes (Turk & Speers, 1983), heart disease (see Krantz, 1980), hypertension (Harrell, 1980), and multiple sclerosis (Mei-Tal, Meyerowitz, & Engel, 1970). As a consequence, stress management programs are increasingly being incorporated into physical treatment regimens for the chronically ill.

Perhaps the greatest problem of physical management involves adherence to treatment. At least half of all patients with chronic disorders do not adhere fully to their treatment regimens (Taylor & Aspinwall, 1990). Moreover, because many of the changes that chronically ill patients must make involve lifestyle change, adherence problems are especially acute. The features that characterize the treatment regimens of chronically ill patients are those typically associated with high levels of nonadherence. Regimens that must be followed over a long period of time, that are complex, that interfere with other desirable life activities, and that involve lifestyle changes such as adding exercise, stopping smoking, or reducing stress show low levels of adherence (Turk & Meichenbaum, 1989).

Physical rehabilitation of chronically ill or disabled patients typically involves several goals: to help them use their bodies as much as possible; to enable them to sense changes in the environment and within themselves so that they can make the appropriate physical accommodations; to learn new physical management skills; to pursue a necessary treatment regimen; and to learn how to control the expenditure of energy. Patients must develop the capacity to read bodily signs that signal the onset of a crisis, know how to respond to that crisis, and maintain whatever treatment regimen is required (Gartner & Reissman, 1976).

Vocational Issues in Chronic Illness

Many chronic illnesses create problems for patients' vocational activities. Some patients need to restrict or change their work activities or learn new ones. Other chronically ill patients, such as those with heart disease, cancer, or AIDS, face potential job discrimination (Davidson, 1983). When these patients return to their jobs, they may be moved into less demanding positions or promoted less quickly because the organization believes they have a poor prognosis and are not worth training for more advanced work.

Related to these issues is the enormous financial impact that chronic illness can have. Many people's insurance coverage is not sufficient to meet the needs created by chronic illness, and patients who must cut back on their work or stop working altogether may lose their insurance, so that enormous financial costs are added to the burden of their care. Thus, the threat to vocation that chronic illness creates can sometimes be a double-whammy: the chronically ill patient's capacity to earn income may be reduced and, simultaneously, the benefits that would have helped shoulder the costs of care may be cut back.

Social Interaction Problems in Chronic Illness

The development of a chronic illness can also create problems of social interaction for many patients. Patients may have trouble reestablishing normal social relations. They may complain of others' pity or rejection, but behave in ways that inadvertently elicit these behaviors. Friends and relatives may have problems adjusting to the patient's altered condition. Acquaintances may give verbal signs of warmth and affection while conveying revulsion or rejection through their gestures, contacts, and body postures (Wortman & Dunkel-Schetter, 1979). These mixed messages may create difficulties for the chronically ill in knowing how to present themselves to others.

In their account of the "victimization" model of reactions to the chronically ill, Wortman and Dunkel-Schetter (1979) suggest that the stressful event of a chronic disease may create fear and aversion in family and friends, but may also evoke a simultaneous awareness of the need to provide social support. These tensions may produce a variety of adverse outcomes, such as physically avoiding the patient, avoiding open communication about the disease, minimizing its impact, or demonstrating forced cheerfulness. Under such conditions, effective social support may be reduced (Stephens, Kinney, Norris, & Ritchie, 1987). Distant relationships with friends and acquaintances appear to be more adversely affected in these ways than intimate relations (Dakor & Taylor, 1990; Fitzpatrick, Newman, Lamb, & Shipley, 1988). However, intimate others may be distressed by the loved one's condition (e.g., Tompkins, Schulz, & Rau, 1988) and be ineffective in providing support because their own social support needs are unmet (e.g. Cassileth et al., 1985; Michela, 1987).

Consistent with these points, it has been said that individuals do not develop chronic illnesses, families do. The reason for this belief is that the family is a social system and disruption in the life of one family member invariably affects the lives of others (Leventhal, Leventhal, & Nguyen, 1985). One of the chief changes brought about by chronic illness is the increased dependency of the chronically ill patient. Consequently, new responsibilities fall to the spouse and children. If family members' resources are already stretched, accommodating to new tasks may be difficult. Young children who are suddenly forced to take on more responsibilities than would normally be expected for their age, for example, may react by rebelling or acting out (Wellisch, 1981).

Despite the many sources of strain that may develop when a member of a family has a chronic illness, there is no evidence that such strains are catastrophic. For example, there is no higher divorce rate among families with a chronic illness, nor do such families appear to show less cohesion (Litman, 1974).

Personal Issues in Chronic Illness

In addition to the physical, vocational, and social adjustments a patient must make, changes in self-perceptions are often required. Physical limitations may lead to a change in one's body image—that is, to a deterioration in the perception and evaluation of one's physical functioning and appearance. At first, the entire body image may take on a negative aura, although over time, most patients appear to adjust to permanent alterations in their physical appearance. An exception appears to be facial disfigurement. Patients whose faces are scarred or disfigured may never accept their altered appearance (Richardson, Goodman, Hastorf, & Dornbusch, 1961).

Achievement through vocational and avocational activities is also an important component of self-esteem and self-concept. To the extent that a chronic illness threatens these valued aspects of the self, self-concept may be damaged. Often, then, patients must offset the damage to valued aspects of the self that are threatened by the chronic illness by placing value on other aspects that remain unthreatened.

The residual core of a patient's identity, his or her ambitions, goals, and desires for the future, also relate to adjustment to chronic illness. For example, adjustment may be impeded because the patient has had an unrealized dream that has been shattered, or at least appears to have been. In such cases, goals may need to be revamped or alternative means to meet the same goals may need to be developed.

Emotional Reactions to Chronic Illness

As the previous sections attest, the impact of chronic illness on the individual can be pervasive, affecting physical well-being, work, sexual functioning, and family life (see Burish & Bradley, 1983, for a review). Consequently, chronic illness and its treatment can produce a variety of adverse emotional effects, such as anxiety and depression (e.g., Burish, Meyerowitz, & Carey, 1987). When left undetected and untreated, these emotional problems may produce a substantial reduction in patients' quality of life and may interfere with physical rehabilitation and return to work, leisure, and social activities. Because of their importance, we give extended consideration to the problems associated with anxiety and depression. In considering these issues, it is useful to remember that those with prior histories of such disorders are at high risk for exacerbated emotional responses to chronic illness inasmuch as chronic illness constitutes yet another stressful event for them (Morris & Raphael, 1987).

Anxiety. Chronically ill patients often experience anxiety (Derogatis et al., 1983; Popkin, Callies, Lentz, Colon, & Sutherland, 1988), and heightened levels of anxiety can interfere with physical and psychosocial functioning. For example, anxiety is associated with poor functioning following radiotherapy (Graydon, 1988), poor glucose control and increased symptom reporting in diabetics (Lustman, 1988), and less likelihood of returning to work in myocardial infarction patients (Maeland & Havik, 1987).

While some anxiety among the chronically ill may be a manifestation of a premorbid propensity for anxiety, there are also specific documented sources of anxiety during rehabilitation and treatment. Waiting for test results, receiving a threatening diagnosis, anticipating or undergoing invasive medical procedures, experiencing side effects of treatments, coming to terms with lifestyle alterations, dependency on health professionals, and fear of recurrence are all documented sources of anxiety (Fallowfield, Baum, & Maguire, 1987; Welch-McCaffrey, 1985). In fact, one study (Scott, 1983) found levels of anxiety among women awaiting breast biopsy results to be comparable to norms for patients with acute anxiety reactions.

The challenges posed by rehabilitation may also produce anxiety. For example, research with myocardial infarction (MI) patients suggests that, while anxiety about a repeat MI decreases in the year following the heart attack, anxiety over complications, the future, return to work, leisure time activities, relations with others, and sexual relations increases (Christman et al., 1988; Thompson, Webster, Cordle, & Sutton, 1987).

Depression. Depression is a common and often disabling reaction to chronic illness. In their review, Rodin and Voshart (1986) concluded that one-third of medical in-patients experience moderate symptoms of depression, while up to one-quarter suffer from severe depression. Some of this depression may represent either premorbid propensity for it or neurological damage, but other instances of depression are clearly associated with the stressors that accompany chronic illness (Derogatis et al., 1983; Popkin et al., 1988; Primeau, 1988). Some theorists have suggested that depression is a reliable stage of responding to chronic illness; however, the notion of a stage of depression has received little empirical support (Silver & Wortman, 1980).

Unlike anxiety, which appears to be episodic, depression can be a long-term reaction. For many illnesses, depression can last a year or longer following initial treatment (e.g., Lustman, Griffith, & Clouse, 1998; Meyerowitz, 1980; Robinson & Price, 1982; Stern, Pascale, & Ackerman, 1977). Accordingly, depression is important not only for the distress it produces but also because it may have an impact on long-term rehabilitation and recovery (Primeau, 1988). Depressed stroke patients have longer hospital stays and are more often discharged to nursing homes than nondepressed patients (Cushman, 1986). They show less motivation to undergo rehabilitation (Thompson, Sobolew-Shubin, Graham, & Janigian, 1989), they are less likely to maintain gains made during rehabilitation (Sinyor et al., 1986), and they are less likely to restore their quality of life to prestroke levels (Niemi, Laaksonen, Kotila, & Waltimo, 1988). Depressed MI patients are less likely to return to work one year later and are more likely to be rehospitalized (Stern, Pascale, & Ackerman, 1977). Depression has also been linked to suicide among the chronically ill (Schneider, Taylor, Hammen, Kemeny, & Dudley, 1991).

Assessment of depression in the chronically ill can be problematic. First, many of the physical signs of depression, such as fatigue, sleeplessness or weight loss, may also be symptoms of the disease or side effects of treatment. If depressive symptoms are attributed to the illness, depression may be infrequently diagnosed (Rodin & Voshart, 1986). Sinyor et al. (1986) found that only one-third of the depressed stroke victims in their sample had been referred for treatment, and Lustman and Harper (1987) reported similar findings for diabetics. These problems are exacerbated in illnesses like cancer, stroke, diabetes, AIDS, and epilepsy that can affect brain function. Only in the last decade have researchers tried to adjust standardized measures of depression to eliminate overlap with somatic symptoms (Clark, Cavanaugh, & Gibbons, 1983).

Another barrier to assessment is that there are no standards for diagnosing depression in the medically ill (Rodin & Voshart, 1986). Depression in the chronically ill often goes untreated because many people believe that one is supposed to be depressed after a diagnosis of chronic illness (Greer, 1987; Robinson, 1986). Clearly, guidelines are needed to distinguish normal dysphoria experienced in coping with a chronic illness from responses severe enough to warrant intervention.

A number of specific factors related to chronic illness have been associated with depression. Generally speaking, the likelihood of depression increases with the severity of illness (e.g., Cassileth et al., 1985; Rodin & Voshart, 1986), and this statistical relation appears to increase over time (Morris & Raphael, 1987; Primeau, 1988). Long-term disability, then, is one of the factors consistently associated with long-term depression. Pain is also a significant predictor of depression (Hawley & Wolfe, 1988). Other negative life events, social stress, and lack of social support are also associated with depression in chronically ill patients (Murphy, Creed, & Jayson, 1988; Thompson et al., 1989).

COPING WITH THE STRESS OF CHRONIC ILLNESS

In the previous sections, we have attempted to identify the major sources of stress that may stem from having a chronic illness. We now turn to the means by which people cope with the stresses raised by chronic illness. Coping consists of "efforts, both action-oriented and intrapsychic, to manage (i.e., master, tolerate, reduce, minimize) environmental and internal demands and conflicts among them" (Lazarus & Launier, 1978:311). Generally, two types of coping efforts have been distinguished: problem-solving efforts and efforts at emotional regulation (Lazarus & Folkman, 1984). Problem-solving efforts are attempts to do something active about the stressful condition; emotion-focused coping involves efforts to regulate its emotional consequences. Generally, however, researchers have found it more useful to go beyond this dichotomy to identify specific coping strategies adopted for managing stressful events.

Coping Strategies

Relatively few investigations have systematically examined coping strategies among chronically ill patient groups. In a study by Dunkel-Schetter, Feinstein, Taylor, and Falke (1992), cancer patients specified their most troublesome cancer-related problem and then completed a sixty-eight-item version of the Ways of Coping Inventory developed by Folkman and Lazarus (1988). Factor analysis of the items yielded five strategies:

1. *Social support/direct problem-solving,* which included items indicating the seeking out and use of social support, as well as other direct problem-solving actions (e.g., "I talked to someone to find out more about the situation.").
2. *Distancing,* which involves effort to detach oneself from the stressful situation (e.g., "I didn't let it get to me. I refused to think about it too much.").
3. *Positive focus,* characterized by efforts to find meaning in the experience by focusing on personal growth (e.g., "I came out of the experience better than I went in.").
4. *Cognitive escape/avoidance,* which involves such efforts as wishful thinking (e.g., "I wished that the situation would go away.").
5. *Behavioral escape/avoidance,* such as efforts to avoid the situation by eating, drinking, smoking, using drugs, or taking medications.

The ways that people cope with chronic disease are not confined to these five strategies, nor would factor analyses of strategies employed by victims of chronic illnesses other than cancer necessarily yield the same structure (cf. Felton & Revenson, 1984; Felton, Revenson, & Hinrichsen, 1984). The cancer patients in the Dunkel-Schetter et al. study rated their coping efforts concerning the aspects of cancer they had found to be the most stressful: fear and uncertainty about the future (41%); limitations in physical abilities, appearance, and lifestyle (24%); and pain management (12%). It is likely that the preponderance of uncontrollable concerns expressed by these patients produced a factor structure that deemphasizes such factors as planful problem solving or confrontative coping, which involve direct action (cf. Lazarus & Folkman, 1984). Among those coping with the aftermath of myocardial infarction, for example, confrontative coping and planful problem solving might emerge, as people actively modify their health habits and lifestyle with the hopes of reducing subsequent risk. Another aspect of chronic illness that may influence coping is prognosis. Felton et al. (1984) found that terminally ill cancer patients were less likely than patients with hypertension, diabetes, or rheumatoid arthritis to cognitively restructure their disease by concentrating on something good that could come out of it.

Because of the limited number of studies that have addressed coping styles and specific chronic diseases, a full analysis of the types of coping strategies employed by the chronically ill is precluded and constitutes an important direction for future research.

Determinants of Successful Coping

A logical next step in the analysis of coping strategies employed by the chronically ill is to identify which strategies facilitate psychological adjustment. That question has yet to be answered definitively. There is some evidence from coping with stressors other than chronic disease that the use of avoidant coping is associated with increased psychological distress and may therefore constitute a psychological risk factor for adverse responses to stress more generally (Aspinwall & Taylor, in press; Cronkite & Moos, 1984; Holahan & Moos, 1986, 1987). Consistent with this argument, Felton et al. (1984) found that cognitive restructuring was associated with good emotional adjustment in patients with hypertension, diabetes, or rheumatoid arthritis; whereas coping by fantasizing, expressing emotion, or blaming oneself was associated with poor adjustment. Information-seeking and threat minimization were not related to adjustment. Similarly, Weisman and Worden (1976–1977) found poor adjustment among cancer patients to be associated with efforts to forget the cancer, fatalistic views of cancer, passive acceptance, withdrawal from others, blaming of others, and self-blame. At least one study has also found avoidant coping to be associated with poor glycemic control among insulin-dependent diabetics (Frenzel, McCaul, Glasgow, & Schafer, 1988).

Correspondingly, research has found lower psychosocial morbidity to be associated with positive confrontative responses to a stress, with optimism (Scheier, Weintraub, & Carver, 1986), with high internal locus of control (Burgess, Morris, & Pettingale, 1988), and with beliefs that one can personally exert direct control over an illness (e.g., Affleck, Tennen, Pfeiffer, & Fifield, 1987; Taylor, Lichtman, & Wood, 1984). Similarly, low helplessness has been associated with superior psychological and behavioral functioning and reduced symptom severity in patients with rheumatoid arthritis (Stein, Wallston, Nicassio, & Castner, 1988).

Some research suggests that hardiness (Kobasa, 1979) is associated with physiologic and psychosocial adaptation to diabetes but not necessarily to hypertension or rheumatoid arthritis (Pollock, 1985). These findings and their generalization to other diseases, however, are complicated by the multidimensional nature of this construct, by the fact that low hardiness may simply reflect a propensity for negative affect (Allred & Smith, 1989), and by questions concerning whether hardiness enables people to combat stressors better or simply influences health practices (Allred & Smith, 1989; Wiebe & McCallum, 1986; see also Funk & House, 1987).

Denial

The role of denial in adjustment to chronic illness has been a particularly controversial issue in the exploration of coping strategies among the chronically ill. Researchers have known for decades that intermittent denial may be useful in enabling people to come to terms gradually with the threatening aspects of stressful events (e.g., Lazarus, 1983; Meyerowitz, 1980). In fact, Hackett and Weisman (1969) argue that denial is an appropriate and adaptive way to deal with stress in the face of a life-threatening illness (see also Meyerowitz, 1983).

Denial may be more adaptive at some points in adjustment to chronic disease than others (Meyerowitz, 1983). For example, among MI patients, Levine and his colleagues

(Levine et al., 1988) found that high denial was associated with fewer days in intensive care and fewer signs of cardiac dysfunction relative to low deniers. However, in the year following discharge, high deniers showed poorer adaptation to disease, were less adherent to treatment, and required more days of rehospitalization. These findings suggest that denial may interfere with effective monitoring of the long-term nature of some chronic condition.

The findings concerning denial imply that coping strategies may be most effective when they are matched to the particular problems or points in time when they may be most useful (i.e., a matching hypothesis). There is evidence that people spontaneously match coping strategies to aspects of a stressful event. For example, people are more likely to use problem-solving strategies for aspects of a stressor that are amenable to direct control and to employ emotion-focused coping for aspects of a stressful event that remain uncontrollable (e.g., Folkman & Lazarus, 1980; Scheier, Weintraub, & Carver, 1986). Also consistent with a matching hypothesis, some research suggests that multiple coping strategies may be most effective in managing some stressful events (Collins, Taylor, Skokan, 1990; Pearlin & Schooler, 1978).

Thus, an answer to the question "Which coping strategies work best?" is likely to be complex and to depend upon which aspects of a stressful event an individual is coping with at a particular point in the adjustment process (Meyerowitz, 1983). Despite this caveat, a general conclusion is that active coping efforts are more consistently associated with good adjustment than avoidant strategies, so long as aspects of the disease are amenable to active coping efforts.

Social Support

Social support appears to be an important coping resource for those suffering from chronic disease. The benefits of social support have generally been grouped into three categories: tangible assistance, information, and emotional support (Schaefer, Coyne, & Lazarus, 1981).

Social support may lower the likelihood of illness initially, although research results are mixed on this point (e.g., Wallston, Alagna, DeVellis, & DeVellis, 1983). Social support does reliably speed recovery from illness, and it reduces the risk of mortality (House, Landis, & Umberson, 1988). Self-reports of good social relationships and positive adjustment to chronic disease are consistently found in the literature for cancer (Fitzpatrick et al., 1988; Siegal, Calsyn, & Cuddihee, 1987; Taylor et al., 1984), arthritis (Fitzpatrick et al., 1988), and end-stage renal disease (Siegal et al., 1987). Social support has been associated with better recoveries from kidney disease (Dimond, 1979), childhood leukemia (Magni, Silvestro, Tamiello, Zanesco, & Carl, 1988), and stroke (Robertson & Suinn, 1968), a reduced likelihood of mortality from myocardial infarction (Wiklund et al., 1988), better diabetes control (Schwartz, Springer, Flaherty, & Kiani, 1986; but see Kaplan & Hartwell, 1987), and less pain among arthritis patients (DeVellis, DeVellis, Sauter, & Cohen, 1986).

Social support may reduce the distress that accompanies chronic illness (e.g., Zich & Temoshok, 1987). Fewer illness-related problems among chronically ill or elderly populations have been documented for those with high levels of social support (Wallston et al., 1983). Social support also appears to affect health habits and, in particular, promotes adherence to medical regimens. People with high levels of social support are usually more compliant with their medication requirements and they are more likely to use health services (e.g., Wallston et al., 1983).

Social support may be most effective when it provides coping assistance (Thoits, 1986). Different stressors create different needs that elicit different coping efforts. Social support efforts may be viewed as assisting these coping efforts and should be most effective when they match the person's needs. Consistent with the view that social support represents coping assistance, Dunkel-Schetter, Folkman, and Lazarus (1987) found that individuals' ways of coping were strongly associated with the types of support they received. Studies with cancer patients suggest a further qualification to this matching hypotheses (Dakof & Taylor, 1990; Dunkel-Schetter, 1984)—namely, that different kinds of support may be valued from different members of the social support network. Each member may have unique abilities to be helpful along particular dimensions. Intimate others may be best able to provide emotional support, but information and advice may be more valuable from experts and actually experienced as aversive when received from intimate others.

COPING INTERVENTIONS AND CHRONIC ILLNESS

As the sources of stress and needs for help among the chronically ill are increasingly being identified, a variety of interventions ranging from informal communication to pharmacological treatments have been proposed to aid coping and alleviate emotional distress in the chronically ill.

Improving Staff-Patient Communication

Informal interventions can be accomplished within the medical setting by improving staff-patient communication. Telling patients and their families what to expect may substantially alleviate anxiety. For example, Maguire (1975) found that women who were warned ahead of time about physical discomfort following surgery were less disturbed by their symptoms. Simply telling patients that anxiety or depression may be related to chronic illness can alleviate patients' and family members' concerns.

Increasing Patient Involvement in Treatment

Increasing patient involvement in treatment has also been found to ameliorate adverse psychological responses. Such interventions can often be easily implemented, for example, by training patients to ask more questions regarding their health care (Greenfield, Kaplan, Ware, Yano, & Frank, 1988). Other studies have given patients responsibility for monitoring their conditions, as in one study by Follick et al. (1988) who instructed MI patients in reading and phoning in electrocardiograph readings to the hospital. Interventions like these may reduce negative affect and improve psychosocial functioning.

Pharmacological Treatment

Pharmacologic treatments for psychosocial sequelae of chronic illness have yet to be extensively researched, but clinical use suggests that antidepressants may be appropriate for at least some patients suffering from depression associated with cancer or stroke (Rodin

& Voshart, 1986). Evans et al. (1988), for example, showed alleviation of depression and improvements in psychosocial functioning in cancer patients receiving antidepressants.

Relaxation Training

Relaxation training is a widely used nonpharmacological intervention to manage distress that arises in response to chronic illness or treatments with adverse side effects. For example, relaxation has been used to decrease anxiety and nausea from chemotherapy and to decrease pain (Carey & Burish, 1988). Various combinations of relaxation training and stress management, biofeedback, or blood pressure monitoring have been used in the treatment of essential hypertension as well (e.g., Agras, Taylor, Kraemer, Southam, & Schneider, 1987).

Psychotherapy

Psychotherapeutic interventions, such as crisis intervention, brief psychotherapy, family therapy, and group therapy, have been shown to reduce emotional distress in patients. However, it has been difficult to compare the effectiveness of these treatments because psychotherapy is typically tailored to individual cases and because investigators have not fully described the treatments (Greer, 1987; Linn, 1988).

Social Support Groups

Social support groups represent an increasingly frequent intervention with the chronically ill. Potentially, such groups may satisfy unmet needs for social support and they may also be viewed as an additional source of support. Some of these groups evolve from rehabilitation programs, and in other cases, linkages between the primary health care setting and established groups (such as I Can Cope for cancer patients) may facilitate entry into such programs.

Chronically ill patients report a variety of positive experiences from such contacts, such as exposure to good role models on whom they can pattern their own coping and the acquisition of useful information. Although researchers have not identified the therapeutic ingredients underlying reported improvements produced by support groups (Telch & Telch, 1985), substantial evidence from a wide range of chronically ill populations suggest that these groups help patients cope (see Taylor & Aspinwall, 1990, for a review).

Perhaps the major problem with support groups as an intervention with the chronically ill at present is their limited appeal. Self-help groups appear to appeal disproportionately to well-educated, middle class white females, a segment of the population that is already served by traditional treatment services (Taylor, Falke, Shoptaw, & Lichtman, 1986). The potential for self-help groups to be a general resource for the chronically ill has yet to be fully realized.

Interventions with Family Members

As previously noted, communication between chronically ill patients and their families may be adversely affected by the illness. In some cases, problems may arise because of misunderstandings and/or lack of information about how to respond to the chronically ill person. Accordingly, researchers are recognizing the potential usefulness of intervening with spouses and other family members to inform them more fully about the nature of the illness, to describe or demonstrate the limitations (or not) placed on the patient by the disease or treatments, and the ways in which family members can help further rehabilitation (Taylor, Bandura, Ewart, Miller, & DeBusk, 1985). Even simple interventions involving the provision of information may be helpful (e.g., Thompson & Cordle, 1988).

Rehabilitation Programs

Comprehensive rehabilitation planning for the chronically ill is a goal toward which many in the health care professions are currently striving. At present, however, the goal is only partially realized for one disorder: myocardial infarction. In this case, patients are often enrolled in rehabilitation programs shortly after discharge from the hospital. Most of these programs heavily emphasize exercise and, generally speaking, they appear to produce modest improvements in cardiac functioning (see Greenland & Chu, 1988, for a review). Other interventions include not only exercise but also efforts to modify type A behavior, a risk factor for cardiovascular disease, and to address psychosocial sequelae of MI more generally. In a review of cardiac rehabilitation programs that include exercise therapy, type A modification, and nonspecific psychological therapeutic interventions, Blumenthal and Emery (1988) concluded that some programs may prolong life or significantly reduce morbidity in post-MI patients, when compared with routine medical care.

POSITIVE LIFE EXPERIENCE AND CHRONIC DISEASE

Throughout this chapter, we have emphasized the stresses that are created by chronic illness and its treatment and the problems the patients experience in attempting to cope with these stressful events. Obscured in such a portrait is the fact that the chronically ill not only usually cope successfully with these stressful events but often use them to bring about positive changes in their lives.

Consider the following paradoxical findings. Two studies have compared the quality of life reported by cancer patients with that of a normal age-matched sample free of disease, and both found that quality of life reported by the cancer patients was higher (Danoff, Kramer, Irwin, & Gottlieb, 1983; Tempelaar et al., in press). In one study of cancer patients (Collins et al., 1990), over ninety percent of the respondents found at least some beneficial changes in their lives as a result of the cancer. These patients reported an increased ability to appreciate each day and the inspiration to do things in their lives immediately instead of postponing them. Respondents also reported that they were putting more effort into their social lives and believed they had acquired greater awareness of others' feelings and increased sympathy and compassion for others. They reported feeling stronger and more self-assured as individuals (see also Taylor, 1983). Similarly, in a study of myocardial infarction patients, a third of the patients felt that their lives had actually improved overall as a result of the MI (Laerum, Jonhsen, Smith, & Larsen, 1987).

Psychological and psychiatric models of mental health and adjustment have left relatively little room for understanding the kinds of positive changes that can be observed in response to chronic illness. When researchers have uncovered these positive changes in response to chronic disease, they have sometimes viewed them with suspicion. Some have regarded these processes as defensive ones; others have implied that these effects may result from response biases, such as a need to say something positive to a research investigator. These criticisms may be somewhat shortsighted. There exists now, among some psychoanalytic theorists, an effort to reexamine the assumptions underlying the imputation of defensiveness to these kinds of processes. For example, Sackeim (1983) has argued persuasively that the creative reconstructions and distortions that one sometimes sees of negative events are actually associated with mental health and should be thought of as offensive rather than defensive processes.

Our own framework for thinking about these changes, which we have termed cognitive adaptation theory (Taylor, 1983; Taylor & Brown, 1988), emphasizes the continuity in the strategies that people use for dealing with everyday stressful events, as well as major threatening events like chronic illness. We argue that people deal with the world generally and with negative events in particular through a set of illusions or biases that represent themselves and the world more positively than may actually be the case. When people encounter damaging information or circumstances, they sometimes selectively distort them to reduce the negative implications for themselves or their world view, or they represent them in as unthreatening a manner as possible. When negative consequences are difficult to deny, a person may attempt to offset them with perceived gains incurred from the event, such as finding meaning through the experience or believing one is a better person for having withstood the event.

In making these claims, we are not suggesting that a chronic illness is a positive experience and that patients should be grateful for having had it for the meaning it can bring to their lives. Clearly, people experiencing a chronic illness report many negative changes as well. However, what does seem evident is that people actively struggle with chronic illness and attempt, often successfully, to derive benefits and value from the event while simultaneously seeking to accommodate their perspectives realistically to the adverse changes in their lives.

REFERENCES

AARONSON, N. K., CALAIS DE SILVA, F., YOSHIDA, O., VAN DAM, F. S. A. M., FOSSA, S. D., MIYAKAWA, M., RAGHAVAN, D., RIEDL, H., ROBINSON, M. R. G., & WORDEN, J. W. Quality of life assessment in bladder cancer clinical trials: Conceptual, methodological and practical issues. *Progress in Clinical and Biological Research,* 1986, *22,* 149–170.

AARONSON, N. K., VAN DAM, F. S. A. M., POLAK, C. E., & ZITTOUN, R. Prospects and problems in European psychosocial oncology: A survey of the EORTC Study Group on Quality of Life. *Journal of Psychosocial Oncology,* 1986, *4,* 43–53.

AFFLECK, G., TENNEN, H., PFEIFFER, C., & FIFIELD, J. Appraisals of control and predictability in adapting to a chronic disease. *Journal of Personality and Social Psychology* 1987, *53,* 273–279.

AGRAS, W. S., TAYLOR, C. B., KRAEMER, H. C., SOUTHAM, M. A., & SCHNEIDER, J. A. Relaxation training for essential hypertension at the worksite: II. The poorly controlled hypertensive. *Psychosomatic Medicine,* 1987, *49,* 264–273.

ALLRED, K. D., & SMITH, T. W. The hardy personality: Cognitive and physiological responses to evaluative threat. *Journal of Personality and Social Psychology,* 1989, *56,* 257–266.

AMERICAN CANCER SOCIETY. *Cancer facts and figures—1989.* Atlanta, GA: American Cancer Society, 1989.

AMERICAN DIABETES ASSOCIATION. *Diabetes: Facts you need to know.* Alexandria, VA: American Diabetes Association, 1986.

AMERICAN HEART ASSOCIATION. *1989 heart facts.* Dallas, TX: American Heart Association, 1988.

ANDERSEN, B. L., ANDERSON, B., & dePROSSE, C. Controlled prospective longitudinal study of women with cancer: I. Sexual functioning outcomes. *Journal of Consulting and Clinical Psychology,* 1989, *57,* 683–691.(a)

————. Controlled prospective longitudinal study of women with cancer: II. Psychological outcomes. *Journal of Consulting and Clinical Psychology,* 1989, *57,* 692–697.(b)

ASPINWALL, L. G., & TAYLOR, S. E. (in press). Modeling cognitive adaptation: A longitudinal investigation of the impact of individual differences and coping on college adjustment and performance. *Journal of Personality and Social Psychology.*

BERGNER, M., BOBBITT, R. A., CARTER, W. B., & GILSON, B. S. The sickness impact profile: Development and final revision of a health status measure. *Medical Care,* 1981, *19,* 787–805.

BLUMENTHAL, J. A., & EMERY, C. F. Rehabilitation of patients following myocardial infarction. *Journal of Consulting and Clinical Psychology,* 1988, *56,* 374–381.

BURGESS, C., MORRIS, T., & PETTINGALE, K. W. Psychological response to cancer diagnosis—II. Evidence for coping styles (coping styles and cancer diagnosis). *Journal of Psychosomatic Research,* 1988, *32,* 263–272.

BURISH, T. C., & BRADLEY, L. A. *Coping with chronic disease: Research and applications.* New York: Academic Press, 1983.

BURISH, T. G., MEYEROWITZ, B. E., & CAREY, M. P. The stressful effects of cancer in adults. In A. Baum & J. Singer (eds.), *Handbook of psychology and health.* Vol. 5. Hillsdale, NJ: Lawrence Erlbaum, 1987.

CAREY, M. P., & BURISH, T. G. Etiology and treatment of the psychological side effects associated with cancer chemotherapy: A critical review and discussion. *Psychological Bulletin,* 1988, *104,* 307–325.

CASSILETH, B. R., LUSK, E. J., STROUSE, T. B., MILLER, D. S., BROWN, L. L., CROSS, P. A. A psychological analysis of cancer patients and their next-of-kin. *Cancer,* 1985, *55,* 72–76.

CHRISTMAN, N. J., McCONNELL, E. A., PFEIFFER, C., WEBSTER, K. K., SCHMITT, M., & RIES, J. Uncertainty, coping, and distress following myocardial infarction: Transition from hospital to home. *Research in Nursing and Health,* 1988, *11,* 71–82.

CLARK, D. C., CAVANAUGH, S., & GIBBONS, R. D. The core symptoms of depression in medical and psychiatric patients. *Journal of Nervous and Mental Disease,* 1983, *171,* 705–713.

COLLINS, R. L., TAYLOR, S. E., & SKOKAN, L. A. A better world or a shattered vision? Changes in perspectives following victimization. *Social Cognition,* 1990, *8,* 263–285.

CRONKITE, R. C., & MOOS, R. H. The role of predisposing and moderating factors in the stress-illness relationship. *Journal of Health and Social Behavior,* 1984, *25,* 372–393.

CUSHMAN, L. A. Secondary neuropsychiatric complications in stroke: Implications for acute care. *Archives of Physical Medicine and Rehabilitation,* 1986, *69,* 877–879.

DAKOF, G. A., & TAYLOR, S. E. Victims' perceptions of social support: What is helpful from whom? *Journal of Personality and Social Psychology,* 1990, *58,* 80–89.

DANOFF, B., KRAMER, S., IRWIN, P., & GOTTLIEB, A. Assessment of the quality of life in long-term survivors after definitive radiotherapy. *American Journal of Clinical Oncology,* 1983, *6,* 339–345.

DAVIDSON, D. M. Return to work after cardiac events: A review. *Journal of Cardiac Rehabilitation,* 1983, *3,* 60–69.

DEROGATIS, L. R., MORROW, G. R., FETTING, J., PENMAN, D., PIASETSKY, S., SCHMALE, A. M., HENRICHS, M., CARNICKE, C. L. M., JR. The prevalence of psychiatric disorders among cancer patients. *Journal of the American Medical Association,* 1983, *249,* 751–757.

DEVELLIS, R. F., DEVELLIS, B. M., SAUTER, S. V. H., & COHEN, J. L. Predictors of pain and functioning in arthritis. *Health Education Research,* 1986, *1,* 61–67.

DIMOND, M. Social support and adaptation to chronic illness: The case of maintenance hemodialysis. *Research in Nursing and Health,* 1979, *2,* 101–108.

DUNKEL-SCHETTER, C. Social support and cancer: Findings based on patient interviews and their implications. *Journal of Social Issues,* 1984, *40,* 77–98.

DUNKEL-SCHETTER, C., FEINSTEIN, L., TAYLOR, S. E., & FALKE, R. Patterns of coping with cancer and their correlates. *Health Psychology,* 1992, *11,* 79–87.

DUNKEL-SCHETTER, C., FOLKMAN, S., & LAZARUS, R. S. Correlates of social support receipt. *Journal of Personality and Social Psychology,* 1987, *53,* 71–80.

EVANS, D. L., McCARTNEY, C. F., HAGGERTY J. J., NEMEROFF, C. B., GOLDEN, R. N., SIMON, J. B., QUADE, D., HOLMES, V., DROBA, M., MASON, G. A., FOWLER, W. C., & RAFT, D. Treatment of depression in cancer patients is associated with better life adaptation: A pilot study. *Psychosomatic Medicine,* 1988, *50,* 71–76.

FALLOWFIELD, L. J., BAUM, M., & MAGUIRE, G. P. Addressing the psychological needs of the conservatively treated breast cancer patient: Discussion paper. *Royal Society of Medicine,* 1987, *80,* 696–700.

FELTON, B. J., & REVENSON, T. A. Coping with chronic illness: A study of illness controllability and the influence of coping strategies on psychological adjustment. *Journal of Consulting and Clinical Psychology,* 1984, *52,* 343–353.

FELTON, B. J., REVENSON, T. A., & HINRICHSEN, G. A. Coping and adjustment in chronically ill adults. *Social Science and Medicine,* 1984, *18,* 889–898.

FITZPATRICK, R., NEWMAN, S., LAMB, R., & SHIPLEY, M. Social relationships and psychological well-being in rheumatoid arthritis. *Social Science and Medicine,* 1988, *27,* 399–403.

FOLKMAN, S., & LAZARUS, R. S. An analysis of coping in a middle-aged community sample. *Journal of Health and Social Behavior,* 1980, *21,* 219–239.

————. *Manual for the Ways of Coping Questionnaire.* Palo Alto, CA: Consulting Psychologists Press, 1988.

FOLLICK, M. J., GORKIN, L., SMITH, T. W., CAPONE, R. J., VISCO, J., & STABLEIN, D. Quality of life post-myocardial infarction: Effects of a transtelephonic coronary intervention system. *Health Psychology,* 1988, *7,* 169–182.

FRENZEL, M. P., McCAUL, K. D., GLASGOW, R. E., & SCHAFER, L. C. The relationship of stress and coping to regimen adherence and glycemic control of diabetes. *Journal of Social and Clinical Psychology,* 1988, *6,* 77–87.

FUNK, S. C., & HOUSE, B. K. A critical analysis of the hardiness scale's validity and utility. *Journal of Personality and Social Psychology,* 1987, *53,* 572–578.

GARTNER, A., & REISSMAN, F. Health care in a technological age. In *Self help and health: A report.* New York: New Human Services Institute, 1976.

GRAYDON, J. E. Factors that predict patients' functioning following treatment for cancer. *International Journal of Nursing Studies,* 1988, *25,* 117–124.

GREENFIELD, S., KAPLAN, S. H., WARE, J. E., YANO, E. M., & FRANK, H. J. L. Patients' participation in medical care: Effects on blood sugar control and quality of life in diabetes. *Journal of General Internal Medicine,* 1988, *3,* 448–457.

GREENLAND, P., & CHU, J. S. Efficacy of cardiac rehabilitation services with emphasis on patients after myocardial infarction. *Annals of Internal Medicine,* 1988, *109,* 650–663.

GREER, S. Psychotherapy for the cancer patient. *Psychiatric Medicine,* 1987, *5,* 267–279.

GRUNBERG, N. E. Specific taste preferences: An alternative explanation for eating changes in cancer patients. In T. G. Burish, S. M. Levy, & B. E. Meyerowitz (eds.), *Cancer, nutrition, and eating behavior: A biobehavioral perspective.* Hillsdale NJ: Lawrence Erlbaum, 1985.

HACKETT, T. P., & WEISMAN, A. D. Denial as a factor in patients with heart disease and cancer. *Annals of the New York Academy of Sciences: Care of Patients with Fatal Illness,* 1969, *164,* 802–817.

HARRELL, J. P. Psychological factors and hypertension: A status report *Psychological Bulletin,* 1980, *87,* 482–501.

HAWLEY, D. J., & WOLFE, F. Anxiety and depression in patients with rheumatoid arthritis: A prospective study of 400 patients. *Journal of Rheumatology,* 1988, *15,* 932–941.

HOLAHAN, C. J., & MOOS, R. H. Personality, coping, and family resources in stress resistance: A longitudinal analysis. *Journal of Personality and Social Psychology,* 1986, *51,* 389–395.

————. Personal and contextual determinants of coping strategies. *Journal of Personality and Social Psychology,* 1987, *52,* 946–955.

HOUSE, J. S., LANDIS, K. R., & UMBERSON, D. Social relationships and health. *Science,* 1988, *241,* 540–545.

JACHUCK, S. J., BRIERLEY, H., JACHUCK, S., & WILLCOX, P. M. The effect of hypotensive drugs on the quality of life. *Journal of the Royal College of General Practitioners,* 1982, *32,* 103–105.

KAPLAN, R. M. Quality of life measurement. In P. Karoly (ed.), *Measurement strategies in health psychology.* New York: Wiley, 1985.

KAPLAN, R. M., & HARTWELL, S. L. Differential effects of social support and social network on physiological and social outcomes in men and women with type II diabetes mellitus. *Health Psychology,* 1987, *6,* 387–398.

KATZ, S. T., FORD, A. B., MOSKOWITZ, R. W., JACKSON, B. A., & JAFFEE, M. W. Studies of illness in the aged: The index of ADL. *Journal of the American Medical Association,* 1983, *185,* 914–919.

KOBASA, S. C. Stressful life events and health: An inquiry into hardiness. *Journal of Personality and Social Psychology,* 1979, *37,* 1–11.

KRANTZ, D. S. Cognitive processes and recovery from heart attack: A review and theoretical analysis. *Journal of Human Stress,* 1980, *6,* 27–38.

LAERUM, E., JOHNSEN, N., SMITH, P., & LARSEN, S. Can myocardial infarction induce positive changes in family relationships? *Family Practice,* 1987, *4,* 302–305.

LAWRENCE, R. C., HOCHBERG, M. C., KELSEY, J. L., McDUFFIE, F. C., MEDSGER, T. A., FELTS, W. R., & SHULMAN, L. E. Estimates of the prevalence of selected arthritis and musculo-skeleto diseases in the U. S. *Journal of Rheumatology,* 1989, *16,* 427–441.

LAZARUS, R. S. The costs and benefits of denial. In S. Breznitz (ed.), *Denial of stress.* New York: International Universities Press, 1983.

LAZARUS, R. S., & FOLKMAN, S. *Stress, appraisal, and coping.* New York: Springer, 1984.

LAZARUS, R. S., & LAUNIER, R. Stress-related transactions between person and environment. In L. A. Pervin & M. Lewis (eds.), *Internal and external determinants of behavior.* New York: Plenum, 1987.

LEVENTHAL, H., LEVENTHAL, E. A., & NGUYEN, T. V. Reactions of families to illness: Theoretical models and perspectives. In D. C. Turk and R. D. Kerns (eds.), *Health, illness, and families: A lifespan perspective.* New York: Wiley, 1985.

LEVINE, M. N., GUYATT, G. H., GENT, M., DE PAUW, S., GOODYEAR, M. D., HRYNIUK, W. M., ARNOLD, A., FINDLAY, B., SKILLINGS, J. R., BRAMWELL, V. H., LEVIN, L., BUSH, H., ABU-ZAHRA, H., & KOTALIK, J. Quality of life in stage II breast cancer: An instrument for clinical trials. *Journal of Clinical Oncology,* 1988, *6,* 1798–1810

LINN, M. W. Psychotherapy with cancer patients. *Advances in Psychosomatic Medicine,* 1988, *18,* 54–65.

LITMAN, T. J. The family as the basic unit in health and medical care: A social behavioral overview. *Social Science and Medicine,* 1974, *8,* 495–519.

LUBECK, D. P., & YELIN, E. H. A question of value: Measuring the impact of chronic disease. *The Millbank Quarterly,* 1988, *66,* 444–464.

LUSTMAN, P. J. Anxiety disorders in adults with diabetes mellitus. *Psychiatric Clinics of North America,* 1988, *11,* 419–432.

LUSTMAN, P. J., GRIFFITH, L. S., & CLOUSE, R. E. Depression in adults with diabetes: Results of a 5-year follow-up study. *Diabetes Care,* 1988, *11,* 605–612.

LUSTMAN, P. J., & HARPER, G. W. Non psychiatric physicians' identification and treatment of depression in patients with diabetes. *Comprehensive Psychiatry,* 1987, *28,* 22–27.

MAELAND, J. G., & HAVIK, O. E. Psychological predictors for return to work after a myocardial infarction. *Journal of Psychosomatic Research,* 1987, *31,* 471–481.

MAGNI, G., SILVESTRO, A., TAMIELLO, M., ZANESCO, L., & CARL, M. An integrated approach to the assessment of family adjustment to acute lymphocytic leukemia in children. *Acta Psychiatrica Scandinavia,* 1988, *78,* 639–642.

MAGUIRE, P. The psychological and social consequences of breast cancer. *Nursing Minor,* 1975, *140,* 54–57.

MEI-TAL, V., MEYEROWITZ, S., & ENGEL, G. I. The role of psychological process in a somatic disorder: M. S. 1. The emotional setting of illness onset and exacerbation. *Psychosomatic Medicine,* 1970, *32,* 67–85.

MEYEROWITZ, B. E. Psychosocial correlates of breast cancer and its treatments. *Psychological Bulletin,* 1980, *87,* 108–131.

————. Postmastectomy coping strategies and quality of life. *Health Psychology,* 1983, *2,* 117–132.

MICHELA, J. L. Interpersonal and individual impacts on a husband's heart attack. In A. Baum and J. E. Singer (eds.), *Handbook of psychology and health.* Vol. 5. Hillsdale, NJ: Lawrence Erlbaum, 1987.

MOOS, R. H. *Coping with physical illness.* New York: Plenum, 1977.

MORRIS, P. L. P., & RAPHAEL, B. Depressive disorder associated with physical illness: The impact of stroke. *General Hospital Psychiatry,* 1987, *9,* 324–330.

MURPHY, S., CREED, F., & JAYSON, M. I. Psychiatric disorder and illness behavior in rheumatoid arthritis. *British Journal of Rheumatology,* 1988, *27,* 357–363.

NAIL, L. M., KING, K. B., & JOHNSON, J. E. Coping with radiation treatment for gynecologic cancer: Mood and disruption in usual function. *Journal of Psychosomatic Obstetrics and Gynaecology,* 1986, *5,* 271–281.

NIEMI, M. L., LAAKSONEN, R., KOTILA, M., & WALTIMO, O. Quality of life 4 years after stroke. *Stroke,* 1988, *19,* 1101–1107.

PEARLIN, L. I., & SCHOOLER, C. The structure of coping. *Journal of Health and Social Behavior,* 1978, *19,* 2–21.

POLLOCK, S. E. Human responses to chronic illness: Physiologic and psychosocial adaptation. *Nursing Research,* 1985, *35,* 90–95.

POPKIN, M. K., CALLIES, A. L., LENTZ, R. D., COLON, E. A., & SUTHERLAND, D. E. Prevalence of major depression, simple phobia, and other psychiatric disorders in patients with long-standing type I diabetes mellitus. *Archives of General Psychiatry,* 1988, *45,* 64–68.

PRIMEAU, F. Post-stroke depression: A critical review of the literature. *Canadian Journal of Psychiatry,* 1988, *33,* 757–765.

RICHARDSON, S. A., GOODMAN, N., HASTORF, A. H., & DORNBUSCH, S. M. Cultural uniformity in reaction to physical disabilities. *American Sociological Review,* 1961, *26,* 241–247.

ROBERTSON, E. K., & SUINN, R. M. The determination of rate of progress of stroke patients through empathy measures of patient and family. *Journal of Psychosomatic Research,* 1968, *12,* 189–191.

ROBINSON, R. G. Post-stroke mood disorder. *Hospital Practice,* 1986, *21,* 83–89.

ROBINSON, R. G., & PRICE, T. R. Post-stroke depressive disorders: A follow-up study of 103 patients. *Stroke,* 1982, *13,* 635–640.

RODIN, G., & VOSHART, K. Depression in the medically ill: An overview. *American Journal of Psychiatry,* 1986, *143,* 696–705.

SACKEIM, H. A. Self-deception, self-esteem and depression: The adaptive value of lying to oneself. In J. Masling (ed.), *Empirical studies of psychoanalytic theories.* Vol. 1. Hillsdale, NJ: Analytic Press, 1983.

SCHAEFER, C., COYNE, J. C., & LAZARUS, R. S. The health-related functions of social support. *Journal of Behavioral Medicine,* 1981, *4,* 381–406.

SCHAG, C. A. C., HEINRICH, R. L., AADLAND, R. L., & GANZ, P. A. Assessing problems of cancer patients: Psychometric properties of the cancer inventory of problem situations. *Health Psychology,* 1990, *9,* 83–102.

SCHEIER, M. F., WEINTRAUB, J. K., & CARVER, C. S. Coping with stress: Divergent strategies of optimists and pessimists. *Journal of Personality and Social Psychology,* 1986, *51,* 1257–1264.

SCHNEIDER, S. G., TAYLOR, S. E., HAMMEN, C., KEMENY, M. E., & DUDLEY, J. Factors influencing suicide intent in gay and bisexual suicide ideators: Differing models for HIV+ and HIV− men. *Journal of Personality and Social Psychology,* 1991, *16,* 776–788.

SCHWARTZ, L. S., SPRINGER, J., FLAHERTY, J. A., & KIANI, R. The role of recent life events and social support in the control of diabetes mellitus. *General Hospital Psychiatry,* 1986, *8,* 212–216.

SCOTT, D. W. Anxiety, critical thinking, and information processing during and after breast biopsy. *Nursing Research,* 1983, *32,* 24–28.

SIEGAL, B. R., CALSYN, R. J., & CUDDIHEE,, R. M. The relationship of social support to psychosocial adjustment in end-stage renal disease patients. *Journal of Chronic Disease,* 1987, *40,* 337–344.

SILVER, R. L., & WORTMAN, C. B. Coping with undesirable life events. In J. Garber and M. E. P. Seligman (eds.), *Human helplessness: Theory and applications.* New York: Academic Press, 1980.

SINYOR, D., AMATO, P., KALOUPEK, D. G., BECKER, R., GOLDENBERG, M., & COOPERSMITH, H. Post-stroke depression: Relationships to functional impairment, coping strategies, and rehabilitation outcomes. *Stroke,* 1986, *17,* 1102–1107.

STEIN, M. J., WALLSTON, K. A., NICASSIO, P. M., & CASTNER, N. M. Correlates of a clinical classification schema for the arthritis helplessness subscale. *Arthritis and Rheumatism,* 1988, *31,* 876–881.

STEPHENS, M. A. P., KINNEY, J. M., NORRIS, V. K., & RITCHIE, S. W. Social networks as assets and liabilities in recovery from stroke by geriatric patients. *Psychology and Aging,* 1987, *2,* 125–129.

STERN, M. J., PASCALE, L., & ACKERMAN, A. Life adjustment postmyocardial infarction: Determining predictive variables. *Archives of Internal Medicine,* 1977, *137,* 1680–1685.

TAYLOR, C. B., BANDURA, A., EWART, C. K., MILLER, N. H., & DEBUSK, R. F. Exercise testing to enhance wives' confidence in their husbands' cardiac capabilities soon after clinically uncomplicated acute myocardial infarction. *American Journal of Cardiology,* 1985, *55,* 635–638.

TAYLOR, S. E. Adjustment to threatening events: A theory of cognitive adaptation. *American Psychologist,* 1983, *38,* 1161–1173.

TAYLOR, S. E., & ASPINWALL, L. G. Psychological aspects of chronic illness. In G. R. VandenBos & P. T. Costa, Jr. (eds.), *Psychological aspects of serious illness.* Washington, DC: American Psychological Association, 1990.

TAYLOR, S. E., & BROWN, J. D. Illusion and well-being: A social psychological perspective on mental health. *Psychological Bulletin,* 1988, *103,* 193–210.

TAYLOR, S. E., FALKE, R. L., SHOPTAW, S. J., & LICHTMAN, R. R. Social support, support groups, and the cancer patient. *Journal of Consulting and Clinical Psychology,* 1986, *54,* 608–615.

TAYLOR, S. E., LICHTMAN, R. R., & WOOD, J. V. Attributions, beliefs about control, and adjustment to breast cancer. *Journal of Personality and Social Psychology,* 1984, *46,* 489–502.

TELCH, C. F., & TELCH, M. J. Psychological approaches for enhancing coping among cancer patients: A review. *Clinical Psychology Review,* 1985, *5,* 325–344.

TEMPELAAR, R., DEHAES, J. C. J. M., DERUITER, J. H., BAKKER, D., VAN DEN HEUVEL, W. J. A., & VAN NIEUWENHIUJZEN, M. G. The social experiences of cancer patients under treatment: A comparative study. *Social Science and Medicine,* in press.

THOITS, P. A. Social support as coping assistance. *Journal of Consulting and Clinical Psychology,* 1986, *54,* 416–423.

THOMPSON, D. R., & CORDLE, C. J. Support of wives of myocardial infarction patients. *Journal of Advanced Nursing,* 1988, *13,* 223–228.

THOMPSON, D. R., WEBSTER, R. A., CORDLE, C. J., & SUTTON, T. W. Specific sources and patterns of anxiety in male patients with first myocardial infarction. *British Journal of Medical Psychology,* 1987, *60,* 343–348.

THOMPSON, S. C., SOBOLEW-SHUBIN, A., GRAHAM, M. A., & JANIGIAN, A. S. Psychosocial adjustment following a stroke. *Social Science and Medicine,* 1989, *28,* 239–247.

TOMPKINS, C. A., SCHULZ, R., & RAU, M. T. Post-stroke depression in primary support persons: Predicting those at risk. *Journal of Consulting and Clinical Psychology,* 1988, *56,* 502–508.

TURK, D. C., & MEICHENBAUM, D. Adherence to self-care regimens: The patient's perspective. In R. H. Rozensky, J. J. Sweet, & S. M. Tovian (eds.), *Handbook of clinical psychology in medical settings.* New York: Plenum, 1989.

TURK, D. C., & SPEERS, M. A. Diabetes mellitus: A cognitive-functional analysis of stress. In T. G. Burish & L. A. Bradley (eds.), *Coping with chronic disease: Research and applications.* New York: Academic Press, 1983.

UNITED STATES BUREAU OF THE CENSUS. *U. S. Bureau of the Census Statistical Abstract of the United States 1989* (109th ed.). Washington, DC: U.S. Government Printing Office, 1989.

WALLSTON, B. S., ALAGNA, S. W., DEVELLIS, B. MCE., & DEVELLIS, R. F. Social support and physical health. *Health Psychology,* 1983, *2,* 367–391.

WEISMAN, A., & WORDEN, J. W. The existential plight in cancer: Significance of the first 100 days. *International Journal of Psychiatry in Medicine,* 1976–1977, *7,* 1–15.

WELCH-MCCAFFREY, S. Cancer, anxiety, and quality of life. *Cancer Nursing,* 1985, *8,* 151–158.

WELLISCH, D. K. Intervention with the cancer patient. In C. K. Prokop & L. A. Bradley (eds.), *Medical psychology: Contributions to behavioral medicine.* New York: Academic Press, 1981.

WIEBE, D. J., & MCCALLUM, D. M. Health practices and hardiness as mediators in the stress-illness relationship. *Health Psychology,* 1986, *5,* 425–438.

WIKLUND, I., ODEN, A., SANNE, H., ULVENSTAM, G., WILHELMSSON, C., & WILHEMSEN, L. Prognostic importance of somatic and psychosocial variables after a first myocardial infarction. *American Journal of Epidemiology,* 1988, *128,* 786–795.

WORTMAN, C. B., & DUNKEL-SCHETTER, C. Interpersonal relationships and cancer: A theoretical analysis. *Journal of Social Issues,* 1979, *35,* 120–155.

ZICH, J., TEMOSHOK, L. Perceptions of social support in men with AIDS and ARC: Relationships with distress and hardiness. *Journal of Applied Social Psychology,* 1987, *17,* 193–215.

29

Stress, Ethyl Alcohol, and Alcoholism

Herbert S. Peyser

THERE IS NO BETTER EVENT than the voluntarily ingestion of ethanol for the examination of the stress-response interaction, for that act is a simple, clearly defined parameter with clean boundaries and easily studied causal, concomitant, and resultant phenomena on both the physiological and behavioral levels. Much the same can be said for other potentially addicting drugs: the closely related sedatives (barbiturates, benzodiazepines, meprobamate, etc.), the narcotics (heroin, morphine, methadone, meperidine, oxycodone, propoxyphene, codeine, etc.), to a lesser degree, the stimulants (cocaine, the amphetamines, methylphenidate, etc.), and, to an even lesser degree, the amphetamines (lysergic acid diethylamide, phencyclidine, mescaline, etc.)

Everyday common sense and clinical observations seem to show that ethanol ingestion is related to stress and tension reduction: e.g., Robert Benchley's "I have to get out of these wet clothes and into a Dry Martini." The literature has many studies supporting this hypothesis, and yet there are equally everyday clinical observations that ethanol is taken at times without a preceding stressful event. In addition, ethanol can often be seen to increase rather than decrease tension, anxiety, and dysphoric states: e.g., the physically ill, agitated, and unhappy drunk. Here, too, the research literature has many studies supporting these observations and indicating that at times other causative factors are at work motivating ethanol ingestion.

These studies have further implications for the problematic elements in stress theory. The ingestion of ethanol demonstrates how a response to stress can also constitute a stress, both behaviorally and physiologically, and can feed back as well into an already existing interaction. This phenomenon can thereby greatly complicate the stress-response picture, which instead of being a simple, one-way process becomes highly complicated, interacting, and dynamic, as can be seen in the clinical disorder of ethanol abuse or dependence (alcoholism).

There is a history to the stress response, tension reduction hypothesis of ethanol ingestion, the emphasis on which varies depending upon the world view of the era: innate or reactive—and, if the latter, in response to stress or what other factors? The hypothesis arose in its contemporary form in the United States in the late nineteenth century where it reflected the social and medical interests of the time in the effects of stress on life in general and on drinking behavior in particular. This was in turn linked to the concerns about the tensions inherent in the rapidly industrializing American society; society itself was seen as stressful (Lender, 1987), and there were similar notions of the stress of industrialization and urbanization as the cause of psychiatric illness in general.

Ethanol had first been seen in the nineteenth century as a central nervous system stimulant that could assist nerves whose energies had been exhausted by a stress, thus causing depression, neurosis, neurasthenia, etc.; the stimulant property could, however, lead to addiction. It was noted later in the same century that the stimulant action was related to lower doses and that ethanol in higher doses caused central nervous system depression with sedation and "narcosis"; this finding was then used to explain another mechanism of response to stress and it, too, was seen as leading to addiction. As the temperance movement grew, and as the partisans of prohibition increased, they seized upon the tension reduction model and used it for social and political purposes, thereby demedicalizing the situation.

Much earlier, however, and prior to the emergence of the disease concept, alcoholism has been viewed not as a medical matter but as innately driven, not a response to stress but a willful act (Peyser, 1989). The notion of a disease process taking place in an organ or organ system began to replace the humoral model of physical illness in the course of the sixteenth through the eighteenth centuries, and by the close of the latter century it was applied to psychiatric illness in England, France, and Italy and soon after in the United States. At the same time, the physicians Thomas Trotter in England and Benjamin Rush in the United States applied that model to alcoholism, another behavioral disorder, with the concept of a disease-driven compulsive urge to drink ethanol taking over the individual's will, despite conflicts with other interests such as family, job, or health. The orientation later in the nineteenth century was to see such matters as resulting from an external cause, some external pathogenic situation—i.e., a stress—in keeping with the discovery of pathogenic micro-organisms and the germ theory of disease.

Another factor in the development of the stress response, tension reduction hypothesis was Freud's influence on the behavioral scientists in the twentieth century. The work on hypnosis and hysteria had shown how an external event, a stressor (a hypnotic command in the experimental situation or a traumatic event in real life) could cause symptoms, actions, and behavioral changes (Mora, 1984). Even when Freud gave up the seduction theory of a traumatic external situation as the cause of abnormal behavior of a part of or the total organism, he still saw conflict as the stress; in his new formulation, however, intrapsychic conflict, arising from internal sources—the ultimately biologically based drives—and played out in the real world, constituted the stressful etiology. This concept was then adapted to ideas concerning the etiology of alcoholism and the other addictive disorders, which could also be seen as behavior arising out of stressful internal conflict played out in the real world to deal with anxiety and tension and to serve as defenses against those dysphoric states. A review of the literature will reveal how these themes were further developed in the present era.

Much of the contemporary experimental work in this area began with the psychoanalyst J. H. Masserman's research in the 1940s in which he attempted to provide a scientific and experimental basis for the developing Freudian theory. His work with experimentally produced conflict in cats (Masserman, 1946) utilized such research to substantiate that theory and to explain phobias and other neurotic behavior on a natural science basis. He applied these ideas to ethanol ingestion and alcoholism (Masserman & Yum, 1946), which he saw as reactions to the stress of internal conflict and as defensive activities to deal with the anxiety and tension resulting from that stressful situation. This work was in keeping with the developing theory of stress, but as further observations came in and as the thinking and the laboratory studies became more exact and more penetrating, an increasing number of qualifications, objections, and negative results began to enter the picture. The view of the relationship between stress, the tension reduction hypothesis, and ethanol has subsequently undergone considerable change, particularly over the last decade and a half.

ETHANOL: PHYSIOLOGY AND PSYCHOLOGY

Ethanol intake has both central nervous system (CNS) depressant and excitatory effects, neurochemically, electrically, and clinically, but the depressant effects predominate in the earliest phases. Ethanol enhances inhibitory transmission across the synapse related to its interactions with gamma aminobutyric acid (GABA) and its receptors and with glycine, both of which are major inhibitory mammalian neurotransmitters (Celentano, Gibbs, & Farb, 1988; Glowa, Crawley, Suzdak, & Paul, 1989). (Genetic factors influence these processes, for rats can be bred for preference or nonpreference for and sensitivity or resistance to the effects of ethanol and benzodiazepines.) Other neurotransmitters such as serotonin are involved as well (McBride, Murphy, Lumeng, & Li, 1988), and ethanol also inhibits the activity of the glutamate neurotransmitter system, a major excitatory transmitter system of the mammalian brain (Watkins & Olverman, 1987). The CNS-depressant endogenous opioid systems are also involved (Reid, Czirr, Bensinger, Hubbell, & Volanth, 1987). Furthermore, the corticotropin releasing factor (CRF) that affects the CNS arousal system by activating CNS and sympathetic systems, thereby contributing not only to stress but also to stress response (Koob & Bloom, 1985), has its stress-related behavioral responses reversed by low doses of ethanol (Koob, Britton, & Ehlers, 1990) and also contributes to the stress response, tension-reducing effects of ethanol.

As regards neuroelectrical factors, these phenomena correlate with electroencephalographic (EEG) findings that show, following a transitory excitatory stage with small doses of ethanol, a CNS depression phase, particularly with higher, more usual doses (Horsey & Akert, 1953), and an increase in percent of time and slowing in alpha frequency (Varga & Nagy, 1960) Similar dose-related effects are seen in the autonomic nervous system in relationship to the cardiovascular system, with low doses facilitating responsiveness and higher doses retarding it (Knott & Beard, 1982).

From the clinical point of view, these EEG effects are correlated with the degree of intoxication and changes in the level of consciousness (Begleiter & Platz, 1974) but not with the quality of the mood changes, which vary depending on the meaning and context to the individual. The positive affective states, which range from mildly pleasant to euphoric (Lukas & Mendelson, 1988), tend to be correlated with increases in EEG alpha and increases in plasma adrenocorticotropic hormone levels (i.e., excitatory changes) during the ascending portion of the blood ethanol curve, but do not occur when the blood ethanol levels are descending. Thus, some of the mood changes are due to the direct CNS effects of ethanol.

Ethanol's CNS excitatory and reinforcing effects relate to the EEG findings of the initial transitory excitatory stage. These effects to a great degree are mediated through ethanol's increase in dopamine release by activation of the firing rate of brain cells containing dopamine (Engel & Liljequist, 1983) as well as through ethanol's effects on serotonin uptake and monoaminergic activity in general (Murphy et al., 1988). Ethanol generally increases catecholamine activity, particularly norepinephrine, and thus contributes to CNS excitatory activity, and catecholaminergic turnover is further increased in the withdrawal period, thus contributing to withdrawal discomfort (Ellingboe, 1978).

This EEG excitatory stage is usually initially suppressed by the CNS depressant phase.

In this latter phase, the midbrain and its reticular activating system, an alerting and arousal system, are depressed, as well as the cortex; these changes result at first in early disinhibition of the cortex and increased amplitude of its electrical activity. The activity of the cortex is, in the first phase, progressively released from integrating controls and cognitive organization (Kalant, 1962), so that disinhibition and release are produced. Subsequently there is cortical depression following the excitation, with CNS depression extending in a progressively downward manner over time, from the cortex through the thalamus and hypothalamic systems (affecting the autonomic functions), further down the brainstem and lower areas, and finally to the medulla and its vital centers, where it ultimately produces the symptoms of shock (Himwich, 1956). Early in this process, higher functions involving praxis and certain psychological activities are first and progressively more and more interfered with. Such psychological functions involve the inhibitory and self-critical activities of what might appear clinically as the functions of the internal moral imperatives and the ideals, and these psychological functions would present themselves on the behavioral level as disinhibition and release during the early phase of intoxication.

Although there is cortical depression and secondary excitation with ethanol (Diperri, Dravid, Schweigerdt, & Himwich, 1968), there is also a direct excitatory cortical effect (Sauerland & Harper, 1970). Recent work has concentrated on this phenomenon, for ethanol is also a stimulant and this function serves as a mechanism for reinforcement, stimulation, novelty, and sensation-seeking and as a stressor itself; it is this stimulant stressor effect that causes the withdrawal symptoms, at least in part. The behavior associated with the euphoriant and excitatory properties of self-administered ethanol in animals (and other drugs of abuse such as cocaine, heroin, etc.) is similar to that seen in animal electrical self-stimulation of the brain stimulation reward areas. Ethanol and electrical stimulation enhance each other in this regard (Bain & Kornetsky, 1989). These brain stimulation reward areas in rats appear to be in the medial forebrain bundle, the rat's mesotelencephalic dopamine system. In humans the location is not as clear, but the dopamine pathway from the ventral tegmental area to the nucleus accumbens and parts of the limbic system are involved. Many types of drugs of abuse—including ethanol, benzodiazepines, and other sedatives—can augment the electrical brain stimulation reward or lower the brain reward thresholds. The opiate antagonist naloxone attenuates that augmentation and thus implicates the endogenous opioid-peptide system in that process along with the GABA system, the serotonin and norepinephrine systems, and other neural circuitry.

These neurophysiological and neurochemical mechanisms constitute the biological substrate of the CNS effects that exist in the organism and are utilized for the purpose of responding to stress and dealing with tension. They have other effects as well and can serve as stressor agents at other times (Vedernikova, Borisova, & Orekhov, 1989) or at the same time that they are being used to deal with stress.

ETHANOL INGESTION AS A RESPONSE TO STRESS

The psychological effects of ethanol have been grouped into three categories: euphoriant, disinhibiting, and anxiety-, tension- and depression-relieving actions (Kissin, 1974). The literature reports alcoholics drinking for the effect on their moods and emotions (Mulford & Miller, 1960). Alcoholics have also reported mood changes, disinhibition with increased aggression and sexuality, and decreased sense of responsibility when intoxicated (Tamerin, Weiner, Popper, Steinglass, & Mendelson, 1971). Sober alcoholics frequently report tension and anxiety reduction following ethanol intake, although they often fail to express these effects while drinking (Nathan & O'Brien, 1971), and similar effects have been reported in nonalcoholics (infra).

The mood changes associated with relief of discomfort often appear with the alcoholic's first drinking episode—long before the drinking becomes a source of further discomfort and dysphoria—and seem almost magical. The individual finds, in the initial phases of the alcoholism process, that he or she can socialize, talk to the opposite sex or to the boss, speak up at school or at parties, dance in public, or have freer sexual activity—all previously inhibited.

These stress response, tension-relieving effects are related in part to ethanol's sedative, CNS-depressant activity, with disinhibition, obtunding of awareness, and decreased alertness directed toward the external world and its influx of noxious stimuli and toward the internal world as well. This latter world involves memory and other internal representatives or reality (denial) and, perhaps more important, the stimuli flowing toward the self from the internal representative of moral authority and the ideals. As a result, one sees disinhibition and release of sexual, aggressive, and assertive tendencies. The lessening of the self-critical, self-judgmental, inhibiting influences helps account for the diminution in anxiety and depression and the development of euphoria, apparent self-esteem, courage, and confidence.

Masserman's work in the 1940s (Masserman et al., 1945; Masserman & Yum, 1946) and Conger's experiments in 1952 were among the earliest experimental animal studies developing the stress response, tension reduction hypothesis of ethanol. On the cross-cultural level Horton (1943) and Bacon (1974) also supported that hypothesis, but Horton's findings were disputed by Field (1945), and Aasved's review (1989) of the literature failed to find evidence that ethanol was used to reduce anxieties in tribal societies.

More recent cultural studies (Drew, 1988; Linsky, Colby, & Straus, 1987) have tended to support the hypothesis that sociological factors have some influence, but only in particular situations and in multifactorial contexts. The dislocation of Native Americans to urban areas and other social stress, when operating in the context of strong cultural support for ethanol use (a significant contributing factor), increased the rates of alcoholism. Heien & Pompelli in 1987 similarly showed how stress factors combined with ethnically determined attitudes toward ethanol to influence ethanol abuse.

Studies involving aging (Finney & Moos, 1983) also show how social stresses appear to increase ethanol intake, but, again, other factors, such as the loss of significant others, were emphasized as contributing factors. Perceived stress is seen as having a role in the etiology of other life cycle stress, such as in adolescent problem drinking (Mitic, McGuire, & Neumann, 1987) where the influence of social relationships and a sense of powerlessness are also present (Labouvie, 1986).

Other life stresses are reported to have increased ethanol consumption in specific situations, such as the increase in drinking in a West Virginia community after a flood (Gleser, Green, & Winget, 1981) and the increase in alcohol problems in terms of court cases, referrals to community alcoholism centers, and police arrests for violation of liquor laws in the seven months following a volcanic eruption (Adams & Adams, 1984). Other work has, however, questioned the buffering effects of ethanol in catastrophic events through revealing buffering effects for ethanol intake only in noncatastrophic events and varying with the amount of drinking (Neff, 1985). Studies of war-induced post-traumatic stress disorder (PTSD) have revealed a positive correlation between stress and ethanol intake and ethanol and substance abuse in World War II and Korean War veterans (Druley & Pashko, 1988).

Robins (1974) showed similar results in Vietnam veterans, with increased ethanol, sedative, and narcotic drug use due to stress in the lower military ranks. Upon returning home, this drug use decreased significantly, thus suggesting a positive relationship to active stress, but also noted was the presence of other factors that had to be taken into consideration, such as substance availability, peer pressure, and general acceptance of drug and ethanol use. Niles (1989) found no relationship in higher ranking officers between the amount of combat and the amount of ethanol abuse, although the former and the latter did each, independently and separately, relate positively to the degree of PTSD.

Job and school stress have been related to ethanol and drug intake (Forney, Forney, Sheets, et al., 1990; Vinyard, 1989), but the findings were also related to the subcultural drinking norms of the co-workers and the psychological orientation of low mastery or control over the outcomes of the various job pressures. Pashko and Druley (1987) found that seeing oneself as controlled by external forces was correlated with the use of substances (including ethanol) to relieve tension under stress. Another related factor positively affecting ethanol use was high job demands with low decision latitude (Bromet, Dew, Parkinson, & Schulberg, 1988). Beliefs regarding the use of ethanol to relieve job stress played an important role in these circumstances (Harris & Fennell, 1988). Beliefs and expectancies concerning the tension-reducing effects of ethanol and drugs play an important role according to several studies (McKirnan & Peterson, 1988; Powers & Kutash, 1985). Other studies conclude that stress response dampening is not so much related in many situations to expectancies but more to pre-alcoholic personality traits (Sher & Walitzer, 1986).

There is marked individual variation in response to stress in terms of ethanol and drug intake (Cappell, 1987; Sher & Levenson, 1983), and there are other reasons for this difference than varying beliefs and personality factors. One element (Lipscom, Nathan, Wilson, et al., 1980) is the greater tolerance capacity of one individual compared to another, but stress can greatly complicate the picture by increasing the rate and magnitude of tolerance (Peris & Cunningham, 1989). Brown and Schafer (1986) and Windle and Barnes (1988) noted gender differences in heterosexual situations, where males showed increased relaxation on ethanol ingestion and females showed increased anxiety. McNair (1990) reported that expectancies and control-vulnerability concerns in women exposed to stress were not correlated with ethanol consumption; rather, ethanol intake seemed related to contextual cues (situation-specific consequences and social perceptions of ethanol consumption and use). The co-existence of psychiatric illness also predisposed to increased ethanol intake upon stress (Miller, Surteen, Kreitman, Ingham, & Sashidharan, 1985), as did the presence of purging in adolescent female bulimics (Killen, Taylor, Telch, et al., 1987).

The understanding of the underlying physiological mechanisms contributes to the understanding of individual variation in ethanol's effects in response to stress. Research (Brick & Pohorecky, 1983; DeTurck & Vogel, 1982) has shown that ethanol has a specific stress-dampening effect on the pituitary-adrenal system in rats but that there was considerable variation among the individual animals. Vogel, Harris, and Taylor (1990) attributed this to a genetic component in the decreased reaction of ethanol-preferring rats to stress; this is related to the brain monamine and adrenal catecholamine systems, whose activity seems in part to be genetically determined (Korpi et al., 1988). Other studies (DeTurck & Pohorecky, 1987) have shown how prenatal stress (maternal handling) can affect rat offspring by decreasing sensitivity to the adrenocortical activating effects of ethanol and increasing the impairment of stressful swimming performance testing.

In rats, ethanol increased sensitivity and decreased maximum responsiveness of the pituitary to CRF by altering the activity of the hypothalamic-pituitary-adrenal axis and thus the response to stress (Rivier, Imaki, & Vale, 1990). Ethanol also protected animals against the effects of stress in terms of the release of beta-endorphins and catecholamines, although ethanol caused beta-endorphin and catecholamine effects similar to, but less pronounced than, those produced by stress (Patel & Pohorecky, 1988) and therefore can act as a stressor itself. Vogel, Miller and Roggendorf (1987) also showed an initial stress-dampening effect of ethanol as reflected in epinephrine and norepinephrine levels, but after a short period of time sensitization took place and the stress-produced catecholamine levels rose even higher, a manifestation of the biphasic effect of ethanol—both stressor and response to stress.

The dosage level of ethanol is a factor: low doses in stressed rats decrease the stress-produced elevation of plasma corticosterone and nonesterified fatty acids as well as some behavioral stress effects, while higher doses appear to increase the effects of stress (Brick & Pohorecky, 1987; Pohorecky & Brick, 1987). Experimentally produced central nervous system lesions involving the limbic system's amygdala and hippocampus potentiate the moderate ethanol dose effect that elevates nonsterified fatty acids and corticosterone. Alcoholics were found to show autonomic dysfunction (on pupillary reaction to light and dark) when free of stress, but low doses of ethanol tended to normalize some of those responses (Rubins, Gottheil, Roberts, et al., 19977).

There is ample evidence of the increased use of ethanol and other substances in response to stress, perceived stress, and stressful interpersonal events (Bry, McKeon, & Pandina, 1982; Dudley, Mules, Roszell, et al., 1976; Higgins & Marlatt, 1975; Miller, Hersen, Eisler, et al., 1974) in alcoholics and social drinkers, in the laboratory situation and in life. However, here, too, considerable individual variation is noted, sometimes related to personality typology (Lehrfeld, 1989); type A personalities are reported to be particularly susceptible to the ethanol stress response dampening effect (Zeichner, Edwards, & Cohen, 1985).

The more recent literature contains many studies supporting the stress response, tension reduction hypothesis (Baer, McLaughlin, Burnside, Pokorney, & Garmezy, 1985; Pohorecky, 1990; Silverman, Eichler, & Williams, 1987). Some studies have uncovered other physiological mechanisms at work, such as the ability of ethanol to prevent stress-increased cytochrome oxidase activity in the cerebral cortex and in the hippocampus (Gulyaeva, Levina, & Levishina, 1985). Also determined were the lessening of stress-induced increase in norepinephrine and serotonin levels and plasma corticosterone, nonesterified fatty acids, and aminoacids and the diminishing of the decline in adrenal catechloamines (Pohorecky, 1990) and its blunting of stress-induced secretion of ACTH and beta-endorphin (Rivier & Vale, 1988). However, often it is not clear whether the physiological and biochemical changes are causal, concomitant, or consequent, and they are apt to vary depending upon the type of stressor (Moore, 1986). Some studies seem to indicate that some catecholamine elevations may be associated with positive changes in mood due to the relief of stress tension rather than to mediating the reduction of the emotional tension per se (Vogel & Netter, 1989).

Many of the studies exhibit significant qualifications and relate the ethanol stress-dampening effect to the presence of co-existing parameters, such as personality, cultural, genetic, pre-natal, and other factors. Comprehensive reviews of the earlier literature (Cappell & Herman, 1972; Lester, 1966; Pohorecky, 1981) appear to have supported the tension reduction hypothesis somewhat more strongly than the recent literature, although inconsistencies were noted even then (Higgins, 1976). Indeed, Cappell in his papers (Cappell, 1975, 1987; Cappell & Herman, 1972) has progressively noted the mixed results and emphasized how ethanol may, in different situations, reduce or increase tension, as indicated by physiological, biochemical, or self-reported behavioral measures. Important roles in the results are played by the expectancies, individual differences, types of stress, dosage of ethanol, and the state of the individual. Tension-increasing effects are noted by Kalant (1990) as well at dosage levels not much higher than those producing tension-relieving effects.

Marlatt (1976), Williams (1976), and George and Marlatt (1983) found mixed evidence for the tension reduction hypothesis and questioned its adequacy. By 1987, Marlatt stated outright that the hypothesis as a unitary model was outmoded, and he stressed ethanol's biphasic effects, with its arousal enhancement effects even preceding its tension-reducing effects. He, along with Cappell (1987) and Powers (1987), also noted the importance of the individual's expectancies concerning ethanol's effects on behavioral changes involving disinhibition (Marlatt & Rohsenow, 1980; Rohsenow & Marlatt, 1981). Marlatt remarked upon ethanol's deleterious effects on certain nonconflict behavior (e.g., motor performance and reaction time) regardless of the expectancies. This was supported by Cappell (1987) and Powers (1987). The stress response is greatly dependent upon the individual's appraisal of the stress as well as the effect of ethanol as a coping mechanism, the context of the situation, and other factors. Ethanol intake can increase as well as decrease tension and anxiety (Mendelson, La Dou, & Solomon, 1964; Vanicelli, 1972).

At least on some occasions, the apparent reduction in tension appears to be due not to actual decreased response to stress caused by ethanol but to decreased attention or diversion of attention from the affective response state—for example, by diversion to other activities. The apparent reduction in tension occurs even when ethanol has increased anxiety and tension or perhaps even because of that increase in tension (Josephs & Steele, 1990; Levenson, Sher, Grossman, et al., 1980; Steele & Josephs, 1988; Steele, Southwick, & Pagano, 1986), or else it occurs when ethanol had caused arousal (Knott & Bulmer, 1985) that could either be seen as helping to confront the stress or as providing self-stimulation to escape boredom. This mechanism of attention diversion is closely related to the denial (Davidge, 1990) seen in ethanol and substance abuse. Conditioning may also play a role (Boyd, Callen, & House, 1989; Stasiewicz, 1990).

The more recent literature, particularly over the past ten to fifteen years, has progressively included a large number of studies and papers outrightly contradicting the ethanol stress-dampening, tension reduction hypothesis and indicating that these other factors are involved: accessibility to ethanol, lifestyle, dosage, peer interaction, sensation seeking, alcoholic predisposition and risk, social influences, beliefs and expectancies, and general arousal (Caplan & Puglisi, 1986; Hammer & Vaglum, 1989; Higgins & Marlatt, 1973; Hingson, Mangione, & Barret, 1981; Holyrod, 1978; Huffine, Folkman, & Lazarus, 1989; Kasl, Ostfeld, Berkman, & Jacobs, 1987; MacAndrew, 1982; Miller, Hersen, Eisler, et al., 1974; Mulford, 1983; Rohsenow, 1982; Sadawa, Thistle, & Forsyth, 1976; Tucker, Vuchinick, Sobell, et al., 1980).

Certain of these factors have received particular attention for the practical purposes of treatment and prevention—for example, peer pressure (Carpalan & Cisin, 1976; Madsen, 1974). However, increasing attention has been paid to the stimulus, novelty, and sensation-seeking motivation (Kilpatrick, Sutker, & Smith, 1976; Zuckerman, 1983). Zuckerman (1987) reported that sensation seeking is related to ethanol's effect on the augmentation of visual and auditory cortical-evoked potentials found in alcoholism and the low monoamine oxidase inhibitor levels.

Sensation seeking has been used by Cloninger (1987) and others (Bohman, Sigvardsson, & Cloninger, 1981; Cloninger, Bohman, & Sigvardsson, 1981; Cloninger, Bohman,

Sigvardsson, & von Knorring, 1985) to characterize the motivation, risk inheritance pattern, and vulnerability to postnatal environmental influence in two genetically predisposed groups of alcoholics. They found a type II group, primarily male and characterized by spontaneous (not stress response) alcohol seeking, earlier onset, polydrug abuse, and tendencies to problem behavior and to paternal criminality. In this group, stimulus, novelty, and sensation seeking through ethanol and drug use constitute a major motivation, as opposed to the type I group, which has a later onset and a more specific ethanol orientation. Type I appears to use the CNS depressant, sedative, and disinhibiting effects more as motivating factors. There appear to be separate inheritance patterns by which the two types are genetically predisposed.

The sensation-seeking motivation of the type II alcoholics, as well as the peer pressure motivation in other situations, appears to contradict the stress-dampening, tension reduction hypothesis. One might, however, say that the lack of stimuli, novelty, and sensation (or, to put it another way, a lack of stimulation to the brain reward mechanisms, particularly where there had been prior stimulation) would, in some, produce a state of boredom tension that could only be relieved by an increase in tension from new stimuli, novelty, and sensations. One could, therefore, define that boredom state as a stress. Or, considering cultural support for drinking and peer pressure, one might say that the threatened diminution in social approval, perhaps even alienation from the group, would constitute the stress. This line of reasoning, however, greatly exposes one to the dangers of overgeneralization, universal rationalization, and overinclusiveness. Anything that could disturb the equilibrium, even life itself, could then become a stress, and the term would become so vague, excessively inclusive, and general as to lose all practical meaning; it would mean everything and nothing. Such an abstract concept could not be pinned down to specific, concrete phenomena that are capable of validation and thus cannot lead to practical prevention or treatment measures. It is best to reserve the concept for specific phenomena and specific situations and to limit it by keeping in mind the effects of the co-existing parameters that greatly influence the responses to stress.

ALCOHOLISM AND STRESS

The pattern, nature, and motivation of drinking differ in alcoholics and in nonalcoholic social drinkers, and the differences throw light on the relationship of ethanol intake to stress. The essence of an addictive disorder lies in the compulsive urge to drink or take drugs (loss of control) in the presence of significant contraindication in an area of life important to the individual: physical or psychological health; one's job, career, or education; or social, intimate, or sexual relationships. The physiological symptoms of tolerance and withdrawal may or may not be present, although they usually are. Tolerance means that the body has physiologically adapted to a level of ethanol or drug intake so that more is required to produce the same effect. Withdrawal stems from the same source, for once the body has become dependent on the ethanol or other substance, abrupt withdrawal produces a specific syndrome. In the case of ethanol and other sedatives, withdrawal involves restlessness, agitation, gross tremor, hyperactivity, tachycardia, hypertension, disturbance of consciousness, nausea, other disturbances of visceral functioning, and diaphoresis; in more severe cases hallucinations and grand mal seizures occur.

These physiological symptoms constitute motives for the alcoholic to continue and even increase drinking to prevent the symptoms of withdrawal and/or to achieve the desired effect without necessarily having the influence of external stressful events. One could extend the concept of stress to include either of those states because of the body's adaptation to ethanol or other drugs, so that the sudden cessation of the drug intake would produce a stressful, intense, physiological state; or, on the other hand, the lack of the desired effect of the drug or ethanol at the usual dosage level would itself constitute a stress. If one does so define stress, however, one runs into a post hoc reasoning that threatens to lead to the previously mentioned overgeneralization and overinclusiveness of one's terms and definitions, which then might become deprived of specificity, value, and meaning. As noted previously, it is best to restrict the term, so that tolerance, perhaps, could be understood to constitute a stress only if the state to be achieved by drinking is clearly stressful and urgently and compulsively driven (and not just strongly desired) on either physiological or psychological grounds, or both.

Inasmuch as the compulsive urge to drink, the essence of the disorder, exists independently of tolerance and withdrawal (although it might be added to by them), it can be seen that other factors can cause one to drink. External events pointed to by the alcoholic as causal (Mulford & Miller, 1960) may be merely historical coincidences used by the alcoholic as rationalization and legitimization of the drinking.

One such internal factor that can cause drinking in alcoholics is related to the predisposition, the addictive diathesis: biological and genetic, environmental and sociocultural, and/or psychological in nature. Each of these elements vary in degree from person to person and from one type of alcoholic to another (Bohman, Sigvardsson, & Cloninger, 1981; Cloninger, Bohman, & Sigvardsson, 1981). The biological and genetic factor in the predisposition is felt by many to be in great part responsible for the origins of the compulsive drive to drink, but alone it may not be sufficient; sociocultural and environmental factors provide supporting elements for the compulsive drive (Cloninger, 1987).

A second element in the disorder is the onset factor. The onset can be insidious and slowly progressive, arising out of heavy social drinking and without any external stress, or it can develop more acutely following some precipitating stress, such as a loss or threatened loss of a spouse or family member, one's job, money, or home; or aging, with the loss of one's powers, abilities, looks, or friends; or even, paradoxically, some success or achievement that violates an internal taboo, albeit an unconscious one.

The third element in this disorder is the endogenous, autonomous, self-perpetuating factor that causes the drinking to go on once it develops and keeps it going regardless of the predisposing or precipitating factors and regardless of any external stressful events. The cause of this factor may be related partly to the reinforcing properties of ethanol and the other drugs (especially, for example, cocaine), but one sees a similar phenomenon in the overeaters who, they start, binge, or in compulsive gamblers who, once they begin to bet and lose, lose control and "chase the money." This phenomenon is something in the nature of the compulsive urge itself and not in some external or even internal stress. This compulsive drive may be related to the biogenetic factors in the predisposition.

It is interesting to note how Alcoholics Anonymous (AA) regards stress. This self-help group, more than fifty-five years old, is generally felt to offer the single most effective program for the treatment of the disorder, either alone or as an adjunct to other therapy. The organization has a pragmatic, empirical program and an ambivalent attitude towards stress. One the one hand, AA conceives of a causal role for stress: for example, "H.A.L.T.; don't be *h*ungry, *a*ngry, *l*onely, or *t*ired"; or, "don't keep resentments; alcoholics can't tolerate resentments without a slip." On the other hand, it also emphasizes the compulsive element and "loss of control" without bringing in the factor of stress: for example, "that's just the bottle trying to get you back"; "once you've been pickled you can never be a cucumber again"; and "one drink is too many and a hundred is never enough." Indeed, apparently stressful events are often seen as rationalizations and excuses for giving in to the ever-present compulsive urge.

Once established, the disorder becomes a stress in itself. On the physiological level it causes all manner of illnesses, medical (Gitlow & Seixas, 1988), pediatric (Clarren & Smith, 1978), and psychiatric (Regier et al., 1990). The disorder can also abet the effects of stress by negatively affecting the immune defense system and the body's ability to fight off infections (MacGregor, 1986). On the behavioral level, alcoholism deleteriously affects work, career, school, family, and various social and other interpersonal relationships. These factors, in turn, can constitute stresses and contribute to more drinking and thereby to the progressive nature of the addiction, until the alcoholic reaches "bottom" and moves toward recovery or until the process either stabilizes at a pathological level or culminates in death.

CONCLUSION

The stress response, tension reduction hypothesis of ethanol use, abuse, and dependence that held sway over the past century and a half and that was set forth in the previous edition of this handbook has given way over the last decade and a half to a less monolithic, more multifactorial concept that bears some resemblance to the earlier view but is far more sophisticated. This transition may be related to a change in the world view, but more immediately it reflects the recent developments in neurophysiology and the more exacting psychological, sociological, behavioral, and clinical research.

The practical consequence of this decrease in emphasis on the role of stress is that the treatment and prevention of ethanol and drug abuse and dependency must not rely solely on stress and coping, although those factors might be useful in specific situations. Attention to the social pressures and the needs for novelty and stimulus, for example, may well be as important and, in certain instances, even more so, as well as attention to availability and to reward-punishment systems.

Attention should also be devoted to determining the diagnostic, etiological, prognostic, prevention, and therapeutic factors in individual situations, separately: under what circumstances the situation occurs, the probability of such occurrences, how to recognize them, and what to do about them. As far as ethanol and drugs are concerned, stress exists and it does something, but it doesn't do everything, and not all the time. These conclusions may be applicable to other parameters as well and could contribute to a re-evaluation of the theory and concept of stress in general.

REFERENCES

AASVED, M. J. Alcohol, drinking, and intoxication in preindustrial society: Theoretical, nutritional, and religious considerations. *Dissertation Abstracts International,* 1989, *49,* 3406-A.

ADAMS, P. R., & ADAMS, G. R. Mount Saint Helen's ashfall: Evidence for a disaster stress reaction. *American Psychologist,* 1984, *39,* 252-260.

BACON, M. K. The dependency conflict hypothesis and the frequency of drunkenness: Further evidence from a cross-cultural study. *Quarterly Journal of Studies on Alcohol,* 1974, *35,* 863-865.

BAER, P. E., MCLAUGHLIN, R. J., BURNSIDE, M. A., POKORNEY, A. D., & GARMEZY, L. B. Stress, the family environment and multiple substance use among seventh graders. In *Alcohol, drugs and tobacco: An international perspective. Past, present and future. Proceedings of the 34th International Congress on Alcohol and Drug Dependence.* Vol. II. Calgary, Can., 1985.

BAIN, G. T., & KORNETSKY, C. Ethanol oral self administration and rewarding brain stimulation. *Alcohol,* 1989, *6,* 499–503.

BEGLEITER, H., & PLATZ, A. The effects of alcohol on the central nervous system in humans. In B. Kissin & H. Begleiter (eds.), *The biology of alcoholism. Vol. 2: Physiology and behavior.* New York: Plenum, 1974.

BOHMAN, M., SIGVARDSSON, S., & CLONINGER, C. R. Maternal inheritance of alcohol abuse: Cross-fostering of adopted women. *Archives of General Psychiatry,* 1981, *38,* 965–969.

BOYD, T. L., CALLEN, E. J., & HOUSE, W. J. Effects of post stress exposure to alcohol upon the development of alcohol consumption in rats. *Behavior Research and Therapy,* 1989, *27,* 35–41.

BRICK, J., & POHORECKY, L. A. The neuroendocrine response to stress and the effects of alcohol. In L. A. Pohorecky & J. Brick (eds.), *Stress and alcohol use.* New York: Elsevier Biomedical, 1983.

————. The limbic system and ethanol induced changes in plasma corticosterone and nonesterified fatty acids. In E. Gottheil, K. A. Druley, S. Pashko, & S. P. Weinstein (eds.), *Stress and addiction.* New York: Brunner/Mazel, 1987.

BROMET, E. J., DEW, M. A., PARKINSON, D. K., & SCHULBERG, H. C. Predictive effects of occupational and marital stress on the mental health of a male work force. *Journal of Organizational Behavior,* 1988, *9,* 1–13.

BROWN, S. A., & SCHAFER, J. Does alcohol reduce tension in heterosexual interaction? In *94th Annual Convention of the American Psychological Association.* Washington, DC, August 1986.

BRY, B., MCKEON, P., & PANDINA, R. L. Extent of drug use as a function of a number of risk factors. *Journal of Abnormal Psychology,* 1982, *91,* 163–164.

CAPLAN, M. A., & PUGLISI, K. Stress and conflict conditions leading to and maintaining voluntary alcohol consumption in rats. *Pharmacology, Biochemistry and Behavior,* 1986, *24,* 271–280.

CAPPELL, H. An evaluation of tension reduction models of alcohol consumption. In R. J. Gibbon (ed.), *Research advances in alcohol and drug problems.* Vol. 2. New York: Wiley, 1975.

————. Alcohol and tension reduction: What's new? In E. Gottheil, K. A. Druley, S. Pashko, & S. P. Weinstein (eds.), *Stress and addiction.* New York: Brunner/Mazel, 1987.

CAPPELL, H., & HERMAN, C. Alcohol and tension reduction: A review. *Quarterly Journal of Studies on Alcohol,* 1972, *33,* 33–64.

CARPALAN, D., & CISIN, I. H. Drinking behavior and drinking problems in the United States. In B. Kissin & H. Begleiter (eds.), *The biology of alcoholism. Vol. 3: Social aspects of alcoholism.* New York: Plenum Press, 1976.

CELENTANO, J. J., GIBBS, T. T., & FARB, D. H. Ethanol potentiates GABA- and glycine-induced chloride currents in chick spinal cord neurons. *Brain Research,* 1988, *455,* 377–380.

CLARREN, S. K., & SMITH, D. W. The fetal alcohol syndrome: A review of the world literature. *New England Journal of Medicine,* 1978, *298,* 1063–1067.

CLONINGER, C. R. Neurogenetic adaptive mechanisms in alcoholism. *Science,* 1987, *236,* 410–416.

CLONINGER, C. R., BOHMAN, M., & SIGVARDSSON, S. Inheritance of alcohol abuse: Cross-fostering analysis of adopted men. *Archives of General Psychiatry,* 1981, *38,* 861–868.

CLONINGER, C. R., BOHMAN, M., SIGVARDSSON, S., & VON KNORRING, A. L. Psychopathology in adopted out children of alcoholics: The Stockholm adoption study. *Recent Developments in Alcoholism,* 1985, *3,* 37–51.

CONGER, J. J. The effects of alcohol in conflict behavior in the albino rat. *Quarterly Journal of Studies on Alcohol,* 1952, *12,* 1–29.

DAVIDGE, A. M. Relationship between stress, coping and adolescent substance use. *Dissertation Abstracts International,* 1990, *50,* 3185-B.

DETURCK, K. H., & POHORECKY, L. A. The effect of maternal handling on ethanol sensitivity in adult offspring. In E. Gottheil, K. A. Druley, S. Pashko, & S. P. Weinstein (eds.), *Stress and addiction.* New York: Brunner/Mazel, 1987.

DETURCK, H., & VOGEL, W. H. Effects of acute plasma and brain catecholamine levels in stressed and unstressed rats: Evidence for an ethanol stress interaction. *Journal of Pharmacology and Experimental Therapeutics,* 1982, *223,* 348-354.

DIPERRI, R. DRAVID, A., SCHWEIGERDT, A., & HIMWICH, H. E. Effects of alcohol on evoked potentials of various parts of the central nervous system of the cat. *Quarterly Journal of Studies on Alcohol,* 1968, *29,* 20.

DREW, L. L. Acculturation stress and alcohol usage among Canadian Indians in Toronto. *Canadian Journal of Public Health,* 1988, *79,* 115-118.

DRULEY, K. A., & PASHKO, S. Post traumatic stress disorder in World War II and Korean combat veterans with alcohol dependence. In M. Galanter (ed.), *Recent developments in alcoholism.* New York: Plenum Press, 1988.

DUDLEY, D. L., MULES, J. E., ROSZELL, D. K., et al. Frequency and magnitude distribution of life changes in heroin and alcohol addicts. *International Journal of the Additions,* 1976, *11,* 977-987.

ELLINGBOE, J. Effects of alcohol on neurochemical processes. In M. A. Lipton, A. D. Masur, & K. F. Killan (eds.), *Psychopharmacology: A generation of progress.* New York: Raven Press, 1978.

ENGEL, J., & LILJEQUIST, S. The involvement of different central neurotransmitters in mediating stimulating and sedative effects of ethanol. In L. A. Pohorecky & J. Brick (eds.), *Stress and alcohol use.* New York: Elsevier Biomedical, 1983.

FADDA, F., MOSCA, E., COLOMBO, G., & GESSA, G. L. Effects of spontaneous ingestion of ethanol on brain dopamine metabolism. *Life Science,* 1989, *44,* 281-287.

FIELD, P. B. A new cross-cultural study of drunkenness. In D. J. Pitman & C. R. Snyder (eds.), *Culture and drinking patterns.* New York: Wiley, 1945.

FINNEY, J. W., & MOOS, R. H. Life stressors and problem drinking among older adults. In M. Galanter (ed.), *Recent developments in alcoholism.* New York: Plenum Press, 1983.

FORNEY, M. A., FORNEY, P. D., SHEETS, K., et al. Relationship between stress and substance use among first year medical students: An exploratory investigation. *Journal of Alcohol and Drug Education,* 1990, *35,* 54-65.

GEORGE, W. H., & MARLATT, G. A. Alcoholism: The evolution of a behavioral perspective. In M. Galanter (ed.), *Recent advances in alcoholism.* Vol. 1. New York: Plenum Press, 1983.

GITLOW, S. E., & SEIXAS, F. The medical complications of alcoholism. In S. E. Gitlow & H. S. Peyser (eds.), *Alcoholism: A practical treatment guide* (2d ed.). Philadelphia: Grune and Stratton, 1988.

GLESER, G. C., GREEN, B. L., & WINGET, C. *Prolonged psychosocial effects of disaster: A study of Buffalo Creek.* New York: Academic Press, 1981.

GLOWA, J. R., CRAWLEY, J., SUZDAK, P. D., & PAUL, S. M. Ethanol and the GABA receptor complex. Studies with the partial inverse benzodiazepine receptor agonist Ro 15-4513. *Pharmacology, Biochemistry and Behavior,* 1989, *31,* 767-772.

GULYAEVA, N. V., LEVINA, O. L., & LEVISHINA, I. P. Action of alcohol on rats with chronic emotional painful stress. *Bulletin of Experimental Biology and Medicine,* 1985, *100,* 1083-1086.

HAMMER, T., & VAGLUM, P. Increase in alcohol consumption among women: A phenomenon related to accessibility or stress? A general population study. *British Journal of Addition,* 1989, *84,* 767-775.

HARRIS, M. M., & FENNELL, M. L. Multivariate model of job stress and alcohol consumption. *Sociological Quarterly,* 1988, *29,* 391–406.

HEIEN, D., & POMPELLI, G. Stress, ethnic and distribution factors in a dichotomous response model of alcohol abuse. *Journal of Studies on Alcohol,* 1987, *48,* 450–455.

HIGGINS, R. L. Experimental investigation of tension reduction models of alcoholism. In G. Goldstein & C. Neuringer (eds.), *Experimental studies of alcoholism.* Cambridge, MA: Ballinger, 1976.

HIGGINS, R. L., & MARLATT, G. A. The effects of anxiety arousal on the consumption of alcohol by alcoholics and social drinkers. *Journal of Consulting and Clinical Psychology,* 1973, *41,* 426–433.

————. Fear of interpersonal evaluation as a determinant of alcohol consumption in male social drinkers. *Journal of Abnormal Psychology,* 1975, *84,* 644–651.

HIMWICH, H. E. Alcohol and brain physiology. In G. Thompson (ed.), *Alcoholism: Clinical and experimental research.* Springfield, IL: Thomas, 1956.

HINGSON, R., MANGIONE, T., & BARRET, J. Job characteristics and drinking practices in the Boston metropolitan area. *Journal of Studies on Alcohol,* 1981, *42,* 735–738.

HOLYROD, K. A. Effects of social anxiety and social evaluation on beer consumption and social interaction. *Journal of Studies on Alcohol,* 1978, *39,* 737–744.

HORSEY, W. J., & AKERT, K. The influence of ethyl alcohol on the spontaneous electrical activity of the cerebral cortex and subcortical structures of the cat. *Quarterly Journal of Studies on Alcohol,* 1953, *14,* 363.

HORTON, D. The functions of alcohol in primitive societies: A cross-cultural study. *Quarterly Journal of Studies on Alcohol,* 1943, *4,* 199–203.

HUFFINE, C. L., FOLKMAN, S., & LAZARUS, R. S. Psychoactive drugs, alcohol, and stress and coping processes in older adults. *American Journal of Drug and Alcohol Abuse,* 1989, *15,* 101–113.

JOSEPHS, R. A., & STEELE, C. M. Two faces of alcohol myopia: Attentional mediation of psychological stress. *Journal of Abnormal Psychology,* 1990, *97,* 196–205.

KALANT, H. Some recent physiological and biochemical investigations on alcohol and alcoholism. *Quarterly Journal of Studies on Alcohol,* 1962, *23,* 52.

————. Stress related effects of ethanol on mammals. *Critical Reviews in Biotechnology,* 1990, *9,* 265–272.

KASL, S. V., OSTFELD, A. M., BERKMAN, L. F., & JACOBS S. C. Stress and alcohol consumption: The role of selected social and environmental factors. In E. Gottheil, K. A. Druley, S. Pashko, & S. P. Weinstein (eds.), *Stress and addiction.* New York: Brunner/Mazel, 1987.

KILLEN, J. D., TAYLOR, C. B., TELCH, M. J., et al. Evidence for an alcohol stress link among normal weight adolescents reporting purging behavior. *International Journal of Eating Disorders,* 1987, *6,* 349–356.

KILPATRICK, D. C., SUTKER, P. B., & SMITH, D. Deviant drug and alcohol use: The role of anxiety, sensation seeking and other personality variables. In M. Zuckerman & C. D. Spielberger (eds.), *Emotions and anxiety: New concepts, methods and implications.* Hillsdale, NJ: Lawrence Erlbaum, 1976.

KISSIN, B. The pharmacodynamics and natural history of alcoholism. In B. Kissin & H. Begleiter (eds.), *The biology of alcoholism. Vol. 3: Clinical pathology.* New York: Plenum Press, 1974.

KNOTT, D. H., & BEARD, J. D. Effects of alcohol ingestion on the cardiovascular system. In E. M. Patterson & E. K. Kaufman (eds.), *Encyclopedic handbook of alcoholism.* New York: Gardner, 1982.

KNOTT, V. J., & BULMER, D. R. Relaxation, noise induced stress, and autonomic responsivity in male alcoholics and normal controls. *International Journal of the Addictions,* 1985, *20,* 623–628.

KOOB, G. F., & BLOOM, F. E. Corticotropin releasing factor and behavior. *Federation Proceedings,* 1985, *44,* 259–263.

KOOB, G. F., BRITTON, K. T., & EHLERS, C. L. Corticotropin releasing factor, stress, and ethanol. In R. A. Deitrich & A. A. Pawlowski (eds.), *NIAAA research monograph no. 20: Initial sensitivity to alcohol.* Rockville, MD: National Institute on Alcohol Abuse and Alcoholism, 1990.

KORPI, E. R., SINCLAIR, J. D., KAHEINEN, P., VIITAMAA, T., HELLEVUO, K., & KIIANMAA, K. Brain regional and adrenal monoamine concentrations and behavior responses to stress in alcohol preferring AA and alcohol avoiding ANA rats. *Alcohol,* 1988, *5,* 417–425.

LABOUVIE, E. W. Alcohol and marijuana use in relation to adolescent stress. *International Journal of the Addictions,* 1986, *21,* 333–345.

LEHRFELD, D. I. Personality configuration, occupational stress, and alcohol usage: Testing a model and its relationship to police performance. *Dissertation Abstracts International,* 1989, *50,* 2157-B.

LENDER, M. B. Alcohol, stress and society: The 19th century origins of the tension reduction hypothesis. In E. Gottheil, K. A. Druley, S. D. Pashko, & S. P. Weinstein (eds.), *Stress and addiction.* New York: Brunner/Mazel, 1987.

LESTER, D. Self selection of alcohol by animals, human variation, and the etiology of alcoholism. A critical review. *Quarterly Journal of Studies on Alcohol,* 1966, *27,* 395–438.

LEVENSON, R. W., SHER, K. J., & GROSSMAN, L., et al. Alcohol and stress response dampening: Pharmacological effects, expectancy, and tension reduction. *Journal of Abnormal Psychology,* 1980, *89,* 528–538.

LINSKY, A. S., COLBY, J. P., & STRAUS, M. A. Social stress, normative constraints and alcohol problems in American states. *Social Science and Medicine,* 1987, *24,* 875–883.

LIPSCOM, T. R., NATHAN, P. E., WILSON, T., et al. Effects of tolerance on the anxiety reducing functions of alcohol. *Archives of General Psychiatry,* 1980, *37,* 577–582.

LISMAN, S. A. Closer to the truth or time to ask some new questions. In E. Gottheil, K. A. Druley, S. Pashko, & S. P. Weinstein (eds.), *Stress and addiction.* New York: Brunner/Mazel, 1987.

LUKAS, S., & MENDELSON, J. H. Behavioral concomitants of ethanol and drug reinforcement. In L. S. Harris (ed.), *Problems of drug dependence 1987* (National Institute on Drug Abuse Research Monograph Series no. 81. DHHS publication no. (ADM)88-1564). Rockville, MD: NIDA, 1988.

MACANDREW, C. Examination of the relevance of the individual differences (A-trait) formulation of the tension reduction theory to the etiology of alcohol abuse in young males. *Addictive Behaviors,* 1982, *7,* 39–45.

MACGREGOR, R. R. Alcohol and immune defense. *Journal of the American Medical Association,* 1986, *256,* 1474–1478.

MADSEN, W. *The American alcoholic: The nature-nurture controversy in alcoholic research and therapy.* Springfield, IL: Charles C Thomas, 1974.

MARLATT, G. A. Alcohol, stress and cognitive control. In I. G. Sarason & C. D. Spielberger (eds.), *Stress and anxiety.* Vol. 3. New York: Wiley, 1976.

————. Alcohol, the magic elixir: Stress, expectancy, and the transformation of emotional states. In E. Gottheil, K. A. Druley, S. Pashko, & S. P. Weinstein (eds.), *Stress and addiction.* New York: Brunner/Mazel, 1987.

MARLATT, G. A., & ROHSENOW, D. R. Cognitive processes in alcohol use: Expectancy and the balanced placebo design. In N. K. Mello (ed.), *Advances in substance abuse.* Vol. 1. Greenwich, CT: JAI Press, 1980.

MASSERMAN, J. H. *Principles of dynamic psychiatry: Including an integrative approach to abnormal and clinical psychology.* Philadelphia: W. B. Saunders, 1946.

MASSERMAN, J. H. JACQUES, M. G., & NICHOLSON, M. R. Alcohol as a preventative of experimental neurosis. *Quarterly Journal of Studies on Alcohol,* 1945, *6,* 281–299.

MASSERMAN, J. H., & YUM, K. S. An analysis of the influence of alcohol on experimental neurosis in cats. *Psychosomatic Medicine,* 1946, *8,* 32–62.

MCBRIDE, W. J., MURPHY, J. M., LUMENG, L., & LI, T. K. Effects of Ro 15-4513, fluoxetine and desipramine on the intake of ethanol, water and food by the alcohol preferring (P) and non preferring (NP) lines of rats. *Pharmacology, Biochemistry and Behavior,* 1988, *30,* 1045–1050.

MCKIRNAN, D. J., & PETERSON, P. L. Stress, expectancies, and vulnerability to substance abuse: A test of a model among homosexual men. *Journal of Abnormal Psychology,* 1988, *97,* 461–466.

MCNAIR, L. D. Alcohol use and stress in college women. *Dissertation Abstracts International,* 1990, *50,* 3707-B.

MENDELSON, J. H., LA DOU, J., & SOLOMON, P. Experimentally induced chronic intoxication and withdrawal in alcoholics, part 3, psychiatric findings. *Quarterly Journal of Studies on Alcohol,* 1964 (suppl. 2), 40–52.

MILLER, P. M., HERSEN, M., EISLER, R. M., et al. Effects of social stress on operant drinking of alcoholics and social drinkers. *Behaviour Research and Therapy,* 1974, *12,* 67–72.

MILLER, P. M., SURTEEN, P. G., KREITMAN, N. B., INGHAM, J. G., & SASHIDHARAN, S. P. Maladaptive coping reactions to stress: A study of illness inception. *Journal of Nervous and Mental Disease,* 1985, *173,* 707–716.

MITIC, W. R., MCGUIRE, D. P., & NEUMANN, B. Adolescent problem drinking and perceived stress. *Journal of Alcohol and Drug Education,* 1987, *33,* 45–54.

MOORE, D. T. Alcohol and stress: New directions in research. *Alcohol Health and Research World,* 1986, *10,* 48–53, 75.

MORA, G. History of psychiatry. In H. I. Kaplan & B. J. Sadock (eds.), *Comprehensive textbook of psychiatry/IV* (4th ed.). Baltimore, MD: Williams and Wilkins, 1984.

MULFORD, H. A. Stress, alcohol intake and problem drinking in Iowa. In L. A. Pohorecky & J. Brick (eds.), *Stress and alcohol use.* New York: Elsevier Biomedical, 1983.

MULFORD, H. A., & MILLER, D. E. Drinking in Iowa: III. A scale of definitions of alcoholism related to drinking behavior. *Quarterly Journal of Studies on Alcohol,* 1960, *21,* 267–278.

MURPHY, J. M., WALLER, M. B., GATTO, G. J., MCBRIDE, W. J., LUMENG, L., & LI, T. K. Effects of acute ethanol administration on monoamine and metabolite content in forebrain regions of ethanol tolerant and nontolerant alcohol preferring (P) rats. *Pharmacology, Biochemistry and Behavior,* 1988, *29,* 169–174.

NATHAN, P. E., & O'BRIEN, J. S. Experimental analysis of the behavior of alcoholics and nonalcoholics during prolonged experimental drinking: A necessary precursor of behavioral therapy. *Behavior Therapy,* 1971, *2,* 455–476.

NEFF, J. A. Evaluating the stress buffering role of alcohol consumption: Variation by type of event and type of symptom. *Alcohol and Alcoholism,* 1985, *20,* 391–401.

NILES, D. P. Relationship between combat experiences, posttraumatic stress disorder symptoms, and alcohol abuse among active duty Vietnam veterans. *Dissertation Abstracts International,* 1989, *49,* 2868-B.

PASHKO, S., & DRULEY, K. A. Anxiety and control issues in substance abusing veterans. In E. Gottheil, K. A. Druley, S. Pashko, & S. P. Weinstein (eds.), *Stress and addiction.* New York: Brunner/Mazel, 1987.

PATEL, V. A., & POHORECKY, L. A. Interaction of stress and ethanol: Effect on beta-endorphins and catecholamines. *Alcoholism: Clinical and Experimental Research,* 1988, *12,* 785–788.

PERIS, J., & CUNNINGHAM, C. L. Stress enhances the development of tolerance to the hypothermic effect of ethanol. *Alcohol and Drug Research,* 1989, *7,* 187–193.

PEYSER, H. S. The problems of accountability and the will in a program for alcohol and drug impaired professionals: The contributions from legal history. *Georgia State Bar Journal,* 1989, *25,* 136–140.

POHORECKY, L. A. The interaction of alcohol and stress. A review. *Neuroscience and Biobehavioral Reviews,* 1981, *5,* 209–229.

—————. Interaction of ethanol and stress: Research with experimental animals: An update. *Alcohol and Alcoholism,* 1990, *25,* 263–276.

POHORECKY, L. A., & BRICK, J. Characteristics of the interaction of ethanol and stress. In E. Gottheil, K. A. Druley, S. Pashko, & S. P. Weinstein (eds.), *Stress and addiction.* New York: Brunner/Mazel, 1987.

POWERS, R. J. Stress as a factor in alcohol use and abuse. In E. Gottheil, K. A. Druley, S. Pashko, & S. P. Weinstein (eds.), *Stress and addiction.* New York: Brunner/Mazel, 1987.

POWERS, R. J., & KUTASH, I. L. Stress and alcohol. *International Journal of the Addictions,* 1985, *20,* 461–482.

REGIER, D. A., FARMER, M. E., RAE, D. S., LOCKE, B. Z., KEITH, S. J., JUDD, L. L., & GOODWIN, F. K. Comorbidity of mental disorders with alcohol and other drug abuse: Results from the Epidemiological Catchment Area (ECA) Study. *Journal of the American Medical Association,* 1990, *264,* 2511–2518.

REID, L. D., CZIRR, S. A., BENSINGER, L. C., HUBBELL, C. L., & VOLANTH, A. J. Morphine and diprenorphine together potentiate intake of alcoholic beverage. *Alcohol: An International Biomedical Journal,* 1987, *4,* 161–168.

RIVIER, C., IMAKI, T., & VALE, W. Prolonged exposure to alcohol: Effect on CRF mRNA levels, and CRF and stress induced ACTH secretion in the rat. *Brain Research,* 1990, *510,* 1–5.

RIVIER, C., & VALE, W. Interaction between ethanol and stress on ACTH and beta-endorphin secretion. *Alcoholism: Clinical and Experimental Research,* 1988, *12,* 206–210.

ROBINS, L. N. *The Vietnam drug user returns* (Special Action Office monograph no. 2, series A). Washington, DC: U. S. Government Printing Office, 1974.

ROHSENOW, D. J. Social anxiety, daily moods, and alcohol use over time among heavy social drinking men. *Addictive Behaviors,* 1982, *7,* 311–315.

ROHSENOW, D. J., & MARLATT, G. A. The balanced placebo design: Methodological considerations. *Addictive Behaviors,* 1981, *6,* 107–122.

RUBINS, L. S., GOTTHEIL, E., ROBERTS, A., et al. Effects of stress on autonomic reactivity in alcoholics. Pupillometric studies: I. *Journal of Studies on Alcohol,* 1977, *38,* 2036–2048.

SADAWA, W. S., THISTLE, R., & FORSYTH, R. Stress, escapism, and patterns of alcohol and drug use. *Journal of Studies on Alcohol,* 1976, *29,* 725–730.

SAUERLAND, E. K., & HARPER, R. M. Effects of ethanol on EEG spectra of the intact brain and isolated forebrain. *Experimental Neurology,* 1970, *27,* 490.

SHER, K. J., & LEVENSON, R. W. Alcohol and tension reduction: The importance of individual differences. In L. A. Pohorecky & J. Brick (eds.), *Stress and alcohol use.* New York: Elsevier Biomedical, 1983.

SHER, K. J., & WALITZER, K. S. Individual differences in the stress response dampening effect of alcohol: A dose response study. *Journal of Abnormal Psychology,* 1986, *95,* 159–167.

SILVERMAN, M. M., EICHLER, A., & WILLIAMS, G. D. Self reported stress: Findings from the 1985 National Health Interview Study. *Public Health Reports,* 1987, *102,* 47–53.

STASIEWICZ, P. R. Relation of conditioned tolerance to the stress response dampening effects of alcohol. *Dissertation Abstracts International,* 1990, *50,* 4237-B.

STEELE, C. M., & JOSEPHS, R. A. Drinking your troubles away. II: An attention allocation model of alcohol's effects on psychological stress. *Journal of Abnormal Psychology,* 1988, *97,* 196–205.

STEELE, C. M., SOUTHWICK, L., & PAGANO, R. Drinking your troubles away: The role of activity in mediating alcohol's reduction of psychological stress. *Journal of Abnormal Psychology,* 1986, *95,* 173–180.

TAMERIN, J. S., WEINER, S., POPPER, R., STEINGLASS, P., & MENDELSON, J. H. Alcohol and memory: Amnesia and short term memory function during experimentally induced intoxication. *American Journal of Psychiatry,* 1971, *127,* 1659–1664.

TUCKER, J. A., VUCHINICK, R. E., SOBELL, M. B., et al. Normal drinkers' alcohol consumption as a function of conflicting motives induced by intellectual performance stress. *Addictive Behaviors,* 1980, *5,* 171–178.

VANICELLI, M. Mood and self perception of alcoholics when sober and intoxicated. *Quarterly Journal of Studies on Alcohol,* 1972, *33,* 341–357.

VARGA, B., & NAGY, T. Analysis of alpha rhythm in the electroencephalogram of alcoholics. *Encephalography and Clinical Neurophysiology,* 1960, *92,* 933.

VEDERNIKOVA, N. N., BORISOVA, I. P., & OREKHOV, S. N. Does ethanol stress rats with established motivation? *Bulletin of Experimental Biology and Medicine,* 1989, *107,* 516–518.

VINYARD, J. L. Alcohol abuse and occupational stress. *Dissertation Abstracts International,* 1989, *49,* 3164-A.

VOGEL, W. H., HARRIS, N., & TAYLOR, J. Alcohol stress interaction: A genetically determined relationship. In R. A. Deitrich & A. A. Pawlowski (eds.), *NIAA research monograph no. 20: Initial sensitivity to alcohol.* Rockville, MD: National Institute on Alcohol Abuse and Alcoholism, 1990.

VOGEL, W. H., MILLER, J., & ROGGENDORF, H. Effects of ethanol and plasma catecholamines and heart rate in unstressed and stressed rats. In E. Gottheil, K. A. Druley, S. Pashko, & S. P. Weinstein (eds.), *Stress and addiction.* New York: Brunner/Mazel, 1987.

VOGEL, W. H., & NETTER, P. Effect of ethanol and stress on catecholamines and their relation to changes in emotional state and performance. *Alcoholism: Clinical and Experimental Research,* 1989, *13,* 284–290.

WATKINS, J. C., & OLVERMAN H. J. Agonists and antagonists for excitatory amino acid receptors. *Trends in Neuroscience,* 1987, *10,* 265–272.

WILLIAMS, A. F. The alcoholic personality. In B. Kissin & H. Begleiter (eds.), *The biology of alcoholism. Vol. 4: Social aspects of alcoholism.* New York: Plenum Press, 1976.

WINDLE, M., & BARNES, G. M. Similarities and differences in correlates of alcohol consumption and problem behaviors among male and female adolescents. *International Journal of the Addictions,* 1988, *23,* 707–728.

ZEICHNER, A., EDWARDS, P., & COHEN, E. Acute effects of alcohol on cardiovascular reactivity to stress in college-age type A (coronary prone) individuals. *Journal of Psychopathology and Behavioral Assessment,* 1985, *7,* 75–89.

ZUCKERMAN, M. Sensation seeking: The initial motive for drug abuse. In E. Gottheil, K. A. Druley, & T. E. Skoloda (eds.), *Etiological aspects of alcohol and drug abuse.* Springfield, IL: Thomas, 1983.

ZUCKERMAN, M. Is sensation seeking a predisposing trait for alcoholism? In E. Gottheil, K. A. Druley, S. Pashko, & S. P. Weinstein (eds.), *Stress and addiction.* New York: Brunner/Mazel, 1987.

30

Stress and Depression: Toward the Development of Integrative Models

Rand J. Gruen

RESEARCH EXAMINING THE RELATIONSHIP between stress and unipolar depression has focused on a number of specific themes. The studies that have been done can be grouped into several broad content areas: factors associated with vulnerability to depression; life stress, coping, and social support; and the role of interpersonal processes in depression. Although there are exceptions to the rule, most of the work has examined the relationship between variables within a specific domain or content area and depression. It is becoming increasingly clear, however, that conceptual and methodological frameworks that have guided research in the past do not address the complexity of the phenomenon we are dealing with. Studies that focus on a narrow range of psychosocial provoking agents, for example, do not adequately explain how depression develops or how it should be treated. In particular, a growing body of evidence suggests that biological factors play an important role in depression. The majority of studies done to date, however, have not been designed to examine the relative contribution of psychosocial, biochemical, and genetic factors.

This chapter examines factors suggested to play an important role in the stress-depression relationship. The potential role of biochemical factors in unipolar depression is discussed, and, in the process, a rationale for the assessment of stress-induced biochemical changes in depressed patients is provided.

VULNERABILITY TO DEPRESSION

Gender

A number of studies have found that women are more likely to become depressed than men. Approximately 10% of men experience a major depressive episode at least once in their life; the lifetime prevalence rate for women is about twice as high (American Psychiatric Association, 1980). In a 9-year longitudinal study, Kaplan, Roberts, Camacho, and Coyne (1987) found that the risk of experiencing high levels of depressive symptoms was 1.5 times greater for women than for men. These gender differences do not appear to reflect differences in symptom reporting (Gove & Geerkin, 1976) or help-seeking behavior (Weissman & Klerman, (1977). Slack and Vaux (1988) studied the relationship between life stress and depressive symptoms in 114 undergraduate student volunteers. Life events were significantly related to depressive symptoms for females ($r = .47$; $p < .001$) but not for males. Turner and Avison (1989) found that women experience more negative life events than men. These differences did not result from the number of events occurring to the respondent however; females reported being exposed to a greater number of events that occurred to others, particularly their spouses.

Age

Age appears to be related to the incidence of depression; younger individuals are more vulnerable to depression than older individuals. Hirschfeld et al. (1989) found that the odds of becoming depressed decreased by one half with each additional 15 years of age. In a large cross-sectional study, Burke, Burke, Regier, and Rae (1990) studied subjects from birth to age 94 and found that risk for unipolar depression was highest from the ages of 15 to 19 and 25 to 29. Incidence rates were significantly higher for females than males in these two groups. Onset rates for depression gradually declined after age 29.

Previous Episodes of Depression

Previous episodes of depression increase one's risk of experiencing subsequent episodes. In a 1-year longitudinal study in which subjects were studied at two time points, Sargeant, Bruce, Florio, and Weissman (1990) found that approximately 20% of patients who were depressed at time 1 (T1) recovered and relapsed within one year. Females aged 30 or older demonstrated a significantly higher rate of persistence than males. Higher persistence rates were found for females who had a history of unstable relationships and less than a high school education. Experiencing a large number of previous episodes of depression prior to T1 increased one's risk of being depressed at time 2 (T2). In a 2-wave, 9-year longitudinal study, Kaplan et al. (1987) found that subjects reporting high levels of depressive symptoms at T1 were 4 times more likely to report high levels of depressive symptoms at T2 than those who reported low levels of symptoms at T1.

Family/Genetic Factors

The study of factors that result in the transmission of depression across generations has become an important area of research (Coyne & Downey, 1991; Downey & Coyne, 1990; Lee & Gotlib, 1989). It appears that both environmental and genetic factors are important. Genetic factors appear to play an important role in some subtypes of unipolar depression but not in others (Blehar, Weissman, Gershon, & Hirschfeld, 1988), and in certain forms of depression, both family and genetic factors contribute (Merikangas, Prusoff, & Weissman, 1988).

Weissman, Leckman, Merikangas, Gammon, and Prusoff (1984) studied the incidence rates of affective and anxiety disorders in children from two groups of probands: those with major depression (assessed using Research Diagnostic Criteria—RDC—and the Schedule for Affective Disorders and Schizophrenia-Lifetime—SADS-L) and a never psychiatrically ill control group. The children of depressed probands had significantly more DSM-III diagnoses than the children whose parents were never ill. Children of parents with both depression and panic disorder had high levels of separation anxiety and major depression. None of the children of normal probands had a major depressive or anxiety disorder. Increased numbers of episodes of depression in the proband significantly increased the risk of illness in the children.

Merikangas et al. (Merikangas, Prusoff, & Weissman, 1988a; Merikangas, Weissman, Prusoff, & John, 1988b) found that parental concordance for affective or anxiety disorders increased the risk of a depressive or anxiety disorder in the child. The type of pathology seen in the child often paralleled the type of pathology seen in the parents. The results of this study suggest that the psychiatric status of both parents must be taken into consideration in examining the impact of these factors on the status of offspring.

Personality

A number of personality variables have been said to increase an individual's vulnerability to depression (Akiskal, Hirschfeld, & Yerevanian, 1983). In evaluating whether an attribute serves as a vulnerability factor, it is important to show that the trait actually predisposes the person to depression as opposed to either co-occuring with depressive symptomatology (i.e., state-dependent traits) or reflecting the sequelae of depression (Akiskal et al., 1983). Reich, Noyes, Hirschfeld, Coryell, and O'Gorman (1987) studied the personality characteristics of depressed, panic disorder, and control subjects before and after treatment. Depressed and panic disorder patients did not differ with respect to the traits assessed, and this finding suggests the possibility of common underlying personality traits. Recovered patients scored significantly lower than controls on emotional stability and objectivity; they scored significantly higher on orality, emotional reliance on another person, and lack of social self-confidence. The results suggest that these attributes are not completely state dependent and may represent stable character traits that predispose to depression.

As part of the National Institute of Mental Health Collaborative Program on the Psychobiology of Depression, Hirschfeld et al. (1989) studied the personality characteristics of 438 never-ill subjects at risk for depression. These subjects were re-evaluated for depression (using RDC and the SADS-L) 6 years later. Of the subjects, 29 had developed a first-onset depressive episode during the 6 year study period. T1 personality attributes were not predictive of onset in subjects aged 17–30. Subjects aged 31–40 who were depressed at T2 scored significantly lower on emotional and ego strength, resiliency, and the ability to respond to stress and significantly higher on emotional lability and interpersonal dependency at T1 compared to never-ill subjects.

The role played by the attributes of dependency and self-criticism in depression have been examined by a number of researchers and theorists (Arieti & Bemporad, 1980; Beck, 1983; Blatt, D'Afflitti, & Quinlan, 1976; Blatt, Quinlan, & Chevron, 1990; Hirschfeld et al., 1977). Dependent individuals show excessive needs for reassurance, approval, love, and respect; they are vulnerable to depression when their needs for gratification are not met. Self-critical individuals are thought to have excessively high standards for themselves; failure to achieve expected goals may lead to guilt, self-blame, and depression. Blatt, Quinlan, Chevron, McDonald, and Zuroff (1982) found that depressed in-patients and out-patients scored higher on dependency and self-criticism than controls, and Hirschfeld et al. (1977) found that psychiatric patients with mixed diagnoses scored significantly higher on dependency. Nietzel and Harris (1990) conducted a meta-analytic study examining findings from studies assessing the relationship between dependency and self-criticism and depression during the period 1976–1989. The mean effect size for dependency and self-criticism was $r = .28$ ($p < .0000000001$) and $.31$ ($p < .0000000001$), respectively.

A number of researchers have attempted to assess whether these attributes increase an individual's vulnerability to depression following stressful life events. If these attributes do increase an individual's vulnerability to depression, then attribute-congruent life stress should be more likely to lead to depression than attribute-incongruent stress. For example, subjects high in dependency should be more vulnerable to depression following loss events than failure events; the converse should be true for highly self-critical subjects. A limited number of studies have attempted to assess the "specificity" hypothesis, but the results have been inconclusive. For example, Robins and Block (1988) found that dependent and self-critical subjects reported high levels of depressive symptoms after experiencing negative social events and negative achievement events. Hammen, Marks, Mayol, and deMayo (1985) found some support for the specificity hypothesis but the results were not consistent across the assessment modalities used in the study. In a more recent study, Hammen, Ellicott, and Gitlin (1989) followed 15 unipolar depressed patients (patients were diagnosed by an admitting psychiatrist using DSM-III criteria) for at least six months after admission to a treatment facility. Although a significant interaction was found between self-criticism and achievement events in the prediction of depressive symptoms, the interaction between dependency and interpersonal events was not significant.

One of the problems with this type of research is that life events are typically categorized as loss events or achievement events on an a priori basis based on the ratings of outside observers. The meaning of an event may differ across subjects however; an event that engenders feelings of loss in one subject may be associated with feelings of failure in another. Future studies will need to address the issue of individual differences in the meaning of events before the specificity hypothesis can be adequately evaluated.

The role of "hardiness" in the stress-depression relationship has also been assessed. The personality attribute of hardiness is intended to identify individuals who possess a sense of commitment, respond positively to challenge, and are stress resilient (Gentry & Kobasa, 1984). Rhodewalt and Zone (1989) found that nonhardy women appraised a significantly higher number of stress events as undesirable and were more likely to experience depressive symptoms following negative life events than hardy women.

Beck (1972, 1976) and Beck, Rush, Shaw, and Emery (1979) have suggested that maladaptive cognitive schema and irrational beliefs play an important role and predispose an individual to depression following environmental stress. The results of studies testing this hypothesis have been inconsistent. Peselow, Robins, Block, Barouche, and Fieve (1990) studied 112 depressed subjects before and 3 to 6 weeks after pharmacotherapy. Dysfunctional attitudes of recovered patients decreased to control levels following treatment, so these attitudes appear to be state dependent. Patients with endogenous features showed significantly lower levels of irrational beliefs than patients in a nonendogenous group; this finding suggests that biological factors may play a greater role in the symptoms experienced by the former group of subjects than irrational beliefs. Evidence suggesting that dysfunctional attitudes are state dependent has also been reported by Persons and Rao (1985) and Dobson and Shaw (1987). Persons and Rao (1985) did not find evidence that irrational beliefs interacted with life events to increase an individual's vulnerability to depression. Olinger, Kuiper, and Shaw (1987), however, found a significant interaction between life events and dysfunctional attitudes in predicting depressive symptoms in a group of normal undergraduates. Vulnerable subjects ascribed more importance and emotional impact to life events and ruminated more about the events they experienced. Wise and Barnes (1986) found a significant interaction between life events and dysfunctional attitudes in the prediction of depressive symptoms in a normal college population but not in a patient sample.

MAJOR AND MINOR LIFE EVENTS AND DEPRESSION

Life Events

The results of a large number of studies suggest that life stress is significantly but moderately related to depression (Billings & Moos, 1984; Brown & Harris, 1978). In an early study, Paykel (1974) found a positive relationship between life stress and depression and Sarason, Hohnson, and Siegel (1978) found that negative life events were positively related to scores on the Beck Depression Inventory (BDI). Mitchell, Cronkite, and Moos (1983) found that depressed patients experienced more negative life events and ongoing chronic strains and less supportive family environments than controls during the 12 months prior to the study. Hammen, Mayol, deMayo, and Marks (1986) studied the relationship between major life events and depression (assessed using the BDI and interviewer ratings) in a 4-month longitudinal study. Life events in the monthly period preceding each monthly assessment were found to contribute to depression after controlling for prior levels of depression. Events assessed more than one month prior to each assessment were not significantly related to depression. Billings and Moos (1985) studied 424 depressed patients 12 months after they entered treatment for major and minor unipolar depression. Although the amount of variance explained was relatively low, negative life events and chronic strains (i.e., negative home environment, family arguments, child illness) were significantly correlated with depressive symptoms, after controlling for stress at intake.

Previous work has suggested that depressed patients can be classified according to whether their symptoms arise in response to life events—so-called reactive depressions—or whether they result from biochemical factors—so-called endogenous depressions. Bebbington et al. (1988) examined the frequency of life events experienced by patients with and without endogenous symptoms. Contrary to expectations, the number of events experienced by patients in the endogenous group did not differ from the number of events experienced by patients in the nonendogenous group. Further, there appeared to be a sharp increase in the number of events experienced by patients in both groups in the month prior to onset, a finding that suggests that an increase in stress may lead to the emergence of symptoms. If these results are replicated in future studies, the idea that environmental events do not play an important role in the emergence of endogenous symptoms may need to be re-evaluated.

Daily Stress

In the last 5 to 10 years, there has been considerable interest in the assessment of daily stress, or "hassles," and ongoing chronic strains and their relationship to psychological symptoms. It has been suggested that daily stress events represent a more proximal measure of stress than major life events and that, as a consequence, they should be more closely related to symptoms (Kanner, Coyne, Schaefer, & Lazarus, 1981). Pearlin and his colleagues (Pearlin & Johnson, 1977; Pearlin & Schooler, 1978) examined the relationship between chronic role strain and depressive symptomatology in a series of early studies. Kanner et al. (1981) reported that the number of daily hassles experienced by subjects was significantly related to psychological symptoms; hassles frequency was more strongly related to symptoms than life events scores. Furthermore, hassles frequency added significantly to the variance in symptoms after the variance associated with life events had been partialled out of the equation. Monroe (1983) used a prospective design to study the impact of daily stress events on psychological symptoms. Hassles were significantly related to symptoms after T1 symptoms had been taken into account and were more strongly related to symptoms than life events. In a recent study, Bolger, DeLongis, Kessler, and Schilling (1989) used a daily diary approach to study the relationship between daily stress and negative mood during a 6-week period. Daily stress ratings accounted for approximately 20% of the variance in negative mood. Among the stresses assessed, interpersonal stresses accounted for 16% of the explained variance; this finding suggests that this type of stress is particularly important in terms of its impact on mood states. Gannon and Pardie (1989) studied the effect of everyday stress on depressive symptoms in a sample of undergraduate men and women. The number of stresses experienced was significantly correlated with symptom levels. Women experienced significantly higher levels of stress and symptoms than men. Social support was negatively related to symptom levels for both men and women but did not act as a buffer in the stress-illness relationship.

Methodological/Conceptual Issues

There are a number of difficult conceptual and methodological issues related to work in this area. Stress has typically been conceptualized as an external stimulus that impinges on the person. A number of life event researchers (Dohrenwend, Dohrenwend, Dodson, & Shrout, 1984) have suggested that the relationship between stress and psychopathology is best studied under conditions in which the measure of stress is completely independent of the person. To accomplish this condition, it would be necessary to demonstrate: (1) that the individual did not play a role in causing the event to occur and (2) that the individual's perception of the event was not mediated by internal or intrapsychic factors. Although it may be possible to isolate events that are not caused by an individual, it is probably not possible to identify a situation in which the person's appraisal of an event does not play a role in shaping the degree of stress experienced. While the notion of stress as an independent variable has utility, the expectation that stress can be completely independent of the person is probably unrealistic. Lazarus, DeLongis, Folkman, and Gruen (1985) and Gruen, Folkman, and Lazarus (1988) have argued that an individual's appraisal of an event is shaped by the beliefs, commitments, resources, and neurotic agendas and conflicts that the individual brings to an encounter. To the extent that this is true, measures of stress and outcome are confounded with one another (Lazarus et al., 1985).

A related issue, alluded to earlier, concerns the question of whether the meaning of stress events differs from subject to subject. Gruen et al. (1988) found that the meaning of daily stress events varied considerably from individual to individual, so that one cannot use normative ratings of meaning to assess the significance of life events. In this study, ratings of *centrality* (a measure of the importance of an event) added significantly to the variance in outcomes beyond that associated with ratings of frequency and severity; this suggests that the impact of an event is mediated, in part, by its salience or importance for the person.

Further examination of individual differences in the appraisal of stressful events may enhance our understanding of the relationship between stress and depression.

STRESS, COPING, AND DEPRESSION

Early investigations examining the relationship between stress and depression were based, at least implicitly, on the idea that life stress may cause depression. In the past decade, bivariate models have been replaced by conceptual frameworks that posit that the relationship between stress and depression is mediated by a number of other variables such as coping and social support. Coping strategies consist of cognitive and behavioral efforts designed to manage the demands of situations that tax or exceed the person's resources (Folkman, Lazarus, Dunkel-Schetter, DeLongis, & Gruen, 1986a; Folkman, Lazarus, Gruen, & DeLongis, 1986). A distinction has been made between strategies that alter the person-environment relationship (problem-focused coping) and strategies used to manage the person's emotional response to the situation (emotion-focused coping) (Folkman et al., 1986a,b).

The coping strategies used by depressed and nondepressed subjects have been examined in a series of studies. Coyne, Aldwin, and Lazarus (1981) found that subjects high in depressive symptoms scored higher on wishful thinking, seeking emotional support, and avoidance than subjects who were not symptomatic. Folkman and Lazarus (1986) assessed the coping and affective responses of subjects dealing with stressful events over a 5-month period. They found that subjects high in depressive symptoms engaged in significantly higher levels of confrontive coping, self-control, escape-avoidance, accepting responsibility, and seeking social support. There were no differences between depressed and nondepressed subjects with regard to planful problem solving, positive reappraisal, or distancing. Depressed subjects reported feeling more angry and disgusted and worried and fearful and less confident and secure than subjects low in depressive symptoms when dealing with stressful events. Mitchell et al. (1983) reported that depressed subjects engaged in significantly higher levels of emotional discharge and significantly lower levels of problem-solving coping than controls. Fondacaro and Moos (1989) studied a sample of 233 depressed subjects meeting RDC for depression and a community sample of 260 controls at 2 time points 12 months apart. T2 stress resulted in an increase in the use of emotional discharge coping at T2 (controlling for coping and level of stress at T1). Gotlib and Whiffen (1989a) studied the coping responses of couples with and without a female diagnosed as having major or minor depression (subjects were diagnosed with the SADS, which was administered over the phone). Couples in which the wife was diagnosed as having major depression reported using more distancing and accepting responsibility compared with couples without a wife with major depression. Couples in which the wife was diagnosed as having either major or minor depression used significantly more confrontation, self-control, and escape-avoidance compared with couples without a depressed member.

There are two clear limitations to the use of self-report inventories to assess coping: (1) they are subject to response bias, and (2) they are limited in terms of their ability to assess coping strategies such as escape-avoidance and distancing, which operate outside subjects' awareness. Observer-based coding systems that examine the coping strategies used by subjects during stressful, laboratory-based tasks can be used to address some of these problems. Self-report strategies, however, allow access to inner thoughts and feelings that might not be observable to outside raters. It appears therefore, that both assessment strategies are necessary.

MARITAL STRESS, INTERPERSONAL PROCESSES, AND DEPRESSION

A number of theorists have suggested that the interpersonal context in which the depressed person lives may play an important role in causing or maintaining the disorder (Barnett & Gotlib, 1988; Coyne, 1976; Coyne, Burchill, & Stiles, 1991). Results from a series of early studies indicated that family or marital stress was related to depressive symptomatology. Paykel (1974) found that depressed patients reported about 3 times as many life events as controls in the 6 months preceding onset; arguments with spouse and marital separation were two of the most commonly reported events. Vaughn and Leff (1976) studied the effects of indexes of expressed emotion (i.e., criticism) on relapse in schizophrenic and neurotic depressed patients after discharge from the hospital. High levels of expressed emotion were found to increase the rate of relapse in both patient groups. Brown and Harris (1978) found that lack of a confidant was one of the factors that predisposed an individual to depression. Ilfeld (1982) found that stress associated with marital or interpersonal issues was more closely associated with depressive symptoms than other types of stressors.

Interpersonal Disturbances and Depression

Paykel and Weissman (1973) studied a sample of 40 depressed females (based on psychiatrist ratings using the Raskin Depression Scale) and 40 nondepressed females 8 months after treatment. Although depressive symptoms had remitted, residual deficits in social functioning remained, the most pronounced involving inhibited communication and interpersonal friction. Bothwell and Weissman (1977) conducted a 4-year follow-up of the same subjects and found that 26% of females who were depressed at T1 were still depressed 4 years later and that an additional 43% exhibited minimal or mild symptoms. Depressed females were significantly more impaired than controls with regard to work performance, anxious rumination, and interpersonal friction. Recovered patients were significantly more impaired than controls in their ability to function in a marital role and they reported higher levels of interpersonal friction. This finding suggests that disturbances in social functioning may represent stable interpersonal attributes that predispose to depression.

Merikangas (1984) studied the divorce rate in 56 couples in which one spouse met RDC for affective disorder at intake and found the incidence of divorce to be 9 times the rate expected in the general population. Crowther (1985) found that depressed patients showed significantly higher levels of marital maladjustment compared with patients with other psychiatric diagnoses. Fredman, Weissman, Leaf, and Bruce (1988), in a sample consisting of 4,913 community participants, found that currently depressed subjects were significantly less likely to get along with or confide in their partners than respondents with other current psychiatric disorders or past depressive episodes. Kahn, Coyne, and Margolin (1985) found that depressed subjects engaged in less constructive problem solving and more withdrawal when dealing with stressful interpersonal events than normal controls.

Marital Satisfaction and Depression

A number of studies have reported a significant negative relationship between marital satisfaction and depressive symptomatology (Crowther, 1985; Gotlib & Whiffen, 1989b; Kahn et al., 1985; Ruscher & Gotlib, 1988). The relationship between marital satisfaction and depression is probably bidirectional. Coyne et al. (1987) studied how a major depressive episode in one member of a dyad affects the partner. Partners of depressed patients reported feeling upset about their partner's lack of energy, they experienced living with the patient to be a burden and a strain, and they worried that their partner would become depressed again. They reported high levels of psychological symptomatology; approximately 41% were suitable for psychological intervention compared with 17% in a control group. Krantz and Moos (1987) found that spouses of depressed patients experienced their families as being more conflictual and less cohesive than families of controls and they used more avoidant coping strategies. The results of these studies suggest that living with a depressed individual is stressful and disturbing. Thus, while disturbances in close interpersonal relationships may precede the onset of depressive symptoms, marital dissatisfaction may also reflect the alienation and estrangement experienced by both members of a couple when one is depressed.

Laboratory-based Studies

A number of researchers have examined the interpersonal interactions of depressed and nondepressed subjects directly in controlled laboratory settings. In an early study, Hinchliffe, Hooper, Roberts, and Vaughan (1975) compared the verbal and nonverbal responses of depressed patients and their spouses with nonpsychiatric surgical patients and their spouses during a dyadic laboratory interaction task. The interaction patterns of couples with a depressed member were characterized by higher levels of tension and negative expression. Linden, Hautzinger, and Hoffman (1983) observed couples with and without a depressed member on eight occasions in a variety of tasks. Depressed subjects displayed a negative future orientation, made more negative self-evaluations and negative comments about their well-being, and made more positive comments about their partners than nondepressed subjects. Kahn et al. (1985) found that depressed subjects and their spouses reported feeling angrier, sadder, and more dissatisfied during an interaction task than control couples. Ruscher and Gotlib (1988) asked couples with and without a depressed member (depression was assessed using the BDI) to discuss 5 areas of conflict in their relationship. Couples with a depressed member gave a lower proportion of positive statements and a greater proportion of negative statements than couples without a depressed member. Gotlib and Whiffen (1989b) found that couples with a depressed member (depression was assessed using DSM-III criteria) experienced each other as significantly more dominant, submissive and hostile than control couples. Biglan et al. (1985) studied 3 groups of couples: couples with a depressed female who were maritally distressed; couples with a depressed female who were not maritally distressed; and nondistressed couples without a depressed member. Nondepressed/nondistressed couples showed significantly higher rates of self-disclosure than couples in the other groups. Depressed/distressed couples showed significantly less facilitative behavior than depressed/nondistressed or control couples. Among depressed/distressed couples, wives' aggressive behavior reduced the probability that the husband would propose a solution to a significantly greater degree than was true among normal couples.

Dyadic-level Processes

With few exceptions (i.e., Biglan et al., 1985), previous research examining the role of interpersonal processes in depression has focused on the individual rather than the couple. From a marital systems perspective, the responses of individuals within a system cannot be completely understood by examining the responses of either partner alone; variables representing the pattern of response between partners must be assessed (Fisher, 1982; Thompson & Walker, 1982). In an attempt to address this issue, Gruen, Folkman, and Lazarus (1987) studied dyadic-level patterns of emotion in couples dealing with a range of stressful events. Levels of depressive symptoms were significantly higher in wives in one group than wives in other groups. The pattern of response of couples in this case was marked by an incongruity of affective response between husbands and wives; wives were disgusted, angry, worried, and fearful, and their husbands were not. The dyadic patterns identified contributed significantly to the variance in wife's depression after controlling for the individual's emotional response. The results suggest that in order to understand the affective responses of partners to a stressful event, one must assess the reactions of subjects at both the individual and dyadic level.

STRESS, BIOCHEMICAL RESPONSE, AND DEPRESSION

In the last fifteen years, evidence has emerged that suggests that unipolar depression is associated with specific transmitter and hormonal disturbances. Recently, it has been suggested that there may be an important relationship between stress, biochemical response, and depression (Gold, Goodwin, & Chrousos, 1988a, 1988b; Paul, 1988). Integration of the results of studies examining biochemical responses to stress into the larger body of research examining the relationship between stress, coping, and depression may greatly enhance our understanding of the factors that cause or maintain the disorder.

Biochemical Responses to Stress

In normal human subjects, stress leads to the activation of a number of different biochemical systems: the sympathetic nervous system, the hypothalamic-pituitary-adrenal (HPA) axis, and the noradrenergic system in the central nervous system (CNS) (Axelrod & Reisine, 1984; Stokes & Sikes, 1987; Ward et al., 1983). Psychological and physical stress results in increases in plasma norepinephrine (NE), epinephrine (E), hypothalamic corticotropin-releasing hormone (CRH), and adrenocorticotropic hormone (ACTH) (Axelrod & Reisine, 1984; Dimsdale & Moss, 1980; Stokes & Sikes, 1987; Ward et al., 1983). Increases in ACTH lead to increases in peripheral plasma cortisol (Stokes & Sikes, 1987).

Evidence for the involvement of the central noradrenergic system in the stress response comes from a variety of sources. 3-methoxy-4-hydroxyphenylethylene glycol (MHPG) is the major metabolite of NE. Levels of MHPG in plasma have been shown to correlate highly with levels of MHPG in the brain (Elsworth, Redmond, & Roth, 1982; Elsworth,

Roth, & Redmond, 1983); thus, assessment of plasma MHPG may provide a reliable and convenient index of CNS functioning. Exposure of phobic patients to a phobic stimulus leads to a significant increase in plasma MHPG (Ko et al., 1983). Similarly, mild hand shock leads to an increase in urinary MHPG in normal subjects (Buchsbaum, Muscettola, & Goodwin, 1981). Electrical stimulation of the locus coeruleus, a primary nucleus of the noradrenergic system in the brain, results in behavioral changes that are nearly identical to those observed in naturally occurring fear states (Charney & Redmond, 1983). Yohimbine, an alpha-2-adrenergic autoreceptor antagonist, leads to increases in noradrenergic transmission and induces anxiety states in normal subjects; increases in the transmission NE in the CNS are significantly correlated with increases in anxiety (Charney & Redmond, 1983).

Biochemical Alterations in Depressed Patients

Patients with unipolar depression show alterations in HPA axis activity and central and peripheral noradrenergic transmission compared to controls. A number of studies have compared levels of NE, E, and MHPG in plasma, cerebral spinal fluid (CSF), and urine in depressed and nondepressed subjects. The most frequently assessed index of HPA axis activity is cortisol.

Results from a majority of studies suggest that levels of NE are higher in depressed that nondepressed subjects under basal conditions (Siever, 1987). In an early study, Wyatt, Portnoy, Kupfer, Snyder, and Engelman (1971) found that levels of NE and E were elevated in depressed compared to nondepressed subjects and Lake et al. (1982) and Roy, Pickar, Linnoila, and Potter (1985) found that plasma NE levels were increased in melancholic depressed patients. Wyatt et al. (1971) suggested that high levels of plasma NE in depressed patients may be associated with states of chronic anxiety.

Results of studies comparing basal levels of MHPG in depressed and nondepressed subjects have been conflicting. Depressive symptomatology has been shown to be significantly negatively correlated with plasma MHPG in nonpatient samples (Ballenger, Post, Jimerson, Lake, & Zuckerman, 1984) and depressed patients have been shown to exhibit lower levels of urinary MHPG at admission (Pickar, Sweeney, Maas, & Heninger, 1978). Sweeney, Maas, and Heninger (1978) proposed that depressed patients with low baseline MHPG may be particularly vulnerable to stress; this vulnerability may lead to increased production of MHPG in response to stress. Koslow et al. (1983), however, found significantly higher levels of CSF MHPG in postmenopausal depressed women compared to premenopausal depressed women and nondepressed controls.

Charney, Heninger, Sternberg, and Roth (1981) and Siever and Uhde (1984) failed to find significant differences in plasma MHPG between depressed and nondepressed subjects. Siever and Uhde (1984) reported that depressed patients showed increased variability in metabolite concentrations compared to controls. This finding suggests the possibility that subgroups of depressed patients exist who display low and high basal MHPG values (Siever, 1987).

Disturbances in HPA axis activity have been reported in depressed compared to nondepressed individuals. Depressed subjects show increased levels of CSF and plasma cortisol compared to nondepressed subjects (Gerner & Wilkins, 1983; Stokes et al., 1984). Depressive symptomatology is significantly positively correlated with urinary free cortisol in nonpatient samples (Ballenger et al., 1984) and depressed patients show elevations in the urinary excretion of cortisol metabolites (Stokes & Sikes, 1987). It has been suggested that increased cortisol secretion rates in depressed subjects may be associated with hyperactivity of the noradrenergic system (Siever, 1987).

Stress-induced Biochemical Alterations in Depressed Patients

The preceding suggests that depressed patients show functional disturbances in primary systems associated with the stress response. This hypothesis raises the possibility that stress or anxiety may play an important role in the pathophysiology of depression and that anxiety disorders and depression are closely associated with one another. Support for this idea comes from various sources. Unipolar depression and anxiety disorders have both been associated with noradrenergic dysfunction (Charney & Redmond, 1983; Paul, 1988; Siever, 1987). Results from clinical and epidemiological studies suggest that patients with depression often present with symptoms of anxiety (Leckman, Weissman, Merikangas, Pauls, & Prusoff, 1983), and a diagnostic subgroup of anxious-depressed patients has been identified (Downing & Rickels, 1974; Paykel, 1971; Roth, Gurney, Garside, & Kerr, 1972). Finally, the fact that antidepressant medications have been found useful in the treatment of patients with panic disorder and obsessive-compulsive disorder suggests a close link between major depression and these disturbances (Hudson & Pope, 1990).

To date, stress-induced biochemical responses in subjects with unipolar depression have not been examined systematically. Heninger, Charney, and Price (1988) found that depressed patients (assessed using DSM-III criteria) experienced a greater increase in somatic symptoms (i.e., palpitations, tremors, hot and cold flashes) and blood pressure following administration of yohimbine than controls; depressed and nondepressed subjects did not differ, however, in yohimbine-induced increases in plasma MHPG. Buchsbaum et al. (1981) found that depressed subjects exhibited a blunting of the normal stress-induced increase in urinary MHPG following hand shock compared to controls. Six out of 12 of the depressed subjects in the Buchsbaum et al. (1981) study were diagnosed as bipolar, however; thus, the generalizability of the findings to unipolar depression may be limited. Clearly, more research needs to be done in this area. Future studies should examine the biochemical responses of depressed and nondepressed subjects to a range of stressors, including psychological and physical stressors.

MULTIVARIATE STUDIES

As noted in the introduction, there is growing recognition of the fact that depression may result from a variety of factors, including interpersonal, psychological, genetic, and biological factors (Bebbington et al., 1988; Kaplan et al., 1987; Lewinsohn, Hoberman, & Rosenbaum, 1988). Although biochemical and genetic factors have not been integrated into the current body of research, a limited number of studies have examined the role played by several psychosocial factors in depression.

Husaini and Von Frank (1985) used a 2-wave panel design (the 2 assessments took place 6 to 18 months apart) to assess the relationship between stress, social support, locus of control, and depression. Life event stress at T2 was significantly related to an increase in depressive symptoms at T2; life stress at T1 was not. It has been suggested that while stress may lead to depression, depression may also lead to an increase in life stress. T1 symptoms were not significantly related to life event stress at T2, however. Internal locus of control at T2 was negatively related to T2 depression. Individuals with more close friends were less depressed. Interestingly, Husaini and Von Frank (1985) found that individuals who utilized supportive others more were more depressed. Depression at T1 was significantly positively related to the use of supportive others at T2. Coyne (1976) has argued that the help-seeking behavior of depressed subjects alienates others in the social environment and leads to an escalation of depressive symptoms. The results of the study by Husaini and Von Frank (1985) support this contention.

Dohrenwend et al. (1987) studied the effects of life stress, social support, and a variety of personality variables in depressed, schizophrenic, and control subjects. Patients were diagnosed using DSM-III criteria. Life events were divided into three categories: fateful losses, physical illnesses and injuries, and nonfateful events likely to disrupt social support networks. Within this framework, fateful losses (events that arise independently of the person, such as death of a child or spouse) are thought to have causal status with regard to symptomatology. Depressed patients reported a significantly higher level of fateful losses than controls in the year preceding the assessment. Schizophrenic patients did not differ from controls on this variable. Both depressed and schizophrenic patients experienced a higher rate of illness and nonfateful events than controls. Schizophrenics showed a significant reduction in the size and extensiveness of their social network and number of social companions compared to controls, while depressed patients showed a significant decrease in the density of their social network and number of social companions compared to controls. Deficits in social network size were especially marked for repeat-episode patient cases. Schizophrenic and depressed patients showed higher levels of external locus of control and denial and lower levels of mastery orientation than controls. Both patient groups were more likely to have a first-degree relative with a mental disorder than controls.

Kaplan et al. (1987) reported the results of a large-scale epidemiological study conducted by the Human Population Laboratory in Alameda, California, between 1965 and 1974. Factors predicting high levels of depressive symptoms in 1974 in subjects who were not depressed at T1 were studied. Nondepressed subjects who reported a physical health disability at T1 were 3 times more likely to become depressed at T2 than subjects who did not report a disability. High levels of stress were related to increased risk of depression at T2. Job loss and financial problems accounted for the largest proportion of variance compared to other types of stress. Increased age was associated with decreased risk. Subjects with less than 12 years of education who reported an inadequate income at T1 were also at increased risk. Subjects reporting social isolation at T1 were at a threefold risk of developing high levels of symptoms at T2.

Lewinsohn et al. (1988) studied 998 subjects at 2 time points approximately 8 months apart. The following characteristics were significantly related to the emergence of depression (assessed using SADS-RDC criteria) at T2: age (younger subjects were more likely to become depressed); gender (females were more likely to become depressed); past episodes of depression; and having a child under the age of 6 at home. Subjects who became depressed during the study period experienced elevated levels of stress compared to those who did not become depressed, they were more likely to be unemployed, and, if married, they were more likely to be experiencing marital conflict.

Swindle, Cronkite, and Moos (1989) studied 424 depressed patients at intake, and at 1 and 4 years following treatment. Level of depression was determined using a self-report instrument based on RDC criteria. In general, patients reported less depression and physical symptoms and an improvement in self-esteem over the 4 years of the study. Although the frequency of social contact or number of friends did not increase over the course of the study, family cohesion and expressiveness increased at both the 1- and 4-year assessments. There was a significant decline in the number of negative life events from the 1- to 4-year follow-up. Compared to intake, levels of problem solving and affective regulation increased and emotional discharge declined at the 4-year follow-up. Levels of information seeking declined from intake to 1 year but then did not change. At the 4-year follow-up, problem-solving coping was negatively correlated with depression and life event stress, and emotional discharge coping and a negative home environment were positively related to depression.

CONCLUSION

The findings reviewed in this chapter suggest that stress and coping processes play an important role in unipolar depression. In future studies, the role of vulnerability and biochemical factors must be examined in greater detail. The development of integrative models that examine the relative contributions of psychosocial and biochemical/genetic factors will enhance our understanding of processes that cause or maintain the disorder.

A number of issues raised in the preceding sections suggest that models used to guide future research must be refined to mirror the complexity of the phenomena we are studying. The first question that must be addressed has to do with the issue of subtypes of depression. Distinctions have been made between major and minor depressions, endogenous and reactive depressions, and typical and atypical depressions. Studies examining the overlap between depression and specific anxiety disorders (Downing & Rickels, 1974; Hudson & Pope, 1990; Paykel, 1971; Roth et al., 1972) suggest that depressions that involve anxiety as a central component may differ from those that do not. It is quite likely that the balance of factors that play a role in different forms of depression differs.

Second, it should be recognized that the relative importance of various contributing factors may differ depending on where the patient is in the course of the illness; biochemical factors may play an important role in the development of the disorder, while interpersonal factors may serve to maintain the symptoms. Alternatively, in some forms of depression, biochemical factors may increase one's vulnerability to depression; symptoms may arise however, only following severe environmental stress.

Third, it was noted that approximately 20% to 25% of patients who experience an initial episode of depression experience recurrent episodes. Factors important in causing first-onset cases may differ from those that are important in causing repeat episodes. Fourth, the type of psychosocial stress or biochemical alteration important in various forms of depression may differ depending on the life stage of the individual (Coyne & Downey, 1991). For example, Koslow et al. (1983) found significantly higher levels of CSF MHPG in postmenopausal depressed women compared to premenopausal depressed women and nondepressed controls. Both pre- and postmenopausal depressed women showed significantly higher levels of CSF 5-hydroxyindoleacetic acid (5-HIAA) compared to controls, however. An examination of issues related to subtype, illness course, and life stage may lead to a more accurate and comprehensive understanding of factors that contribute to unipolar depression. This, in turn, may enhance our ability to treat patients more effectively.

REFERENCES

AKISKAL, H. S., HIRSCHFELD, R. M. A., & YEREVANIAN, B. I. The relationship of personality to affective disorders. *Archives of General Psychiatry,* 1983, *40,* 801–810.

AMERICAN PSYCHIATRIC ASSOCIATION. *Diagnostic and statistical manual of mental disorders,* (3rd ed.). Washington, DC: APA, 1980.

ARIETI, S., & BEMPORAD, J. R. The psychological organization of depression. *American Journal of Psychiatry,* 1980, *137,* 1360–1365.

AXELROD, J., & REISINE, T. D. Stress hormones: Their interaction and regulation. *Science,* 1984, *224,* 452–459.

BALLENGER, J. C., POST, R. M., JIMERSON, D. C., LAKE, C. R., & ZUCKERMAN, M. Neurobiological correlates of depression and anxiety in normal individuals. In R. M. Post & J. C. Ballenger (eds.), *Neurobiology of mood disorders.* Baltimore, MD: Williams and Wilkins, 1984.

BARNETT, P. A., & GOTLIB, I. H. Psychosocial functioning and depression: Distinguishing among antecedents, concomitants, and consequences. *Psychological Bulletin,* 1988, *104,* 97–126.

BEGGINGTON, P. E., BRUGHA, T., MACCARTHY, B., POTTER, J., STURT, E., WYKES, T., KATZ, R., & McGUFFIN, P. The Camberwell collaborative depression study; I. Depressed probands: adversity and the form of depression. *British Journal of Psychiatry,* 1988, *152,* 754–765.

BECK, A. T. *Depression: Causes and treatment.* Philadelphia: University of Pennsylvania Press, 1972.

————. *Cognitive therapy and the emotional disorders.* New York: International Universities Press, 1976.

BECK, A. T. Cognitive therapy of depression; New perspectives. In P. Clayton & J. Barrett (eds.), *Treatment of depression: old and new perspectives* (1983) 265–290.

BECK, A. T., RUSH, A. J., SHAW, B. F., & EMERY, G. *Cognitive therapy of depression.* New York: Guilford Press, 1979.

BIGLAN, A., HOPS, H., SHERMAN, L., FRIEDMAN, L., ARTHUR, J., & OSTEEN, V. Problem-solving interactions of depressed women and their husbands. *Behavior Therapy,* 1985, *16,* 431–451.

BILLINGS, A. G., & MOOS, R. H. Coping, stress, and social resources among adults with unipolar depression. *Journal of Personality and Social Psychology,* 1984, *46,* 877–891.

————. Psychosocial processes of remission in unipolar depression: Comparing depressed patients with matched community controls. *Journal of Consulting and Clinical Psychology,* 1985, *53,* 314–325.

BLATT, S. J., D'AFFLITTI, J. P., & QUINLAN, D. M. Experiences of depression in normal young adults. *Journal of Abnormal Psychology,* 1976, *85,* 383–389.

BLATT, S. J., QUINLAN, D. M., & CHEVRON, E. Empirical investigations of a psychoanalytic theory of depression. In J. Masling (ed.), *Empirical studies of psychoanalytic theory.* Vol. 3, 1990, 89–147.

BLATT, S. J., QUINLAN, D. M., CHEVRON, E. S., McDONALD, C., & ZUROFF, D. Dependency and self-criticism: Psychological dimensions of depression. *Journal of Consulting and Clinical Psychology,* 1982, *50,* 113–124.

BLEHAR, M. C., WEISSMAN, M. M., GERSHON, E. S., & HIRSCHFELD, R. M. A. Family and genetic studies of affective disorders. *Archives of General Psychiatry,* 1988, *45,* 289–292.

BOLGER, N., DELONGIS, A., KESSLER, R. C., & SCHILLING, E. A. Effects of daily stress on negative mood. *Journal of Personality and Social Psychology,* 1989, *57,* 808–818.

BOTHWELL, S., & WEISSMAN, M. M. Social impairments four years after an acute depressive episode. *American Journal of Orthopsychiatry,* 1977, *47,* 231–237.

BROWN, G. W., & HARRIS, T. *Social origins of depression: A study of psychiatric disorder in women.* New York: Free Press, 1978.

BUCHSBAUM, M. S., MUSCETTOLA, G., & GOODWIN, F. K. Urinary MHPG, stress response, personality factors and somatosensory evoked potentials in normal subjects and patients with major affective disorders. *Neuropsychobiology, 1981, 7, 212–224.*

BURKE, K. C., BURKE, J. D., JR., REGIER, D. A., & RAE, D. S. Age at onset of selected mental disorders in five community populations. *Archives of General Psychiatry, 1990, 47, 511–518.*

CHARNEY, D. S., HENINGER, G. A., STERNBERG, D. E., & ROTH, R. H. *Psychiatry Research, 1981, 5, 2117–2129.*

CHARNEY, D. S., & REDMOND, D. E. Neurobiological mechanisms in human anxiety: Evidence supporting central noradrenergic hyperactivity. *Neuropharmacology, 1983, 22, 1531–1536.*

COYNE, J. C. Toward an interactional description of depression. *Psychiatry, 1976, 39, 28–40.*

COYNE, J. C., ALDWIN, C., & LAZARUS, R. S. Depression and coping in stressful episodes. *Journal of Abnormal Psychology, 1981, 90, 439–447.*

COYNE, J. C., BURCHILL, S. A. L., & STILES, W. B. An interactional perspective on depression. In C. R. Snyder & D. O. Forsyth (eds.), *Handbook of social and clinical psychology: The health perspective.* New York: Pergamon 1991, in press. 327–349.

COYNE, J. C., & DOWNEY, G. Social factors and psychopathology: Stress, social support and coping processes. *Annual Review of Psychology, 1991, 42, 401–425.*

COYNE, J. C., KESSLER, R. C., TAL, M., TURNBULL, J., WORTMAN, C. B., & GREDEN, J. F. Living with a depressed person. *Journal of Consulting and Clinical Psychology, 1987, 55, 347–352.*

CROWTHER, J. H. The relationship between depression and marital maladjustment: A descriptive study. *Journal of Nervous and Mental Disease, 1985, 173, 227–231.*

DIMSDALE, J. E., & MOSS, J. Plasma catecholamines in stress and exercise. *Journal of American Medical Association, 1980, 243, 340–342.*

DOBSON, K. S., & SHAW, B. F. Specificity and stability of self-referent encoding in clinical depression. *Journal of Abnormal Psychology, 1987, 96, 34–40.*

DOHRENWEND, B. S., DOHRENWEND, B. P., DODSON, M., & SHROUT, P. E. Symptoms, hassles, social supports and life events: The problem of confounded measures. *Journal of Abnormal Psychology, 1984, 93, 222–230.*

DOHRENWEND, B. P., LEVAV, I., SHROUT, P. E., LINK, B. G., SKODOL, A. E., & MARTIN, J. L. Life stress and psychopathology: Progress on research begun with Barbara Snell Dohrenwend. *American Journal of Community Psychology, 1987, 15, 677–715.*

DOWNEY, G., & COYNE, J. C. Children of depressed parents: An integrative review. *Psychology Bulletin, 1990, 50–76.*

DOWNING, R. W., & RICKELS, K. Mixed anxiety-depression: Fact or myth? *Archives of General Psychiatry, 1974, 30, 312–317.*

ELSWORTH, J. D., REDMOND, D. E., & ROTH, R. H. Plasma and cerebrospinal fluid 3-methoxy-4-hydroxyphenylethylene glycol (MHPG) as indices of brain norepinephrine metabolism in primates. *Brain Research, 1982, 235, 115–124.*

ELSWORTH, J. D., ROTH, R. H., & REDMOND, D. E. Relative importance of 3-methoxy-4-hydroxyphenylglycol and 3,4-dihydroxyphenylglycol as norepinephrine metabolites in rat and monkey, and humans. *Journal of Neurochemistry, 1983, 41, 786–793.*

FISHER, L. Transactional theories but individual assessment: A frequent discrepancy in family research. *Family Process, 1982, 21, 313–320.*

FOLKMAN, S., & LAZARUS, R. S. Stress processes and depressive symptomatology. *Journal of Abnormal Psychology, 1986, 95, 107–113.*

FOLKMAN, S., LAZARUS, R. S., DUNKEL-SCHETTER, C., DeLONGIS, A., GRUEN, R. S. Dynamics of a stressful encounter; cognitive appraisal, coping, and encounter outcomes. *Journal of Personality and Social Psychology. 1986a, 50, 992–1003.*

FOLKMAN, S., LAZARUS, R. S., GRUEN, R. J., & DELONGIS, A. Appraisal, coping, health status, and psychological symptoms. *Journal of Personality and Social Psychology,* 1986b, *50,* 571–579.

FONDACARO, M. R., & MOOS, R. H. Life stressors and coping: A longitudinal analysis among depressed and nondepressed adults. *Journal of Community Psychology,* 1989, *17,* 330–340.

FREDMAN, L., WEISSMAN, M. M., LEAF, P. J. & BRUCE, M. L. Social functioning in community residents with depression and other psychiatric disorders: Results of the New Haven Epidemiologic Catchment Area study. *Journal of Affective Disorders,* 1988, *15,* 103–112.

GANNON, L., & PARDIE, L. The importance of chronicity and controllability of stress in the context of stress-illness relationships. *Journal of Behavioral Medicine,* 1989, *12,* 347–372.

GENTRY, W. D., & KOBASA, S. C. O. Social and psychological resources mediating stress-illness relationships in humans. In W. D. Gentry (ed.), *Handbook of behavioral medicine.* New York: Guilford Press, 1984.

GERNER, R. H., & WILKINS, J. N. CSF cortisol in patients with depression, mania, or anorexia nervosa and in normal subjects. *American Journal of Psychiatry,* 1983, *140,* 92–94.

GOLD, P. W., GOODWIN, F. K., & CHROUSOS, G. P. Clinical and biochemical manifestations of depression: Relation to the neurobiology stress. Pt. 1. *New England Journal of Medicine,* 1988, *319,* 346–353.(a)

————. Clinical and biochemical manifestations of depression: Relation to the neurobiology stress. Pt. 2. *New England Journal of Medicine,* 1988, *319,* 413–420.(b)

GOTLIB, I. H., & WHIFFEN, V. E. Depression and marital functioning: An examination of specificity and gender differences. *Journal of Abnormal Psychology,* 1989, *98,* 23–30.(a)

————. Stress, coping, and marital satisfaction in couples with a depressed wife. *Canadian Journal of Behavioral Science,* 1989, *21,* 401–418.(b)

GOVE, W. R., & GEERKIN, M. R. Response bias in surveys of mental health: An empirical investigation. *American Journal of Sociology,* 1976, *82,* 1289–1317.

GRUEN, R. J., FOLKMAN, S., & LAZARUS, R. S. Dyadic response patterns in married couples, depressive symptoms, and somatic dysfunction. *Journal of Family Psychology,* 1987, *1,* 168–186.

————. Centrality and individual differences in the meaning of daily hassles. *Journal of Personality,* 1988, *56,* 743–762.

HAMMEN, C., ELLICOTT, A., & GITLIN, M. Vulnerability to specific life events and prediction of course of disorder in unipolar depressed patients. *Canadian Journal of Behaviorial Science,* 1989, *21,* 377–388.

HAMMEN, C., MARKS, T., MAYOL, A., & DEMAYO, R. Depressive self-schemas, life stress, and vulnerability to depression. *Journal of Abnormal Psychology,* 1985, *94,* 308–319.

HAMMEN, C., MAYOL, A., DEMAYO, R., & MARKS, T. Initial symptom levels and the life-event-depression relationship. *Journal of Abnormal Psychology.* 1986, *95,* 114–122.

HENINGER, G. R., CHARNEY, D. S., & PRICE, L. H. α_2-adrenergic receptor sensitivity in depression: The plasma MHPG, behavioral, and cardiovascular responses to yohimbine. *Archives of General Psychiatry,* 1988, *45,* 718–726.

HINCHLIFFE, M., HOOPER, D., ROBERTS, F. J., & VAUGHAN, P. W. A study of the interaction between depressed patients and their spouses. *British Journal of Psychiatry,* 1975, *126,* 164–172.

HIRSCHFELD, R. M., KLERMAN, G. L., GOUGH, H. C., BARRETT, J., KORCHIN, S. J., & CHODOFF, P. A measure of interpersonal dependency. *Journal of Personality Assessment,* 1977, *41,* 611–618.

HIRSCHFELD, R. M. A., KLERMAN, G. L., LAVORI, P., KELLER, M. B., GRIFFITH, P., & CORYELL, W. Premorbid personality assessments of first onset of major depression. *Archives of General Psychiatry,* 1989, *46,* 345–350.

HUDSON, J. I., & POPE, H G., JR. Affective spectrum disorder: Does antidepressant response identify a family of disorders with a common pathophysiology? *American Journal of Psychiatry,* 1990, *147,* 552–564.

HUSAINI, B. A., & VON FRANK, A. Life events, coping resources, and depression: A longitudinal study of direct, buffering and reciprocal effects. *Research in Community and Mental Health,* 1985, *5,* 111–136.

ILFELD, F. W., JR. Marital stressors, coping styles, and symptoms of depression. In L. Goldberger & S. Breznitz (eds.), *Handbook of stress.* New York: Free Press, 1982.

KAHN, J. P., COYNE, J. C., & MARGOLIN, G. Depression and marital disagreement: The social construction of despair. *Journal of Social and Personal Relationships,* 1985, *2,* 447–461.

KANNER, A. D., COYNE, J. C., SCHAEFER, C., & LAZARUS, R. S. Comparison of two modes of stress measurement: Daily hassles and uplifts versus major life events. *Journal of Behavioral Medicine,* 1981, *4,* 1–39.

KAPLAN, G. A., ROBERTS, R. E., CAMACHO, T. C., & COYNE, J. C. Psychosocial predictors of depression: Prospective evidence from the human population laboratory studies. *American Journal of Epidemiology,* 1987, *125,* 206–220.

KO, G. N., ELSWORTH, J. D., ROTH, R. H., RIFKIN, B. G., LEIGH, H., & REDMOND, D. E., JR. Panic-induced elevation of plasma MHPG levels in phobic-anxious patients: Effects of clonidine and imipramine. *Archives of General Psychiatry,* 1983, *40,* 425–430.

KOSLOW, S. H., MAAS, J. W., BOWDEN, C. L., DAVIS, J. M., HANIN, T., & JAVAID, J. CSF and urinary biogenic amines and metabolites in depression and mania. *Archives of General Psychiatry,* 1983, *40* 999–1010.

KRANTZ, S. E., & MOOS, R. H. Functioning and life context among spouses of remitted and nonremitted depressed patients. *Journal of Consulting and Clinical Psychology,* 1987, *55,* 353–360.

LAKE, C. R., PICKAR, D., ZIEGLER, M. G., LIPPER, S., SLATER, S., & MURPHY, D. L. High plasma norepinephrine levels in patients with major affective disorder. *American Journal of Psychiatry,* 1982, *139,* 1315–1318.

LAZARUS, R. S., DELONGIS, A., FOLKMAN, S., & GRUEN, R. Stress and adaptational outcomes: The problem of confounded measures. *American Psychologist,* 1985, *40,* 770–776.

LECKMAN, J. F., WEISSMAN, M. M., MERIKANGAS, K. R., PAULS, D. L., & PRUSOFF, B. A. Panic disorder and major depression. *Archives of General Psychiatry,* 1983, *40,* 1055–1060.

LEE, C. M., & GOTLIB, I. H. Maternal depression and child adjustment: A longitudinal analysis. *Journal of Abnormal Psychology,* 1989, *98,* 78–85.

LEWINSOHN, P. M., HOBERMAN, H. M., & ROSENBAUM, M. A prospective study of risk factors for unipolar depression. *Journal of Abnormal Psychology,* 1988, *97,* 251–264.

LINDEN, M., HAUTZINGER, M., & HOFFMANN, N. Discriminant analysis of depressive interactions. *Behavior Modification,* 1983, *7,* 403–422.

MERIKANGAS, K. R. Divorce and assortative mating among depressed patients. *American Journal of Psychiatry,* 1984, *141,* 74–76.

MERIKANGAS, K. R., PRUSOFF, B. A., & WEISSMAN, M. M. Parental concordance for affective disorders: psychopathology in offspring. *Journal of Affective Disorders,* 1988a, *15,* 279–290.

MERIKANGAS, K. R., WEISSMAN, M. M., PRUSOFF, B. A., & JOHN, K. Assortative mating and affective disorders: Psychopathology in offspring. *Psychiatry,* 1988b, *51,* 48–57.

MITCHELL, R. E., CRONKITE, R. C., & MOOS, R. H. Stress, coping, and depression among married couples. *Journal of Abnormal Psychology,* 1983, *92,* 433–448.

MONROE, S. M. Major and minor life events as predictors of psychological distress: Further issues and findings. *Journal of Behavioral Medicine,* 1983, *6,* 189–205.

NIETZEL, M. T., & HARRIS, M. J. Relationship of dependency and achievement/autonomy to depression. *Clinical Psychology Review,* 1990, *10,* 279–297.

OLINGER, L. J., KUIPER, N. A., & SHAW, B. F. Dysfunctional attitudes and stressful life events: An interactive model of depression. *Cognitive Therapy and Reserach,* 1987, *11,* 25–40.

PAUL, S. M. Anxiety and depression: A common neurobiological substrate? *Journal of Clinical Psychiatry,* 1988 (suppl. 10), *49,* 13–16.

PAYKEL, E. S. Classification of depressed patients: A cluster analysis derived grouping. *British Journal of Psychiatry,* 1971, *188,* 275–288.

————. Life stress and psychiatric disorder. In B. S. Dohrenwend & B. P. Dohrenwend (eds.), *Stressful life events: Their nature and effects.* New York: John Wiley, 1974.

PAYKEL, E. S., & WEISSMAN, M. M. Social adjustment and depression: A longitudinal study. *Archives of General Psychiatry,* 1973, *28,* 659–663.

PEARLIN, L. I., & JOHNSON, J. S. Marital status, life-strains and depression. *American Sociological Review,* 1977, *42,* 704–715.

PEARLIN, L. I., & SCHOOLER, C. The structure of coping. *Journal of Health and Social Behavior,* 1978, *19,* 2–21.

PERSONS, J. B., & RAO, P. A. Longitudinal study of cognitions, life events, and depression in psychiatric inpatients. *Journal of Abnormal Psychology,* 1985, *94,* 51–63.

PESELOW, E. D., ROBINS, C., BLOCK, P., BAROUCHE, F., & FIEVE, R. R. Dysfunctional attitudes in depressed patients before and after clinical treatment and in normal control subjects. *American Journal of Psychiatry,* 1990, *147,* 439–444.

PICKAR, D., SWEENEY, D. R., MAAS, J. W., & HENINGER, G. R. Primary affective disorder, clinical state change, and MHPG excretion: A longitudinal study. *Archives of General Psychiatry,* 1978, *35,* 1378–1383.

REICH, J., NOYES, R., HIRSCHFELD, R., CORYELL, W., & O'GORMAN, T. State and personality in depressed and panic patients. *American Journal of Psychiatry,* 1987, *144,* 181–187.

RHODEWALT, F., & ZONE, J. B. Appraisal of life change, depression, and illness in hardy and non-hardy women. *Journal of Personality and Social Psychology,* 1989, *56,* 81–88.

ROBINS, C. J., & BLOCK, P. Personal vulnerability, life events, and depressive symptoms: A test of the specific interactional model. *Journal of Personality and Social Psychology,* 1988, *54,* 847–852.

ROTH, M., GURNEY, C., GARSIDE, R. F., & KERR, T. A. Studies in the classification of affective disorders: The relationship between anxiety states and depressive illnesses—I. *British Journal of Psychiatry,* 1972, *121,* 147–161.

ROY, A., PICKAR, D., LINNOILA, M., & POTTER, W. Z. Plasma norepinephrine level in affective disorders. *Archives of General Psychiatry,* 1985, *42,* 1181–1185.

RUSCHER, S. M., & GOTLIB, I. H. Marital interaction patterns of couples with and without a depressed partner. *Behavior Therapy,* 1988, *19,* 455–470.

SARASON, I. G., HOHNSON, J. H., & SIEGEL, J. M. Assessing the impact of life changes: Development of the Life Experiences Survey. *Journal of Consulting and Clinical Psychology,* 1978, *46,* 932–946.

SARGEANT, J. K., BRUCE, M. L., FLORIO, L. P., & WEISSMAN, M. M. Factors associated with 1-year outcome of major depression in the community. *Archives of General Psychiatry,* 1990, *47,* 519–526.

SIEVER, L. J. Role of noradrenergic mechanisms in the etiology of the affective disorders. In H. Y. Meltzer (ed.), *Psychopharmacology: The third generation of progress.* New York: Raven Press, 1987.

SIEVER, L. J., & UHDE, T. W. New studies and perspectives on the noradrenergic receptor system in depression: Effects of the alpha$_2$-adrenergic agonist clonidine. *Biological Psychiatry,* 1984, *19,* 131–156.

SLACK, D., & VAUX, A. Undesirable life events and depression: The role of event appraisals and social support. *Journal of Social and Clinical Psychology,* 1988, *7,* 290–296.

STOKES, P. E., & SIKES, C. R. Hypothalamic-pituitary-adrenal axis in affective disorders. In H. Y. Meltzer (eds.), *Psychopharmacology: The third generation of progress.* New York: Raven Press, 1987.

STOKES, P. E., STOLL, P. M., KOSLOW, S. H., MAAS, J. W., DAVIS, J. M., SWANN, A. C., & ROBINS, E. Pretreatment DST and hypothalamic-pituitary-adrenocortical function in depressed patients and comparison groups. *Archives of General Psychiatry,* 1984, *41,* 257–267.

SWEENEY, D. R., MAAS, J. W., & HENINGER, G. R. State anxiety, physical activity, and urinary 3-methoxy-4-hydroxyphenethylene glycol excretion. *Archives of General Psychiatry,* 1978, *35,* 1418–1423.

SWINDLE, R. W., CRONKITE, R. C., & MOOS, R. H. Life stressors, social resources, coping, and the 4-year course of unipiolar depression. *Journal of Abnormal Psychology,* 1989, *98,* 468–477.

THOMPSON, L., & WALKER, A. J. The dyad as the unit of analysis: Conceptual and methodological issues. *Journal of Marriage and the Family,* 1982, *44,* 889–900.

TURNER, R. J., & AVISON, W. R. Gender and depression: Assessing exposure and vulnerability to life events in a chronically strained population. *Journal of Nervous and Mental Disease,* 1989, *177,* 443–455.

VAUGHN, C. E., & LEFF, J. P. The influence of family and social factors on the course of psychiatric illness: A comparison of schizophrenic and depressed neurotic patients. *British Journal of Psychiatry,* 1976, *129,* 125–137.

WARD, M. M., MEFFORD, I. N., PARKER, S. D., CHESNEY, M. A., TAYLOR, B., KEEGAN, D. L., & BARCHAS, J. D. Epinephrine and norepinephrine responses in continuously collected human plasma to a series of stressors. *Psychosomatic Medicine,* 1983, *45,* 471–486.

WEISSMAN, M. M., & KLERMAN, G. K. Sex differences and the epidemiology of depression. *Archives of General Psychiatry,* 1977, *34,* 98–111.

WEISSMAN, M. M., LECKMAN, J. F., MERIKANGAS, K. R., GAMMON, G. D., & PRUSOFF, B. A. Depression and anxiety disorders in parents and children: Results from the Yale family study. *Archives of General Psychiatry,* 1984, *41,* 845–852.

WISE, E. H., & BARNES, D. R. The relationship among life events, dysfunctional attitudes, and depression. *Cognitive Therapy and Research,* 1986, *10,* 257–266.

WYATT, R. J., PORTNOY, B., KUPFER, D. J., SNYDER, F., & ENGELMAN, K. Resting plasma catecholamine concentrations in patients with depression and anxiety. *Archives of General Psychiatry,* 1971, *24,* 65–70.

PART VII

EXTREME STRESSORS

31

Interpersonal Violence and Traumatic Stress Reactions

Robert S. Pynoos   Susan B. Sorenson   Alan M. Steinberg

INTERPERSONAL VIOLENCE COVERS A BROAD RANGE of human experiences that involve harm, coercion, or threat. It entails injury or threat to the physical and/or psychological well-being of the individual, family, or group. The impact of interpersonal violence has developmental implications in that the safety and security of one's interpersonal life, expectations about the world, and sense of personal integrity are affected. Stress from violent life threats rests on the extreme of a spectrum of life stresses, from those of daily hassles (DeLongis, Coyne, Dakof, Folkman, & Lazarus, 1982); to negative life events such as divorce, unemployment, and death (Dohrenwend & Dohrenwend, 1974; Holmes & Rahe, 1967); to chronic role strain (Pearlin & Lieberman, 1979). Exposure to violence also carries a risk for depressive, anxiety, and post-traumatic stress reactions. Despite the intense personal efforts of victims to alleviate the psychological distress in the aftermath of these extreme situations, if it is to remain reality based, ongoing reappraisal only serves to confirm the original threat.

Traumatic stress reaction and *victimization* refer to complementary aspects of exposure to violence. The former refers to the subjective distress and disruption of normal adaptive functioning. Such reactions may range from a heightened sense of vulnerability and helplessness to a specific constellation of symptoms constituting psychiatric disturbance or dysfunction, such as post-traumatic stress disorder (PTSD). Victimization refers to the abrogation of expectations of the social contract within or outside the family. A victim is sanctioned to assume a social role that warrants restitution and/or special treatment and to expect society to bring the perpetrator to judicial accountability. Thus, victimization differs from other experiences in which violence may be anticipated, expected, and socially sanctioned—for example, athletic competition or military combat.

Issues of human accountability are difficult to resolve and entail additional sources of distress. These issues may encompass attributions of responsibility to the perpetrator, oneself, and others, including third party intervenors and social institutions. When the perpetrator is a stranger, responsibility may be easier to assign than when the agent is a family member, a situation in which issues of betrayal and conflicts of loyalty arise. Adjudication

The writing of this chapter was supported, in part, by the UCLA Program in Trauma, Violence and Sudden Bereavement, the Bing Fund, David Hockney, and the Southern California Injury Prevention Research Center (Centers of Disease Control grant R49/CCR903622).

of blame generally requires bringing a distressing private experience into the public domain; this step raises many secondary concerns for the victim and, thereby, links societal attitudes and action with the individual's attempt at trauma resolution.

A person may be victimized in a variety of ways, all of which involve the violation of social norms and moral standards. (1) A person may be the victim of intentional violence directed against the individual per se (rape, incest, or child, sibling, or spousal abuse). Intentional violence may occur within a discrete episode or may be repeated over time. (2) Violence may be directed against an individual as a representative of a group (racially, sexually, religiously, or politically motivated violence). (3) Violence may be instrumental— that is, based on the threat or use of violence against the individual as a means to achieve an end (armed robbery, or extortion involving kidnapping, hijacking, or terrorism). (4) Finally, violence may be the result of happenstance (drive-by shooting or drunk driving accident) in which the perpetrator's actions are reckless and endanger others.

Interpersonal violence involves several sources of stress. The most immediate source is the individual's experience of the violent situation. The individual's experience is influenced by a number of circumstantial factors, including the type of victimization, proximity to the violent threat, event intensity (as measured by the perceived or actual degree of life threat), the unexpectedness and duration of the experience, the use of a weapon, injury to oneself, injury or death to another, the number of threats during a particular episode, the nature of the relationship to the assailant and others under threat, and the perceived personal impact. One aspect of the components of the victimization experience has been described by Ochberg (1986) as including feelings of shame, self-blame, subjugation, morbid hatred, defilement, and resignation.

In the aftermath of a violent trauma, a number of secondary stressors are set in motion. These include medical attention for physical injury or forensic examinations, continued medical procedures and physical rehabilitation, participation in criminal proceedings from the initial police investigation to trial and sentencing, engagement with social agencies (for example, victim-witness programs, workman's compensation, or disability), and the need to learn new social skills to respond to social questioning, stigmatization, and altered role performance. These post-trauma stressors commonly generate additional adverse emotional reactions and practical problems. The term *secondary victimization* refers to how the social response can go badly awry in the aftermath of interpersonal violence (Symonds, 1980).

Victims of a violent crime need to rely on appropriate social supports, especially within the immediate family or community. However, family members and close friends of persons who have been victimized also may experience a series of stresses that generate emotional reactions that disturb their psychological and social functioning. While they are contending with their reactions, those close to the victim are expected by others, as well as themselves, to provide special support to the victim. Family members may witness the violence or receive graphic information about how a family member has been, for example, violently mutilated. They may have to endure an extended period of waiting until they know a family member is safe—for example, in a hostage or kidnapping situation or in the case of postassault emergency or surgical care. Worry about a significant other may constitute a severe stress with correspondingly high levels of fear and anxiety. Family and friends may assume supportive roles that tax their emotional resources. The sense that their own lives have been intruded upon and adversely changed by the actions of the perpetrator is implied in the term, *indirect victimization* (Friedman, Bischoff, Davis, & Person, 1982).

The psychological sequelae of criminal victimization has received increased recognition and scientific investigation. Traditionally, interest in mental health aspects of violence focused on the profile of the perpetrators and the genesis of violent behavior. Social interest began to change with the acknowledgment of the extent of physical injuries that result from child abuse (Kempe, Silverman, Steele, Droegemueller, & Silver, 1963) and the psychological concomitants of being raped (Burgess & Holmstrom, 1979). Mental health research has increasingly documented the stress of victimization as a risk factor for mental health problems (Burnam et al., 1988; Winfield, George, Swartz, & Blazer, 1990).

Recent legislation and judicial decisions also reflect increased acknowledgment of the stress of violent victimization. At one time, women who made an allegation of rape were commonly required to undergo a psychiatric evaluation. Results from the examination could then be used to call into question the veracity of the charge. The use of psychiatric testimony to impugn a woman victim has been sharply curtailed following reform of rape laws in the 1970s. Many states have enacted "rape shield" statutes that limit the use of evidence relating to an accuser's sexual history in rape trials. Recently, appellate court decisions have reinforced the admissibility and importance of expert psychiatric testimony for the purpose of "disabusing the jury about some widely held misconceptions about rape and rape victims," (Court of Appeal of the State of California, 1991).

Within this overall schema of various types of victimization and the historical context of victim mental health, we review patterns of individual victimization within a developmental framework. We then discuss psychological sequelae and the social implications of violent interpersonal victimization.

PATTERNS OF VICTIMIZATION THROUGH THE COURSE OF LIFE

Characteristics of interpersonal violence (e.g., type, frequency, and duration of the exposure) and adaptive resources are strongly related to developmental phase, age, sex, ethnicity, and socioeconomic status. Exposure to chronically dangerous situations has also been noted to be related to housing, educational, and employment factors (Breslau, Davis, Andreski, & Peterson, 1991). The type and nature of the personal relationship between the assailant and the victim (e.g., stranger or family member), as well as their relative social roles (e.g., female or male, white or African-American), are also related to both risk and recovery.

Both the varieties of events and the cumulative risk for victimization change over the individual's life time. Although crime surveys indicate that only 1 in 600 women is raped in a given year (U. S. Department of Justice, 1991a), a cumulative incidence approach to the data suggests that more than 1 in every 10 will be raped during her lifetime.

Child Victimization

Over the past several decades, there has been increasing recognition of the degree to which children are exposed to violence. As dependent members of a family, children's risk of violent traumatic events is strongly linked to the social, emotional, and physical environment of the family. Criminal victimization of children is more commonly due to sexual molestation or physical abuse than, for instance, to armed assault. Physical or sexual abuse of children usually does not involve a circumscribed violent experience but rather a pattern of multiple molestations or beatings within a disturbed environment. Rates of abuse of children are distressingly high; for example, each year 1 out of every 10 children is severely physically abused (i.e., kicked, bitten, hit with an object, beaten, threatened with a gun or knife, or had a gun or knife used against them) by their parents (Straus, Gelles, & Steinmetz, 1985). Children also are at special risk of witnessing violence to a family member— e.g., rape, murder, suicidal behavior (Malmquist, 1984; Pynoos & Eth, 1985), spousal abuse (Carlson, 1984), or abuse of a sibling (Pfouts, Schopler, & Henley, 1982).

The extent to which children and adolescents are direct victims of physical or sexual abuse or witness violence has only recently begun to be fully appreciated. Estimates indicate that each year there are 150,000 to 200,000 new cases of sexual abuse of a child (Finkelhor & Hotaling, 1984). Even at the lowest estimates of prevalence (see, Peters, Wyatt, & Finkelhor, 1986), as Conte (1991) has noted, it is clear that sexual abuse is a common experience affecting a large number of children. The sexual abuse of boys is gradually being recognized as more common than once thought (Bolton, Morris, & MacEachron, 1989; Hunter, 1990).

Specific family circumstances may be associated with increased risk of violent experiences for children—for example, parental psychopathology, lack of supervision, marital discord, maladaptive assortative mating, recent unemployment, and alcohol or other substance abuse by adult caretakers. The same factors that place a child at risk of direct victimization may contribute to exposure to witnessing other forms of violence. In addition, societal conditions influence the type of traumatic events to which children are likely to be exposed; for example, girls are at higher risk of sexual molestation from stepfathers than from biological fathers (Russell, 1983, 1984). Furthermore, social policies may lead to removing children from a disturbed family setting and placing them in foster or institutional care, thereby increasing the risk of further traumatization. Changing social conditions also have led to significant exposure to extrafamilial violence; for example, children in inner cities are at risk at younger ages (Richters & Saltzman, 1990). As children mature, their own personality may contribute to risk of exposure. For example, those with pre-existing conduct disturbances or substance abuse may place themselves in situations in which there is an added risk of violence.

Initially, in the area of child abuse, the recognition of physical injury preceded the acknowledgment of psychological harm. Our understanding of the psychological consequences of violent traumatic experiences for children and adolescents has considerably advanced. This change has resulted, in part, from a quiet revolution in research strategies to include age-appropriate and reliable methods of interviewing children in addition to the traditional use of parent, teacher, and other informants. Investigators have found important influences on the psychological, interpersonal, emotional, cognitive, and neurobiological development of children.

A major difference between child and adult victimization is that traumatic events in childhood occur during critical periods of personality formation, including the evolution of the internal representation of the self and others and the constant revision of the inner model of the world. Key developmental tasks or transitions may be adversely affected by violent experiences. Early violent trauma may have a far-reaching influence on attachment behavior. In preschool-aged children, traumatic experiences may reappear in the form of behavioral or play re-enactments, which are not readily assimilated into verbal communication even with increasing maturity. By comparison, trauma during adolescence may interfere with the task of integrating past, present, and future orientation; exacerbate moral confusion; and compromise the development of symbolic thinking and expression (Pynoos & Nader, 1992a). The developmental level of the child, prior life experience, and family response mediates the degree to which these traumas are integrated into the personality or become a major theme in character structure.

Chronic or repetitive violent trauma in childhood is associated with profound restrictions in emotional responsiveness, pervasive interpersonal avoidant behavior, atypical modulation of aggression, and increased frequency of dissociative responses. Chronic sexual abuse is associated with many of these symptoms also, including nightmares, phobic/avoidant behaviors, and repetitive/inappropriate sexual behaviors (Friedrich, Urquiza, & Beilke, 1986). Sexual abuse appears to be more highly associated with post-traumatic stress disorder than physical abuse (Deblinger, McLeer, Atkins, Ralphe, & Foa, 1989). The cumulative effects may lead to severe disturbances in object relations, affect tolerance, and impulse control (including self-injurious behavior). The violent exposure may serve as one of several complex antecedents to borderline personality disorder (Herman, Perry, & van der Kolk, 1989) or, in the extreme, to multiple personality or other dissociative disorders (Putnam, 1985). By the time these traumatized children reach adulthood, there may be a multiplicity of clinical presentations.

Adult Victimization

Victimization of adults, like the victimization of children, includes violence by known persons and is expanded by street and other violent crimes. Criminal victimization is surprisingly common. According to law enforcement data, 17% of households experienced at least one attempted or completed theft, and 5% of households had at least one member who was the victim of a violent crime against persons (rape, robbery, or aggravated or simple assault) in 1990 (U. S. Department of Justice, 1991b). Only 34% of the victimizations were reported to police (U. S. Department of Justice, 1991c). Risk varies significantly by race/ethnicity and gender.

Two forms of victimization are relatively common for adult women—sexual assault and battering. One in 12 college women is the victim of a rape or attempted raped each year; more than 1 in 4 is sexually victimized in some other form (Koss, Gidycz, & Wisniewski, 1987). Research has shown that nearly 1 out of every 5 women emergency department patients is seeking treatment for injuries sustained at the hands of her male intimate (Stark et al., 1981). The cause of most of these injuries goes undetected (McCleer & Anwar, 1989); without such identification an opportunity for an appropriate intervention and referral is lost. Battered women, by definition, are at higher risk for injury and for spontaneous abortion. Emergency departments, obstetric and gynecological services, and prenatal care services provide excellent settings in which physical injury and risk of injury can be detected.

Psychological understandings of battering are grounded in research on learned helplessness and have been used, along with social role explanations (e.g., differential pay, status within society), to describe why battered women return to their male batterers. The Stockholm syndrome, in which victims identify with and protect aggressors on whom their existence depends, recently has been applied to situations of battering (Graham, Rawlings, & Rimini, 1989).

Models of victimization have not always sufficiently considered the interaction between violent experiences and adult development. The impact of a violent experience occurs within the context of the current developmental challenges in an adult's life. Developmental spheres encompass interpersonal and occupational functioning, financial and health status, and personal goals related to psychological stability, self-efficacy, and personal gratification. To illustrate, sexual assault can occur in the course of the development of a relationship, from dating to serious involvement and commitment. If a rape occurs in early to middle adolescence, there may be a prolonged delay in dating behavior that may interfere with the acquisition of certain interpersonal skills. Perhaps rape by a stranger may jeopardize an intimate relationship that is in transition from being casual to serious, whereas there may be less interpersonal risk in the context of a longstanding stable commitment.

In contrast to young children, who typically respond to violent trauma with alarm, adults frequently respond with an acknowledged sense of surrendering to a moment of unavoidable danger. The experience of traumatic helplessness is inconsistent with perceptions of adult competency and can lead to subsequent changes in ambition, initiative, and assertiveness (Krystal, 1991). Violent trauma or loss may lead to reactivation of latent negative self-images that challenge adult adaptive functioning (Horowitz, Wilner, Marmar, & Krupnick, 1980). The attribution of meaning to the experience and secondary behavioral changes may depend on well-formed personality traits and may reflect exaggerations or inhibitions, more than discontinuities, in internal mechanisms of emotional regulation and cognitive processing. In addition, the adult must accommodate or assimilate the extreme, violent nature of the experience into an already well-formed schematization of the world (Horowitz & Kaltreider, 1979).

Elder Victimization

An often-neglected and unrecognized form of victimization is that perpetrated against elders. Four major types of abuse specifically against elders have been identified: physical, material, medical, and emotional (Finkelhor & Hotaling, 1984). Physical abuse of elders appears to be spousal abuse grown old (Pillemer & Finkelhor, 1988). Caretaker and family violence toward the elderly highlight the need for further exploration of the interface between societal and personal responsibility for frail elders (Select Committee on Aging, 1990).

The elderly face unique developmental issues in addressing violence. The violent trauma occurs at a time in life when they are coming to terms with loss of social status, loss of relatives and friends, restricted income, reduced social role function, and increased dependency on others. As a result, coping and adjustment resources may be more limited and compromised. Victimization of this group has been highlighted by the recent exposure of a number of financial fraud schemes aimed at the retirement savings of the elderly.

The elderly face particular fears regarding their own vulnerability to criminal assault and, although they are at lower risk (U.S. Department of Justice, 1987), their reaction to an assault may be to engage in future avoidant behaviors that adversely restrict and change the quality of their daily lives. Perception of self-efficacy in meeting and coping with violent threat may be low among the elderly. A large percentage of elders are widows living alone, without spousal financial and social support and with other sources of family support often at a distance. Elders may circumscribe their behavior out of fear of victimization, regardless of whether they have been the direct victim of a crime (Fattah & Sacco, 1989).

Elders, due to vulnerabilities associated with osteoporosis, unsteady gait, failing eyesight, and other physiological declines related to aging, are at relatively high risk of physical injury from a violent event. Thus, a violent victimization would place them at special health risk. In addition, there is some evidence that the elderly are vulnerable to depression secondary to victimization, especially when accompanied by physical injury and property or financial loss (Maida, Gordon, Steinberg, & Gordon, 1989). As the U.S. population ages, the health, mental health, and social sequelae of violence against the elderly will require increased investigation and attention.

PATTERNS OF STRESSORS ACROSS THE LIFE SPAN

A model of violence-related traumatic stress or victimization needs to include an interactive historical perspective that can examine the interplay of previous and current trauma on adaptive functioning. The developmental consequences of childhood victimization carry potential risk for further adult victimization and, at the same time, may contribute to diminished resistance or resilience when confronted with adult traumas. For example, young men with a history of child abuse who leave home prematurely by volunteering for the armed services and who receive high exposure to combat may be more prone to negative and chronic postwar outcomes. Women who were sexually abused as children appear to be at higher risk for adult sexual assault and may not resist or be as self-protective in certain situations as a woman without such a history (Wyatt, Guthrie, & Notgrass, in press). Traumatic experiences across the life course may therefore serve to influence one another and subsequent coping. Current violent exposures can serve as powerful reminders of past traumatic experiences, compound psychological distress, and further compromise efforts to adapt. Traumatic experiences, human development, and social context comprise a complex matrix.

PSYCHOLOGICAL SEQUELAE

Violence-induced post-traumatic stress reactions are difficult to categorize along the traditional spectrum of normal to pathological responses. The acute reactions can be conceptualized as understandable and expected; thus, professional and societal care must be taken not to impose psychopathological labels that can result in the attribution of additional psychopathology and stigma. Alternatively, acute reactions may involve severe subjective distress, altered behaviors, or neurophysiological dysregulation that do not recede naturally. Early identification and intervention may be critical to prevent these symptoms from becoming chronic and disabling.

Violent situations involve intense perceptual experiences, internal moment-to-moment appraisals of threat, and continuous outcome assessment, including thoughts and fantasies of intervention. The central emotion is often fear, ranging to terror, horror, and helpless despair (Kolb & Mutalipassi, 1982), violation, or deep betrayal. Following the episode, the person is left with the challenge of tolerating an intensity of emotional reaction that necessitates increased efforts at emotional regulation. The event may remain in prolonged active memory and constantly threaten to intrude upon and disrupt normal information processing (Horowitz, 1986). Reminders of the violence stimulate intrusive thoughts and images and generate renewed emotional distress and physiological reactivity, which secondarily result in trauma-related behaviors such as efforts to prevent recurrence of the trauma and to avoid reminders. Traumatic reminders renew physiological and psychological reactivity and account for some of the phasic nature of the course of symptoms.

The extreme intensity of some situations will lead to an initial set of negative reactions in virtually anyone, whereas under less extreme exposure individual vulnerability factors will exert more influence (Hocking, 1970). After extreme situations, a person may immediately experience generalized anxiety, narrowing of attention, apparent disorientation, anger or verbal aggression, despair or hopelessness, inappropriate or purposeless overactivity, outrage at the intrusion, and a profound sense of ineffectualness (Weisaeth, 1989). Especially when there has been death or injury to others, these acute reactions may include uncontrollable and excessive grief and intense guilt over behaviors of omission or commission specific to the event (Weisaeth, 1989).

Individuals vary in the ability to tolerate and respond to acute disturbances in psychological functioning, to adversities consequent to the event, and to the subsequent challenge to their self-concept, meaning, and future orientation. Outcome may range from a relatively successful adaptation that includes restored psychological, interpersonal, and occupational functioning, to severe trauma-related pathology and pervasive functional impairment. The set of trauma-related reactions may constitute recognizable patterns of psychiatric disorder, including depression, alcohol and drug abuse, and phobic, generalized anxiety, obsessive-compulsive, dissociative, or post-traumatic stress disorders (Winfield, George, Swartz, & Blazer, 1990).

The clinical diagnostic criteria for PTSD include symptoms of re-experiencing, avoidance and withdrawal, and increased arousal (American Psychiatric Association, 1987). Re-experiencing phenomena include recurrent intrusive distressing recollections of the trauma, dreams or nightmares of the event, flashbacks, and psychological reactivity to reminders of the event. Symptoms of avoidance and withdrawal include efforts to avoid feelings or thoughts of the trauma and activities or situations that provoke such recollections and feeling detached or estranged from others. Symptoms of increased arousal include hypervigilance, exaggerated startle reactions, sleep disturbance, dysregulation of aggression, and physiologic reactivity to reminders. Disturbances of memory can include omissions, distortions, and amnestic or dissociative reactions.

The functional impact of arousal symptoms is related to developmental stage and interplay with current daily activities. Hypervigilance and exaggerated physiological reactivity may alter a child's usual behavior by leading to chronic efforts to ensure personal security or the safety of others. These recurrent "bouts" of fear may adversely alter a child's emerging self-concept. Temporary or chronic difficulties in the modulation of aggression may alter peer relationships and lead to unusual acts of aggression or social withdrawal. In adults, irritability may interfere with interactions at work and place a strain on intimate personal relationships. A chronic sleep disturbance may interfere with a child's learning and school performance or impair an adult's job performance and decisionmaking. Changing societal values determine to what degree these impairments are socially recognized as meriting special consideration or compensation.

The risk of PTSD is related to a number of circumstantial factors. For example, rape by a stranger, use of physical force, display of a weapon, and injury to the victim are associated with increased risk of PTSD in rape victims (Bownes, O'Gorman, & Sayers, 1991). Similar findings have been reported for battered women, where the risk for PTSD has been shown to be linked with characteristics of the battery experience (Kemp, Rawlings, & Green, 1991). Kilpatrick et al. (1985) reported that suicide attempts were higher for crime victims than nonvictims. Dahl (1989) reported that rape victims suffer more acute guilt, shame, and suicidal ideation as compared with individuals who experience civilian accidents or industrial disaster. In a community sample, Sorenson and Golding (1990) found that individuals who were mugged, sexually assaulted, or experienced multiple victimizations during the previous six months were at greatest risk for current depression. Longitudinal studies have indicated that a proportion of victims of violence remain symptomatic for years, and that if anxiety and/or PTSD symptoms persist beyond three months, they are not likely to remit without intervention (Kilpatrick, Veronen, & Resick, 1979).

The rate of comorbidity may represent an interplay between specific trauma-related reactions and those associated with the accumulation of secondary adversities following the violent experience. For example, intense depressive reactions may be associated with repeated hospitalization, reconstructive surgery, or temporary and sometimes permanent disability. At the same time, these medical procedures or disabilities may also act as unavoidable, recurrent reminders of the circumstances of the trauma and thus require additional emotional effort to contend with post-traumatic reactions.

The interplay of trauma and grief constitutes another dimension to victimization. Psychosocial responses to exposure to events in which there is unnatural death have been described. Rynearson (1990) has emphasized three important aspects of unnatural death, including violence (injury), violation (transgression), and volition (willful intention or negligence), to which family members or friends must adjust. He notes that compulsive inquiry, undertaken to provide a frame of meaning for an irrational death, is intensified in homicide or accidental death where the perpetrator is not found and in survivors of those who have died by suicide and that the combination of post-traumatic stress reactions, victimization and compulsive inquiry are associated with unnatural death. Pynoos (1992) has pointed out that violent death complicates the bereavement process by keeping attention focused to the circumstances of the death, including a mutilated image of the deceased and issues of accountability. These preoccupations interfere with efforts to address the meaning of the loss by impeding positive reminiscing and remembering of the deceased. These traumatic sequelae may increase the risk of pathological bereavement, depression, and chronic PTSD.

Self-revelation, disclosure, and social communication have been noted to be important factors that mediate even the psychosomatic repercussions of trauma. Inhibition of disclosure may serve as a cumulative stressor that adversely affects physical and psychological well-being (Pennebaker & Susman, 1988).

LEARNING, MEMORY, AND PHYSIOLOGICAL REACTIVITY

A comprehensive explanatory framework for understanding the formation, content, and course of post-traumatic stress reactions to violence will incorporate a multifaceted model that encompasses a variety of principles of learning and memory. This framework will also include consideration of the acute neurophysiological responses and the more prolonged neurochemical, hormonal, and neuroanatomical changes that can result from exposure to extreme stress.

Different models of learning provide alternative vantage points on aspects of traumatic memory and post-trauma behavior. For example, one-trial learning models may be critical to understanding the encoding and storage of information related to experiences of extreme danger or life threat and the evolutionary significance of memories that are resistent to extinction. One-trial learning may be related to a hard-wired neuromechanism (neuro convergence) that marks memories as important (Garcia, Lasiter, Bermudez-Rattoni, & Deems, 1986). Given the fight-or-flight response associated with highly aversive experience, one-trial learning may involve hormonal influences (particularly peripheral release of adrenaline and/or adrenocorticotrophic hormone that increase brain glucose and thus facilitate memory (Gold, 1987; McGaugh, 1983).

Classical models of conditioning and instrumental learning (Mowrer, 1947) suggest ways that continued exposure to traumatic cues can lead to chronic avoidant behavior and increased efforts at emotional regulation. State-dependent learning (Weingartner, 1978) may explain the greater likelihood of the occurrence of re-experiencing phenomena under conditions of renewed anxiety, stress, or dysphoria, as well as the inaccessibility of aspects of the traumatic experience in post-trauma conscious memory.

Traumatic memories may lead to a constricted associative network that widely tags traumatic details that were previously neutral or positive with negative, trauma-related meaning. Theories of memory retrieval as a memory modifier (Bjork & Richardson-Klavehn, 1989) suggest that distortions, omissions, and spatial misrepresentations of threat may occur during the retrieval process, as opposed to being associated with an encoding or storage error (Pynoos & Nader, 1992b). Under the right contextual conditions, retrieval mechanisms may be initiated even years later, when highly charged traumatic cues produce a full stimulus completion and recall of the experience.

In addition to learning theories, traditional psychoanalytic theories can provide a framework in which to examine the attribution of meaning to special details of the event (Freud, 1966), the unique configuration of traumatic meaning that derives from past experience and current context (Lindy, 1985), the internal representation of catastrophic emotions (Rangell, 1991), the disruption of the synthetic functions of the ego (Bernstein, 1990), and vulnerability to future life stresses (Greenacre, 1952). Current psychodynamic models provide another perspective to examine cognitive and affective regulation and the interplay of unconscious and conscious schematization of internal and external threats (Horowitz, 1986).

Traumatic stress may initiate significant alterations in a number of neurophysiological and neurochemical processes that underlie clinically observable symptoms. Exposure to extreme life threat appears to elicit physiological stress responses in the brain, autonomic nervous system, and the hypothalamic-pituitary adrenocortical (HPA) axis (see Perry, 1992). Although the preponderance of biological studies of exposure to violence have focused on veterans of combat (Pitman, 1988), preliminary work suggests that similar biological disturbances can be found among victims of civilian trauma (Ornitz & Pynoos, 1989; Shalev, Orr, Peri, Schreiber, & Pitman, 1991).

Increases in noradrenergic activity in the locus coeruleus (which regulates a number of functions including affect, irritability, arousal, attention, and startle) and in the central nucleus of the amygdala (involved in the regulation of fear) may be associated with exposure to extreme stress. There may be increases in catecholamine activity in the brain that result in increased reactivity to future stressful events. Abnormal patterns of catecholamine activity associated with prolonged "alarm reactions" may result in abnormal brain stem functioning, including altered cardiovascular regulation, increased anxiety, increased startle response, and sleep abnormalities (Perry, in press). Altered responsivity to trauma-related reminders may represent both central adrenergic and peripheral sympathetic nervous system dysregulation (Krystal et al. 1989).

Potential Treatment Issues

Although the field lacks comparative treatment studies, a sufficient body of clinical knowledge has emerged to suggest a number of therapeutic guidelines. The type and duration of intervention often depend on the amount of therapeutic attention needed to address trauma-associated external and internal dangers and related individual factors and secondary adversities (Pynoos & Nader, 1992b). Despite advances in treatment, the primary public health concern should remain that of preventing the precipitating events.

The goal of psychological first aid is to provide important emotional relief through immediate psychological and social services and age-appropriate interventions. After catastrophic community violence, school classrooms, workplaces, and religious and cultural centers are settings in which to: (1) provide information about typical post-trauma reactions and expectations about the recovery process; (2) minimize the fear of recurrence and its continued interference with everyday activities or tasks; and (3) identify children and adults at risk for post-trauma stress and grief reactions.

Early intervention also permits contextual understanding of the violent experience within the life situation and culture of the individual, family, and community. In monitoring the acute disturbances, the clinician can attend to the impact on phase-specific narcissistic vulnerabilities and to cognitive, interpersonal, and psychosexual disturbances. By remaining attentive to secondary changes in the person's life, the clinician can help the individual and his or her family to choose appropriate practical responses.

Most therapeutic approaches to violence-induced post-traumatic stress reactions incorporate cognitive and emotional reprocessing of the traumatic memories. The traumatic cues, the emotional meaning of the event, and its personal impact are embedded in the details of the experience. The clinician must be prepared to hear everything, however horrifying or sad (Haley, 1974). The unexpected nature of reminders and the lack of understanding of their association to the trauma may re-evoke a sense of unpreparedness and a lack of control. The victim can be assisted to identify traumatic reminders that elicit intrusive imagery, intense affective responses, and psychophysiological reactions. All therapy approaches targeted at the resolution of trauma share a number of goals: to enhance tolerance for the feelings of fear, helplessness, and vulnerability generated by the experience; to permit the traumatic memories to recede in their influence on thinking and daily behavior; and to promote a sense of courage, rather than fear, in the task of assimilating the violent experience.

Although immediate consultation and crisis intervention may prove adequate for some victims, many severely exposed and other at-risk children and adults will require further therapeutic interventions. The violent experience may involve a complex succession of traumatic moments, even within a short period of time, that generate a wide spectrum of trauma-related cues and associations. Therefore, cognitive-behavioral or psychodynamic brief therapy may be needed to permit adequate exploration and reworking (Foy, Resnick, Carroll, & Osato, 1991; Horowitz, 1986), with therapeutic attention progressing toward the most terrifying and irreversibly damaging moments. To assist in complete emotional processing (Rachman, 1980), special attention should be paid to omissions, spatial misrepresentations, memory disturbances, cognitive shifts, and altered focus, which indicate a suppression of normal fears.

Cognitive-behavioral approaches rely on learning theories of fear acquisition and the role of re-exposure and cognitive restructuring in reducing the intensity and frequency of fear and anxiety reactions. These approaches take account of the complicated hierarchy of fearful moments that emerge or evolve from traumatic events (Saigh, 1988) and the need to include reworking of the meaning of the event as dangerous (Foa & Kozak, 1986). There have been recent efforts to develop an accelerated extinction paradigm for traumatic memories (Shapiro, 1989).

Psychodynamic approaches emphasize a hierarchy of internal dangers and the complex affective states that characterize the victim's experience and subsequent response. They recognize that meaningful associations are linked to each moment within the traumatic event and its aftermath; these associations recruit unconscious conflict from pre-existing developmental issues and self-regulatory mechanisms. Furthermore, the demands on prior mental schemas of danger, protection, and intervention are likely to elicit concerns from childhood and adolescence regarding safety, risk, injury, loss, and parental protection or supervision and similar adult worries about independence and parenting.

Preliminary psychopharmacological studies are beginning to provide data about the relative efficacy of a variety of medications in treating different sets of symptoms seen in patients with PTSD. Re-experiencing symptoms (e.g., flashbacks and nightmares) and hyperarousal symptoms (e.g., hypervigilence, insomnia, irritability, and exaggerated startle) may be selectively treated with pharmacological agents. Symptoms that have been most resistant to pharmacotherapy include: emotional numbing, affective constriction, avoidance, memory disturbances, and impulse control. However, some of these symptoms may improve secondarily when levels of arousal and re-experiencing are diminished. At the same time, reduction of tonic and phasic physiological activity may facilitate psychotherapy by permitting fuller registration and tolerance of traumatic reminders and better cognitive discrimination.

Personal adaptation can be aided or hampered by the nature and timing of social support. Relatively little social training prepares one for the role of victim of interpersonal violence. Nonetheless, persons who have been victimized are likely to need to guide others as to how to provide the most helpful support. Such guidance is included under the umbrella of learning appropriate assertion, where the person gives legitimate affective expression within the context of current personal needs. As individuals develop greater facility in the role of victim, they may need to develop skills to differentiate when to simply acknowledge offers of supportive interest or to respond fully to specific queries; such responses are likely to trigger reminders of the event that would not be helpful in the person's attempt to develop a greater sense of, for example, on-the-job competence. Furthermore, the victim must deal with the incongruity between what others believe to be helpful and what they express (Lehman, Ellard, & Wortman, 1986).

The family provides a key context for reinstating a sense of safety and security. This goal is inherently jeopardized when the agent and victim of the violence are members of the same family. Other family members may require their own therapeutic intervention before they can adequately provide ongoing support to a spouse, parent, child, or sibling who was the immediate victim. A primary goal of family therapy is to help family members validate and legitimize each other's psychological tasks, thereby facilitating continued mutual support. Because of different degrees of exposure, family members may experience estrangement or impatience with one another. The skills of family members can be enhanced through education on post-traumatic stress reactions, realistic expectations about the course of recovery, differing psychological agendas, the management of temporary behavioral alterations or regressions, and the importance of encouraging open communications. Likewise, group therapy offers the opportunity to reinforce the normative nature of reactions and recovery, to share mutual concerns, to address common fears and traumatic reminders and avoidant behaviors, to increase tolerance for disturbing emotions, to provide early attention to depressive reactions, and to aid recovery through age-appropriate and situation-specific problem solving.

A pulsed intervention model may serve as an intermediary between brief and long-term intervention strategies. In this model, an acute phase of treatment is followed by planned periods of consultation (Budman & Gurman, 1988). After initial treatment, the individual will be seen by the clinician at certain critical junctures, determined by anticipated or reported reminders, including judicial proceedings, and at important life transitions or challenges that may be compromised by renewed symptoms.

Long-term treatment of violence-related psychological disturbance involves techniques and goals in common with other forms of long-term psychotherapy. However, recognition that emotional meaning remains embedded in the violent experience remains a constant feature of therapeutic work with persons who have experienced violence. Attention is given to revised intrapsychic schemas or conflicts, narcissistic accommodations, and traumatic influences on personality. Previous trauma, including chronic or repetitive trauma, may lead to oscillations between past and present experiences. Intrafamilial violence requires attention to the pre-existing relationship with the perpetrator, to issues of identification and conflict of loyalty, to vulnerabilities secondary to a chronically impulse-ridden environment, and to the stigma and legacy of domestic violence. When the trauma is violent and massive, a central goal is to alleviate dangerous unconscious re-enactment behavior and to address conscious and unconscious intervention fantasies, especially unresolved revenge fantasies and accompanying preoccupations with rescue or reparative roles. Resolution of associated psychosexual disturbances also may require more extended therapeutic intervention.

Social Ramifications

Numerous social issues regarding victimization extend beyond the immediate physical and psychological concerns of the victim and victim's family. The social and financial costs of victimization, in terms of medical and psychological care, loss of productive time, chronic disability, loss of function, and loss of life and property are enormous. The federal and state mandated victim-witness assistance programs are a public legislated response to the burden of these costs for the individual and community.

The evidence of an epidemic of violence in the United States has been recognized for more than two decades (West, 1982). More recently, former Surgeon-General C. Everett Koop, M.D., pronounced victimization by violence to be a major public health problem in the United States (Health Resources and Services Administration, 1986). The epidemic of violence is having differential effects on different segments of our population. For example, for persons born in the United States in 1989, the lifetime probability of becoming a homicide victim varies from 1 in 496 for a white female to 1 in 29 for a black male (U.S. Department of Justice, 1990). School-based conflict resolution programs aimed at adolescents (Prothrow-Stith, 1987) have originated as a response to this alarming rate of violent death among the young.

In some respects, attention to childhood trauma has rested on recognition of the potential societal cost in terms of maladaptive adult behavior. Much of the concern about child abuse has centered on the transgenerational implications for perpetuating a cycle of violence (Widom, 1989). In the current discussions of homelessness and prostitution among adolescents, the change to referring to the children as "throw-aways" rather than as "runaways" more fully acknowledges that these children are often escaping from intolerable abuse and neglect rather than simply being wayward youth.

The prospect of victimization has a broader influence on the social structure of society. Fear of victimization functions as an anticipatory mechanism and governs attitudinal, behavioral, and economic dimensions. This phenomenon is widely recognized by the general public; media headlines highlight how urban dwellers who have installed multiple locks on doors and windows, put bars on their windows, set up sophisticated electronic security systems, and contracted for private security surveillance are "prisoners in their own homes." The fear of being victimized is so strong that they have taken numerous and sometimes extreme methods to protect themselves from an environment perceived as hostile and threatening (New York Times, 1992).

Ironically, such measures have been linked to increased exposure to victimization. Criminal behavior responds to changes in available citizen protection technology. Sophisticated automobile alarm systems appear to thwart vehicle theft from parking lots; however, according to police reports, criminal behavior has changed in order to steal such cars. Robbers now identify the vehicle and follow the owner to his or her residence, where the auto is taken. Thus, what in the past would have been an automobile theft with no threat of personal harm has become what the media is calling "in your face" crime, with increased risk of personal injury and trauma (New York Times, 1992).

Fear of victimization is also recognized to function as a form of social control. Feminists have emphasized how the fear of rape serves to keep women "in their place" (Brownmiller, 1975). Women are taught that they should not go out late at night, should not walk alone, should not get in their car without checking the back seat first, etc. The constant concern for physical safety can limit women's efforts to assume a broad range of social roles and to fully function without self-imposed or outside restrictions. In addition, such social expectations serve to raise questions about whether women are responsible for their own victimization.

Victimization engenders strong emotions, conflicts, and fears throughout society. Heinous crimes evoke powerful, irrational demands and moral necessities to obtain justice far beyond the utilitarian purpose of punishment and deterrence (Ehrenzweig, 1971). The increased demand for retributive justice and the compelling psychological need to rid society of possible threats shape elements of the social system, as reflected in current public debates over capital punishment and the right to bear arms.

REFERENCES

AMERICAN PSYCHIATRIC ASSOCIATION. *Diagnostic and statistical manual of mental disorders* (3d ed., rev.) Washington, DC: APA, 1987.

BERNSTEIN, A. E. The impact of incest trauma on ego development. In H. B. Levine (ed.), *Adult analysis and childhood sexual abuse*. Hillsdale, NJ: Analytic Press, 1990.

BJORK, R. A., & RICHARDSON-KLAVEHN, A. On the puzzling relationship between environmental context and human memory. In C. Izawa (ed.), *Current issues in cognitive processes: The Tulane Flowertree symposium on cognition*. Hillsdale, NJ: Lawrence Erlbaum, 1989.

BOLTON, F. G., MORRIS, L. A., & MACEACHRON, A. A. *Males at risk*. Newbury Park, CA: Sage, 1989.

BOWNES, I. T., O'GORMAN, E. C., & SAYERS, A. Assault characteristics and post-traumatic stress disorder in rape victims. *Acta Psychiatrica Scandinavica*, 1991, *83*, 27–30.

BRESLAU, N., DAVIS, G. C., ANDRESKI, P., & PETERSON, E. Traumatic events and posttraumatic stress disorder in an urban population of young adults. *Archives of General Psychiatry*, 1991, *48*, 216–222.

BROWNMILLER, S. *Against our will: Men, women and rape*. New York: Simon and Schuster, 1975.

BUDMAN, S. H., & GURMAN, A. S. *Theory and practice of brief therapy.* New York: Guilford Press, 1988.

BURGESS, A. W., & HOLMSTROM, L. L. *Rape: Crisis and recovery.* Bowie, MD: Robert S. Brady, 1979.

BURNAM, A., STEIN, J. A., GOLDING, J. M., SIEGEL, J. M., SORENSON, S. B., FORSYTHE, A. B., & TELLES, C. A. Sexual assault and mental disorders in a community population. *Journal of Consulting and Clinical Psychology,* 1988, *56,* 843–850.

CARLSON, B. E. Children's observations of interparental violence. In A. R. Roberts (ed.), *Battered women and their families: Intervention strategies and treatment programs.* New York: Springer, 1984.

CONTE, J. Overview of child sexual abuse. In A. Tasman & S. M. Goldfinger (eds.), *Review of Psychiatry.* Washington, DC: American Psychiatric Press, 1991.

COURT OF APPEAL OF THE STATE OF CALIFORNIA. Second Appellate District, Div. II, A739258, May 7, 1991.

DAHL, S. Acute response to rape—a PTSD variant. *Acta Psychiatrica Scandinavica* 1989 (suppl. 355), *80,* 56–62.

DEBLINGER, E., MCLEER, S. V., ATKINS, M. S., RALPHE, D., & FOA, E. Post-traumatic stress in sexually abused, physically abused, and nonabused children. *Child Abuse and Neglect,* 1989, *13,* 403–408.

DOHRENWEND, B. S., & DOHRENWEND, B. P. (eds.) *Stressful life events: Their nature and effects.* New York: Wiley, 1974.

DELONGIS, A., COYNE, J. C., DAKOF, G., FOLKMAN, S., & LAZARUS, R. S. Relationship of daily hassles, uplifts, and major life events to health status. *Health Psychology,* 1982, *1,* 119–136.

EHRENZWEIG, A. A. *Psychoanalytic jurisprudence.* New York: Oceana Publications, 1971.

FATTAH, E. A., & SACCO, V. F. *Crime and victimization of the elderly.* New York: Springer-Verlag, 1989.

FINKLEHOR, D., & HOTALING, G. T. Sexual abuse in the National Incidence Study of Child Abuse and Neglect: An appraisal. *Child Abuse and Neglect,* 1984, *8,* 23–32.

FOA, E. B., & KOZAK, M. S. Emotional processing of fear: Exposure to corrective information. *Psychological Bulletin,* 1986, *99,* 20–35.

FOY, D. W., RESNICK, H. S., CARROLL, E. M., & OSATO, S. S. Behavior therapy. In A. S. Bellack & M. Hersen (eds.), *Handbook of comparative treatments for adult disorders.* New York: Guilford Press, 1991.

FREUD, A. Comments on psychic trauma. In *The writings of Anna Freud.* Vol 5. New York: International Universities Press, 1966.

FRIEDMAN, K., BISCHOFF, H., DAVIS, R. K., & PERSON, A. *Samaritan blues. Victims and helpers: Reactions to crime* (Summary of grant report, National Institute of Justice, grant 79-N1AX0059). New York: Victims Services Agency, 1982.

FRIEDRICH, W. N., URQUIZA, A. J., & BEILKE, R. L. Behavior problems in sexually abused young children. *Journal of Pediatric Psychology,* 1986, *2,* 47–57.

GARCIA, J., LASITER, P. S., BERMUDEZ-RATTONI, F., & DEEMS, A. A general theory of aversion learning. *Annals of the New York Academy of Sciences,* 1986, *43,* 8–21.

GOLD, P. E. Sweet memories. *American Scientist,* 1987, *75,* 151–155.

GRAHAM, D. L. R., RAWLINGS, E., & RIMINI, N. Survivors of terror: Battered women, hostages and the Stockholm syndrome. In K. Yllo & M. Bograd (eds.), *Feminist perspectives on wife abuse.* Newbury Park, CA: Sage, 1989.

GREENACRE, P. The predispostion to anxiety. In P. Greenacre (ed.), *Trauma, growth and personality.* New York: International Universities Press, 1952.

HALEY, S. A. When the patient reports atrocities. *Archives of General Psychiatry,* 1974, *30,* 191–196.

Health Resources and Services Administration. *Surgeon General's workshop on violence and public health report* (Publication no. HRS-D-MC 86-1). Washington, DC: Department of Health and Human Services, 1986.

Herman, J. L., Perry, J. C., & van der Kolk, B. A. Childhood trauma in borderline personality disorder. *American Journal of Psychiatry,* 1989, *146,* 490–495.

Hocking, F. Extreme environmental stress and its significance for psychopathology. *American Journal of Psychotherapy,* 1970, *24,* 4–26.

Holmes, T. H., & Rahe, R. H. The Social Readjustment Rating Scale. *Journal of Psychosomatic Research,* 1967, *11,* 213–218.

Horowitz, M. J. *Stress response syndomes* (2d ed.). Northvale, NJ: Aronson, 1986.

Horowitz, M. J., & Kaltreider, N. B. Brief therapy of the stress response syndrome. *Psychiatric Clinics of North America,* 1979, *2,* 365–377.

Horowitz, M. J., Wilner, N., Marmar, C., & Krupnick, J. Pathological grief and the activation of latent self-images. *American Journal of Psychiatry,* 1980, *137,* 1157–1162.

Hunter, M. *Abused boys: The neglected victims of sexual abuse.* Lexington, MA: Lexington Books, 1990.

Kemp, A., Rawlings, E. I., & Green, B. L. Post-traumatic stress disorder (PTSD) in battered women: A shelter sample. *Journal of Traumatic Stress,* 1991, *4,* 137–148.

Kempe, C. H., Silverman, F. N., Steele, B. F., Droegemueller, W., & Silver, H. K. The battered child syndrome. *Journal of the American Medical Association,* 1963, *181,* 17–24.

Kilpatrick, D. G., Best, C. L., Veronen, L. J., Amick, A. E., Villeponteaux, L. A., & Ruff, G. A. Mental health correlates of criminal victimization: A random community survey. *Journal of Consulting Clinical Psychology,* 1985, *53,* 866–873.

Kilpatrick, D. G., Veronen, L. J., & Resick, P. A. The aftermath of rape: Recent empirical findings. *American Journal of Orthopsychiatry,* 1979, *49,* 658–659.

Kolb, L. C., & Mutalipassi, L. The conditioned emotional response: A subclass of the chronic and delayed post-traumatic stress disorder. *Psychiatric Annals,* 1982, *12,* 979–987.

Koss, M. P., Gidycz, C. A., & Wisniewski, N. The scope of rape: Incidence and prevalence of sexual aggression and victimization in a national sample of higher education students. *Journal of Consulting and Clinical Psychology,* 1987, *55,* 162–170.

Krystal, H. Integration and self-healing in post-traumatic states: A ten year retrospective. *American Imago,* 1991, *48,* 93–118.

Krystal, J. H., Kosten, T. R., Perry, B. D., Southwick, S., Mason, J. W., & Giller, E. L. Neurobiological aspects of PTSD: Review of clinical and preclinical studies. *Behavioral Therapy* 1989, *20,* 177–198.

Lehman, D. R., Ellard, J. H., & Wortman, C. B. Social support for the bereaved: Recipients' and providers' perspectives on what is helpful. *Journal of Consulting and Clinical Psychology,* 1986, *54,* 438–446.

Lindy, J. D. The trauma membrane and other clinical concepts derived from psychotherapeutic work with survivors of natural disasters. *Psychiatric Annals,* 1985, *15,* 153–160.

Maida, C., Gordon, N., Steinberg, A., & Gordon, G. Psychosocial impact of disasters: Victims of the Baldwin Hills fire. *Journal of Traumatic Stress,* 1989, *2,* 37–48.

Malmquist, C. P. Children who witness parental murder: Post-traumatic and legal issues. *Journal of the American Academy of Child Psychiatry,* 1984, *25,* 320–325.

McCleer, S. V., & Anwar, R. A study of women presenting in an emergency department. *American Journal of Public Health,* 1989, *79,* 65–67.

McGaugh, J. L. Hormonal influences on memory. *American Review of Psychology,* 1983, *34,* 297–323.

MOWRER, O. H. On the dual nature of learning: A reinterpretation "of conditioning" and "problem solving." *Harvard Educational Review,* 1947, *17,* 102–148.

NEW YORK TIMES. Crime and its amplifed echoes are rearranging people's lives. February 9, 1992, 1–4.

OCHBERG, F. M. *Posttraumatic therapy with the victim of violence.* New York, Brunner/Mazel, 1986.

ORNITZ, E. M., & PYNOOS, R. S. Startle modulation in children with post-traumatic stress disorder. *American Journal of Psychiatry,* 1989, *147,* 866–870.

PEARLIN, L. I., & LIEBERMAN, M. Social sources of emotional distress. In R. Simmons (ed.), *Research in community and mental health.* Greenwich, CT: JAI Press, 1979.

PENNEBAKER, J. W., & SUSMAN, J. R. Disclosure of traumas and psychosomatic processes. *Social Science and Medicine,* 1988, *26,* 327–332.

PERRY, B. D. Neurobiological sequelae of childhood trauma. Post-traumatic stress disorders in children. In M. Murberg (ed.), *Catecholamine function in post-traumatic stress disorder: Emerging concepts.* Washington, DC: American Psychiatric Press.

PETERS, S. D., WYATT, G. E., & FINKELHOR, D. Prevalence. In D. Finkelhor (ed.), *A sourcebook on child sexual abuse.* Beverly Hills, CA: Sage, 1986.

PFOUTS, J., SCHOPLER, J., & HENLEY, H. C. Forgotten victims of family violence. *Social Work,* 1982, *27,* 367–368.

PILLEMER, K., & FINKELHOR, D. The prevalence of elder abuse: A random sample survey. *The Gerontologist,* 1988, *28,* 51–57.

PITMAN, R. K. Post-traumatic stress disorder, conditioning, and network theory. *Psychiatric Annals* 1988, *18,* 182–189.

PROTHROW-STITH, D. *Violence prevention. Curriculum for adolescents.* Newton, MA: Education Development Center, 1987.

PUTNAM, F. W. Dissociation as a response to extreme trauma. In R. P. Kluft (ed.), *The childhood antecedents of multiple personality.* Washington, DC: American Psychiatric Press, 1985.

PYNOOS, R. S. New perspective on grief and trauma in children and adolescents. *Bereavement Care,* 1992, *11*:(1); 2–10.

PYNOOS, R. S., & ETH, S. Children traumatized by witnessing acts of personal violence: Homicide, rape and suicide behavior. In S. Eth & R. Pynoos (eds.), *Post-traumatic stress disorder in children.* Washington, DC: American Psychiatric Press, 1985.

PYNOOS, R. S., & NADER, K. Post-traumatic stress disorder in adolescents. In E. McAnarney, R. Kreipe, D. Orr, & G. Comerci (eds.), *The textbook of adolescent medicine.* Philadelphia: W. B. Saunders, 1992.(a)

PYNOOS, R. S., & NADER, K. Issues in the treatment of post-traumatic stress in children and adolescents. In: J. P. Wilson & B. Raphael (eds.) *The international handbook of traumatic stress syndromes.* New York & London: Plenum Press, 1992.(b)

RACHMAN, S. Emotional processing. *Behavior Research and Therapy,* 1980, *18,* 51–60.

RANGELL, L. Castration. *Journal of the American Psychoanalytic Association,* 1991, *39,* 3–23.

RICHTERS, J. E., & SALTZMAN, W. *Survey of children's exposure to community violence: Parent report.* Rockville, MD: National Institute of Mental Health, 1990.

RUSSELL, D. E. H. The incidence and prevalence of intrafamilial and extrafamilial sexual abuse of female children. *Child Abuse and Neglect,* 1983, *7,* 133–146.

————. The prevalence and seriousness of incestuous abuse: Stepfathers vs biological fathers. *Child Abuse and Neglect,* 1984, *8,* 15–22.

RYNEARSON, E. K. Psychological adjustment to unnatural dying. In S. Zisook (ed.), *Biopsychosocial aspects of bereavement.* Washington, DC: American Psychiatric Press, 1990.

SAIGH, P. A. The use of an in vitro flooding package in the treatment of traumatized adolescents. *Journal of Developmental Behavioral Pediatrics,* 1988, *10,* 17–21.

SELECT COMMITTEE ON AGING. *Elder abuse: A decade of shame and inaction* (House of Representatives, comm. pub. no. 101-752). Washington, DC: U.S. Government Printing Office, 1990.

SHALEV, A. Y., ORR, S. P., PERI, T., SCHREIBER, S., & PITMAN, R. K. *Non-habituation of the startle response in post-traumatic stress disorder.* Paper presented at the American Psychiatric Association annual meeting, New Orleans, 1991.

SHAPIRO, F. Efficacy of the eye movement desensitization procedure in the treatment of traumatic memories. *Journal of Traumatic Stress,* 1989, *2,* 199–223.

SORENSON, S. B., & GOLDING, J. M. Depressive sequelae of recent criminal victimization. *Journal of Traumatic Stress,* 1990, *3,* 337–350.

STARK, E., FLITCRAFT, A., ZUCKERMAN, D., GREY, A., ROBISON, J., & FRAZIER, W. Wife abuse in the medical setting. *Domestic Violence,* 1981, *7,* 7–41.

SYMONDS, M. The "second injury" to victims. *Evaluation and Change,* 1980 (special issue), 36–38.

STRAUS, M., GELLES, R., & STEINMETZ, S. *Behind closed doors: Violence in the American family.* New York; Anchor Books, 1985.

U.S. DEPARTMENT OF JUSTICE. *Elderly victims* (Bureau of Justice statistics, bulletin NCJ-107676). Washington, DC: U.S. Department of Justice, 1987.

————. *Uniform crime reports 1989.* Washington, DC: U.S. Department of Justice, 1990.

————. *Crime and the nation's households, 1990* (Bureau of Justice statistics, bulletin NCJ-130302). Washington, DC: U.S. Department of Justice, 1991.(a)

————. *Criminal victimization in the United States, 1989* (Bureau of Justice statistics, National Crime Survey report NCJ-129391). Washington, DC: U.S. Department of Justice, 1991.(b)

————. *Female victims of violent crime* (Bureau of Justice statistics, bulletin NCJ-126826). Washington, DC: U.S. Department of Justice, 1991.(c)

WEINGARTNER, H. Human state dependent learning. In B. T. Ho, D. W. Richards, & D. C. Chute (eds.), *Drug discrimination and state dependent learning.* New York: Academic Press, 1978.

WEISAETH, L. The stressors and the post-traumatic stress syndrome after an industrial disaster. *Acta Psychiatrica Scandinavica,* 1989 (suppl. 355), *80,* 25–37.

WEST, L. J. Foreword. In M. M. Nagler (eds.), *America without violence.* Covelo, CA: Island Press, 1982.

WIDOM, C. S. The cycle of violence. *Science,* 1989, *244L,* 160–166.

WINFIELD, I., GEORGE, L. K., SWARTZ, M., & BLAZER, D. G. Sexual assault and psychiatric disorders among a community sample of women. *American Journal of Psychiatry,* 1990, *147,* 335–341.

WYATT, G. E., GUTHRIE, D., & NOTGRASS, C. M. The differential effects of women's child sexual abuse and subsequent sexual assault. *Journal of Consulting and Clinical Psychology,* 1992, *60:* 167–173.

32

Disasters: Psychological and Psychiatric Aspects

Lars Weisæth

THE SCOPE OF THE PROBLEM

Natural disasters, such as those caused by earthquakes, windstorms, tsunamis, floods, land-slides, volcanic eruptions, wildfires, and other calamities, have killed 3 million people worldwide over the past two decades, adversely affected the lives of at least 800 million more people, and resulted in immediate economic damage exceeding 23 billion U.S. dollars. The smallest and poorest countries are affected most severely by natural disasters, and the poorest and most disadvantaged members of a disaster-affected community are likely to experience the most serious consequences. Therefore, in the majority of developing countries, disasters, because of their severity and frequency, represent a real public health priority (World Health Organization, 1992).

However, there has been a general tendency in the past to consider that the basic needs of the populations affected by a disaster could be met essentially by providing shelter, food, sanitation, and immunization against epidemics. People's psychosocial needs were seen as too secondary to attract the attention of relief agencies and relief workers. But considering the vast number of people involved, any prevalence of mental disorder caused by natural disaster would be significant in terms of health. Unfortunately, the pioneer research on communities struck by such disasters was carried out almost exclusively in the United States (Penick, Powell, & Sieck, 1976; Perry & Lindell, 1978), where minimal emotional effects of natural disaster were found (Quarantelli, 1985). There findings, mainly from sociological studies, were later challenged (Frederick, 1980).

Recent studies using adequate research methods do find mental health effects in U.S. communities after natural disasters (e.g., Shore, Tatum, & Vollmer, 1986), although nowhere near the high prevalence of postdisaster psychopathology recently reported after massive disasters in the third world. For example, the prevalence of emotional distress was as high as 78%, and fivefold higher than for the nondistressed group, among survivors living in a tent camp 2 years after a mudslide in Columbia had killed 80%, or 30,000, of the town's inhabitants (Lima, 1987, 1990a, 1990b, 1991). Six months after an earthquake in China and 12 months after a major Australian bushfire, epidemiological studies (McFarlane, 1988; McFarlane & Hua, 1992) showed twice the prevalence of psychiatric morbidity anticipated.

Berz (1989), studying 109 natural disasters that occurred between 1960 and 1987, found that the number of deaths from the 41 disasters that had occurred in developing countries was 758,850 compared to only 11,441 in developed countries. In general, the number of deaths and injuries is closely related to the prevailing level of economic development. The vast majority of these lives could have been saved by better technology, warning systems, evacuation capacity, building constructions, etc. As a consequence, UN General Assembly Resolution 42/169, adopted on December 11, 1987, designated the 1990s as a decade for natural disaster reduction (World Health Organization, 1988). Consequently, the World Health Organization's (WHO) role has gradually shifted from the provision of emergency relief to disaster preparedness and response, including involvement in training, assessment of health situation and needs, and coordination of large-scale disaster operations. Disaster preparedness is a significant part of the overall strategy for achieving the goals of the Health for All by the Year 2000 program. By 1995, the WHO's target for the Eighth General Program of Work is that 70% of all countries will have developed master plans to deal with the health aspects of emergency and disaster situations. These master plans should include a mental health component (World Health Organization, 1992a).

In the industrial countries, the concentration of industrial complexes, advanced technology, and the density of population in the urban centers have increased the possibility of disasters and magnified their potential destruction. In Western society, people are more concerned about potential disasters caused by failed technology, the man-made disasters. However, in developing countries, technological disasters have even worse effects (Sethi, Sharma, Singh, & Singh, 1987). As never before, humankind, also on the global level, is threatened by self-destruction from pollution, population growth, the armament race, and technological disasters of almost unimaginable magnitude.

MYTHS OF DISASTER

Since ancient times, people have ascribed supernatural meaning to the sudden, violent acts of nature. In our time, the causes have been scientifically explained and are generally understood. Nonetheless, when it comes to the expected effects of a disaster, myth still often overwhelms reality. Group panic is wrongly believed to be a frequent response to disaster. Stereotypes of the victim and helper roles (Short, 1979) may distortedly view the victims as only weak and helpless, the helper as all-powerful and effective. Neither scenario is supported by research findings (Raphael, 1986). In few areas does a full understanding of the psychology of helping have such importance as in disaster relief work. Relief activities based on misconceptions may be wasteful, useless, and often counterproductive; the actual recovery of the population may be hampered rather than hastened, so that a "second disaster" or "second trauma" is produced.

Tenacious misbeliefs widely held by the affected population are also part of the problem: "Dead bodies will lead to catastrophic outbreaks of communicable diseases." This fear-driven belief, which leads to rapid mass burials of unidentified bodies, causes many families great uncertainty about the fate of their missing members and deprives them of a place to mourn. (In fact, a body is rarely a risk until 72 hours after death. Unnecessary vaccination campaigns and international assistance are frequently put in action while the affected people are wrongly expected to be too shocked and helpless to take responsibility for their own survival.

Psychological factors also play a role in postdisaster decisions—for example, the reluctance to resettle in a new site after a natural disaster (Oliver-Smith, 1991).

DEFINING DISASTER: CONSEQUENCES FOR MENTAL HEALTH

Why should it be necessary to discuss formal characteristics of an event so full of tragedy and misery? In the first place, declaring an event to be a "disaster" may influence, among other things, the amount of help offered. Second, the disaster concept also has emotional, political, and value loadings that will in various ways influence the public in general and the victims themselves. Third, and most important, the sheer magnitude of a disaster, in contrast to other severe and traumatic events, creates needs that outrun the available resources. Probably no event so severely tests the adequacy of a nation's health infrastructure as the occurrence of a sudden natural disaster such as an earthquake, hurricane, or flood. Most definitions, and those of medicine, psychology, and sociology, which are of most relevance for our purpose, stress that a disaster is a severe destruction that exceeds the coping capacity of the affected community. Thus the adjustment capacity and the psychosocial and physical resources of a community are essential aspects in defining when a destructive event leads to disaster.

There is no upward limit on the magnitude of a disaster, but there is difficulty involved when trying to draw a line between disasters and accidents. What is the difference between an accident and a disaster for those affected? Kinston and Rosser (1974) emphasize the "massive collective stress," thus distinguishing the victims of disaster from those suffering from single traumas, which otherwise can carry many of the same stresses as a disaster trauma. Raphael (1986) uses the term personal disaster for such severe single traumas. From the psychiatric viewpoint, the possibly different degree of risk to the mental health of the victim of collective versus single trauma has not been adequately researched but would be of considerable theoretical and practical importance to society, which is responsible for the allocation of mental health services. After all, only 5% of unnatural deaths in most Western countries are lost in destructive events that cost 5 or more lives.

Despite the lack of empirical research, it is possible to speculate on the differences that distinguish collective trauma from individual trauma. For example, by virtue of the sheer number of people involved, is there more likely a warning before a disaster trauma than an accident trauma? During the event, the disaster victim is likely to experience enormous destruction, suffer multiple losses, witness mass injuries and deaths, and may have to make difficult choices between ensuring personal survival and possibly helping others. The presence of others, however, also increases the opportunity for leadership and one's own rescue. On the whole, however, a disaster victim probably experiences more intense feelings of powerlessness than the accident victim. Again, because of magnitude, in the immediate aftermath, the disaster victim is more likely to suffer from the inadequacy of emergency operations compared to the accident victim, who normally benefits from an intact framework.

As far as psychological reactions are concerned, research observations indicate that the collective situation may synchronize post-traumatic stress reactions, reinforce individual reactions, and shorten the shock phase (Berle, Haver, & Karterud, 1991); in children, post-traumatic symptom contagion has been reported (Terr, 1985). The group situation opens many possibilities for working through the trauma that a single accident victim does not have. Sociological findings have emphasized the positive effects upon health of the development of an "altruistic community" after disasters (Barton, 1969) and, according to Quarantelli (1985), Prince in his 1920 study noted that the blow was softened for the individual because many shared the suffering. Finally, disaster victims in Western society become the focus of public sympathy and thus receive the participation and support of society's leaders and enormous media attention; this response is in stark contrast to the lonely fate of many experiencing single trauma.

As for scientific definitions, Korver (1987) found more than forty different definitions of disaster in the literature. The apparent disagreements reflect the diverse interests of scientists dealing with the destructive events from the perspectives of medicine, psychology, sociology, political science, ecology, engineering, or economics. From the vantage point of each discipline, an event may be a disaster along one or some dimensions but not along others. Thus, the disaster concept is a very complex, multidimensional phenomenon. The definition adopted usually reflects the role of the particular organization, but it may also depend upon the event itself or solely on the consequences of the event.

For example, the accident at the Chernobyl nuclear plant would be termed a disaster by all of the disciplines listed above. "Silent disasters," such as toxic and radiation disasters, may occur without producing the massive destruction traditionally associated with the term disaster. But do the estimated 400 cancer deaths expected in the long-term in Norway because of Chernobyl constitute a disaster? Perhaps new terms are needed to describe far-off effects. The Three Mile Island nuclear plant accident did not qualify as a disaster from a medical viewpoint, although moderate long-term physiological disturbances were recorded in the local community (Baum, 1986), but from a sociological point of view, the 200,000 who took to the roads in the acute aftermath made the accident a disaster, and many would say it was catastrophic for the nuclear energy industry.

The concept of disaster can also change over time and among different cultures (Girolamo, 1992). A high frequency of catastrophic events may raise the threshold for an event to be considered a disaster, a phenomenon mirrored by "the disaster fatigue" observed in the populations of the industrialized world at times when the mass media flood the public with reports of several simultaneous catastrophic events in the third world. Stereotypes of human reactions to huge numbers come into play. People are unable to differentiate in consciousness and emotions between, say, half a million, 1 million, and 2 million deaths. The geographical distance from the scene of the disaster also appears to play an important part in this response.

The focus of disaster medicine on victims who are so numerous that their treatment needs far outweigh the resources available serves to emphasize the need to bring in immediately extra resources—for example, all the resources of the hospital or region. The mobilization of a hospital's disaster plan will therefore depend on the number of patients that a particular hospital can handle during an emergency. Until recently, however, the number of injured or acutely ill patients was the only criterion taken into consideration. Since hospitals, with their continuous preparedness, have been the basis for the health services offered during and after disasters, this very narrow operationalization of the disaster definition has had some unfortunate consequences: Only if physical injuries or illnesses occur will a hospital mobilize. In other words, if every victim perished, as is frequently the case in modern accidents like air crashes, no resources would be sent in to alleviate the psychological problems of bereaved families, rescue workers, body handlers, and other disaster workers. This orientation is one reason why the stress problems of these groups went almost unnoticed for many years. And if everyone survived without physical harm, no help would be offered, even to those who experienced extremely narrow escapes.

The medical definition of disasters also fails to differentiate between mass injury situations and disasters in the sociological sense—i.e., the destruction or disruption of a large social system. If the victims of an air crash, for example, come from the same area, where many deaths imply a breakdown of social structure, a wider sociological perspective should be employed. Such societal breakdowns may result in the opposite of the altruistic or thera- peutic community, namely a "loss of communality" (Erikson, 1976), as observed after the Buffalo Creek flood. This loss can damage the bonds attaching people together and, again, may have negative consequences for health. In any case, the medical definition of disaster is too narrow for the mental health disaster worker.

DEVELOPMENTS IN PSYCHOSOCIAL DISASTER RESEARCH

There are several reasons for studying the psychiatric aspects of disaster. At one level, such study could be equated to basic applied research on a stress model. The effects of studying disaster behavior might improve survival, preparation for disasters, and management of victims and others affected by the disaster. Furthermore, it is of great importance to study postdisaster morbidity, health, and adaptation, as well as the effects of intervention (Ra- phael, Lundin, & Weisæth, 1989).

Historically, the impacts of man-made major accidents involving technology—such as railway collisions, mine catastrophes, and explosions—were the first to be studied. Disputes about the nature and etiology of traumatic neurosis was an important stimulus for this research (Erichsen, 1866). The new unsafe technology caused horrifying accidents, and there were almost epidemic occurrences of some "new" kinds of illness; the survivors started to press for compensation through the courts of law. The misinterpretation of the many facets of post-traumatic anxiety symptoms led the doctors into believing the disorder could be organically explained. Gradually, an awareness of, and focus on, the demonstrated psychic changes replaced the hypothesis of physical injury to the brain caused by "chocs nerveux" (Fischer-Homberger, 1975; Merskey, 1991).

In the first decade of this century, the Swiss psychiatrist Eduard Stierlin (1909, 1911), the first and usually overlooked researcher in disaster psychiatry, investigated both man- made (mining and railway) and natural disasters. Of 135 persons who had experienced the earthquake in Messina in 1908, he found that 25% suffered from traumatic sleep distur- bances, including nightmares. Stierlin considered violent emotions and fright the most im- portant etiological factors. He postulated that emotions create a state of lowered resistance within the nervous system that forms the basis for the development of a neurosis. Later research has confirmed several of his findings, such as that unfortunate social conditions and personal disposition can contribute to the development of post-traumatic psychopath- ology.

Hesnard's study (1914) of two ship explosions in France in 1907 and 1909 illustrates the interest at the time in the devastating effects of failing technology. Hesnard recorded symptoms of post-traumatic psychological responses that have been repeatedly observed in later wars and catastrophes. His study was the first to describe post-traumatic stress symp- toms in rescuers that last for weeks after the rescue operation. This knowledge of emotional changes after explosions quickly became part of the contemporary climate of ideas and paved the way for recognition of the true nature of the numerous cases of "shell shock" in World War I, which reflected people's vulnerability to shock trauma and inescapable shock.

The first sociological study (Prince, 1920) typically covered a man-made disaster and focused on the social changes subsequent to the Halifax munition explosion, which killed two thousand, injured six thousand, and was at that time the greatest single explosion in history.

During the interwar period there was no progress in the study of traumatic stress and disaster; the insight gained during World War I about trauma as the main etiological agent was weakened and replaced by a stronger emphasis on unconscious intrapsychic processes. The post-traumatic sequelae were seen as irrational, neurotic, and not truly reflecting real traumatic experiences. It took another war to put stress researchers onto the right trail, and wartime psychiatry had an important influence on disaster psychiatry, as evidenced by the pioneering studies of Fraser, Leslie, & Phelps. (1942/1943) on London bomb victims, Lindemann (1944) on loss trauma after a nightclub fire in Boston, and Tyhurst (1951, 1957a, 1957b) on disaster behavior and the phases of postdisaster responses.

Even so, most of the research of the 1950s and 1960s suffered from methodological weaknesses or did not deal with disaster as such. In a critical review of research on 103 disasters, Barton (1963) found that only the studies of the Arkansas tornado and the Holland flood satisfied methodological demands.

As stated previously, most of the planned disaster research before the 1970s was carried out by sociologists in the United States. Their research mainly focused on the effects of disruption of communities and organizations by natural disasters. Severe disorganization was found to result only rarely. As far as psychological functioning was studied, their findings challenged the traditional beliefs of the public and the authorities. The response to warnings was found not to be automatic and adaptive, contrary to the somewhat naive conceptions many had about the warning process (Dynes, 1974; Fritz, 1961). On the other hand, these studies demonstrated that group panic is rare and should not be expected except under specific circumstances (Fritz & Marks, 1954; Quarantelli, 1954), such as when there is an immediate threat coupled with the belief that escape is possible but fast diminishing. These findings have been supported by later research (see subsequently).

According to Quarantelli (1985), two opposing positions were taken in the United States toward postdisaster mental health effects. The sociologists maintained that, although there were immediate widespread effects, much of the reaction was superficial, nonpersistent, of short duration, and not behaviorally dysfunctional; they argued that disasters could even engender significant positive psychological effects. In their view, the relatively unimportant behavioral difficulties resulted not from the experience of disaster trauma but from the social setting in which postdisaster relief and recovery services were obtained. The mental health field, on the other hand, held that effects of community disasters were widespread, deep, persistent, long-lasting, and dysfunctional. In reality, however, psychiatry was very reluctant to accept stress as a cause of psychiatric disorder, and only as late as 1980 was post-traumatic stress disorder (PTSD) introduced into the diagnostic system.

Unfortunately, there has been very little overlap between the sociological and mental health research on community disasters in the United States, so the possible differences between the two positions cannot be wholly accounted for. Some of the explanation may be that different researchers tended to generalize from the particular type of disaster trauma they studied; for example, they might have applied findings from natural disasters to manmade disasters. Many U.S. natural disasters caused a limited number of deaths and did not expose victims to high-risk trauma dimensions to the same degree as man-made disasters. Frederick (1980) pointed out that because skilled clinicians had not been involved in disaster research or service, there was a lack of awareness about the presence of mental health problems.

A review of the research shows that among the main methodological weaknesses were nonclinical procedures that failed to measure the relevant psychological reactions as those of traumatic neurosis—e.g., PTSD. Instead, community-level data were often used because of their availability, not because of their validity: rates of juvenile delinquency, calls to the police because of domestic trouble, reports of child abuse, attempted and actual suicides, drunken driving, infant mortality, overall death rates, and numbers of prescriptions for tranquillizers. None of these rates are valid measures of post-traumatic psychopathology; nor is the use of admission rates to psychiatric institutions or to other health services, for the simple reason that traumatized people often avoid seeking help. In fact, studies of admission rate to psychiatric institutions during World War II in an occupied country in Europe (Ødegård, 1975) failed to pick up the thousands suffering from traumatic syndromes because of war stress. Researchers who lack intimate knowledge of the cognitive, affective, and behavioral responses to psychic trauma are likely to make such methodological errors.

The pertinent psychiatric literature of that time appears to be periodic and unintegrated. Clearly, disaster psychiatry needed an institutional structure for planning studies. Most of these inadequacies were rectified from the mid-1970s onward. Whole disaster populations or representative samples were studied with adequate control or comparison groups, in prospective designs with long observation periods, with high response rates, and with adequate clinical methods, such as structured interviews and standardized rating instruments (Alexander & Wells, 1991; Gleser, Green, & Winget, 1978; Green, 1982; Herlofsen, in press; Holen, 1990; McFarlane, 1988; Raphael, 1986; Raphael, Lundin & Weisæth, 1989; Shore, Tatum & Wollmer, 1986; Solomon, 1989; Sund, Holen, & Weisæth, 1983; Weisæth, 1984).

Finally, disaster researchers were helped by the introduction of the diagnostic criteria for PTSD in the DSM-III in 1980. These criteria provided a more reliable tool for measuring perhaps the most important mental disorder after disaster stress. During the subsequent decade, the diagnostic system was perfected by further revisions of the DSM-III and the latest proposals of the ICD-10 (International Classification of Diseases, 10th edition) on acute stress reactions, PTSD and "Enduring personality change after catastrophic experience" (World Health Organization, 1992b).

GUIDELINES FOR A RESEARCH DESIGN

A standardized core methodology has been proposed by Raphael et al. (1989). International comparisons between disasters can thus be made, so that the long-awaited cross-cultural studies are now feasible. The procedure recommended by Raphael et al. (1989) is demonstrated in Table 32–1.

From a research point of view, the collective nature of disaster trauma offers the researcher a cost-effective opportunity to study variance within a population exposed to the

TABLE 32–1
Prospective Intervention Studies of Disasters

Procedure	Method	Time
Brief screening	Questionnaire	Within 2 weeks
Early interview	Personal interview and rating scales	2–4 weeks
Follow-ups	Personal interviews/ questionnaires/ rating scales	3–4 months 12–13 months 2, 5, 10 years

same trauma, thus pinpointing factors that account for differences in response such as level of training, personality, social networks, etc. If the exposed group is relatively homogeneous, such as employees in the same company or soldiers from the same unit, the researcher should be in a better position to carry out controlled intervention studies. The limiting factor so far has been ethical objections to having an untreated control group. After the King's Cross fire in the London subway, waiting list patients were used as controls (Rachel Rosser, personal communication), and a European Community group of researchers has proposed to compare effects of optimal interventions versus the ordinary, thus avoiding the ethical dilemma (Schüffel, Lopez-Ibor, Rosser, & Weisæth, 1990).

Controlled intervention studies—trying to measure the effects of preventive and therapeutic interventions—should be encouraged because trauma research has some advantages compared to other psychiatric studies. In disaster studies (1) the risk group is well defined, (2) the presence/absence of the main illnesses in question, such as PTSD, can reliably be assessed, (3) the observation period necessary to establish the illness risk can be relatively brief, (4) the illness risk is usually very high (somewhere between 10% to 50% depending mainly upon the severity of the trauma), and (5) the interventions can be reasonably well described.

From the literature it is apparent that disaster studies frequently have foundered on lack of cooperation from the subjects who were to be studied (Bennet, 1973; Lindy, Grace, & Green, 1981). Because subjects wish to avoid re-experiencing the trauma, they will often defend themselves by displaying resistance, including toward investigators. The implication for studies of the aftereffects of trauma is that response rates need to be high. One study (Weisæth, 1989a) found that the resistance related to the severity of exposure as well as to outcome. Thus, a potential loss of follow-up would reduce the prevalence rates of PTSD (even an 82% response rate would have missed 42% of the PTSD cases) and the predictor value of belonging to the severely exposed group. For primary and secondary prevention, the implication may be that early outreach must be very active.

Basic guidelines for a research design of proven success are:

1. Establishing a "we-project," a partner-like relationship with the social group that was struck by the disaster. It is important that victims of trauma feel that they are in control.
2. Combining research and interventions. Although offers of help distort the natural course of the postdisaster reactions, the response rate and the quality of the data will improve when the researcher is also seen as a helper.
3. Applying a stress-crisis frame of reference, emphasizing prevention not illness, and dealing with subjects, not patients.
4. Keeping a low media profile

RESEARCH ON CHILDREN AFTER DISASTER

It has been pointed out (Yule & Williams, 1990) that several of the early studies of children's response to disaster trauma suffered methodologically from the use of research instruments, such as the Rutter scales and the Quay and Peterson Behavior Problem Checklist, that were never intended to measure the effects of trauma on children or have a poor validity for this purpose. There is a consensus in recent literature that teachers report less psychopathology among child survivors than parents do, and that both teachers and parents report far less than the children themselves. The conclusion is that screening scales used on their own, without detailed interviews with the children, are of limited value. In combination, however, these two methods reveal a considerable amount of postdisaster stress reaction in children (Pynoos et al., 1987). Regressive behaviors, with clinging to parents and heightened dependency, are frequent findings.

The early studies showed that, in the majority of cases, the disturbances are short-lived (Garmezy & Rutter, 1985); however, these studies rarely dealt with major disasters in which the children had been exposed to life-threatening factors. In the aftermath of the Buffalo Creek disaster, Newman (1976) found that children under 12 exhibited vulnerability to future stress, an altered sense of power over the self, and an early awareness of fragmentation and death. The effects on the children depended upon the children's developmental level at the time of the trauma, their perceptions of reactions in the family to the catastrophic event, and direct exposure of the children themselves to the trauma. The first studies of children (Bloch, Silber, & Perry, 1956) found that children tend to reflect the reactions of their parents.

As in the PTSD of many adult survivors of acute trauma (Weisæth, 1989b), psychic numbing was difficult to detect in children and adolescents, in whom it often takes the form of withdrawal into uncustomary behavioral patterns (Frederick, 1985). The sense of a foreshortened future, which is a symptom of PTSD, resulting from the exposure to mass death may have particularly severe effects on children by causing them to give up their involvement in education, their expectation of having their own families in the future, etc.

TYPOLOGIES OF DISASTER: CONSEQUENCES FOR COPING AND MENTAL HEALTH

A satisfactory classification system should be able to categorize neatly the way people react, the types of help required, and measures needed for prevention and preparedness. Broadly speaking, disasters can be divided into two types: natural and man-made.

Natural disasters include floods, tidal waves, storms, cyclones, hurricanes, tornadoes, tsunamis, earthquakes, volcanic eruptions, landslides, avalanches, droughts, and wildfires. Such events are often familiar to the victims, because they tend to occur only in certain areas. Through their long and intimate relationship with nature, people have had to cope with the natural dangers and come to accept them. Perhaps human genetic apparatus has become uniquely adapted to cope with such threats. While the onset of a natural disaster may be sudden, the ability to forecast has made some of them relatively predictable, so that warnings can be issued. The disaster impact is often extremely powerful and causes substantial destruction, social disruption, and a number of secondary disaster stressors. Usually it is possible to define a low point—that is, when "the worst is over" (Baum, 1986).

Man-made disasters include fires in great buildings and cities, the collapse of man-made structures (bridges, mines, dams, buildings, roads), crashes of transportation systems (ship, railway, airplane, motor transport), and technological accidents (oil, toxic, chemical, or nuclear explosions). (War, the greatest of all catastrophes, and other forms of intended disasters caused by violence, such as genocide, are excluded from our discussion).

Man-made or technological disasters are rarely preceded by warnings and, therefore, often have a sudden onset, thus producing shock traumas. Sometimes these disasters are preceded by a critical situation in which crisis management failed to avert the disaster. The impact of such disasters is extremely powerful, the destruction is often concentrated and cause less social disintegration. These events occur in man-made environments and some observations indicate human fight/flight/freezing responses may be less adaptive in such circumstances and, sometimes, even costly in terms of life. Since technological disasters imply the breakdown of man-made products or result from human failure, they are seen as preventable events. They result from a loss of control that someone is responsible for and can be blamed for.

A multitude of further classifications have been proposed for disasters and their victims (Berren, Beigel, & Barker, 1982; Dynes, 1974; Taylor, 1987). Comparative research on types of disaster is still in its infancy, and the possible differential psychosocial effects on each disaster type have not yet been described systematically. Furthermore, according to Quarantelli (1985), to focus solely on the disaster agent results in the omission of a very important aspect of the situation—the organized attempt to respond to the occasion. Organizational response to a disaster is crucial because it provides the structure for possible individual responses and thus affects level and type of psychiatric morbidity.

It is usually claimed that the mental consequences of man-made disasters are more severe and persistent than the effects of natural disasters (Frederick, 1980; Baum, 1986; Luchterhand, 1971). There are no truly comparable disaster studies of mental health effects, so one has to compare across many differences, such as between the Rapid City flood and the man-made Buffalo Creek flood (Gleser, Green, & Winget, 1981). There are more well-designed psychiatric studies of man-made disasters than of comparable natural disasters.

The distinction between the forces of nature and the forces of humanity cannot always be made and may be blurred. Human actions that upset the ecological balance may introduce a partly human causation into what was earlier a previously natural disaster.

The 1991 Bangladesh floods, which claimed 200,000 lives, illustrate the case in point. The uneducated believed that the floods signalled God's anger with them. Others blamed the authorities for allowing settlement in this densely populated country where floods are periodic and for poor warning, evacuation, and rescue procedures (although 300,000 lives were spared that would have been lost a decade ago). Educated citizens saw other human actions as contributory causes to the floods, such as the deforestation of the Himalayas, the weakening of the ozone layer, etc. A professor of meteorology in Bangladesh stated that while they drowned, people in the industrialized countries quarreled about the greenhouse effect.

As the world grows smaller, people in developing countries will probably alter their attitude toward death from natural disasters from a resignation and fatalism to despair: It could have been prevented. The traditional understanding and acceptance of the natural disaster through a religious and fatalistic lens may be lost. Changing perceptions of who is responsible or who is to blame for disasters will in all likelihood have psychological consequences. Nature can do harm, but nature has no evil intent. Only humanity has this capability. The human context, often with attacks on people's integrity and self-respect, differs from natural trauma. Nature does not threaten a person's self-respect, even if it is deadly. Technological disasters, however, are not necessary, but avoidable; therefore, they produce aggression rather than acceptance.

There are no comparative studies of responses to a technological disaster perceived as truly accidental and one seen as due to negligence. However, a comparison between the former and a collective violence trauma demonstrated marked differences. The violence produced a higher prevalence of PTSD; the content of the symptoms was interpersonal and threatening, in contrast to material/technological dangers; there was social isolation rather than circumscribed phobias; and the anger was a direct reaction to the violence. No aggressive symptoms of this nature was found in the victims of the technological disaster (Weinsæth, 1989b, 1989d).

A special type of man-made disaster is the toxic disaster. Exposure to radiation and toxic chemicals may not be an acute, time-limited event but rather a sequence of events that continues to unfold over several years. The belief that one has been exposed to toxic substances may cause long-term uncertainty and stress, as well as pose a threat to one's health (Baum, 1986). The toxic disaster may have no clearly defined low point, and if the dangerous substance is invisible or otherwise impossible to detect for the exposed individual, a particularly difficult stressful situation is at hand.

Time Phases

An abundance of classifications of phases of disaster exist that are more or less variations on the same theme (Raphael, 1986). Either the classification is based on the external event or on the response of the individual, or both, such as in distinguishing between the following phases with their corresponding coping tasks: the steady state (preparedness), crisis (warning, crisis management), impact (survival and rescue), and shock and reaction phases (prevention of post-traumatic stress problems). Frederick (1986) distinguishes between impact/shock, heroic, honeymoon, disappointment, and reorganization/recovery responses, terms that well indicate certain characteristics of the victims' reactions. The psychosocial responses of the preceding phase will strongly affect the response of the next. One challenge of the pre-impact phase, both to the individual and to the authorities, is to create the optimal level of anxiety, balancing between maladaptive blanket reassurance at one extreme and indiscriminate vigilance at the other. In some disasters, an isolation phase occurs, a period after impact when the disaster survivors are on their own before outside help arrives.

Geographical Zones

A disaster area can be divided into zones, some of which become the location of predictable behavioral problems. For example, the filter zone, where people, material, and information are to be filtered in and out of the destroyed area, is often bothered by the convergence phenomenon, the aggregation of people searching for their missing relatives, professional helpers, volunteers, and curious spectators.

PSYCHIATRIC RISK FACTORS IN DISASTER

Disaster trauma usually contains multiple stressors and is not unidimensional; it includes both an acute event and a chronic one (Green et al., 1990). The primary disaster stressors are those experienced during impact, and they increase in severity the nearer one is to the center of impact. Such stressors include physical injuries, objective risk to life, witnessing the death and suffering of others, and having to make difficult choices between escape and rescue. Most studies that attempted to scale disaster exposure found a correlation between intensity of exposure and likelihood of psychiatric after-effects (Green, Grace, & Gleser,

1986; Holen, 1990; Shore et al., 1986; Weisæth, 1984, 1985). The severity of the primary stressors depends on the amount of mastery possible, the speed of onset, the level of preparedness and warning, the geographical and numerical scope of impact, duration of impact, level of control, predictability, leadership, competence, social cohesion, etc. and will determine whether traumatic degrees of helplessness, anxiety, emotional storm, hopelessness, inhibition, or conflict develop. These responses are decisive as to whether postdisaster psychiatric morbidity will develop, and they reflect the primary stressors, such as danger to life, loss trauma conflicts. In this case, the main psychiatric outcome is likely to be post-traumatic stress disorder. Thus the whole literature on psychic trauma and PTSD is relevant to disaster psychiatry.

We have seen an important exception to the notion that severity of exposure is the worst stressor. In a natural disaster that strikes and kills more than half of a closely knit group (for example, a military unit hit by an avalanche), among those not directly exposed the post-traumatic stress reactions in the acute period were more pronounced than for those who barely survived (Herlofsen, in press). The interpretation is that in this particular disaster, for those on the periphery, uncertainty about the fate of their friends and lack of a possibility to act and help contributed more severe stressors than the impact of the experience on those directly exposed.

Naturally, most disasters have several secondary stressors caused by the destruction, such as loss of home or job. Sometimes these secondary disaster stressors become the main cause of new morbidity (Veltro et al., 1990). This consequence makes the whole literature on stressful life events relevant to disaster psychology. If the primary disaster stressors were not severe, the postdisaster psychiatric disorders may not reflect the initial disaster experience, and theoretically any type of stress-inuced disorder may develop.

Uncertainty on a catastrophic scale has been created by the Chernobyl nuclear disaster, so that the event has been termed "the Chernobyl psychiatric disaster"; proponents of this view have interpreted the mass response as irrational and have coined the psychiatric label "radiophobia." This term is very unfortunate, because it labels as psychiatric and fear-driven a response that probably is more motivated by distrust and protest in people who have previously been seriously misinformed about the fallout by people in authority who have lost their credibility. Recent reports (personal communication) indicate that half of the population living in contaminated areas suffers from psychological stress symptoms; eventually these stress reactions will produce psychosomatic and somatic illness in some cases. There is no doubt that Chernobyl is a textbook example on how to create a second disaster.

Awareness of individual health status has increased enormously since the Chernobyl accident, and anxiety and its concomitant physiological reactions have spread far beyond the heavily contaminated areas. Shortly after the disaster, many subjective and objective symptoms were attributed to radiation exposure. Except for independent sources, media had low credibility, and understanding of the consequences of exposure to radiation was incomplete in the public as well as among community physicians. Dissatisfaction with medical advice and the public administration was considerable. As a 1990 WHO report stated:

> In order to cope with general anxiety and uncertainty about the possible health effects of exposure to radiation, people focus on the more tangible aspects of their physical state of health, seeking out the health care system and requesting explanations. In the absence of reliable data about the health effects of the accident, the medical profession lacks adequate explanations and responds predictably with more extensive and intensive diagnostic screening of population and

individual patients. As a result, hitherto unobserved morbidity patterns and individual variations emerge which are without explanation and which confuse the situation further.

The invisible nature of radiation reduces the subject's possibility of detecting and controlling the risk. Even in far-off countries, populations experienced stress and information crisis (Weisæth, 1991b) after the Chernobyl disaster. In other circumstances, invisible dangers are more easily accepted or denied.

A disaster affects individuals, groups, and the community at the macro level. For the mental health professional, an important unit to focus on to understand disaster responses is the family. Were the family members together when the disaster struck, were they split up and exposed, or were only some members affected? In the latter two cases search behavior usually predominates throughout the family, both during the impact and in the immediate aftermath.

IMPACT RESPONSES: DISASTER BEHAVIOR

The first systematic attempt to study disaster impact behavior was made by Tyhurst (1957a,b). More recently, Weisæth categorized the impact behavior of survivors of a factory explosion into *optimal, adaptive,* and *maladaptive* disaster behavior by using seven response variables. Because the accident was industrial, very few families were jointly exposed, so the typical desperate search for close ones by split families was not a problem. Categorizing disaster impact responses was difficult and not without value choices. The behavioral responses had to be rated in terms of their desirability from a biological, psychological, social, and ethical point of view. It was not always easy to decide what was optimal behavior; the response that could be desirable for one individual was not necessarily desirable from another's point of view. For example, escape was a rational response in the face of danger, but for those who were injured and unable to move it was vital that someone stopped, went back, and brought them out.

All but one of these seven response variables were behavioral and could be observed by others; thus, the reliability of the self-reported data could be controlled by cross interviews. To an increasing extent documentary evidence on how disaster victims cope can also be supplied by video recordings of the disaster event made by the victims themselves, onlookers, or the media. The physical responses to disaster trauma can be rated on a scale from loss of mobility on the one extreme to uncontrolled flight behavior on the other. But the acute response to disaster is undoubtedly a complex biopsychosocial response that may fluctuate from moment to moment and that constitutes a multifaceted phenomenon.

While about 70% of the high stress exposure group had some reduction in cognitive control—and half of these suffered severe reductions—only about 20% displayed some degree of inadequate behavior, usually motor paralysis; 15% needed help from others to overcome psychological blocks; 33% demonstrated leadership; about 50% were able to engage in cooperative activities; and only 38% of the severe exposure group made no or insignificant rescue efforts. In all, 37% displayed optimal disaster behavior in this occupational disaster (Weisæth, 1989d). In his studies of disasters in Canada, Tyhurst found that 12–25% of survivors are what he called "cool and collected" and able to retain their awareness, make an appreciation of the situation, formulate some plan of action, and carry it through. In the study of the factory explosion, previous level of training and experience of physically dangerous situations had a strong modulating effect on whether or not traumatic helplessness developed. The disaster training/experience variable alone yielded an overall correct prediction rate of 63.6%. A high level of training/experience had a high sensitivity (81%), specificity (85.9%), and positive predictive power (70.7%) in its relationship with optimal disaster behavior. Among personality types, the unremarkable and the compulsive/overcontrolled appeared to have an advantage in coping with the impact stress.

The modelling effect of those who coped well may go a long way toward explaining why there were few inadequate actions compared with the high frequency of disturbed cognitive functions. A tendency during critically dangerous situations to follow the person in authority has been observed (Abe, 1976), and experiments on simulated emergency situations have demonstrated the presence of an initial period of social influence in people faced with an urgent and uncommon situation (Py, 1978).

Adaptive disaster behavior was seen in 34%, who needed no help to survive and who contributed to rescue activities when recruited for such activities by one of those who took charge. Tyhurst reports that about three-quarters of the survivors were stunned and bewildered, while about 10 to 25% showed manifest inappropriate responses: states of confusion, paralyzing anxiety, inability to move, or "hysterical" crying or screaming. Only a few, 1 to 2%, exhibited psychotic reactions. In the study of the factory explosion, 29% showed maladaptive responses, compared to 5% reported from household fires (Wood, 1980). While flight was frequent (and usually wrongly termed panic by the media), a few cases of individual panic did occur, with loss of cognitive function and evidence of egocentric thinking, overwhelming fear, and uncontrolled flight. Psychotic reactions were only seen in the severely injured (burn and crush injuries), while other disaster researchers have reported reactive psychoses (Ploeger, 1968; Popovic & Petrovic, 1964).

The immediate responses to the disaster impact were found to frequently determine the individual's chances of survival, the ability to rescue other victims, and whether the individual contributed to rational collective behavior. Maladaptive or psychiatric reactions to a severe danger, such as immobilizing fright, uncontrolled flight behavior, or breakdown of reality testing, may be incompatible with survival in situations in which immediate rational action is mandatory. However, the exact proportion of deaths caused by maladaptive responses to a danger trauma has never been established. Disturbed behavior also taxed rescue resources and negatively affected the behavior of others. Group panic did not occur, although the risk factor for the development of panic when perceiving possible entrapment was widely present. Human factors (leadership, group cohesion, competence, motivation) neutralized the unfavorable physical circumstances. While group panic may be an infrequent phenomenon (Quarantelli, 1954), when it occurs, it has devastating consequences for survival.

As regards the long-term effects, it was found that the subjects' responses during the impact phase, and how they viewed them in the aftermath, deeply affected the type and intensity of their post-traumatic reactions. Thus, PTSD after this disaster exposure was to a large extent the result of a failure to cope with the primary disaster stressors and not mainly a failure to recover from post-traumatic stress reactions.

The mediating variable was probably the amount of control that the well-trained individual was able to feel during the disaster impact; this factor reduced the intensity of helplessness that was otherwise strongly associated with a high risk of illness. Similar findings have been made in studies of PTSD in soldiers after combat (Solomon, Weisen, Schwarzwald, & Mikulincer, 1987), in which combat stress reactions were found to be strongly associated with PTSD.

These and other findings from similar studies of duty-related disaster stress demonstrate that selection and training for disaster are important preventive measures in term of post-disaster stress. Promising results in increasing stress tolerance and coping capacity have been achieved from teaching coping skills (stress inoculation training) in occupations with a high risk of accidents or disasters (Hytten, Jensen, & Skauli, 1990).

IMMEDIATE AFTERMATH

The disaster syndrome—absence of emotion, lack of response to external stimuli, inhibition of outward activity and random movements, besides being "stunned," "shocked," or "dazed"—has repeatedly been reported by observers of disaster victims immediately after the event. After the Arkansas tornado, 14% were reported to be in a state of shock (Fritz & Marks, 1954), with women somewhat over-represented.

After the Skopje earthquake, stupor engulfed more than half the population (Popovic & Petrovic, 1964). In the immediate aftermath of the factory explosion described previously, 21% displayed marked derealization and apathy, 17% reacted with disorganized flight behavior, and 3% showed confusional-excitational states. In several, a shocked reaction turned into uncontrolled flight or highly agitated uncontrolled behavior. Still, about 30% were undisturbed during the aftermath of this single impact shock trauma. Taking part in rescue work was a very useful way of coping with these stress reactions and reduced risk of PTSD. In the absence of consciously experienced emotions, manifest physical changes appropriate to fear or psychophysiological symptoms made themselves felt. Severe tremors, palpitations, hyperventilation, breathing difficulty, nausea, vomiting, etc. may (1) interfere with actions that are important to survivors such as talking, calling on the phone, etc., (2) serve as the starting point of a somatization process, or (3) be misinterpreted as signs of some toxic agent. After this particular disaster trauma, 90% of those who experienced significant anxiety reactions did so within 5 hours.

THE HEALTH EFFECTS OF DISASTER STRESS

Mortality has been shown to increase after disasters (Adams & Adams, 1984; Bennet, 1970), although not approaching the rates experienced after concentration camp imprisonment (Eitinger & Strøm, 1973). Mortality rates among the severely handicapped in institutions will soar if quality of care decreases for a considerable period of time because of disaster or war (personal observation). After the mass death of children, sharp increases in birth rates have been noted (Williams & Parkes, 1975). With regard to studying general morbidity, the methodological problems are difficult to overcome, particularly securing a perfect control group. Holen (1991), who studied survivors of an oil rig disaster, found an increase in psychosomatic diagnoses during the first eight years after, but not in general somatic diagnoses. Physical symptoms are frequently reported and health care utilization and hospital admission may increase or decrease; the level of morbidity is only one factor of many that influences the figures.

THE MENTAL HEALTH EFFECTS OF DISASTER STRESS

The new ICD-10 (World Health Organization, 1992) has introduced the diagnosis of "acute stress reaction" (F.43.0), which demands exposure to "an exceptional mental or physical stressor" and immediate (within one hour) onset of symptoms. The reaction is graded as mild if two criteria of symptoms for generalized anxiety disorder are met. The reaction is ranked as moderate if two of the following symptoms are found: narrowing of attention, apparent disorientation, anger or verbal aggression, despair or hopelessness, inappropriate or purposeless overactivity, or uncontrollable and excessive grief. Finally, a severe rating is given if four of the preceding symptoms are present or if dissociative stupor is found. After transient stressors, the symptoms must begin to diminish after not more than 8 hours; after continuous stressors, after 48 hours.

PTSD, with its cognitive, affective, and behavioral symptoms and characteristic changes, is the most frequent psychiatric consequence of disaster. In addition—often comorbid with PTSD—a variety of psychological and psychiatric disorders have been found: depression, phobias, dissociative disorders, alcohol and drug abuse, family disturbances, accident proneness, etc.

The ICD-10 proposes a new diagnostic category: "Enduring personality change after catastrophic experience." The stress exposure must be so extreme that is not necessary to consider personal vulnerability in order to explain its profound effect on the personality. Usually the personality change has to be confirmed by a key informant. The definite and persistent change in the person's pattern of perceiving, relating to, and thinking about the environment and him or her self should be significant and represent inflexible and maladaptive features present for at least three years. Symptoms consist of at least two of the following: permanently hostile or distrustful attitudes toward the world; social withdrawal; constant feelings of emptiness and/or hopelessness; enduring feelings of "being on edge" or being threatened without any external cause, as evidenced by an increased vigilance and irritability; and, finally, permanent feelings of being changed or being different from others (estrangement). The personality change meeting the above criteria is often preceded by a post-traumatic stress disorder and must not be related to episodes of any other mental disorder.

INDIVIDUAL VULNERABILITY FACTORS

Few studies have systematically examined individual vulnerability factors in victims of disaster. As described previously, a low level of disaster training constituted a risk factor for PTSD after a factory explosion, a finding that partly explained the greater risk in the female industrial employees, who had less training than the males. In the same study, it was possible to collect data on predisaster physical health from various independent sources. It was found that only one-third of the PTSD cases, 7 months postdisaster, at some point in their lives had previously suffered from a psychological problem (Weisæth, 1985). The sum of personal vulnerability factors increased in importance as a prognostic risk factor during the 4-year follow-up period. In the main there seemed to be a broad and nonspecific type of psychological vulnerability, like the ordinary psychiatric risk factors, to the disaster stress. Persons with a proneness for anxiety reactions or strong dependency traits were particularly vulnerable. But chronic PTSD was almost exclusively found in the group exposed to high disaster stress. Thus, severe exposure was sufficient to produce an acute PTSD and necessary to produce a disorder of long duration. No correlation to illness risk and prognostic risk was provided by age, civil status, education, secondary disaster stressors, or independent life events after this disaster. Gleser et al. (1981) found more disaster-related pathology in women and noted a curvilinear relationship between age and psychopathology in the population of Buffalo Creek, with the age range of 25–54 being most affected—the group, perhaps, that had most to lose from the massive destructions. While low education in men related to pathology, this was not the case among the women. After a volcano disaster in the United States, women with high exposure had twice the rate of anxiety, depression, and PTSD (Shore et al., 1986) as men.

Green et al. (1986) found that vulnerability factors played a minor role in accounting for PTSD after a catastrophic fire, while Holen (1990) reported that, respectively, occupational dysfunction and distress in survivors of an oil rig disaster were more severe in subjects with a history of previous psychiatric problems or neurotic character traits. Also, McFarlane (1989) found that the acute PTSD group among the firefighters he studied had no major vulnerability factors, whereas the chronic PTSD group scored significantly higher on vulnerability factors.

All the above studies were of severe but brief exposures to disaster stressors. It appears that the degree of exposure plays a dominating role in the onset of PTSD, while premorbid factors play an important prognostic role in long-term PTSD, although less than in general psychiatric disorders.

LONG-TERM PSYCHIATRIC MORBIDITY AFTER DISASTERS

A series of studies have established morbidity levels from about 20% to 50% one year after disaster (Gleser et al., 1981; Green, Grace, Lindy, Titchener, & Lindy, 1983; Powell & Penick, 1983; Shore et al., 1986; Tierney & Baisden, 1979; Weisæth, 1985). In spite of the brief duration of the exposure, man-made disasters with high shock showed persisting levels of over 30% morbidity, with PTSD the most frequent disorder, followed by depressions. Considering that some of the populations studied are positive samples in terms of prior health compared to the general population, and even trained to cope with disaster, such as industrial shift workers (Weisæth, 1985) or offshore oil rig employees (Holen, 1990), these morbidity rates are impressive. However, after an avalanche accident, no case of PTSD has developed from the post-traumatic stress reactions within 5 years after the event (Herlofsen, in press). Intensive preventive work has been offered as explanation, in combination with absence of pronounced individual vulnerability factors.

In the third world, victims of low socioeconomic status exposed to devastating natural disasters followed by severe secondary stressors may have even higher morbidity rates of PTSD and a higher proportion of major depressions (Lima et al. 1991).

There are different findings on the natural course of the stress response. In one study, neurasthenic irritability caused by longstanding post-traumatic anxiety symptoms was the only stress reaction that increased during the first year (Weisæth, 1989b). In another, hostility increased significantly 1 to 2 years after (Green et al., 1983). Such aggressive symptoms complicate the PTSD and frequently reduce motivation for treatment and produce family conflicts. Most of the studies show a gradual decrease in the various types of pathology over time. For example, the PTSD prevalence rates decreased from 36% (after 7 months) to 27% (after 2 years), 22% (after 3 years), and 19% (after 4 years) in the high exposure group after the factory explosion; in the medium exposure group the decrease was from 17% at 7 months to 2% after 4 years; and in the low exposure group the decrease went from 4% to 3% (Weisæth, 1985). However, cases of severe PTSD at 7 months did not improve significantly during the 4-year observation period, and hardly any of the 7-month PTSD cases became asymptomatic during the next 3 years.

Delayed PTSD is reported by most studies, but after exposure to brief disaster traumas this form of PTSD is the exception rather than the rule. Probably this finding is related to the invasive property of the shock trauma, which leaves no time for psychological defenses to be mobilized.

Leopold and Dillon (1963) found that the majority of sailors who had survived a ship's collision/explosion suffered appreciable deterioration in mental health during the next years, with 71% being severely impaired 4 years later. At the time, the high persisting morbidity was ascribed to the nature of the disaster and to the subsequent return to sea of the middle-aged sailors. However, in retrospect one can question whether these sailors were a not high-risk group before the disaster, because many of them had served in the wartime merchant marine. Such war service has since (Askevold, 1976/1977) been shown to produce chronic post-traumatic stress syndromes in a high proportion of those who survived.

As regards very long term follow-ups, Ploeger (1977) found chronic personality changes in the majority of survivors 10 years after a mine accident. A 14-year follow-up of Buffalo Creek survivors (Green et al., 1990) established a PTSD rate of 28%, down from 44% at the 2-year follow-up. There were no differences between men and women. The chronic PTSD cases had experienced more extreme and prolonged life-threatening experiences and loss of close family members in the disaster.

IDENTIFYING INDIVIDUALS AND GROUPS AT RISK

Assessment of traumatization in victim groups can in principle, be carried out in three ways, by identifying:

1. High-risk situations—the presence of particularly severe trauma dimensions.
2. High-risk persons—the presence of high-risk factors (vulnerability) in exposed persons.
3. High-risk reactions—the presence of early response variables that predict later illness.

The number of disaster-affected persons may be large, whereas the interventive resources may be limited, as may be the time available to prevent psychiatric cases from developing. In practical preventive work, ways to address the three groups of risk factors often have to be applied in combination. Screening instruments have been developed for this purpose (Raphael et al., 1989). In prospectively designed studies, prediction of long-term PTSD has been made by early response variables (sensitivity 0.96, specificity 0.89 in predicting PTSD 7 months later). Discriminant analysis using background variables and a measure of the degree of disaster exposure predicted correctly in 91% of the cases whether the subject would develop a PTSD or not (Weisæth, 1985). It is, however, less likely that such strong predictions can be achieved in disasters followed by severe secondary stressors.

GROUPS AT RISK

A disaster of some magnitude can affect the mental health of various groups in the aftermath:

1. the next-of-kin
2. the injured survivors and their close ones

   3. the uninjured survivors
   4. onlookers (the helpless helpers are particularly at risk)
   5. rescuers
   6. body handlers
   7. health personnel (mass injury situations that demand difficult prioritizing)
   8. persons holding responsibility
   9. workmates (in company disasters) (Weisæth, 1989b)
  10. evacuees (Milne, 1977)

Of these groups, a family may include all of the first three. The other groups need to be considered, but they usually have less pressing needs.

Next-of-Kin

There are many reasons why disaster death constitutes a risk to the health of next-of-kin (Lundin, 1987, 1990; Raphael, 1983, 1986): the unexpected and sudden nature of the death; the tragic and terrible circumstances of the death, which was perhaps witnessed by family members; or the uncertainty, despair, and hope that the family must endure while waiting to be informed about a death in a far-away place. The bereaved may not be able to travel to the site, may not be able to view their dead, the remains cannot always be identified, or the missing body may never be found. In preventive work after disasters, emphasis is put on conveying the message of death correctly and compassionately. Furthermore, the family is helped to make a last farewell to their dead ones, informed about the circumstances of death, and encouraged to visit the site of disaster and meet survivors, rescuers, or identification experts. All of these steps will enable them to grasp the reality of death and accept what has happened. The confrontation with reality evokes strong feelings and support may be needed.

Rescue Workers

In disasters with a high death toll, the helplessness of the victim may be mirrored by the powerlessness of disaster rescuers. In one study of rescuers, a high correlation was found between a low level of training, suffering severe stress reactions during the rescue operation, and the risk of developing post-traumatic stress problems. (Ersland, Weisæth, & Sund, 1989).

A great deal of evidence shows that disasters pose a more severe risk to the mental health of rescuers and other disaster workers than single accidents (Bartone, Ursano, Wright, & Ingraham, 1989; Durham, McCammon, & Allison, 1985; Ersland & Weisæth, 1989; Lundin, 1990; McFarlane, 1986). Inexperienced body handlers seem to be at greater risk (Taylor & Frazer, 1982; Ursano & McCarrol, 1990). Group debriefing has become increasingly applied after exposure to duty-related stress and beneficial effects have been postulated, but there is as yet little evidence (Mitchell, 1983; Shalev & Ursano, 1990) of its effectiveness.

INTERVENTIONS AFTER DISASTER-GROUP APPROACHES

In all disasters, those in the social network of the victims will be important support providers. In developing countries, the disaster and health workers should be given a care curriculum for mental health training in dealing with victims of disaster (Lima et al., 1989; World Health Organization, 1991). Another level of intervention that could be implemented is giving professional advice to decisionmakers at high level, thus ensuring that decisions made in the aftermath of disaster take mental health issues into consideration.

In the industrialized countries, the chain of care from which one can mobilize support at different levels runs in this way:

1. self-help—advice to victims about intrapsychic, interpersonal, and activity-related coping techniques
2. social network—mobilizing support from family, friends, workmates, and neighbors
3. helpers outside the health care and social services—leaders, clergy, police, rescuers, firemen, volunteer organizations, etc.
4. general and specialized somatic health care services
5. mental health professionals
6. specific disaster psychiatric teams for the bereaved, injured, survivors, debriefing teams, and disaster workers

Because of the different social contexts of the community, company, and communication disasters (the three Cs), in Norway there has been a recognition of the need to design specific models for psychiatric interventions in each of these cases. The geographical distance from the home and whether or not the victims constituted an established group or just happened to be together at the site are related to Green's (1982) dimension of a disaster as being central or peripheral to the community. The agencies with which one should establish a working relationship in order to be an effective catalyst of support services will vary in each case. For example, in the communication category, people who die or are severely injured are often far away from home. Their social network is not there, and so close ones need to be brought in from outside. The family comes in to give, but also to take. They give what they have of social support; they take, in cases of bereavement, what they can only receive from those with firsthand knowledge of the tragedy.

ESTABLISHING AN INFORMATION-SUPPORT CENTER

The psychosocial organization can be located either at a hospital or at a convenient place not too far from the disaster area, (hotel, school, etc.), or both. If the identities of the dead are uncertain (as is frequently the case), or the number of dead is unknown for a time, a great many families will be affected until they ascertain whether their missing family member is safe. Establishing an information-support center has proven useful (Weisæth, 1991a,c), particularly after transport or communication disasters in which people have died far away from their homes. The existence of such a center and its telephone numbers should be distributed by radio and television. Families who suspect their members are missing should be invited to come to the center, and survivors may also be asked to gather there. The center gives the bereaved a chance to meet survivors and get a firsthand report about what happened to their loved ones—how they died, perhaps even what they said before they perished, where, why, etc.—and what efforts were made to rescue them. The survivors, and possibly onlookers and rescuers, have information that often cannot be given by others. Frequently, such information will be crucial in helping the bereaved to understand, and finally to accept, the new reality. For the survivors it is often an important experience to help the bereaved.

The main functions of such an information-support center are:

1. to provide rapid, authoritative information about tragic news that can be conveyed in a humane, direct way and given in a setting sheltered from public and media attention
2. to provide support and a holding environment for the affected persons (health personnel, clergy, police, and others)
3. to serve as a forum or meeting place where affected individuals and families can support each other and, possibly, create Self-help groups or organizations
4. to be a place where the police can collect identification data about missing and dead persons from their close ones
5. to be used, at times, by the police for interrogating survivors, of the chain of events that led to the disaster
6. to help reduce the convergence of people on the disaster site that may otherwise create congestion and, therefore, mobility problems for rescuers
7. to provide links to local helpers when initial assessment indicates that some kind of help or service will be needed in the long term

A meeting may be organized for everyone affected (this may be possible for up to 1,000 people), or at least one or two representatives from each affected family can attend and be given information about rescue, identification, investigation of causes, insurance, psychosocial support services, and religious services.

REFERENCES

ABE, K. The behaviour of survivors and victims in a Japanese nightclub fire: A descriptive research note. *Mass Emergencies,* 1976, *1,* 119–124.

ADAMS, P. R., & ADAMS, G. R. Mount St. Helens' ashfall: Evidence for a disaster stress reaction. *American Psychologists,* 1984, *39,* 252–260.

ALEXANDER, D. A., & WELLS, A. Reactions of police officers to body handling after a major disaster. A before-and-after comparison. *British Journal of Psychiatry,* 1991, *159,* 547–555.

ASKEVOLD, F. War sailor syndrome. *Psychotherapy and Psychosomatics,* 1976/1977, *27,* 133–138.

BARTON, A. H. Social organization under stress. Washington, DC: National Research Council, 1963.

BARTON, A. H. *Communities in disaster: A sociological analysis of collective stress situations.* Garden City, NY: Doubleday, 1969.

BARTONE, P. T., URSANO, R. J., WRIGHT, K. M., & INGRAHAM, L. H. The impact of a military air disaster on the health of assistance workers. *Journal of Nervous and Mental Disease,* 1989, *177,* 317–328.

BAUM, A. Toxins, technology, disasters. In G. R. Vanden Bos & B. K. Bryant (eds.), *Cataclysms, crisis, and catastrophes: Psychology in action.* Washington, DC: American Psychological Association, 1986

BENNET, G. Bristol floods 1968: Controlled survey of effects on health of local community disaster. *Br Med J,* 1970, *3,* 454–458.

————. Community disaster in Britain. In K. Jones (ed.) *The year book of social policy in Britain 1973.* London: Routledge and Kegan Paul, 1973.

BERLE, J. Ø., HAVER, B., & KARTERUD, S. Group reactions as observed in crisis intervention programs in hospitals. *Nordisk Psykiatrisk Tidsskr,* 1991, *45,* 329–335.

BERREN, M. R. BEIGEL, A., & BARKER, G. A typology for the classification of disasters: Implications for intervention. *Community Mental Health Journal,* 1982, *18,* 120–134.

BERZ, G. List of major natural disasters, 1960–1987. *Earthquakes and Volcanoes,* 1989, *20,* 226–228.

BLOCH, D. A., SILBER, E., PERRY, S. E. Some factors in the emotional reaction of children to disaster. *American Journal of Psychiatry,* 1956, *113,* 416–422.

DURHAM, T. W., MCCAMMON, S. L., & ALLISON, E. J. The psychological impact of disaster on rescue personnel. *Annals of Emergency Medicine,* 1985, *14,* 664–668.

DYNES, R. R. *Organized behavior in disaster.* Columbus: Ohio State University, Disaster Research Center, 1974.

EITINGER, L., & STRØM, A. *Mortality and morbidity after excessive stress.* Oslo: Universitetsforlaget, 1973.

ERICHSEN, J. E. On railway and other injuries of the nervous system. London: Walton and Moberly; Philadelphia: H. C. Lea, 1866.

ERIKSON, K. T. Loss of communality at Buffalo Creek. *American Journal of Psychiatry,* 1976, *133,* 302–304.

ERSLAND, S., WEISÆTH, L., & SUND, A. The stress upon rescuers involved in an oil rig disaster. "Alexander L. Kielland" 1980. *Acta Psychiatrica Scandinavica,* 1989 (suppl. 355); *80,* 38–49.

FISCHER-HOMBERGER, E. *Die Traumatische Neurose, vom somatischen zum soziale Leiden.* Bern: Verlag Hans Huber, 1975.

FRASER, L., LESLIE, I. M., & PHELPS, D. Psychiatric effects of personal experience during bombing. *Proceedings of the Royal Society of Medicine,* 1942/1943, *36,* 119–123.

FREDERICK, C. J. Effects of natural vs. human-induced violence upon victims. *Evaluation and Change,* 1980, special issue, 71–75.

————. Children traumatized by catastrophic situations. In S. Eth & R. S. Pynoos (eds.), *Post-traumatic Stress Disorder in Children.* Washington, DC: American Psychiatric Press, 1985.

————. Psychic trauma in victims of crime and terrorism. In G. R. Vanden Bos & B. K. Bryant (eds.), *Cataclysms, crisis and catastrophes:* Psychology in action. Washington, D.C: American Psychological Association, 1986.

FRITZ, C. E. Disaster. In R. K. Merton & R. A. Nisbet (eds.), *Contemporary social problems.* New York: Harcourt, Brace and World, 1961.

FRITZ, C. E., & MARKS, E. S. The NORC studies of human behavior in disaster. *Journal of Social Issues,* 1954, *10,* 26–41.

GARMEZY, N., & RUTTER, M. Acute reactions to stress. In M. Rutter & L. Hersov (eds.), *Child and adolescent psychiatry: Modern approaches.* Oxford: Blackwell, 1985.

GIROLAMO, G. International perspectives on the treatment and prevention of post-traumatic stress disorders. In J. P. Wilson & B. Raphael (eds.), *International handbook of traumatic stress syndromes.* New York: Plenum, 1992.

GLESER, G. C., GREEN, B. L., & WINGET, C. N. Quantifying interview data on psychic impairment of disaster survivors. *Journal of Nervous and Mental Disease,* 1978, *166,* 209–216.

————. *Prolonged psychosocial effects of disaster: A study of Buffalo Creek.* New York: Academic Press, 1981.

GREEN, B. L. Assessing levels of psychosocial impairment following disaster: Consideration of actual and methodological dimensions. *Journal of Nervous and Mental Disease,* 1982, *170,* 544–552.

GREEN, B. L., GRACE, M. C., & GLESER, G. C. Identifying survivors at risk: Longterm impairment following the Beverly Hills Supper Club fire. *J Consulting Clinical Psychology,* 1986, *53,* 672–678.

GREEN, B. L., GRACE, M. C., LINDY, J. D., TITCHENER, J. L., & LINDY, J. G. Levels of functional impairment following a civilian disaster: The Beverly Hills Supper Club fire. *J Consulting Clinical Psychology,* 1983, *51,* 563–80.

GREEN, B. L., LINDY, J. D., GRACE, M. C., GLESER, G. C., LEONARD, B. A., KOROL, M., & WINGET, C. Buffalo Creek survivors in the second decade: stability of stress symptoms. *American Journal of Ortho-psychiatry,* 1990, *60,* 43–54.

HERLOFSEN, P. Individual and group reactions to an avalanche trauma. In R. J. Ursano, B. McCaughey, & C. S. Fullerton (eds.), *Individual and community response to disaster.* New York: Cambridge University Press, in press.

HESNARD, A. Les troubles nerveux et psychiques consecutifs aux catastrophes navales. *Revue de Psychiatrie,* 1914, *18,* 139–151.

HOLEN, A. *A long-term outcome study of survivors from a disaster.* Oslo: University of Oslo, 1990.

————. A longitudinal study of the occurrence and persistence of post-traumatic health problems in disaster survivors. *Stress Medicine,* 1991, *7,* (11):17.

HYTTEN, K., JENSEN, A., & SKAULI, G. Stress inoculation training for smoke divers and free fall lifeboat passengers. *Aviation Space Environmental Medicine,* 1990, *61,* 983–988.

KINSTON, W., & ROSSER, R. Disaster effects on mental and physical state. *Journal of Psychosomatic Research,* 1974, *18,* 437–456.

KORVER, A. J. H. What is a disaster? *Prehospital and Disaster Medicine,* 1987, *2,* 152–153.

LEOPOLD, R. L., & DILLON, H. Psycho-anatomy of a disaster: A long term study of post-traumatic neuroses in survivors of a marine explosion. *American Journal of Psychiatry,* 1963, *119,* 913–921.

LIMA, B. R. The emotional consequences of two Latin American disasters: Colombia and Ecuador. In Stefanis et al. (eds.), *Psychiatry: a world perspective.* Vol 4. Elsevier, 1990.

LIMA, B. R., CHAVEZ, H., SAMANIEGO, N., POMPEI, S., PAI, S., SANTACRUZ, H., & LOZANO, J. Disaster severity and emotional response: Implications for primary mental health care in developing countries. *Acta Psychiatrica Scandinavica,* 1989, *79,* 74–82.

LIMA, B. R., PAI, S., LOZANO, J., & SANTACRUZ, H. The stability of emotional symptoms among disaster victims in a developing country. *Journal of Traumatic Stress,* 1976, *3,* 497–505.

LIMA, B. R., PAI, S., SANTACRUZ, H., LOZANO, J., & LUNA, J. Screening for the psychological consequences of a major disaster in a developing country: Armero, Colombia. *Acta Psychiatrica Scandinavica,* 1987, *76,* 561–567.

LIMA, B. R., SHAILA, P., SANTACRUZ, H., & LOZANO, J. Psychiatric disorders among poor victims following a major disaster: Armero, Colombia. *Journal of Nervous and Mental Disease,* 1991, *179,* 420–427.

LINDEMANN, E. Symptomatology and management of acute grief. *American Journal of Psychiatry,* 1944, *101,* 141–148.

LINDY, J. D., GRACE, M. C., & GREEN, B. L. Survivors: Outreach to a reluctant population. *American Journal of Orthopsychiatry,* 1981, *51,* 468–478.

LUCHTERHAND, E. G. Sociological approaches to massive stress in natural and man-made disasters. In H. Krystal & W. G. Niederland (eds.), *Psychiatric traumatization: After-effects in individuals and communities.* Boston: Little, Brown 1977.

LUNDIN, T. The stress of unexpected bereavement. *Stress Medicine,* 1987, *4,* 109–114.

LUNDIN, T. The rescue personnel and the disaster stress. In Lundeberg J. E., Otto U, Rybeck B (eds.) Wartime Medical Services. Stockholm: FOA, 1990, 208–216.

————. The rescue personnel and the disaster stress. In J. E. Lundeberg, U. Otto, & B. Rybeck (eds.), *Wartime medical services.* Stockholm: FOA, 1991.(a)

McFARLANE, A. C. Long-term psychiatric morbidity after a natural disaster. *Medical Journal of Australia,* 1986, *145,* 561–563.

————. The longitudinal course of post-traumatic morbidity: The range of outcomes and their predictors. *Journal of Nervous and Mental Disease,* 1988, *179,* 406–411.

————. The aetiology of post-traumatic morbidity: Predisposing, precipitating and perpetuating factors. *British Journal of Psychiatry,* 1989, *154,* 221–228.

McFARLANE, A. C., & HUA, C. The study of a major disaster in the People's Republic of China: The Yunnan earthquake. In J. Wilson & B. Raphael (eds.), *International handbook of traumatic stress syndromes.* New York: Plenum, 1992.

MERSKEY, H. Shell shock. In G. E. Berrios, & H. Freeman (eds.), *150 Years of British psychiatry 1841–1991.* London: The Royal College of British Psychiatrists, 1991.

MILNE, G. Cyclone Tracy: I. Some consequences of the evacuation for adult victims. *Australian Psychology,* 1977, *12,* 39–54.

MITCHELL, J. When disaster strikes . . . The critical incident stress debriefing process. *Journal of Emergency Medical Services,* 1983, *8,* 36–39.

NEWMAN, C. J. Children of disaster: Clinical observations at Buffalo Creek. *American Journal of Psychiatry,* 1976, *133,* 306–316.

ØDEGÅRD, Ø. Extreme stress. In K. P. Kisker, J. E. Meyer, C. Müller, & E. Strømberg (eds.), *Psychiatrie der Gegenwart. 2 Aufl.* Berlin: Springer, 1975

OLIVER-SMITH, A. Success and failures in post-disaster resettlement. *Disasters,* 1991, *15,* 12–23.

PENICK, E. C., POWELL, B. J., & SIECK, W. A. Mental health problems and natural disaster: Tornado victims. *Journal of Community Psychology,* 1976, *4,* 64–67.

PERRY, R. W., & LINDELL, M. K. The psychological consequences of natural disaster: A review of research on American communities. *Mass Emergencies,* 1978, *3,* 105–115.

PLOEGER, A. Persönlichkeitseigentümliche Angstabwehr durch psychogene Halluzinose: Die "Realangst-Halluzinose": Weitere Untersuchungen an den Geretteten der Bergwerkskatastrophe von Lengede 1963. *Zeitschrift für Psychotherapic und Medizinische Psychologie,* 1968, *18,* 134–140.

————. A 10 year follow up of miners trapped for 2 weeks under threatening circumstances. In C. D. Spielberger & I. G. Sarason (eds.), *Stress and anxiety.* Vol. 4. New York: Wiley, 1977.

POPOVIC, M., & PETROVIC, D. After the earthquake. *Lancet,* 1964, *2,* 1169–1171.

POWELL, B. J., & PENICK, E. C. Psychological distress following a natural disaster: A one-year follow-up of 98 flood victims. *Journal of Community Psychology,* 1983, *2,* 269–276.

PRINCE, S. H. *Catastrophe and social change.* New York: Columbia University, 1920.

PY, Y. Comportements dans un cas de secours d'urgence. *Travail Humain,* 1978, *41,* 67–80.

PYNOOS, R. S., FREDERICK, C., NADER, K., ARROYO, W., STEINBERG, A., ETHS, S., NUNEZ, F., & FAIRBANKS, L. Life threat and post-traumatic stress in school-age children. *Archives of General Psychiatry,* 1987, *44,* 1056–1063.

QUARANTELLI, E. L. The nature and conditions of panic. *American Journal of Sociology,* 1954, *60,* 267–275.

————. An assessment of conflicting views on mental health: The consequences of traumatic events. In C. R. Figley (ed.), *Trauma and its wake.* New York: Brunner, 1985.

RAPHAEL, B. *The anatomy of bereavement.* New York: Basic Books, 1983.

————. *When disaster strikes. How individuals and communities cope with catastrophe.* New York: Basic Books, 1986.

RAPHAEL,, B., LUNDIN, T., & WEISÆTH, L. A research method for the study of psychological and psychiatric aspects of disaster. *Acta Psychiatrica Scandinavica,* 1989, (suppl. 353) 1–60.

SCHÜFFEL, W., LOPEZ-IBOR, J. J., ROSSER, R., & WEISÆTH, L. (eds.). *A concerted European action for coping with disaster.* Brussels: E. C. Research and Development Coordination Programme, 1990.

SETHI, B. B., SHARMA, M., SINGH, T., & SINGH, H. Psychiatric morbidity of patients attending clinics in gas affected areas in Bhopal. *Indian Journal of Medical Research,* 1987 (suppl.) 45–50.

SHALEY, A., & URSANO, R. J. Group debriefing following exposure to traumatic stress. In J. E. Lundeberg, U. Otto, & B. Rybeck (eds.), *Wartime medical services.* Stockholm: FOA, 1990.

SHORE, J. H., TATUM, E., & VOLLMER, W. M. Evaluation of mental health effects of disaster. *American Journal of Public Health,* 1986, *76,* 76–83.

SHORT, P. Victims and helpers. In R. L. Heathcote & B. G. Tong, (eds.), *Natural hazards in Australia.* Canberra: Australian Academy of Science, 1979.

SOLOMON, S. Research issues in assessing disasters' effects. In R. Gist, & B. Lubin (eds.), *Psychological aspects of disaster.* New York: Wiley, 1989.

SOLOMON, Z., WEISEN, M., SCHWARZWALD, J., & MIKULINCER, M. Post-traumatic stress disorder among frontline soldiers with combat stress reactions: The 1982 Israeli experience. *American Journal of Psychiatry,* 1987, *144,* 448–454.

STIERLIN, E. *Über psychoneuropathische Folgezustände bei den Überlebenden der Katastrophe von Courriere am 10. Marz 1906.* Doctoral dissertation, University of Zürich, 1909.

————. Nervöse und psychische Störungen nach Katastrophen. *Deutsches Medizinisches Wochenschrift,* 1911, *37,* 2028–2035.

SUND, A., HOLEN, A., & WEISÆTH, L. *The Alexander Kielland oil rig disaster, March 27, 1980. Report to Ministry of Health.* Oslo: Division of Disaster Psychiatry, University of Oslo, 1983.

TAYLOR, A. J. A taxonomy of disasters and their victims. *Journal of Psychosomatic Research,* 1987, *31,* 535–544.

TAYLOR, A. J. W., & FRAZER, A. G. The stress of post-disaster body handling and victim identification work. *Journal of Human Stress,* Vol. 8, 1982, 4–12.

TERR, L. C. Children traumatized in small groups. In S. Eth & R. Pynoos (eds.), *Post-traumatic stress disorder in children.* Washington DC: American Psychiatric Press, 1985.

TIERNEY, K. J., & BAISDEN, B. *Crisis intervention programs for disaster victims: a source book and manual for smaller communities.* Rockville, MD: National Institute of Mental Health, 1979.

TYHURST, J. S. Individual reactions to community disaster. *American Journal of Psychiatry,* 1951, *107,* 764–769.

TYHURST, J. S. Psychological and social aspects of civilian disaster. *Canadian Medical Association Journal;* 1957a, *76,* 385–393.

TYHURST, J. S. (1957b) The role of transition states, including disasters, in mental illness. In *Symposium on preventive and social psychiatry,* 15–17 April, 1957. Washington: Walter Reed Army Institute of Research, 1958.

URSANO, R. J., & McCARROL, J. E. The nature of the traumatic stressors: Handling dead bodies. *The Journal of Nervous and Mental Disease,* 1990, *178,* 396–398.

VELTRO, F., LOBRACE, S., STARACE, F., MAJ, M., & KEMALI, D. Prevalence of mental disorders among subjects exposed to seismic phenomena in Naples Province. 1990. In Stefanis, C. N. et al. (eds.) A World Perspective, *4,* pp. 415–419.

WEISÆTH, L. *Stress reactions to an industrial disaster.* Oslo: Medical Faculty, University of Oslo, 1984.

————. Post-traumatic stress disorder after an industrial disaster: Point prevalences, etiological and prognostic factors. In P. Pichot, P. Berner, R. Wolf, & K. Thau (eds.), *Psychiatry - the state of the art*. New York: Plenum Press, 1985.

————. Importance of high response rates in traumatic stress research. *Acta Psychiatrica Scandinavica,* 1989 (suppl. 355), *80,* 131–137.(a)

————. The stressors and the post-traumatic stress syndrome after an industrial disaster. *Acta Psychiatrica Scandinavica,* 1989 (suppl. 355), *80,* 25–37.(b)

————. Torture of a Norwegian ship's crew. *Acta Psychiatrica Scandinavica,* 1989 (suppl. 355), *80,* 63–72.(d)

————. A study of behavioural responses to an industrial disaster, *Acta Psychiatrica Scandinavica,* 1989 (suppl. 355), *80,* 13–24.(c)

————. The psychiatrist's role in preventing psychopathological effects of disaster trauma. In A. Seva (ed.), *The European handbook of psychiatry and mental health.* Barcelona: Editorial Anthropos, 1991.(a)

————. Psychosocial reactions in Norway to nuclear fallout from the Chernobyl disaster. In S. R. Couch & J. S. Kroll-Smith (eds.), *Communities at risk. Collective responses to technological hazards.* New York: Peter Lang, 1991.(b)

————. The information and support centre. Preventing the after-effects of disaster trauma. In Sørensen, T., Abrahamsen, P., Torgersen, S. (eds), *Psychiatric disorders in the social domain.* Oslo: Norwegian University Press, 50–58, 1991.(c)

WILLIAMS, R. M., & PARKES, C. M. Psychosocial effects of disaster: Birth rate in Aberfan. *British Medical Journal,* 1975, *2,* 303–304.

WOOD, P. G. A survey of behaviour in fires. In D. Canter (ed.), *Fires and human behaviour.* Chichester, Eng.: John Wiley, 1980.

WORLD HEALTH ORGANIZATION. *Resolution on the international Decade for Natural Disaster Reduction.* Geneva: WHO, 1988.

————. *Working Group on Psychological Effects of Nuclear Accidents. Summary Report. EUR/ICP June 21, 1990.* Geneva: WHO Regional Office for Europe, 1990.(b)

————. Psychosocial consequences of disasters: Prevention and management. WHO, unpublished document, 1992a. Geneva. WHO/MNH/PSF/91.3

————. *The ICD-10 Classification of Mental and Behavioural Disorders Clinical descriptions and diagnostic guidelines,* Geneva, WHO, 1992b.

YULE, W., & WILLIAMS, R. M. Post-traumatic stress reactions in children. *Journal of Traumatic Stress,* 1990, *2,* 279–295.

33

Stress of the Holocaust

Leo Eitinger   Ellinor F. Major

IT IS TODAY GENERALLY ACCEPTED that about 50 million people had to pay with their lives on account of World War II. About 6 million of these victims were Jews, or somewhat more than 10%. Although in this chapter we apply the term *Holocaust* only to the Jewish persecuted and killed, we well know that the populations in almost all the countries occupied by the Nazis were exposed to suppression, persecution, arrests, and executions. There are many reasons for choosing this limited use of the term; the main reason is that of all those who perished during World War II, the Jewish people were the only ones defined as a group to be exterminated by all possible means. The plans for the wholesale murder of the Jewish people were begun and nearly completed without Allied attempts at intervention.

However, even in Nazi Germany it was not possible to kill millions of people without long-term and detailed preparations. There is no proof that Hitler already had planned the Holocaust when he came to power on January 30, 1933, but there is no doubt that he and his government had a clear aim to eliminate the Jews of Germany (and Europe) in one way or other. Although the Holocaust proper—i.e., the wholesale killing of the Jews—took place mainly after World War II had been started by Hitler's invasion of Poland, Jews had been exposed to all kinds of persecutions and harassments from 1933, first in Germany and later on in Austria, the so-called Sudetenland of Czechoslovakia, and in the Protectorate Bohemia and Moravia after they had been occupied by the Nazis without war. However, no publications in the literature refer to the long-lasting effects of these particular stress experiences. The explanation is probably that most of these early traumatized people were later exposed either to much more serious traumatizations or—and this is undoubtedly the rule—they were later killed during the following stages of the persecution that led to wholesale massacres of Jews. This genocidal destruction is known as the Holocaust. In this chapter it is impossible to give a detailed description of the step-by-step evolution from January 1933 to September 1939 when the war started and the system of mass murder was implemented. Only a few essentials can be mentioned as an introduction, to hint at the stress reactions that the Holocaust induced in its victims.

Among the most important tools for the completion of the Holocaust were the concentration camps, an integral part of the Nazi regime. Much deliberation, planning, organization, and classification were devoted to their perfection. For a time after the Nazis rose to power in Germany in 1933, the concentration camps were unorganized places where the different groups in the National Socialist Party were allowed to vent their aggression against

Jews and to wreak vengeance on their political enemies. Later the camps became well-organized institutions run by the highest authorities in the SS; the official aim was described as the re-education of the inmates, who would be transformed into new individuals better suited to live and cooperate with the new regime. In reality, the inmates were never considered worthy of reeducation. In all the camps, the prisoners were treated with utmost brutality and sadism, resulting in a high rate of mortality and suicide. But the possibility existed, though in most cases only theoretically, that the inmates could or should be freed sooner or later. This principle also applied—though to a far lesser degree—to Jewish concentration camp prisoners before the war. This situation radically changed after the beginning of World War II and altered still more after the infamous Wannsee Conference, where the Nazis decided to kill the entire Jewish population wherever the German military power enabled them to do so. To accomplish this aim, the so-called annihilation camps in Poland were established (Auschwitz, Treblinka, Majdanek, Sobibor, etc.).

Among these camps, Auschwitz was unique. It was both an annihilation camp, with gas chambers and crematoria where between 3 and 4 million people were killed, and at the same time a vast labor camp that provided manpower for many branches of the German industry (coal mining, chemical industries, weaponry, and many, many others). This double function of Auschwitz—the organization of mass murder on the one hand and the providing of a workforce on the other—put the inmates of Auschwitz in an extraordinary psychological situation.

STRESS OUTSIDE THE CONCENTRATION CAMPS

An unknown number of Jews managed through their own efforts to keep themselves out of the concentration camps. Some were able to go into hiding, in spite of all the actions of the SS to find and arrest them and in spite of the fact that the punishment for helping Jewish fugitives was extreme, from internment in concentration camps to immediate execution. The Jews who lived under these extremely insecure conditions, in permanent danger of being discovered and often in dreadful physical conditions, were exposed to stress situations whose effects (both immediate and long-term) we still know far too little about. It was relatively easier to hide children, but successfully saving their lives led in turn to serious consequences that can only be hinted at: The identity problems of these children during and after the war, their emotional relations with their foster parents, and eventually the dissolution of those relations. Furthermore, the few parents who survived the war and tried to find their children had to face difficulties in mutual understanding and complications arising from their different experiences. All these human tragedies cannot be dealt with in detail here.

Some Jews who escaped and organized themselves into different groups of partisans managed to fight against German troops for longer or shorter periods. They either cooperated with the national underground movements and partisans, like the French, Italian, Greek, and Russian, or they operated as independent groups, especially in White Russia, under highly gruesome circumstances (Levin, 1968). Nevertheless, the stress situations endured by the partisans cannot be compared with those that the concentration camp survivors or people in hiding had to suffer. The partisans were active fighters and had a certain degree of control over their fate; they were not defenseless victims. Their monument can be found in the belletristic literature (Levi, 1987), but there has been no scientific examination on the sequelae of their wartime experiences.

The greatest number of Jews who were not delivered to the concentration camps, however, were killed almost immediately after the Germans caught them. They were either shot dead by the so-called *Einsatzgruppen* in "actions," or killed shortly after in gas vans specially constructed for this purpose, or finally gassed in the huge gas chambers in the annihilation camps. Their remains were processed as if on conveyor belt: the gold of their teeth was sent to the German National Bank, the hair of the women was used for mattresses, the fat of those incinerated on pyres was made into soap, and the ashes from the crematories served as manure. Could mankind's ethics ever sink lower?

INSIDE THE CONCENTRATION CAMPS

Living Conditions

After the usually nightmarish journey in cattle trucks to the camps, the admittance procedures signalled to even the most naive prisoner that something exceptional was happening. The prisoners had to hand over all their personal belongings, not only their luggage and valuables, but also all their personal clothing, their wedding rings—everything. The SS did not give any receipt for these belongings, so it was not difficult for the prisoners to imagine what fate was in store for them. After the selection procedure, those not sent directly to the gas chambers were ushered naked into showers that alternated between ice cold and scalding. Finally, still completely naked, they came into the camp itself. All the Jewish prisoners (and later others also) had prisoner numbers tattooed on their left forearms immediately after their admittance to the camps, and this number replaced their names and their personalities. A prisoner was literally only a number and a triangle. The latter designated the nationality and the category of prisoner that the inmate belonged to—political, criminal, asocial, homosexual, or, the worst crime, Jewish).

Having arrived at the "block," one of the first things the newcomers heard was that there was only one way out of the camp: through the chimney of the crematorium. The prisoner could hear this either brutally from a Kapo (overseer), or more fatalistically from a fellow prisoner, who would just say "here everybody is killed—sooner or later." In some cases detailed information about the total death machinery in the camps was received from better-informed fellow prisoners. Even in retrospective evaluation, one must say that the only rational reaction to this situation, especially during the years before the ultimate defeat of the German armies was obvious, would have been to take one's life.

Starvation and Diseases. Extreme nutritional insufficiency dominated the prisoners' life completely. The hunger that ravaged the inmates is almost incomprehensible; it took them beyond the limits of normal human endurance. For example, in one camp a highly intellectual former official fell to his knees and licked up a few drops of soup that had run out of the soup kettle onto the ground.

Over extended periods extreme starvation causes mental changes, the most usual being impaired memory, reduced initiative, fatigue, drowsiness, irritability, and finally indifference, dullness, and apathy. The last characteristic phase produced by famine in the camps is known as the Mussulman state, in which all mental processes are retarded and normal reactions cease (Helweg-Larsen, Hoffmeyer, Kieler, et al., 1952). However, sometimes the origin of this condition seemed to be largely psychic. In many cases, death resulted when people simply ceased clinging actively to life—that is, when they gave up hope.

Filth and lack of hygiene combined with lowered resistance were the main reasons for the numerous epidemic diseases that brought many inmates to what was called the camp hospital. Every prisoner knew that arriving there was very dangerous because it could lead to immediate extermination (in Auschwitz, with injection of carbolic acid directly into the heart) or to selection for the gas chamber if the disease was not cured very quickly. People unable to work for more than two weeks had no chance to live.

Extremely hard forced labor under the constant and ruthless supervision of the so-called kapos was usually combined with beatings and other kinds of ill-treatment. In addition, the prisoners endured the psychic stress caused by witnessing the continual macabre deaths and by the constant threat of their own extermination. Older, weak, and sick prisoners were selected, sometimes daily, for execution. Death permeated the atmosphere of the camps and, especially in Auschwitz and Birkenau, the stench of death was quite literal in the acid smoke from the ovens.

Stress Reactions. Even a sketchy review of the total literature on the direct observations and the different theories concerning the prisoners' behavior in the camps is impossible within the limits of this chapter. Only a few reports can be mentioned here. Bettelheim (1943), in his observations of the prewar camps, found only regression and identification with the aggressor. Cohen (1954), at that time a young physician from the Netherlands, also observed mostly negative behavior—regression, resignation, and extreme egoism. However, he also described prisoners who were altruistic and compassionate toward their fellow prisoners. Similar observations were reported by Adelsberger (1956), a psychologist imprisoned in Auschwitz-Birkenau and Ravensbrück. She describes both positive and negative aspects of human reactions and relations, a relapse to the animal state, as well as a sublimation of the highest level. For example, they might themselves be on the verge of starvation, yet they would sell their own bread ration, in order to buy potatoes for a dying comrade. According to Frankl (1961), only a few prisoners were able to preserve their humanity, but they set an example for the others, an example that started a chain reaction. For these people, life in the camp was not a regression but a test and a moral progression—in some cases, even a religious revelation.

Observations by prisoners without medical or psychological training often seem contradictory. However, this discrepancy may be explained by the incredible number of prisoners. The average population in the camps of Nazi Germany and the occupied territories was about one million at any given time (Kogon, 1946). Any attempt to generalize psychological reactions and changes of personality in a such a huge population without being able to measure individual observations scientifically must therefore be undertaken with the greatest caution.

G. W. Allport (1961) states that even under condition of social anomie (disintegration of values) an individual will retain his or her personality system more or less intact, but only up to a certain point. When the pressure increases to an intolerable extent, as it did for the victims of Nazi concentration camps, the personality may change and conform to a completely different value system. There is a breaking point for most people—some earlier, some later. Fortunately the ultimate limit is rarely tested.

Coping Mechanisms of the Prisoners

We consider a positive coping mechanism to be any reaction that not only helped the individual to survive but also to maintain mental health. However, one must take a complex set of circumstances into consideration when trying to answer how people coped or why some survived. The individual prisoner saw only his or her own small circle, the daily battle, in the most literal sense, for a piece of bread, the orders it was necessary to obey, and the small amount of help that might be possible. An inmate's horizon was narrow and the possibility of appraisal very small.

Furthermore, a certain minimum of survival possibilities had to be present in order to differentiate the problems of coping mechanisms. The first theory of coping with aggression in concentration camps was set forth by Bettelheim (1943). He maintained that most of the long-term prisoners tried to cope with the violence and aggression by identifying themselves with the aggressors. Obviously, this coping mechanism would be a negative one. However, Bettelheim's description was based on a camp experience that has nothing to do with the realities of the wartime concentration camps. There is no doubt that identification with the aggressor was used by some prisoners. This identification was encouraged by the fact that the SS guards delegated some of their power to certain carefully selected prisoners. But any shift of the regime in the camp or any transfer to another camp or subcamp would result in the dethronement of these "superprisoners," often drastically or fatally. Interviews conducted by Eitinger (1964) with about 1,500 former prisoners in Norway and Israel proved that identification with the aggressor, as far as it occurred, was a negative coping mechanism, because it led to the destruction of those involved or—in the few individuals who survived—to deep pathological personality changes.

In contrast to Bettelheim, Frankl (1959) stressed that those who have something to live for can endure suffering practically without limits. During his camp imprisonment, Frankl clung to the belief that every misfortune, every trauma that he was subjected to would spare his beloved in another camp the same sort of misfortune—a "contract with fate." How far such a coping strategy can help a person when he or she finally is confronted with the hard realities is difficult to say. None of the survivors we (Eitinger, 1964; Major, 1990) interview referred to such a coping mechanism, so we presume that it was not frequently used.

The prisoners able to mobilize the most adequate coping mechanisms were those who, for one reason or another, could maintain their personalities and systems of values more or less intact, even under conditions of nearly complete social anomie (Eitinger, 1964; Eitinger & Askevold, 1968). In this respect, the most successful individuals were those who, thanks to their profession, could show and practice interest in others and thus retain their norms and values inside the camp. The few, fortunate individuals were doctors, nurses, social workers, and priests—as described by Kral (1951) in Theresienstadt (Terezin)—who were more preoccupied with the problems of their fellow prisoners than with their own. These prisoners came through their trials in better mental condition than the average inmate of the camps.

Our interviews showed that prisoners who resisted best had been able to stay together with some members of their family, to remain in contact with some of their prewar peers, to help others, and to get help, as shown by Luchterhand (1970), among others.

There were other coping mechanisms, too. One of them, also described by Bettelheim (1943), was to adopt the attitude of a detached observer. A few managed to convince themselves that life in the camps was no concern of theirs—they were just spectators of a terrible drama in which their own bodies happened to be the actors. Or, as Bettelheim put it: "This torture is happening to my body and not to me." (p. 431) Less than 1% of all the survivors we interviewed, however, referred to this coping mechanism. This finding suggests that the mechanism was either very demanding or not very successful. Those who regarded their surroundings as unreal became unavoidably isolated and slowly lost contact with others and with reality. Rage was yet another survival mechanism: the strong wish to tell the world about what happening in the camps and the determined refusal to be defeated by the brutal kapos (Schmolling, 1984).

One of the most important and, probably, most used mechanisms was denial (Eitinger, 1983). This reaction was necessary to the fatalism that would lead to "the only possible consequence" in the camp—suicide. Thus, in some cases denial had immediate life-saving value by helping the inmates to behave as though the most dangerous situations and severe anxieties did not exist and thus allowing some of them to survive. Denial was especially prevalent at the beginning of the uphill struggle experienced by newcomers. The first few weeks and sometimes even months were the most difficult, dangerous, and devastating for the inmates. Only after being put to some sort of better work or gaining a position in the camp where the immediate danger of death was relatively small was it rational to harbor the hope that something unforeseen would happen and that one would be able to survive in spite of the negative odds. At a later stage in the war, the very few who could occasionally get hold of bits of news and thus follow the steady retreat of the German military forces had a small additional encouragement of this faint hope. At this stage of the war, the psychological situation had already changed somewhat. One could afford to be more aware of the life-threatening situation, to assess it more rationally, and to do everything possible to stay alive to become a witness and to tell the story. The transition in awareness from complete denial to a more differentiated degree of understanding, which implies an emotional assessment of the real possibilities of surviving, was not always easy to bear. This process demonstrated to the experienced self-observer the difference between a rigid defense mechanism of total denial and the pains and pleasures of living emotions and of orientation to reality. On the other extreme, prisoners who completely denied their life-threatening situation, who escaped into daydreams, and who did not try to find a more operative adaptational mechanism quickly made themselves more vulnerable to harm.

Nobody in the camp, for instance, could avoid knowing about the deadly danger of typhus and how it is spread by lice. Denial of this danger by neglecting the not very delicate, but absolutely life-saving daily lice inspection was a nearly pathognomonic symptom giving up and of the imminent end of a prisoner's life. The usefulness of denial was thus rather complex. Denying death could be lifesaving under certain circumstances, but denying the small, seemingly unimportant struggles of daily life could result in certain premature death. Also, Dimsdale (1974, 1978) has shown, though in a different context, that the effects of a coping style in the camps may have been beneficial in the short run but ominous in the long run. More generally, denial can be of positive in situations in which there is no possibility of influencing one's fate, while denying situations that offer this possibility is usually detrimental.

Preserving the ability to make some decisions was also an important coping mechanism. In some cases it was only deciding how to apportion one's daily ration of bread, in other cases it was how to keep up personal hygiene. The decisive factor was always not to become completely passive and not to lose one's reasoning power and ability to plan and put plans into action. One proved this by continuing to administering the diminutive remains of one's right to decide for oneself, by refusing to be overwhelmed completely by circumstances, and by remaining an individual and an individualist.

Of course, quite a number of survivors readily admitted that they merely survived by chance, without exercising any decisive personal coping mechanisms. Many of these survived because the war ended before the ultimate stage of the "Final Solution to the Jewish Problem" could be put into effect against these few. This failure was mainly because able-bodied individuals were increasingly needed for the war effort, but also because the extermination machinery could not keep up with the supply (particularly in the case of the annihilation of the Hungarian Jews during the last months of 1944).

When comparing groups of survivors who more or less consciously and actively mobilized coping mechanisms with those who ascribed their survival to mere luck, it appeared, on a statistically significant level, that the former had less psychiatric complications than the latter. In other words, coping mechanisms that enhanced the individual's contact with a group and that were based on intact and positive value systems and on retaining self-respect as a human being proved to be important not only for immediate survival. Such coping also promoted long-term survival without too many psychological disturbances and with one's personality intact—when possible (Eitinger, 1974).

Suicide in the Concentration Camps

In different discussions of suicide in the concentration camps it has been stated that it occurred rather infrequently. This conclusion, however, is by no means certain. There are no acceptable quantitative studies. Nobody knows how many of the prisoners who were "shot while trying to escape" were suicides, or how many threw themselves onto the electrically charged barbed wire fences around the camps, or how many sought a medical examination in order to be killed. The investigations performed after the war are not representative of all the inmates, so the problem can not be dealt with here.

THE POSTWAR PERIOD

When liberation came, most of the Jewish prisoners were too weak to move or recognize what was happening. Prisoners were not immediately restored to health by liberation; three weeks after liberation in Bergen-Belsen deaths had been reduced to 200 per day and only after six weeks could most of the remaining prisoners be considered as saved (Kolb, 1962).

Awakening from the nightmare was perhaps even more painful than captivity. After the first physical improvement, the ability to feel and think returned, and many realized the completeness of their isolation. They could no longer repress what had happened, and the reality was agonizing. Studies of survivors living in Israel show that 80 to 90% had lost most of their closest relatives; 3 out of 4 had lost their entire family (Eitinger, 1964). Studies in Norway show that out of nearly 700 deported Norwegian-born Jews, only 11 survived; 6 of these were sole survivors of their immediate families, and all had lost at least two close relatives (Eitinger, 1979).

The newly released prisoners had no one left and nowhere to go: their old life was complete gone, and they had no idea of what to do with the new life that had so unexpectedly been given to them. They remained in camps, now called Displaced Persons (DP) camps, where new international organizations took care of them, provided for them, and tried to put new meaning into their lives. The effort made by these organizations must not be belittled in any way; however, the former prisoners still had very little personal autonomy. They had no right to decide for themselves or to determine their own fates. The former prisoners, now known as displaced persons, were brought up before boards from different countries, who decided whether or not they could be admitted into the country in question. Many displaced persons, however, had no desire to depend upon others' decisions and conclusions; instead, they tried to make their way to Palestine, where they expected to find a solution to all their problems. Some were admitted, but the majority were stopped and put into yet another internment camp on Cyprus. Only when the state of Israel was established was it possible for all those who wished it to go there and start a new life (Eitinger, 1980).

The former prisoners who left the camps and attempted to return to their home towns in Eastern Europe, were, in most cases, confronted with rejection and hatred, and in some cases, as in Poland, they met direct persecution and pogroms. Their homes were in ruins, and the possibility of finding new means of existence were minimal. The returnees, often the only survivors of large families, were isolated and had no means of contact with hostile neighbors, who showed no understanding of their plight. On the other hand, the returnees were not capable of understanding their new surroundings, which were so different from the world they had dreamed of in the camps. Thus it is not surprising that many sought a new country where they could start a new life, and Israel, for many of them, seemed to be the place designated by fate as a solution to all their difficulties and problems. Many of the new immigrants had very unrealistic ideas of the possibilities Israel had to offer, and their awakening to reality was by no means easy, especially because of their reduced mental elasticity.

A comparison between Jewish and Norwegian concentration camp survivors shows that, of the latter, 60 to 86% were in regular work again before December 31, 1945; the corresponding figures for Jewish survivors was 0 to 47%. A year later the Norwegian figures had risen to 85 to 99%, while among the Jews there were still groups without the capacity to work (Eitinger, 1964).

The traumatization of the Jewish survivors thus seemed to last much longer than that of the Norwegians, but this is not the only, and perhaps not the most important, difference. Most non-Jewish concentration camp survivors could return to their countries and homes, even if these were often in ruins, while the greatest part of the Jewish survivors had no home to go to and nobody to come back to. They were bound to remain dependent.

Aftereffects of Concentration Camp Life

The survivors from the DP camps mainly emigrated either to the new world (Australia, the United States, and Canada) or to Israel. Both groups had to adjust to strange surroundings, learn new languages and new laws, and build new lives. The breakdown of former family and community ties inevitably caused radical changes in each individual's conception of self and environment.

None of the helpers the survivors met in the overseas countries—whether general practitioners, psychiatrists, psychologists, social workers, etc.—knew much of the later sequelae of traumas like the survivors had endured. Those who heard what had happened just "couldn't believe it." Danieli (1981a) describes how a conspiracy of silence evolved between the therapists and their patients. Hertz and Freyberger (1982) pointed out how many different factors influenced the experts' evaluation of the psychological and psychosomatic reactions of the survivors. The survivors who went to Israel came to a country at war. Even if they felt that they finally had reached their home, the situation in Israel in its early years did not permit a proper discussion of concentration camp experiences, and this continued to be the case until the Eichmann trial in 1961–1962. However, the majority adapted to their positions adequately in newly founded families, jobs, or kibbutzim. Still, many suffered from chronic anxiety, sleep disturbances, nightmares, emotional lability, and depression.

Feelings of Guilt

Several authors (Chodoff, 1970; Niederland, 1961; Pedersen, 1949) have pointed out the guilt borne by the survivors because they lived, unlike their families and comrades.

In the highly emotional atmosphere of the first postwar years, when the annihilation of the Jewish people in Europe and the passivity of the Allies (and of much of the Jewry in Great Britain and the United States) slowly became common knowledge, the objectivity of Jewish psychiatrists seems doubtful. It is, of course, impossible to prove, but it seems likely that the importance that has been attached (especially in the first papers published) to the "severe and persisting guilt complex" as a central symptom of the survivor syndrome is rooted in the unconscious guilt that some therapists may have projected onto these patients, who fell outside any previous clinical experience.

Studies in Europe and Israel show a varied picture. Scandinavian former prisoners often noted that, in spite of all the advantages, it was not always pleasant to belong to the privileged group of prisoners who received parcels and could gain advantages through them—sometimes to the detriment of less-privileged prisoners. Others upbraided themselves for their forced passivity while witnessing the sufferings of others, like the floggings or hangings of comrades. However, these experiences very seldom formed the core of neurotic feelings of guilt. On the other hand, there were cases of self-reproach for yielding during interrogations and torture. The psychological situation was especially complicated where situations of this kind forced the victims to make revelations that may have resulted in more arrests and new death sentences. These experiences often created very complex guilt responses, with secondary reactions, that were extremely difficult to treat by therapeutic means.

Among the Israeli survivors were those who reproached themselves, mostly irrationally, for not sharing the fate of the others. In some cases, after repeated interviews had collected sufficient information about the survivor, one occasionally could find a neurotic reason for this self-reproach. For example, a daughter, whose mother concealed her during a raid to find Jewish children and the next day, was taken in a new round-up, felt that she "could never forgive" herself, because if she had let herself be arrested then, perhaps, her mother would have lived. There were also patients, although very few, whose guilt can be considered rational. For example, a woman who was being transported to Auschwitz with her younger sister and her own one-year-old child became ill, so her younger sister took care of the child. Upon their arrival in Auschwitz, the sister was assumed to be the child's mother, and both were put into the long line that led directly to the gas-chambers; however, the patient, who was designated as an able-bodied woman with no children, came to the camp and survived. During numerous interviews with doctors, including narcoanalysis, this experience was found to be the core of her self-reproach.

These two cases illustrate very clearly that the bases for guilt varied the apparently irrational to the concrete and realistic.

The Problem of Compensation

Many survivors felt that their doctors and psychiatrists could not understand them, and this feeling was often intensified when the problem of compensation from the German government became a dominating issue. This debate transformed the relationship between patient and doctor to that of victim and expert.

When the survivors became entitled to compensation from the West German government for damage suffered under the Nazis, many were examined intensively by specialists in internal and neurological medicine. In most cases, these experts found no ill-effects directly attributable to detainment in the camps. The reason for this absence was the repeated selection of Jewish victims for extermination; in the ghettos, on arrival at the camps, at the frequent medical examinations, in the sick-bays, and at every transfer, those showing signs of physical disease were eliminated. Particularly, during the long, infamous death marches at the end of the war—which took a horrifying toll of lives—everyone unable to follow was shot on the spot. Those who survived despite everything and who were later examined by doctors in the United States or Australia were thus an extremely select group. Their main problems were emotional, which the German authorities did not consider as sufficient cause for compensation.

In an accusatory article, Meerlo (1963) commented upon this distorted view of the aftereffects of concentration camp experiences. " . . . When a psychic trauma has enough impact and lasts long enough it alters the personality . . ." and " . . . no reflex hammer can help here in our judgement". Meerloo's appeal had no influence. Several years later he repeated his accusations of the decisions of German psychiatrists (Merloo, 1969). "There are physicians who still deny the existence of psychic trauma and immense psychological damage. . . . German authorities try to deny the impact of life experiences on man as long as no brain damage is found. This, of course, is contradictory to all we know." (p. 1187)

The official school of German psychiatry strictly kept to the Jaspers's criteria on psychogenesis, which accepted that substantial psychological trauma could produce serious psychological reactions. However, it was argued, with the cessation of the cause, the reaction should disappear too, like the so-called jail psychosis. But Jaspers never evaluated such extreme psychological traumas as imprisonment in concentration camps. Still, for a very long time his pupils in Germany did not dare change their master's teaching.

Only a few psychiatrists in West Germany, like von Baeyer (1958, 1961; von Baeyer, Haefner, & Kisker, 1964), Kluge (1958), and Venzlaff (1958), understood that this attitude was unreasonable and were ready to accept the overwhelming findings of serious mental post-traumatic disturbances published by other Western psychiatrists. Peters (1989) describes the nearly hopeless situation of German postwar psychiatry; its psychological and political background is explained best by Müller-Hill (1988) and Pross (1990).

Nevertheless, the findings made during the whole postwar period, and especially in elderly survivors during the last few years, have proved the correctness of the demand for financial compensation for psychological damages. The rationale for these demands were not only the demonstrated medical and psychiatric changes, but also social and moral considerations. Ultimately, however, financial compensation—even though needed—could never compensate for the losses of the survivors.

The Pathology of the Survivors

The first and most obvious pathological change among survivors was extreme loss of weight and the resulting general weakness (Helweg-Larsen, et al., 1952; Targowla, 1954). Helweg-Larsen and colleagues believed that they could prove a direct correlation between loss of weight and degree of the concentration camp syndrome. In briefly summarizing the main symptoms of the Holocaust survivors, one must first mention anxiety, sleep disturbances, and nightmares, which were very often combined. Affective disturbances, with emotional lability, dysphoria, and depression, were also very common symptoms and were found in more than 80% of those investigated by Strøm (1968). Hyperirritability and feelings of inner tension, with hyperalertness and exaggerated startle response, were common, as were recollections of concentration camp experiences.

In other cases, apathy developed in the camps continued in the form of reduction of affect and loss of initiative. Most observers agreed that the survivors did not dramatize or make hysterical appeals; rather, the most common impression was that the survivors were no longer capable of enjoying life. In more extreme cases, the individuals seemed to be merely existing; they did what work had to be done, but their joy in life, their spark, was gone. They were not the same after the war as they had been before; something essential had changed.

Psychosomatic diseases were relatively frequent among camp survivors as were a tendency to develop diarrhoea and peptic ulcers. The diarrhoea was mostly functional, so that any situation involving stress, unusual food, large meals, psychic difficulties, interrecurrent infections, or even other diseases could provoke diarrhoeal reactions. Most former prisoners connected this tendency with digestive disturbances and diarrhoea that they had suffered during imprisonment (Eitinger, 1969).

Peters (1989) has called attention to some specific and otherwise not sufficiently described traits of the Holocaust survivors' stress problems (both etiological and symptomatological). After the war there were numerically few Jewish survivors left in Europe and they felt unprecedented isolation. There were no graves to commemorate the deceased, who had disappeared literally without any trace. (Parenthetically, we would like to remark that the opposition of many Jews the erection of a cloister on the grounds of the Auschwitz camp probably was because this camp has become a symbol for all the nonexistent graves and tomb stones.)

The Holocaust resulted in the loss of both the homelands and the cultures in which the survivors had grown up. This loss was especially painful for the German Jews, who had cherished and admired German culture, and it caused overwhelming narcissistic trauma that they had serious difficulties in overcoming.

Degradation, defamation, loss of all social positions and of citizens' rights—i.e., loss of individuality—were also specific stress-provoking factors during the Holocaust. Venzlaff (1958) described some typical cases and observed that the individuals had undergone what he described as personality changes caused by life experiences. Peters (1989) called attention to other factors: the continual threat of death during many years of persecution, the depression caused by uprooting, and maltreatment in everyday life, even before arrest.

Theories about the etiology of the concentration camp or survivors' syndrome have varied among authors of the postwar literature (Eitinger, 1964, 1973; Helweg-Larsen, et al., 1952; Herman & Thygesen, 1954; Krystal, 1968; Niederland, 1968; Strøm, 1961, 1968; Szwarc, 1985). It is futile to discuss which author has found the correct etiology or symptoms of the concentration camp syndrome. These authors' varied findings can be accounted for by the selection of the former prisoners examined (Eitinger, 1985) and by the theoretical orientations of the investigators (Chodoff 1963, 1970; Hoppe, 1971; Kestenberg, 1981; Krystal, 1968; Matussek, 1971). Furthermore, the complexity of the populations in question and their different degrees of trauma and loss also explain some of the differences in the published findings. The same principle applies to the many uncontrolled case studies in which unrelated or common character traits were ascribed to the effect of the survivors' stay in a concentration camp. Sometimes not even the term *survivor* is properly delineated. To compare people who endured the hell of concentration camps for years with those who escaped Germany in 1933 or those who lived safely in the United States during the war but felt like "vicarious survivors," is to underestimate grossly the impact of long-lasting and excessive traumatization, the effect of which has been proved by numerous investigations worldwide.

Most of the studies of concentration camp survivors have had a selective bias that leaves some uncertainty about the possibility of generalizing the findings. However, the relatively few studies of large, unselected samples of survivors that were conducted in a context unrelated to benefit seeking (Eaton, Sigal, & Weinfeld, 1982; Levav & Abramson, 1984) conclude that there are long-term consequences of the stress of the Holocaust. The literature on the survivors has grown so large that it is impossible to quote individual authors; instead, we must refer to bibliographies (Eitinger, 1981; Eitinger, Krell, & Rieck, 1985).

Davidson (1979) points out that the syndrome became a somewhat stereotyped diagnostic construct with established internationally accepted criteria for recommending compensation payments based on percentages of psychiatric disability. Slowly and reluctantly even the German authorities accepted the view that also quite normal personalities reacted with chronic pathological changes after the excessive traumatization they had been exposed to during the Holocaust and especially in the concentration camps. A large literature grew out of the examination of tens of thousands of survivors for the purpose of the compensation certificates and from the survivors seen in psychiatric clinics and hospitals.

PRESENT STATUS OF THE SURVIVORS

Unfortunately, the findings of gross pathology in survivors were misinterpreted and construed to mean that the pathological reactions—or, rather, the survivors' normal reactions to pathological situations—would persist, unchanged and unchangeable. Such a view completely disregarded not only the human adaptability, but also the regenerative powers of the ego, one of the most fascinating aspects of human nature. Many of the survivors acquired coping mechanisms in their new surroundings, found a new place in their adopted societies, and gave the impression that they had integrated their massive traumatization into their psychic functioning and their present reality. The individual survivor's desire to once again be an active part of a family and a community, to belong, and to create must not be underestimated. However, many of the survivors' difficulties were only repressed, not resolved. Investigations that uncovered subconscious ideas were able to demonstrate clearly that the scars were still present.

The extreme trauma of the camps inflicted deep wounds that have healed very slowly, so that even today the scars are still present. The experiences still hurt and sometimes surface to influence the psychic life of the former prisoners. The strength to deny or fight old memories diminishes during serious diseases or when vitality is reduced by other causes—for instance, old age.

The problems of aging survivors have been dealt with in several studies. Krystal (1981) surveyed the difficulties of integration, psychoanalytical treatment, and self-healing in a classic essay discussed by Danieli (1981b). She concluded with the ever-crucial questions of human beings: Who loves me? Who cares if I live? Who will remember me? These questions are perhaps more important for Holocaust survivors than for any other people. Steinitz (1982) surveyed papers on 550 noninstitutionalized survivor patients and found that the clinicians had diagnosed a higher frequency of depression, paranoid reactions, sleep disturbances, and feelings of loneliness and isolation among them than in the average population. Eaton and co-workers (1982) compared the psychiatric status of 135 survivors with that of control subjects. Both groups were generated by a random sample survey of all heads of households in a community. Survivors were more likely to have mild psychiatric symptoms, and the level of these symptoms was greatly amplified in respondents who perceived recent increases in anti-semitism in their communities.

In an unselected sample of 380 Israeli concentration camp survivors, Levav & Abramson (1984) found a higher prevalence of emotional distress and more psychiatric symptoms than in other European-born members of the same community (controlled for age and education). Robinson, et al. (1990) found that although Holocaust survivors had coped and adjusted, had achieved success at work and in society, and had managed to raise families, they still suffered from the results of persecution; and death camp survivors suffered more than those subjected to other forms of persecution. These conclusions are based on interviews with 86 survivors from a nonclinical population.

Fenig and Levav (1991) examined 76 Polish-born married women who went through World War II between the ages of 15 and 20, and compared them with 69 Polish-born married women of the same age who lived in Tel Aviv during the war. The findings again demonstrated the prolonged aftermath of the Holocaust. All the respondents had living spouses and all were members of the local community, but in the survivor group psychological scars were found in form of low self-esteem, helplessness, hopelessness, sadness, anxiety, etc. The authors of earlier publications considered social support to be a buffer of stressful life events. In Fenig and Levav's study the women's social support was found to be satisfactory, yet psychological scars were nevertheless present, although inversely according to how much social support they received. The degree of stressfulness of the World War II experiences correlated positively with the pathological findings.

Rosen, Reynolds, Yeager, Houck, and Hurwitz (1991) showed that for many survivors of the Holocaust impaired sleep remained a problem even forty-five years after the liberation. The authors studies the sleep quality of survivors, depressed patients, and healthy comparison subjects. Based on the Pittsburgh Sleep Quality Index, they found that the survivors reported significantly more sleep disturbances than the comparison subjects. The profile of sleep disturbances was different for the survivors than for all the others examined, and the severity of sleep disturbances and frequency of nightmares were related to the number of years spent in an annihilation camp. Although the response rate of survivors is very low (25%), the results correlate with other clinical findings that impaired sleep is a hallmark of post-traumatic stress disorder (Ross, Ball, Sullivan, & Caroff, 1989).

CHILD SURVIVORS

Davidson (1987) often has stressed that social support makes survivors less vulnerable that the majority of the survivors, especially those who were relatively young at the liberation, did not decompensate clinically in their later encounters with stressful life events. This response is quite understandable when one considers that these young survivors were extremely selected individuals. Probably the best proof is the description by Pinsky (1955) of the liberated and uprooted children in 1945; their behavior and appearance were indistinguishable from the adults. However, Pinsky differentiated between several categories of these children. The most striking group were those from the concentration camps, who were easy to recognize by their prison haircuts, emaciation, listless facial expressions, and numbers tattooed on their forearms. The next group Pinsky identified were children who had successfully evaded the Nazis and remained in hiding. In order to survive, these children, left to their own devices, had to use an ingenuity that surpasses imagination. Many sheltered in forests or in caves and survived the severest physical and mental tests. Like hunted animals, they were exposed to storms, frost, and hunger. After the way, these children, and those who had joined the underground movement, displayed more courage, ingenuity, and initiative than all the other child survivors. They had learned many devices to outwit and outmaneuver their persecutors, and after looking death in the eye to eye nothing encountered afterward could faze them. Nevertheless, one should not underestimate the social support this incredible band of survivors needed—and some got—after the war.

One of the most touching examples concerns the "90 Buchenwald boys" who came to the Chateau de Taverny, which was administered by Judith Hemmendinger. They were described (Minkowski, 1946) as an undifferentiated mass of youths with no hair, faces swollen from hunger, and uniform clothes; all of them were apathetic, unconcerned, and indifferent, and they never laughed or smiled. They were aggressive toward the doctors and staff, and were suspicious and mistrustful. Hemmendinger's account (1980, 1981) of how this "mass" changed into the young men, who later invited her to celebrate the twenty-fifth anniversary of the liberation of Buchenwald at a dinner party in New York, is a highly moving and human documents. She can state proudly that "these boys were rehabilitated and well rehabilitated, and no one ever applied for psychological help or treatment." (Hemmendinger, 1980, p. 133) Not all the children were so fortunate. Keilson (1980) found that a poor postwar environment exacerbated the effects of the traumatic events.

The problem of children survivors is not easy (Krell, 1985a, 1985b). Moskowitz (1983, 1985) traced the children who came to England after World War II and who lived in the Lingfield orphanage under the direction of Alice Goldberger, with the counsel of Anna Freud (Freud & Dann, 1951). Moskowitz was impressed by the children's development into adulthood and stressed that one can hardly overestimate the importance of learning from child survivors how massive trauma in early life reverberates across the life span and what factors may have been helpful, irrelevant, or detrimental. These findings make it more than depressing to read (Wangh, 1971) that the German courts denied most applications on behalf of the child survivors on the grounds that their persecution took place before they were "aware," so they could not remember what had taken place during that time.

Child survivors who were hospitalized did not demonstrate the resilience of nonclinical groups. Robinson (1979) reported on 106 patients who were under age 17 at the time of Nazi occupation. Over half were diagnosed as psychotic, whether they had been in hiding or in camps. Of the 9 children under age 7 at the time, 7 were diagnosed as psychotic. All three under age 3 were psychotic.

The specific stress problems of the children in hiding resurfaced at a conference recently attended by about 500 children who spent World War II in hiding. From the only account, by a journalist (Shenitz, 1991), it is obvious that in spite of their resilience, adaptation, and success, the need to tell their story is just as important for these survivors as for the concentration camp survivors.

PROBLEMS OF THERAPY

The sequelae of the stress of Holocaust were complex, unknown, and incomprehensible to the medical and psychological community. As a consequence, mutual misunderstandings and difficulties developed when therapy was started. Experience in the psychotherapeutic treatment of persecution victims had to be discussed and evaluated in many countries, perhaps mainly in the United States and Israel (Chodoff, 1980; Hoppe, 1965).

Theories had to be changed. Traumatic experiences in early childhood cannot be considered as the only or the main causes of subsequent mental disturbances. At a more advanced age, the personality and its functions may be so weakened that irreversible mental disturbances result, even if no psychoses or organic damage are present.

The introduction of the diagnosis of post-traumatic stress disorder in the DSM-III (American Psychiatric Association, 1987) is the most important proof of this new knowledge. In terms of therapy, this knowledge means that a complete sociopsychotherapy is required to thoroughly understand a patient's background and specific needs, including supportive and somatic therapy. The therapeutic approach should not be limited by the orthodoxy of one school or other; it must always be based on the individual patient's experiences, losses, and needs.

The stress of Holocaust also has taught us that human beings can undergo extremely traumatic experiences, become deeply impaired, and yet retain the ability to rehabilitate their ego drives—to all appearances, at least. The survivors of the Holocaust continue to have, as noted previously, an increased vulnerability to stress situations, but also a greater sensitivity toward fellow humans, capacity for empathy, appreciation for the higher values in life (Dasberg, 1987). Unfortunately, with decreasing vitality, physical and psychological burdens can no longer be denied. Memories that have never ceased to haunt the victims may return, reinforced. The physical constitution weakens, mental capabilities dwindle, emptiness fills the hearts of the survivors, and life increasingly loses its meaning. Nearly fifty years after the Holocaust, psychosocial help is therefore more important now than ever.

THE CHILDREN OF HOLOCAUST SURVIVORS

By the end of the 1960s, an unforeseen long-term effect was described by some authors: The children of survivors also seemed to be affected adversely by their parents' Holocaust experiences (Rakoff, Sigal, & Epstein, 1966), and these children showed symptoms similar to those of people who had experienced the Holocaust (Barocas & Barocas, 1973, 1979, 1980). In the following years, several publications called attention to the psychopathology observed in these children, and there was debate over the existence or nonexistence of a "second generation syndrome" or complex (Barocas & Barocas 1973; de Graaf, 1975; Kestenberg, 1982; Levine, 1982; Mussaph, 1981). Some publications have even called attention to possible adverse effects of the Holocaust in the third generation (Rosenthal & Rosenthal, 1980; Sigal, Dinicola, & Buonvino, 1988; Sigal & Rakoff, 1971).

Most investigators agree that the Holocaust seems to be the frame of reference for the identity of a large number of the second generation. Hadar (1989) put it this way: "The starting point of the second generation after the Holocaust is in the Holocaust itself. . . . The second generation has no possibility to see their world in a way where no Holocaust exists, whether their parents spoke about the Holocaust or not. . . . Their beginning is in the Holocaust" (pp. 5–6).

The growing interest among clinicians and investigators in the second generation and in a possible transmission of the effects of their parents' trauma has been displayed in conferences and in a steadily growing number of publications. As the children of survivors became adults, many of them became involved in the Holocaust trauma—for example, as investigators, therapists, or artists. Thus many of the recent investigations of the effects of the Holocaust upon the second generation are carried out by the children themselves.

In the following discussion, the term *second generation* is applied only to survivors' children who were born after World War II. Within the limits of this chapter, the different areas of research dealing with the second generation can only be alluded to.

Childrearing Practices and Pathology

The survivors from Eastern Europe who came as immigrants to the United States or Canada were, as described, often the only remaining members of their families. Having been exposed to the same experiences, two single survivors often married; as a rule, these couples did not marry for love but because they were from the same community, city, or even country of origin. These "marriages of despair" were formed on short acquaintance, and their main aim was to recreate a family in order to compensate for the losses of the Holocaust (Danieli, 1985). According to Krell (1979), the postwar marriages of the survivors—whether or not to other survivors—would carry the Holocaust tragedy into new homes.

Clinical Studies. Rakoff, et al. (1966) observed disorganization in survivor families treated at their clinic in Montreal. The limit setting in these families was either rigid or chaotic and rarely related to the needs of the children. Specifically, the parents seemed to lack emotional engagement with their children because of their preoccupation with the past and reliving of the horrors of the Holocaust. The children were evaluated as deprived, with symptoms of emptiness, depression, apathy, or agitated hyperactivity.

In his treatment of adolescent students, Trossman (1968) found that the most detrimental parental attitude was making the children feel that they had to provide a justification for their parents' sufferings. Such parents placed so many unrealistic demands upon their children that they gave up in despair or became rebellious. Where the family was dominated by one strong parent, this pressure often resulted in examination anxiety and impotence.

Sigal and Rakoff (1971) suggested that problems in survivor families follow an identifiable pattern—a familial survivor syndrome. The concentration camp families they investigated complained more of excessive sibling rivalry, overvaluation of the children, and difficulties in controlling the behavior of the children. In a later study, Sigal, Silver, Rakoff, and Ellin (1973) found that parental preoccupation with the past was a contributing factor to behavioral and other disturbances in a clinical sample of adolescents in Canada.

Rosenberger (1973) postulated two types of survivor parents. First are those who disregarded their children's emotional needs and instead were preoccupied with providing food and goods so that their children would never suffer from the hunger and material deprivation they had experienced in Europe. The second category comprises those who almost totally identified themselves with their children. Through their children they relived their own childhoods. These parents lacked emotional maturity and so used their children to meet their own narcissistic needs.

Barocas and Barocas (1973, 1979, 1980) stated that children of survivors seeking psychotherapeutic help presented symptoms that were strikingly similar to the concentration camp families: During pregnancy the mothers feared giving birth to an abnormal or unhealthy child or felt unable to nurture the child. Later on they became extremely protective. This overprotection, as well as the mother's domineering role, led to many identification problems for both male and female children. The fathers were mostly ineffective parents—

weak, withdrawn, quiet, and passive. Furthermore, these parents often had exaggerated expectations of their children's achievements in school. As units, these families presented "even more than the expected doublebinds, skews and schisms, destructive dyadic and triadic alliances, incongruencies, dysfunctional communication patterns, and maladaptive behavioral sequences."

As shown previously, the clinical studies seemed not only to stress pathological findings but also tended to generalize them. This tendency led to serious criticisms of these studies, as described by Solkoff (1981): "we will continue to be overwhelmed with anecdotes and unsupported findings, unnecessarily stigmatizing a very substantial group of the children of survivors." This criticism also found outlet at a 1979 conference at which participating children of survivors reacted against the stigmatizing label of pathology and declared that nothing was wrong with them (Peskin, 1981; Sigal, 1989).

Nonclinical Studies. During the 1980s several nonclinical studies were performed that did not find the same amount of pathological childrearing practices or pathology. Last and Klein (1984) evaluated the impact of parental Holocaust traumatization using the offspring's reports of childrearing practices. The aim of the study was twofold: to evaluate these practices in survivor families and to examine a possible relationship between severity of parental Holocaust stress and childrearing practices. The results yielded only a very few specific differences in perceived childrearing practices the children of survivors and the control groups. However, the relationship between the severity of parental traumatization and childrearing practices was complex and depended on the parent's and the child's gender. For instance, deficient paternal nurturance of their sons seemed to be a function of the degree of traumatization that the fathers had suffered.

In a study of 47 second generation adults, Keinan, Mikulincer, and Rybnicki (1988) (using the Semantic Differential Instrument by Osgood, Suci, and Tannenbaum) showed that offspring of Holocaust survivors perceived their parents as more tense and anxious, but also as having more attractive traits than the control group. Thus, the authors concluded that the second generation's perception of their parents is not consistently negative.

Major (1990) examined both the survivor fathers and their children and did not find significant differences between them and the control groups: survivors' children did not perceive their fathers to be more overprotective, anxious, aggressive, or achievement-oriented than did the controls. Neither were there significant differences between the two groups of fathers when they reported on these parental characteristics. The only difference was that the children of survivors perceived their fathers as more pessimistic and felt more attached to them than did the comparison children.

Other nonclinical studies have focused on the healthy and adaptive sides of belonging to the second generation. Gay and Shulman (1978) investigated children of survivors and control groups who applied for admission to a university. The study confirmed the authors' hypothesis that, despite the pathological atmosphere in which the children of survivors may have been brought up, some would display adaptabilities that would enable them to cope successfully and remain healthy.

Zlotogorski (1985) studied levels of ego functioning in 73 children of survivors and 68 control children by administering the Washington University Sentence Completion Test and the Satisfaction with Well-Being Questionnaire and found that levels of functioning and self-determined well-being scores were uniformly distributed in the two groups. There were no significant correlations between length of parental internment or parental age at internment and levels of functioning of their offspring.

Russell, Plotkin, and Heapy (1985) investigated family dynamic and social development factors considered to contribute to positive adaptations in the second generation. The authors concluded that these children drew on positive factors in their families or their environments. The children felt strongly that they had to be high achievers in order to compensate for what had been lost during the Holocaust and were compelled to help others altruistically. This group displayed a strong tendency to engage in mental health work.

Rieck and Eitinger (1983) did not find any differences in the proportion of children of survivors and a control group who were referred by their parents to a psychoeducational clinic for emotional or behavioral problems.

Communication about the Holocaust

Other authors (Kav-Venaki, Nadler, & Gershoni, 1983; Krell, 1979; Major, 1990; Robinson & Winnik, 1981) focused on the association between communication about the Holocaust and the development of mental disturbances in the children. A preliminary finding is that children benefit most when there is not too much communication and yet the Holocaust is not a taboo subject. Communication about the Holocaust also seems to be affected by whether the parents were concentration camp survivors. Parents who were partisans or otherwise managed to escape the camps by own efforts were considered as heroes by their children, so communication between the generations was much easier. Concentration camp survivors were considered victims, and this perception made communication more difficult and led to more mental disturbances in the children. Another important decision turned out to be how much, when, and how to tell the children.

The Influence of Being Immigrants' Children

Several of the earlier studies did not differentiate between the children of survivors and the children of immigrants. Thus, some of all of the pathological findings could be an effect of the parents' immigrant problems. Recent studies, therefore, have tried to control for this immigration factor.

Weiss, O'Connell, and Siiter (1986) did not find differences between the children of Holocaust survivors and the children of immigrants on measures such as alienation, guilt, and mental health. Sigal and Weinfeld (1985), who compared the children of survivors, the children of other immigrants, and children of native-born parents, concluded that parents' exposure to prolonged, severe victimization does not necessarily have negative effects on the second generation's ability to control aggression.

Also, Rose and Garske (1987) attempted to discriminate between the children of Jewish Holocaust survivors and the children of parents (Jewish and non-Jewish) who belonged to other "target" populations by using measures such as the California Psychological Inventory, the Beck Depression Inventory, and the Moos Family Environment Scale. No differences in psychopathology were found; thus, the authors concluded that the children of Holocaust survivors, as a group, seemed to be well adjusted.

Major (1990) compared children of Jewish Norwegian-born Holocaust survivors to a control group in terms of symptoms considered to be part of a second generation syndrome. The former did not exhibit signs of gross pathology, although they scored somewhat higher on most symptoms. As found by Russell, et al. (1985), these children also showed a considerable interest in taking part in different helping organizations or professions.

Problems of Methodology

As mentioned previously, the rather one-sided focus of the clinical studies on gross psychopathology led to the labeling of the children of survivors. Trossman (1968) stated that "These children . . . could not fail to be adversely affected if one or both of their parents suffer from even mild degrees of the syndrome" (p. 121).

Because these studies were based mainly on disturbed families or individuals who had sought treatment, it is not surprising that the authors found pathology, symptoms, and problems. The results, however, cannot be generalized to all Holocaust families, whether in the United States, Canada, Europe, or Israel.

The conditions into which the second generation children were born were extremely varied. Some important factors are the age at which the parents were released, whether the parents had lost a spouse or children in the camps, the socioeconomic and cultural surroundings in which they finally settled, and the personality of the parents. Most studies have failed to take such factors into account when trying to generalize their findings.

Most of the studies using nonclinical and nonselected samples have failed to find gross pathology. However, one limitation applies to both clinical and nonclinical studies of the survivors and their children: the often very small samples and low participation rates make it difficult to generalize the results obtained.

A controversial issue has been the hypothesized transmission of Holocaust-related pathology from parents to children. While there is no disagreement that the effect of the Holocaust on the survivors may have influenced the second generation in many and different ways, the controversy concerns the *transmission* of symptoms from parents to children. Although several studies have focused on such transmission (Barocas & Barocas, 1979; Davidson, 1980a, 1980b; Herzog, 1982; Kestenberg, 1982; Klein, 1973; Levine, 1982), no systematic comparison between the symptoms or behavior of the survivor parents and those of their children has been carried out. Only by investigating the parents' symptoms and comparing them with those of their children will the transmission question be resolved.

The continued growth of the literature on the health of the survivors and their children shows that people are still concerned with the Holocaust and its long-term consequences, in both from a humanist and a scientific perspective. Moreover, this ongoing interest demonstrates that there are still unclarified problems to be investigated.

REFERENCES

ADELSBERGER, L. *Auschwitz, ein tatsachenbericht.* Berlin: Lettner, 1956.

ALLPORT, G. W. *Pattern and growth in personality.* New York: Holt, Rinehart, and Winston, 1961.

AMERICAN PSYCHIATRIC ASSOCIATION. *Diagnostic and statistical manual of mental disorders. DSM-III-R.* Washington, DC: American Psychiatric Association, 1987.

BAROCAS, H. A., & BAROCAS, C. B. Manifestations of concentration camp effects on the second generation. *American Journal of Psychiatry,* 1973, *130,* 820–821.

—————. Wounds of the fathers: The next generation of Holocaust victims. *International Review of Psycho-Analysis,* 1979, *6,* 331–339.

—————. Separation-individuation conflicts in children of Holocaust survivors. *Journal of Contemporary Psychotherapy,* 1980, *11,* 6–14.

Bettelheim, B. Individual and mass behavior in extreme situations. *Journal of Abnormal Social Psychology,* 1943, *38,* 417–452.

Chodoff, P. Late effects of the concentration camp syndrome. *Archives of General Psychiatry,* 1963, *8,* 323–333.

—————. Depression and guilt among concentration camp survivors. *Existential Psychiatry,* 1970, *7,* 19–26.

Chodoff, P. Psychotherapy of the survivor. In J. E. Dimsdale (ed.), *Survivors, victims and perpetrators.* Washington, DC: Hemisphere Publishing, 1980, 205–216.

Cohen, E. A. *Human behavior in the concentration camp.* London: Jonathan Cape, 1954.

Danieli, Y. *Therapists' difficulties in treating survivors of the Nazi Holocaust and their children.* Ph.D. dissertation, New York University, 1981.(a)

—————. The aging survivor of the Holocaust. Discussion: On the achievement of integration in aging survivors of the Nazi Holocaust. *Journal of Geriatric Psychiatry,* 1981, *14,* 191–210.(b)

—————. The treatment and prevention of long-term effects and intergenerational transmission of victimization: A lesson from Holocaust survivors and their children. In C. R. Figley, (ed.), *Trauma and its wake.* New York: Brunner/Mazel, 1985.

Dasberg, H. Trauma in Israel. In H. Dasberg, S. Davidson, G. L. Durlacher, B. C. Filet, & E. de Wind (eds.), *Society and trauma of war.* Assen/Maastricht, Neth.: Van Gorcum, 1987.

Davidson, S. Massive psychic traumatization and social support. *Journal of Psychosomatic Research,* 1979, *23,* 395–402.

—————. The clinical effects of massive psychic trauma in families of Holocaust survivors. *Journal of Marital and Family Therapy,* 1980, *6,* 11–21.(a)

—————. Transgenerational transmission in the families of Holocaust survivors. *International Journal of Family Psychiatry,* 1980, *1,* 95–112.(b)

—————. Trauma in the life cycle of the individual and the collective consciousness in relation to war and persecution. In H. Dasberg, S. Davidson, G. L. Durlacher, B. C. Filet, E. de Wind (eds.), *Society and trauma of war.* Assen/Maastricht, Neth.: Van Gorcum, 1987.

de Graaf, Pathological pattern of identification in families of survivors of the Holocaust. *Israel Annals of Psychiatry and Related Disciplines,* 1975, *13,* 335–363.

Dimsdale, J. E. The coping behavior of Nazi concentration camp survivors. *American Journal of Psychiatry,* 1974, *131,* 792–799.

—————. Coping—every man's war. *American Journal of Psychotherapy,* 1978, *32,* 402–413.

Eaton, W. W., Sigal, J. J., & Weinfeld, M. Impairment in Holocaust survivors after 33 years: Data from an unbiased community sample. *American Journal of Psychiatry,* 1982, *139,* 773–777.

Eitinger, L. *Concentration camp survivors in Norway and Israel.* Oslo: Oslo University Press, 1964.

—————. Psychosomatic problems in concentration camp survivors. *Journal of Psychosomatic Research,* 1969, *13,* 183–189.

—————. A follow-up study of the Norwegian concentration camp survivors' mortality and morbidity. *Israeli Annals of Psychiatry and Related Disciplines,* 1973, *11,* 199–208.

—————. Coping with aggression. *Mental Health and Society,* 1974, *1,* 297–301.

—————. On being a psychiatrist and a survivor. In A. H. Rosenfeld & I. Greenberg (eds.), *Confronting the Holocaust. The impact of Elie Wiesel.* Bloomington: Indiana University Press, 1979.

—————. Jewish concentration camp survivors in the post-war world. *Danish Medical Bulletin,* 1980, *27,* 232–235.

—————. Psychological and medical effects of concentration camps. *Research bibliography.* Haifa: Ray D. Wolfe Centre, University of Haifa, 1981.

————. Denial in concentration camps. In S. Breznitz (eds.), *The denial of stress*. New York: International University Press, 1983.

————. The concentration camp syndrome: An organic brain syndrome? *Integrative Psychiatry,* 1985, *3,* 115-119.

EITINGER, L., & ASKEVOLD, F. In A. Strøm (ed.), *Norwegian concentration camp survivors*. Oslo: Oslo University Press, 1968.

EITINGER, L., KRELL, R., & RIECK, M. *The psychological and medical effects of concentration camps and related persecutions. A research bibliography.* Vancouver: University of British Columbia Press, 1985.

FENIG, S., & LEVAV, I. Demoralization and social supports among Holocaust survivors. *Journal of Nervous and Mental Disease,* 1991, *179,* 167-172.

FRANKL, V. E. *From death-camp to existentialism*. Boston: Beacon Press, 1959.

FRANKL V. E. Psychologie und psychiatrie des konzentrationslagers. In *Psychiatrie der Gegenwart III*. Berlin, Göttingen, Heidelberg: Springer Verlag, 1961.

FREUD, A., DANN, S. *An experiment in group upbringing*. New York: International University Press, 1951.

GAY, M., & SHULMAN, S. Comparison of children of Holocaust survivors with children of the general population in Israel. *Mental health and Society,* 1978, *5,* 252-256.

HADAR, Y. *Second generation of the Holocaust survivor—existential experience or a mental syndrome?* Paper presented to the conference on Psychological and Psychiatric Sequelae of Nazi-Terror on Aging Survivors and their Offspring, Hannover, Germany, 1989.

HELWEG-LARSEN, P., HOFFMEYER, H., KIELER, J., et al. Famine disease in German concentration camps. Complications and sequels. *Acta Psychiatrica et Neurologica Scandinavica,* 1952 (suppl. 83).

HEMMENDINGER, J. Readjustment of young concentration camp survivors through a surrogate family experience. *Interaction,* 1980, *3,* 127-134.

————. A la sortie des camps de la mort: Reinsertion dans la vie. *Israel Journal of Psychiatry and Related Sciences,* 1981, *18,* 331-334.

HERMAN, K., & THYGESEN, P. Kz-syndromet. *Ugeskrift for læger,* 1954, *116,* 825-836.

HERTZ, D. G., & FREYBERGER, H. Factors influencing the evaluation of psychological and psychosomatic reactions in survivors of the Nazi persecution. *Journal of Psychosomatic Research,* 1982, *26,* 83-89.

HERZOG, J. World beyond metaphor: Thoughts on the transmission of trauma. In M. S. Bergmann & M. E. Jucovy, (eds.), *Generations of the Holocaust*. New York: Basic Books, 1982.

HOPPE, K. D. Psychotherapy of concentration camp victims. *Psyche,* 1965, *19,* 290-319.

————. Chronic reactive aggression in survivors of severe persecution. *Comprehensive Psychiatry,* 1971, *12,* 230-237.

KAV-VENAKI, S., NADLER, A., & GERSHONI, H. Sharing past traumas: A comparison of communication behaviors in two groups of Holocaust survivors. *International Journal of Social Psychiatry,* 1983, *29,* 49-59.

KEILSON, H. Sequential traumatization of children. *Danish Medical Bulletin,* 1980, *27,* 235-237.

KEINAN, G., MIKULINCER, M., & RYBNICKI, A. Perception of self and parents by second-generation Holocaust survivors. *Behavioral Medicine,* 1988, *14,* 6-12.

KESTENBERG, J. The psychological consequences of punitive institutions. *Israel Journal of Psychiatry and Related Sciences,* 1981, *18,* 15-30.

————. Survivor-parents and their children. In M. S. Bergmann & M. E. Jucovy (eds.), *Generations of the Holocaust*. New York: Basic Books, 1982.

KLEIN, H. Children of the Holocaust: Mourning and bereavement. In J. Anthony & C. Koupernik (eds.), *The child in his family. Yearbook of the International Association for Child Psychiatry and Allied Professions.* New York: Wiley, 1973.

Kluge, E. Über die Folgen schwerer Haftzeiten. *Nervenarzt,* 1958, *29,* 462–465.

Kogon, E. *Der SS-Staat.* Frankfurt: Europäische Verlagsanstalt, 1946.

Kolb, E. *Bergen-Belsen.* Hannover: Verlag für Literatur und Zeitgeschehen, 1962.

Kral, V. A. Psychiatric observation under severe chronic stress. *American Journal of Psychiatry,* 1951, *108,* 185–192.

Krell, R. Holocaust families: The survivors and their children. *Comprehensive Psychiatry,* 1979, *20,* 560–568.

————. Child survivors of the Holocaust: 40 years later. *Journal of the American Academy of Child Psychiatry,* 1985, *24,* 378–380.(a)

————. Therapeutic value of documenting child survivors. *Journal of the American Academy of Child Psychiatry,* 1985, *24,* 397–400.(b)

Krystal, H. *Massive psychic trauma.* New York: International Universities Press, 1968.

————. The aging survivor of the Holocaust. Integration and self-healing in post-traumatic states. *Journal of Geriatric Psychiatry,* 1981, *14,* 165–189.

Last, U., & Klein, H. Impact of parental Holocaust traumatization on offsprings' reports of parental child-rearing practices. *Journal of Youth and Adolescence,* 1984, *13,* 267–283.

Levav, I., & Abramson, J. H. Emotional distress among concentration camp survivors—a community study in Jerusalem. *Psychological Medicine,* 1984, *14,* 215–218.

Levi, P. Besøkelsestid [If not now, when?]. Oslo: Gyldendal, 1987.

Levin, N. *The Holocaust. The destruction of European Jewry, 1933–1945.* New York: Crowell, 1968.

Levine, H. B. Toward a psychoanalytic understanding of children of survivors of the Holocaust. *Psychoanalytic Quarterly,* 1982, *51,* 70–92.

Luchterhand, E. G. Early and late effects of imprisonment in Nazi concentration camps; Conflicting interpretations in survivor research. *Social Psychiatry,* 1970, *5,* 102–110.

Major, E. F. *The effect of Holocaust on the second generation: A controlled investigation of Norwegian-born Holocaust survivors and their children.* Dissertation, University of Oslo, 1990.

Major, E. The second generation of Norwegian Jewish Holocaust survivors: Mental health and identity conflicts. *Acta Psychiatrica Scandinavica,* in press.

Matussek, P. *Die Konzentrationslagerhaft und ihre Folgen.* Berlin: Springer Verlag, 1971.

Meerloo, J. A. M. Neurologism and denial of psychic trauma in survivors. *American Journal of Psychiatry,* 1963, *120,* 65–66.

————. Persecution trauma and the reconditioning of emotional life: A brief survey. *American Journal of Psychiatry,* 1969, *125,* 1187–1195.

Minkowski, E. *Les enfants de Buchenwald.* Geneva: Union O.S.E., 1946.

Moskowitz, S. *Love despite hate: Child survivors of the Holocaust and their adult life.* New York: Schocken, 1983.

————. Longitudinal follow-up of child survivors of the Holocaust. *Journal of the American Academy of Child Psychiatry,* 1985, *24,* 401–407.

Müller-Hill, B. *Murderous science.* Oxford: Oxford University Press, 1988.

Mussaph, H. The second generation of war victims: Psychopathological problems. *Israel Journal of Psychiatry and Related Sciences,* 1981, *18,* 3–14.

Niederland, W. G. The problem of the survivor. Journal *Hillside Hospital,* 1961, *10,* 233–247.

Niederland, W. G. Clinical observations on the ''Survivor'' Syndrome. *International Journal of Psychoanalysis,* 1968, *49,* 313–315.

PEDERSEN, S. Psychopathological reactions to extreme social displacement. *Psychoanalytical Review,* 1949, *36,* 344–354.

PESKIN, H. Observations on the first international conference on children of Holocaust survivors. *Family Process,* 1981, *20,* 391–394.

PETERS, U. H. Die psychischen folgen der verfolgung. Das überlebenden-syndrom. *Fortschritte der Neurologie-Psychiatrie,* 1989, *57,* 169–218.

PINSKY, L. The children. In H. B. M. Murphy, et al. (eds.), *Flight and resettlement.* Paris: UNESCO, 1955.

PROSS, C. *Breaking through the post-war coverup of Nazi physicians in Germany.* Paper presented to the International Symposium on Torture and the Medical Profession, University of Tromsø, Norway, 1990.

PROSS, C. Breaking through the postwar coverup of Nazi doctors in Germany. Proceedings of the International Symposium on torture and the medical profession. *Journal of Medical Ethics,* 1991 (supplement), *17,* 13–16.

RAKOFF, V., SIGAL, J. J., & EPSTEIN, N. B. Children and families of concentration camp survivors. *Canada's Mental Health,* 1966, *14,* 24–26.

RIECK, M., & EITINGER, L. *Psychological investigations of Holocaust survivors' offspring.* Paper given at the 7th biennial meeting of the ISSBD, Munich, 1983.

ROBINSON, S. Late effects of persecution in persons as children or young adolescents survived the Nazi occupation in Europe. *Israeli Annals of Psychiatry and Related Diciplines,* 1979, *17,* 209–214.

ROBINSON, S., RAPAPORT, J., DURST, R., RAPAPORT, M., ROSCA, P., METZER, S., & SILBERMAN, L. The late effects of Nazi persecution among elderly Holocaust survivors. *Acta Psychiatrica Scandinavica,* 1990, *82,* 311–315.

ROBINSON, S., & WINNIK, H. Second generation of the Holocaust. Holocaust survivors' communication of experience their children, and its effects. *Israel Journal of Psychiatry and Related Sciences,* 1981, *18,* 99–107.

ROSE, S. L., & GARSKE, J. Family environment, adjustment, and coping among children of Holocaust survivors: A comparative investigation. *American Journal of Orthopsychiatry,* 1987, *57,* 332–344.

ROSEN, J., REYNOLDS, C. F., YEAGER, A. L., HOUCK, P. R., & HURWITZ, L. F. Sleep disturbances in survivors of the Nazi Holocaust. *American Journal of Psychiatry, 1991, 148,* 62–66.

ROSENBERGER, L. Children of survivors. In E. J. Anthony & C. Koupernik, (eds.), *The child in his family: The impact of disease and death. Yearbook of the International Association for Child Psychiatry and Allied Professions.* New York: Wiley, 1973.

ROSENTHAL, P. A., & ROSENTHAL, S. Holocaust effect in the third generation: Child of another time. *American Journal of Psychotherapy,* 1980, *34,* 572–580.

ROSS, R. J., BALL, W. A., SULLIVAN, K. A., & CAROFF, S. N. Sleep disturbances as the hallmark of post-traumatic stress disorder. *American Journal of Psychiatry,* 1989, *146,* 697–707.

RUSSELL, A. Late psychosocial consequences in concentration camp survivor families. *American Journal of Orthopsychiatry,* 1974, *44,* 611–619.

RUSSELL, A., PLOTKIN, D., & HEAPY, N. Adaptive abilities in nonclinical second-generation Holocaust survivors and controls: A comparison. *American Journal of Psychotherapy,* 1985, *39,* 564–579.

SCHMOLLING, P. Human reactions to the Nazi concentration camps. *Journal of Human Stress,* 1984, *10,* 108–120.

SHENITZ, B. Hidden children speak out. *Newsweek,* April 15, 1991, 52.

SIGAL, J. J. *Retrospective roles of clinical and empirical studies of the intergenerational effects of the Holocaust.* Paper presented to the conference on Psychological and Psychiatric Sequelae of the Nazi-Terror in Aging Survivors and Their Offspring, Hannover, Germany, 1989.

SIGAL, J. J., DINICOLA, V. F., & BUONVINO, M. Grandchildren of survivors: Can negative effects of prolonged exposure to excessive stress be observed two generations later? *Canada Journal of Psychiatry,* 1988, *33,* 207–212.

SIGAL, J. J., & RAKOFF, V. Concentration camp survival. A pilot study of the effects on the second generation. *Canada Psychiatry Association Journal,* 1971, *16,* 393–397.

SIGAL, J. J., SILVER, D., RAKOFF, V., & ELLIN, B. Some second-generation effects of survival of the Nazi persecution. *American Journal of Orthopsychiatry,* 1973, *43,* 320–327.

SIGAL, J. J., & WEINFELD, M. Control of aggression in adult children of survivors of the Nazi persecution. *Journal of Abnormal Psychology,* 1985, *94,* 556–564.

SOLKOFF, N. Children of survivors of the Nazi Holocaust: A critical review of the literature. *American Journal of Orthopsychiatry,* 1981, *51,* 29–42.

STEINITZ, L. Y. Psycho-social effects of the Holocaust on aging survivors and their families. *Journal of Gerontological Social Work,* 1982, *4,* 145–152.

STRØM, A. Undersøkelse av norske tidligere konsentrasjonsleirfanger. *Tidsskrift for Den Norske Lægeforening,* 1961, *81,* 803–804.

————. *Norwegian concentration camp survivors.* Oslo: Oslo University Press; New York: Humanities Press, 1968.

SZWARC, H. The premature ageing of former KZ-prisoners. *Zeitscrift für Altersforschung,* 1985, *40,* 209–212.

TARGOWLA, R. Les séquelles pathologiques de la déportation dans les camps de concentration allemands pendant la deuxième guerre mondiale. *Presse Médicale,* 1954, *62,* 611–613.

TROSSMAN, B. Adolescent children of concentration camp survivors. *Canadian Psychiatric Association Journal,* 1968, *13,* 121–123.

VENZLAFF, U. Die psychoreaktiven Störungen nach entschädigungspflichtigen Ereignissen. Berlin: Springer, 1958.

VON BAEYER, W. Erlebnisreaktive Störungen und ihre Bedeutung für die Begutachtung. *Deutsche Medizinische Wochenschrift,* 1958, *83,* 2317–2322.

VON BAEYER, W. Erlebnisbedingte verfolgungsschäden. *Nervenarzt,* 1961, *32,* 534–538.

VON BAEYER, W., HAEFNER, H., & KISKER, K. P. *Psychiatrie der verfolgten.* Berlin: Springer, 1964.

WANGH, U. Die Bedeutung der Wiedergutmachungsanprüche der als Kleinkinder Verfolgten. In H. J. Herberg. *Spätschäden nach Extremebelastungen.* Herford, Ger.: Nicolaische Verlagsbuchhandlung, 1971.

WEISS, E., O'CONNELL, A. N., & SIITER, R. Comparisons of second-generation Holocaust survivors, immigrants, and non-immigrants on measures of mental health. *Journal of Personality and Social Psychology,* 1986, *50,* 828–831.

ZLOTOGORSKI, Z. Offspring of concentration camp survivors: A study of levels of ego functioning. *Israel Journal of Psychiatry and Related Sciences,* 1985, *22,* 201–209.

34

Migration and Stress

Judith T. Shuval

THE RELATIONSHIP BETWEEN STRESS AND MIGRATION may be considered on two levels that differ analytically in terms of the assumed direction of cause and effect. On the one hand, stress of various sorts may be said to cause migration; on the other, stress may be viewed as an outcome of migration. As noted, this distinction is essentially analytical, because both processes may occur with regard to any specific stream of migration. This chapter focuses primarily on stress as a potential outcome of migration, although some attention is also given to the causative role of stress in stimulation that process.

MIGRATION: SOME THEORETICAL CONSIDERATIONS

Before considering the relationship between migration and stress, it is useful to present a theoretical view of migration as a general social process. Because the large number of descriptive studies that have been carried out in the past twenty to thirty years have not yielded a single, coherent model of migration (Brody, 1970; Davis, 1974; Jackson, 1969; Jansen, 1970; Lee, 1969; Price, 1969; Richmond, 1969), I will draw together several theoretical themes and attempt to integrate them into a comprehensive model of the migration process (Shuval, 1982).

Migration may be viewed as a dynamic process that involves a decision to leave one place of residence for another. In the most general sense, migration refers to moves of any distance, ranging from one block to the next or from one continent to another. The intention of the move is long-term, if not permanent, residence in the new social setting, so that nomadic wanderings are generally not considered a category of migration. Relatively inexpensive means of transportation and the transferability of many occupational skills have made postmodern migration less of a permanent commitment than resettlement was in the past. Thus, a new location may be viewed as tentative for a period of time and, under certain conditions, migration may continue to another, more attractive destination or even back to the migrant's original location.

This paper was prepared under the auspices of the Rose Programme in Medical Sociology at the Hebrew University Hadassah Medical School. I am grateful to Paula Feder for her assistance in updating and revising the paper.

On the macrolevel, migration may be said to have implications and repercussions not only for the individuals involved but for two social systems as well—at the place of origin and at the destination. Departure or entry of groups requires readjustment in each of the two social systems (Mangalam & Schwarzweller, 1970). The extent of these readjustments depends on the size of the migrating population relative to the populations at the origin and the destination. The greater the proportion of each of these groups, the more far-reaching the social adaptation required of the total social system at the relevant point.

The number of persons involved is associated with the position they occupied or will occupy at either end of the migration process. "Brain drain" is a type of migration that depletes the society of origin of highly trained persons and may require redeployment in the occupational structure. Migration of dissidents from the Soviet Union eased the potential tension they generated in that society and improved social control (Gitelman, 1972, 1977). At the destination, a process of readjustment takes place when specific racial, ethnic, or occupational groups enter the social system and precipitate a shift in the balance of relationships in that society. Thus, viewed on the macrolevel, migration may be said to be a process generating social change in at least two social systems.

The decision to migrate is made, in the final analysis, on an individual level but, like other decisions, within a context of social norms and salient reference groups. On the whole, the social networks in which individuals are embedded tend to tie them to a given locus of residence (Hull, 1979). But when such groups see migration as desirable or even as normative, pressure is generated to encourage individuals to move. Thus, migration may become a norm in certain social situations and sweep along individuals whose inclination to migrate is initially low. On the other hand, the decision to migrate may run counter to prevailing norms and therefore require tenacity and nonconformity in the individual.

The decision to leave a given location has been described as a product of complementary push and pull factors (Lee, 1969). These vary in their relative intensity, but when a decision to migrate is reached, the overall balance is such as to make the destination appear more attractive than the place of origin to the potential migrant. Given the inertia of most people, the place of origin needs to present situational or value factors that are perceived as undesirable, and these must be sufficiently sapient to motivate people to disengage from the social context in which they are embedded. Classically, these factors have included religious or political persecution, physical or environmental disasters, economic deprivation, physical or environmental disasters, economic deprivation, ideological rejection of the dominant norms, or other forms of alienation. Refugees are migrants for whom the push factors in the place of origin are drastic or traumatic, so that departure is not a matter of choice. In all cases, the negative factors at the origin are subjectively defined by the potential migrant, and include situations of relative deprivation in which the objective status of the individual may appear quite satisfactory to others.

The mutual dependence of the push and pull factors is seen in the fact that even the strongest push will fail to disengage individuals from their place of origin unless they can identify an alternative accessible location in which the relevant negative factor is absent, markedly weaker, or avoidable. Therefore, there is a symmetrical relationship between factors that motivate people to leave a permanent residence and those that attract them to another specific locus (e.g., unemployment versus job opportunities, religious persecution versus religious freedom, marginal status versus social acceptance). From this viewpoint, push and pull factors are frequently opposite sides of the same coin.

A lack of symmetry occurs when the destination appears to the potential migrant to be characterized by special, salient attractive qualities, so that even if certain negative qualities of his place of origin persist at the destination, these attractive qualities play a powerful role in decisionmaking.

A decision to migrate is mediated by the individual's resources. However negative the perceived conditions in the place of origin and however attractive the destination, a decision to move requires material means, as well as skills that include initiative, organizational abilities, and knowledge.

Needless to say, all migrants are not equal participants in the decisionmaking process. When an unaccompanied adult migrates, most of the decisionmaking is individual. But some migrants may be passive participants in a decision reached by others. The most evident of these are dependents, such as children and elderly persons. When a marriage is characterized by asymmetrical power relations, wives tend to be less actively involved in the decisionmaking process. Such participation is related to the subsequent process of adjustment in the new social setting because of the motivational and cognitive-perceptual patterns such participation generates.

All migration is selective. The population moving from one setting to another is rarely representative of the population from which it is drawn; however, the criteria of selection vary (Lee, 1969). In some cases, the selection will be "positive"—resulting in highly educated, ambitious, adventurous, and adaptable migrants (Kuo & Tsai, 1986). It has been suggested that many Holocaust survivors had an exceptional ability to cope with stress and that these skills assisted them in adjusting to employment and social life after migrating to Israel (Aviram, Silverberg, & Carel, 1987). In other cases, migrants may be characterized by failure in their place of origin, low education, present or potential social or psychological pathology, lack of occupational skills, or susceptibility to illness. A mixture of these two selection conditions often occurs, although it is usually possible to discern a dominant pattern of positive or negative selection. Processes of selection determine the kinds of personal resources migrants bring with them in the form of education, skills, and personality traits. Their level of sensitivity and susceptibility to different stresses is also a function of selection processes.

The self-selection process of migrants is mediated by formal restrictions and preferential admission policies of gatekeepers at the origin and destination, respectively. On a formal level, there are often barriers to leaving and requirements—health, educational, or occupational—for entry.

An example of the two-stage process of selection at the origin may be seen in the example of Jewish emigration from the Soviet Union during the 1970s. The first stage was self-determined: individuals or families made a decision, which was expressed in their formal application for a permit to emigrate. For this application to be considered, a *vyzov* was required—that is, an affidavit attesting to an invitation from a family member in Israel. Between 1968 and 1978, 318,914 such affidavits were sent from Israel, but only a third were utilized for emigration (Insight, 1977). The limited use of the affidavits can be explained by a variety of restrictions imposed by the Soviet authorities, by a change of mind on the part of potential emigrants, or by the decision among some of the latter to keep the *vyzov* in case of later need (Gitelman, 1972, 1977). Applying to emigrate from the Soviet Union during that period entailed considerable risk, and often led to job loss, expulsion of children from school or university, ostracism by colleagues and friends, threats and open hostility, condemnation in the media, and the need to move to other housing. The Soviet authorities demanded that applicants for permits provide a character reference from their place of employment, permission from their parents, permission from a former spouse (in cases of divorce), and certification from their house committee. Self-selection at this first stage, therefore, involved courage, determination, alienation from Soviet society, self-confidence, Jewish identity, or some combination of these factors (Shuval, 1982).

The second stage of selection was imposed by the Soviet authorities, who granted exit permits to a subgroup of would-be emigrants (Insight, 1977). Those most likely to obtain exit permits included people viewed as less skilled, older people, people whose work was not considered essential or secret, people who did not have relatives in the security establishment or in high party positions, dissidents, and troublemakers. It has been suggested that some local officials may have been eager to grant exit permits to Jews, who generally assimilated into Russian culture rather than into that of local ethnic groups: emigration thus removed "agents" of Russification. Such emigration also freed jobs for local people and broadened the opportunities for occupational mobility. In the 1970s, the Soviet Union's need for expanded trade relations with the West made the USSR particularly sensitive to the Jackson Amendment, which linked free emigration of Soviet citizens with most favored nation recognition by the United States (Shuval, 1982).

Selection processes are applied to immigrants by virtually all sovereign states or administrative authorities to which admission is sought (Kuo & Tsai, 1986). These policies differ in their restrictiveness and are directly geared to the needs of the host society. In extreme (but frequent) cases, borders are closed and would-be immigrants are prevented from entering. Such closure stems from fears, beliefs, prejudices, or self-interested considerations that cause decisionmakers to view immigrants as a potentially disruptive element in the society. The most widespread selection criterion for admission relates to occupational skills. When a society is short of specific types of workers, it admits immigrants with the appropriate skills. Ideological and humanitarian criteria sometimes play a role in selection processes, especially with regard to refugees.

An immigrant's entry into a new society is a gradual process. The length of time that is relevant depends on the parameters being considered. At what point in time does an immigrant turn into a veteran? The critical time span may be defined in months, years, or even generations. What seems to be important is the dynamic quality of the process.

Different stages in the integration process have different characteristics, so that issues that are important at one stage may disappear at another. For example, knowledge of a new language has a different meaning in terms of behavior and interaction with others when an immigrant has been in a new country six months, five years, or twenty years. The same is true for primary relations between immigrants and veteran members of the host society; these generally develop relatively late in the integration process (Gordon, 1964). Even unemployment, downward mobility, and poverty may be perceived for a short period as transitional stages in the immigration process and, therefore, as acceptable (Munroe-Blum, Boyle, Offord, & Kates, 1989). Although the orderly progression described by Park and Burgess (1921) from contact to competition and conflict and finally to accommodation does not seem to characterize all situations, the migrant experience undoubtedly varies by stage (Hertz, 1988).

There are a variety of approaches to the conceptual definition of integration into a new social system (Richmond, 1984). Terms such as socialization, resocialization, acculturation, accommodation, and normative behavior have been widely used but, in most cases, inadequately spelled out either conceptually or empirically (Price, 1969). Does the term *integration* refer to the dispersal of immigrants in the institutional structure? To their conformity to the prevalent norms of the society? To an absence of pathological behavior among them? To their feelings of identification, well-being, familiarity, acceptance, hopefulness? To their interaction on a primary level with other members of the society? To lack of conflict between them and other groups? These issues refer to a variety of contents of the integration concept.

It is essential to establish what point of view on the integration of immigrants is being considered. Several are undoubtedly relevant. One salient point of view is, of course, that of the immigrants themselves. How do they feel about the new society? Do they see it as their permanent home, or is it more of a waystation in a series of moves? Another point of view is that of veteran residents. Do they accept newcomers or do they view them with hostility—as potential competitors or disrupters of the status quo? Are they apathetic? Finally, one may consider the viewpoint of the society as a whole in terms of its dominant values and their relationship to the issue of immigration. These values have both manifest and latent components that are expressed by more and less formal means.

It seems essential to view integration into a new society as a multidimensional process that can be considered in terms of a variety of subprocesses, each focusing on a different aspect of life in the new society. Thus, immigrants can enter a new social system by means of many pathways and mechanisms. At any point in time, integration in one area of life is not necessarily correlated with integration in others; some areas are more highly correlated with each other than are others, but there seems to be no consistency across populations or situations to permit one to establish necessary correlations. Furthermore, change in one area of life may not be correlated with change in other areas (Shuval, Markus, & Dotan, 1973, 1975).

The implication of such a multidimensional approach is that there is little to be gained from seeking one overall measure of integration. The problem is to establish which points of view are to be considered, which content areas are relevant for understanding the process, and to seek the empirical relationships among them at various points in time. Composite indexes of integration, such as the one used by Rose (1969), which involve arbitrary weighting of the measures from which the composite is derived are, therefore, of limited use. It seems preferable to focus on different meanings and factors depending on the temporal stage in a group's process of entry into the social system. Focusing on one specific area—for example, the occupational sphere—is, of course, legitimate, provided one bears in mind that, despite its centrality, work is only one of several areas of life that could be considered. While behavior in this area is not positively correlated with behavior in all other areas, it is generally highly correlated with morale, identification, and feelings about the new society, so that employment has special sapience in the overall process of migration (Shuval, Markus, & Dotan, 1973).

The integration process in all its dimensions may involve conflict no less than solidarity. The process does not necessarily re-establish an earlier equilibrium, but may result in a redefinition of the social environment in terms quite different from those that initially characterized the society (Mangalam & Schwarzweller, 1970). Indeed, the differing interests and values that inhere in the meeting of groups and subgroups suggest that the process is unlikely to be smooth. One can assume that various groups have different interests and goals as a result of their different positions in the social system and that these may not always be complementary. No less important are value conflicts inherent in the orientation of any one group.

Immigrants are just as likely to come into contact with the problems and pathologies of the institutional structure of the host society as they are to encounter its more stable elements. Chronic problems to which veterans have accommodated often plague newcomers during their initial stages in the society. It has even been suggested that acceptance of certain chronic pathologies of a society be used as one index of integration. Furthermore, weak or imperfectly functioning institutional structures may be strained by the arrival of an immigrant population, so that the migrants may contribute further to the institutional dysfunction. An example of this difficulty would be a social service that was overutilized before the arrival of an immigrant group (Shuval, 1982).

In a rapidly changing society, newcomers generally are not presented with a coherent set of norms to which conformity is expected. Differentiation of the host society in terms of ethnic, social, regional, occupation, or political subgroups results in a variety of norms to which immigrants are differentially exposed depending on the groups with which they come into contact.

By channeling newcomers into specific subgroups or locations, a pluralistically structured society allows immigrants to learn the norms of one group but remain ignorant of the norms of others or of those held in common by all members of the society. If that subgroup happens to consist of other immigrants from the same place of origin, the familiarity and intimacy may provide a positive cushioning effect for some period, but separation from broader segments of the host society may intensify feelings of isolation or conflict (Mavreas & Bebbington, 1989).

In the case of migrant professionals, such as physicians, who are familiar with and share professional norms with members of that profession in the host society, acculturation is ostensibly comparatively simple. If both the country of origin and the host society belong to the same overall cultural and professional tradition, professional practice in the country of origin is controlled by norms similar to those prevalent in the new society. Thus, if Western medicine is practiced in both societies, little acculturation should be required for physicians, because the same norms were presumably learned and followed. However, because the broader cultural context, the history, and the structure of professional practice impinge on role performance, one can expect professionals to behave somewhat differently in two similar societies. To the extent that the general values of the social system impinge on professional performance and to the extent that these values differ across countries, a process of acculturation will be necessary. The cultural distance between the groups determines the pace and quality of this process (Shuval, 1982; Stevens, Goodman, & Mick, 1978).

Whichever dimension of integration is considered, the process involves interaction between immigrants and the host society. There is a mutual process of adaptation in which immigrants and veterans respond to each other in a variety of patterns. It is, therefore, just as important to understand attitudes and orientations of members of the host society toward immigrants as it is to understand the attitudes of the immigrants. Focusing on the host society, Rose (1969) referred to the degree of societal openness as expressed, on the one hand, by formal rules and regulations concerning admission or granting of privileges and, on the other, by informal attitudes expressed by members of the host society toward immigrants. The latter include fear of competition, xenophobia, stereotyping, and the extent to which the host culture is able to tolerate deviance.

STRESS: A DEFINITION

The stress model that appears to be most useful in the present context is the one proposed by Levine and Scotch (1970). House (1974) noted that "stress occurs when an individual confronts a situation where his usual modes of behavior are insufficient and the consequences of not adapting are serious" (p. 12). Stated most generally, this theory proposes a multilinked chain among potential stressor situations, subjectively determined perception variables, and the availability and usability of personal and social coping mechanisms (French, Rodgers, & Cobb, 1974; Scott & Howard, 1970). Thus, homeostasis on the individual level will be disrupted when a person perceives a given situation to be disturbing, alarming, or threatening. If the individual is unable to mobilize personal or social resources to cope with the situation and restore homeostasis, his or her energy will be bound up in dealing with this perceived disturbance. This preoccupation defines a stressful condition (Scott & Howard, 1970).

Levine and Scotch's (1970) approach emphasizes the subjective definition of stress by making it clear that situations are not objectively stressful but are socially or psychologically defined as such by individuals in terms of social and cultural norms. Thus, bereavement or divorce may be subjectively defined as extremely disturbing but also, by some and under certain circumstances, as a relief or even as a positive challenge (House, 1974). The conditional quality of the stress model also emphasizes the importance of coping mechanisms, which may be individual (personal skills, personality traits, intelligence, knowledge) or social (formal institutions, informal groups, social norms and values). The availability and usability of coping mechanisms constitute the link that determines whether a situation that is perceived as disturbing will result in stress for the individual (Pearlin & Schooler, 1978).

Mechanic (1978) distinguished between two types of coping: *defense processes,* which are psychological mechanisms that redefine, deny, repress, or possibly distort a disturbing reality; and *instrumental coping behavior,* which utilizes skills and knowledge for problem solving is an effort to change or ameliorate the stressful situation. Defense processes may enable the individual to live with a difficult situation—e.g., chronic illness—but in the long run neurotic or more serious consequences are likely to accompany this form of coping. In contrast, instrumental coping seeks to alter or modify a disturbing situation. Clearly, coping depends on early socialization and on prior experiences with the given situation or with settings perceived as similar.

In sum, stress is said to exist to the extent that an individual defines a salient situation as disturbing and is unable to recruit effective coping mechanisms to remove or reduce the disturbance. Two simultaneous conditions are necessary for stress to be present or to increase: a subjective definition of a situation as disturbing and an inability—for whatever reason—to cope with the condition. The centrality of social and psychological factors in determining stress is seen in the fact that both these conditions (i.e., what one defines as disturbing and what resources one can utilize for coping) are largely socially determined.

CHANGE AS A STRUCTURAL CHARACTERISTIC OF MIGRATION

Change is inherent in migration and may be considered a structural characteristic of the process. Such change may, under the circumstances proposed in the model just outlined, be viewed as a potential stressor. Three forms of change characterize the migration process: physical, social, and cultural.

Physical Change

Migration involves movement from one geographical location to another. The migrant may experience changes in climate, level of sanitation, and dietary habits, as well as exposure to pollution, new pathogens, and endemic diseases. Changes in climate, in conjunction with the new culture, may induce changes in lifestyle that express themselves in altered patterns of sleep, nutrition, timing of meals (e.g., when the main meal of the day is taken), clothing, housing, or general pace of activity. All these physical changes may, under certain circumstances, serve as stressors (Hull, 1979; Wessen, 1971).

Social Change

All migrants disengage from a network of social relations in the society they are leaving. In the case of migration of whole kin groups, disengagement may be minimal, but in other cases there are numerous breaks in social relationships. Disruption of longstanding ties may or may not be perceived as disturbing by the migrant; accordingly, disengagement will cause the migrant to feel isolated and unsupported or relieved and unencumbered. Separation may be viewed as permanent (e.g., leaving behind aged parents in a society to which access is closed) or as temporary if the people left behind can visit the migrant in the new residence or the migrant can revisit the original home. In some cases the disengagement may become disturbing only after a lapse of time: a young migrant, initially exhilarated by the freedom from ties to parents and other kin, may begin to feel disturbed by their absence after a period of separation. Experiences in the host society—difficulties in establishing new social networks, employment problems, or other frustrations—may sharpen the sense of loneliness at a later stage (Laffrey, Meleis, Lipson, Solomon, & Omidian, 1989; MacCarthy & Craissati, 1989).

The relevant coping mechanism for feelings of isolation is a new social network that serves as a functional alternative to the earlier one. Immigrants experience different levels of difficulty in developing such alternative relations in their new location. When entire kin groups or whole communities migrate, membership within such groups provides considerable support (Kuo & Tsai, 1986; Mavreas & Bebbington, 1989), but meaningful primary relations with veterans in a new social context generally develop slowly (Gordon, 1964; Haour-Knipe, 1989). In many cases, social relations develop among migrants of the same origin, either because of residential proximity or because of deliberate choice. But when migrants seek to move into the larger social context of the host society, their success will be determined by its receptiveness to newcomers (Rose, 1969).

Cultural Change

All migrants need to learn new norms and values and to abandon or adapt their old ones. The extent of the culture gap between the place of origin and destination determines the amount of learning that must be undergone. But even when the gap is minimal, as in the case of migration from one part of a city to another, the sensitive migrant will nevertheless feel subtle culture changes. Learning skills, youth, flexibility, and readiness for change serve as individual coping mechanisms for dealing with cultural changes. Individual coping by immigrants is mediated by the attitudes and behavior of the host population, which may range from acceptance, tolerance, and encouragement to disdain, ridicule, or hostility toward immigrants' efforts to learn the new language, norms, and values. Some host societies in which the culture gap is considered large may provide formal institutions for instruction in the local language and culture, but most acculturation takes place informally.

Styles of interpersonal relations are culturally defined and often require a process of readjustment. For example, expected levels of intimacy among friends, relations with officials in bureaucratic settings, and styles of politeness vary widely from society to society and may require migrants to change many patterns of behavior. An immigrant from the Soviet Union poignantly expressed the issue of the expected level of intimacy in his new home.

[In the Soviet Union] life is hopeless and dark. So the relationship among people, relations of the "soul", is very developed and this adorns (*ykrashchaet*) the life of the individual. In America a man is free but alone in his little corner. In Russia there is no freedom, so in order to escape the influence of the environment, people hide in groups of two or twenty or thirty people. . . . When life became unbearable we banded together in groups and such strong friendships developed in these groups and there was so much self-sacrifice that spiritual contact was stronger than in family relations. This was the natural defence of the soul against tyranny. . . . This cannot be repeated in a free country. . . . Here life is too multi-faceted (*mnogo-granna*), but that's the price you pay for freedom in the West. (Gitelman, 1982, p. 215)

MIGRATION AND COPING

The theoretical model associating migration and stress notes the critical role of individual perception in defining any situation, as well as of the existence of effective and appropriate coping mechanisms to deal with stressors. Each of these elements may be affected by the migration process.

Expectations are crucial in determining perception. Realistic expectations based on accurate information about the new situation tend to buffer negative definitions of conditions at the destination. Highly educated migrants tend to have more knowledge of the destination than do less educated migrants.

Migrants' coping mechanisms are affected by the migration process in a number of ways. First, as noted, selection patterns determine the type and effectiveness of resources migrants bring with them; these resources include material possessions but also skills, status, knowledge, and personality traits (flexibility, adaptive capacity, readiness for change, etc.). When selection is negative, migrants may have low levels of such resources and, consequently, poor coping capacity. But regardless of the type or effectiveness of resources that migrants import into the host society, the structural processes of change described earlier may affect coping mechanisms in diverse ways. For example, the migrants may find their existing coping mechanisms inadequate to deal with new stressors. Unless they can strengthen them or develop alternative, more suitable coping mechanisms, stress will result. Change—physical, social, and cultural—may weaken coping mechanisms that functioned effectively in the past, so that they no longer are effective in the new situation. Finally, social change processes may subject the migrants to new stresses for which they have no prior coping mechanisms. New strategies must then be developed if stress is to be avoided.

Stress is not easy to measure directly, and proxy variables viewed as outcomes of stress are frequently used instead. If a phenomenon such as illness (physical or mental) or social deviance is linked to migration, it is often assumed that stress is the mediating variable, although it eludes identification or measurement. Heightened blood pressure levels have been found among immigrants, especially those experiencing less success in entering the host society (Aviram, et. al., 1987; Walsh & Walsh, 1986). Considerable evidence links migration with both infectious and chronic diseases and especially with mental illness (Abramson, 1966; Antonovsky, 1971; Aviram & Levav, 1975; Halevi, 1963; Hull, 1979; Kuo,

1976; Odegaarde, 1932; Scotch, 1943; Shuval, 1981; Stromberg, Peyman, & Dowd, 1974; Syme, Hyman, & Enterline, 1964; Wessen, 1971). Suicide among unemployed young male migrants has been reported (Trovato, 1986).

VULNERABILITY OF MIGRANTS

Refugees who migrate as a result of persecution, terror, or war carry a burden of stress with them into the host society. On a psychological level, the aftermath of such experiences is a source of ongoing stress with which individuals must cope, over and above the problems encountered by all immigrants. The coping ability of persons who have previously experienced trauma may be seriously impaired as a result of those experiences. Some research suggests that, in the short run, refugees who previously suffered traumatic persecution show relatively high morale in the host society, possibly because their present situation, however difficult, is much more favorable than the past experiences from which they escaped (Franks & Faux, 1990). However, it is not unusual for earlier traumatic experiences, such as the Holocaust, to have long-term effects not only on the survivors but also on the second generation (Aviram, Silverberg, & Carel, 1987; Rose & Garske, 1987).

At the same time, it is clear that migration as a social process does not inevitably induce stress. While social change is structurally built into the process, a variety of subjective responses and definitions of the situation may take place. In accordance with the theoretical model, stress occurs when migrants define some aspect of their situation as disturbing and when they are unable to recruit significant personal or social resources to cope with that disturbance. Such a combination of circumstances may occur in some migration situations but not in all.

In the host society, migrants are differentially exposed to stressors; their coping abilities are often directly affected by the process of migration, their entry into a new social setting, and their location in it. The status of migrant may result in exposure to special stressors by virtue of the position accorded to that status in the host society. I consider this issue on both a structural and a normative level.

Structural Issues

In general, migrants are not dispersed at random in a social system but tend to be located in specific occupational and geographical niches that determine their socioeconomic status in the society. On the occupational level, migrants' distribution often reflects the host society's need for particular types of labor; much migration takes place in response to demands for specific skills or types of workers. Accordingly, migrants tend to be located in particular occupational areas, frequently in high concentrations and sometimes to the exclusion of nonmigrant workers. The types of jobs available vary widely, from unskilled laborers to skilled technicians or professionals. This process is often accompanied by local geographical concentration. The nonrandom residence patterns of migrants reflect both their location in specific occupational niches in a social system that requires residence in certain areas and the availability of suitable housing at an appropriate price level. Housing shortages may force migrants into undesirable neighborhoods or into substandard housing. In some situations, housing is provided by employers. Thus, the structural location of the migrant in the social system exposes him or her to different stressors depending on the characteristics of the location.

Occupational and geographical concentration contributes to the visibility of migrants, which affects both the migrant group and other populations in the society. Insofar as the migrants are concerned, a common structural location carries implications for self-identity, solidarity, and feelings of commonality. A sense of cohesion may result that promotes positive group identification and social support, which are mechanisms that alleviate stress (Mavreas and Bebbington, 1989). In some cases, such feelings may exacerbate stress by encouraging or reinforcing collective perceptions of exploitation and deprivation.

Attitudes of groups in the host society toward migrants range from acceptance and tolerance to hostility and overt aggression. In any case, the visibility of the migrants makes possible a clearer focus on them by the host population or by subgroups in it. Expressions of prejudice, intolerance, aggression, or xenophobia may serve as stressors, especially when the migrant group is perceived as competing with, or advantaged relative to, longtime members of the society. Conversely, positive and accepting attitudes by host groups alleviate stress (Rose, 1969).

Another structural dimension on which migrants are not randomly distributed is the power and influence hierarchy in the host society. At the time of entry, migrants tend to be low on this hierarchy. Even professional immigrants, whose socioeconomic status is relatively high, are likely to have little power and influence as a result of being new to the society. The accumulation of power is generally a function of time, so that veterans or natives are, by definition, able to mobilize more of it. For migrants who enjoyed and weilded power before their move, its absence may be a stressor in the new society.

Absence of power may express itself on the simplest level by lack of citizenship. For a period of time, the migrant may be unable to vote, hold office, acquire property, or qualify for certain jobs. Once formal citizenship has been acquired, migrants may still encounter barriers in the economic and political spheres, where positions of power are occupied by veterans, who have little interest in relinquishing such influence to newcomers. In open, democratic societies, political organizations of migrant groups may provide channels for members to acquire power and influence within such groups and through them, eventually, within the broader political context.

On the informal level, migration often results in a shift in the balance of power within families and other informal social contexts. Thus, persons who traditionally have wielded power in the family—e.g., grandparents or fathers—may find themselves stripped of their accustomed roles as a result of different patterns of family life in the new society. Unless alternative rewards are found for the demoted traditional leaders, they are likely to experience stress (Haour-Knipe, 1989).

There is a dynamic quality to structurally determine stressors. As noted earlier, migrants may be located in vulnerable or deprived positions in the new social system, which in itself exposes them to stress. However, the length of time they remain in this location varies. Migrants often accept low status or deprivation as inevitable or even as justifiable during their initial period in the new environment; however, there is generally a strong underlying expectation of change for the better. When the host society's culture includes such values as equality, achievement, and social mobility, these expectations are reinforced, and if improvement is perceived as slow or absent, lack of such change may be a stressor. In such a social context, any subgroup that feels it is not succeeding or is not attaining as much as relevant others tends to be under stress. Migrants are especially vulnerable to such feelings when they have been in the host society for longer periods of time and particularly when they see themselves as approaching or entering veteran status (Vega, Kolodny, Valle, & Hough, 1986).

Normative Issues

The potential for stress varies directly with the magnitude of the differences between norms and values in the place of origin and those in the new setting. In an effort to minimize such differences, migrants often seek locations that are relatively similar culturally to their place of origin or settle near compatriots who migrated earlier (Murphy, 1955). Thus, culture shock, or the confrontation between very different norms and values, may be viewed as a stressor; response to this stress depends, as in other cases, on the coping mechanisms available to the migrant.

Expectations also function as a mediating variable controlling the immigrant's response to new norms and values. Realistic expectations and accurate knowledge—however different the new culture may be from the old—tend to moderate the effect of such differences.

Different norms may serve as stressors not only because they are unfamiliar and put pressure on the immigrant to change, but also because they run counter to familiar guidelines—for example, norms of greater assertiveness for people socialized to nonaggressive behavior, norms of restraint and control for people socialized to expressiveness, and norms of a future orientation for people socialized to an orientation to the past.

Furthermore, the content of certain norms or values may be especially problematic for migrants because of their migrant status. Thus, norms of achievement may be stressors for migrants who are blocked from conforming to that norm by language barriers or ignorance of social niceties. Merton (1949) described the forms of anomie that occur when there is a gap between values and the means to attain them. This model is undoubtedly appropriate for migrants confronting norms for which there are structural barriers to conformity.

Norms concerning the migration process also play a role in stress. When migration is a norm—as, for example, in Israel—the migrant is not in a deviant role. In societies that see migration as unusual, the entering migrant is a stranger who has deviated from prevailing norms merely by relocating. Stevens, Goodman, and Mick (1978) dramatized this issue by noting that immigrant physicians in the United States are referred to as aliens, even though their professional practice norms are close to those of their professional colleagues. In Israel, on the other hand, large segments of the population immigrated in the recent past, so that foreign accents and lack of familiarity with certain elements of the culture are widespread and readily accepted. Other things being equal, there is likely to be less stress when the host population is composed largely of recent migrants than when the resident population is composed predominantly of natives.

A combination of structural and normative issues impinge on certain types of migrants to increase their vulnerability. One such group consists of young children of migrants, who are often exposed to contradictory norms and values: those of their parents, who still adhere to the culture of origin, and those of the host culture, represented by the school and peers. When migration is from a traditional to a modern society, these conflicts are intensified by cultural disparities and by the transition from an extended family to a nuclear family structure, in which support mechanisms are of necessity more limited. But for all migrants, the move from society to society entails disengagement from social ties in the country of origin and the need to rebuild a social network in a new setting. Thus, immigrant families are frequently isolated during their early period in the host society and the stress associated with such isolation is likely to radiate to infants and young children. Among immigrant children, impaired school performance and lowered self-esteem are associated with learning a new language and different social skills. Some research indicates a relatively high frequency of behavioral disorders among such children (Aronowitz, 1984; Gokalp, 1984; Haour-Knipe, 1989).

The developmental problems of normal adolescence are exacerbated by migration. The ubiquitous difficulties—issues of identity, conflicts with parents, sense of alienation, self-concepts, and establishment of social credentials—are frequently intensified in a situation of culture change and value conflict. Immigrant parents, who are also seeking a new identity, are less able to provide adolescent children with the stability and support that can help them deal successfully with these normal problems. Drug use among immigrant adolescents from Puerto Rico is one example of a response to the stress experienced by these young people in New York (Aronowitz, 1984; Haour-Knipe, 1989; Velez & Ungemack, 1989).

Another group with a high vulnerability to stress is elderly immigrants, who generally move with their adult children. In many cases, the decision to migrate was not their own, so that their motivation to adapt to the new social context is ambivalent. Uprooting from a social network and re-establishing a new one in an unfamiliar setting is more difficult for the elderly, especially when traditional norms and values are no longer appropriate. Relations with their adult children become more difficult as a result of the elderly immigrants' increased dependence. Because of their age, such immigrants are more likely to have suffered from chronic illness before moving and to be more susceptible to illness as a result of exposure to a new environment (Gelfand, 1989; Hull, 1979).

Some Research Issues

Much of the research on migration has focused on migrants at their destination and has addressed the issue of stress or its pathological outcomes at that geographical location. Many investigators have asked whether migrants exhibit relatively high rates of illness, hospitalization, crime, or other social pathology. If it can be demonstrated that migrants generally display high levels of social or physical pathology, interested groups in the host society can make a strong case for limiting entry.

The constraint of studying migrants at their destination naturally stems from the fact that migrants can be conclusively identified only after they have left their place of origin and arrived at their destination. The alternative strategy is to study self-declared potential migrants—people who have registered for exit visas or otherwise demonstrated an intention to leave. For logistic reasons this procedure, despite the useful findings it could yield, has rarely been followed.

Focusing on migrants in the host setting and attempting to link migration with stress require consideration of the selection mechanisms at the place of origin to determine the different susceptibilities of the migrants to stress. Testing this hypothesis requires data on populations in the place of origin as well as at the destination. Odegaarde's (1932) early work comparing Norwegian migrants to Minnesota with residents of Norway and Minnesota was a classic test of this hypothesis (see also Malzberg & Lee, 1956).

In order to demonstrate that selection influences migrants' relative susceptibility to stress, it is necessary to determine what criteria of selection affect susceptibility and to show that migrants differ significantly on these measures from the population at the point of origin. For example, compared to controls at the place of origin, are migrants more prone to mental or physical illness, more deviant in behavior, or less able to cope? Such negative selection could explain relatively high stress at the destination. The difficulty in testing this hypothesis is considerable. At best, demographic data on the population at the original location may be available, but psychological or social indicators of comparative susceptibility generally are neither collected nor reliably recorded.

Using migrant populations at the destination as the data base makes it difficult to identify the motivational and decisionmaking patterns that preceded migration. After migration has taken place, such information is by definition retrospective and suffers from all the weaknesses of this type of data.

One fruitful strategy is to look at migrants from one origin who have opted for different destinations. A number of studies have considered migrants from the Soviet Union in the United States and in Israel. The research sheds light on assimilation processes of similar groups in two host societies (Flaherty, Kohn, Levav, & Birz, 1988; Simon, 1985).

Ideally, several research issues could be addressed by a longitudinal, multistage design that started at the place of origin and included various population groups at different times: samples of the base population from which migrants were self-selected at the place of origin; the subset of persons who formally identified themselves as potential migrants at the place of origin; actual migrants at the place of origin prior to leaving; migrants in the host society shortly after arrival and at subsequent points in time; and samples of nonmigrants in the host society. All these groups would need to be evaluated with regard to motivations, decisionmaking, expectations, available resources, norms, values, perceptions, feelings about host and migrant population, and evidence of stress or its outcomes. Such a design poses formidable logistic problems. During the 1970s Israel's Ministry of Absorption shed considerable light on the migration experience in the host society by systematically monitoring the process of absorption in a longitudinal investigation (Israel Ministry of Immigrant Absorption, 1975, 1976, 1977, 1978, 1979, 1980). Because entry into a new social system is a prolonged process, during which levels of stress may vary considerably, such longitudinal research deems necessary if this area is to be addressed appropriately.

REFERENCES

ABRAMSON, J. H. Emotional disorder, status inconsistency, and migration. *Milbank Memorial Fund Quarterly,* 1966, *44,* 23–48.

ANTONOVSKY, A. Social and cultural factors in coronary heart disease: An Israel-North American sibling study. *Israel Journal of Medical Sciences,* 1971, *7,* 1578–1583.

ARONOWITZ, M. The social and emotional adjustment of immigrant children: A review of literature. *International Migration Review,* 1984, *18,* 237–257.

AVIRAM, U., & LEVAV, I. Psychiatric epidemiology in Israel: Analysis of community studies. *Acta Psychiatrica Scandinavica,* 1975, *52,* 295–311.

AVIRAM, A., SILVERBERG, D. S., & CAREL, R. S. Hypertension in European immigrants to Israel—the possible effect of the Holocaust. *Israel Journal of Medical Sciences,* 1987, *23,* 257–263.

BRODY, E. B. (ed.), *Behavior in new environments.* Beverly Hills, CA: Sage, 1970.

CASSEL, J. T. Social science theory as a source of hypotheses in epidemiological research. *American Journal of Public Health,* 1964, *54,* 1482–1488.

DAVIS, K. The migration of human populations. *Scientific American,* 1974, *231,* 93–107.

FLAHERTY, J. A., KOHN, R., LEVAV, I., & BIRZ, S. Demoralization in Soviet-Jewish immigrants to the United States and Israel. *Comprehensive Psychiatry,* 1988, *29,* 588–597.

FRANKS, F., & FAUX, S. Depression, stress, mastery and social resources in four ethnocultural womens' groups. *Research in Nursing and Health,* 1990, *13,* 283–292.

FREID, M. Deprivation and migration. In E. B. Brody (ed.), *Behavior in new environments.* Beverly Hills, CA: Sage, 1970.

FRENCH, J. P. R., JR., RODGERS, W., & COBB, S. Adjustment as person-environment fit. In G. V. Coelho, D. A. Hamburg, & J. E. Adams (eds.), *Coping and adaptation: Interdisciplinary perspectives.* New York: Basic Books, 1974.

GELFAND, D. E. Immigration, aging and intergenerational relationships. *The Gerontologist,* 1989, *29,* 366–372.

GITELMAN, Z. *Jewish nationality and Soviet politics.* Princeton, NJ: Princeton University Press, 1972.

————. Soviet Jewish emigrants: Why are they choosing America? *Soviet Jewish Affairs,* 1977, *7,* 31–46.

————. *Becoming Israeli: Political resocialization of Soviet and American immigrants in Israel.* New York: Praeger, 1982.

GOKALP, A. Migrants' children in Western Europe: Differential socialization and multicultural problems *International Social Science Journal,* 1984, *36,* 487–500.

GORDON, M. *Assimilation in American life.* New York: Oxford University Press, 1964.

HALEVI, H. S. Frequency of mental illness among Jews in Israel. *International Journal of Social Psychiatry,* 1963, *9,* 268–282.

HAOUR-KNIPE, M. International employment and children: Geographical mobility and mental health among children of professionals. *Social Science and Medicine,* 1989, *28,* 197–205.

HERTZ, D. G. Identity lost and found: Patterns of migration and psychological and psychosocial adjustment of migrants. *Acta Psychiatrica Scandinavica,* 1988, (suppl.), *344,* 159–165.

HOUSE, J. S. Occupational stress and coronary heart disease: A review. *Journal of Health and Social Behavior,* 1974, *15,* 12–27.

HULL, D. Migration, adaptation, and illness: A review. *Social Science and Medicine,* 1979, *13A,* 25–36.

HULL, D. Migration, adaptation, and illness: A review.
Insight, 1977, 5(3).

ISRAEL MINISTRY OF ABSORPTION. *Immigrant absorption.* Jerusalem: IMA, 1975, 1976, 1977, 1978, 1979, 1980.

JACKSON, J. A. (ed.), *Migration.* New York: Cambridge University Press, 1969.

JANSEN, C. J. *Readings in the sociology of migration.* New York: Pergamon Press, 1970.

KANTOR, M. B. *Mobility and mental health.* Springfield, IL: Charles C. Thomas, 1965.

KUO, W. Theories of migration and mental health: An empirical testing on Chinese Americans. *Social Science and Medicine,* 1976, *10,* 297–306.

KUO, W. H., & TSAI, Y. M. Social networking, hardiness and immigrants' mental health. *Journal of Health and Social Behavior,* 1986, *27,* 133–149.

LAFFREY, S. C., MELEIS, A. I., LIPSON, J. G., SOLOMON, M., & OMIDIAN, P. A. Assessing Arab-American health care needs. *Social Science and Medicine,* 1989, *29,* 877–883.

LEE, E. A theory of migration. In J. A. Jackson (ed.), *Migration.* New York: Cambridge University Press, 1969.

LEVINE, S., & SCOTCH, N. A. (eds.), *Social stress.* Chicago: Aldine, 1970.

MACCARTHY, B., & CRAISSATI, J. Ethnic differences in response to adversity: A community sample of Bangladeshis and their indigenous neighbors. *Social Psychiatry and Psychiatric Epidemiology,* 1989, *24,* 196–201.

MALZBERG, B., & LEE, E. *Migration and mental disease.* New York: Social Science Research Council, 1956.

MANGALAM, J., & SCHWARZWELLER, H. Some theoretical guidelines toward a sociology of migration. *International Migration Review,* 1970, *4,* 5–21.

MAVREAS, V., BEBBINGTON, P. Does the act of migration provoke psychiatric breakdown? A study of Greek Cypriot immigrants. *Acta Psychiatrica Scandinavica,* 1989, *80,* 469–473.

MECHANIC, D. *Medical sociology.* New York: Free Press, 1978.

MERTON, R. K. *Social theory and social structure.* New York: Free Press, 1949.

MUNROE-BLUM, H., BOYLE, M. H., OFFORD, D. R., & KATES, N. Immigrant children: Psychiatric disorder, school performance and service utilization. *American Journal of Orthopsychiatry,* 1989, *59,* 510–519.

MURPHY, H. B. M. *Flight and resettlement.* Paris: UNESCO, 1955.

ODEGAARDE, O. Emigration and insanity. *Acta Psychiatrica et Neurologica,* 1932, (suppl. 4), 1–206.

PARK, R., & BURGESS, E. *Introduction to the science of sociology.* Chicago: University of Chicago Press, 1921.

PEARLIN, L. I., & SCHOOLER, C. The structure of coping. *Journal of Health and Social Behavior,* 1978, *19,* 2–21.

PRICE, C. The study of assimilation. In J. A. Jackson (ed.), *Migration.* New York: Cambridge University Press, 1969.

RICHMOND, A. Migration in industrial societies. In J. A. Jackson (ed.), *Migration.* New York: Cambridge University Press, 1969.

————. Socio-cultural adaptation and conflict in immigrant-receiving countries, *International Social Science Journal,* 1984, *36,* 519–536.

ROSE, A. *Migrants in Europe.* Minneapolis: University of Minnesota Press, 1969.

ROSE, S. L., & GARSKE, J. Family environment, adjustment and coping among children of Holocaust survivors: A comparative investigation. *American Journal of Orthopsychiatry,* 1987, *57,* 332–344.

SCOTCH, N. A. Socio-cultural factors in the epidemiology of Zulu hypertension. *American Journal of Public Health,* 1943, *53,* 1205–1213.

SCOTT, R., & HOWARD, A. Models of stress. In S. Levine & N. A. Scotch (eds.), *Social stress.* Chicago: Aldine, 1970.

SHUVAL, J. T. The contribution of social and psychological phenomena to an understanding of the aetiology of disease and illness. *Social Science and Medicine,* 1981, *15,* 337–342.

————. *Newcomers and colleagues: Soviet immigrant physicians in Israel.* New York: Academic Press, 1982.

SHUVAL, J. T., MARKUS, E. J., & DOTAN. J. *Patterns of adjustment of Soviet immigrants to Israel.* Jerusalem: Israel Institute of Applied Social Research, 1973.

————. *Patterns of integration over time: Soviet immigrants in Israel.* Jerusalem: Israel Institute of Applied Social Research, 1975.

SIMON, R. J. (ed.), *New lives: The adjustment of Soviet Jewish immigrants in the United States and Israel.* Lexington, MA: Lexington Books, 1985.

STEVENS, R., GOODMAN, L. W., & MICK, S. S. *The alien doctors.* New York: Wiley, 1978.

STROMBERG, J., PEYMAN, N. M., & DOWD, J. E. Migration and health: Adaptation experiences of Iranian immigrants to the city of Teheran. *Social Science and Medicine,* 1974, *8,* 309–323.

SYME, L. S., HYMAN, M. M., & ENTERLINE, P. E. Some social and cultural factors associated with the occurrence of coronary heart disease. *Journal of Chronic Diseases,* 1964, *17,* 277–289.

TROVATO, F. A time series analysis of international immigration and suicide mortality in Canada. *International Journal of Social Psychiatry,* 1986, *32,* 38–46.

VEGA, W. A., KOLODNY, B., VALLE, R., & HOUGH, R. Depressive symptoms and their correlates among immigrant Mexican women in the United States. *Social Science and Medicine,* 1986, *22,* 645–652.

VELEZ, C. N., & UNGEMACK, J. A. Drug use among Puerto Rican youth: An exploration of generational status and status differences. *Social Science and Medicine,* 1989, *29,* 779–789.

WALSH, A., & WALSH, P. O. The effects of immigration, stigma and stress on biological effective blood pressure levels. *International Review of Modern Sociology,* 1986, *16,* 353–366.

WESSEN, A. E. The role of migrant studies in epidemiological research. *Israel Journal of Medical Sciences,* 1971, *7,* 1584–1591.

35

Psychosocial Effects of HIV Infection

Susan Folkman

THE HUMAN IMMUNODEFICIENCY VIRUS (HIV) HAS CAUSED one of the most tragic epidemics of recent times. The World Health Organization estimates that there may be a cumulative total of 15 to 20 million HIV-infected adults and 10 million infected infants and children in the world (WHO Press, 1991), In the United States, it is estimated that approximately 1 million people are infected with this virus. As of February 1991, infection with HIV had progressed to AIDS in 218,301 people (Centers for Disease Control, 1992). Although some of the manifestations of HIV disease can be managed medically for a time, there is no cure. Of the adults and adolescents who were diagnosed with AIDS between 1981 and 1990, 111,778 or 63% were dead as of March, 1992 (Centers for Disease Control, 1992).

HIV disease evolves over many years. Although its course can wax and wane during much of that time, its end stages are usually devastating physically, mentally, and emotionally. This chapter deals with just one aspect of HIV disease, its psychosocial effects, including psychological distress, depression, anxiety, and risky sexual behavior for HIV transmission. I have constrained the scope of the discussion in two ways. First, the discussion focuses on the psychosocial effect of HIV infection in homosexual men living in the United States, who comprise the majority of HIV-infected persons in the United States (Centers for Disease Control, 1992). The article does not discuss groups among whom HIV infection is transmitted heterosexually, through shared injection needles, or through transfusion of blood products. Second, the review of the literature is illustrative rather than exhaustive within any given category, and with a few exceptions, the review is limited to empirical studies that have appeared since 1987.

The psychosocial effects of HIV disease cannot be understood without some knowledge of the disease itself. Therefore, the chapter begins with a brief overview of its clinical course. The discussion of psychosocial effects that follows the overview is organized according to markers of the HIV disease process, beginning with the decision to be tested for HIV antibodies and proceeding through the diagnosis of full-blown AIDS. Investigators from diverse disciplines, including epidemiology, sociology, psychology, psychiatry, anthropology, nursing, and social work, have contributed to knowledge of the psychosocial effects

This chapter was supported in part by a grant from the National Institute of Mental Health (MH44045). I would like to thank Margaret Chesney, Richard Lazarus, Honey Nashman, and Robert Weiss for their comments on an earlier version of this chapter, and Lynae Darbes for her assistance with the literature search.

of HIV disease. Although I draw on these diverse disciplines, the orientation of the discussion is primarily psychological, with a focus on the individual's cognitive, emotional, and behavioral responses to the psychosocial demands of HIV disease.

THE CLINICAL COURSE OF HIV DISEASE

HIV is transmitted through three primary paths: sexual contact with an infected individual, exposure to infected blood or blood products, and perinatally from an infected mother to her child. This very brief overview summarizes the physical course of HIV disease in order to familiarize the reader with what the infected individual contends with insofar as the physical aspects of the disease are concerned and then reviews its psychoneurological course because what appear to be psychosocial effects of HIV disease may instead be neurotropic or central nervous system effects of the virus.

Physical Course

Infection with HIV begins a disease process that can vary widely in its physical course. McCutchan (1990) provides an excellent description of the course of HIV disease that is particularly suited to a nonmedical audience: Within a few weeks of infection, many people develop a self-limited acute illness that is like mononucleosis, with fever, sore throat, lymphadenopathy (swelling of lymph nodes), malaise, skin rash, headache, and other less frequent symptoms. Following this illness, there is in many people a prolonged incubation or latent period, which in adults can be as short as one year or as long as ten years. The estimated average is seven to eight years. During this period there are minimal symptoms, such as diffuse lymphadenopathy, mild fatigue, recurrent low-grade fevers, and other nonspecific symptoms. Many people have no physical or laboratory abnormality during this period.

The next stage involves minor infections such as oral candidiasis (thrush), zoster (shingles), or frequent recurrences of herpes simplex virus (fever blisters) on the lips or genitals. Nonspecific symptoms, including fever, weight loss, fatigue, diarrhea, or skin rashes, also might occur. Further disease progression and deterioration of cell-mediated immunity is signaled by the appearance of opportunistic infections, tumors, neurological illnesses, or nonspecific symptoms such as fever, diarrhea, and wasting. Occurrence of any of a number of AIDS-defining conditions establishes the diagnosis of AIDS. (See McCutchan, 1990, for a list of these conditions.)

Most patients die with multiple opportunistic infections involving the lungs, gastrointestinal tract, and brain. The period of survival after AIDS is diagnosed varies. Before the widespread use of azidothymidine (AZT), survival was estimated at about one year following diagnosis, with a small percentage surviving longer than four years. Current data suggest that AZT delays opportunistic infections and death up to about twelve months. People with a diagnosis of Kaposi's sarcoma, a tumor of the skin and internal organs that occurs more frequently in homosexual men than in other risk groups, have a slightly better prognosis because it often presents at a less advanced stage of immune deficiency than do the opportunistic infections and may progress more slowly.

The pattern of HIV disease over time, especially the period free of physical reminders of the infection, has important implications for cognitive coping and psychological well-being. As long as symptoms are not evident, the infected individual is likely to believe that he has time on his side during which a drug to control or even halt the course of the disease may become available. The enormous resources that are being directed toward developing effective pharmacological therapies for HIV disease help support these beliefs. The long asymptomatic period can also help support the individual's coping efforts to avoid thinking about the threatening implications of HIV disease. Together, beliefs that focus on positive outcomes and cognitive coping processes that help avoid threatening outcome support hope, which in turn sustains morale (Breznitz, 1983). However, the beliefs and coping processes that may help sustain hope and morale throughout the asymptomatic period are likely to be challenged once symptoms appear. The infected individual may no longer feel he has time on his side, and the presence of symptoms is likely to make it more difficult for him to avoid thinking about the threatening implications of the disease. These and other psychological implications of the pattern of HIV disease are discussed later.

Neuropsychological Course

Neuropsychological dysfunction has been observed in individuals with HIV infection since the beginning of the epidemic (e.g., Holland & Tross, 1985). The extent to which clinically significant signs of neuropsychological dysfunction—such as difficulty with memory, concentration, and psychomotor speed and neuromotor deficits such as ataxia, tremor, and affected handwriting—are evident in HIV-positive asymptomatic individuals is not clear. Most studies suggest that neuropsychological impairment is ambiguous (e.g., Claypoole et al., 1990; Grant et al., 1987; Janssen et al., 1989; Lunn et al., 1991; McArthur et al., 1989; Perry, Belsky-Barr, Barr, & Jacobsberg, 1989; Stern et al., 1991; Wilkie, Eisdorfer, Morgan, Lowenstein, & Szapocznik, 1990). Wilkins and colleagues (1990) caution that effects that have been detected may be confounded with other conditions, such as head injury, pre-existing severe psychiatric disease, or past substance abuse. In their study of 40 persons with HIV disease, of the 9 patients who were asymptomatic and had no confounding factors, Wilkins, et al. found that 78% were normal and none was markedly impaired. However, when all 28 asymptomatic subjects were examined without regard to confounding factors, only 39% were normal and 14% were markedly impaired.

Neuropsychological impairment is not only detectable, but often clinically significant by the time individuals progress to AIDS in that it impairs daily functioning. Compared to people who are asymptomatic, people with AIDS have been found to perform significantly worse on tests measuring concentration, memory, and psychomotor speed (Lunn et al, 1991; Tross and Hirsh, 1987), and these deficits are likely to interfere with normal social and occupational functioning. The most thoroughly documented syndrome of neuropsychological impairment in persons with advanced HIV disease is AIDS dementia complex (ADC), a specific diagnosis that implies failing mental capacity and global intellectual impairment, which are commonly associated with symptoms such as generalized motoric slowing and behavioral complications such as social withdrawal. ADC is estimated to occur by the preterminal phase in up to two-thirds of patients (O'Dowd, 1988). The term ADC is limited to those HIV-infected individuals whose symptoms interfere with occupational and social function and who show only cortical atrophy (Boccellari & Dilley, in press). Price and his colleagues, who have conducted a number of studies of ADC, describe its clinical features (Price et al., 1988) as including slowing and loss of precision in mentation and motor control. Mental slowing is accompanied by loss of interest in work as well as in social and recreational activities. This growing apathy is frequently mistaken for depression, yet dysphoria is often absent. Early complaints include exaggerated tremor or mild gait unsteadiness, and examination may reveal slowing of rapid alternating eye and extremity movements and abnormal "release" reflexes. Over time intellectual impairment becomes more pervasive and affects nearly all aspects of cognition. Performance slows and becomes more inaccurate. Increasing apathy, slowing of speech, and mental impoverishment may progress to near or absolute mutism and severe dementia, and unsteady gait gives way to frank weakness, general hypokinesia, and incontinence (Price et al., 1988).

Neurological impairment, even the threat of neurological impairment, may well be one of the most frightening aspects of HIV disease. We need to know more about the salience of this threat throughout the various stages of HIV disease and how individuals appraise and cope with this threat over time, especially after neurological or psychoneurological symptoms appear.

THE ANTIBODY TEST

The test for the presence of HIV antibodies involves a blood draw. Sera are first tested for antibodies to HIV by an enzyme-linked immunosorbent assay (ELISA)., Samples that are reactive are rested, and repeatedly reactive ELISA tests are confirmed by Western blot testing, or sometimes by an immunofluorescent antibody test. The test for HIV antibodies is thus physically relatively unintrusive. However, the decisions about whether to be tested, and if tested, whether to learn the results, can be psychologically extremely intrusive and difficult to make.

There are two points in the decisionmaking process at which individuals have a choice as to whether or not they want to know their HIV status. The first point is the decision to take the test. The second point is the decision to learn the results.

Deciding Whether to Take the Test

The decision to take the test involves weighing the potential costs of testing against its potential benefits. On the cost side, those who volunteer for testing must identify themselves as at risk for a fatal and stigmatizing illness for which there is currently no cure; undergo a relatively long waiting period for test results; publicly admit, at least to strangers, by undergoing the testing process that they are at risk for this disease; and confront the social and psychological implications of a possible positive test (Coates et al., 1988). Confidentiality may be breached, which can have significant psychological, social, and financial effects. Knowledge that an individual has been tested can be used to limit or deny insurance to infected individuals and in other ways cause psychological, social, financial, and legal damage (Avins & Lo, 1989). Although California law mandates that HIV antibody status cannot be used to deny insurance coverage, insurance carriers have attempted to circumvent this law by demanding counts of T-helper cells or by denying insurance to persons with histories of sexually transmitted diseases (Coates et al., 1988).

Fears about loss of confidentiality may help explain why many people who seek anonymous HIV antibody testing would avoid testing if anonymity were not secure. Kegeles, Catania, Coates, Pollack, and Lo (1990) reported that over 40% of the respondents at an anonymous testing site stated that they would have avoided testing if it had not been conducted anonymously. Over 60% stated that they would not have taken the HIV antibody test if positive results had to be reported to health officials. Additional reasons for not being tested reported by Siegel, Levine, Brooks, and Kern (1989) in their study of 120 homosexual men living in New York City include to avoid the adverse psychological impact of a positive test result, to avoid an ambiguous and unreliable test result, and to avoid having to make undesired lifestyle changes.

On the other hand, people also identify benefits of testing. Reasons people give for choosing to be tested include to learn if they have been infected, to cope better with fear of AIDS, to promote change in sexual behavior (Lyter, Valdiserri, Kingsley, Amoroso, & Rinaldo, 1987), to enable medical treatments for HIV infection, to become motivated to make needed health and lifestyle changes, to clarify an ambiguous medical condition, and to inform sexual decisionmaking (Siegel, et al., 1989). These respondents also expressed concern about whether they had been exposed through past sexual activities, desire for information about their future health, and concern about exposing sexual partners (Ostrow, Joseph, et al., 1989). The advent in the late 1980s of pharmacological therapies such as zidovudine (AZT) and aerosol pentamadine that can help control some symptoms of HIV infection has provided additional incentive for being tested.

In general, the benefits of testing seem to outweigh the costs, in that a majority of homosexual men have decided to be tested in most major cities. However, for the substantial minority who remain untested, the costs seem to outweigh the benefits. In San Francisco, for example, of the 490 men in the AIDS Behavioral Research Project as of November 1989, 90 (18%) were untested (Folkman, Chesney, Pollack, & Coats, 1991); and of the 752 men in the San Francisco Men's Health Study as of 1989, 25% stated they had not ever received results of the HIV antibody test (Coates, personal communication, 1991). Of 144 self-identified homosexual men surveyed in 1988 and 1989 as part of the AIDS in Multi-Ethnic Neighborhoods (AMEN) study, 39% were untested (Peterson, et al., 1990). In their study of 120 homosexual men, Siegel et al. (1989) found that 41% (49) were untested. In a survey conducted in late 1989 in Chicago, Oakland, Minneapolis, and Birmingham, 38% of 55 white men who had same-sex patterns in the past year had not been tested (Berrios et al., 1992). The proportion of untested homosexual men in the communities in which these studies were conducted may be conservative because the findings are based on reports from men who chose to be in research studies and because the selected communities may be more AIDS-aware than communities elsewhere in the country.

Deciding Whether to Learn the Test Results

The decision about whether or not to learn the test results involves yet another consideration of costs and benefits. A compelling benefit of obtaining test results is that they give a clear direction about health care and eliminate anxiety caused by uncertainty about HIV status. However, knowledge of a positive HIV serostatus also involves costs. People who find out they are positive have to deal with long-term treatment (with unknown consequences) for chronic disease, the threat of imminent death, and repeated crises resulting from fear, discrimination, and illnesses (Batchelor, 1987). The most frequently cited reasons given by the participants in the Pittsburgh Cohort of the Multicenter AIDS Cohort Studies (MACS) for not wanting to learn their HIV status were because the test was not considered predictive of AIDS; because, if positive, they would be too worried about developing AIDS; because they would be unable to cope with a positive results; and because the test is inaccurate (Lyter et al., 1987).

The perceived psychological, social, and economic costs of a positive HIV test result may account for the fact that sizable minorities of people who choose to be tested choose not to learn their antibody status. In a study of 1007 people seeking HIV antibody testing at a free anonymous test site in California, 75% completed anonymous self-administered questionnaires and were given numbered identity cards to permit anonymous tracking over time. Twenty-eight percent of the respondents did not return for their results (Catania, Kegeles, & Coates, 1990). In the San Francisco AMEN study, of the 144 self-identified homosexual men who had been tested for HIV, 9% had not learned their results (Peterson et al., 1990), and in a study of 270 homosexual men at a Boston community health center, 21% elected to remain unaware of their test results (McCusker et al., 1988).

Mental Health Effects of Positive HIV Test

We would expect that the profound practical, social, economic, and existential implications of learning that one is infected with HIV would lead to psychosocial disturbance, including increased symptoms of anxiety, depression, and general psychological distress. Findings from the Chicago cohort of the Multicenter AIDS Cohort Study are consistent with this expectation. As of June 1987, 170 of the 585 men in this cohort had requested their HIV antibody test results. Subjects who learned they were seropositive showed significant increases in psychological symptoms following notification; in contrast, seropositive men who had not received their test results exhibited general improvement in mental health (Ostrow et al., 1989). McCusker and her colleagues (1988) studied the effects of HIV antibody test knowledge in a cohort of initially physically asymptomatic homosexually active male clients of a Boston community health center. At the six-month visit of those who were seropositive, those who had been notified of their status reported more depression and anger than those who were unaware of their status.

The expectation of increased psychosocial disturbance in individuals who learn they are seropositive for HIV, however, is not supported by a longitudinal study reported by Perry, et al. (1990). In their study of 218 physically asymptomatic adults in New York City, Perry, et al. report that the 39 adults who were seropositive did not have significant increases in distress following notification, and their distress scores were significantly lower at ten weeks after notification. Perry, et al. offer three possible explanations for their counterintuitive findings: (1) the study focused only on the immediate and intermediate emotional impact of notifying physically asymptomatic subjects, and long-term effects may be different; (2) all subjects received pretest and posttest counseling in private offices, thereby simulating the potential support inherent in a physician-patient relationship, which may not have been comparable to standard practice HIV test counseling; and (3) the distress of being at risk for HIV infection and not knowing one's serological status may be inherently greater than the short-term effect of learning that one is infected with HIV.

The findings of these studies provide only a preliminary sense of the psychosocial impact of test results. We know little about the impact of test results on the individual's sense of his future, his perception of his psychological and physical vulnerability, his values beliefs and goals, and changes in these cognitions during the days, weeks, months, and years following testing.

Behavioral Effects of Positive HIV Test

A major public health concern is the effects of HIV testing on sexual behaviors that place people at risk for HIV infection. Public health officials want to use the test to help prevent the spread of HIV and ultimately slow the epidemic. This motive is not limited to public health officials. Individuals, too, report that they hope the HIV test will motivate them to modify risky sexual behavior (Siegel et al., 1989). Significant declines between the mid 1980s and the late 1980s in risk indexes for high-risk sexual behavior, including unprotected receptive and insertive anal intercourse, have been charted in homosexual communities across the country, including San Francisco (e.g., Doll et al., 1990; Ekstrand & Coates, 1990; Winkelstein et al., 1988), New York (e.g. Martin, Dean, Garcia, & Hall, 1989; Siegel, Bauman, Christ, & Krown, 1988); Michigan (Joseph et al., 1987), and Washington, D.C. (Fox, Odaka, Brookmeyer, & Polk, 1987). For a review of these effects, see also Stall, Coates, and Hoff (1988).

It would be encouraging to find that knowledge of serostatus has been responsible for, or at least associated with, observed reduced risk behavior in homosexual men. The evidence linking changes in behavior to knowledge of one's HIV status is mixed. On the one hand, Coates, Morin, and McKusick (1987), in their study of the San Francisco AIDS Behavioral Research Project, found as of November 1986 that knowledge of serostatus was associated with reductions in risk behavior, with 12% of the seropositive group reporting unprotected anal intercourse versus 18% of the seronegative group and 27% of the untested group. Fox, et al., (1987), who studied 1,001 homosexual men living in the Baltimore-Washington, D.C., metropolitan area, reported that seropositive individuals who were notified of their status decreased specific risk behaviors more than did seropositive individuals who were not notified, whereas seronegative individuals who were notified decreased specific risk behaviors less than did seronegative individuals who were not notified. In their prospective study of 270 homosexual men, McCusker, et al. (1988) found no relationship between awareness of test results and reduction of unprotected receptive anogenital contact, either in seropositive or seronegative men. However, individuals who learned of a positive antibody result were more likely to eliminate unprotected insertive anogenital contact than either unaware seropositive men or men who learned of a negative antibody result. No relationship between declines in risk indexes for unprotected receptive and insertive anal intercourse and knowledge of HIV status and actual serostatus reported by Doll, et al. (1990), and Ostrow, Joseph, et al. (1989) found no relationship between disclosure of HIV antibody status and sexual behavior change. (For a review of methodological issues involved in these studies see Jacobsen, Perry, & Hirsch, 1990).

A pilot study by Kegeles, Catania, and Coates (1988) provided disquieting information about the behavioral intentions of individuals at an anonymous testing site. Although a large majority of the approximately 300 respondents in their study intended to communicate a seropositive status to their sexual partners, 12% said they would not tell their primary sexual partner and 27% said they would not tell their nonprimary partners. Since questionnaires were completed prior to the participants obtaining their test results, the extent to which these intentions predicted actual behavior among those who tested seropositive is not known.

THE ASYMPTOMATIC AND EARLY SYMPTOMATIC STAGE

The antibody test can be followed by a period of many years during which the infected person is relatively asymptomatic. The absence of symptoms marks a time that can be though of as a latent period. From a psychological perspective this is a particular interesting period because its stressful demands usually are not directly related to physical and mental deterioration caused by HIV, but rather to psychological and social sequelae of knowledge that one is infected.

The individual has a great deal of latitude in the extent to which he focuses on HIV infection and the psychological and social demands of this latent period. At a very concrete level, there are a number of decisions for the individual who has tested positive for HIV, including whom to tell about his serostatus, whether to modify sexual behaviors to reduce the risk of transmission, and whether to be proactive about maintaining physical and emotional health. At a more abstract, existential level, the individual may need (or want) to deal with stigmatization, uncertainty as to when he will begin to experience the first symptoms of the disease, the possibility of suffering, and the ultimate threats—a shortened life and death at an unnaturally early age. Whether the tasks are to make concrete decisions or to confront existential issues, all are potentially highly stressful because they represent profound threats to the individual's well-being for which there is no immediate solution.

Adaptive Tasks

Several studies discuss adaptive tasks associated with HIV disease, including disclosing HIV status, modifying sexual behavior, and maintaining physical and emotional health. The findings of these studies help illustrate the complexity and psychological and social implications of these tasks.

Disclosing HIV Status. The decision to disclose HIV status is usually not a single decision, but rather a series of decisions that the seropositive individual makes with respect to each person or group of persons in his social network. In their interviews with 55 seropositive homosexual men, Siegel and Krauss (1991) found that four considerations influenced the decision about whom to tell about their infected status: fears of rejection, the wish to avoid others' pity, the wish to spare loved ones emotional pain, and concerns about discrimination. These considerations may help explain why some individuals decide not to disclose their status even to their primary partner. As noted earlier, Kegeles and her colleagues (1988) found that 12% of the approximately 300 persons tested at an anonymous testing site said they would not tell their primary sexual partner, and 27% said they would not tell their nonprimary partners. One fifth (20%) did not intend to tell their nonprimary partners if they were seropositive and had engaged in high-risk sex with multiple partners during the previous month.

It is not known whether these intentions regarding disclosure were translated into behavior following testing. It may be that when confronted with confirmation of a seropositive HIV status, those who had previously said they would not disclose their status to those with whom they were intimate changed their minds. The extent to which individuals disclose a positive serostatus to friends, family, and colleagues has not been studied. However, the findings reported by Kegeles, et al. (1988) suggest that many people who are seropositive tell only those closest to them, and even then infected individuals undoubtedly vary in their willingness to disclose.

In disclosing HIV antibody status, the individual is confronted with delivering bad news. He risks losing the relationships that are most important to him in terms of his identity and sense of belonging, including relationships with parents, siblings, spouse, children, and old friends. Disclosure may also exact a price in the settings where the individual spends his time away from home, including the workplace or school. We need to increase our understanding of the factors that influence to whom the individual chooses to disclose his serostatus, the responses that are helpful and harmful, and changes over time in the effects of disclosure on the individual and his relationship with those close to him.

Modifying Risky Sexual Behaviors. As noted earlier, as a group homosexual men in major urban settings significantly reduced risky sexual practices by the late 1980s. (For reviews, see Becker & Joseph, 1988; Stall, Coates, & Hoff, 1988). These impressive changes suggest that practicing safer sex became normative and widely socially supported at the community level in these urban settings. However, even in the late 1980s, a sizable proportion of homosexual men still engaged in risky sexual behavior, including a sizable minority of this group who relapsed from previously established safer sexual practices (Ekstrand & Coates, 1990; Saltzman, Stoddard, McCusker, & Mayer, 1989; Stall, Ekstrand, Pollack, McKusick, & Coates, 1990). Stall, et al. report that relapse was predicted by interpersonal variables, including having a good-looking partner, being afraid that a partner might leave unless the respondent agreed to unprotected anal intercourse, having a partner who claimed HIV antibody negativity, feeling there was a lot of stress in their lives, and being sad or upset. The persistence of risky sexual behavior, especially among those who had previously practiced safer sexual behavior, suggests that the perceived psychological and social costs associated with modification of these practices persist, even though knowledge of the risks to oneself and others is now widespread.

Maintaining Physical Health. The development of strategies for maintaining physical health was one of the adaptive tasks for persons infected with HIV identified by Siegel and Krauss (1991) in their interviews with HIV-positive men. One set of strategies their subjects reported had to do with taking control of their health by aggressively seeking medical treatment options, learning about the efficacy and side effects of such treatments, and promoting health by avoiding tobacco, alcohol, and drugs, eating well, and getting adequate rest. A second set of strategies had to do with maintaining vigilance about health by monitoring physical symptoms and CD4 T lymphocyte counts. A third set of strategies had to do with decisions on treatment, including when to begin treatment, and whether to get involved with healing therapies such as visualization, meditation, yoga, macrobiotic diets, and megavitamins.

Individuals who are active with respect to their health are likely to believe that health-related behaviors are efficacious. Otherwise, why do them? This belief in the efficacy of the behavior is generally associated with good mental health (e.g., Bandura, 1982). Thus, there may be an important link between taking active steps to maintain physical health and emotional well-being.

Maintaining Emotional Health. Given the range of psychological and social threats to which people who are infected with HIV are potentially vulnerable, we might expect elevated levels of anxiety and depression among HIV-infected individuals not yet diagnosed with AIDS. A fascinating finding from studies of asymptomatic seropositive homosexual males is that their levels of distress are much closer to the levels of distress in the general community than they are to the levels of distress in clinical samples (e.g., Blaney, Millon, Morgan, Eisdorfer, & Szapocznik, 1990; Kessler, O'Brien, Joseph, et al., 1988; Martin, Dean, Garcia, & Hall, 1989; Rabkin, Williams, Neugebauer, Remien, & Goetz, 1990).

When general anxiety and depressive symptoms have been examined separately from AIDS-related depression and anxiety, general anxiety and depressive symptoms tends to remain at the same level over time (Joseph, et al., 1990) or even decrease (Martin, Dean, Garcia, & Hall, 1989), whereas AIDS-related worries and concerns increase.

At some point, symptoms of HIV infection appear, including diarrhea, night sweats, oral hairy leukoplakia, and rashes. These symptoms generally do not interfere with the activities of daily living, but they are a signal that the disease is progressing. Thus, we would expect increases in anxiety and depression during the period in which these symptoms appear. Findings from two studies that compared levels of psychological distress in asymptomatic and symptomatic homosexual men with HIV infection are not consistent. In a study of homosexual men in the Michigan cohort of the MACS, the depressive symptom scores of men who reported more than three possible HIV-related symptoms were twice as high as the scores of those not reporting any symptoms (Ostrow, Monjan, et al., 1989). However, symptomatic men in the San Francisco AIDS Behavioral Research Project were not more depressed or anxious than their asymptomatic counterparts (Folkman, Chesney, Pollack, & Coates, 1991).

The differences in the findings of these studies might be a function of when in the epidemic the data were collected. The subjects in the study reported by Ostrow, Monjan, et al. (1989) were interviewed in 1984 and 1985, before they knew their antibody status. Because symptoms were the only way the individual might know he was infected, and because treatment was not yet available, the appearance of symptoms may have had a much greater psychological impact on the subjects in the Ostrow, et al. study than on the subjects in the Folkman, Chesney, Pollack, and Coates (1991) study, who were surveyed in 1989, by which time the antibody test and treatment were both available.

Psychiatric Disorder

Clinical depression and anxiety are frequently mentioned as common in HIV illness, but the prevalence of psychiatric disorder in people infected with HIV has been systematically examined in only a few studies. These studies suggest that it is not easy to determine whether psychiatric disorder is an effect of HIV or instead has its origins prior to HIV infection.

Tross, Hirsch, Rabkin, Berry, and Holland (1987) studied 149 homosexual men prior to the availability of the HIV antibody test. They classified subjects as presumably healthy, having ARC, and having AIDS. They found the rates of *any* current DSM-III Axis I disorder to be two to four times those in the general population. However, since the HIV antibody test was not available at the time of this study, the association between HIV disease and psychiatric disorder is difficult to evaluate.

A study by Atkinson, et al. (1988) used structured diagnostic interviews and rating scales to assess lifetime prevalence of psychiatric disorders of 56 homosexual men in four groups: men with AIDS, men with AIDS-related complex (ARC), men asymptomatic or mildly symptomatic but HIV positive, and men who were HIV negative. Atkinson and his colleagues used as a comparison group 22 healthy heterosexual men. They also studied recent diagnoses in the seropositive groups to determine whether serious HIV-related medical diagnoses were associated with greater recent psychiatric morbidity. The authors reported that ambulatory homosexual men had a high lifetime prevalence of major psychiatric disorders, including increased generalized anxiety disorder and major depression. The majority of these men developed a diagnosable psychiatric syndrome preceding their HIV-related illness or seropositivity; a substantial proportion of this group also reported symptoms meeting criteria for a diagnosable psychiatric condition within the preceding six months. Psychiatric disorder was unrelated to cognitive impairment.

A different picture is painted by Williams, Rabkin, Remien, Gorman, and Ehrhardt (1991), who administered standardized clinical interviews to 208 homosexual men, of whom 124 were HIV positive and 84 were HIV negative. People with diagnosed AIDS were excluded. The authors found low rates of current syndromal depressive and anxiety disorders in their cohort of men with and without HIV infection, compared with the results of previous studies. In contrast, lifetime "pre-AIDS" rates for depressive disorder and substance abuse/dependence disorders were much higher than those in the general population and were consistent with the reports of other investigators. Williams and her colleagues point out that it is important to distinguish between mood changes (feeling sad, worried, or anxious) and the presence of syndromal disorders in this population of men "who are realistically concerned about debilitating disease and premature death" (p. 129).

These findings highlight the importance of understanding the context of psychiatric symptoms, especially depression and anxiety (cf. Brown & Harris, 1978). Williams and her colleagues point out that current depressive symptoms need to be understood in the context of HIV infection. It is also important to learn more about the context of earlier periods of clinical depression in the lives of gay men. At some point, most gay men go through a period during which they wrestle with the personal significance of their homosexuality and its significance for family and friends. There is also the "coming out" process, through which the gay man discloses (or does not disclose) his sexual orientation to others. It is possible, even probable, that wrestling with the meaning of one's sexual orientation in terms of identity, affiliations, and life goals and disclosing sexual orientation to others will have significant psychosocial effects, especially if the individual is living in a family or community where homosexuality is stigmatized and homophobia is common. Thus, like the current symptoms that Williams, et al. suggest may be realistic to responses to concerns about debilitating disease and premature death in men who are infected with HIV, earlier clinical depression may have been triggered by stresses associated with changes of expectations regarding identity, life goals and commitments, close personal relationships, and community membership.

Stress-mediating Processes

The findings in the preceding studies contain two important messages: HIV disease poses profound psychological changes, and most people seem somehow to manage or tolerate them. I deliberately used the words *manage* and *tolerate* as opposed to *master* or *eliminate* out of respect for the significant, intractability, and pervasiveness of the psychological challenges associated with HIV disease. Effective coping with challenges of this sort implies management or toleration, not mastery or elimination (Lazarus & Folkman, 1984). The findings of these studies do show evidence of management and tolerance of these psychological challenges. Even when symptoms of HIV infection appear, anxiety and depression do not necessarily become more intense. As Blaney, Moran, et al. (1990) point out, we may be doing a disservice to seropositive individuals if we suggest that emotional turmoil and disruption are the norm rather than the converse; the psychosocial effects of HIV infection can be managed effectively, at least for a time.

The question then becomes: What do people who are infected with HIV think and do to manage the psychological challenges associated with their disease? How do they adapt psychologically over time? The literature on psychological stress highlights two processes that mediate the effects of stressful situations and conditions: coping and social support. A few studies provide some information about these processes in HIV-infected individuals.

Coping. As noted earlier, the physical course of HIV disease has implications for coping processes. In general, the more ambiguous a situation is, the easier it is to engage in denial-like coping that supports hopeful beliefs or illusions (Lazarus & Folkman, 1984). Thus, throughout the asymptomatic period and early symptomatic period, when there is still ambiguity about when the disease will progress to full-blown AIDS, we would expect that cognitive coping processes that support hopeful beliefs and illusions helping to screen out negative implications and focus on the positive implications would play a particularly important role.

Only a few studies have examined the stress-mediating effects of coping in seropositive homosexual men not yet diagnosed with AIDS. In a study of Dutch individuals infected with HIV, Storosum, Van den Boom, Van Beuzekom, and Sno (1990) report that avoidant coping does not protect people from distress, whereas active coping/positive reinterpretation correlates negatively with distressful feelings. (It is not clear whether the subjects in this study were asymptomatic or symptomatic.) In a study of 89 HIV-positive men, Nicholson and Long (1990) found that avoidant coping was positively associated with psychological distress, but that time since the diagnosis of HIV serostatus was negatively associated with distressed.

On the basis of their study of the Chicago cohort of the MACS, Joseph, et al. (1990) suggest that most people who are infected with HIV are not denying the reality of their infection, but rather are compartmentalizing their worries and concerns, so that while AIDS-related anxiety and depression increase over time, general anxiety and depression do not. Rabkin, et al. (1990) examined the maintenance of hope in 124 seropositive men who were not diagnosed with AIDS and 84 seronegative homosexual men. They found that men with a stronger sense of control over the events that they experienced and who reported stronger social supports had higher levels of hope. Hart, Taylor, Kemeny, & Dudley (1990), in a study from the Los Angeles cohort of the MACS, studied three groups: HIV-negative men, HIV-positive men with normal CD4 cell levels, and HIV-positive men with depleted CD4 cell levels. Hart, et al. asked how the threat of AIDS changed five domains of life: daily activities/priorities, view of the future, view of the self, view of the world, and interpersonal relationships in. On average, daily activities, priorities, and interpersonal relations were characterized by positive changes, whereas view of the world was characterized by negative changes. Negative changes in view of the self were most evidence in the CD4-depleted HIV-positive men. Men with normal CD4 levels described few negative changes, even compared to HIV-negative men.

Although studies of coping with HIV disease are few and differ in their methodologies, the pattern of findings is consistent in two regards: First, avoidant coping does not seem to protect HIV-infected individuals from distress. This finding is consistent with reports in the general coping literature (e.g., Aldwin & Revenson, 1987; Billings & Moos, 1984; Manne & Sandler, 1984; Vitaliano, et al., 1987). What we do not know is whether the situations that call for avoidant coping are typically more stressful than other kinds of situations. If this is the case, it is possible that avoidant coping might not be able to reduce distress, because the situation is so bad that inevitably it will intrude, but it may keep distress from becoming even more intense. An alternative explanation is that avoidant coping is inherently maladaptive. The interesting question about the relationship between the conditions under which avoidant coping is used and its efficacy in managing distress needs further exploration. Second, cognitive coping strategies that help the individual focus on the positive seem to help promote psychological well-being throughout the disease's course. Cognitive coping strategies mentioned previously that fall into this category include positive reinterpretation (Storosum et al., 1990), sense of control over events (Rabkin, Remien, Katoff, & Williams, 1991), and positive changes in daily life (Hart et al., 1990).

The pattern of findings further suggests that avoidant coping and cognitive coping strategies that focus on positive aspects of the situation may be incompatible. Avoidance coping deflects the individual's attention from the situation, whereas focusing on the positive directs the person's attention to the situation, albeit selectively (Folkman & Lazarus, 1988). Possibly one cannot try to avoid a situation and simultaneously selectively attend to the same situation.

Social Support. As noted earlier, Rabkin, et al. (1991) found that men with strong social support had higher levels of hope. A study from the San Francisco AIDS Behavioral Research Project (Hays, Catania, McKusick, & Coates, 1990) provides elaboration about sources of social support. Hays, et al. found that regardless of the men's serostatus, peers were perceived to be the most helpful source of support, and family members were perceived as least helpful in dealing with AIDS-related concerns. Hays, et al. ascribe this pattern, which is the obverse of the pattern found in heterosexuals, to the fact that peers can easily empathize, are readily accessible, share a common culture, and offer the opportunity to reciprocate the help received. (As will be discussed later, when diagnosed with AIDS, men turned to their families for support.) The reluctance of homosexual men who were not diagnosed with AIDS to seek support for AIDS concerns from family members may be due to feeling estranged from their families, a desire to avoid the topic of AIDS with their families because of its association with homosexuality, a desire to protect their family members from worry, or a concern that heterosexual family members may not have sufficient information or understanding about AIDS and gay culture to provide helpful support (Hays et al. 1990). In addition, physical distance from their families may have contributed to the perceived lack of family support.

AIDS

The diagnosis of AIDS marks the next stage of the disease process. In many ways, a diagnosis of AIDS brings dreaded news of significant disease progression and threats of serious physical and possibly neurological deterioration. Weitz (1989), who studied 23 homosexual and bisexual men diagnosed with AIDS, found that a diagnosis of AIDS raises questions about why this terrible thing has happened to them, whether they will be able to carry out long-range or even short-range plans, and whether they will be able to live with dignity, "beat the odds," and die with dignity. Diagnosed individuals may also feel the burden of the stigma associated with AIDS. AIDS is a likely candidate for stigmatization because its symptoms are often visible and perceived by others as repellent, ugly, or upsetting, and because its routes of transmission are perceived as intentional (Herek, 1990).

Despite the negative impact of an AIDS diagnosis, it is not unusual for people to experience some positive affect when they hear the diagnosis. Individuals may greet the news with a sense of relief because it ends a long period of uncertainty (Weitz, 1989). At last they have something concrete to fight, and their AIDS diagnosis may open up the way to obtain promising experimental drugs (Miller, 1988).

Anxiety and Depression

Findings are mixed regarding anxiety and depression among people diagnosed with AIDS. On the other hand, in their study of 65 gay or bisexual men infected with HIV, of whom 24 were asymptomatic, 22 were symptomatic, and 19 were diagnosed with AIDS, Chuang, Devins, Hunsely, and Gill (1989) reported that the asymptomatic and symptomatic groups were significant more depressed than the group diagnosed with AIDS. Rabkin, Remien, Katoff, and Williams (1991) were interested in the attitudinal and psychological characteristics of long-term survivors of AIDS, whom they defined as men who were alive at least three years after the diagnosis of an opportunistic infection. They interviewed 53 clients of the Gay Men's Health Crisis in New York City. Nearly all of these long-term survivors had experienced one or more episodes of life-threatening illness. Most were unable to work, and many had been led to believe that they had only months to live. Yet these long-term survivors had low aggregate rates of syndromal mood disorders and psychiatric distress, and nearly all maintained the conviction that "good times lay ahead and that their lives were worthwhile" (p. 9). On the other hand, as of November, 1989, among 490 men in the San Francisco AIDS Behavioral Research Project—of whom 90 were untested, 237 were seronegative, 76 were seropositive asymptomatic, 53 were seropositive symptomatic, and 34 were diagnosed with AIDS—those diagnosed with AIDS were significantly more depressed and anxious than were the other groups (Folkman, Chesney, Pollack, & Coates, 1991).

Coping with an AIDS Diagnosis

The mixed findings in the preceding studies suggest that over time many people adjust to living with AIDS. One reason is that, because AIDS is a disease that is likely to go on for years, its meaning can change over time as the result of news about treatment that generates hope and optimism about the future. Even in the absence of news about treatment, the meaning of the illness can be modified through cognitive coping processes (cf. Folkman & Lazarus, 1988; Pearlin & Schooler, 1978; Taylor & Aspinwall, 1989). Sheridan and Sheridan (1988) write that persons who are diagnosed with AIDS "review their lives, put regrets that cannot be undone in the past, and make mental lists of what they want to do for themselves and for others about whom they care. . . . They gain new respect for their physical selves and, with productive aggression, do what they can to retard the disease process. They investigate therapies, approved and experimental, and alternative drugs. They question and confront their physicians (and psychotherapists) with new findings and promising trends. They make decisions regarding potential guardianship arrangement and end-stage care" (p. 534). For example, in her study of 23 men with AIDS, Weitz (1989) found that over time the men made uncertainty an accepted part of their lives. "Stress had decreased because the men had learned both to assert control over some aspects of their lives and to accept that they could not control other aspects" (p. 277).

An important theme in these reports is the changing nature of personal control. Early in the disease process an individual may believe he has control over the course of his disease.

He may believe, for example, that by staying in good condition, eating well, getting enough rest, and otherwise living a healthy life he can delay the onset of symptoms. However, as the disease progresses, symptoms appear, and AIDS is diagnosed, this belief is likely to be altered. The challenge is to yield control when control is no longer realistic and to accept what cannot be controlled or changed. But it is not enough to give up control. At the same time, it is important to assert control in another area where control is feasible by substituting new goals for old ones. For example, the individual may decide that he cannot control the course of his disease, but he can decide that each day he will do at least one activity that brings him satisfaction. Because HIV disease evolves over time, the individual needs to be prepared to reappraise his goals in light of disease progression and modify them as necessary.

Information about specific strategies that people use to cope with AIDS is provided by Namir, Wolcott, Fawzy, and Alumbaugh (1987), who studied the coping of 50 homosexual or bisexual men who had been diagnosed with AIDS during the previous three months. They assessed eight coping strategies: active-positive involvement, active-expressive/information seeking, active-reliance on others, cognitive-positive understanding/create meaning, cognitive-passive/ruminative, distraction, passive resignation, and avoidance-solitary/passive behaviors. The strategy labeled *cognitive-positive/create meaning* was used most frequently compared to the seven other coping strategies. Items denoting this strategy included "Prayed hard for a good ending to the situation," "Thought about it one day at a time," and "Thought about the positive changes in me since the illness" (p. 314). Following this, the most frequently used strategy was active-behavioral, which included items such as "Went out more socially," "Talked to people, just to be able to talk about it," and "Went to a friend, or professional, for advice on how to change things in the situation." (p. 312). Further, the use of these strategies, as compared to avoidance strategies, was associated with lower mood disturbances and higher self-esteem. A similar pattern was found in the AIDS Behavioral Research Project (Folkman, Chesney, et al., 1991). Coping that involved positive reappraisal, planful problem-solving, and social support seeking was negatively associated with increases in depression between November 1988 and November 1989 in 490 subjects, including those diagnosed with AIDS.

These studies suggest a second theme for successful management of psychosocial distress: the maintenance of hope and morale over the disease's course. The challenge is to maintain hope about the future (e.g., Rabkin, et al., 1991) while controlling the intrusion of threatening thoughts and feelings. It would seem that to achieve this goal a delicate balance is required between cognitive coping strategies through which the individual selectively attends to those aspects of a situation that promote hope and coping strategies that allow the individual to minimize the meaning of threatening information (cf. Breznitz, 1983). Just how this delicate balance can be achieved and maintained is a subject about which we need to know more.

DO PSYCHOSOCIAL VARIABLES AFFECT HIV DISEASE?

The emphasis of this chapter is on the psychosocial effects of HIV disease. A question that follows naturally is: To what extent might psychosocial variables in turn affect HIV disease? The extent to which the psychosocial characteristics of the person and his environment influence HIV disease progression has been given little attention thus far. Kessler, et al. (1991) asked whether or not stressful life events predicted illness onset in the Chicago component of the MACS. Life events, including AIDS-related events and more general stressors, were used to predict illness progression (CD4 percentage and onset of thrush and/or fever lasting a minimum of two weeks between examinations) among initially asymptomatic HIV positive men. No relationship was found between stressful live events and illness onset, at least during the first five waves of data collection that were conducted semiannually from 1984 through 1987.

A second study by Blaney, et al. (1990) evaluated cynical hostility as a characteristic that might influence HIV disease progression through its relationship to psychosocial vulnerability. They chose cynical hostility because two prospective studies had shown it to be a significant predictor of deaths from all causes, independent of other risk factors (Barefoot, Dahlstrom, & Williams, 1983; Shekelle, Gale, Ostfeld, & Paul, 1983). In a cross-sectional analysis with both HIV-negative and HIV-positive individuals, cynical hostility was found to be associated with psychosocial deficits, including externality and a lack of social support, as well as with emotional distress. The authors also found that cynical hostility was associated with deficits in coping styles, including a lack of problem-focused coping for HIV-negative individuals and the use of potentially maladaptive emotion-focused coping in HIV positives. Unfortunately, the cross-sectional design of this study limits its ability to determine whether cynical hostility predicts HIV disease progression.

Given the dearth of research, it is not possible to way whether psychosocial characteristics influence HIV disease progression. One study shows no evidence of such effects, and another study shows only an indirect relationship, and this relationship is not demonstrated prospectively. Research about this question still in its infancy. Future studies of the effects of psychosocial characteristics on disease progression need to take into account when in the disease process such effects might occur. It seems likely that psychosocial factors may have more influence early in the disease process, before the infection runs rampant. Investigators also need to use sophisticated conceptualizations of psychosocial processes that, among other variables, include psychological vulnerability and psychological, social, and material resources for coping in order to understand the mechanisms through which psychosocial factors might influence the disease process.

PSYCHOSOCIAL INTERVENTIONS

The findings described previously indicate that coping may have an important role in maintaining morale and controlling depression throughout the course of HIV disease. Training people with AIDS how to cope more effectively with the stressful conditions and events of their day-to-day lives may help them maintain morale in the face of this disease. In the absence of a cure for the disease or evidence that psychological and social processes can affect the disease's course, the maintenance of morale takes on additional significance because it is one of the few outcomes of this disease that the individual may be able to control, at least to a certain extent.

Most HIV-related interventions to date have focused on reducing risk behavior (for a review, see St. Lawrence & Kelly, 1989; also see Franzini, Sideman, Dexter, & Elder, 1990). A few interventions have focused on maintaining morale by training in techniques for coping or stress management. Fawzy, Namir, and Wolcott (1989), for example, describe a structured group intervention for AIDS patients. Fifty patients were divided into groups consisting of seven to ten members who met for two-hour sessions for ten weeks. Patients were taught stress management techniques, relaxation training, problem-solving skills, and effective coping skills. Those involved in the intervention had decreases in distressed mood states, whereas nonparticipants had increases in their distressed mood states. Perry, Fishman, Jacobsberg, Young, and Frances (1991) evaluated three psychoeducational interventions to help reduce distress after voluntary HIV antibody testing. The interventions included standard counseling, counseling plus a three-session interactive video program, and counseling plus six individual sessions of stress prevention training. The stress prevention training took place in six weekly, hour-long individual sessions. The material was based on stress inoculation training and cognitive-behavioral techniques for treatment of depression, stress, and anxiety. Among the 103 subjects who were HIV positive, those in the counseling with stress prevention showed decreased distress at a three-month follow-up, and the distress of those in the other two conditions did not significantly increase. Perry and his colleagues concluded that stress prevention training is particularly helpful after notification of an HIV-positive status.

My colleagues and I (Folkman, Chesney, McKusick, et al., 1991) pilot tested a theory-based coping intervention with 20 mildly depressed HIV-negative and 20 mildly depressed HIV-positive gay men. The program, which is based on stress and coping theory (Lazarus & Folkman, 1984) and principles of cognitive-behavioral therapy, consisted of eight weekly two-hour group sessions. Participants were stratified by serostatus and randomly assigned to treatment or control conditions. Those in the treatment group decreased their use of self-blame coping compared to those in the control group. Analysis of six-week follow-up scores for positive morale and depression showed that the treatment groups had increased positive morale and decreased depression compared to the control groups. A full-scale controlled study is now underway to evaluate this model compared to a social support intervention.

The number of people needing psychosocial interventions is going to increase as the epidemic unfolds. To meet the needs created by this epidemic, it is important that interventions to help individuals infected with HIV maintain morale (1) be theory-based, so that we can test pathways through which changes in depression and positive morale take place; (2) be brief, so that many people can have the opportunity to benefit from them; (3) be effective in teaching skills for coping with chronic stress; (4) include techniques to help individuals maintain their skills once the intervention is complete; and (5) have manuals, so that mental health workers across the country can learn the interventions with relative ease.

THE EFFECTS OF HIV-RELATED BEREAVEMENT

The death of a spouse, child, lover, or close friend is never easy, and is usually considered to be among the most stressful events people experience. However, the meaning of the death of someone important can vary, depending on the circumstances of that death. The death of a person who has lived to an old age, for example, has a different meaning that does the death of a child or young adult. And the expected death of someone who has suffered through a long and painful illness has a different meaning than does a sudden, unexpected death.

Three circumstances help shape the meaning of the deaths of gay men from AIDS. First, death from HIV occurs at an unnaturally early age. As of March, 1992, for example, 75% of white men diagnosed with AIDS were between the ages of 25 and 44 (Centers for Disease Control, 1992). Second, those who are seropositive for HIV have the additional burden of grieving for someone who died from the disease for which the survivor is himself at risk. Third, as the epidemic progresses, more and more people are experiencing not just the loss of someone close to them, but the loss of many who are close to them.

In a study of 745 gay men living in New York City in 1985, Martin (1988) found a significant association between numbers of bereavements and traumatic stress response, demoralization, and sleep problems. In another study from this cohort, Martin and Dean (1989) demonstrated that bereavement was not a random event in this sample. Factors that predicted bereavement, including a history of a high number of different sexual partners, a history of frequent receptive anal intercourse, the presence of the HIV antibody, and the experience of one or more ARC symptoms, also predicted compromised health. Martin (1988) controlled for these potentially confounding variables and found that being bereaved of one or more close friends or a lover because of AIDS remained a strong predictor of psychological distress. Further, he reported a significant dose-response relationship between number of bereavements and indicators of psychological distress, including the use of recreational drugs and prescription sedative drugs taken specifically for sleep or to ease tension.

Theoretically, social support and coping should help bereaved individuals recover from grief. Lennon, Martin, and Dean (1990) examined the relationship between instrumental and emotional support and the experience of grief reaction in a study of a subsample of 180 gay men from the New York cohort who had lost a lover or close friend to AIDS during the first five years of the epidemic. They found that the perceived adequacy of instrumental and emotional support reduced the impact of bereavement on subsequent psychological distress.

As noted earlier, the death of a lover might have an even greater impact on men who are themselves infected with HIV. The extent to which this is the case, and how HIV serostatus affects recovery from bereavement over time, are among the questions we are addressing in a prospective study of bereavement in the caregiving partners of men with AIDS now under way in San Francisco. By the conclusion of the study there will be a group of seropositive bereaved partners and a group of seronegative bereaved partners whom we will have followed prospectively for two years from the time they were caregivers. The study will increase knowledge about the effects of HIV serostatus, caregiving, and bereavement on mental and physical health, and the extent to which these effects are mediated by stress, coping, and social support processes.

CONCLUSION

This chapter has drawn on epidemiological, sociological, psychological, and psychiatric perspectives. Each discipline addresses a different aspect of the overall question of the psychosocial effects of HIV infection. Although the boundaries between disciplines are often blurred, in general, epidemiologists and sociologists describe patterns of psychosocial effects in the population of HIV-infected people, while psychologists and psychiatrists focus on the motivational, cognitive, and behavioral factors that help explain individual differences in psychosocial effects.

A consistent finding across disciplines is that, as a group, people with HIV infection seem to manage the psychological challenge of the disease relatively well. Thus, we must be careful not to assume that people who are infected with HIV uniformly will be psychologically overwhelmed by the disease, especially in the stages before the development of full-blown AIDS. The research to date directs us to begin with the premises that there are wide individual differences in psychosocial adjustment and that many people are not psychologically overwhelmed. If we begin with this premise, the focus of our research will broaden to include the study of how people manage the diverse and incredibly powerful psychological challenges that are inherent in being infected with HIV. In contrast, if we assume that as a rule people are psychologically overwhelmed, our research efforts will continue to focus primarily on psychological morbidity in HIV-infected individuals. While this research direction is important, it is not sufficient for understanding psychosocial adjustment during HIV disease.

We need to know more about how HIV-infected people appraise the significance of what is happening to them and how they understand their illness, its meaning, its effects on their day-to-day lives, and its effects on their long-term goals and aspirations. We need to know more about how people cope with the psychological challenges posed by HIV disease and the ways in which coping processes facilitate or impede the maintenance of morale and reduction in risk behaviors, and we need to know more about social support, the conditions under which it is helpful and the conditions under which it makes things worse.

Answers to these questions will have significant practical application. In the absence of a cure for HIV disease, psychological support is important at every stage of the disease process, from antibody testing through death. We must use knowledge about how people manage the psychological challenges of HIV disease to help those who have difficulty managing. The knowledge will also be important for mental health professionals and home care providers on whom those with advanced HIV disease depend for psychological support as well as for health care.

REFERENCES

ALDWIN, C., & REVENSON, T. Does coping help? *Journal of Personality and Social Psychology,* 1987, *53,* 337–348.

ATKINSON, J. H., GRANT, I., KENNEDY, C. J., RICHMAN, D. D., SPECTOR, S. A., & MCCUTCHAN, J. A. Prevalence of psychiatric disorders among men infected with human immunodeficiency virus. *Archives of General Psychiatry,* 1988, *45,* 859–864.

AVINS, A., & LO, B. To tell or not to tell: The ethical dilemmas of HIV test notification in epidemiologic research. *American Journal of Public Health,* 1989, *79,* 1544–1548.

BANDURA, A. Self efficacy mechanism in human agency. *American Psychologist,* 1982, *37,* 122–147.

BAREFOOT, J. C., DAHLSTROM, W. G., & WILLIAMS, R. B. Hostility, CHD incidence, and total mortality: A 25-year follow-up study of 255 physicians. *Psychosomatic Medicine,* 1983, *45,* 59–63.

BATCHELOR, W. F. Real fears, false hopes: The human costs of AIDS antibody testing. *AIDS and Public Policy Journal,* 1987, *2,* 25–30.

BECKER, M. H., & JOSEPH, J. G. AIDS and behavioral change to reduce risk: A review. *American Journal of Public Health,* 1988, *78,* 394–410.

BERRIOS, D. C., HEARST, N., PERKINS, L., BURKE, G. L., SIDNEY, S., MCREATH, H. E., & HULLEY, S. B. HIV antibody testing in young, urban adults. *Archives of Internal Medicine,* 1992, *152,* 397–402.

BILLINGS, A. G., & MOOS, R. H. Coping, stress, and social resources among adults with unipolar depression. *Journal of Personality and Social Psychology,* 1984, *46,* 877–891.

BLANEY, N. T., MILLON, C., MORGAN, R., EISDORFER, C., & SZAPOCZNIK, J. Emotional distress,

stress-related disruption and coping among health HIV-positive gay males. *Psychology and Health,* 1990, *4,* 259–273.

BLANEY, N. T., MORGAN, R. O., FEASTER, D., MILLON, C., SZAPOCZNIK, J., & EISDORFER, C. Cynical hostility: A risk factor in HIV-1 infection? Unpublished manuscript, Miami, FL: University of Miami School of Medicine, 1990.

BOCCELLARI, A., & DILLEY, J. W. HIV related cognitive impairment in San Francisco: Associated management and residential placement problems. *Journal of Hospital and Community Psychiatry,* in press.

BREZNITZ, S. Denial versus hope. In S. Breznitz (ed.), *The denial of stress.* New York: International Universities Press, 1983.

BROWN, G. W., & HARRIS, T. *The social origins of depression: The study of psychiatric disorder in women.* New York: Free Press, 1978.

CATANIA, J., KEGELES, S. M., & COATES, T. J. Psychosocial predictors of people who fail to return for their HIV test results. *AIDS,* 1990, *4,* 262–282.

CENTERS FOR DISEASE CONTROL. *HIV/AIDS Surveillance.* Atlanta: U.S. Department of Health and Human Services, 1992.

CHUANG, J. T., DEVINS, G. M., HUNSLEY, J., & GILL, M. J. Psychosocial distress and well-being among gay and bisexual men with human immunodeficiency virus infection. *American Journal of Psychiatry,* 1989, *146,* 876–880.

CLAYPOOLE, K. H. J., TOWNES, B. D., WHITE, D., HANDSFIELD, H. H., LONGSTRETH, W., MARAVILLA, K., MURPHY, V., & COLLIER, A. C. Neuropsychological aspects of early HIV infection. *Journal of Clinical Experimental Neuropsychology,* 1990, *12,* 72.

COATES, T. J., MORIN, S. F., & MCKUSICK, L. Behavioral consequences of AIDS antibody testing among gay men. *Journal of the American Medical Association,* 1987, *258,* 1889.

COATES, T. J., STALL, R. D., KEGELES, S. M., LO, B., MORIN, S., & MCKUSICK, L. AIDS antibody testing: Will it stop the epidemic? Will it help people infected with HIV? *American Psychologist,* 1988, *43,* 859–864.

DOLL, L. S., O'MALLEY, P. M., PERSHING, A. L., DARROW, W. W., HESSOL, N. A., & LIFSON, A. R. High-risk sexual behavior and knowledge of HIV antibody status in the San Francisco City Clinic Cohort. *Health Psychology,* 1990, *9,* 253–265.

EKSTRAND, M. L., & COATES, T. J. Maintenance of safer sexual behaviors and predictors of risky sex: The San Francisco Men's Health Study. *American Journal of Public Health,* 1990, *80,* 973–977.

FAWZY, I. F., NAMIR, S., & WOLCOTT, D. L. Group intervention with newly diagnosed AIDS patients. *Psychiatric Medicine,* 1989, *7,* 35–46.

FOLKMAN, S., CHESNEY, M. A., MCKUSICK, L., IRONSON, G., JOHNSON, D., & COATES, T. J. Translating coping theory into an intervention. In J. Eckenrode (ed.), *The social context of stress.* New York: Plenum Press, 1991

FOLKMAN, S., CHESNEY, M. A., POLLACK, L, & COATES, T. J. Stress, coping, and changes in depression in homosexual men. Manuscript in preparation, 1991.

FOLKMAN, S., & LAZARUS, R. S. The relationship between coping and emotion: Implications for theory and research. *Social Science and Medicine,* 1988, *26,* 309–317.

FOX, R., ODAKA, N. J., BROOKMEYER, R., & POLK, B. F. Effect of HIV antibody disclosure on subsequent activity in homosexual men. *AIDS,* 1987, *1,* 241–246.

FRANZINI, L. R., SIDEMAN, L. M., DEXTER, K. E., & ELDER, J. P. Promoting AIDS risk reduction via behavioral training. *AIDS Education and Prevention,* 1990, *2,* 313–321.

GRANT, I., ATKINSON, J. H., HESSELINK, J. R., KENNEDY, C. J., RICHMAN, D. D., SPECTOR, S. A., & MCCUTCHAN, J. A. Evidence for early central nervous system involvement in the acquired immunodeficiency syndrome (AIDS) and other human immunodeficiency virus (HIV) infections. *Annals of Internal Medicine,* 1987, *107,* 828–836.

HART, C. B., TAYLOR, S. E., KEMENY, M. E., & DUDLEY, J. Positive and negative changes in response to the threat of AIDS: Psychological adjustment as a function of severity of threat and life domain. In *Program and abstracts: VI International Conference on AIDS,* San Francisco: Abstract S.B.371, 1990.

HAYS, R. B., CATANIA, J. A., MCKUSICK, L., & COATES, T. J. Help-seeking for AIDS-related concerns: A comparison of gay men with various HIV diagnoses. *American Journal of Community Psychology,*, 1990, *18,* 743–755.

HEREK, G. M. Illness, stigma, and AIDS. In P. T. Costa, Jr., & G. R. VandenBos (eds.), *Psychological aspects of serious illness: Chronic conditions, fatal diseases, and clinical care.* Washington, DC: American Psychological Association, 1990.

HOLLAND, J. C., & TROSS, S. The psychosocial and neuropsychiatric sequelae of the acquired immunodeficiency syndrome and related disorders. *Annals of Internal Medicine,* 1985, *103,* 760–764.

JACOBSEN, P. B., PERRY, S. W., & HIRSCH, D. A. Behavioral and psychological responses to HIV antibody testing. *Journal of Consulting and Clinical Psychology,* 1990, *58,* 31–37.

JANSSEN, R. S., SAYKIN, A. J., CANNON, L., CAMPBELL, M. A., PINSKY, P. F., HESSOL, N. A., O'MALLEY, P. M., LIFSON, A. R., DOLL, L. S., RUTHERFORD, G. W., & KAPLAN, J. E. Neurological and neuropsychological manifestations of HIV-1 infection: Association with AIDS-related complex but not asymptomatic HIV-1 infection. *Annals of Neurology,* 1989, *26,* 589–600.

JOSEPH, J. G., CAUMARTIN, S. M., TAL, M., KIRSCHT, J. P., KESSLER, R. C., OSTROW, D. G., & WORTMAN, C. B. Psychological functioning in a cohort of gay men at risk for AIDS: A three-year descriptive study. *Journal of Nervous and Mental Disease,* 1990, *178,* 607–615.

JOSEPH, J. G., MONTGOMERY, S. B., EMMONS, C. A., KESSLER, R. C., OSTROW, D. G., WORTMAN, C. B., O'BRIEN, K., ELLER, M., & ESHLEMAN, S. Magnitude and determinants of behavioral risk reduction: Longitudinal analysis of a cohort at risk for AIDS. *Psychology and Health,* 1987, *1,* 73–96.

KEGELES, S. M., CATANIA, J. A., & COATES, T. J. *A comparison of current and early utilization of alternative test sites for HIV antibody testing.* Paper presented to the fourth International Conference on AIDS, Stockholm, 1988.

KEGELES, S. M., CATANIA, J., COATES, T. J., POLLACK, L. M., & LO, B. Many people who seek anonymous HIV-antibody testing would avoid it under other circumstances. *AIDS,* 1990, *4,* 588–595.

KESSLER, R. C., FOSTER, C., JOSEPH, J., OSTROW, D., WORTMAN, C. B., PHAIR, J., & CHMIEL, J. Stressful life events as predictors of symptoms onset in HIV infection. *American Journal of Psychiatry,* 1991, *145,* 733–738.

KESSLER, R. C., O'BRIEN, K., JOSEPH, J. G., et al. Effects of HIV infection, perceived health and clinical status on a cohort at risk for AIDS. *Social Science and Medicine,* 1988, *27,* 569–578.

LAZARUS, R. S., & FOLKMAN, S. *Stress, appraisal, and coping.* New York: Springer, 1984.

LENNON, M. C., MARTIN, J. L., & DEAN, L. The influence of social support on AIDS-related grief reaction among gay men. *Social Science and Medicine,* 1990, *31,* 477–484.

LUNN, S., SKYDSBJERG, M., SCHULSINGER, H., PARNAS, J., PEDERSEN, C., & MATHIESEN, L. A preliminary report on the neuropsychologic sequelae of human immunodeficiency virus. *Archives of General Psychiatry,* 1991, *48,* 139–142.

LYTER, D. W., VALDISERRI, R. O., KINGSLEY, L. A., AMOROSO, W. P., & RINALDO, C. R. The HIV antibody test: Why gay and bisexual men want or do not want to know their results. *Public Health Reports,* 1987, *102,* 468–474.

MANNE, S., & SANDLER, I. Coping and adjustment to genital herpes. *Journal of Behavioral Medicine,* 1984, *7,* 391–410.

MARTIN, J. Psychological consequences of AIDS-related bereavement among gay men. *Journal of Consulting and Clinical Psychology,* 1988, *56,* 856–862.

MARTIN, J. L., & DEAN, L. Risk factors for AIDS-related bereavement in a cohort of homosexual men in New York City. In B. Cooper & T. Helgason (eds.), *Epidemiology and the prevention of mental disorders.* London: Routledge, 1989.

MARTIN, J. L., DEAN, L., GARCIA, M. A., & HALL, W. The impact of AIDS on a gay community: Changes in sexual behavior, substance use, and mental health. *American Journal of Community Psychology,* 1989, *17,* 269–293.

MCARTHUR, J. K. C., COHEN, B. A., SELNES, O. A., KUMAR, A. J., COOPER, K., MCARTHUR, J. H., SOUCY, G., CORNBLATH, D. R., CHMIEL, J. S., WANG, M., STARKEY, D. L., GINZBURG, H., OSTROW, D. G., JOHNSON, R. T., PHAIR, J. P., & POLK, F. Low prevalence of neurological and neuropsychological abnormalities in otherwise health HIV-1 infected individuals: Results from the Multicenter AIDS Cohort Study. *Annals of Neurology,* 1989, *26,* 601–611.

MCCUSKER, J., STODDARD, A. M., MAYER, K. H., ZAPKA, J., MORRISON, C., & SALTZMAN, M. Effects of HIV antibody test knowledge on subsequent sexual behaviors in a cohort of homosexually active men. *American Journal of Public Health,* 1988, *78,* 462–467.

MCCUTCHAN, J. A. Virology, immunology, and clinical course of HIV infection. *Journal of Consulting and Clinical Psychology,* 1990, *58,* 5–12.

MILLER, D. HIV and social psychiatry. *British Medical Bulletin,* 1988, *44,* 130–148.

NAMIR, S., WOLCOTT, D. L., FAWZY, I. F., & ALUMBAUGH, M. J. Coping with AIDS: Psychological and health implications. *Journal of Applied Social Psychology,* 1987, *17,* 309–328.

NICHOLSON, W. D., & LONG, B. C. Self-esteem, social support, internalized homophobia, and coping strategies of HIV + gay men. *Journal of Consulting and Clinical Psychology,* 1990, *58,* 873–876.

O'DOWD, M. A. Psychosocial issues in HIV infection. *AIDS,* 1988 (suppl. 1), *2,* S201–S205.

OSTROW, D. G., JOSEPH, J. G., KESSLER, R., SOUCY, J., TAL, M., ELLER, M., CHMIEL, J., & PHAIR, J. P. Disclosure of HIV antibody status: Behavioral and mental health correlates. *AIDS Education and Prevention, 1989, 1,* 1–11.

OSTROW, D. G., MONJAN, A., JOSEPH, J., VANRADEN, M., FOX, R., KINGLSEY, L., DUDLEY, J., & PHAIR, J. HIV-related symptoms and psychological functioning in a cohort of homosexual men. *American Journal of Psychiatry,* 1989, *146,* 737–742.

PEARLIN, L. I., & SCHOOLER, K. The structure of coping. *Journal of Health and Social Behavior,* 1978, *19,* 2–21.

PERRY, S., BELSKY-BARR, W., & JACOBSBERG, L. Neuropsychological function in physically asymptomatic, HIV-seropositive men. *Journal of Neuropsychiatry,* 1989, *1* 296–302.

PERRY, S., FISHMAN, B., JACOBSBERG, L., YOUNG, J., & FRANCES, A. Effectiveness of psychoeducational interventions in reducing emotional distress after human immunodeficiency virus antibody testing. *Archives of General Psychiatry,* 1991, *48,* 143–147.

PERRY, S., JACOBSBERG, L. B., FISHMAN, B., WEILER, P. H., GOLD, J. W. M., & FRANCES, A. J. Psychological responses to serological testing for HIV. *AIDS,* 1990, *4,* 145–152.

PETERSON, J. L., COATES, T. J., CATANIA, J., KEGELES, S., DRUES, J., FULLILOVE, M., & HULLEY, S. To be or not to be tested? Racial, ethnic and sexual orientation differences in obtaining HIV antibody testing and receiving test results. *VI international Conference on AIDS,* San Francisco. Abstract S.C.101.

PRICE, R. W., BREW, B., SIDTIS, J., ROSENBLUM, M., SCHECK, A., & CLEARY, P. The brain in AIDS; central nervous system HIV-1 infection and AIDS dementia complex. *Science,* 1988, *239,* 586–592.

RABKIN, J. G., REMIEN, R. H., KATOFF, L., & WILLIAMS, J. B. W. *AIDS long term survivors: A clinical assessment.* Paper presented to the American Psychiatric Association annual meetings, New Orleans, May, 1991.

RABKIN, J. G., WILLIAMS, J. B. W., NEUGEBAUER, R., REMIEN, R. H., & GOETZ, R. Maintenance of hope in HIV-spectrum homosexual men. *American Journal of Psychiatry,* 1990, *147,* 1322–1326.

SALTZMAN, S., STODDARD, A., McCUSKER, J., & MAYER, K. *Factors associated with recurrence of unsafe sex practices in a cohort of gay men previously engaging in "safer sex."* Paper presented to the fifth International Conference on AIDS, Montreal, 1989.

SHEKELLE, R. B., GALE, M., OSTFELD, A. M., & PAUL, O. Hostility, risk of coronary heart disease, and mortality. *Psychosomatic Medicine,* 1983, *45,* 109–114.

SHERIDAN, K., & SHERIDAN, E. P. Psychological consultation to persons with AIDS. *Professional Psychology: Research and Practice,* 1988, *19,* 532–535.

SIEGEL, K., BAUMAN, L. J., CHRIST, G. H., & KROWN, S. Patterns of change in sexual behavior among gay men in New York City. *Archives of Sexual Behavior,* 1988, *17,* 481–497.

SIEGEL, K., & KRAUS, B. J. Living with HIV infection. *Journal of Health and Social Behavior,* 1991, *32,* 17–32.

SIEGEL, K., LEVINE, M. P., BROOKS, C., & KERN, R. The motives of gay men for taking or not taking the HIV antibody test. *Social Problems,* 1989, *36,* 368–383.

ST. LAWRENCE, J. S., & KELLY, J. A. AIDS Prevention: Community and behavioral interventions. In M. Hersen, R. M. Eisler, & P. M. Miller (eds.), *Progress in behavioral modification, 24.* Newbury Park, CA: Sage, 1989.

STALL, R. D., COATES, T. J., & HOFF, C. Behavioral risk reduction for HIV infection among gay and bisexual men. *American Psychologist,* 1988, *43,* 878–885.

STALL, R., EKSTRAND, M., POLLACK, L., McKUSICK, L., & COATES, T. J. Relapse from safer sex: The next challenge for AIDS prevention efforts. *Journal of Acquired Immune Deficiency Syndrome,* 1990, *3,* 1181–1187.

STERN, Y., MARDER, K., BELL, K., CHEN, J., DOONEIEF, G., GOLDSTEIN, S., MINDRY, D., RICHARDS, M., SANO, M., WILLIAMS, J., GORMAN, J., EHRHARDT, A., & MAYEAUX, R. Multidisciplinary baseline assessment of homosexual men with and without human immunodeficiency virus infection. *Archives of General Psychiatry,* 1991, *48,* 131–138.

STOROSUM, J., VAN DEN BOOM, F., VAN BEAUZEKOM, M., & SNO, H. Stress and coping in people with HIV infection. In *Program and abstracts of the VI International Conference on AIDS.* San Francisco: Abstract:S.B.365.

TAYLOR, S. E., & ASPINWALL, K. G. Psychological aspects of chronic illness. Master lecture presented to the annual meetings of the American Psychological Association, New Orleans, 1989.

TROSS, S. & HIRSCH, D. A., Psychological distress and neuropsychological complications of HIV infection and AIDS. *American Psychologist,* 1988, 929–934.

TROSS, S., HIRSCH, D., RABKIN, J., BERRY, C., & HOLLAND, J. C. B. Determinants of current psychiatric disorder in AIDS spectrum patients. In Program and abstracts of the Third International Conference on AIDS: June 1–5, 1987; Washington, DC: Abstract T.10.5.

VITALIANO, P. P., KATON, W., RUSSO, J., MAIURO, R. D., ANDERSON, K., & JONES, M. Coping as an index of illness behavior in panic disorder. *Journal of Nervous and Mental Disease,* 1987, *175,* 78–84.

WEITZ, R. Uncertainty and the lives of persons with AIDS. *Journal of Health and Social Behavior,* 1989, *30,* 270–281.

WILKIE, F. L., EISDORFER, C. E., MORGAN, R., LOWENSTEIN, D. A., & SZAPOCZNIK, J. Cognition in early human immunodeficiency virus infection. *Archives of Neurology,* 1990, *47,* 433–440.

WILKINS, J. W., ROBERTSON, K. R., VAN DER HORST, C., ROBERTSON, W. T., FRYER, J. G., & HALL, C. D. The importance of confounding factors in the evaluation of neuropsychological changes in patients infected with human immunodeficiency virus. *Journal of Acquired Immune Deficiency Syndrome,* 1990, *3,* 938–942.

WILLIAMS, J. B. W., RABKIN, J. B., REMIEN, R. H., GORMAN, J. M., & EHRHARDT, A. A. Multidisciplinary baseline assessment of homosexual men with and without human immunodeficiency virus infection. *Archives of General Psychiatry,* 1991, *48,* 124–130.

WINKELSTEIN, W., WILEY, J., PADIAN, N. S., SAMUEL, M., SHOBOSKI, S., ASCHER, M. S., & LEVY, J. A. The San Francisco Men's Health Study: Continued decline in HIV seroconversion rates among homosexual/bisexual men. *American Journal of Public Health,* 1988, *78,* 1472–1474.

WHO PRESS. Press Release WHO/17. Geneva: World Health Organization, 1991.

PART **VIII**

TREATMENT AND SUPPORTS

36

Social Support: Social Resources and Social Context

Stevan E. Hobfoll   Alan Vaux

WHEN STRESS RESEARCHERS ORIGINALLY SET ABOUT THEIR TASK of exploring the effects of stress on psychological and physical health, they expected that stress would be a major cause of psychological distress and even physical illness. Such thinking was largely a product of the strong environmental viewpoint that dominated psychology in the 1960s and early 1970s. This viewpoint held that the current environment, not genetics or early childhood, was mainly responsible for psychopathology and physical malaise. This world view was consistent with popular Kennedy-era political philosophies that to a large extent were represented in psychology but were not necessarily grounded in data.

When empirical evidence clearly began to show that stress only played a modest role in the onset of psychopathology or physical illness (Rabkin & Streuning, 1976), it was only natural for researchers to look for another environmental explanation for the unexpectedly modest contribution of stress to distress. One variable that intrigued researchers was, and remains, social support. Just as early expectations about stress were overzealous, likewise, social support was viewed as a social panacea. Clearly, it was hoped that social support might explain why some people who experience stress do surprisingly well, while others who experience stress do as poorly as early thinking on stress had expected (Hobfoll & Stokes, 1988).

Research on social support has not met the original expectations that social support could be a cure for all ills. Indeed, like stress, social support has a complex effect on well-being. Overall, social support is a valuable social commodity and those who are endowed with social support are better off in most instances than those who are not. However, the averaged effect of social support across stressful events is modest, it is not always helpful, and it sometimes has a paradoxically negative effect on the recipient (Sarason, Sarason, & Pierce, 1990; Vaux, 1988a).

This chapter begins with a review of various definitions of social support that have been proffered. For perhaps the first time in a review, we feel that there is a reasonable accumulation of evidence on factors that contribute to the receipt of social support, and we review the early studies that have pioneered this new research focus. Next, we focus on

This chapter was made possible, in part by the National Institute of Health (#1 R01 HD24901-01A2) and the National Institute of Mental Health (#1 R01 MH45669-01) and Kent State's Applied Psychology Center. We also thank Sarah Chisholm for assistance with the review of the literature.

outcomes of studies that address the effects of social support on well-being. With these empirical findings in mind, we outline theoretical models that have developed and are consistent with research findings. In particular, we address a general ecological model (cf. Vaux, 1988a) that emphasizes the person-in-environment nature of social support, and we outline how conservation of resource theory (Hobfoll, 1988, 1989) may explain the motivation to seek support and the ability to utilize it successfully. Finally, we suggest future important research directions.

DEFINITIONS OF SOCIAL SUPPORT

In defining the construct, Caplan (1974) suggested that social support is the product of social activities that enhance people's sense of mastery through sharing tasks, giving material and cognitive assistance, and providing emotional comfort. Other early social support theorists, such as Cobb (1976) and Weiss (1974), emphasized that social support is the product of beliefs that one is esteemed and cared for. Cassel (1974) saw a lack or breakdown of significant social attachments as resulting in disequilibrium and heightened susceptibility to disease. While these notions carried a common thread, they are not synonymous with one another, nor are they very specific. They did, nonetheless, spur a flurry of research, and what followed was a great increase of interest and investigation in social support that was marked by a wide spectrum of visions of what constituted social support.

Complexity may be the product of a complex underlying construct or of a lack of clear thinking. While one may find studies that are conceptually weak, our review of the literature suggests that many of the conceptualizations of social support are equally valid, well thought out, and, yet, quite divergent. For these reasons, Vaux (1988a) suggested that it is best to view social support as a metaconstruct—that is, a higher-order theoretical construct comprised of several legitimate and distinguishable theoretical constructs (see Cook & Campbell, 1979). Three social support constructs were distinguished by Vaux under the grand metaconstruct of social support: (1) support network resources, (2) supportive behavior, and (3) the subjective appraisals of support. Let us now define each of these.

Support Network Resources

Bowlby (1969) suggested that links to strong social attachments are a prerequisite of health and well-being. Those who belong to a strong social network have access to support in fulfilling the needs of both everyday and dramatic events. Some cognitively oriented theorists have suggested that it is not the availability or the receipt of support that is important, but its perception; however, work by Bowlby suggests that even this belief is the product of being strongly attached to significant others both early in life and throughout life's course. We would define social network resources as the available social relationships that objectively may be called upon for help in times of need and that offer stable attachment to a social group.

Supportive Behavior

Shumaker and Brownell (1984) offer a good definition of supportive behavior. Although they used their definition to define all social support, we find their definition to apply more specifically to supportive behavior. As such, supportive behavior would be seen as "an exchange of resources between at least two individuals perceived by the provider or the recipient to be intended to enhance the well-being of the recipient" (p. 17). These interactions tend to be viewed as supportive when they are intended to gratify people's needs (Thoits, 1982). An important distinction here is that, although the intention is to help, the outcome may not be beneficial.

The subjective appraisals of support are "subjective, evaluative assessments of a person's supportive relationships and the supportive behavior that occurs within them" (Vaux, 1988a:29). Subjective appraisals are important indicators of support for two reasons, but only the first has been generally recognized. Cognitively oriented psychologists have emphasized that perceptions of support are important because people are affected by how they interpret their world, not necessarily by how their world is (Heller & Swindle, 1983; Turner, Frankel, & Levin, 1983). Consequently, an act of kindness may not be interpreted as such, and an act of treachery may be seen as helpful. Clearly, when perceptions diverge from reality to a marked degree, perceptions will have great importance. Sarason, Sarason, and Shearin (1986) argued in this vein that social support is in large part a reflection of aspects of the self, rather than the environmental construct that was originally envisioned.

Hobfoll (1988) has taken a second tack that is otherwise not addressed in the literature. Specifically, he sees the concept of perceptions, as it has been used, as misleading because measurement that falls under the rubric or perceptions contains much objective information that is not tapped by what are called objective assessments of supportive behavior. Typical support behavior inventories tap, perhaps twenty-five to thirty behaviors. The individual, in contrast, may catalog thousands of behaviors. Moreover, individuals' evaluative synthesis incorporates features of supportive behavior such as quality, timing, and fit (Vaux, 1988a) that are measurable in principle, though rarely measured for practical reasons. So, where perceptions are found not to be highly correlated with behaviors or are found to be superior predictors of outcome than assessments of supportive behavior, these differences may mainly be a product of sampling differences and not interpretation.

Gotlib and Hooley (1988) provide insight into how what appear to be ideographic perceptions may reflect actual supportive behavior at the same time that they appear to be a distortion. For example, suppose that a husband is observed sharing the child care. This behavior, however, may be correctly viewed as unsupportive by his wife, if she knows that in his view that a successful housewife would not need such help. This difference between her perception and a rater's objective report of the behavior is not a difference of perception, but of fuller knowledge of (objective) background history. This situation is quite different than if she were to distort his help that was intended to be fully participative and not a mask for his discontent. This distortion is what cognitively oriented social support researchers argue is responsible for the differential and more powerful effect of perceptions (see Kobasa, Maddi, & Courington, 1981; Lazarus & Folkman, 1984).

CONSERVATION OF RESOURCES AND SOCIAL SUPPORT: AN ECOLOGICAL VIEWPOINT

Although definitions are important in clarifying common concepts, the lack of a unifying theory has also limited work on social support. Hobfoll's (1988, 1989) conservation of resources (COR) theory has been applied to work on social support and may prove useful in this regard.

COR theory is based on the motivational tenet *that people strive to obtain, retain, and protect what they value.* The things they value are termed resources and include objects (e.g., car, house), personal characteristics (e.g., sense of mastery, social skills), conditions (e.g., seniority, good marriage), and energies (e.g., money, knowledge) that are goal objects or that are valuable in meeting goals. From this principle, it follows that stress will occur under any of three conditions: (1) when resources are lost, (2) when resources are threatened with loss, or (3) where individuals invest resources without consequent and consummate gain of resources. For example, self-esteem could be lost owing to failure, could be threatened by potential failure, or people could risk their self-esteem (e.g., by self-disclosure of love) and fail to meet their intended goals (e.g., by finding out that their love is unrequited). All three of these instances are seen as stressful.

A number of axioms follow from COR theory. First, individuals use resources to offset loss of other resources or to enhance gain. Second, this coping demands resources and comes at certain cost (Schonpflug, 1985). Related to these first two axioms or corollaries, COR envisions individuals as active players, not passive responders, in the stress process. They shape their resources, determine how to best employ them, and influence environmental circumstances in ways that they hope will maximize gain and minimize loss. Fourth, both the objective circumstances and appraisals are seen as important, but appraisals are seen primarily as based on actual, objective circumstances. Nevertheless, we should not underestimate the influence of interpretation, over and above accurate appraisal, as suggested by Lazarus and Folkman (1984) and Kobasa, et al. (1981). Finally, because stress follows from loss and resources must be spent in coping, those who lack resources will be more vulnerable to loss spirals and those who possess resources will be more likely to experience gain spirals (see also Holahan & Moos, 1991).

Two additional axioms relate more specifically to social support (Hobfoll, Freedy, Lane, & Geller, 1990). First, "social support is the major vehicle by which individuals' resources are widened outside the limited domain of resources that are contained in the self . . . [and] personal and social resources are two integral aspects of people's identities" (p. 467). Thus, people will strive to maintain social support both to protect their resources and in order to protect their identity (see Swann & Brown, 1990).

Social support may best be viewed as a dynamic process of transactions between people and their social networks that takes place in an ecological context (Vaux, 1988a). People use the social support process to assist them both in dealing with demands and in achieving goals. They actively develop and maintain support network relationships to supplement, enhance, and actuate their personal resources and their capacity to function. Ideally, these relationships represent a rich and reliable source of resources, including affection, caring, wisdom, money, energy, specialized skills, and opportunities to socialize. People seek or receive assistance with life tasks through transfers of resources, often observable as supportive behavior. Such transactions take place routinely within continuing relationships and distinctly during support incidents. People actively evaluate these transactions and ongoing relationships to form general support appraisals. This process does not occur in a vacuum, but is shaped by an ecology of personal and social context factors.

Support Networks

We can begin to understand this complex process by examining support networks, which are the source of extrapersonal resources. Are some kinds of networks more beneficial than others? It appears that the structure and composition of networks is less important than how well their resultant capability fits short- and long-term needs. For example, large and less dense networks should provide many advantages, including accessibility, stamina in the face of chronic demand, varied expertise, breadth of information, and diverse perspectives on life's problems and challenges (Vaux, 1988a).

Yet empirical evidence is mixed. Diverse networks may counter loneliness and promote positive support appraisals (Vaux, 1988b; Vaux & Harrison, 1985), but sometimes only for some groups, some networks, or some support appraisals (Cutrona, 1986; Vaux & Athanassopoulou, 1987). The benefits appear most valuable (and detectable) when stressors involve life transitions and role-exploration, as in divorce (Wilcox, 1981), widowhood, or college re-entry (Hirsch, 1979). In other contexts, a smaller or denser network may be less costly to maintain and more efficient for most needs, and sometimes denser networks may provide more supportive behavior (Hirsch, 1979; Stokes, 1985).

Network density is complicated because it also reflects network composition—particularly the proportion of family. A preponderance of family members in the network may have functional advantages or disadvantages, including a paucity of close friends (Mitchell, 1982), greater commitment to support but also more obligations (Hobfoll, Nadler, & Lieberman, 1986), and greater potential for conflict (Hirsch, 1979). Moreover, for better or worse, family members may represent a particular point of view. Thus, they may constrain adjustment following divorce (Wilcox, 1981), but counter the tendency of peer socializing to encourage substance use among adolescents (Vaux, 1981; Wills, 1990). Among adolescents, links between family and peer networks may be beneficial generally, but harmful when a family member is psychologically disordered (Hirsch & Reischl, 1985).

The quality of network relationships is also critical to their function. Intimate relationships play a key role in social support (Reis, 1990) and perhaps fulfill basic human needs essential to well-being (Cobb, 1976; Weiss, 1974). Moreover, intimates and close friends would seem more likely to provide high quality support for several reasons. They are more likely to be responsive to one's distress, to be motivated to expend energy to help, to be accurate about the nature and degree of one's difficulties, and to provide help appropriate to one's needs, at the least cost in self-esteem (Vaux, 1988a). Close, confiding, reciprocal, and complex network relationships have been linked to more supportive behavior, more positive support appraisals, less loneliness, and greater life satisfaction (Antonucci, Fuhrer, & Jackson, 1990; Stokes, 1983; Stokes & Wilson, 1984; Vaux & Harrison, 1985; Vaux & Athanassopoulou, 1987; Vaux & Wood, 1987).

Relationships of high quality also imply relative freedom from conflict and negative interactions—a factor seriously underplayed in the support literature (Coyne & Bolger, 1990) and clearly of importance (Barrera, 1981; Barrera & Baca, 1990; La Gaipa, 1990; Rook, 1990). Too much might be made of the distinction between negative and positive interactions here, because both may be involved in the transfer of intangible resources, but clearly we need a better understanding of their joint role in the support process.

According to COR theory, the social support task that individuals face is to develop network resources with a sufficient sustainable yield that are most appropriate to their needs (i.e., given their demands, goals, and personal resources) and to access and use these resources skillfully to maximize net gain or, or least, to minimize net loss of personal and social resources. In execution, this task is extremely challenging and is constrained by a host of social and personal factors. Moreover, those with greater need and fewer personal resources are likely to have support of lower quality from more conflicted relationships and generally to be at greater risk for resource loss cycles (Hobfoll, 1988; Vaux, 1988a).

Provisions of Social Support

With the definitions of social support, our ecological view of COR theory, and some knowledge of support networks in mind, we now turn to factors that lead to the acquisition of social support (see also, Hobfoll, 1990). Unfortunately, our knowledge of these factors is still limited, because the first ten to fifteen years of social support research considered social support as a predictor variable and interest was focused on the effects of social support. It was simply assumed that some people had support and some lacked it, and little attention was paid to how support came about. More recently, there has been a call to discover the factors related to the receipt of support (Hobfoll, 1985; Vaux & Harrison, 1985). This focus also raises the point that for one to receive support, another has to provide support so that the two are probably in some kind of relationship. Thus, a more interactive, interpersonal viewpoint is emerging.

House (1981) outlined three categories that affect the proffering of support: (1) characteristics of individuals that facilitate or impede the ability to give and receive support, (2) properties of relationships that facilitate or impede the commerce of support, and (3) sociocultural factors that foster or discourage support provision. As COR they would have it, House is outlining the importance of individual, relational, and sociocultural resources. Others have suggested that the current environment, especially stress and resultant mood, may be a fourth factor contributing to the give and take of help (Barbee, Gulley, & Cunningham, 1990; Dunkel-Schetter & Skokan, 1990). In this way, resources are seen as becoming activated when situations threaten loss, when losses are incurred, or when individuals choose to seek the challenge of achieving some new goal.

Recipient Characteristics. The characteristics of those receiving aid may be subsumed in large part under the rubric of relational competence, a broad constellation of personal resources that shape the support process (Hansson, Jones, & Carpenter, 1984). Those who have greater relational competence tend to be more capable of appropriate social behavior and to act in a manner that is likely to be successful. Competence and coping are also related to greater receipt of support, and those who project that they are actively problem solving and not overly depressed are more likely to elicit help than those who use avoidant forms of coping or who become depressed (Gurtman, 1986; Schwarz, 1977; Staub, 1974). People who are described as coping well and not to blame for their malaise are more likely to elicit support (Schwarzer & Weiner, 1991).

Other recipient characteristics include possessing strong personal resources. In particular, hardiness (Kobassa & Puccetti, 1983), internal locus of control (Lefcourt, Martin, & Selah, 1984; Sandler & Lakey, 1982), self-esteem (Hobfoll, Nadler, & Leiberman, 1986), and mastery (Hobfoll, Shoham, & Ritter, 1991) have been examined. In general, it has been shown that those who possess strong personal resources have greater access to a supportive network and activate and utilize support from others more successfully than do those who lack these personal resources (Caldwell & Reinhart, 1988). It has also been suggested that these positive personal traits make them more attractive to others and that the kinds of relations such individuals develop are healthier and are with stronger people (Hansson et al., 1984). These examples support the COR axiom concerning the loss and gain spirals that link resources with stress resistance and lack of resources with stress vulnerability.

Network orientation may either act as a hindrance or a resource depending on the nature of that orientation. Individuals who are willing to seek support and feel comfortable interacting with others and discussing problems are also more likely to be involved in the support process. This general principle may underlie gender differences in the use and benefit of social support. Kessler, McLeod, and Wethington (1985) suggest that women are much more involved than men in social support interactions and others have found evidence that women are more adept than men in the support process (Sarason & Sarason, 1985; Sarason, et al., 1986). This facility may, in part, explain women's greater intimacy with others and their larger support networks (Hobfoll, 1986; Lootens & Strube, 1985). Compared to men, women have been found to spend more time interacting with others in their social networks and sharing feelings and personal concerns, and they report receiving more support (Burke & Weir, 1978; Hirsch, 1979). Women also benefit more from very close ties (Cohen & Wills, 1985; Sarason, et al., 1986; Stokes & Wilson, 1984). In particular, women report receiving more emotional support than men, but not necessarily more guidance or material aid (Burda, Vaux, & Schill, 1984; Stokes & Wilson, 1984). Finding comfort and sustenance in their social interactions may correspondingly create an increased motivation to seek and obtain more support (Hobfoll, 1991; Sarason & Sarason, 1985).

This caring may also engender greater costs for women, who by providing support are open to stress contagion and who may not receive adequate return on their investment of their own resources (Riley & Eckenrode, 1986). The significantly higher rate of depression among women compared to men is statistically cancelled out if one controls for differences in men's and women's numbers of close ties (Kessler, et al., 1985). A poignant example of sex differences was found in a study of recovering heart patients, among whom it was found that men went home and received support, while women went home and again became support providers (Coyne, Ellard, & Smith, 1990). One interpretation of these data is that women are burdened by the giving of support, without receiving adequate comfort in their receipt of support.

Regardless of gender, social network orientation may also explain differences in receipt of aid (Hill, 1991; Hobfoll & Lerman, 1988; Tolsdorf, 1976; Vaux, 1988a). Those who are more open and comfortable with seeking help are more likely to involve themselves in active support interactions and to benefit from them. Hill (1991) also found that those who are open to support may be attracted to nurturant others. Race may also play a role, and some theorists have suggested that communal orientation is more consistent with an Africentric than a Eurocentric viewpoint, but little empirical research is yet available on this important question (Jackson, Antonucci, & Gibson 1990).

Stress and Support Provision.   Although it was seldom stated directly, an assumption of the stress-buffering hypothesis (that social support is most influential under high stress) is that support is mobilized under high stress conditions. Evidence supports this notion that when stress increases people seek and report more social support behavior (Dunkel-Schetter, Folkman, & Lazarus, 1987; Schwarz, 1977; Staub, 1974). Stress may signal a need to seek help or to offer help, or both (Revenson & Majerovitz, 1990).

In a recent study, Hobfoll, et al. (1991) found that women who had strong personal resources were more likely to receive instrumental support under high stress conditions, but that under low stress conditions they were more likely to rely on their personal resources. It was also found that weak personal resources were easily depleted and that those with weak resources were unlikely to receive help when they needed it most. Chronic illness has also been found to increase patients' anger and their anger, in turn, was found to anger and alienate potential supporters (Lane & Hobfoll, in press). Depression in response to illness, in contrast, was not found to alienate supporters, perhaps because the depression was seen as understandable given the individual's malady (Revenson & Majerovitz, 1990).

Furthermore, findings suggest that when a potential supporter shares the stressful experience, his or her own distress may be an obstacle to providing effective support (Hobfoll & London, 1986; Revenson & Majerovitz, 1990; Stephens, Crowther, Hobfoll, & Tennenbaum, 1990).

Support Providers, Relationships, and Sociocultural Factors and Support. Much less research has appeared concerning how provider variables, relationship variables, and sociocultural variables may affect support provision. Findings on these three variables have been rather intertwined, and to some extent they should be. Support providers are affected by the nature of their relationship with the support recipient and by the background sociocultural factors that broadly influence behavior in relationships.

Perhaps the firmest evidence on relationship factors that relate to support provision involves findings regarding intimacy. Intimate relationships are more likely to yield support than those that are more distant (Dunkel-Schetter & Skokan, 1990; Hobfoll & Lerman, 1988). When relationships are not so close, norms of social responsibility may be more important than relational qualities (Berkowitz, 1972). In close relations, in contrast, individuals may help because they feel as if the event is happening to them. The pain of the victim arouses empathy, on one hand, and guilt if one does not act, on the other hand (Carlson & Miller, 1987). Unfortunately, myths about coping and difficulty in providing support because the provider is anxious may interfere with successful support provision, even if it is intended (Wortman & Silver, 1987). Nevertheless, on the balance, support from more distant ties cannot compensate for a lack of support from intimate others (Brown & Harris, 1978; Coyne & Smith, 1991).

Conflict within a relationship, on the other hand, may contribute more to distress than to relief (Rook, 1984; Stephens, Kinney, Norris, & Ritchie, 1987). However, others have found that high levels of support can be beneficial, even when the relationship is conflicted (Barrera & Baca, 1990; Pagel, Erdly, & Becker, 1987). Clearly, more work will be necessary to disentangle how intimacy and conflict interact. Coyne & Smith (1991) emphasize that relationships are based on interdependence and, as such, are characterized by varying degrees and quality of caring. Helping, conflict, shared goals, and divergent goals are all part of a relationship and the unidimensional receipt or lack of support may be more stereotype than reality.

Unsolicited support may be even more difficult to study. This type of support may be a significant but subtle part of close relationships that is hidden in routine and mundane everyday interactions (Burleson, 1990; Leatham & Duck, 1990). Indeed, within marriage, support may be most effective when not noticed by the recipient (Bolger, DeLongis, Kessler, & Shilling, 1989). Though unsolicited support can be intrusive and unwelcome (Wortman & Dunkel-Schetter, 1979), it may involve less threat to esteem or competence and reflect a sensitive helper—often one who is more competent, committed, and knowledgeable. Indeed, unsolicited support may be the norm in well-functioning relationships (Eckenrode & Wethington, 1990).

Within relationships, the norms of support are affected by broader sociocultural norms, but there are only glimmers of empirical evidence on this issue (Antonucci et al., 1990; Dressler, 1985). One interesting avenue of sociocultural social support research involves the study of the interaction between support and nontraditional economic structures among economically disadvantaged groups, but again empirical knowledge in this area is still scanty (Jackson et al., 1990). How relationships fulfill social-economic interactions, however, has exciting potential for researchers.

Models of Social Support's Effect

Traditional Models. Despite its abundance during the last fifteen years, research on social support has had a remarkably narrow and simple focus. In his seminal paper, Cobb (1976) planted an apparently simple idea that grew into a peculiar blend of hypothesis and dogma over a decade—that is, social support acts to protect individuals from stressful conditions. This buffer hypothesis was particularly appealing for two reasons: (1) it promised to revive the flagging research on life events, which had generated consistent but small results, and (2) it suggested an attractive foundation for preventive social interventions.

The buffer model was generally interpreted to mean that the association between stressful experiences and psychological distress would be diminished under conditions of greater social support. A second model, termed *direct effect,* was recognized somewhat reluctantly. This model stated that social support had effects on well-being independently of the stress process. As we shall see, these general models hide almost as much as they reveal.

At first glance, it would seem straightforward to test these models. They seem to imply, respectively, the interaction and main effects of social support and stress on well-being. Yet, for a decade, conceptual confusion, methodological problems, and inappropriate statistical tests were quite common (see discussions by Dooley, 1985; Kessler & McLeod, 1985; Wheaton, 1985). Consequently, reviewers of the literature reached very different conclusions. Empirical evidence for the model was seen as adequate (Gottlieb, 1981; House, 1981), dubious (Heller & Swindle, 1983; Lin, 1986), or mixed (Cohen & Wills, 1985; Kessler & McLeod, 1985; Mitchell, Billings, & Moos, 1982). Many factors contributed to inconsistencies in findings and in reviewers' conclusions, but these are not easily resolved (Vaux, 1988a).

Two thorough and widely cited reviews warrant further discussion. Cohen and Wills (1985) attempted to account for inconsistencies in findings through a modified buffer hypothesis proposed by Cohen and McKay (1984), who proposed that support will buffer stress when it matches the functional coping requirements of the stressor. Support measures were classified on two dimensions: specific versus global and structural versus functional. The classification of measures was problematic, the pattern of findings was not entirely in line with expectations, and post hoc arguments were necessary to explain exceptions. Nevertheless, consistent with the modified model, the majority of buffer effects were observed for functional support measures, particularly global functional measures. We will return to this issue later in the section on specificity models.

Kessler and McLeod (1985) conducted perhaps the most careful and systematic review of relevant literature to date, though limited to life event studies of community samples. Again, sorting of studies by type of support measure clarified inconsistencies. They found evidence of stress-buffering effects for emotional support and perceived availability of support measures (i.e., support appraisals), but not for measures of affiliative networks for which direct effects were observed in several strong studies. With respect to these direct effects, the reviewers note that, if robust, a large literature that they excluded (because support but not stress was examined) provides additional evidence.

While these reviews help to bring some order to a complex literature, several problems persist. First, why do some support measures show buffer effects? The modified buffer model probably is relevant, but it does not provide a clear and simple answer. Second, most studies (all in the latter review) involved heterogeneous life events as stressors and thus were a test of a pervasive buffer effect; they may tell us little about how support relates to particular stressors (Hobfoll, 1985). Third, many of these carefully selected studies involved poor support measures. A third of those in the Kessler and McLeod (1985) review contained three or fewer items. Fourth, most of these studies were published in or before 1983. Vaux (1988a) examined another nineteen studies specifically with the solutions of these reviews in mind. The pattern of findings was not consistent with the conclusions of either review. Moreover, in several studies, buffer effects were observed not only for just some support measures, but also for just some subsamples, or for just some measures of distress. These and the issues raised later all converge to suggest the same conclusion: the general buffer model may have outlived its usefulness. Future progress will require greater specification of stressors, support, process, and context, consistent with the more elaborate ecological model proposed in this paper.

Quantitative reviews present some of this confusion quite starkly (Schwarzer & Leppin, 1989, 1991). For example, Schwarzer and Leppin (1991) reviewed 80 studies on support and physical health and found correlations that varied from $-.43$ to $+.17$ (they did not examine stress-support interactions). While physical symptoms were negatively related to social integration ($-.07$), emotional support ($-.11$), instrumental support ($-.18$), and support satisfaction ($-.25$), they were positively related to enacted support ($+.12$). Findings for psychological distress are likely to be comparable and point out the urgent need for differentiated constructs and measures. Further, more elaborate models are needed to account for these varied associations.

Alternative Models.   The buffer and direct models hardly exhaust the possible relationships between stress, support, and distress. Barrera (1986), Lin (1986), Vaux (1988a), and Wheaton (1985) have discussed a variety of other models. Most relevant here are models that do not assume independence of stress and support—an implicit assumption of the buffer and direct models as typically tested. An alternative buffer model, termed counteractive (Lin, 1986) or suppressor (Wheaton, 1985), suggests that, in addition to their direct positive effect on distress, stressors also lead to support that in turn diminishes distress. Though rarely tested, this model is consistent with COR theory's resource activation notions (see also Billings & Moos, 1981; Eckenrode & Wethington, 1990), and such support mobilization can explain the otherwise paradoxical positive associations between support and distress noted in the preceding meta-analysis.

A proactive buffer model, termed suppressant (Lin, 1986) or stress-deterrent (Wheaton, 1985), suggests that, in addition to a negative effect on distress, support diminishes stressors that lead to distress. Consistent with this effect, Lin, Dean, and Ensel (1986) found that strong tie support was associated with fewer negative life events a year later. In short, support might buffer by mediating or preventing stressors as well as by moderating their effects, yet these models have received little attention. Moreover, the various models are not mutually exclusive and may coexist. It is by no means clear that we can disentangle them with passive research designs, whether cross-sectional or longitudinal.

Specificity Models.   A serious problem with research on the buffer model is that it tells us little about some extremely important questions: when, why, and how does support influence the stress process? Specificity models begin to address these issues, particularly that of when buffering will occur.

One of the first explicit statements of a specificity model was by Cohen and McKay (1984). They argued that particular stressors elicit different coping demands and will be buffered only by support that meets those demands. Specifically, stressors arising from resource deficits, subjective interpretations of events, internal attributions of inadequacy, and loss of important relationships should be buffered, respectively, by tangible, appraisal, esteem, and belonging support. The notion of a match between stressors and support was also evident in efforts to distinguish different forms or modes of support (Barrera & Ainlay, 1983; Vaux, Riedel, & Stewart, 1987). Vaux (1988a) drew a macabre image to highlight this point; Consider a man who stands at the edge of a lake to offer sympathy to a drowning friend and who, later, provides the man's grieving widow with a rope. The fact that such incompetent help is rare spotlights the point that support must match the stressor in some sense.

Specificity models face some major challenges. They must develop relevant taxonomies of stressors and of support and develop hypotheses regarding appropriateness of fit. Early studies found very limited evidence for specificity regardless of whether appropriate forms of support were identified theoretically (Tetzloff & Barrera, 1987) or empirically through subjective (Cohen & Hoberman, 1983) or normative ratings (Rosenberg & Vaux, 1987).

The most extensive and systematic work on specificity models has been conducted by Cutrona and her colleagues (Cutrona, 1990; Cutrona & Russell, 1990). In her model of optimal matching, two dimensions of stressors are viewed as important: controllability and life domain. It is predicted that controllable stressors are best matched by instrumental support (especially information), but also by esteem support (to sustain efficacy), whereas uncontrollable stressors allow only the management of emotion and thus are best matched by emotional support (cf. Thoits, 1986; Vaux & Burda, 1981; see also subsequently). Based in part of COR theory (Hobfoll, 1988), the life domain dimension is broken down into losses involving assets, relationships, achievement, and social roles. Optimal support for these losses involve, respectively, tangible support, attachment or network support (for loss of intimate or more casual relationships), esteem support, and network support.

Empirical support for optimal matching is considerable, if post hoc. Cutrona and Russell (1990) reviewed almost forty studies that examined particular components of support in the context of a wide range of specific life events. In about two-thirds of the studies, significant associations were observed between well-being and the appropriate form of support, with controllability predictions faring better than life domain predictions. This review also highlighted some complications, however. First, many events (e.g., bereavement, unemployment) are complex; in COR terms, they involve losses in several domains. As a result, no single form of support is optimal, and several modes showed a relationship to well-being. Second, the importance of various losses related to a complex life event will be a function of personal factors (e.g., commitments) and contextual factors (e.g., available alternatives) in ways that might be difficult to predict. Third, although distinct forms of support can be conceptualized (Barrera & Ainlay, 1983) and measured (Cutrona & Russell, 1987; Vaux, Riedel, & Stewart, 1987), most measures of support make these distinctions poorly, if at all (for a review of measures, see Vaux, 1988a). Despite these difficulties, this impressive review and the model underlying it will set the stage for future theory and research on stress buffering.

Specificity models go a long way toward countering the simplicity of early buffer models and take into account distinctions between different forms and functions of social support. As such, they help us better understand when buffer effects might occur. But they, too, leave questions of mechanism unanswered—specifically, how support might affect the stress process. Several authors have outlined possible mechanisms (Thoits, 1986; Vaux, 1988a; Vaux & Burda, 1981).

Briefly, support might prevent the occurrence of stressors, inoculate against them, facilitate accurate appraisal of an ambiguous encounter, facilitate reappraisal as an encounter unfolds, act directly to meet the demand, suggest coping options and sustain efficacy, or facilitate recovery of emotional equilibrium through either emotional support or diversion (see Vaux, 1988a, for a more complete discussion). Though plausible, empirical evidence for these paths is slim because they rarely have been subject to explicit empirical testing (see Billings & Moos, 1982; Gore, 1978; Rosenberg & Vaux, 1987; Slack & Vaux, 1988).

Clearly the latitude for influence through these various pathways is shaped by numerous features of the context, which include the nature of the stressor (e.g., its complexity and ambiguity), whether it is a threat or an already sustained loss, and the degree to which a threat is controllable or inevitable. Other factors include the resources available to the individual and the support network, the network orientation of the individual, the responsiveness of the network, and the timing of assistance as the encounter unfolds.

To summarize, the global buffer and direct models have been the focus of a voluminous empirical literature on social support. Yet they have serious limitations, both as a guide to research and as a context within which to synthesize findings. Clearly we need more complex models that address the fit of support to stressor-related needs, that examine the process by which support influences the stress process, and that take context into account. These more complex models seem to follow more directly from our ecological COR model, and from Cutrona's fit mode, than from the simpler notions that set the stage for the testing of the direct versus the stress-buffering effect.

A brief list and description of measures of social support are appended at the end of this chapter.

Fitting Resources, Not Fit of Resources

The importance of the fit of resources to need has been raised by a number of social support theorists (Cohen & Wills, 1985; Cutrona & Russell, 1990; Hobfoll, 1985). The basic concept of fit is that when resources match need, then the resources will aid stress resistance. Conversely, when resources do not match need and the fit is poor, resources will fail to aid stress resistance.

Based on the ecological model we have presented and COR theory, we would modify fit theory radically. The concept of fit, as it is now used, is passive—that is, it is assumed that if individuals possess the right resources, that there will be fit. In contrast, fit can be seen as a verb, such that those who can fit their resources to their need will experience positive outcomes.

If individuals have the task of fitting resources to need, a number of very different predictions follow. First, as COR theory predicts, those rich in resources will have an array of resources from which to choose. They can select, adjust, and modify resources to a large extent. For example, a healthy intimate significant other will be more likely than a weak or troubled one to help when needed and when called for. Having a few confidants may similarly translate into the ability to choose and select the kind of support demanded by different situations (Hirsch, 1980). Where personal resources are more appropriate, those who possess them may call on these first and only turn to others for support when they truly require it (Hobfoll et al., 1990).

Those who are weak in resources, in contrast, are less likely to possess the resource that could be best fit to need. Furthermore, if the resources they possess are of poor quality, even the resource that might meet need might not meet it well. Moreover, since stressors are seen as depleting resources, these individuals would be increasingly less likely to have the appropriate resource. In such cases, we would predict that individuals will still try to cope, but will use poorer and poorer strategies for doing so. Considerable research suggests that hopelessness follows this "grasping at straws" stage (Abramson, Seligman, & Teasdale, 1978), but, while there is much work on hopelessness, little work has investigated this probably more common intermediate stage of coping (i.e.., grasping at straws). In this regard, we suggest that investigators study how those weak in resources nevertheless manage to cope as well as they do. In a sense, we can learn more from how a poor single mother lives reasonably than by how a rich man lives well.

It should also be emphasized that certain resources are more robust than others. Hobfoll (1988) and Thoits (1986) suggest that sense of mastery may be an overarching resource that regulates the appropriate use of other resources, including social support. Emotional support also may be a key social resource, because a broad array of events results in loss of self-esteem and sense of mastery. Emotional support seems critical in rebuilding feelings of competency, control, and well-being (Cutrona & Russell, 1990; Vaux, 1988a). Antonovsky (1979) referred to such grand resources as general resistance resources, and those who possess these may have the key that fits many diverse situational demands. Further, since resources tend to lead to other resources, these grand resources will be possessed along with a chain of other valuable resources.

CONCLUSIONS

Social support will continue to be an exciting area of research. Future work, however, will need to focus on the process of social support, how social support interacts with different aspects of the self and the environment, and the limitations of social support's contribution. Social support is important not only because it is a link to mental and physical health, but because the establishment and maintenance of close ties is an important aspect of well-being.

Research will gain insights by examining the waxing and waning of social support during periods of acute and chronic stress. Rather than a static picture of social support, these investigations can lead us to a living picture of social support. We must come to know how and when it succeeds, when it disappoints and frustrates, and when it causes further grief and despair. What we must accept as given is that people are players in the stress and social support process; the view of people as passive victims or mere reactors to stress has been passed by.

MEASURES OF SOCIAL SUPPORT

The following is a list of measures of social support with brief descriptions. These instruments vary dramatically in length, complexity, conceptual base, and available reliability and validity data. For a more complete discussion see Vaux (1988).

Support Network Resources

SOCIAL NETWORK QUESTIONNAIRE (SNQ). Hirsch, 1979. Designed to yield data on the size and structure (especially density and boundary density) of the social network.

SOCIAL RELATIONSHIP SCALE (SRS). McFarlane, Neale, Norman, Roy, & Streiner, 1981. Designed to assess the size and helpfulness of networks providing support (specifically, discussing problems, or guidance support) in each of six potentially stressful areas: home and family, work, money and finances, personal and social, health, and society in general.

SOCIAL SUPPORT QUESTIONNAIRE (SSQ). Sarason, Levine, Basham, & Sarason, 1983. Designed to assess support resources and appraisals across a range of situations; specifically, it provides data on support network size and support satisfaction.

SOCIAL SUPPORT NETWORK INTERVIEW (SSNI). Fischer, 1982. Developed as part of a large community survey of social exchange and support networks, it provides data on counseling, companionship, and practical help (cf. advise/guidance, socializing, and practical assistance).

ARIZONA SOCIAL SUPPORT INTERVIEW SCHEDULE (ASSIS). Barrera, 1981. Developed to assess network resources with respect to six modes of support: material aid, physical assistance, intimate interaction, guidance, feedback, and social participation. Focuses on the size of this network, the size of the conflicted network, the need for support, and satisfaction with level of support.

SOCIAL SUPPORT RESOURCES (SSR). Vaux, 1982. Designed to assess networks providing five modes of support (emotional, socializing, practical, financial, and advice/guidance) and to yield data on the structure, composition, and relationship quality of these networks (both total and mode-specific).

Supportive Behavior

INVENTORY OF SOCIALLY SUPPORTIVE BEHAVIOR (ISSB). Barrera, Sandler, & Ramsay, 1981. Designed to assess six modes of enacted supportive behavior; reports of actual assistance are provided.

SOCIAL SUPPORT BEHAVIORS (SSB). Vaux, Riedel, & Stewart, 1987. Designed to assess five modes of available supportive behavior: emotional, socializing, practical assistance, financial assistance, and advice/guidance. Yields total and mode-specific scores, and an enacted behavior version is available.

Support Appraisals

ASSIS. Described previously, this measure also includes ratings of whether each of six modes of support provided by the network was insufficient, excessive, or optimal.

SSR. Described previously, this measure also includes satisfaction ratings for each of five modes of support.

SRS. McFarlane, et al., 1981; McFarlane, Norman, Streiner, & Roy, 1983. An integral part of the SRS, described previously, is appraisals of the helpfulness or unhelpfulness of network support in relation to six life domains.

DAILY INTERACTION RATING FORM (DIRF). Hirsch, 1979, 1980. Used with the SNQ, participants list network members with whom they have interacted during the day, note the duration of interactions, and rate their (dis)satisfaction with the interactions in terms of five modes of support: cognitive guidance, social reinforcement, tangible assistance, socializing, and emotional support.

SSQ. Described previously, this measure includes ratings of satisfaction with support in twenty-seven situations, yielding the SSQ-S score.

PERCEIVED SOCIAL SUPPORT (PSS). Procidano & Heller, 1983. Designed to assess the extent to which an individual perceives that family and friends fulfill needs for support, information, and feedback.

FAMILY RELATIONSHIP INDEX (FRI). Holahan & Moos, 1981, 1982. Combines three scales from the Family Environment Scales: cohesion—the degree to which family members are helpful and supportive of each other; expressiveness—the extent to which family members are encouraged to act openly and to express their feelings directly; and conflict—the extent to which the open expression of anger, aggression, and other conflictual interactions are characteristic of the family.

WORK RELATIONSHIP INDEX (WRI). Holahan & Moos, 1981, 1982. Combines three scales from the Work Environment Scales: involvement—the extent to which employees are concerned and committed to their jobs; peer cohesion—the extent to which employees are friendly to, and supportive of, one another; and supervisor support—the extent to which management is supportive of employees and encourages supportiveness among employees.

INTERPERSONAL SUPPORT EVALUATION LIST (ISEL). Cohen & Hoberman, 1983; Cohen, Mermelstein, Kamarck, & Hoberman 1985. Designed (as a population-specific measure for college samples) to assess the perceived availability of four separate functions of support: self-esteem—perceived availability of a positive comparison when comparing one self to others; appraisal—perceived availability of someone to talk to about problems; belongingness—perceived availability of people one can do things with; and tangible—perceived availability of material aid. Yields separate scores for these functions.

PROVISION OF SOCIAL RELATIONS (PSR). Turner, 1981; Turner, Frankel, & Levin, 1983. Based explicitly on Weiss's (1974) conceptualization of the provisions of social relationships, it was designed to assess five such provisions. Total, family, and friend scales are scored.

SOCIAL PROVISIONS SCALE (SPS). Russell & Cutrona, 1984. Designed to assess six social provisions: attachment, integration, opportunity for nurturance, reassurance of worth, reliable alliance, and guidance. Yields separate scores for these provisions.

REVISED KAPLAN SCALE (RKS). Turner, 1981; Turner, Frankel, & Levin, 1983. Developed from an earlier measure that used a novel vignette method. Scores reflecting love/esteem and network involvement are derived.

SOCIAL SUPPORT APPRAISALS. Vaux, Phillips, Holly, Thomson, Williams & Stewart, 1986. Based explicitly on Cobb's (1976) conceptualization of social support and designed to measure the degree to which a person feels cared for, respected, and involved.

Help Seeking and Support Mobilization

EFFICACY OF HELP SEEKING (EHS). Eckenrode, 1983. Designed to assess beliefs in the benefits versus the costs of seeking and accepting help from others.

NETWORK ORIENTATION SCALE (NOS). Vaux, Burda, & Stewart, 1986. Twenty items assessing a set of expectations or beliefs that it is inadvisable, impossible, useless, or potentially dangerous to draw on network resources.

REFERENCES

ABRANSOM, L., SELIGMAN, M. E. P., & TEASDALE, J. P. Learned helplessness in humans: Critique and reformulation. *Journal of Abnormal Psychology,* 1978, *87,* 49–74.

ANTONOVSKY, A. *Health, stress, and coping.* San Francisco: Jossey-Bass, 1979.

ANTONUCCI, T. C., FUHRER, R., & JACKSON, J. S. Social support and reciprocity: A cross-ethnic and cross-national perspective. *Journal of Social and Personal Relationships,* 1990, *7,* 519–530.

BARBEE A. P., GULLEY, M. R., & CUNNINGHAM, M. R. Support seeking in personal relationships. *Journal of Social and Personal Relationships,* 1990, *7,* 531–540.

BARRERA, M., JR. Social support in the adjustment of pregnant adolescents: Assessment issues. In B. H. Gottlieb (ed.), *Social networks and social support.* Beverly Hills, CA: Sage, 1981.

————. Distinctions between social support concepts, measures, and models. *American Journal of Community Psychology,* 1986, *14,* 413–445.

BARRERA, M., JR. & AINLAY, S. L. The structure of social support: A conceptual and empirical analysis. *Journal of Community Psychology,* 1983, *11,* 133–143.

BARRERA, M., JR., & BACA, L. M. Recipient reactions to social support: Contributions of enacted support, conflicted support and network orientation. *Journal of Social and Personal Relationships,* 1990, *7,* 541–551.

BARRERA, M., JR., SANDLER, I. N., & RAMSAY, T. B. Preliminary development of a scale of social support: Studies on college students. *American Journal of Community Psychology,* 1981, *9,* 435–447.

BERKOWITZ, L. Social norms, feelings, and other factors affecting helping and altruism. In L. Berkowitz (ed.), *Advances in experimental social psychology.* Vol. 6. New York: Academic Press, 1972.

BILLINGS, A. G., & MOOS, R. H. The role of coping responses and social resources in attenuating the stress of life events. *Journal of Behavioral Medicine,* 1981, *4,* 139–157.

————. Social support and functioning among community and clinical groups: A panel model. *Journal of Behavioral Medicine,* 1982, *5,* 295–311.

BOLGER, N., DeLONGIS, A., KESSLER, R. C., & SCHILLING, E. A. Effects of daily stress on negative mood. *Journal of Personality and Social Psychology,* 1989, *57,* 808–818.

BOWLBY, J. *Attachment and loss. Vol. 1: Attachment.* London: Hogarth Press, 1969.

BROWN, G. W., & HARRIS, T. *The social origins of depression: The study of psychiatric disorder in women.* New York: Free Press, 1978.

BURDA, P. C., JR., VAUX, A., & SCHILL, T. Social support resources: Variations across sex and sex-role. *Personality and Social Psychology Bulletin,* 1984, *10,* 119–126.

BURKE, R. J., & WEIR, T. Sex differences in adolescent life stress, social support, and well-being. *Journal of Psychology,* 1978, *98,* 277–288.

BURLESON, B. R. Comforting as social support: Relational consequences of supportive behaviors. In S. Duck (ed.), *Personal relationships and social support.* Beverly Hills, CA: Sage, 1990.

CALDWELL, R. A., & REINHART, M. A. The relationships of personality to individual differences in the use of type and source of social support. *Journal of Social and Clinical Psychology,* 1988, *6,* 140–146.

CAPLAN, G. *Support systems and community mental health: Lectures on concept development.* New York: Behavioral Publications, 1974.

CARLSON, M., & MILLER, N. Explanation of the relation between negative mood and helping. *Psychological Bulletin,* 1987, *102,* 91–108.

CASSEL, J. Psychosocial processes and "stress": Theoretical formulations. *International Journal of Health Services,* 1974, *4,* 471–482.

COBB, S. Social support as a moderator of life stress. *Psychosomatic Medicine,* 1976, *38,* 300–314.

COHEN, S., & HOBERMAN, H. M. Positive events and social supports as buffers of life change stress. *Journal of Applied Social Psychology,* 1983, *13,* 99–125.

COHEN, S., & McKAY, G. Social support, stress, and the buffering hypothesis: A theoretical analysis. In A. Baum, S. E. Taylor, & J. E. Singer (eds.), *Handbook of Psychology and Health. Vol. 4: Social psychological aspects of health.* Hillsdale, NJ: Lawrence Erlbaum, 1984.

COHEN, S., MERMELSTEIN, R., KAMARCK, T., & HOBERMAN, H. Measuring the functional components of social support. In I. G. Sarason & B. R. Sarason (eds.), *Social support: Theory, research, and application.* The Hague: Martinus Nijhoff, 1985.

COHEN, S., & WILLS, T. A. Stress, social support, and the buffering hypothesis. *Psychological Bulletin,* 1985, *98,* 310–357.

COOK, T. D., & CAMBELL, D. T. *Quasi-experimentation: Design and analysis issues for field settings.* Boston: Houghton Mifflin, 1979.

COYNE, J. C., & BOLGER, N. Doing without social support as an explanatory concept. *Journal of Social and Clinical Psychology,* 1990, *9,* 148–158.

COYNE, J. C., ELLARD, J. H., & SMITH, D. A. F. Social support, interdependence, and the dilemmas of helping. In B. R. Sarason, I. G. Sarason, & G. R. Pierce (eds.), *Social support: An interactional view.* New York: Wiley, 1990.

COYNE, J. C., & SMITH, D. A. F. Couples coping with a myocardial infarction: A contextual perspective on wives' distress. *Journal of Personality and Social Psychology,* 1991, *61,* 404–412.

CUTRONA, C. E. Objective determinants of perceived social support. *Journal of Personality and Social Psychology,* 1986, *50,* 349–355.

————. Stress and social support: In search of optimal matching. *Journal of Social and Clinical Psychology,* 1990, *9,* 3–14.

CUTRONA, C. E., & RUSSELL, D. The provisions of social relationships and adaptation to stress. In W. H. Jones & D. Perlman (eds.), *Advances in personal relationships.* Greenwich, CT: JAI Press, 1987.

————. Type of social support and specific stress: Toward a theory of optimal matching. In B. R. Sarason, I. G. Sarason, & G. R. Pierce (eds.), *Social support: An interactional view.* New York: Wiley, 1990.

DOOLEY, D. Causal inferences in the study of social support. In S. Cohen & S. L. Syme (eds.), *Social support and health.* Orlando, FL: Academic Press, 1985.

DRESSLER, W. W. Extended family relationships, social support and mental health in a southern black community. *Journal of Health and Social Behavior,* 1985, *26,* 39–48.

DUNKEL-SCHETTER, C., FOLKMAN, S., & LAZARUS, R. S. Social support received in stressful situations. *Journal of Personality and Social Psychology,* 1987, *53,* 71–80.

DUNKEL-SCHETTER, C., & SKOKAN, L. A. Determinants of social support provision in personal relationships. *Journal of Social and Personal Relationships,* 1990, *7,* 437–450.

ECKENRODE, S. The mobilization of social supports: Some individual constraints. *American Journal of Community Psychology,* 1983, *11,* 509–520.

ECKENRODE, J., & WETHINGTON, E. The process and outcome of mobilizing social support. In S. Duck (ed.), *Personal relationships and social support.* Beverly Hills, CA: Sage, 1990.

FISCHER, S. C. *To dwell among friends.* Chicago: University of Chicago Press, 1982.

GORE, S. The effect of social support in moderating the health consequences of unemployment. *Journal of Health and Social Behavior,* 1978, *19,* 157–165.

GOTLIB, I. H., & HOOLEY, J. M. Depression and marital distress: Current status and future directions. In S. Duck, D. F. Hay, S. E. Hobfoll, W. Ickes, & B. M. Montgomery (eds.) *Handbook of personal relationships: Theory, research and interventions.* Chichester, Eng.: Wiley, 1988.

GOTTLIEB, B. H. Social networks and social support in community mental health. In B. H. Gottlieb (ed.), *Social networks and social support.* Beverly Hills, CA: Sage, 1981.

GURTMAN, M. B. Depression and the response of others: Re-evaluating the evaluation. *Journal of Abnormal Psychology,* 1986, *95,* 99–101.

HANSSON, R. O., JONES, W. H., & CARPENTER, B. N. Relationship competence and social support. In P. Shaver (ed.), *Review of personality and social psychology.* Vol. 5. Beverly Hills, CA: Sage, 1984.

HELLER, K., & SWINDLE, R. W. Social networks, perceived support, and coping with stress. In R. D. Felner, L. A. Jason, J. N. Moritsugu, & S. S. Farber (eds.), *Preventive psychology.* New York: Pergamon Press, 1983.

HILL, C. A. Seeking emotional support: The influence of affiliative need and partner warmth. *Journal of Personality and Social Psychology,* 1991, *60,* 112–121.

HIRSCH, B. J. Psychological dimensions of social networks: A multimethod analysis. *American Journal of Community Psychology,* 1979, *7,* 263–277.

————. Natural support systems and coping with major life changes. *American Journal of Community Psychology,* 1980, *8,* 159–172.

HIRSCH, B. J., & REISCHL, T. M. Social networks and developmental psychopathology: A comparison of adolescent children of a depressed, arthritic, or normal parent. *Journal of Abnormal Psychology,* 1985, *94,* 272–281.

HOBFOLL, S. E. Limitations of social support in the stress process. In I. G. Sarason & B. R. Sarason (eds.), *Social support: Theory, research, and applications.* The Hague: Martinus Nijhoff, 1985.

————. *Stress, social support, and women.* Washington, DC: Hemisphere, 1986.

————. *The ecology of stress.* New York: Hemisphere, 1988.

————. Conservation of resources: A new attempt at conceptualizing stress. *American Psychologist,* 1989, *44,* 513–524.

————. Social support. Special issue of the *Journal of Social and Personal Relationships,* 1990, *7.*

————. Gender differences in stress reactions: Women filling the gaps. *Psychology and Health,* 1991, *5,* 95–109.

HOBFOLL, S. E., FREEDY, J., LANE, C., & GELLER, P. Conservation of social resources: Social support resource theory. *Journal of Social and Personal Relationships,* 1990, *7,* 465–478.

HOBFOLL, S. E., & LERMAN, M. Personal relationships, personal attributes, and stress resistance: Mothers' reactions to their child's illness. *American Journal of Community Psychology,* 1988, *16,* 565–589.

HOBFOLL, S. E., & LONDON, P. The relationship of self-concept and social support to emotional distress among women during war. *Journal of Social and Clinical Psychology,* 1986, *4,* 189–203.

HOBFOLL, S. E., NADLER, A., & LEIBERMAN, J. Satisfaction with social support during crisis: Intimacy and self-esteem as critical determinants. *Journal of Personality and Social Psychology,* 1986, *51,* 296–304.

HOBFOLL, S. E., SHOHAM, S. B., & RITTER, C. Women's satisfaction with social support and their receipt of aid. *Journal of Personality and Social Psychology,* 1991, *61,* 332–341.

HOBFOLL, S. E., & STOKES, J. P. The processes and mechanics of social support. In S. Duck, D. F. Hay, S. E. Hobfoll, W. Ickes, & B. M. Montgomery (eds.), *Handbook of personal relationships: Theory, research and interventions.* Chichester, Eng.: Wiley, 1988.

HOLAHAN, C. J., & MOOS, R. H. Social support and psychological distress: A longitudinal analysis. *Journal of Abnormal Psychology,* 1981, *90,* 365–370.

————. Social support and adjustment: Predictive benefits of social climate indices. *American Journal of Community Psychology,* 1982, *10,* 403–413.

————. Life stressors, personal and social resources, and depression: A 4-year structural model. *Journal of Abnormal Psychology,* 1991, *100,* 31–38.

HOUSE, J. S. *Work stress and social support.* Reading, MA: Addison-Wesley, 1981.

JACKSON, J. S., ANTONUCCI, T. C., & GIBSON, R. C. Social relations, productive activities, and coping with stress in late life. In M. A. P. Stephens, J. H. Crowther, S. E. Hobfoll, & D. L. Tennenbaum (eds.), *Stress and coping in later-life families.* New York: Hemisphere, 1990.

KESSLER, R. C., & McLEOD, J. D. Social support and mental health in community samples. In S. Cohen & S. L. Syme (eds.), *Social support and health.* Orlando, FL: Academic Press, 1985.

KESSLER, R. C., McLEOD, J. D., & WETHINGTON, E. The costs of caring: A perspective on the relationship between sex and psychological distress. In I. G. Sarason & B. R. Sarason (eds.), *Social support: Theory, research, and applications.* The Hague: Martinus Nijhoff, 1985.

KOBASA, S. C., MADDI, S. R., & COURINGTON, S. Personality and constitution as mediators in the stress-illness relationship. *Journal of Health and Social Behavior,* 1981, *22,* 368-378.

KOBASA, S. C., & PUCCETTI, M. C. Personality and social resources in stress resistance. *Journal of Personality and Social Psychology,* 1983, *45,* 839-850.

LA GAIPA, J. J. The negative effects of informal support systems. In S. Duck (ed.), *Personal relationships and social support.* Beverly Hills, CA: Sage, 1990.

LANE, C. & HOBFOLL, S. E. How loss affects anger and alienates potential supporters. *Journal of Consulting and Clinical Psychology,* in press.

LAZARUS, R. S., & FOLKMAN, S. *Stress, appraisal, and coping.* New York: Springer, 1984.

LEATHAM, G., & DUCK S. Conversations with friends and the dynamics of social support. In S. Duck (ed.), *Personal relationships and social support.* Beverly Hills, CA: Sage, 1990.

LEFCOURT, H. M., MARTIN, R. A., & SELAH, W. E. Locus of control and social support: Interactive moderators of stress. *Journal of Personality and Social Psychology,* 1984, *47,* 378-389.

LIN, N. Modeling the effects of social support. In N. Lin, A. Dean, & W. Ensel (eds.), *Social support, life events, and depression.* Orlando, FL: Academic Press, 1986.

LIN, N., DEAN, A., & ENSEL, W. *Social support, life events, and depression.* Orlando, FL: Academic Press, 1986.

LOOTENS, A. L., & STRUBE, M. J. *Daily hassles, social support, and psychological well-being.* Paper presented at the annual meeting of the American Psychological Association, Los Angeles, California, August, 1985.

MCFARLANE, A. H., NEALE, K. A., NORMAN, G. R., ROY, R. G., & STREINER, D. L. Methodological issues in developing a scale to measure social-support. *Schizophrenia Bulletin,* 1981, *7,* 90-100.

MCFARLANE, A. H., NORMAN, G. R., STREINER, D. L., & ROY, R. J. The process of social stress: Stable, reciprocal, and mediating relationships. *Journal of Health and Social Behavior,* 1983, *14,* 160-173.

MITCHELL, R. E. Social networks of psychiatric clients: The personal and environmental context. *American Journal of Community Psychology,* 1982, *10,* 387-432.

MITCHELL, R. E., BILLINGS, A. G., & MOOS, R. H. Social support and well-being: Implications for prevention programs. *Journal of Primary Prevention,* 1982, *3,* 77-97.

PAGEL, M. D., ERDLY. W. W., & BECKER, J. Social networks: We get by with (and in spite of) a little help from our friends. *Journal of Personality and Social Psychology,* 1987, *53,* 793-804.

PROCIDANO, M., & HELLER, K. Measures of perceived social support from friends and from family: Three validational studies. *American Journal of Community Psychology,* 1983, *11,* 1-24.

RABKIN, J. G., & STREUNING, E. L. Life events, stress, and illness. *Science,* 1976, *194,* 1013-1020.

REIS, H. T. The role of intimacy in interpersonal relations. *Journal of Social and Clinical Psychology,* 1990, *9,* 15-30.

REVENSON T. A., & MAJEROVITZ, S. D. Spouses' support provision to chronically ill patients. *Journal of Social and Personal Relationships,* 1990, *7,* 575-586.

RILEY., & ECKENRODE, J. Social ties: Subgroup differences in costs and benefits. *Journal of Personality and Social Psychology,* 1986, *51,* 770-778.

ROOK, K. S. The negative side of social interaction: Impact on psychological well-being. *Journal of Personality and Social Psychology,* 1984, *46,* 1097-1108.

————. Parallels in the study of social support and social strain. *Journal of Social and Clinical Psychology,* 1990, *9,* 118-132.

ROSENBERG, M. R., & VAUX, A. *Social support: Mechanisms of action and stressor-support specificity.* Unpublished paper, Southern Illinois University, Carbondale, IL, 1987.

RUSSELL, D., & CUTRONA, D. *The provisions of social relationships and adaptation to stress.* Paper presented at the American Psychological Association meeting, Toronto, August 1984.

SANDLER, I. N., & LAKEY, B. Locus of control as a stress moderator: The role of control perceptions and social support. *American Journal of Community Psychology,* 1982, *10,* 65–80.

SARASON, B. R., SARASON, I. G., & PIERCE, G. R. (eds.), *Social support: An interactional view.* New York: Wiley, 1990.

SARASON, I. G., LEVINE, H. M., BASHAM, R. B., & SARASON, B. R. Assessing social support: The Social Support Questionnaire. *Journal of Personality and Social Psychology,* 1983, *44,* 127–139.

SARASON, I. G., & SARASON, B. R. (eds.), *Social support: Theory, research and applications:* The Hague: Martinus Nijhoff, 1985.

SARASON, I. G., SARASON, B. R., & SHEARIN, E. N. Social support as an individual difference variable: Its stability, origins, and relational aspects. *Journal of Personality and Social Psychology,* 1986, *50,* 845–855.

SCHONPFLUG, W. Goal directed behavior as a source of stress: Psychological origins and consequences of inefficiency. In M. Frese & J. Sabini (eds.), *The concept of action in psychology.* Hillsdale, NJ: Lawrence Erlbaum, 1985.

SCHWARZ, S. H. Normative influences on altruism. In L. Berkowitz (ed.), *Advances in experimental social psychology.* Vol. 10. New York: Academic Press, 1977.

SCHWARZER, R., & LEPPIN, A. Social support and health: A meta-analysis. *Psychology and Health: An International Journal,* 1989, *3,* 1–15.

————. Social support and health: A theoretical and empirical overview. *Journal of Social and Personal Relationships,* 1991, *8,* 99–127.

SCHWARZER, R., & WEINER, B. Stigma controllability and coping as predictors of emotions and social support. *Journal of Social and Personal Relationships,* 1991, *8,* 133–140.

SHUMAKER, S. A., & BROWNELL, A. Toward a theory of social support: Closing the conceptual gaps. *Journal of Social Issues,* 1984, *40,* 11–36.

SLACK, D., & VAUX, A. Undesirable life events and depression: The role of event appraisals and social support. *Journal of Social and Clinical Psychology,* 1988, *7,* 290–296.

STAUB, E. Helping a distressed person: Social, personality and stimulus determinants. In L. Berkowitz (ed.), *Advances in experimental social psychology.* Vol. 7. New York: Academic Press, 1974.

STEPHENS, M. A. P., CROWTHER, J. H., HOBFOLL, S. E., & TENNENBAUM, D. L. *Stress and coping in later-life families.* New York: Hemisphere, 1990.

STEPHENS, M. A. P., KINNEY, J. M., NORRIS, V. K., & RITCHIE, S. W. Social networks as assets and liabilities in recovery from stroke by geriatric patients. *Psychology and Aging,* 1987, *2,* 125–129.

STOKES, J. P. Predicting satisfaction with social support from social network structure. *American Journal of Community Psychology,* 1983, *11,* 141–152.

————. The relation of social network and individual difference variables to loneliness. *Journal of Personality and Social Psychology,* 1985, *48,* 981–990.

STOKES, J. P., & WILSON, D. G. The inventory of socially supportive behaviors: Dimensionality, prediction, and gender differences. *American Journal of Community Psychology,* 1984, *12,* 53–69.

SWANN, W. B., JR., & BROWN, J. D. From self to health: Self-verification and identity disruption. In B. R. Sarason, I. G. Sarason, & G. R. Pierce (eds.), *Social support: An interactional view.* New York: Wiley, 1990.

TETZLOFF, C. E., & BARRERA, M., JR. Divorcing mothers and social support: Testing the specificity of buffering effects. *American Journal of Community Psychology,* 1987, *15,* 19–34.

THOITS, P. A. Conceptual, methodological, and theoretical problems in studying social support as a buffer against life stress. *Journal of Health and Social Behavior,* 1982, *23,* 145–159.

————. Social support as coping assistance. *Journal of Consulting and Clinical Psychology,* 1986, *54,* 416–423.

TOLSDORF, C. C. Social networks, support, and coping: An exploratory study. *Family Process,* 1976, *15,* 407–417.

TURNER, R. J. Experienced social support as a contingency in emotional well-being. *Journal of Health and Social Behavior,* 1981, *22,* 357–367.

TURNER, R. J., FRANKEL, B. G., & LEVIN, D. M. Social support: Conceptualization, measurement, and implications for mental health. In J. R. Greenley (ed.), *Research in community and mental health.* Greenwich, CT: JAI Press, 1983.

VAUX, A. *Psychological, health, and behavioral consequences of adolescent life stress and social support.* Paper presented at the Western Psychological Association meeting, Los Angeles, April 1981.

————. *Measures of three levels of social support: Resources, behavior, and feelings.* Unpublished manuscript, 1982.

————. *Social support: Theory, research, and intervention.* New York: Praeger, 1988. (a)

————. Social and personal factors in loneliness. *Journal of Social and Clinical Psychology,* 1988, *6,* 462–471. (b)

VAUX, A., & ATHANASSOPOULOU, M. Social support appraisals and network resources. *Journal of Community Psychology,* 1987, *15,* 537–556.

VAUX, A., & BURDA, P. *Mechanisms of social support.* Paper presented at the Midwestern Eco-Community Psychology meeting, Chicago, 1981.

VAUX, A., BURDA, P., JR., & STEWART, D. Orientation towards utilizing support resources. *Journal of Community Psychology,* 1986, *14,* 159–170.

VAUX, A., & HARRISON, D. Support network characteristics associated with support satisfaction and perceived support. *American Journal of Community Psychology,* 1985, *13,* 245–268.

VAUX, A., PHILLIPS, J., HOLLY, L., THOMSON, B., WILLIAMS, D., & STEWART, D. The Social Support Appraisals (SSA) Scale: Studies of reliability and validity. *American Journal of Community Psychology,* 1986, *14,* 195–220.

VAUX, A., RIEDEL S., & STEWART, D. Modes of social support: The Social Support Behaviors (SSB) Scale. *American Journal of Community Psychology,* 1987, *15,* 209–237.

VAUX, A., & WOOD, J. Social support resources, behavior, and appraisals: A path analysis. *Social Behavior and Personality: An International Journal,* 1987, *15,* 107–111.

WEISS, R. S. The provisions of social relationships. In Z. Rubin (ed.), *Doing unto others.* Englewood Cliffs, NJ: Prentice-Hall, 1974.

WHEATON, B. Models for the stress-buffering functions of coping resources. *Journal of Health and Social Behavior,* 1985, *26,* 352–364.

WILCOX, B. Social support in adjusting to marital disruption: A network analysis. In B. H. Gottlieb (ed.), *Social networks and social support.* Beverly Hills, CA: Sage, 1981.

WILLS, T. A. Multiple networks and substance use. *Journal of Social and Clinical Psychology,* 1990, *9,* 78–90.

WORTMAN, C. B., & DUNKEL-SCHETTER, C. A. Interpersonal relationships and cancer: A theoretical analysis. *Journal of Social Issues,* 1979, *35,* 120–155.

WORTMAN, C. B., & SILVER, R. C. Coping with irrevocable loss. In G. R. Vanden Bos & B. K. Bryant (eds.), *Cataclysms, crises and catastrophes: Psychology in action.* Washington, DC: American Psychological Association, 1987.

37

A Constructivist Narrative Perspective on Stress and Coping: Stress Inoculation Applications

Donald Meichenbaum   **Deborah Fitzpatrick**

The need to make our life coherent, to make a story out of it, is probably so basic that we are unaware of its importance. (Fuller, 1979: 224)

The initial draft of this chapter was written in August, 1991, as Hurricane Bob bore down on Cape Cod, Massachusetts. This tranquil, cozy holiday and retirement setting was bracing itself for the frightening onslaught and resultant aftermath of a potentially devastating storm. As a precaution, the authorities had evacuated residents from low-lying areas.

I (the first author) had just completed a week-long workshop on the cape on the use of Stress Inoculation Training (SIT) as a preventive and treatment approach. Now a firsthand opportunity had presented itself for me and my family to practice all that I had taught. Because we had taken all the necessary precautions and were "hunkered down" in a rented house for the duration of the storm, this seemed like a good occasion to put together my notes on stress and coping. Little did I realize that by nightfall I would be attempting to complete my reflections by candlelight, as all electrical power to the cape was lost—in some areas for over a week.

The next morning, the immensity of the destruction from Hurricane Bob emerged. The cape had suffered over $1 billion in damage. The ferocity of the storm had ripped 100-year-old trees from the ground, toppled houses, and lifted 40-foot boats from their moorings and deposited them in people's yards. Fortunately, because of adequate warning there were few instances of personal injury and death. It soon became apparent from news reports that Hurricane Bob had not only shattered people's property (home, businesses, possessions), but also their dreams and beliefs.

Such stressful natural disasters, however, are not unusual. For instance, between 1974 and 1980 there were 37 major natural catastrophies in the United States, and in 1979–1980 alone, some 688,000 persons in the United States received emergency care following a disaster (Ursano & Fullerton, 1990). It has been estimated that 6% to 8% of the population of North America (or nearly 17 million people) annually will be exposed to traumatic, dangerous, sudden, and overwhelming natural disasters. Another indicator of the widespread occurrence of natural disasters comes from a survey in one Kentucky community where 39% of an elderly population had survived a natural disaster during their lifetime, 12% had survived a serious fire, and 15% described exposure to similarly terrifying events (Wilson & Raphael, in press). Although such traumatic events are often short-lived, their effects can last for years, often creating secondary changes such as personal, social, and financial disruptions. Such traumatic events can also have negative implications on the loss of both important aspects of the survivors' past and their future. As Tait and Silver (1989) observe, the occurrence of a negative stressful event may preclude the realization of dreams, opportunities, or aspirations in which individuals may be heavily invested, as well as rob them of their past.

To the litany of natural disasters we could add the traumas that are produced by human intention, such as wars, accidents, and various forms of victimization (abuse, torture, crimes) that have even more devastating psychological effects than do impersonal stressors (Epstein, 1990). Traumatic events, personal loss, as well as cumulative daily hassles can each take a physical and psychological toll, as documented by many authors (Baum, 1990; Lazarus & Cohen, 1977; Lazarus & Folkman, 1984; Ursin, Baade, & Levine, 1978). But not all individuals who are exposed to stressors suffer long-term negative consequences.

This chapter provides a constructivist narrative perspective to help explain these individual differences and to further explicate how distressed individuals cope with stress. Moreover, the constructivist narrative perspective provides a framework for understanding the multitude of interventions that laypeople and health care providers—whether natural social support agents, clergy, or mental health workers—use to help individuals cope more effectively with stress. More specifically, following a brief discussion of the constructivist and narrative perspectives, we will use these perspectives to interpret the chronic effects of stress, explain naturally occurring efforts at coping, and describe treatment interventions.

THE CONSTRUCTIONIST NARRATIVE PERSPECTIVE

The Constructivist Perspective

The constructivist perspective is founded on the idea that humans actively construct their personal realities and create their own representational models of the world. There is a long tradition of philosophers and psychologists who have argued that the paradigms, models, assumptive worlds, and schemas that individuals actively create determine and, in some instances, constrain how they perceive reality. The constructivist perspective finds root in the philosophical writings of Immanuel Kant, Ernst Cassirer, and Nelson Goodman, and in the psychological writings of Wilhelm Wundt, Alfred Adler, George Kelly, Jean Piaget, Viktor Frankl, and Jerome Frank. More recently, the constructivist perspective has been advocated by Epstein and Erskine (1983), Mahoney and Lyddon (1988), McCann and Perlman (1990), Neimeyer and Feixas (1990), and Meichenbaum (1992). Common to each of these proponents is the tenet that the human mind is a product of constructive symbolic activity and that reality is a product of the personal meanings that individuals create. Individuals do not merely respond to events in and of themselves, but they respond to their interpretation of these events and to their perceived implications of these events. How individuals create such meanings and realities, how they construct their world view, is the subject of narrative psychology.

Narrative Psychology

Narrative psychology is the study of the stories we tell about ourselves to others, as well as to ourselves. Authors such as Bruner (1986, 1990), Sarbin (1986), Schafer (1981), and Spence (1984), each highlight the observation that individuals construct meaning, offer explanations, and provide narrative accounts of events. As Meichenbaum (1977) has argued, individuals tend to engage in internal and external dialogues that fabricate meaning when the automacity of their acts and scripted routines is interrupted, and when readjustment is required—especially when their physical or psychological well-being is judged to be at stake. A prime occasion for narrative construction, or what Bruner (1990) calls "meaning making," is the exposure to stressful events that call for readjustment, as in the case of Hurricane Bob. Even near misses can provide the occasion for narrative construction, as this chapter attests.

It is proposed that how individuals and groups engage in such narrative constructions is critical to their adjustment to stressful events. Moreover, it is proposed that a major mechanism of psychological change that follows from various psychotherapeutic interventions is that of what Shafer (1981) called "narrative repair." An examination of some of the immediate and long-term effects of exposure to stressful events illustrates the role that constructive narratives play in the adjustment process.

THE EFFECTS OF STRESS

Exposure to stressful life events not only has physiological effects that influence catabolic processes, as documented by Mason (1975), Selye (1976) and others, but it also has psychological effects. A number of investigators (Epstein, 1990; Horowitz, 1979; Janoff-Bulman, 1985; 1990; Lecky, 1945; Marris, 1986; Silver & Wortman, 1980; and Wilson, 1980) have reported that exposure to traumatic stressful events can threaten, destabilize, invalidate, and even shatter an individual's fundamental beliefs and implicit assumptions about him- or herself and about the world. The basic tacit rules or implicit beliefs that guide a person's life can be challenged and/or nullified by stressful events. These rules include:

1. the belief in one's own invulnerability (i.e., maintaining an optimistic bias by underestimating the probability that major negative events would be likely to happen)
2. the belief that events are predictable, controllable and just
3. the belief that the world is benign and benevolent
4. the belief that life is meaningful
5. the belief in the worth of oneself

As Epstein (1990) observed, "threatening events invalidate at a deep experiential level the most fundamental beliefs in a personal theory of reality . . . [moreover], recovery is contingent upon building a new assumptive world that can assimilate the victimization experience in an adaptive manner" (p. 80).

What Epstein is referring to is the narrative that individuals construct in making sense of and reframing their experience with stressful events. In the instance of Hurricane Bob, what appeared to be secure and benign at one moment was capriciously destroyed the next moment. The hurricane not only shattered houses, but survivors' beliefs. As Janoff-Bulman (1990) observed, "post traumatic stress following victimization is largely due to the shattering of basic assumptions victims hold about themselves and their world, whether the stressful event is a life-threatening disease, criminal assault, technological or natural disaster" (p. 1). Tait and Silver (1989) add to this list such major negative life events as incest; the accidental, suicidal or homicidal death of a loved one; loss of a limb; forced relocation due to urban renewal; and a variety of natural or human-caused disasters that go beyond the range of common experience. Each of these stressful events shares a common experience of a loss, either literal (e.g., a person, environment, relationship) and/or symbolic (e.g., loss of goals, hopes, plans, possibilities). These events constitute the loss of one's past and future and of one's beliefs, assumptions, and expectations about oneself, others, and the world.

When such beliefs are radically altered, they often leave individuals feeling weak, helpless, demoralized, hopeless, and, in some instances, also responsible and culpable. These affective states influence and are, in turn, influenced by the narratives individuals construct.

There are many examples in the stress literature of how individuals continually struggle to make sense (that is, construct narratives) of what has happened and why. Silver, Boon, and Stones (1983) report that incest victims often continue to wonder painfully for many years why an adult took advantage of them as they continue to find the perpetrator's behavior incomprehensible. Baumeister, Stillwell, and Wotman (1990) and McAdams (1985) have highlighted the intimate link between the personal narrative recollections that individuals offer and their readjustment. For example, whether individuals define their roles in their narrative as that of victim or perpetrator influences the content of their narrative and the nature of their distress.

Individuals not only offer narratives of what happened, but they also provide causal explanations (attributions) and accompanying justifications. The research on attribution of blame indicates that the content of a survivor's narrative influences the quality of adaptation to stressful events. When an individual's causal explanation for his or her response to a stressful life event is attributed to a behavioral characteristic that conveys the illusion of control, when it conveys personal responsibility and avoids blaming others, better adjustment is evident. As Baum, O'Keefe, and Davidson (1990) observed, after reviewing research on breast cancer patients, accident victims, children with diabetes, and residents living near Three Mile Island, "those individuals who assume some personal responsibility and avoided blaming others for their misfortune exhibited better adjustments than those who do not assume responsibility or who focus blame on others" (p. 1645).

Baum et al. (1990) also raise one other set of findings that have important implications for the present constructivist narrative perspective on stress and coping. They observe that while most individuals who experience natural disasters, combat, and other major stressors, cope adequately, a percentage of the population (estimated to be between 20% to 40% depending on the nature of the stressor) experiences continual chronic distress. Their review suggests that those individuals who report unwanted or uncontrollable thoughts about past stressors, intrusive imagery, and/or dreams, nightmares, and daydreams about past stressors exhibit the highest level of stress symptoms. Such instances of re-experiencing the stressful event, reliving the stressful event long after it has ended, result in the stressful event lasting longer. As Baum (1990) notes, the more frequent, vivid, uncontrolled, and intrusive such images and recollections of the stressor appear to be, the more chronic the stress reactions. For example, in Baum's (1990) data on Three Mile Island residents, the strength of the relationship between the level of chronic stress and the frequency and emotional intensity of experienced intrusions increased as the time since the initial stressor lengthened. Such intrusions tend to keep the stressful event alive, in a manner of speaking, as Baum conjectures.

While Baum (1990) attempts to explain the relationship between intrusive imagery and chronic stress in terms of conditioning and information-processing concepts, an alternative explanation derives from the constructivist narrative perspective. Intrusive imagery can be viewed as an attempt by an individual to make sense of or to construct meaning about a stressful event or to formulate a narrative account of what happened and why.

Tait and Silver (1989) have also reported on the narrative features of individuals' efforts to come to terms with major negative life events. Using interviews and questionnaires, they asked 45 individuals between the ages of 60 to 93 to report on the ongoing psychological effects of the most stressful or the "worst things" that had ever happened to them. The results indicated that the psychological impact of major life events persisted for many years for a significant proportion of their population. How the event was experienced and how individuals came to terms with the major stressful life event was more relevant to the psychological impact than was the event itself. As expected, people responded very differently to the same type of stressful events. Tait and Silver (1989) found that the experience of ruminations (i.e., intense, involuntary, intrusive thoughts, mental images, and memories) was correlated positively with both the degree of reported distress and with the level of negative affect, and inversely related to indexes of positive emotion. For many individuals, the past stressful event still had an "existence for them." As Tait and Silver (1989) summarize, "a persistent search for meaning was inversely related to psychological recovery and positively related to the occurrence of involuntary, intrusive, distressing event-related ruminations" (p. 355). Such a persistent search for meaning was often evident in the individuals' need to discuss with others the stressful events and their responses to them. This working through process reflects the survivors' attempts to put their experiences into words and to validate their reactions. Such discussions can also foster useful insight, nurture a sense of personal control, and serve as a way of clarifying and conveying coping needs (Tait & Silver, 1989). In terms of the present perspective, such discussions also provide occasions for individuals to construct meaningful narratives. But when such discussions and narrative construction do not lead to a resolution and the search for meaning persists, recovery does not readily follow. Moreover, the stress literature indicates that not all narrative accounts are equally effective in fostering adaptation.

NARRATIVE FEATURES OF COPING

Investigators who have examined the cognitive and affective components of coping have each highlighted different aspects of the complex narrative that follows exposure to major negative stressful life events. Some researchers have focused on appraisal processes (Lazarus & Folkman, 1984), social comparison processes (Wood, 1989), attributional processes (Janoff-Bulman & Frieze, 1983), and perceptions of personal control (Lefcourt, 1980). Other investigators have highlighted process variables such as optimistic biases (Scheier & Carver, 1987), positive illusions (Taylor & Brown, 1988), search for meaning (Tait & Silver, 1989; Thompson, 1985, 1991), and striving for coherence (Antononsky, 1979). A somewhat different tack was taken by Foa and Kozak (1986) and Rachman (1980), who highlighted the significance of the accompanying affect and emotional processing that contribute to and are elicited by specific narrative accounts.

Given the variety of stressful life events, the heterogeneity of distressed populations, and the complexity and dynamic changes for the stress response, it is little wonder that investigators would parse the coping narrative processes into different component parts. The present integrative approach highlights the need to bring these diverse features into a coherent narrative perspective.

An examination of the literature on coping with stress suggests that individuals and groups who have difficulty adjusting to major stressful life events will construct narratives that have the following features.[1] Distressed individuals tend to:

1. make unfavorable comparisons between life as it is and as it might have been had the distressed event not occurred
2. engage in comparisons between aspects of life after the stressful event versus how it was before, and also continually pine for what was lost
3. see themselves as victims, with little expectation or hope that things will change or improve
4. blame others for distress and fail to take on any personal responsibility
5. fail to find any meaning or significance in the stressful event
6. dwell on the negative implications of the stressful event
7. see themselves as continually at risk or vulnerable to future stressful events
8. feel unable to control the symptoms of distress (i.e., viewing intrusive images, nightmares, ruminations, psychic numbing, avoidant behaviors, hyperarousal, and exaggerated startle reactions as being uncontrollable and unpredictable)
9. remain vigilant to threats and obstacles

In examining this list of proposed narrative features, it is necessary to keep one important caveat in mind. Individuals who adjust more effectively to stressful life events may also, on some occasions, engage in similar narrative activities and experience distressing symptoms. After reviewing the literature on cognition and coping, Kendall (in press) has recently concluded, that it is not the absence of negative thinking per se, but rather the ratio of positive to negative thinking (2 to 1, respectively) that correlates with adaptive coping. In other words, what various coping efforts achieve is the reduction of negative thinking, or "maladaptive dysfunctional narratives." Kendall (in press) proposes that the "power of non-negative thinking" is a central feature of adaptive coping narratives. Baumeister (1989) has similarly argued that one's narrative should reflect an optional margin of illusion. As he notes, "it may be most adaptive to hold a view of self that is a little better than the truth—neither too inflated nor too accurate" (Baumeister, 1989: 184).

Thus, it is not the mere presence or absence of the negative narrative, but rather the frequency, timing, accompanying affect, meaning, and significance attached to stress symptoms and reactions that most significantly influence the adjustment process. It is what survivors say to themselves and others about their intrusive thoughts, ruminations, and nightmares that figures most prominently in the adjustment process.

In contrast to individuals experiencing difficulty coping, those who are coping more effectively develop meaningful and acceptable interpretations for stressful events by integrating them into coherent, stable, and adaptive conceptual frameworks that provide a source of predictability and control. Those who cope more adequately are likely to find or construct positive meaning for the stressful events. As we will see, health care providers help clients construct such coherent frameworks in order to reframe their perceptions of their stressful experiences and their reactions to them. Illustrative of these adaptive processes are the findings by Taylor, Wood, and Lichtman (1983) and Thompson (1991), who found that those individuals who adapt more effectively find and focus upon positive aspects or beneficial side effects of their stressful experience (e.g., how the stressful event brought family closer together, elicited support and caring from relatives and friends, made one more aware of the precariousness of life, helped them "find God," etc.).

A major constructive technique in formulating such adaptive narratives is the use of social comparison processes in which distressed individuals convince others, as well as themselves, that things could be worse. As Taylor et al. (1983) have enumerated, these social comparison processes may take several forms including:

1. comparing oneself with others who are less fortunate or who are not doing as well, thereby conveying a pride in one's own ability to handle a difficult situation
2. creating hypothetical worst-world scenarios of what might have happened
3. imagining a worse alternative or possible outcome, thus bolstering feelings of being fortunate, even under distressing circumstances
4. manufacturing normative standards of adjustment (e.g., constructing a scenario as to how most people would cope) in order to make one's own adjustment appear more acceptable or exceptional

Other narrative techniques are available to survivors of stressful experiences as they begin to script or rescript their reactions. Like a good storyteller, survivors can redefine what they expect or want from a given situation, and/or they can adopt a stance of resigned acceptance in the form of a fatalistic philosophy that such stress is a natural byproduct of life. The narrator may also selectively focus his or her attention on one aspect of the stressful event in order to view it in a more favorable light. The narrator can also choose to forget or not attend to specific negative events by simply putting them out of his or her mind. Clearly, some stressful situations are more amenable to these attentional and cognitive narrative maneuvers than others.

It is proposed that how individuals go about constructing narrative accounts influences their ability to cope with their distress. The following sections of this chapter illustrates some specific examples of such narrative constructions.

Naturally Occurring Examples of Narrative Constructions

An example of how individuals fabricate an understanding of stressful life events and how they bolster their coping efforts is reflected in the widely held practice of using religious beliefs and religious rituals as a means of coping. Pargament (1990) has reported that 42% to 62% of people who have emotional problems resulting from stressful events first turn to clergy for counsel. In North America, 50% of individuals indicated that religious beliefs were important to their coping efforts, while only 15% indicated that religious beliefs had little or no significance in how they coped with stress (Pargament et al. 1990).

Religious coping may take various forms, including turning to God as a basis of trust, faith, engaging in prayer, confession, turning to clergy or to a congregation for support, and focusing on the world to come. As Pargament (1990) found, religious belief, faith, and rituals:

1. make stressful events more bearable by providing a meaningful, coherent explanation and orderliness to events in the universe
2. provide a source of hope and comfort, as well as established guidelines on how to handle stressful events
3. nurture a sense of belonging as by promoting identity and a sense of intimacy and support with both God and with the religious community.

In short, religion and other forms of spirituality, provide the frame of reference or literary genre in which to construct a narrative story line that helps individuals understand, predict, and control their reactions to stressful events (Ochberg, 1991).

Quite often such religious narrative can be positive and aid the coping process (e.g., when individuals believe in a just, benevolent God whom they experience as a supportive partner in the coping process). The following items, taken from Pargament et al.'s (1990) Religious Coping Activities Scale, illustrate the narrative manner in which distressed religious individuals reframe and rescript stressful events:

1. I trusted that God would not let anything terrible happen to me.
2. I realized that God was trying to strengthen me.
3. I realized that I didn't have to suffer because Jesus suffered for me.
4. I took control over what I could, and I gave the rest up to God.
5. My faith showed me different ways to handle the problem.
6. I used my faith to help me decide how to cope with the situation.

The endorsement of such items reflects the spiritually based narrative that some distressed individuals employ. While in many instances individuals automatically use religious or spiritual rituals to cope, such forms of coping are not limited to the religious domain. Visits to the site of a stressful event such as North Vietnam, Auschwitz, Pearl Harbor, the Vietnam memorial in Washington, D.C., and the like are restorative attempts to rewrite the coping narrative. For some, dramatic steps are required to alter what they say to themselves and to others about what they have experienced and about their ability to cope.

Therapists can also aid in this narrative repair process. For example, torture victims have been asked to give testimony at real or mock trials condemning their perpetrators. Abused individuals have been asked to engage in an imagery reconstruction exercise in which they mentally revisit abusive incidents that occurred in their childhood and then distance themselves by acting as a reporter to convey what happened and how the abused child felt (Wilson & Raphael, in press). Foa and her colleagues (Foa, Rothbaum, Riggs, & Murdock, 1991) have asked rape victims to engage repeatedly in prolonged imagery exposure of the traumatic scenes. The rape victims are also asked to listen at home to audiotape recordings of their narrative accounts, to defuse or uncouple the intense affect that accompanies such storytelling.

Another example of abreactive narrative repair efforts was offered by Silver and Wilson (1988), who described the Native American purification practices that have been used to treat individuals who experience combat stress. An analysis of the Indian sweat lodge rituals, the purification ceremonies, and the spiritual exercises indicates the variety of ingenious procedures that native healers use to help veterans and their families (who also experience war stress). These religious rituals allow survivors to (1) recognize and validate their distressing experiences, (2) acknowledge combat realities, (3) redefine and reframe their stress, and (4) restructure the survivor's role in the family and in the community. These religious healing ceremonies convey a central message that, as a result of the combat experience, the veteran is to be recognized as holding uniquely acquired wisdom. As Silver and Wilson (1988) observe, "There is wisdom in survivorship worth salvaging" (p. 345). Even dreams and trance states are incorporated into the religious rituals, and they contribute to the rescripting process. When distress is severe and chronic, the ascribed healer's rescripting activities or narrative repair efforts need to be elaborate and different in kind in order to be perceived by the survivors as commensurate to the distress they feel.

In this regard, we are reminded of occasions when we treated chronic pain patients with muscular relaxation exercises, which in some instances proved to be insufficient to insure change. However, once we brought in a biofeedback machine as part of the relaxation training process, improvement emerged promptly. With biofeedback, we had introduced a form of treatment with all the aura of science that was truly commensurate with the patient's perception of the seriousness of the problem. This speculation was supported when we learned that one of the major changes that followed from biofeedback was not usually a change in the patient's physiological reactivity per se, but a reduction in the frequency of negative thinking (Turk & Rudy, in press; Turk, Meichenbaum, & Genest, 1983). Thus, once again, the "power of non-negative thinking" emerged as a plausible mediator of behavior change.

Whether distressed individuals spontaneously use religious beliefs, or participate in religious healing rituals, or receive specific treatments such as biofeedback, each procedure shares the common outcome of nurturing a different, more adaptive personal narrative. However, such narrative activity does not occur merely in one's head, nor does it always follow stressful events. There is a clear interpersonal plane in the development of such narrative construction. Individuals are active in selectively creating and eliciting from significant others the data that will be incorporated into their story lines. Moreover, individuals often engage in narrative construction prior to stressful events in order to inoculate themselves to possible stressful consequences. Like the Native American preparatory ceremonies and rites of passage prior to combat, individuals also engage in preparatory narrative constructions before confronting stressful encounters. We have been studying how these proactive constructive narrative efforts are employed as individuals cope with the everyday stress that accompanies receiving personal criticism.

A Constructivist Narrative Analysis of Coping with Criticism

Thus far, we have argued, first, that information about oneself is organized in terms of stories that individuals construct about themselves. Second, that negative stressful life events that call for major readjustment can significantly affect the basic assumptions and implicit belief systems that provide the framework and basis for our story making and narrative constructions. Third, how we rescript our stories or construct our narratives is an important determinant of how effectively we cope with stress. Fourth, the stress literature has begun to establish what are adaptive and maladaptive narratives.

But narrative reconstructive efforts are not limited to only major stressful events. Daily occurring stressors can also cause individuals to engage in narrative repair efforts. Most of the time we do not wish to alter our stories about ourselves because these stories usually cast us in a favorable light. However, when we are confronted with input that challenges our view of ourselves, that threatens our self-esteem—as in the instance of receiving unfavorable criticism—we engage in a number of narrative and behavioral maneuvers to preserve a benign view of ourselves and to maintain a positive self-image. In our laboratory, we have been studying how individuals engage in such narrative repairs.

Research on the effects of criticism indicates that it is an important area to examine. For instance, several investigators have reported that interpersonal criticism from family members and from one's spouse is a predictor of such clinical problems as relapse of depression (Beach & O'Leary, 1986, Hooley & Teasdale, 1989), relapse of schizophrenia (Vaugh & Leff, 1976), exacerbation of rheumatoid arthritis (Manne & Zautra, 1990), and proneness to initial episodes of depression (Blatt, Quinlan, Chevron, McDonald, & Zuroff, 1982).

We have developed a self-report scale to identify people who are particularly vulnerable to the negative effects of criticism and have examined how such individuals and their less susceptible counterparts cope with criticism (Fitzpatrick, 1991). Subjects were asked to identify "the worst criticism they had received within the last three months" and to indicate how they handled the effects of such criticism. An analysis of these answers revealed a broad array of constructive coping efforts. Table 37-1 summarizes the array of narrative repair efforts, which include interpersonal, behavioral, cognitive, and affective regulation coping procedures. The recipient of criticism is not passive in the story creation process; rather he or she often actively seeks information that questions the basis of the criticism, cognitively reframes it, or solicits information from others that reconfirms the recipient's original narrative account.

Interestingly, individuals also inoculate themselves to criticism before it is offered by preparing explanations, reasons, justifications, and excuses. For example, individuals who were performing in the theater indicated how they fortified themselves beforehand against possible criticism from a theater critic when they noted, "The theater critic never liked this playwright"; "He has an axe to grind with the director because his girlfriend was rejected for a role"; "Some of the best shows have had the worst reviews," and the like.

Probably you can think of a time when a manuscript, grant proposal, oral presentation, or interaction with a loved one resulted in what was judged to be unfair, unjustified, and unexpected criticism. What were the maneuvers that you used to handle such criticism? Compare your coping techniques to those listed in Table 37-1 and consider the multiple ways in which individuals can construct narrative explanations to cope with criticism, with some ways being potentially more adaptive than others.

How adaptive different constructive narrative maneuvers will be surely depends on the situation and varies over time and across cultural settings. In some instances, challenging and protesting the criticism may be most appropriate and effective, while on other occa-

TABLE 37-1
Constructive Narrative Responses to Criticism

When Presented with Criticism Individuals Can

Challenge the critic (verbally, physically)	Offer other explanations as the basis of the criticism (e.g., task too difficult, not
Protest or ignore criticism (verbally, physically)	enough time, not put in enough effort, coerced to respond)
Withdraw (physically, cognitively, affectively— e.g., "Forget it," "I won't think about it")	Engage in comparative processes contrasting present incident of criticism with:
Modify behavior in area of criticism or in some other area	how others would have behaved in a similar situation
Accept criticism—engage in problem solving, weighing positive features of criticism	worst world senario
Distract oneself (cognitively, behaviorally— e.g., engage in wishful thinking, sleep more, jog)	what could have happened
	how one has behaved in the past
Question the source of the criticism (e.g., person, test) as to validity, appropriateness, ulterior motives	one's own concurrent behavior
	less fortunate others
Seek information and/or solace from others, thus confirming one's self-worth	Make light of the criticism, use humor
	Vent and regulate emotions
See positive aspects in criticism (e.g., "At least he was interested in my work")	Use religious beliefs and rituals
Alter one's perspective (e.g., see criticism in larger perspective or assume critic's perspective)	Blame oneself, others, the situation, the institution, the world order ("It's a dog-eat-dog world"), fate
	Criticize oneself more, not let go of criticism
Reframe criticism as a "pocket of incompetence"	Experience and convey bodily complaints
	Engage in addictive behaviors (self-medication, smoking, consuming too much alcohol, or food)

sions withdrawal and engaging in social comparison may work best. Moreover, what works at one time may not prove most adaptive at a later time. Thus, the *transactional fit* between the demands of the situation and the appropriateness of the selected coping efforts will determine the adaptiveness of the constructive narrative response.

We have come to view these adaptive and maladaptive coping efforts in response to criticism from the metaphorical perspective of a jury trial or, to paraphrase Mickey Spillane's thriller, we all play the role of, "I, the Jury," in our own personal scripts. When confronted with criticism, an individual may take on the role of the defense attorney in the mental courtroom drama:

1. challenging the validity of the data (criticism)
2. questioning the credentials and ulterior motives of the critic
3. dismissing or reframing the criticism as unimportant
4. characterizing the criticism as being in an arena that the individual doesn't expect to do well in anyway, or what Taylor (1989) characterizes as "protective pockets of incompetence"
5. calling expert or character witnesses to mind or actually seeking them out
6. admitting fault, but highlighting extenuating circumstances by offering self-handicapping excuses (e.g., not feeling well, drank too much, felt coerced), thus denying responsibility
7. employing other narrative maneuvers listed in Table 37–1.

On the other hand, the individual who has been criticized can also act as prosecutor, offering self-criticism that is even more damning and ego-challenging than that offered by the critic. The expression "you are your own worst critic" conveys the prosecutorial flavor of these narrative constructions. Since the criticized individual is privy to information that the critic does not have, the criticized individual can selectively attend and retrieve information that challenges his or her self-worth, competence, and self-esteem, thus insuring a "guilty" verdict. We hypothesize that the depressive stacks the deck in favor of the individual's evidential prosecution.

One can extend this trial metaphor by noting that we each also act as judge and jury, weighing the evidence offered by both the defense attorney and the prosecutor. What are the rules of evidence we use to form a verdict, what about possible appeals we might conduct as we reconsider the event at a later time, what verdict do we offer, as well as what reprieve do we seek?

Weiner (1991) has also offered the metaphor of "the person as judge," who passes an emotional sentence based on the narrative causal ascriptions that he or she draws. As part of their constructive narrative, individuals seek a causal understanding of their world and make inferences about intentionality, responsibility, and blame. These ascriptions or causal explanations can influence how individuals cope with the stress of criticism. For individuals who have difficulty coping with criticism, some form of criticism inoculation training may prove helpful (see Kirschenbaum, Wittrock, Smith, & Monson, 1984). Guidelines of what should be included in such intervention programs can come from the work on self-handicapping, excuse theory, positive illusions, and how individuals reconcile events with their desired self-concepts (e.g., see Baumeister et al., 1990; Kihlstrom et al., 1988; Snyder, Higgins, & Stucky, 1985; Taylor, 1989; Weiner, Figueroa-Munoz, & Kakihara, 1991) and from the work on coping effectiveness training (Folkman et al., 1991) and on stress inoculation training (Epstein, 1983; Meichenbaum, 1985), to which we now turn our attention.

STRESS INOCULATION TRAINING AS A FORM
OF NARRATIVE RECONSTRUCTION

For the last twenty years, investigators have been working on the development and assessment of stress inoculation training (SIT) (see Meichenbaum, 1992). Since its initial introduction, there have been some 200 studies evaluating the relative effectiveness of SIT with a variety of distressed populations, including those who have:

1. difficulty adjusting to life transitions, such as unemployment or entering the military
2. to cope with medical or psychiatric illness and the accompanying treatments, such as surgery or hospitalization
3. difficulty dealing with anger, as in the case of handling criticism or dealing with anxiety in evaluative situations
4. stressful occupations, such as police officers, nurses, teachers, soldiers, and employees of other high-risk jobs

In each instance, the trainees have been provided with cognitive behavioral interventions on either a preventive or a treatment basis.

A major concept underlying SIT is *inoculation,* a term that has been used in medicine to describe immunization to illness and in social psychological research to explain such interventions as inoculating subjects against attitude change. In both areas, the central notion is that bolstering an individual's repertoire for coping with milder stressors can reduce the likelihood of maladaptive coping responses to later exposure to more intense stressors. Like medical inoculation, a person's resistance is enhanced by exposure to a stimulus strong enough to arouse defenses without being so powerful that it overcomes the individual.

In order to enhance an individual's or group's coping repertoire and to empower each person to use already existing coping skills, an overlapping three-phase SIT intervention approach is employed: (1) a reconceptualization phase, (2) a coping skills acquisition and rehearsal phase, and (3) an application and follow-through phase. Since the clinical features of SIT have already been described in detail (see Meichenbaum, 1985, 1992; Meichenbaum & Deffenbacher, 1988; Meichenbaum & Jaremko, 1983; Meichenbaum & Novaco, 1978; Turk, Meichenbaum, & Genest, 1983), the focus of this chapter is on illustrating the various treatment phases of SIT from a constructive narrative perspective.

The first phase of SIT is for the therapist or trainer to *establish a nurturant, compassionate, nonjudgmental set of conditions in which distressed clients can tell their story at their own pace.* A number of clinical techniques, including reflective listening, Socratic dialogue, sensitive probes, imagery reconstruction of stressful experiences, client self-monitoring, and the like, are employed to help the client(s) relate what happened and why from their perspective. Such exchanges help clients begin to make sense of their experiences, as they often search to determine not only what happened, but why it happened, who (if anyone) is to be held responsible, and what meaning does the stressful event have for them, their family, and their view of the world. Timely clinically sensitive questioning can also influence what clients attend to in their narrative account. For instance, Thompson (1985) suggests that clinicians ask the following questions about possible positive outcomes that might come from the client's stressful encounter.

Has anything positive come out of this experience for you?
Compared to others who have had this experience, do you feel you are in a better or worse situation?

Has anything that has happened made you feel particularly lucky or fortunate?
Was the stressful experience as bad as it could have been, or could it have been worse?
Is this experience as negative as you would have imagined before going through it?

Such probes not only solicit an individual's narrative, but they also begin the process of rescripting the survivor's account and collaboratively transforming the meaning of the stressful experience.

This type of narrative repair continues as the SIT trainer helps to *normalize* the distressed individual's reactions. As noted, it is not the symptoms per se but what individuals say to themselves about those symptoms that is important to the adaptive process. The therapist/trainer not only helps to validate the survivors' distressing reactions, but the therapist indicates that such symptoms are normal by saying something like "Given what you have been through, if you didn't have such stressful reactions, then I'd be really concerned." The therapist helps clients appreciate that the stress they experience is not abnormal and not a sign of "going crazy"; rather, their distressing symptoms reflect a normal reaction to a difficult situation. The trainer helps the clients reframe their stressful symptoms as a normal spontaneous reconstructive or natural rehabilitative adaptive process and not a sign of weakness or failure. Thus, such symptoms as intrusive images and nightmares are reframed as signaling both conscious (deliberate) and unconscious (automatic) efforts to work through stressful events and as ways to search for personal meaning. Emotional numbing, denial, and avoidance are characterized as ways individuals who have experienced traumatizing events dose or pace themselves so they can deal with only a limited amount of stress at a given time. As Epstein (1983) metaphorically characterizes this process, "the mind is taking a time out from overstimulation."

Based on the biographical data and narrative accounts, the rehabilitative process continues through the first phase as the therapist collaboratively develops a *reconceptualization* of the distress process with the client and significant others. Figley (1989) describes this reconceptualization process with veterans and their families as their formulating or constructing a "healing theory," or explanation, of what happened and why. Meichenbaum (1985) has described a similar reconceptualization process in which the SIT therapist helps distressed clients develop a more differentiated and integrated view of their stress by helping them break their complex distressing reactions into manageable component parts that go through different phases and that vary across situations and over time. By objectifying their stressful reactions, clients are made aware of low-intensity prodromal cues that can be viewed as reminders to use their coping efforts, rather than being viewed as harbingers of further distressful reactions. The reconstructive processes also provide what Frank (1987) describes as "articles of faith" that act as the basis for hope. The adoption of a reconstructive system also conveys the series of coping efforts that clients can employ that follow naturally from the specific new narrative.

There are two important features to recognize about this reconceptualization or new narrative reconstruction process. First, the scientific validity of the specific healing theory that is developed is less important than is its plausibility or credibility to the client. Secondly, this entire narrative repair effort is conducted in a collaborative inductive fashion and not imposed upon nor didactly taught to distressed individuals. As Meichenbaum (1977) has often noted, the therapist or trainer is at his or her therapeutic best when the client is one step ahead, offering the suggestion, the new narrative, that the therapist would otherwise offer. The distressed client must come to develop and accept a reconceptualization of the distress that he or she has helped cocreate.

In the second phase, the SIT trainer helps distressed clients rescript what they say to themselves by encouraging them to *break down or disaggregate their global stress descriptions into specific concrete, behaviorally prescriptive stressful situations.* As Folkman et al. (1991) observe, distressed individuals during appraisal training are taught the difference between changeable and unchangeable aspects of stressful situations and how to fit problem-focused and emotion-focused coping efforts with their perceived demands of the situation. In addition, during the skills phase, the SIT trainer teaches clients a variety of cognitive, behavioral, and interpersonal coping skills, if these coping skills are not already in the clients' repertoire. Clients are encouraged to practice these coping skills in vivo so they can collect "data" and review the results of their personal experiments as evidence to unfreeze or change the views of themselves and the world. In this way, SIT contributes to the clients' experiential rescripting of their narratives.

But the stories we tell ourselves and others can be readily put aside if stressors are unexpectedly re-experienced. If recovery is going to result in the building of a new assumptive world that assimilates victimization in an adaptive manner, it must be based on *experientially meaningful occurrences.* The third, critical feature of SIT is to have distressed clients gradually, at their own pace, perform personal experiments (e.g., engage in an activity that they would not otherwise think possible, test the limits on how they will respond by re-entering the stressful situation, and participate in graded exposure both in the training setting by means of imagery rehearsal, prolonged exposure imagery, behavioral rehearsal, and, gradually, in personal experiments performed in real situations). Such repetitive intense re-experiencing of stressful reactions will provide distressed clients with experientially meaningful data (as a result of their personal experiments) that they can take as evidence to unfreeze or alter their views of themselves and the world. Thus, distressed clients can learn that even though a particular situation may prove to be dangerous, they don't have to conclude that all of life is dangerous. As Epstein (1990) observed, "they can accept life with its imperfections." SIT helps clients view stressful events as problems to be solved rather than as a series of personal threats. But this significant reformulation may take repetitive trials, because clients (like scientists) do not readily accept data as evidence when it changes their hypotheses.

The SIT trainer does not leave this evidential step to chance. A central feature of SIT is to ensure that clients and distressed survivors *take credit for positive outcomes of their coping efforts*—i.e., engage in self-attributions that bolster a sense of personal efficacy (Bandura, 1986)—and do not "catastrophize"—i.e., engage in self-blaming negative narratives when things do not work out as planned. The SIT therapist not only provides the conditions for attribution training, but also encourages clients to share their new narrative with others (e.g., help others in a similar situation).

Finally, because not all experiments (personal or scientific) work, the SIT trainer *includes relapse prevention* in the training process (Marlatt & Gordon, 1985) as a way of anticipating high-risk situations, possible setbacks, obstacles, stressors. Clients/survivors are taught ways to anticipate, accept, and cope with such lapses so that they don't escalate into relapse. By anticipating and rehearsing for such possible lapses and setbacks, clients/survivors can be inoculated to possible future stressful events. By including relapse prevention into the training regimen, the clients/survivors' symptoms and stressful reactions are more likely to be perceived as predictable, controllable, and meaningful. Some clients/survivors may also benefit from training in specific coping skills (e.g., relaxation, parenting skills, assertiveness, and so forth).

In most instances, however, the narrative repair is the prime focus of SIT intervention.

Whatever specific coping techniques are taught, the therapist/trainer helps clients/survivors construct narratives that fit their particular present circumstances and that are coherent and adequate in capturing and explaining the individuals' personal difficulties. As Shafer (1981) indicates, therapy allows clients to retell their tale "in a way that allows them to understand the origins, meanings and significance of present difficulties and moreover to do so in a way that makes change conceivable and attainable" (p. 38). What matters most about this storytelling or narrative construction is not its "historical truthfulness," as Spence (1984) observes, but its "narrative truthfulness."

Hurricane Bob has subsided, but the survivor's efforts at narrative construction continue. The stories we tell ourselves and others about what happened and why will influence how we cope.

NOTE

1. We recognize that the determination of what constitutes effective and poor coping is complex. Effective modes of coping in the short term may not prove effective in the long term, and vice versa. Also, the relationship among various indexes of coping (e.g., self-report, physiological indexes, behavioral measures) vary over time; thus, it is impossible to derive one overall index of coping effectiveness. Nevertheless, for the sake of argument, we have drawn a general distinction between those who cope more effectively versus those who are less effective.

REFERENCES

ANTONOVSKY, A. *Health, stress and coping.* San Francisco: Jossey-Bass, 1979.

BANDURA, A. *Social foundations of thought and action: A social cognitive theory.* Englewood Cliffs, NJ.: Prentice Hall, 1986.

BAUM, A. Stress, intrusive imagery and chronic distress. *Health Psychology,* 1990, *9,* 653–675.

BAUM, A., O'KEEFE, M. K., & DAVIDSON, L. M. Acute stressors and chronic response: The case of traumatic stress. *Journal of Applied Social Psychology,* 1990, *20,* 1643–1654.

BAUMEISTER, R. F. The optimal margin of illusion. *Journal of Social and Clinical Psychology,* 1989, *8,* 176–189.

BAUMEISTER, R. F., STILWELL, A., & WOTMAN, S. R. Victim and perpetrator accounts of interpersonal conflict: Autobiographical narratives about anger. *Journal of Personality and Social Psychology,* 1990, *59,* 994–1005.

BEACH, S. R., & O'LEARY, K. D. 1986. The treatment of depression occurring in the context of marital discord. *Behavior Therapy,* 1986, *17,* 43–99.

BLATT, S. J., QUINLAN, D. M., CHEVRON, E. S., McDONALD, C., & ZUROFF, D. Dependence and self-criticism: Psychological dimensions of depression. *Journal of Consulting and Clinical Psychology,* 1982, *50,* 113–124.

BRUNER, J. S. *Actual minds, possible worlds.* Cambridge, MA: Harvard University Press, 1986.

————. *Acts of meaning.* Cambridge, MA: Harvard University Press, 1990.

CASSIRER, E. *The philosophy of symbolic forms. Vol. 3: The phenomenology of knowledge.* New Haven, CT: Yale University Press, 1987.

EPSTEIN S. Natural healing processes of the mind. Graded stress inoculation as an inherent coping mechanism. In D. Meichenbaum & M. Jaremko (eds.), *Stress prevention and management.* New York: Plenum Press, 1983.

————. The self-concept, the traumatic neurosis and the structure of personality. In D. Ozer, J. N. Healy, & A. J. Stewart (eds.), *Perspectives on personality.* Vol. 3. Greenwich, CT.: JAI Press, 1990.

EPSTEIN, S., & ERKSINE, N. The development of personal theories of reality. In D. Magnusson & V. Allen (eds.), *Human development: An interactional perspective.* New York: Academic Press, 1983.

FIGLEY, C. R. *Helping traumatized families.* San Francisco: Josey Bass, 1989.

FITZPATRICK, D. *Criticism as a vulnerability factor of depression.* Paper presented at Canadian Psychology Association, Calgary, Alberta, 1991.

FOA, E. B., & KOZAK, M. J. Emotional processing of fear: Exposure to corrective information. *Psychological Bulletin,* 1986, *99,* 20–35.

FOA, E. B., ROTHBAUM, B. O., RIGGS, D. S., & MURDOCK, T. B. *Treatment of PTSD in rape victims: A comparison between cognitive behavioral procedures and counseling.* Unpublished manuscript, Medical College of Pennsylvania, Philadelphia, 1991.

FOLKMAN, S., CHESNEY, M., McKUSIK, L., IRONSON, G., JOHNSON, D. S., & COATES, T. J. Translating coping theory into an intervention. In J. Eckenrode (ed.), *The social context of coping.* New York: Plenum Press, 1991.

FRANK, J. D. Psychotherapy, rhetoric, and hermeneutics: Implications for practice and research. *Psychotherapy,* 1987, *24,* 293–302.

FRANKL, V. E. *Man's search for meaning: An introduction to logotherapy.* New York: Washington Square Press, 1963.

FULLER, R. Teaching reading with stories versus cognitive hierarchy. *Journal of Suggestive-Accelerative Learning and Teaching,* 1979, *4,* 220–226.

GOODMAN, N. *Ways of worldmaking.* Indianapolis, IN: Hackett, 1978.

HOOLEY, J. M., & TEASDALE, J. D. Predictors of relapse in unipolar depressives: Expressed emotion, marital distress, and perceived criticism. *Journal of Abnormal Psychology,* 1989, *98,* 229–235.

HOROWITZ, M. *Stress response syndromes.* New York: Jason Aronson, 1979.

JANOFF-BULMAN, R. The aftermath of victimization: Rebuilding shattered assumptions. In C. R. Figley (ed.), *Trauma and its wake.* New York: Brunner/Mazel, 1985.

————. Understanding people in terms of their assumptive worlds. In D. J. Ozer, J. M. Healy, & A. J. Stewart (eds.), *Perspectives in personality: Self and emotion.* Greenwich, CT: JAI Press, 1990.

JANOFF-BULMAN, R., & FRIEZE, I. H. A theoretical perspective for understanding responses to victimization. *Journal of Social Issues,* 1983, *39,* 1–17.

KENDALL, P. Healthy thinking. *Behavior Theory,* in press.

KIHLSTROM, J. F., CANTOR, N., ALBRIGHT, J. S., CHEW, B. R., KLEIN, S. B., & NIEDENTHAL, P. M. Information processing and the study of the self. In L. Berkowitz (ed.), *Advances in experimental social psychology.* Vol. 21. San Diego, CA: Academic Press, 1988.

KIRSCHENBAUM, D. S., WITTROCK, D. A., SMITH, R. A., & MONSON, W. Criticism inoculation training: Concept in search of strategy. *Journal of Sport Psychology,* 1984, *6,* 77–93.

LAZARUS, R. S., & COHNE, J. B. Human behavior and the environment. In I. Ahman & J. F. Wohlwill (eds.), *Human behavior and the environment: Current theory and research.* Vol. 2. New York: Plenum Press, 1977.

LAZARUS, R. S., & FOLKMAN, S. *Stress, appraisal and coping.* New York: Springer, 1984.

LECKY, P. *Self-consistency: A theory of personality.* Long Island, NY: The Island Press, 1945.

LEFCOURT, H. Locus of control and coping with life events. In E. Staub (ed.), *Personality: Basic aspects and current research.* Englewood Cliffs, NJ: Prentice Hall, 1980.

MAHONEY, M. J. Psychotherapy and human change process. In J. H. Harvey & M. M. Parks (eds.), *Psychotherapy research and behavior change*. Washington, DC: APA Press, 1981.

MAHONEY, M. J., & LYDDON, W. J. Recent developments in cognitive approaches to counseling and psychotherapy. *The Counseling Psychologist*, 1988, *16*, 190–234.

MANNE, S. L., & ZAUTRA, A. J. Couples coping with chronic illness: Women with rheumatoid arthritis and their healthy husbands. *Journal of Behavioral Medicine*, 1990, *13*, 327–342.

MARLATT, G. A., & GORDON, J. R. *Relapse prevention: Maintenance strategies in the treatment of addictive behaviors*. New York: Guilford Press, 1985.

MARRIS, P. *Loss and change*. London: Routledge & Kegan Paul, 1986.

MASON, J. W. Emotion as reflected in patterns of endocrine integration. In L. Leve (ed.), *Emotions: Their parameters and measurement*. New York: Raven, 1975.

McADAMS, D. P. *Power, intimacy and life story: Personalogical inquiries into identity*. Homewood, IL: Dorsey, 1985.

McCANN, I. L., & PERLMAN, L. A. *Psychological trauma and the adult survivor*. New York: Brunner/Mazel, 1990.

MEICHENBAUM, D. *Cognitive behavior modification: An integrative approach*. New York: Plenum Press, 1977.

————. *Stress inoculation training*. New York: Pergamon Press, 1985.

————. Evolution of cognitive behavior therapy: Origins, tenets and clinical examples. In J. Zeig (ed.), *The evaluation of psychotherapy: II*. New York: Brunner/Mazel, 1990.

————. Stress inoculation training. A twenty year update. In R. L. Woolfolk & P. M. Lehrer (eds.), *Principles and practices of stress management*. New York: Guilford Press, 1992.

MEICHENBAUM, D., & DEFFENBACHER, J. L. Stress inoculation training. *Counseling Psychologist*, 1988, *16*, 69–90.

MEICHENBAUM, D., & JAREMKO, M. (eds.), *Stress prevention and management: A cognitive-behavioral approach*. New York: Plenum Press, 1983.

MEICHENBAUM, D., & NOVACO, R. Stress inoculation: A preventative approach. In C. Spielberger & I. Sarason (eds.), *Stress and anxiety*. Vol. 5. Washington, DC: Hemisphere, 1978.

NEIMEYER, R., & FEIXAS, G. Constructivist contributions to psychotherapy integration. *Journal of Integrative and Eclectic Psychotherapy*, 1990, *9*, 4–20.

OCHBERG, F. M. Post-traumatic therapy. *Psychotherapy*, 1991, *28*, 5–15.

PARGAMENT, K. I. God help me: Toward a theoretical framework of coping for the psychology of religion. *Research in the Social Scientific Study of Religion*, 1990, *2*, 195–224.

PARGAMENT, K. I., ENSING, D. S., FALGOUT, K., OLESN, H., REILLY, B., VAN HARTSMA, K., & WARREN, R. God help me (I): Religious coping efforts as predictors of the outcomes to significant negative life events. *American Journal of Community Psychology*, 1990, *18*, 793–824.

PARGAMENT, K. I., KENNELL, J., HATHAWAY, L., GREVENGOED, N., NEWMAN, J., & JONES, W. Religion and the problem-solving process: Three styles of coping. *Journal for the Scientific Study of Religion*, 1988, *27*, 90–104.

RACHMAN, S. Emotional processing. *Behaviour Research and Therapy*, 1980, *18*, 51–60.

SARBIN, T. R. (ed.), *Narrative psychology: The storied nature of human conduct*. New York: Praeger, 1986.

SCHAFER, R. *Retelling a life: Narration and dialogue in psychoanalysis*. New York: Basic Books, 1992.

SCHEIER, M. F., & CARVER, C. S. Dispositional optimism and well-being. *Journal of Personality*, 1987, *55*, 169–210.

SELYE, H. *The stress of life*. New York: McGraw Hill, 1976.

SILVER, R. C., BOON, C., & STONES, M. H. Searching for meaning in misfortune: Making sense of incest. *Journal of Social Issues,* 1983, *39,* 81–102.

SILVER, S. M., & WILSON, J. P. Native American healing and participation rituals for war stress. In J. P. Wilson, Z. Harel, & B. Kahana (eds.), *Human adaptation to external stress.* New York: Plenum Press, 1988.

SILVER, R. C., & WORTMAN, C. B. Coping with undesireable life events. In J. Garber & M. E. Seligman (eds.), *Human helplessness.* New York: Academic Press, 1980.

SNYDER, C. R., HIGGINS, R. L., & STUCKY, R. J. *Excuses.* New York: Wiley, 1985.

SPENCE, D. *Narrative truth and historical truth: Meaning and interpretation in psychoanalysis.* New York: Norton, 1984.

TAIT, R., & SILVER, R. C. Coming to terms with major negative life events. In J. S. Uleman & J. A. Bargh (eds.), *Unintended thought.* New York: Guilford Press, 1989.

TAYLOR, S. E. *Positive illusions.* New York: Basic Books, 1989.

TAYLOR, S. E., & BROWN, J. Illusion and well-being: A social psychological perspective on mental health. *Psychology Bulletin,* 1988, *103,* 193–210.

TAYLOR, S. E., WOOD, J. V., & LICHTMAN, R. R. It could be worse: Selective evaluation as a response to victimization. *Journal of Social Issues,* 1983, *39,* 19–40.

THOMPSON, S. C. Finding positive meaning in a stressful event and coping. *Basic and Applied Social Psychology,* 1985, *6,* 279–285.

————————. The search for meaning following a stroke. *Basic and Applied Social Psychology,* 1991, *12,* 81–96.

TURK, D., MEICHENBAUM, D., & GENEST, M. *Pain and behavioral medicine.* New York: Guilford Press, 1983.

TURK, D., & RUDY, T. E. Cognitive factors and persistent pain: A glimpse into Pandora's Box. *Cognitive Therapy and Research,* in press.

URSANO, R. J., & FULLERTON, C. Cognitive and behavioral responses to trauma. *Journal of Applied Social Psychology,* 1990, *20,* 1766–1775.

URSIN, H., BAADE, E., & LEVINE, S. *Psychology of stress.* New York: Academic Press, 1978.

VAUGH, C. E., & LEFF, J. P. The influences of family and social factors on the course of psychiatric illness. *British Journal of Psychiatry,* 1976, *129,* 125–135.

WEINER, B. Metaphors in motivation and attribution. *American Psychologist,* 1991, *46,* 921–930.

WEINER, B., FIGUEROA-MUNOZ, A., & KAKIHARA, C. The goals of excuses and communication strategies related to causal perceptions. *Personality Social Psychological Bulletin,* 1991, *17,* 4–13.

WILSON, J. P. Conflict, stress and growth: The effects of war on psychological development among Vietnam veterans. In C. Figley & S. Leveutan (eds.), *Strangers at home: Vietnam veterans since the war.* New York: Praeger Press, 1980.

WILSON, J., & RAPHAEL, B. (eds.), *Handbook of traumatic stress.* New York: Plenum Press, in press.

WOOD, J. V. Theory and research concerning social comparisons of personal attributes. *Psychological Bulletin,* 1989, *106,* 231–248.

38

A Coping/Rest Model of Relaxation and Stress Management

Johann M. Stoyva   John G. Carlson

INTRODUCTION

One's first reaction to the term *stress management* is likely to be one of skepticism: perhaps this is simply another of those shimmering illusions conjured up by the ebullient and indefatigable purveyors of pop psychology. Indeed, there are some genuine problems with the term. To begin with, quite a mix of techniques seems to be involved. Do these various techniques have anything in common? Do they possess any theoretical coherence? Moreover, the term *stress* itself is not the clearest of concepts. Nearly as large as life itself, it has been applied to virtually anything we don't like. One wonders, too, with something this amorphous, exactly how to go about managing it.

Despite these difficulties, we believe that stress management is a legitimate field of endeavor. It is an area taking shape in response to widely perceived needs and problems in our society and is evolving quickly. Consequently, an asessment of the area should be a useful undertaking. In this assessment, we first present a point of view regarding the term *stress,* with particular reference to the distinction between coping and rest. Second, we describe and briefly evaluate a number of procedures currently utilized in stress management.

An Oscillation Between Activity and Rest

Considering the nebulous character of the stress concept, it is useful to remind ourselves that a time-honored method for dealing intellectually with global and amorphous phenomena is the Cartesian strategy of first splitting them into components.[1] There is then a search for regularities in the behavior of the individual components. After some promising regularities have been identified, it becomes possible to begin experimenting with interventions, and combinations of interventions, likely to favorably alter the action (and interaction) of the components.

In the case of stress-related disorders, certain major components can be proposed. One of these is the coping/rest dimension. (Here it should be noted that the term *coping* refers to the active coping efforts of daily living.) In our view, the individual's reaction to stress can be regarded as consisting of two major phases: an active coping phase and a rest phase. Both are necessary, as is a fairly frequent alternation between the two phases. In fact, our daily existence can be thought of as a series of shifts from one mode to the other. (See Figure 38–1). Sometimes the shifts are difficult to accomplish—that is, the transition becomes sticky.

It can further be noted that this alternation between coping endeavors and rest is reflected at many different levels of behavioral and physiological organization. At the gross behavioral level, the fundamental and dramatic contrast between wakefulness and sleep may be noted, a shift that is especially clear in the higher forms of life such as birds and mammals. Waking is the time of active coping efforts; sleep is the time of behavioral quiescence.[2] A coping/rest alternation is also seen in the three major bodily effector systems. In the *skeletal muscle system,* there is an alternation between muscular contraction (involved in active coping efforts) and muscular relaxation, an alternation that is at the core of how this system operates. In the *autonomic nervous system,* the action of the heart may be observed as it alternates rapidly between contraction (systole) and relaxation (diastole). In the autonomic nervous system as a whole, we see a division between two great branches, the sympathetic nervous system and the parasympathetic nervous system. The former supports high energy production and vigorous physical action (the catabolic phase); the latter promotes digestion, relaxation, sleep, and the replenishing of energy sources (the anabolic phase).

Similarly, in the *neuroendocrine system* there is considerable evidence of the occurrence of periods of activation and nonactivation, as, for example, in the case of hormone responses to various psychological stressors (Mason, 1972). According to Mason, pituitary-adrenal cortical activity is increased under conditions in which there appears to be an undifferentiated state of arousal, alerting, or involvement—"perhaps in anticipation of activity or coping" (1972:23). (See also Goldstein, 1990.) Particularly effective in triggering pituitary-adrenal cortical activity are situations involving novelty, uncertainty, suspenseful anticipation, or "trying." A related series of experiments by Frankenhaeuser (1978) indicates that the neuroendocrine system in humans is highly responsive to perceived stress. In particular, situations requiring a marked degree of active coping behavior generate large increases in catecholamine levels. In her later work, Frankenhaeuser (1983) emphasizes the importance of personal control as a key factor in modulating neuroendocrine responses. As the sense of control increases, secretion rates of catecholamines and cortisol decrease. Similarly, in his review of the neuroendocrine patterns of emotion, Henry (1986) contrasts

FIGURE 38–1. The oscillation between activity and rest at different levels of organization

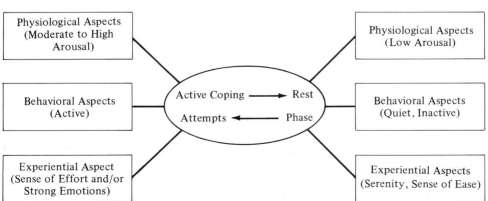

fear and serenity in terms of levels of increases in catecholamine and cortisol levels as well as in amygdalar basal nucleus activity. In the fear condition, increases in these three parameters support flight and effort, while decreases in the two hormones and in amygdalar activity accompany states of serenity—for example, in meditation.

Finally, when we consider the experiential level, it may be noted that during active coping attempts the individual is likely to sense excitement, exhibit focused attention, or be aware of feelings of mental effort. During relaxation, one is likely to experience tranquility, an absence of striving, or even drowsiness as a shift toward sleep occurs. Many of these experiential conditions are indexed (approximately) by characteristic electroencephalogram (EEG) wave forms. Mental effort and excitement, for example, are accompanied by fast, low-voltage, desynchronized EEG patterns; drowsiness by an abundance of theta rhythms; and profound sleep by slow, synchronized, high-voltage delta waves.

Central to our position is the idea that a high proportion of patients with stress-related disorders have entered an excessively active coping mode. (More conservatively put, this pattern is very common among the sample of patients ordinarily seen in the practice of stress management.) Moreover, an important manifestation of this pattern is an impaired ability to shift readily from the coping mode to the resting mode. There is a certain rigidity to these patients. In one way or another, they are stuck in a pattern of active coping. The insomniac complains of an inability to "switch off thoughts"; the type A individual leads a life of frenetic activity and unending struggle; the anxious patient is excessively vigilant and highly prone to startle reactions.

A closely related characteristic is the "vicious circle" phenomenon reported by many patients with stress disorders. A perceived threat or challenge sets off anxiety-evoking thoughts. The latter then trigger a physiological reaction, which is especially evident in the principally disturbed system—for example, the cramping and accelerated bowel motility that occur in irritable bowel syndrome. Sensations arising from these peripheral reactions then feed back to the central nervous system and exacerbate the flow of anxiety-evoking thoughts, in turn intensifying the physiological reaction. In other words, a positive feedback loop has been set up. Patients find themselves caught in the vicious circle, which often leaves them feeling exasperated, agitated, and out of control. (Interestingly, in German, such a positive feedback loop is referred to as a *Teufelskreis* or "devil's circle.")

Examples of Arousal

Many examples can be noted of the stress patient's tendency to manifest heightened or sustained arousal.

Generalized Anxiety. Patients suffering from chronic generalized anxiety show many signs of high physiological arousal, as listed in DSM-III-R (American Psychiatric Association, 1987). There are motor signs—such as, trembling, twitching, and restlessness. There are many symptoms of autonomic hyperactivity—shortness of breath, palpitations, tachycardia, sweating, cold and clammy hands, lightheadedness, nausea, or abdominal distress. There are symptoms of excessive vigilance—feeling "wired," difficulties in concentration, an exaggerated startle response.

Post-traumatic Stress Disorder (PTSD). Of particular recent interest, both clinically and experimentally, is PTSD. Victims of trauma, such as that occurring in combat, natural disasters, or other threats to personal physical and psychological well-being, may exhibit a classic syndrome of reactions that also signal arousal along several dimensions. Characteristics of the disorder include (1) re-experiencing the traumatic event (e.g., intrusive thoughts), (2) numbing or feelings of detachment, and (3) a variety of autonomic and behavioral indicators of arousal, including hyperalertness and other signs of sympathetic arousal, along the dimensions of generalized anxiety cited above (American Psychiatric Association, 1987).

Response Specificity. When stressed, patients with psychosomatic disorders react more strongly in their symptomatic system than do normal people. This phenomenon, a principal finding in psychophysiological research over the past several decades, has been noted in many different psychosomatic disorders: essential hypertension, Raynaud's syndrome, migraine headache, peptic ulcers, asthma, and rheumatoid arthritis (Sternbach, 1966).

Poor Sleep and Insomnia. In a study comparing poor sleepers versus good sleepers, Monroe (1967) noted that the poor sleepers showed various indicators of elevated physiological arousal during their time asleep. Compared to the good sleepers, they showed heightened levels of heart rate, respiration, and electrodermal activity. Working with insomniacs, Hauri (1991) observes that many, but not all, of these individuals manifest excessive arousal.

Type A Behavior Pattern. The type A behavior pattern—or certain components of it—may be a significant risk factor in coronary artery disease (see Chapter 25). The type A individual, as depicted by Friedman and Rosenman (1974) and Friedman and Ulmer (1984) shows many signs of being strongly in the coping mode, a characteristic true of both men and women (e.g., Haynes, Feinleib, & Kannel, 1980). The more notable attributes of the pattern include a generalized competitiveness, time urgency, hostility, irritableness, polyphasic thinking, and, overall, an abiding sense of struggle. It has further been documented (Glass, 1977) that such individuals not only react very strongly to various stressors but also place great emphasis upon achieving control over their environment.

To summarize, we can state that patients with psychosomatic or stress-linked disorders:

1. are likely to complain of arousal that is excessive or sustained for too long—that is, experience a surfeit of the active coping mode in response to stress
2. are likely, under stress, to react strongly in the symptomatic system—that is, show response specificity
3. show signs of being deficient in the ability to shift from the coping to the rest mode—that is, a slowness of habituation and recovery from stressful stimulation.

A corollary inference is that such patients, if studied on a round-the-clock basis, would show activity in the symptomatic system for a higher percentage of the time than do normal subjects. We also hypothesize that this defect in the capacity to shift to a rest condition is the principal reason why various relaxation procedures have so often proved successful in the alleviation of stress-related symptoms.

A THREE-SYSTEMS EXTENSION OF THE COPING/REST MODEL

A Tripartite Conception of Anxiety

As has already been hypothesized, the individual's reaction to stress may be viewed as a process occurring over time; there is an oscillation between episodes of rest and episodes of active coping attempts. We further propose that each wing of the coping/rest dimension can again be partitioned in a way that reflects the complex and multidimensional nature of the stress response. In other words, the coping/rest alternation, as suggested earlier in this section is not only a physiological phenomenon, but is manifest in behavior and cognition as well (see Figure 38–1).

Such a tripartite conceptualization of the individual's reaction to threat was proposed by Rachman (1978) with regard to anxiety, and was an idea first elaborated by Lang (1968). In arguing for a three-level or three-systems approach to anxiety, these researchers maintain that anxiety is not a "unified lump" but a phenomenon with physiological, verbal, and behavioral manifestations. The same thesis, we think, can be developed for stress management. As we consider the various procedures commonly employed in stress reduction, it will become apparent that they reflect the multidimensional nature of the stress response. Some techniques, such as relaxation training and biofeedback, emphasize modification of physiological responses. Others, such as the self-statements approach and imagery techniques, focus on cognitive changes. In assertiveness training and social skills learning, behavior change is emphasized. In other words, present clinical practice in stress management already reflects a three-systems view of the reactions to stress.

The foregoing conception should further a more sophisticated approach to stress management because it reminds the therapist not to overlook significant etiological factors in favor of some monolithic strategy, whether this be relaxation training, cognitive reassessment, or some other intervention. Furthermore, as Rachman (1978) has emphasized, a three-systems conception raises questions and stimulates research. Although the various indicators of anxiety may often be discrepant, this need not be an occasion for hand wringing; rather, it can help us to deal more resourcefully with the patient's disorder. For example, one patient may state that he does not feel afraid, yet he manifests the behavioral as well as the physiological signs of fear—a pattern suggesting that strong denial mechanisms are at work or that he is deficient in perceiving (or labeling) his own emotional reactions. Another individual may show the physiological and cognitive signs of fear, yet she gamely proceeds to grapple with the source of the threat in what might be called the courage model. In yet another case, discrepancies among our measures may lead us to refine or substitute our clinical instruments for assessing fear. In such cases, a three-systems analysis reduces our chances of overlooking observations and relationships that may prove to be turning points in the course of therapy.

Empirical work by behavior therapists on the three-systems approach to anxiety has been reported by Öst and colleagues in Sweden and by Michelson and associates at the University of Pittsburgh. In a group of 32 agoraphobics, Jansson, Jerremalm, and Öst found that a physiological measure (heart rate) lagged behind behavioral changes at the end of treatment (Öst & Jansson, 1987). However, through the 7-month and 15-month follow-ups, heart rate continued to shift in a downward direction. In other words, the physiological component at first lagged behind the other measures, becoming concordant with them only during the follow-up periods. Michelson, Mavissakalian, and Marchione (1988) employed a combination of behavioral, self-report, and psychophysiological measures in a comparison of cognitive and behavioral treatments of agoraphobia. Patients displaying concordance among the three measures at the end of treatment also showed superior clinical outcome. Among patients identified as concordant, 88% met previously established criteria for high functioning, compared to only 12% of those who did not show concordance. Concordance was also associated with superior functioning at the three-month follow-up.

Stress Defined as a Three-systems Phenomenon

A three-systems approach can also be applied to stress, for the latter is clearly a multidimensional phenomenon involving cognitive as well as physiological and behavioral components. This cognitive component runs through current definitions of psychological stress. Frankenhaeuser (1983:91), for example, defines psychological stress as involving a cognitive appraisal of the balance between situational demands, on the one hand, and personal coping resources, on the other. The greater the perceived difference between the two, then the more psychosocial factors are implicated in arousing the pituitary-adrenocortical and the sympathetic-adrenal systems. Similarly, Fisher (1984), who emphasizes the "mental load" aspects of stress, makes perception of control central to her definition of psychological stress. For Goldstein (1990:258), as well, stress involves the perception of a discrepancy between what is expected and the coping resources available to the individual. Stress is seen as an intervening variable that sets off a coordinated pattern of compensatory responses having behavioral, autonomic, and experiential aspects.

Summarizing the three preceding definitions, we might say that psychological stress centrally refers to a situation in which the challenges or threats facing the individual exceeds his or her estimated coping resources. The individual perceives a gap between the challenge and the physical and psychological resources he or she judges to be available. The perception of this discrepancy sets off a coordinated pattern of physiological, behavioral, and psychological reactions.

Implicit in the foregoing conception of stress is a key role for cognition. Because psychological stress involves the perception of a discrepancy, cognitive factors are clearly involved. And it then becomes an empirical question as to what type and level of intervention yields the strongest result. Is it a change in the response? Can this change be effected by relaxation training or behavior changes? Or is it a change in the thinking pattern that precedes the stress reaction?

The preceding definition also implies the idea of control, or sense of mastery, as a key factor in psychological stress and in stress management. The topic of perceived control is pursued in our concluding section.

THE COPING/REST DIMENSION IN RELATED TRADITIONS

Techniques arising from a number of different cultural and intellectual traditions also support the idea that the coping/rest dimension may be a fruitful way of thinking about both the stress response and its modification. Note, too, that many of these examples parallel our three-systems approach.

Biobehavioral Methods in Anxiety Management

Systematic Desensitization of Anxiety. As developed by Wolpe (1958), the method of anxiety reduction known as systematic desensitization consists of three phases: relaxation training; the visualization of increasingly potent anxiety-evoking scenes while maintaining good relaxation; finally, actually confronting and coping with the anxiety-arousing situation, a task that generally requires repeated encounters. What we see, in other words, is a phase of learning to master relaxation (rest) followed by a phase of actually encountering the feared situation (coping).

Implosion Therapy with Relaxation. Implosion therapy (or "flooding") for anxiety disorders consists of the repetitive presentation of feared stimuli—usually repeated imaginings of the feared event by the client (Levis, 1980; Stampfl & Levis, 1967). This method has been shown to be particularly effective in application to anxiety disorders and compares favorably with systematic desensitization (Marks, 1977). In recent applications to treatment of PTSD in combat veterans (Keane, Fairbank, Caddell, & Zimering, 1989), implosion therapy has been effectively alternated with relaxation. In Keane et al.'s approach, clients were first taught relaxation prior to the implosion therapy itself. Then during sessions in which they were intensively encouraged to visualize traumatic combat scenes, clients displaying extreme agitation were instructed to stop visualization and to practice their relaxation exercises. Additional periods of relaxation were introduced at the beginning and the end of the session. Keane et al. argue that this provides the PTSD sufferer with respite from periods of anxiousness during therapy, a return to lowered arousal at the conclusion of a treatment session and, interestingly, a heightening of the effects of traumatic imagery during flooding, thus enhancing therapeutic gains.

Electromyographic Feedback, Autogenic Training, and Meditation Combined. A set of training procedures developed in our Colorado laboratory and regularly utilized in treating various disorders of hyperarousal, including anxiety reactions, explicitly draws from several independent traditions (Stoyva, 1989). For laboratory sessions, electromyographic (EMG) feedback is used—first from the forearm extensors, then from a forehead placement (for teaching relaxation of the frontal musculature). A particular value of the feedback technology is that it offers not only some quantification of the learning process, but the patient is also taught what is meant by shifting into a "noneffort" or "nonstriving" mode. This latter ability is a crucial skill running through various relaxation and meditative techniques. For home practice exercises, patients learn autogenic heaviness and warmth exercises, then, subsequently, two meditative exercises (Stoyva, 1989). About 70% of patients achieve good heaviness sensations, at least in their arms; while about 40% report strong warmth sensations, mainly in hands and arms, and sometimes in the feet. Physiologically, the autogenic exercises promote a shift from sympathetic to parasympathetic response patterns (Luthe, 1970). In addition, the exercises dampen mental activity, something many patients find especially valuable.

An important additional component we have added in recent years is the regular use of two meditative exercises that are often helpful to patients who have enjoyed little success at the autogenic exercises. The first meditative exercise, physically, involves a shift to abdominal (diaphragmatic) breathing. Mentally, the patient learns to pay quiet attention to the movement sensations accompanying the rise and fall of the stomach. The second meditative exercise also involves first shifting to abdominal breathing. In addition, the patient is asked to quietly focus attention on the sensation of cool air in the nostrils that accompanies every in-breath. "On every in-breath, swing your attention back to the cool-air sensation. This helps to break up the chains of thoughts." As patients become skilled in this maneuver, they have at their disposal a potent tool for achieving a mentally quiet condition and one that can be carried along into many everyday stressful situations.

The Stanislavski System of Acting

A different but complementary perspective on stress and anxiety reactions can be seen in the thought of Stanislavski. Probably the most influential theater director of the twentieth century, Stanislavski, is best remembered for the system of acting he created, the American variant of which became known simply as "The Method." Though containing much of psychological interest, this body of techniques seems to have been ignored by psychologists.

In the decade prior to the 1920s, Stanislavski evolved a number of methods designed to assist the actor in the task of affecting the controlled evocation of emotion on stage. A key part of his method was unlocking the "affective memory," a goal that the actor attains by the use of appropriate physical actions. As Stanislavski put it, "the physical action is the bait for the emotion." By developing precise and finely modulated ensembles of behavior— including movements, gestures, words, and facial expression—the emotion connected with the ensemble can be voluntarily called forth on stage. Through using this system, the actor becomes more than simply a performer with a bag of tricks. He or she becomes a creator who fashions a character and, especially, the emotional life of that character, before the gaze of an audience (Moore, 1976). Interestingly, Stanislavski's thesis is consistent with the Darwinian view that the autonomic concomitants of emotion are intimately connected to its expressive aspects (Darwin, 1965:364).

While a detailed consideration of Stanislavski's ideas would take us a little far afield, it is worth noting that certain of his techniques are highly pertinent to the form of stress we call stage fright, or performance anxiety. In dealing with this principal *bête noire* of the actor, his methods have stood the test of time. Two of these techniques are of particular interest because they relate to the coping/rest dichotomy.

On the basis of observations of himself, and fellow members of the Moscow Art Theatre, Stanislavski formulated a number of precepts designed to guide the actor in the re-creation of emotional experience before an audience. Interestingly, his first major observation was that muscular tension was associated with anxiety and that even in small amounts this tension disrupted a finely modulated performance. His second major observation concerned the importance of concentration. The better the actor's concentration, the less his anxiety about the audience and the more accomplished his performance (Magarshack, 1950). For Stanislavski, anxiety and concentration were inversely related—more of one meant less of the other. In Stanislavski's view, anxiety is the archenemy of the actor; it, more than anything, interferes with a convincing and finely wrought performance. He also declared that, in combating this anxiety, the actor has two main weapons to draw upon: "relaxation and concentration." Accordingly, actors are taught to relax their muscles, a skill that should become near-automatic. They are also taught ways to improve their concentration. In the words of Moore, a student of Stanislavski, "Think of your action, not of your feelings. You will feel at ease and relaxed if you concentrate on action" (Moore, 1976:26).

The Mindfulness Tradition

Over the centuries, a major reservoir of methods and ideas for the modification of stress reactions has emerged in the meditative traditions of the Far East. Admittedly, the fundamental orientation of these various traditions is spiritual, and their practices are embedded in a whole system of religious meanings. Nonetheless, many of the practices involved in these teachings are surprisingly operational. These skills can be learned and can sometimes be put to clinical use.

The *mindfulness* tradition is of special interest because it embodies techniques for carrying a more tranquil and composed mental state into daily activities, thereby bridging the gap between rest and coping. Historically, this vehicle of meditation is linked with the

Therevada tradition, or the southern branch of Buddhism, which flourishes in Sri Lanka, Burma, Thailand, and Indochina.

Mindfulness refers to a state of relaxed attentiveness characterized by quiet concentration and heightened awareness. The individual is very much absorbed in the here and now and what he or she is presently doing, whether this is walking, chopping wood, washing dishes, or carrying on a conversation. He or she is neither dwelling on the past nor preoccupied with the future. Practitioners sometimes refer to a mental state of "bare attention."

As the individual attains proficiency at becoming highly absorbed in the present task, this skill appears to serve as a powerful reducer of stress responses. The more one's attention is focused on the specifics of the present situation, the less it is available for being anxious—a conception of the relation between anxiety and concentration similar to that proposed by Stanislavski.

An interest in mindfulness, or in phenomena closely related to it, has appeared in various contexts, both Eastern and Western. By way of illustration, let us discuss briefly one of the Oriental martial arts (Tai Chi), the practice of mindfulness meditation, and two Western approaches to the idea—the "experience of flow" and the activity of task-involvement.

Martial Arts.   Many of the practices observed in Oriental martial arts implicitly embody the coping/rest distinction. The various martial arts that grew up in the Far East, nearly always placed some emphasis on cultivating the skills of relaxation. There was also an emphasis on developing concentration skills useful in the martial context. In the Samurai teaching of swordsmanship, for example, relaxation formed a definite part of the tradition, as did the skill of concentrating well during the martial encounter. This concentration, moreover, was to be effortless.

Awareness of the coping/rest distinction can also be seen very clearly in Tai Chi. Originating in Chinese Taoism, Tai Chi Chuan is the best-known of China's martial arts, but it is also more than a martial art. If practiced seriously, Tai Chi affects a very large part of thought and behavior. Tai Chi is of particular interest for the coping/rest model because it emphasizes not only relaxation but also the goal of "stillness in motion" (Adler, 1983). When Tai Chi is practiced correctly, the mind is said to be still even when the body is moving.

A principal method for improving concentration is to pay continuous attention to one's movements during the performance of particular physical exercises. Those exercises are as much mental as physical, and one's movements should be fluid, slow, and gentle. During an exercise, one focuses attention continuously on bodily movements; if attention is deflected, one must be aware of this, then return attention to the movement. With increasing skill, the experience becomes one of meditation in action.

In addition to stillness in motion, there is also the teaching of relaxation for when the individual is not engaged in movement. This ability is taught in various ways, for example, by means of certain breathing exercises, which are in addition to those used in Tai Chi *per se,* and which also involve quiet concentration. Overall, it is clear that Tai Chi focuses on both rest and action. Moreover, its emphasis on maintaining steady attention on movements echoes mindfulness meditation.

Mindfulness Meditation.   A leading present-day proponent of the mindfulness tradition is the Vietnamese Zen master and poet, Thich Nhat Hanh. In his short but impressive book, the *Miracle of Mindfulness* (1987), Thich Nhat Hanh offers a variety of practical exercises, many of which involve paying quiet attention to one's breathing. Focusing on the breath becomes an anchor and a resting place for one's attention, a way to subdue the "chattering monkey brain." Characteristic of many of these exercises is an alternation between the practice of mindfulness and paying attention to the breath. For example, some-one on a hike in the mountains allows herself to be absorbed in the natural setting surrounding her. But when she finds her thoughts wandering away to what is not present, she re-sumes paying attention to her breathing sensations. As her attention settles, and the wandering thoughts disappear, she again turns her attention to the nature around her. Thich Nhat Hanh (1987) goes on to suggest a great many other exercises. Overall, one might characterize these exercises as designed to foster a kind of tranquility in action. In terms of the coping/rest model, we might say that a collected and calm consciousness is no longer confined to the behaviorally quiescent condition of formal meditation, but is transferred into action as well.

It must be admitted that becoming skilled at mindfulness meditation takes a great deal of practice. Yet, its potential for managing stress reactions, for decreasing anxiety and pain, and for improving performance seems substantial enough to warrant extensive investigation. In their stress-reduction and relaxation program at the University of Massachusetts Medical Center, Kabat-Zinn and his associates have applied mindfulness meditation to chronic pain as well as to a variety of stress-related disorders. Kabat-Zinn, Lipworth, and Burney (1985), for example, report on 90 chronic pain patients who received mindfulness meditation training in a 10-week stress reduction and relaxation program. Significant de-creases in pain and pain-related affect were observed, as were decreases in drug utilization. A comparison group of 21 pain patients given customary medical treatments did not show significant improvement on any of the measures.

The Experiences of Flow and Task Involvement. Reports from several Western sources suggest that mindfulness—or activities that appear closely related to it—may not only buffer the effects of stress, but even change it into something beneficial to health and well-being.

Mihaly Csikszentmihalyi at the University of Chicago writes of the "flow experience," a phenomenon he has studied over several decades in athletes, artists, scientists, mathemati-cians, dancers, mountain climbers, and others engaged in pursuits highly demanding of mental and physical resources (Csikszentmihalyi, 1990). Csikszentmihalyi speaks of the flow experience as a state of concentration so intense that it amounts to absolute absorption in an activity. Body and mind are stretched to their limits. A kind of self-forgetfulness occurs, in which the distinction between self and object dissolves during the time of intense concentration on the task at hand.

Another observation pertinent to the concept of mindfulness comes from research on the type A coronary-prone behavior pattern. Part of the type A pattern is a high degree of involvement in work. In fact, the expressions "workaholic" and "type A" often occur in the same breath. Yet it seems that job involvement may be a characteristic that acts against the risk of coronary events (Dembroski, Weiss, Shields, Haynes, & Feinleib, 1978).

Work in the areas of stress research and health psychology has also brought out the importance of a capacity for task involvement—a characteristic, incidentally, that White (1959) regarded as a significant aspect of general competence. Thus, Flannery (1987), in summarizing much empirical work on the coping strategies of stress-resistant individuals, discerns four main categories: (1) *task* involvement, (2) a sense of personal control, (3) the presence of positive health practices—regular exercise and relaxation, and low use of stimu-lant substances such as caffeine and nicotine, and (4) utilization of social supports.

SOME COMMON STRESS DISORDERS:
RELAXATION AS A CORE PROCEDURE

Over the past twenty years, a major landmark to emerge in the nonpharmacological treatment of stress-related disorders has been the often-successful application of relaxation methods. In terms of the coping/rest dimension, the various relaxation techniques can be thought of as allowing the stressed client—in whom the capacity to rest has become defective or little used—to recapture this ability. The relaxation response is a way of breaking up the stress reaction by anticipating and/or inhibiting it, by moderating its intensity, or by assisting in post-stress recovery to resting (baseline) levels (Stoyva & Budzynski, 1974).

During this century, many systems of relaxation training have been developed. Among those more widely used in Western countries have been: the progressive relaxation of Jacobson (1938); autogenic training (Linden, 1990; Luthe & Schultz, 1969; Schultz, 1932); EMG feedback, especially from the frontal (forehead) area (Budzynski & Stoyva, 1969; Budzynski, Stoyva, & Peffer, 1980); and the modified transcendental meditation of Benson (1975).

The differences in emphasis from one technique to the other suggest that they may tap different aspects of relaxation (see Woolfolk & Lehrer, 1984, for a discussion of this issue). But these differences notwithstanding, considerable evidence has accumulated showing that relaxation procedures (especially those involving a whole-body relaxation response) can be used in diminishing stress-related symptoms such as sleep-onset insomnia, tension headache, migraine headache, high blood pressure, and chronic anxiety. These procedures can be useful as well for localized muscular tension and cramping involved in dysphagia and sometimes for temporomandibular joint syndrome (TMJ) (see Rugh, Perlis, & Disraeli, 1977).

We should also note the important long-term trend in the increasing use of combined procedures in stress management. For each of the disorders discussed, interventions targeted at different components of the stress response have been formulated and put to experimental test. This development reflects a recognition that stress is a multidimensional phenomenon with behavioral, cognitive, and physiological aspects. Clinically, it suggests that the tools available for modifying the stress reaction will continue to grow in usefulness, particularly as we experiment with combinations of procedures.

Combined Interventions

In day-to-day practice with stress-related disorders, we often find that the impact of one intervention by itself yields only a marginal treatment effect. But if two or three techniques are used in combination, there may occur a summated effect large enough to be quite significant clinically. In the future, we can expect more work on combinations of techniques—for example, biofeedback plus cognitive interventions plus behavior change techniques, such as assertiveness training or anger control. Overall, such combinations are likely to prove more effective than one technique by itself. Valuable work along these lines has been done by Blanchard and his associates. In one such study (Blanchard et al., 1982), patients with tension headache or migraine headache were first given 10 sessions of nonbiofeedback relaxation training over an 8-week period. This intervention produced decreased headache levels in 52% of tension headache patients and 30% of the migraineurs. Treatment failures were then given biofeedback: frontal EMG feedback in the case of the tension headache patients, hand temperature feedback for the migraineurs. Treatment successes then increased to 73% for the tension headache group, and to 50% for the migraineurs. Biofeedback, in other words, increased the proportion of treatment successes by roughly 50% in both conditions over that achieved by relaxation alone.

Another obvious candidate for a combined approach is essential hypertension. Here it is known that several procedures used singly can have limited use in lowering blood pressure. Weight reduction and lowering salt intake have been known for some time. In recent years, evidence for the utility of the following interventions also has accumulated: reducing alcohol intake, regular physical exercise, and relaxation training. Clearly, at this juncture, a logical next step will be to examine carefully the impact of other combinations of techniques. One possible regimen would be to combine weight reduction, decreased alcohol consumption, relaxation training, and aerobic exercise—a combination that amounts to a total fitness program.

Studies of this type are arduous because many comparison conditions need to be examined (see Borkovec, Johnson, & Block, 1984, for a fine discussion of this point). Yet, once we have begun to isolate individual components in a given disorder, it becomes reasonable to ask whether relevant interventions can be combined. Are they additive, or is one simply equivalent in effect to the other? It is our conviction, moreover, that in research concerning the various stress-reduction techniques, the main question now is not so much whether a particular technique enjoys an edge over another, but whether the respective techniques tap into differing dimensions of the stress reaction. When they do, their effects are likely to be additive.

The following sections provide examples of some common stress-related disorders in which retraining the capacity to rest can be usefully applied. The first four are medical disorders considered to have a stress component—primary insomnia, tension headache, essential hypertension, and irritable bowel syndrome. The fifth disorder, performance anxiety, involves some of the most widely experienced stress-related reactions. In treating each of these disturbances, there is usually a core emphasis on acquiring an effective relaxation response. There is also—varying somewhat with the disorder—attention paid to modifying the active coping behavior of the individual.

Insomnia

A good example of the coping/rest paradigm can be found in the evolving body of techniques utilized in treating primary insomnia. Prominent among these techniques are methods for reducing physical and mental activity in a way to facilitate sleep—that is, relaxation skills are emphasized. Also, methods are emerging for altering waking behavior that impinges upon sleep (Hauri & Linde, 1990).

Sleep researchers have identified three main types of insomnia: sleep-onset insomnia, fragmented or intermittent sleep, and insomnia characterized by early morning awakenings and a failure to return to sleep. The psychophysiological methods described here are frequently useful for the first two types. For early morning insomnia, the results are variable and less robust (Hauri, 1991).

It is important to note that persisting early morning awakenings are often associated with clinical depression and have become recognized as one of its clinical markers. In such cases, the principal focus devolves onto the treatment of the depression (Hauri, 1991). We should note, too, that early morning awakenings are often a natural part of aging.

For the first two types of insomnia mentioned previously, a number of interventions are now available. Hauri and Linde (1990) describe an impressive body of empirically grounded procedures. In our Colorado laboratory, we have found a combination of three techniques to be often useful. For relaxation purposes, as described earlier, we begin with a combination of EMG feedback in the laboratory and the autogenic heaviness exercise for the home practice part of the regimen. Later, we add an exercise drawn from Vipassana meditation: "Pay quiet attention to your respiratory sensations; on every in-breath, notice the cool air sensations in your nose" (Hart, 1987). The better the patient becomes at this exercise, the more the flow of ideation is reduced. The two foregoing exercises strengthen the skills needed for the voluntary induction of sleep onset. Often, patients report that mastery of the autogenic heaviness exercise by itself is enough to produce substantial remission of their insomnia.

A third strategy can be added to the two preceding exercises: cutting down on the hours spent in bed (see later). This technique appears to potentiate the impact of the two quieting exercises. As Hauri notes, it is frequently the first major strategy recommended to the insomniac.

Although relaxation skills were first emphasized in the treatment of insomnia, there is increasing evidence that various kinds of active waking behavior can also affect sleep (Hauri & Linde, 1990), probably through interactions with various biological stress processes. This new knowledge, much of it related to the idea of sleep as a biological rhythm, leads to a number of recommendations as to how the insomniac can change daytime behavior in ways that promote better sleep. The patient may be told to (1) stabilize the daily time of rising, a practice that helps induce sleepiness at the usual bedtime; (2) avoid naps, a practice likely to hinder falling asleep at the usual bedtime; (3) engage in quiet activities during the last hour prior to bedtime to reduce the level of central arousal; (4) engage in regular physical exercise, preferably aerobic, during the day and (in line with point 3) not during the several hours preceding sleep; (5) cut down on time in bed—that is, practice *sleep consolidation.* This last procedure may seem counterintuitive. Usually, the person who has slept badly begins to spend more time in bed in an attempt to catch up, a practice that aggravates th original difficulty because sleep becomes more fitful and more shallow. A larger percentage of time in bed is spent simply lying awake, fidgeting, tossing, and feeling exasperated. The bed and the bedroom have become conditioned stimuli for high arousal and wakefulness. Such patients are told to cut down on the time spent in bed (e.g., from eight to seven hours, or even to five hours). After two or three weeks, when sleep has consolidated, the time in bed can be extended gradually back to a normal duration (e.g., seven and a half hours).

Tension Headache

Psychophysiological and behavioral interventions have by now established a recognized place for themselves in the treatment of tension headache. Several nonpharmacological interventions are now at hand that were not available fifteen or twenty years ago or that had not yet been subjected to systematic evaluation.

Our initial work with EMG biofeedback was prompted by the prevailing medical opinion at the time that tension headache arises from sustained muscle contractions in the head, scalp, and neck. This view, based primarily on the work of Harold Wolff (1963) found expression in the judgment of the American Medical Association's Ad Hoc Committee on the Classification of Headache (1962) that tension headache is muscular in origin and can be properly referred to as "muscle contraction" headache.

During our initial observations with a group of five patients, a combination of frontal EMG feedback in the laboratory along with the home practice of muscle relaxation led to a substantial reduction in both the intensity and duration of headache pain (Budzynski, Stoyva, & Adler, 1970). This observation was subsequently confirmed and elaborated in a controlled study (Budzynski, Stoyva, Adler, & Mullaney, 1973).

It is worth recalling that the foregoing studies were initiated against a backdrop of some skepticism. There was doubt as to whether a psychological or psychophysiological intervention would have any reliable effect at all upon tension headache, one of the most commonly encountered disorders in medical practice. Considering this climate of opinion, the importance of first demonstrating a reliable treatment effect is worth emphasizing. During the 1970s and 1980s, the existence of a useful treatment effect from relaxation training was amply confirmed. Nuechterlein and Holroyd (1980) summarized 20 investigations carried out in the decade subsequent to the original report from the Colorado laboratory (Budzynski et al., 1970). Nearly half of these were controlled studies. All but one or two of the 20 investigations indicated that relaxation training brought significant reductions in headache activity. Controversy remained, however, this time about whether EMG feedback is necessary for the requisite degree of relaxation. Nuechterlein and Holroyd (1980) concluded that verbally induced relaxation works about as well and is somewhat more cost effective.

As a clinical area, headache treatment has advanced both in ingenuity and sophistication. Budzynski (1989), for example, describes an impressive array of procedures now available for use in the psychophysiological treatment of tension headache. And in a wide-ranging volume, Adler, Adler, and Packard (1987) explore the psychiatric aspects of headache and their relevance to treatment.

To summarize, we can say with some confidence that relaxation techniques produce a reliable decrement in tension headache. In some ways, however, the situation has become more complex than it was previously. Various controversies have sprung up that, basically, turn on the question of what exactly are the pathological factors in tension headache. In a valuable review, Olton and Noonberg (1980) point out that the idea of equating tension headache with muscular tension needs qualification and is open to criticism on several counts. For example, there is evidence that a vasoconstrictive component may contribute to the headache pain, although this evidence has remained a neglected feature of the disorder. Other observers draw attention to the role of cognitive factors, which may be much more important etiologically than previously thought (e.g, Bakal, 1982). This recognition has been a principal spur to the development of new psychological approaches to treatment.

One body of observations points to the conclusion that muscular tension (usually measured by EMG levels in the frontal area) correlates rather poorly with degree of headache pain. Muscular tension may be only a part of the disorder. In a study focusing on the acquisition of cognitive coping strategies, Reeves (1976) found a lack of parallelism between reductions in headache pain and decreases in frontal EMG activity. Holroyd, Andrasik, and Westbrook (1977) compared cognitive and EMG feedback strategies in the control of tension headache. As with the Reeves (1976) study, no relationship was found between headache improvement and frontal EMG levels.

In the Holroyd et al. (1977) study, cognitive strategies proved superior to the biofeedback intervention. Subjects in the cognitive group were taught coping strategies, such as ways to countermand negative self-statements and the use of imagery to cope with stressful situations. Cognitive subjects showed significantly greater improvement than did the biofeedback group and also showed a greater consistency of improvement. Andrasik and Holroyd (1980) have suggested that control of EMG levels may be less important in moderating headache activity than is learning to attenuate excessive stress response. In their view, the crucial skill may be not so much learning to modify EMG activity as it is to "learn to monitor the insidious onset of headache symptoms and engage in some sort of coping response incompatible with the further exacerbation of symptoms" (p. 584).

Recognition of cognitive factors is also explicit in Bakal's (1982) psychobiological approach to headache. In a program developed by Bakal, Demjen, and Kaganov (1981), strong emphasis was placed on teaching long-term headache sufferers ways to alter the sensory and distress reactions associated with their headache attacks. A combination of procedures was devised that included brief relaxation training, the learning of cognitive skills—such as attention focusing and attention diversion—the use of imagery, and thought management techniques. The program proved highly successful, except for those patients whose headache pain was continuous or nearly continuous.

In summary, we can say that both relaxation and cognitive treatments have demonstrated their usefulness in tension headache (Andrasik, 1986). Furthermore, a major etiological development over the past decade has been the recognition of the role played by cognitive factors in the genesis of this type of headache.

Essential Hypertension

The search for a behavioral treatment of essential hypertension has something of a Holy Grail quality to it, in that the object of the quest seems to be forever receding. Although the earlier literature of both progressive relaxation and autogenic training contains many references to the successful use of relaxation methods in essential hypertension (Jacobson, 1938; Luthe & Schultz, 1969:69–76), these investigations consist almost uniformly of uncontrolled studies. In this context, we should note that the use of psychological interventions in essential hypertension is beset with vexatious methodological difficulties. One major problem is that a surprisingly high proportion of hypertensives will return to normotensive levels even in the absence of treatment. For example, in the large-scale Australian Therapeutic Trial in Mild Hypertension (1982), at least one-third of those receiving placebo medication had decreased to less than 90 mm Hg diastolic pressure when they were measured again a year later. Another vexatious problem, especially for psychological interventions, is whether the decrements in pressure observed in the laboratory generalize to the rest of the patient's diurnal cycle. To answer this question, the use of ambulatory blood pressure monitoring devices will be increasingly important. Such devices are now used fairly frequently by clinical hypertension laboratories as well as in the scientific evaluation of new antihypertensive drugs.

In recent years, several review articles have appeared. Blanchard (1990), summarizing a series of investigations by his own and other groups, sounds a note of guarded optimism. Recently, a meta-analysis of 75 treatment groups and 41 control groups of hypertensives from a large number of behavioral treatment studies seemingly demonstrated "marked superiority" of relaxation or meditation treatment (Jacob, Chesney, Williams, Ding, & Shapiro, 1991). Unfortunately, the largest effects were seen in the most poorly controlled studies. Jacob et al. (1991) conclude that, overall, the more vigorously controlled the studies, the smaller the effect was likely to be.

Similarly, in two other meta-analyses only very modest effects of relaxation treatments were obtained (Kaufman et al., 1988; Ward, Swan, & Chesney, 1987). These two investigations made use of quite sophisticated methods, including stringent analysis and design evaluation. The Kaufman et al. (1988) report is of particular interest since its authors addressed the question of "fugitive studies,"—that is, studies not submitted for publication because of negative outcomes. In this carefully conducted investigation, all of the principal investigators of the twelve major outcome projects then being funded through the National Heart, Lung and Blood Institute committed themselves to providing outcome data when their research was still at an early stage—before it was known whether the outcome would be positive or negative. Known as the Hypertension Intervention Pooling Project (HIPP), and the most encompassing study so far conducted on the outcome topic, this investigation yielded only modest results. No effects of treatment on systolic pressures and only very modest effects on diastolic pressure were observed.

In an additional analysis, however, the results were more encouraging. An analysis of the slopes of regression lines of blood pressure decreases for both systolic and diastolic levels showed significant decreases at the end of intervention, but not at the one-year follow-up. Significant results were noted only for the nonmedicated patients. Pressure decreases in the controls failed to reach significance. In other words, with this group of relaxation interventions, patients with higher starting pressures showed the greatest decreases (with favorable effects at about 130 mm Hg/94 mm Hg and above).

Among the more positive recent hypertension treatment studies, in a unique approach, Blanchard and colleagues (Blanchard et al., 1986) evaluated the relative effects of thermal (hand temperature) biofeedback and progressive muscle relaxation in relaxation training on altering hypertensive medication usage. Rather than use blood pressure reduction as the dependent variable, Blanchard and his co-workers looked at the number of trained subjects who, though starting on second-stage medications, were able to cut back to first-stage medications (diuretics) alone after training. The two forms of relaxation training were each provided for eight weeks. The results indicated that a greater percentage of subjects in the thermal biofeedback group was able to discontinue second-stage drugs than in the progressive muscle relaxation group, both at post-treatment (65% versus 27%, respectively), and at a three-month follow-up (47% versus 23%, respectively). Blanchard et al.'s results are particularly interesting in light of one of the conclusions of Jacob et al.'s (1991) summary of the hypertension treatment literature: patients with the highest blood pressures, and therefore those most likely to be medicated, may benefit the most from relaxation therapies.

Combining relaxation procedures has also been recently successfully employed in treating essential hypertension. McGrady, Woerner, Bernal, and Higgins (1987) provided both progressive muscle relaxation and frontal EMG biofeedback training to achieve significant reductions in systolic and diastolic blood pressures (14 mm Hg and 8.9 mm Hg at post-treatment, respectively). Interestingly, reductions in urinary cortisol (-20%) and plasma cortisol (-23%) were significantly correlated with blood pressure decreases, a finding that supports the role of relaxation in coping with this disorder in terms of reduction in sympathetic arousal.

In our Hawaii laboratory, efforts to research the role of relaxation in the reduction of blood pressure currently focus on a procedure in which progressive muscle relaxation is alternated with temperature EMG training from session to session. Preliminary results with six unmedicated subjects with borderline hypertension (blood pressures > 140/90) showed normalizing of levels in all but one subject at post-treatment following five or more sessions of training. (The effects of longer-term incorporation of relaxation with daily coping will be assessed in follow-ups at several months.)

Finally, we should note that individuality of response is likely to be an important factor in developing behavioral treatments of this disorder. Essential hypertension is a complex phenomenon, so it is unlikely that any single kind of intervention will prove helpful to all. McGrady and Higgins (1989) found that hypertensives showing signs of high sympathetic arousal were most likely to respond favorably to a regimen of EMG feedback-assisted relaxation training (pre-post treatment decreases $\geq$ 5 mm Hg in mean arterial pressure). The successful responders showed high state and trait anxiety, high heart rate, high levels of EMG activity, and low peripheral temperature. As a group, these patients could be characterized as strong stress responders.[3]

Irritable Bowel Syndrome

Another surprisingly common disorder is irritable bowel syndrome (IBS). The syndrome is usually defined by the presence of abdominal pain along with a change in bowel habits, diarrhea, or constipation (Latimer, 1983). Known under a great many different names—functional diarrhea, spastic colon, coloric enterospasm, and others—IBS is the most common of all presenting complaints in the gastrointestinal (GI) clinic. Switz (1976), for example, estimates that 30 to 50% of gastroenterological consultations involve this disorder.

Nevertheless, diagnosis of IBS is not a simple matter. Evidence for the diagnostic decision rests heavily on a patient's reports of symptoms as well as on the physical examination and laboratory reports undertaken to rule out other graver possibilities. Typical symptoms of IBS include abdominal pain and tenderness, diarrhea, constipation, flatulence, belching, and nausea along with an absence of organic pathology in the GI system. IBS patients also show a wide range of nongastrointestinal symptoms, such as fatigue, muscle pains, insomnia, dizziness, and headache. It has been noted, too, that affective disturbances, such as anxiety or depression, are often present (Latimer, 1983).

Two characteristics of the syndrome make it of great psychological interest. First, it is very much a multidimensional disorder, with affective as well as physiological and behavioral components. Second, exacerbation of bowel symptoms is frequently linked to psychologically stressful events (Whitehead & Schuster, 1985).

Latimer (1983:86–94) has developed a theoretical framework for analyzing IBS that is quite explicitly a three-systems (and behavioral) model. In his analysis, Latimer proposes that the disorder involves symptoms at three levels, consisting of: (1) verbal behavior (e.g., reports of abdominal pain); (2) motoric behavior (e.g., pill-taking or trips to the toilet); and (3) physiological activity (e.g., colonic segmental contractions).

Latimer emphasizes that these three components are often desynchronous; that is, they can be negatively as well as positively correlated with one another (apropos our earlier section regarding a three-systems version of the coping/rest model). For example, a patient may report an increase in abdominal pain (verbal behavior), but at the same time not show any increase in the strength or frequency of colonic contractions (physiological activity) or any increase in the frequence of defecation (motoric behavior).

Traditional medical treatments of IBS have usually consisted of dietary changes or various drug therapies. Typically, these treatments have had modest effects or have been of short duration (Drossman, Powell, & Sessions, 1977). In recent years, however, treatments reflecting the psychological aspects of IBS have begun to emerge. Several controlled studies involving psychological interventions are now available (Giles, 1978; Svedlund, Sjodin, Ottosson, & Dotevall, 1983; Whitehead & Schuster, 1985). However, evidence for the long-term efficacy of psychological interventions has been skimpy. Consequently, a series of investigations conducted at the Center for Stress and Anxiety Disorders (SUNY, Albany) is of special interest.

Neff and Blanchard (1987), in an earlier multicomponent intervention program focusing on both the psychological and the physiological aspects of the disorder, compared a treatment group to a symptom-monitoring control group. Patients in the treatment group received 12 individual 1-hour training sessions over an 8-week period. Components of the training included (1) progressive relaxation, (2) temperature biofeedback for a hand-warming response, (3) cognitive stress-coping techniques, and (4) education about normal bowel functioning and the symptomatology and etiology of IBS.

Before patients could be included in the study, a confirmed diagnosis by their physicians was required, as was the completion of an assessment battery including personal, medical, and social histories, psychological testing, and a psychophysiological evaluation. Following training, the combined treatment group proved significantly better than the controls as regards alleviation of five major IBS symptoms. Subsequently, the symptom-monitoring group was also offered the treatment. Altogether a total of 17 patients completed the training.

A commendable addition to this investigation was the inclusion of a year-long follow-up period (Schwarz, Blanchard, & Neff, 1986). At 12 months after the end of training, all 17 patients were asked to keep a symptom diary for a 2-week period. These diaries were filled out on a daily basis, and principal GI symptoms were rated on a 5-point scale. The diary data were then compared with a similar diary from an earlier 2-week period. For the 14 patients who completed the diaries, there were significant reductions in IBS symptoms. In the immediate post-training period (i.e., after the initial study) there had been significant reductions in five symptoms—abdominal pain and tenderness, diarrhea, constipation, flatulence and nausea (Neff & Blanchard, 1987). At the 12-month follow-up, improvement levels were not as marked, although three of the key symptoms in IBS still maintained significant reductions: abdominal pain and tenderness, diarrhea, and flatulence (Schwarz, Blanchard, & Neff, 1986).

At the end of the study, 15 patients reported themselves to be still using the techniques learned earlier. Overall, these studies lend support to the view that stress management procedures are effective for reducing the subjective distress and the bowel symptoms associated with IBS. As Whitehead and Schuster (1985) propose, such interventions could become the treatment of choice for most IBS patients.

Performance Anxiety

Systematic desensitization, the first major clinical technique to emerge in behavior therapy, focuses on active coping behavior as well as on relaxation. The patient is first taught relaxation, a condition Wolpe (1958, 1980) regarded as being incompatible with anxiety. Next, scenes related to the feared stimulus are visualized at the same time that relaxation is maintained. The various scenes are worked on one-by-one and on the basis of graduated intensity (similarity to the feared stimulus). After patients have learned to visualize the scenes successfully (by the criterion of relaxation), they are encouraged to seek out and actively encounter the situations that arouse fear—again, on the basis of graduated levels of intensity.

A frequent use of systematic desensitization has been in the treatment of performance anxiety, such as in the case of test anxiety or public speaking anxiety (classified under social phobia in DSM-III-R); and its efficacy has been strongly documented in scores of studies. Building on this knowledge base, we find that various useful additions to the core technique can be made in daily clinical practice. Three of these procedural innovations follow.

Abdominal Breathing Exercise. While the efficacy of desensitization has been well demonstrated, a weakness of the procedure is that it does not provide the patient with any specific tool for moderating anxiety in the situation itself. For this difficulty, we have found an abdominal (diaphragmatic) breathing maneuver to be a useful addition. At least 50% of patients report this technique to be useful, either in the situation or during the anticipatory phase, when mounting anxiety often becomes nearly intolerable. (For a description of this exercise, see "Retraining of Respiratory Patterns," subsequently.)

Multisite EMG Feedback. At the University of Hawaii, we have experimented with multisite EMG feedback training based on the rationale that EMG feedback from a number of sites—rather than, say, from the frontalis muscle alone—should lead to more extensive relaxation. In one study (Kim, 1991), experimental subjects (previously selected on the basis of high cardiovascular reactivity) were provided with auditory feedback based on an equally weighted average of four muscle sites—frontalis, masseter, sternomastoid, and forearm flexor. A second group received only frontalis EMG feedback. The third group simply listened to a steady tone in lieu of feedback. Only the multisite group showed significantly lowered EMG levels averaged from the four sites across training sessions. Moreover, skin conductance levels (but not heart rate) reflected lower arousal in the multisite group than in the other groups.

We have recently successfully extended this technique to several individuals with performance anxiety. One client, for example, was phobic about being in crowded places, especially city buses; another feared eating in front of others. Multisite EMG training was provided in a number of clinic sessions. Both clients reported reductions of incidents in which anxiety was experienced. However, these benefits cannot be solely attributed to the EMG training because both individuals also received a standard relaxation tape for home practice, as well as in vivo exposure to the fear stimuli later in training. Nonetheless, the multisite training technique does show promise, and both clients and therapist seem to find it a plausible step.

Acquiring Task-related Skills. Frequently, patients with performance anxiety can also be taught various practical, active coping procedures. Often, they can be encouraged to suggest some of these strategies themselves, a process that gives them a sense of creative participation in their own treatment. For example, in public speaking phobia, various active coping strategies can be recommended. The patient may be told to tape record a practice talk, then to practice relaxing while listening to the tape playback—and, also, to keep an eye on both delivery and content. "Is the tempo too slow or too fast? Too much in a monotone? Too much mumbling? Is the presentation well organized? Is it clear? Practice the talk in a place and manner similar to the actual speaking situation. It may be necessary to practice by writing on the blackboard or using the slide projector." One of our patients, a young pediatrician, used her slides as a reminder to maintain abdominal breathing during a much-dreaded Grand Rounds presentation. Each of her thirty slides served as a reminder to check her breathing pattern. In this way, she successfully moderated both her tendency to hyperventilate and the associated fear that she would faint midway through her lecture.

Similar recommendations can be made in cases of examination anxiety. To summarize, we might say that, in performance anxiety, the learning of relaxation skills and the learning of active coping skills are complementary enterprises.

ADDITIONAL TECHNIQUES FOR MODIFYING THE STRESS-COPING RESPONSE

Recent decades have witnessed a steady evolution of procedures designed to alter various components of the stress response. This incremental growth will no doubt continue so that we can expect to see an expanding body of practical procedures at our disposal. This growth also means that additional specific techniques will be available for the development of combined interventions. Such combinations should allow an increasingly better fit between our ministrations and the needs of the individual patient.

Several of the new techniques, which range from the physical to the cognitive, are discussed in the section that follows. These three techniques—the retraining of breathing patterns, physical exercise, and the cognitive behavior therapy technique of anger control—are good illustrations of specific procedures designed to change significant components of the active coping response.

Retraining of Respiratory Patterns

Respiratory disturbances are increasingly being seen as key antecedents of certain anxiety reactions, especially panic disorders. Furthermore, there is evidence that an easily-learned abdominal breathing exercise can often be successful in countering such reactions. We now make such a manuever a regular part of the training given to our stress patients. Indeed, the advent of this technique in recent years illustrates one of our leading themes: stress management is not a static technology, but an evolving body of knowledge and techniques.

A hyperventilation theory of panic disorder and agoraphobia has been advanced by Ley (1987). In his view, hyperventilation is the crucial event in panic attacks and in most, if not all, of the sensations, dizziness, lightheadedness, paresthesias, and feelings of unreality. If one feels unable to breathe, and if one's heart beats wildly for no apparent reason, then heart failure and death may well seem imminent. Under the circumstances, intense fear is a natural reaction.

When overbreathing occurs, the body suffers an excess loss of carbon dioxide. This loss leads to an increase in blood alkalosis and a decrease in arterial CO_2 tension. Arterial diameter is reduced and there is less blood flow to body tissue. Consequently, the heart begins to pump more vigorously; there is a shortness of breath as well as a host of other reactions particularly affecting the autonomic nervous system and metabolic processes.

Over the past several years, evidence has mounted that respiratory retraining—usually in the form of learning abdominal (diaphragmatic) breathing—has some definite merits in the modification of stress and anxiety reactions. The rationale for such training is that hyperventilation generates drastic physiological changes that, in turn, set the stage for the onset of powerful anxiety.

At St. Bartholomew's Hospital in London, Bonn, Readhead, and Timmons (1984) successfully used breathing retraining in treating clinically diagnosed agoraphobics. A group of 21 patients was first subjected to a 3-minute hyperventilation test in which they panted through both mouth and nose at a rate of over 60 breaths per minute. Of the 21 patients, 20 reported their hyperventilation symptoms as being similar to those occurring in their panic attacks, although not as severe. Fourteen of the patients were unable to complete the full 3-minute test because they were overcome by dizziness or other distress.

Twelve of the agoraphobics then entered a treatment program and 7 received two 1-hour breathing retraining sessions followed by seven weekly 2-hour sessions of real-life exposure to the feared situation(s). Breathing retraining consisted of instruction in diaphragmatic respiration—that is, abdominal breathing—which was maintained at a rate of 8 to 10 breaths per minute. The 5 patients in the comparison group—who received the best-documented standard treatment, a behavioral therapy—were simply given nine 2-hour sessions of real-life exposure but without any breathing retraining.

At the end of training, both groups showed a large drop in panic attack frequency (from about 4 per week to less than 1) and in resting breathing rate as well. At the 6-month follow-up, however, the comparison group showed some resurgence in panic attacks, while those in the treatment group had further decreased virtually to zero.

The course of resting breathing rates was also quite illuminating. At the start of treatment, rates were 28 per minute for both groups. At the 6-month follow-up, levels had dropped to 14 per minute in the breathing retraining group (a 50% decrease), but only to 22 per minute in the comparison group—a figure still well above the normal range of 8 to 17 breaths per minute.

Two Dutch investigators used respiratory feedback for 25 carefully chosen patients suffering from hyperventilation syndrome (Defares & Grossman, 1988). Auditory feedback told the patients when their breathing exceeded a desired preset rate. In addition, auditory stimuli concerning the correct breathing pattern to follow were simultaneously provided. Patients also practiced at home with the feedback device for 30 minutes per day over the 8-week training period. Control patients were likewise exposed to respiratory feedback, but no attempt was made to alter their breathing patterns, although they did practice relaxation at home twice a day.

Tests conducted one month after training showed an interesting pattern of differences between feedback and nonfeedback patients. Experimental patients were significantly lower on physiological measures: breathing rate and a CO_2 measure. They also measured lower on trait anxiety, state anxiety, and on neurosomatic instability. In the judgment of Defares and Grossman, this shift in trait (long-term) anxiety indicated that a fundamental change in organismic functioning had occurred.

The particular variant of abdominal breathing taught in our Colorado laboratory is patterned on a meditative technique commonly employed in the Vipassana Buddhist tradition of Sri Lanka (Hart, 1987). An important advantage of this technique is that it provides the user with quite specific instructions about what to do mentally as well as physically during the exercise.

The first part of the exercise consists of a shift to relaxed, abdominal breathing. The second part focuses on an attentional component. On every in-breath, the patient returns attention to the muscular sensations that accompany the gentle expansion of the stomach. This second part is reported by patients as helping them to interrupt trains of thought, thereby quieting down mental noise. In other words, this exercise becomes more than simply a respiratory maneuver. With increasing skill, it also becomes a tool for dampening the cognitive processes likely to set off stress and anxiety reactions.

In clinical work with performance anxiety, we find that about 50% of patients report the breathing exercise to be useful during the feared situation. And about 33% say that this exercise was the single most useful maneuver during their encounter with the anxiety-arousing situation.

Physical Exercise

Another technique that appears destined for a lasting place in the pantheon of stress management interventions is the regular use of physical exercise. Some 25 years ago, jogging was a lonely pursuit, an activity that sometimes awakened the suspicions of the police. But during the 1970s, jogging not only became a mass movement, but a movement that has endured. Participation has remained at surprisingly high levels. For example, in Boulder, Colorado, a town of 80,000, the Memorial Day 10-kilometer footrace attracts more than 30,000 contestants annually.

Overall, it is fair to say that over the past couple of decades, millions of people have discovered the stress-reducing properties of regular physical exercise. By now, a formidable body of evidence underscoring the long-term benefits of exercise has accumulated, such as the following:

1. In their Alameda County $5\frac{1}{2}$-year prospective study of 7,000 individuals, Belloc and Breslow (1972) concluded that regular physical exercise was a major factor in health status and longevity. Men with the lowest level of physical activity experienced twice the mortality of those with the highest activity, an effect more pronounced in those under fifty.

2. More recently, in an 8-year prospective study at the Cooper Aerobics Institute in Dallas, Blair and colleagues found a very wide gap in the health status of those who exercised regularly and those who did not (Blair, Kohl, Paffenbarger, Clark, Cooper, & Gibbons, 1989). Some 13,300 patients (10,200 men and 3,100 women) were carefully tested for fitness and health status, then followed for 8 years. Only patients without signs of disease were included in the original sample. Over the 8-year period, sedentary individuals showed far higher mortality rates than those who exercised regularly. Mortality levels for women in the lowest quintile for exercise were 4.6 times higher than those of women in the highest quintile. For men, there were 3.4 times more deaths in the lowest than in the highest quintile. Interestingly, the reduced mortality levels in the physically fit groups were due primarily to their lower rate of cardiovascular disease and cancer.

This study also brought encouraging news to those not especially attracted to the more fanatical aspects of athletics. It was found that the greatest increment in fitness came in the step from the lowest quintile level in exercise to the next one. Among women, the all-cause mortality rates for quintiles 1 (least physically active) through 5 (most active), in order, over the 8-year study, were 39.5, 20.5, 12.2, 6.5, and 8.5. For the men, the corresponding figures were 64.0, 25.5, 27.1, 21.7, and 18.6. Translated into amount of exercise, the step from the first to the second quintile would amount roughly to going from a sedentary status to one involving 30 to 60 minutes of brisk walking each day. Beyond this moderate level of exercise, the gains in health status were not large, although additional exercise of the aerobic type is known to enhance the sense of well-being as well as augment cardiovascular fitness measures. As noted in an accompanying *Journal of the American Medical Association* editorial, this long-term study showed that an impressive improvement in the health status of the U.S. population could be effected simply by encouraging sedentary individuals (about 30% of adults) to indulge regularly in a moderate amount of brisk walking or its equivalent.

3. In a similar vein, in the realm of mental health, Stephens (1988) has recently reported secondary analyses of the results of 4 surveys in the United States and Canada conducted across a 10-year period. These analyses yielded positive relationships between physical activity—swimming, walking, jogging, bicycling, and others—and six measures of mental health, including general well-being, positive and negative affects, and several measures of anxiety and depression. However, it is rightly pointed out by Brown (1990) that the direction of this association is not established—that is, does exercise promote self-reports consistent with mental health, or are mentally healthy people more likely to engage in physical activities? Since most of the existing research on the role of exercise in mental health is correlational, a definite answer to this question is not yet available, but the accumulating research on the two most prevalent emotional disorders, anxiety and depression, is encouraging. Let us look briefly at these areas.

Anxiety and Exercise. In an important review article, Brown (1990) concludes that a substantial body of data indicates a positive correlation between physical exercise and lowered levels of acute (state) measures of anxiety. For chronic (trait) anxiety, however, it has not been possible to document a similar positive relationship. Brown further notes that studies in both areas have been plagued by a variety of methodological flaws, often including nonrandom subject assignment, the use of nonclinical populations, and the absence of measures of aerobic fitness to independently document the effects of exercise.

Two recent studies by Raglin and Morgan (1987) are illustrative of the role that exercise may play in modulating state anxiety. In the first experiment, males who regularly exercised were observed on alternate days of quiet rest and exercise (of several varieties, including jogging, swimming, cycling). Both state anxiety and blood pressure were measured at baseline and at several points up to three hours post-treatment. A significant effect on anxiety reduction due to exercise, but not to rest, was obtained. Moreover, blood pressure reductions due to exercise persisted for three hours, whereas those due to rest did not. In the second experiment, male hypertensives (controlled with medications) served as subjects. Similar effects were obtained, although the effects of effects of rest were more positive in this group. On the other hand, the effects on blood pressure reduction were more persistent in these subjects following exercise than following rest. The authors conclude from these studies that the anti-anxiety effects of exercise are more lasting than those of quiet rest.

In a study conducted at a Norwegian psychiatric hospital, Martinsen, Hoffart, and Solberg (1989) compared the effect of aerobic versus nonaerobic exercise on anxiety. All 79 in-patients met the DSM-III-R criteria for one of the anxiety disorders, and 71% were diagnosed as panic disorder with agoraphobia.

Each patient received three 1-hour sessions of exercise per week of either aerobic or nonaerobic exercise over an 8-week training period. An important inclusion in this study as a VO_2 max test, showing that the aerobic group achieved significant increases in fitness relative to the nonaerobic group as a result of training. Both groups achieved significant decrements in anxiety as measured by three different tests, a result in line with earlier experiments on nonpsychiatric populations. In this study, however, it was found that while both types of exercise reduced reported anxiety, the aerobic form of exercise did not accentuate the reductions, despite the successful impact on VO_2 max levels. This lack of a dose-response relationship led the authors to conclude that the mechanism of action of exercise on anxiety may be more psychological than biological. For example, processes such as the experience of mastery or being distracted from anxiety-producing stimuli may have been operating.

Depression and Exercise. By contrast with the mixed results of research linking exercise and reduction of chronic anxiety, a wealth of studies fairly consistently documents a positive relationship between physical activity and reductions in depression (Brown, 1990). Moreover, the correlations extend to both clinical and nonclinical populations. Unfortunately, again, a wide range of methodological difficulties afflict much of this research, including a common failure to document measures of fitness as a function of training (see review by Brown, 1990).

A relatively early and important study documenting the use of running in treating clinical depression was conducted by Greist and his colleagues (Greist et al., 1979). These investigators compared the effects of running with those of psychotherapy. To be included, patients had to score at the 50th percentile level or above on the SCL-90 depression cluster, not be at significant risk for suicide, not be suffering from psychosis, and not be in need of antidepressant medication. Ten patients received the running treatment, 6 patients received time-limited psychotherapy, and 12 patients received time-unlimited psychotherapy.

Patients in the running group ran 3 to 4 times per week, 1 hour each time, over a 10-week training period. Outcome comparisons for the three groups showed the running treatment to be just as effective in reducing depressive symptoms as the psychotherapy. For the study group as a whole, ratings of depression dropped from a baseline level of "quite a bit" down to "a little bit" by the end of treatment. Over the 9-month follow-up period, this reduced level of depression was well-maintained, especially in the exercise group. Klein et al., (1985) essentially replicated these results and showed, in addition, advantages for exercise over meditation-relaxation and group psychotherapy in treating depression.

Assertiveness Training and Anger Management

While our emphasis in this paper has been primarily psychophysiological, two important cognitive-behavioral techniques should be mentioned because they are often useful in altering significant components of the stress response. These are assertiveness training and anger control.

Some patients with stress-related disorders show an impaired ability to express emotions. This defect has been postulated to be a causative factor in psychosomatic illness by the psychoanalyst Sifneos (1973) as well as by other writers. It seems reasonable to think that if the inability to express affect—that is, "bottling up emotions"—is a contributing factor in a psychosomatic or stress-related disorder, then procedures aimed at correcting this difficulty could be useful therapeutically.

One sure procedure is assertiveness training, a technique that focuses on both the behavioral and cognitive aspects of the stress response. Initially developed by the behavior therapists Salter (1949) and Wolpe (1958), this procedure essentially involves learning the expression of appropriate affect as well as the assertion of one's reasonable rights. It should be emphasized that assertiveness training is not a training in aggression, either verbal or physical. Rather, it may be viewed as learning the skills of emotional expression. An extensive discussion of the technique, along with descriptions of many specific procedures and situations, can be found in *Your Perfect Right* by Alberti and Emmons (1990). It is no exaggeration to say that since its first publication in the early 1970s, this book has become one of the most widely read and influential in contemporary psychology.

To give one example of the technique, we may consider the study by Brooks and Richardson (1980) in which "emotional skills training" was utilized in the alleviation of duodenal ulcer. Anxiety management training was used to moderate strong anxiety and stress reactions, while assertiveness training was employed to alter the inhibited expression of emotion and nonsupportive behavior.

Experimental patients first received four sessions of anxiety management training that included restructuring of irrational beliefs, replacement of worry-type self-statements with more positive self-statements, and progressive relaxation. During the assertiveness training phase, patients focused on learning prudent self-expression to replace feelings of chronic resentment. Patients were also instructed in the daily rehearsal of the new behavior in both home and work situations.

Treatment subjects showed reduced levels of anxiety, fewer days of ulcer pain, and reduced levels of antacid consumption compared to the controls. Most dramatic was the much lower rate of ulcer recurrence in the experimental group. At a follow-up more than 3 years later, only 1 of the 9 available treatment patients had shown a recurrence, but 5 of the 8 controls had suffered recurrence of their ulcer condition. Admittedly, since a mix of procedures was used, the exact role played by assertiveness training cannot be specified, but the study is encouraging nonetheless.

A particular variant of assertiveness training, designed to alter anger responses, has been developed by Novaco (1975; 1980). It should be noted that anger, hate, and suppressed rage are prominent features of many psychosomatic disturbances.

Novaco's method emphasizes a three-systems approach and includes cognitive, emotional (physiological), and behavioral components. Its phases of training parallel Meichenbaum's (1976) stress inoculation technique (see Chapter 37). In the first step of Novaco's method, the cognitive preparation phase, clients are educated concerning the functions of anger and their own patterns of anger. Triggers of anger—persons and situations, multiple determinants of anger, interpersonal interactions, and other cognitive aspects of anger—are identified in discussions between the client and therapist. An anger interview is conducted, and clients develop a diary of anger events and reactions that is used throughout treatment.

In the skill acquisition and rehearsal phase, clients are taught to focus on their expectations concerning others' behavior and on their appraisals of events. For example, clients are urged to "not take things personally." They are encouraged to focus on desirable outcomes in anger situations and to engage in behavior that will enable them to obtain these outcomes using an individually tailored self-instructional package. Clients are also taught specific behavioral skills in the areas of assertiveness, effective communication skills, and problem solving. In this phase, clients are also taught relaxation, encouraged to develop an exercise program, or trained in other techniques designed to reduce physiological arousal.

In the third phase of the anger management procedure, application training, clients practice their skills in situations that are graded hierarchically in terms of level of provocation. Beginning with situations that evoke the least anger and anxiety, and progressing through those that provoke the greatest anger response, clients are encouraged to apply their skills in ways that most effectively enable them to cope with their anger.

Evidence of the effectiveness of anger management training includes Novaco's own applications of the method to psychiatric patients with severe anger (Novaco, 1977a), and to certain groups of individuals with high occupational risk for anger, such as police officers (Novaco, 1977b). Other demonstrations of the usefulness of anger management training were reported by Nomellini and Katz (1983) for families with child-abusing parents and by Moon and Eisler (1983) for male undergraduates. The latter investigators reported that problem-solving and social skills training reduced anger-related cognitions and increased assertiveness and social skills. On the other hand, while cognitive training by itself reduced the level of anger-provoking cognitions, it did not favorably affect assertiveness.

THE PERCEPTION OF CONTROL

A somewhat neglected aspect of stress management, but one that may be central to the whole endeavor, is the matter of controllability—the individual's feeling of influence over the situation or his or her reaction to it. Indeed, the phrase *stress management* implies some degree of controllability. In many stress management procedures, the idea of increasing control, or even the sense of it, can be seen quite clearly—as, for instance, in relaxation training, biofeedback, and assertiveness training.

The sense of control is emerging as a salient concept not only in stress management but in both behavioral and psychodynamic therapies as well (Strupp, 1970). Recall Freud's dictum, "Where Id was, there Ego shall be." Rachman (1978), in an extensive review of behavioral approaches to anxiety, has stressed the importance of a sense of controllability as a major determinant of both anxiety and courage. He suggests that anxiety is likely to appear when we face situations that are both important as well as of uncertain outcome.

In World War II studies of courage and fear in military flyers (summarized by Rachman, 1978), the controllability factor emerged as a major dimension, along with a sense of competence and group membership ("not letting your buddies down"). Studies later conducted on the original Project Mercury astronauts arrived at similar conclusions. For the Mercury astronauts—all of whom were military test pilots—the element of controllability was a principal determinant of their attitude toward the whole enterprise. Indeed, several leading test pilots declined to participate in the Mercury program because the pilot's role in it was obviously modest—not unlike that of an experimental monkey. The original vehicle was simply a windowless capsule. According to the novelist Tom Wolfe (1980), virtuoso test pilots were quite reluctant to assume the status of "spam in a can." At the astronauts' insistence, mission scientists added manual controls and a window to the capsule and renamed it a "spacecraft."

The perception of control has been found to play a role in the development of physiological change through biofeedback and, in turn, biofeedback has been shown to influence the individual's perception of self-control. Carlson (1982) summarizes a number of studies showing that the degree to which persons perceive themselves to be in control over significant outcomes of their performance, measured in terms of "internality" on Rotter's (1966) "locus of control" scale or related scales of perceived self-control, determines the rate at which they will acquire control using biofeedback over heart rate speeding, frontal EMG relaxation, and alpha production. Additionally, in the EMG training setting, some tendency for subjects to shift in the direction of greater perceived self-control following training has been documented (e.g., Carlson, 1977; Stern & Berrenberg, 1977).

The former study is illustrative. Subjects, who tested either at a high level of perceived control ("internals") or a relatively low level of control ("externals"), were then randomly assigned in equal numbers either to a group that received auditory feedback for frontal EMG levels or to a control group that received a noncontingent auditory signal. While there were no differences in EMG levels between the internally and externally oriented subjects during baseline sessions (prior to biofeedback), the former subjects attained somewhat lower EMG levels more rapidly during biofeedback. Moreover, following biofeedback training, the externally oriented subjects had shifted significantly in the internal direction, as reflected by retesting on the scale for perceived control.

While research in this area has been predominantly with nonclinical populations, among the obvious implications is the possibility that clients with generalized beliefs in personal control may be the best candidates for biofeedback treatment for stress disorders. Moreover, biofeedback (and perhaps other relatively focused forms of treatment as well) may generate important effects beyond changes in the biological processes themselves. When self-regulation training is successful, it may promote the more generalized belief and expectation that one can successfully modify one's own reaction patterns in ways that lead to better coping with environmental stress.

Evidence from several sources indicates that the sense of control is an important factor not only in coping with stress, but for health more generally. Antonovski, the Israeli medical sociologist, has developed a concept he terms the "sense of coherence" (Antonovski, 1989). Those imbued with this sense see their world as a coherent, structured place as opposed to one that is chaotic and unstructured. This world is also seen as reasonably predictable: it is one in which effort is rewarded, in contrast to a world that is unpredictable and the consequences of effort capricious. In Antonovski's view, the sense of coherence directly affects one's adaptation to stress. It leads one to engage in particular sorts of behavior, including the adoption of attitudes, that promote health.

The sense of coherence is made up of three components: (1) *comprehensibility:* one's world can be understood in the cognitive sense; (2) *manageability:* resources are available for one to meet the demands posed by the world; (3) *meaning:* the challenges one faces are worthy of effort and emotional commitment. (This component differs from the comprehensibility dimension, which is strictly a cognitive matter.) Antonovski's ideas are especially pertinent to the self-regulatory methods described in this chapter. Each of these techniques involves personal effort in modifying some aspect of an aberrant stress reaction (manageability). Prior to such effort, there must be a degree of understanding regarding the technique (comprehensibility. And the proposed intervention must make emotional sense to patients before they are willing to make an effort to apply it (meaning). Indeed, in daily clinical practice with stress management procedures, patients frequently refer to a sense of mastery and to their increased sense of confidence that they can deal effectively with the problems that confront them.

Independent work by Taylor (1983) similarly points to meaning and controllability as key factors in the individual's ability to cope with stress. Taylor examined the reactions of women diagnosed as having breast cancer. From a psychological point of view, a patient's reactions to learning about the presence of a potentially fatal illness proved to be surprisingly robust. The women, who came from various walks of life, showed a remarkable ability to weather successfully the catastrophic news implied by the diagnosis of cancer. Taylor (1983) noted that her patients' efforts at psychological adaptation to the presence of life-threatening illness focused around three themes: a search for understanding, an attempt to gain mastery over the disease and over their lives in general, and efforts to enhance their self-esteem, to feel positive about themselves despite the reversal of fortune. Some attempt to grapple with these three issues was present in virtually all the patients.

Taylor also offers the surprising suggestion that an important underpinning of the search for meaning and controllability is the capacity to generate and maintain illusions in both these areas (which is a view similar to that advanced earlier by Lefcourt, 1973). On the basis of her observations with cancer patients, Taylor (1983) reached the surprising conclusion that a successful resolution of the issues of meaning, mastery, and self-enhancement depended to a large degree on the capacity to create and nourish illusions—beliefs without factual support. One might think that adaptive strategies based on illusions would be fragile creations, highly vulnerable to disconfirmation by the realities of degenerative neoplastic disease. Yet, this seems not to have been the case. Although their three major coping strategies were frequently based on illusions, for the women in the study disconfirmation of an optimistic belief was a less shattering experience than might have been expected. The demise of one illusion was followed by the birth of another. A particular interpretation generated by a patient seemed less a fixed and precise matter, such as a bookkeeping entry, than an expression of a general need or theme pertaining to meaning or controllability. And if a particular explanation for their disease became discredited, patients would readily generate a new one. If control efforts with a particular technique proved obviously ineffectual, patients would turn to another technique or to something they could control, such as participating in the management of their own treatment.

In this view, the capacity for illusion around the issues of meaning and controllability is of central importance in our adaptation to stress and may even have evolutionary significance: it helps us to continue to think and act in a collected fashion, even under conditions of great adversity.

NOTES

1. Even sleep can be subdivided into quiet and active phases. In infants, rapid eye movement (REM) sleep is sometimes called active sleep because of the child's vigorous activity, both behavioral and physiological. Non-REM sleep is often called quiet sleep.

2. An often-overlooked advantage of the Cartesian approach to problems is that it stimulates invention. Specifically, once a phenomenon has been broken into components, it may then prove possible to combine and recombine these in novel ways, thereby creating new effects. Such a process of discovering and documenting new effects can fairly be called invention.

3. It seems likely that further work will tell us more about what sort of hypertensive responds to what sort of interventions. Duncan et al. (1985), for example, showed that hypertensives with high catecholamine levels benefited more from an aerobic exercise program than did low catecholamine patients. Martin and Calfas (1989), found that regular aerobic exercise reduced diastolic pressures by 9.6 mm Hg in a group of mild hypertensives. A control group spending an equal amount of time at slow calisthenics and stretching exercises did not show any change in pressure.

REFERENCES

AD HOC COMMITTEE ON CLASSIFICATION OF HEADACHE. Classification of headache. *Journal of the American Medical Association,* 1962, *179,* 717–718.

ADLER, C. S., ADLER, S. M., & PACKARD, R. C. *Psychiatric aspects of headache.* Baltimore, MD: Williams & Wilkins, 1987.

ADLER, S. S. Seeking stillness in motion: An introduction to Tai Chi for seniors. *Activities, Adaptation, and Aging,* 1983, *3,* 1–14.

ALBERTI, R. E., & EMMONS, M. L. *Your perfect right: A guide to assertive living.* New York: Impact Publications, 1990.

AMERICAN PSYCHIATRIC ASSOCIATION. *Diagnostic and statistical manual of mental disorders* (3d rev. ed.). Washington, DC: American Psychiatric Association, 1987.

Andrasik, F. Relaxation and biofeedback for chronic headaches. In A. D. Holzman & D. C. Turk (eds.), *Pain management*. New York: Pergamon Press, 1986.

Andrasik, F., & Holroyd, K. A. A test of specific and nonspecific effects in the biofeedback treatment of tension headache. *Journal of Consulting and Clinical Psychology*, 1980, *48*, 575–586.

Antonovski, A. A somewhat personal odyssey in studying the stress process. *Stress Medicine*, 1989, *6*, 71–80.

Australian Therapeutic Trial in Mild Hypertension. Untreated mild hypertension. *The Lancet*, 1982, *1*, 185–191.

Bakal, D. A. *The psychobiology of chronic headache*. New York: Springer, 1982.

Bakal, D. A., Demjen, S., & Kaganov, J. A. Cognitive behavioral treatment of chronic headache. *Headache*, 1981, *21*, 81–86.

Belloc, H. B., & Breslow, L. Relationship of physical health status and health practice. *Preventive Medicine*, 1972, *1*, 409–421.

Benson, H. *The relaxation response*. New York: Morrow Press, 1975.

Blair, S. N., Kohl, H. W., Paffenbarger, R. S., Clark, D. G., Cooper, K. H., & Gibbons, L. W. Physical fitness and all-cause mortality: A prospective study of healthy men and women. *Journal of the American Medical Association*, 1989, *262*, 2395–2401.

Blanchard, E. B. Biofeedback treatment of essential hypertension. *Biofeedback and Self-Regulation*, 1990, *15*, 209–228.

Blanchard, E. B., Andrasik, F., Neff, D. F., Teders, S. J., Pallmeyer, T. P., Arena, J. B., Jurish, S. E., Saunders, N. L., Ahles, T. A., & Rodichok, L. D. Sequential comparison of relaxation training and biofeedback in the treatment of three kinds of chronic headache or, the machines be necessary some of the time. *Behavior Research and Therapy*, 1982, *20*, 1–13.

Blanchard, E. B., McCoy, G. C., Musso, A., Gerardi, M. A., Pallmeyer, T. P., Gerardi, R. J., Cotch, P. A., Siracusa, K., & Andrasik, F. A controlled comparison of thermal biofeedback and relaxation training in the treatment of essential hypertension: I. Short-term and long-term outcome. *Behavior Therapy*, 1986, *17*, 563–579.

Bonn, J. A., Readhead, C. P., & Timmons, B. H. Enhanced adaptive behavioral response in agoraphobic patients pretreated with breathing retraining. *The Lancet*, 1984, *2*, 665–669.

Borkovec, T. D., Johnson, M. C., & Block, D. L. Evaluating experimental designs in relaxation research. In R. L. Woolfolk & P. M. Lehrer (eds.), *Principles and practice of stress management*. New York: Guilford Press, 1984.

Brooks, G. R., & Richardson, F. C. Emotional skills training: A treatment program for duodenal ulcer. *Behavior Therapy*, 1980, *11*, 198–207.

Brown, D. R. Exercise, fitness, and mental health. In C. Bourchard, R. J. Shephard, T., Stephens, J. R. Sutton, & B. D. McPherson (eds.), *Exercise, fitness, and health*. Champaign, IL: Human Kinetics Books, 1990.

Budzynski, T. H. Biofeedback strategies in headache treatment. In J. V. Basmajian (ed.), *Biofeedback: Principles and practice for clinicians* (3d ed.). Baltimore, MD: Williams & Wilkins, 1989.

Budzynski, T. H., & Stoyva, J. M. An instrument for producing deep muscle relaxation by means of analog information feedback. *Journal of Applied Behavior Analysis*, 1969, *2*, 231–237.

Budzynski, T. H., Stoyva, J. M., & Adler, C. S. Feedback-induced muscle relaxation: Application to tension headache. *Behavior Therapy and Experimental Psychiatry*, 1970, *1*, 205–211.

Budzynski, T. H., Stoyva, J. M., Adler, C. S., & Mullaney, D. J. EMG biofeedback and tension headache: A controlled outcome study. *Psychosomatic Medicine*, 1973, *35*, 484–496.

Budzynski, T. H., Stoyva, J. M., & Peffer, K. E. Biofeedback techniques in psychosomatic disorders. In A. Goldstein & E. Foa (eds.) *Handbook of behavioral interventions*. New York: Wiley, 1980.

CARLSON, J. G. Locus of control and frontal electromyographic response training. *Biofeedback and Self-regulation,* 1977, *2,* 259–271.

————. Some concepts of perceived control and their relationship to bodily self-control. *Biofeedback and Self-regulation,* 1982, *7,* 341–375.

CSIKSZENTMIHALYI, M. *Flow: The psychology of optimal experience.* New York: Harper & Row, 1990.

DARWIN, C. *The expression of emotion in man and animals.* Chicago: University of Chicago Press, 1965.

DEFARES, P. B., & GROSSMAN, P. Hyperventilation, anxiety, and coping with stress. In P. B. Defares (ed.), *Stress and anxiety, 11.* New York: Hemisphere, 1988.

DEMBROSKI, T. M., WEISS, S., SHIELDS, J. L., HAYNES, S., & FEINLEIB, M. (eds.), *Coronary-prone behavior.* New York: Springer-Verlag, 1978.

DROSSMAN, D. A., POWELL, D. W., & SESSIONS, J. T. The irritable bowel syndrome. *Gastroenterology,* 1977, *73,* 811–822.

DUNCAN, J. J., FARR, J. E., UPTON, J., HAGAN, R. D., OGELSBY, M. E., & BLAIR, S. N. The effects of aerobic exercise on plasma catecholamines and blood pressure in patients with mild essential hypertension. *Journal of the American Medical Association,* 1985, *254,* 2609–2613.

FISHER, G. S. *Stress and the perception of control.* London: Lawrence Erlbaum, 1984.

FLANNERY, R. B. From victim to survivor: A stress management approach in the treatment of learned helplessness. In B. A. van der Kolk, *Psychological trauma.* Washington, DC: American Psychiatric Press, 1987.

FRANKENHAEUSER, M. Psychoneuroendocrine approaches to the study of emotion as related to stress and coping. In H. E. Howe & R. A. Dienstbier (eds.), *1978 Nebraska Symposium on Motivation.* Lincoln: University of Nebraska Press, 1978.

————. The sympathetic-adrenal and pituitary-adrenal responses to challenge. In T. M. Dembroski, T. H. Schmidt, & G. Blumchen (eds.), *Biobehavioral bases of coronary heart disease.* Basel: Karger, 1983.

FRIEDMAN, M., & ROSENMAN, R. *Type A behavior and your heart.* New York: Knopf, 1974.

FRIEDMAN, M., & ULMER, D. *Treating type A behavior and your heart.* New York: Fawcett Cress/ Ballantine, 1984.

GILES, S. L. Separate and combined effects of biofeedback training and brief individual psychotherapy in the treatment of gastrointestinal disorders. *Dissertation Abstracts International,* 1978, *39,* 2495-B.

GLASS, D. C. Stress, behavior patterns, and coronary disease. *American Scientist,* 1977, *65,* 177–187.

GOLDSTEIN, D. S. Neurotransmitters and stress. *Biofeedback and Self-regulation,* 1990, *15,* 243–271.

GOLDSTEIN, J. *The experience of insight: A simple and direct guide to Buddhist meditation.* Boston: Shambhala, 1983.

GREIST, J. H., KLEIN, M. H., EISCHENS, R. R., FARIS, J., GURMAN, A. S., & MORGAN, W. P. Running as a treatment for depression. *Comprehensive Psychiatry,* 1979, *20,* 41–54.

HART, W. *Vipassana meditation: As taught by S. N. Goenka.* San Francisco: Harper & Row, 1987.

HAURI, P. *Case studies in insomnia.* New York: Plenum Press, 1991.

HAURI, P., & LINDE, S. *No more sleepless nights.* New York: Wiley, 1990.

HAYNES, S. G., FEINLEIB, M., & KANNEL, W. B. The relationship of psychosocial factors to coronary heart disease in the Framingham study. Pt. 3: Eight-year incidence of coronary heart disease. *American Journal of Epidemiology,* 1980, *111,* 37–58.

HENRY, J. P. Neuroendocrine patterns of emotional response. In R. Plutchik & H. Kellerman (eds.), *Emotion: Theory, research, and experience.* Vol. 3. New York: Academic Press, 1986.

HIRAI, T. *Zen meditation and psychotherapy.* Tokyo, New York: Japan Publications, 1989.

Holroyd, K. A., Andrasik, F., & Westbrook, T. Cognitive control of tension headache. *Cognitive Therapy and Research,* 1977, *1,* 121–133.

Jacob, R. G., Chesney, M. A., Williams, D. M., Ding, Y., & Shapiro, A. P. Relaxation therapy for hypertension: Design effects and treatment effects. *Annals of Behavioral Medicine,* 1991, *13,* 5–17.

Jacobson, E. *Progressive relaxation.* Chicago: University of Chicago Press, 1938.

Kabat-Zinn, J., Lipworth, L., & Burney, R. The clinical use of mindfulness meditation for the self-regulation of chronic pain. *Journal of Behavioral Medicine,* 1985, *8,* 163–190.

Kaufmann, P. G., Jacob, R. G., Ewart, C. K., Chesney, M. A., Muenz, L. R., Doub, H., Mercer, W., & Hipp Investigators. Hypertension intervention pooling project. *Health psychology,* 1988, 7(Suppl.), 209–224.

Keane, T. M., Fairbank, J. A., Caddell, J. M., & Zimering, R. T. Implosive (flooding) therapy reduces symptoms of PTSD in Vietnam combat veterans. *Behavior Therapy,* 1989, *20,* 245–260.

Kim, K. *The efficacy of multi-site EMG biofeedback in producing a generalized relaxation effect.* Unpublished master's thesis, University of Hawaii, Honolulu, 1991.

Klein, M. H., Greist, J. H., Gurman, A. S., Neimeyer, R. A., Lesser, D. P., Bushnell, N. J., & Smith, R. E. A comparative outcome study of group psychotherapy vs. exercise treatments for depression. *International Journal of Mental Health,* 1985, *13,* 148–176.

Koplan, J. K., Caspersen, C. J., & Powell, K. E. Physical activity, physical fitness, and health: Time to act. (Editorial). *Journal of the American Medical Association,* 1989, *262,* 2437.

Lang, P. J. Fear reduction and fear behavior: Problems in treating a construct. *Research in Psychotherapy,* 1968, *3,* 90–102.

Latimer, P. R. *Functional gastrointestinal disorders: A behavioral medicine approach.* New York: Springer, 1983.

Lefcourt, H. M. The function of the illusions of control and freedom. *American Psychologist,* 1973, *28,* 417–425.

Levis, D. J. Implementing the technique of implosive therapy. In A. Goldstein & E. B. Foa (eds.), *Handbook of behavioral interventions: A clinical guide.* New York: Wiley, 1980.

Ley, R. Panic disorder: A hyperventilation interpretation. In L. Michelson & L. M. Ascher (eds.), *Anxiety and stress disorders: Cognitive-behavioral assessment and treatment.* New York: Guilford Press, 1987.

Linden, W. *Autogenic training: A clinical guide.* New York: Guilford Press, 1990.

Luthe, W. *Autogenic therapy. Vol. IV: Research and therapy.* New York: Grune & Stratton, 1970.

Luthe, W., & Schulz, J. H. *Autogenic therapy. Vol. II: Medical applications.* New York: Grune & Stratton, 1969.

Magarshack, D. *Stansilavski on the art of the stage.* London: Faber & Faber, 1950.

Marks, I. M. Phobias and obsessions. In J. Maser & M. Seligman (eds.), *Experimental psychopathology.* New York: Wiley, 1977.

Martin, J. E., & Calfas, K. J. Is it possible to lower blood pressure with exercise? Efficacy and adherence issues. *Applied Sport Psychology,* 1989, *1,* 109–131.

Martinsen, E. W., Hoffart, A., & Solberg, Ø. Y. Aerobic and non-aerobic forms of exercise in the treatment of anxiety disorders. *Stress Medicine,* 1989, *5,* 115–120.

Mason, J. W. Organization of psychoendocrine mechanisms. In N. S. Greenfield & R. A. Sternbach (eds.), *Handbook of psychophysiology.* New York: Holt, Rinehart & Winston, 1972.

McGrady, A., & Higgins, J. T. Prediction of response to biofeedback-assisted relaxation in hypertensives: Development of a hypertensive predictor profile (HYPP). *Psychosomatic Medicine,* 1989, *51,* 277–284.

McGrady, A., Woerner, M., Bernal, G. A., & Higgins, J. T. Effect of biofeedback-assisted relaxation on blood pressure and cortisol levels in normotensives and hypertensives. *Journal of Behavioral Medicine,* 1987, *10,* 301–310.

MEICHENBAUM, D. Cognitive factors in biofeedback therapy. *Biofeedback and Self-regulation,* 1976, *1,* 201–216.

MICHELSON, L., MAVISSAKALIAN, M., & MARCHIONE, K. Cognitive, behavioral, and psychophysiological treatments of agoraphobia: A comparative outcome investigation. *Behavior Therapy,* 1988, *19,* 97–120.

MONROE, L. J. Psychological and physiological differences between good and poor sleepers. *Journal of Abnormal Psychology,* 1967, *72,* 255–264.

MOON, J. R., & EISLER, R. M. Anger control: An experimental comparison of three behavioral treatments. *Behavior Therapy,* 1983, *14,* 493–505.

MOORE, S. *The Stanislavski system: The professional training of an actor.* New York: Penguin, 1976.

NEFF, D. F., & BLANCHARD, E. B. A multi-component treatment for irritable bowel syndrome. *Behavior Therapy,* 1987, *18,* 70–83.

NHAT HANH, T. *The miracle of mindfulness: A manual on meditation.* Boston: Beacon Press, 1987.

NOMELLINI, S., & KATZ, R. C. Effects of anger control training on abusive parents. *Cognitive Therapy and Research,* 1983, *7,* 57–68.

NOVACO, R. W. *Anger control: The development and evaluation of an experimental treatment.* Lexington, MA.: Lexington Books, 1975.

————. Stress inoculation: A cognitive therapy for anger and its application to a case of depression. *Journal of Consulting and Clinical Psychology,* 1977, *45,* 600–608. (a)

————. A stress innoculation approach to anger management in the training of law enforcement officers. *American Journal of Community Psychology,* 1977, *5,* 327–346. (b)

————. The training of probation counselors as anger therapists. *Journal of Counseling Psychology,* 1980, *27,* 385–390.

NUECHTERLEIN, K. H., & HOLROYD, J. C. Biofeedback in the treatment of tension headache. *Archives of General Psychiatry,* 1980, *37,* 866–873.

OLTON, D. S., & NOONBERG, A. R. *Biofeedback: Clinical applications in behavioral medicine.* Englewood Cliffs, NJ: Prentice-Hall, 1980.

ÖST, L. G., & JANSSON, L. Methodological issues in cognitive-behavioral treatments of anxiety disorders. In L. Michelson & L. M. Ascher (eds.), *Anxiety and stress disorder: Cognitive-behavioral assessment and treatment.* New York: Guilford Press, 1987.

RACHMAN, S. J. *Fear and courage.* San Francisco: W. J. Freeman, 1987.

RAGLIN, J. S., & MORGAN, W. P. Influence of exercise and quiet rest on state anxiety and blood pressure. *Medicine and Science in Sports and Exercise,* 1987, *19,* 456–463.

REEVES, J. L. EMG-biofeedback reduction of tension headache: A cognitive skills-training approach. *Biofeedback and Self-regulation,* 1976, *1,* 217–225.

ROTTER, J. Generalized expectancies for internal versus external control of reinforcement. *Psychological Monographs,* 1966, *80.*

RUGH, J., PERLIS, D., & DISRAELI, R. (eds.), *Biofeedback in dentistry.* Pheonix, AZ: Semantodontics, 1977.

SALTER, A. *Conditioned reflex therapy.* New York: Capricorn Books, 1949.

SCHULTZ, J. H. *Das autogene training: Konzentrative selbstentspannung. [Autogenic training: Self-induced relaxation.]* Stuttgart: Thieme Verlag, 1932.

SCHWARZ, S. P., BLANCHARD, E. B., & NEFF, D. F. Behavioral treatment of irritable bowel syndrome: A 1-year follow-up study. *Biofeedback and Self-regulation,* 1986, *11,* 189–198.

SIFNEOS, P. E. The prevalence of "Alexithymic" characteristics in psychosomatic patients. *Psychotherapy and Psychosomatics,* 1973, *22,* 255–262.

STAMPFL, T. G., & LEVIS, D. J. Essentials of implosive therapy: A learning theory-based psychodynamic behavioral therapy. *Journal of Abnormal Psychology,* 1967, *72,* 496–503.

STEPHENS, T. Physical activity and mental health in the United States and Canada: Evidence from four population surveys. *Preventive Medicine,* 1988, *17,* 35–47.

STERN, G. S., & BERRENBERG, J. L. Biofeedback training in frontalis muscle relaxation and ehancement of belief in personal control. *Biofeedback and Self-regulation,* 1977, *2,* 173–182.

STERNBACH, R. A. *Principles of psychophysiology.* New York: Academic Press, 1966.

STOYVA, J. M. Autogenic training and biofeedback combined: A reliable method for the induction of general relaxation. In J. V. Basmajian (ed.), *Biofeedback: Principles and practice for clinicians.* (3d ed.). Baltimore, MD: Williams & Wilkins, 1989.

STOYVA, J. M., & BUDZYNSKI, T. H. Cultivated low arousal—an anti-stress response? In L. V. DiCara (ed.), *Recent advances in limbic and autonomic nervous systems research.* New York: Plenum Press, 1974.

STRUPP, H. Specific versus nonspecific factors in psychology and the problem of control. *Archives of General Psychiatry,* 1970, *23,* 393–401.

SVEDLUND, J., SJODIN, I., OTTOSON, J. O., & DOTEVALL, G. Controlled study of psychotherapy of irritable bowel syndrome. *The Lancet,* 1983, *2,* 589–591.

SWITZ, D. M. What the gastroenterologist does all day. *Gastroenterology,* 1976, *70,* 1048–1050.

TAYLOR, S. E. Adjustment to threatening events: A theory of cognitive adaptation. *American Psychologist,* 1983, *38,* 1161–1173.

WARD, M. M., SWAN, G. E., & CHESNEY, M. A. Arousal-reduction treatments for mild essential hypertension: A meta-analysis of recent studies. In S. Julius & D. Basset (eds.), *Handbook of hypertension. Vol. 9: Behavioral factors in hypertension.* New York: Elsevier/North Holland Biomedical Press, 1987.

WHITE, R. W. Motivation reconsidered: The conceptualization of competence. *Phychological Review,* 1959, *66,* 297–333.

WHITEHEAD, W. E., & SCHUSTER, M. M. *Gastrointestinal disorders: Behavioral and physiological basis for treatment.* New York: Academic Press, 1985.

WOLFE, T. *The right stuff.* New York: Bantam Books, 1980.

WOLFF, H. G. *Headache and other head pain.* New York: Oxford University Press, 1963.

WOLPE, J. *Psychotherapy by reciprocal inhibition.* Stanford, CA: Stanford University Press, 1958.

——————. Behavior therapy for psychosomatic disorders. *Psychosomatics,* 1980, *21,* 379–385.

WOOLFOLK, R. L., & LEHRER, P. M. (eds.), *Principles and practice of stress management.* New York: Guilford Press, 1984.

39

Stress Response Syndromes and Their Treatment

Mardi J. Horowitz   Nigel P. Field   Catherine C. Classen

THE EXPERIENCE OF RECURRENT INTRUSIVE IMAGES, ideas, and feelings related to a previous traumatic experience has long been recognized as a cardinal symptom of stress response syndromes. The tendency toward the compulsive repetition of traumatic perceptions and the repression of equivalent memories was first observed and documented by Breuer and Freud (1895) in their work on hysteria. These clinical observations on intrusive repetitions and avoidance were further verified in field studies on the impact of life events, such as combat reactions (Grinker & Spiegel, 1945), nuclear holocaust (Lifton, 1967), disasters (Keiser, 1968), and bereavement (Lindemann, 1944; Parkes, 1970). Following systematic studies of the dramatic increase in intrusive and omissive conscious experiences after a variety of stressful life events, the centrality of these symptoms led to the DSM-III diagnosis of post-traumatic stress disorder (PTSD), which was subsequently revised for DSM-III-R (see Table 39–1).

UNBIDDEN IMAGES: CLINICAL OBSERVATIONS

Unbidden images are experienced consciously as the loss of voluntary control over the flow of information. Intrusiveness is of special interest because it is a formal rather than conceptual quality that ranges across hallucinations, illusions, nightmares, obsessive thought images, flashbacks, and altered body images. Careful description and explanation of such unbidden images shed some light on visual thinking, regulation of thinking, and failures of control processes (Horowitz, 1983).

The contents, genesis, and changes of recurrent unbidden imagery experiences are multicausal, as are the reasons for cessation of a recurrent image, alteration of its contents, and appearance of greater volitional control (Horowitz, 1978). One finding is that the contents of unbidden images are frequently based upon previous perceptual realities of a serious life event and that intrusion is an important index of stress.

Work on this chapter was funded through the John D. and Catherine T. MacArthur Foundation's Program on Conscious and Unconscious Mental Processes.

TABLE 39-1
PTSD Criteria According to DSM-III-R

Diagnostic Criteria for 309.89 Post-traumatic Stress Disorder

A. The person has experienced an event that is outside the range of usual human experience and that would be markedly distressing to almost anyone, e.g., serious threat to one's life or physical integrity; serious threat or harm to one's children, spouse, or other close relatives and friends; sudden destruction of one's home or community; or seeing another person who has recently been, or is being, seriously injured or killed as the result of an accident or physical violence.

B. The traumatic event is persistently reexperienced in at least one of the following ways:

    (1) recurrent and intrusive distressing recollections of the event (in young children, repetitive play in which themes or aspects of the trauma are expressed)
    (2) recurrent distressing dreams of the event
    (3) sudden acting or feeling as if the traumatic event were recurring (includes a sense of reliving the experience, illusions, hallucinations, and dissociative [flashback] episodes, even those that occur upon awakening or when intoxicated)
    (4) intense psychological distress at exposure to events that symbolize or resemble an aspect of the traumatic event, including anniversaries of the trauma

C. Persistent avoidance of stimuli associated with the trauma or numbing of general responsiveness (not present before the trauma), as indicated by at least three of the following:

    (1) efforts to avoid thoughts or feelings associated with the trauma
    (2) efforts to avoid activities or situations that arouse recollections of the trauma
    (3) inability to recall an important aspect of the trauma (psychogenic amnesia)
    (4) markedly diminished interest in significant activities (in young children, loss of recently acquired developmental skills such as toilet training or language skills)
    (5) feeling of detachment or estrangement from others
    (6) restricted range of affect, e.g., unable to have loving feelings
    (7) sense of foreshortened future, e.g., does not expect to have a career, marriage, or children, or a long life

D. Persistent symptoms of increased arousal (not present before the trauma), as indicated by at least two of the following:

    (1) difficulty falling or staying asleep
    (2) irritability or outbursts of anger
    (3) difficulty concentrating
    (4) hypervigilance
    (5) exaggerated startle response
    (6) physiologic reactivity upon exposure to events that symbolize or resemble an aspect of the traumatic event (e.g., a woman who was raped in an elevator breaks out in a sweat when entering any elevator)

E. Duration of the disturbance (symptoms in B, C, and D) of at least one month.

Specify delayed onset if the onset of symptoms was at least six months after the trauma.

Source: American Psychiatric Association: *Diagnostic and Statistical Manual of Mental Disorders, Third Edition, Revised,* Washington, DC, American Psychiatric Association, 1987.

EXPERIMENTAL WORK ON INTRUSIVE THINKING AFTER PERCEPTION OF STRESS-INDUCING STIMULI

In light of such clinical observations of intrusive images following a stressful life event, Horowitz carried out a series of experimental studies in an attempt to demonstrate the generality of intrusive conscious representations as a cardinal sign of a psychological state of stress (for a review, see Horowitz, 1975). This undertaking involved showing stress-inducing films to subjects, such as films depicting bodily injury threats to evoke fear and anger and neutral films that functioned as controls. This paradigm was based on work by Lazarus and Opton (1966), who demonstrated that fear-inducing films are effective in eliciting stressful responses in a laboratory setting.

Following exposure to a stressful or neutral film, subjects participated in a signal detection task, modelled on a paradigm utilized by Antrobus, Singer, and Greenberg (1966) for sampling a subject's ongoing conscious thought. Subjects were required to judge whether two tones, separated by a brief temporal interval, were of the same pitch. Successful performance of this task required mental rehearsal of the previous tone throughout the interval prior to the subsequent tone, thus involving utilization of attentional resources. Subjects were also instructed to try to avoid attending to task-irrelevant thoughts, as these might impede performance.

After engaging in the sound-matching task for one or two minutes, subjects were asked to write down the thoughts they had while performing the task. This sequence of sound matching and written recall was repeated several times over the course of the session. The signal detection task was included in order to create a conflict situation between a conscious intention to inhibit task irrelevant thoughts in order to perform well on the task and an unconscious motive toward conscious representation of incompletely processed stress-related information.

The main dependent measure consisted of the extent of intrusive thought contained in subjects' written recall of the thoughts they had while engaged in the sound-matching task. In the context of these studies, an intrusive thought was defined as "any thought that implies nonvolitional entry into awareness, requires suppressive effort or is hard to dispel, occurs perseveratively, or is experienced as something to be avoided" (Horowitz, 1975:1458). As predicted, subjects exposed to the stressful films exhibited a significantly greater frequency of intrusive thought relative to neutral film subjects. Also, for subjects within the stressful film condition, those who experienced greater emotional arousal during the film, as indicated on an affect self-report measure administered immediately following the film, exhibited a greater frequency of intrusion. These results were replicated across different stressful films and demand set manipulations (Horowitz, 1975).

In a subsequent study utilizing the stress film paradigm, Horowitz and Wilner (1976) found preliminary support for the role of individual difference factors in stress responses. In this experiment, a film showing the abandonment of a young boy by his father was included. This film tended to induce feelings of anger and sadness. Subjects were also asked to complete an inventory of life events prior to viewing the film (Horowitz, Schaefer, & Cooney, 1974). Because a history of exposure to stressful experiences was expected to make a person more prone to exhibiting stress reactions in response to subsequent stressors, those with such a history were expected to evidence greater reactivity to the stressful film relative to those with a less stressful history. This would be especially likely if the nature of the current stressor were of a type similar to previous stressors.

No correlation was found between response to the films and the overall stress score on the life events questionnaire. However, people who had the highest frequency of deaths and separations in the past experienced the most sadness and fear after the separation film. This provided some support to the hypothesis that earlier stressful life events make one more vulnerable to stress reactions to later stressful life events of the same type. Thus, while a general index of life stress did not predict the extent of stress reactions, similarity between a previous stressor and a current stressor did so.

A study by Klos and Singer (1981) provides further support for the hypothesis that intrusive and repetitive thought is a general stress response tendency. In addition, it extends Horowitz and Wilner's (1976) preliminary findings that earlier stress experiences increase one's vulnerability to having subsequent stress reactions in response to stressors of the same type.

In their study, Klos and Singer (1981) examined the impact of a simulated stressful interaction with a parent on subsequent repetitive cognitions related to the stressor. They defined repetitive cognition as "the persistence or recurrence of particular thoughts, fantasies, or imagery pertaining to past experience; these cognitions are independent of the present situation of the person and are experienced as attention demanding" (p. 975).

An improvisational technique was used with undergraduate subjects by asking them to simulate interactions with the same-sexed parent. Subjects were instructed to enact three dialogues with the parent utilizing the "empty chair" method, in which they were to imagine their parent sitting in an empty chair facing them. They were instructed to role-play both sides of the interaction by switching chairs so that one chair represented the self and the other represented the parent. While role-playing their parent, subjects were asked to make the simulation as realistic as possible by trying to use the same words, gestures, and tone of voice as that of the parent.

Subjects were randomly assigned to one of three conditions representing different levels of interpersonal stress. The high stress condition involved a coercive confrontation with the parent in which the parent appeared unwilling to listen or showed no attempt to take the perspective of the son or daughter but, instead, was motivated to "win" the argument. The moderately stressful collaborative confrontation condition had the parent showing greater willingness to consider the son or daughter's point of view and more openness to compromise. For these two confrontation conditions, the interactions were based on conflict situations commonly experienced by college students in relation to their parents, such as conflict over family obligations. The collaborative decisionmaking control condition constituted a dialogue between the parent and child involving a shared problem that was external to the dyadic relationship.

Immediately after participating in the dialogues, subjects completed a number of affect scales in order to assess the emotional impact of the roleplay and then engaged in a 20-minute thought sampling session. During the thought sampling session, subjects were seated alone next to a microphone and instructed to report out loud whatever thoughts, images, feelings, or fantasies they were experiencing each time a buzzer sounded.

The role of personality factors on subjective distress in response to the simulation was assessed by having subjects complete a questionnaire prior to the simulation. This questionnaire measured the extent to which subjects experienced conflict and a sense of estrangement, as well as the degree of acceptance and support, with the same-sexed parent.

As predicted, the coercive condition evoked more frequent simulation-related thought relative to the collaborative confrontation and the collaborative decisionmaking conditions. Longstanding conflict with a parent was found to be an important mediator of the effects of type of interpersonal interaction on simulation-related repetitive thought, particularly within the coercive confrontation condition. Within the coercive confrontation condition, subjects with longstanding parental relationship stress exhibited as much as 50% simulation-related thought, whereas subjects with low longstanding parental stress experienced less than 10%. This study demonstrates the importance of personality and situational variables and their interaction in accounting for intrusion as an index of current states of psychological stress. Furthermore, it shows the importance of the match between the situational stressor events and longstanding internalized meaning systems, or person schemas (Horowitz, 1991; Singer & Salovey, 1991).

EMPIRICAL INVESTIGATIONS OF SUBJECTIVE STRESS IN RESPONSE TO A LIFE EVENT

Impact of Event Scale

In addition to the laboratory investigations of intrusive thinking, Horowitz and his colleagues conducted a series of clinical and field studies that provided additional valid and convergent evidence for the centrality of intrusion in stress response. A self-rating instrument, the Impact of Event Scale (IES), was developed from the frequent signs and symptoms observed in the clinical studies (Horowitz, Wilner, & Alvarez, 1979). This scale could be anchored to specific constellations of life events, such as natural disasters, assaults, illnesses, injuries, and losses. It thus provided a means for measuring subjective distress across any kind of stress-inducing life event and could be repeatedly used to track response over time in longitudinal studies and in psychotherapy research for assessing outcome of treatments. The instrument, as it is focused on the formal properties of thought, permits comparison of the impact of different kinds of life events and individual differences in response to them.

Extensive clinical observations indicated that subjective distress in response to life events is comprised of two independent forms of felt experience: intrusion and avoidance. Intrusion involves the involuntary entry into awareness of ideas, memories, and emotions associated with the event. Avoidance is the conscious attempt to divert attention from cognitions and feelings related to the life event. The IES was developed to measure both dimensions. It cannot, however, measure pure repression, denial, and disavowel in which there is not the experience of avoidance.

A 20-item version of the IES was given to a sample of 66 adults who sought psychotherapy as a result of a serious life event. Approximately half of these subjects had experienced bereavement and the remainder had suffered from personal injuries. Because all items were endorsed frequently, it seemed that an appropriate pool of items had been selected. A cluster analysis was conducted in which separate clusters were identified via a correlational measure of association and an average linkage algorithm (Sokall & Sneath, 1973). Four separate clusters were identified. The primary and secondary clusters included 15 of the 20 items, with two smaller residual clusters containing 5 items. The primary cluster contained items from the clinically derived intrusion subset, while the second cluster was composed of clinically derived avoidance items. Thus, this finding provided support for the separate existence of the intrusion and avoidance classifications.

The number of items was reduced by including only those items that empirically clustered and had significant item-to-subscale correlations beyond the .01 level of significance. The revised scale consisted of 15 items, where 7 of the items described episodes of intrusion and 8 items described episodes of avoidance. The revised form of the IES is in Table 39-2.

As indicated in Table 39-2, the investigator or the subject enters at the top of the form the life event that will serve as a referent for each statement on the scale. The subject is asked to estimate the frequency to which each item describes his or her experience over the past week on a 4-point scale ranging from "not at all" to "often". A score for each item is obtained by assigning the weights 0, 1, 3, and 5 to the frequency categories. The time period of the previous week is used, as it was found to provide the most clinically valid reports of a person's current response level (Horowitz et al., 1979).

Using the revised IES, the data on the original sample of 66 adults was recalculated.

TABLE 39–2
Revised Impact of Event Scale

On _____ you experienced _____.
    (date)   (life event)

Below is a list of comments made by people after stressful life events. Please check each item, indicating how frequently these comments were true for you *DURING THE PAST SEVEN DAYS.* If they did not occur during that time, please mark the "not at all" column.

	FREQUENCY		
Not at All	Rarely	Sometimes	Often

1. I thought about it when I didn't mean to.
2. I avoided letting myself get upset when I thought about it or was reminded of it.
3. I tried to remove it from memory.
4. I had trouble falling asleep or staying asleep, because of pictures or thoughts about it that came into my mind.
5. I had waves of strong feelings about it.
6. I had dreams about it.
7. I stayed away from reminders of it.
8. I felt as if it hadn't happened or it wasn't real.
9. I tried not to talk about it.
10. Pictures about it popped into my mind.
11. Other things kept making me think about it.
12. I was aware that I still had a lot of feelings about it, but I didn't deal with them.
13. I tried not to think about it.
14. Any reminder brought back feelings about it.
15. My feelings about it were kind of numb.

Intrusion subset = 1, 4, 5, 6, 10, 11, 14; avoidance subset = 2, 3, 7, 8, 9, 12, 13, 15.

Source: M. J. Horowitz, N. Wilner, & W. Alvarez. The impact of event scale: A measure of subjective stress. *Psychosomatic Medicine 41*(3), 209–218, 1979, © by American Psychosomatic Society.

The split half reliability of the scale was high ($r = 0.86$). Internal consistency of the subscales, calculated using Cronbach's alpha, was also high (intrusion = .78, avoidance = .82). A correlation of .42 ($p < 0.0002$) between intrusion and avoidance subscale scores indicated that the two subscales were associated but did not measure identical dimensions.

The sensitivity of the IES was demonstrated with a subsample of 32 patients from the original sample of 66 adults. Subjects completed the scale immediately before and after a brief therapy. The marked decline in subscale scores that was noted at the end of therapy provides support for its sensitivity to change over time. This subsample was also compared to a sample of medical students who had completed the IES after their first experience with cadaver dissection. As expected, the patient subsample had significantly higher scores on the IES than the medical students; thus the IES also has the ability to discriminate between persons who have experienced life events of different severities.

Further evidence for the psychometric soundness of the IES was obtained in a study of grief response to the loss of a parent (Zilberg, Weiss, & Horowitz, 1982). Thirty-five subjects were out-patients who sought psychotherapy after the death of their parent. A sample of 37 field subject volunteers, who had also recently experienced the death of a parent, comprised the comparison group. That all items were endorsed frequently by both patient and field subjects provides support for the relevance of the item pool and the similarity in the pattern of stress responses across patient and nonpatient groups. The similarity in endorsement of IES items is consistent with Horowitz's position that it is more useful to think of normal and pathological levels of stress as differing in degree rather than kind, as shown for bereavement reactions in Table 39-3 (Horowitz, 1990).

Confirmation of the validity of item assignments to the intrusion and avoidance subscales was obtained in a factor analysis of the combined patient and field groups data. The IES subscales were found to remain internally consistent in both patient and field groups, as well as across time (Cronbach's alpha ranging from .79 to .92). The ability of the IES to differentiate between populations, as well as change over time, was again demonstrated. The patient subscales were of significantly higher magnitude than the subscales for the field subjects. Changes in subscale scores over time was noted in both patient and nonpatient samples.

A cross-validation of the IES in relation to combat stress was conducted by Schwarzwald, Solomon, Weisenberg, and Mikulincer (1987). The purpose of the study was to validate the IES in the context of a population different from those previously studied. The goals were to validate the IES scale structure, determine the relevance of the items to a combat population, examine its ability to discriminate between groups of soldiers who had various levels of exposure and stress reactions, and examine the effects of treatment on IES scores. The results of the study were consistent with previous findings in regard to the validity of the IES. This finding suggests the utility of the IES in measuring stress reactions in diverse populations.

Since its inception, a large body of research across diverse traumatic events has been undertaken utilizing the IES. Its ease of administration, relevance to any stressful life event, and its capacity to measure two central characteristics of PTSD have resulted in the IES becoming a widely used instrument.

A selective listing of IES intrusion and avoidance subscale scores across different subject populations and types of life events is shown in Table 39-4. It highlights the sensitivity of the IES in distinguishing the relative impacts of different life events on subjective distress, the time course of the stress response, and group differences in severity of stress response to the same life event. The reader should note that this is a selective and not an exhaustive review.

In terms of the relative severity of the life event, the IES allows events to be compared according to the degree of subjective distress engendered by them. In comparing the intrusion and avoidance mean scores across events in Table 39-3, it is evident that certain types of events tend to be experienced as more stressful than others. Clearly, the least stressful event in this table is the dissection of a cadaver, followed surprisingly closely by breast biopsy for possible cancer and the actual diagnosis of cancer. IES scores tend to be significantly higher for events involving loss of a significant other, disaster, and violence.

Even though the IES intrusion and avoidance scores provide some information regarding the severity of a life event, it is also important to take the number of weeks elapsed into account. The IES scores, taken in the context of time elapsed since the event, may provide a more accurate reflection of the severity of the life event. In this vein, high IES scores derived shortly after a stressful event, followed by low scores some time afterward, reflect either a less traumatic event or greater progressive mastery of the personal meanings of the event over time relative to events for which the high IES scores persist over time. For example, Steinglass and Gerrity (1990) found that female survivors of a tornado had high IES scores at 17 weeks but relatively low scores 68 weeks later. This natural disaster has

TABLE 39-3
Common Experiences During Grief and Their Pathological Intensification

Phase	Normal Response	Pathological Intensifications
Dying	Emotional expression and immediate coping with the dying process	Avoidant; over-whelmed, dazed, confused; self-punitive; inappropriately hostile
Death and outcry	Outcry of emotions with news of the death and turning for help to others or isolating self with self-succoring	Panic; dissociative reactions; reactive psychoses
Warding off (denial)	Avoidance of reminders, social withdrawal, focusing elsewhere, emotional numbing, not thinking of implications to self or certain themes	Maladaptive avoidances of confronting the implications, of the death. Drug or alcohol abuse, counterphobic frenzy, promiscuity, fugue states, phobic avoidance, feeling dead or unreal
Re-experience (intrusion)	Intrusive experiences including recollections of negative relationship experiences with the deceased, bad dreams, reduced concentration, compulsive enactments	Flooding with negative images and emotions, uncontrolled ideation, self-impairing compulsive reenactments, night terrors, recurrent nightmares, distraught from intrusion of anger, anxiety, despair, shame or guilt themes, physiological exhaustion from hyperarousal
Working through	Recollections of the deceased and contemplations of self with reduced intrusiveness of memories and fantasies, increased rational acceptance, reduced numbness and avoidance, more "dosing" of recollections and a sense of working it through	Sense that one cannot integrate the death with a sense of self and continued life. Persistent warded off themes may manifest as anxious, depressed, enraged, shame-filled or guilty moods, and psychophysiological syndromes.
Completion	Reduction in emotional swings with a sense of self coherence and readiness for new relationships. Able to experience positive states of mind	Failure to complete mourning may be associated with inability to work, create, to feel emotion or positive states of mind

Source: M. J. Horowitz, A model of mourning: Change in schemas of self and others. *Journal of the American Psychoanalytic Association,* 1990, *38*(2), 297–324.

TABLE 39-4
Impact of Event Subscale Scores for Different Populations

Population (Author)	Event	N	Weeks Mean (SD)	Intrusion Mean (SD)	Avoidance Mean (SD)
Israeli soldiers with PTSD (Solomon, 1989)	1982 Lebanon war	382	52 —	17.4 (9.7)	17.7 (12.8)
		285	104 —	14.6 (9.5)	16.1 (12.6)
		213	156 —	13.0 (9.3)	14.4 (12.3)
Israeli soldiers without PTSD (Solomon, 1989)	1982 Lebanon war	334	52 —	6.8 (6.2)	8.4 (9.7)
		198	104 —	4.9 (6.1)	7.0 (9.8)
		116	156 —	4.3 (6.0)	6.8 (9.3)
American soldiers with PTSD before thenelzine (Frank, et al., 1988)	Vietnam war	11	>500 —	22.0 (11.3)	19.0 (5.6)
American soldiers with PTSD after thenelzine (Frank, et al., 1988)	Vietnam war	12	>500 —	9.0 (9.3)	11.0 (6.0)
Disaster victims (Laube, 1986)	Earthquake, Kalamata, Greece	83	5 (0)	27.3 (7.5)	21.1 (7.7)
Shoppers (Foreman, 1988)	Plane Crash into Sun Valley mall	17	27 —	25.7 (9.8)	21.9 (10.5)
		11	82 —	19.4 (10.2)	18.9 (11.4)
Rescue Workers (Foreman, 1988)	Plane crash into Sun Valley mall	20	27 —	11.8 (10.1)	9.2 (10.4)
		15	82 —	8.3 (10.7)	5.2 (7.3)
Female disaster survivors (Steinglass & Gerrity, 1990)	Tornado	18	17 —	17.9 (7.4)	15.6 (8.9)
		20	68 —	8.9 (6.6)	12.0 (10.0)
Male disaster survivors (Steinglass & Gerrity, 1990)	Tornado	15	17 —	9.6 (9.0)	11.4 (11.5)
		19	68 —	7.0 (8.5)	5.4 (7.4)
Family survivors of violence (Amick-McMullan, et al., 1989)	Homicide of family member	16	130 (130)	24.6 —	16.9 —
Rape survivors (Kilpatrick & Veronen, 1984)	Rape	23	104 —	11.2 —	16.0 —
Stress clinic patients (Horowitz, Weiss, et al., 1984)	Death of a parent	35	26 (20)	20.1 (7.8)	20.8 (10.6)
		35	66 (17)	8.4 (6.2)	6.2 (8.2)
Bereaved nonpatient controls (Horowitz, Weiss, et al., 1984)	Death of a parent	37	8 (2)	13.5 (9.5)	9.3 (9.6)
		37	58 (9)	6.9 (7.9)	5.8 (8.2)
Surgical patients (Horowitz, 1982)	Breast biopsy for possible cancer	68	1 (0)	7.2 (7.5)	7.5 (9.0)
Medical patients (Horowitz, 1982)	Cancer diagnosis	54	5 (3)	8.4 (8.2)	9.2 (8.1)
Medical students (Horowitz, et al., 1979)	First exposure to and dissection of cadaver	69	2 (0)	4.0 (4.4)	6.0 (6.3)

an acute stress reaction profile. In contrast, the Amick-McMullan, Kilpatrick, Vernonen, & Smith (1989) study of family survivors of homicide victims illustrates the profile of chronic stress reaction. The IES scores of these subjects, obtained on average 130 weeks after the event, were extremely high. In this case, the event has the enduring effects of both horror and extreme loss.

Group differences in the severity of stress responses to the same life event and in readiness to report conscious experiences to others must also be taken into account. These differences include such factors as sex, age, cultural background, education, and personality. The influence of gender is exemplified in the Steinglass and Gerrity (1990) study, in which the females reported an acute stress response to the tornado disaster, while the males did not. In the Foreman (1988) study of the aftermath of a plane crash into a shopping mall, a difference in IES scores between shoppers and rescue workers was noted in that IES scores were higher in shoppers. In contrast to the shoppers, the rescue workers were trained and more experienced in dealing with disasters, and the shoppers were present when the disaster occurred, while the rescue workers arrived on the scene shortly afterwards. The initial high IES subscale scores of the clinic patients with pathological grief reactions relative to the lower IES score of bereaved nonpatient controls (Horowitz, Weiss, et al., 1984) is also likely to be partially a function of personality factors (see Table 39–4). The same should also partly account for the differences between war veterans with PTSD and those without.

Group differences due to treatment effects is reflected in the studies by Frank and Horowitz. Frank and colleagues compared Vietnam war veterans with PTSD before a psychotropic drug treatment program of thenelzine and after treatment (Frank, Kosten, Giller, & Elisheva, 1988). A significant drop in IES scores was noted following treatment. Similarly, Horowitz, Weiss, et al. (1984) reported a lowering of IES scores for patients who sought and received psychotherapy following the death of a parent.

Thematic Contents of Intrusive Thoughts and Feelings

Although the IES is a relatively sensitive measure of the degree of psychological distress in response to a life event, it does not address the content of intrusions. The content of intrusions usually consists of memories, ideas, and feelings evoked by the stressful event. The constellation of contents that make up these intrusions take the form of recurrent themes, which represent the implications the event has to the person. Although each individual will respond in his or her unique way to the stressful event, it has been noted in the clinical literature that certain common themes emerge across individuals.

While the recurrence of general themes has long been recognized in the clinical literature on stress reactions, an important step was to provide empirical evidence for their existence and the extent of occurrence. Krupnick and Horowitz (1981) developed content analysis manuals for raters and thereby demonstrated the frequency with which the ten most common themes emerged (outlined in Horowitz, 1976, 1986). Krupnick and Horowitz examined 15 cases in which the stress event was the death of a loved one and 15 in which it was a personal injury such as an amputation, an assault, or a near-fatal experience. The frequency of conflicts involving the common themes in stress-response syndromes, as agreed upon by two judges, is reported in Table 39–5. All themes were present in both groups, although some themes were noted more frequently than others. The themes of discomfort over vulnerability, rage at the source, and feelings of responsibility occurred at a high level of frequency for both groups. For some themes, however, they were found to

TABLE 39–5
Frequency of Themes

	No. (%) of Cases		
	Bereavement *(n = 15)*	*Personal Injury* *(n = 15)*	*Combined* *(n = 30)*
Discomfort over vulnerability	13 (87)	11 (73)	24 (80)
Rage at the source	12 (80)	11 (73)	23 (77)
Guilt over responsibility	9 (60)	12 (80)	21 (70)
Fear of repetition	7 (47)	13 (87)	20 (67)
Sadness over loss	14 (93)	4 (27)	18 (60)
Discomfort over aggressive impulses	7 (47)	9 (60)	16 (53)
Fear of loss of control over aggressive impulses	6 (40)	7 (47)	13 (43)
Fear of similarity to victim	9 (60)	2 (13)	11 (37)
Rage at those exempted	6 (40)	4 (27)	10 (33)
Survivor guilt	3 (20)	3 (20)	6 (20)

Source: J. Krupnick & M. J. Horowitz, Stress response syndromes: Recurrent themes. *Archives of General Psychiatry,* 1981, 38, 428–435. Copyright © 1981, American Medical Association.

be prevalent in one group but not so prevalent in the other. In the bereavement group, sadness over loss was noted in 14 out of 15 cases, but was present in only 4 out of 15 personal injury cases. On the other hand, fear of repetition was present in 13 personal injury cases and in only 7 bereavement cases.

Their status as common themes has also been demonstrated in a study by Armsworth (1988) on incest survivors. Armsworth developed a themes of stressful events questionnaire based on the ten themes described by Krupnick and Horowitz (1981). It examined the extent to which the theme was present in the subject's life. All themes were frequently endorsed in her sample of 42 adult incest survivors. A study by Roth and Lebowitz (1988) on rape and incest, although not examining these ten themes directly, provides further evidence that these are commonly expressed themes.

While providing some support for the universality of these themes, the study by Roth and Lebowitz (1988) suggests that themes that are more specific to the type of event will also be frequently expressed. The themes they report that may be more unique for rape and incest survivors include feelings of isolation and alienation and issues with mothers. An extensive analysis of themes across different types of events may provide a means of examining the universal implications stressful life events have for the self as well as the unique implications of various types of traumatic events to the self.

In regard to these common themes, it should be noted that they have been identified in clinical samples. That is, these are subjects who have experienced an excessive stressful reaction to the traumatic event. What remains to be determined is whether these are common themes for individuals who have a normal stress reaction to a traumatic event. For such individuals there may be qualitative differences in the content or in the degree of intrusiveness of these themes.

EXPLANATION OF INTRUSIVE IDEAS AND FEELINGS

Horowitz (1976, 1986) introduced a theoretical framework to explain intrusion, informed by Freud's ego-psychological explanatory account of the compulsive repetition of warded-off ideas and associated emotions. Freud (1920) regarded compulsive repetition as an expression of an attempt on the part of the ego to master and assimilate traumatic experiences. This mastery was gained through repeated reviewing of the event and its implications.

Elaborating on this ego-psychological explanation, Horowitz (1976) explained the motive to repeat as based on a "completion tendency," or an intrinsic cognitive motive to reduce the discrepancy between new information elicited by the life event, as retained in an active form of memory storage, and pre-existing inner models of meaning, or schemata. This disequilibrium is reduced through the processes of assimilation and accommodation (Piaget, 1954).

Active memory was seen as a recurrent re-entry of long-term memories into short-term memory modules, and so into modes of repeated conscious representation. In this theory, the contents in active memory would have an intrinsic property of repeated review unless these contents were inhibited by control processes in order to focus attention on other topics of concern. Information in active memory would remain "in line" for processing until processing was complete. Then the contents would be a part of current enduring schemas and various forms of long-term memory. Stressful topics would be those that contain information that cannot readily be assimilated into pre-existing schemata. So long as information in active memory is open to conscious review in sufficient dosages, it will eventually become fully processed and lead to reschematization. For highly discrepant information, however, this process may take considerable time in light of working memory capacity constraints and competition with other programs for access to these limited processing resources. Moreover, the completion process will be prolonged by affective factors. The traumatic memories would activate negative emotion and might be inhibited in order to ward off entry into dreaded states of mind: states anticipated to be too emotional, too painful, too out of control, and/or too hopeless.

Complete processing of this information generally involves a series of progressive steps. Each time active memory content is represented in working memory, processing will resume at the point where it last left off. This process is repeated until the discrepancy between active memory contents and schemata no longer exists.

Stress events are defined as a notable discrepancy between the implications of the event and the person's schema for understanding and reacting to events. For example, news of the death of a significant other is highly incongruent with the person's inner models of attachment to this person. The person's representation of the other as always present for routine activities such as meals will conflict with the new reality of the other as permanently absent. Such a serious life event will take considerable time to become assimilated.

In order to explain the prototypical oscillations between episodes of intrusion and denial in stress disorders, Horowitz (1976) built upon Freud's (1926) insights into the role of signal anxiety in defense. Freud viewed anxiety as a motivating factor in the regulation of mental content entering consciousness. Applying Freud's insights into the role of signal anxiety in defense, in conjunction with cognitive perspectives on the role of appraisal in emotional arousal and coping (e.g., Janis, 1967; Lazarus, 1964). Horowitz characterized emotions as capable of influencing cognitive controls that, in turn, affect subsequent cognitive processes. In other words, a reciprocal relationship exists between cognitive appraisal, emotion, and control. Moreover, it was hypothesized that cognitive appraisal could take place without conscious memory or intentionality and, also, in parallel processing channels.

Individual differences are shown in both the meaning assigned to the inciting event and the nature of the control processes utilized. The meaning appraisal may be realistic or unrealistic and will have a direct bearing on the quality and intensity of emotion aroused.

The state of mind of emotionality can be unconsciously anticipated and thus, in turn, can affect controls.

According to this theory, the individual may be regarded as exhibiting two opposing categories of motives in response to a stressful event. These consist of an approach motive toward conscious review and assimilation of discrepant information in active memory, and an avoidance motive toward warding off this information from conscious representation in order to avoid entering dreaded states of mind. In attempting to assimilate a stressful experience, the completion tendency may become disrupted by defenses instigated in response to threat of entry into overwhelmingly painful states.

The nature of a stressful event is such that the person may become or anticipate becoming overwhelmed whenever he or she consciously contemplates its implications. Whenever the level of painful emotion (or anticipated threat of entry into such a state) reaches a certain point, controls will become operative and modify conscious experience by inhibiting active memory contents from entering any mode of representation. This is expressed in states of mind characterized by numbing, attention constriction, and mental or communicative acts of disavowel, suppression, or denial. However, the resulting decrease in accessibility of stress-related information in active memory will be accompanied by a reduction in anxiety that, in turn, will lead to a relaxation of controls. The relaxation of controls will again result in the increased accessibility and conscious representation of stress-related information in light of the completion tendency, thus returning the system to its initial position. This kind of marginal instability explains rapid oscillations between intrusion and denial in some states of mind (see Horowitz, 1991).

The same event may set in motion a number of "programs" of ideation, or themes. The degree of fit between pre-existing inner models and the various aspects of new information will determine the intensity and quality of the resultant emotions. For instance, fear may be generated by an appraisal of threat that exceeds the person's coping capacity, whereas shame may be induced by the discrepancy between new information and the person's ideals. Because some of these programs will be more easily assimilated than others, there will be differences in the amount of time needed for completion of each. For example, the theme of discomfort over vulnerability might be a recurrent intrusive experience appearing early after the traumatic event, whereas survivor guilt may initially be completely warded off and only allowed to enter consciousness at a later time, such as in the context of a safe therapeutic relationship. In this case, the theme of discomfort over vulnerability would be expected to become fully processed earlier than the survivor guilt theme. As this example illustrates, a single stressful event can have multiple emotional repercussions as a result of its implications and can lead to a complex of themes that the person must work through.

TREATMENT OF STRESS RESPONSE SYNDROMES

Treatment can be conceptualized as an effort to assist patients in their own natural completion process. This undertaking usually involves efforts to work through conflicts that have stymied the patient's own attempts toward this goal. It also involves examination of latent conflicts that have been activated by association to this recent event and its present implications.

A pattern of phases that individuals tend to progress through in normal responses to serious life events has been identified (Horowitz, 1986). A pathological phasic response to extreme stress can be thought of as an intensification of the normal phasic response, as shown for bereavement in Table 39-3 and in general in Figure 39-1. This model of normal and pathological phasic responses provides a framework from which a treatment model was developed.

The patient enters therapy as a result of a delayed, protracted, or overwhelming stress response to a traumatic life stressor. The initial aim is to establish a working alliance quickly. The vehicle used to establish the collaborative relationship is to have the patient recount the circumstances of and surrounding the traumatic event. Following this introduction, the therapist and patient jointly decide on an appropriate focus for the therapy.

For traumatized patients, the development of a trusting relationship, as well as the

FIGURE 39-1. Normal and pathological phases of poststress response. *Source:* Stress Response Syndromes, *2d ed., by Mardi J. Horowitz.* © *1986 by Mardi J. Horowitz. Reprinted with permission of the publisher, Jason Aronson, Inc.*

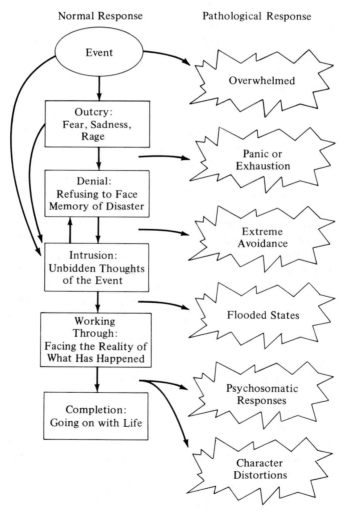

therapy itself, may activate issues arising directly from the traumatic event. For patients suffering from a pathological grief response, there may be a reluctance to enter into a significant relationship that is destined to end for fear of being retraumatized by separation or—as it is often experienced—abandonment.

With the establishment of a working alliance and the identification of a mutually agreed-upon focus, the patient can begin the process of working through the thoughts and feelings in terms of the focus. This process involves a reappraisal of the serious life event, the meanings associated with it, and its intersection with pre-existent features of personality. With the support and guidance of the therapist, the patient is helped to examine, in tolerable doses, aspects of the traumatic experience and its personal implications to the patient. The overall aim of this phase is to move the patient from either a rigidly overcontrolled orientation or undermodulated intrusive reactions to an affectively manageable exploration of the meanings the traumatic event has for the patient.

The relationship of therapy technique to traumas and to personality features is described in case examples reported elsewhere (Horowitz, 1986, 1987; Horowitz, Marmar, et al., 1984). In general, loss of this supportive relationship may lead to reactivation of the emotions related to the losses involved in the traumatic event, perhaps accompanied by a return of symptoms. In therapy, however, termination can be anticipated well in advance, as emphasized by Mann (1973). Loss can be faced gradually, actively rather than passively, and in the context of a helping relationship. Frequently, transference reactions occur most intensively in anticipation of termination. These reactions can be linked back to the treatment focus and provide a context to further work through any incompletely resolved responses to the traumatic event and any personality features that led to problems in working through the event.

At termination, the patient may still have symptoms, partly because of the time needed to work through a major loss but also because of anxiety about the loss of the therapeutic relationship. The patient is encouraged to view the post-termination phase as a continuation of the working-through process, which will now take place in the context of other personal relationships and episodes of self-reflection.

Medications, if necessary, should be prescribed only on an interim basis rather than for maintenance of the traumatized patient. Adaptive working through of the meaning of the stressful event requires that the patient consciously be able to process the emotionally painful material. The over-use of medications may stymie this natural working-through process.

CONCLUSION

Experimental, field, and clinical investigations of stress have provided convergent support for intrusion and avoidance or omission as important signs of current psychological stress in response to a stressful life event. The Impact of Event Scale has provided an efficient way of measuring degree of intrusion and has led to large body of research on the extent and time course of intrusion in response to a wide range of stressful life events. It has also highlighted individual differences in response to the same event. Important work has also been conducted on the thematic content of intrusive ideas. Common conflictual themes associated with a variety of types of stressful life events have been identified and investigated empirically through the development of text analytic and questionnaire methods. In light of the role of such themes in the evocation and maintenance of symptomatology following a stressful event, a greater understanding of themes has important implications for distinguishing normal and pathological stress responses as well as having implications for treatment. Further research on the interaction of personality features such as person schemas and habitual control processes with stressful life events is required to enhance our understanding of pathological stress responses.

REFERENCES

AMERICAN PSYCHIATRIC ASSOCIATION. *Diagnostic and statistical manual of mental disorders,* (3d ed., rev.). Washington, DC: American Psychiatric Association, 1987.

AMICK-MCMULLAN, A., KILPATRICK, D. G., VERONEN, L. J., & SMITH, S. Family survivors of homicide victims: Theoretical perspectives and an exploratory study. *Journal of Traumatic Stress,* 1989, *2,* 21–35.

ANTROBUS, J. S., SINGER, J. L., & GREENBERG, S. Studies in the stream of consciousness: Experimental enhancement and suppression of spontaneous cognitive processes. *Perceptual and Motor Skills,* 1966, *23,* 399–417.

ARMSWORTH, M. *Posttraumatic stress and incest.* Unpublished manuscript, Department of Educational Psychology, University of Houston, Houston, TX, 1989.

BREUER, J., & FREUD, S. Studies on hysteria. In *Standard edition.* Vol. 2. Reprinted, London: Hogarth Press, 1954. Original edition 1895.

FOREMAN, C. *Sun Valley disaster study.* Unpublished manuscript, Contra Costa Health Services, Martinez, CA, 1988.

FRANK, J. B., KOSTEN, T. R., GILLER, E. L., & ELISHEVA, D. A randomized clinical trial of phenelzine and imipramine for posttraumatic stress disorder. *American Journal of Psychiatry,* 1988, *145,* 1289–1291.

FREUD, S. Beyond the pleasure principle. In *Standard edition.* Vol. 18. Reprinted, London: Hogarth Press, 1962. Original edition 1920.

————. Inhibitions, symptoms and anxiety. In *Standard edition.* Vol. 18. Reprinted, London: Hogarth Press, 1959. Original edition 1926.

GRINKER, K., & SPIEGEL, S. *Men under stress.* Philadelphia: Blackston, 1945.

HOROWITZ, M. J. Intrusive and repetitive thoughts after experimental stress: A summary. *Archives of General Psychiatry,* 1975, *32,* 1457–1463.

————. *Stress response syndromes.* New York: Aronson, 1976.

————. *Image formation and cognition* (2d ed.). New York: Appleton, 1978.

————. Stress response syndromes and their treatment. In L. Goldberger & S. Breznitz (eds.), *Handbook of stress: Theoretical and clinical aspects.* New York: Free Press, 1982.

————. *Image formation and psychotherapy* (rev. ed.). New York: Aronson, 1983.

————. *Stress response syndromes* (2d ed.). New York: Aronson, 1986.

————. *States of mind* (2d ed.). New York: Plenum Press, 1987.

————. A model of mourning: Change in schemas of self and others. *Journal of the American Psychoanalytic Association,* 1990, *38,* 297-324.

————. Person schemas. In M. J. Horowitz (ed.), *Person schemas and maladaptive interpersonal patterns.* Chicago: University of Chicago Press, 1991.

HOROWITZ, M. J., MARMAR, C., KRUPNICK, J., WILNER, N., KALTREIDER, N., & WALLTERSTEIN, R. *Personality styles and brief psychotherapy.* New York: Basic Books, 1984.

HOROWITZ, M. J., SCHAEFER, C., & COONEY, P. Life event scaling for recency of experience. In E. Gunderson & R. Rahe (eds.), *Life stress and illness.* Springfield, IL: Thomas, 1974.

HOROWITZ, M. J., WEISS, D. S., KALTREIDER, N., KRUPNICK, J., MARMAR, C., WILNER, N., & DEWITT, K. Reactions to the death of a parent: Results from patients and field subjects. *Journal of Nervous and Mental Disease,* 1984, *172,* 383–392.

HOROWITZ, M. J., & WILNER, N. Stress films, emotions and cognitive response. *Archives of General Psychiatry,* 1976, *30,* 1339–1344.

HOROWITZ, M. J., WILNER, N., & ALVAREZ, W. Impact of Event Scale: A measure of subjective stress. *Psychosomatic Medicine,* 1979, *41,* 209–218.

JANIS, I. L. Effects of fear arousal on attitude change: Recent development in theory and experimental research. In L. Berkowitz (ed.), *Advances in experimental social psychology.* Vol. 3. New York: Academic Press, 1967.

KEISER, L. *The traumatic neuroses.* Philadelphia: Lippincott, 1968.

KILPATRICK, D. G., & VERONEN, L. J. *Treatment of fear and anxiety in victims of rape.* Rockville, MD: National Institute of Mental Health, 1984.

KLOS, D. S., & SINGER, J. L. Determinants of the adolescent's ongoing thought following simulated parental confrontation. *Journal of Personality and Social Psychology,* 1981, *41,* 975–987.

KRUPNICK, J. L., & HOROWITZ, M. J. Stress response syndromes: Recurrent themes. *Archives of General Psychiatry,* 1981, *38,* 428–435.

LAUBE, J. *Kalamata earthquake 1986: Psychological reactions and a look at health care workers.* Unpublished manuscript, School of Nursing, University of Southern Mississippi, Hattiesburg, MI, 1986.

LAZARUS, R. S. A laboratory approach to the dynamics of psychological stress. *American Psychologist,* 1964, *19,* 400–411.

LAZARUS, R. S., & OPTON, E. M. The use of motion picture films in the study of psychological stress: A summary of experimental studies and theoretical formulations. In C. Spielberger (ed.), *Anxiety and behavior.* New York: Academic Press, 1966.

LIFTON, R. J. *History and human survival.* New York: Vantage Books, 1967.

LINDEMANN, E. Symptomatology and management of acute grief. *American Journal of Psychiatry,* 1944, *101,* 141–148.

MANN, J. *Time limited psychotherapy.* Cambridge, MA: Harvard University Press, 1973.

PARKES, C. M. The first year of bereavement: A longitudinal study of the reaction of London widows to the death of their husbands. *Psychiatry,* 1970, *33,* 444–467.

PIAGET, J. *The construction of reality in the child.* New York: Basic Books, 1954.

ROTH, S., & LEBOWITZ, L. The experience of sexual trauma. *Journal of Traumatic Stress,* 1988, *1,* 79–107.

SCHWARZWALD, J., SOLOMON, Z., WEISENBERG, M., & MIKULINCER, M. Validation of the Impact of Event Scale for psychological sequaelae of combat. *Journal of Consulting and Clinical Psychology,* 1987, *55,* 251–256.

SINGER, J. L., & SALOVEY, P. Organized knowledge structures and personality: Person schemas, prototypes, and scripts. In M. J. Horowitz (ed.), *Person schemas and maladaptive interpersonal patterns.* Chicago: University of Chicago Press, 1991.

SOKALL, R. R., & SNEATH, P. *Numerical taxonomy: The principles and practice of numerical classifications.* San Francisco: Freeman, 1973.

SOLOMON, Z. Psychological sequelae of war. *Journal of Nervous and Mental Disease,* 1989, *177,* 342–346.

STEINGLASS, P., & GERRITY, E. Natural disasters and post-traumatic stress disorder: Short-term versus long-term recovery in two disaster-affected communities. *Journal of Applied Social Psychology,* 1990, *20,* 1746–1765.

ZILBERG, N. J., WEISS, D. S., & HOROWITZ, M. J. Impact of Event Scale: A cross-validation study and some empirical evidence supporting a conceptual model of stress response syndromes. *Journal of Consulting and Clinical Psychology,* 1982, *50,* 407–414.

Author Index

Subject Index